Yorkshire and the Humber Region
Pages 366–399

Northumbria
Pages 400–415

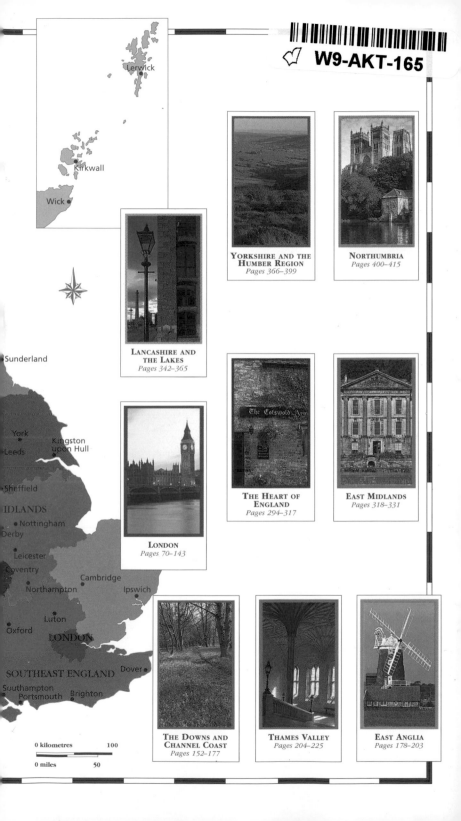

Lancashire and the Lakes
Pages 342–365

The Heart of England
Pages 294–317

East Midlands
Pages 318–331

London
Pages 70–143

Sunderland
York
Kingston upon Hull
Leeds
Sheffield
IDLANDS
Nottingham
Derby
Leicester
Coventry
Cambridge
Northampton
Ipswich
Luton
Oxford
LONDON
SOUTHEAST ENGLAND
Dover
Southampton
Portsmouth
Brighton

The Downs and Channel Coast
Pages 152–177

Thames Valley
Pages 204–225

East Anglia
Pages 178–203

0 kilometres 100

0 miles 50

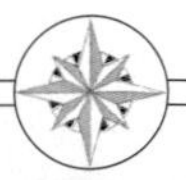

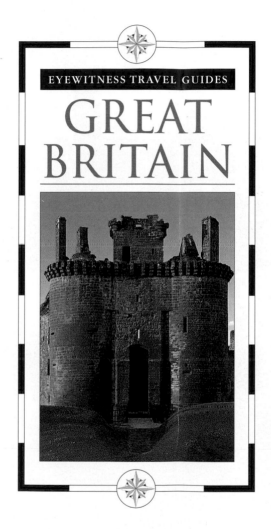

EYEWITNESS TRAVEL GUIDES

GREAT BRITAIN

EYEWITNESS TRAVEL GUIDES

GREAT BRITAIN

Main contributor: MICHAEL LEAPMAN

LONDON, NEW YORK,
MELBOURNE, MUNICH AND DELHI
www.dk.com

ART EDITOR Stephen Bere
PROJECT EDITOR Marian Broderick
EDITORS Carey Combe, Sara Harper, Elaine Harries, Kim Inglis, Ella Milroy, Andrew Szudek, Nia Williams
US EDITOR Mary Sutherland
DESIGNERS Susan Blackburn, Elly King, Colin Loughrey, Andy Wilkinson

CONTRIBUTORS
Josie Barnard, Christopher Catling, Juliet Clough, Lindsay Hunt, Polly Phillimore, Martin Symington, Roger Thomas

MAPS
Jane Hanson, Phil Rose, Jennifer Skelley (Lovell Johns Ltd)
Gary Bowes (Era-Maptec Ltd)

PHOTOGRAPHERS
Joe Cornish, Paul Harris, Rob Reichenfeld, Kim Sayer

ILLUSTRATORS
Richard Draper, Jared Gilby (Kevin Jones Assocs), Paul Guest, Roger Hutchins, Chris Orr & Assocs, Maltings Partnership, Ann Winterbotham, John Woodcock

Reproduced by Colourscan (Singapore)
Printed and bound by South China Printing Co. Ltd., China

First American edition 1995
10 9
Published in the United States by
DK Publishing, Inc.,
375 Hudson Street, New York, NY 10014
Reprinted with revisions 1996, 1997, 1999, 2000, 2001, 2002, 2003, 2004

Published in Great Britain by Dorling Kindersley Limited.

ISSN 1542-1554
ISBN 0-7894-9385-3

THROUGHOUT THIS BOOK, FLOORS ARE REFERRED TO IN ACCORDANCE WITH EUROPEAN USAGE, I.E., THE "FIRST FLOOR" IS ONE FLIGHT UP.

The information in this Dorling Kindersley Travel Guide is checked annually.
Every effort has been made to ensure that this book is as up-to-date as possible at the time of going to press. Some details, however, such as telephone numbers, prices, gallery hanging arrangements and travel information, are liable to change. The publishers cannot accept responsibility for any consequences arising from the use of this book, nor for any material on third-party websites, and cannot guarantee that any website address in this book will be a suitable source of travel information. We value the views and suggestions of our readers highly. Please write to: Publisher, DK Eyewitness Travel Guides, Dorling Kindersley, 80 Strand, London WC2R 0RL, Great Britain.

CONTENTS

HOW TO USE THIS GUIDE *6*

A 14th-century illustration of two knights jousting

INTRODUCING GREAT BRITAIN

PUTTING GREAT BRITAIN ON THE MAP *10*

A PORTRAIT OF GREAT BRITAIN *16*

THE HISTORY OF GREAT BRITAIN *38*

GREAT BRITAIN THROUGH THE YEAR *62*

Beefeater at the Tower of London

LONDON

INTRODUCING LONDON *72*

WEST END AND WESTMINSTER *78*

SOUTH KENSINGTON AND HYDE PARK *96*

Eilean Donan Castle on Loch Duich in the Scottish Highlands

REGENT'S PARK AND BLOOMSBURY *104*

THE CITY AND SOUTHWARK *110*

FURTHER AFIELD *130*

STREET FINDER *135*

SOUTHEAST ENGLAND

INTRODUCING SOUTHEAST ENGLAND *146*

THE DOWNS AND CHANNEL COAST *152*

EAST ANGLIA *178*

THAMES VALLEY *204*

THE WEST COUNTRY

INTRODUCING THE WEST COUNTRY *228*

WESSEX *234*

DEVON AND CORNWALL *260*

THE MIDLANDS

INTRODUCING THE MIDLANDS *286*

THE HEART OF ENGLAND *294*

EAST MIDLANDS *318*

Jacobean "Old House" in Hereford

THE NORTH COUNTRY

INTRODUCING THE NORTH COUNTRY *334*

LANCASHIRE AND THE LAKES *342*

YORKSHIRE AND THE HUMBER REGION *366*

NORTHUMBRIA *400*

WALES

INTRODUCING WALES *418*

NORTH WALES *426*

SOUTH AND MID-WALES *442*

SCOTLAND

INTRODUCING SCOTLAND *464*

THE LOWLANDS *476*

THE HIGHLANDS AND ISLANDS *510*

TRAVELLERS' NEEDS

WHERE TO STAY *538*

WHERE TO EAT *574*

SURVIVAL GUIDE

PRACTICAL INFORMATION *614*

TRAVEL INFORMATION *632*

GENERAL INDEX *644*

View of the Usk Valley and the Brecon Beacons, Wales

How to Use this Guide

THIS GUIDE helps you to get the most from your holidays in Great Britain. It provides both detailed practical information and expert recommendations. *Introducing Great Britain* maps the country and sets it in its historical and cultural context. The six regional chapters, plus *London*, describe important sights, using maps, pictures and illustrations. Features cover topics from houses and famous gardens to sport. Hotel, restaurant, and pub recommendations can be found in *Travellers' Needs*. The *Survival Guide* has practical information on everything from transport to personal safety.

London

The centre of London has been divided into four sightseeing areas. Each has its own chapter, which opens with a list of the sights described. The last section, *Further Afield,* covers the most attractive suburbs. All sights are numbered and plotted on an area map. The information for each sight follows the map's numerical order, making sights easy to locate within the chapter.

Sights at a Glance lists the chapter's sights by category: Historic Streets and Buildings; Museums and Galleries; Churches and Cathedrals; Shops; Parks and Gardens.

All pages relating to London have red thumb tabs.

A locator map shows where you are in relation to other areas of the city centre.

1 Area Map
For easy reference, the sights are numbered and located on a map. Sights in the city centre are also marked on the Street Finder *on pages 135–43.*

2 Street-by-Street Map
This gives a bird's-eye view of the key areas in each chapter.

Stars indicate the sights that no visitor should miss.

A suggested route for a walk is shown in red.

3 Detailed information
The sights in London are described individually. Addresses, telephone numbers, opening hours, admission charges, tours and wheelchair access are also provided, as well as public transport links.

SCOTLAND 477

THE LOWLANDS

CLYDE VALLEY · CENTRAL SCOTLAND · FIFE · THE LOTHIANS
AYRSHIRE · DUMFRIES AND GALLOWAY · THE BORDERS

Southeast of the Highland boundary fault line lies a part of Scotland very different in character from its northern neighbour. If the Highlands embody the romance of Scotland, the Lowlands have traditionally been her powerhouse. Lowlanders have always prospered in agriculture and, more recently, in industry and commerce.

Being the region of Scotland closest to the English border, the Lowlands inevitably became the crucible of Scottish history. For centuries after the Romans built the Antonine Wall (see p44) across the Forth-Clyde isthmus, the area was engulfed in conflict. The Borders are scattered with the castles of a territory in uneasy proximity to rapacious neighbours, and the ramparts of Stirling Castle overlook no fewer than seven different battlefields fought over in the cause of independence.

The ruins of medieval abbeys, such as Melrose, also bear witness to the dangers of living on the invasion route from England, though the woollen trade founded by their monks still flourishes in Peebles and Hawick.

North of the Borders lies Edinburgh, the cultural and administrative capital of Scotland. With its Georgian squares dominated by a medieval castle, it is one of Europe's most elegant cities. While the 18th and 19th centuries saw a great flowering of the arts in Edinburgh, the city of Glasgow became a merchant city second only to London. Fuelled by James Watt's development of the steam engine in the 1840s, Glasgow became the cradle of Scotland's Industrial Revolution, which created a prosperous cotton industry and launched the world's greatest ships.

Both cities retain this dynamism today: Edinburgh annually hosts the world's largest arts festival, and Glasgow is acclaimed as a model of industrial renaissance.

1 Introduction

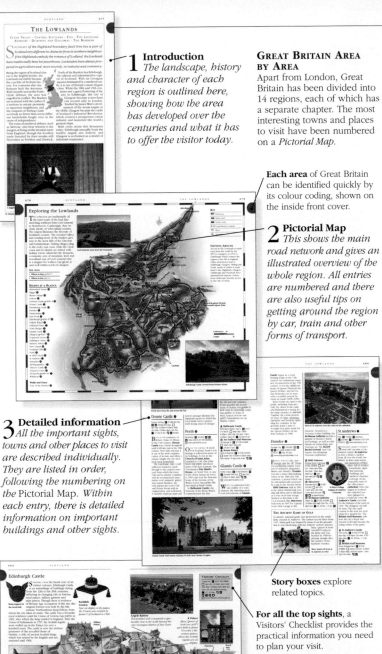

The landscape, history and character of each region is outlined here, showing how the area has developed over the centuries and what it has to offer the visitor today.

Great Britain Area by Area

Apart from London, Great Britain has been divided into 14 regions, each of which has a separate chapter. The most interesting towns and places to visit have been numbered on a *Pictorial Map*.

Each area of Great Britain can be identified quickly by its colour coding, shown on the inside front cover.

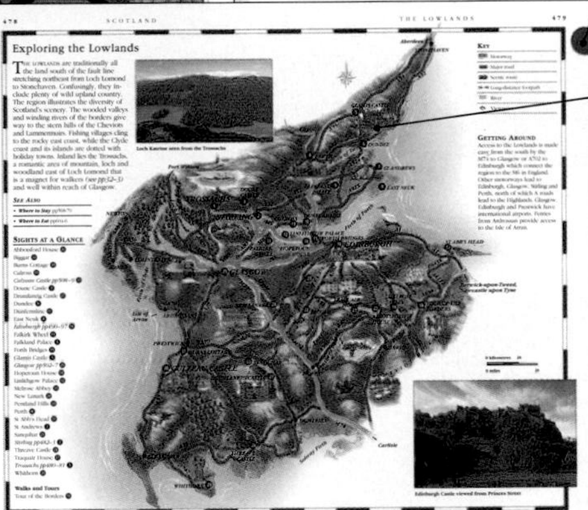

2 Pictorial Map

This shows the main road network and gives an illustrated overview of the whole region. All entries are numbered and there are also useful tips on getting around the region by car, train and other forms of transport.

3 Detailed information

All the important sights, towns and other places to visit are described individually. They are listed in order, following the numbering on the Pictorial Map. *Within each entry, there is detailed information on important buildings and other sights.*

Story boxes explore related topics.

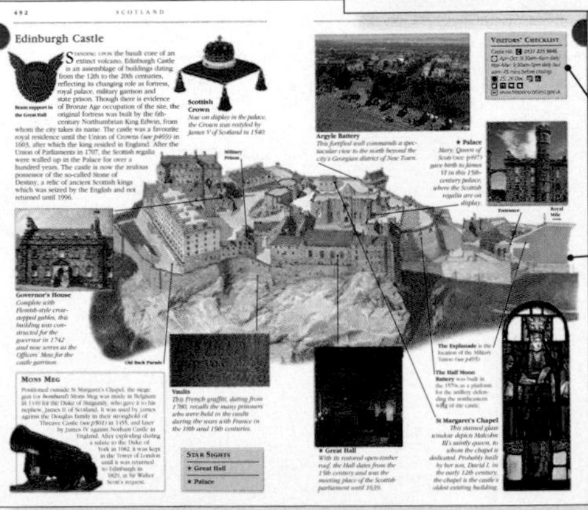

For all the top sights, a Visitors' Checklist provides the practical information you need to plan your visit.

4 The top sights

These are given one or more full pages. Three-dimensional illustrations reveal the interiors of historic buildings. Interesting town and city centres are given street-by-street maps, featuring individual sights.

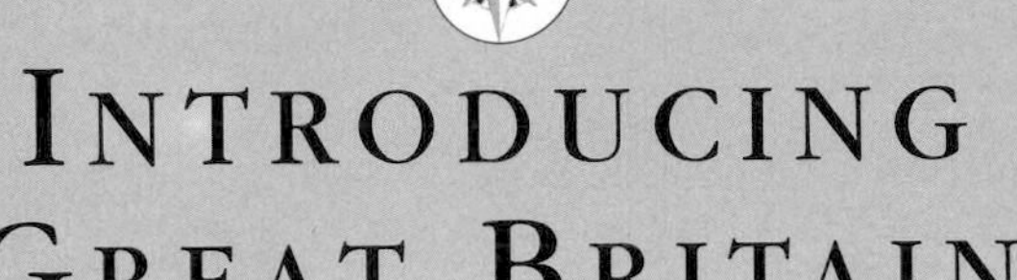

Introducing Great Britain

Putting Great Britain on the Map 10-15

A Portrait of Great Britain 16-37

The History of Great Britain 38-61

Great Britain through the Year 62-69

Putting Great Britain on the Map

LYING IN NORTHWESTERN EUROPE, Great Britain is bounded by the Atlantic Ocean, the North Sea and the English Channel. The island's landscape and climate are varied, and it is this variety that even today affects the pattern of settlement. The remote shores of the West Country peninsula and the inhospitable mountains of Scotland and Wales are less populated than the relatively flat and fertile Midlands and Southeast, where the vast majority of the country's 58 million people live. Due to this population density, the south is today the most built-up part of the country.

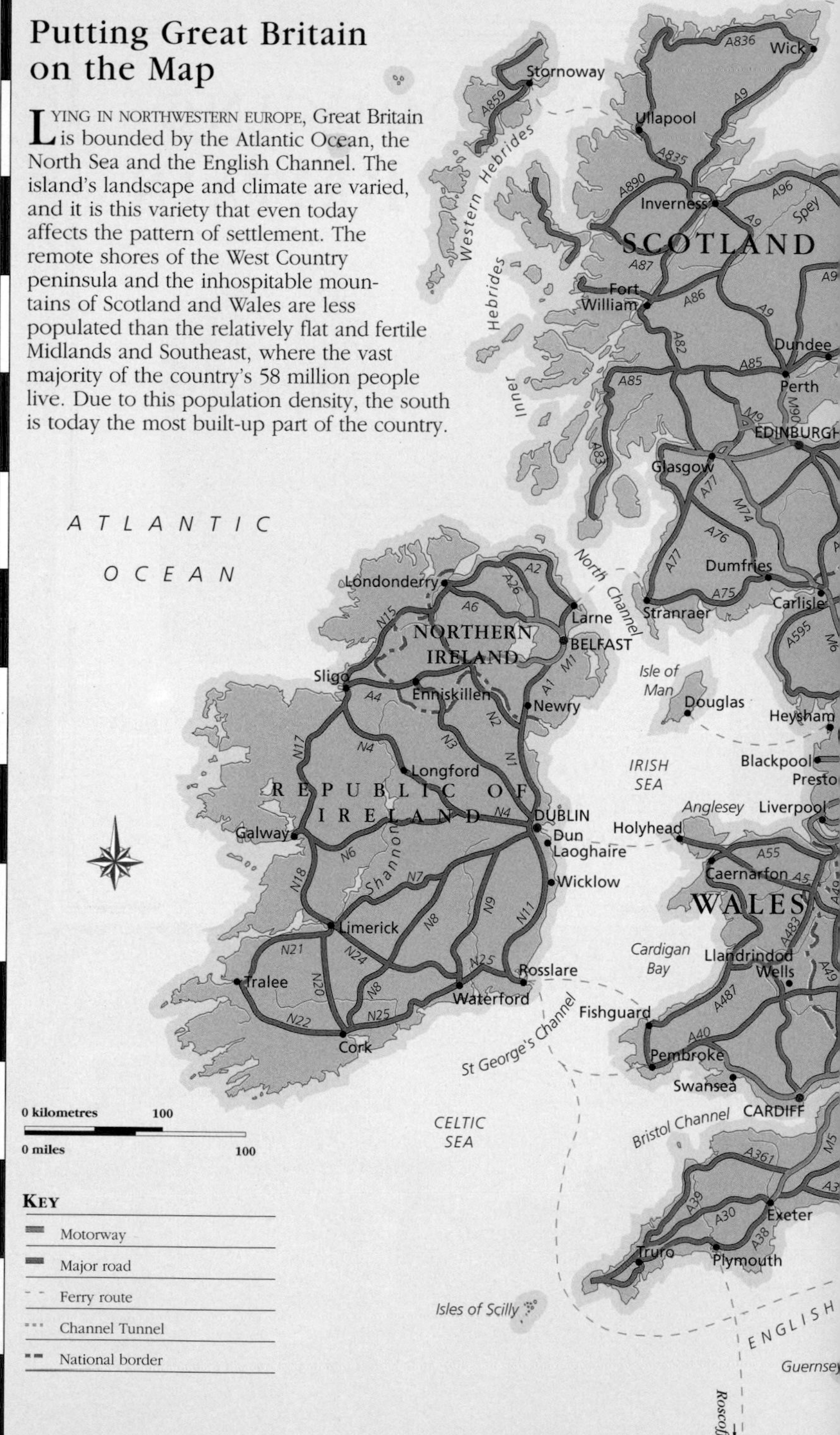

◁ ***Salisbury Cathedral: from the meadows*** **by John Constable (1776–1837)**

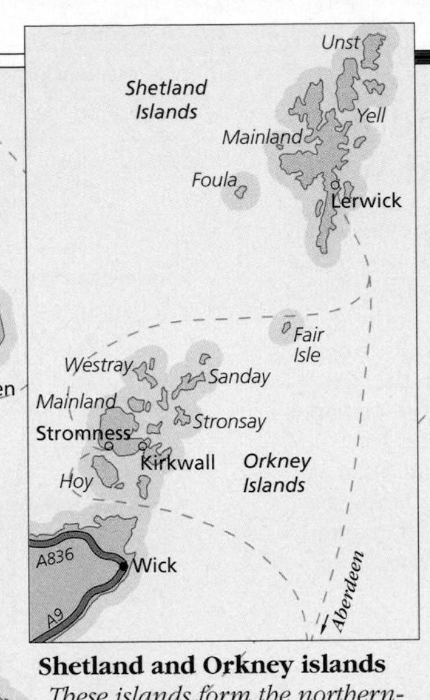

Shetland and Orkney islands

These islands form the northern-most part of Great Britain, with the Shetlands lying six degrees south of the Arctic Circle. There are transport links to the mainland.

Europe

Great Britain is situated in the northwest corner of Europe. Its nearest neighbours are Ireland to the west, and the Netherlands, Belgium and France across the Channel. Denmark, Norway and Sweden are also easily accessible.

Regional Great Britain: London, the South, the Midlands and Wales

GREAT BRITAIN has airline connections with most cities in the world. London is the main transport hub with two major international airports, including Heathrow, the world's busiest. Southern England, Britain's most populous area, is divided, within this book, into four regions – Southeast England, the West Country, Wales and the Midlands – with a separate chapter for London. Road and rail links to the North and Scotland *(see pp14–15)* are plentiful, as are links between all main towns.

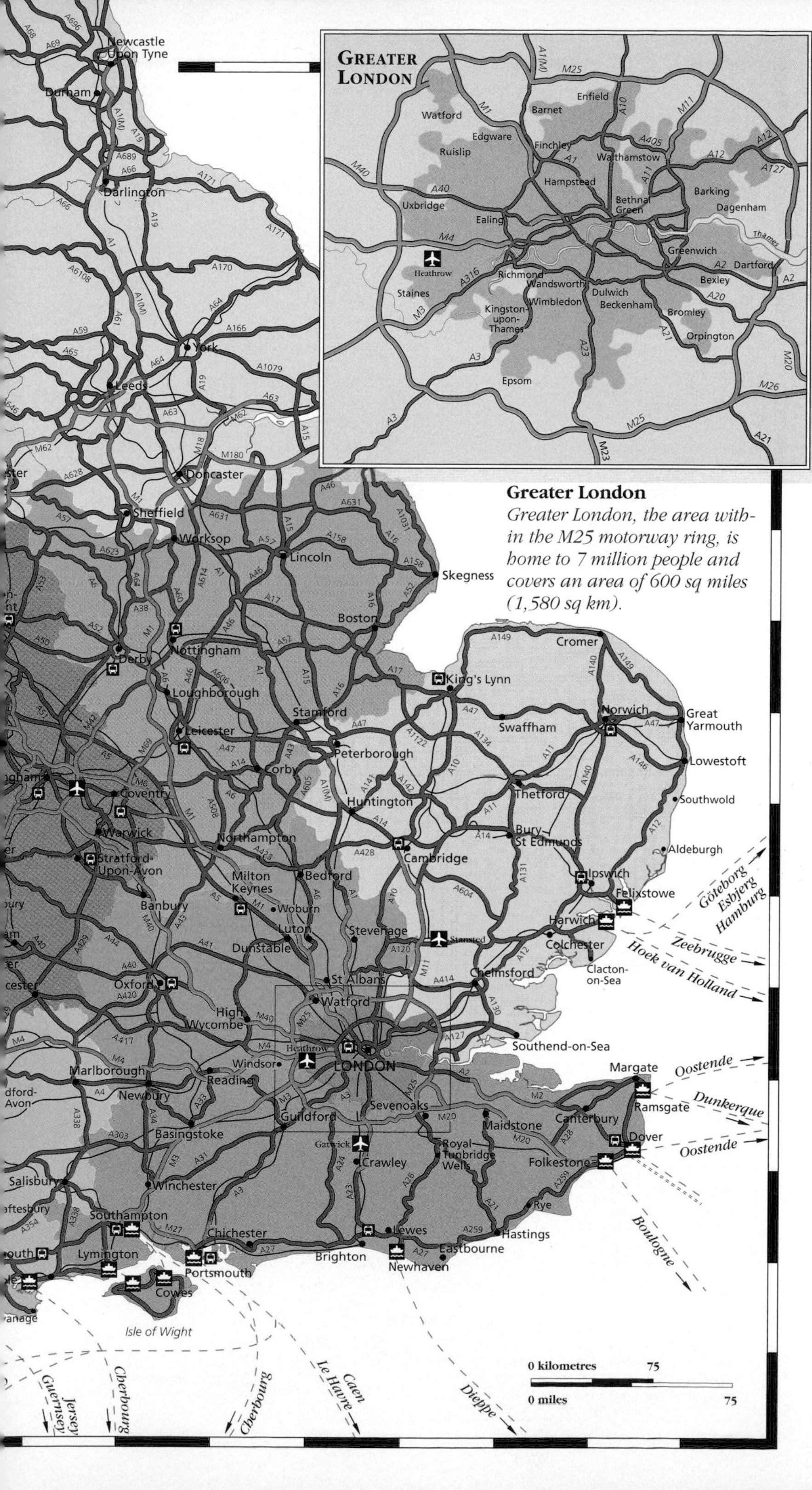

Greater London

Greater London, the area within the M25 motorway ring, is home to 7 million people and covers an area of 600 sq miles (1,580 sq km).

Regional Great Britain: The North and Scotland

THIS PART OF GREAT BRITAIN is divided into two sections in this book. Although it is far less populated than the southern sector of the country, there are good road and rail connections, and ferry services link the islands with the mainland.

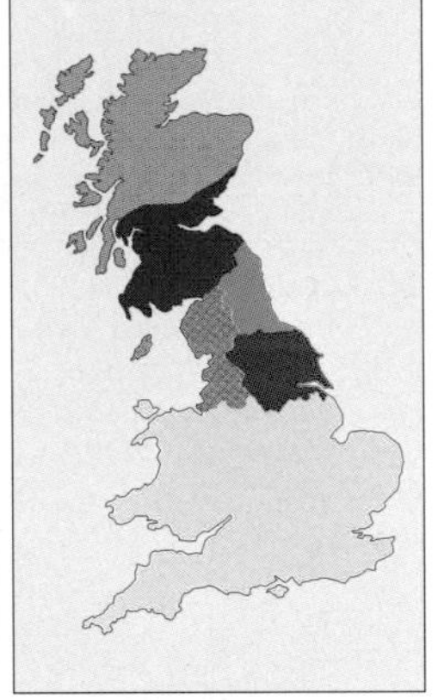

Key to Colour-Coding

The North Country

- Lancashire and the Lakes
- Yorkshire and Humber Region
- Northumbria

Scotland

- The Lowlands
- The Highlands and Islands

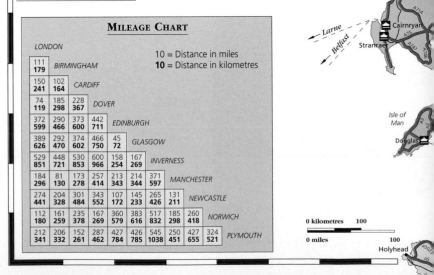

Mileage Chart

10 = Distance in miles
10 = Distance in kilometres

	LONDON	BIRMINGHAM	CARDIFF	DOVER	EDINBURGH	GLASGOW	INVERNESS	MANCHESTER	NEWCASTLE	NORWICH
BIRMINGHAM	111 **179**									
CARDIFF	150 **241**	102 **164**								
DOVER	74 **119**	185 **298**	228 **367**							
EDINBURGH	372 **599**	290 **466**	373 **600**	442 **711**						
GLASGOW	389 **626**	292 **470**	374 **602**	466 **750**	45 **72**					
INVERNESS	529 **851**	448 **721**	530 **853**	600 **966**	158 **254**	167 **269**				
MANCHESTER	184 **296**	81 **130**	173 **278**	257 **414**	213 **343**	214 **344**	371 **597**			
NEWCASTLE	274 **441**	204 **328**	301 **484**	343 **552**	107 **172**	145 **233**	265 **426**	131 **211**		
NORWICH	112 **180**	161 **259**	235 **378**	167 **269**	360 **579**	383 **616**	517 **832**	185 **298**	260 **418**	
PLYMOUTH	212 **341**	206 **332**	152 **261**	287 **462**	427 **784**	426 **785**	545 **1038**	250 **451**	427 **655**	324 **521**

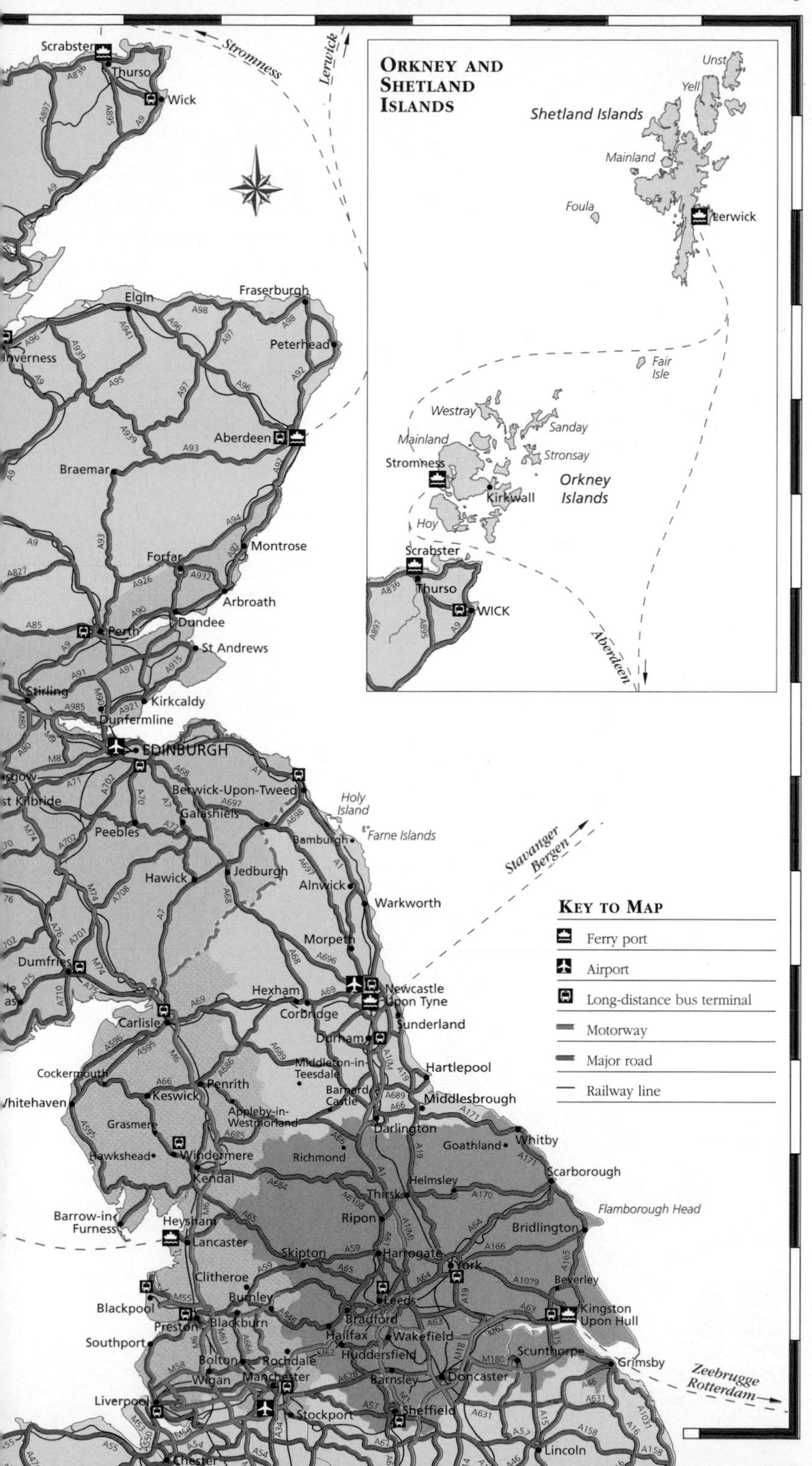
Orkney and Shetland Islands
Unst
Yell
Shetland Islands
Mainland
Foula
Lerwick
Fair Isle
Westray
Sanday
Mainland
Stronsay
Stromness
Orkney Islands
Kirkwall
Hoy
Scrabster
Thurso
WICK
Aberdeen
Key to Map
Ferry port
Airport
Long-distance bus terminal
Motorway
Major road
Railway line
Scrabster
Thurso
Wick
Stromness
Lerwick
Elgin
Fraserburgh
Peterhead
Inverness
Aberdeen
Braemar
Montrose
Forfar
Arbroath
Dundee
Perth
St Andrews
Stirling
Kirkcaldy
Dunfermline
EDINBURGH
Berwick-Upon-Tweed
Holy Island
Galashiels
Peebles
Farne Islands
Bamburgh
Hawick
Jedburgh
Alnwick
Warkworth
Stavanger Bergen
Morpeth
Dumfries
Hexham
Newcastle Upon Tyne
Corbridge
Sunderland
Carlisle
Durham
Middleton-in-Teesdale
Hartlepool
Cockermouth
Penrith
Barnard Castle
Middlesbrough
Whitehaven
Keswick
Appleby-in-Westmorland
Darlington
Grasmere
Goathland
Whitby
Hawkshead
Windermere
Richmond
Kendal
Helmsley
Scarborough
Thirsk
Flamborough Head
Barrow-in-Furness
Heysham
Ripon
Bridlington
Lancaster
Skipton
Harrogate
York
Clitheroe
Beverley
Burnley
Blackpool
Leeds
Kingston Upon Hull
Preston
Blackburn
Bradford
Halifax
Wakefield
Southport
Huddersfield
Scunthorpe
Bolton
Rochdale
Grimsby
Wigan
Manchester
Barnsley
Doncaster
Zeebrugge Rotterdam
Liverpool
Stockport
Sheffield
Chester
Lincoln

A Portrait of Great Britain

Britain has been assiduous *in preserving its traditions, but offers the visitor much more than stately castles and pretty villages. A diversity of landscape, culture, literature, art and architecture, as well as its unique heritage, results in a nation balancing the needs of the present with those of its past.*

Britain's character has been shaped by its geographical position as an island. Never successfully invaded since 1066, its people have developed their own distinctive traditions. The Roman invasion of AD 43 lasted 350 years but Roman culture and language were quickly overlain with those of the northern European settlers who followed. Ties with Europe were loosened further in the 16th century when the Catholic church was replaced by a less dogmatic established church.

Tudor rose

Although today a member of the European Union, Britain continues to delight in its non-conformity, even in superficial ways such as driving on the left-hand side of the road instead of the right. The opening of the rail tunnel to France is a topographical adjustment that does not necessarily mark a change in national attitude.

The British heritage is seen in its ancient castles, cathedrals and stately homes with their gardens and Classical parklands. Age-old customs are renewed each year, from royal ceremonies to Morris dancers performing on village greens.

For a small island, Great Britain encompasses a surprising variety in its regions, whose inhabitants maintain distinct identities. Scotland and Wales are separate countries from England with their own legislative assemblies.

Walking along the east bank of the River Avon, Bath

◁ Punting, a popular pastime on the River Cam, Cambridge

Widecombe-in-the-Moor, a Devon village clustered round a church and set in hills

They have different customs, traditions, and, in the case of Scotland, different legal and educational systems. The Welsh and Scots Gaelic languages survive and are sustained by their own radio and television networks. In northern and West Country areas, English itself is spoken in a rich variety of dialects and accents, and these areas maintain their own regional arts, crafts, architecture and food.

The landscape is varied, too, from the craggy mountains of Wales, Scotland and the north, through the flat expanses of the Midlands and eastern England to the soft, rolling hills of the south and west. The long, broad beaches of East Anglia contrast with the picturesque rocky inlets along much of the west coast.

Scottish coat of arms at Edinburgh Castle

Lake and gardens at Petworth House, Sussex

Despite the spread of towns and cities over the last two centuries, rural Britain still flourishes. Nearly three-quarters of Britain's land is used for agriculture. The main commercial crops are wheat, barley, sugar beet and potatoes, though what catches the eye in early summer are the fields of bright yellow rape or slate-blue flax.

The countryside is dotted with farms and charming villages, with picturesque cottages and lovingly tended gardens – a British passion. A typical village is built around an ancient church and a small, friendly pub. Here the pace of life slows. To drink a pint of ale in a cosy, village inn and relax before a fire is a time-honoured British custom. Strangers will be welcomed cordially, though perhaps with caution; for even if strict formality is a thing of the past, the British have a tendency to be reserved.

In the 19th and early 20th centuries, trade with the extensive British Empire, fuelled by abundant coal supplies, spurred manufacturing and created wealth. Thousands of people moved from the countryside to towns and cities near mines, mills and factories. By 1900 Britain was the world's strongest industrial nation. Now many of these old industrial centres have declined, and today manufacturing employs only 22 per cent of the labour force, while 66 per cent work in the growing service sector. These service industries are located mainly in the southeast, close to London, where modern office buildings bear witness to comparative prosperity.

Crowds at Petticoat Lane market in London's East End

Society and Politics

British cities are melting-pots for people not just from different parts of the country but also from overseas. Irish immigration has long ensured a flow of labour into the country, and since the 1950s hundreds of thousands have come from former colonies in Africa, Asia and the Caribbean, many of which are now members of the Commonwealth. Nearly five per cent of Britain's 58 million inhabitants are from non-white ethnic groups – and about half of these were born in Britain. The result is a multi-cultural society that can boast a wide range of music, art, food and religions. However, prejudice does exist and in some inner-city areas where poorer members of different communities live, racial tensions can occasionally arise. Even though discrimination in housing and employment on the grounds of race is against the law, it does occur in places.

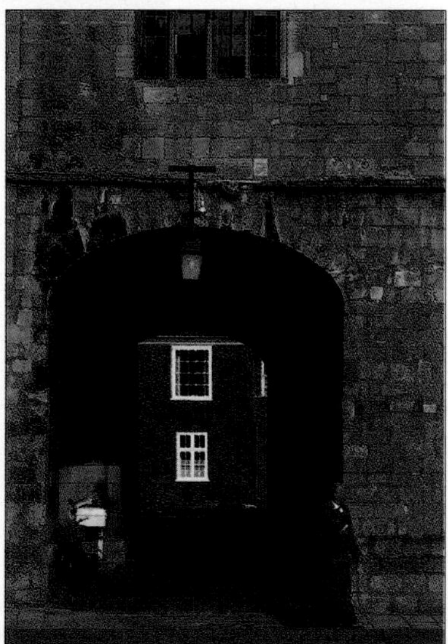
Priest in the Close at Winchester Cathedral

Britain's class structure still intrigues and bewilders many visitors, based as it is on a subtle mixture of heredity and wealth. Even though many of the great inherited fortunes no longer exist, some old landed families still live on their large estates, and many now open them to the public. Class divisions are further entrenched by the education system. While more than 90 per cent of children are educated free by the state, richer parents often opt for private schooling, and the products of these private schools are disproportionately represented in the higher echelons of government and business.

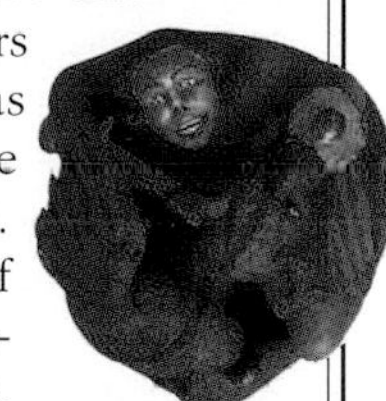
Bosses in Norwich Cathedral cloisters

The monarchy's position highlights the dilemma of a people seeking to preserve its most potent symbol of national unity in an age that is suspicious of inherited privilege. Without real political power, though still head of the Church of England, the Queen and her family are subject to increasing public scrutiny. Following a spate of personal scandals, some citizens advocate the abolition of the monarchy.

Democracy has deep foundations in Britain: there was even a parliament of sorts in London in the 13th century.

Yet with the exception of the 17th-century Civil War, power has passed gradually from the Crown to the people's elected representatives. A series of Reform Acts between 1832 and 1884 gave the vote to all male citizens, though women were not enfranchised on an equal basis until 1928. Margaret Thatcher – Britain's first woman Prime Minister – held office for 12 years from 1979. During the 20th century, the Labour (left wing) and Conservative (right wing) parties have, during their periods in office, favoured a mix of public and private ownership for industry and ample funding for the state health and welfare systems.

Afternoon tea on the back lawn at the Thornbury Castle Hotel, Avon

The position of Ireland has been an intractable political issue since the 17th century. Part of the United Kingdom for 800 years, but divided in 1921, it has seen conflict between Catholics and Protestants for many years. The Good Friday Peace Agreement of 1998 was a huge step forward but the path to lasting peace is a rocky one.

Culture and the Arts

Britain has a famous theatrical tradition stretching back to the 16th century and William Shakespeare. His plays have been performed on stage almost continuously since he wrote them and the works of 17th- and 18th-century writers are also frequently revived. Contemporary British playwrights such as Tom Stoppard, Alan Ayckbourn and David Hare draw on this long tradition with their vivid language and by using comedy to illustrate serious themes. British actors such as Vanessa Redgrave, Ian McKellen, Ralph Fiennes and Anthony Hopkins have international reputations.

The House of Lords, in Parliament

While London is the focal point of British theatre, fine drama is to be seen in many other parts of the country. The Edinburgh Festival and its Fringe are the high point of Great Britain's cultural calendar with theatre and music to suit all tastes. Other music festivals are held across the country, chiefly in summer, while there are annual festivals of literature at Hay-on-Wye and Cheltenham. Poetry has had an enthusiastic following since Chaucer wrote the *Canterbury Tales* in the 14th century: poems from all eras can even be read on the London Underground, where they are interspersed with the advertisements in the carriages and on the station platforms.

Schoolboys at Eton, the famous public school

In the visual arts, Britain has a strong tradition in portraiture, caricature, landscape and watercolour. In modern times David Hockney and Lucian Freud, and sculptors Henry Moore and Barbara Hepworth, have enjoyed worldwide recognition. Architects including

Reading the newspaper in Kensington Gardens

Christopher Wren, Inigo Jones, John Nash and Robert Adam all created styles that define British cities; and today, Norman Foster and Richard Rogers carry the standard for Post-Modernism. Britain is becoming famous for its innovative fashion designers, many of whom now show their spring and autumn collections in Paris.

The British are avid newspaper readers. There are 11 national newspapers published from London on weekdays: the standard of the broadsheets is very high and newspapers such as *The Times* are read the world over because of their reputation for strong international reporting. Most popular, however, are the tabloids packed with gossip, crime and sport, which account for some 80 per cent of the total.

Naomi Campbell, a British supermodel

The indigenous film industry, although squeezed by Hollywood, produces occasional international hits such as *Four Weddings and a Funeral* and *The Full Monty*. British television is famous for the high quality of its serious news, current affairs and nature programmes as well as for its drama. The publicly funded British Broadcasting Corporation (BBC), which controls five national radio networks and two terrestrial television channels, is widely admired.

The British are great sports fans, and soccer, rugby, cricket and golf are popular. An instantly recognizable English image is that of the cricket match on a village green. Nationwide, fishing is the most popular sporting pastime, and the British make good use of their national parks as keen walkers.

British food used to be derided for a lack of imagination. The cuisine relied on a limited range of quality ingredients, plainly prepared. But recent influences from abroad have introduced a wider range of ingredients and more adventurous techniques. Typical English food – plain home cooking and regional dishes – can still be found but they are being supplemented by a tastier modern British cuisine.

In this, as in other respects, the British are doing what they have done for centuries: accommodating their own traditions to influences from other cultures, while leaving the essential elements of their national life and character intact.

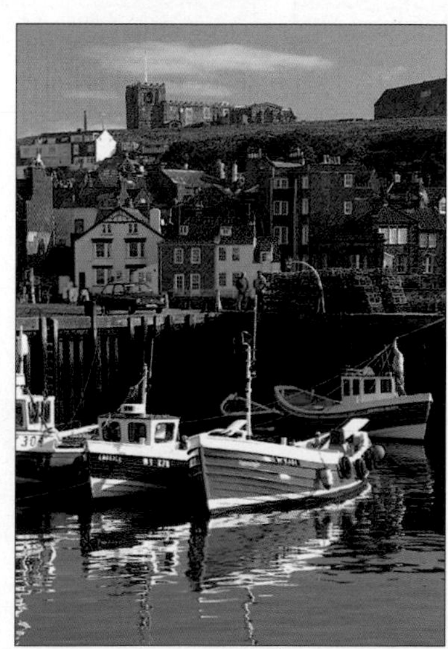

Whitby harbour and St Mary's Church, Yorkshire

Gardens Through the Ages

STYLES OF GARDENING in Britain have expanded alongside architecture and other evolving fashions. The Elizabethan knot garden became more elaborate and formal in Jacobean times, when the range of plants greatly increased. The 18th century brought a taste for large-scale "natural" landscapes with lakes, woods and pastures, creating the most distinctively English style to have emerged. In the 19th century, fierce debate raged between supporters of natural and formal gardens, developing into the eclecticism of the 20th century when "garden rooms" in differing styles became popular.

Capability Brown (1715–83) *was Britain's most influential garden designer, favouring the move away from formal gardens to man-made pastoral settings.*

Monumental column
A grotto and cascade brought romance and mystery.
Blackthorn
Classical temples were a much appreciated feature in 18th-century gardens and were often exact replicas of buildings that the designers had seen in Greece.
Maple
Winding paths were carefully planned to allow changing vistas to open out as visitors strolled around the garden.

Elaborate parterres *were a feature of aristocratic gardens of the 17th century, when the fashion spread from Europe. This is the Privy Garden at Hampton Court Palace, restored in 1995 to its design under William III.*

Ideal Landscape Garden

Classical Greece and Rome inspired the grand gardens of the early 18th century, such as Stourhead and Stowe. Informal clumps of trees played a critical part in the serene, manicured landscapes.

Design and Formality

A flower garden is a work of artifice, an attempt to tame nature rather than to copy it. Growing plants in rows or regular patterns, interspersed with statues and ornaments, imposes a sense of order. Designs change to reflect the fashion of the time and the introduction of new plants.

Medieval gardens usually had a herber (a turfed sitting area) and a vine arbour. A good reconstruction is Queen Eleanor's Garden, Winchester.

Tudor gardens featured edged borders and sometimes mazes. The Tudor House Garden, Southampton, also has beehives and heraldic statues.

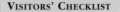

Herbaceous borders*, full of lush plants, are the glory of the summer garden. Gertrude Jekyll (1843–1932), was high priestess of the mixed border, with her eye for seductive colour combinations.*

The Palladian bridge was a favourite feature, often decorative rather than practical.

Knot Gardens *were in vogue in the 1500s. Intersecting lines of lavender or box were filled with flowers, herbs or vegetables, as in this restoration at Pitmedden in Scotland.*

VISITORS' CHECKLIST

The "yellow book", Gardens of England and Wales, *the annual guide to the National Gardens Scheme, lists gardens open to the public.*

DEVELOPMENT OF THE MODERN PANSY

All garden plants derive from wild flowers, bred over the years to produce qualities that appeal to gardeners. The story of the pansy, one of our most popular flowers, is typical.

The wild pansy *(Viola tricolor)* native to Britain is commonly known as heartsease. It is a small-flowered annual which can vary considerably in colour.

The mountain pansy (*Viola lutea)* is a perennial. The first cultivated varieties resulted from crossing it with heartsease in the early 19th century.

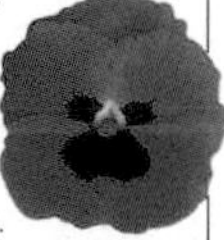

The Show Pansy was bred by florists after the blotch appeared as a chance seedling in 1840. It was round in form with a small, symmetrical blotch.

The Fancy Pansy, developed in the 1860s, was much larger. The blotch covered all three lower petals save for a thin margin of colour.

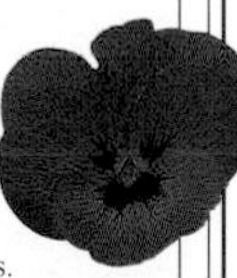

Modern hybrids of pansies, violas and violettas, developed by selective breeding, are varied and versatile in a wide range of vibrant new colours.

17th-century gardening was more elaborate. Water gardens like those at Blenheim were often combined with parterres of exotic foreign plants.

Victorian gardens, their formal beds a mass of colour, were a reaction to the landscapes of Capability Brown. Alton Towers has a good example.

20th-century gardens mix historic and modern styles, as at Hidcote Manor, Gloucestershire. Growing wild flowers is becoming a popular choice.

Stately Homes

Adam sketch (c.1760) for ornate panel

The grand country house reached its zenith in the 18th and 19th centuries, when the old landed families and the new captains of industry enjoyed their wealth, looked after by a retinue of servants. The earliest stately homes date from the 14th century, when defence was paramount. By the 16th century, when the opulent taste of the European Renaissance spread to England, houses became centres of pleasure and showplaces for fine art *(see pp290–91)*. The Georgians favoured chaste Classical architecture with rich interiors, the Victorians flamboyant Gothic. Due to 20th-century social change many stately homes have been opened to the public, some administered by the National Trust.

The saloon, a domed rotunda based on the Pantheon in Rome, was designed to display the Curzon family's Classical sculpture collection to 18th-century society.

The Drawing Room, the main room for entertaining, contains the most important pictures and some exquisite plasterwork.

The Marble Hall *is where balls and other social functions took place among Corinthian columns of pink alabaster.*

The Family Wing is a self-contained "pavilion" of private living quarters; the servants lived in rooms above the kitchen. The Curzon family still live here.

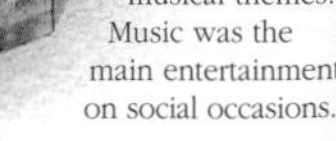

The Music Room is decorated with musical themes. Music was the main entertainment on social occasions.

Timeline of Architects

1650 — 1750

Sir John Vanbrugh *(see p384)* was helped by **Nicholas Hawksmoor** (1661–1736) on Blenheim Palace *(see pp216–17)*

Colen Campbell (1676–1729) designed Burlington House *(see p83)*

William Kent (1685–1748) built Holkham Hall *(see p185)* in the Palladian style

Castle Howard (1702) by Sir John Vanbrugh

Robert Adam (1728–92), who often worked with his brother James (1730–94) was as famous for decorative details as for buildings

John Carr (1723–1807) designed the Palladian Harewood House *(see p396)*

Henry Holland (1745–1806) designed the Neo-Classical south range of Woburn Abbey *(see p218)*

Adam fireplace, Kedleston Hall, adorned with Classical motifs

NATIONAL TRUST

National Trust oak leaf design

At the end of the 19th century, there were real fears that burgeoning factories, mines, roads and houses would obliterate much of Britain's historic landscape and finest buildings. In 1895 a group that included the social refomer Octavia Hill formed the National Trust, to preserve the nation's valuable heritage. The first building acquired by the trust was the medieval Clergy House at Alfriston in Sussex, in 1896 *(see p168)*. Today the National Trust is a charity that runs many historic houses and gardens, and vast stretches of countryside and coastline *(see p617)*. It is supported by more than two million members nationwide.

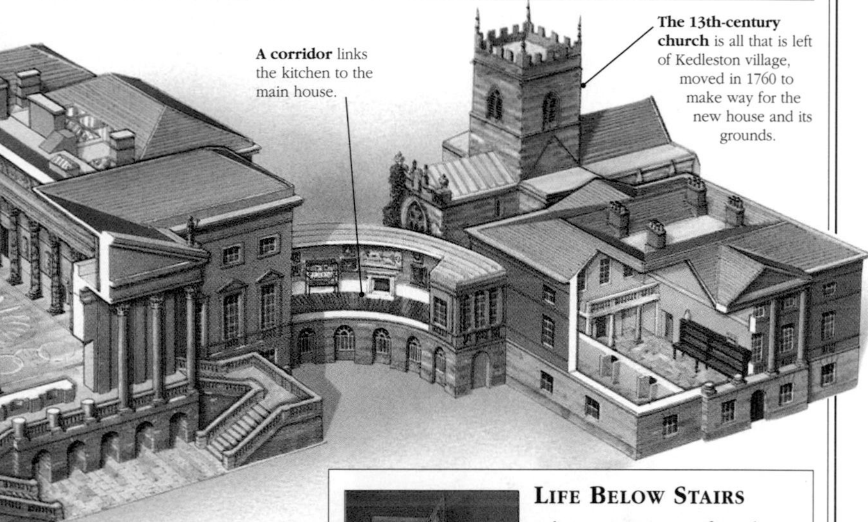

A corridor links the kitchen to the main house.

The 13th-century church is all that is left of Kedleston village, moved in 1760 to make way for the new house and its grounds.

KEDLESTON HALL

This Derbyshire mansion *(see p324)* is an early work of the influential Georgian architect Robert Adam, who was a pioneer of the Neo-Classical style derived from ancient Greece and Rome. It was built for the Curzon family in the 1760s.

LIFE BELOW STAIRS

***Life Below Stairs* by Charles Hunt (c.1890)**

A large community of resident staff was essential to run a country house smoothly. The butler was in overall charge, ensuring that meals were served on time. The housekeeper supervised uniformed maids who made sure the place was clean. The cook ran the kitchen, using fresh produce from the estate. Ladies' maids and valets acted as personal servants.

1800	1850

Dining Room, Cragside, Northumberland

Norman Shaw (1831–1912) was an exponent of Victorian Gothic, as in Cragside (above), and a pioneer of the Arts and Crafts movement *(see p316)*

Philip Webb (1831–1915) was a leading architect of the influential Arts and Crafts movement *(see p316)*, whose buildings favoured the simpler forms of an "Old English" style, instead of flamboyant Victorian Gothic

Sir Edwin Lutyens (1869–1944) designed the elaborate Castle Drogo in Devon *(see p283)*, one of the last grand country houses

Standen, West Sussex (1891–94) by Philip Webb

Heraldry and the Aristocracy

Order of the Garter medal

The British aristocracy has evolved over 900 years from the feudal obligations of noblemen to the Norman kings, who conferred privileges of rank and land in return for armed support. Subsequent monarchs bestowed titles and property on their supporters, establishing new aristocratic dynasties. The title of "earl" dates from the 11th century; that of "duke" from the 14th century. Soon the nobility began to choose their own symbols, partly to identify a knight concealed by his armour: these were often painted on the knight's coat (hence the term "coat of arms") and also copied onto his shield.

The College of Arms, London: housing records of all coats of arms and devising new ones

Royal Coat of Arms

The most familiar British coat of arms is the sovereign's. It appears on the royal standard, or flag, as well as on official documents and on shops that enjoy royal patronage. Over nearly 900 years, various monarchs have made modifications. The quartered shield in the middle displays the arms of England (twice), Scotland and Ireland. Surrounding it are other traditional images including the lion and unicorn, topped by the crown and the royal helm (helmet).

***Edward III** (1327–77) was the founder of the chivalric Order of the Garter. The garter, bearing the motto,* Honi soit qui mal y pense *(evil be to him who thinks of evil), goes round the central shield.*

The lion is the most common beast in heraldry.

The red lion is the symbol of Scotland.

The unicorn is a mythical beast, generally regarded as a Scottish royal beast in heraldry.

HONI SOIT QUI MAL Y PENSE

DIEU ET MON DROIT

***Henry II** (1154–89) formalized his coat of arms to include three lions. This was developed by his son Richard I to become the "Gules three lions passant guardant or" seen on today's arms.*

The royal helm with gold protective bars was introduced to the arms by Elizabeth I (1558–1603).

Dieu et mon droit (God and my right) has been the royal motto since the reign of Henry V (1413–22).

***Henry VII** (1485–1509) devised the Tudor rose, joining the white and red roses of York and Lancaster.*

Admiral Lord Nelson

When people are ennobled they may choose their own coat of arms if they do not already have one. Britain's naval hero (1758–1805) was made Baron Nelson of the Nile in 1798 and a viscount in 1801. His arms relate to his life and career at sea; but some symbols were added after his death.

A seaman supports the shield.

The motto means "Let him wear the palm (or laurel) who deserves it".

A tropical scene shows the Battle of the Nile (1798).

The San Joseph was a Spanish man o'war that Nelson daringly captured.

Tracing your Ancestry

Records of births, deaths and marriages in England and Wales since 1837 are at the **Family Records Centre,** 1 Myddelton St, London (020-8392 5300 Enquiries), and in Scotland at **New Register House**, Edinburgh (0131 334 0380). For help in tracing family history, consult **Society of Genealogists**, 14 Charterhouse Buildings, London (020-7251 8799).

***Inherited titles** usually pass to the eldest son or the closest male relative, but some titles may go to women if there is no male heir.*

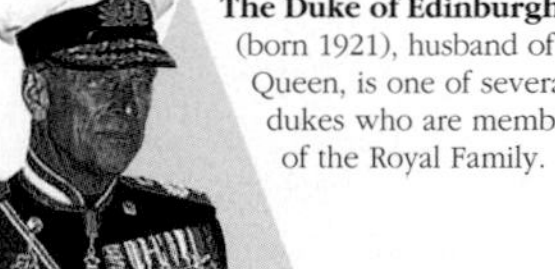

The Duke of Edinburgh (born 1921), husband of the Queen, is one of several dukes who are members of the Royal Family.

The Marquess of Salisbury (1830–1903), Prime Minister three times between 1885 and 1902, was descended from the Elizabethan statesman Robert Cecil.

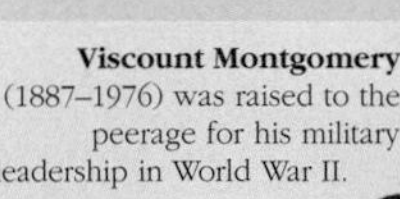

Earl Mountbatten of Burma (1900–79) was ennobled in 1947 for diplomatic and military services.

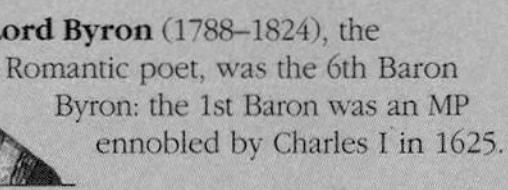

Viscount Montgomery (1887–1976) was raised to the peerage for his military leadership in World War II.

Lord Byron (1788–1824), the Romantic poet, was the 6th Baron Byron: the 1st Baron was an MP ennobled by Charles I in 1625.

Peers of the Realm

There are nearly 1,200 peers of the realm. In 1999 the process began to abolish the hereditary system in favour of life peerages which expire on the death of the recipient *(see left and below)*. All peers are entitled to sit in the House of Lords, including the Lords Spiritual – archbishops and senior bishops of the Church of England – and the Law Lords. In 1958 the Queen expanded the list of life peerages to honour people who had performed notable public service. From 1999 the system of "peoples peerages" began to replace inherited honours.

Key to the Peers

- 25 dukes
- 35 marquesses
- 175 earls and countesses
- 100 viscounts
- 800+ barons and baronesses

The Queen's Honours List

Twice a year several hundred men and women nominated by the Prime Minister and political leaders for outstanding public service receive honours from the Queen. Some are made dames or knights, a few receive the prestigious OM (Order of Merit), but far more receive lesser honours such as OBEs or MBEs (Orders or Members of the British Empire).

***Mother Theresa** received the OM in 1983 for her work in India.*

***Terence Conran,** founder of Habitat, was knighted for services to industry.*

***The Beatles** were given MBEs in 1965. Paul McCartney was knighted in 1997.*

Rural Architecture

FOR MANY, THE ESSENCE OF BRITISH LIFE is found in villages. Their scale and serenity nurture a way of life envied by those who live in towns and cities. The pattern of British villages dates back some 1,500 years, when the Saxons cleared forests and established settlements, usually centred around a green or pond. Most of today's English villages existed at the time of the *Domesday Book* in 1086, though few actual buildings survive from then. The settlements evolved organically around a church or manor; the cottages and gardens were created from local materials. Today, a typical village will contain structures of various dates, from the Middle Ages onward. The church is usually the oldest, followed perhaps by a tithe barn, manor house and cottages.

Abbotsbury, in Dorset – a typical village built up around a church

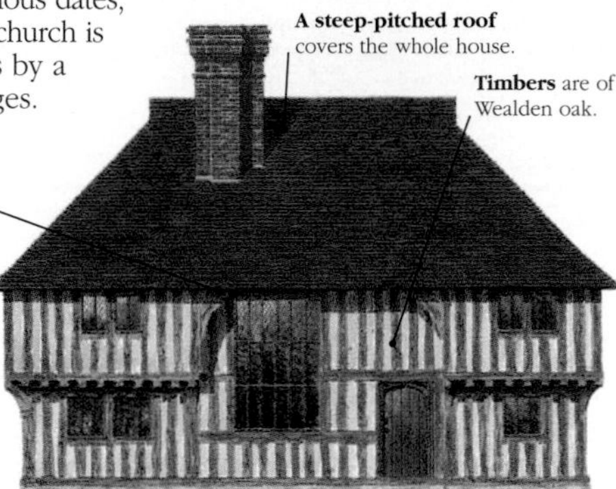

A steep-pitched roof covers the whole house.

Timbers are of Wealden oak.

Eaves are supported by curved braces.

Wealden Hall House *in Sussex is a medieval timber-framed house, of a type found in southeast England. It has a tall central open hall flanked by bays of two floors and the upper floor is "jettied", overhanging the ground floor.*

A tiled roof keeps the grain dry.

The entrance is big enough for ox-wagons.

Holes let in air – and birds.

Walls and doors are weatherboarded.

The medieval tithe barn *stored produce for the clergy – each farmer was required to donate one tenth (tithe) of his annual harvest. The enormous roofs may be supported by crucks, large curved timbers extending from the low walls.*

THE PARISH CHURCH

The church is the focal point of the village and, traditionally, of village life. Its tall spire could be seen – and its bells heard – by travellers from a distance. The church is also a chronicle of local history: a large church in a tiny village indicates a once-prosperous settlement. A typical church contains architectural features from many centuries, occasionally as far back as Saxon times. These may include medieval brasses, wall paintings, misericords *(see p329)*, and Tudor and Stuart carvings. Many sell informative guide books inside.

Slender spire from the Georgian era

West elevation

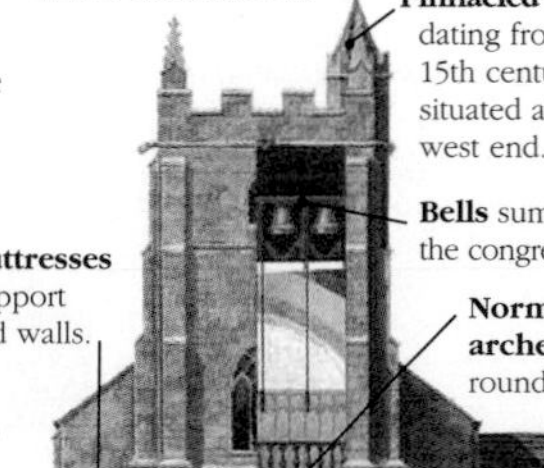

Pinnacled towers dating from the 15th century are situated at the west end.

Bells summon the congregation.

Buttresses support old walls.

Norman arches are rounded.

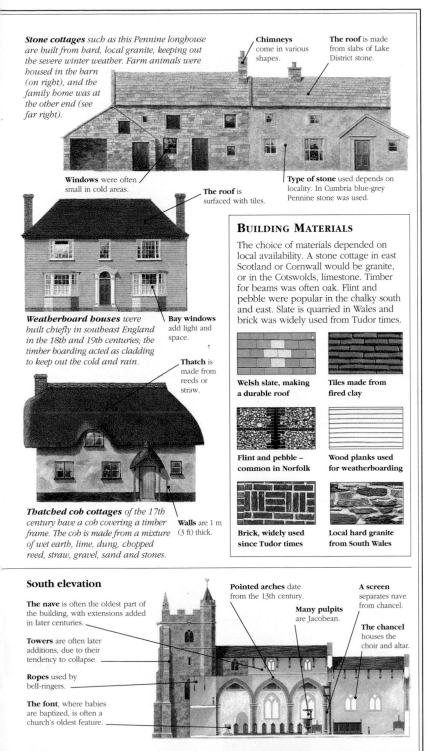

__Stone cottages__ such as this Pennine longhouse are built from hard, local granite, keeping out the severe winter weather. Farm animals were housed in the barn (on right), and the family home was at the other end (see far right).

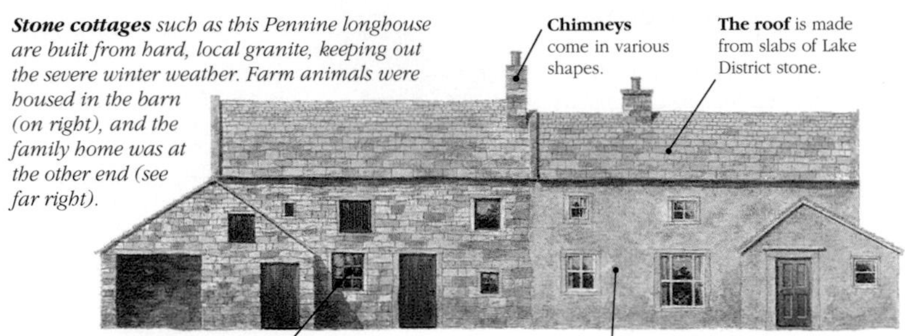

Chimneys come in various shapes.

The roof is made from slabs of Lake District stone.

Windows were often small in cold areas.

Type of stone used depends on locality. In Cumbria blue-grey Pennine stone was used.

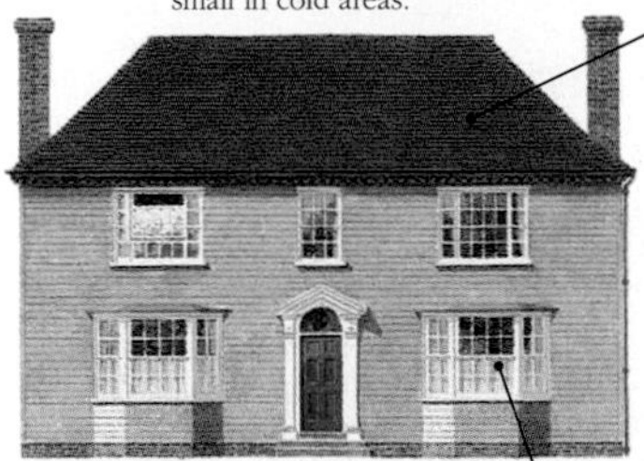

The roof is surfaced with tiles.

__Weatherboard houses__ were built chiefly in southeast England in the 18th and 19th centuries; the timber boarding acted as cladding to keep out the cold and rain.

Bay windows add light and space.

Thatch is made from reeds or straw.

__Thatched cob cottages__ of the 17th century have a cob covering a timber frame. The cob is made from a mixture of wet earth, lime, dung, chopped reed, straw, gravel, sand and stones.

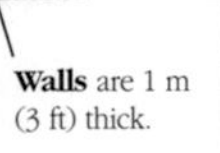

Walls are 1 m (3 ft) thick.

Building Materials

The choice of materials depended on local availability. A stone cottage in east Scotland or Cornwall would be granite, or in the Cotswolds, limestone. Timber for beams was often oak. Flint and pebble were popular in the chalky south and east. Slate is quarried in Wales and brick was widely used from Tudor times.

Welsh slate, making a durable roof

Tiles made from fired clay

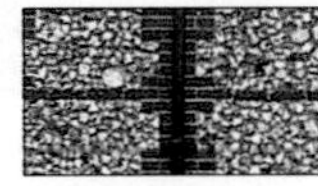

Flint and pebble – common in Norfolk

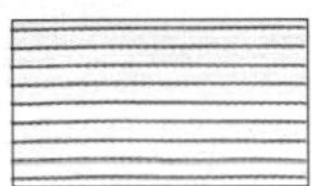

Wood planks used for weatherboarding

Brick, widely used since Tudor times

Local hard granite from South Wales

South elevation

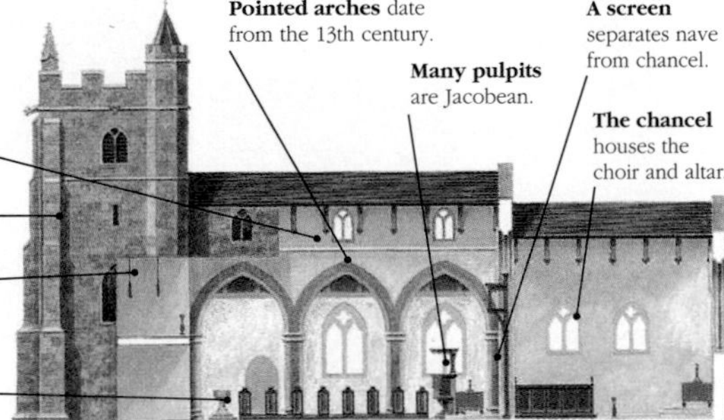

The nave is often the oldest part of the building, with extensions added in later centuries.

Towers are often later additions, due to their tendency to collapse.

Ropes used by bell-ringers.

The font, where babies are baptized, is often a church's oldest feature.

Pointed arches date from the 13th century.

Many pulpits are Jacobean.

A screen separates nave from chancel.

The chancel houses the choir and altar.

The Countryside

For its size, Britain contains an unusual variety of geological and climatic conditions that have shaped diverse landscapes, from treeless windswept moorland to boggy marshes and small hedged cattle pastures. Each terrain nurtures its typical wildlife and displays its own charm through the seasons. With the reduction in farming and the creation of footpaths and nature reserves, the countryside is becoming more of a leisure resource.

Common Blue butterfly

Indigenous Animals and Birds

There are no large or dangerous wild animals in Britain but a wealth of small mammals, rodents and insects inhabit the countryside, and the rivers and streams are home to many varieties of fish. For bird-watchers there is a great range of songbirds, birds of prey and seabirds.

Livestock graze on low pastures.

Trees provide shelter and protection for wildlife.

Higher land is uncultivated.

Wooded Downland

Chalk downland, seen here at Ditchling Beacon on the Downs *(see p169)*, has soil of low fertility and is grazed by sheep. However crops are sometimes grown on the lower slopes. Distinctive wild flowers and butterflies thrive here, while beech and yew predominate in the woods.

***Spear thistle** has pink heads in summer that attract several species of butterfly.*

***The dog rose** is one of Britain's best-loved wild flowers; its pink single flower is widely seen in hedgerows.*

***Hogweed** has robust stems and leaves with large clusters of white flowers.*

Bushes and trees grow between rocks.

Streams flow over a stony bed from mountain springs.

The highest ground is often covered in snow until spring.

Wild Hillside

Large tracts of Britain's uplands remain wild terrain, unsuitable for crops or forestry. Purple heather is tough enough to survive in moorland, the haunt of deer and game birds. The highest craggy uplands, such as the Cairngorms *(see p530–31)* in Scotland, pictured here, are the habitat of birds of prey, such as the golden eagle.

***Ling**, a low-growing heather with tiny pink bell-flowers, adds splashes of colour to peaty moors and uplands.*

***Meadow cranesbill** is a wild geranium with distinctive purple flowers.*

***Tormentil** has small yellow flowers. It prefers moist, acid soil and is found near water on heaths and moors in summer.*

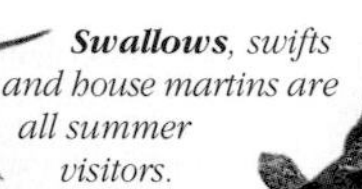

***Swallows**, swifts and house martins are all summer visitors.*

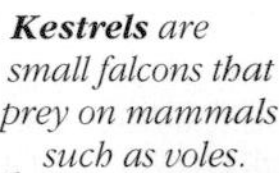

***Kestrels** are small falcons that prey on mammals such as voles.*

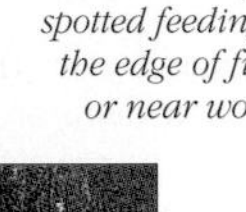

***Rabbits** are often spotted feeding at the edge of fields or near woods.*

***Robins**, common in gardens and hedgerows, have distinctive red breast feathers.*

***Foxes**, little bigger than domestic cats, live in hideaways in woods, near farmland.*

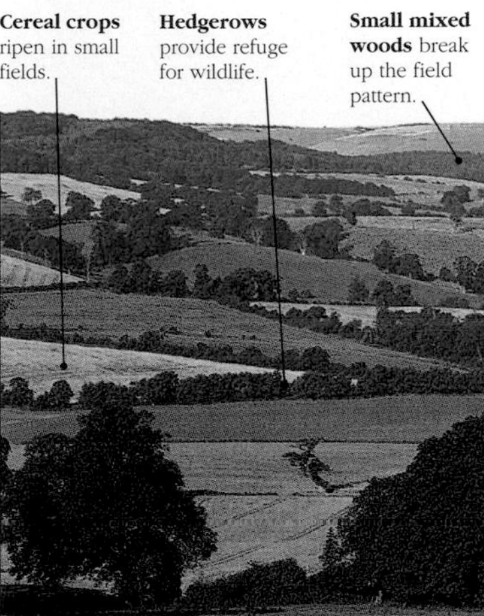
Cereal crops ripen in small fields.
Hedgerows provide refuge for wildlife.
Small mixed woods break up the field pattern.

TRADITIONAL FIELDS

The patchwork fields here in the Cotswolds *(see p292)* reflect generations of small-scale farming. A typical farm would produce silage, hay and cereal crops, and keep a few dairy cows and sheep in enclosed pastures. The tree-dotted hedgerows mark boundaries that may be centuries old.

Sheep graze on salty marshes.
Culverts drain water from the field.
Reed beds edge the water.

MARSHLAND

Flat and low-lying wetlands, criss-crossed with dykes and drainage canals, provide the scenery of Romney Marsh *(see also p170)* as well as much of East Anglia. Some areas have rich, peaty soil for crops, or salty marshland for sheep, but there are extensive uncultivated sections, where reed beds shelter wildlife.

***The oxeye daisy** is a larger relative of the common white daisy, found in grassland from spring to late summer.*

***Orchids** are among the rarer wild flowers. This species is the Common Spotted Orchid.*

***Cowslips** belong to the primrose family. In spring they are often found in the grass on open meadowlands.*

***Sea lavender** is a saltmarsh plant that is tolerant of saline soils. It flowers in late summer.*

***Poppies** glow brilliant red in cornfields.*

***Buttercups** are among the most common wild flowers. They brighten meadows in summer.*

Walkers' Britain

Walkers of all levels of ability and enthusiasm are well served in Britain. There is an unrivalled network of long-distance paths through some spectacular scenery, which can be tackled in stages with overnight stays en route, or dipped into for a single day's walking. For shorter walks, Britain is dotted with signposts showing public footpaths across common or private land. You will find books of walk routes in local shops and a large map will keep you on track. Choose river routes for easy walking or take to the hills for a greater challenge.

Walker resting on Scafell Pike, Lake District

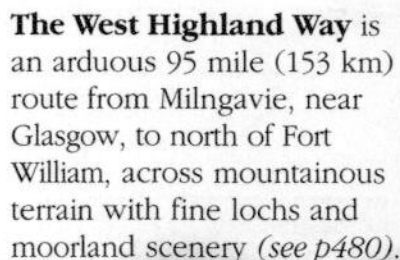

The West Highland Way is an arduous 95 mile (153 km) route from Milngavie, near Glasgow, to north of Fort William, across mountainous terrain with fine lochs and moorland scenery *(see p480)*.

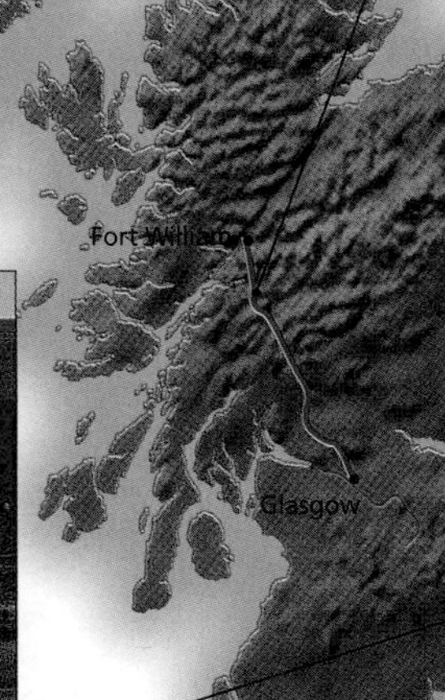

***The Pennine Way** was Britain's first designated long-distance path. The 256 mile (412 km) route from Edale in Derbyshire to Kirk Yetholm on the Scottish border is a challenging upland hike, with long, lonely stretches of moorland. It is only for experienced hill walkers.*

***Offa's Dyke Footpath** follows the boundary between Wales and England. The 168 mile (270 km) path goes through the beautiful Wye Valley* (see p447) *in the Welsh borders.*

Dales Way runs from Ilkley in West Yorkshire to Bowness-on-Windermere in the Lake District, 81 miles (130 km) of delightful flat riverside walking and valley scenery.

***Pembrokeshire Coastal path** is 186 miles (229 km) of rugged cliff-top walking from Amroth on Carmarthen Bay to the west tip of Wales at Cardigan.*

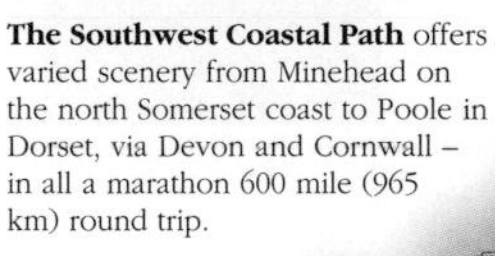

The Southwest Coastal Path offers varied scenery from Minehead on the north Somerset coast to Poole in Dorset, via Devon and Cornwall – in all a marathon 600 mile (965 km) round trip.

Ordnance Survey Maps

The best maps for walkers are published by the Ordnance Survey, the official mapping agency. Out of a wide range of maps the most useful are the green-covered *Pathfinder* series, on a scale of 1:25,000, and the *Landranger* series at 1:50;000. The *Outdoor Leisure and Explorer* series are maps of the more popular regions and cover a larger area.

Signposts

Long-distance paths are well signposted, some of them with an acorn symbol (or with a thistle in Scotland). Many shorter routes are marked with coloured arrows by local authorities or hiking groups. Local councils generally mark public footpaths with yellow arows. Public bridleways, marked by blue arrows, are paths that can be used by both walkers and horse riders – remember, horses churn up mud. Signs appear on posts, trees and stiles.

Tips for Walkers

Be prepared: *The weather can change very quickly: dress for the worst. Always take a compass, a proper walking map and get local advice before undertaking any ambitious walking. Pack some food and drink if the map does not show a pub en route.*
On the walk: *Always keep to the footpath and close gates behind you. Never feed or upset farm animals, leave litter, pick flowers or damage plants.*
Where to stay: *The International Youth Hostel Federation (see pp616–17) has a network of hostels which cater particularly for walkers. Bed-and-breakfast accommodation is also available near most routes (see p539).*
Further information: *The Ramblers' Association (tel: 020-7339 8500) is a national organization for walkers, with a magazine and a guide to accommodation.*

The Coast to Coast Walk *crosses the Lake District, Yorkshire Dales and North York Moors, on a 190 mile (306 km) route. This demanding walk covers a spectacular range of North Country landscapes. All cross-country routes are best walked from west to east to take advantage of the prevailing wind.*

The Ridgeway *is a fairly easy path that follows an ancient track once used by cattle drovers. Starting near Avebury* (see p251) *it covers 85 miles (137 km) to Ivinghoe Beacon.*

Peddars Way and the Norfolk Coast Path together make 94 miles (151 km) of easy lowland walking, from Thetford, north to the coast then east to Cromer.

Icknield Way, the most ancient prehistoric road in Britain, is 105 miles (168 km) long and links the Ridgeway to Peddars Way.

The Thames Path follows the river for 213 miles (341 km) from central London to Kemble, its source in Gloucestershire.

The South Downs Way *is a varied 106 mile (171 km) walk from Eastbourne on the south coast to Winchester* (see p158-9). *It can be completed in a week.*

The Isle of Wight Coastal Path circles the entire island on an easy 65 mile (105 km) footpath.

The North Downs Way is an ancient route through 141 miles (227 km) of low-lying hills from Farnham in Surrey to Dover or Folkestone in Kent.

The Traditional British Pub

Beer label c.1900

EVERY COUNTRY HAS ITS BARS, but Britain is famous for its pubs or "public houses". Ale was brewed in England in Roman times – mostly at home – and by the Middle Ages there were inns and taverns which brewed their own. The 18th century was the heyday of the coaching inn as stage coaches brought more custom. In the 19th century came railway taverns for travellers and "gin palaces" for the new industrial workers. Today, pubs come in all styles and sizes and many cater to families, serving food as well as drink *(see pp608–11)*.

Early 19th-century coaching inn – also a social centre and post office

The Victorian Pub

A century ago, many pubs in towns and cities had smart interiors, to contrast with the poor housing of their clients.

***Pub games**, such as cribbage, bar billiards, pool and dominoes are part of British pub culture. Here some regular customers are competing against a rival pub's darts team.*

***Beer gardens** outside pubs are a favourite venue for family summer treats.*

Pint glasses (containing just over half a litre) are used for beer.

The Red Lion pub name is derived from Scottish heraldry *(see p26)*.

Elaborately etched glass is a feature of many Victorian interiors.

Old-fashioned cash register contributes to the period atmosphere of the bar.

Pewter tankards, seldom used by drinkers today, add a traditional touch.

What to Drink

Draught bitter is the most traditional British beer. Brewed from malted barley, hops, yeast and water, and usually matured in a wooden cask, it varies from region to region. In the north of England the sweeter mild ale is popular, and lagers served in bottles or on tap are also widely drunk. Stout, made from black malt, is another variation.

Beer pump

Draught bitter is drunk at room temperature.

Draught lager is a light-coloured, carbonated beer.

Guinness is a thick, creamy Irish stout.

Pavement tables, crowded with city drinkers during the summer months

A village pub, offering a waterside view and serving drinks in the garden

Bottles of spirits, as well as the popular port and sherry, are ranged behind the bar.

Glass lamps imitate the Victorian style.

Wine, once rarely found in pubs, is now increasingly popular.

A deep-toned mahogany bar forms part of the traditional setting.

Draught beer, served from pumps or taps, comes from national and local brewers.

Optics dispense spirits in precise measures.

Mild may be served by the pint or in a half-pint tankard (as above).

Top cocktails are gin-and-tonic (right) and Pimm's.

PUB SIGNS

Early medieval inns used vines or evergreens as signs – the symbol of Bacchus, the Roman god of wine. Soon pubs acquired names that signalled support for monarchs or noblemen, or celebrated victories in battle. As many customers could not read, pub signs had vivid images.

The George *may derive from one of the six English kings of that name, or, as here, from England's patron saint.*

The Bat and Ball *celebrates cricket, and may be sited near a village green where the game can be played.*

The Green Man *is a woodland spirit from pagan mythology, possibly the basis for the legend of Robin Hood* (see p324).

The Magna Carta *sign commemorates and illustrates the "great charter" signed by King John in 1215* (see p48).

The Bird in Hand *refers to the ancient country sport of falconry, traditionally practised by noblemen.*

A Flavour of British Food

BRITAIN'S UNIQUE contributions to gastronomy include its cooked breakfasts, afternoon teas and satisfying puddings. Fast food and takeaways were pioneered here with fish and chips, the sandwich and the Cornish pasty. Modern British cuisine is innovative and varied, but it is also worth seeking out traditional dishes which use first-rate ingredients: beef, lamb and game figure prominently. As an island, Britain has historically been a fish-eating nation, although shellfish, once cheap, has become pricier.

Fish and chips *(French fries) are made from white sea fish, batter-coated and fried in oil, with chipped potatoes, salt and vinegar.*

A full English breakfast *can include fried bacon and egg, mushrooms, sausage, tomatoes, fried bread and black pudding.*

Cockles and whelks *remain cheap compared with larger shellfish. They are sold from small stalls outside pubs, and can be awkward to eat.*

Laverbread *is a Welsh speciality made from dark-coloured seaweed. It is served cold with seafood, or, as here, hot with bacon, toast and tomato.*

Cornish pasties *are filled with meat and vegetables baked in a pastry crust. They originated as a handy way for farm labourers to take their lunch to work.*

TEA TIME

Afternoon tea, taken at around 4pm, is a British tradition enacted daily in homes, tea-shops and grand hotels. The tea is usually from India or Sri Lanka, served with optional milk and sugar; but it could be scented China or herbal tea served with or without lemon. Small, delicately cut sandwiches are eaten first: fish paste and cucumber are traditional fillings. These may be followed by scones, jam and cream, especially in the west of England *(see p275)*. Other options include buttered toast or crumpets, but leave room for a slice of fruit cake or jam sponge, a chocolate éclair or a regional speciality such as Scottish shortbread.

Ploughman's lunch *is served in many pubs. It consists of bread, cheese (often Cheddar), and pickles, garnished with salad. Ham or pâté may be substituted for cheese.*

Roast beef *is Britain's traditional Sunday lunch. It usually comes with Yorkshire pudding (savoury batter baked with the meat), roast potatoes and seasonal vegetables. A rich gravy enhances the flavour, and horseradish sauce is a favourite relish.*

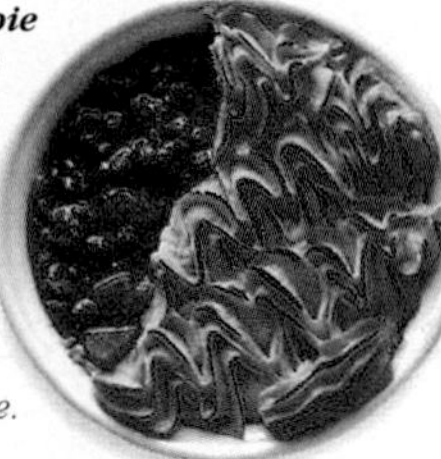

Shepherd's pie *is made from minced lamb baked with a potato topping. If minced (ground) beef is used, the dish is called cottage pie.*

Dover sole *is Britain's most prized flat fish. Served on the bone or filleted, it is firm fleshed and delicately flavoured.*

Cumberland sausage*, a regional speciality, is in a coil. Sausages and mashed potatoes are called "bangers and mash".*

Steak and kidney pie *is beef and kidney in thick gravy baked in pastry or in a suet crust, when it is known as a pudding.*

Strawberries and cream *are the delight of early summer, associated with outdoor social occasions of all types. Later, raspberries come into season. Both fruits make excellent jam.*

Cheese *is often served to finish lunch and dinner. Mature Cheddar is one of the most popular regional varieties. Blue-veined cheeses such as Stilton are an acquired taste.*

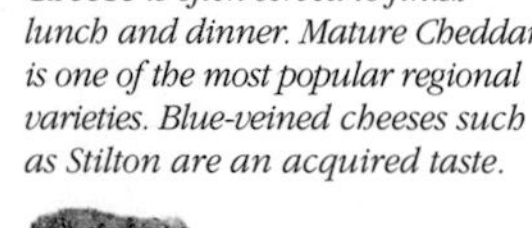

Stilton

Cheddar

Cornish Yarg

Sage Derby

Cheshire

Red Leicester

Treacle pudding *is a steamed sponge pudding, topped with syrup and served with custard. It is a popular dessert in winter.*

Sherry trifle *was originally sponge cake soaked in sweet sherry and served with custard. Modern versions may include sponge fingers covered with fruit, jelly and a layer of cream, and decorated with angelica and cherries.*

The History of Great Britain

Britain began to assume a cohesive character as early as the 7th century, with the Anglo-Saxon tribes absorbing Celtic and Roman influences and finally achieving supremacy. They suffered repeated Viking incursions and were overcome by the Normans at the Battle of Hastings in 1066. Over centuries, the disparate cultures of the Normans and Anglo-Saxons combined to form the English nation, a process nurtured by Britain's position as an island. The next 400 years saw English kings involved in military expeditions to Europe, but their control over these areas was gradually wrested from them. As a result they extended their domain over Scotland and Wales. The Tudor monarchs consolidated this control and laid the foundations for Britain's future commercial success. Henry VIII recognized the vital importance of sea power and under his daughter, Elizabeth I, English sailors ranged far across the world, often coming into conflict with the Spanish. The total defeat of the Spanish Armada in 1588 confirmed Britain's position as a major maritime power. The Stuart period saw a number of internal struggles, most importantly the Civil War in 1641. But by the time of the Act of the Union in 1707 the whole island was united and the foundations for representative government had been laid. The combination of this internal security with continuing maritime strength allowed Britain to seek wealth overseas. By the end of the Napoleonic Wars in 1815, Britain was the leading trading nation in the world. The opportunities offered by industrialization were seized, and by the late 19th century, a colossal empire had been established across the globe. Challenged by Europe and the rise of the US, and drained by its leading role in two world wars, Britain's influence waned after 1945. By the 1970s almost all the colonies had become independent Commonwealth nations.

Medieval knights, masters of the arts of war

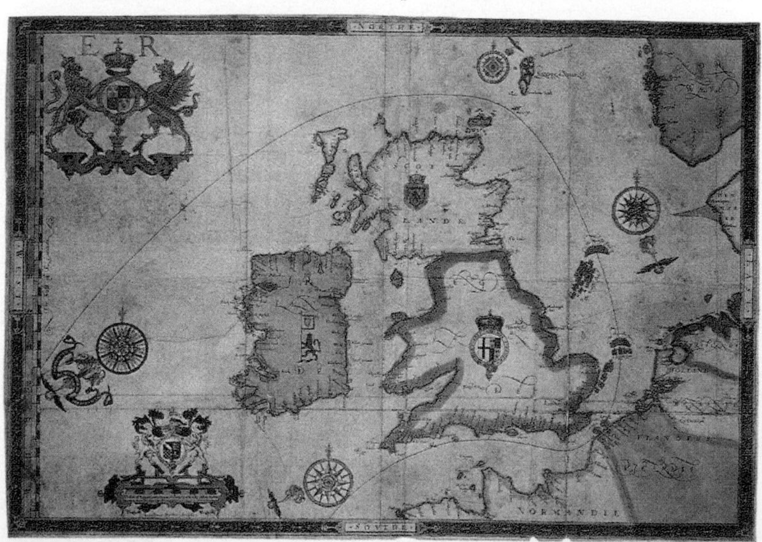

Contemporary map showing the defeat of the Armada (1588), making Britain into a world power

◁ **Henry VIII, founder of the British navy, seen here with his children Edward and Mary**

Kings and Queens

All English monarchs since the Norman Conquest in 1066 have been descendants of William the Conqueror. Scottish rulers, until James VI and the Union of Crowns in 1603 *(see pp468–9)*, have been more diverse. When the Crown passes to someone other than the monarch's eldest son, the name of the ruling family usually changes. The rules of succession have been precisely laid down and strongly favour men over women, but Britain has still had six queens since 1553. In Norman times the monarchy enjoyed absolute power, but today the position is largely symbolic.

Matthew Paris's 13th-century chronicle showing clockwise from top left, Richard I, Henry II, John and Henry III

1660–85 Charles II
1685–8 James II
1689–1702 William III and Mary II
1702–14 Anne
1714–27 George I
1553–8 Mary I
1603–25 James I
1727–60 George II
1837 1897
1837–1901 Victoria
1936 Edward VIII
1901–10 Edward VII
1952– Elizabeth II
50 1600 1650 1700 1750 1800 1850 1900 1950 2000
STUART
HANOVER
SAXE-COBURG
WINDSOR
50 1600 1650 1700 1750 1800 1850 1900 1950 2000
1830–37 William IV
1649–60 Commonwealth under Lord Protector Oliver Cromwell
1936–52 George VI shown on the George Medal
1820–30 George IV
1910–36 George V
1625–49 Charles I
1558–1603 Elizabeth I
1760–1820 George III
47–53 Edward VI

Prehistoric Britain

BRITAIN WAS PART of the European landmass until the end of the last Ice Age, around 6000 BC, when the English Channel was formed by melting ice. The earliest inhabitants lived in limestone caves: settlements and farming skills developed gradually through the Stone Age. The magnificent wooden and stone henges and circles are masterworks from around 3000 BC, but their significance is a mystery. Flint mines and ancient pathways are evidence of early trading and many burial mounds (barrows) survive from the Stone and Bronze Ages.

Axe Heads
Stone axes, like this one found at Stonehenge, were used by Neolithic men.

Cup and ring marks were carved on standing stones, such as this one at Ballymeanoch.

MAPPING THE PAST

Monuments from the Neolithic (New Stone), Bronze and Iron Ages, together with artifacts found from these periods, provide a wealth of information about Britain's early settlers, before written history began with the Romans.

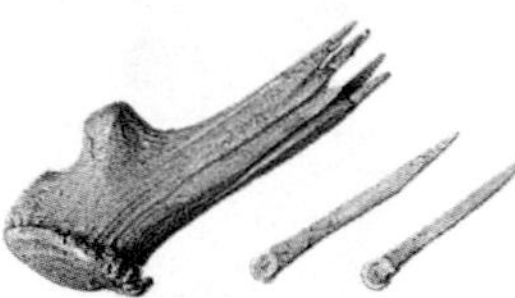

Neolithic Tools
Antlers and bones were made into Neolithic leather-working tools. These were found at Avebury (see p251).

Pottery Beaker
The Beaker People, who came from Europe in the early Bronze Age, take their name from these drinking cups often found in their graves.

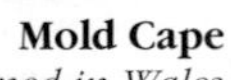

Gold Breast Plate
Made by Wessex goldsmiths, its spectacular pattern suggests it belonged to an important chieftain.

Pentre Ifan, an impressive Neolithic burial chamber in South Wales, was once covered with a huge earth mound.

Mold Cape
Gold was mined in Wales and Cornwall in the Bronze Age. This intricately worked warrior's cape was buried in a grave at Mold, Clwyd.

This gold cup, found in a Cornish barrow, is evidence of the wealth of Bronze Age tribes.

TIMELINE

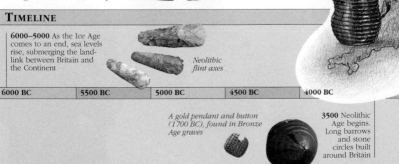

6000–5000 As the Ice Age comes to an end, sea levels rise, submerging the land-link between Britain and the Continent

Neolithic flint axes

6000 BC	5500 BC	5000 BC	4500 BC	4000 BC

A gold pendant and button (1700 BC), found in Bronze Age graves

3500 Neolithic Age begins. Long barrows and stone circles built around Britain

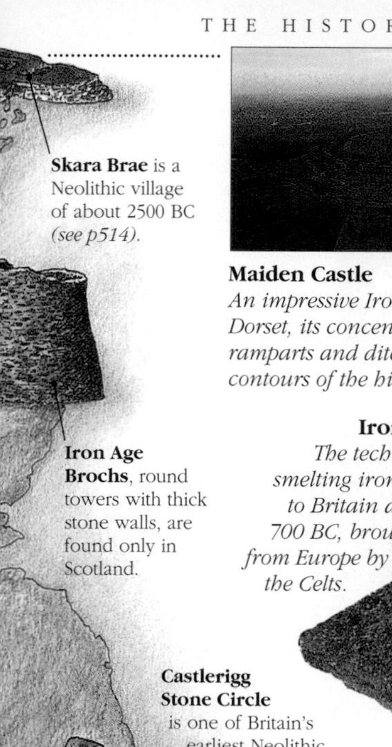

Skara Brae is a Neolithic village of about 2500 BC *(see p514)*.

Iron Age Brochs, round towers with thick stone walls, are found only in Scotland.

Maiden Castle
An impressive Iron Age hill fort in Dorset, its concentric lines of ramparts and ditches follow the contours of the hill top (see p257).

Iron Age Axe
The technique of smelting iron came to Britain around 700 BC, brought from Europe by the Celts.

Where to See Prehistoric Britain

Wiltshire, with Stonehenge *(p250)* and Avebury *(p251)*, has the best group of Neolithic monuments, and the Uffington White Horse is nearby *(p209)*. The Scottish islands have many early sites and the British Museum *(pp108–9)* houses a huge collection of artefacts.

A circular bank *with over 180 stones encloses the Neolithic site at Avebury* (see p251).

Castlerigg Stone Circle is one of Britain's earliest Neolithic monuments *(see p349)*.

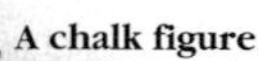

Uffington White Horse
Thought to be 3,000 years old, the shape has to be "scoured" to keep grass at bay (see p209).

A chalk figure, thought to be a fertility goddess, was found at Grimes Graves *(see p182)*.

This bronze Celtic helmet (50 BC) was found in the River Thames, London.

Stonehenge was begun around 3,500 years ago *(see pp250–51)*.

Snettisham Torc
A torc was a neck ring worn by Celtic men. This one, found in Norfolk, dates from 50 BC and is made from silver and gold.

2500 Temples, or henges, are built of wood or stone

2100–1650 The Bronze Age reaches Britain. Immigration of the Beaker People, who make bronze implements and build ritual temples

1650–1200 Wessex is at the hub of trading routes between Europe and the mines of Cornwall, Wales and Ireland

Chieftain's bronze sceptre (1700 BC)

1200 Small, self-sufficient villages start to appear

1000 First farmsteads are settled

550–350 Migration of Celtic people from southern Europe

500 Iron Age begins. Hill forts are built

150 Tribes from Gaul begin to migrate to Britain

)00 BC | 2500 BC | 2000 BC | 1500 BC | 1000 BC | 500 BC

Roman Britain

Roman jasper seal

THROUGHOUT the 350-year Roman occupation, Britain was ruled as a colony. After the defeat of rebellious local tribes, such as Boadicea's Iceni, the Romans remained an unassimilated occupying power. Their legacy is in military and civil construction: forts, walls, towns and public buildings. Their long, straight roads, built for easy movement of troops, are still a feature of the landscape.

Cavalry Sports Helmet
Found in Lancashire, it was used in tournaments by horsemen. Cavalry races and other sports were held in amphitheatres near towns.

Silver Jug
This 3rd-century jug, the earliest known silver item with Christian symbols, was excavated near Peterborough.

Exercise corridor

Main baths

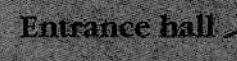
Entrance hall

Fishbourne Palace was built at the site of a natural harbour and ships could moor here.

Hadrian's Wall
Started in 120 as a defence against the Scots; it marked the northern frontier of the Roman Empire and was guarded by 17 forts housing over 18,500 foot-soldiers and cavalry.

Mithras
This head of the god Mithras was found on the London site of a temple devoted to the cult of Mithraism. The sect demanded of its Roman followers loyalty and discipline.

TIMELINE

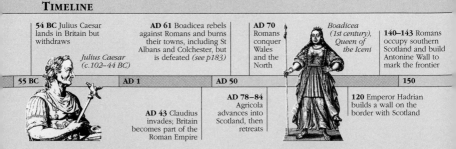

54 BC Julius Caesar lands in Britain but withdraws

AD 61 Boadicea rebels against Romans and burns their towns, including St Albans and Colchester, but is defeated *(see p183)*

AD 70 Romans conquer Wales and the North

140–143 Romans occupy southern Scotland and build Antonine Wall to mark the frontier

55 BC | AD 1 | AD 50 | 150

Julius Caesar (c.102–44 BC)

AD 43 Claudius invades; Britain becomes part of the Roman Empire

AD 78–84 Agricola advances into Scotland, then retreats

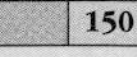
Boadicea (1st century), Queen of the Iceni

120 Emperor Hadrian builds a wall on the border with Scotland

Flavian Mosaic
Roman floors of the 1st century used patterns in black and white stone. More mosaics survive at Fishbourne than at any other British site.

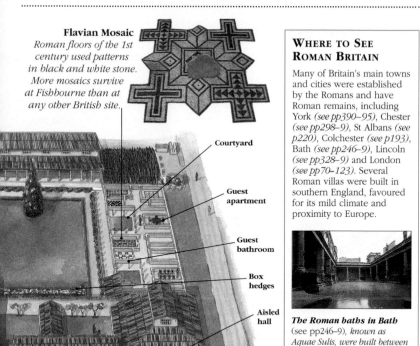

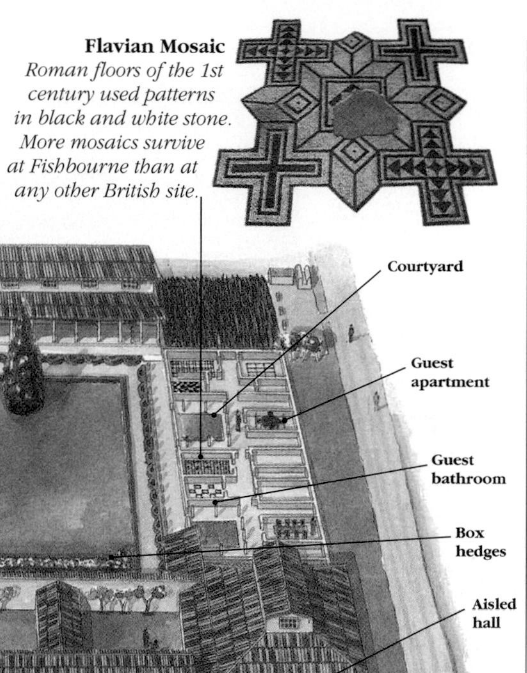

Fishbourne Palace

Built during the 1st century for Togidubnus, a pro-Roman governor, the palace (here reconstructed) had sophisticated functions such as underfloor heating and indoor plumbing for baths *(see p159)*.

Where to See Roman Britain

Many of Britain's main towns and cities were established by the Romans and have Roman remains, including York *(see pp390–95)*, Chester *(see pp298–9)*, St Albans *(see p220)*, Colchester *(see p193)*, Bath *(see pp246–9)*, Lincoln *(see pp328–9)* and London *(see pp70–123)*. Several Roman villas were built in southern England, favoured for its mild climate and proximity to Europe.

The Roman baths in Bath (see pp246–9), *known as Aquae Sulis, were built between the 1st and 4th centuries around a natural hot spring.*

Battersea Shield
Found in the Thames near Battersea, the shield bears Celtic symbols and was probably made at about the time of the first Roman invasion. Archaeologists suspect it may have been lost by a warrior while crossing the river, or offered as a sacrifice to one of the many river gods. It is now at the British Museum (see pp108–9).

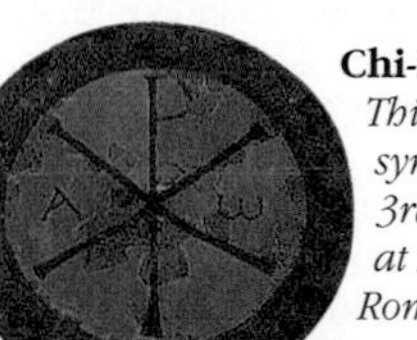

Chi-Rho Symbol
This early Christian symbol is from a 3rd-century fresco at Lullingstone Roman villa in Kent.

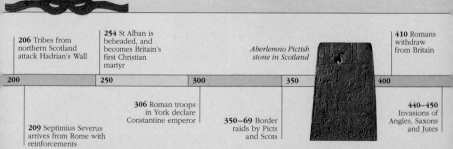

206 Tribes from northern Scotland attack Hadrian's Wall

209 Septimius Severus arrives from Rome with reinforcements

254 St Alban is beheaded, and becomes Britain's first Christian martyr

306 Roman troops in York declare Constantine emperor

350–69 Border raids by Picts and Scots

Aberlemno Pictish stone in Scotland

410 Romans withdraw from Britain

440–450 Invasions of Angles, Saxons and Jutes

200 | 250 | 300 | 350 | 400

Anglo-Saxon Kingdoms

King Canute (1016–35)

By the mid-5th century, Angles and Saxons from Germany had started to raid the eastern shores of Britain. Increasingly they decided to settle, and within 100 years Saxon kingdoms, including Wessex, Mercia and Northumbria, were established over the entire country. Viking raids throughout the 8th and 9th centuries were largely contained, but in 1066, the last invasion of England saw William the Conqueror from Normandy defeat the Anglo-Saxon King Harold at the Battle of Hastings. William then went on to assume control of the whole country.

Viking Axe

The principal weapons of the Viking warriors were spear, axe and sword. They were skilled metal-workers with an eye for decoration, as seen in this axe-head from a Copenhagen museum.

Vikings on a Raiding Expedition

Scandinavian boat-building skills were in advance of anything known in Britain. People were terrified by these large, fast boats with their intimidating figureheads, which sailed up the Thames and along the coasts.

Anglo-Saxon Calendar

These scenes from a chronicle of seasons, made just before the Norman invasion, show life in late Anglo-Saxon Britain. At first people lived in small farming communities, but by the 7th century towns began to spring up and trade increased. Saxon kings were supported by nobles but most of the population were free peasants.

Timeline

450 | 500 | 550 | 600 | 650 | 700 | 750

450 Saxons first settle in Kent

c.470–495 Saxons and Angles settle in Essex, Sussex and East Anglia

c.556 Saxons move across Britain and set up seven kingdoms

563 St Columba lands on Iona

597 St Augustine sent by Rome to convert English to Christianity

St Augustine (d.604)

617–85 Supremacy of Northumbrian kingdom

635 St Aidan establishes a monastery on Lindisfarne

730–821 Supremacy of Mercia, whose king, Offa (d.796), builds a dyke along the Mercia–Wales border

Mercian coin which bears the name of King Offa

Ox-drawn plough for tilling

Minstrels entertaining at a feast

Hawks, used to kill game

Harold's Death
This 14th-century illustration depicts the victorious William of Normandy after King Harold was killed with an arrow in his eye. The Battle of Hastings (see p169) *was the last invasion of Britain.*

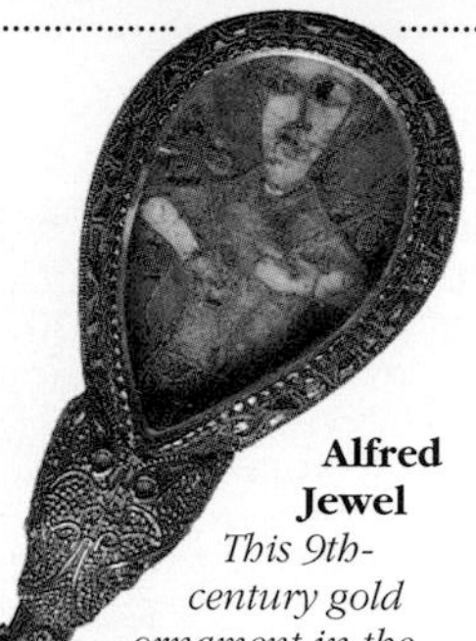

Alfred Jewel
This 9th-century gold ornament in the Ashmolean Museum (see p212) *has the inscription: "Alfred ordered me made". This may refer to the Saxon King Alfred.*

Edward the Confessor
In 1042, Edward – known as "the Confessor" because of his piety – became king. He died in 1066 and William of Normandy claimed the throne.

Where to See Anglo-Saxon Britain

The best collection of Saxon artefacts is from a burial ship unearthed at Sutton Hoo in Suffolk in 1938 and now on display at the British Museum *(see pp108–9)*. There are fine Saxon churches at Bradwell in Essex and Bosham in Sussex *(see p159)*. In York the Viking town of Jorvik has been excavated *(see p394)* and actual relics are shown alongside models of people and dwellings.

***The Saxon church** of St Laurence* (see p243) *was built in the late 8th century.*

Legend of King Arthur
Arthur is thought to have been a chieftain who fought the Saxons in the early 6th century. Legends of his knights' exploits appeared in 1155 (see p273).

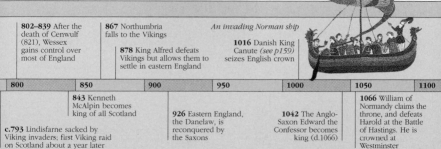

An invading Norman ship

802–839 After the death of Cenwulf (821), Wessex gains control over most of England

867 Northumbria falls to the Vikings

878 King Alfred defeats Vikings but allows them to settle in eastern England

1016 Danish King Canute *(see p159)* seizes English crown

800 | 850 | 900 | 950 | 1000 | 1050 | 1100

c.793 Lindisfarne sacked by Viking invaders; first Viking raid on Scotland about a year later

843 Kenneth McAlpin becomes king of all Scotland

926 Eastern England, the Danelaw, is reconquered by the Saxons

1042 The Anglo-Saxon Edward the Confessor becomes king (d.1066)

1066 William of Normandy claims the throne, and defeats Harold at the Battle of Hastings. He is crowned at Westminster

The Middle Ages

Noblemen stag hunting

REMAINS OF Norman castles on English hill tops bear testimony to the military might used by the invaders to sustain their conquest – although Wales and Scotland resisted for centuries. The Normans operated a feudal system, creating an aristocracy that treated native Anglo-Saxons as serfs. The ruling class spoke French until the 13th century, when it mixed with the Old English used by the peasants. The medieval church's power is shown in the cathedrals that grace British cities today.

Magna Carta
To protect themselves and the church from arbitrary taxation, the powerful English barons compelled King John to sign a "great charter" in 1215 (see p223). *This laid the foundations for an independent legal system.*

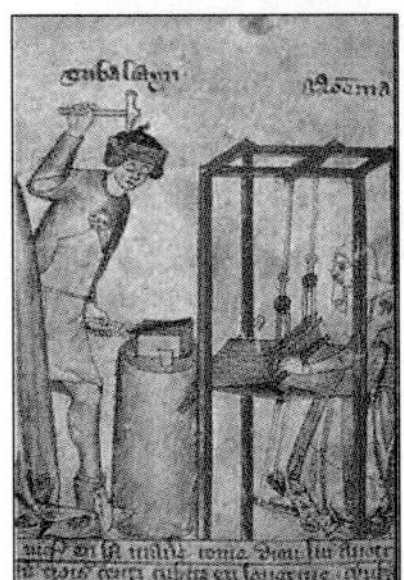

Craft Skills
An illustration from a 14th-century manuscript depicts a weaver and a copper-beater – two of the trades that created a wealthy class of artisans.

Becket is received into heaven.

Henry II's knights murder Becket in Canterbury Cathedral.

Murder of Thomas à Becket

The struggle between church and king for ultimate control of the country was brought to a head by the murder of Becket, the Archbishop of Canterbury. After Becket's canonization in 1173, Canterbury became a major centre of pilgrimage.

Ecclesiastical Art
Nearly all medieval art had religious themes, such as this window at Canterbury Cathedral (see pp174–5) *depicting Jeroboam.*

Black Death
A plague swept Britain and Europe several times in the 14th century, killing millions of people. This illustration, in a religious tract, produced around 100 years later, represents death taking its heavy toll.

Timeline

1071 Hereward the Wake, leader of the Anglo-Saxon resistance, defeated at Ely

1154 Henry II, the first Plantagenet king, demolishes castles, and exacts money from barons instead of military service

1170 Archbishop of Canterbury, Thomas à Becket, is murdered by four knights after quarrelling with Henry II

1100 | 1150 | 1200 | 1250

1086 The *Domesday Book*, a survey of every manor in England, is compiled for tax purposes

Domesday Book

1215 Barons compel King John to sign the *Magna Carta*

1256 Firs[t] Parliament t[o] includ[e] ordinar[y] citizen[s]

Battle of Agincourt
In 1415, Henry V took an army to France to claim its throne. This 15th-century chronicle depicts Henry beating the French army at Agincourt.

This casket (1190), in a private collection, is said to have contained Becket's remains.

Becket takes his place in Heaven after his canonization.

Two clergymen look on in horror at Becket's murder.

Richard III
Richard, shown in this 16th-century painting, became king during the Wars of the Roses: a bitter struggle for power between two factions of the royal family – the houses of York and Lancaster.

John Wycliffe *(1329–84)*
This painting by Ford Madox Brown (1821–93) shows Wycliffe with the Bible he translated into English to make it accessible to everyone.

Where to See Medieval Britain

The university cities of Oxford *(pp210–15)* and Cambridge *(pp198–203)* contain the largest concentrations of Gothic buildings. Magnificent cathedrals rise high above many historic cities, among them Lincoln *(pp326–7)* and York *(pp390–93)*. Both cities still retain at least part of their ancient street pattern. Military architecture is best seen in Wales *(pp424–5)* with the formidable border castles of Edward I.

***All Souls College** in Oxford* (see p214), *which only takes graduates, is a superb blend of medieval and later architecture.*

Castle Life
Every section of a castle was allotted to a baron whose soldiers helped defend it. This 14th-century illustration shows the coats of arms (see p26) *of the barons for each area.*

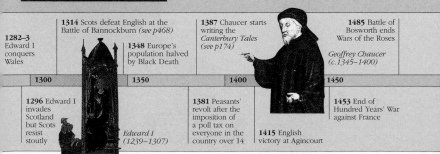

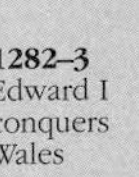

1282–3 Edward I conquers Wales

1296 Edward I invades Scotland but Scots resist stoutly

1300

1314 Scots defeat English at the Battle of Bannockburn *(see p468)*

Edward I (1239–1307)

1348 Europe's population halved by Black Death

1350

1381 Peasants' revolt after the imposition of a poll tax on everyone in the country over 14

1387 Chaucer starts writing the *Canterbury Tales (see p174)*

1400

Geoffrey Chaucer (c.1345–1400)

1415 English victory at Agincourt

1450

1453 End of Hundred Years' War against France

1485 Battle of Bosworth ends Wars of the Roses

Tudor Renaissance

Hawking, a popular pastime

AFTER YEARS OF DEBILITATING civil war, the Tudor monarchs established peace and national self-confidence, reflected in the split from the church of Rome – due to Henry VIII's divorce from Catherine of Aragon – and the consequent closure of the monasteries. Henry's daughter, Mary I, tried to re-establish Catholicism but under her half-sister, Elizabeth I, the Protestant church secured its position. Overseas exploration began, provoking clashes with other European powers seeking to exploit the New World. The Renaissance in arts and learning spread from Europe to Britain, with playwright William Shakespeare adding his own unique contribution.

Curtains behind the queen are open to reveal scenes of the great English victory over the Spanish Armada in 1588.

Sea Power
Henry VIII laid the foundations of the powerful English navy. In 1545, his flagship, the Mary Rose (see p157), *sank before his eyes in Portsmouth harbour on its way to do battle with the French.*

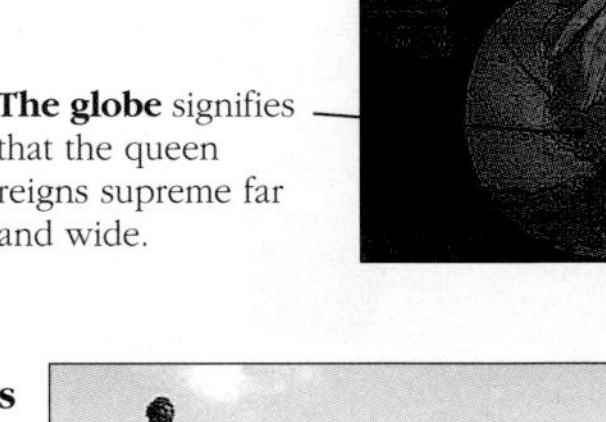

The globe signifies that the queen reigns supreme far and wide.

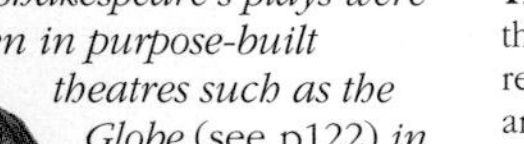

Theatre
Some of Shakespeare's plays were first seen in purpose-built theatres such as the Globe (see p122) *in south London.*

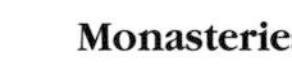

Monasteries
With Henry VIII's split from Rome, England's religious houses, like Fountains Abbey (see pp376–7), *were dissolved. Henry stole their riches and used them to finance his foreign policy.*

TIMELINE

1497 John Colet denounces the corruption of the clergy, supported by Erasmus and Sir Thomas More

1533–4 Henry VIII divorces Catherine of Aragon and is excommunicated by the Pope. He forms the Church of England

1542–1567 Mary, Queen of Scots rules Scotland

1490 | 1510 | 1530

1497 John Cabot *(see p244)* makes his first voyage to North America

1513 English defeat Scots at Flodden *(see p468)*

Henry VIII (1491–1547)

1535 Act of Union with Wales

1536–40 Dissolution of the Monasteries

1549 First Book o Common Praye introduce

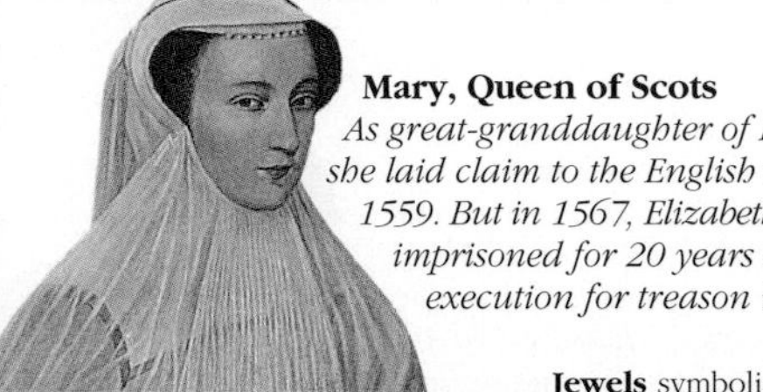

Mary, Queen of Scots
As great-granddaughter of Henry VII, she laid claim to the English throne in 1559. But in 1567, Elizabeth I had her imprisoned for 20 years until her execution for treason in 1587.

Jewels symbolize triumph.

Defeat of the Armada

Spain was England's main rival for supremacy on the seas, and in 1588 Philip II sent 100 powerfully armed galleons towards England, bent on invasion. The English fleet – under Lord Howard, Francis Drake, John Hawkins and Martin Frobisher – sailed from Plymouth and destroyed the Spanish navy in a famous victory. This commemorative portrait of Elizabeth I by George Gower (d.1596) celebrates the triumph.

Where to See Tudor Britain

Hampton Court Palace *(p161)* has been altered over the centuries but remains a Tudor showpiece. Part of Elizabeth I's former home at Hatfield *(p219)* still survives. In Kent, Leeds Castle, Knole *(pp176–7)* and Hever Castle *(p177)* all have connections with Tudor royalty. Burghley House *(pp330–31)* and Hardwick Hall *(p290)*, both Midlands mansions, retain their 16th-century character.

***This astronomical clock** at Hampton Court* (see p161), *with its intriguing zodiac symbols, was installed in 1540 by Henry VIII.*

Protestant Martyrs
Catholic Mary I reigned from 1553 to 1558. Protestants who opposed her rule were burned, such as these six churchmen at Canterbury in 1555.

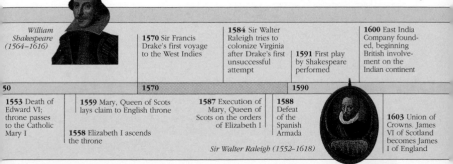

William Shakespeare (1564–1616)

1570 Sir Francis Drake's first voyage to the West Indies

1584 Sir Walter Raleigh tries to colonize Virginia after Drake's first unsuccessful attempt

1591 First play by Shakespeare performed

1600 East India Company founded, beginning British involvement on the Indian continent

50 | 1570 | 1590

1553 Death of Edward VI; throne passes to the Catholic Mary I

1558 Elizabeth I ascends the throne

1559 Mary, Queen of Scots lays claim to English throne

1587 Execution of Mary, Queen of Scots on the orders of Elizabeth I

1588 Defeat of the Spanish Armada

Sir Walter Raleigh (1552–1618)

1603 Union of Crowns. James VI of Scotland becomes James I of England

Stuart Britain

THE END of Elizabeth I's reign signalled the start of internal turmoil. The throne passed to James I, whose belief that kings ruled by divine right provoked clashes with Parliament. Under his son, Charles I, the conflict escalated into Civil War that ended with his execution. In 1660 Charles II regained the throne, but after his death James II was ousted for Catholic leanings. Protestantism was reaffirmed with the reign of William and Mary, who suppressed the Catholic Jacobites *(see p469)*.

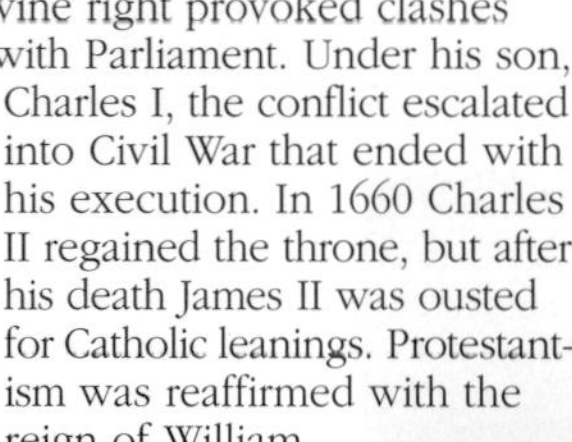

A 17th-century barber's bowl

Science
Sir Isaac Newton (1642–1727) invented this reflecting telescope, laying the foundation for a greater understanding of the universe, including the law of gravity.

Oliver Cromwell
A strict Protestant and a passionate champion of the rights of Parliament, he led the victorious Parliamentary forces in the Civil War. He became Lord Protector of the Commonwealth from 1653 to 1658.

Charles I stayed silent at his trial.

On the way to his death, the king wore two shirts for warmth, so onlookers should not think he was shivering with fright.

EXECUTION OF CHARLES I

Cromwell was convinced there would be no peace until the king was dead. At his trial for treason, Charles refused to recognize the authority of the court and offered no defence. He faced his death with dignity on 30 January 1649, the only English king to be executed. His death was followed by a republic known as the Commonwealth.

Theatre
After the Restoration in 1660, when Parliament restored the monarchy, theatre thrived. Plays were performed on temporary outdoor stages.

TIMELINE

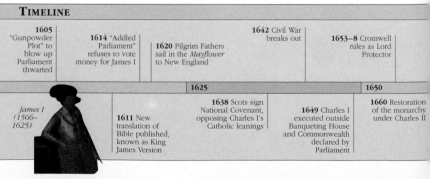

1605 "Gunpowder Plot" to blow up Parliament thwarted

1611 New translation of Bible published, known as King James Version

1614 "Addled Parliament" refuses to vote money for James I

1620 Pilgrim Fathers sail in the *Mayflower* to New England

1625

1638 Scots sign National Covenant, opposing Charles I's Catholic leanings

1642 Civil War breaks out

1649 Charles I executed outside Banqueting House and Commonwealth declared by Parliament

1650

1653–8 Cromwell rules as Lord Protector

1660 Restoration of the monarchy under Charles II

James I (1566–1625)

Restoration of the Monarchy
This silk embroidery celebrates the fact that Charles II escaped his father's fate by hiding in an oak tree. There was joy at his return from exile in France.

Where to See Stuart Britain

The best work of the two leading architects of the time, Inigo Jones and Christopher Wren, is in London, and includes St Paul's Cathedral *(pp116–17)*. In the southeast two classic Jacobean mansions are Audley End *(p196)* and Hatfield House *(p219)*. The Palace of Holyrood *(p496)*, in Edinburgh, is another example.

Hatfield House (p219) *is a splendid Jacobean mansion.*

The headless body kneels by the block.

The axeman holds the severed head of Charles I.

Onlookers soaked up the king's blood with their handkerchiefs to have a memento.

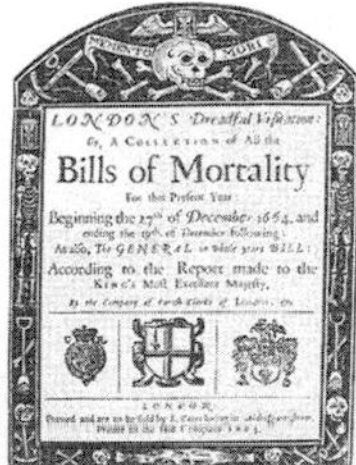

Plague
Bills of mortality showed the weekly deaths as bubonic plague swept London in 1665. Up to 100,000 Londoners died.

Anatomy
By dissecting corpses, physicians began to gain an understanding of the working of the human body – a crucial step towards modern surgery and medicine.

Pilgrim Fathers
In 1620 a group of Puritans sailed to America. They forged good relations with the native Indians; here they are shown being visited by the chief of the Pokanokets.

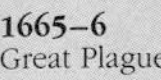

1665–6 Great Plague

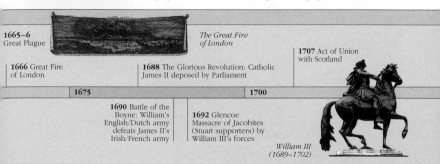

The Great Fire of London

1666 Great Fire of London

1675

1688 The Glorious Revolution: Catholic James II deposed by Parliament

1690 Battle of the Boyne: William's English/Dutch army defeats James II's Irish/French army

1692 Glencoe Massacre of Jacobites (Stuart supporters) by William III's forces

1700

1707 Act of Union with Scotland

William III (1689–1702)

Georgian Britain

Actress Sarah Siddons (1785), Gainsborough

THE 18TH CENTURY saw Britain, now recovered from the trauma of its Civil War, develop as a commercial and industrial powerhouse. London became a centre of banking, and a mercantile and professional class grew up. Continuing supremacy at sea laid the foundations of an empire; steam engines, canals and railways heralded the Industrial Revolution. Growing confidence was reflected in stately architecture and elegant fashions but, as cities became more crowded, conditions for the underclass grew worse.

Slate became the preferred tile for Georgian buildings. Roofs became less steep to achieve an Italian look.

A row of sash windows is one of the most characteristic features of a Georgian house.

Oak was used in the best dwellings for doors and stairs, but pine was standard in most houses.

The saloon was covered in wallpaper, a cheaper alternative to hanging walls with tapestries or fabrics.

The drawing room was richly ornamented and used for entertaining visitors.

The dining room was used for all family meals.

Steps led to the servants' entrance in the basement.

Battle of Bunker Hill
In 1775 American colonists rebelled against British rule. The British won this early battle in Massachusetts, but in 1783 Britain recognized the United States of America.

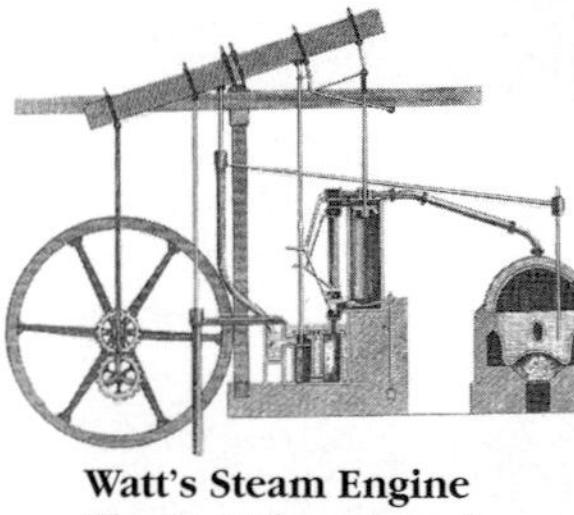

Watt's Steam Engine
The Scottish engineer James Watt (1736–1819) patented his engine in 1769 and then developed it for locomotion.

Lord Horatio Nelson
Nelson (see p27) *became a hero after his death at the Battle of Trafalgar fighting the French.*

TIMELINE

1714 George, Elector of Hanover, succeeds Queen Anne, ending the Stuart dynasty and giving Britain a German-speaking monarch

1715

1720 "South Sea Bubble" bursts: many speculators ruined in securities fraud

1721 Robert Walpole (1646–1745) becomes the first Prime Minister

George I (1660–1727)

1730

Satirical engraving about the South Sea Bubble, 1720

1745

1746 Bonnie Prince Charlie *(see p521)*, Jacobite claimant to throne, defeated at the Battle of Culloden

1757 Britain's first canal completed

1760

The attics were where children and servants slept.

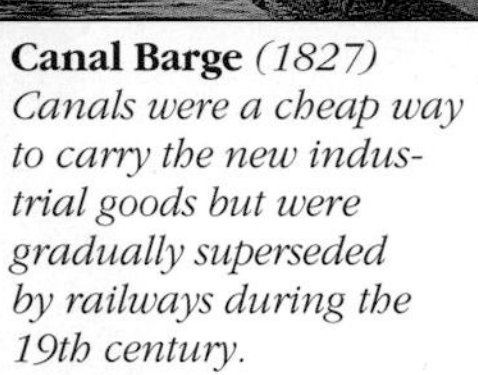

Canal Barge *(1827)*
Canals were a cheap way to carry the new industrial goods but were gradually superseded by railways during the 19th century.

WHERE TO SEE GEORGIAN BRITAIN

Bath *(see pp246–9)* and Edinburgh *(see pp490–7)* are two of Britain's best-preserved Georgian towns. The Building of Bath Museum in Bath *(see p249)* has a real Georgian flavour and Brighton's Royal Pavilion *(see pp166–7)* is a Regency extravaganza by John Nash.

Charlotte Square (see p490) *in Edinburgh has fine examples of Georgian architecture.*

The master bedroom often had a mahogany four-poster bed.

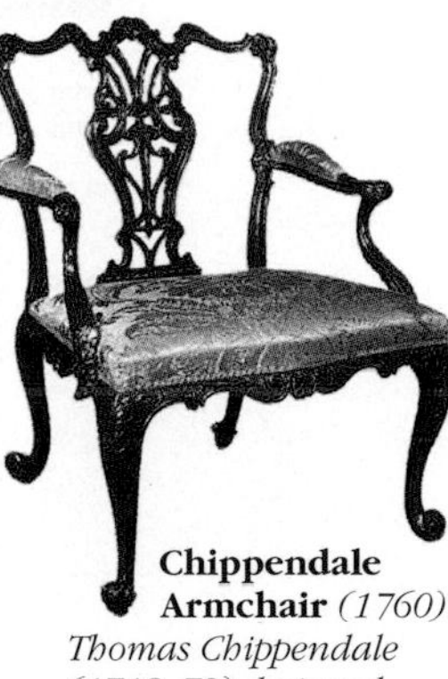

Chippendale Armchair *(1760)*
Thomas Chippendale (1718–79) designed elegant furniture in a style still popular today.

Furniture was often carved, depicting animal heads and legs.

Hogarth's Gin Lane
Conditions in London's slums shocked William Hogarth (1694–1764), who made prints like this to urge social reform.

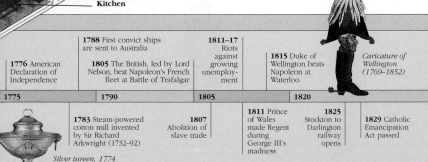

GEORGIAN TOWN HOUSE

Tall, terraced dwellings were built to house wealthy families. The main architects of the time were Robert Adam *(see p24)* and John Nash *(see p107)*.

The servants lived and worked in the basement during the day.

Kitchen

1775 | 1790 | 1805 | 1820

- **1776** American Declaration of Independence
- **1783** Steam-powered cotton mill invented by Sir Richard Arkwright (1732–92)
- **1788** First convict ships are sent to Australia
- **1805** The British, led by Lord Nelson, beat Napoleon's French fleet at Battle of Trafalgar
- **1807** Abolition of slave trade
- **1811** Prince of Wales made Regent during George III's madness
- **1811–17** Riots against growing unemployment
- **1815** Duke of Wellington beats Napoleon at Waterloo
- **1825** Stockton to Darlington railway opens
- **1829** Catholic Emancipation Act passed

Caricature of Wellington (1769–1852)

Silver tureen, 1774

Victorian Britain

When Victoria became Queen in 1837, she was only 18. Britain was in the throes of its transformation from an agricultural country to the world's most powerful industrial nation. The growth of the Empire fuelled the country's confidence and opened up markets for Britain's manufactured goods. The accelerating growth of cities created problems of health and housing and a powerful Labour movement began to emerge. But by the end of Victoria's long and popular reign in 1901, conditions had begun to improve as more people got the vote and universal education was introduced.

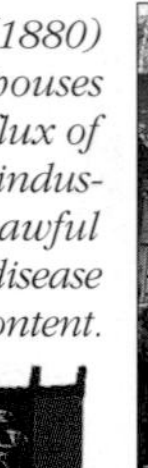

Victoria and Disraeli, 1887

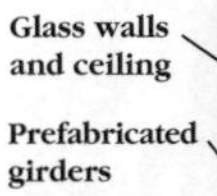

Florence Nightingale *(1820–1910)* *Known as the Lady with the Lamp, she nursed soldiers in the Crimean War and pioneered many improvements in army medical care.*

Newcastle Slum *(1880)* *Rows of cheap houses were built for an influx of workers to the major industrial cities. The awful conditions spread disease and social discontent.*

Union Banner *Trade unions were set up to protect industrial workers against unscrupulous employers.*

Glass walls and ceiling

Prefabricated girders

As well as silk textiles exhibits included carriages, engines, jewels, glass, plants, cutlery and sculptures.

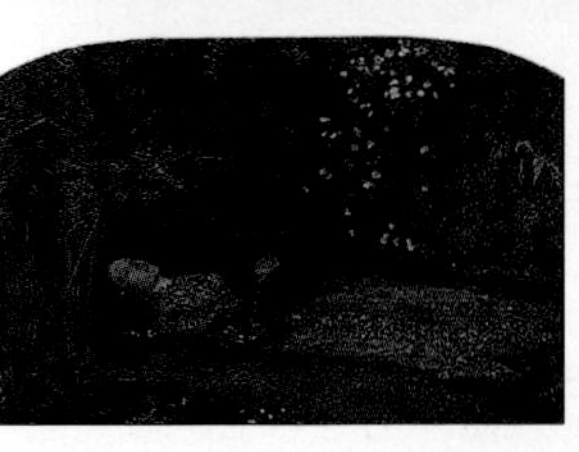

Ophelia by Sir John Everett Millais *(1829–96)* *The Pre-Raphaelite painters chose Romantic themes, reflecting a desire to escape industrial Britain.*

Timeline

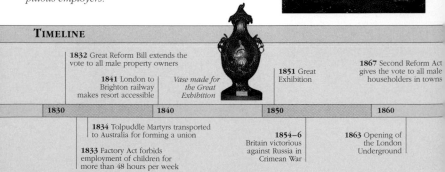

- 1830
- **1832** Great Reform Bill extends the vote to all male property owners
- **1833** Factory Act forbids employment of children for more than 48 hours per week
- **1834** Tolpuddle Martyrs transported to Australia for forming a union
- 1840
- **1841** London to Brighton railway makes resort accessible
- 1850
- **1851** Great Exhibition
- **1854–6** Britain victorious against Russia in Crimean War
- 1860
- **1863** Opening of the London Underground
- **1867** Second Reform Act gives the vote to all male householders in towns

Vase made for the Great Exhibition

Triumph of Steam and Electricity
This picture from the Illustrated London News *(1897) sums up the feeling of optimism engendered by industrial advances.*

Elm trees were incorporated into the building along with sparrows, and sparrow hawks to control them.

GREAT EXHIBITION OF 1851

The brainchild of Prince Albert, Victoria's consort, the exhibition celebrated industry, technology and the expanding British Empire. It was the biggest of its kind held up till then. Between May and October, six million people visited Joseph Paxton's lavish crystal palace, in London's Hyde Park. Nearly 14,000 exhibitors brought 100,000 exhibits from all over the world. In 1852 it was moved to south London where it burned down in 1936.

WHERE TO SEE VICTORIAN BRITAIN

The industrial cities of the Midlands and the North are built around grandiose civic, commercial and industrial buildings. Notable Victorian monuments include the Manchester Museum of Science and Industry *(p361)* and, in London, the vast Victoria and Albert Museum *(pp100–101)*.

The Rotunda, Manchester *is a stately Victorian building.*

Cycling Craze
The bicycle, invented in 1865, became immensely popular with young people, as illustrated by this photograph of 1898.

1870 Education Act makes school compulsory for children up to the age of 11

1872 The Ballot Act introduces secret voting

1874 Benjamin Disraeli becomes Prime Minister

1877 Queen Victoria created Empress of India

1884 Telephones introduced

Early telephone

1892 First Labour MP elected

1893 Gladstone's Irish Home Rule Bill defeated

1899–1902 Britain defeats South African Dutch settlers in Boer War

1901 Queen Victoria dies

Cartoon of Gladstone, Vanity Fair *(1869).*

Britain from 1900 to 1950

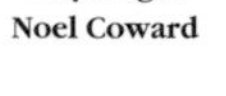

Playwright Noel Coward

When Queen Victoria's reign ended in 1901, British society threw off many of its 19th-century inhibitions, and an era of gaiety and excitement began. This was interrupted by World War I. The economic troubles that ensued, which culminated in the Depression of the 1930s, brought misery to millions. In 1939 the ambitions of Germany provoked World War II. After emerging victorious from this conflict, Britain embarked on an ambitious programme of social, educational and health reform.

Suffragettes
Women marched and chained themselves to railings in their effort to get the vote; many went to prison. Women over 30 won the vote in 1919.

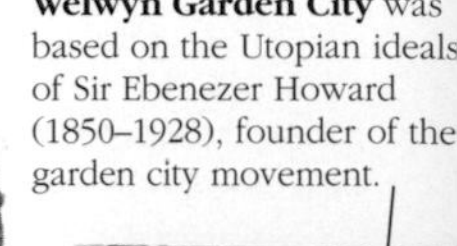

Welwyn Garden City was based on the Utopian ideals of Sir Ebenezer Howard (1850–1928), founder of the garden city movement.

The Roaring Twenties
Young flappers discarded the rigid social codes of their parents and instead discovered jazz, cocktails and the Charleston.

New Towns

A string of new towns was created on the outskirts of London, planned to give residents greenery and fresh air. Welwyn Garden City was originally founded in 1919 as a self-contained community, but fast rail links turned it into a base for London commuters.

World War I
British troops in Europe dug into deep trenches protected by barbed wire and machine guns, only metres from the enemy, in a war of attrition that cost the lives of 17 million.

Wireless
Invented by Guglielmo Marconi, radios brought news and entertainment into homes for the first time.

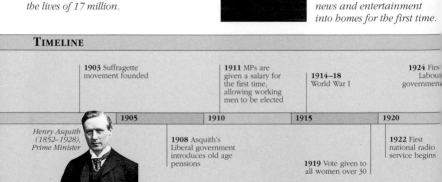

Timeline

1905 | 1910 | 1915 | 1920

1903 Suffragette movement founded

Henry Asquith (1852–1928), Prime Minister

1908 Asquith's Liberal government introduces old age pensions

1911 MPs are given a salary for the first time, allowing working men to be elected

1914–18 World War I

1919 Vote given to all women over 30

1922 First national radio service begins

1924 First Labour government

Marching for Jobs
These men were among thousands who marched for their jobs after being put out of work in the 1920s. The stock market crash of 1929 and the ensuing Depression caused even more unemployment.

Garden cities all had trees, ponds and open spaces.

Cheap housing and the promise of a cleaner environment attracted many people to these new cities.

World War II
German night-time air raids targeted transport, military and industrial sites and cities, such as Sheffield, in what was known as the "Blitz".

Modern Homes
Labour-saving devices, such as the vacuum cleaner, invented by William Hoover in 1908, were very popular. This was due to the virtual disappearance of domestic servants, as women took jobs outside the home.

Family Motoring
By the middle of the century, more families could afford to buy mass-produced automobiles, like the 1950s Hillman Minx pictured in this advertisement.

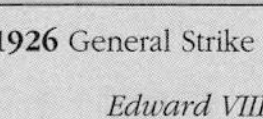

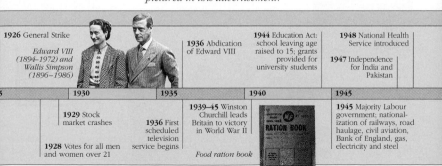

1926 General Strike

Edward VIII (1894–1972) and Wallis Simpson (1896–1986)

1928 Votes for all men and women over 21

1929 Stock market crashes

1930

1936 Abdication of Edward VIII

1936 First scheduled television service begins

1935

1939–45 Winston Churchill leads Britain to victory in World War II

1940

Food ration book

1944 Education Act: school leaving age raised to 15; grants provided for university students

1945

1945 Majority Labour government; nationalization of railways, road haulage, civil aviation, Bank of England, gas, electricity and steel

1947 Independence for India and Pakistan

1948 National Health Service introduced

Britain Today

WITH THE DEPRIVATIONS of war receding, Britain entered the Swinging Sixties, an explosion of youth culture characterized by the mini-skirt and the emergence of pop groups. The Age of Empire came to an end as most colonies gained independence by the 1970s – although Britain went to war again in 1982 when Argentina sought to annexe the tiny Falkland Islands.

People were on the move; immigration from the former colonies enriched British culture – though it also gave rise to social problems – and increasing prosperity allowed millions of people to travel abroad. Britain joined the European Community in 1973, and forged a more tangible link when the Channel Tunnel opened in 1994.

Designer Vivienne Westwood and Naomi Campbell

1960s The mini-skirt takes British fashion to new heights of daring – and Flower Power arrives from California

1951 Winston Churchill comes back as Prime Minister as Conservatives win general election

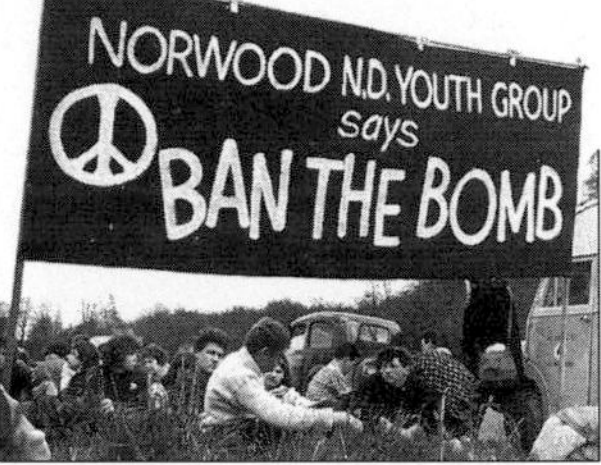

1958 Campaign for Nuclear Disarmament launched, reflecting young people's fear of global annihilation

1965 Death penalty is abolished

1950	1955	1960	1965	1970

1950	1955	1960	1965	1970

1953 Elizabeth II crowned in first televised Coronation

1951 Festival of Britain lifts postwar spirits

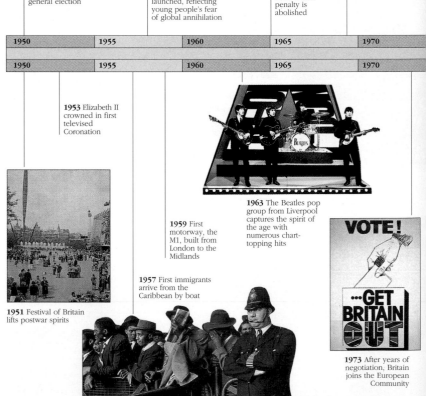

1963 The Beatles pop group from Liverpool captures the spirit of the age with numerous chart-topping hits

1959 First motorway, the M1, built from London to the Midlands

1957 First immigrants arrive from the Caribbean by boat

1973 After years of negotiation, Britain joins the European Community

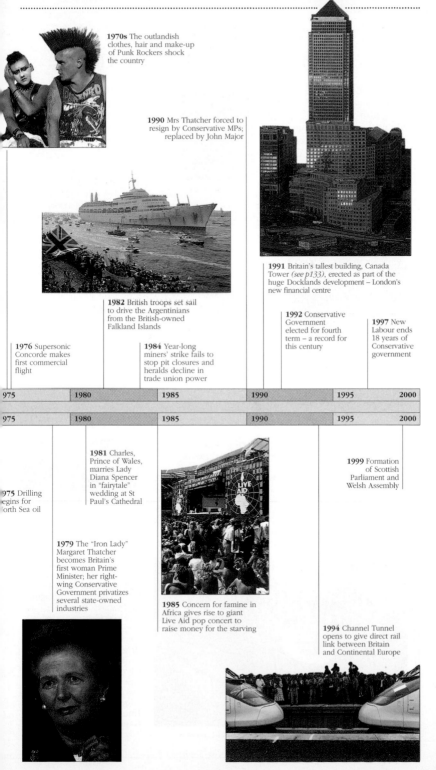

1970s The outlandish clothes, hair and make-up of Punk Rockers shock the country

1990 Mrs Thatcher forced to resign by Conservative MPs; replaced by John Major

1991 Britain's tallest building, Canada Tower *(see p133)*, erected as part of the huge Docklands development – London's new financial centre

1982 British troops set sail to drive the Argentinians from the British-owned Falkland Islands

1992 Conservative Government elected for fourth term – a record for this century

1997 New Labour ends 18 years of Conservative government

1976 Supersonic Concorde makes first commercial flight

1984 Year-long miners' strike fails to stop pit closures and heralds decline in trade union power

975 | 1980 | 1985 | 1990 | 1995 | 2000

975 | 1980 | 1985 | 1990 | 1995 | 2000

1981 Charles, Prince of Wales, marries Lady Diana Spencer in "fairytale" wedding at St Paul's Cathedral

1999 Formation of Scottish Parliament and Welsh Assembly

975 Drilling egins for orth Sea oil

1979 The "Iron Lady" Margaret Thatcher becomes Britain's first woman Prime Minister; her right-wing Conservative Government privatizes several state-owned industries

1985 Concern for famine in Africa gives rise to giant Live Aid pop concert to raise money for the starving

1994 Channel Tunnel opens to give direct rail link between Britain and Continental Europe

Great Britain Through the Year

Every British season has its particular charms. Most major sights are open all year round, but many secondary attractions may be closed in winter. The weather is changeable in all seasons and the visitor is as likely to experience a crisp, sunny February day as to be caught in a cold, heavy shower in July. Long periods of adverse weather and extremes of temperature are rare. Spring is characterized by daffodils and bluebells, summer by roses and autumn by the vivid colours of changing leaves. In wintertime, country vistas are visible through the bare branches of the trees. Annual events and ceremonies, many stemming from age-old traditions, reflect the attributes of the seasons.

Film festival sign

Bluebells in spring in Angrove woodland, Wiltshire

Spring

As the days get longer and warmer, the countryside starts to come alive. At Easter many stately homes and gardens open their gates to visitors for the first time, and during the week before Whit Sunday, or Whitsun (the seventh Sunday after Easter), the Chelsea Flower Show takes place. This is the focal point of the gardening year and spurs on the nation's gardeners to prepare their summer displays. Outside the capital, many music and arts festivals mark the middle months of the year.

March

Ideal Home Exhibition *(second week),* Earl's Court, London. New products and ideas for the home.
Crufts Dog Show *(second week),* National Exhibition Centre, Birmingham.
International Book Fair *(third week),* Olympia, London.
St Patrick's Day *(17 March).* Musical events in major cities celebrate the feast day of Ireland's patron saint.

Yeomen of the Guard conducting the Maundy money ceremony

April

Maundy Thursday (Thursday before Easter), the Queen gives money to pensioners.
St George's Day *(23 April),* English patron saint's day.
British International Antiques Fair *(last week),* National Exhibition Centre, Birmingham.

Water garden exhibited at the Chelsea Flower Show

May

Furry Dancing Festival *(8 May),* Helston, Cornwall. Spring celebration *(see p268).*
Well-dressing festivals *(Ascension Day),* Tissington, Derbyshire *(see p325).*
Chelsea Flower Show *(mid-May),* Royal Hospital, London.
Brighton Festival *(last three weeks).* Performing arts.
Glyndebourne Festival Opera Season *(mid-May–end Aug),* near Lewes, East Sussex. Opera productions.
International Highland Games *(last weekend),* Blair Atholl, Scotland.

SUMMER

LIFE MOVES OUTDOORS in the summer months. Cafés and restaurants place tables on the pavements and pub customers take their drinks outside. The Queen holds garden parties for privileged guests at Buckingham Palace while, more modestly, village fêtes – a combination of a carnival and street party – are organized. Beaches and swimming pools become crowded and office workers picnic in city parks at lunch. The rose, England's national flower, bursts into bloom in millions of gardens. Cultural treats include open-air theatre performances, outdoor concerts, the Proms in London, the National Eisteddfod in Wales, Glyndebourne's opera festival, and Edinburgh's festival of the performing arts.

Deck chair at Brighton

JUNE

Royal Academy Summer Exhibitions *(Jun–Aug)*. Large and varied London show of new work by many artists.
Bath International Festival *(19 May–4 Jun)*, various venues. Arts events.
Beaumaris Festival *(27 May–4 Jun)*, various venues. Concerts, craft fairs plus fringe activities.
Trooping the Colour *(Sat closest to 10 Jun)*, Whitehall, London. The Queen's official birthday parade.
Glastonbury Festival *(23–25 June)*, Somerset.
Aldeburgh Festival *(second and third weeks)*, Suffolk. Arts festival with concerts and opera.
Royal Highland Show *(third week)*, Ingliston, near Edinburgh. Scotland's agricultural show.
Leeds Castle *(last week)*. Open-air concerts.
Glasgow International Jazz Festival *(last weekend)*. Various venues.

Assessment of sheep at the Royal Welsh Show, Builth Wells

Glastonbury music festival, a major event attracting thousands of people

JULY

Royal Show *(first week)*, near Kenilworth, Warwickshire. National agricultural show.
International Eisteddfod *(first week)*, Llangollen, North Wales. International music and dance competition *(see p436)*.
Hampton Court Flower Show *(early July)*, Hampton Court Palace, Surrey.
Summer Music Festival *(third weekend)*, Stourhead, Wiltshire.
International Henley Royal Regatta *(first week)*, Henley-on-Thames. Rowing regatta on the Thames.
Cambridge Folk Festival *(last weekend)*. Music festival with top international artists.
Royal Welsh Show *(last weekend)*, Builth Wells, Wales. Agricultural show.
International Festival of Folk Arts *(late Jul–early Aug)*, Sidmouth, Devon *(see p277)*.

AUGUST

Royal National Eisteddfod *(early in month)*. Traditional arts competitions, in Welsh *(see p421)*. Various locations.

Reveller in bright costume at the Notting Hill Carnival

Henry Wood Promenade Concerts *(mid-Jul–mid-Sep)*, Royal Albert Hall, London. Famous concert series popularly known as the Proms.
Edinburgh International Festival *(mid-Aug–mid-Sep)*. The largest festival of theatre, dance and music in the world *(see p495)*.
Edinburgh Festival Fringe. Alongside the festival, there are 400 shows a day.
Brecon Jazz *(mid-Aug)*, jazz festival in Brecon, Wales.
Beatles Festival *(last weekend)*, Liverpool. Music and entertainment related to the Fab Four *(see p363)*.
Notting Hill Carnival *(last weekend)*, London. West Indian street carnival with floats, bands and stalls.

Boxes of apples from the autumn harvest

AUTUMN

AFTER THE HEADY escapism of summer, the start of the new season is marked by the various party political conferences held in October and the royal opening of Parliament. All over the country on 5 November, bonfires are lit and fireworks let off to celebrate the foiling of an attempt to blow up the Houses of Parliament by Guy Fawkes and his co-conspirators in 1605. Cornfields become golden, trees turn fiery yellow through to russet and orchards are heavy with apples and other autumn fruits. In churches throughout the country, thanksgiving festivals mark the harvest. The shops stock up for the run-up to Christmas, their busiest time of the year.

SEPTEMBER

Blackpool Illuminations *(beg Sep–end Oct).* A 5 mile (8 km) spectacle of lighting along Blackpool's seafront.
Royal Highland Gathering *(first Sat)*, Braemar, Scotland. Kilted clansmen from all over the country toss cabers, shot putt, dance and play the bagpipes. The royal family usually attends.
International Sheepdog Trials *(14–16 Sep)*, all over Britain, with venues changing from year to year.
Great Autumn Flower Show *(third weekend)*, Harrogate, N Yorks. Displays by nurserymen and national flower organizations.
Horse of the Year Show *(last weekend)*, Wembley, London *(see p67).*
Oyster Festival *(Sat at beginning of oyster season)*, Colchester. Lunch hosted by the mayor to celebrate the start of the oyster season.

Shot putting at Braemar

OCTOBER

Harvest Festivals *(whole month)*, all over Britain especially in farming areas.
Nottingham Goose Fair *(second weekend).* One of Britain's oldest traditional fairs now has a funfair.
Canterbury Festival *(second and third weeks).* Music, drama and the arts.
Aldeburgh Britten Festival *(third weekend).* Concerts with music by Britten *(see p189)* and other composers.
Hallowe'en *(31 Oct)*, "trick or treat" games countrywide.

Procession leading to the state opening of Parliament

NOVEMBER

Opening of Parliament *(Oct or Nov).* The Queen goes from Buckingham Palace to Westminster in a state coach, to open the new parliamentary session.
Lord Mayor's Procession and Show *(second Sat).* Parade in the City, London.
Remembrance Day *(second Sun).* Services and parades at the Cenotaph in Whitehall, London, and all over Britain.
RAC London to Brighton Veteran Car Rally *(first Sun).* A 7am start from Hyde Park, London to Brighton, East Sussex.
Guy Fawkes Night *(5 Nov)*, fireworks and bonfires all over the country.
London Film Festival *(first two weeks).* Forum for new films, various venues.
Regent Street Christmas Lights *(mid-Nov)*, London.

Fireworks over Edinburgh on Guy Fawkes Night

Winter landscape in the Scottish Highlands, near Glencoe

WINTER

BRIGHTLY COLOURED fairy lights and Christmas trees decorate Britain's principal shopping streets as shoppers rush to buy their seasonal gifts. Carol services are held in churches across the country, and pantomime, a traditional entertainment for children deriving from the Victorian music hall, fills theatres in major towns.

Brightly lit Christmas tree at the centre of Trafalgar Square

Many offices close between Christmas and the New Year. Shops reopen for the January sales on 27 December – a paradise for bargain-hunters.

DECEMBER

Christmas Tree *(first Thu)*, Trafalgar Square, London. The tree is donated by the people of Norway and is lit by the Mayor of Oslo; this is followed by carol singing.
Carol concerts *(whole month)*, all over Britain.
Grand Christmas Parade *(beg Dec)*, London. Parade with floats to celebrate myth of Santa Claus.
Midnight Mass *(24 Dec)*, in churches everywhere around Britain.
Allendale Baal Festival *(31 Dec)*, Northumberland. Parade by villagers with burning tar barrels on their heads to celebrate the New Year.

Sprig of holly

JANUARY

Hogmanay and **New Year** *(31 Dec, 1 Jan)*, Scottish celebrations. **Burns Night** *(25 Jan)*. Scots everywhere celebrate poet Robert Burns' birth with poetry, feasting and drinking.

FEBRUARY

Chinese New Year *(late Jan or early Feb)*. Lion dances, firecrackers and processions in Chinatown, London.

PUBLIC HOLIDAYS

New Year's Day (1 Jan).
2 Jan (Scotland only).
Easter weekend (March or April). In England it begins on **Good Friday** and ends on **Easter Monday**; in Scotland there is no Easter Monday holiday.
May Day (usually first Mon in May).
Late Spring Bank Holiday (last Mon in May).
Bank Holiday (first Mon in August, Scotland only).
August Bank Holiday (last Mon in August, except Scotland).
Christmas and Boxing Day (25–26 December).

Morris dancing on May Day in Midhurst, Sussex

The Sporting Year

MANY OF THE WORLD'S major competitive sports, including soccer, cricket and tennis, were invented in Britain. Originally devised as recreation for the wealthy, they have since entered the arena of mass entertainment. Some, however, such as the Royal Ascot race meeting and Wimbledon tennis tournament, are still valued as much for their social prestige as for the sport itself. Other delightful sporting events in Britain take place at a local level: village cricket, point-to-point racing and the Highland Games are all popular amateur events.

Ewan Thomas

Royal Ascot *is the four-day social highlight of the horse racing year. The high class of the thoroughbreds is matched by the high style of the fashions, with royalty attending*

Oxford and Cambridge Boat Race*, first held in 1829 at Henley, has become a national event, with the two university eights now battling it out between Putney and Mortlake on the Thames.*

The FA Cup Final *is the apex of the football season.*

Derby Day horse races, Epsom

January	February	March	April	May	June

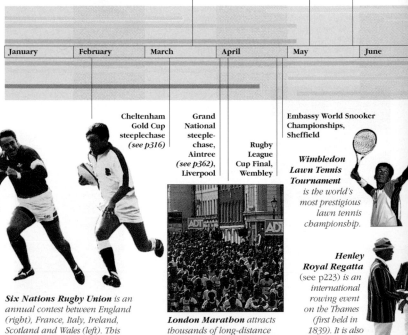

Cheltenham Gold Cup steeplechase *(see p316)*

Grand National steeplechase, Aintree *(see p362)*, Liverpool

Rugby League Cup Final, Wembley

Embassy World Snooker Championships, Sheffield

Six Nations Rugby Union *is an annual contest between England (right), France, Italy, Ireland, Scotland and Wales (left). This league-based competition runs through winter ending in March.*

London Marathon *attracts thousands of long-distance runners, from the world's best to fancy-dressed fund raisers.*

Wimbledon Lawn Tennis Tournament *is the world's most prestigious lawn tennis championship.*

Henley Royal Regatta (see p223) *is an international rowing event on the Thames (first held in 1839). It is also a glamorous social occasion.*

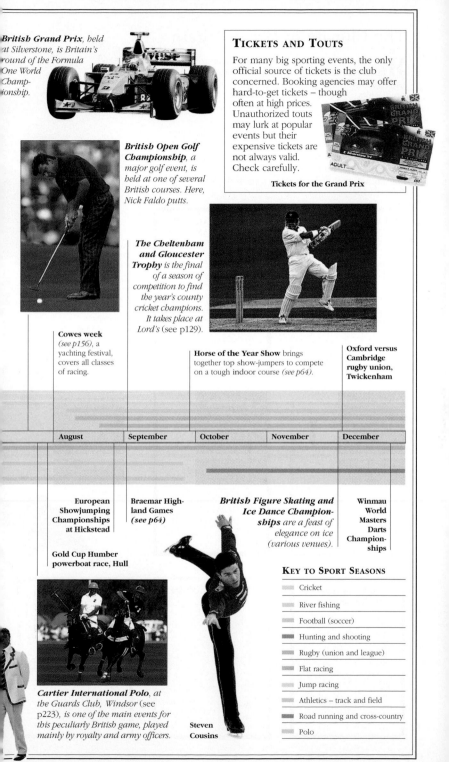

***British Grand Prix**, held at Silverstone, is Britain's round of the Formula One World Championship.*

Tickets and Touts

For many big sporting events, the only official source of tickets is the club concerned. Booking agencies may offer hard-to-get tickets – though often at high prices. Unauthorized touts may lurk at popular events but their expensive tickets are not always valid. Check carefully.

Tickets for the Grand Prix

***British Open Golf Championship**, a major golf event, is held at one of several British courses. Here, Nick Faldo putts.*

***The Cheltenham and Gloucester Trophy** is the final of a season of competition to find the year's county cricket champions. It takes place at Lord's* (see p129).

Cowes week *(see p156)*, a yachting festival, covers all classes of racing.

Horse of the Year Show brings together top show-jumpers to compete on a tough indoor course *(see p64)*.

Oxford versus Cambridge rugby union, Twickenham

August	September	October	November	December

European Showjumping Championships at Hickstead

Braemar Highland Games (see p64)

***British Figure Skating and Ice Dance Championships** are a feast of elegance on ice (various venues).*

Winmau World Masters Darts Championships

Gold Cup Humber powerboat race, Hull

***Cartier International Polo**, at the Guards Club, Windsor* (see p223), *is one of the main events for this peculiarly British game, played mainly by royalty and army officers.*

Steven Cousins

Key to Sport Seasons

- Cricket
- River fishing
- Football (soccer)
- Hunting and shooting
- Rugby (union and league)
- Flat racing
- Jump racing
- Athletics – track and field
- Road running and cross-country
- Polo

The Climate of Great Britain

Britain has a temperate climate. No region is far from the sea, which exerts a moderating influence on temperatures. Seldom are winter nights colder than -15°C, even in the far north, or summer days warmer than 30°C in the south and west: a much narrower range than in most European countries. Despite Britain's reputation, the average annual rainfall is quite low – less than 100 cm (40 inches) – and heavy rain is rare. The Atlantic coast is warmed by the Gulf Stream, making the west slightly warmer, though wetter, than the east.

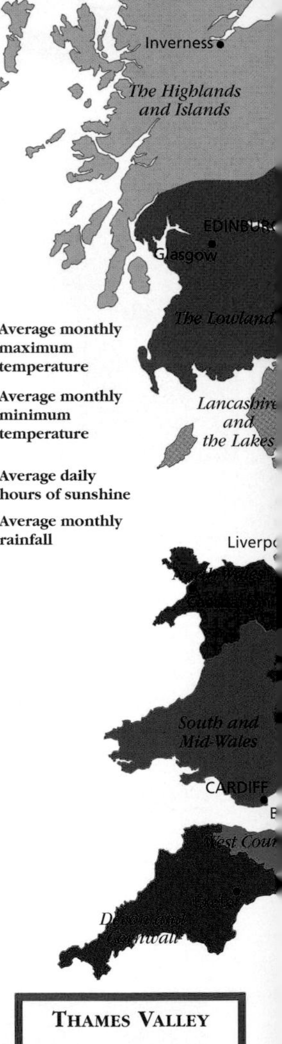

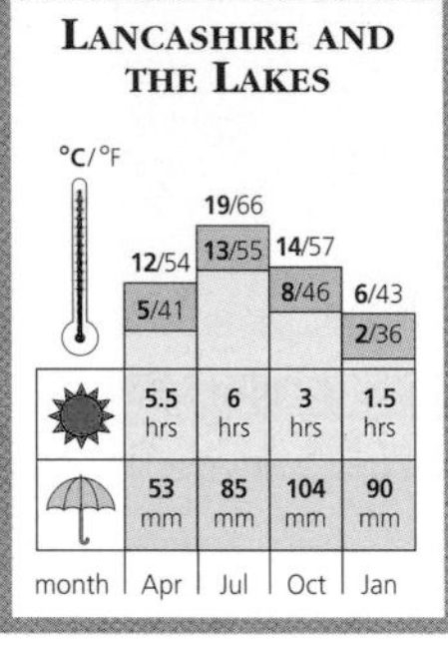

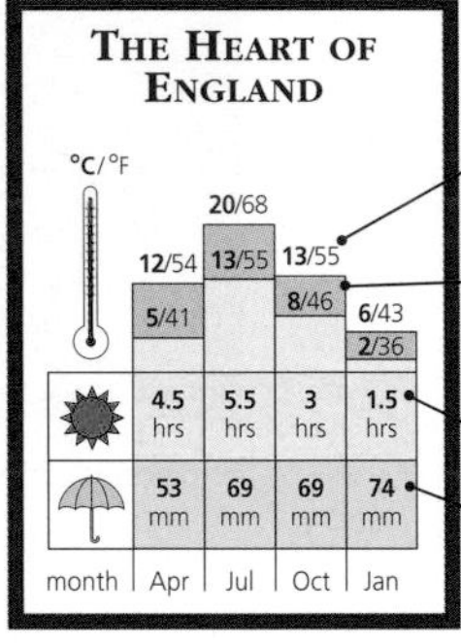

South and Mid-Wales

	Apr	Jul	Oct	Jan
°C/°F max	13/55	20/68	14/57	7/45
°C/°F min	5/41	13/55	8/46	2/36
Sunshine	5.5 hrs	6 hrs	3.5 hrs	1.5 hrs
Rainfall	65 mm	89 mm	109 mm	108 mm

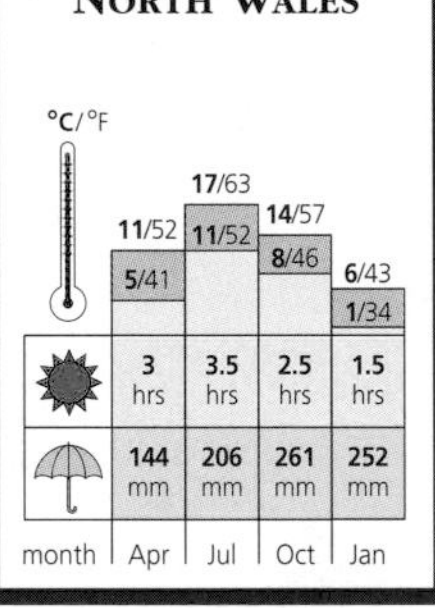

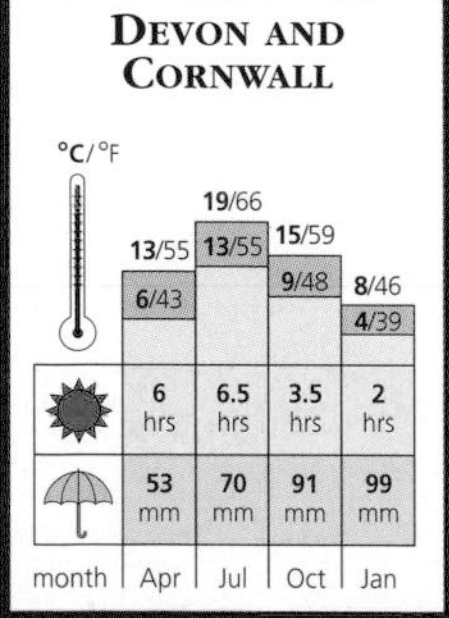

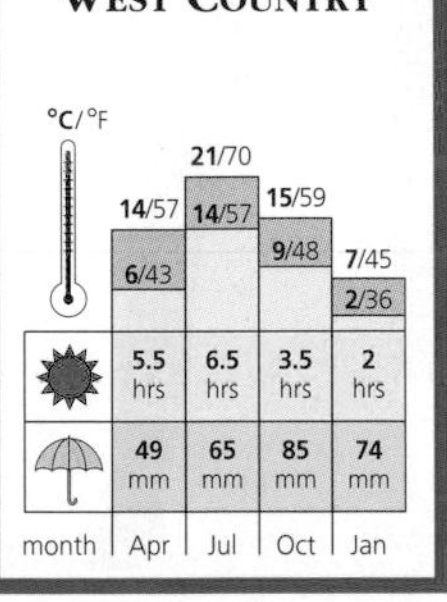

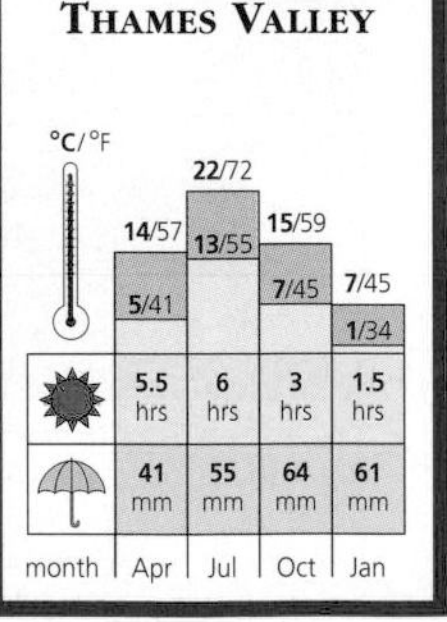

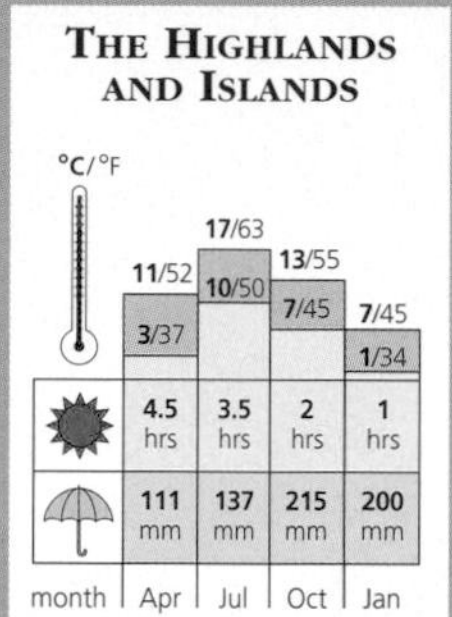
THE HIGHLANDS AND ISLANDS
°C/°F
11/52
3/37
17/63
10/50
13/55
7/45
7/45
1/34
4.5 hrs
3.5 hrs
2 hrs
1 hrs
111 mm
137 mm
215 mm
200 mm
month
Apr
Jul
Oct
Jan

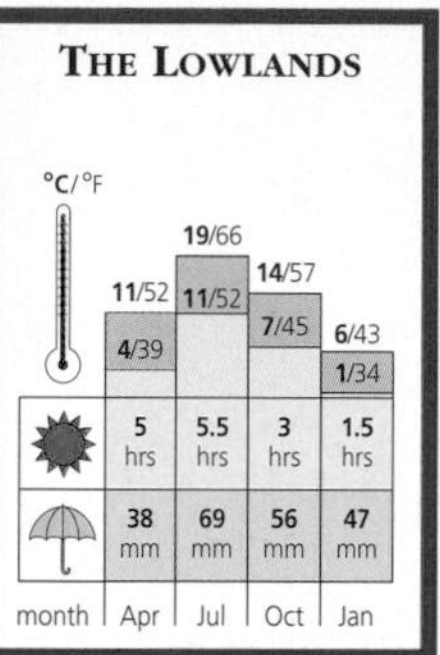
THE LOWLANDS
°C/°F
11/52
4/39
19/66
11/52
14/57
7/45
6/43
1/34
5 hrs
5.5 hrs
3 hrs
1.5 hrs
38 mm
69 mm
56 mm
47 mm
month
Apr
Jul
Oct
Jan

York
East Midlands
Norwich
Cambridge
East Anglia
Thames Valley
Oxford
Downs and Channel Coast
Dover
Portsmouth

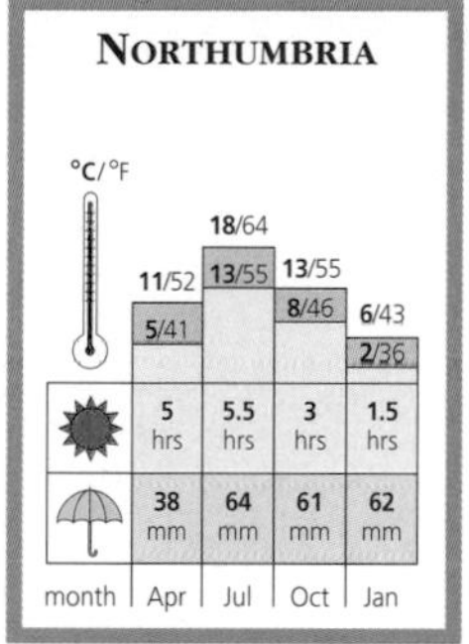
NORTHUMBRIA
°C/°F
11/52
5/41
18/64
13/55
13/55
8/46
6/43
2/36
5 hrs
5.5 hrs
3 hrs
1.5 hrs
38 mm
64 mm
61 mm
62 mm
month
Apr
Jul
Oct
Jan

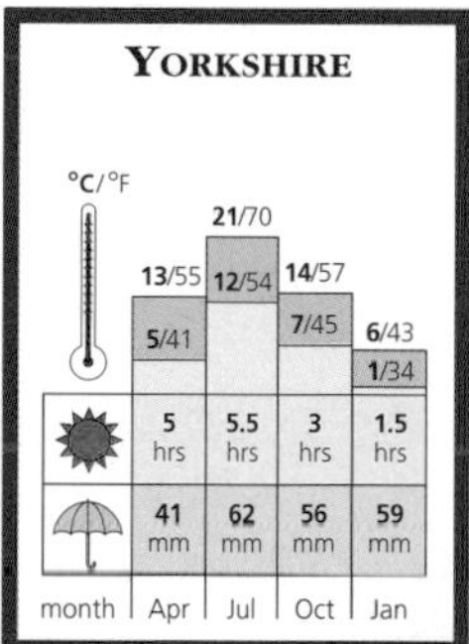
YORKSHIRE
°C/°F
13/55
5/41
21/70
12/54
14/57
7/45
6/43
1/34
5 hrs
5.5 hrs
3 hrs
1.5 hrs
41 mm
62 mm
56 mm
59 mm
month
Apr
Jul
Oct
Jan

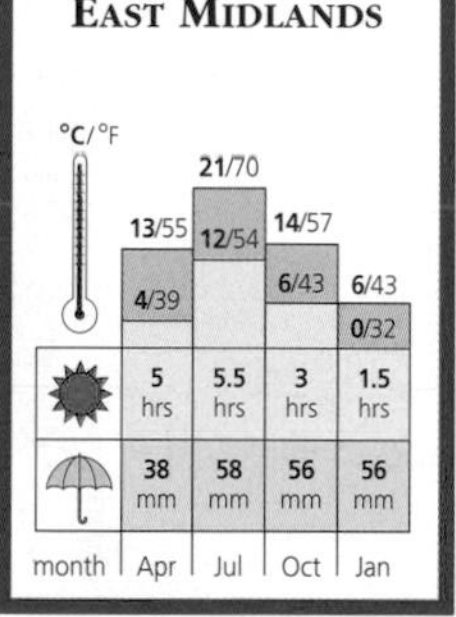
EAST MIDLANDS
°C/°F
13/55
4/39
21/70
12/54
14/57
6/43
6/43
0/32
5 hrs
5.5 hrs
3 hrs
1.5 hrs
38 mm
58 mm
56 mm
56 mm
month
Apr
Jul
Oct
Jan

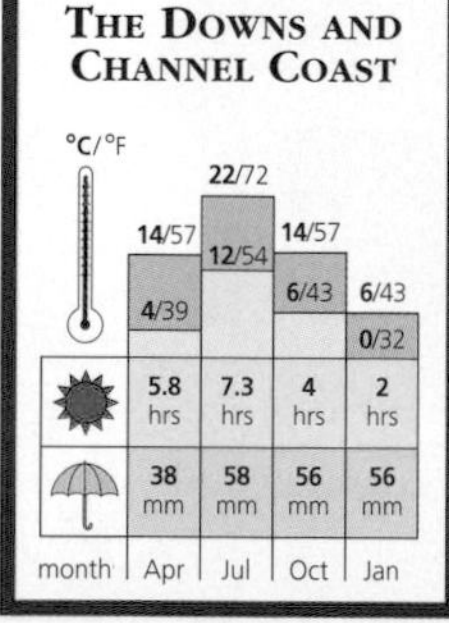
THE DOWNS AND CHANNEL COAST
°C/°F
14/57
4/39
22/72
12/54
14/57
6/43
6/43
0/32
5.8 hrs
7.3 hrs
4 hrs
2 hrs
38 mm
58 mm
56 mm
56 mm
month
Apr
Jul
Oct
Jan

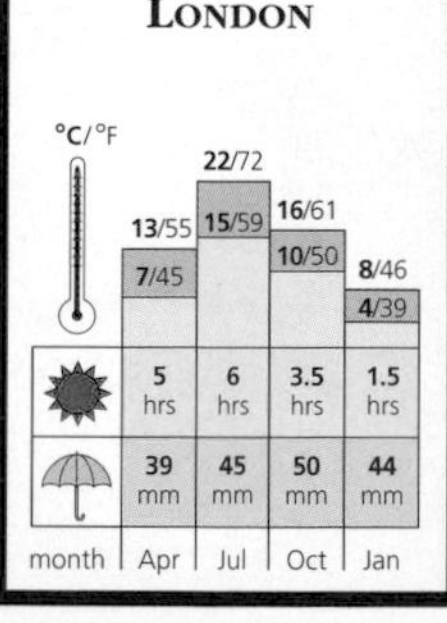
LONDON
°C/°F
13/55
7/45
22/72
15/59
16/61
10/50
8/46
4/39
5 hrs
6 hrs
3.5 hrs
1.5 hrs
39 mm
45 mm
50 mm
44 mm
month
Apr
Jul
Oct
Jan

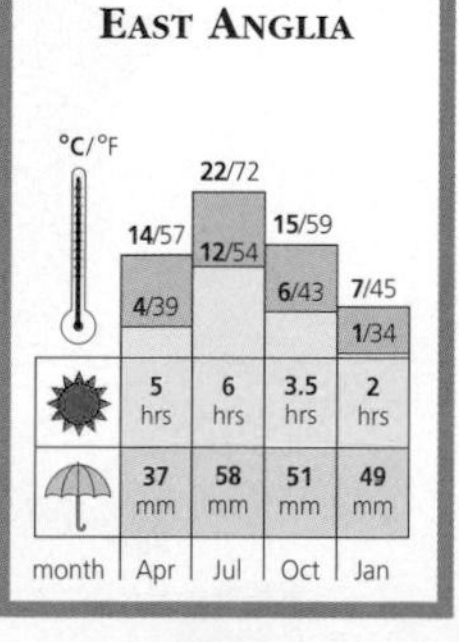
EAST ANGLIA
°C/°F
14/57
4/39
22/72
12/54
15/59
6/43
7/45
1/34
5 hrs
6 hrs
3.5 hrs
2 hrs
37 mm
58 mm
51 mm
49 mm
month
Apr
Jul
Oct
Jan

LONDON

INTRODUCING LONDON 72-77

WEST END AND WESTMINSTER 78-95

SOUTH KENSINGTON AND HYDE PARK 96-103

REGENT'S PARK AND BLOOMSBURY 104-109

THE CITY AND SOUTHWARK 110-123

SHOPS AND MARKETS 124-125

ENTERTAINMENT IN LONDON 126-129

FURTHER AFIELD 130-134

STREET FINDER 135-143

London at a Glance

THE LARGEST CITY IN EUROPE, London is home to about seven million people and covers 625 sq miles (1,600 sq km). The capital was founded by the Romans in the first century AD as a convenient administrative and communications centre and a port for trade with Continental Europe. For a thousand years it has been the principal residence of British monarchs as well as the centre of business and government, and it is rich in historic buildings and treasures from all periods. In addition to its diverse range of museums, galleries and churches, London is an exciting contemporary city, packed with a vast array of entertainments and shops. The attractions on offer are virtually endless but this map highlights the most important of those described in detail on the following pages.

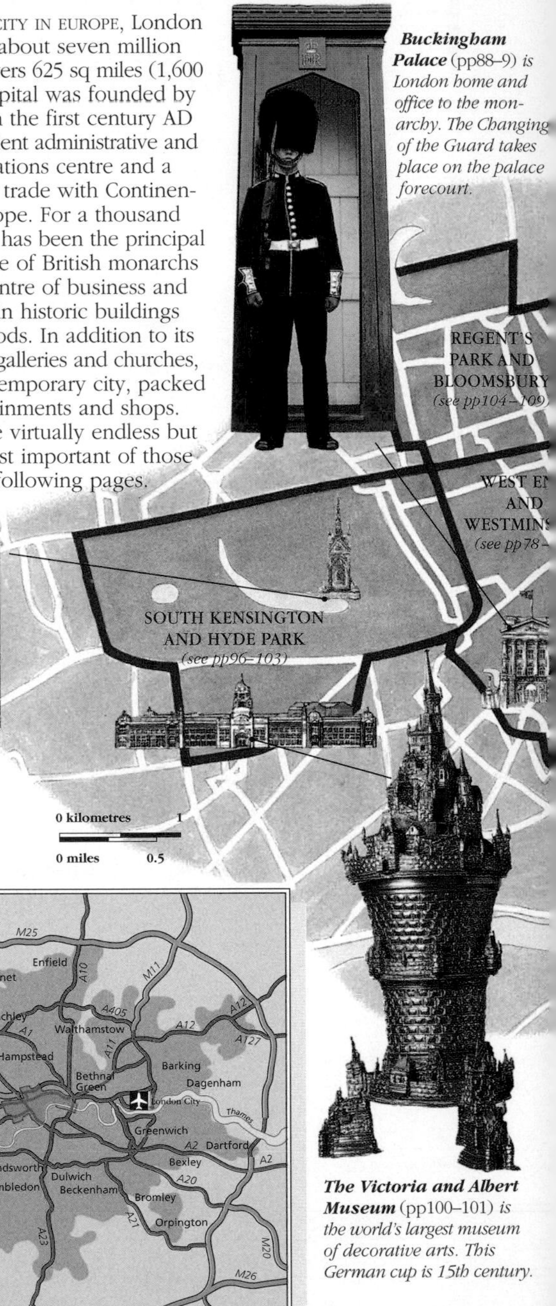

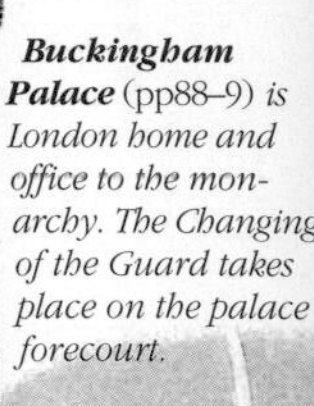

Buckingham Palace (pp88–9) *is London home and office to the monarchy. The Changing of the Guard takes place on the palace forecourt.*

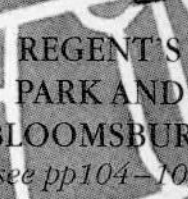

Hyde Park (p77)*, the largest central London park, boasts numerous sports facilities, restaurants, an art gallery and Speakers' Corner. The highlight is the Serpentine Lake.*

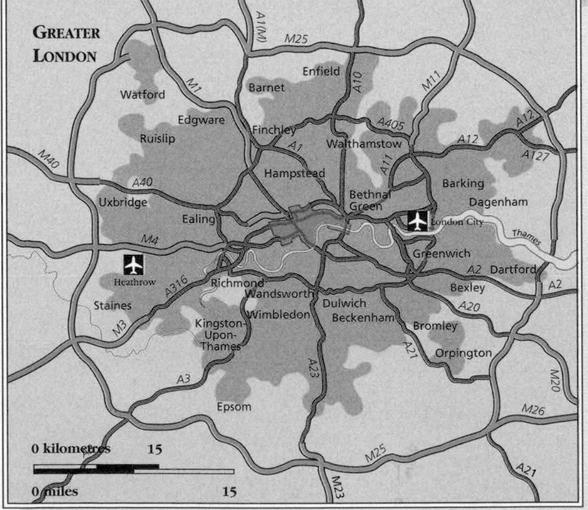

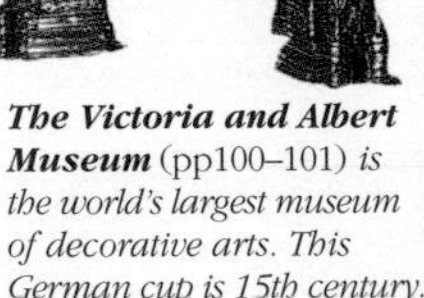

The Victoria and Albert Museum (pp100–101) *is the world's largest museum of decorative arts. This German cup is 15th century.*

KEY

Main sightseeing area

◁ **Nelson's Column (1843) and the National Gallery, Trafalgar Square**

The British Museum's (pp108–9) *vast collection of antiquities from all over the world includes this Portland Vase from the 1st century BC.*

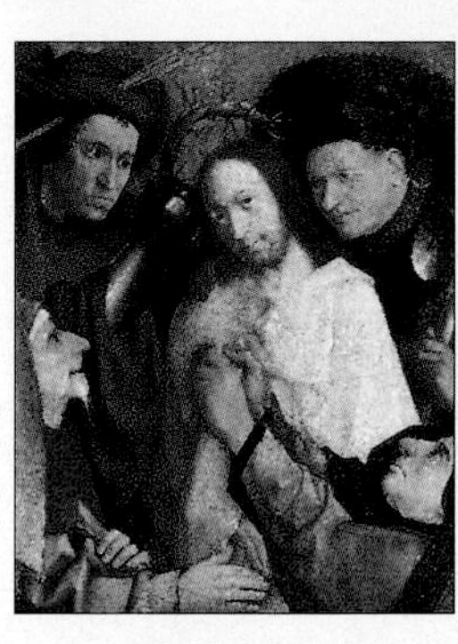

The National Gallery's (pp84–5) *world-famous collection of paintings includes works such as* Christ Mocked *(c.1495) by Hieronymus Bosch.*

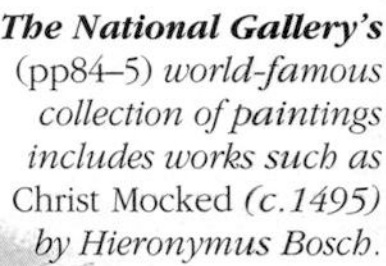

St Paul's (pp116–17) *huge dome is the cathedral's most distinctive feature. Three galleries around the dome give spectacular views of London.*

Westminster Abbey (pp94–5) *has glorious medieval architecture and is crammed with impressive tombs and monuments to some of Britain's greatest public figures.*

Tate Britain (p93) *displays an outstanding collection of British art ranging from stylized Elizabethan portraiture, such as* The Cholmondeley Sisters, *to cutting edge installation and film.*

The Tower of London (pp120–21) *is most famous as the prison where enemies of the Crown were executed. The Tower houses the Crown Jewels, including the Imperial State Crown.*

A River View of London

THE RIVER THAMES was the artery for much of the country's commerce from Roman times until the 1950s. Today the river is one of London's foremost leisure amenities, with wharves and warehouses converted into riverside marinas, bars and restaurants. One of the most enjoyable ways to see the capital is by boat, and the most popular river trips travel downstream from the Houses of Parliament to Tower Bridge. This 30-minute cruise gives a different perspective on some of London's historic buildings and sights.

St Paul's Cathedral (pp116–17), *Wren's masterpiece, dominates the north bank of the river.*

Shell Mex House *was built in 1931 on the site of the vast Cecil Hotel.*

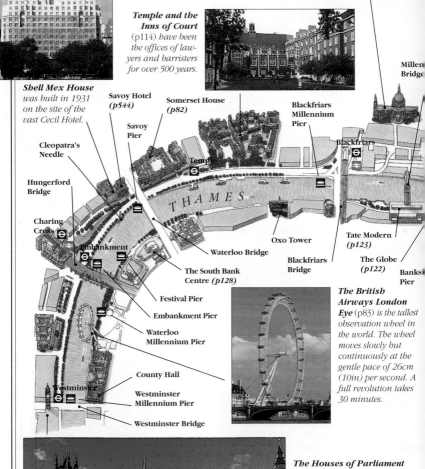

Temple and the Inns of Court (p114) *have been the offices of lawyers and barristers for over 500 years.*

Savoy Hotel ***(p544)***

Somerset House ***(p82)***

Savoy Pier

Cleopatra's Needle

Hungerford Bridge

Charing Cross

Embankment

Temple

THAMES

Blackfriars Millennium Pier

Blackfriars

Millen Bridge

Oxo Tower

Waterloo Bridge

The South Bank Centre ***(p128)***

Festival Pier

Embankment Pier

Waterloo Millennium Pier

County Hall

Westminster

Westminster Millennium Pier

Westminster Bridge

Blackfriars Bridge

Tate Modern ***(p123)***

The Globe ***(p122)***

Banksi Pier

The British Airways London Eye (p83) *is the tallest observation wheel in the world. The wheel moves slowly but continuously at the gentle pace of 26cm (10in) per second. A full revolution takes 30 minutes.*

The Houses of Parliament (p92) *were designed by Charles Barry after a fire burnt down the 14th-century Palace of Westminster in 1834. The tall tower housing Big Ben dominates the skyline.*

Thames Cruises

The most popular boat trips run through central London round the year, with reduced schedules in winter. During the summer, sailing times are frequent between Westminster *(pp90–91)* and Greenwich *(p133)*, with a boat arriving every half hour to an hour. Often accompanied by witty commentary, a cruise along this fascinating stretch of the Thames should not be missed.

Trips can also be taken further afield, with launches heading downstream from Greenwich to the Thames Barrier, an awe-inspiring work of modern engineering. The cruise takes 30 minutes one-way and sails past industrial sites. Heading upstream to picturesque Kew *(p134)* from Westminster (2 hrs) leaves the city behind, after sailing through Hammersmith and passing some of the city's most startling landmarks, including Battersea Power Station and the MI6 building, headquarters of the internal security service. It's possible to head even further upstream to Richmond *(p134)* and Hampton Court *(p161)*, but be forewarned that tidal conditions can hamper the journey.

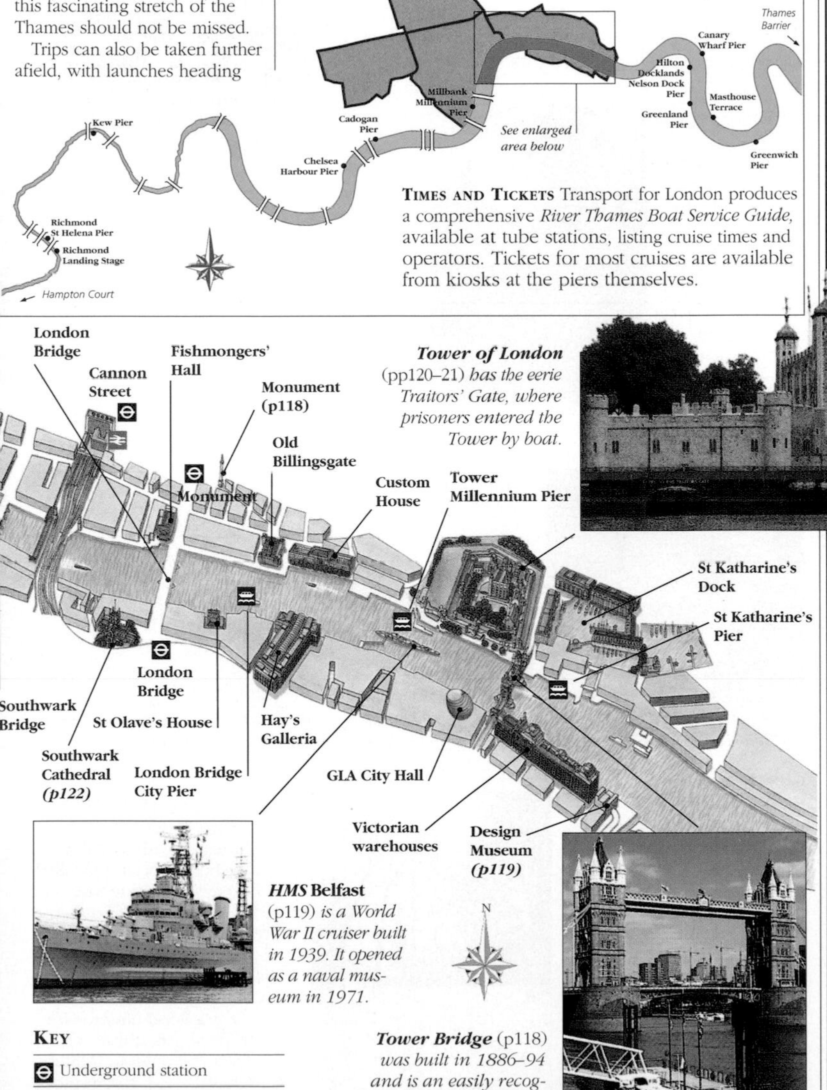

Times and Tickets Transport for London produces a comprehensive *River Thames Boat Service Guide,* available at tube stations, listing cruise times and operators. Tickets for most cruises are available from kiosks at the piers themselves.

Tower of London (pp120–21) *has the eerie Traitors' Gate, where prisoners entered the Tower by boat.*

***HMS* Belfast** (p119) *is a World War II cruiser built in 1939. It opened as a naval museum in 1971.*

Tower Bridge (p118) *was built in 1886–94 and is an easily recognized landmark. It still opens to allow tall ships to pass underneath.*

Key

- Underground station
- Railway station
- River boat pier

London's Parks and Gardens

Camellia japonica

LONDON HAS ONE OF THE WORLD'S greenest city centres, full of tree-filled squares and large expanses of grass, some of which have been public land since medieval times. From the elegant terraces of Regent's Park to the botanic gardens of Kew, every London park and garden has its own charm and character. Some are ancient crown or public land, while others were created from the grounds of private houses or disused land. Londoners make the most of these open spaces: for exercise, listening to music, or simply escaping the bustle of the city.

Holland Park (see pp130–31) *offers acres of peaceful woodland, an open-air theatre* (see p127) *and a café.*

Kew Gardens (see p134) *are the world's premiere botanic gardens. An amazing variety of plants from all over the world is complemented by an array of temples, monuments and a landscaped lake.*

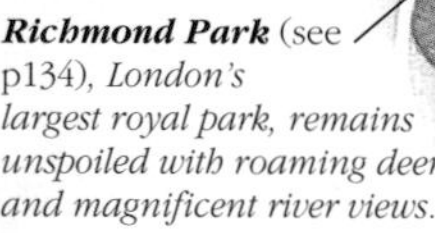

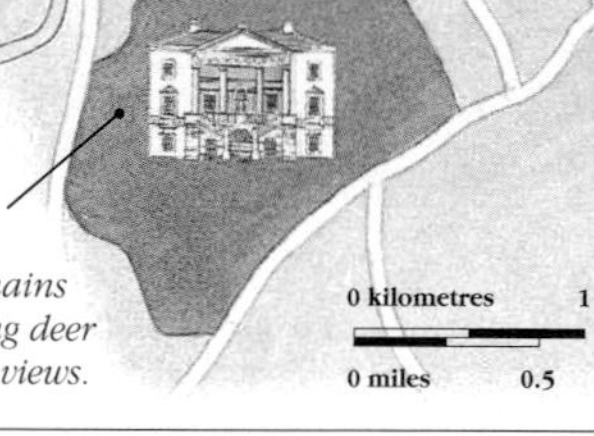

Richmond Park (see p134), *London's largest royal park, remains unspoiled with roaming deer and magnificent river views.*

SEASONAL BEST

As winter draws to a close, spectacular drifts of crocuses, daffodils and tulips are to be found peeping above the ground in Green Park and Kew. Easter weekend marks the start of outdoor events with funfairs on many commons and parks. During the summer months the parks are packed with picnickers and sunbathers and you can often catch a free open-air concert in St James's or Regent's parks. The energetic can play tennis in most parks, swim in Hyde Park's Serpentine or the ponds on Hampstead Heath, or take rowing boats out on the lakes in Regent's and Battersea parks. Autumn brings a different atmosphere, and on 5 November firework displays and bonfires celebrate Guy Fawkes Night *(see p64)*. Winter is a good time to visit the tropical glasshouses and the colourful outdoor winter garden at Kew. If the weather gets really cold, the Round Pond in Kensington Gardens may be fit for ice-skating.

Winter in Kensington Gardens, adjoining Hyde Park

Hampstead Heath *(see p132)* is a breezy open space embracing a variety of landscapes.

Regent's Park (see p105) *has a large boating lake, an open-air theatre* (see p127) *and London Zoo. Surrounded by Nash's graceful buildings, it is one of London's most civilized retreats.*

St James's Park*, in the heart of the city, is a popular escape for office workers. It is also a reserve for wildfowl.*

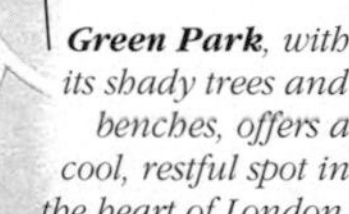

Green Park*, with its shady trees and benches, offers a cool, restful spot in the heart of London.*

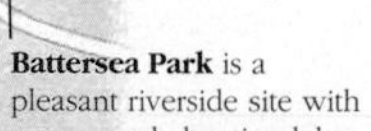

Battersea Park is a pleasant riverside site with a man-made boating lake.

Greenwich Park (see p133) *is dominated by the National Maritime Museum. There are fine views from the Old Royal Observatory on the hill top.*

Hyde Park and Kensington Gardens (see p103) *are both popular London retreats. There are sporting facilities, a lake and art gallery in Hyde Park. This plaque is from the ornate Italian Garden in Kensington Gardens.*

HISTORIC CEMETERIES

In the late 1830s, a ring of private cemeteries was established around London to ease the pressure on the monstrously overcrowded and unhealthy burial grounds of the inner city. Today the cemeteries, notably **Highgate** *(see p132)* and **Kensal Green,** are well worth visiting for their flamboyant Victorian monuments.

Kensal Green cemetery on the Harrow Road

WEST END AND WESTMINSTER

THE WEST END is the city's social and cultural centre and the London home of the royal family. Stretching from the edge of Hyde Park to Covent Garden, the district bustles all day and late into the night. Whether you're looking for art, history, street- or café-life, it is the most rewarding area in which to begin an exploration of the city.

Horse Guard on Whitehall

Westminster has been at the centre of political and religious power for a thousand years. In the 11th century, King Canute founded Westminster Palace and Edward the Confessor built Westminster Abbey, where all English monarchs have been crowned since 1066. As modern government developed, the great offices of state were established in the area.

SIGHTS AT A GLANCE

Historic Streets and Buildings

Banqueting House 18
Buckingham Palace pp88–9 13
Cabinet War Rooms 16
Downing Street 17
Houses of Parliament pp92–3 19
Piccadilly Circus 8
Ritz Hotel 10
Royal Mews 15
The Mall 12
The Piazza and Central Market 1

Museums and Galleries

London's Transport Museum 2
National Gallery pp84–5 6
National Portrait Gallery 7
Queen's Gallery 14
Royal Academy 9
Somerset House 4
Tate Britain 21
Theatre Museum 3

Churches

Queen's Chapel 11
Westminster Abbey pp94–5 20

Attractions

British Airways London Eye 5

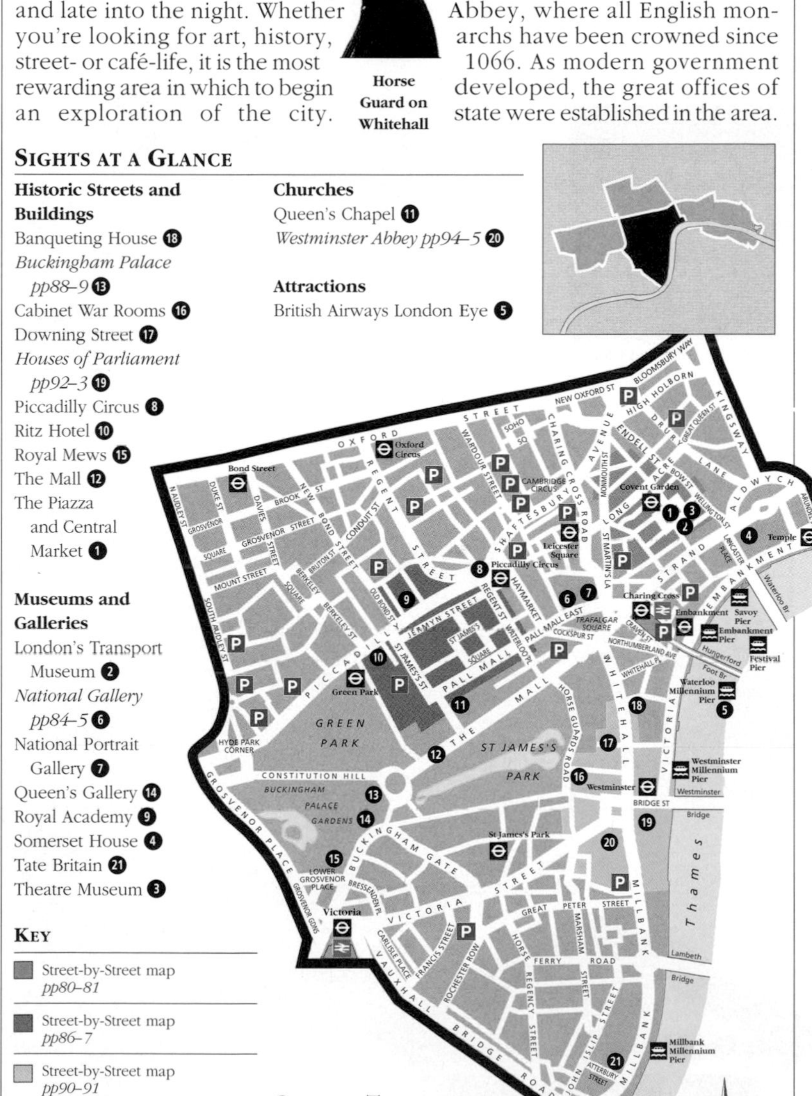

KEY

Street-by-Street map *pp80–81*
Street-by-Street map *pp86–7*
Street-by-Street map *pp90–91*
Underground station
Railway station
Parking
River boat pier

GETTING THERE

This area is the hub of the city's public transport system, served by virtually all tube lines and scores of buses *(see pp642–3)*. The most convenient tube and railway station is Charing Cross.

Street-by-Street: Covent Garden

Until 1973, covent garden was an area of decaying streets and warehouses, which only came alive after dark when the fruit and vegetable market traders packed up for the day. Since then the Victorian market and elegant buildings nearby have been converted into stylish shops, restaurants, bars and cafés, creating an animated district which attracts a lively young crowd, night and day.

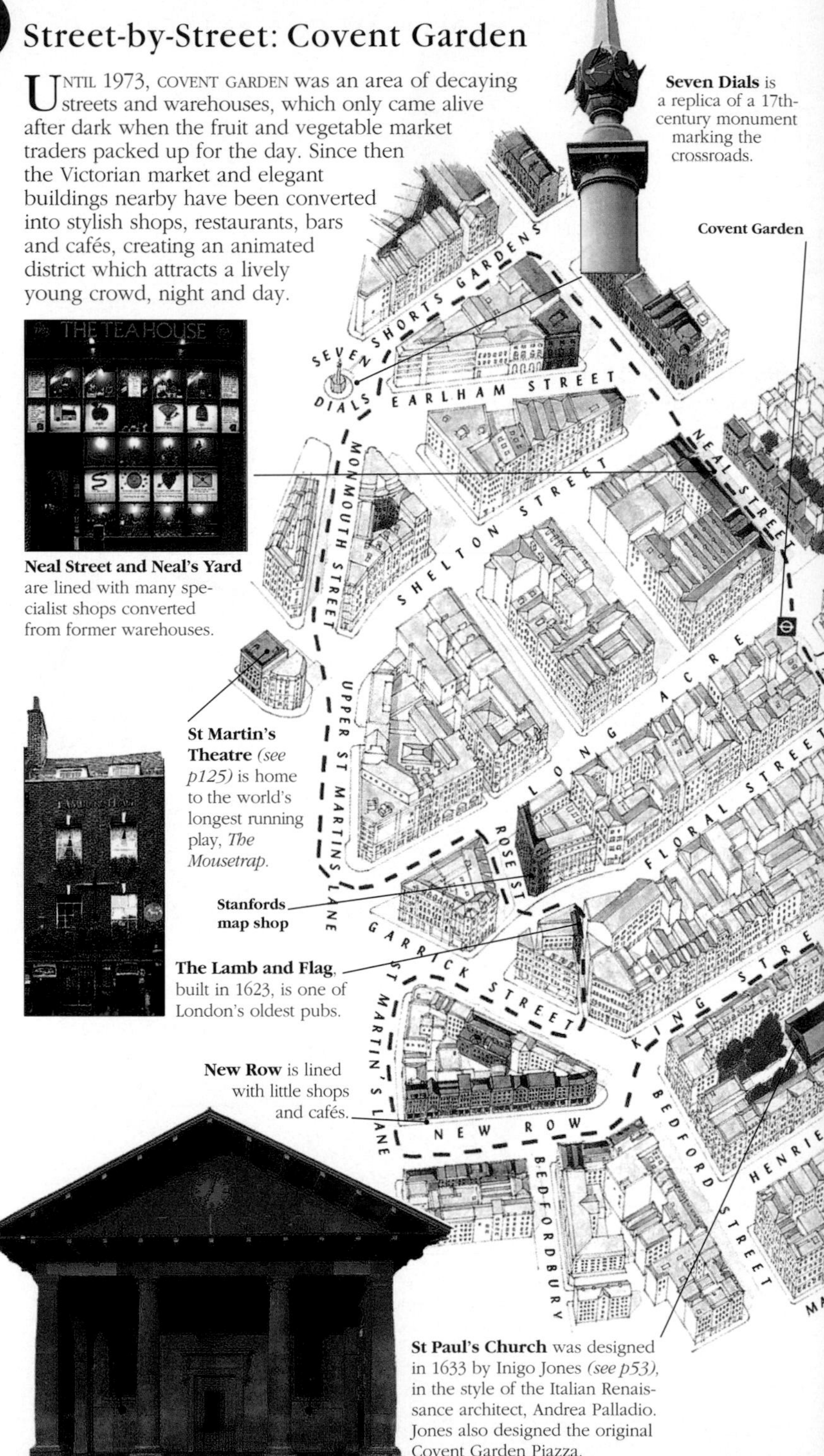

Seven Dials is a replica of a 17th-century monument marking the crossroads.

Covent Garden

Neal Street and Neal's Yard are lined with many specialist shops converted from former warehouses.

St Martin's Theatre *(see p125)* is home to the world's longest running play, *The Mousetrap*.

Stanfords map shop

The Lamb and Flag, built in 1623, is one of London's oldest pubs.

New Row is lined with little shops and cafés.

St Paul's Church was designed in 1633 by Inigo Jones *(see p53)*, in the style of the Italian Renaissance architect, Andrea Palladio. Jones also designed the original Covent Garden Piazza.

Theatre Museum
This houses a collection of theatrical memorabilia ❸

The Royal Opera House *(see p128)* is where many of the greatest opera singers and ballet dancers have performed.

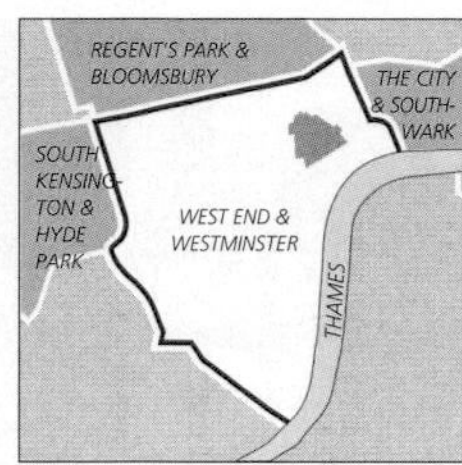

Locator Map
See Street Finder map 4

Key

— — — Suggested route

0 metres 100

0 yards 100

London's Transport Museum
This museum's intriguing collection brings to life the history of the city's tubes, buses and trains. It also displays examples of 20th-century commercial art ❷

Jubilee Market

★ Piazza and Central Market
One of the Piazza's many cafés ❶

Star Sights

★ Piazza and Central Market

The Piazza and Central Market ❶

Covent Garden WC2. **Map** 4 F5.
Covent Garden. *cobbled streets.* **Street performers in Piazza:** *10am–dusk daily.*

The 17th-century architect Inigo Jones *(see p53)* planned the Piazza in Covent Garden as an elegant residential square, modelled on the piazza in the Tuscan town of Livorno, which he had seen under construction during his travels in Italy. For a brief period, the Piazza became one of the most fashionable addresses in London, but it was superseded by the even grander St James's Square *(see p87)* which lies to the southwest.

Decline accelerated when a fruit and vegetable market developed. By the mid-18th century, the Piazza had become a haunt of prostitutes and most of its houses had turned into seedy lodgings, gambling dens, brothels and taverns.

A mid-18th-century view of Covent Garden's Piazza

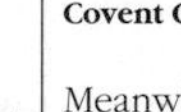

Meanwhile the wholesale produce market became the largest in the country and in 1828 a market hall was erected to ease congestion. The market, however, soon outgrew its new home and despite the construction of new buildings, such as Floral and Jubilee halls, the congestion grew worse. In 1973 the market moved to a new site in south London, and over the next two decades Covent Garden was redeveloped. Today only St Paul's Church remains of Inigo Jones's buildings, and Covent Garden, with its many small shops, cafés, restaurants, market stalls and street entertainers, is one of central London's liveliest districts.

London's Transport Museum ❷

The Piazza, Covent Garden WC2. **Map** 4 F5. *020-7379 6344.* *Covent Garden.* *10am–6pm Sat–Thu; 11am–6pm Fri (last adm 5:15pm).* *24–26 Dec.* *phone in advance.* www.ltmuseum.co.uk

THIS COLLECTION of buses, trams and underground trains ranges from the earliest horse-drawn omnibuses to a present-day Hoppa bus. Housed in the Victorian Flower Market of Covent Garden built in 1872, the museum is particularly good for children, who can put themselves in the driver's seat of a bus or an underground train, operate signals and chat to an actor playing the part of a 19th-century tube-tunnel miner.

London's bus and train companies have long been prolific patrons of artists, and the museum holds a fine collection of 19th- and 20th-century commercial art. Copies of some of the best posters and works by distinguished artists, such as Paul Nash and Graham Sutherland, are on sale at the museum shop.

Poster by Michael Reilly (1929), London Transport Museum

Theatre Museum ❸

Russell St WC2. **Map** 4 F5. *020-7943 4700.* *Covent Garden.* *10am–6pm Tue–Sun.* *public hols.* www.theatremuseum.org

CHILDREN CAN BE MADE UP with gruesome wounds in this museum, and find out how Cyrano de Bergerac's nose was created for the film. An exhibition reveals how a theatre production is mounted, from cast readings of the author's original script, through videoed rehearsals and backstage procedures, to the first staged performance.

More conventionally, the intriguing history of show business is traced through a collection of memorabilia – playbills, programmes, props and costumes.

Somerset House ❹

Strand WC2. **Map** 4 F5. *020-7845 4600.* *Temple (closed Sun), Embankment, Charing Cross.* *10am–6pm daily.* *1 Jan, 24–26 Dec.* **Outdoor ice rink** *two months in winter.* **Courtauld Institute** *020-7848 2526.* **Gilbert Collection** *020-7420 9400.* **Hermitage Rooms** *020-7413 3398.* *all galleries.* www.somerset-house.org.uk

DESIGNED IN 1770 by William Chambers, Somerset House is home to three great collections of art, the **Courtauld Institute**, the **Gilbert Collection** and the **Hermitage Rooms**. The courtyard forms an attractive piazza (which becomes an ice rink in the winter), and the riverside terrace has a café. Located in Somerset House but famous in its own right is the Courtauld Institute. Its collection includes important Impressionist and Post-Impressionist paintings. The Gilbert Collection is a major museum of decorative arts, made up of 800 pieces dating from the 16th century, including gold snuff boxes and European silverware. The Hermitage Rooms recreate, in miniature, the splendour of the Winter Palace and its various wings which now

Somerset House: Strand façade

SOHO AND CHINATOWN

Soho has been renowned for pleasures of the table, the flesh and the intellect ever since it was first developed in the late 17th century. At first a fashionable residential area, it declined when high society shifted west to Mayfair and immigrants from Europe moved into its narrow streets. Furniture-makers and tailors set up shop here and were joined in the late 19th century by pubs, nightclubs, restaurants and brothels. In the 1960s, Hong Kong Chinese moved into the area around Gerrard and Lisle streets and they created an aromatic Chinatown, packed with many restaurants and food shops. Soho's raffish reputation has long attracted artists and writers, ranging from the 18th-century essayist Thomas de Quincey to poet Dylan Thomas and painter Francis Bacon. Although strip joints and peep shows remain, Soho has enjoyed something of a renaissance, and today is full of stylish and lively bars and restaurants.

Lion dancer in February's Chinese New Year celebrations

The opulent Palm Court of the Ritz Hotel

comprise the State Hermitage Museum, St Petersburg, and exhibitions are mounted from the museum's collections.

British Airways London Eye ❺

Jubilee Gardens, South Bank SE1. **Map** 6 F2. *0870 5000 600 for information and 24-hr advance booking service.* *Waterloo, Westminster.* *Apr–May: 10am–8pm; June–Aug: 10am–10pm; Sep: 10am–8pm; Oct–Mar: 10am–7pm.* *1 Jan, 25, 31 Dec.*
www.ba-londoneye.com

The British Airways London Eye is a 135-m (443-ft) observation wheel that was installed on the South Bank to mark the Millennium. Its enclosed passenger capsules offer a gentle, 30-minute ride as the wheel makes a full turn, with breathtaking views over London and for up to 42 km (26 miles) around. Towering over one of the world's most familiar riverscapes, it has understandably captured the hearts of Londoners and visitors alike, and is one of the city's most popular attractions. Advance reservation is strongly recommended, by phone (but must be three days in advance) or in person at the ticket office in County Hall. "Flights" are on the hour and half-hour.

National Gallery ❻

See pp84–5.

National Portrait Gallery ❼

2 St Martin's Place WC2. **Map** 6 E1. *020-7306 0055.* *Charing Cross, Leicester Sq.* *10am–6pm Sat–Wed, 10am–9pm Thu & Fri.* *1 Jan, Good Fri, May Day, 24, 25 Dec.*
www.npg.org.uk

This museum celebrates Britain's history through portraits, photographs and sculptures; subjects range from Elizabeth I to Margaret Thatcher. The 20th-century section contains paintings and photographs of the royal family, politicians, rock stars, designers, artists and writers.

The Statue of Eros

Piccadilly Circus ❽

W1. **Map** 6 D1. *Piccadilly Circus.*

Dominated by garish neon advertising hoardings, Piccadilly Circus is a hectic traffic junction surrounded by shopping malls. It began as an early 19th-century crossroads between Piccadilly and John Nash's *(see p107)* Regent Street. It was briefly an elegant space, edged by curving stucco façades, but by 1910 the first electric advertisements had been installed. For years people have congregated at its centre, beneath the delicately poised figure of Eros, erected in 1892.

Royal Academy ❾

Burlington House, Piccadilly W1. **Map** 6 D1. *020-7300 8000.* *Piccadilly Circus, Green Park.* *10am–6pm daily, 10am–10pm Fri.* *24–25 Dec, Good Fri.* *by appointment.*
www.royalacademy.org.uk

Founded in 1768, the Royal Academy is best known for its summer exhibition, which has been an annual event for over 200 years and comprises a rewarding mix of around 1,200 new works by established and unknown painters, sculptors and architects. During the rest of the year, the gallery shows prestigious touring exhibitions from around the world, and the courtyard in front of Burlington House, one of the West End's few surviving mansions from the early 18th century, is often filled with people waiting to get in. Quite apart from its aesthetic delights, the Royal Academy provides the weary traveller with a little lacuna of tranquillity. Its interior decoration inspires calm, and seems to be cut off from the stresses and strains of modern city life.

Ritz Hotel ❿

Piccadilly W1. **Map** 5 C1. *020-7493 8181.* *Green Park.* *See **Where to Stay** p540.*
www.theritzlondon.com

Cesar Ritz, the Swiss hotelier who inspired the word "ritzy", had virtually settled down to a quiet retirement by 1906 when this hotel was built and named after him. The colonnaded front of the château-style building was erected in 1906 to suggest just the merest whiff of Paris, where the grandest hotels were to be found at the turn of the century. It still maintains its Edwardian air of *fin de siècle* opulence and sophisticated grandeur, and is a popular venue for afternoon tea (reservations are required). A touch of *soigné* danger may be found in the casino.

National Gallery ❻

THE NATIONAL GALLERY is London's leading art museum, with over 2,300 paintings, most on permanent display. It has flourished since 1824 when George IV persuaded the government to purchase 38 major paintings. These became the core of a national collection of European art that now ranges from Cimabue in the 13th century to 19th-century Impressionists. The gallery's particular strengths are in Dutch, Italian Renaissance and 17th-century Spanish painting. In 1991 the Sainsbury Wing was added to hold the Early Renaissance collection. During 2004–5 rooms may be closed for renovation.

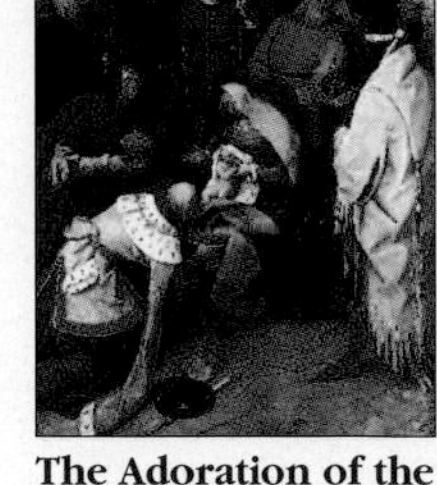

The Adoration of the Kings *(1564)*
This realistic work is by Flemish artist Pieter Brueghel the Elder (1520–1569).

★ The Leonardo Cartoon
(c.1499–1500)
The genius of Leonardo da Vinci glows through this picture of the Virgin and Child, St Anne and John the Baptist.

Orange Street entrance

Stairs to lower floor

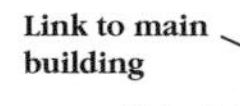

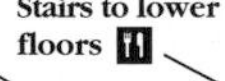

KEY TO FLOORPLAN

- Painting 1260–1510
- Painting 1510–1600
- Painting 1600–1700
- Painting 1700–1900
- Special exhibitions
- Non-exhibition space

Arnolfini Portrait
Jan van Eyck (1389–1441), one of the pioneers of oil painting, shows his mastery of colour, texture, and minute detail in this portrait of 1434.

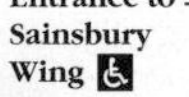

The Annunciation
This refined work of the late 1450s, by Fra Filippo Lippi, forms part of the gallery's exceptional Italian Renaissance collection.

★ Rokeby Venus
This is Velázquez's only surviving female nude (1647–51).

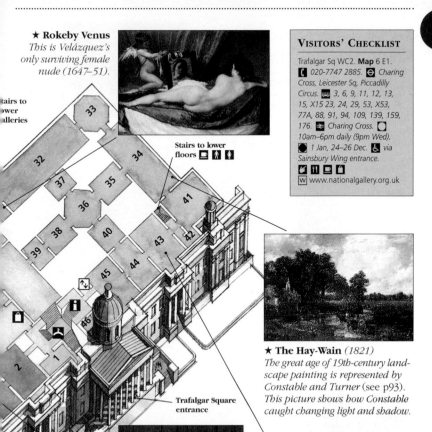

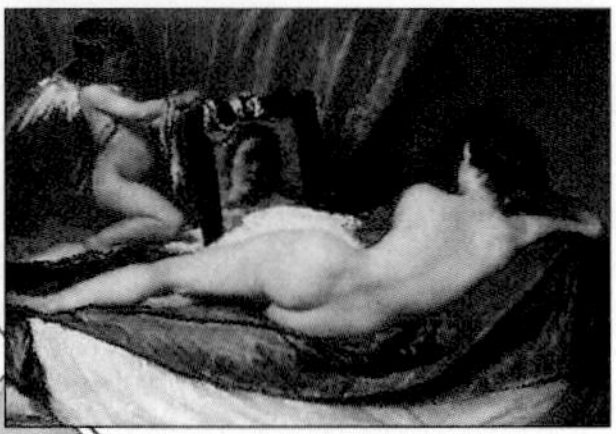

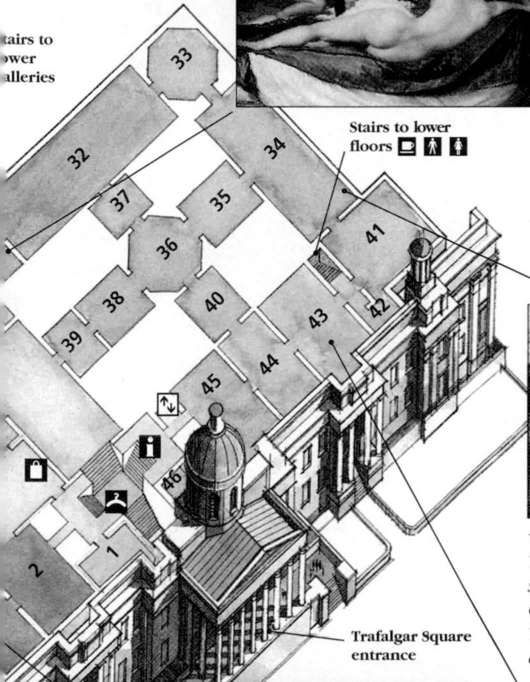

tairs to ower alleries

Stairs to lower floors

Visitors' Checklist

Trafalgar Sq WC2. **Map** 6 E1. *020-7747 2885. Charing Cross, Leicester Sq, Piccadilly Circus. 3, 6, 9, 11, 12, 13, 15, X15 23, 24, 29, 53, X53, 77A, 88, 91, 94, 109, 139, 159, 176. Charing Cross. 10am–6pm daily (9pm Wed). 1 Jan, 24–26 Dec. via Sainsbury Wing entrance.*
www.nationalgallery.org.uk

★ The Hay-Wain *(1821)*
The great age of 19th-century landscape painting is represented by Constable and Turner (see p93)*. This picture shows how Constable caught changing light and shadow.*

Trafalgar Square entrance

The Neo-Classical façade is made of Portland stone.

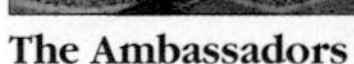

The Ambassadors
The strange shape in the foreground of this Hans Holbein portrait (1533) is a foreshortened skull, a symbol of mortality.

At the Theatre *(1876–7)*
Renoir was one of the greatest painters to be influenced by the Impressionist movement. The theatre was a popular subject among artists of the time.

Gallery Guide

Most of the collection is housed on the first floor, divided into four wings. The paintings hang chronologically, with the earliest works, notably the Italian Renaissance collection (1260–1510), in the Sainsbury Wing. Lesser paintings of all periods are displayed on the lower floor of the main building. The better of the two restaurants is on the first floor in the Sainsbury Wing.

Star Paintings

- **★ Cartoon by Leonardo da Vinci**
- **★ Rokeby Venus by Diego Velázquez**
- **★ The Hay-Wain by John Constable**

Street-by-Street: Piccadilly and St James's

As soon as Henry VIII built St James's Palace in the 1530s, the surrounding area became the centre of fashionable court life. Today Piccadilly forms a contrast between the bustling commercial district full of shopping arcades, eateries and cinemas, with St James's, to the south, which is still the domain of the wealthy and the influential.

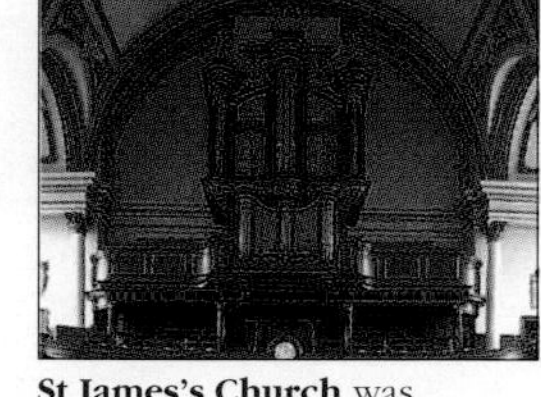

St James's Church was designed by Sir Christopher Wren in 1684.

★ Royal Academy
The permanent art collection here includes this Michelangelo relief of the Madonna and Child (1505) ❾

Burlington Arcade, an opulent covered walk, has fine shops and beadles on patrol.

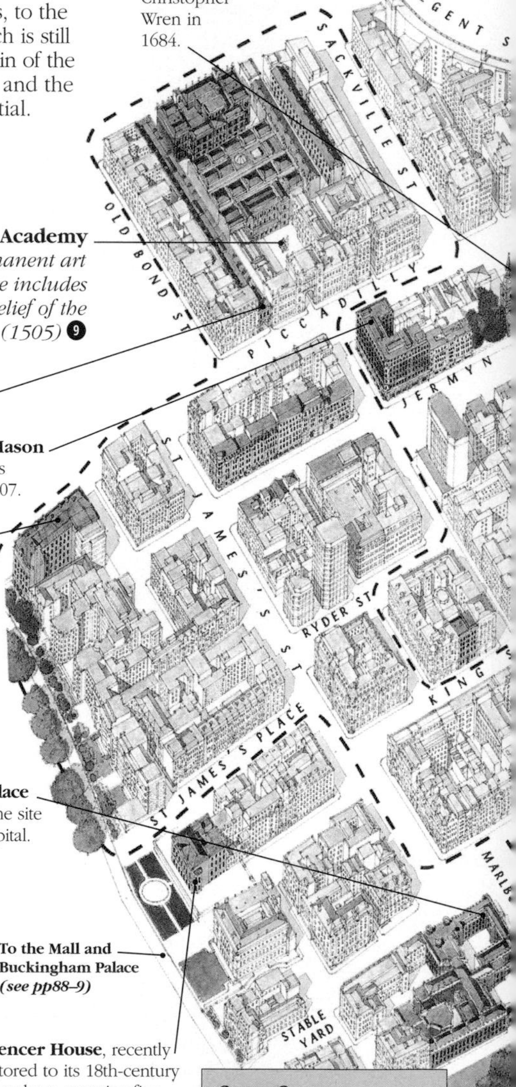

Fortnum & Mason *(see p124)* was founded in 1707.

The Ritz
César Ritz founded one of London's most famous hotels in 1906 ❿

St James's Palace was built on the site of a leper hospital.

To the Mall and Buckingham Palace ***(see pp88–9)***

Spencer House, recently restored to its 18th-century splendour, contains fine period furniture and paintings. This Palladian palace was completed in 1766 for the 1st Earl Spencer, an ancestor of the late Princess of Wales.

Star Sights

★ **Piccadilly Circus**

★ **Royal Academy**

★ Piccadilly Circus
The crowds and dazzling neon lights make this the West End's focal point ❽

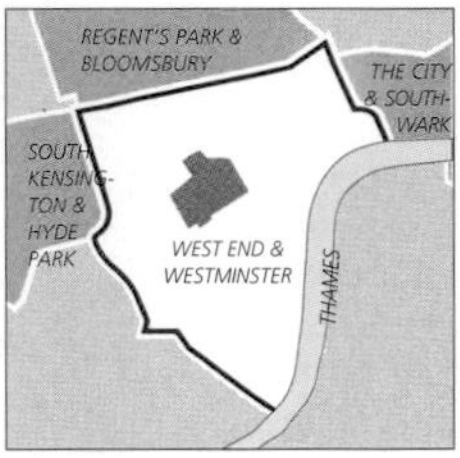

Locator Map
See Street Finder map 5, 6

Key

— — — Suggested route

0 metres 100

0 yards 100

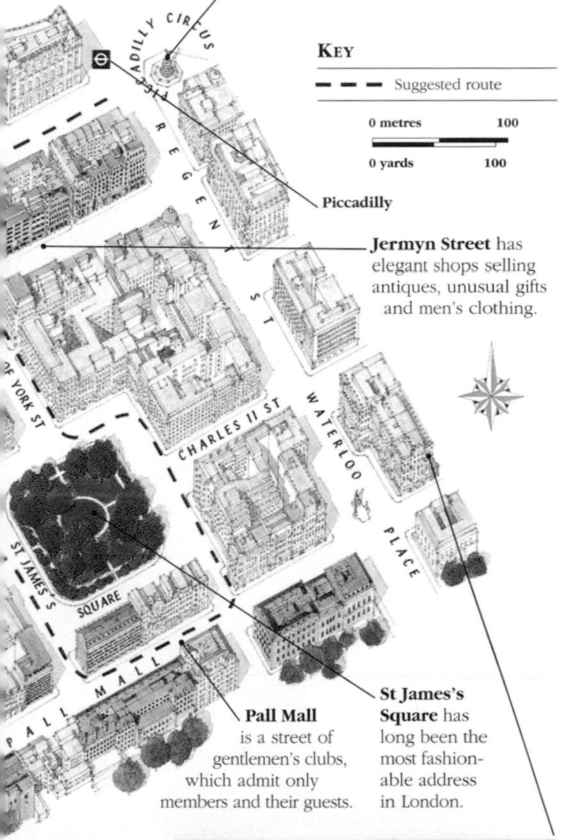

Piccadilly

Jermyn Street has elegant shops selling antiques, unusual gifts and men's clothing.

Pall Mall is a street of gentlemen's clubs, which admit only members and their guests.

St James's Square has long been the most fashionable address in London.

Queen's Chapel
This was the first Classical church in England ⓫

Royal Opera Arcade is lined with quality shops. Designed by John Nash, it was completed in 1818.

Queen's Chapel ⓫

Marlborough Rd SW1. **Map** 6 D1. *020-7930 4832.* *Green Park.* *to the public Sun services (Easter–end Jul) and major Saints' Days only.*

THE SUMPTUOUS Queen's Chapel was designed by Inigo Jones for the Infanta of Spain, the intended bride of Charles I (*see pp52–3*). Work started in 1623 but ceased when the marriage negotiations were shelved. The chapel was finally completed in 1627 for Charles's eventual queen, Henrietta Maria. It was the first church in England to be built in a Classical style, with a coffered ceiling based on a reconstruction by Palladio of an ancient Roman temple.

Interior of Queen's Chapel

The Mall ⓬

SW1. **Map** 6 D2. *Charing Cross, Green Park.*

THIS BROAD TRIUMPHAL approach from Trafalgar Square to Buckingham Palace was created by Aston Webb when he redesigned the front of the palace and the Victoria Monument in 1911. The spacious tree-lined avenue follows the course of an old path at the edge of St James's Park. The path was laid out in the reign of Charles II, when it became London's most fashionable and cosmopolitan promenade. The Mall is used for royal processions on special occasions. Flagpoles down both sides fly the national flags of foreign heads of state during official visits. The Mall is closed to traffic on Sundays.

Buckingham Palace ⓭

Queen Elizabeth II

OPENED TO VISITORS for the first time in 1993 to raise money for repairing fire damage to Windsor Castle *(see pp224–5)*, the Queen's official London home and office is an extremely popular attraction in August and September. John Nash *(see p107)* began converting the 18th-century Buckingham House into a palace for George IV in 1826 but was taken off the job in 1831 for overspending his budget. The first monarch to occupy the palace was Queen Victoria, just after she came to the throne in 1837. The tour takes visitors up the grand staircase and through the splendour of the State Rooms, but not into the royal family's private apartments.

Music Room
State guests are presented and royal babies christened in this room.

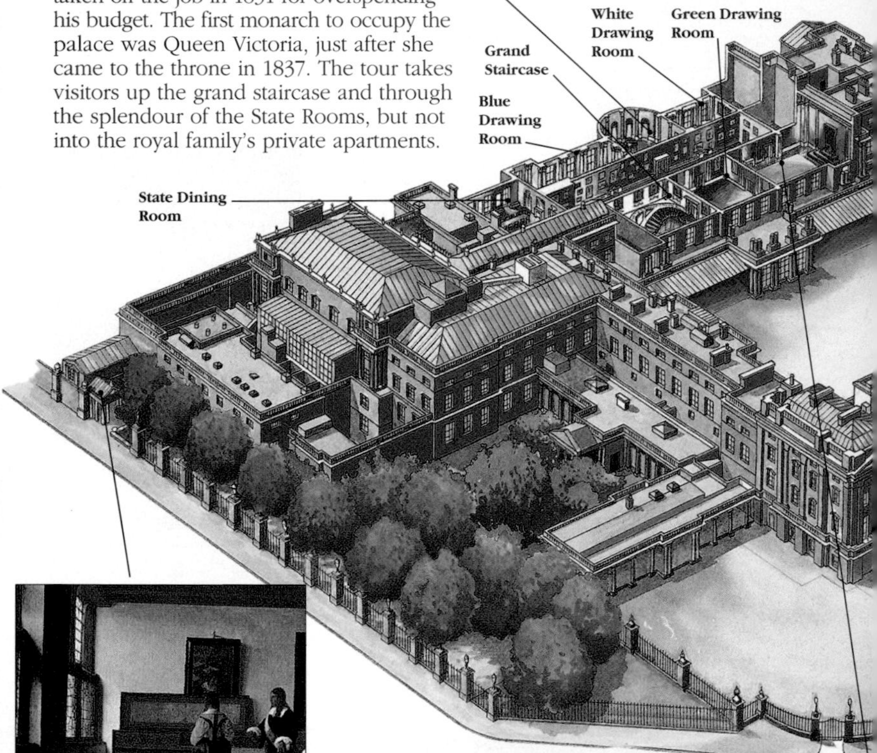

White Drawing Room

Green Drawing Room

Grand Staircase

Blue Drawing Room

State Dining Room

Queen's Gallery
Masterpieces from the Royal Collection, such as Vermeer's The Music Lesson *(c.1660), are displayed here in a series of changing exhibitions.*

Throne Room
The Queen carries out many formal ceremonial duties here, under the richly gilded ceiling.

View over the Mall
On special occasions the Royal Family wave to crowds from the balcony.

Visitors' Checklist

SW1. **Map** 5 C2. *020-7321 2233.* *St James's Park, Victoria.* *11, 16, 24, 25, 28, 36, 38, 52, 73, 135, C1.* *Victoria.* **State Rooms** *Aug–Sep: 9:30am–5:30pm daily (last adm: 4:15pm). The ticket office is located in Green Park by Canada Gate. Each ticket has a set entry time.* *phone first.* **Changing of the Guard**: *11:30am daily or alternate days. Subject to change without notice.* *020-7321 2233.* www.royal.gov.uk

The Royal Standard flies while the Queen is in residence.

The East Wing façade was added by Aston Webb in 1913.

The Changing of the Guard takes place on the palace forecourt.

The Changing of the Guard

Dressed in brilliant scarlet tunics and tall furry hats called bearskins, the palace guards stand in sentry boxes outside the Palace. Crowds gather in front of the railings to watch the colourful and musical military ceremony as the guards march down the Mall from St James's Palace, parading for half an hour while the palace keys are handed by the old guard to the new.

Queen's Gallery ⓮

Buckingham Palace Rd SW1. **Map** 5 C2. *020-7321 2233.* *St James's Park, Victoria.* *10am–5:30pm daily (last adm for exhibitions: 4:30pm).* *25, 26 Dec.* www.royal.gov.uk

The Queen's art collection is one of the finest and most valuable in the world, rich in the works of old masters such as Vermeer and Leonardo. A recent major expansion programme has increased the display space for the Collection, enabling the virtual year-round display of many masterpieces, as well as special exhibitions of drawings and decorative arts.

Detail: The Gold State Coach (1762), Royal Mews

Royal Mews ⓯

Buckingham Palace Rd SW1. **Map** 5 C3. *020-7321 2233.* *Victoria.* *Mar–Oct: 11am–4pm daily (last adm: 3:15pm). Extended opening hrs may operate Aug–Sep.* *open 9:30am–5pm daily all year (closed 25, 26 Dec).* www.royal.gov.uk

Lovers of horses and royal pomp should not miss this working stable and coach house. Designed by John Nash in 1825, it houses horses and state coaches used on official occasions. Among them is the glass coach used for royal weddings and foreign ambassadors. The star exhibit is the ornate gold state coach, built for George III in 1762, which was used by the Queen during the Golden Jubilee celebrations in 2002. The shop sells interesting merchandise.

Street-by-Street: Whitehall and Westminster

THE BROAD AVENUES of Whitehall and Westminster are lined with imposing buildings that serve the historic seat of both government and the established church. On weekdays the streets are crowded with civil servants whose work is based here, while at weekends the area takes on a different atmosphere with a steady flow of tourists.

Downing Street
Sir Robert Walpole was the first Prime Minister to live here in 1732 ⑰

Cabinet War Rooms
Now open to the public, these were Winston Churchill's World War II headquarters ⑯

St Margaret's Church is a favourite venue for political and society weddings.

★ Westminster Abbey
The abbey is London's oldest and most important church ⑳

Central Hall (1911) is a florid example of the Beaux Arts style.

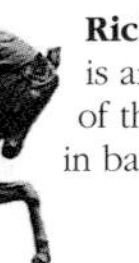

Richard I's Statue is an 1860 depiction of the king, killed in battle in 1199.

Dean's Yard is a secluded grassy square surrounded by picturesque buildings from different periods, many used by Westminster School.

The Burghers of Calais is a cast of Auguste Rodin's 1886 original in France.

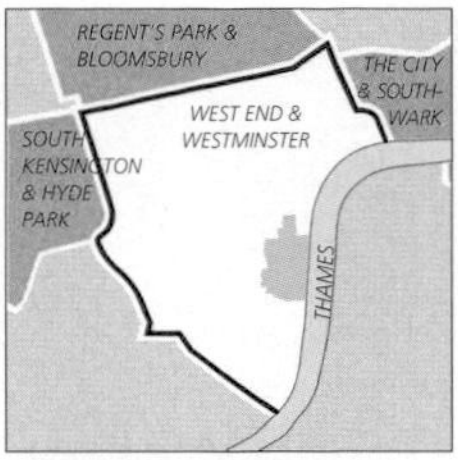

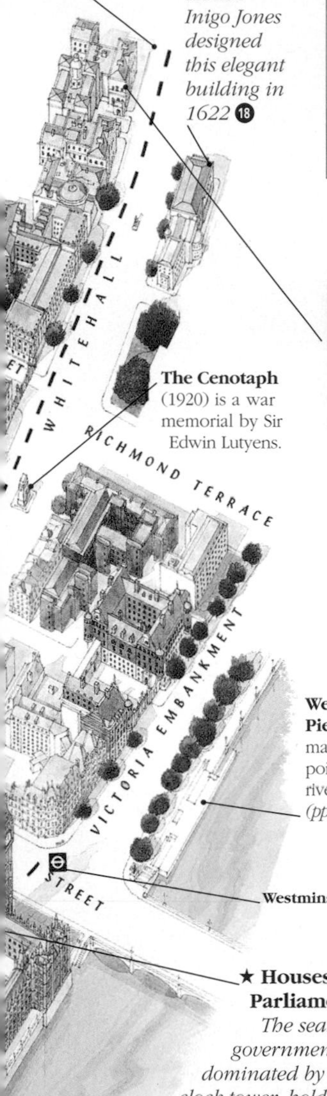

To Trafalgar Square

Banqueting House *Inigo Jones designed this elegant building in 1622* ⓲

The Cenotaph (1920) is a war memorial by Sir Edwin Lutyens.

WHITEHALL
RICHMOND TERRACE
VICTORIA EMBANKMENT
STREET

Locator Map
See Street Finder map 6

Horse Guards is a parade ground protected by a guard, changed twice each day.

Westminster Pier is the main starting point for river trips *(pp74–5)*.

Westminster

★ Houses of Parliament *The seat of government is dominated by the clock tower, holding the 14-tonne bell Big Ben, hung in 1858. Its deep chimes are broadcast daily on BBC radio* ⓳

Key

Suggested route

0 metres 100

0 yards 100

Star Sights

★ Westminster Abbey

★ Houses of Parliament

Cabinet War Rooms ⓰

Clive Steps, King Charles St SW1. **Map** 6 E2. 020-7930 6961. *Westminster.* *Apr–Sep: 9:30am– 6pm; Oct –Mar: 10am–6pm.* *24–26 Dec.* www.iwb.org.uk

This warren of cellars below a government office building is where the War Cabinet – first under Neville Chamberlain, then Winston Churchill from 1940 – met during World War II when German bombs were falling on London. The rooms include living quarters for ministers and military leaders and a sound-proofed Cabinet Room, where strategic decisions were taken. All rooms are protected by a concrete layer about a metre (3 ft) thick and are laid out as they were when the war ended, complete with Churchill's desk, communications equipment, and maps with markers for plotting battles and strategies.

Telephones in the Map Room, Cabinet War Rooms

Downing Street ⓱

SW1. **Map** 6 E2. *Westminster.* *to the public.*

Number 10 Downing Street has been the official residence of the British Prime Minister since 1732. It contains a Cabinet Room in which government policy is decided, an impressive State Dining Room and a private apartment; outside is a well-protected garden.

Next door at No. 11 is the official residence of the Chancellor of the Exchequer, who is in charge of the nation's financial affairs. In 1989, iron gates were erected at the Whitehall end of Downing Street for security purposes.

Banqueting House ⑱

Whitehall SW1. **Map** 6 E1. ☎ *020-7839 8919.* ⊖ *Charing Cross.* ◯ *10am–5pm Mon–Sat.* ● *public hols & for functions.* 🛍 ♿ www.hrp.org.uk

COMPLETED BY Inigo Jones *(see p53)* in 1622, this was the first building in central London to embody the Palladian style of Renaissance Italy. In 1629 Charles I commissioned Rubens to paint the ceiling with scenes exalting the reign of his father, James I. They symbolize the divine right of kings, disputed by the Parliamentarians, who executed Charles I outside the building in 1649 *(see pp52–3)*.

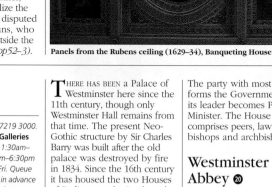

Panels from the Rubens ceiling (1629–34), Banqueting House

Houses of Parliament ⑲

SW1. **Map** 6 E2. ☎ *020-7219 3000.* ⊖ *Westminster.* **Visitors' Galleries** ◯ *2:30–10:30pm Mon; 11:30am–7:30pm Tue, Wed; 11:30am–6:30pm Thu; 9:30am–3pm sitting Fri. Queue or UK residents may apply in advance to local MP.* ● *frequently for parliamentary recesses.* ♿ *8 every 15 mins during summer opening hours. Call 0870-906 3773 for more info.* 🛍 www.parliament.uk

THERE HAS BEEN a Palace of Westminster here since the 11th century, though only Westminster Hall remains from that time. The present Neo-Gothic structure by Sir Charles Barry was built after the old palace was destroyed by fire in 1834. Since the 16th century it has housed the two Houses of Parliament, the Lords and the Commons. The House of Commons consists of elected Members of Parliament (MPs). The party with most MPs forms the Government, and its leader becomes Prime Minister. The House of Lords comprises peers, law lords, bishops and archbishops.

Westminster Abbey ⑳

See pp94–5.

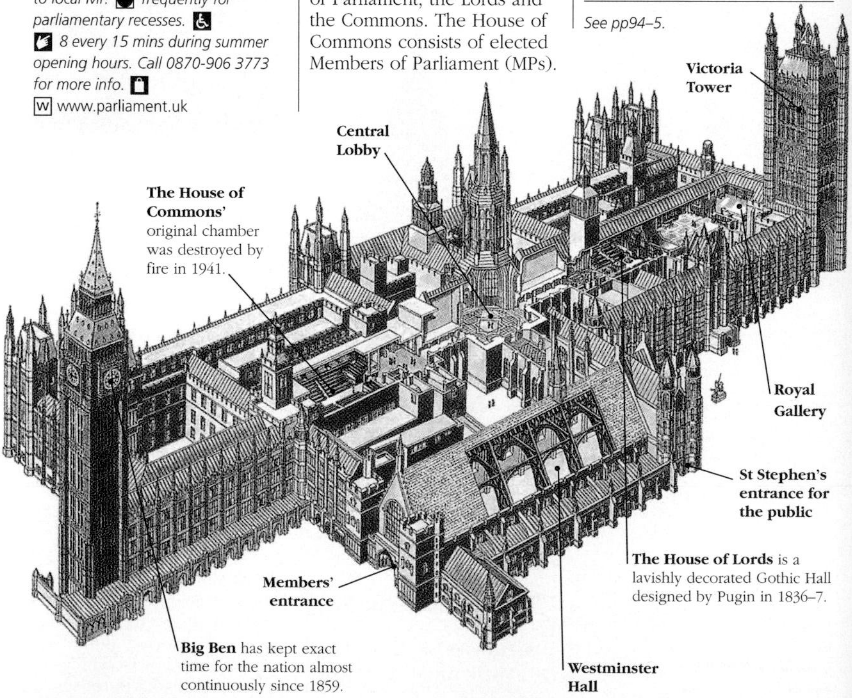

Victoria Tower

Central Lobby

The House of Commons' original chamber was destroyed by fire in 1941.

Royal Gallery

St Stephen's entrance for the public

The House of Lords is a lavishly decorated Gothic Hall designed by Pugin in 1836–7.

Members' entrance

Big Ben has kept exact time for the nation almost continuously since 1859.

Westminster Hall

Portico of Tate Britain

Tate Britain ㉑

Millbank SW1. **Map** 6 E4. *020-7887 8000. Pimlico. 77a, 88, C10. Victoria, Vauxhall. to Tate Modern every 40 mins. 10am–5:50pm daily. 24–26 Dec. for major exhibitions. Atterbury St.* www.tate.org.uk

FORMERLY THE Tate Gallery, Tate Britain is the national gallery of British art, and includes works from the 16th to the 21st century. Displays draw on the enormous Tate Collection, which also includes the international modern art seen at Tate Modern *(p123)*. A new boat, Tate to Tate, takes visitors between the two galleries. Located in the adjoining Clore Gallery is the Turner Bequest (see box).

The permanent collection displays occupy three-quarters of the main floor. The displays follow a broad chronological sweep from the early 16th century to the present. The size of the collection necessitates some rotation of displays, which are organized in various imaginative and innovative ways. Major themes change on a three yearly basis, solo artists rooms and smaller themed rooms more frequently. Loan exhibitions are installed in the ground floor galleries and part of the main floor.

The section on the years 1500–1800 is dominated by portraiture, as seen in an exquisite portrait of Elizabeth I (c.1575) by the miniaturist Nicholas Hilliard, as well as the lively works of William Hogarth and the grand portraiture of Joshua Reynolds and Thomas Gainsborough. The section concludes with the visionary paintings of William Blake.

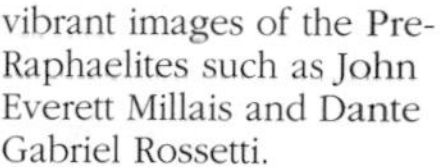

***Recumbent Figure* (1938) by Henry Moore**

The 19th-century section is rich in the great landscape works of John Constable, as well as the vibrant images of the Pre-Raphaelites such as John Everett Millais and Dante Gabriel Rossetti.

The period 1900–1960 includes the war imagery of C R W Nevinson, the landscapes of Paul Nash, and the British modernist works of Henry Moore, Barbara Hepworth and Ben Nicholson.

The Tate Collection is outstanding in its wealth of British art from 1960 to the present, and the displays in this section are changed on a regular basis. Works range from the 1960s Pop artists David Hockney, Richard Hamilton and Peter Blake, through the works of Gilbert and George and the landscape artist Richard Long, to the 1980s paintings of Lucian Freud, Howard Hodgkin and R B Kitaj. The so-called Young British Artists (YBAs) are well represented by the leading figures Damian Hirst, Tracey Emin and Sarah Lucas, as is the contemporary movement of British artists such as Tacita Dean and Douglas Gordon, who use film and video as their medium.

***Mr. and Mrs. Clark and Percy* (1970–71) by David Hockney**

***Captain Thomas Lee* (1594) by Marcus Gheeraerts II**

THE TURNER BEQUEST

The Turner Bequest comprises some 300 oil paintings and 20,000 watercolours and drawings, left to the nation by the great landscape painter J M W Turner on his death in 1851. Turner's will had specified that a special gallery be built to house his pictures and this was finally done in 1987 with the opening of the Clore Gallery, a south-east extension of Tate Britain. The oils are on view in the main galleries, and the wonderful watercolours are the subject of changing displays.

***The Scarlet Sunset: A Town on a River* (c.1830–40)**

Westminster Abbey ⓴

WESTMINSTER ABBEY has been the burial place of Britain's monarchs since the 11th century and the setting for many coronations and royal weddings. It is one of the most beautiful buildings in London, with an exceptionally diverse array of architectural styles, ranging from the austere French Gothic of the nave to the astonishing complexity of Henry VII's chapel. Half national church, half national museum, the abbey aisles and transepts are crammed with an extraordinary collection of tombs and monuments honouring some of Britain's greatest public figures, ranging from politicians to poets.

North Entrance
The mock-medieval stonework is Victorian.

Statesmen's Aisle

Flying buttresses help redistribute the great weight of the roof.

★ Nave
At a height of 31 m (102 ft), the nave is the highest in England. The ratio of height to width is 3:1.

Cloisters
Tombs here include those of several medieval abbots.

CORONATION

The coronation ceremony is over 1,000 years old and since 1066, with the crowning of William the Conqueror on Christmas Day, the abbey has been its sumptuous setting. The coronation of Queen Elizabeth II, in 1953, was the first to be televised.

STAR FEATURES

- ★ **Nave**
- ★ **Henry VII Chapel**
- ★ **Chapter House**

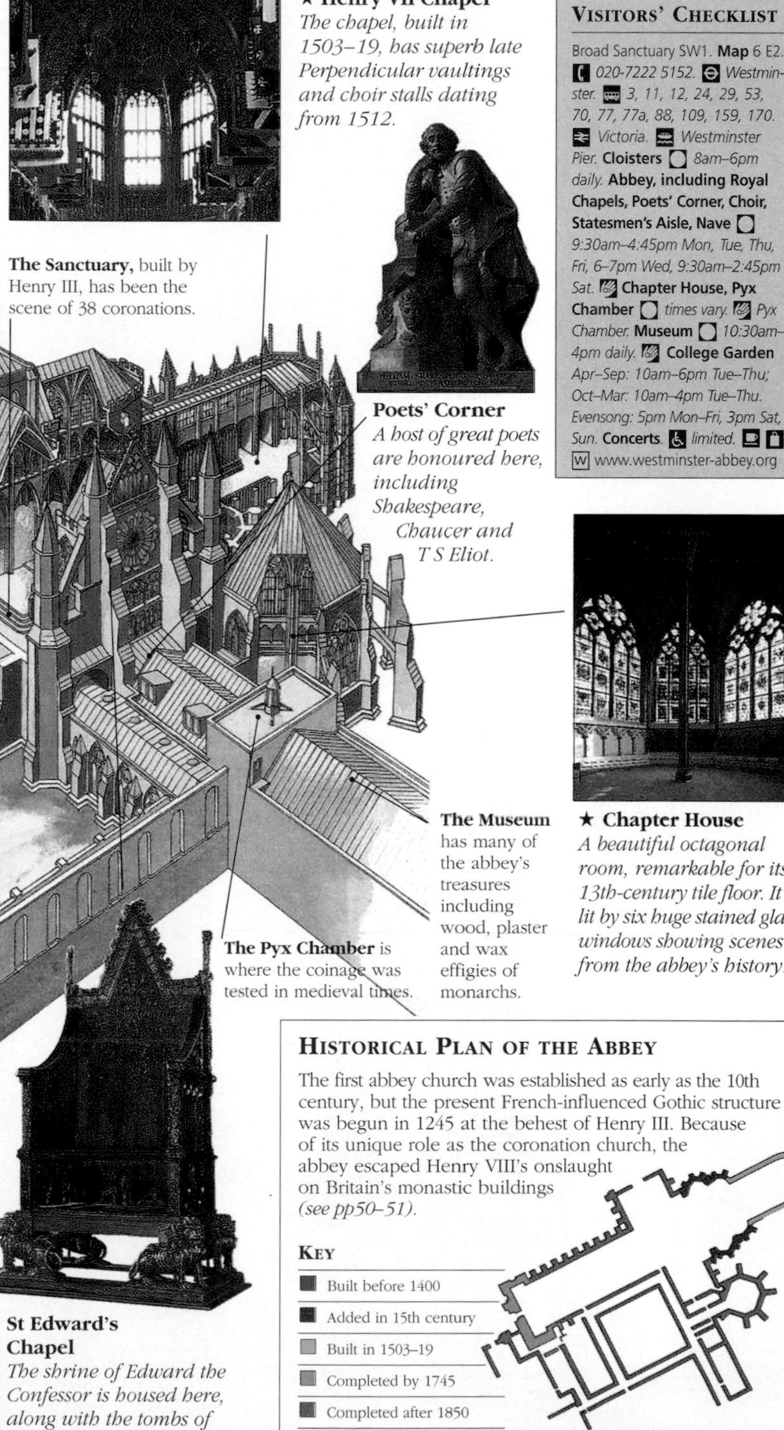

★ Henry VII Chapel
The chapel, built in 1503–19, has superb late Perpendicular vaultings and choir stalls dating from 1512.

The Sanctuary, built by Henry III, has been the scene of 38 coronations.

Poets' Corner
A host of great poets are honoured here, including Shakespeare, Chaucer and T S Eliot.

The Museum has many of the abbey's treasures including wood, plaster and wax effigies of monarchs.

★ Chapter House
A beautiful octagonal room, remarkable for its 13th-century tile floor. It is lit by six huge stained glass windows showing scenes from the abbey's history.

The Pyx Chamber is where the coinage was tested in medieval times.

St Edward's Chapel
The shrine of Edward the Confessor is housed here, along with the tombs of many medieval monarchs.

Visitors' Checklist

Broad Sanctuary SW1. **Map** 6 E2. *020-7222 5152. Westminster.* *3, 11, 12, 24, 29, 53, 70, 77, 77a, 88, 109, 159, 170.* *Victoria.* *Westminster Pier.* **Cloisters** *8am–6pm daily.* **Abbey, including Royal Chapels, Poets' Corner, Choir, Statesmen's Aisle, Nave** *9:30am–4:45pm Mon, Tue, Thu, Fri, 6–7pm Wed, 9:30am–2:45pm Sat.* **Chapter House, Pyx Chamber** *times vary.* *Pyx Chamber.* **Museum** *10:30am–4pm daily.* **College Garden** *Apr–Sep: 10am–6pm Tue–Thu; Oct–Mar: 10am–4pm Tue–Thu.* *Evensong: 5pm Mon–Fri, 3pm Sat, Sun.* **Concerts.** *limited.* www.westminster-abbey.org

Historical Plan of the Abbey

The first abbey church was established as early as the 10th century, but the present French-influenced Gothic structure was begun in 1245 at the behest of Henry III. Because of its unique role as the coronation church, the abbey escaped Henry VIII's onslaught on Britain's monastic buildings *(see pp50–51)*.

Key

- Built before 1400
- Added in 15th century
- Built in 1503–19
- Completed by 1745
- Completed after 1850

South Kensington and Hyde Park

This exclusive district embraces one of London's largest parks and some of its finest museums, shops, restaurants and hotels. Until the mid-19th century it was a genteel, semi-rural backwater of large houses and private schools lying to the south of Kensington Palace. In 1851, the Great Exhibition, until then the largest arts and science event ever staged *(see pp56–7)*, was held in Hyde Park, transforming the area into a celebration of Victorian learning and self-confidence.

Peter Pan statue in Kensington Gardens

The brainchild of Queen Victoria's husband, Prince Albert, the exhibition was a massive success and the profits were used to buy 35 ha (87 acres) of land in South Kensington. Here, Prince Albert encouraged the construction of a concert hall, museums and colleges devoted to the applied arts and sciences; most of them survive. The neighbourhood soon became modish, full of flamboyant red-brick mansion blocks, garden squares and the elite shops still to be found in Knightsbridge.

Sights at a Glance

Historic Buildings
Kensington Palace 7

Churches
Brompton Oratory 2

Shops
Harrods 1

Parks and Gardens
Hyde Park and Kensington Gardens 6

Museums and Galleries
Natural History Museum 5
Science Museum 4
Victoria and Albert Museum pp100–101 3

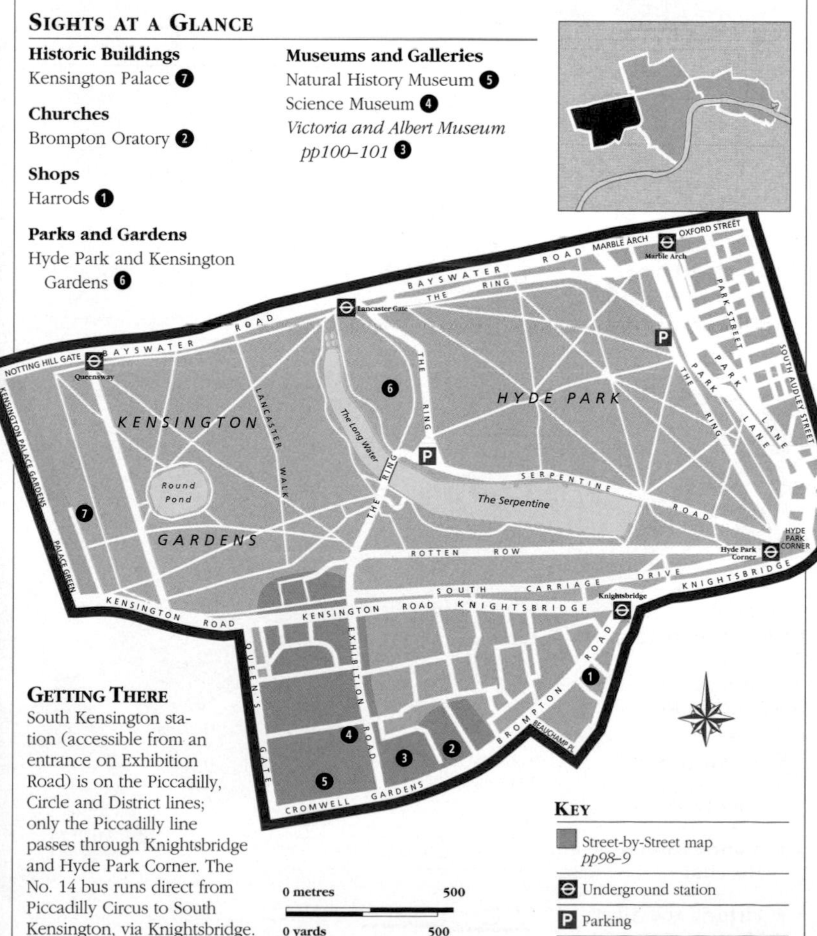

Getting There

South Kensington station (accessible from an entrance on Exhibition Road) is on the Piccadilly, Circle and District lines; only the Piccadilly line passes through Knightsbridge and Hyde Park Corner. The No. 14 bus runs direct from Piccadilly Circus to South Kensington, via Knightsbridge.

0 metres 500
0 yards 500

Key

Street-by-Street map *pp98–9*
Underground station
Parking

◁ **Ennismore Mews in South Kensington, built 1843–6**

Street-by-Street: South Kensington

THE NUMEROUS MUSEUMS and colleges created in the wake of the Great Exhibition of 1851 *(see pp56–7)* continue to give this neighbourhood an air of leisured culture. Visited as much by Londoners as tourists, the museum area is liveliest on Sundays and on summer evenings during the Royal Albert Hall's famous season of classical "Prom" concerts *(see p128)*.

The Royal Albert Hall opened in 1870 and was modelled on Roman amphitheatres.

The Memorial to the Great Exhibition is surmounted by a bronze statue of its instigator, Prince Albert.

The Royal College of Music, founded in 1882, exhibits historic musical instruments such as this harpsichord dating from 1531.

★ Science Museum
Visitors can experiment with over a thousand interactive displays ❹

★ Natural History Museum
The Creepy Crawlies exhibition has proved highly popular ❺

Entrance to South Kensington tube

KEY

— — — Suggested route

0 metres 100

0 yards 100

STAR SIGHTS

- ★ Science Museum
- ★ Natural History Museum
- ★ Victoria and Albert Museum

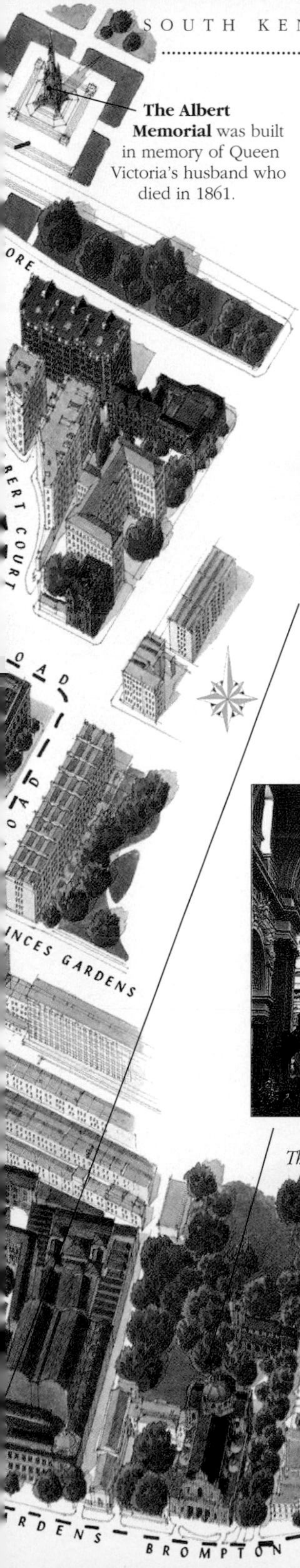

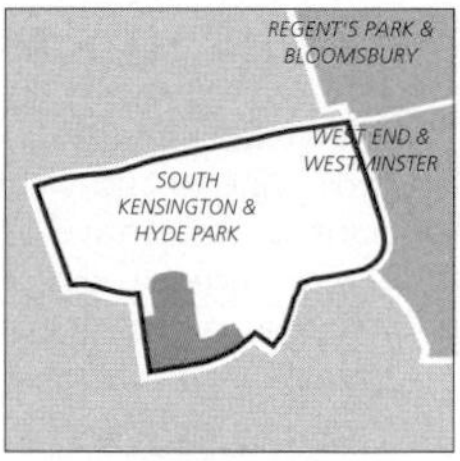

The Albert Memorial was built in memory of Queen Victoria's husband who died in 1861.
ORE
RERT COURT
ROAD
NCES GARDENS
RDENS
BROMPTON ROAD
Brompton Square (1821)
To Knightsbridge and Harrod's

REGENT'S PARK & BLOOMSBURY
WEST END & WESTMINSTER
SOUTH KENSINGTON & HYDE PARK

LOCATOR MAP
See Street Finder map 2

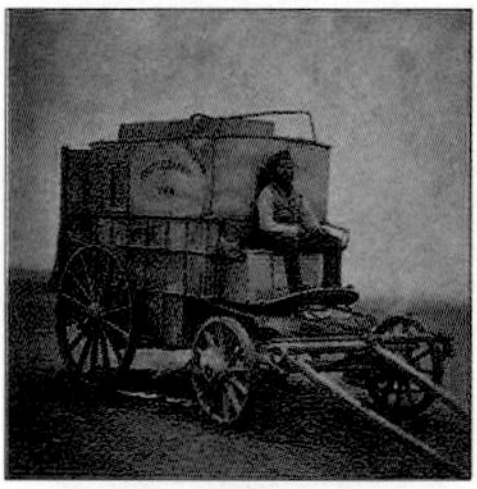

★ Victoria and Albert Museum
The museum has a fine collection of applied arts and photography from around the world ❸

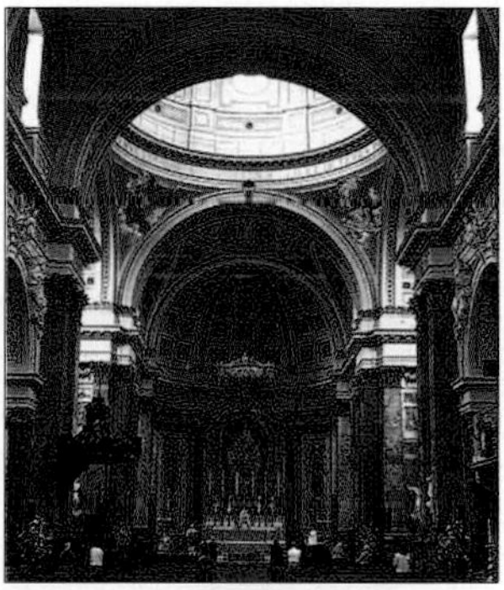

Brompton Oratory
This ornate Baroque church is famous for its splendid musical tradition ❷

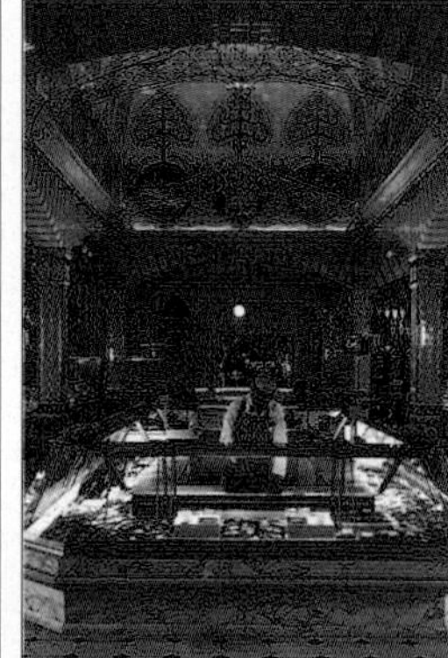

Harrods Food Hall

Harrods ❶

Knightsbridge SW1. **Map** 5 A3. *020-7730 1234.* *Knightsbridge.* *10am–7pm Mon–Sat.* See ***Shops and Markets*** *pp122–3.* www.harrods.com

IN 1849 HENRY CHARLES HARROD opened a small grocery shop on Brompton Road, which soon became famous for its impeccable service and quality. The store moved into these extravagant premises in Knightsbridge in 1905.

Brompton Oratory ❷

Brompton Rd SW7. **Map** 2 F5. *020-7808 0900.* *South Kensington.* *6:30am–8pm daily.* www.bromptonoratory.org.uk

THE ITALIANATE ORATORY is a lavish monument to the 19th-century English Catholic revival. It was established as a base for a community of priests by John Henry Newman (later Cardinal Newman), who introduced the Oratorian movement to England in 1848. The church was opened in 1884, and the dome and façade added in the 1890s.

The sumptuous interior holds many fine monuments. The 12 huge 17th-century statues of the apostles are from Siena Cathedral, the elaborate Baroque Lady Altar (1693) is from the Dominican church at Brescia, and the 18th-century altar in St Wilfred's Chapel is from Rochefort in Belgium.

Victoria and Albert Museum ❸

The Glass Gallery, room 131

The Victoria and Albert Museum (the V&A) contains one of the world's widest collections of decorative arts, ranging from early Christian devotional objects and the mystical art of southeast Asia to cutting-edge furniture design. Originally founded in 1852 as the Museum of Manufactures to inspire students of design, it was renamed by Queen Victoria in 1899 in memory of Prince Albert. The museum is embarking on a dramatic redisplay of much of its collection and a major new contemporary space, the Spiral, designed by Daniel Libeskind, is currently under construction.

Whiteley Silver Galleries
Radiant pieces such as the Burgess Cup (Britain, 1863) fill these stunning galleries.

★ British Galleries
The Great Bed of Ware has been a tourist attraction since 1601, when Shakespeare sparked interest in it by making reference to it in Twelfth Night.

★ Dress Court
In this popular gallery, European clothing from the mid-1500s to the present day is displayed. This dress dates from 1880.

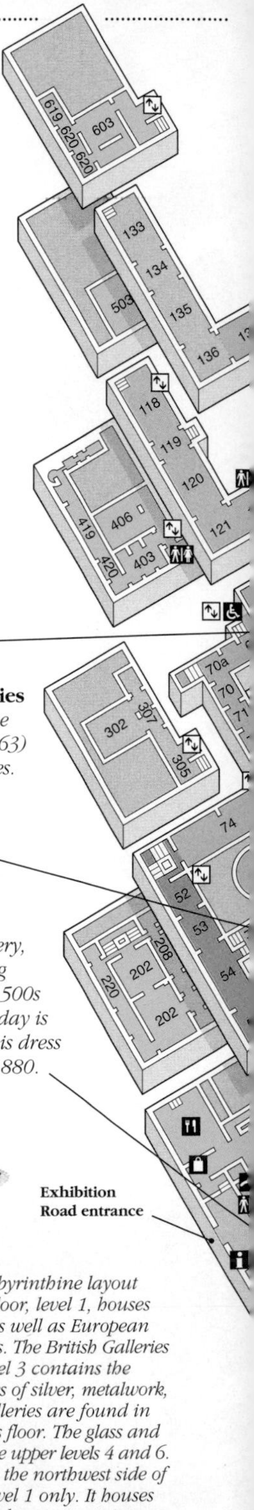

Exhibition Road entrance

Key to Floorplan

- Level 0
- Level 1
- Level 2
- Level 3
- Level 4
- Level 6
- Henry Cole Wing
- Non-exhibition space

Star Exhibits

- ★ **British Galleries**
- ★ **Dress Court**
- ★ **Medieval Treasury**
- ★ **Nehru Gallery of Indian Art**

Gallery Guide

The V&A has a 7-mile (11-km) labyrinthine layout spread over six levels. The main floor, level 1, houses the Asian and Islamic galleries, as well as European Medieval and Renaissance displays. The British Galleries are located on levels 2 and 4. Level 3 contains the 20th Century galleries and displays of silver, metalwork, arms and jewellery; the textile galleries are found in the far north-eastern corner of this floor. The glass and ceramics displays are located on the upper levels 4 and 6. The Henry Cole Wing, situated on the northwest side of the building, is accessible from level 1 only. It houses galleries on Frank Lloyd Wright and portrait miniatures.

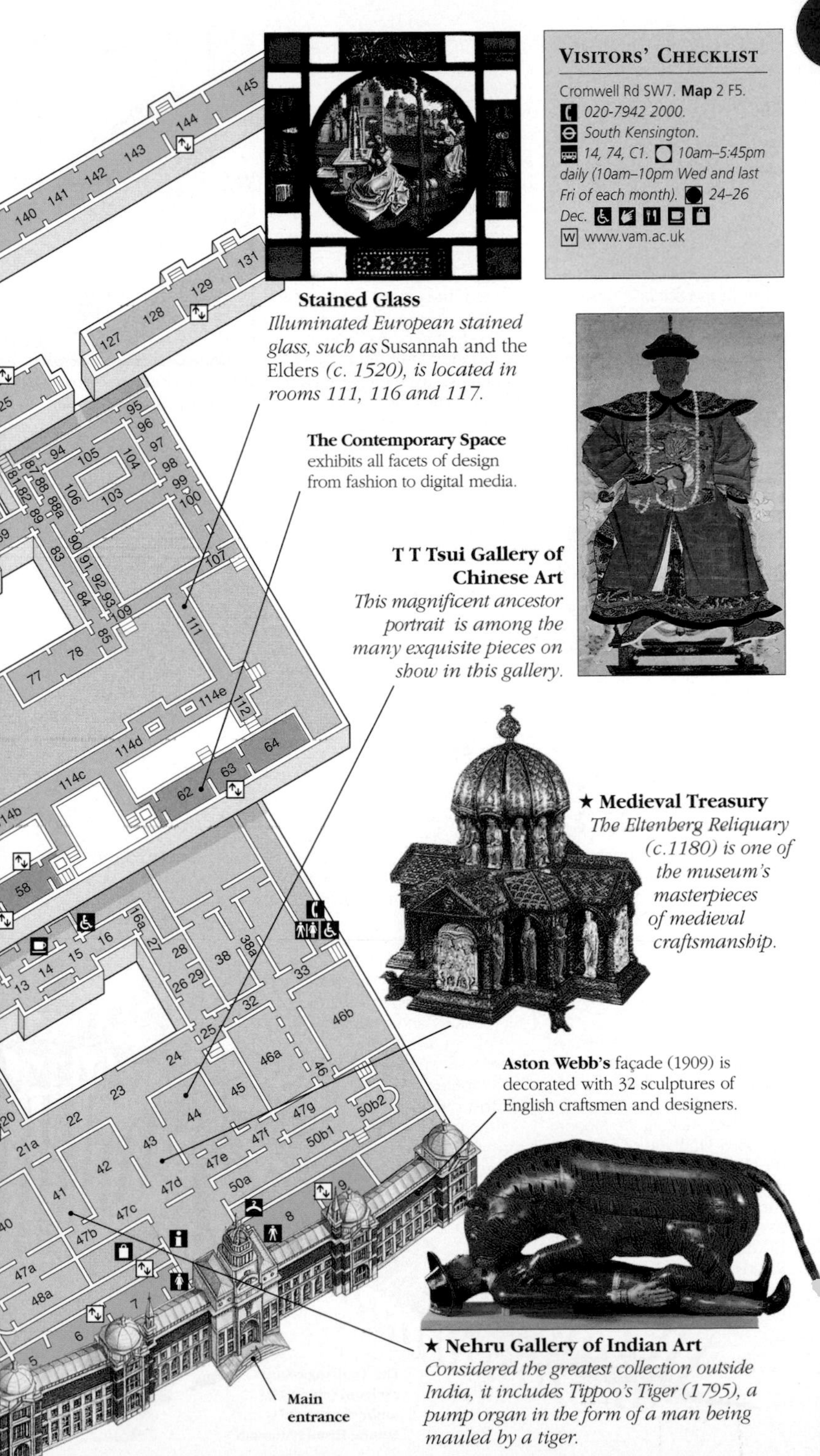

Stained Glass
Illuminated European stained glass, such as Susannah and the Elders *(c. 1520), is located in rooms 111, 116 and 117.*

The Contemporary Space exhibits all facets of design from fashion to digital media.

T T Tsui Gallery of Chinese Art
This magnificent ancestor portrait is among the many exquisite pieces on show in this gallery.

★ **Medieval Treasury**
The Eltenberg Reliquary (c.1180) is one of the museum's masterpieces of medieval craftsmanship.

Aston Webb's façade (1909) is decorated with 32 sculptures of English craftsmen and designers.

★ **Nehru Gallery of Indian Art**
Considered the greatest collection outside India, it includes Tippoo's Tiger (1795), a pump organ in the form of a man being mauled by a tiger.

VISITORS' CHECKLIST

Cromwell Rd SW7. **Map** 2 F5.
020-7942 2000.
South Kensington.
14, 74, C1. 10am–5:45pm daily (10am–10pm Wed and last Fri of each month). 24–26 Dec.
www.vam.ac.uk

Science Museum ❹

Exhibition Rd SW7. **Map** 2 E5. 020-7942 4000. South Kensington. 10am–6pm daily. 24–26 Dec. for IMAX and special exhibitions only. www.sciencemuseum.org.uk

CENTURIES OF continuing scientific and technological development lie at the heart of the Science Museum's massive collections. The hardware displayed is magnificent: from steam engines to aero-engines; spacecraft to the very first mechanical computers. Equally important is the social context of science – what discoveries and inventions mean for day-to-day life – and the process of discovery itself. There are many interactive and hands-on displays which are very popular with children.

Newcomen's Steam Engine (1712), Science Museum

The museum is spread over seven floors and includes the recent Wellcome Wing at the west end of the museum. The basement features the excellent hands-on galleries for children, including the Launch Pad and Garden. Power dominates the ground floor, and is dedicated to steam power, with the still-operational Harle Syke Mill Engine of 1903. Here too are Space and Making the Modern World, a highlight of which is the display of the scarred Apollo 10 spacecraft, which carried three astronauts to the moon and back in May 1969. In Challenge of Materials, located on the first floor, our expectations of materials are confounded with exhibits such as a bridge made of glass and a steel wedding dress.

The Flight gallery on the third floor is packed with early flying contraptions, fighter planes and aeroplanes, many of them suspended as if in mid-flight. The fourth and fifth floors house the medical science galleries, where Glimpses of Medical History has a 17th-century Italian vase for storing snake bite potion.

The high-tech Wellcome Wing offers four floors of interactive technology, including the digital landscape of Digitopolis, where the curious can explore a virtual world of sound and vision. With an IMAX 3D Cinema and a motion simulator, Virtual Voyages, it is a breathtaking addition to the museum.

Natural History Museum ❺

Cromwell Rd SW7. **Map** 2 E5. 020-7942 5000. South Kensington. 10am–5:50pm Mon–Sat, 11am–5:50pm Sun & public hols. 25, 26 Dec. www.nhm.ac.uk

THIS VAST CATHEDRAL-LIKE building is the most architecturally flamboyant of the South Kensington museums. Its richly sculpted stonework conceals an iron and steel frame; this building technique was revolutionary when the museum opened in 1881. The imaginative displays tackle fundamental issues such as the ecology and evolution of the planet, the origin of species and the development of human beings – all explained through a dynamic combination of the latest technology, interactive techniques and traditional displays.

Relief from a decorative panel in the Natural History Museum

The museum is divided into the Life and Earth Galleries. In the former, the Ecology exhibition begins its exploration of the complex web of the natural world, and man's role in it, through a convincing replica of a moonlit rainforest buzzing with the sounds of insects. The most popular exhibit is the Dinosaur Gallery, which has a new, robotic *Tyrannosaurus rex* in the Dinosaur Pavilion. The state-of-the-art Earth Galleries explore the history of Earth and its wealth of natural resources, and the Power Within offers the opportunity to experience the rumblings of an earthquake.

The Tuojiangasaurus skeleton (about 150 million years old), Natural History Museum

Statue of the young Queen Victoria outside Kensington Palace, sculpted by her daughter, Princess Louise

Hyde Park and Kensington Gardens ❻

W2. **Map** 2 F2. *020-7298 2100.* **Hyde Park** *Hyde Park Corner, Knightsbridge, Lancaster Gate, Marble Arch.* *dawn–midnight daily.* **Kensington Gardens** *020-7298 2117.* *Queensway, Lancaster Gate.* *dawn–dusk daily.* *See also pp76–7.* **Diana, Princess of Wales Memorial Playground** *Queensway, Bayswater.* *10am–dusk daily.* www.royalparks.gov.uk

THE ANCIENT MANOR of Hyde was part of the lands of Westminster Abbey seized by Henry VIII at the Dissolution of the Monasteries in 1536 *(see pp50–51)*. James I opened the park to the public in the early 17th century, and it was soon one of the city's most fashionable public spaces. Unfortunately it also became popular with duellists and highwaymen, and consequently William III had 300 lights hung along Rotten Row, the first street in England to be lit up at night. In 1730, the Westbourne River was dammed by Queen Caroline in order to create the Serpentine, an artificial lake that is today used for boating and swimming, and Rotten Row for horse riding. The park is also a rallying point for political demonstrations, while at Speaker's Corner, in the northeast, anyone has had the right to address the public since 1872. Sundays are particularly lively, with many budding orators and a number of eccentrics revealing their plans for the betterment of mankind.

Adjoining Hyde Park is Kensington Gardens, the former grounds of Kensington Palace. Three great attractions for children are the innovative Diana, Princess of Wales Memorial Playground, the bronze statue of J M Barrie's fictional Peter Pan (1912), by George Frampton, and the Round Pond where people sail model boats. Also worth seeing is the dignified Orangery (1704), once used by Queen Anne as a "summer supper house" and now a summer café.

Detail of the Coalbrookdale Gate, Kensington Gardens

Kensington Palace ❼

Kensington Palace Gdns W8. **Map** 2 D3. *020-7937 9561.* *High St Kensington, Queensway.* *Nov–Feb: 10am–5pm daily; Mar–Oct: 10am–6pm daily (last adm: 1 hr before closing).* *1 Jan, 24–26 Dec.* *ground floor.* www.hrp.org.uk

KENSINGTON PALACE was the principal residence of the royal family from the 1690s until 1760, when George III moved to Buckingham Palace. Over the years it has seen a number of important royal events. In 1714 Queen Anne died here from a fit of apoplexy brought on by over-eating and, in June 1837, Princess Victoria of Kent was woken to be told that her uncle William IV had died and she was now queen – the beginning of her 64-year reign. Half of the palace still holds royal apartments, but the other half is open to the public. Among the highlights are the 18th-century state rooms with ceilings and murals by William Kent *(see p24)*. After the death of Princess Diana in 1997, the palace became a focal point for mourners who gathered in their thousands at its gates and turned the area into a field of bouquets.

Regent's Park and Bloomsbury

Cream stuccoed terraces built by John Nash *(see p107)* fringe the southern edge of Regent's Park in London's highest concentration of quality Georgian housing. The park, named for the Prince Regent, was also designed by Nash, as the culmination of a triumphal route from the Prince's house in St James's *(see pp86–7)*. Today it is the busiest of the royal parks and boasts a zoo, an open air theatre, boating lake, rose garden, cafés and London's largest mosque. To the northeast is Camden Town *(see p132)* with its popular market, shops and cafés, reached by walking, or taking a boat, along the picturesque Regent's Canal.

Ancient Greek vase, British Museum

Bloomsbury, an enclave of attractive garden squares and Georgian brick terraces, was one of the most fashionable areas of the city until the mid-19th century, when the arrival of large hospitals and railway stations persuaded many of the wealthier residents to move west to Mayfair, Knightsbridge and Kensington. Home to the British Museum since 1753 and the University of London since 1828, Bloomsbury has long been the domain of artists, writers and intellectuals, including the Bloomsbury Group *(see p151)*, George Bernard Shaw, Charles Dickens and Karl Marx. Traditionally a centre for the book trade, it remains a good place for literary browsing.

Sights at a Glance

Historic Streets
Bloomsbury 5

Museums and Galleries
British Museum pp108–9 4

Madame Tussaud's and the Planetarium 1
Sherlock Holmes Museum 2
Wallace Collection 3

Getting There

For most of Regent's Park, the nearest tube stations are Regent's Park, Great Portland Street and Baker Street. Buses 13, 139 and 159 run from Trafalgar Square to near Baker Street. The closest station to the zoo is Camden Town. Russell Square tube station is in the heart of Bloomsbury.

Key

Underground station

Parking

0 metres 500
0 yards 500

◁ **St Andrew's Place, Regent's Park**

Madame Tussaud's and the Planetarium ❶

Marylebone Rd NW1. **Map** 3 B3. *0870 400 3000.* *Baker St.* **Planetarium** *9am–5:30pm daily.* **Tussaud's** *10am–5:30pm daily.* *25 Dec.* *phone first.* www.madame-tussauds.com

MADAME TUSSAUD began her wax-modelling career making death masks of victims of the French Revolution. She moved to England and in 1835 set up an exhibition of her work in Baker Street, near the present site. Traditional techniques are still used to create figures of royalty, politicians, actors, pop stars and sporting heroes. The main sections of the exhibition are: the Garden Party, where visitors mingle with models of celebrities; Première Night, devoted to the giants of the entertainment world; and the Grand Hall, a collection of various royalty, statesmen, world leaders, writers and artists, from Shakespeare to Picasso.

Wax figure of Elizabeth II

The Chamber of Horrors is the most renowned part of Madame Tussaud's. Alongside some of the original French Revolution death masks are recreations of murders and executions. In the Spirit of London finale, visitors travel in stylized taxi-cabs through the city's history to "witness" events, from the Great Fire of 1666 to the Swinging 1960s. Next door, the Planetarium, built in 1958, has spectacularly exciting star and laser shows.

Wax model of Luciano Pavarotti (1990), Madame Tussaud's

Conan Doyle's fictional detective Sherlock Holmes

Sherlock Holmes Museum ❷

221b Baker St NW1. **Map** 3 A3. *020-7935 8866.* *Baker St.* *9:30am–6pm daily.* *25 Dec.* www.sherlock-holmes.co.uk

SIR ARTHUR CONAN DOYLE'S fictional detective was supposed to live at 221b Baker Street, which did not exist. The museum, labelled 221b, actually stands between Nos. 237 and 239, and is the only surviving Victorian lodging house in the street. There is a reconstruction of Holmes's front room, and memorabilia from the stories decorate every room. Visitors can buy plaques, Holmes hats, Toby jugs and meerschaum pipes.

Wallace Collection ❸

Hertford House, Manchester Sq W1. **Map** 3 B4. *020-7563 9500.* *Bond St, Baker St.* *10am–5pm Mon–Sat, noon–5pm Sun.* *24–26 Dec, Good Fri, 1 Jan.* *phone first.* www.wallace-collection.org.uk

ONE OF THE WORLD'S finest private collections of European art, it has remained intact since 1897. The product of passionate collecting by four generations of the Seymour-Conway family who were Marquesses of Hertford, it was bequeathed to the state on the condition that it would go on permanent public display with nothing added or taken away. Hertford House still retains the atmosphere of a grand 19th-century house, and the recent Centenary Project has created more gallery space and a stunning high-level glass roof for the central courtyard, which now contains a sculpture garden and an elegant restaurant.

The 3rd Marquess (1777–1842), a flamboyant London figure, used his Italian wife's fortune to buy works by Titian and Canaletto, along with numerous 17th-century Dutch paintings including works by Van Dyck. The collection's particular strength is 18th-century French painting, sculpture and decorative arts, acquired by the 4th Marquess (1800–70) and his natural son, Sir Richard Wallace (1818–90).

A 16th-century Italian majolica dish from the Wallace Collection

The Marquess had a taste for lush romanticism, and notable among his acquisitions are Watteau's *Champs Elysées* (1716–17), Fragonard's *The Swing* (1766) and Boucher's *The Rising and Setting of the Sun* (1753).

Other highlights at the Wallace Collection include Rembrandt's *Titus, the Artist's Son* (1650s), Titian's *Perseus and Andromeda* (1554–6) and Hals's famous *Laughing Cavalier* (1624). There is also an important collection of Renaissance armour, and superb examples of Sèvres porcelain and Italian majolica.

John Nash's Regency London

JOHN NASH, the son of a Lambeth millwright, was designing houses from the 1780s. However, it was not until the 1820s that he also became known as an inspired town planner, when his "royal route" was completed. This took George IV from his Pall Mall palace, through Piccadilly Circus and up the elegant sweep of Regent Street to Regent's Park, which Nash bordered with rows of beautiful Neo-Classical villas, such as Park Crescent and Cumberland Terrace. Though many of his plans were never completed, this map of 1851, which unusually places the south at the top, shows Nash's overall architectural impact on London. His other work included the revamping of Buckingham Palace *(see pp88–9)*, and the building of several theatres and churches.

Statue of John Nash (1752–1835)

The Theatre Royal Haymarket *has retained Nash's 1821 Corinthian portico, but its interior was totally rebuilt in 1905.*

All Souls, Langham Place *is shown in this 1824 cartoon which lampoons Nash for his unorthodox design.*

***Cumberland Terrace**, the longest and most ornate of the stuccoed terraces surrounding Regent's Park, was intended to face a royal palace, which was never built.*

Park Crescent *was designed by Nash to be the southern half of a circle, but the northern half was never built. The interiors were refurbished in the 1960s but the dramatic façade was kept intact.*

British Museum ❹

Helmet from Sutton Hoo ship burial

The oldest public museum in the world, the British Museum was established in 1753 to house the collections of the physician Sir Hans Sloane (1660–1753). Sloane's collection has been added to by gifts and purchases from all over the world, and the museum now contains artifacts spanning thousands of years of culture. The main part of the building (1823–50) is by architect Robert Smirke, but the architectural highlight is the modern Great Court, with the Reading Room at its centre.

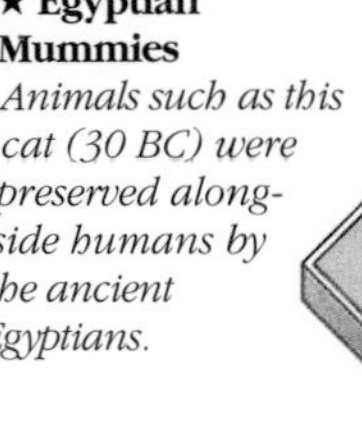

★ Egyptian Mummies
Animals such as this cat (30 BC) were preserved alongside humans by the ancient Egyptians.

Bronze Figure Shiva Nataraja
This statue of the Hindu God Shiva Nataraja (c.1100) from South India forms part of the fine collection of Oriental art.

The Egyptian Gallery on the main floor houses the Rosetta Stone, the inscription that enabled 19th-century scholars to decipher Egyptian hieroglyphs.

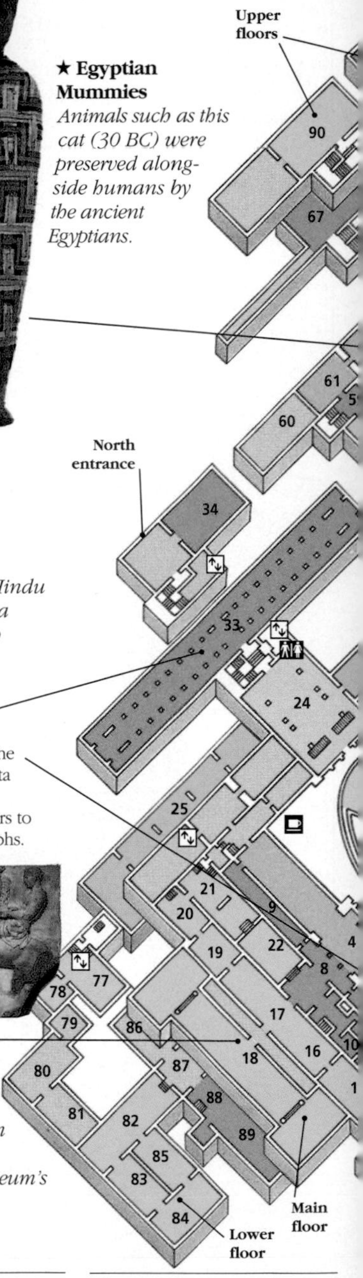

★ Elgin Marbles
These 5th-century BC reliefs from the Parthenon in Athens were brought to London by Lord Elgin around 1802 and are the museum's most famous treasure.

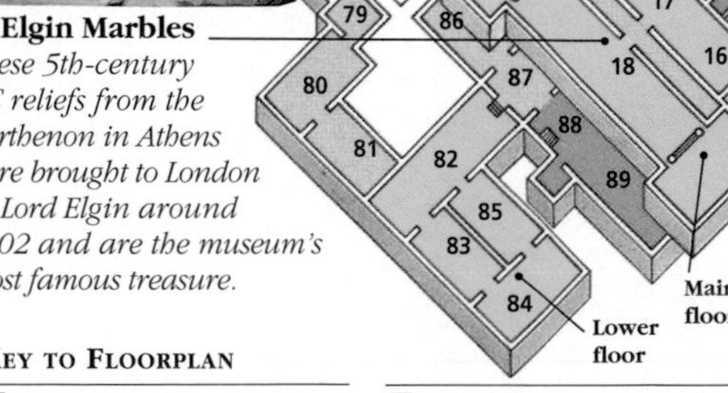

Gallery Guide

The Greek and Roman, and Ancient Near Eastern collections are found on all three levels of the museum, predominantly on the west side. The African collection is located on the lower floor, while Asian exhibits are found on the main and upper floors at the rear of the museum. The Americas collection is located in the northeast corner off the main floor. Egyptian artifacts are found in the large gallery to the west of the Great Court and on the first floor.

Key to Floorplan

- Asian collection
- Americas collection
- Coins, medals, prints and and drawings
- Greek and Roman collections
- Egyptian collection
- Ancient Near Eastern collection
- Prehistory collection
- European collection
- African collection
- Temporary exhibitions
- Non-exhibition space

Star Exhibits

- ★ Egyptian Mummies
- ★ Elgin Marbles
- ★ Lindow Man

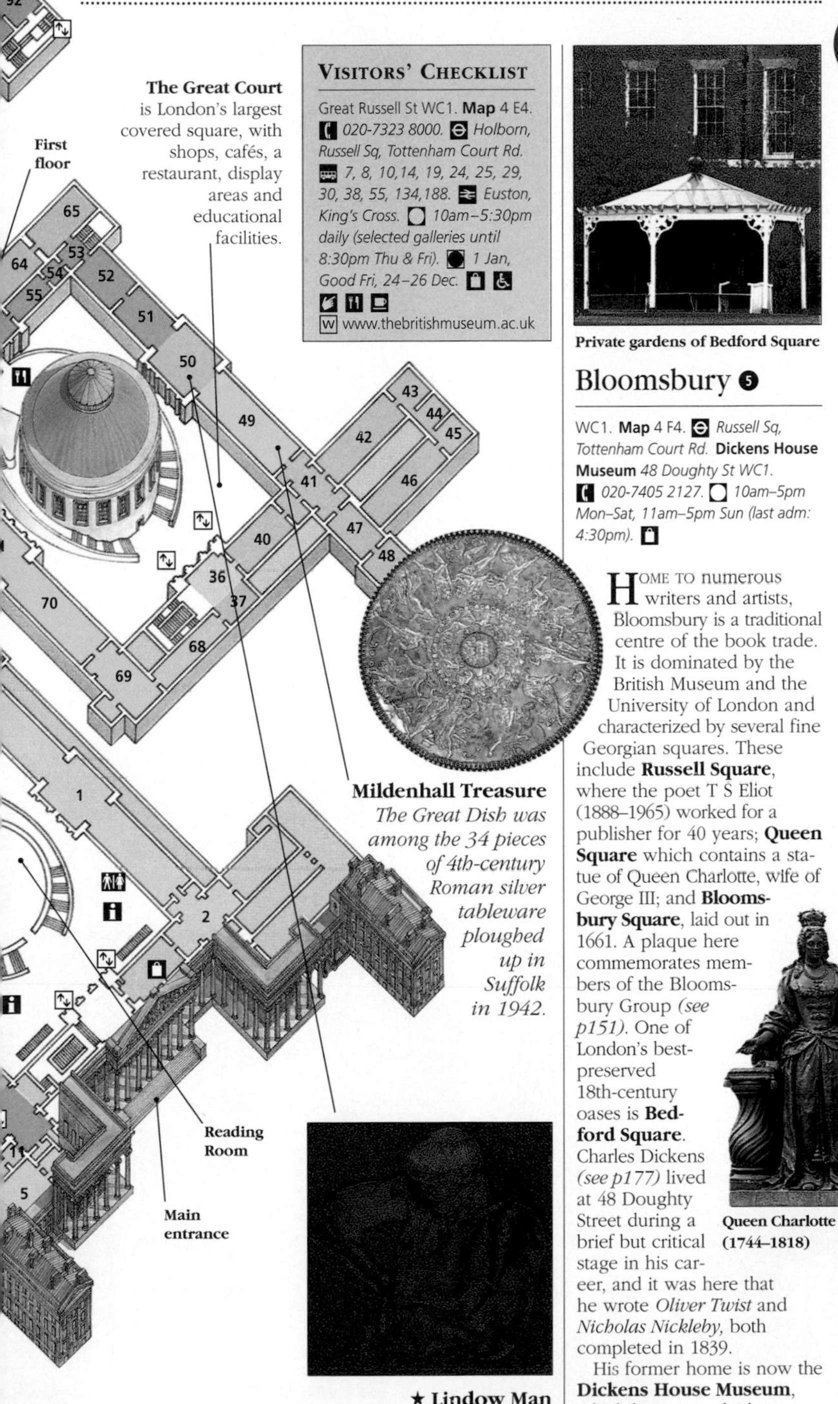

The Great Court is London's largest covered square, with shops, cafés, a restaurant, display areas and educational facilities.

Mildenhall Treasure
The Great Dish was among the 34 pieces of 4th-century Roman silver tableware ploughed up in Suffolk in 1942.

★ Lindow Man
The skin on this 2,000-year-old human body was preserved by the acids of a peat-bog in Cheshire. He was probably killed in an elaborate ritual.

Visitors' Checklist

Great Russell St WC1. **Map** 4 E4. *020-7323 8000. Holborn, Russell Sq, Tottenham Court Rd. 7, 8, 10,14, 19, 24, 25, 29, 30, 38, 55, 134,188. Euston, King's Cross. 10am–5:30pm daily (selected galleries until 8:30pm Thu & Fri). 1 Jan, Good Fri, 24–26 Dec.*
www.thebritishmuseum.ac.uk

Private gardens of Bedford Square

Bloomsbury ❺

WC1. **Map** 4 F4. *Russell Sq, Tottenham Court Rd.* **Dickens House Museum** *48 Doughty St WC1. 020-7405 2127. 10am–5pm Mon–Sat, 11am–5pm Sun (last adm: 4:30pm).*

Home to numerous writers and artists, Bloomsbury is a traditional centre of the book trade. It is dominated by the British Museum and the University of London and characterized by several fine Georgian squares. These include **Russell Square**, where the poet T S Eliot (1888–1965) worked for a publisher for 40 years; **Queen Square** which contains a statue of Queen Charlotte, wife of George III; and **Bloomsbury Square**, laid out in 1661. A plaque here commemorates members of the Bloomsbury Group *(see p151)*. One of London's best-preserved 18th-century oases is **Bedford Square**. Charles Dickens *(see p177)* lived at 48 Doughty Street during a brief but critical stage in his career, and it was here that he wrote *Oliver Twist* and *Nicholas Nickleby,* both completed in 1839.

Queen Charlotte (1744–1818)

His former home is now the **Dickens House Museum**, which has rooms laid out as they were in Dickens's time, with objects taken from his other London homes and first editions of many of his works.

The City and Southwark

Dominated today by glossy office blocks, the City is the oldest part of the capital. The Great Fire of 1666 obliterated four-fifths of its buildings. Sir Christopher Wren rebuilt much of it and many of his churches survived World War II *(see pp58–9)*. Commerce has always been the City's lifeblood, and the power of its merchants and bankers secured it a degree of autonomy from state control. Humming with activity in business hours, it empties at night.

In the Middle Ages Southwark, on the south bank of the Thames, was a refuge for pleasure-seekers, prostitutes, gamblers and criminals. Even after 1550, when the area fell under the jurisdiction of the City, its brothels and taverns thrived. There were also several bear-baiting arenas in which plays were staged until the building of theatres such as the Globe (1598), where many of Shakespeare's works were first performed. Relics of old Southwark are mostly on the waterfront, which has been imaginatively redeveloped and provided with a pleasant walkway.

Old bank sign on Lombard Street

Sights at a Glance

Historic Sights and Buildings
- HMS Belfast 12
- Lloyd's Building 7
- Monument 8
- The Old Operating Theatre 14
- Temple 3
- Tower Bridge 10
- *Tower of London pp120–21* 9

Pubs
- George Inn 15

Museums and Galleries
- Design Museum 11
- London Dungeon 13
- Museum of London 6
- Shakespeare's Globe 18
- Sir John Soane's Museum 4
- Tate Modern 19

Markets
- Borough Market 16

Churches and Cathedrals
- St Bartholomew-the-Great 5
- *St Paul's Cathedral pp116–17* 2
- St Stephen Walbrook 1
- Southwark Cathedral 17

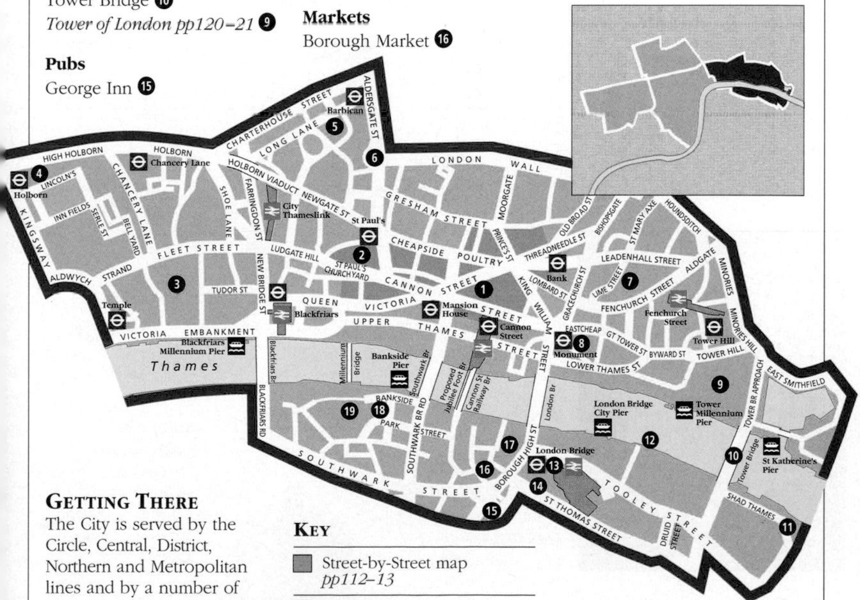

Getting There

The City is served by the Circle, Central, District, Northern and Metropolitan lines and by a number of buses. London Bridge is the main station for Southwark – served by the Northern and Jubilee lines and by trains running from Charing Cross, Cannon Street and Waterloo.

Key
- Street-by-Street map *pp112–13*
- Underground station
- Railway station
- Parking
- River boat pier

0 metres 500
0 yards 500

◁ **St Paul's Cathedral in the heart of the City, with the NatWest Tower (1980) to the left**

Detail: St Paul's Cathedral

Street-by-Street: The City

THIS IS THE FINANCIAL HEART of London and has been ever since the Romans set up a trading post here 2,000 years ago. For years it was London's main residential area but today very few people live here. The City was severely bombed in World War II and the main clues to its past are streets named after vanished inns and markets. Its numerous churches, many built after the Great Fire of 1666 by the architect Sir Christopher Wren *(see p116)*, are now dwarfed by lavish banks and post-modern developments.

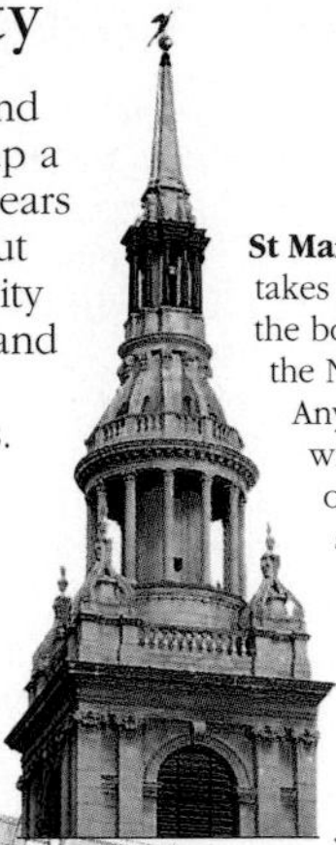

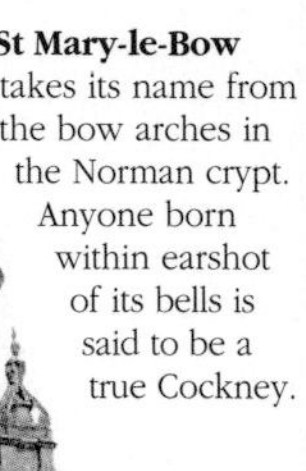

St Mary-le-Bow takes its name from the bow arches in the Norman crypt. Anyone born within earshot of its bells is said to be a true Cockney.

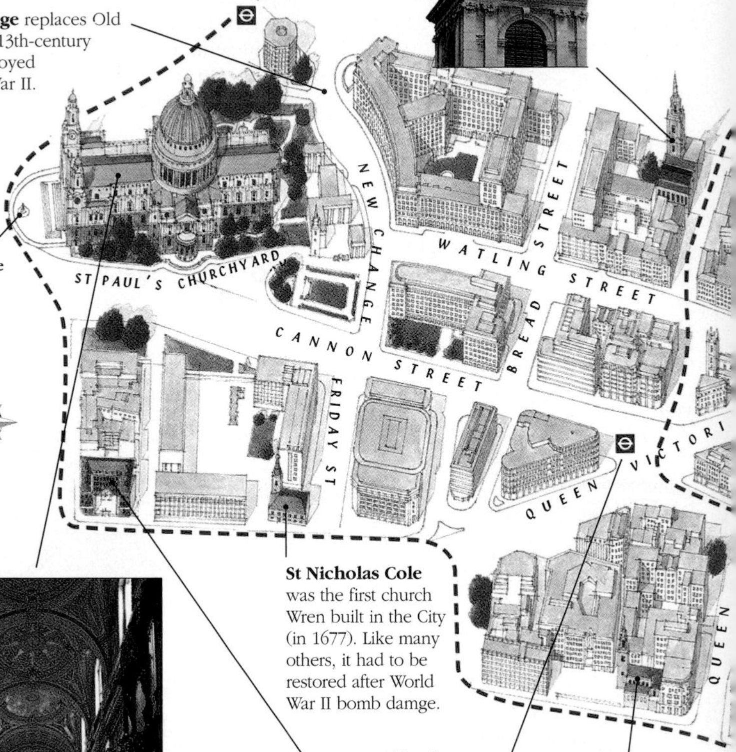

St Paul's station

New Change replaces Old Change, a 13th-century street destroyed in World War II.

Statue of Queen Anne

ST PAUL'S CHURCHYARD

NEW CHANGE

WATLING STREET

BREAD STREET

CANNON STREET

FRIDAY ST

QUEEN VICTORIA

QUEEN

N

St Nicholas Cole was the first church Wren built in the City (in 1677). Like many others, it had to be restored after World War II bomb damge.

★ St Paul's Cathedral
Built after the Great Fire of 1666, Wren's masterpiece was funded by a tax on coal ❷

Mansion House station

St James Garlickhythe contains unusual sword rests and hat stands, beneath Wren's elegant spire of 1717.

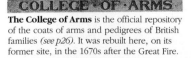

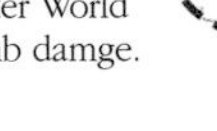

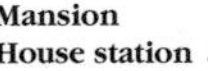

The College of Arms is the official repository of the coats of arms and pedigrees of British families *(see p26)*. It was rebuilt here, on its former site, in the 1670s after the Great Fire.

STAR SIGHTS

★ St Paul's Cathedral

★ St Stephen Walbrook

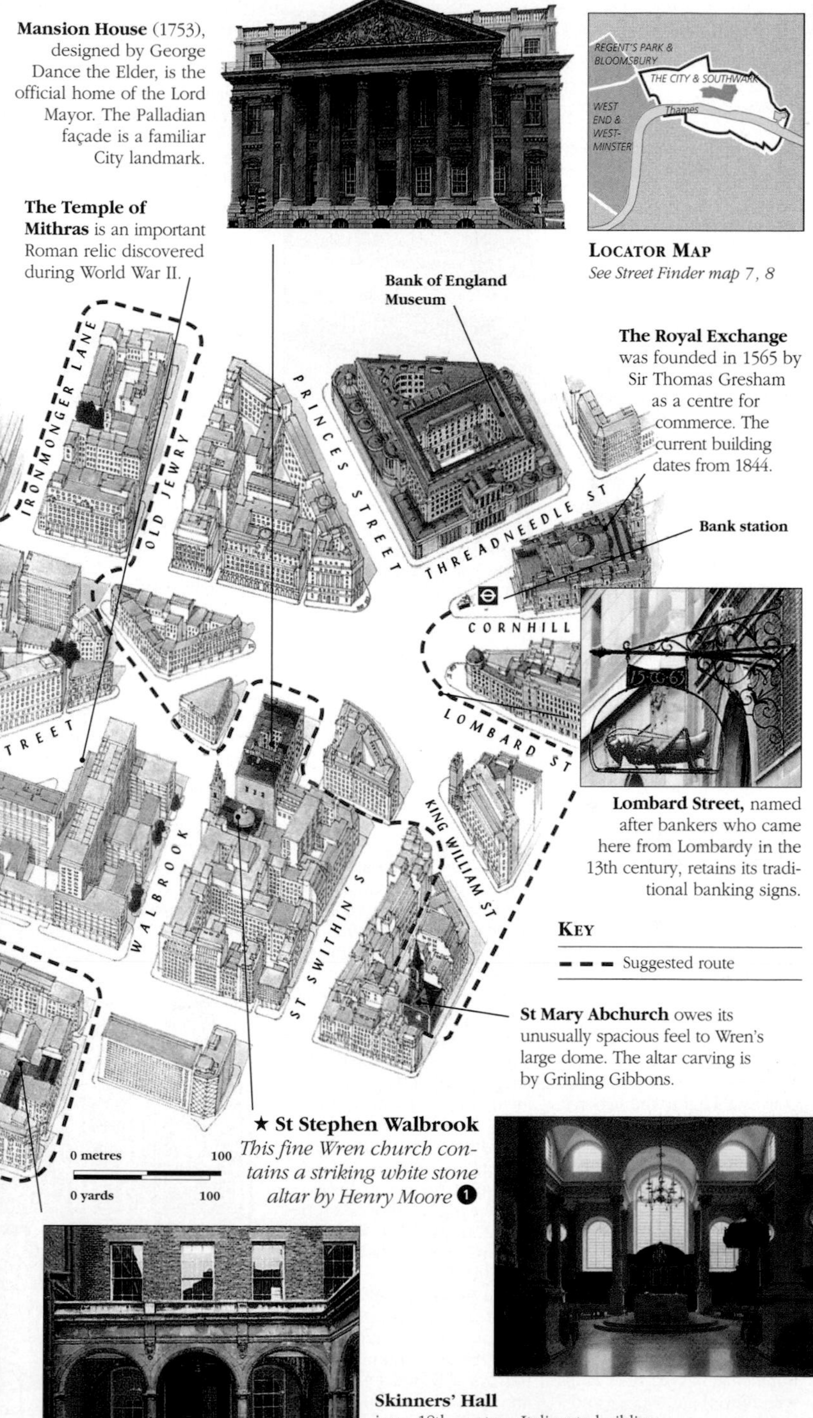

Mansion House (1753), designed by George Dance the Elder, is the official home of the Lord Mayor. The Palladian façade is a familiar City landmark.

The Temple of Mithras is an important Roman relic discovered during World War II.

Locator Map
See Street Finder map 7, 8

Bank of England Museum

The Royal Exchange was founded in 1565 by Sir Thomas Gresham as a centre for commerce. The current building dates from 1844.

Bank station

Lombard Street, named after bankers who came here from Lombardy in the 13th century, retains its traditional banking signs.

Key

Suggested route

St Mary Abchurch owes its unusually spacious feel to Wren's large dome. The altar carving is by Grinling Gibbons.

★ St Stephen Walbrook
This fine Wren church contains a striking white stone altar by Henry Moore ❶

Skinners' Hall is an 18th-century Italianate building constructed for the ancient guild that controlled trade in fur and leather.

St Stephen Walbrook ❶

39 Walbrook EC4. **Map** 8 D3. *020-7626 8242.* *Bank, Cannon St.* *10am–4pm Mon–Thu, 10am–3pm Fri.* *public hols.*

THE LORD MAYOR'S parish church was built by Sir Christopher Wren in the 1670s and is among the finest of all his City churches. The bright, airy interior is flooded with light by a huge dome that appears to float above the eight columns and arches that support it. The dome, deep and coffered with ornate plasterwork, was a forerunner of St Paul's. Original fittings, such as the highly decorative font cover and pulpit canopy, contrast with the stark simplicity of Henry Moore's massive white stone altar (1987). The best time to see the church is during one of its free organ recitals (on Fridays) or lunchtime concerts.

St Paul's ❷

See pp116–17.

Effigies in Temple Church

Temple ❸

Inner Temple, King's Bench Walk EC4. *020-7797 8250.* **Map** 7 A3. *Temple.* *10am–4pm Mon–Fri (grounds only).* **Middle Temple Hall**, Middle Temple Lane EC4. *020-7427 4800.* *10–11:30am, 3–4pm Mon–Fri.* **Temple Church** *020-7353 8559.* *11am–4pm daily.*

A CLUSTER of atmospheric squares form the Inner and Middle Temples, two of London's four Inns of Court, where law students are trained. The name Temple derives from the medieval Knights Templar, a religious order which protected pilgrims to the Holy Land and was based here until 1312 when it was suppressed by the Crown. Marble effigies of knights lie on the floor of the circular Temple Church, part of which dates from the 12th century. Middle Temple Hall has a fine Elizabethan interior.

St Bartholomew-the-Great ❺

West Smithfield EC1. **Map** 7 B1. *020-7606 5171.* *Barbican, St Paul's.* *8:30am–5pm Tue–Fri (mid-Nov–mid-Feb: 8:30am–4pm), 10:30am–1:30pm Sat.* *25, 26 Dec, 1 Jan.* *(call to arrange).* www.greatstbarts.com

THE HISTORIC AREA of Smithfield has witnessed a number of bloody events over the years, among them the execution of rebel peasant leader Wat Tyler in 1381, and, in the reign of Mary I (1553–58), the burning of scores of Protestant martyrs.

Sir John Soane's Museum ❹

13 Lincoln's Inn Fields WC2. **Map** 4 F4. *020-7405 2107.* *Holborn.* *10am–5pm Tue–Sat, 6–9pm 1st Tue of month.* *1 Jan, 24–26 Dec, public hols.* *ground floor only.* *Sat 2:30pm.* www.soane.org

ONE OF THE MOST eccentric museums in London, this house was left to the nation by Sir John Soane in 1837, with a stipulation that nothing should be changed. The son of a bricklayer, Soane became one of Britain's leading late Georgian architects developing a restrained Neo-Classical style of his own. After marrying the niece of a wealthy builder, whose fortune he inherited, he bought and reconstructed No. 12 Lincoln's Inn Fields. In 1813 he and his wife moved into No. 13 and in 1824 he rebuilt No. 14, adding a picture gallery and the mock medieval Monk's Parlour. Today, true to Soane's wishes, the collections are much as he left them – an eclectic gathering of beautiful, instructional and often simply peculiar artifacts. There are casts, bronzes, vases, antique fragments, paintings and a selection of bizarre trivia which ranges from a giant fungus from Sumatra to a scold-bridle, a device designed to silence nagging wives. Highlights include the sarcophagus of Seti I, Soanes's own designs, including those for the Bank of England, models by leading Neo-Classical sculptors and the *Rake's Progress* series of paintings (1734) by William Hogarth, which Mrs Soane bought for £520.

The building itself is full of architectural surprises and illusions. In the main ground floor room, cunningly placed mirrors play tricks with light and space, while an atrium stretching from the basement to the glass-domed roof allows light on to every floor.

A glass dome lets light on to all the floors.

A vast sarcophagus (1300 BC) stands on the floor of the crypt.

Hidden in a quiet corner behind Smithfield meat market (central London's only surviving wholesale food market), St Bartholomew-the-Great is one of London's oldest churches. It once formed part of a priory founded in 1123 by a monk named Rahere, whose tomb is here. He was Henry I's court jester until he dreamed that St Bartholomew had saved him from a winged monster. As prior, he would sometimes revert to his former role, entertaining crowds with juggling tricks at the annual Bartholomew Fair. The 13th-century arch, now topped by a Tudor gatehouse, used to be the entrance to the church until the old nave was pulled down during the Dissolution of the Monasteries *(see pp50–51).*

St Bartholomew's gatehouse

Museum of London ❻

London Wall EC2. **Map** 7 C2.
020-7600 3699. Barbican, St Paul's. 10am–5:50pm Mon–Sat & public hols, noon–5:50pm Sun.
1 Jan, 24–26 Dec.
www.museumoflondon.org.uk

THIS MUSEUM traces life in London from prehistoric times to the outbreak of World War I. Displays of archaeological finds and domestic objects alternate with reconstructed street scenes and interiors. The World City galleries chart the birth of modern London from the French Revolution to World War I, and display Nelson's bejewelled sword.

Delft plate made in London 1600, Museum of London

The Roman London gallery has a brightly coloured 2nd-century fresco from a Southwark bath house, while the 17th-century section holds the shirt that Charles I wore on the scaffold *(see pp52–3).* Popular exhibits are the Lord Mayor's State Coach, built in 1757 and still used for the Lord Mayor's Show in November, and the working model of the Great Fire of 1666.

Every wall is covered and every room filled with artifacts from Soane's voluminous collection.

In the picture gallery, panels covered with paintings unfold to reveal more works of art hidden behind them.

The Monk's Parlour is full of grotesque Gothic casts.

St Paul's Cathedral ❷

THE GREAT FIRE OF LONDON in 1666 left the medieval cathedral of St Paul's in ruins. Wren was commissioned to rebuild it, but his design for a church on a Greek Cross plan (where all four arms are equal) met with considerable resistance. The authorities insisted on a conventional Latin cross, with a long nave and short transepts, which was believed to focus the congregation's attention on the altar. Despite the compromises, Wren created a magnificent Baroque cathedral, which was built between 1675 and 1710 and has since formed the lavish setting for many state ceremonies.

★ Dome
At 111 m (360 ft), the elaborate dome is one of the highest in the world.

The balustrade along the top was added in 1718 against Wren's wishes.

★ West Front and Towers
Inspired by the Italian Baroque architect, Borromini, the towers were added by Wren in 1707.

The West Portico consists of two storeys of coupled Corinthian columns, topped by a pediment carved with reliefs showing the Conversion of St Paul.

The Nave
An imposing succession of massive arches and saucer domes open out into the vast space below the cathedral's main dome.

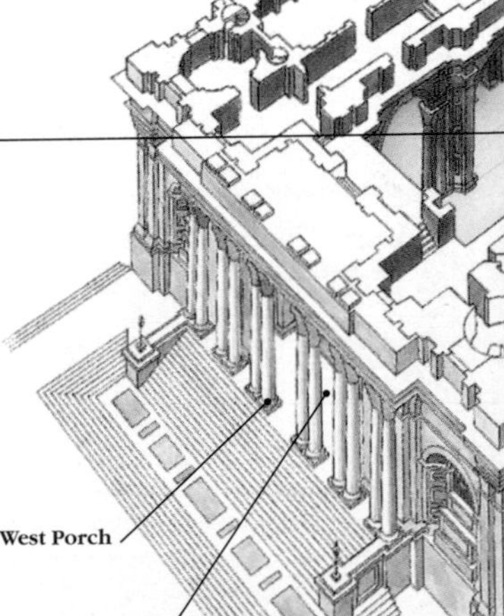

West Porch

Main entrance approached from Ludgate Hill

CHRISTOPHER WREN

Trained as a scientist, Sir Christopher Wren (1632–1723) began his impressive architectural career at the age of 31. He became a leading figure in the rebuilding of London after the Great Fire of 1666, building a total of 52 new churches. Although Wren never visited Italy, his work was influenced by Roman, Baroque and Renaissance architecture, as is apparent in his masterpiece, St Paul's Cathedral.

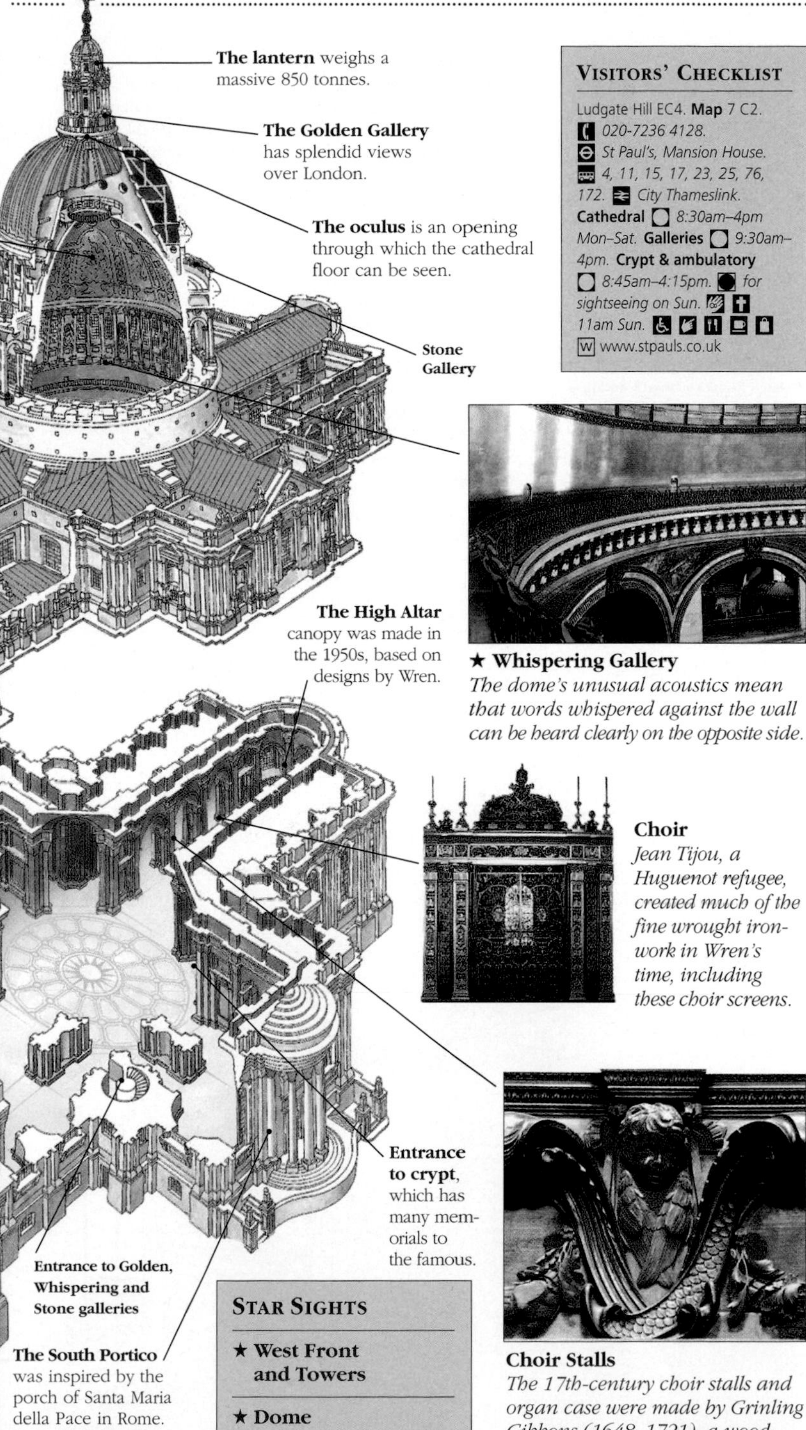

The lantern weighs a massive 850 tonnes.
The Golden Gallery has splendid views over London.
The oculus is an opening through which the cathedral floor can be seen.
Stone Gallery
The High Altar canopy was made in the 1950s, based on designs by Wren.
Entrance to crypt, which has many memorials to the famous.
Entrance to Golden, Whispering and Stone galleries
The South Portico was inspired by the porch of Santa Maria della Pace in Rome. Wren absorbed the detail by studying a friend's collection of architectural engravings.

Visitors' Checklist

Ludgate Hill EC4. **Map** 7 C2.
020-7236 4128.
St Paul's, Mansion House.
4, 11, 15, 17, 23, 25, 76, 172. *City Thameslink.*
Cathedral *8:30am–4pm Mon–Sat.* **Galleries** *9:30am–4pm.* **Crypt & ambulatory** *8:45am–4:15pm.* *for sightseeing on Sun.* *11am Sun.*
www.stpauls.co.uk

★ Whispering Gallery
The dome's unusual acoustics mean that words whispered against the wall can be heard clearly on the opposite side.

Choir
Jean Tijou, a Huguenot refugee, created much of the fine wrought ironwork in Wren's time, including these choir screens.

Choir Stalls
The 17th-century choir stalls and organ case were made by Grinling Gibbons (1648–1721), a woodcarver from Rotterdam. He and his team of craftsmen worked on these intricate carvings for two years.

Star Sights

- ★ West Front and Towers
- ★ Dome
- ★ Whispering Gallery

Richard Rogers's Lloyd's building

Lloyd's Building ⑦

1 Lime St EC3. **Map** 8 E2. *020-7327 1000.* *Monument, Bank, Aldgate.* *to the public.*

Lloyd's was founded in the late 17th century and soon became the world's main insurers, issuing policies on everything from oil tankers to Betty Grable's legs. The present building, designed by Richard Rogers, dates from 1986 and is one of the most interesting modern buildings in London. Its exaggerated stainless steel external piping and high-tech ducts echo Roger's forceful Pompidou Centre in Paris. Lloyds' is well worth seeing floodlit at night.

Monument ⑧

Monument St EC3. **Map** 8 D3. *020-7626 2717.* *Monument.* *9:30am–5pm daily (last adm: 4:40pm).* *25, 26 Dec, 1 Jan.*

This Doric column, designed by Wren to commemorate the Great Fire of London that devastated the original walled city in September 1666, was, in 1681, the tallest isolated stone column in the world. Topped with a bronze flame, the Monument is 62 m (205 ft) high; the exact distance west to Pudding Lane, where the fire is believed to have started. Reliefs around the column's base show Charles II restoring the city after the tragedy.

The 311 tightly-spiralled steps lead to a tiny, claustrophobia-inducing viewing platform. (In 1842, it was enclosed with an iron cage to prevent suicides.) The steep climb is well worth the effort as the views from the top are spectacular and visitors are rewarded with a certificate.

Tower of London ⑨

See pp120–21.

Tower Bridge ⑩

SE1. **Map** 8 F4. *020-7940 3985.* *Tower Hill.* **The Tower Bridge Experience** *Apr–Oct: 9am–6pm daily; Nov–Mar: 9:30am–6pm daily (last adm: 5pm).* *1 Jan, 24–26 Dec.*
www.towerbridge.org.uk

This flamboyant piece of Victorian engineering, designed by Sir Horace Jones, was completed in 1894 and soon became a symbol of London. Its two Gothic towers contain the mechanism for raising the roadway to permit large ships to pass through. The towers are made of a supporting steel framework clad in stone, and are linked by two high level walkways which were closed between 1909 and 1982 due to their popularity with suicides and prostitutes. The bridge now houses The Tower Bridge Experience, with interactive displays bringing the bridge's history to life. There are fine river views from the walkways, and a look at the steam engine room that powered the lifting machinery until 1976, when the system was electrified.

Walkways, open to the public, give panoramic views over the Thames and London.

The roadway, when raised, creates a space 40 m (135 ft) high and 60 m (200 ft) wide, big enough for large cargo ships.

Engine room

South Bank

Lifts and 300 steps lead to the top of the towers.

The Victorian wind ing machinery wa originally powere by steam.

Entran

North Bank

Design Museum ⓫

Butlers Wharf, Shad Thames SE1. **Map** 8 F4. *0870-909 9009.* *Tower Hill, London Bridge.* *10am–5:45pm daily (last adm: 5:15pm), late Fri opening to 9pm Jun–Aug.* *24, 26 Dec.* *020-7378 7031 (booking advised).* www.designmuseum.org

THIS MUSEUM is the first in the world to be dedicated solely to 20th- and 21st-century design. Its permanent collection of design classics features everyday objects, product design, fashion, creative technology and architecture, and it also mounts temporary exhibitions, ranging from retrospectives on the work of great designers such as Charles Eames and Manolo Blahnik, to thematic shows on such subjects as the Bauhaus Dessau. It hosts the new series of European Design Biennials and the annual exhibition and award for Designer of the Year. As well as exploring the history of modern design and architecture, the museum showcases the most innovative contemporary designs and technologies that will shape our future.

The museum is arranged over two floors, with the gallery on the first floor showing several displays simultaneously. Along the river front outside the museum, the Design Musem Tank features installations from leading contemporary designers and artists.

Located on the first floor of the museum is the well-known Blueprint Café restaurant, which is a great place to get wonderful views of the Thames, especially after dark.

Austin Mini in the Design Museum

The now familiar sight of the naval gunship HMS Belfast on the Thames

HMS Belfast ⓬

Morgan's Lane, Tooley St SE1. **Map** 8 E4. *020-7940 6300.* *London Bridge, Tower Hill.* *Mar–Oct: 10am–6pm daily; Nov–Feb: 10am–5pm daily (last adm: 45 mins before closing).* *24–26 Dec.* *limited.* www.iwm.org.uk

ORIGINALLY LAUNCHED in 1938 to serve in World War II, the 11,500-ton battle ship HMS *Belfast* was instrumental in the destruction of the German battle cruiser *Scharnhorst* in the battle of North Cape, and also played an important role in the Normandy Landings.

After the war, the battle cruiser, designed for offensive action and for supporting amphibious operations, was sent to work for the United Nations in Korea. The ship remained in service with the British navy until 1965.

Since 1971, the cruiser has been used as a floating naval museum. Part of it has been atmospherically recreated to show what the ship was like in 1943, when it participated in sinking the German battle cruiser. Other displays portray life on board during World War II, and there are also general exhibits which relate to the history of the Royal Navy.

As well as being a great family day out, it is also possible for children to take part in the educational activity weekends that take place on board the ship.

London Dungeon ⓭

Tooley St SE1. **Map** 8 D4. *020-7403 7221.* *London Bridge.* *Jul–Sep 9:30am–8pm daily; Oct-Jun 10am–5:30pm daily (last adm: 30 mins before closing).* *25 Dec.* www.thedungeons.com

IN EFFECT a much expanded version of the chamber of horrors at Madame Tussaud's *(see p106)*, this museum is a great hit with children. It illustrates the most bloodthirsty events in British history. It is played strictly for terror, and screams abound as Druids perform a human sacrifice at Stonehenge, Anne Boleyn is beheaded on the orders of her husband Henry VIII, and a room full of people die in agony during the Great Plague. Other displays include torture, murder and witchcraft.

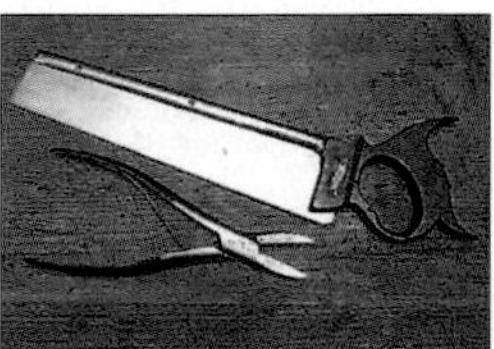

19th-century surgical tools

The Old Operating Theatre ⓮

9a St Thomas St SE1. **Map** 8 D4. *020-7955 4791.* *London Bridge.* *10:30am–5pm daily.* *15 Dec–5 Jan.* www.thegarret.org.uk

ST THOMAS'S HOSPITAL stood here from its foundation in the 12th century until it was moved west in 1862. At this time most of its buildings were demolished to make way for the railway. The women's operating theatre (The Old Operating Theatre Museum and Herb Garret) survived only because it was located away from the main buildings, in a garret over the hospital church. It lay, bricked up and forgotten, until the 1950s. Britain's oldest operating theatre, dating back to 1822, it has now been fitted out as it would have been in the early 19th century.

Tower of London ❾

SOON AFTER HE BECAME KING in 1066, William the Conqueror built a fortress here to guard the entrance to London from the Thames Estuary. In 1097 the White Tower, standing today at the centre of the complex, was completed in sturdy stone; other fine buildings have been added over the centuries. The Tower has served as a royal residence, armoury, treasury and most famously as a prison for enemies of the crown. Many were tortured and among those who met their death there were the "Princes in the Tower", the sons and heirs of Edward IV. Today the tower is a popular attraction, housing the Crown Jewels and other exhibits. Its most celebrated residents are seven ravens whose presence is protected by the legend that the kingdom will fall if they desert the tower.

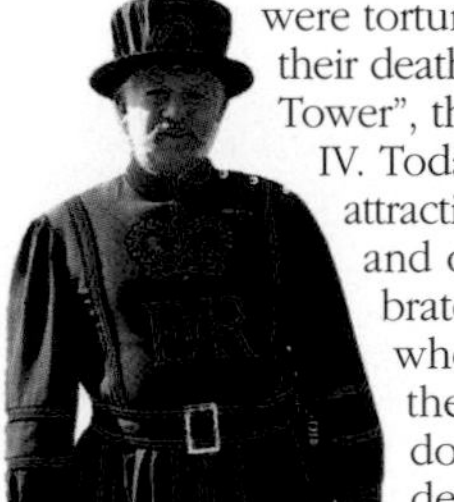

"Beefeaters"
Thirty-seven Yeoman Warders guard the Tower and live here. Their uniforms hark back to Tudor times.

Beauchamp Tower
Many high-ranking prisoners were held here, often with their own retinues of servants. The tower was built by Edward I around 1281.

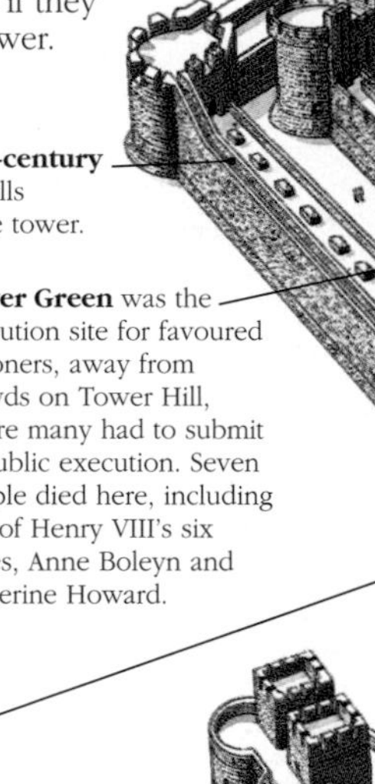

Two 13th-century curtain walls protect the tower.

Tower Green was the execution site for favoured prisoners, away from crowds on Tower Hill, where many had to submit to public execution. Seven people died here, including two of Henry VIII's six wives, Anne Boleyn and Catherine Howard.

Queen's House
This Tudor building is the sovereign's official residence at the Tower.

Main entrance from Tower Hill

THE CROWN JEWELS

The world's best-known collection of precious objects, now displayed in a splendid exhibition room, includes the gorgeous regalia of crowns, sceptres, orbs and swords used at coronations and other state occasions. Most date from 1661, when Charles II commissioned replacements for regalia destroyed by Parliament after the execution of Charles I *(see pp52–3)*. Only a few older pieces survived, hidden by royalist clergymen until the Restoration – notably, Edward the Confessor's sapphire ring, now incorporated into the Imperial State Crown *(see p73)*. The crown was made for Queen Victoria in 1837 and has been used at every coronation since.

The Sovereign's Ring (1831)

The Sovereign's Orb (1661), a hollow gold sphere encrusted with jewels

★ Jewel House
Among the magnificent Crown Jewels is the Sceptre with the Cross (1660), which now contains the world's biggest diamond.

★ White Tower
When the tower was finished in 1097, it was the tallest building in London at 27 m (90 ft) high.

VISITORS' CHECKLIST

Tower Hill EC3. **Map** 8 E3. *0870-756 6060. Tower Hill; Tower Gateway (DLR). RV1, 15, X15, 25, 42, 78, 100, D1, D9, D11. Fenchurch Street. from Westminster to Tower Pier. Mar–Oct: 9am–6pm Tue–Sat, 10am–6pm Sun; Nov–Feb: 9am–5pm Tue–Sat, 10am–5pm Sun & Mon. 1 Jan, 24–26 Dec. limited, except Jewel House.* **Ceremony of the Keys**: *9:30pm daily (book in advance).* www.tower-of-london.org.uk

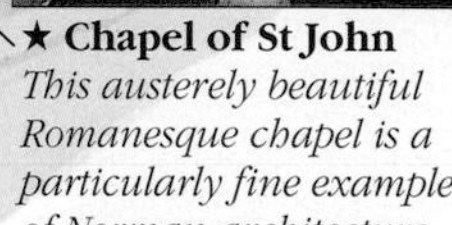

★ Chapel of St John
This austerely beautiful Romanesque chapel is a particularly fine example of Norman architecture.

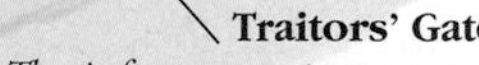

Traitors' Gate
The infamous entrance was used for prisoners brought from trial in Westminster Hall.

Bloody Tower
Edward IV's two sons were put here by their uncle, Richard of Gloucester (subsequently Richard III), after their father died in 1483. The princes, depicted here by John Millais (1829–96), disappeared mysteriously and Richard was crowned later that year. In 1674 the skeletons of two children were found nearby.

STAR SIGHTS

- ★ Jewel House
- ★ White Tower
- ★ Chapel of St John

The George Inn, now owned by the National Trust

George Inn ⓯

77 Borough High St SE1. **Map** 8 D4. *020-7407 2056.* *London Bridge, Borough.* *11am–11pm Mon–Sat, noon–10:30pm Sun.*

DATING FROM THE 17th century, this building is the only traditional galleried coaching inn left in London and is mentioned in Dickens's *Little Dorrit*. It was rebuilt after the Southwark fire of 1676 in a style that dates back to the Middle Ages. There were originally three wings around a courtyard, where plays were staged in the 17th century. In 1889 the north and east wings were demolished, so there is only one wing remaining.

The inn is still a restaurant and a popular pub with a well-worn, comfortable atmosphere, perfect on a cold, damp day. In the summer, the yard fills with picnic tables and patrons are occasionally entertained by actors and morris dancers. The house bitter is highly recommended.

Borough Market ⓰

8 Southwark St SE1. **Map** 8 D4. *London Bridge.* **Retail market** *Fri noon–6pm, Sat 9am–4pm.*

BOROUGH MARKET was until recently an exclusively wholesale fruit and vegetable market, which had its origins in medieval times, and moved to its current atmospheric position beneath the railway tracks in 1756. A popular and fine food market has now become well established, selling gourmet foods from Britain and abroad, as well as quality fruit and vegetables, to locals and tourists alike.

Shakespeare window (1954), Southwark Cathedral

Southwark Cathedral ⓱

Montague Close SE1. **Map** 8 D4. *020-7367 6700.* *London Bridge.* *8am–6pm daily.* www.dswark.org.uk

ALTHOUGH SOME PARTS OF this building date back to the 12th century, it was not until 1905 that it became a cathedral. Many original medieval features remain, notably the superb Gothic choir, and the tomb of the poet John Gower (c.1325–1408), a contemporary of Chaucer *(see p172)*. There is a monument to Shakespeare, carved in 1912, and a memorial window *(above)* installed in 1954.

Shakespeare's Globe ⓲

New Globe Walk SE1. **Map** 7 C3. *020-7902 1400. Box office: 020-7401 9919.* *London Bridge, Mansion House.* **Exhibition** *May–Sep: 9am–noon daily; Oct–Apr: 10am–5pm daily.* *24, 25 Dec.* *every 30 mins.* **Performances** *May–Sep.* *limited.* www.shakespeares-globe.org

OPENED IN 1997, this circular building is a faithful reproduction of an Elizabethan theatre, close to the site of the original Globe where many of Shakespeare's plays were first performed. It was built using handmade bricks and oak laths, fastened with wooden pegs rather than metal screws, and has the first thatched roof allowed in London since the Great Fire of 1666. The theatre was erected thanks to a heroic campaign, waged for over two decades, by the American actor and director Sam Wanamaker. Open to the elements (although the seats are protected), it operates only in the summer, and seeing a play here can be a lively experience, with the "groundlings" standing just in front of the stage encouraged to cheer or jeer.

A basement exhibition, in the Underglobe, is open all year and covers many aspects of Shakespeare's work and the world of Elizabethan theatre.

Groups of 15 or more may book ahead via the Globe to see an exhibition about the nearby Rose Theatre, Bankside's very first playhouse.

Shakespeare's *Henry IV* (performed at the Globe Theatre around 1600)

Tate Modern ⑲

Holland St, SE1. **Map** 7 C3. *020-7887 8000.* *Blackfriars, Southwark.* *to Tate Britain every 40 mins.* *Blackfriars* *10am–6pm Sun–Thu, 10am–10pm Fri & Sat.* *24–26 Dec.* *major exhibitions.* www.tate.org.uk

LOOMING OVER the southern bank of the Thames, Tate Modern occupies the converted Bankside power station, a dynamic space for one of the world's premier collections of modern art. Tate Modern draws its main displays from the expansive Tate Collection – also drawn from by the other Tate galleries: Tate St Ives *(p265)*, Tate Liverpool *(p363)* and Tate Britain *(p93)*. A new boat, Tate to Tate, transports visitors between Tate Modern and Tate Britain. The rotation of pieces and numerous special exhibitions result in compelling displays that change constantly.

The gallery's west entrance leads straight into the massive Turbine Hall. Each year an artist is commissioned to install in this space. Louise Bourgeois was the first to install here, creating three giant towers and a gargantuan 9-m high spider, *Maman* (2000). Her installations were followed by those of Juan Muñoz and Anish Kapoor.

A two storey escalator whisks visitors from the Turbine Hall, up to level 3 where the main galleries are located. In a break with convention, Tate Modern organizes its displays by theme rather than chronology or school – a practice that cuts across movements and mixes up media. Four themes based on traditional genres reveal how traditions have been confronted, extended or rejected by artists throughout the 20th and into the 21st centuries.

Still Life/Object/Real Life on level 3 includes work ranging from Cézanne's paintings to Claes Oldenberg's extraordinary objects. Landscape/Matter/Environment, also on Level 3, looks at how artists have taken up the challenge of representing our environment. In one room in these galleries, "land artist" Richard Long and the Impressionist Claude Monet, who seem to have opposing approaches to representation, are displayed together, giving startling insights into the similarites between the two artists.

In Nude/Action/Body on level 5, artists who have attempted to reshape the body, such as Lucian Freud, are on display. Also on level 5 is History/Memory/Society. These galleries contain 20th-century works by artists such as Piet Mondrian and Joseph Beuys who engage with the social and political world.

To complement its collection displays, Tate Modern presents a dynamic programme of temporary exhibitions including three large-scale shows per year.

***Death* from *Death Hope Life Fear* (1984) by Gilbert and George**

***Standing by the Rags* (1988-89) by Lucian Freud**

***Soft Drainpipe – Blue (Cool)* (1967) by Claes Oldenburg**

BANKSIDE POWER STATION

This forbidding fortress was designed in 1947 by Sir Giles Gilbert Scott, the architect of Battersea Power Station, Waterloo Bridge and London's famous red telephone boxes. The power station is of a steel-framed brick skin construction, comprising over 4.2 million bricks. The Turbine Hall was designed to accommodate huge oil-burning generators and three vast oil tanks are still in situ, buried under the ground just south of the building. The tanks are to be employed in a future stage of Tate Modern development. The power station itself was converted by Swiss architects Herzog and de Meuron who designed the two-storey glass box, or lightbeam, which runs the length of the building. This serves to flood the upper galleries with light and also provides wonderful views of London.

The façade, chimney and light beam of Tate Modern

Shops and Markets

London is one of the great shopping cities of Europe, with bustling, lively street markets, world-famous department stores, and a wide variety of eclectic shops selling clothes, crafts and antiques *(see p627)*. The best shopping areas range from elegant, upmarket districts such as Knightsbridge and Bond Street, which sell expensive designer clothes, to the busy, chaotic stretch of Oxford Street, and the colourful, noisy markets of Covent Garden *(see p81)*, Berwick Street and Brick Lane. The city is best known, however, for its huge range of clothes shops selling everything from traditional tweeds to the latest zany designs of the ever-changing high-street fashions.

Bags from two famous London department stores

Chain and Department Stores

Façade of Liberty (1925)

The most famous of London's many department stores is **Harrods**, with some 300 departments, 4,000 staff, and a spectacular Edwardian food hall. Nearby **Harvey Nichols** stocks high fashion and boasts the city's most stylish food hall. Gourmets should make a pilgrimage to **Fortnum & Mason** which has stocked high-quality food for nearly 300 years. Traditional teas are available in the café.

Selfridges sells virtually everything from international fashion labels to household gadgets, while **John Lewis** and its Chelsea partner **Peter Jones** specialize in fabrics, china, glass and household items. **Liberty**, set in a beautiful Tudor-style building, still sells the silks and Oriental goods for which it was famous when it first opened in 1875, as well as contemporary fashion design. **Marks & Spencer** has long been known for its high quality own-label clothes, and also has many good food stores.

The best chain store record shops are **Virgin Megastore**, **Tower Records** and **HMV**.

Clothes and Shoes

British designers range from elegant **Jasper Conran** to **Vivienne Westwood**, doyenne of the punkish avant-garde. Top British fashion designers **Margaret Howell** and **Paul Smith** sell stylish fashion for men and women, while shops such as **Urban Outfitters** stock adventurous young designer ware for trendy clubbers. More established international designers are stocked at **Browns** and the department stores **Harvey Nichols**, **Liberty** and **Selfridges** (which also has a Top Shop concession with great fashion for girls).

Traditional English clothing – Barbour jackets and Burberry trench coats – is found in outlets such as **The Scotch House, Burberry** and **Gieves & Hawkes**. Shoes range from traditional mens at **Church's Shoes** and **John Lobb**, to the stylish designs of **Emma Hope** and the more affordable **Hobbs** and **Pied à Terre**.

Markets

London's markets sell everything from street fashion and vintage clothes to fine food, antiques and cheap household goods.

The fashionable markets are **Camden Lock**, **Greenwich**, **Portobello Road** and **Covent Garden** where you can find handmade crafts, old clothes and antiques. For those more serious about antique collecting, go early on a Friday to

Harrods at night, illuminated by 11,500 lights

Bermondsey Market in South London. **Petticoat Lane** is worth a visit for the sheer volume of leather goods and fabric. **Brick Lane** is another authentic East End market where stalls and sheds are piled high with tatty furniture and bric-a-brac. Nearby is **Old Spitalfields Market,** a mecca for the latest street fashions. For a glimpse of spirited costermongers head for **Berwick Street**, which is lined with fruit and vegetables, fabrics and household goods. **Borough Market** is a thriving fine food and farmer's market with a great atmosphere *(see p122)*.

Bustling Petticoat Lane market, officially known as Middlesex Street

Directory

Chain and Department Stores

Fortnum & Mason
181 Piccadilly W1.
Map 6 D1.
020-7734 8040.

Harrods
87–135 Brompton Rd SW1.
Map 5 A3.
020-7730 1234.

Harvey Nichols
109–125 Knightsbridge SW1.
Map 5 B2.
020-7235 5000.

HMV
150 Oxford St W1.
Map 4 D4.
020-7631 3423.

John Lewis
278–306 Oxford St W1.
Map 3 C5.
020-7629 7711.

Liberty
210–20 Regent St W1.
Map 3 C5.
020-7734 1234.

Marks & Spencer
173 & 458 Oxford St W1.
Map 3 C5/3 B5.
020-7935 7954.
Two of many branches.

Peter Jones
Sloane Square SW1.
Map 5 A4.
020-7730 3434.

Selfridges
400 Oxford St W1.
Map 3 B5.
0870-837 7377.

Tower Records
1 Piccadilly Circus W1.
Map 6 D1.
020-7439 2500.

Virgin Megastore
14–16 Oxford St W1.
Map 4 E4.
020-7631 1234.

Clothes and Shoes

Browns
23–27 South Molton St W1.
Map 3 B5.
020-7514 0000.
One of several branches.

Burberry
21–23 New Bond St W1.
Map 3 C5.
020-7930 3343.
One of three branches.

Church's Shoes
163 New Bond St W1.
Map 3 C5.
020-7499 9449.
One of several branches.

Gieves & Hawkes
1 Savile Row W1. **Map** 3 C5.
020-7434 2001.

Hobbs
47 South Molton St W1.
Map 3 C5.
020-7629 0750.
One of several branches.

Emma Hope
53 Sloane Sq SW1.
Map 5 B4.
020-7259 9566.
One of three branches.

Jasper Conran
6 Burnsall St SW3.
020-7717 8440.

John Lobb
9 St James's St SW1.
Map 6 D1.
020-7930 3664.

Margaret Howell
34 Wigmore St W1.
Map 3 B4.
020-7009 9009.

Paul Smith
40–44 Floral St WC2.
Map 4 E5.
020-7379 7133.
One of several branches.

Pied à Terre
19 South Molton St W1
Map 3 B5.
020-7629 1362.
One of several branches.

The Scotch House
2 Brompton Rd SW1.
Map 5 A2.
020-7581 2151.
One of several branches.

Vivienne Westwood
6 Davies St W1.
Map 3 B5.
020-7629 3757.

Urban Outfitters
36–38 Kensington High St W8. **Map** 1 C4.
020-7761 1001.

Markets

Bermondsey
Long Lane & Bermondsey St SE1. **Map** 8 E5.
5am–2pm Fri.

Berwick Street
Berwick St W1. **Map** 4 D5.
9am–6pm Mon–Sat.

Borough
8 Southwark St SE1.
Map 8 D4. *Fri noon–6pm, Sat 9am–4pm.*

Brick Lane
Brick Lane E1.
Liverpool St, Aldgate East. *dawn–1pm Sun.*

Camden Lock
Chalk Farm Rd NW1. *Camden Town, Chalk Farm.*
9:30am–5:30pm daily.

Covent Garden
The Piazza WC2.
Map 4 F5. *9am–5pm daily (antiques: Mon).*

Greenwich
College Approach SE10.
Greenwich.
9am–6pm Sat, Sun.

Old Spitalfields
Commercial St E1.
Liverpool St.
9:30am–5:30pm Sun.

Petticoat Lane
Middlesex St E1.
Map 8 E2 *Liverpool St.*
9am–2pm Sun.

Portobello Road
Portobello Rd W10.
Notting Hill Gate.
7am–5:30pm Sat.

Entertainment in London

London has the enormous variety of entertainment that only the great cities of the world can provide. The historical backdrop and the lively bustling atmosphere add to the excitement. Whether dancing the night away at a famous disco or making the most of London's varied arts scene, the visitor has a bewildering choice. A trip to London is not complete without a visit to the theatre which ranges from glamorous West End musicals to experimental Fringe plays. There is world-class ballet and opera in fabled venues such as Sadler's Wells and the Royal Opera House. The musical menu covers everything from classical, jazz and rock to rhythm and blues performed in atmospheric basement clubs, old converted cinemas and outdoor venues such as Wembley. Movie buffs can choose from hundreds of films each night. Sports fans can watch cricket at Lord's or participate in a host of activities from water sports to ice skating.

Many London cafés have free live music

Time Out, published every Tuesday, is the most comprehensive guide to what's on in London, with detailed weekly listings and reviews. *The Evening Standard*, *The Guardian* (Saturday) and *The Independent* also have reviews and information on events. If you buy tickets from booking agencies rather than direct from box offices, do compare prices – and only buy from ticket touts if you're desperate.

West End and National Theatres

Palace Theatre poster (1898)

The glamorous, glittering world of West End theatreland, emblazoned with the names of world-famous performers, offers an extraordinary range of entertainment.

West End theatres (see Directory for individual theatres) survive on their profits and rely on financial backers, known as "angels". Consequently, they tend to stage commercial productions with mass appeal: musicals, classics, comedies and plays by bankable contemporary playwrights which can, if successful, run for years.

The state-subsidized **Royal National Theatre** is based in the South Bank Centre *(see p128)*. Its three auditoriums – the large, open-staged Olivier, the proscenium-arched Lyttelton, and the small but flexible studio space of the Cottesloe – make a diversity of productions possible.

The **Royal Shakespeare Company** (RSC) regularly stages plays by Shakespeare, but its large repertoire includes Greek tragedies, Restoration comedies and modern works. Based at Stratford-upon-Avon *(see pp313–15)*, its major productions also come to London. Its London base used to be the Barbican Centre *(see p128)*, but it now performs at West End theatres as well. The RSC ticket hotline has information.

Theatre tickets generally cost from £5 to £30 and can be bought direct from box offices, by telephone or by post. The "tkts" discount theatre ticket booth in Leicester Square sells tickets for a wide range of shows on the day of performance. It is open Monday to Saturday (10am–7pm) for matinees and evening shows, and Sundays (noon–3pm) for matinees only (cash or credit card only).

Off-West End and Fringe Theatres

Off-West End theatre is a middle category bridging the gap between West End and Fringe theatre. It includes venues that, regardless of location, have a permanent management team and often provide the opportunity for established directors and actors to turn their hands to more adventurous works in a smaller, more intimate, environment. Fringe theatres, on the other hand, are normally venues hired out to visiting companies. Both offer a vast array of innovative productions, serving as an outlet for new, often experimental writing.

Venues (too numerous to list – see newspaper listings),

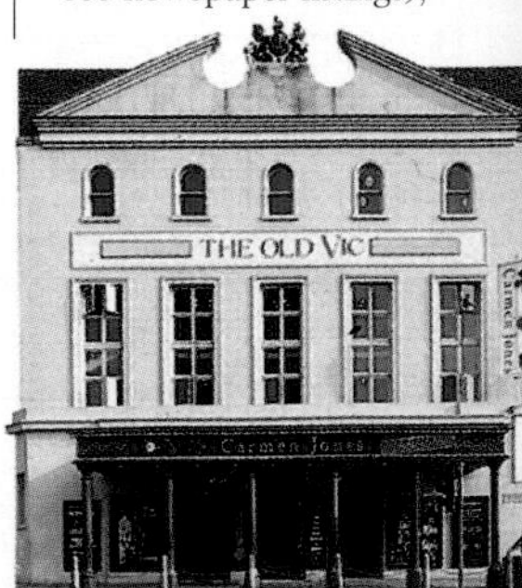

The Old Vic, the first home of the National Theatre from 1963

Open-air theatre at Regent's Park

range from tiny theatres or rooms above pubs such as the Gate, which produces neglected European classics, to theatres such as the Donmar Warehouse, which attracts major directors and actors.

Open-Air Theatre

In summer, a performance of one of Shakespeare's airier creations such as *A Midsummer Night's Dream*, takes on an atmosphere of pure enchantment among the green vistas of Regent's Park (020-7935 5756) or Holland Park (020-7602 7856). Open-air performances of a different kind are to be had at Shakespeare's Globe *(see p122)*, an authentic reproduction of an Elizabethan theatre.

Cinemas

The West End abounds with multiplex cinema chains (MGM, Odeon, UCI) which show big budget Hollywood films, usually in advance of the rest of the country, although release dates tend to lag well behind the US and many other European countries.

The Odeon Marble Arch has the largest commercial screen in Europe, while the Odeon Leicester Square boasts London's biggest auditorium with almost 2,000 seats.

Londoners are well-informed cinema-goers and even the larger cinema chains include some low-budget and foreign films in their repertoire. The majority of foreign films are subtitled, rather than dubbed. A number of independent cinemas, such as the Metro, Renoir and Prince Charles in central London, and the Curzon in Mayfair, show foreign-language and slightly more offbeat art films.

The largest concentration of cinemas is in and around Leicester Square although there are local cinemas in most areas. Just off Leicester Square, the Prince Charles is the West End's cheapest cinema. Elsewhere in the area you can expect to pay between £6 and £9 for an evening performance – almost twice the price of the local cinemas. Monday and afternoon performances in the West End are often cheaper.

IMAX Cinema, at Waterloo

The National Film Theatre (NFT), on the South Bank, is London's flagship repertory cinema. Subsidized by the British Film Institute, it screens a wide range of films, old and new, from all around the world. Nearby at Waterloo is the IMAX, with one of the world's largest screens.

Directory

Adelphi
Strand. **Map** 4 F5. *020-7344 0055.*

Albery
St Martin's Lane. **Map** 4 E5. *020-7369 1730.*

Aldwych
Aldwych. **Map** 4 F5. *020-7379 3367.*

Apollo
Shaftesbury Ave. **Map** 4 E5. *020-7494 5070.*

Cambridge
Earlham St. **Map** 4 E5. *020-7494 5080.*

Comedy
Panton St. **Map** 6 E1. *020-7369 1731.*

Criterion
Piccadilly Circus. **Map** 4 D5. *020-7413 1437.*

Dominion
Tottenham Court Rd. **Map** 4 E4. *0870-607 7460.*

Duchess
Catherine St. **Map** 4 F5. *020-7494 5075.*

Duke of York's
St Martin's Lane. **Map** 4 E5. *020-7369 1791.*

Fortune
Russell St. **Map** 4 F5. *020-7836 2238.*

Garrick
Charing Cross Rd. **Map** 4 E5. *020-7494 5085.*

Gielgud
Shaftesbury Ave. **Map** 4 D5. *020-7494 5065.*

Her Majesty's
Haymarket. **Map** 6 E1. *020-7494 5400.*

Lyceum
Wellington St. **Map** 4 F5. *0870 243 9000.*

Lyric
Shaftesbury Ave. **Map** 4 D5. *0870-890 1107.*

New London
Drury Lane. **Map** 4 E5. *020-7405 0072.*

Palace
Shaftesbury Ave. **Map** 4 E5. *020-7434 0909.*

Phoenix
Charing Cross Rd. **Map** 4 E5. *020-7369 1733.*

Piccadilly
Denman St. **Map** 4 D5. *020-7369 1734.*

Prince Edward
Old Compton St. **Map** 4 D5. *020-7447 5400.*

Prince of Wales
Coventry St. **Map** 4 D5. *020-7839 5972.*

Queen's
Shaftesbury Ave. **Map** 4 E5. *0870-890 1110.*

Royal National
(Olivier, Lyttelton, Cottesloe) South Bank. **Map** 7 A4. *020-7452 3000.*

Royal Shakespeare Company
0870 609 1110.

Shaftesbury
Shaftesbury Ave. **Map** 4 E4. *020-7379 3345.*

Strand
Aldwych. **Map** 4 F5. *0870-901 3356.*

St Martin's
West St. **Map** 4 E5. *020-7836 1443.*

Theatre Royal:
– Drury Lane
Catherine St. **Map** 4 F5. *020-7494 5000.*
– Haymarket
Haymarket. **Map** 6 E1. *0870-901 3356.*

Vaudeville
Strand. **Map** 4 F5. *020-7836 9987.*

Wyndham's
Charing Cross Rd. **Map** 4 E5. *020-7369 1736.*

Royal Festival Hall, South Bank Centre

Classical Music, Opera and Dance

London is one of the world's great centres for classical music, with five symphony orchestras, internationally renowned chamber groups such as the Academy of St-Martin-in-the-Fields and the English Chamber Orchestra, as well as a number of contemporary groups. There are performances virtually every week by major international orchestras and artists, reaching a peak during the summer Proms season at the **Royal Albert Hall** *(see p63)*. The newly restored **Wigmore Hall** has excellent acoustics and is a fine setting for chamber music, as is the converted Baroque church (1728) of **St John's, Smith Square**.

Although televised and outdoor performances by major stars have greatly increased the popularity of opera, prices at the **Royal Opera House** are still aimed at corporate entertainment but the policy now is to keep a few cheaper seats. The refurbished building is elaborate and productions are often extremely lavish. English National Opera, based at the **London Coliseum**, has more adventurous productions, appealing to a younger audience (nearly all operas are sung in English). Tickets range from £5 to £200 and it is advisable to book in advance.

The Royal Opera House is also home to the Royal Ballet, and the London Coliseum to the English National Ballet, the two leading classical ballet companies in Britain. Visiting ballets also perform in both. There are numerous young contemporary dance companies, and **The Place** is a dedicated contemporary dance theatre where many companies perform. Other major dance venues are **Sadler's Wells**, the **ICA**, the **Peacock Theatre** and the **Chisenhale Dance Space**.

The **Barbican Concert Hall** and **South Bank Centre** (comprising the Royal Festival Hall, Queen Elizabeth Hall and Purcell Room) host an impressive variety of events ranging from touring opera and classical music performances to free foyer concerts.

Elsewhere in London many outdoor musical events take place in summer *(see pp62–3)* at venues such as **Kenwood House**. Events to look out for are: the London Opera Festival (June) with singers from all over the world; the City of London Festival (July) which hosts a range of varied musical events; and contemporary dance festivals Spring Loaded (February–April) and Dance Umbrella (October) – see *Time Out* and newspaper listings.

Kenwood House on Hampstead Heath *(see p132)*

Directory

Classical Music, Opera and Dance

Barbican Concert Hall
Silk St EC2. **Map** 7 C1. *020-7638 8891.* www.barbican.org.uk

Chisenhale Dance Space
64–84 Chisenhale Rd E3. *Bethnal Green, Mile End.* *020-8981 6617.*

ICA
The Mall SW1. **Map** 6 E1. *020-7930 3647.* www.ica.org.uk

Kenwood House
Hampstead Lane NW3. *Archway.* *020-8233 7435.*

London Coliseum
St Martin's Lane WC2. **Map** 4 E5. *020-7632 8300.* www.eno.org

Peacock Theatre
Portugal St WC2. **Map** 4 F5. *020-7863 8000.*

The Place
17 Duke's Rd WC1. **Map** 4 E2. *020-7387 0031.*

Royal Albert Hall
Kensington Gore SW7. **Map** 2 E4. *020-7589 3203.* www.royalalberthall.com

Royal Opera House
Bow St WC2. **Map** 4 F5. *020-7304 4000.* www.royalopera.org

Sadler's Wells
Rosebery Ave EC1. *Angel.* *020-7863 8000.* www.sadlerswells.com

St John's, Smith Square
Smith Sq SW1. **Map** 6 E3. *020-7222 1061.* www.sjss.org.uk

South Bank Centre
SE1. **Map** 6 F1. *020-7921 0600.* www.southbank.com

Wigmore Hall
Wigmore St W1. **Map** 3 B4. *020-7935 2141.*

Rock, Pop, Jazz and Clubs

100 Club
100 Oxford St W1. **Map** 4 D5. *020-7636 0933.*

Brixton Academy
211 Stockwell Rd SW9. *Brixton.* *0870-771 2000.*

Forum
9–17 Highgate Rd NW5. *Kentish Town.* *020-7344 0044.*

Fridge
Town Hall Parade, Brixton Hill SW2. *Brixton.* *020-7326 5100.*

The Hippodrome, Leicester Square

Rock, Pop, Jazz and Clubs

An ordinary week night in London features scores of concerts, ranging from rock and pop, to jazz, Latin, world, folk and reggae. Artists guaranteed to fill thousands of seats play large venues such as **Wembley Arena** or the **Royal Albert Hall**. However, many major bands prefer to play the **Brixton Academy** and the **Forum**, both former cinemas.

The number of jazz venues has increased over the last few years. Best of the old crop is **Ronnie Scott's**, while of the newcomers the **100 Club**, **Jazz Café** and **Pizza on the Park** have good reputations.

London's club scene is one of the most innovative in Europe, particularly since 1990, when all-night clubbing (though not drinking) was legalized. It is dominated by big-name DJs, who host different nights in different clubs, and some of the best clubs are one-nighters (see *Time Out* and newspaper listings). The world-famous mainstream discos **Stringfellows** and the **Hippodrome** are glitzy, expensive and very much part of the tourist circuit, as is the **Limelight** nearby. In contrast the New York-style **Ministry of Sound**, the camp cabaret of **Madame Jojo's**, the trendy Shoreditch club **333**, and a host of other venues ensure that you will never be short of choice. Alternatives are the excellent laser and light shows at **Heaven**, the glamorous super-club **Pacha London**, or the ska, classic soul and R'n'B at **Gossips** on Thursdays. Heaven and the **Fridge** are among the most popular of London's gay clubs.

Opening times are usually 10pm–3am, but on weekends many clubs open until 6am.

Ticket agency, Shaftesbury Avenue

Sports

An impressive variety of public sports facilities are to be found in London and they are generally inexpensive to use. Swimming pools, squash courts, gyms and sports centres, with an assortment of keep-fit classes, can be found in most districts, and tennis courts hired in most parks. Water sports, ice skating and golf are among the variety of activities on offer. Spectator sports range from football and rugby at various club grounds to cricket at **Lord's** or the **Oval**, and tennis at the **All England Lawn Tennis Club**, Wimbledon. Tickets for the most popular matches can often be hard to come by *(see p67)*. More traditional sports include polo at **Guards**, croquet at **Hurlingham** and medieval tennis at **Queen's Club Real Tennis**. See pages 630 to 631 for more information on sporting activities.

Gossips
69 Dean St W1. **Map** 4 D4.
020-7434 4480.

Heaven
Under the Arches, Villiers St WC2. **Map** 6 E1.
020-7930 2020.

Hippodrome
Leicester Square WC2.
Map 4 E5.
020-7437 4311.

Jazz Café
3-5 Parkway NW1.
Camden Town.
020-7916 6060.

Limelight
136 Shaftesbury Ave, W1.
Map 4 E5.
020-7434 0572.

Madame Jojo's
8–10 Brewer St W1.
Map 4 D5.
020-7734 3040.

Ministry of Sound
103 Gaunt St SE1. **Map** 7 C5. *020-7378 6528.*

Pacha London
Terminus Place, SW1.**Map** 5 C3. *020-7834 4440.*

Pizza on the Park
11 Knightsbridge SW1.
Map 5 B2. *020-7235 5550.* www.pizzaonthepark.com

Ronnie Scott's
47 Frith St W1. **Map** 4 D5.
020-7439 0747.
www.ronniescotts.uk

Stringfellows
16–19 Upper St Martin's Lane WC2. **Map** 4 E5.
020-7240 5534.

333
333 Old St EC1.
020-7739 5949.
www.333mother.com

Sports

All England Lawn Tennis Club
Church Rd, Wimbledon SW19. *Southfields.*
020-8946 2244.

Guards Polo Club
Windsor Great Park, Englefield Green, Egham, Surrey. *Egham.*
01784 434212.

Hurlingham Club
Ranelagh Gdns SW6.
Map 5 B5.
020-7736 8411.

Lord's Cricket Ground
St John's Wood NW8.
St John's Wood.
020-7289 1611.

Oval Cricket Ground
The Oval, Kennington SE11.
Oval.
020-7582 6660.

Queen's Club Real Tennis
Palliser Rd W14.
Barons Court.
020-7385 3421.

Further Afield

Over the centuries London has steadily expanded to embrace the scores of villages that surrounded it, leaving the City as a reminder of London's original boundaries. Although now linked in an almost unbroken urban sprawl, many of these areas have maintained their old village atmosphere and character. Hampstead and Highgate are still distinct enclaves, as are artistic Chelsea and literary Islington. Greenwich, Chiswick and Richmond have retained features that hark back to the days when the Thames was an important artery for transport and commerce, while just to the east of the City the wide expanses of the former docks have, in the last 20 years, been imaginatively rebuilt as new commercial and residential areas.

Sights at a Glance

Camden and Islington 7
Chelsea 1
Chiswick 10
East End and Docklands 8
Greenwich 9
Hampstead 4
Hampstead Heath 5
Highgate 6
Holland Park 2
Notting Hill and Portobello Road 3
Richmond and Kew 11

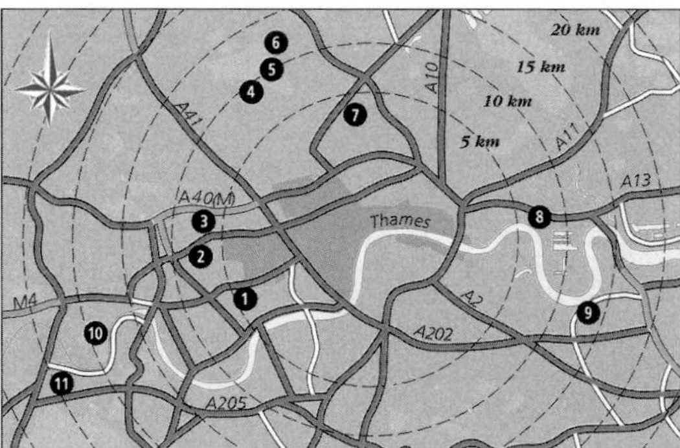

Key

- Main sightseeing areas
- Greater London
- Parks
- Motorway
- Major road
- Minor road

10 miles = 15 km

Chelsea 1

SW3. *Sloane Square.*

Riverside Chelsea has been fashionable since Tudor times when Sir Thomas More, Henry VIII's Lord Chancellor *(see p50)*, lived here. The river views attracted artists and the arrival of the historian Thomas Carlyle and essayist Leigh Hunt in the 1830s began a literary connection. Blue plaques on the houses of **Cheyne Walk** celebrate former residents such as J M W Turner *(see p93)* and writers George Eliot, Henry James and T S Eliot.

Statue of Sir Thomas More (1478–1535), Cheyne Walk

Chelsea's artistic tradition is maintained by its galleries and antique shops, many of them scattered among the clothes boutiques on **King's Road**. This begins at **Sloane Square**, named after the physician Sir Hans Sloane, who bought the manor of Chelsea in 1712. Sloane expanded the **Chelsea Physic Garden** (1673) along Swan Walk to cultivate plants and herbs.

Wren's **Royal Hospital**, on Royal Hospital Road was built in 1692 as a retirement home for old soldiers and still houses 400 Chelsea Pensioners.

Arab Hall, Leighton House (1866)

Holland Park 2

W8, W14. *Holland Park.*

This small but delightful park is more intimate than the large royal parks such as Hyde Park *(see p103)*. It was opened in 1952 on the grounds of **Holland House**, a centre of social and political intrigue in its 19th-century heyday.

Around the park are some magnificent late Victorian

houses. **Linley Sambourne House** was built about 1870 and has received a much-needed facelift, though it remains much as Sambourne furnished it, in the Victorian manner, with china ornaments and heavy velvet drapes. He was a political cartoonist for the satirical magazine *Punch* and drawings cram the walls.

Leighton House, built for the Neo-Classical painter Lord Leighton in 1866, has been preserved as an extraordinary monument to the Victorian Aesthetic movement. The highlight is the Arab Hall, which was added in 1879 to house Leighton's stupendous collection of 13th- to 17th-century Islamic tiles. The best paintings include some by Leighton himself and by his contemporaries Edward Burne-Jones and John Millais.

Georgian house, Hampstead

Linley Sambourne House
18 Stafford Terrace W8. *020-7602 3316. High St Kensington. 10am–5:30pm Sat & Sun. mandatory. Tours every hr; last tour 4pm.*

Leighton House
12 Holland Park Rd W14. *020-7602 3316. High St Kensington. 11am–5:30pm Sun–Mon. public hols.*

Notting Hill and Portobello Road ❸

W11. *Notting Hill Gate.*

In the 1950s and 60s, Notting Hill became a centre for the Caribbean community and today it is a vibrant cosmopolitan part of London. It is also home to Europe's largest street carnival *(see p63)* which began in 1966 and takes over the entire area on the August bank holiday weekend, when costumed parades flood through the crowded streets.

Nearby, Portobello Road market *(see pp124–5)* has a bustling atmosphere with hundreds of stalls and shops selling a variety of collectables.

Hampstead ❹

NW3, N6. *Hampstead. Hampstead Heath.*

Positioned on a high ridge north of the metropolis, Hampstead has always remained aloof from London. Essentially a Georgian village with many perfectly maintained mansions and houses, it is one of London's most desirable residential areas, home to a community of artists and writers since Georgian times.

Situated in a quiet Hampstead street, **Keats House** (1816), is an evocative and memorable tribute to the life and work of the poet John Keats (1795–1821). Keats lived here for two years before his tragic death from consumption at the age of 25, and it was under a plum tree in the garden that he wrote his celebrated *Ode to a Nightingale*. Mementoes of Keats and of Fanny Brawne, the neighbour to whom he was engaged, are on display.

The **Freud Museum**, which opened in 1986, is dedicated to the dramatic life of Sigmund Freud (1856–1939), the founder of psychoanalysis. At the age of 82, Freud fled from Nazi persecution in Vienna to this Hampstead house where he lived and worked for the last year of his life. His daughter Anna, pioneer of child psychoanalysis, continued to live here until her death in 1982. Inside, Freud's rich Viennese-style consulting rooms remain unaltered, and 1930s home movies show moments of Freud's life, including scenes of the Nazi attack on his home in Vienna.

Keats House
Keats Grove NW3.
020-7435 2062. Hampstead, Belsize Park. noon–5pm Tue–Sun. www.keatshouse.org

Freud Museum
20 Maresfield Gdns NW3.
020-7435 2002. Finchley Rd. noon–5pm Wed–Sun. limited. www.freud.org.uk

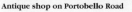

Antique shop on Portobello Road

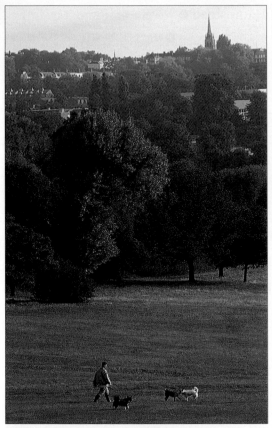

View east across Hampstead Heath to Highgate

Hampstead Heath ❺

N6. Ⓤ *Hampstead, Highgate.* ⇌ *Hampstead Heath.*

SEPARATING the hill-top villages of Hampstead and Highgate, the open spaces of Hampstead Heath are a precious retreat from the city. There are meadows, lakes and ponds for bathing and fishing, and fine views over the capital from **Parliament Hill**, to the east.

Situated in landscaped grounds high on the edge of the Heath is the magnificent **Kenwood House**, where classical concerts *(see p128)* are held by the lake in summer. The house was remodelled by Robert Adam *(see p24)* in 1764 and most of his interiors have survived, the highlight of which is the library. The mansion is filled with Old Master paintings, such as works by Van Dyck, Vermeer, Turner *(see p93)* and Romney; the star attraction is Rembrandt's self-portrait of 1663.

Kenwood House
Hampstead Lane NW3. 020-8348 1286. *daily.* *Nov–Dec.*
www.english-heritage.org.uk

Handmade crafts and antiques, Camden Lock indoor market

Highgate ❻

N6. Ⓤ *Highgate, Archway.*

A SETTLEMENT since the Middle Ages, Highgate, like Hampstead, became a fashionable aristocratic retreat in the 16th century. Today, it still has an exclusive rural feel, aloof from the urban sprawl below, with a Georgian high street and many expensive houses.

Highgate Cemetery *(see p77),* with its monuments and hidden overgrown corners, has an extraordinary, magical atmosphere. Tour guides (daily in summer, weekends in winter) tell of the many tales of intrigue, mystery and vandalism connected with the cemetery since it opened in 1839. In the eastern section is the tomb of Victorian novelist George Eliot (1819–80) and of the cemetery's most famous incumbent, Karl Marx (1818–83).

Highgate Cemetery
Swains Lane N6. 020-8340 1834.
Ⓤ *Archway, Highgate.* *daily.*
during burials, 25–26 Dec.
www.highgate-cemetery.org

Camden and Islington ❼

NW1, N1. **Camden** Ⓤ *Camden Town, Chalk Farm.* **Islington** Ⓤ *Angel, Highbury & Islington.*

CAMDEN IS A LIVELY AREA packed with restaurants, shops and a busy **market** *(see p124–5).* Thousands of people come here each weekend to browse among the wide variety of stalls or simply to soak up the atmosphere of the lively cobbled area around the canal, which is enhanced by the buskers and street performers.

Neighbouring Islington was once a fashionable spa but the rich moved out in the late 18th century and the area deteriorated rapidly. In the 20th century, writers such as Evelyn Waugh, George Orwell and Joe Orton lived here. In recent decades, Islington has been rediscovered and is again fashionable as one of the first areas in London to become "gentrified", with many professionals buying the old houses.

East End and Docklands 8

E1, E2, E14. **East End** *Aldgate East, Liverpool St, Bethnal Green.* **Docklands** *Canary Wharf.*

IN THE MIDDLE AGES the East End was full of craftsmen practising noxious trades such as brewing, bleaching and vinegar-making, which were banned within the City. The area has also been home to numerous immigrant communities since the 17th century, when French Huguenots, escaping religious persecution moved into Spitalfields, and made it a silk-weaving centre. Even after the decline of the silk industry, textiles and clothing continued to dominate, with Jewish tailors and furriers setting up workshops in the 1880s, and Bengali machinists sewing in cramped premises from the 1950s.

A good way to get a taste of the East End is to explore its Sunday street markets *(see p125)*, and sample freshly baked bagels and spicy Indian food. By way of contrast, anyone interested in contemporary architecture should visit the **Docklands**, an ambitious redevelopment of disused docks, dominated by the Canada Tower; at 250 m (800 ft) it is London's tallest building. Other attractions include the **Bethnal Green Museum of Childhood,** a toy museum with a good display of toys and dolls' houses and **Dennis Severs' House**, in which you are taken on a historic journey from the 17th to the 19th centuries.

Canada Tower, Canary Wharf

Royal Naval College framing the Queen's House, Greenwich

Bethnal Green Museum of Childhood
Cambridge Heath Rd E2. *020-8983 5200.* *10am–5:50pm Sat–Thu.* *1 Jan, 24, 25 Dec.* www.museumofchildhood.org.uk

Dennis Severs' House
18 Folgate St E1. *020-7247 4013.* *1st Sun & Mon of month.* www.dennisevershouse.co.uk

Greenwich 9

SE10. *Greenwich, Maze Hill.* *Cutty Sark (DLR).*

THE WORLD'S TIME has been measured from the **Royal Observatory Greenwich** (now housing a museum) since 1884. The area is full of maritime and royal history, with Neo-Classical mansions, a park, many antique and book shops and various markets *(see pp124–5)*. The **Queen's House**, designed by Inigo Jones for James I's wife, was completed in 1637 for Henrietta Maria, the queen of Charles I. It has now been restored to its original state. The highlights of the Queen's House include the perfectly cubic main hall and the unusual spiral "tulip staircase".

The adjoining **National Maritime Museum** has exhibits that range from primitive canoes, through Elizabethan galleons, to modern ships. Anyone interested in naval history should visit the **Old Royal Naval College**, which was designed by Christopher Wren *(see p116)* in two halves so that the Queen's House could retain its river view. It began as a royal palace, became a hospital in 1692, and in 1873 the Old Royal Naval College moved its premises here. The Rococo chapel and the 18th-century *trompe l'oeil* Painted Hall are open to the public.

An 18th-century compass, National Maritime Museum

Royal Observatory Greenwich
Greenwich Park SE10. *020-8312 6535.* *daily.* *24–26 Dec.* www.rog.nmm.ac.uk

Queen's House and National Maritime Museum
Romney Rd SE10. *020-8312 6565.* *daily.* *24–26 Dec.* *limited.* www.nmm.ac.uk

Old Royal Naval College
King William Walk, Greenwich SE10. *020-8269 4747.* *10am–5pm Mon–Sat; 12:30–5pm Sun.* *public hols.*

Chiswick ⑩

W4. Chiswick.

CHISWICK IS A PLEASANT suburb of London, with pubs, cottages and a variety of birdlife, such as herons, along the picturesque riverside. One of the main reasons for a visit is **Chiswick House**, a magnificent country villa inspired by the Renaissance architecture of Andrea Palladio. It was designed in the early 18th century by the 3rd Earl of Burlington as an annexe to his larger house (demolished in 1758), so that he could display his collection of art and entertain friends. The gardens, with their Classical temples and statues, are now restored to their former glory.

Heron

Chiswick House
Burlington Lane W4. *020-8995 0508.* *Apr–Oct: daily.*

Richmond and Kew ⑪

SW15. *Richmond.*

THE ATTRACTIVE village of Richmond took its name from a palace built by Henry VII (the former Earl of Richmond in Yorkshire) in 1500, the remains of which can be seen off the green. Nearby is the expansive **Richmond Park** *(see p76)*, which was once Charles I's royal hunting ground. In summer, boats sail down the Thames from Westminster Millennium Pier, making a pleasant day's excursion from central London *(see pp74–5)*.

The nobility continued to favour Richmond after royalty had left, and some of their mansions have survived. The Palladian villa, **Marble Hill House**, was built in 1724–9 for the mistress of George II and has been restored to its original appearance. On the opposite side of the Thames, the brooding **Ham House**, built in 1610, had its heyday later that century when it became the home of the Lauderdales. The Countess of Lauderdale inherited the house from her father, who had been Charles I's "whipping boy" – meaning that he was punished whenever the future king misbehaved. He was rewarded as an adult by being given a peerage and the lease of Ham estate.

A little further north along the Thames, **Syon House** has been inhabited by the Dukes and Earls of Northumberland for over 400 years. Numerous attractions here include a butterfly house, a museum of historic cars and a spectacular conservatory built in 1830. The lavish Neo-Classical interiors of the house, created by Robert Adam in the 1760s *(see p24)*, remain the highlight.

Brewers Lane, Richmond

On the riverbank to the south, **Kew Gardens** *(see p76)*, the most complete botanic gardens in the world, are flawlessly maintained, with examples of nearly every plant that can be grown in Britain. There are also conservatories where thousands of exotic tropical blooms are on display.

Marble Hill House
Richmond Rd, Twickenham. *020-8892 5115.* *Apr–Sep: daily; Oct: Wed–Sun.* *limited.*

Ham House
Ham St, Richmond. *020-8940 1950.* *Apr–Oct: Sat–Wed.*

Syon House
London Rd, Brentford. *020-8560 0881.* **House** *mid-Mar–Oct: Wed, Thu, Sun.* **Gardens** *daily.* *Nov–mid-Mar.* *gardens only.* www.syonpark.co.uk

Kew Gardens
Royal Botanic Gdns, Kew Green, Richmond. *020-8332 5655.* *daily.* *25 Dec, 1 Jan.* www.kew.org

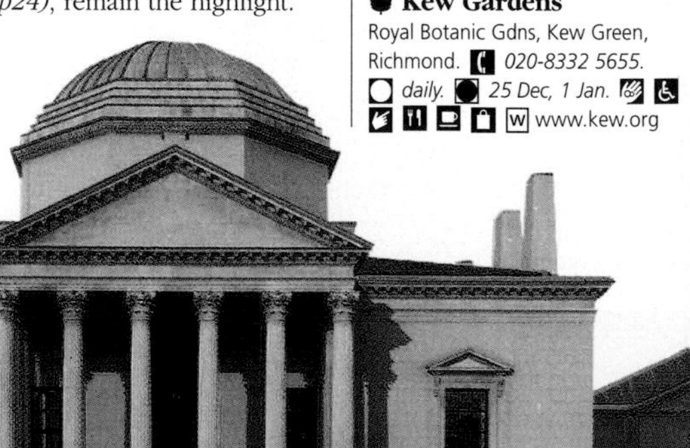
Chiswick House

Street Finder

The map references given with the sights, hotels, restaurants, shops and entertainment venues based in central London refer to the following four maps. All the main places of interest within the central area are marked on the maps in addition to useful practical information, such as tube, railway and coach stations. The key map below shows the area of London that is covered by the *Street Finder*. The four main city-centre areas (colour-coded in pink) are shown in more detail on the inside back cover.

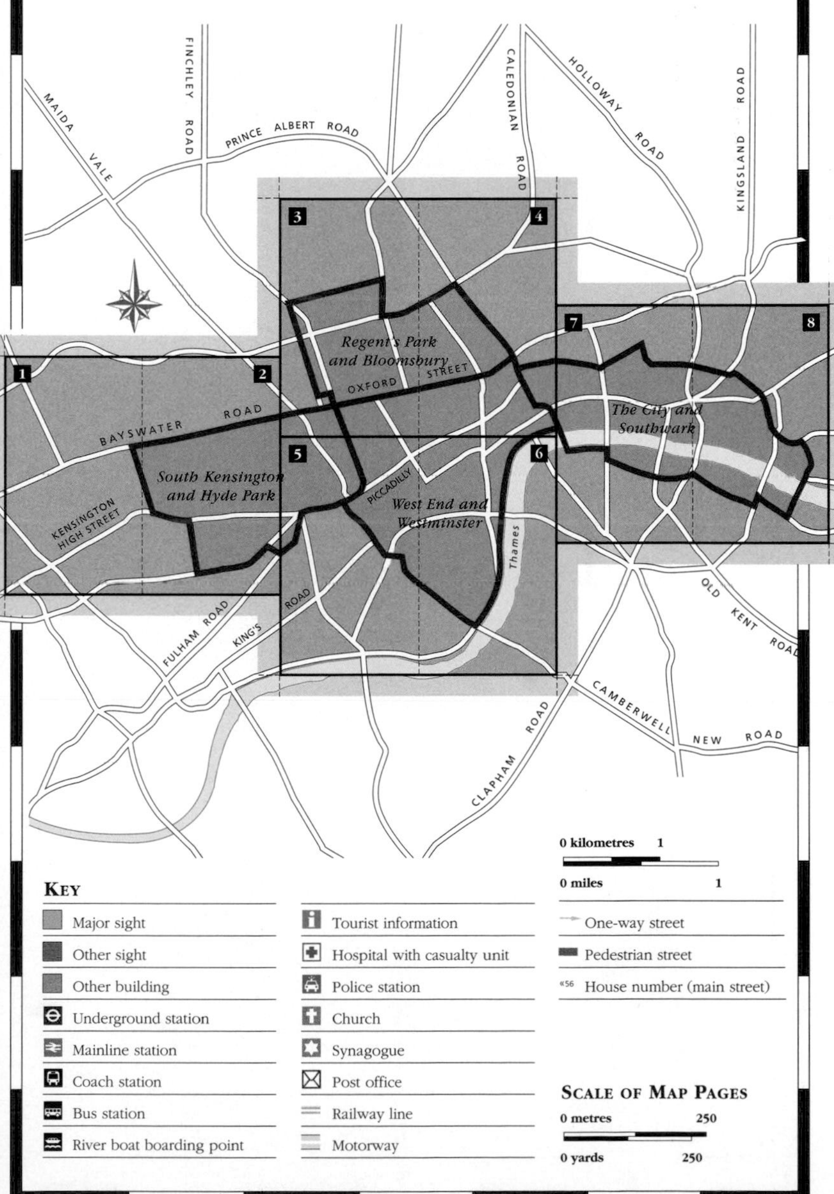

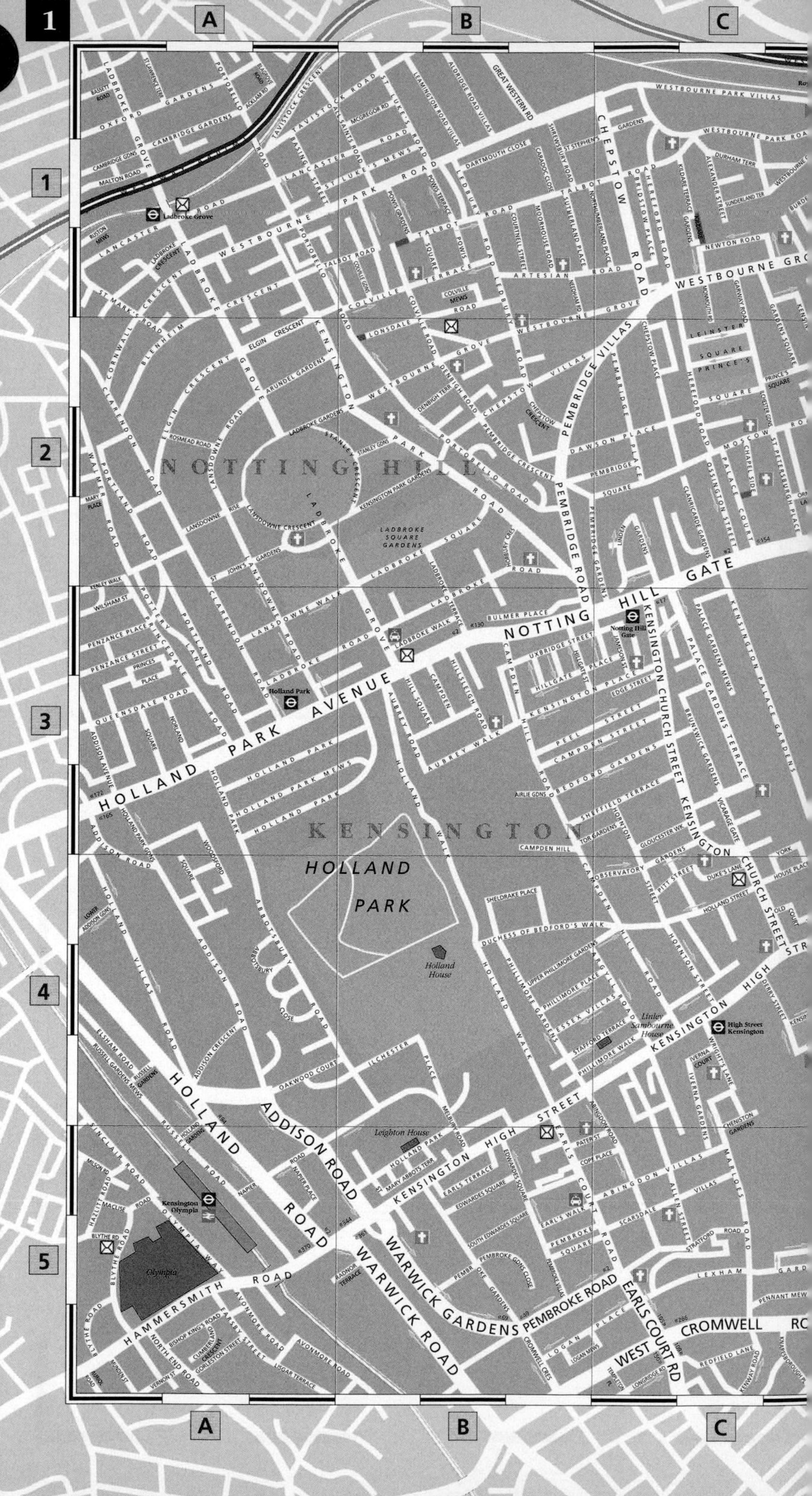

1
A
B
C
1
2
3
4
5
NOTTING HILL
KENSINGTON
HOLLAND PARK
Holland House
Linley Sambourne House
Leighton House
Olympia
Ladbroke Grove
Notting Hill Gate
Holland Park
High Street Kensington
Kensington Olympia
LADBROKE SQUARE GARDENS
WESTBOURNE PARK VILLAS
WESTBOURNE PARK ROAD
WESTBOURNE GROVE
GREAT WESTERN RD
CHEPSTOW ROAD
CHEPSTOW VILLAS
CHEPSTOW PLACE
CHEPSTOW CRESCENT
PEMBRIDGE VILLAS
PEMBRIDGE ROAD
PEMBRIDGE SQUARE
PEMBRIDGE CRESCENT
PEMBRIDGE GARDENS
PORTOBELLO ROAD
LADBROKE GROVE
LADBROKE ROAD
LADBROKE SQUARE
LADBROKE GARDENS
LADBROKE CRESCENT
LANCASTER ROAD
TALBOT ROAD
ELGIN CRESCENT
ARUNDEL GARDENS
LANSDOWNE CRESCENT
LANSDOWNE ROAD
STANLEY CRESCENT
KENSINGTON PARK ROAD
KENSINGTON PARK GARDENS
BLENHEIM CRESCENT
CORNWALL CRESCENT
CLARENDON ROAD
PORTLAND ROAD
POTTERY LANE
PENZANCE PLACE
PENZANCE STREET
PRINCES PLACE
QUEENSDALE ROAD
ADDISON AVENUE
NORLAND SQUARE
HOLLAND PARK AVENUE
HOLLAND PARK
HOLLAND PARK MEWS
HOLLAND PARK GDNS
HOLLAND VILLAS ROAD
HOLLAND WALK
HOLLAND ROAD
ADDISON ROAD
ADDISON CRESCENT
ABBOTSBURY ROAD
ABBOTSBURY CLOSE
OAKWOOD COURT
ILCHESTER PLACE
MELBURY ROAD
CAMPDEN HILL
CAMPDEN HILL ROAD
CAMPDEN HILL SQUARE
CAMPDEN STREET
AUBREY ROAD
AUBREY WALK
HILLSLEIGH ROAD
PEEL STREET
BEDFORD GARDENS
SHEFFIELD TERRACE
KENSINGTON PLACE
KENSINGTON CHURCH STREET
KENSINGTON PALACE GARDENS
PALACE GARDENS TERRACE
BRUNSWICK GARDENS
VICARAGE GATE
NOTTING HILL GATE
BULMER PLACE
UXBRIDGE STREET
HILLGATE PLACE
HORNTON STREET
OBSERVATORY GARDENS
DUKE'S LANE
HOLLAND STREET
SHELDRAKE PLACE
DUCHESS OF BEDFORD'S WALK
PHILLIMORE GARDENS
PHILLIMORE PLACE
UPPER PHILLIMORE GARDENS
PHILLIMORE WALK
ESSEX VILLAS
STAFFORD TERRACE
ARGYLL ROAD
KENSINGTON HIGH STREET
WRIGHT'S LANE
IVERNA COURT
IVERNA GARDENS
DERRY STREET
ABINGDON ROAD
ABINGDON VILLAS
EARLS COURT ROAD
EARLS TERRACE
EDWARDES SQUARE
SOUTH EDWARDES SQUARE
PEMBROKE ROAD
PEMBROKE SQUARE
PEMBROKE GARDENS
WARWICK GARDENS
WARWICK ROAD
ALLEN STREET
SCARSDALE VILLAS
MARLOES ROAD
STRATFORD ROAD
LEXHAM GARDENS
CROMWELL ROAD
WEST CROMWELL ROAD
LOGAN PLACE
REDFIELD LANE
HAMMERSMITH ROAD
AVONMORE ROAD
NORTH END ROAD
BLYTHE ROAD
OLYMPIA WAY
RUSSELL ROAD
ELSHAM ROAD
SINCLAIR ROAD
A
B
C

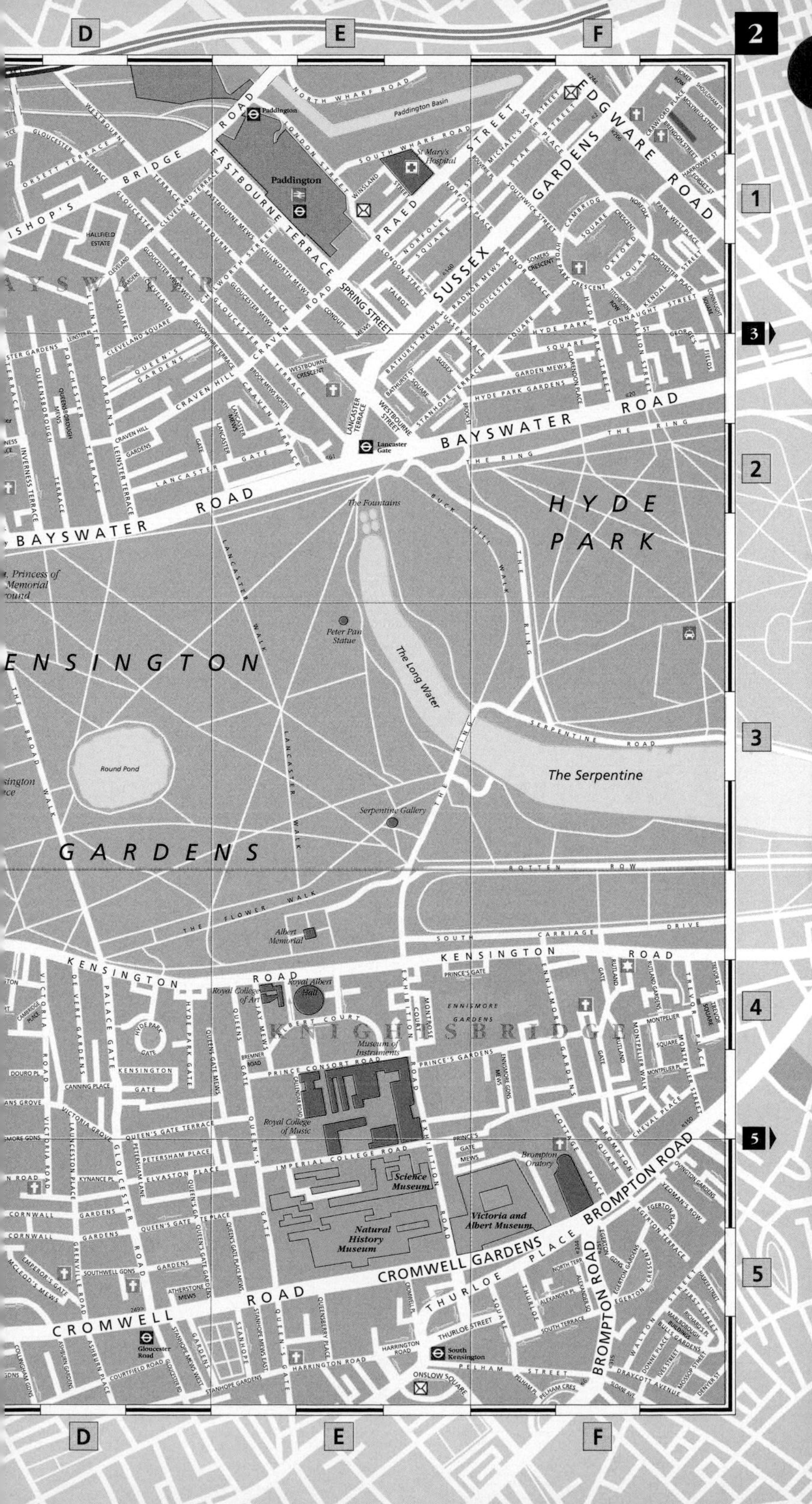

2
D
E
F
1
2
3
4
5
Paddington
St Mary's Hospital
Paddington Basin
North Wharf Road
South Wharf Road
Edgware Road
Sussex Gardens
Praed Street
Eastbourne Terrace
Bishop's Bridge Road
Westbourne Terrace
Hallfield Estate
Bayswater
Spring Street
Craven Hill
Lancaster Gate
Bayswater Road
The Ring
Hyde Park
The Fountains
Buck Hill Walk
Lancaster Walk
Peter Pan Statue
The Long Water
Kensington Gardens
Round Pond
The Broad Walk
The Serpentine
Serpentine Road
Serpentine Gallery
Rotten Row
The Flower Walk
Albert Memorial
South Carriage Drive
Kensington Road
Royal College of Art
Royal Albert Hall
Knightsbridge
Ennismore Gardens
Museum of Instruments
Prince Consort Road
Exhibition Road
Royal College of Music
Imperial College Road
Science Museum
Natural History Museum
Victoria and Albert Museum
Brompton Oratory
Brompton Road
Cromwell Gardens
Cromwell Road
Thurloe Place
Gloucester Road
South Kensington
Pelham Street
Onslow Square
Queen's Gate
Harrington Road
Palace Gate
Hyde Park Gate
Victoria Road
Montpelier Square
Trevor Square
Egerton Crescent
Walton Street
Draycott Avenue

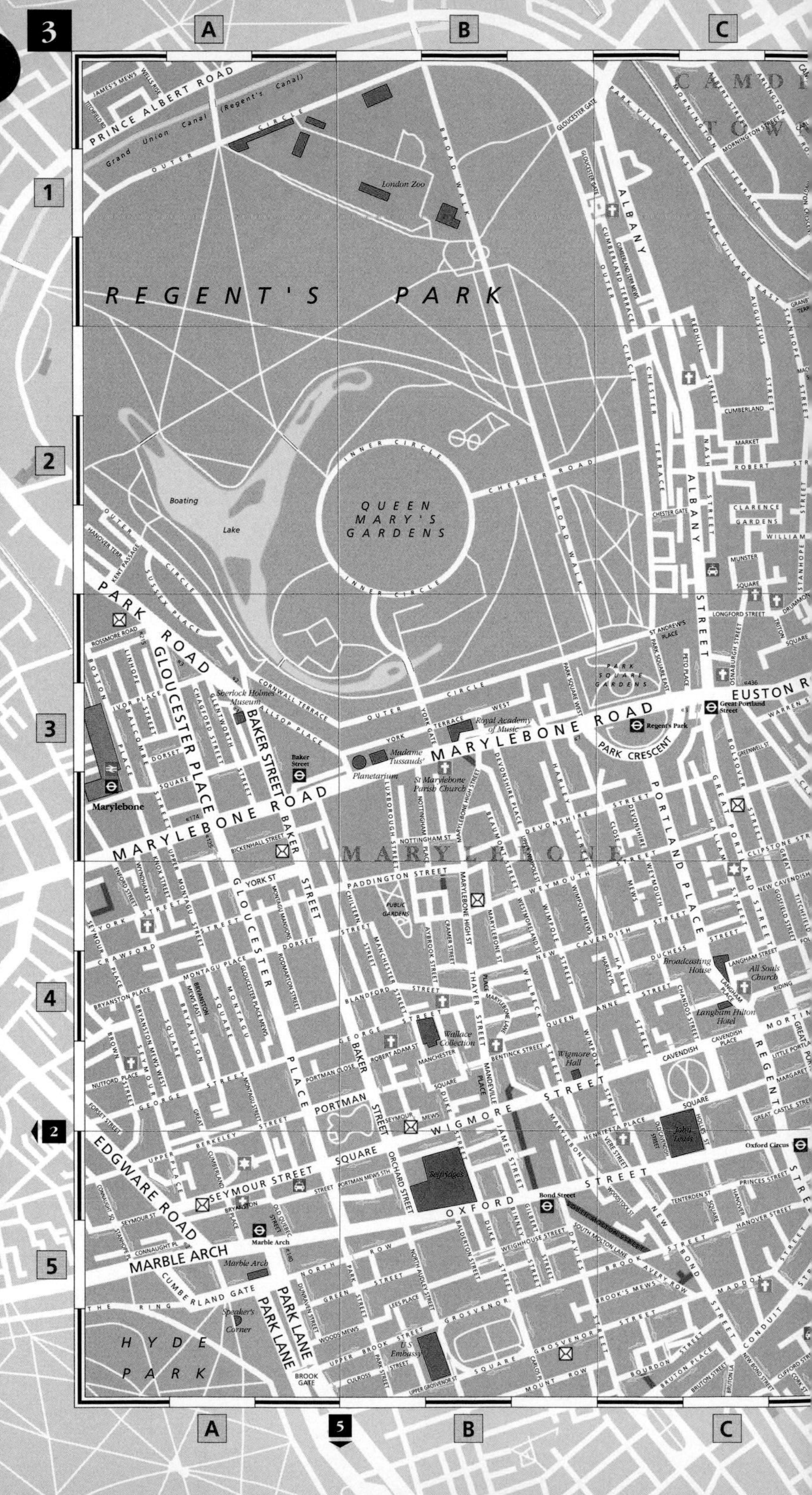
3
A
B
C
1
2
3
4
5
2
5
REGENT'S PARK
PRINCE ALBERT ROAD
Grand Union Canal (Regent's Canal)
OUTER CIRCLE
London Zoo
BROAD WALK
GLOUCESTER GATE
PARK VILLAGE EAST
ALBANY STREET
CUMBERLAND TERRACE
CHESTER TERRACE
Boating Lake
QUEEN MARY'S GARDENS
INNER CIRCLE
CHESTER ROAD
CHESTER GATE
PARK ROAD
GLOUCESTER PLACE
BAKER STREET
Sherlock Holmes Museum
CORNWALL TERRACE
ALLSOP PLACE
PARK SQUARE GARDENS
PARK CRESCENT
Regent's Park
Great Portland Street
EUSTON ROAD
MARYLEBONE ROAD
Royal Academy of Music
Madame Tussauds'
Planetarium
Baker Street
St Marylebone Parish Church
Marylebone
MARYLEBONE
PORTLAND PLACE
HARLEY STREET
WIMPOLE STREET
Broadcasting House
All Souls Church
Langham Hilton Hotel
Wallace Collection
Wigmore Hall
WIGMORE STREET
CAVENDISH SQUARE
John Lewis
Oxford Circus
REGENT STREET
PORTMAN SQUARE
Selfridges
OXFORD STREET
Bond Street
NEW BOND STREET
EDGWARE ROAD
SEYMOUR STREET
Marble Arch
MARBLE ARCH
CUMBERLAND GATE
PARK LANE
Speaker's Corner
HYDE PARK
BROOK GATE
US Embassy
GROSVENOR SQUARE
UPPER BROOK STREET
MOUNT ROW
BRUTON PLACE
CONDUIT STREET
MADDOX

D
E
F
4
1
2
3
4
5
7
6
Euston
British Library
St Pancras
King's Cross
King's Cross St Pancras
King's Cross Thameslink
St Pancras Church
Euston Square
University College
University College Hospital
Percival David Foundation
Foundling Museum
Russell Square
The Dickens House Museum
British Museum
St George's Bloomsbury
Holborn
Sir John Soane's Museum
Pollock's Toy Museum
Goodge Street
Tottenham Court Road
Covent Garden
Royal Opera House
Theatre Museum
Theatre Royal
London Transport Museum
Central Market
St Paul's Church
Leicester Square
Palace Theatre
Photographers' Gallery
Trocadero Centre
The London Coliseum
Adelphi Theatre
The Savoy
Savoy Chapel
The Waldorf Hotel
St Mary-le-Strand
Bush House
Australia House
Courtauld Gallery
Somerset House
EUSTON ROAD
PENTONVILLE ROAD
CALEDONIAN ROAD
YORK WAY
PANCRAS ROAD
GRAY'S INN ROAD
KING'S CROSS ROAD
EVERSHOLT STREET
GOWER STREET
TOTTENHAM COURT ROAD
WOBURN PLACE
SOUTHAMPTON ROW
THEOBALD'S ROAD
HIGH HOLBORN
NEW OXFORD STREET
OXFORD STREET
CHARING CROSS ROAD
SHAFTESBURY AVENUE
KINGSWAY
ALDWYCH
STRAND
BLOOMSBURY WAY
CROWNDALE ROAD

5
A
B
C
3
2
1
2
3
4
5
HYDE PARK
The Serpentine
SERPENTINE ROAD
ROTTEN ROW
SOUTH CARRIAGE DRIVE
PARK LANE
GROSVENOR GATE
UPPER GROSVENOR STREET
REEVES MEWS
MOUNT STREET
SOUTH AUDLEY STREET
ALDFORD STREET
SOUTH STREET
ST GEORGE'S GARDENS
FARM STREET
CHARLES STREET
HILL STREET
HAY'S MEWS
CURZON STREET
TILNEY ST
STANHOPE GATE
SHEPHERD MARKET
HERTFORD STREET
SHEPHERD STREET
MARKET MEWS
BRICK STREET
DOWN STREET
OLD PARK LANE
HAMILTON PLACE
PICCADILLY
BERKELEY SQUARE
BERKELEY STREET
CLARGES STREET
HALF MOON STREET
BOLTON STREET
STRATTON STREET
HAY HILL
DOVER STREET
ALBEMARLE STREET
Faraday Museum
Green Park
GREEN PARK
CONSTITUTION HILL
Buckingham Palace
BUCKINGHAM PALACE GARDENS
Queen's Gallery
Royal Mews
Apsley House
HYDE PARK CORNER
Wellington Arch
Hyde Park Corner
DUKE OF WELLINGTON PLACE
KNIGHTSBRIDGE
Knightsbridge
GROSVENOR PLACE
GROSVENOR CRESCENT
WILTON ROW
WILTON CRESCENT
WILTON PLACE
BELGRAVE MEWS NORTH
HALKIN STREET
HEADFORT PLACE
MONTROSE PLACE
CHAPEL STREET
BELGRAVE SQUARE
CHESTER STREET
CHESTER MEWS
LITTLE CHESTER MEWS
UPPER BELGRAVE STREET
HOBART PL
LOWER GROSVENOR PLACE
BUCKINGHAM PALACE ROAD
BRESSENDEN
ALLINGTON STREET
GROSVENOR GARDENS
BEESTON PL
EATON LANE
Victoria
TERMINUS PL
VICTORIA
WILTON ROAD
BROMPTON ROAD
Harrods
SLOANE STREET
HANS CRESCENT
HANS ROAD
HANS PLACE
HANS ST
BASIL STREET
RAPHAEL STREET
LANCELOT PLACE
TREVOR SQ
SEVILLE ST
WILLIAM ST
KINNERTON STREET
LOWNDES SQUARE
WILMINGTON MEWS
HARRIET WALK
PAVILION ROAD
MOTCOMB STREET
LOWNDES STREET
BELGRAVE MEWS WEST
CADOGAN PL
CHESHAM STREET
CHESHAM PLACE
PONT STREET
CADOGAN PLACE
CADOGAN LANE
EATON PLACE
EATON SQUARE
LOWNDES PLACE
LYALL STREET
EATON MEWS NORTH
BELGRAVE PLACE
ECCLESTON MEWS
ECCLESTON SQUARE
ECCLESTON STREET
LOWER BELGRAVE STREET
ELIZABETH STREET
EBURY MEWS
EBURY STREET
ECCLESTON PLACE
CHESTER SQUARE
CHESTER ROW
EATON TERRACE
EATON MEWS WEST
SOUTH EATON PLACE
GERALD ROAD
MINERA MEWS
CLIVEDEN PL
WEST EATON PLACE
BROMPTON PL
BEAUFORT GDNS
BEAUCHAMP PL
WALTON PL
WALTON STREET
SHAFTO MEWS
LENNOX GARDENS
LENNOX GARDENS MEWS
CLABON MEWS
CADOGAN SQUARE
OVINGTON STREET
MILNER STREET
MOORE STREET
HALSEY STREET
CADOGAN GATE
CADOGAN GARDENS
RAWLINGS STREET
ROSEMOOR ST
CADOGAN STREET
DRAYCOTT TERR
DRAYCOTT AVENUE
DRAYCOTT PLACE
CULFORD GDNS
SYMONS STR
SLOANE SQUARE
Sloane Square
Peter Jones
SLOANE AVENUE
BRAY PLACE
COULSON STREET
ANDERSON ST
ELYSTAN PLACE
KING'S ROAD
CHELTENHAM TERRACE
WALPOLE STREET
MARKHAM SQUARE
ROYAL AVENUE
WELLINGTON SQUARE
SMITH STREET
ST LEONARD'S TERRACE
FRANKLIN'S ROW
BURTON'S COURT
ROYAL HOSPITAL ROAD
Chelsea Royal Hospital
RANELAGH GARDENS
National Army Museum
TEDWORTH SQUARE
ORMONDE GATE
TITE STREET
RADNOR WALK
REDESDALE ST
REDBURN STREET
CHRISTCHURCH STREET
CAVERSHAM STREET
PARADISE WALK
SWAN WALK
DILKE STREET
FLOOD STREET
FLOOD WALK
CHELSEA PHYSIC GARDEN
EMBANKMENT GARDENS
CHELSEA EMBANKMENT
Chelsea Bridge
CHELSEA BRIDGE ROAD
LOWER SLOANE STREET
SLOANE COURT EAST
SLOANE GARDENS
HOLBEIN PLACE
CAROLINE TERR
BOURNE STREET
GRAHAM TERRACE
PIMLICO ROAD
BLOOMFIELD TERR
ST BARNABAS STREET
RANELAGH GROVE
BRIDGE ROAD
EBURY BRIDGE ROAD
WELLINGTON BUILDINGS
GATLIFF ROAD
SEMLEY PLACE
CUNDY ST
Victoria Coach Station
BUCKINGHAM PALACE ROAD
Eccleston Bridge
Elizabeth Bridge
Ebury Bridge
BELGRAVE ROAD
BRIDGE PLACE
HUGH STREET
ECCLESTON SQUARE
CAMBRIDGE STREET
ALDERNEY STREET
WARWICK WAY
WINCHESTER STREET
SUTHERLAND STREET
CLARENDON STREET
CUMBERLAND STREET
WESTMORELAND TERRACE
WESTMORELAND PL
TURPENTINE LANE
PEABODY AVENUE
LUPUS STREET
CHURCHILL GARDENS
GROSVENOR
Grosvenor Bridge

6
4
7
D
E
F
1
2
3
4
5
REGENT ST
PICCADILLY
Piccadilly Circus
Theatre Royal Haymarket
JERMYN ST
HAYMARKET
St James's Church
Royal Academy of Arts
National Gallery
WILLIAM IV STREET
St Martin-in-the-Fields
STRAND
Savoy Pier
Waterloo Bridge
Cleopatra's Needle
VICTORIA EMBANKMENT
VICTORIA EMBANKMENT GARDENS
New Zealand House
PALL MALL EAST
TRAFALGAR SQUARE
Nelson's Column
Canadian Embassy
Charing Cross
Embankment
Embankment Pier
National Film Theatre
Festival Pier
COCKSPUR STREET
Admiralty Arch
NORTHUMBERLAND AVENUE
Hungerford Foot Bridge
ST JAMES'S SQUARE
WATERLOO PLACE
CARLTON HOUSE TERRACE
Whitehall Theatre
Institute of Contemporary Arts
Royal Festival Hall
PALL MALL
The Admiralty
WHITEHALL
HORSEGUARDS AVENUE
Queen's Chapel
Marlborough House
Banqueting House
Horse Guards
Ministry of Defence
Thames
JUBILEE GARDENS
Waterloo Millennium Pier
British Airways London Eye
ST JAMES'S PARK
THE MALL
DUCK ISLAND
DOWNING STREET
RICHMOND TERRACE
St James's Park Lake
Foreign & Commonwealth Office
Cenotaph
KING CHARLES STREET
Cabinet War Rooms
The Treasury
PARLIAMENT ST
London Aquarium
County Hall
CHICHELEY ST
YORK ROAD
Westminster Millennium Pier
Westminster
Westminster Bridge
GREAT GEORGE STREET
PARLIAMENT SQUARE
BRIDGE STREET
WESTMINSTER BRIDGE ROAD
BIRDCAGE WALK
Big Ben
OLD QUEEN STREET
ANNE'S GATE
Florence Nightingale Museum
Guards Museum
St Margaret's Church
Houses of Parliament
TOTHILL STREET
BROAD SANCTUARY
St James's Park
PETTY FRANCE
Westminster Abbey
Jewel Tower
St Thomas' Hospital
ALBERT EMBANKMENT
ROYAL ST
Blewcoat School
New Scotland Yard
DEAN'S YARD
BUCKINGHAM GATE
CAXTON STREET
VICTORIA STREET
ABBEY ORCHARD STREET
OLD PYE STREET
GREAT COLLEGE STREET
VICTORIA TOWER GARDENS
LAMBETH PALACE ROAD
ARCHBISHOP'S PARK
WESTMINSTER
MILLBANK
HOWICK PLACE
ARTILLERY ROW
GREAT PETER STREET
MARSHAM STREET
St John's Smith Square
SMITH SQUARE
Lambeth Palace
ROMNEY STREET
Lambeth Bridge
LAMBETH ROAD
HORSEFERRY ROAD
Museum of Garden History
Westminster Hospital
PAGE STREET
OLD PARADISE STREET
WESTMINSTER SCHOOL PLAYING FIELDS
VINCENT SQUARE
LAMBETH HIGH STREET
WHITGIFT STREET
REGENCY STREET
Millbank Millennium Pier
LAMBETH
Tate Britain
VAUXHALL BRIDGE ROAD
ATTERBURY STREET
JOHN ISLIP STREET
TACHBROOK STREET
PONSONBY PLACE
JONATHAN STREET
TINWORTH STREET
Pimlico
BESSBOROUGH STREET
GLASSHOUSE WALK
TYERS TERRACE
Vauxhall Bridge
BRIDGEFOOT
Vauxhall
KENNINGTON LANE
HARLEYFORD ROAD
DURHAM ST
GROSVENOR ROAD
WANDSWORTH ROAD
NINE ELMS LANE
PARRY STREET
SOUTH LAMBETH ROAD
LANGLEY LANE
LAWN LANE

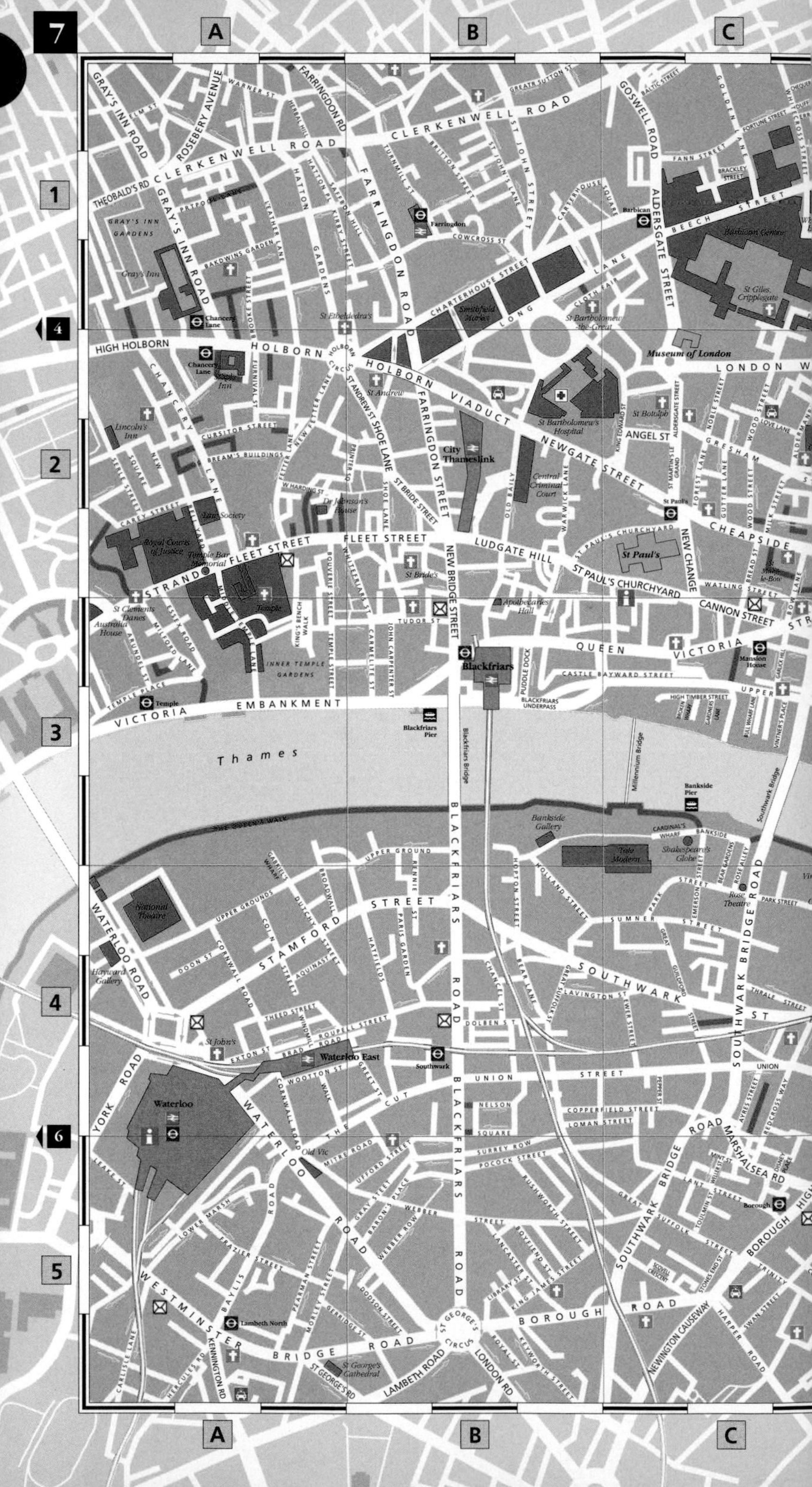
7
A
B
C
1
2
3
4
5
6
Thames
Victoria Embankment
Clerkenwell Road
Holborn
Holborn Viaduct
Fleet Street
Strand
Ludgate Hill
Newgate Street
Cheapside
Cannon Street
Queen Victoria Street
Farringdon Road
Farringdon Street
New Bridge Street
Blackfriars Road
Blackfriars Bridge
Southwark Street
Stamford Street
Waterloo Road
Borough Road
Westminster Bridge Road
Southwark Bridge Road
Aldersgate Street
Goswell Road
Gray's Inn Road
Chancery Lane
Farringdon
Barbican
Barbican Centre
Museum of London
St Paul's
City Thameslink
Blackfriars
Mansion House
Temple
Chancery Lane
Royal Courts of Justice
Temple Bar Memorial
Central Criminal Court
St Bartholomew's Hospital
Smithfield Market
Tate Modern
Shakespeare's Globe
Bankside Pier
Blackfriars Pier
Millennium Bridge
Southwark Bridge
National Theatre
Hayward Gallery
Waterloo
Waterloo East
Southwark
Old Vic
Lambeth North
St George's Cathedral
Borough
St George's Circus

8
D
E
F
1
2
3
4
5
CITY ROAD
BUNHILL FIELDS
BONHILL STREET
WORSHIP STREET
CHRISTOPHER STREET
PRIMROSE STREET
SUN STREET
ELDON STREET
FINSBURY CIRCUS
MOORGATE
LIVERPOOL STREET
Liverpool Street Station
Broadgate Centre
Liverpool Street
LONDON WALL
BISHOPSGATE
NORTON FOLGATE
FOLGATE STREET
Dennis Severs's House
SPITAL SQUARE
Spitalfields Market
BRUSHFIELD STREET
WHITE'S ROW
FASHION STREET
COMMERCIAL STREET
PLAYING FIELDS
Shoreditch
QUAKER STREET
BUXTON STREET
CALVIN STREET
BRICK LANE
WOODSEER STREET
HANBURY STREET
Spitalfields Centre Museum of Immigration
PRINCELET STREET
Jamme Masjid
FOURNIER STREET
Christ Church, Spitalfields
HENEAGE STREET
CHICKSAND STREET
OLD MONTAGUE STREET
MIDDLESEX STREET
WENTWORTH STREET
CUTLERS GARDENS
HOUNDSDITCH
Whitechapel Art Gallery
WHITECHAPEL RD
WHITECHAPEL HIGH STREET
Aldgate East
COMMERCIAL ROAD
BRAHAM STREET
LEMAN STREET
Aldgate
ALDGATE HIGH STREET
ST BOTOLPH STREET
OLD BROAD STREET
THROGMORTON STREET
Stock Exchange
Bank of England
THREADNEEDLE STREET
Royal Exchange
CORNHILL
Bank
LEADENHALL STREET
St Helen's Bishopsgate
St Katherine Cree
ALDGATE
MINORIES
MANSELL STREET
Lloyd's of London
KING WILLIAM STREET
LOMBARD STREET
GRACECHURCH STREET
Leadenhall Market
FENCHURCH STREET
Fenchurch Street
HAYDON STREET
PORTSOKEN STREET
GOODMANS YARD
PRESCOT ST
DOCK STREET
CHAMBER STREET
EASTCHEAP
Monument
St Margaret Pattens
GREAT TOWER STREET
PEPYS STREET
Tower Gateway DLR
Tower Hill
MINORIES HILL
ROYAL MINT STREET
Fishmongers' Hall
KING WILLIAM ST
BYWARD ST
TOWER HILL
LOWER THAMES STREET
St Magnus the Martyr
Billingsgate
All Hallows by the Tower
EAST SMITHFIELD
TOWER BRIDGE APPROACH
St Katharine's Dock
Tower of London
Tower Millennium Pier
Thames
London Bridge
London Bridge City Pier
HMS Belfast
Southwark Cathedral
DUKE ST HILL
London Dungeon
London Bridge
Old St Thomas's Operating Theatre
Greater London Authority Headquarters
St Katharine's Pier
ST KATHARINE'S WAY
Tower Bridge
TOOLEY STREET
ST THOMAS STREET
Guy's Hospital
TOWER BRIDGE ROAD
SHAD THAMES
Design Museum
CRUCIFIX LANE
Fashion & Textile Museum
BERMONDSEY STREET
SNOWSFIELDS
SOUTHWARK
DRUID STREET
JAMAICA ROAD
LONG LANE
Bermondsey Antiques Market
ABBEY STREET
TANNER STREET
WESTON STREET

Southeast England

Introducing Southeast England 146-151
The Downs and Channel Coast 152-177
East Anglia 178-203
Thames Valley 204-225

Southeast England at a Glance

THE OLD SAXON KINGDOMS covered the areas surrounding London, and today, while their accessibility to the capital makes them a magnet for commuters, each region retains a character and history of its own. The attractions include England's oldest universities, royal palaces, castles, stately homes and cathedrals, many of which played critical roles in the nation's early history. The landscape is soft, with the green and rounded hills of the south country levelling out to the flat fertile plains and fens of East Anglia, fringed by broad, sandy beaches.

Blenheim Palace (see pp216–17) *is a Baroque masterpiece. The Mermaid Fountain (1892) is part of the spectacular gardens.*

Oxford University's *buildings* (see pp210–15) *amount to a textbook of English architecture from the Middle Ages to the present. Christ Church College (1525) is the largest in the university.*

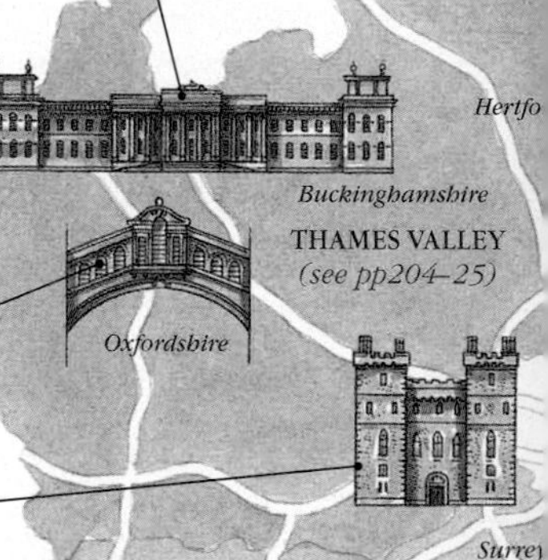

Windsor Castle (see pp224–5) *is Britain's oldest royal residence. The Round Tower was built in the 11th century when the palace guarded the western approaches to London.*

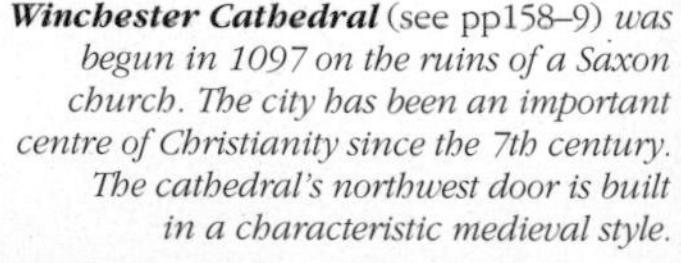

Winchester Cathedral (see pp158–9) *was begun in 1097 on the ruins of a Saxon church. The city has been an important centre of Christianity since the 7th century. The cathedral's northwest door is built in a characteristic medieval style.*

◁ **The white cliffs of Dover, Kent**

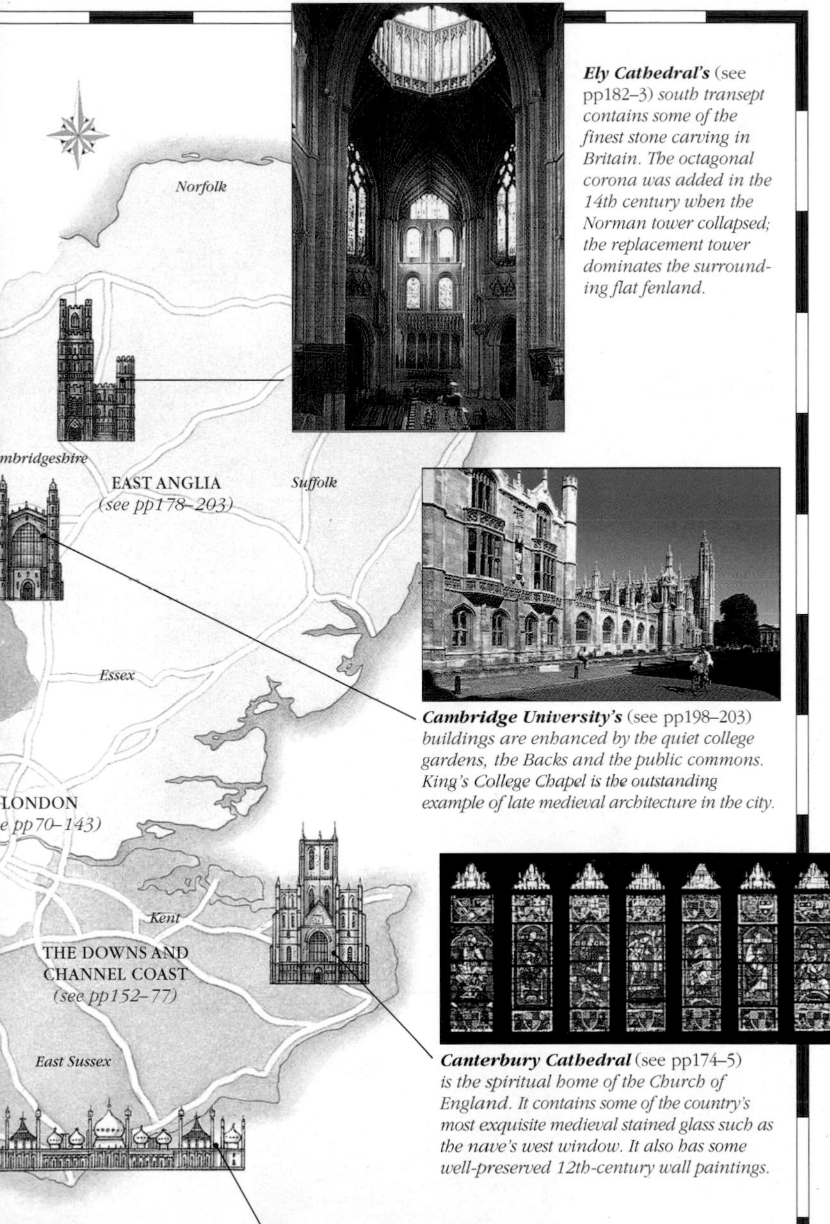

Ely Cathedral's (see pp182–3) *south transept contains some of the finest stone carving in Britain. The octagonal corona was added in the 14th century when the Norman tower collapsed; the replacement tower dominates the surrounding flat fenland.*

Cambridge University's (see pp198–203) *buildings are enhanced by the quiet college gardens, the Backs and the public commons. King's College Chapel is the outstanding example of late medieval architecture in the city.*

Canterbury Cathedral (see pp174–5) *is the spiritual home of the Church of England. It contains some of the country's most exquisite medieval stained glass such as the nave's west window. It also has some well-preserved 12th-century wall paintings.*

Brighton's Royal Pavilion (see pp166–7) *was built for the Prince Regent and is one of the most lavish buildings in the land. Its design by John Nash (see p107) is based on Oriental themes and it has recently been restored to its original splendour.*

0 kilometres 25

0 miles 25

The Garden of England

White wine from the southeast

With its fertile soil, mild climate and regular rainfall, the Kentish countryside has flourished as a fruit-growing region ever since its first orchards were planted by the Romans. There has been a recent boom in wine-making, as the vine-covered hillsides around Lamberhurst show, and several vineyards may be visited. The orchards are dazzling in the blossom season, and in the autumn the branches sag with ripening fruit – a familiar sight which inspired William Cobbett (1762–1835) to describe the area as "the very finest as to fertility and diminutive beauty in the whole world". Near Faversham, the fruit research station of Brogdale is open to the public, offering orchard walks, tastings and informative displays.

Hops and Hopping

Hop-picking, a family affair

Oast houses, topped with distin tive angled cowls, are a commo feature of the Kentish landscape and many have now been turne into houses. They were original

Seasonal Fruit

This timeline shows the major crops in each month of the farming year. The first blossoms may appear when the fields are still dusted with snow. As the petals fall, fruit appears among the leaves. After ripening in the summer sun, the fruit is harvested in the autumn.

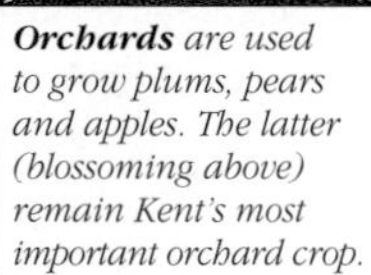

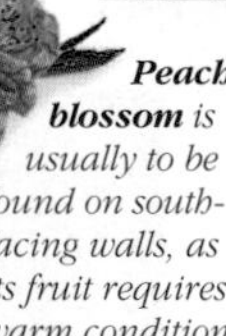

***Peach blossom** is usually to be found on south-facing walls, as its fruit requires warm conditions.*

***Orchards** are used to grow plums, pears and apples. The latter (blossoming above) remain Kent's most important orchard crop.*

***Raspberries** are a luscious soft frui Many growers allo you to pick your o from the fields, an then pay by weig*

MARCH | APRIL | MAY | JUNE | JU

***Sour cherry blossom** is the earliest flower. Its fruit is used for cooking.*

***Pear blossom** has creamy white flowers which appear two or three weeks before apple blossom.*

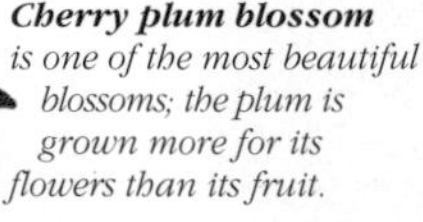

***Cherry plum blossom** is one of the most beautiful blossoms; the plum is grown more for its flowers than its fruit.*

***Srawberries** are Britain's favourite and earliest soft frui New strains allow them to be picked all summer.*

***Gooseberries** are not always sweet enough to eat raw, though all types are superb in pies and other desserts.*

ilt to dry hops, an ingredient brewing beer *(see pp34–5)*. .ny are still used for that, for hough imports have reduced mestic hop-growing, more ın four million tonnes are ɔduced in Britain annually, ɔstly in Kent.

n summer, the fruiting plants ı be seen climbing the rect- gular wire frames in fields by ː roadside. Until the middle of ː 20th century thousands of nilies from London's East End ɔuld move to the Kentish hop lds every autumn for working lidays harvesting the crop and nping in barns. That tradition s faded, because now the ps are picked by machine.

Oast House

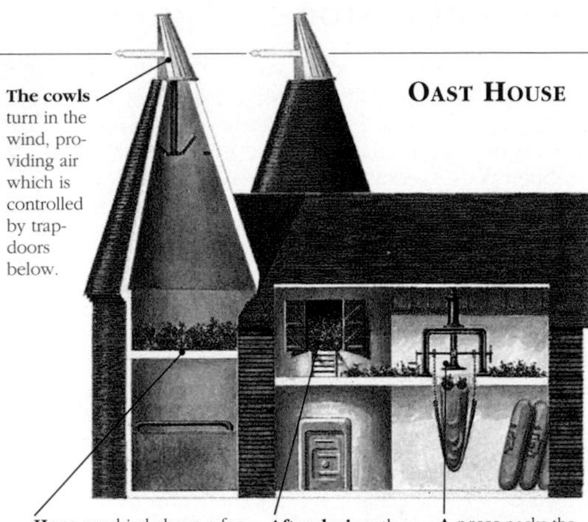

The cowls turn in the wind, providing air which is controlled by trapdoors below.

Hops are dried above a fan which blows hot air from the underlying radiators.

After drying, the hops are cooled and stored.

A press packs the hops into bags, ready for the breweries.

Cherries *are the sweetest of Kent's fruit: two popular varieties are Stella (top) and Duke.*

Plums *are often served stewed, in pies, or dried into prunes. The Victoria plum (left) is the classic English dessert plum and is eaten raw. The Purple plum is also popular.*

Greengages *are green plums. They have a distinctive taste and can be made into jam.*

Bramley Seedling *is one of the best cooking apples, but it is not sweet enough to eat raw.*

Pears*, such as the William (left), should be eaten at the height of ripeness. The Conference keeps better.*

AUGUST | SEPTEMBER | OCTOBER | NOVEMBER

urrants *are nong the most assertively avoured fruit and are sed in desserts and jams.*

Peaches*, grown in China 4,000 years ago, came to* *ɜngland in the 19th century.*

Dessert apples*, such as Cox's Orange Pippin (right), are some of England's best-loved fruits. The newer Discovery is easier to grow.*

The Kentish cob*, a variety of hazelnut, is undergoing a revival, having been eclipsed by European imports. Unlike many nuts, it is best picked fresh from the tree.*

Vineyards *are now a familiar sight in Kent (as well as Sussex and Hampshire). Most of the wine produced, such as Lamberhurst, is white.*

Houses of Historical Figures

VISITING THE HOMES OF ARTISTS, writers, politicians and royalty is a rewarding way of gaining an insight into their private lives. Southeast England, near London, boasts many historic houses that have been preserved as they were when their illustrious occupants were alive. All these houses, from large mansions such as Lord Mountbatten's Broadlands to the more modest dwellings, like Jane Austen's House, contain exhibits relating to the life of the famous people who lived there.

***Florence Nightingale** (1820–1910), the "Lady with the Lamp", was a nurse during the Crimean War* (see p56). *She stayed at Claydon with her sister, Lady Verney.*

***Nancy Astor** (1879–1964) was the first woman to sit in Parliament in 1919. She lived at Cliveden until her death and made it famous for political hospitality.*

Claydon House, Winslow, nr Milton Keynes

***The Duke of Wellington** (1769–1852) was given this house by the nation in 1817, in gratitude for leading the British to victory at Waterloo* (see p55).

THAMES VALLEY
(see pp204–25)

Cliveden House, nr Maidenhead

Stratfield Saye, Basingstoke, nr Windsor

***Jane Austen** (1775–1817) wrote three of her novels, including* Emma, *and revised the others at this house where she lived for eight years until shortly before her death* (see p160).

Jane Austen's House, Chawton, nr Winchester

Broadlands, nr Southampton

Osborne House, Isle of Wight

Lord Mountbatten (1900–79), a British naval commander and statesman, was the last Viceroy of India in 1947. He lived here all his married life and remodelled the original house considerably.

Queen Victoria (1819–1901) and her husband, Prince Albert, built Osborne House *(see p156)* in 1855 as a seaside retreat for their family because they never truly warmed to the Royal Pavilion in Brighton.

Bloomsbury Group

A circle of avant-garde artists, designers and writers, many of them friends as students, began to meet at a house in Bloomsbury, London, in 1904 and soon gained a reputation for their Bohemian lifestyle. When Duncan Grant and Vanessa Bell moved to Charleston in 1916 *(see p168)*, it became a Sussex outpost of the celebrated group. Many of the prominent figures associated with the circle, such as Virginia Woolf, EM Forster, Vita Sackville-West and JM Keynes paid visits here. The Bloomsbury Group was also known for the Omega Workshops, which made innovative ceramics, furniture and textiles.

***Vanessa Bell at Charleston* by Duncan Grant (1885–1978)**

Gainsborough's House, Sudbury, nr Ipswich

***Thomas Gainsborough** (1727–88), one of Britain's greatest painters, was born in this house* (see p194). *He was best known for his portraits, such as this one of* Mr and Mrs Andrews.

EAST ANGLIA
(see pp178–203)

***Charles Darwin** (1809–82), who developed the theory that man and apes have a common ancestor, wrote his most famous book,* On the Origin of Species, *at the house where he lived.*

Down House, Downe, nr Sevenoaks

THE DOWNS AND CHANNEL COAST
(see pp152–77)

Bleak House, Broadstairs, nr Margate

Charles Dickens (1812–70), the prolific and popular Victorian novelist *(see p177)*, had many connections with Kent. He took holidays at Bleak House, later named after his famous novel.

Chartwell, Westerham, nr Sevenoaks

Batemans, Burwash, nr Hastings

Winston Churchill (1874–1965), Britain's inspirational Prime Minister in World War II *(see p177)*, lived here for 40 years until his death. He relaxed by rebuilding parts of the house.

***Rudyard Kipling** (1865–1936), the poet and novelist, was born in India, but lived here for 34 years until his death. His most famous works include* Kim, *the two* Jungle Books *and the* Just So Stories.

Charleston, Lewes

Vanessa Bell (1879–1961), artist and member of the Bloomsbury Group, lived here until her death in 1961. The 18th-century farmhouse reflects her unusual decorative ideas and is filled with murals, paintings and painted furniture.

THE DOWNS AND CHANNEL COAST

HAMPSHIRE · SURREY · EAST SUSSEX · WEST SUSSEX · KENT

WHEN SETTLERS, *invaders and missionaries came from Europe, the southeast coast was their first landfall. The wooded chalk ridges and lower-lying weald beyond them made an ideal base for settlement and proved to be productive farmland.*

The Romans were the first to build major fortifications along the Channel Coast to discourage potential attackers from the European mainland. The remains of many of these can be seen today, and some, like Portchester Castle just outside Portsmouth, were incorporated into more substantial defences in later centuries. There also exists substantial evidence of Roman domestic buildings, such as Fishbourne Palace, in coastal areas and further inland.

The magnificence of cathedrals such as Canterbury and Winchester bear witness to their role as important bases of the medieval church, then nearly as powerful as the state. Many Kent and Sussex ports grew prosperous on trade with the Continent – as did the hundreds of smugglers who operated from them. From Tudor times on, monarchs, noblemen and courtiers acquired estates and built manor houses in the countryside between London and the coast, appreciating the area's moderate climate and proximity to the capital. Many of these survive and are popular attractions for visitors.

Today the southeast corner of England is its most prosperous and populous region. Parts of Surrey and Kent, up to 20 miles (32 km) from the capital, are known as the Stockbroker Belt: the area has many large, luxurious villas belonging to wealthy people prominent in business and the professions, attracted by the same virtues that appealed to the Tudor gentry.

The fertile area of Kent has long been known as the Garden of England, and despite the incursion of bricks and mortar, it is still a leading area for growing fruit *(see pp148–9)*, being in a prime position for the metropolitan market nearby.

Aerial view of the medieval and moated Leeds Castle

◁ **A lush covering of bluebells in the deciduous woodlands of Kent**

Exploring the Downs and Channel Coast

The North and South Downs, separated by the lower-lying Weald are ideal walking country as well as being the site of many stately homes. From Tudor times, wealthy, London-based merchants and courtiers built their country residences in Kent, a day's ride from the capital, and many are open to the public. On the coast are the remains of sturdy castles put up to deter invaders from across the Channel. Today, though, the seashore is largely devoted to pleasure. Some of Britain's earliest beach resorts were developed along this coast, and sea bathing is said to have been invented in Brighton.

Oast houses at Chiddingstone near Royal Tunbridge Wells

View of Brighton's Palace Pier from the promenade

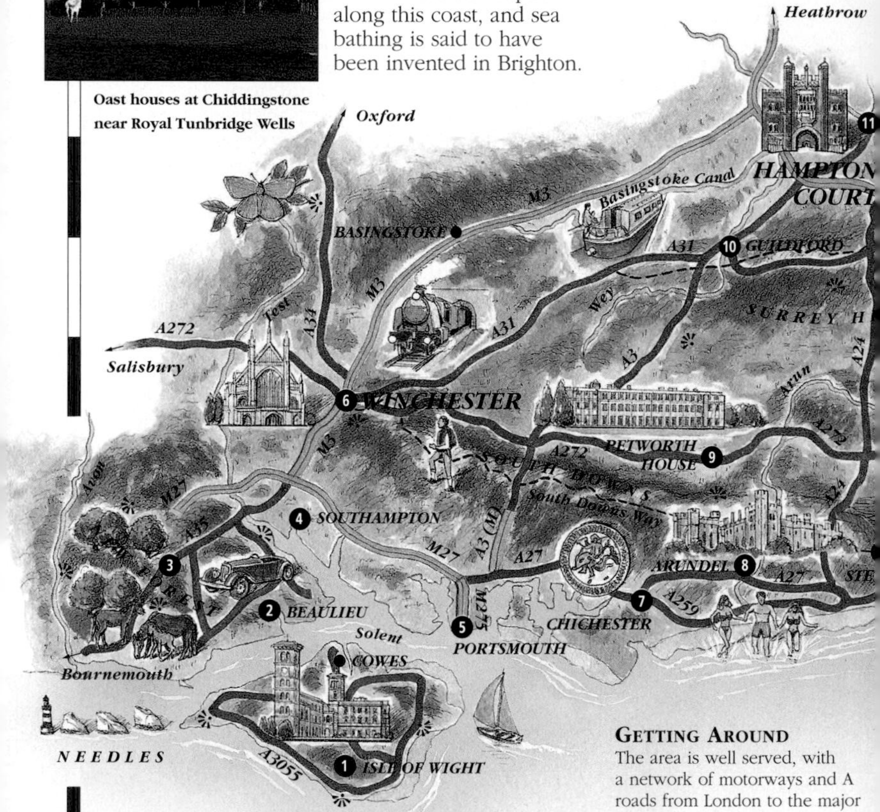

Heathrow
Oxford
11 HAMPTON COURT
Basingstoke Canal
M3
BASINGSTOKE
A31
10 GUILDFORD
Wey
SURREY H
Test
A272
A34
Salisbury
A3
Arun
A24
6 WINCHESTER
A272
PETWORTH HOUSE 9
SOUTH DOWNS
South Downs Way
Avon
M27
M3
A35
4 SOUTHAMPTON
M27
A3 (M)
A27
ARUNDEL 8
A27
3
2 BEAULIEU
M275
7
A259
Solent
5 PORTSMOUTH
CHICHESTER
COWES
Bournemouth
NEEDLES
A3055
1 ISLE OF WIGHT

0 kilometres 20

0 miles 10

Getting Around

The area is well served, with a network of motorways and A roads from London to the major towns. The A259 is a scenic coast road which offers fine views over the English Channel. Bus and rail transport is also good, with a number of coach companies providing regular tours to the major sites. An InterCity train service runs to all the major towns.

See Also

- ***Where to Stay*** pp545–7
- ***Where to Eat*** pp582–4

Sights at a Glance

- Arundel 8
- Beaulieu 2
- Bodiam Castle 18
- *Brighton pp162–7* 13
- *Canterbury pp174–5* 23
- Chichester 7
- Dover 21
- The Downs 16
- Eastbourne 15
- Guildford 10
- *Hampton Court p161* 11
- Hastings 17
- Hever Castle 27
- Isle of Wight 1
- Knole 26
- Leeds Castle 24
- Lewes 14
- Margate 22
- Rochester 25
- New Forest 3
- Petworth House 9
- Portsmouth 5
- Romney Marsh 20
- Royal Tunbridge Wells 28
- *Rye pp172–3* 19
- Southampton 4
- Steyning 12
- *Winchester pp158–9* 6

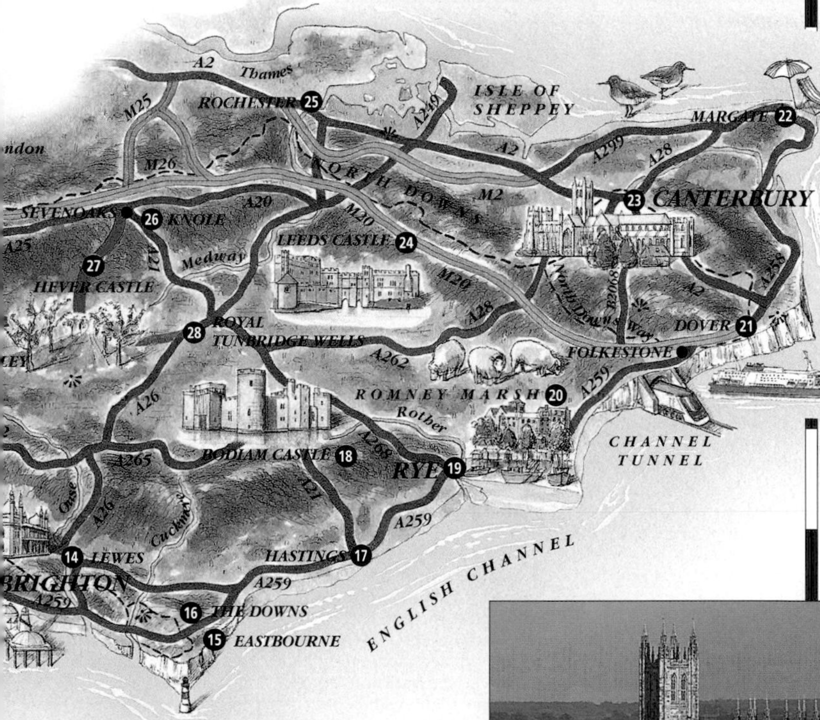

Key

- Motorway
- Major road
- Minor road
- Scenic route
- Scenic path
- River
- Viewpoint

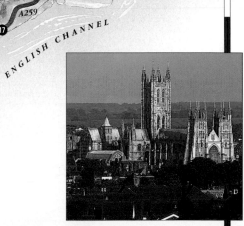

Canterbury Cathedral's spire, dominating the skyline

The Victorian Osborne House, Isle of Wight

Isle of Wight 1

Isle of Wight. 133,000. from Lymington, Southampton, Portsmouth. Westridge Centre, Brading Road, Ryde (01983 813818). www.islandbreaks.co.uk

A visit to **Osborne House**, the favoured seaside retreat of Queen Victoria and Prince Albert *(see p148)*, is alone worth the ferry ride from the mainland. Furnished much as they left it, the house provides a marvellous insight into royal life and is dotted with family mementoes.

The **Swiss Cottage** was built for the royal children to play in. It is now a museum attached to Osborne House. Adjacent to it you can see the bathing machine used by the queen to preserve her modesty while taking her to the edge of the sea *(see p383)*.

The other main sight on the island is **Carisbrooke Castle**, built in the 11th century. A walk on its outer wall and the climb to the top of its keep provides spectacular views. It was here that Charles I *(see pp52–3)* was held prisoner in 1647; an attempt to escape was foiled when he got stuck between the bars of a window.

The island is a base for ocean sailing, especially during Cowes Week *(see p67)*. The scenic highlight is the **Needles** – three towers of rock jutting out of the sea at the island's western end. This is only a short walk from Alum Bay, famous for its multi-coloured cliffs and sand.

Osborne House
(EH) East Cowes. 01983 200022. Apr–Oct: daily; Nov–Mar: open some days for only, phone for details. limited. (also in Swiss Cottage Apr–Oct only)

Carisbrooke Castle
Newport. 01983 522107. daily. 1 Jan, 24–26 Dec. limited.

Beaulieu 2

Brockenhurst, Hampshire. 01590 612345. Brockenhurst then taxi. daily. 25 Dec. by arrangement. www.beaulieu.co.uk

Palace House, once the gatehouse of Beaulieu Abbey, has been the home of Lord Montagu's family since 1538. It now contains the finest collection of vintage cars in the country at the **National Motor Museum**, along with boats used in the James Bond films.

There is also an exhibition of monastic life in the ruined ancient **abbey**, founded in 1204 by King John *(see p48)* for Cistercian monks. The original abbey church now serves as the parish church.

Environs: Just south is the maritime museum at **Buckler's Hard**, telling the story of shipbuilding in the 18th century. The yard employed 4,000 men at its peak but declined when steel began to be used.

Buckler's Hard
Beaulieu. 01590 616203. daily. 25 Dec. limited.

New Forest 3

Hampshire. Brockenhurst. Lymington then bus. main car park, Lyndhurst (023 8028 2269). www.thenewforest.co.uk

This unique expanse of heath and woodland is, at 145 sq miles (375 sq km), the largest area of unenclosed land in southern Britain.

William the Conqueror's "new" forest, despite its name, is one of the few primeval oak woods in England. It was the popular hunting ground of Norman kings, and in 1100 William II was fatally wounded here in a hunting accident.

Today it is enjoyed by up to seven million visitors a year who share it with the New Forest ponies, unique to the area, and over 1,500 fallow deer.

Southampton 4

Hampshire. 220,000. 9 Civic Centre Road (023 8083 3333). www.southampton.gov.uk

For centuries this has been a flourishing port. The *Mayflower* sailed from here to America in 1620 with the

A 1909 Rolls-Royce Silver Ghost at Beaulieu's National Motor Museum

Pilgrim Fathers, as did the *Titanic* on its maiden and ultimately tragic voyage in 1912.

The **Maritime Museum** has exhibits about both these ships, along with displays on the huge romantic liners that sailed from the port in the first half of the 20th century.

There is a walk around the remains of the medieval city wall. At the head of the High Street stands the old city gate, **Bargate**, the most elaborate gate to survive in England. It still has its 13th-century drum towers and is decorated with intricate, 17th-century armorial carvings. **God's House Tower Museum of Archaeology** consists of a 13th-century gatehouse and 15th-century gallery and tower, and includes displays from the Roman to medieval periods.

The luxurious liner the *Titanic*, which sank in 1912

Maritime Museum
Town Quay Rd. 023 8063 5904. *Tue–Sun (closed 1–2pm).* *1 Jan, 25, 26 Dec, public hols.* *limited.*

God's House Tower Museum
Winkle St. 023 8063 5904. *Tue–Sat (closed noon–1pm), 2–5pm Sun.* *foyer & shop only.*

Portsmouth 5

Hampshire. *190,000.* *The Hard (023 9282 6722).* *Thu–Sat.* www.portsmouthand.co.uk

ONCE A VITAL naval port, with all the nightlife that entails, Portsmouth is today a much quieter town but fascinating for those interested in English naval history.

Under the banner of **Flagship Portsmouth Victorygate**, the city's historic dockyard is the hub of Portsmouth's most important sights. Among these is the hull of the ***Mary Rose***, the favourite of Henry VIII *(see p50)*, which capsized on its maiden voyage as it left to fight the French in 1545. It was recovered from the sea bed in 1982 along with thousands of 16th-century objects now on display nearby, giving an absorbing insight into life at sea in Tudor times.

Alongside it is **HMS *Victory***, the English flagship on which Admiral Nelson was killed at Trafalgar *(see p27)* and now restored to its former glory. You can also visit the **Royal Naval Museum** which deals with naval history from the 16th century to the Falklands War, the 19th-century **HMS *Warrior***, and galleries telling the story of Nelson.

Portsmouth's other military memorial is the **D-Day Museum**. This is centred on the *Overlord Embroidery*, a masterpiece of needlework which was commissioned in 1968 from the Royal School of Needlework and took five years to complete. At 83 m (272 ft), its 34 panels are 12 m (41 ft) longer than the *Bayeux Tapestry* in France, and it depicts the World War II Allied landing in Normandy in 1944.

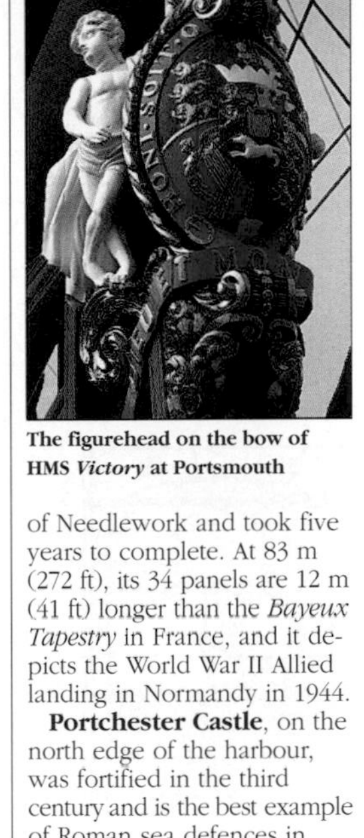

The figurehead on the bow of HMS *Victory* at Portsmouth

Portchester Castle, on the north edge of the harbour, was fortified in the third century and is the best example of Roman sea defences in northern Europe. The Normans later used the Roman walls to enclose a castle – only the keep survives – and a church. Henry V used the castle as a garrison to assemble his army before the Battle of Agincourt *(see p49)*. In the 18th–19th centuries it was a prisoner-of-war camp and you can still see where the prisoners carved their names on the walls.

Among less warlike attractions is the **Charles Dickens Museum** *(see p177)*. The house where the author was born in 1812 is furnished in the style of that time.

Flagship Portsmouth Victorygate
The Hard. 023 9286 1512. *daily.* *25 Dec.*

D-Day Museum
Clarence Esplanade. 023 9282 7261. *daily.* *24–26 Dec.*

Portchester Castle
Castle St, Porchester. 023 9237 8291. *daily.* *24–26 Dec, 1 Jan.* *by arrangement.*

Charles Dickens Museum
393 Old Commercial Rd. 023 9282 7261. *Apr–Oct: daily, 7 Feb (Dickens's birthday).*

A wild pony and her foal roaming freely in the New Forest

Winchester ❻

Hampshire. 36,000.
Guildhall, The Broadway (01962 840500). Wed–Sat.
www.visitwinchester.com

Capital of the ancient kingdom of Wessex, the city of Winchester was also the headquarters of the Anglo-Saxon kings until the Norman Conquest *(see p47)*.

William the Conqueror built one of his first English castles here. The only surviving part of the castle is the **Great Hall**, erected in 1235 to replace the original. It is now home to the legendary Round Table. The story behind the table is a mix of history and myth. King Arthur *(see p273)* had it shaped so no knight could claim precedence. It was said to have been built by the wizard Merlin but was actually made in the 13th century.

The **Westgate Museum** is one of the two surviving 12th-century gatehouses in the city wall. The room (once a prison) above the gate has a 16th-century painted ceiling. It was moved here from Winchester College, England's oldest fee-paying, or "public" school. Winchester has been an ecclesiastical centre for many centuries. **Wolvesey Castle** (built around 1110) was the home of the **cathedral's** bishops after the Conquest. The **Hospital of St Cross** is an almshouse built in 1446.

The 13th-century Round Table, Great Hall, Winchester

Author Izaac Walton *(1593–1683) is depicted in the stained glass Anglers' Window made in 1914.*

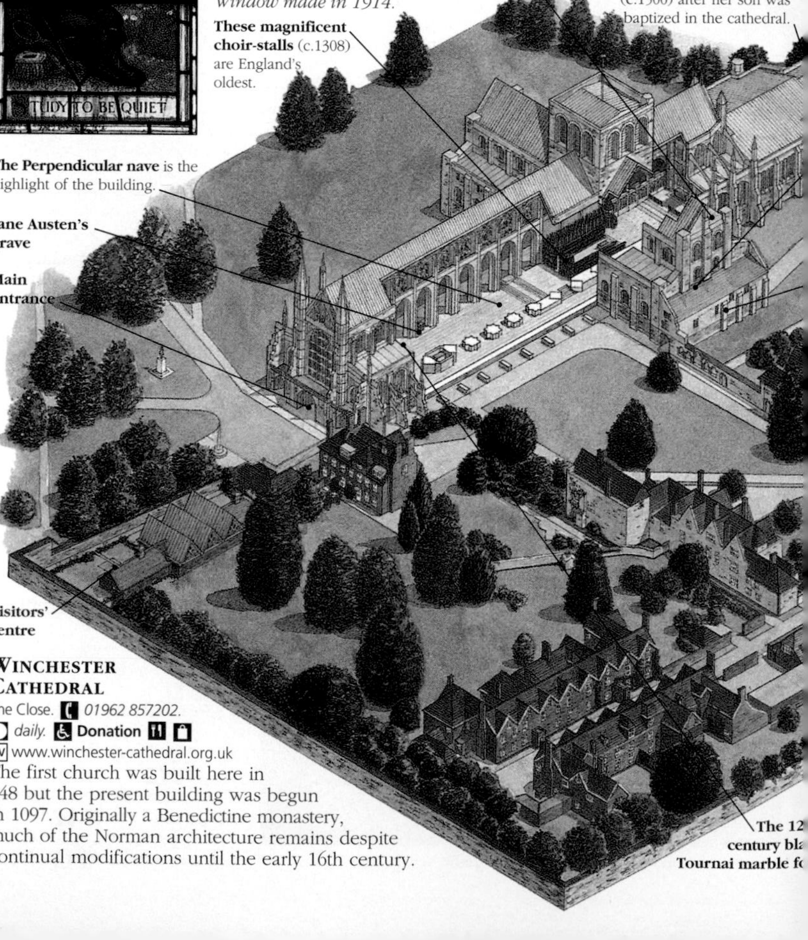

These magnificent choir-stalls (c.1308) are England's oldest.

The Lady Chapel was rebuilt by Elizabeth of York (c.1500) after her son was baptized in the cathedral.

The Perpendicular nave is the highlight of the building.

Jane Austen's grave

Main entrance

Visitors' centre

The 12 century bl Tournai marble f

Winchester Cathedral

The Close. 01962 857202.
daily. Donation
www.winchester-cathedral.org.uk

The first church was built here in 648 but the present building was begun in 1097. Originally a Benedictine monastery, much of the Norman architecture remains despite continual modifications until the early 16th century.

Weary strangers may claim the "Wayfarer's Dole" a horn (cup) of ale and bread, given out since medieval times.

Great Hall & Visitor Centre Castle Ave. *01962 846476.* *daily.* *25, 26 Dec.*

Westgate Museum
High St. *01962 848269.* *Feb, Mar: Tue–Sun; Apr–Oct: Mon–Sun.*

Hospital of St Cross
St Cross Rd. *01962 851375.* *Mon–Sat.* *25 Dec.* www.stcrosshospital.co.uk

***The Library** has over 4,000 books. This "B" from Psalm 1 is found in the Winchester Bible, an exquisite work of 12th-century illumination.*

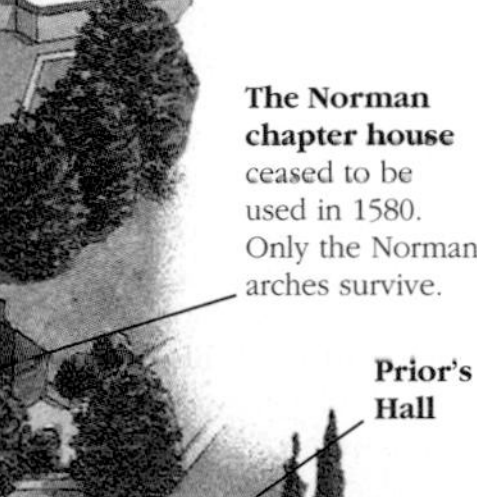

The Norman chapter house ceased to be used in 1580. Only the Norman arches survive.

Prior's Hall

The Close originally contained the domestic buildings for the monks of the Priory of St Swithun – the name before it became Winchester Cathedral. Most of the buildings, such as the refectory and cloisters, were destroyed during the Dissolution of the Monasteries *(see p50)*.

Chichester 7

West Sussex. *26,000.* *29A South St (01243 775888).* *Wed, Sat.* www.visitsussex.org

THIS WONDERFULLY preserved market town, with an elaborate early 16th-century market cross at its centre, is dominated by its **cathedral**, consecrated in 1108. The exterior is a lovely mix of greenish limestone and Caen stone and its graceful spire, said to be the only English cathedral spire visible from the sea, dominates the town. The cathedral still contains much of interest, including a unique detached bell tower dating from 1436.

There are two carved stone panels in the choir, dating from 1140. Modern works include paintings by Graham Sutherland (1903–80), and a stained-glass window by Marc Chagall (1887–1985).

ENVIRONS: Just west at Bosham is the Saxon **Holy Trinity Church,** thought to have been used by King Canute *(see p46)*. Myth has it that this was where Canute failed to stop the incoming tide and so proved to his courtiers that his powers had limits. The church appears in the *Bayeux Tapestry,* held in France, because Harold heard mass here in 1064 before he was shipwrecked off Normandy and then rescued by William the Conqueror *(see p47)*.

Fishbourne Roman Palace *(see p45)*, between Bosham and Chichester, is the largest Roman villa in Britain. It covers 3 ha (7 acres) and was discovered in 1960 by a workman digging for drains. Constructed

Chagall's stained glass window (1978), Chichester Cathedral

from AD 75, it was destroyed by fire in 285. The north wing has some of the finest mosaics in Britain, including one of Cupid.

To the north is the 18th-century **Goodwood House**. Its magnificent art collection features works by Canaletto (1697–1768) and Stubbs (1724–1806). This impressive house, home to the Earl of March, has a racecourse on the Downs.

Chichester Cathedral
West St. *01243 782595.* *daily.* *during services.*

Fishbourne Roman Palace
Fishbourne. *01243 785859.* *Feb–mid-Dec: daily; mid-Dec–Jan (café closed): Sat, Sun.* www.sussexpast.co.uk

Goodwood House
Goodwood. *01243 755048.* *01243 755040.* *Apr–Sep: Sun–Mon (pm); Aug: Sun–Thu (pm).* *special events.*

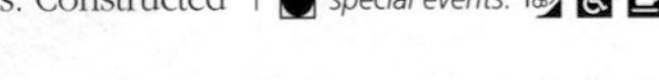

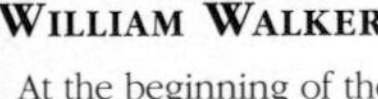

WILLIAM WALKER

At the beginning of the 20th century, the cathedral's east end seemed certain to collapse unless its foundations were underpinned. But because the water table lies only just below the surface, the work had to be done under water. From 1906 to 1911, Walker, a deep-sea diver, worked six hours a day laying sacks of cement beneath the unsteady walls, until the building was safe.

William Walker in his diving suit

The dominating position of Arundel Castle, West Sussex

Arundel Castle ❽

Arundel, West Sussex. *01903 883136.* *Arundel.* *Apr–Oct: Sun–Fri.* *Good Fri.* *by arrangement.*
www.arundelcastle.org

DOMINATING the small riverside town below, this vast, grey hill-top castle, surrounded by castellated walls, was first built by the Normans.

During the 16th century it was acquired by the powerful Dukes of Norfolk, the country's senior Roman Catholic family, whose descendants still live here. They rebuilt it after the original was virtually destroyed by Parliamentarians in 1643 *(see p52)*, and restored it again in the 19th century.

In the castle grounds is the parish church of **St Nicholas**. The small Catholic Fitzalan chapel (c.1380) was built into its east end by the castle's first owners, the Fitzalans, and can only be entered from the grounds.

Petworth House ❾

(NT) Petworth, West Sussex. *01798 342207.* *Pulborough then bus.* **House** *Mar–Nov: Sat–Wed.* **Park** *daily.* *limited.*
www.nationaltrust.org.uk/petworth

THIS LATE 17th-century house was immortalized in a series of famous views by the painter J M W Turner *(see p93)*. Some of his best paintings are on display here and are part of Petworth's outstanding art collection which also includes works by Titian (1488–1576), Van Dyck (1599–1641) and Gainsborough *(see p151)*. Also extremely well represented is ancient Roman and Greek sculpture, such as the 4th-century BC *Leconfield Aphrodite,* widely thought to be by Praxiteles.

The Carved Room is decorated with intricately carved wood panels of birds, flowers and musical instruments, by Grinling Gibbons (1648–1721).

The large deer park includes some of the earliest work of Capability Brown *(see p22)*.

The Restoration clock on the Tudor Guildhall, Guildford

Guildford ❿

Surrey. *63,000.* *14 Tunsgate (01483 444333).* *Fri, Sat.*
www.guildford.gov.uk

THE COUNTY TOWN of Surrey, settled since Saxon times, incorporates the remains of a small Norman **castle**. The attractive High Street is lined with Tudor buildings, such as the impressive **Guildhall**. But it is the huge modern red-brick cathedral, completed in 1954, that dominates the town's skyline.

ENVIRONS: Guildford stands on the end of the North Downs, a range of chalk hills which are popular for walking *(see p33)*. The area also has two famous beauty spots: **Leith Hill** – the highest point in southeast England – and **Box Hill**. The view from the latter is well worth the short, gentle climb from West Humble.

Just to the south of the town is the perfect red brickwork of **Clandon Park**. This 18th-century house has a sumptuous interior, especially the Marble Hall – one of the grandest English interiors of the period. It has an intricate Baroque ceiling, and the hall's side lamps are supported by black ivory forearms jutting from the wall, which represent the Park's West Indian servants.

Southwest is Chawton, where **Jane Austen's House** *(see p150)* is located. This small red-brick house is where she wrote most of her gentle, witty comedies of middle-class manners in Georgian England, such as *Pride and Prejudice.*

Clandon Park
(NT) West Clandon, Surrey. *01483 222482.* *Apr–Oct: Tue–Thu, Sun; public hols.* *limited.*

Jane Austen's House
Alton, Hants. *01420 83262.*
Jan–Feb: Sat, Sun; Mar–Dec: daily.
25, 26 Dec. *limited.*

Hampton Court ⓫

East Molesey, Surrey. *0870-752 7777.* *Hampton Court.* *daily.* *24–26 Dec.* www.hampton-court-palace.org.uk

The powerful chief minister and Archbishop of York to Henry VIII *(see pp50–51)*, Cardinal Wolsey, leased a small manor house in 1514 and transformed it into a magnificent country residence. In 1528, to retain royal favour, Wolsey gave it to the king. After the royal takeover, Hampton Court was extended twice, first by Henry himself and in the 1690s by William and Mary, who used Christopher Wren *(see p116)* as the architect. From the outside the palace is a harmonious blend of Tudor and English Baroque; inside there is a striking contrast between Wren's Classical royal rooms, which include the King's Apartments, and Tudor architecture, such as the Great Hall. Many of the state apartments are decorated with paintings and furnishings from the Royal Collection.

Ceiling decoration, Hampton Court

The Baroque gardens, with their radiating avenues of majestic limes, collections of rare plants and formal plant beds, have been painstakingly restored.

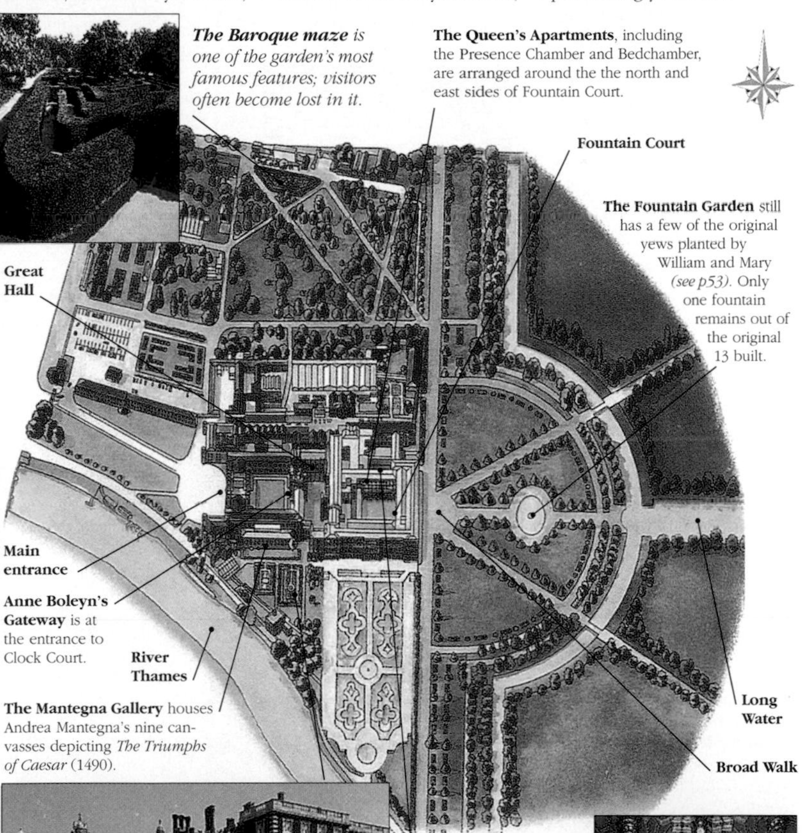
The Baroque maze *is one of the garden's most famous features; visitors often become lost in it.*
The Queen's Apartments, including the Presence Chamber and Bedchamber, are arranged around the the north and east sides of Fountain Court.
Fountain Court
The Fountain Garden still has a few of the original yews planted by William and Mary *(see p53)*. Only one fountain remains out of the original 13 built.
Great Hall
Main entrance
Anne Boleyn's Gateway is at the entrance to Clock Court.
River Thames
The Mantegna Gallery houses Andrea Mantegna's nine canvasses depicting *The Triumphs of Caesar* (1490).
Long Water
Broad Walk

The Tudor Chapel Royal *was completed by Henry VIII. But the superb woodwork, including the massive reredos by Grinling Gibbons, all date from a major refurbishment by Queen Anne (c.1711).*

The Pond Garden*, a sunken water garden, was part of Henry VIII's elaborate designs. The small pond in the middle contains a single-jet fountain.*

Steyning ⓬

West Sussex. 5,000 9 The Causeway, Horsham (01403 211661).

THIS LOVELY little town in the lee of the Downs is packed with timber-framed houses from the Tudor period and earlier, with some built of flint and others in sandstone.

In Saxon times, Steyning was an important port and ship-building centre on the River Adur: King Ethelwulf, father of King Alfred *(see p47)*, was buried here in 858; his body was later moved to Winchester. The *Domesday Book (see p48)* records that Steyning had 123 houses, making it one of the largest towns in the south. The 12th-century church is spacious and splendid, evidence of the area's ancient prosperity: the tower, of chequered stone and flint, was added around 1600.

In the 14th century the river silted up and changed course away from the town, putting an end to its days as a port. Later it became an important coaching stop on the south coast road: the **Chequer Inn** recalls this prosperous period, with its unusual 18th-century flint and stone façade.

ENVIRONS: The remains of a **Norman castle** can be visited at Bramber, east of Steyning. This small, pretty village also contains the timber-framed **St Mary's House** (1470). It has fine panelled rooms, including the Elizabethan Painted Room, and one of the oldest trees in the country, a *Ginkgo biloba*.

Chanctonbury Ring and **Cissbury Ring**, on the hills west of Steyning, were Iron Age forts and the latter has the remains of a Neolithic flint mine. Worthing is the resort where Oscar Wilde (1854–1900) wrote *The Importance of Being Earnest*.

St Mary's House
Bramber. 01903 816205. Easter–Sep: Sun, Thu (pm), public hols.

Street-by-Street: Brighton ⓭

A stick of Brighton rock

AS THE NEAREST south coast resort to London, Brighton is perennially popular, but has always been more refined than its boisterous rivals further east, such as Margate *(see p171)* and Southend. The spirit of the Prince Regent *(see p167)* lives on, not only in the magnificence of his Royal Pavilion, but in the town's reputation as a venue for adulterous weekends in discreet hotels. Brighton has always attracted actors and artists – Laurence Olivier made his final home here.

KING'S ROAD

BLACK LION

GRAND JUNCTION ROAD

Old Ship Hotel
Built in 1559, it was later bought by Nicholas Tettersells, with the money given to him by Charles II as a reward for taking him to France during the Civil War (see p52).

★ Palace Pier
Built in 1899, this typical late-Victorian pier now caters for today's visitors with amusement arcades.

KEY

– – – Suggested route

STAR SIGHTS

★ Palace Pier

★ Royal Pavilion

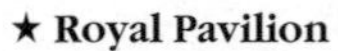

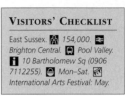

★ Royal Pavilion
The Prince Regent's fantastic Oriental palace helped turn Brighton into a fashionable resort, and is today its principal attraction.

Visitors' Checklist

East Sussex. 154,000. *Brighton Central.* *Pool Valley.* *10 Bartholomew Sq (0906 7112255).* *Mon–Sat.* *International Arts Festival: May.*

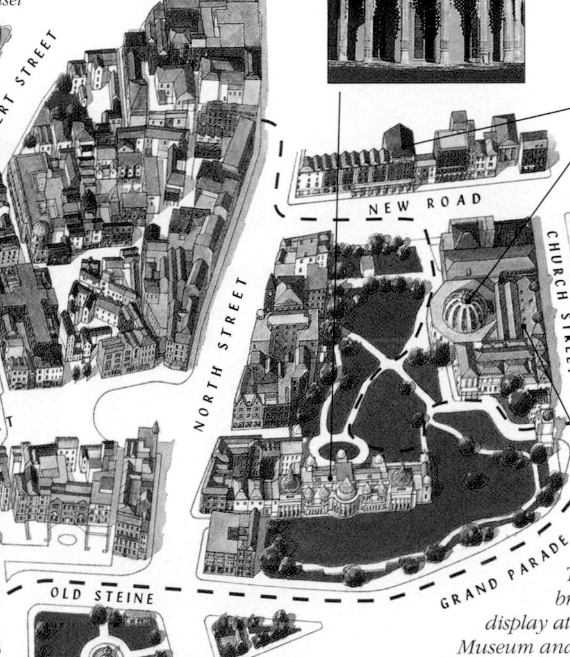

Many new plays are first staged in the charming Theatre Royal, established in 1807, before they move to the West End of London.

The Dome, an Indian-style building opposite the Royal Pavilion and once George IV's stables, is now a venue for arts and exhibitions.

Art Deco
This 1920s Art Deco bronze lamp is on display at the Brighton Museum and Art Gallery.

Sea Life Centre
Built in 1872 as a menagerie, it became an aquarium in 1929. Don't miss the sharks and other British marine life.

The Lanes
Today an engrossing maze of antique shops, the Lanes were the original streets of the village of Brighthelmstone.

Brighton: Royal Pavilion

As sea bathing became fashionable in the mid-18th century, Brighton was transformed into England's first seaside resort. Its gaiety soon appealed to the rakish Prince of Wales, who became George IV in 1820. When, in 1785, he secretly married Mrs Fitzherbert, it was here that they conducted their liaison. He moved to a farmhouse near the shore and had it enlarged by Henry Holland *(see p24)*. As his parties grew more lavish, George needed a suitably extravagant setting for them, and in 1815 he employed John Nash *(see p107)* to transform the house into a lavish Oriental palace. Completed in 1822, the exterior has remained largely unaltered. Queen Victoria sold the Pavilion to the town of Brighton in 1850.

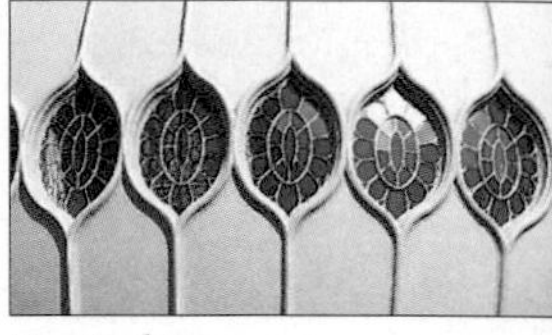

Central Dome
Nash adopted what he called the Hindu Style, as in this delicate tracery on one of the imposing turban domes.

★ Banqueting Room
Fiery dragons feature in many of the interior schemes. This colourful one dominates the centre of the Banqueting Room's extraordinary ceiling, and has a huge crystal chandelier suspended from it.

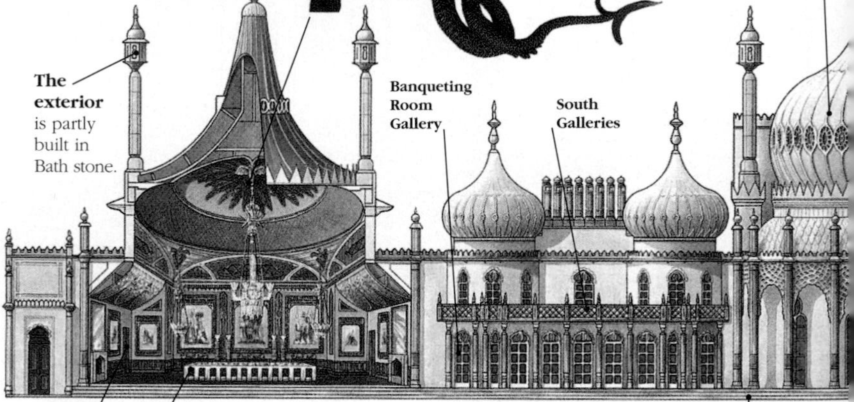

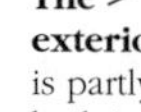

The exterior is partly built in Bath stone.

Banqueting Room Gallery

South Galleries

The banqueting table, which seats 24 people, is laid as for a splendid feast.

The eastern façade of the Pavilion

Standard Lamps
More dragons, along with dolphins and lotus flowers, figure on the Banqueting Room's eight original standard lamps, made of porcelain, ormolu and gilded wood.

Star Sights

★ Banqueting Room

★ Great Kitchen

★ Great Kitchen
The Prince's epic banquets required a kitchen of huge proportions. The vast ranges and long shelves of gleaming copper pans were used by famous chefs of the day.

◁ **Front façade of George IV's extravagant Royal Pavilion, Brighton**

Saloon
The gilded wall decorations were designed on Indian themes, but the Chinese wallpaper harks back to an earlier decorative scheme. The long couch mimics an Egyptian river boat.

VISITORS' CHECKLIST

Old Steine, Brighton. *01273 290900.* *Apr–Sep: 10am–5:15pm; Oct–Mar: 9:30am–5:45pm (last adm: 45 mins before closing); daily.* *25, 26 Dec.* *limited.* www.royalpavilion.org.uk

Long Gallery
Mandarin figures, which can nod their heads, line the pink and blue walls of this 49 m (162 ft) gallery.

Queen Victoria's Bedroom
This reproduction four-poster is on display in the upper floor apartments that were used by Queen Victoria (see pp56–7).

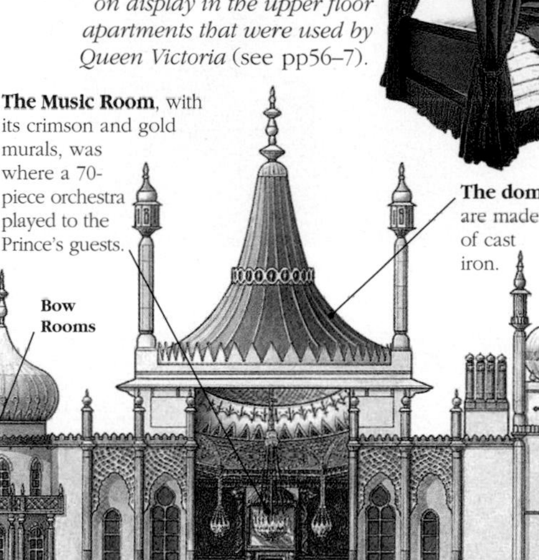

The Music Room, with its crimson and gold murals, was where a 70-piece orchestra played to the Prince's guests.

The domes are made of cast iron.

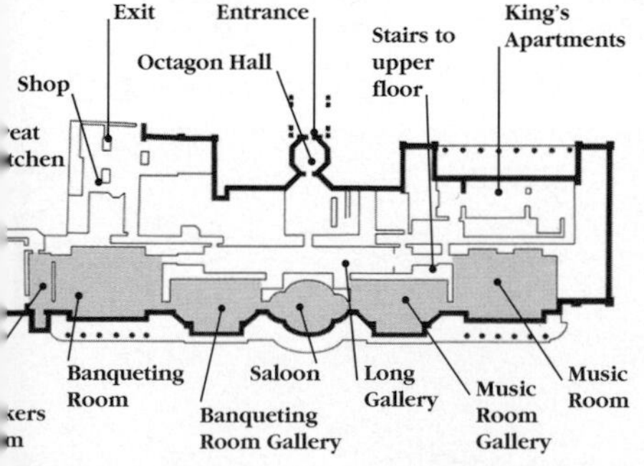

PLAN OF THE ROYAL PAVILION

Both Holland and Nash made additions and changes to the original farmhouse. The upper floor contains bedrooms, such as the Bow Rooms, which George's brothers used. The shaded areas represent the artwork above.

PRINCE OF WALES AND MRS FITZHERBERT

The Prince of Wales was only 23 years old when he fell in love with Maria Fitzherbert, a 29-year-old Catholic widow, and secretly married her. They lived in the farmhouse together and were the toast of Brighton society until George's official marriage took place to Caroline of Brunswick in 1795. Mrs Fitzherbert moved into a small house nearby.

Upstairs interior of Anne of Cleves House, Lewes

Lewes ⓮

East Sussex. 16,000. 187 High St (01273 483448). www.visit-lewes.co.uk

The ancient county town of Sussex was a vital strategic site for the Saxons, because of its high vantage point looking out over the coastline. William the Conqueror built a wooden castle here in 1067 but this was soon replaced by a large stone structure whose remains can be visited today.

In 1264 it was the site of a critical battle in which Simon de Montfort and his barons defeated Henry III, enabling them to establish the first English Parliament.

The Tudor **Anne of Cleves House** is a museum of local history, although Anne of Cleves, Henry VIII's fourth wife, never actually lived here.

On Guy Fawkes Night *(see p64)* lighted tar barrels are rolled to the river and effigies of the pope are burned instead of the customary Guy Fawkes. This commemorates the town's 17 Protestant martyrs burnt at the stake by Mary I *(see p51)*.

Environs: Nearby are the 16th-century **Glynde Place**, a fine courtyard house, and the charming **Charleston**, home to the Bloomsbury Group *(see p151)*.

Anne of Cleves House
Lewes. 01273 474610. *Mar–Oct: daily; Nov–Feb: Tue–Sat.*

Glynde Place
Lewes. 01273 858224. *call for details.* www.glyndeplace.com

Charleston
Lewes. 01323 811265. *Apr–Oct: Wed–Sun, Bank Hol Mon.* www.charleston.org.uk

Eastbourne ⓯

East Sussex. *93,000.* *Cornfield Rd (01323 411400).* *Tue, Sat.* www.eastbourne.org

This Victorian seaside resort is a popular place for retirement, as well as a first-rate centre for touring the Downs. The South Downs Way *(see p33)* begins at **Beachy Head**, the spectacular 163 m (536 ft) chalk cliff just on the outskirts of the town. From here it is a bracing walk to the cliff top at Birling Gap, with views to the **Seven Sisters**, the chalk hills that end abruptly as they meet the sea.

Environs: To the west of Eastbourne is **Seven Sisters Country Park**, a 285 ha (700 acre) area of chalk cliffs and Downland marsh. The **Park Visitor's Centre** contains information on the local area, history and geology.

Just north is the pretty village of **Alfriston**, with an ancient market cross and a 15th-century inn, **The Star**, in its quaint main street. Near the church is the 14th-century **Clergy House** that, in 1896, became the first National Trust property *(see p25)*. To the east is the huge prehistoric chalk carving, the **Long Man of Wilmington** *(see p209)*.

Park Visitor's Centre
Exceat, Seaford. *01323 870280.* *Apr–Oct: daily; Nov–Mar: Sat, Sun.* *25 Dec.*

Clergy House
(NT) Alfriston. *01323 870001.* *Mar: Sat, Sun; Apr–Oct: Sat–Mon, Wed, Thu; Nov, Dec: Wed–Sun.*

The lighthouse (1902) at the foot of Beachy Head, Eastbourne

The meandering River Cuckmere flowing through the South Downs to the beach at Cuckmere Haven

The Downs ⓰

East Sussex. Eastbourne.
Cornfield Rd, Eastbourne (01323 411400).

THE NORTH and South Downs are parallel chalk ridges that run from east to west all the way across Kent, Sussex and Surrey, separated by the lower-lying and fertile Kent and Sussex Weald.

The smooth Downland hills are covered with springy turf, kept short by grazing sheep, making an ideal surface for walkers. The hill above the precipitous **Devil's Dyke**, just north of Brighton, offers spectacular views for miles across the Downs. The legend is that the Devil cut the gorge to let in the sea and flood the countryside, but was foiled by divine intervention. The River Cuckmere runs through one of the most picturesque parts of the South Downs.

Located at the highest point of the Downs is **Uppark House**. This neat square building has been meticulously restored to its mid-18th-century appearance after a fire in 1989.

Uppark House

(NT) Petersfield, West Sussex.
01730 825857. Apr–Oct: Sun–Thu (pm).

Hastings ⓱

East Sussex. 83,000.
Queens Square , Priory Meadow (01424 781111).
www.hastings.gov.uk

THIS FASCINATING seaside town was one of the first Cinque Ports *(see p170)* and is still a thriving fishing port. The town is characterized by the unique tall wooden "net shops" on the beach, where for hundreds of years fishermen have stored their nets. In the 19th century, the area to the west of the Old Town was built up as a seaside resort, which left the narrow, characterful streets of the old fishermen's quarter intact. There are two cliff railways and smugglers' caves displaying where contraband used to be stored *(see p268)*.

The wooden net shops, on Hastings' shingle beach

ENVIRONS: Seven miles (11 km) from Hastings is Battle. The centre square of this small town is dominated by the gatehouse of **Battle Abbey**. William the Conqueror built this on the site of his great victory, reputedly placing the high altar where Harold fell, But the abbey was destroyed in the Dissolution *(see p50)*. There is an evocative walk around the actual battlefield.

Battle Abbey

High St, Battle. 01424 773792.
Easter–Sep: 10am–6pm; Oct: 10am–5pm; Nov–Easter: 10am–4pm daily. 1 Jan, 24–26 Dec.

BATTLE OF HASTINGS

In 1066, William the Conqueror's *(see p47)* invading army from Normandy landed on the south coast, aiming to take Winchester and London. Hearing that King Harold and his army were camped just inland from Hastings, William confronted them. He won the battle after Harold was mortally wounded by an arrow in his eye. This last successful invasion of England is depicted on the *Bayeux Tapestry* in Normandy, France.

King Harold's death, *Bayeux Tapestry*

The fairy-tale 14th-century Bodiam Castle surrounded by its moat

Bodiam Castle ⓲

(NT) Nr Robertsbridge, East Sussex. 📞 *01580 830436.* 🚆 *Robertsbridge then taxi.* ◯ *mid-Feb–Oct: daily; Nov–mid-Feb: Sat–Sun.* ● *24–26 Dec.* 🅿 ♿ *limited.* ☕ 🛍

Surrounded by its wide, glistening moat, this late 14th-century castle is one of the most romantic in England.

It was previously thought to have been built as a defence against French invasion, but is now believed to have been intended as a home for a Sussex knight. The castle saw action during the Civil War *(see p52)*, when it was damaged in an assault by Parliamentary soldiers. They removed the roof to reduce its use as a base for Charles I's troops. It has been uninhabited since, but its grey stone has proved indestructible. With the exception of the roof, it was restored in 1919 by Lord Curzon who gave it to the nation.

Environs: To the east is **Great Dixter**, a 15th-century manor house restored by Sir Edwin Lutyens in 1910. Christopher Lloyd created a magnificent garden with an Edwardian blend of terraces and borders.

Great Dixter
Northiam, Rye. 📞 *01797 252878.* ◯ *Apr–Oct: 2–5:30pm Tue–Sun & public hols.* 🅿 🛍
W www.greatdixter.co.uk

Rye ⓳

See pp170–71.

Romney Marsh ⓴

Kent. 🚆 *Ashford.* 🚌 *Ashford, Hythe.* ℹ *Magpies Church Approach, New Romney (01797 364044).*

Until Roman times Romney Marsh and its southern neighbour Walland Marsh were entirely covered by the sea at high tide. The Romans drained the Romney section, and Walland Marsh was gradually reclaimed during the Middle Ages. Together they formed a large area of fertile land, particularly suitable for the bulky Romney Marsh sheep bred for the quality and quantity of their wool.

Dungeness, a desolate and lonely spot at the southeastern tip of the area, is dominated by a lighthouse and two nuclear power stations that

Coastal Defence and the Cinque Ports

Before the Norman Conquest *(see pp46–7)*, national government was weak and, with threats from Europe, it was important for Saxon kings to keep on good terms with the Channel ports. So, in return for keeping the royal fleet supplied with ships and men, five ports – Hastings, Romney, Hythe, Sandwich and Dover – were granted the right to levy taxes; others were added later. "Cinque" came from the old French word for five. The privileges were revoked during the 17th century. In 1803, in response to the growing threat from France, 74 fixed defences were built along the coast. Only 24 of these Martello towers still exist.

The cliff-top position of Dover Castle

A Martello tower, built as part of the Channel's defences

break up the skyline. It is also the southern terminus of the popular **Romney, Hythe and Dymchurch Light Railway** which was opened in 1927. During the summer this takes passengers 14 miles (23 km) up the coast to Hythe on trains a third the conventional size.

The northern edge of the marsh is crossed by the Royal Military Canal, built to serve both as a defence and supply line in 1804, when it was feared Napoleon was planning an invasion *(see p55)*.

Dover 21

Kent. 30,000. Old Town Jail, Biggin St (01304 205108). Sat. www.dover.gov.uk

ITS PROXIMITY to the European mainland makes Dover, with its neighbour Folkestone (now the terminal for the Channel Tunnel, *see p632*), the leading port for cross-Channel travel. Its famous white cliffs exert a strong pull on returning travellers.

Dover's strategic position and large natural harbour mean the town has always had an important role to play in the nation's defences.

Built on the original site of an ancient Saxon fortification, **Dover Castle**, superbly positioned on top of the high cliffs, has helped defend the town from 1198, when Henry II first built the keep, right up to World War II, when it was used as the command post for the Dunkirk evacuation. Exhibits in the castle and in the labyrinth of tunnels beneath made by prisoners in the Napoleonic Wars *(see p55)* cover all these periods.

ENVIRONS: One of the most significant sites in England's early history is the ruin of **Richborough Roman Fort**. Now a large grassy site two miles (3 km) inland, this was where, in AD 43, Claudius's Roman invaders *(see p44)* made their first landing. For hundreds of years afterwards, Rutupiae, as it was known, was one of the most important ports of entry and military bases in the country.

Dover Castle
Castle Hill. 01304 211067. *Mar: Wed–Sun; Apr–Oct: daily; Nov–Feb: Sat, Sun. 1 Jan, 24–26 Dec.*

Richborough Roman Fort
Richborough. *01304 612013. Oct–Mar: Sat, Sun; Apr–Nov: daily.*

Margate 22

Kent. *40,000.* *17 Albert St (01843 583334).* www.tourism.thanet.gov.uk

TRADITIONALLY the most boisterous of the three seaside resorts on the Isle of Thanet (the other two are Ramsgate and Broadstairs), Margate has long been a popular destination for Londoners, travelling in Victorian times by steam boat and later by train. The town has theme parks and fairground rides.

ENVIRONS: Just south is a 19th-century gentleman's residence, **Quex House,** which has two unusual towers in its grounds. The adjoining museum has a fine collection of African and Oriental art, as well as unique dioramas of tropical wildlife.

Visitors relaxing on Margate's popular sandy beach

To the west is a Saxon church, built within the remains of the bleak Roman coastal fort of **Reculver**. Dramatic twin towers, known as the Two Sisters, were added to the church in the 12th century – these were luckily saved from destruction in 1809 because they were a useful navigational aid for shipping. The church now stands at the centre of a very pleasant, if rather windy, 37 ha (91 acre) camp site.

Quex House
Birchington. *01843 842168. Apr–Oct: Tue–Thu, Sun & public hols (Museum only: Nov, Mar: Sun).* *for groups.*

Reculver Fort
Reculver. *01227 361911 (Herne Bay Tourist Information). daily.*

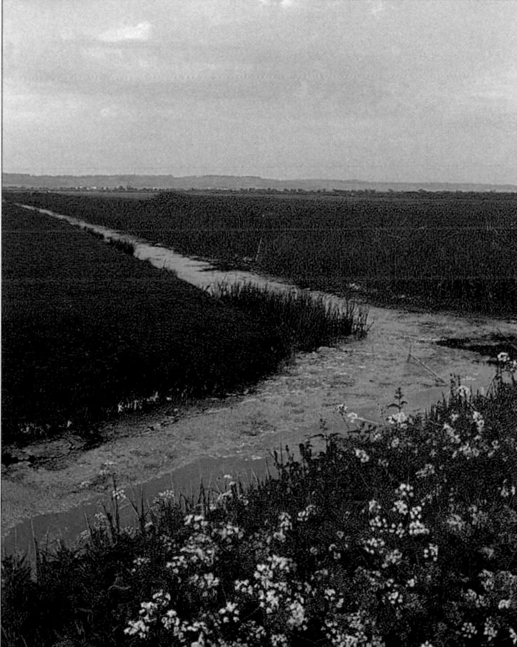

A drainage dyke running through the fertile plains of Romney Marsh

Street-by-Street: Rye 19

The Mermaid Inn sign

THIS ANCIENT and delightful fortified town was added to the original Cinque ports *(see p170)* in the 11th century. A huge storm in 1287 diverted the River Rother so that it met the sea at Rye, and for more than 300 years it was one of the most important channel ports. However, in the 16th century the harbour began to silt up and the town is now 2 miles (3 km) inland. Rye was frequently attacked by the French, culminating in 1377 when it was burnt to the ground.

★ Mermaid Street
This delightful cobbled street, its huddled houses jutting out at unlikely angles, has hardly altered since it was rebuilt in the 14th century.

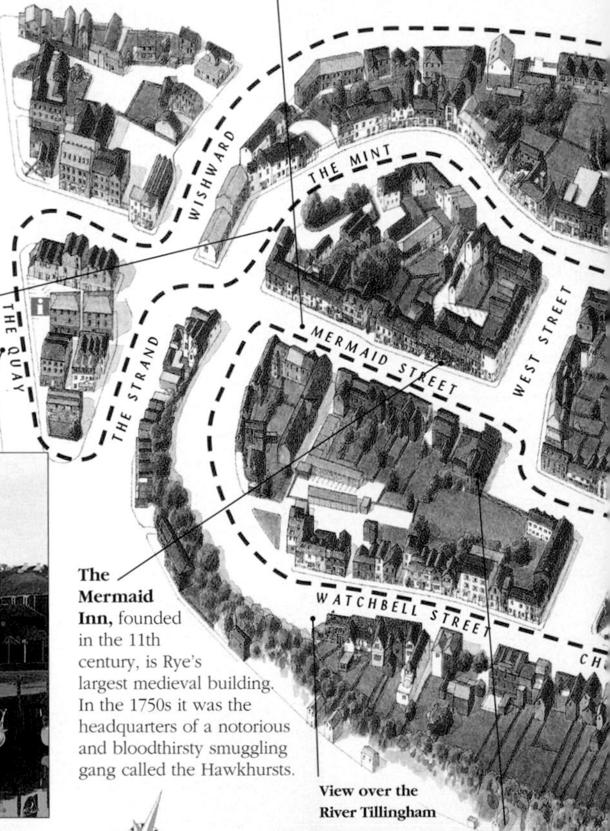

TILLINGHAM
WISHWARD
THE MINT
THE QUAY
THE STRAND
MERMAID STREET
WEST STREET
WATCHBELL STREET
CH

The Mint got its name from the 17th-century minting of tokens.

The Mermaid Inn, founded in the 11th century, is Rye's largest medieval building. In the 1750s it was the headquarters of a notorious and bloodthirsty smuggling gang called the Hawkhursts.

View over the River Tillingham

Strand Quay
The brick and timber warehouses survive from the prosperous days when Rye was a thriving port.

Lamb House
This fine Georgian house was built in 1722. George I stayed here when stranded in a storm, and author Henry James (1843–1916) lived here.

STAR SIGHTS

- ★ Mermaid Street
- ★ Ypres Tower

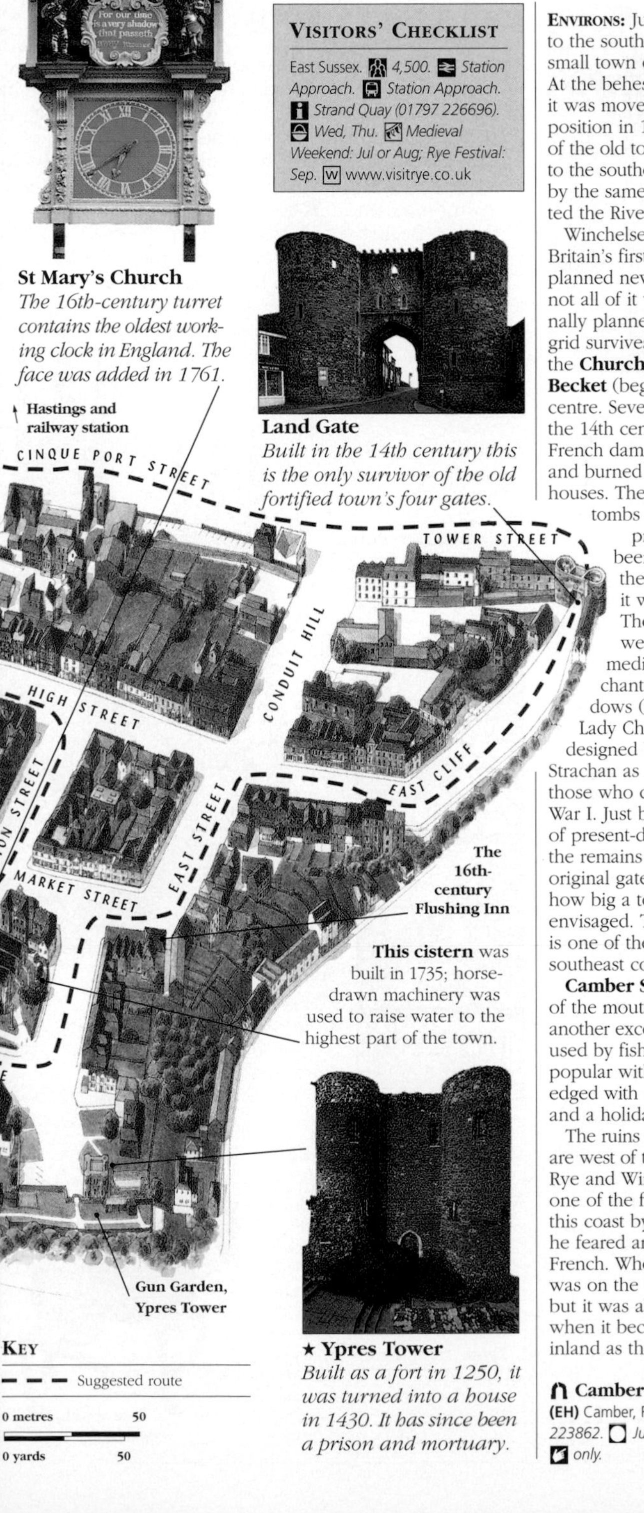

Visitors' Checklist

East Sussex. 4,500. Station Approach. Station Approach. Strand Quay (01797 226696). Wed, Thu. Medieval Weekend: Jul or Aug; Rye Festival: Sep. www.visitrye.co.uk

St Mary's Church
The 16th-century turret contains the oldest working clock in England. The face was added in 1761.

Land Gate
Built in the 14th century this is the only survivor of the old fortified town's four gates.

This cistern was built in 1735; horse-drawn machinery was used to raise water to the highest part of the town.

★ Ypres Tower
Built as a fort in 1250, it was turned into a house in 1430. It has since been a prison and mortuary.

Key

– – – Suggested route

0 metres 50

0 yards 50

Environs: Just 2 miles (3 km) to the south of Rye is the small town of **Winchelsea**. At the behest of Edward I, it was moved to its present position in 1288, when most of the old town on lower land to the southeast, was drowned by the same storm that diverted the River Rother in 1287.

Winchelsea is probably Britain's first coherently planned new town. Although not all of it was built as originally planned, its rectangular grid survives today, as does the **Church of St Thomas Becket** (begun c.1300) at its centre. Several raids during the 14th century by the French damaged the church and burned down scores of houses. The church has three tombs that probably predate it, having been rescued from the old town before it was submerged. There are also two well-preserved medieval tombs in the chantry. The three windows (1928–33) in the Lady Chapel were designed by Douglas Strachan as a memorial to those who died in World War I. Just beyond the edges of present-day Winchelsea are the remains of three of the original gates – showing just how big a town was first envisaged. The beach below is one of the finest on the southeast coast.

Camber Sands, to the east of the mouth of the Rother, is another excellent beach. Once used by fishermen it is now popular with swimmers and edged with seaside bungalows and a holiday camp.

The ruins of **Camber Castle** are west of the sands, between Rye and Winchelsea. This was one of the forts built along this coast by Henry VIII when he feared an attack by the French. When it was built it was on the edge of the sea but it was abandoned in 1642 when it became stranded inland as the river silted up.

Camber Castle
(EH) Camber, Rye. *01797 223862.* *Jul–Sep: Sat, Sun pm for only.*

Jesus on Christ Church Gate, Canterbury Cathedral

Canterbury ㉓

Kent. 50,000. Sun St, Buttermarket (01227 455600). Wed, Fri. www.canterbury.co.uk

Its position on the London to Dover route meant Canterbury was an important Roman town even before the arrival of St Augustine in 597, sent by the pope to convert the Anglo-Saxons to Christianity. The town rose in importance, soon becoming the centre of the Christian Church in England.

With the building of the **cathedral** and the martyrdom of Thomas à Becket *(see p48)*, Canterbury's future as a religious centre was assured.

Adjacent to the ruins of **St Augustine's Abbey**, destroyed in the Dissolution *(see p50)*, is **St Martin's Church**, the oldest in England. This was where St Augustine first worshipped and it has impressive Norman and Saxon work.

West Gate Museum, with its round towers, is an imposing medieval gatehouse. It was built in 1381 and contains a display of arms and armoury.

The Poor Priests' Hospital, founded in the 12th century, now houses the **Museum of Canterbury.**

West Gate Museum
St Peter's St. *01227 452747. Mon–Sat. 23 Dec–1 Jan, Good Fri.*

Museum of Canterbury
Stour St. *01227 452747. Jun–Oct: daily; Nov–May: Mon–Sat.*
www.canterbury-museum.co.uk

Canterbury Cathedral

To match Canterbury's growing ecclesiastical rank as a major centre of Christianity, the first Norman archbishop, Lanfranc, ordered a new cathedral to be built on the ruins of the Anglo-Saxon cathedral in 1070. It was enlarged and rebuilt many times and as a result embraces examples of all styles of medieval architecture. The most poignant moment in its history came in 1170 when Thomas à Becket was murdered here *(see p48)*. Four years after his death a fire devastated the cathedral and Trinity Chapel was built to house Becket's remains. The shrine quickly became an important religious site and until the Dissolution *(see p50)* the cathedral was one of Christendom's chief places of pilgrimage.

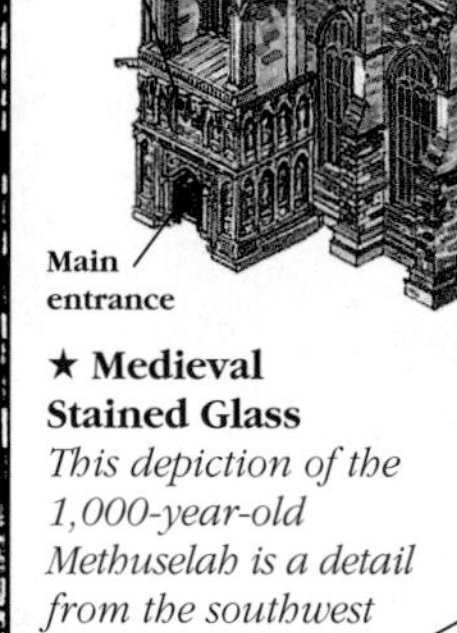

The nave at 60 m (188 ft) makes Canterbury one of the longest medieval churches.

The South West Porch (1426) may have been built to commemorate the victory at Agincourt *(see p49)*.

Main entrance

★ Medieval Stained Glass
This depiction of the 1,000-year-old Methuselah is a detail from the southwest transept window.

Geoffrey Chaucer

Considered to be the first great English poet, Geoffrey Chaucer (c.1345–1400), a customs official by profession, wrote a rumbustious and witty account of a group of pilgrims travelling from London to Becket's shrine in 1387 in the *Canterbury Tales*. The pilgrims represent a cross-section of 14th-century English society and the tales remain one of the greatest and most entertaining works of early English literature.

Wife of Bath, *Canterbury Tales*

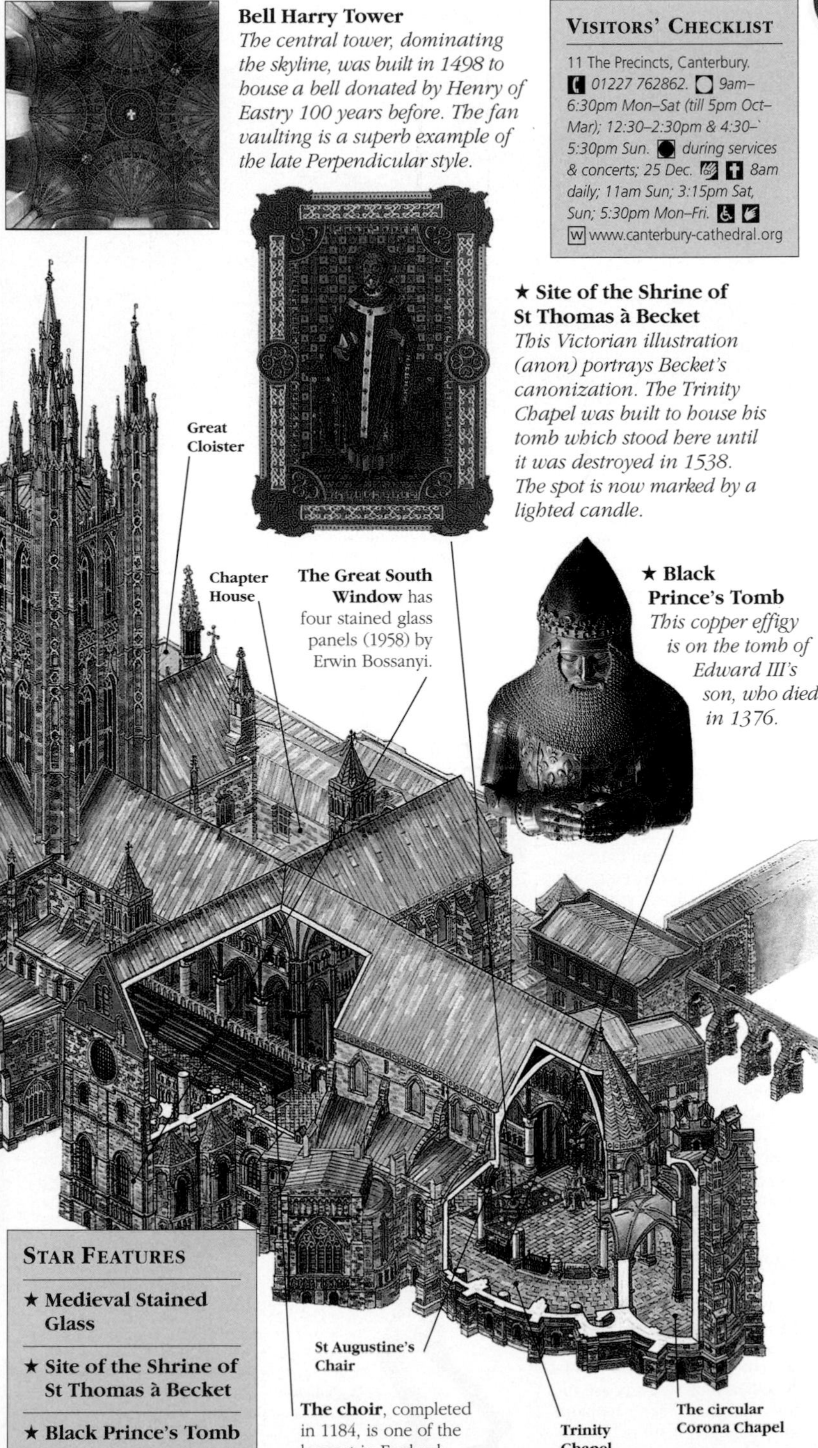

Bell Harry Tower
The central tower, dominating the skyline, was built in 1498 to house a bell donated by Henry of Eastry 100 years before. The fan vaulting is a superb example of the late Perpendicular style.

Visitors' Checklist

11 The Precincts, Canterbury. 01227 762862. 9am–6:30pm Mon–Sat (till 5pm Oct–Mar); 12:30–2:30pm & 4:30–5:30pm Sun. during services & concerts; 25 Dec. 8am daily; 11am Sun; 3:15pm Sat, Sun; 5:30pm Mon–Fri.
www.canterbury-cathedral.org

★ Site of the Shrine of St Thomas à Becket
This Victorian illustration (anon) portrays Becket's canonization. The Trinity Chapel was built to house his tomb which stood here until it was destroyed in 1538. The spot is now marked by a lighted candle.

★ Black Prince's Tomb
This copper effigy is on the tomb of Edward III's son, who died in 1376.

The Great South Window has four stained glass panels (1958) by Erwin Bossanyi.

The choir, completed in 1184, is one of the longest in England.

Star Features

- ★ **Medieval Stained Glass**
- ★ **Site of the Shrine of St Thomas à Becket**
- ★ **Black Prince's Tomb**

The keep of Rochester Castle, dominating Rochester and the Medway Valley

Leeds Castle ㉔

Maidstone, Kent. 01622 765400. Bearsted then bus. daily. for concerts & 25 Dec. www.leeds-castle.com

SURROUNDED BY A LAKE that reflects the warm buff stone of its crenellated turrets, Leeds is often considered to be the most beautiful castle in England. Begun in the early 12th century, it has been continuously inhabited and its present appearance is a result of centuries of rebuilding and extensions, most recently in the 1930s. Leeds has royal connections going back to 1278, when it was given to Edward I by a courtier seeking favour.

Henry VIII loved the castle and visited it often, escaping from the plague in London. It contains a life-sized bust of Henry from the late 16th century. Leeds passed out of royal ownership when Edward VI gave it to Sir Anthony St Leger in 1552 as a reward for helping to pacify the Irish.

Rochester ㉕

Kent. 145,000. 95 High Street (01634 843666).

CLUSTERED AT THE MOUTH of the River Medway are the towns of Rochester, Chatham and Gillingham, all rich in naval history, but none more so than Rochester, which occupied a strategic site on the London to Dover road.

England's tallest Norman keep is at **Rochester Castle,** worth climbing for the views over the Medway. The town's medieval history is still visible, with the original city walls – which followed the lines of the Roman fortifications – on view in the High Street, and some well-preserved wall paintings in the **cathedral**, built in 1088.

ENVIRONS: In Chatham, the **Historic Dockyard** is now a museum of shipbuilding and nautical crafts. **Fort Amherst** nearby was built in 1756 to protect the dockyard and river entrance from attack, and has 1,800 m (5,570 ft) of tunnels to explore that were hewn by Napoleonic prisoners of war.

Rochester Castle
The Esplanade. 01634 402276. *daily.* *1 Jan, 24–27, 31 Dec.* *grounds only.*

Historic Dockyard
Dock Rd, Chatham. *01634 823800.* *mid-Feb–Oct: daily; Nov: Sat, Sun.*

Fort Amherst
Dock Rd, Chatham. *01634 847747.* *call for details.*

Knole ㉖

(NT) Sevenoaks, Kent. *01732 462100.* *Sevenoaks then taxi.* **House** *Mar–Nov: Wed–Sun (pm), Good Fri & public hols.* **Park** *daily.* *limited.* *by arrangement.*

THIS HUGE TUDOR MANSION was built in the late 15th century, and was seized by Henry VIII from the Archbishop of Canterbury at the Dissolution *(see p50)*. In 1566 Queen Elizabeth I gave it to her cousin Thomas Sackville. His descendants have lived here ever since, including the writer Vita Sackville-West, (1892–1962). The house is well known for its 17th-century furniture, such as the elaborate bed made for James II. The 405-ha (1,000-acre) park has deer and lovely walks.

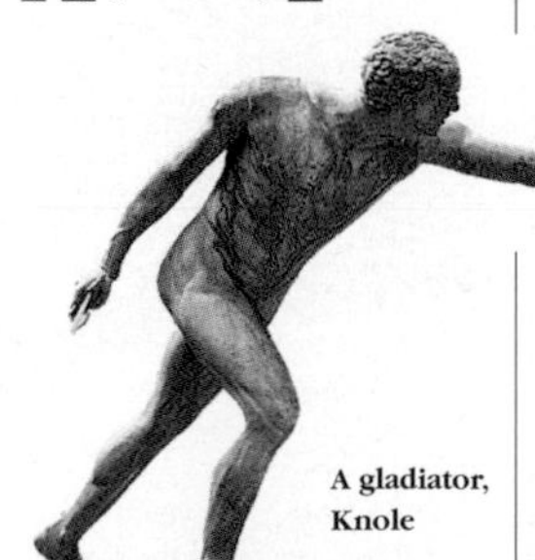

A gladiator, Knole

ENVIRONS: A small manor house, **Ightham Mote**, east of Knole, is one of the finest examples of English medieval architecture. Its 14th-century timber-and-stone building encloses a central court and is encircled by a moat.

At **Sissinghurst Castle Garden** are gardens created by Vita Sackville-West and her husband Harold Nicolson in the 1930s.

Ightham Mote
(NT) Ivy Hatch, Sevenoaks. *01732 810378.* *Apr–Oct: Wed–Fri, Sun, Mon & public hols.*

Sissinghurst Castle Garden
(NT) Cranbrook. *01580 710700.* *Apr–Oct: 11am–6:30pm Mon, Tue, Fri; 10am–6:30pm Sat, Sun, Good Fri.* *limited.*

Hever Castle 27

Edenbridge, Kent. *01732 865224.* *Edenbridge Town.* *Mar–Nov: daily;* **Gardens** *11am–6pm;* **Castle** *noon–6pm.* *limited.* *groups by arrangement.* www.hevercastle.co.uk

THIS SMALL, MOATED CASTLE is famous as the 16th-century home of Anne Boleyn, the doomed wife of Henry VIII, executed for adultery. She lived here as a young woman and the king often visited her while staying at Leeds Castle. In 1903 Hever was bought by William Waldorf Astor, who undertook a restoration programme, building a Neo-Tudor village alongside it to accommodate guests and servants. The moat and gatehouse date from around 1270.

ENVIRONS: To the northwest of Hever is **Chartwell**, the family home of Sir Winston Churchill *(see p59)*. It remains furnished as it was when he lived here. Some 140 of his paintings are on display.

Chartwell
(NT) Westerham, Kent. *01732 866368.* *mid-Mar–Jun, Sep–Nov: 11am–5pm Wed–Sun & public hols; Jul–Aug: 11am–5pm Tue–Sun & public hols.* *limited.*

The façade of Chartwell, Winston Churchill's home

Royal Tunbridge Wells 28

Kent. *55,000.* *Old Fish Market, The Pantiles (01892 515675).* *Wed.* www.heartofkent.org.uk

HELPED BY ROYAL patronage, the town became a popular spa in the 17th and 18th centuries after mineral springs were discovered in 1606. The Pantiles – the colonnaded and paved promenade – was laid out in the 1700s.

ENVIRONS: Nearby is a superb manor house, **Penshurst Place**. Built in the 1340s, it has an 18 m (60 ft) high Great Hall.

Penshurst Place
Tonbridge, Kent. *01892 870307.* *Apr–Oct: daily; Mar: Sat, Sun:* **House** *noon–5:30pm;* **Gardens** *10:30am–6pm;* **Toy Museum** *noon–5pm.* *limited.*

An early 18th-century astrolabe to measure the stars, Hever Castle garden

CHARLES DICKENS

Charles Dickens (1812–70), a popular writer in his own time, is still widely read today. He was born in Portsmouth but moved to Chatham aged five. As an adult, Dickens lived in London but kept up his Kent connections, taking holidays in Broadstairs, just south of Margate – where he wrote *David Copperfield* – and spending his last years at Gad's Hill, near Rochester. The town celebrates the famous connection with an annual Dickens festival.

EAST ANGLIA

NORFOLK · SUFFOLK · ESSEX · CAMBRIDGESHIRE

THE BULGE OF LAND *between the Thames Estuary and the Wash, flat but far from featureless, sits aside from the main north–south axis through Britain, and for that reason it has succeeded in maintaining and preserving its distinctive architecture, traditions and rural character in both cities and countryside.*

East Anglia's name derives from the Angles, the people from northern Germany who settled here during the 5th and 6th centuries. East Anglians have long been a breed of plain-spoken and independent people. Two prominent East Anglians – Queen Boadicea in the 1st century and Oliver Cromwell in the 17th century – were famous for their stubbornness and their refusal to bow to constituted authority. During the Civil War, East Anglia was Cromwell's most reliable source of support. The hardy people who made a difficult living hunting and fishing in the swampy fens, which were drained in the 17th century, were called the Fen Tigers. After draining, the peaty soil proved ideal for arable farming, and today East Anglia grows about a third of Britain's vegetables. The rotation of crops, heralding Britain's agricultural revolution, was perfected in Norfolk in the 18th century. Many of the region's towns and cities grew prosperous on the agricultural wealth, including Norwich. The sea also plays a prominent role in East Anglian life. Coastal towns and villages support the many fishermen who use the North Sea, rich in herring in former days but now known mainly for flat fish.

In modern times, the area has become a centre of recreational sailing, both off the coast and on the inland waterway system known as the Norfolk Broads. East Anglia is also home to one of Britain's top universities: Cambridge.

Lavender fields in full bloom in July, Heacham, Norfolk

◁ **Cley windmill overlooking the sea marshes on the north Norfolk coast**

Exploring East Anglia

As you move away from London, you soon reach the countryside immortalized by the painter Constable *(see p192)* and in many ways unchanged since his day, scattered with churches, windmills and medieval agricultural barns. Nature lovers will find it fruitful territory, especially North Norfolk with its bird reserves and seal colonies. Boating enthusiasts, too, are well catered for in this, Britain's driest and sunniest region. The local architecture ranges from a mix of medieval to modern. The distinctive pink-washed cottages in Suffolk, flint cottages in Norfolk and thatched roofs everywhere, are also much in evidence.

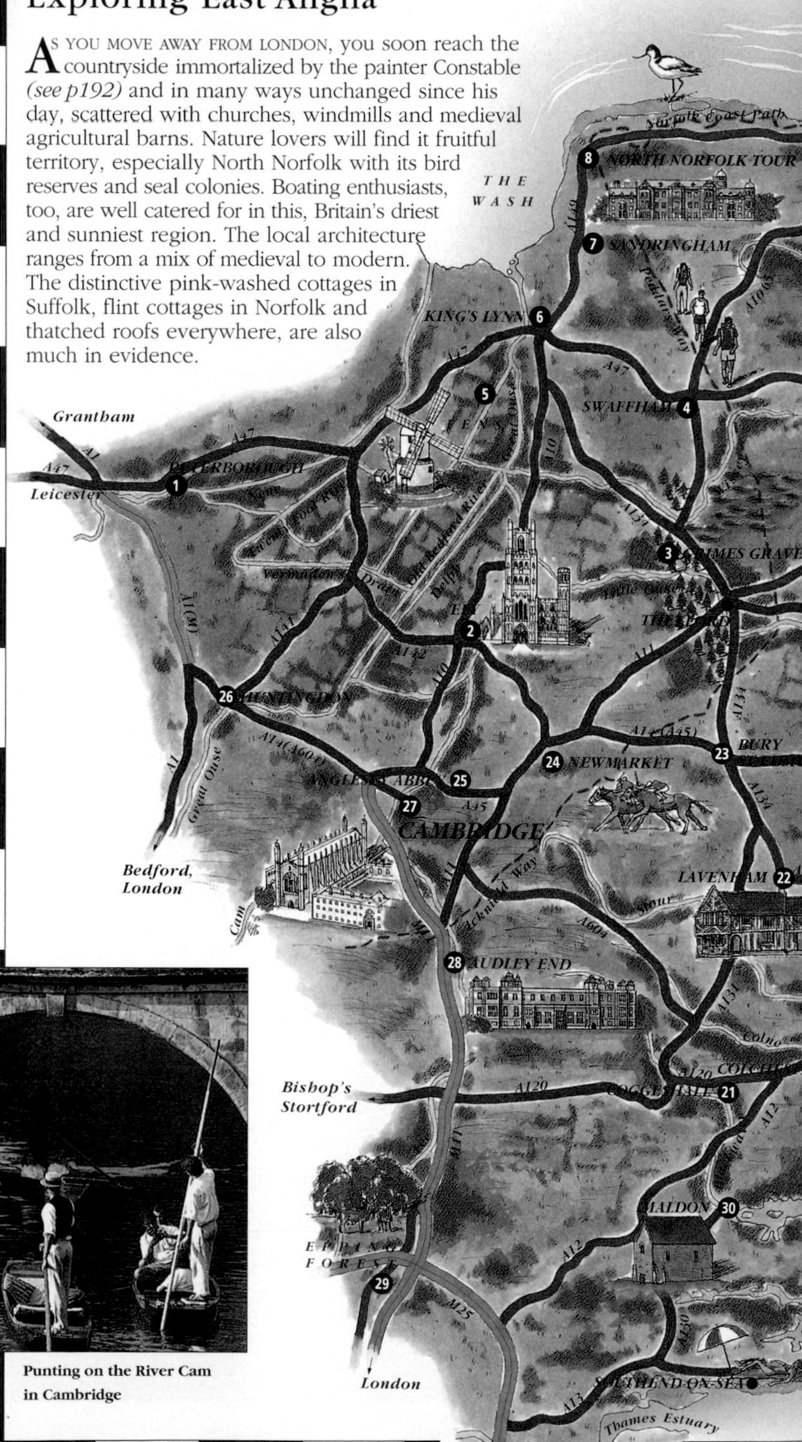

Punting on the River Cam in Cambridge

Key

- Motorway
- Major road
- Minor road
- Scenic route
- Scenic path
- River
- Viewpoint

Getting Around

The region's more isolated sights can be very difficult to reach by public transport and, for a few people, car rental may be a cheaper and more efficient method of travelling around. The M11 motorway runs from London to Cambridge. The coast road from Aldeburgh to King's Lynn takes you through some of the best countryside in the area. There are frequent mainline trains to Norwich, Ipswich and Cambridge although the local trains are more sporadic. There is an international and domestic airport at Norwich.

See Also

- ***Where to Stay*** pp547–9
- ***Where to Eat*** pp584–5

Beach huts on Wells-next-the-Sea beach, north Norfolk

Sights at a Glance

Aldeburgh 16
Anglesey Abbey 25
Audley End 28
Blickling Hall 9
Broads 11
Bury St Edmunds 23
Cambridge pp198–203 27
Coggeshall 21
Colchester 20
Dunwich 15
Ely 2
Epping Forest 29
Fens 5
Framlingham Castle 17
Great Yarmouth 12
Grimes Graves 3
Huntingdon 26
Ipswich 18
King's Lynn 6
Lavenham 22
Lowestoft 13
Maldon 30
Newmarket 24
Norwich 10
Peterborough 1
Sandringham 7
Southwold 14
Swaffham 4

Walks and Tours

Constable Walk 19
North Norfolk Tour 8

0 kilometres 10

0 miles 10

Peterborough ❶

Cambridgeshire. 156,000.
3 Minster Precinct (01733 452336). Tue–Sat.
www.peterborough.gov.uk

ALTHOUGH ONE OF the oldest settlements in Britain, Peterborough was designated a New Town in 1967, and is now a mixture of ancient and modern.

The city centre is dominated by the 12th-century **St Peter's Cathedral** which gave the city its name. The interior of this classic Norman building, with its vast yet simple nave, was badly damaged by Cromwell's troops *(see p52)*, but its unique painted wooden ceiling (1220) has survived intact. Catherine of Aragon, the first wife of

Peterborough's coat of arms with a Latin inscription: Upon this Rock

Henry VIII, is buried here, although Cromwell's troops also destroyed her tomb.

ENVIRONS: The oldest wheel in Britain (1,300 BC) was found preserved in peat at **Flag Fen Bronze Age Centre**. The site provides a fascinating glimpse into prehistory.

Flag Fen Bronze Age Centre

The Droveway, Northey, Peterborough. 01733 313414. daily 10am–5pm. Christmas wk.

Grimes Graves ❸

(EH) Lynford, Norfolk. 01842 810656. Brandon then taxi. daily. 1 Jan, 24–26 Dec.

ONE OF THE MOST important Neolithic sites in England, this was once an extensive complex of flint mines – 433 shafts have been located – dating from before 2000 BC.

Using antlers as pickaxes, Stone Age miners hacked through the soft chalk to extract the hard flint below to make axes, weapons and tools. It is possible that the flint was transported long distances around England on the prehistoric network of paths. You can descend 9 m (30 ft) by ladder into one of the shafts and see the galleries

Ely ❷

Cambridgeshire. 14,000.
29 St Mary's St (01353 662062). Thu (general), Sat (craft & antiques).
www.elyeastcambs.co.uk

BUILT ON A chalk hill, this small city is thought to be named after the eels in the nearby River Ouse. The hill was once an inaccessible island in the then marshy and treacherous Fens *(see p184)*. It was also the last stronghold of Anglo-Saxon resistance, under Hereward the Wake *(see p48)*, who hid in the cathedral until the Normans crossed the Fens in 1071.

Today this small prosperous city, totally dominated by the huge **cathedral**, is the market centre for the rich agricultural area surrounding it.

This painted wooden angel *is one of hundreds of bosses that were carved all over the south and north transepts in the 13th and 14th centuries.*

The lantern's glass windows admit light into the dome.

Stained glass museum

The tomb is that of Alan de Walsingham, designer of the unique Octagon.

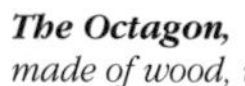

The Octagon, *made of wood, was built in 1322 when the Norman tower collapsed. Its roof, the lantern, took an extra 24 years to build and weighs 200 tonnes.*

Octagon

Area of cutaway

ELY CATHEDRAL

Ely. 01353 667735.
daily. special events.

Begun in 1083, the cathedral took 268 years to complete. It survived the Dissolution *(see p50)* but was closed for 17 years by Cromwell *(see p52)* who lived in Ely for a time.

where the flint was mined. During excavations, unusual chalk models of a fertility goddess *(see p43)* and a phallus were discovered.

Environs: Nearby, at the centre of the once fertile plain known as the Breckland, is the small market town of **Thetford**.

Once a prosperous trading town, its fortunes dipped in the 16th century, when its priory was destroyed *(see p50)* and the surrounding land deteriorated due to excessive sheep grazing. The area was later planted with pine trees. A mound in the city marks the site of a pre-Norman castle.

The revolutionary writer and philosopher Tom Paine, author of *The Rights of Man,* was born here in 1737.

***The huge cathedral spire** dominates the flat Fens countryside surrounding Ely.*

The south aisle has 12 classic Norman arches at its foot, with pointed Early English windows above.

Oxburgh Hall surrounded by its medieval moat

Swaffham ❹

Norfolk. 6,700. Apr–Oct: Market Place (01760 722255). Sat. www.aroundswaffham.co.uk

The best-preserved Georgian town in East Anglia and a fashionable resort during the Regency period, Swaffham is at its liveliest on Saturdays when a market is held in the square around the market cross of 1783. In the centre of the town is the 15th-century **Church of St Peter and St Paul**, with a small spire added in the 19th century. It has a magnificent Tudor north aisle, said to have been paid for by John Chapman, the Pedlar of Swaffham. He is depicted on the two-sided town sign near the market place. Myth has it that he went to London and met a stranger who told him of hidden treasure at Swaffham. He returned, dug it up and used it to embellish the church, where he is shown in a window.

Environs: Castle Acre, north of the town, has the remains of a massive Cluniac **priory**. Founded in 1090, its stunning Norman front still stands.

A short drive south is **Oxburgh Hall and Garden**, built by Sir Edmund Bedingfeld in 1482. The hall, entered through a huge 24 m (80 ft) fortified gatehouse, displays the velvet Oxburgh Hangings, embroidered by Mary, Queen of Scots *(see p497)*.

Swaffham town sign

Castle Acre Priory
(EH) Castle Acre. *01760 755394.* *Apr–Oct: daily; Nov–Mar: Wed–Sun.* *24-26 Dec, 1 Jan.* *limited.*

Oxburgh Hall & Garden
(NT) Oxborough. *01366 328258.* *Mar–Nov: Sat–Wed (garden also Dec: Sat, Sun).* *limited.*

Boadicea and the Iceni

When the Romans invaded Britain, the Iceni, the main tribe in East Anglia, joined forces with them to defeat the Catuvellauni, a rival tribe. But the Romans then turned on the Iceni, torturing Queen Boadicea (or Boudicca). In AD 61, she led a revolt against Roman rule: her followers burned down London, Colchester and St Albans. The rebellion was put down and the queen took poison rather than submit. At Cockley Cley, near Swaffham, an Iceni camp has been excavated.

Illustration of Queen Boadicea leading her Iceni followers

A windmill on Wicken Fen

The Fens ❺

Cambridgeshire/Norfolk. Ely. *29 St Mary's St, Ely (01353 662062).* www.eastcambs.gov.uk

THIS IS THE OPEN, flat, fertile expanse that lies between Lincoln, Cambridge, Bedford and King's Lynn. Up until the 17th century it was a swamp, and settlement was possible only on "islands", such as Ely *(see p182)*, raised above their low-lying surroundings.

Through the 17th century, speculators, recognizing the value of the peaty soil for farmland, brought in Dutch experts to drain the fens. However, as the peat dried it contracted, and the fens have slowly been getting lower. Powerful electric pumps now keep it drained.

Nine miles (14 km) from Ely is Wicken Fen, 243 ha (600 acres) of undrained fen providing a habitat for water life, wildfowl and wild flowers.

King's Lynn ❻

Norfolk. 42,000. *Custom House, Purfleet Quay (01553 763044).* *Tue, Fri, Sat.* www.west-norfolk.gov.uk

FORMERLY BISHOP'S LYNN, its name was changed at the Reformation *(see p50)* to reflect the changing political reality. In the Middle Ages it was one of England's most prosperous ports, shipping grain and wool from the surrounding countryside to Europe. There are still a few warehouses and merchants' houses by the River Ouse surviving from this period. At the north end of the town is **True's**

Trinity Guildhall, King's Lynn

North Norfolk Coastal Tour ❽

THIS TOUR TAKES YOU THROUGH some of the most beautiful areas of East Anglia; nearly all of the north Norfolk coast has been designated an Area of Outstanding Natural Beauty. The sea has dictated the character of the area. With continuing deposits of silt, once busy ports are now far inland and the shingle and sand banks that have been built up are home to a huge variety of wildlife. Do bear in mind when planning your journey that this popular route can get congested during summer.

Tips for Drivers

Tour length: *28 miles (45 km).*
Stopping-off points: *Holkham Hall makes a pleasant stop for a picnic lunch. There are some good pubs in Wells-next-the-Sea. (See also pp636–7.)*

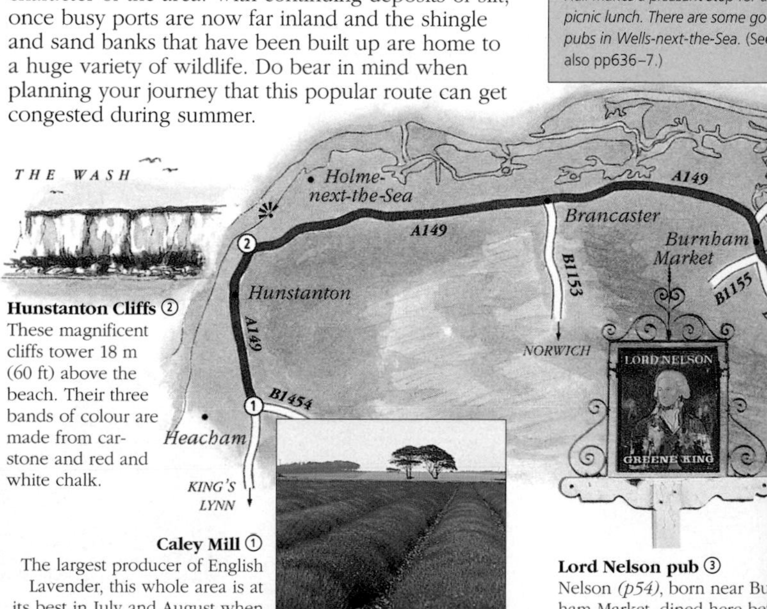

Hunstanton Cliffs ②
These magnificent cliffs tower 18 m (60 ft) above the beach. Their three bands of colour are made from carstone and red and white chalk.

Caley Mill ①
The largest producer of English Lavender, this whole area is at its best in July and August when the fields are a blaze of purple.

Lord Nelson pub ③
Nelson *(p54)*, born near Burnham Market, dined here before he went to sea for the last time

Yard, a relic of the old fishermen's quarter.

The **Trinity Guildhall**, located in the Saturday Market Place, dates back to the 15th century and was formerly a prison. The handsome **Customs House**, overlooking the river, was built in the 17th century as a merchant exchange. It is now a museum dedicated to the town's colourful maritime history. The Tourist Information Centre is also located here. **St Margaret's Church**, on the Market Place, dates back to 1101, and the interior includes a fine Elizabethan screen. In 1741 the tall spire on the southwest tower collapsed in a storm.

Customs House
Purfleet Quay. 01553 763044. *daily. ground floor.*

Sandringham House, where the Royal Family spend every Christmas

Sandringham ❼

Norfolk. *01553 772675. from King's Lynn. Easter–Oct: daily. two wks Jul–Aug.* www.sandringhamestate.co.uk

THIS SIZEABLE NORFOLK estate has been in royal hands since 1862 when it was bought by the Prince of Wales, who later became Edward VII. The 18th-century house was elaborately embellished and refurbished by the prince and now retains an appropriately Edwardian atmosphere.

The large stables are now a museum and contain several trophies that relate to hunting, shooting and horse racing – all favourite royal activities. A popular feature is a display of royal motor cars spanning nearly a century. In the park there are scenic nature trails.

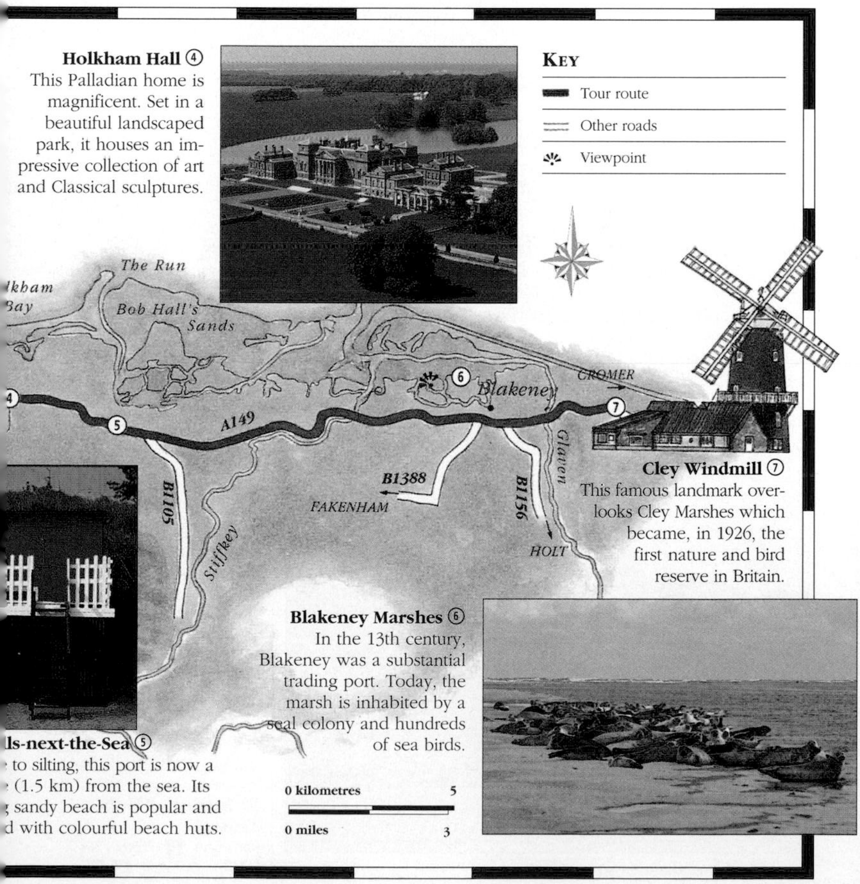

Holkham Hall ④
This Palladian home is magnificent. Set in a beautiful landscaped park, it houses an impressive collection of art and Classical sculptures.

Key
Tour route
Other roads
Viewpoint

The Run
Bob Hall's Sands
Blakeney
CROMER
A149
B1105
B1388
FAKENHAM
B1156
HOLT
Glaven
Stiffkey

Cley Windmill ⑦
This famous landmark overlooks Cley Marshes which became, in 1926, the first nature and bird reserve in Britain.

Blakeney Marshes ⑥
In the 13th century, Blakeney was a substantial trading port. Today, the marsh is inhabited by a seal colony and hundreds of sea birds.

…ls-next-the-Sea ⑤
… to silting, this port is now a … (1.5 km) from the sea. Its … sandy beach is popular and … d with colourful beach huts.

0 kilometres 5
0 miles 3

The symmetrical red-brick façade of the 17th-century Blickling Hall

Blickling Hall ⑨

(NT) Aylsham, Norfolk. *01263 738030.* *Norwich, then bus.* **House** *Apr–Oct: 1–5pm Wed–Sun & public hols.* **Garden** *Apr–Oct: 10:15am–5:15pm Wed–Sun & public hols; Aug daily.* **Park** *daily.*

APPROACHED FROM the east, its symmetrical Jacobean front framed by trees and flanked by two yew hedges, Blickling Hall offers one of the most impressive vistas of any country house in the area.

Anne Boleyn, Henry VIII's tragic second queen, spent her childhood here, but very little of the original house remains. Most of the present structure dates from 1628, when it was home to James I's Chief Justice Sir Henry Hobart. Later in 1767 the 2nd Earl of Buckinghamshire, John Hobart, celebrated the Boleyn connection with reliefs in the Great Hall depicting Anne and her daughter, Elizabeth I.

The Long Gallery is the most spectacular room to survive from the 1620s. Its ceiling depicts symbolic representations of learning.

The Peter the Great Room marks the 2nd earl's service as ambassador to Russia and was built to display a huge spectacular tapestry (1764) of the tsar on horseback, a gift from, Catherine the Great. It also has portraits (1760) of the ambassador and his wife by Gainsborough *(see p151).*

Norwich ⑩

See pp188–9.

The Broads ⑪

Norfolk. *Hoveton, Wroxham.* *Norwich, then bus.* *Station Rd, Hoveton (01603 782281) Apr–Oct.* www.broads/authority.gov.uk

THESE SHALLOW LAKES and waterways south and north-east of Norwich, joined by six rivers – the Bure, Thurne, Ant, Yare, Waveney and Chet – were once thought to have been naturally formed, but in actual fact they are medieval peat diggings which flooded when the water level rose in the 13th century.

During summer the 125 miles (200 km) of open waterways, uninterrupted by locks, teem with thousands of boating enthusiasts, from devotees of pure sail to those who prefer motorboats. You can either hire a boat yourself or take one of the many trips on offer to view the plants and wildlife of the area. Look out for Britain's largest butterfly, the swallowtail. Wroxham, the unofficial capital of the Broads, is the starting point for many of these excursions.

The waterways support substantial beds of strong and durable reeds, much in demand for thatching *(see p29)*. They are cut in winter and carried to shore in the distinctive Broads punts.

For a more detailed look at the origins of the Broads and their varied wildlife, visit the **Norfolk Wildlife Trust** – a large thatched floating information centre on Ranworth Broad, with displays on all aspects of the area, and a bird-watching gallery.

In the centre of Ranworth is **St Helen's Church** which has a painted medieval screen, a well-preserved 14th-century illuminated manuscript and spectacular views over the entire area from its tower.

Norfolk Wildlife Trust

Ranworth. *01603 270479.* *Apr–Oct: daily.*

Sailing boat, Wroxham Broad, Norfolk

Great Yarmouth ⓬

Norfolk. 90,000. Town Hall (01493 846345); Apr–Oct: Marine Parade (01493 842195). Wed, Fri (summer), Sat.
www.great-yarmouth.co.uk

HERRING FISHING was once the major industry of this port, with 1,000 boats engaged in it just before World War I. Over-fishing led to a depletion of stocks and, for the port to survive, it started to earn its living from servicing container ships and North Sea oil rigs.

It is also the most popular seaside resort on the Norfolk coast and has been since the 19th century, when Dickens *(see p177)* gave it useful publicity by setting part of his novel *David Copperfield* here.

The **Elizabethan House Museum** has a large, eclectic display which illustrates the social history of the area.

In the old part of the town, around South Quay, are a number of charming houses including the 17th-century **Old Merchant's House**. It retains its original patterned plaster ceilings as well as examples of old ironwork and architectural fittings from nearby houses, which were destroyed during World War II. The guided tour of the house includes a visit to the adjoining cloister of a 13th-century friary.

Fishing trawlers at Lowestoft's quays

Elizabethan House Museum
(EH) 4 South Quay. *01493 855746.*
Apr–Oct: daily.

Old Merchant's House
(NT) South Quay. *01493 857900.*
Apr–Oct: daily.

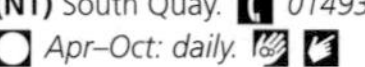

Lowestoft ⓭

Suffolk. 55,000.
East Point Pavilion, Royal Plain (01502 533600). Tue, Fri, Sat.
www.visit/lowestoft.co.uk

THE MOST EASTERLY TOWN in Britain was long a rival to Great Yarmouth, both as a holiday resort and a fishing port. Its fishing industry has only just survived.

The coming of the railway in the 1840s gave the town an advantage over other resorts, and the solid Victorian and Edwardian boarding houses are evidence of its popularity.

Lowestoft Museum, in a 17th-century house, has a good display of the fine porcelain made here in the 18th century, as well as exhibits on local archaeology and domestic life.

ENVIRONS: Somerleyton Hall is built in Jacobean style on the foundations of a smaller mansion. Its gardens are a real delight, and there is a genuinely baffling yew hedge maze.

Lowestoft Museum
Oulton Broad. *01502 568560.*
Mar (last Mon)–Oct (1st Sun) 10:30am–5pm Mon–Fri, 2–5pm Sat & Sun. *limited.* *by arrangement.*

Somerleyton Hall
(EH) On B1074. *01502 730224.*
Easter Sun–Oct: Thu, Sun & public hols (Jul–Aug: Tue–Thu, Sun & public hols). *by arrangement.*
www.somerleyton.co.uk

WINDMILLS ON THE FENS AND BROADS

Corn mill at Saxtead Green, near Framlingham

Herringfleet Smock Mill, near Lowestoft

The flat, open countryside and the stiff breezes from the North Sea made windmills an obvious power source for East Anglia well into the 20th century, and today they are an evocative and recurring feature of the landscape. On the Broads and Fens, some were used for drainage, while others, such as that at Saxtead Green, ground corn. On the boggy fens they were not built on hard foundations, so few survived, but elsewhere, especially on the Broads, many have been restored to working order. The seven-storey Berney Arms Windmill is the tallest on the Broads. Thurne Dyke Drainage Mill is the site of an exhibition about the occasionally idiosyncratic mills and their more unusual mechanisms.

Norwich 10

IN THE HEART of the fertile East Anglian countryside, Norwich, one of the best-preserved cities in Britain, is steeped in a relaxed provincial atmosphere. The city was first fortified by the Saxons in the 9th century and still has the irregular street plan of that time. With the arrival of Flemish settlers in the early 12th century and the establishment of a textile industry, the town soon became a prosperous market and was the second city of England until the Industrial Revolution in the 19th century *(see pp56–7)*.

One of over a thousand carved bosses in the cathedral cloisters

The cobbled street, Elm Hill

Exploring Norwich

The oldest parts of the city are Elm Hill, one of the finest medieval streets in England, and Tombland, the old Saxon market place by the cathedral. Both have well-preserved medieval buildings, which are now incorporated into pleasant areas of small shops.

With a trading history spanning hundreds of years, the colourful market in the city centre is well worth a visit. A good walk meanders around the surviving sections of the 14th-century flint city wall.

Norwich Cathedral

The Close. 01603 218321.
daily. **Donations.**
www.cathedral.org.uk

This magnificent building was founded in 1096 by Bishop Losinga and built with stone from Caen in France and Barnack.

The precinct originally included a monastery, and the surviving cloister is the most extensive in England. The thin cathedral spire was added in the 15th century, making it, at 96 m (315 ft), the second tallest in England after Salisbury *(see pp252–3)*. In the majestic nave, soaring Norman pillars and arches support a 15th-century vaulted roof whose stone bosses, many of which illustrate well-known Bible stories, have recently been beautifully restored.

Easier to appreciate at close hand is the elaborate wood carving in the choir – the canopies over the stalls and the misericords beneath the seats, one showing a small boy being smacked. Not to be missed is the 14th-century Despenser Reredos in St Luke's Chapel. It was hidden for years under a carpenter's table to prevent its destruction by Puritans.

Two gates to the cathedral close survive: **St Ethelbert's**, a 13th-century flint arch, and the **Erpingham Gate** at the west end, built by Sir Thomas Erpingham, who led the triumphant English archers at the Battle of Agincourt in 1415 *(see p49)*.

Beneath the east outer wall is the grave of Edith Cavell, the Norwich-born nurse who was arrested and executed in 1915 by the Germans for helping Allied soldiers escape from occupied Belgium.

Castle Museum

Castle Meadow. *01603 493648.*
daily (Sun pm only). *1 Jan, 25, 26 Dec.* www.norfolk.gov.uk/tourism/museums

The brooding keep of this 12th-century castle has been a museum since 1894, when it ended 650 years of service as a prison. The most important Norman feature is a carved door that used to be the main entrance.

Exhibits include significant collections of archaeology,

A view of Norwich Cathedral's spire and tower from the southeast

Colman's Mustard

It was said of the Colmans that they made their fortune from what diners left on their plate. In 1814 Jeremiah Colman started milling mustard at Norwich because it was at the centre of a fertile plain where mustard was grown. Today at 15 Royal Arcade a shop sells mustard and related items, while a small museum illustrates the history of the company.

A 1950s advertisement for Colman's Mustard

natural history, fine art as well as the world's largest collection of ceramic teapots.

The art gallery is dominated by works from the Norwich School of painters. This group of early 19th century landscape artists painted directly from nature, getting away from the stylized studio landscapes that had been fashionable up to then. Chief among the group were John Crome (1768–1821), whom many compare with Constable *(see p192)*, and John Sell Cotman (1782–1842), known for his watercolours. There are also regular exhibitions held here which are brought from the Tate Gallery in London.

Church of St Peter Mancroft

Market Place. 01603 610443. *10am–4pm Mon–Sat; 10am–4pm Sat (summer), 10am–1pm (winter); Sun (services only).* **Donations.**

This imposing Perpendicular church, built around 1455, so dominates the city centre that many visitors assume it is the cathedral. John Wesley *(see p267)* wrote of it, "I scarcely ever remember to have seen a more beautiful parish church".

The large windows make the church very light, and the dramatic east window still has most of its 15th-century glass. The roof is unusual in having wooden fan tracery – it is normally in stone – covering the hammerbeam construction. The famous peal of 13 bells rang out in 1588 to celebrate the defeat of the Spanish Armada *(see p51)* and is still heard every Sunday.

Its name derives from the Latin *magna crofta* (great meadow) which described the area in pre-Norman times.

Bridewell Museum

Bridewell Alley. 01603 629127. *10am–5pm Mon–Sat.*

One of the oldest houses in Norwich, this 14th-century flint-faced building was for years used as a jail. It now houses an exhibition of local industries, with displays of old machines, advertisements and reconstructed shops.

Guildhall

Gaol Hill.

Above the city's ancient market place is the imposing 15th-century flint and stone Guildhall with its gable of checkered flushwork (now a café).

Visitors' Checklist

Norfolk. *125,000.* *Thorpe Road.* *Surrey St.* *Millennium Plane (01603 727927).* www.visitnorwich-area.co.uk

Strangers' Hall

Charing Cross. *Wed, Sat for only. Tickets from Castle Museum (01603 493648).*

This 14th-century merchant's house gives a glimpse into English domestic life through the ages. The costume display features a unique collection of underwear. The house was lived in by immigrant weavers – the "strangers". It has a fine 15th-century Great Hall.

The Sainsbury Centre for Visual Arts

University of E Anglia (on B1108). *01603 593199.* *Tue–Sun.* *23 Dec–2 Jan.* *by arrangement.* www.uea.ac.uk/scva

This important art gallery was built in 1978 to house the collection of Robert and Lisa Sainsbury given to the University of East Anglia in 1973.

The collection's strength is in its modern European paintings, including works by Modigliani, Picasso and Bacon, and in its sculptures by Giacometti and Moore. There are also displays of ethnographic art from Africa, the Pacific and the Americas.

The centre, designed by Lord Norman Foster, one of Britain's leading and most innovative architects, was among the first to display its steel structure openly.

***Back of the New Mills* (1814) by John Crome of the Norwich School**

Purple heather in flower on Dunwich Heath

Southwold 14

Suffolk. 3,900. High Street (01502 724729). Mon, Thu.
www.visit-southwold.co.uk

This picture-postcard seaside resort, with its charming white-washed villas clustered around grassy slopes, has, largely by historical accident, remained unspoiled. The railway line which connected it with London was closed in 1929, which effectively isolated this Georgian town from an influx of day-trippers.

That this was also once a large port can be judged from the size of the 15th-century **St Edmund King and Martyr Church**, worth a visit for the 16th-century painted screens. On its tower is a small figure dressed in the uniform of a 15th-century soldier and known as Jack o'the Clock. **Southwold Museum** tells the story of the Battle of Sole Bay, which was fought offshore between the English and Dutch navies in 1672.

Jack o'the Clock, Southwold

Environs: The rail closure in Southwold also cut the link with the pretty village of **Walberswick**, across the creek. By road it is a long detour and the only alternative is a rowing-boat ferry across the harbour. Just inland at Blythburgh, the 15th-century **Holy Trinity Church** dominates the surrounding land. Cromwell's troops *(see p52)* used it as a stable.

In 1944 a US bomber blew up over the church, killing Joseph Kennedy Jr, brother of the future American president.

Southwold Museum
9–11 Victoria St. *Easter–Oct: 2–4pm daily.*

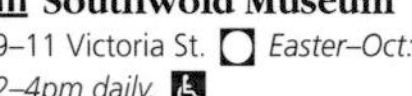

Dunwich 15

Suffolk. *1,400.*

This tiny village is all that remains of a "lost city" consigned to the sea by erosion. In the 7th century Dunwich was the seat of the powerful East Anglian kings. In the 13th century it was still the biggest port in Suffolk and some 12 churches were built. But the land was being eroded at about a metre (3 ft) a year, and the last original church collapsed into the sea in 1919.

Dunwich Heath, to the south, runs down to a sandy beach and is an important nature reserve. **Minsmere Reserve** has observation hides for watching a huge variety of birds.

Dunwich Heath
(NT) Nr Westleton. *01728 648505.* *phone for details.*

Minsmere Reserve
Minsmere, Westleton. *01728 648281.* *Wed–Mon.* *25, 26 Dec.* www.rspb.org.uk

Aldeburgh 16

Suffolk. *2,500.* *High St (01728 453637).*
www.aldeburgh-uk.com

Best known today for the music festivals at Snape Maltings just up the River Alde, Aldeburgh has been a

Intricate carving on the exterior of the Tudor Moot Hall, Aldeburgh

port since Roman times (the Roman area is under water).

Erosion has resulted in the fine Tudor **Moot Hall**, once far inland, now being close to the beach and promenade. Its ground floor, originally the market, is now a museum. The large timbered court room above can only be reached by the original outside staircase.

The **church**, also Tudor, contains a large stained glass window placed in 1979 as a memorial to Benjamin Britten.

Moot Hall
Market Cross Pl. *Apr, May: Sat, Sun (pm); Jun: daily (pm); Jul, Aug: daily.*

Framlingham Castle 17

(EH) Framlingham, Suffolk. *01728 724189. Wickham Market then taxi. daily. 24–26 Dec, 1 Jan.*

PERCHED ON A HILL, the small village of Framlingham has long been an important strategic site, even before the present castle was built in 1190 by the Earl of Norfolk.

Little of the castle from that period survives except the powerful curtain wall and its towers; walk round the top of it for fine views of the town.

Mary Tudor, daughter of Henry VIII, was staying here in 1553 when she heard she was to become queen.

ENVIRONS: To the southeast, on the coast, is the 27 m (90 ft) keep of **Orford Castle**, built for Henry II as a coastal defence at around the same time as Framlingham. It is an early example of an English castle with a 16-sided keep; earlier they were square and later round. A short climb to the top of the castle gives fantastic views.

Orford Castle
(EH) Orford. *01394 450472. Apr–Oct: daily; Nov–Mar: Wed–Sun. 24– 26 Dec, 1 Jan.*

ALDEBURGH MUSIC FESTIVAL

Composer Benjamin Britten (1913–76), born in Lowestoft, Suffolk, moved to Snape in 1937. In 1945 his opera *Peter Grimes* – inspired by the poet George Crabbe (1754–1832), once a curate at Aldeburgh – was performed in Snape. Since then the area has become the centre of musical activity. In 1948, Britten began the Aldeburgh Music Festival, held every June *(see p63)*. He acquired the Maltings at Snape and converted it into a music venue opened by the Queen in 1967. It has since become the focus of an annual series of East Anglian musical events in churches and halls throughout the entire region.

Benjamin Britten in Aldeburgh

Ipswich 18

Suffolk. *120,000.* *St Stephen's Lane (01473 258070). Tue, Fri, Sat.* www.ipswich.gov.uk

SUFFOLK'S COUNTY TOWN has a largely modern centre but several buildings remain from earlier times. It rose to prominence after the 13th century as a port for the rich Suffolk wool trade *(see p195)*. Later, with the Industrial Revolution, it began to export coal.

The **Ancient House** in Buttermarket has a superb example of pargeting – the ancient craft of ornamental façade plastering. The town's museum and art gallery, **Christchurch Mansion**, is a Tudor house from 1548, where Elizabeth I stayed in 1561. It also boasts the best collection of Constable's paintings out of London *(see p192)*, including four marvellous Suffolk landscapes, as well as pictures by the Suffolk-born painter Gainsborough *(see p151)*.

Ipswich Museum contains replicas of the Mildenhall and Sutton Hoo treasures, the originals being in the British Museum *(see pp108–9)*.

In the centre of the town is **St Margaret's**, a 15th-century church built in flint and stone with a double hammerbeam roof and 17th-century painted ceiling panels. **Wolsey's Gate**, a Tudor gateway of 1527, provides a link with Ipswich's most famous son, Cardinal Wolsey *(see p161)*. He started to build an ecclesiastical college in the town, but fell from royal favour before it was finished.

Pargeting on the Ancient House in Ipswich

Christchurch Mansion
Soane St. *01473 433554. 10am–5pm Tue–Sat & public hols; 2:30–4:30pm Sun. 1 Jan, Good Fri, 24–26 Dec. limited. by arrangement.*

Ipswich Museum
High St. *01473 433550. Tue–Sat.*

Constable Walk ⓳

THIS WALK in Constable country follows one of the most picturesque sections of the River Stour. The route taken would have been familiar to the landscape painter John Constable (1776–1837). Constable's father, a wealthy merchant, owned Flatford Mill, which was depicted in many of the artist's important paintings. Constable claimed to know and love "every stile and stump, and every lane" around East Bergholt.

Tips for Walkers

Starting point: *Park off Flatford Lane, East Bergholt (charge to park).* *01206 299460;* **(NT)** *Bridge Cottage (01206 298260).* ***Getting there:*** *A12 to Ipswich, then B1070 to East Bergholt, follow signs to Flatford.* *Manningtree is within walking distance of Flatford.* *from Ipswich or Colchester.* ***Stopping-off point:*** *Dedham.* ***Length:*** *3 miles (5 km).* ***Difficulty:*** *Flat trail along riverside footpath with kissing gates.*

The River Stour, used as a backdrop for Constable's *Boatbuilding* (1814)

Viewpoint ⑤
The view over the valley from the top of the hill shows Constable country at its best.

Car Park ①
Follow the signs to Flatford Mill then cross the footbridge.

Dedham Mill
Stour
B1029
A12
④
Dedham
B1029
COLCHESTER
③
EAST BERGHOLT
⑤
Gosnalls Farm
P ①
Ram Lock
Flatford Mill
②

Fen Bridge ③
This modern footbridge replaced one that Constable used as a focus for many of his paintings.

Dedham Church ④
The tall church tower appears in many of Constable's pictures including the *View on the Stour near Dedham* (1822).

Key

- Route
- B road
- Minor road
- Viewpoint
- P Parking

0 metres 500
0 yards 500

Willy Lott's Cottage ②
This cottage remains much the same as it did when featured in Constable's painting *The Hay-Wain* *(see p85)*.

Colchester 20

Essex. 150,000. Queen St (01206 282920). Fri, Sat.

THE OLDEST recorded town in Britain, Colchester was the effective capital of south-east England when the Romans invaded in AD 43, and it was here that the first permanent Roman colony was established.

After Boadicea *(see p183)* burnt the town in AD 60, a 2 mile (3 km) defensive wall was built, 3 m (10 ft) thick and 9 m (30 ft) high, to deter any future attackers. You can still see these walls and the surviving Roman town gate, which is the largest in Britain.

During the Middle Ages Colchester developed into an important weaving centre. In the 16th century, a number of immigrant Flemish weavers settled in an area west of the castle, known as the **Dutch Quarter**, which still retains the original tall houses and steep, narrow streets.

Colchester was besieged for 11 weeks during the Civil War *(see p52)* before being captured by Cromwell's troops.

Tymperleys

Trinity St. 01206 282943. *Apr–Oct: Tue–Sat.*

Clock-making was an important craft in Colchester, and it is celebrated in this restored half-timbered, 15th-century mansion, also worth visiting for its formal Tudor garden.

Hollytrees Museum

Castle Park. *01206 282940.* *daily.* *24–26 Dec, 1 Jan.*

www.colchestermuseums.org.uk

This elegant Georgian town-house was built in 1719. Now a charming museum of social history, you can experience the day-to-day lives of Colchester people and changing technology over 300 years.

Castle Museum

High St. *01206 282939.* *daily; 11am–5pm Sun.* *24–27 Dec.*

www.colchestermuseums.org.uk

This is the oldest and largest Norman keep still standing in England. Twice the size of the White Tower at the Tower of London *(see pp120–21)*, it was

The Norman keep of the Castle Museum, Colchester

built in 1076 on the platform of a Roman temple dedicated to Claudius *(see p44)*, using stones and tiles from other Roman buildings. Today, the museum is packed full of exhibits relating the story of the town from prehistoric times to the Civil War. You can also visit the medieval prison.

Layer Marney Tower

Off B1022. *01206 330784.* *Apr–Sep: Sun–Fri (pm).* *limited.* *by arrangement.*

www.layermarneytower.co.uk

This remarkable Tudor gate-house is the tallest in Britain: its pair of six-sided, eight-storey turrets reach to 24 m (80 ft). It was intended to be part of a larger complex but the designer, Sir Henry Marney, died before it was completed. The brickwork and terracotta ornamentation around the roof and windows are models of Tudor craftsmanship.

Beth Chatto Garden

Elmstead Market. *01206 822007.* *Mar–Oct: 9am–5pm Mon–Sat; Nov–Feb: 9am–4pm Mon–Fri.* *24 Dec–6 Jan.*

www.bethchatto.co.uk

One of Britain's most eminent gardening writers began this experiment in the 1960s to test her belief that it is possible to create a garden in the most adverse conditions. The dry and windy slopes, boggy patches, gravel beds and wooded areas all support an array of plants best suited to that particular environment.

Coggeshall 21

Essex. *4,000.* *Thu.*

THIS SMALL TOWN has two of the most important and best-preserved medieval and Tudor buildings in the country. Dating from 1140, **Coggeshall Grange Barn** is the oldest surviving timber-framed barn in Europe. Inside is a display of historic farm wagons. The half-timbered merchant's house, **Paycocke's**, was built around 1500 and has a beautifully panelled interior. There is a display of Coggeshall lace.

Coggeshall Grange Barn

(NT) Grange Hill. *01376 562226.* *Apr–Oct: Tue, Thu, Sun & public hols (pm).* *Good Fri.*

Paycocke's

(NT) West St. *01376 561305.* *Apr–Oct: Tue, Thu, Sun & public hols (pm).* *Good Fri.*

Beth Chatto Garden, Colchester, in full summer bloom

Lavenham ㉒

Suffolk. 1,700. *Lady St (01787 248207).*

OFTEN CONSIDERED the most perfect of all English small towns, Lavenham is a treasure trove of black and white timber-framed houses ranged along streets whose pattern is virtually unchanged from medieval times. For 150 years, between the 14th and 16th centuries, Lavenham was the prosperous centre of the Suffolk wool trade. It still has many outstanding and well-preserved buildings; indeed no less than 300 of the town's buildings are listed, including the magnificent **Little Hall**.

ENVIRONS: Gainsborough's House, Sudbury, is a museum on this painter *(see p151)*.

Little Hall Market Place. *01787 247179.* *Apr–Oct: Wed, Thu, Sat, Sun (all pm); public hols.*

Gainsborough's House Sudbury. *01787 372958.* *Tue–Sun.* *24 Dec–1 Jan, Good Fri.* www.gainsborough.org

LITTLE HALL

The solar bedroom was the best and sunniest room in the house.
Communal dormitory
The crown-post roof is a superb feat of medieval engineering.
An Egyptian bronze cat represents the Goddess Bastet.
Library
Entrance
Dining room
The herringbone-style timber on the exterior was used often in the 14th century.

Bury St Edmunds ㉓

Suffolk. 34,000. *Angel Hill (01284 764667).* *Wed, Sat.* www.stedmundsbury.gov.uk

ST EDMUND was the last Saxon king of East Anglia, decapitated by Danish raiders in 870. Legend has it that a wolf picked up the severed head – an image that appears in a number of medieval carvings. Edmund was canonized in 900 and buried in Bury, where in 1014 King Canute *(see p159)* built an **abbey** in his honour, the wealthiest in England until its destruction in the Dissolution of the Monasteries *(see p339)*. The abbey ruins now lie in the town centre.

Nearby are two large 15th-century churches, built when the wool trade made the town wealthy. **St James's** was designated a cathedral in 1914. The best features of **St Mary's** are the north porch and the hammerbeam roof over the nave. A stone slab in the north-east corner marks the tomb of Mary Tudor *(see pp50–51)*.

Illustration of St Edmund

Just below the **market cross** in Cornhill – remodelled by Robert Adam *(see p24)* in 1714 – stands the large 12th-century **Moyse's Hall**, a merchant's house that serves as the local history museum, displaying archaeology from the area.

ENVIRONS: Three miles (5 km) southwest of Bury is the late 18th-century **Ickworth House**. This eccentric Neo-Classical mansion features an unusual rotunda with a

The 18th-century rotunda of Ickworth House, Bury St Edmunds

domed roof flanked by two huge wings. The art collection includes works by Reynolds and Titian. There are also fine displays of silver, porcelain and sculpture, for example, John Flaxman's (1755–1826) moving *The Fury of Athamas*. The house is set in a large park.

Moyse's Hall
Cornhill. 01284 706183. daily. 24–26 Dec, Good Fri.

Ickworth House
Horringer. 01284 735270. Apr–Nov: Fri–Tue, public hols (pm).

Newmarket 24

Suffolk. 17,000.
Palace House, Palace St (01638 667200). Tue, Sat.

A WALK DOWN the short main street tells you all you need to know about this busy and wealthy little town. The shops sell horse feed and all manner of riding accessories; the clothes on sale are tweeds, jodhpurs and the soft brown hats rarely worn by anyone except racehorse trainers.

Newmarket has been the headquarters of British horse racing since James I decided that its open heaths were ideal for testing the mettle of his fastest steeds against those of his friends. The first ever

The stallion unit at the National Stud, Newmarket

recorded horse race was held here in 1622. Charles II shared his grandfather's enthusiasm and after the Restoration *(see p53)* would move the whole court to Newmarket, every spring and summer, for the sport – he is the only British king to have ridden a winner.

A horse being exercised on Newmarket Heath

The modern racing industry began to take shape here in the late 18th century. There are now over 2,500 horses in training in and around the town, and two racecourses staging regular race meetings from around April to October *(see pp66–7)*. Training stables are occasionally open to the public but you can view the horses being exercised on the heath in the early morning. Tattersall's, the auction house for thoroughbreds, is in the centre of Newmarket.

The **National Stud** can also be visited. You will see the five or six stallions on stud, mares in foal and if you are lucky a newborn foal – most likely in April or May.

The **National Horseracing Museum** tells the history of the sport and contains many offbeat exhibits such as the skeleton of Eclipse, one of the greatest horses ever, unbeaten in 18 races and the ancestor of most of today's fastest performers. It also has a large display of sporting art.

National Stud
Newmarket. 01638 663464 Mar–Sep: daily.
www.nationalstud.co.uk

National Horseracing Museum
99 High St, Newmarket. 01638 667333. Apr–Oct: Tue–Sun.
www.nhrm.co.uk

St Mary's Church, Stoke-by-Nayland, southeast of Bury St Edmunds

The Rise and Fall of the Wool Trade

Wool was a major English product from the 13th century and by 1310 some ten million fleeces were exported every year. The Black Death *(see p48)*, which swept Britain in 1348, perversely provided a boost for the industry: with labour in short supply, land could not be cultivated and was grassed over for sheep. Around 1350 Edward III decided it was time to establish a home-based cloth industry and encouraged Flemish weavers to come to Britain. Many settled in East Anglia, particularly Suffolk, and their skills helped establish a flourishing trade. This time of prosperity saw the construction of the sumptuous churches, such as the one at Stoke-by-Nayland, that we see today – East Anglia has more than 2,000 churches. The cloth trade here began to decline in the late 16th century with the development of water-powered looms. These were not suited to the area, which never regained its former wealth. Today's visitors are the beneficiaries of this decline, because the wool towns such as Lavenham and Bury St Edmunds never became rich enough to destroy their magnificent Tudor halls and houses and construct new buildings.

The façade of Anglesey Abbey

Anglesey Abbey ㉕

(NT) Lode, Cambridgeshire. *01223 810080.* *Cambridge then bus.* **House** *Apr–Oct: Wed–Sun;* **Garden** *Wed–Sun.* *limited.*

THE ORIGINAL ABBEY was built in 1135 for an Augustinian order. But only the crypt – also known as the monks' parlour – with its vaulted ceiling on marble and stone pillars, survived the Dissolution *(see p50)*.

This was later incorporated into a manor house whose treasures include furniture from many periods and a rare seascape by Gainsborough *(see p194)*. The superb garden was created in the 1930s by Lord Fairhaven as an ambitious, Classical landscape of trees, sculptures and borders.

Huntingdon ㉖

Cambridgeshire. *18,000.* *Princes St (01480 388588).* *Wed, Sat.* www.huntsleisure.org

MORE THAN 300 YEARS after his death, Oliver Cromwell *(see p52)* still dominates this small town. Born here in 1599, a record of his baptism can be seen in the County Records Office in Huntingdon. You can see his name and traces of ancient graffiti scrawled all over it which says "England's plague for five years". **Cromwell Museum**, his former school, traces his life with pictures and mementoes, including his death mask.

Cromwell remains one of the most disputed figures in British history. An MP before he was 30, he quickly became embroiled in the disputes between Charles I and Parliament over taxes and religion. In the Civil War *(see p52)* he proved an inspired general and – after refusing the title of king – was made Lord Protector in 1653, four years after the King was beheaded. But just two years after his death the monarchy was restored by popular demand, and his body was taken out of Westminster Abbey *(see pp94–5)* to hang on gallows.

There is a 14th-century bridge across the River Ouse which links Huntingdon with Godmanchester, the site of a Roman settlement.

Cromwell Museum
Grammar School Walk. *01480 375830.* *Apr–Oct: Tue–Sun; Nov–Mar: Tue–Sun (pm only except Sat).* *24–27 Dec, 1 Jan, some public hols.*

Cambridge ㉗

See pp198–203.

Audley End ㉘

Saffron Walden, Essex. *01799 522842.* *Audley End then taxi.* *Apr–Sep:Wed–Sun & public hols noon–5pm ; Oct: 11am–3pm.* *24–26 Dec.* *limited.*

THIS WAS THE largest house in England when built in 1614 for Thomas Howard, Lord Treasurer and 1st Earl of Suffolk. James I joked that Howard's house was too big for a king but not for a Lord Treasurer. Charles II, his grandson, disagreed and bought it in 1667 as an extra palace; but he and his successors seldom went there and in 1701 it was given back to the Howards, who demolished two thirds of it to make it more manageable.

What remains is a Jacobean mansion, retaining its original hall and many fine plaster ceilings. Robert Adam *(see p24)* remodelled most of the interior in the 1760s and many rooms have been restored to his original designs. At the same time, Capability Brown *(see p22)* landscaped the magnificent 18th-century park.

***The Chapel** was completed in 1772 to a Gothic design. The furniture was made to complement the wooden pillars and vaulting which are painted to imitate stone.*

The painted window, built in 1768, represents the Last Supper.

Main entrance

***The Great Hall,** hung with family portraits, is the highlight of the house, with the massive oak screen and elaborate hammerbeam roof surviving in their Jacobean form.*

Epping Forest 29

Essex. Chingford. Loughton, Theydon Bois. High Beach, Loughton (020-8508 0028).

As one of the large open spaces near London, the 2,400 ha (6,000 acre) forest is popular with walkers, just as, centuries ago, it was a favourite hunting ground for kings and courtiers – the word forest denoted an area for hunting.

Epping Forest contains oaks and beeches up to 400 years old

A depiction of the Battle of Maldon (991) on the *Maldon Embroidery*

Henry VIII had a lodge built in 1543 on the edge of the forest. His daughter Elizabeth I, also a keen hunter, often used the lodge and it soon became known as **Queen Elizabeth's Hunting Lodge**.

This three-storey timbered building has been fully renovated and now houses an exhibition explaining the lodge's history and other aspects of the forest's life.

The tracts of open land and woods interspersed with a number of lakes, make an ideal habitat for a variety of plant, bird and animal life: deer roam the northern part, many of a special dark strain introduced by James I. The Corporation of London bought the forest in the mid-19th century to ensure it remained open to the public.

Queen Elizabeth's Hunting Lodge

Rangers Rd, Chingford. 020-8529 6681. Wed–Sun (pm). 24–26 Dec, 1 Jan. limited. by appointment.

Maldon 30

Essex. 21,000. Chelmsford then bus. Coach Lane (01621 856503). Thu, Sat. www.maldon.gov.uk

This delightful old town on the River Blackwater, its High Street lined with shops and inns from the 14th century on, was once an important harbour. One of its best-known industries is the production of Maldon sea salt, panned in the traditional way.

A fierce battle here in 991, when Viking invaders defeated the Saxon defenders, is told in *The Battle of Maldon,* one of the earliest known Saxon poems. The battle is also celebrated in the *Maldon Embroidery* on display in the **Maeldune Centre**. This 13 m (42 ft) long embroidery, made by locals, depicts the history of Maldon from 991 to 1991.

Environs: East of Maldon at Bradwell-on-Sea is the sturdy Saxon church of **St Peter's-on-the-Wall**, a simple stone building that stands isolated on the shore. It was built in 654, from the stones of a former Roman fort, by St Cedd, who used it as his cathedral. It was restored in the 1920s.

Maeldune Centre

High St. 01621 851628. Oct–Mar: Thu–Sat; Apr–Sep: Mon–Sat; pm only. 24–26 Dec, 1 Jan.

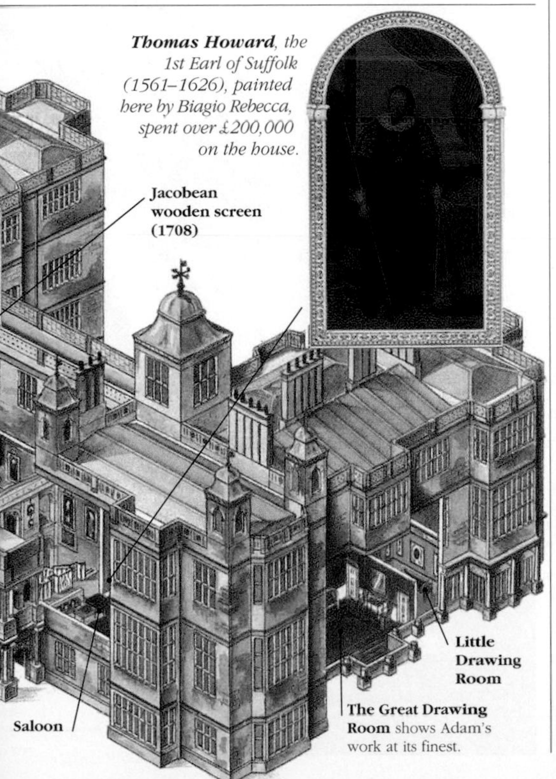
Thomas Howard, the 1st Earl of Suffolk (1561–1626), painted here by Biagio Rebecca, spent over £200,000 on the house.
Jacobean wooden screen (1708)
Little Drawing Room
The Great Drawing Room shows Adam's work at its finest.
Saloon

Street-by-Street: Cambridge 27

Carving, King's College Chapel

CAMBRIDGE HAS BEEN an important town since Roman times as it was sited at the first navigable point on the River Cam. In the 11th century religious orders began to be established in the town and, in 1209, a group of religious scholars broke away from Oxford University *(see pp210–15)* after academic and religious disputes and came here. Student life dominates the city but it is also a thriving market centre serving a rich agricultural region.

Cyclists in Cambridge

Magdalene Bridge carries Bridge Street across the Cam from the city centre to Magdalene College.

St John's College has superb Tudor and Jacobean architecture.

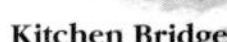
Kitchen Bridge

★ Bridge of Sighs
Built in 1831 in imitation of its namesake in Venice, it is best viewed from the Kitchen Bridge.

Trinity College

Trinity Avenue Bridge

The Backs
This is the name given to the grassy strip lying between the backs of the big colleges and the banks of the Cam – a good spot to enjoy this classic view of King's College Chapel.

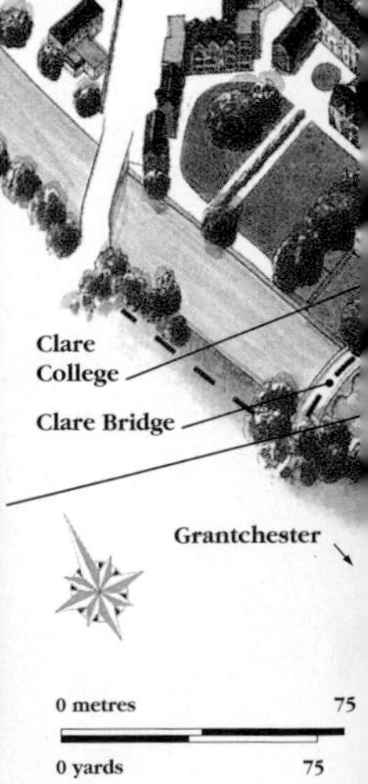

Clare College

Clare Bridge

Grantchester

KEY

— — — Suggested route

0 metres 75

0 yards 75

STAR SIGHTS

★ Bridge of Sighs

★ King's College Chapel

Round Church
The 12th-century Church of the Holy Sepulchre has one of the few round naves in the country. Its design is based on the Holy Sepulchre in Jerusalem.

St Mary's Church
This clock is over the west door of the university's official church. Its tower offers fine views.

Visitors' Checklist

Cambridgeshire. *120,000.* *Stansted.* *Cambridge.* *Station Rd.* *Drummer St.* *Wheeler St (0906 5862526).* *daily.* *Folk Festival: July; Strawberry Fair: June.* www.tourismcambridge.com

Gonville and Caius (pronounced "keys"), founded in 1348, is one of the oldest colleges.

★ King's College Chapel
This late medieval masterpiece took 70 years to build (see pp200–1).

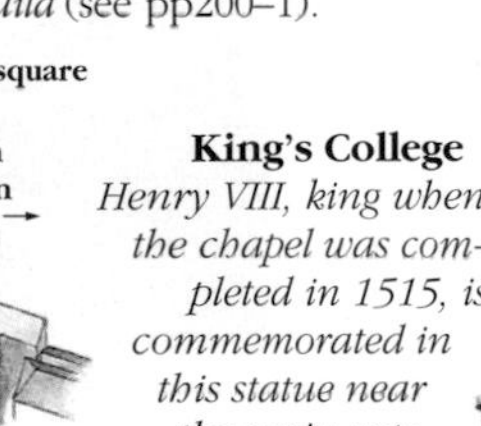

King's College
Henry VIII, king when the chapel was completed in 1515, is commemorated in this statue near the main gate.

Queens' College
Its Tudor courts are among the university's finest. This 17th-century sundial is over the old chapel – now a reading room.

Corpus Christi College

To London and railway station

Mathematical Bridge
Linking the two parts of Queens' College across the Cam, the bridge was first built without nuts or bolts.

Fitzwilliam Museum
Trumpington St. 01223 332900. Tue–Sun; public hols. 24 Dec–1 Jan. Good Fri, May Day. **Donation**. Sun pm.
www.fitzmuseum.cam.ac.uk

One of Britain's oldest public museums, this massive Classical building has works of exceptional quality and rarity, especially antiquities, ceramics, paintings and manuscripts.

The core of the collection was bequeathed in 1816 by the 7th Viscount Fitzwilliam. Other gifts have since greatly added to the exhibits.

Works by Titian (1488–1576) and the 17th-century Dutch masters, including Hals, Cuyp and Hobbema's *Wooded Landscape* (1686), stand out among the paintings. French Impressionist gems include Monet's *Le Printemps* (1866) and Renoir's *La Place Clichy* (1880), while Picasso's *Still Life* (1923) is notable among the modern works. Most of the important British artists are represented, from Hogarth in the 18th century through Constable in the 19th to Ben Nicholson in the 20th.

The miniatures include the earliest surviving depiction of Henry VIII. In the same gallery are some dazzling illuminated manuscripts, notably the 15th-century *Metz Pontifical*, a French liturgical work.

The impressive Glaisher collection of European earthenware and stoneware includes a unique display of English delftware from the 16th and 17th centuries.

Handel's bookcase contains folios of his work, and nearby is Keats's original manuscript for *Ode to a Nightingale* (1819).

Portrait of Richard James (c.1740s) by William Hogarth

Cambridge: King's College

King's College Coat of Arms

Henry VI founded this college in 1441. Work on the chapel – one of the most important examples of late medieval English architecture – began five years later, and took 70 years to complete. Henry himself decided that it should dominate the city and gave specific instructions about its dimensions: 88 m (289 ft) long, 12 m (40 ft) wide and 29 m (94 ft) high. The detailed design is thought to have been by master stonemason Reginald Ely, although it was altered in later years.

★ Fan Vaulted Ceiling
This awe-inspiring ceiling, supported by 22 buttresses, was built by master stonemason John Wastell in 1515.

The Fellows' Building was designed in 1724 by James Gibbs, as part of an uncompleted design for a Great Court.

Henry VI's statue
This bronze statue of the college's founder was erected in 1879.

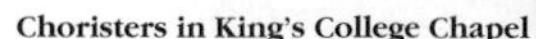

King's College Choir

When he founded the chapel, Henry VI stipulated that a choir of six lay clerks and 16 boy choristers – educated at the College school – should sing daily at services. This still happens in term time but today the choir also gives concerts all over the world. Its broadcast service of carols has become a much-loved Christmas tradition.

Choristers in King's College Chapel

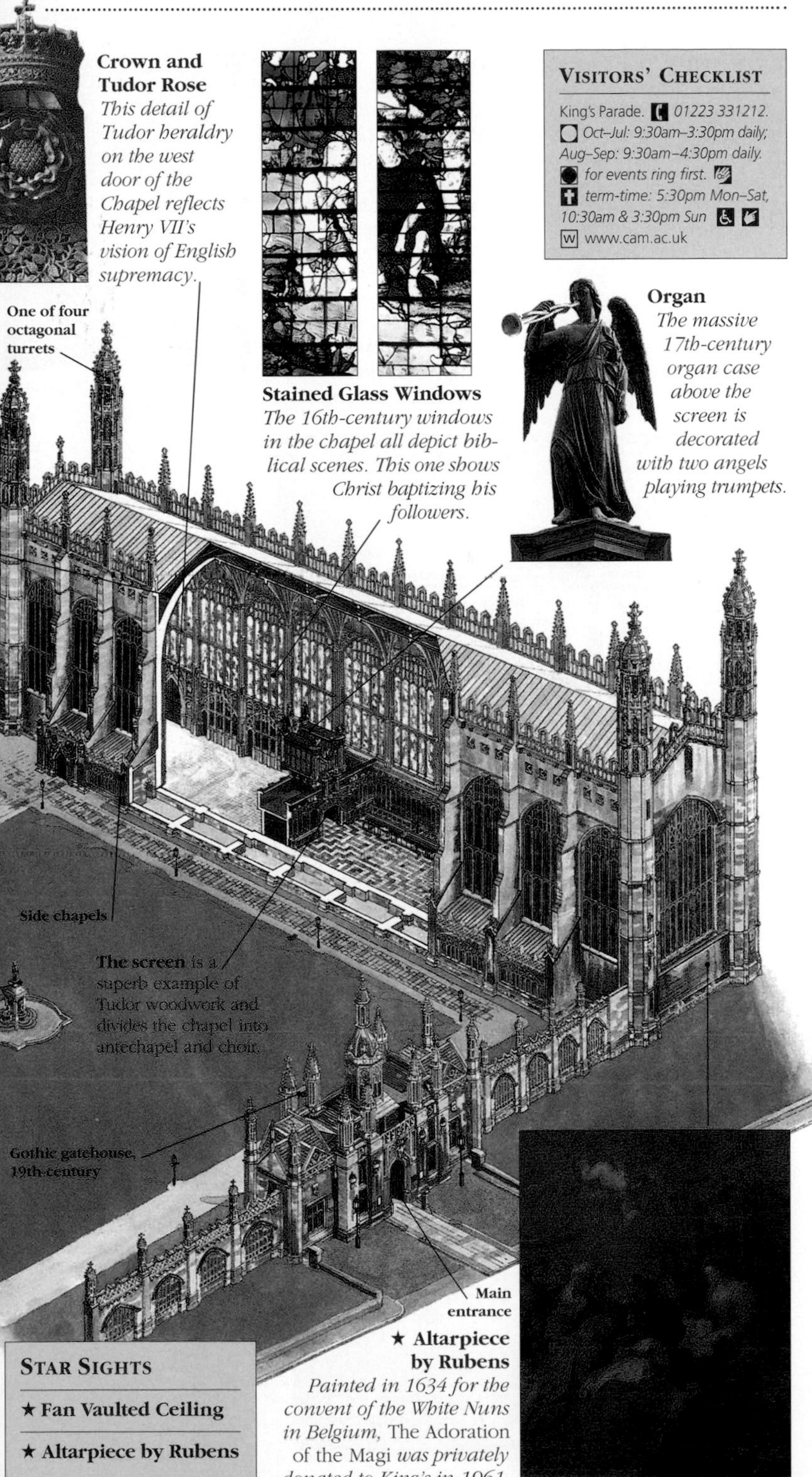

Crown and Tudor Rose
This detail of Tudor heraldry on the west door of the Chapel reflects Henry VII's vision of English supremacy.

Stained Glass Windows
The 16th-century windows in the chapel all depict biblical scenes. This one shows Christ baptizing his followers.

Organ
The massive 17th-century organ case above the screen is decorated with two angels playing trumpets.

The screen is a superb example of Tudor woodwork and divides the chapel into antechapel and choir.

★ Altarpiece by Rubens
Painted in 1634 for the convent of the White Nuns in Belgium, The Adoration of the Magi *was privately donated to King's in 1961.*

Visitors' Checklist

King's Parade. 01223 331212.
Oct–Jul: 9:30am–3:30pm daily; Aug–Sep: 9:30am–4:30pm daily.
for events ring first.
term-time: 5:30pm Mon–Sat, 10:30am & 3:30pm Sun
www.cam.ac.uk

Star Sights

★ **Fan Vaulted Ceiling**

★ **Altarpiece by Rubens**

Exploring Cambridge University

CAMBRIDGE UNIVERSITY HAS 31 COLLEGES *(see also pp198–9)*, the oldest being Peterhouse (1284) and the newest being Robinson (1979). Clustered around the city centre, many of the older colleges have peaceful gardens backing onto the River Cam, which are known as the "Backs". The layout of the older colleges, as at Oxford *(see pp214–15)*, derives from their early connections with religious institutions, although few escaped heavy-handed modification in the Victorian era. The college buildings are generally grouped around squares called courts and offer an unrivalled mix of over 600 years of architecture from the late medieval period through Wren's masterpieces and up to the present day.

The imposing façade of Emmanuel College

Emmanuel College

Built in 1677 on St Andrew's Street, Sir Christopher Wren's *(see p116)* chapel is the highlight of the college. Some of the intricate interior details, particularly the plaster ceiling and Amigoni's altar rails (1734), are superb. Founded in 1584, the college has a Puritan tradition. One notable graduate was the clergyman John Harvard, who emigrated to America in 1636 and left all his money to the Massachusetts college that now bears his name.

Senate House

King's Parade is the site of this Palladian building, which is used primarily for university ceremonies. It was designed by James Gibbs in 1722 as part of a grand square of university buildings – which was never completed.

Corpus Christi College

Just down from Senate House, this was founded in 1352 by the local trade guilds, anxious to ensure that education was not the sole prerogative of church and nobility. Its Old Court is remarkably well preserved and looks today much as it would have done when built in the 14th century.

The college is connected by a 15th-century gallery of red brick to St Bene't's Church (short for St Benedict's), whose large Saxon tower is the oldest structure in Cambridge.

The nave of the Wren Chapel at Pembroke College

King's College

See pp200–1.

Pembroke College

The college chapel was the first building completed by Wren *(see pp116–17)*. A formal classical design, it replaced a 14th-century chapel that was turned into a library. The college, just off Trumpington Street, also has fine gardens.

Jesus College

Although founded in 1497, some of its buildings on Jesus Lane are older, as the college took over St Radegond's nunnery, built in the 12th century. There are traces of Norman columns, windows and a well-preserved hammerbeam roof in the college dining hall.

The chapel keeps the core of the original church but the stained glass windows are modern and contain work by William Morris *(see pp208–9)*.

Queens' College

Built in 1446 on Queens' Land, the college was endowed in 1448 by Margaret of Anjou, queen of Henry VI, and again in 1465 by Elizabeth Woodville, queen of Edward IV, which explains the position of the apostrophe. Queens' has a

PUNTING ON THE CAM

Punting captures the essence of carefree college days: a student leaning on a long pole, lazily guiding the flat-bottomed river craft along, while others stretch out and relax. Punting is still popular both with students and visitors, who can hire punts from boatyards along the river – with a chauffeur if required. Punts do sometimes capsize, and novices should prepare for a dip.

Punting by the King's College "Backs"

marvellous collection of Tudor buildings, notably the half-timbered President's Gallery, built in the mid-16th century on top of the brick arches in the charming Cloister Court. The Principal Court is 15th century, as is Erasmus's Tower, named after the Dutch scholar.

Pepys Library in Magdalene College

The college has buildings on both sides of the Cam, linked by the bizarre Mathematical Bridge, built in 1749 to hold together without the use of nuts and bolts – although they have had to be used in subsequent repairs.

Magdalene College

Pronounced "maudlin" – as is the Oxford college *(see p214)* – the college, on Bridge Street, was established in 1482. The diarist Samuel Pepys (1633–1703) was a student here and left his large library to the college on his death. The 12 red-oak bookcases have over 3,000 books. Magdalene was the last all-male Cambridge college and it admitted women students only in 1987.

St John's College

Sited on St John's Street, the imposing turreted brick and stone gatehouse of 1514, with its colourful heraldic symbols, provides a fitting entrance to the second largest Cambridge college and its rich store of 16th- and 17th-century build-s. Its hall, most of it lizabethan, has portraits of the college's famous alumni, such as the poet William Wordsworth *(see p354)* and the statesman Lord Palmerston. St John's spans the Cam and boasts two bridges, one built in 1712 and the other, the Bridge of Sighs, in 1831, based on its Venetian namesake.

Peterhouse

The first Cambridge college, on Trumpington Street, is also one of the smallest. The hall still has original features from 1286 but its best details are later – a Tudor fireplace which is backed with 19th-century tiles by William Morris *(see pp208–9)*. A gallery connects the college to the 12th-century church of St Mary the Less, which used to be called St Peter's Church – hence the college's name.

William Morris tiles, Peterhouse

> **Visitors' Checklist**
>
> **Cambridge Colleges** can usually be visited from 2–5pm daily, but there are no set opening hours. See noticeboards at each college for daily opening times. Some colleges charge admission.

Trinity College

The largest college, situated on Trinity Street, was founded by Henry VIII in 1547 and has a massive court and hall. The entrance gate, with statues of Henry and James I (added later), was built in 1529 for King's Hall, an earlier college incorporated into Trinity. The Great Court features a late Elizabethan fountain – at one time the main water supply. The chapel, built in 1567, has life-size statues of college members, notably Roubiliac's statue of the scientist Isaac Newton (1755).

University Botanic Garden

A delightful place for a leisurely stroll, just off Trumpington Street, as well as an important academic resource, the garden has been on this site since 1846. It has a superb collection of trees and a sensational water garden. The winter garden is one of the finest in the country.

The Bridge of Sighs over the River Cam, linking the buildings of St John's College

THAMES VALLEY

BUCKINGHAMSHIRE · OXFORDSHIRE · BERKSHIRE
BEDFORDSHIRE · HERTFORDSHIRE

THE MIGHTY TIDAL RIVER *on which Britain's capital city was founded has modest origins, meandering from its source in the hills of Gloucestershire through the lush countryside towards London. Almost entirely agricultural land in the 19th century, the Thames Valley maintains its pastoral beauty despite the incursion of modern industry.*

There are ancient royal connections with the area. Windsor Castle has been a residence of kings and queens for more than 900 years, and played a critical role in history in 1215, when King John set out from here to sign the *Magna Carta* at Runnymede on the River Thames. Further north, Queen Anne had Blenheim Palace built for her military commander, the 1st Duke of Marlborough. Elizabeth I spent part of her childhood at Hatfield House, and part of the Tudor palace still stands.

Several towns in this region, most notably Burford in Oxfordshire, developed as coach staging posts on the important trunk routes between London and the West Country. With the introduction of commuter transportation in the early 20th century, much of the area became an extension of suburbia and saw some imaginative experiments in Utopian town planning such as the garden city of Welwyn and the Quaker settlement at Jordons.

Oxford, the Thames Valley's principal city, owes its importance to the foundation of Britain's first university there in 1167; many of its colleges are gems of medieval architecture. In the 17th century, a number of battles during the Civil War *(see p52)* were fought around Oxford, which for a time was the headquarters of King Charles I, who was supported by the students. When the royalists were forced to flee Oxford, Cromwell made himself chancellor of the university.

Punting on the River Cherwell, Oxford

◁ **Medieval staircase in Christchurch College, Oxford**

Exploring the Thames Valley

THE PLEASANT COUNTRYSIDE of the Chiltern Hills and of the Thames Valley itself appealed to aristocrats who built stately homes close to London. Many of these are among the grandest in the country, including Hatfield House and Blenheim. Around these great houses grew picturesque villages, with half-timbered buildings and, as you move towards the Cotswolds, houses built in attractive buff-coloured stone. That the area has been inhabited for thousands of years is shown by the number of prehistoric remains, including the most remarkable chalk hillside figure, the White Horse of Uffington.

Sights at a Glance

Blenheim Palace pp216–17 6
Burford 2
Gardens of the Rose 14
Great Tew 1
Hatfield House 12
Hughendon Manor 15
Kelmscott 3
Knebworth House 11
Oxford pp210–15 5
St Albans 13
Stowe 7
Vale of the White Horse 4
Waddesdon Manor 9
Whipsnade Wild Animal Park 10
Windsor pp223–5 17
Woburn Abbey 8

Walks and Tours

Touring the Thames 16

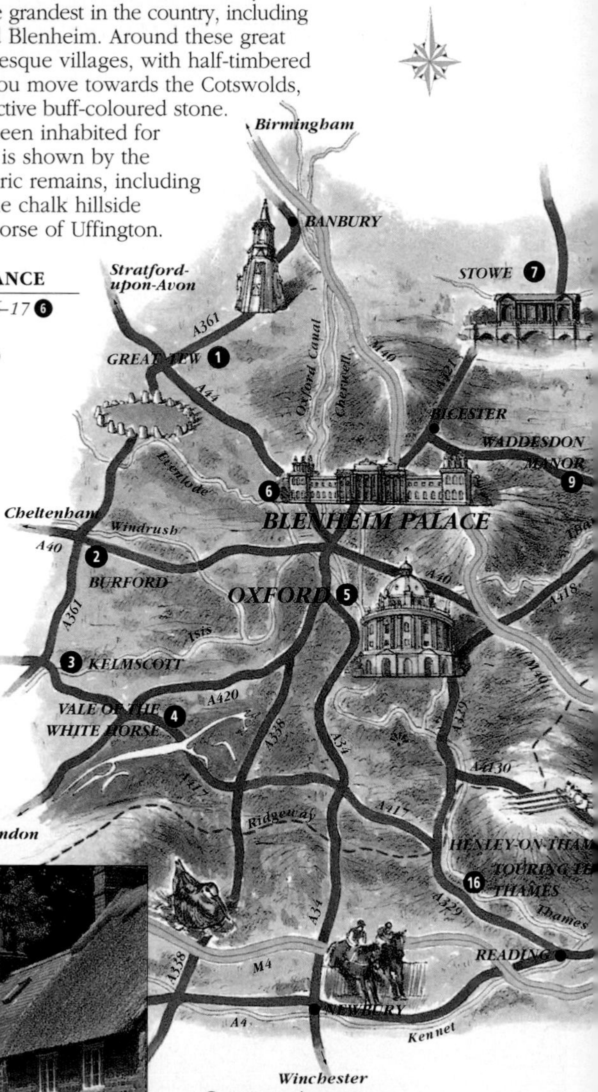

A thatched cottage, Upper Swarford, Banbury

Getting Around

As an important commuter belt, the Thames Valley is well served by public transport, as well as a good network of motorways and major roads into London. Mainline trains travel to all the major towns and there are many coach services that run from London to the major sights and attractions.

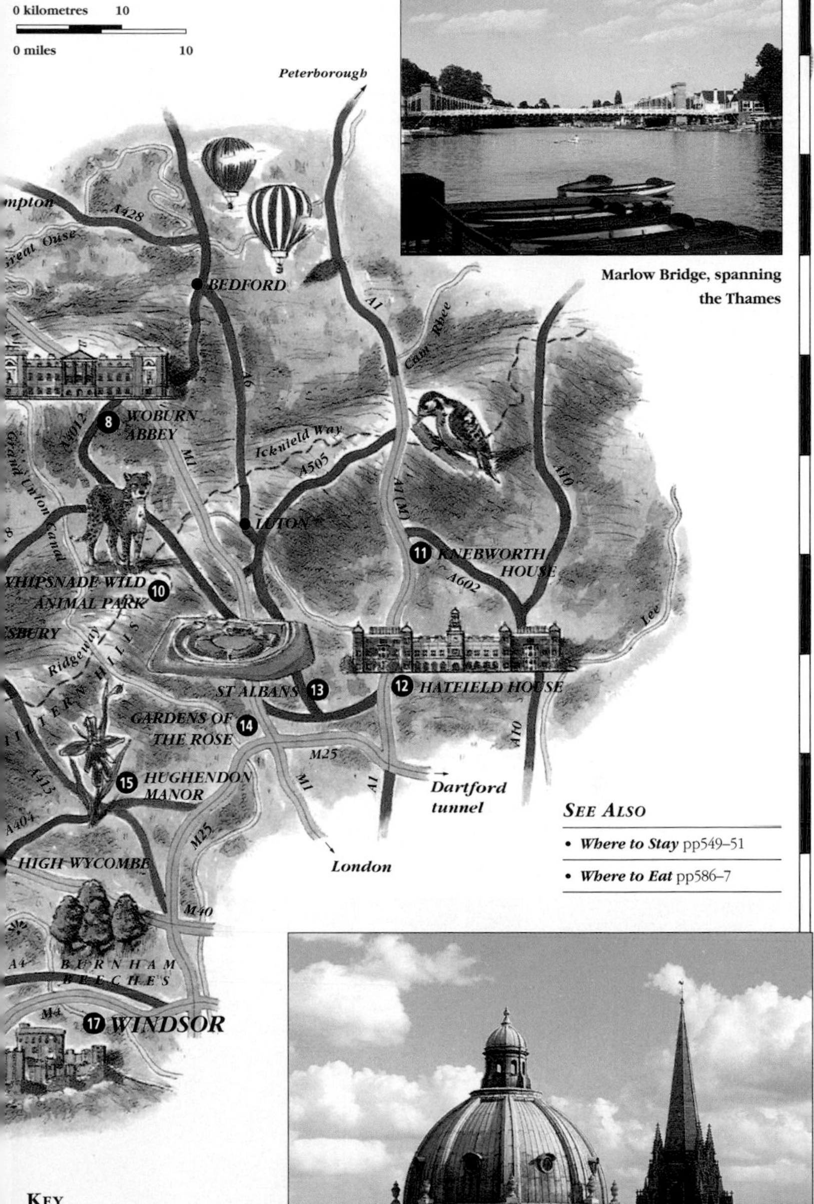

Marlow Bridge, spanning the Thames

SEE ALSO

- ***Where to Stay*** pp549–51
- ***Where to Eat*** pp586–7

KEY

- Motorway
- Major road
- Scenic route
- Scenic path
- River
- Viewpoint

Radcliffe Camera, surrounded by Oxford's spires

Great Tew ❶

Oxfordshire. 250. *Oxford or Banbury then taxi.* *Spiceball Park Rd, Banbury (01295 259855).* www.banburytown.co.uk

THIS SECLUDED village of ironstone was founded in the 1630s by Lord Falkland for estate workers. It was heavily restored between 1809 and 1811 in the Gothic style. Thatched cottages stand in gardens with clipped box hedges, and in the centre of the village is the 16th-century pub, the **Falkland Arms**, which retains its original period atmosphere.

ENVIRONS: Five miles (8 km) west are the **Rollright Stones**, three Bronze Age monuments. They comprise a stone circle of 77 stones, about 30 m (100 ft) in diameter, known as the King's Men; the remains of a burial chamber called the Whispering Knights; and the solitary King Stone.

Further north is **Banbury**, well known for its spicy flat cakes and its market cross, immortalized in the nursery rhyme, *Ride a Cock-horse to Banbury Cross*. The original medieval cross was destroyed but it was replaced in 1859.

The 19th-century Banbury Cross

Falkland Arms
Great Tew. *01608 683653.* *daily.* *25 Dec.*

Burford ❷

Oxfordshire. *1,000.* *Sheep St (01993 823558).*

A CHARMING SMALL town, Burford has hardly changed from Georgian times, when it was an important coach stop between Oxford and the West Country. Cotswold stone houses, inns and shops, many built in the 16th century, line its main street. **Tolsey Hall** is a Tudor house with an open ground floor where stalls are still set up. The house is located on the corner of Sheep Street, itself a reminder of the importance of the medieval wool trade *(see p195)*.

ENVIRONS: Just east of Burford is **Swinbrook**, whose church contains the Fettiplace Monuments, six carved figures from the Tudor and Stuart periods. Two miles (3 km) beyond are the ruins of **Minster Lovell Hall**, a 15th-century manor house whose unusual dovecote survives intact.

Witney, further west, has a town hall dating from 1730. On its outskirts lies **Cogges Manor Farm**, a working farm and museum of rural life, restored to its Victorian state.

Minster Lovell Hall
Minster Lovell. *daily.*

Cogges Manor Farm
Witney. *01993 772602.* *mid-Mar–Nov: Tue–Sun (Sat & Sun pm) & public hols.* *limited.*

Kelmscott ❸

Oxfordshire. *100.* *7a Market Place, Faringdon (01367 242191).* www.faringdon.org

THE IMAGINATIVE designer and writer William Morris lived in this pretty Thameside village from 1871 until his death in 1896. He shared his house, the classic Elizabethan **Kelmscott Manor**, with fellow painter Dante Gabriel Rossetti (1828–82), who left after an affair with Morris's wife Jane – the model for many pre-Raphaelite paintings.

Morris and his followers in the Arts and Crafts movement were attracted by the

Cotswold stone houses, Burford, Oxfordshire

The formal entrance of the Elizabethan Kelmscott Manor

medieval feel of the village and several cottages were later built in Morris's memory.

Today Kelmscott Manor has works of art by members of the movement – including some William de Morgan tiles. Morris is buried in the village churchyard, with a tomb designed by Philip Webb.

Two miles (3 km) to the east is **Radcot Bridge**, thought to be the oldest bridge still standing over the Thames. Built in the 13th century from the local Taynton stone, it was a strategic river crossing, and in 1387 was damaged in a battle between Richard II and his barons.

Kelmscott Manor
Kelmscott. 01367 252486.
Apr–Jun, Sep: Wed, 3rd Sat; Jul–Aug: Wed, 1st & 3rd Sat. *limited.*
www.kelmscottmanor.co.uk

Vale of the White Horse ❹

Oxfordshire. *Didcot.* *25 Bridge St, Abingdon (01235 522711); 19 Church St, Wantage (01235 760176).*

This lovely valley gets its name from the huge chalk horse, 100 m (350 ft) from nose to tail, carved into the hillside above Uffington. It is believed to be Britain's oldest hillside carving and has sparked many legends: some say it was cut by the Saxon leader Hengist (whose name means stallion in German), while others believe it is to do with Alfred the Great, thought to have been born nearby.

It is, however, a great deal older than either of these stories suggest, having been dated at around 1000 BC.

Nearby is the Celtic earth ramparts of the Iron Age hill fort, **Uffington Castle**. A mile (1.5 km) west along the Ridgeway, an ancient trade route, *(see p33)*, is an even older monument, a large Stone Age burial mound which is known as **Wayland's Smithy**. This is immersed in legends that Sir Walter Scott *(see p498)* used in his novel *Kenilworth*.

The best view of the horse is to be had from Uffington village, which is also worth visiting for the **Tom Brown's School Museum**. This 17th-century school house contains exhibits devoted to the author Thomas Hughes (1822–96). Hughes set the early chapters of his Victorian novel, *Tom Brown's Schooldays*, here. The museum also contains material about excavations on White Horse Hill.

Tom Brown's School
Broad St, Uffington. *01367 820259.* *Easter–Oct: Sat, Sun & public hols (pm).* *limited.*
www.uffington.net/museum

Hillside Chalk Figures

It was the Celts who first saw the potential for creating large-scale artworks on the chalk hills of southern England. Horses – held in high regard by both the Celts and later the Saxons, and the objects of cult worship – were often a favourite subject, but people were also depicted, notably Cerne Abbas, Dorset *(see p257)* and the Long Man of Wilmington *(see p168)*. The figures may have served as religious symbols or as landmarks by which tribes identified their territory. Many chalk figures have been obliterated, because without any attention they are quickly overrun by grass. Uffington is "scoured", to prevent encroachment by grass, a tradition once accompanied by a fair and other festivities. There was a second flush of hillside carving in the 18th century, especially in Wiltshire. In some cases – for instance at Bratton Castle near Westbury – an 18th-century carving has been superimposed on an ancient one.

Britain's oldest hillside carving, the White Horse of Uffington

Street-by-Street: Oxford 5

Oxford has long been a strategic point on the western routes into London – its name describes its position as a convenient spot for crossing the river (a ford for oxen). The city's first scholars, who founded the university, came from France in 1167. The development of England's first university created the spectacular skyline of tall towers and "dreaming spires".

Old Ashmolean
Now the Museum of the History of Science, this resplendent building was designed in 1683 to show Elias Ashmole's collection of curiosities. The displays were moved in 1845.

The Ashmolean Museum displays one of Britain's foremost collections of fine art and antiquities.

Martyrs' Memorial
This commemorates the three Protestant martyrs, Latimer, Ridley and Cranmer, who were burned at the stake for heresy.

0 metres 100

0 yards 100

Key

– – – Suggested route

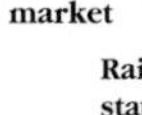

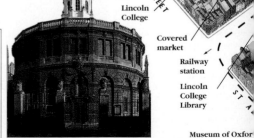

Sheldonian Theatre
The first building designed by Wren (see p116) *is the scene of Oxford University's traditional graduation ceremonies.*

Percy Bysshe Shelley

Shelley (1792–1822), one of the Romantic poets *(see p354)*, attended University College, Oxford, but was expelled after writing the revolutionary pamphlet *The Necessity of Atheism*. Despite that disgrace, the college has put up a marble memorial to him.

Star Sights

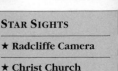

★ **Radcliffe Camera**

★ **Christ Church**

★ Radcliffe Camera
This Classical rotunda is Oxford's most distinctive building and is now a reading room of the Bodleian. It was one of the library's original buildings (see p215).

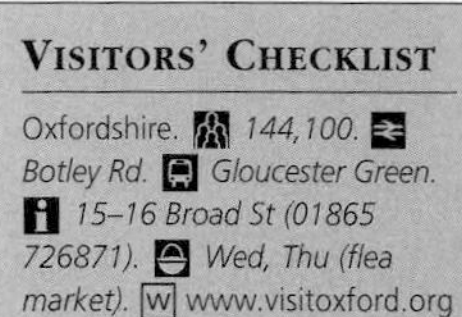

Visitors' Checklist

Oxfordshire. 144,100. Botley Rd. Gloucester Green. 15–16 Broad St (01865 726871). Wed, Thu (flea market). www.visitoxford.org

Bridge of Sighs
A copy of the steeply arched bridge in Venice, this picturesque landmark, built in 1914, joins the old and new buildings of Hertford College.

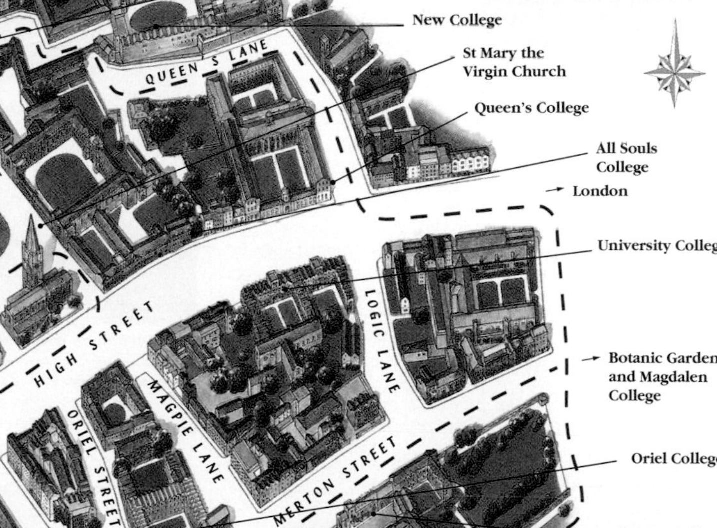

★ Christ Church
Students still eat at long tables in all the college halls. Senior academics sit at the high table and grace is always said in Latin.

A bust on the Sheldonian Theatre

Exploring Oxford

Oxford is more than just a university city; it has one of Britain's most important car factories in the suburb of Cowley. Despite this, Oxford is dominated by institutions related to its huge academic community: like Blackwell's bookshop which has over 20,000 titles in stock. The two rivers, the Cherwell and the Isis (the name given to the Thames as it flows through the city), provide lovely riverside walks, or you can hire a punt and spend an afternoon on the Cherwell.

Ashmolean Museum

Beaumont St. 01865 278000. *Tue–Sun (Sun pm only) & public hols.* *1 Jan, Good Fri, 25–28 Dec.* *Tue, Fri, Sat.* www.ashmole.ox.ac.uk

One of the best museums in Britain outside London, the Ashmolean – the first purpose-built museum in England – opened in 1683, based on a display known as "The Ark" collected by the two John Tradescants, father and son.

On their many voyages to the Orient and the Americas they collected stuffed animals and tribal artifacts, the like of which had never before been displayed in England. The collection was acquired on their death by the antiquarian Elias Ashmole, who donated it to the university and had a building made for the exhibits on Broad Street – the Old Ashmolean, now the Museum of the History of Science.

During the 19th century part of the Tradescant collection was moved to the University Galleries, a magnificent Neo-Classical building of 1845. This greatly expanded museum is now known as the Ashmolean.

However, what is left of the original curio collection is overshadowed by the other exhibits in the museum, in particular the paintings and drawings. These include Bellini's *St Jerome Reading in a Landscape* (late 15th century); Raphael's *Heads of Two Apostles* (1519); Turner's *Venice: The Grand Canal* (1840); Rembrandt's *Saskia Asleep* (1635); Michelangelo's *Crucifixion* (1557), Picasso's *Blue Roofs* (1901) and a large group of Pre-Raphaelites, including Rossetti, Millais and Holman Hunt. There are also fine Greek and Roman carvings and a collection of stringed musical instruments.

The entrance to the Ashmolean Museum

Items of more local interest include a Rowlandson watercolour of Radcliffe Square in about 1790 and the Oxford Crown. This silver coin was minted here during the Civil War in 1644 *(see p52)* when Charles I was based in Oxford, and forms part of the second largest coin collection in Britain. Perhaps the single most important item is the gold enamelled ring known as the Alfred Jewel *(see p47)*, which is over 1,000 years old.

Botanic Garden

Rose Lane. *01865 286690.* *daily.* *25 Dec, Good Fri.* *Apr–Aug.* **Donation** *Sep–Mar.* www.botanic-garden.ox.ac.uk

Britain's oldest botanic garden was founded in 1621 – one ancient yew tree survives from that period. The entrance gates were designed by Nicholas Stone in 1633 and paid for, like the garden itself, by the Earl of Danby. His statue adorns the gate, along with those of Charles I and II. This small garden is a delightful spot for a stroll, with well-labelled flower beds in the original walled garden and a newer section with a herbaceous border and rock garden.

The 17th-century Botanic Gardens

Carfax Tower

Carfax Sq. *01865 792653.* *Apr–Oct daily.*

The tower is all that remains of the 14th-century Church of St Martin, demolished in 1896 so that the adjoining road could be widened. Be there to watch the clock strike the quarter hours, and climb to the top for a panoramic view of the city. Carfax was the crossing point of the original north-to-south and east-to-west routes through Oxford and the word comes from the French *quatre voies*, or "four ways".

Holywell Music Room

Holywell St. *concerts only.*

This was the first building in Europe designed, in 1752, specifically for public musical performances. Previously, concerts had been held in private houses for invited guests only. Its two splendid chandeliers originally adorned Westminster Hall at the coronation of George IV in 1820, and were given by the king to Wadham College, of which the music room technically forms a part. The room is regularly used for contemporary and classical concerts.

Museum of Oxford

St Aldate. *01865 815559.* *Tue–Sun.* *25, 26 Dec, 1 Jan.*

A well-organized display in the Victorian town hall illustrates the long history of Oxford and its university. Exhibits include a Roman pottery kiln and a town seal from 1191.

The main features are a series of well-reconstructed rooms, including one from an Elizabethan inn and an 18th-century student's room.

Martyrs' Memorial

Magdalen St.

This commemorates the three Protestants burned at the stake on Broad Street – Bishops Latimer and Ridley in 1555, and Archbishop Cranmer in 1556. On the accession of Queen Mary in 1553 *(see p51)*, they were committed to the Tower of London, then sent to Oxford to defend their views before the doctors of divinity who, after the hearing, condemned them as heretics.

The memorial was designed in 1843 by George Gilbert Scott and based on the Eleanor crosses erected in 12 English towns by Edward I (1239–1307) to honour his queen.

Oxford Story

6 Broad St. *01865 728822.* *daily.* *25 Dec.* *limited.*

This audio-visual account of the city's history has a train ride through exhibits which are brought to life with animated, life-size models of major historical characters.

St Mary the Virgin Church

High St. *01865 279111.* *daily.* *Good Fri, 25, 26 Dec.*

www.university-church.ox.ac.uk

This, the official church of the university, is said to be the most visited parish church in England. The oldest parts date from the early 13th century and include the tower, from the top of which you can enjoy a fine view. Its Convocation House, of the same date, served as the university's first library until the Bodleian was founded in 1488 *(see p215)*. The church is where the three Oxford Martyrs were pronounced heretics in 1555. An architectural highlight of the church is the Baroque south porch.

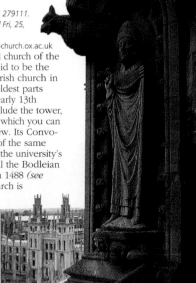

Thomas Cranmer statue, St Mary the Virgin Church

University Museum

Parks Rd. *01865 272950.* *daily (pm).* *24–26 Dec, Easter.*

www.oum.ox.ac.uk

Pitt Rivers Museum

Parks Rd. *01865 270927.* *daily (pm).* *24–26 Dec, Easter.*

www.prm.ox.ac.uk

Two of Oxford's most interesting museums adjoin each other. The first is a museum of natural history containing relics of dinosaurs as well as a stuffed dodo. This flightless bird has been extinct since the 17th century, but was immortalized by Lewis Carroll (an Oxford mathematics lecturer whose real name was Charles Dodgson) in his book *Alice in Wonderland (see p387)*. The exhibits are housed in a large Victorian building with cast-iron columns which support a glass roof leading to a cavernous interior. This leads into the Pitt Rivers Museum, which has one of the world's most extensive ethnographic collections – masks and totems from Africa and the Far East – and archaeological displays, including exhibits collected by the explorer Captain Cook.

Sheldonian Theatre

Broad St. *01865 277299.* *call for details.* *Christmas period, Easter & public hols.* *limited.*

www.sheldon.ox.ac.uk

Completed in 1669, this building was designed by Sir Christopher Wren *(see p116)*. It was paid for by Gilbert Sheldon, the Archbishop of Canterbury, as a place to hold university degree ceremonies. The Classical design of the D-shaped building is based on the Theatre of Marcellus in Rome. The octagonal cupola – larger than the original – was built in 1838 and there is a very famous view from its huge Lantern. In the theatre the beautifully painted ceiling depicts the triumph of religion, art and science over envy, hatred and malice.

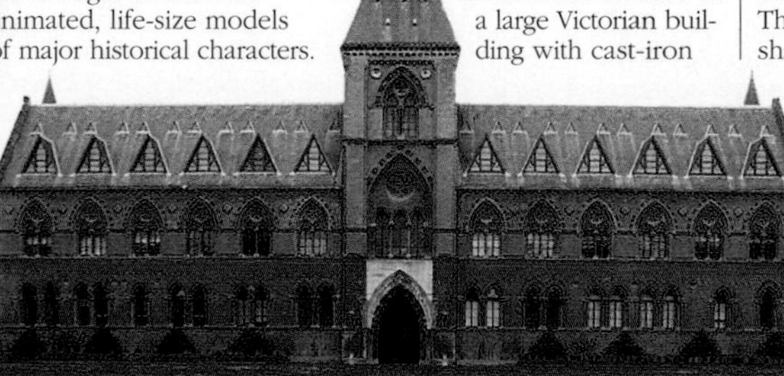

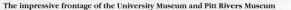

The impressive frontage of the University Museum and Pitt Rivers Museum

Exploring Oxford University

MANY OF THE 36 COLLEGES which go to make up the university were founded between the 13th and 16th centuries and cluster around the city centre. As scholarship was then the exclusive preserve of the church, the colleges were designed along the lines of monastic buildings but were often surrounded by beautiful gardens. Although most colleges have been altered over the years, many still incorporate a lot of their original features.

The spectacular view of All Souls College from St Mary's Church

All Souls College
Founded in 1438 on the High Street by Henry VI, the chapel on the college's north side has a classic hammerbeam roof, unusual misericords *(see p329)* on the choir stalls and 15th-century stained glass.

Christ Church College
The best way to view this, the largest of the Oxford colleges, is to approach through the meadows from St Aldate's. Christ Church dates from 1525 when Cardinal Wolsey founded it as an ecclesiastical college to train cardinals. The upper part of the tower in Tom Quad – a rectangular courtyard – was built by Wren *(see p116)* in 1682 and is the largest in the city. When its bell, Great Tom, was hung in 1648, the college had 101 students, which is why the bell is rung 101 times at 9:05pm, to mark the curfew for students (which has not been enforced since 1963). The odd timing is because night falls here five minutes later than at Greenwich *(see p133)*. Christ Church has produced 16 British prime ministers in the last 200 years. Beside the main quad is the 12th-century Christ Church Cathedral, one of the smallest in England.

Lincoln College
One of the best-preserved of the medieval colleges, it was founded in 1427 on Turl Street, and the front quad and façade are 15th century. The hall still has its original roof, including the gap where smoke used to escape. The Jacobean chapel is notable for its stained glass. John Wesley *(see p267)* was at college here and his rooms, now a chapel, can be visited.

Magdalen College
At the end of the High Street is perhaps the most typical and beautiful Oxford college. Its 15th-century quads in contrasting styles are set in a park by the Cherwell, crossed by Magdalen Bridge. Every May Day at 6am, the college choir sings from the top of Magdalen's bell tower (1508) – a 16th-century custom to mark the start of summer.

New College
One of the grandest colleges, it was founded by William of Wykeham in 1379 to educate clergy to replace those killed by the Black Death of 1348 *(see p49)*.

Magdalen Bridge spanning the River Cherwell

Its magnificent chapel on New College Lane, restored in the 19th century, has vigorous 14th-century misericords and El Greco's (1541–1614) famous painting of *St James*.

Queen's College
Most of the college buildings date from the 18th century and represent some of the finest work from that period in Oxford. Its superb library was built in 1695 by Henry Aldrich (1647–1710) The front screen with its bell-topped gatehouse is a feature of the High Street.

Student Life

Students belong to individual colleges and usually live in them for the duration of their course. The university gives lectures, sets exams and awards degrees but much of the students' tuition and social life is based around their college. Many university traditions date back hundreds of years, like the graduation ceremonies at the Sheldonian which are still held in Latin.

Graduation at the Sheldonian *(see p212)*

Merton College seen from Christ Church Meadows

St John's College
The impressive frontage on St Giles dates from 1437, when it was founded for Cistercian scholars. The old library has lovely 17th-century bookcases and stained glass, while the Baylie Chapel has a display of 15th-century vestments.

Trinity College
The oldest part of the college on Broad Street, Durham Quad, is named after the earlier college of 1296 which was incorporated into Trinity in 1555. The late 17th-century chapel has a magnificent reredos and wooden screen.

Corpus Christi College
The whole of the charming front quad on Merton Street dates from 1517, when the college was founded. The quad's sundial, topped by a pelican – the college symbol – bears an early 17th-century calendar. The chapel has a rare 16th-century eagle lectern.

Visitors' Checklist

Oxford Colleges can usually be visited from 2–5pm daily all year, but there are no set opening hours. See noticeboards outside each college entrance to check opening times.
Bodleian Library (Duke Humphrey's Library & Divinity School), Broad St. *01865 277224. 9am–4:30pm Mon–Fri, 9am–12:30pm Sat. 24 Dec–2 Jan, Easter, last week Aug.* www.bodley.ox.ac.uk

Merton College
Off Merton Street, this is the oldest college (1264) in Oxford. Much of its hall dates from then, including a sturdy decorated door. The chapel choir contains allegorical reliefs representing music, arithmetic, rhetoric and grammar. Merton's Mob Quad served as a model for the later colleges.

Bodleian Library

Founded in 1320, the library was expanded in 1426 by Humphrey, Duke of Gloucester (1391–1447) and brother of Henry V, when his collection of manuscripts would not fit into the old library. It was refounded in 1602 by Thomas Bodley, a wealthy scholar, who insisted on strict rules: the keeper was forbidden to marry. The library is one of the six copyright deposit libraries in the country – it is entitled to receive a copy of every book published in Britain.

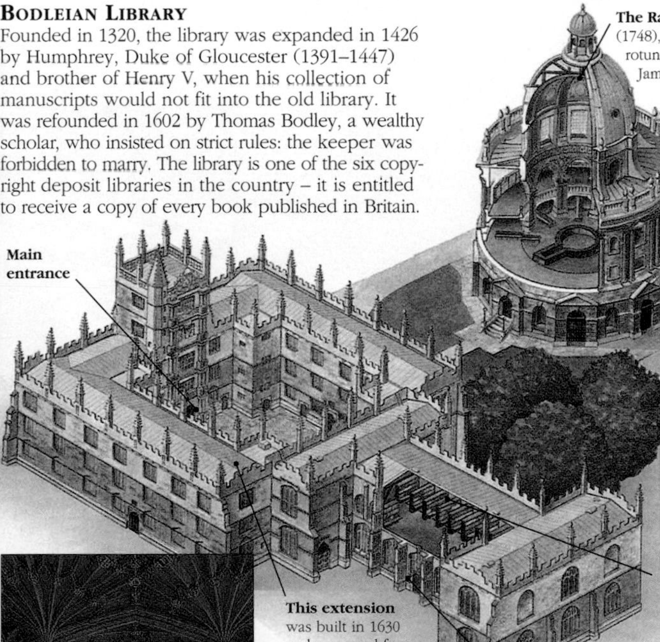

The Radcliffe Camera (1748), a domed Baroque rotunda, was built by James Gibbs as a memorial to the physician Dr John Radcliffe (1650–1714).

Main entrance

This extension was built in 1630 and was used for university exams until 1880.

The Divinity School *(1488) has a unique vaulted ceiling with 455 carved bosses representing biblical scenes and both mythical and real beasts – one of the country's finest Gothic interiors.*

Duke Humphrey's Library *(1602) has ceiling panels that carry the university crest and Latin motto* Dominus Illuminatio Mea – *the Lord, my Light.*

Blenheim Palace 6

After John Churchill, the 1st Duke of Marlborough, defeated the French at the Battle of Blenheim in 1704, Queen Anne gave him the Manor of Woodstock and had this palatial house built for him in gratitude. Designed by both Nicholas Hawksmoor and Sir John Vanbrugh *(see p384)*, it is a Baroque masterpiece. It was also the birthplace of Britain's World War II leader, Winston Churchill, in 1874.

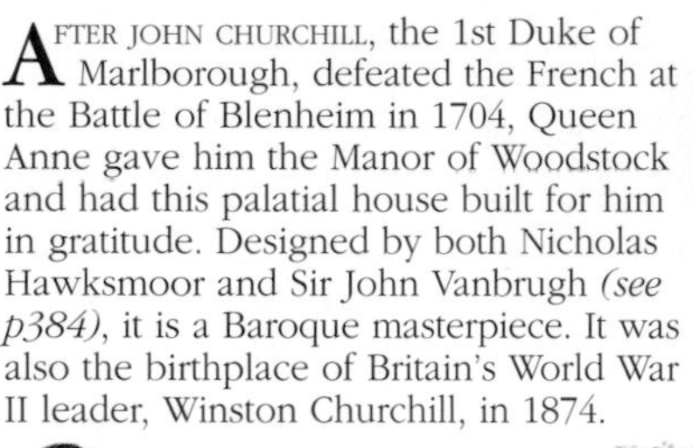

★ Long Librar
This 55 m (183
room was desig
by Vanbrugh a
picture gallery.
portraits includ
of Queen Anne
Sir Godfrey Kn
(1646–1723).
stucco on the
ceiling is by Isa
Mansfield (172

Winston Churchill and his wife, Clementine

The Grand Bridge was built in 1708. It has a 31 m (101 ft) main span and contains rooms within its structure.

Chapel
The marble monument to the 1st Duke of Marlborough and his family was sculpted by Michael Rysbrack in 1733.

Water Terrace Gardens
These magnificent gardens were laid out in the 1920s by French architect Achille Duchêne in 17th-century style, with detailed patterned beds and fountains.

Star Sights

- ★ **Long Library**
- ★ **Saloon**
- ★ **Park and Gardens**

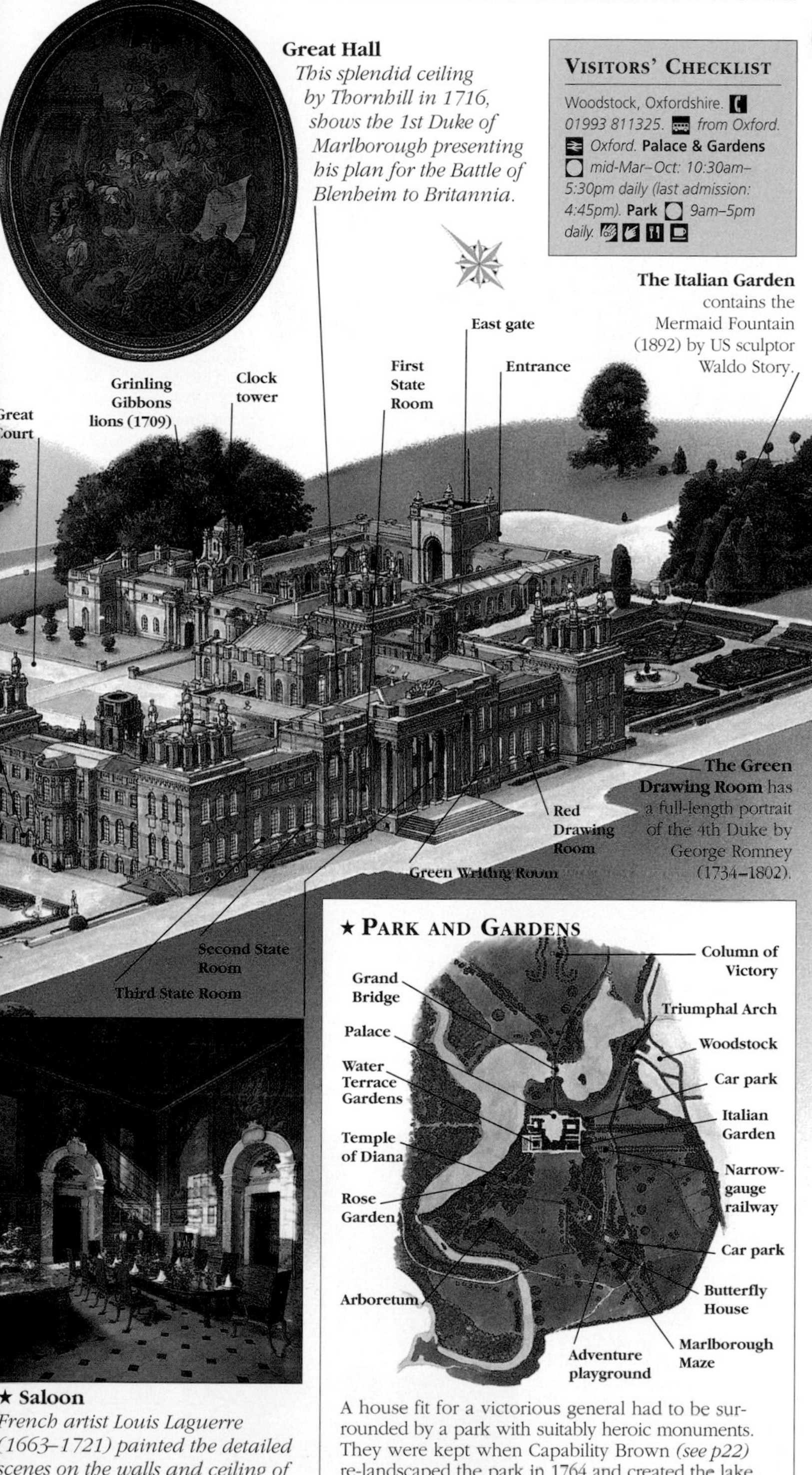

Great Hall
This splendid ceiling by Thornhill in 1716, shows the 1st Duke of Marlborough presenting his plan for the Battle of Blenheim to Britannia.

VISITORS' CHECKLIST
Woodstock, Oxfordshire. 01993 811325. *from Oxford.* *Oxford.* **Palace & Gardens** *mid-Mar–Oct: 10:30am–5:30pm daily (last admission: 4:45pm).* **Park** *9am–5pm daily.*

The Italian Garden contains the Mermaid Fountain (1892) by US sculptor Waldo Story.

The Green Drawing Room has a full-length portrait of the 4th Duke by George Romney (1734–1802).

★ Saloon
French artist Louis Laguerre (1663–1721) painted the detailed scenes on the walls and ceiling of the state dining room.

A house fit for a victorious general had to be surrounded by a park with suitably heroic monuments. They were kept when Capability Brown *(see p22)* re-landscaped the park in 1764 and created the lake.

Canaletto's *Entrance to the Arsenal* (1730) hangs at Woburn Abbey

Stowe 7

(NT) Buckingham, Buckinghamshire. *01280 822850. Milton Keynes then bus. Mar–22 Dec: Wed–Sun, public hols.* *limited.* www.nationaltrust/stowegardens

This is the most ambitious and important landscaped garden in Britain, as well as being one of the finest examples of the 18th-century passion for improving on nature to make it conform to fashionable notions of taste.

In the space of nearly 100 years the original garden, first laid out around 1680, was enlarged and transformed by the addition of monuments, Greek and Gothic temples, grottoes, statues, ornamental bridges, artificial lakes and "natural" tree plantings.

Most of the leading designers and architects of the period contributed to the design, including Sir John Vanbrugh, James Gibbs and Capability Brown *(see p22)*, who was head gardener at Stowe for 10 years, at the start of his career.

From 1593 to 1921 the huge property was owned by the Temple and Grenville families – later the Dukes of Buckingham – until the large Palladian house at its centre was sold and converted into an elite boys' public school (tours can be arranged in school holidays).

The family were soldiers and politicians in the liberal tradition, and many of the buildings and sculptures in the garden symbolize Utopian ideals of democracy and freedom. There are temples of British Worthies, of Ancient Virtue and the Fane (temple) of Pastoral Poetry. Some features deteriorated in the 19th century and statues were sold. But a major restoration programme has meant that statues have been bought back and copies made of others.

Woburn Abbey 8

Woburn, Bedfordshire. *01525 290666. Flitwick then taxi. Apr–Sep: daily; Jan–Mar, Oct: Sat, Sun.* *ring first.* *by arrangement.* www.woburnabbey.co.uk

The Dukes of Bedford have lived here for over 350 years and were among the first owners of an English stately home to open their house to the public some 40 years ago.

The abbey was built in the mid-18th century on the foundations of a large 12th-century Cistercian monastery. Its mix of styles range from Henry Flitcroft and Henry Holland *(see p24)*. It is also popular for its 142 ha (350 acre) safari park and attractive deer park with nine species including the Manchurian Sika deer from China.

Its magnificent state apartments house an important private art collection with works by Reynolds (1723–92) and Canaletto (1697–1768).

Waddesdon Manor 9

nr Aylesbury, Buckinghamshire. *01296 653 203. Aylesbury then taxi.* **House** *Apr–Oct: 11am–4pm Wed–Sun & bank hol Mon.* **Grounds** *Mar–23 Dec: 10am–5pm Wed–Sun & bank hol Mon.* **Bachelors' Wing** *Mar–Oct: 11am–4pm Wed–Fri.* www.waddesdon.org.uk

Waddesdon Manor was built between 1874–89 by Baron Ferdinand de Rothschild and designed by French architect Gabriel-Hippolyte Destailleur. The garden was originally laid out by French landscape gardener Elie Lainé.

Built in the style of a French 16th-century chateau, Waddesdon Manor houses one of the world's finest collections of French 18th-century decorative art. It also contains renowned collections of French furniture, Savonnierie carpets, Sèvres porcelain and 17th-century paintings.

The garden is renowned for its seasonal displays and over the next five years, displays are being designed by contemporary artists. Wine tasting events are also hosted in the comprehensive Wine Cellars.

The 17th-century Palladian bridge over the Octagon Lake in Stowe Park

Hatfield House, one of the largest Jacobean mansions in the country

Whipsnade Wild Animal Park ⓾

Nr Dunstable, Bedfordshire. *01582 872171. Hemel Hempsted then bus or Whipsnade (from Victoria Station, London) daily.* www.whipsnade.co.uk

THE RURAL BRANCH of London Zoo, this was one of the first zoos to minimize the use of cages, confining animals safely but without constriction.

At 240 ha (600 acres), it is Europe's largest conservation park, with more than 2,500 species. You can drive through some areas or go by steam train. Also popular are the adventure playground and sea lions' underwater display.

Knebworth House ⓫

Knebworth, Hertfordshire. *01438 812661. Stevenage then taxi. Sat, Sun; two weeks at Easter: daily; Jul–Sep: daily. limited.* www.knebworthhouse.com

A NOTABLE TUDOR mansion, with a beautiful Jacobean banqueting hall, Knebworth was overlain with a 19th-century Gothic exterior by Lord Lytton, the head of one of the most colourful families in Victorian England.

His eldest son, the 1st Earl of Lytton, was Viceroy of India, and several exhibits illustrate the Delhi Durbar of 1877, when Queen Victoria became Empress of India.

Hatfield House ⓬

Hatfield, Hertfordshire. *01707 287010. Hatfield. Easter Sat–Sep: daily.* www.hatfield-house.co.uk

ONE OF ENGLAND'S finest Jacobean houses, it was built between 1607 and 1611 for the powerful statesman Robert Cecil.

Its chief historical interest, though, lies in the surviving wing of the original Tudor Hatfield Palace, where Queen Elizabeth I *(see pp50–51)* spent much of her childhood. She held her first Council of State here when she was crowned in 1558. The palace was partly demolished in 1607 to make way for the new house, which contains mementoes of her life, including the *Rainbow* portrait painted around 1600 by Isaac Oliver. Visitors can attend medieval banquets in the old palace's Great Hall.

Originally laid out by Robert Cecil with help from John Tradescant, the gardens have been restored to reflect these Jacobean origins.

FAMOUS PURITANS

18th-century engraving of John Bunyan

Three major figures connected with the 17th-century Puritan movement are celebrated in the Thames area. John Bunyan (1628–88), who wrote the allegorical tale *The Pilgrim's Progress*, was born at Elstow, near Bedford. A passionate Puritan orator, he was jailed for his beliefs for 17 years. The Bunyan Museum in Bedford is a former site of Puritan worship. William Penn (1644–1718), founder of Pennsylvania in the USA, lived, worshipped and is buried at Jordans, near Beaconsfield. A bit further north at Chalfont St Giles is the cottage where the poet John Milton (1608–74) stayed to escape London's plague. There he completed his greatest work, *Paradise Lost*. The house is now a museum based on his life and works.

William Penn, founder of Pennsylvania

John Milton painted by Pieter van der Plas

St Albans ⓭

The martyr St Albans

TODAY A THRIVING MARKET TOWN and a base for London commuters, St Albans was for centuries at the heart of some of the most stirring events in English history. A regional capital of ancient Britain, it became a major Roman settlement and then a key ecclesiastical centre – so important that during the Wars of the Roses *(see p49)*, two battles were fought for it. In 1455 the Yorkists drove King Henry VI from the town and six years later the Lancastrians retook it.

Exploring St Albans

Part of the appeal of this ancient and fascinating town, little more than an hour's drive from London, is that its 2,000-year history can be traced vividly by visiting a few sites within easy walking distance of one another. There is a large car park within the walls of the Roman city of Verulamium, between the museum and St Michael's Church and across the road from the excavated theatre. From there it is a pleasant lakeside walk across the park, passing more Roman sites, Ye Olde Fighting Cocks inn, the massive cathedral and the historic High Street. Marking the centre of the town, the High Street is lined with several Tudor buildings and a clock tower dating from 1412, from which the curfew bell used to ring at 4am in the morning and 8:30pm at night.

Verulamium

Just outside the city centre are the walls of Verulamium, one of the first British cities the Romans established after their invasion of Britain in AD 43. Boadicea *(see p183)* razed it to the ground during her unsuccessful rebellion against the Romans in AD 62, but its position on Watling Street, an important trading route, meant that it was quickly rebuilt on an even larger scale and the city flourished until 410.

Verulamium Museum

St Michael's. 01727 751810.
daily. 25, 26 Dec.
www.stalbansmuseum.org.uk

This excellent museum tells the story of the city, but its main attraction is its splendid collection of well-preserved Roman artefacts, notably some breathtaking mosaic floors, including one depicting the head of a sea god, and another of a scallop shell. Other finds included burial urns and lead coffins.

On the basis of excavated plaster fragments, a Roman room has been painstakingly recreated, its walls painted in startlingly bright colours and geometric patterns.

Between here and St Albans Cathedral are a bath house with a mosaic, remnants of the ancient city wall and one of the original gates.

A scallop shell, one of the mosaic floors at the Verulamium Museum

Ye Olde Fighting Cocks

Abbey Mill Lane. 01727 869152.
daily. 25 Dec.

Believed to be England's oldest surviving pub, Ye Olde Fighting Cocks is certainly, with its octagonal shape, one of the most unusual. It originated as the medieval dovecote of the old abbey and moved here after the Dissolution *(see p50)*.

One of the oldest surviving pubs in England

Roman Theatre

St Michael's. 01727 835035.
daily. 25, 26 Dec.
www.romantheatre.co.uk

Just across the road from the museum are the foundations of the open-air theatre, first built around AD 140 but enlarged several times. It is one of only six known to have been built in Roman Britain. Alongside it are traces of a row of Roman shops and a house, from which many of the museum's treasures – such as a bronze statuette of Venus – were excavated in the 1930s.

St Michael's Church

St Michael's. 01727 835037.
Apr–Sep: phone for details.

This church was first founded during the Saxon reign and is built partly with bricks taken from Verulamium, which by then was in decline. Numerous additions have been made since then, including a truly splendid Jacobean pulpit.

The church contains an early 17th-century monument to the statesman and writer Sir Francis Bacon; his father owned nearby Gorhambury, a large Tudor house, now in ruins.

VISITORS' CHECKLIST

Hertfordshire. *125,000.*
Market Pl. (01727 864511).
www.stalbans.gov.uk

St Albans Cathedral

Sumpter Yard. *01727 860780.* *daily.* *11:30am & 2:30pm.*

This outstanding example of medieval architecture has some classic features such as the 13th- and 14th-century wall paintings on the Norman piers.

It was begun in 793, when King Offa of Mercia founded the abbey in honour of St Alban, Britain's first Christian martyr, put to death by the Romans in the third century for sheltering a priest. The oldest parts, which still stand, were first built in 1077 and are easily recognizable as Norman by the round-headed arches and windows. They form part of the 84 m (276 ft) nave – the longest in England.

The imposing west side of St Albans Cathedral

The pointed arches further east are Early English (13th century), while the decorated work of the 14th century was added when some of the Norman arches collapsed.

East of the crossing is what remains of St Alban's shrine – a marble pedestal made up of more than 2,000 tiny fragments. Next to it is the tomb of Humphrey, Duke of Gloucester *(see p215)*.

It was also here at the cathedral that the English barons drafted the *Magna Carta* document *(see p48)*, which King John was then forced to sign.

The splendour of the Gardens of the Rose in June

Gardens of the Rose 14

Chiswell Green, Hertfordshire. *01727 850461.* *St Albans then bus.* *Jun–Sep: 9am–5pm Mon–Sat, 10am–6pm Sun & public hols.* www.rosesociety.org.uk

As well as being England's national symbol, the rose is the most popular flower with British gardeners.

The 5 ha (12 acre) garden of the Royal National Rose Society, with over 30,000 plants and 1,700 varieties, is at its peak in late June. The gardens trace the history of the flower as far back as the white rose of York, the red rose of Lancaster *(see p49)* and the Rosa Mundi – named by Henry II for his mistress Fair Rosamond after she was poisoned by Queen Eleanor in 1177. The nuns who buried Rosamond implied in verse on her tomb that her reputation did not smell of roses.

Hughenden Manor 15

High Wycombe, Buckinghamshire. *01494 755565.* *High Wycombe then bus.* *Mar: Sat, Sun; Apr–Nov: Wed–Sun & public hols.* *Good Fri.* *limited.*

The Victorian statesman and novelist Benjamin Disraeli, Prime Minister from 1874 to 1880, lived here for 33 years until his death. Originally a Georgian villa, Disraeli adapted it in 1862 to the Gothic style. Furnished as it was in his day, the house gives an idea of the life of a wealthy Victorian gentleman and shows some portraits of his contemporaries.

GEORGE BERNARD SHAW

Although a controversial playwright and known as a mischievous character, the Irish-born George Bernard Shaw (1856–1950) was a man of settled habits. He lived near St Albans in a house at Ayot St Lawrence, now called Shaw's Corner, for the last 44 years of his life, working until his last weeks in a summer-house at the bottom of his large garden. His plays, combining wit with a powerful political and social message, still seem fresh today. One of the most enduring is *Pygmalion* (1913), on which the musical *My Fair Lady* is based. The house and garden are now a museum of his life and works.

Touring the Thames ⑯

The Thames between Pangbourne and Eton is leafy and romantic and best seen by boat. But if time is short, the road keeps close to its bank for much of the way. Swans glide gracefully below ancient bridges, voles dive into the water for cover, and elegant herons stand impassive at the river's edge. Huge beech trees overhang the banks which are lined with fine houses, their gardens sloping to the water. The tranquil scene has inspired painters and writers through the ages as well as operating, until recently, as an important transport link.

Hambledon Mill ⑥
The white weather-boarded mill, which was operational until 1955, is one of the largest on the Thames as well as one of the oldest in origin. There are traces of the original 16th-century mill.

Beale Park ①
The philanthropist Gilbert Beale (1868–1967) created a 10 ha (25 acre) park to preserve this beautiful stretch of river intact and breed endangered birds like owls, ornamental water fowl, pheasants and peacocks.

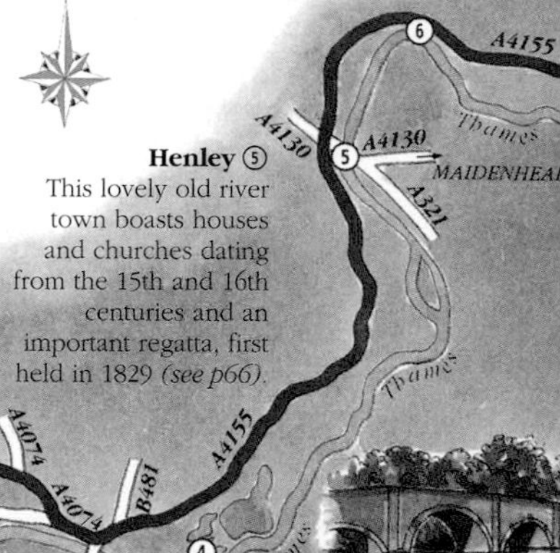

Henley ⑤
This lovely old river town boasts houses and churches dating from the 15th and 16th centuries and an important regatta, first held in 1829 *(see p66)*.

Pangbourne ②
Kenneth Grahame (1859–1932), author of *The Wind in the Willows*, lived here. Pangbourne was used as the setting by artists Ernest Shepard in 1908 and Arthur Rackham in 1951 to illustrate the book.

Sonning Bridge ④
The 18th-century bridge is made up of 11 brick arches of varying width.

Whitchurch Mill ③
This charming village, linked to Pangbourne by a Victorian toll bridge, has a picturesque church and one of the many disused watermills that once harnessed the power of this stretch of river.

Tips for Drivers

Tour length: *50 miles (75 km).*
Stopping-off points: *The picturesque town of Henley has a large number of riverside pubs which will make good stops for lunch. If you are boating you can often moor your boat alongside the river bank.* (See also pp636–7.)

Cookham ⑦
This is famous as the home of Stanley Spencer (1891–1959), one of Britain's leading 20th-century artists. The former Methodist chapel, where Spencer worshipped as a child, has been converted into a gallery that contains some of his paintings and equipment. This work, entitled *Swan Upping* (1914–19), recalls a Thames custom.

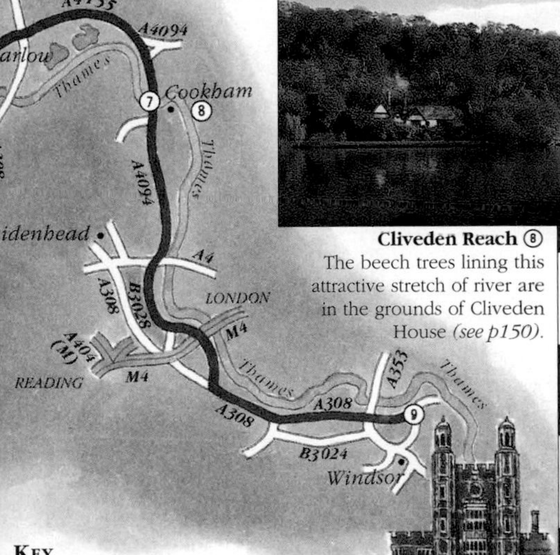

Cliveden Reach ⑧
The beech trees lining this attractive stretch of river are in the grounds of Cliveden House *(see p150)*.

Key

Tour route

Other roads

Viewpoint

0 kilometres 10

0 miles 5

Eton College ⑨
Founded by Henry VI in 1440, Eton is Britain's most famous public school. It has a superb Perpendicular chapel (1441) with a series of English wall paintings (1479–88).

Boating Tours

Salter Bros hire boats, moored at Henley

In summer, scheduled river services run between Henley, Windsor, Runnymede and Marlow. Several companies operate from towns along the route. You can hire boats by the hour or the day or, for a longer tour, you can rent cabin cruisers and sleep on board *(see also p641)*. Ring Salter Bros on 01753 865 832 for more information.

Windsor ⑰

Berkshire. *30,000.*
HighSt (01753 743900).
www.windsor.gov.uk

The town of Windsor is dwarfed by the enormous **castle** *(see pp224–5)* on the hill above – appropriately enough because its original purpose was to serve the castle's needs. The town is full of quaint Georgian shops, houses and inns. The most prominent building on the High Street is the **Guildhall** completed by Wren *(see p116)* in 1689. The **Household Cavalry Museum** has an extensive collection of arms and uniforms.

The huge 1,940-ha (4,800-acre) **Windsor Great Park** stretches straight from the castle three miles (5 km) to Snow Hill, where there is a statue of George III.

Environs: Four miles (7 km) to the southeast is the level grassy meadow known as **Runnymede**. This is one of England's most historic sites, where in 1215 King John was forced by his rebellious barons to sign the *Magna Carta (see p48)*, thereby limiting his royal powers. The dainty memorial pavilion at the top of the meadow was erected in 1957.

Household Cavalry Museum
St Leonard's Rd. *01753 755112.* *Mon–Fri.* *public hols.* **Donation**

King John signing the *Magna Carta*, Runnymede

Windsor Castle

Henry II rebuilt the castle

THE OLDEST CONTINUOUSLY inhabited royal residence in Britain, the castle, originally made of wood, was built by William the Conqueror in 1070 to guard the western approaches to London. He chose the site because it was on high ground and just a day's journey from his base in the Tower of London. Successive monarchs have made alterations that render it a remarkable monument to royalty's changing tastes. King George V's affection for it was shown when he chose Windsor for his family surname in 1917. The castle is an official residence of the Queen and her family who stay here many weekends.

Albert Memorial Chapel
First built in 1240, it was rebuilt in 1485 and finally converted into a memorial for Prince Albert in 1863.

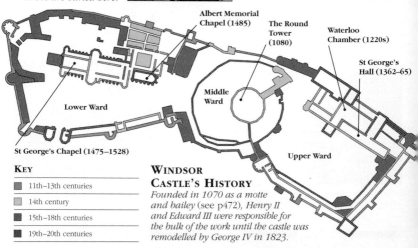

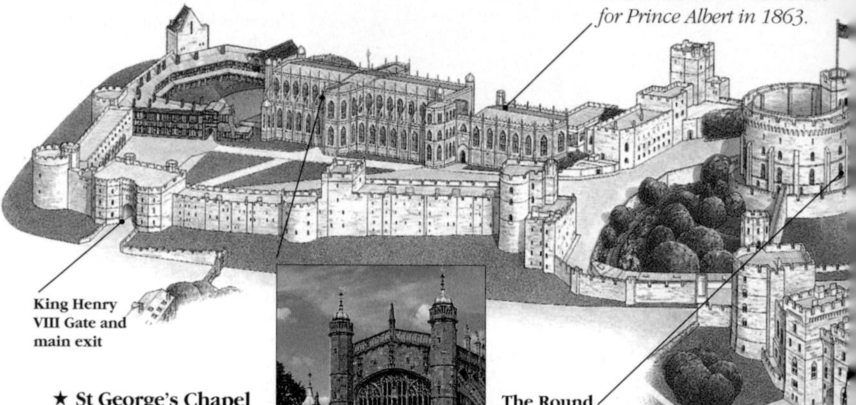

King Henry VIII Gate and main exit

★ St George's Chapel
The architectural highlight of the castle, it was built between 1475 and 1528 and is one of England's outstanding Perpendicular churches. Ten monarchs are buried here.

The Round Tower was first built in wood by William the Conqueror. In 1170 it was rebuilt in stone by Henry II *(see p48)*. It now houses the Royal Archives and Photographic Collection.

Statue of Charles II

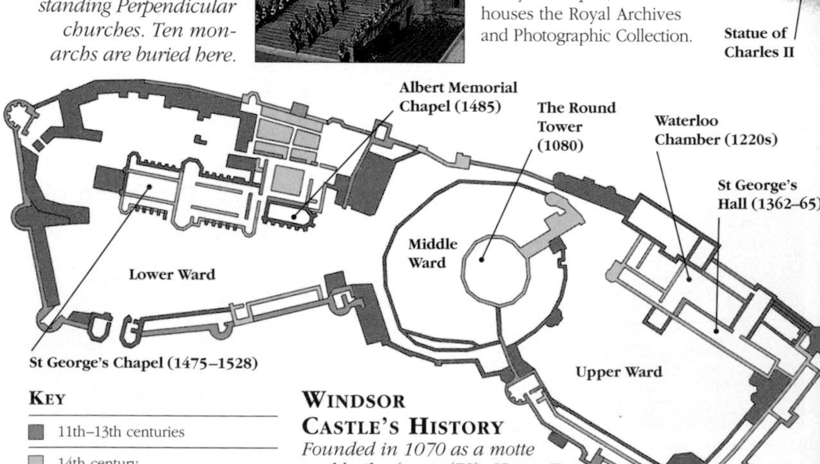

KEY

- 11th–13th centuries
- 14th century
- 15th–18th centuries
- 19th–20th centuries

WINDSOR CASTLE'S HISTORY
Founded in 1070 as a motte and bailey (see p472)*, Henry II and Edward III were responsible for the bulk of the work until the castle was remodelled by George IV in 1823.*

Drawings Gallery
This chalk etching of hrist by Michelangelo is part of the Royal Collection. Various pieces in the collection are on display here in changing exhibitions, including works by Holbein among others.

Visitors' Checklist

Castle Hill. 020-7321 2233. Mar–Oct: 9:45am–5:15pm; Nov– Feb: 9:45am–4:15pm daily (last adm: 3:15pm). 25, 26 Dec, Good Fri. St Georges Chapel: 5:15pm Mon–Sat, 8:30/10:45/11:45am, 5:15pm Sun.

Waterloo Chamber
The walls of this banqueting hall, first built in the 13th century, are lined with portraits of the leaders who played a part in Napoleon's defeat (see p55).

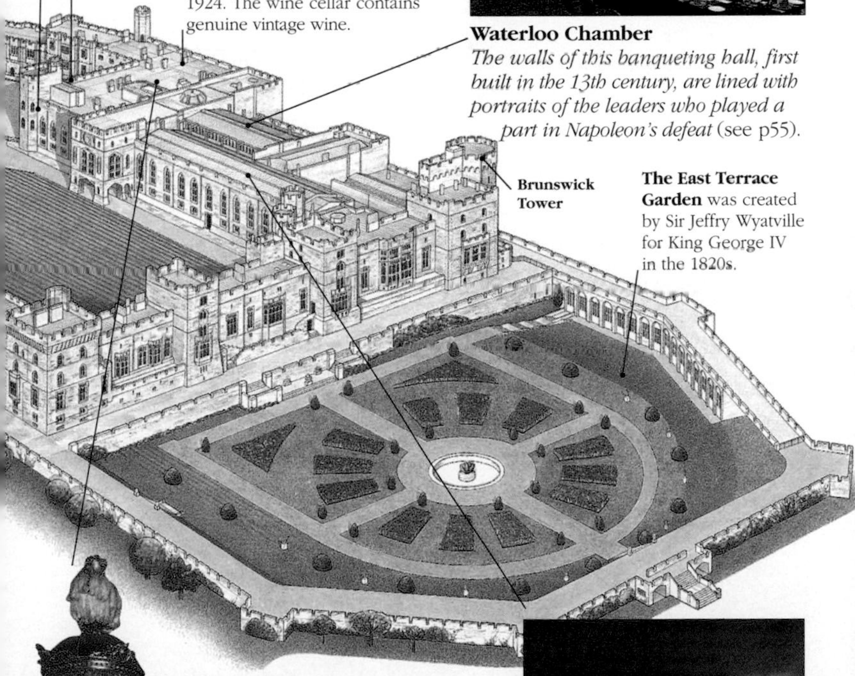

The Audience Chamber is where the Queen greets her guests.

The Queen's Ballroom

Queen Mary's Dolls' House, designed by Sir Edwin Lutyens, was given to Queen Mary in 1924. The wine cellar contains genuine vintage wine.

Brunswick Tower

The East Terrace Garden was created by Sir Jeffry Wyatville for King George IV in the 1820s.

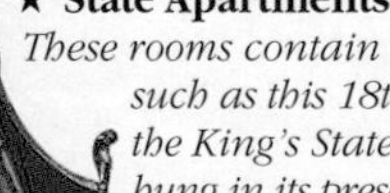

★ State Apartments
These rooms contain many treasures, such as this 18th-century bed in the King's State Bedchamber, hung in its present splendour for the visit in 1855 of Napoleon III.

Star Sights

- ★ **St George's Chapel**
- ★ **State Apartments**

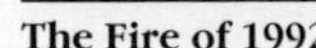

The Fire of 1992
A devastating blaze began during maintenance work on the State Apartments. St George's Hall was destroyed but has been rebuilt.

THE WEST COUNTRY

INTRODUCING THE WEST COUNTRY 228-233

WESSEX 234-259

DEVON AND CORNWALL 260-283

The West Country at a Glance

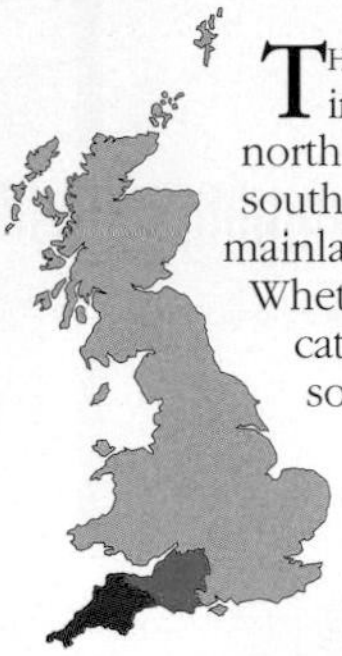

THE WEST COUNTRY forms a long peninsula bounded by the Atlantic to the north and the English Channel to the south, tapering down to Land's End, mainland Britain's westernmost point. Whether exploring the great cities and cathedrals, experiencing the awesome solitude of the moors and their prehistoric monuments, or simply enjoying the miles of coastline and mild climate, this region has an enduring appeal for holiday-makers.

***Wells** (see pp240–41) is a charming town nestling at the foot of the Mendip Hills. It is famous for its exquisite three-towered cathedral with an ornate west façade, featuring an array of statues. Alongside stand the moated Bishop's Palace and the 15th-century Vicar's Close.*

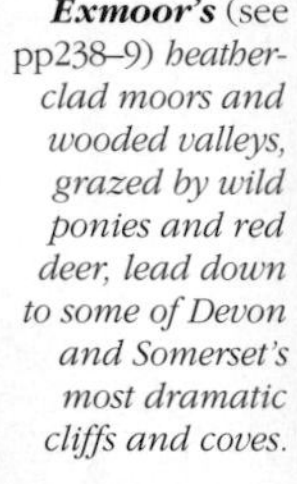

***Exmoor's** (see pp238–9) heather-clad moors and wooded valleys, grazed by wild ponies and red deer, lead down to some of Devon and Somerset's most dramatic cliffs and coves.*

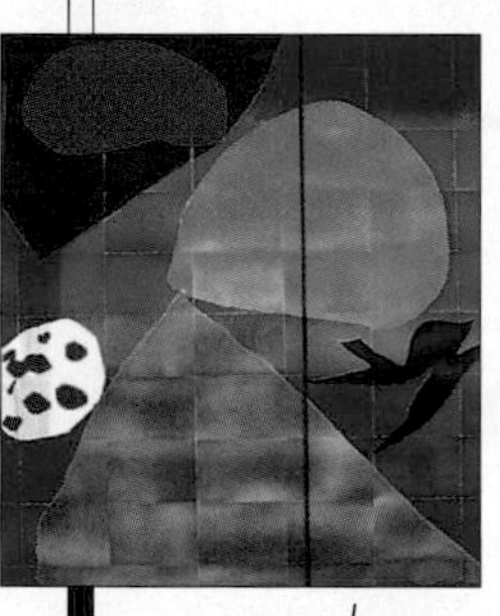

***St Ives** (see p265) has a branch of the Tate Gallery that shows modern works by artists associated with the area. Patrick Heron's bold coloured glass (1993) is on permanent display.*

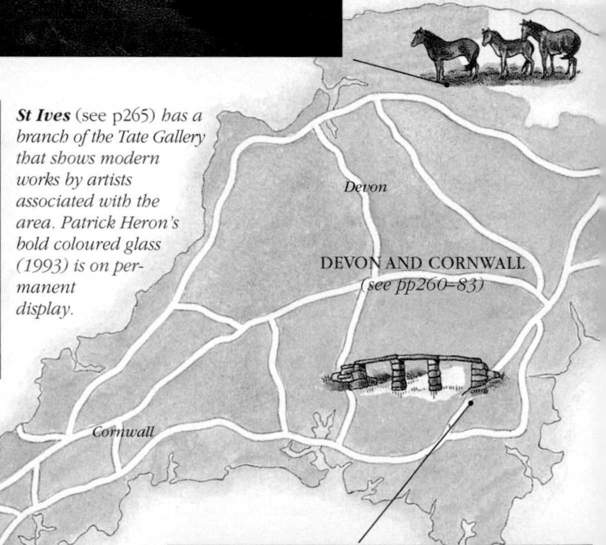

Devon

DEVON AND CORNWALL
(see pp260–83)

Cornwall

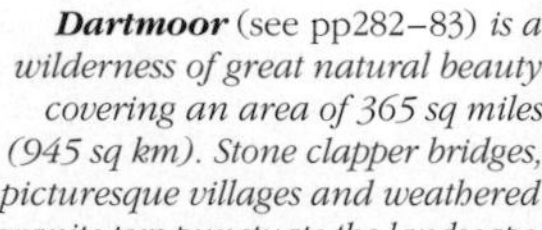

***Dartmoor** (see pp282–83) is a wilderness of great natural beauty covering an area of 365 sq miles (945 sq km). Stone clapper bridges, picturesque villages and weathered granite tors punctuate the landscape.*

◁ **Stunning views of the Lizard Peninsula**

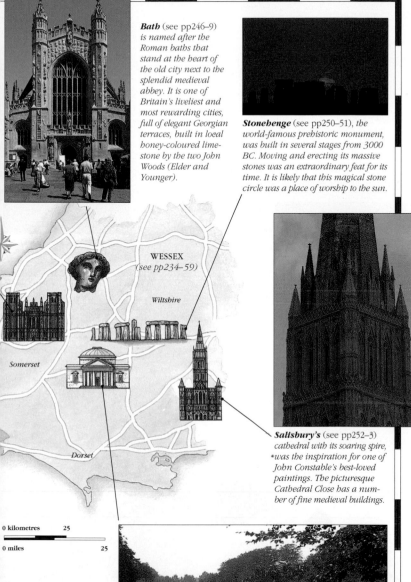

Bath (see pp246–9) *is named after the Roman baths that stand at the heart of the old city next to the splendid medieval abbey. It is one of Britain's liveliest and most rewarding cities, full of elegant Georgian terraces, built in local honey-coloured limestone by the two John Woods (Elder and Younger).*

Stonehenge (see pp250–51), *the world-famous prehistoric monument, was built in several stages from 3000 BC. Moving and erecting its massive stones was an extraordinary feat for its time. It is likely that this magical stone circle was a place of worship to the sun.*

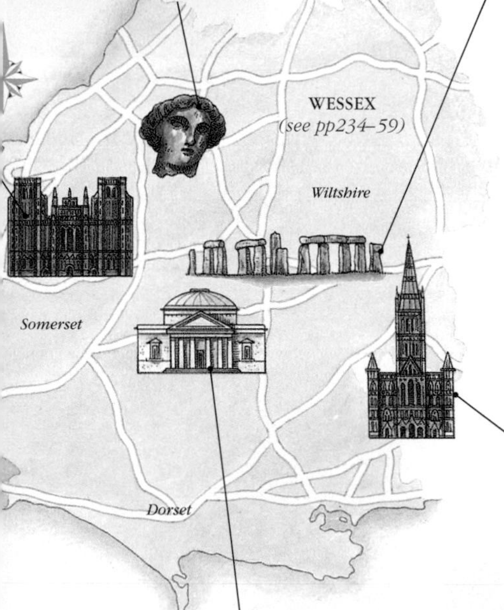

Salisbury's (see pp252–3) *cathedral with its soaring spire, was the inspiration for one of John Constable's best-loved paintings. The picturesque Cathedral Close has a number of fine medieval buildings.*

Stourhead *garden* (see pp254–5) *was inspired by the paintings of Claude and Poussin. Created in the 18th century, the garden is itself a work of art. Contrived vistas, light and shade and a mixture of landscape and gracious buildings, such as the Neo-Classical Pantheon at its centre, are vital to the overall effect.*

Coastal Wildlife

THE LONG AND VARIED West Country coastline, ranging from the stark, granite cliffs of Land's End to the pebble-strewn stretch of Chesil Bank, is matched with an equally diverse range of wildlife. Beaches are scattered with colourful shells, while rock pools form miniature marine habitats teeming with life. Caves are used by larger creatures, such as grey seals, and cliffs provide nest sites for birds. In the spring and early summer, an astonishing range of plants grow on the foreshore and cliffs which can be seen at their best from the Southwest Coastal Path *(see p32)*. The plants in turn attract numerous moths and butterflies.

Cliff-tops of Land's End with safe ledges for nesting birds

***Chesil Bank** is an unusual ridge of pebbles* (see p256) *stretching 18 miles (29 km) along the Dorset coast. The bank was created by storms and the pebbles increase in size from northwest to southeast due to varying strengths of coastal currents. The bank encloses a lagoon called the Fleet, habitat of the Abbotsbury swans, as well as a large number of wildfowl.*

***The Painted Lady**, often se[en] on cliff-top coastal plants, migrates to Brita[in] in the spring.*

High tides wash driftwood and she[lls]

Cliff-top turf contains many species of wild flowers.

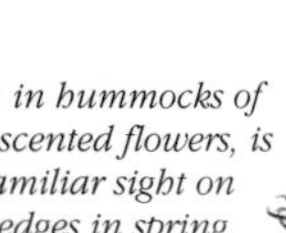

***Thrift**, in hummocks of honey-scented flowers, is a familiar sight on cliff ledges in spring.*

***Yellowhammers** are to be seen perched on cliff-top bushes.*

Marram grass roots help hold back sand against wind erosion.

***Grey seals** come on land to give birth to their young. They can be spotted on remote beaches.*

A BEACHCOMBER'S GUIDE

The best time to observe the natural life of the s[ea]shore is when the tide begins to roll back, befo[re] the scavenging seagulls pick up the stranded cr[abs,] fish and sandhoppers, and the seaweed dries u[p.] Much plant and marine life can be found in the secure habitat provided by rock pools.

***Durdle Door** was formed by waves continually eroding the weaker chalk layers of this cliff* (see p258) *in Dorset, leaving the stronger oolite to create a striking arch, known in geology as an eyelet.*

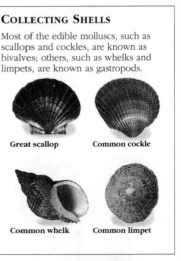

Collecting Shells

Most of the edible molluscs, such as scallops and cockles, are known as bivalves; others, such as whelks and limpets, are known as gastropods.

Great scallop

Common cockle

Common whelk

Common limpet

***Oystercatchers** have a distinctive orange beak. They hunt along the shore, feeding on all kinds of shellfish.*

***Seaweed**, such as bladder wrack, can resemble coral or lichen when in water.*

Rocks are colonized by clusters of barnacles, mussels and limpets.

***Starfish** can be aggressive predators on shellfish. The light-sensitive tips of their tentacles help them to "see" the way.*

***Mussels** are widespread and can be harvested for food.*

Rock pools teem with crabs, mussels, shrimps and plant life.

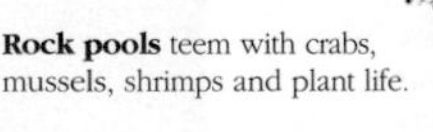

***The Velvet Crab**, often found hiding in seaweed, is covered with fine downy hair all over its shell.*

***Grey mullet**, when newly hatched, can often be seen in rock pools.*

West Country Gardens

GARDENERS HAVE LONG BEEN ATTRACTED to the West Country. Its mild climate is perfect for growing tender and exotic plants, many of which were brought from Asia in the 19th century. As a result, the region has some of England's finest and most varied gardens, covering the whole sweep of garden styles and history *(see pp22–3)*, from the clipped formality of Elizabethan Montacute, to the colourful and crowded cottage-garden style of East Lambrook Manor.

Lanhydrock's (p272) *clipped yews and low box hedges frame a blaze of colourful annuals.*

Trewithen (p269) *is renowned for its rare camellias, rhododendrons and magnolias, grown from seed collected in Asia. The huge garden is at its most impressive in March and June.*

Cotehele *(p281)* has a lovely lush valley garden.

Trelissick *(p269)* has memorable views over the Fal Estuary through shrub-filled woodland.

Glendurgan *(p269)* is a plant-lover's paradise set in a steep, sheltered valley.

Mount Edgcumbe *(p280)* preserves its 18th-century French, Italian and English gardens.

Trengwainton (p264) *has a fine stream garden, whose banks are crowded with moisture-loving plants, beneath a lush canopy of New Zealand tree ferns.*

Overbecks *(near Salcombe) enjoys a spectacular site overlooking the Salcombe Estuary. There are secret gardens, terraces and rocky dells.*

Creative Gardening

Gardens are not simply collections of plants; they rely for much of their appeal on man-made features. Whimsical topiary, ornate architecture, fanciful statuary and mazes help to create an atmosphere of adventure or pure escapism. The many gardens dotted around the West Country offer engaging examples of the vivid imagination of designers.

Mazes *were created in medieval monasteries to teach patience and persistence. This laurel maze at Glendurgan was planted in 1833.*

Fountains *and flamboyant statuary have adorned gardens since Roman times. Such eye-catching embellishments add poetic and Classical touches to the design of formal gardens, such as Mount Edgcumbe.*

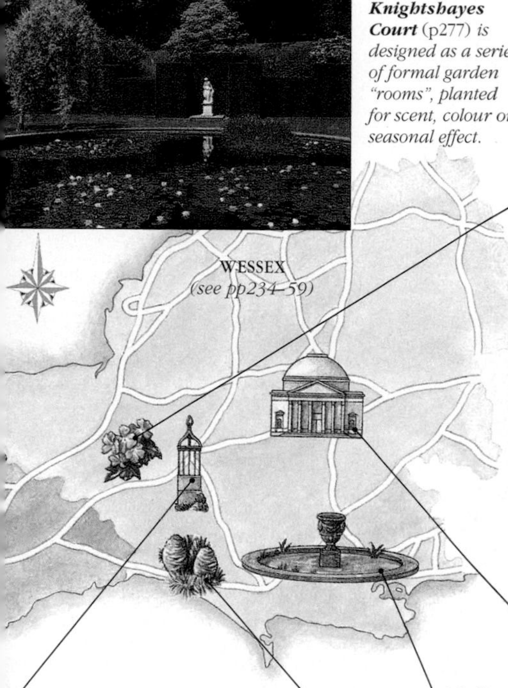

Knightshayes Court *(p277) is designed as a series of formal garden "rooms", planted for scent, colour or seasonal effect.*

East Lambrook Manor *(near South Petherton) is a riot of colours, as old-fashioned cottage plants grow without restraint.*

Stourhead *(see pp254–5)* is a magnificent example of 18th-century landscape gardening.

Athelhampton's *(p257)* gardens make use of fountains, statues, pavilions and columnar yews.

Montacute House *(p256)* has pavilions and a centuries-old yew hedge, and is renowned for its collection of old roses.

Parnham *(near Beaminster), like many West Country gardens, has several parts devoted to different themes. Here conical yews complement the formality of the stone balustrade; elsewhere there are woodland, kitchen, shade and Mediterranean gardens.*

Many garden buildings *are linked by an element of fantasy; while country houses had to conform to eryday practicalities, the design of many smaller uildings gave more scope for imagination. This fanciful Elizabethan pavilion on the forecourt at Montacute House was irst and foremost decora-ive, but sometimes served as a lodging house.*

Topiary *can be traced back to the Greeks. Since that time the sculpting of trees into unusual, often eccentric shapes has been developed over the centuries. The yew topiary of 1920s Knightshayes features a fox being chased by a pack of hounds. The figures form a delightful conceit and come into their own in winter when little else is in leaf.*

WESSEX

WILTSHIRE · SOMERSET · DORSET

THE NATURAL AND DIVERSE BEAUTY *of this predominantly rural region is characterized by rolling hills and charming villages. The area is enriched by a wealth of historical and architectural attractions, ranging from the prehistoric stone circle of Stonehenge to the Roman baths and magnificent Georgian townscape of Bath.*

Vast swathes of bare windswept downland give way to lush river valleys, and the contrast between the two may explain the origin in medieval times of the saying, "as different as chalk and cheese". The chalk and limestone hills provided pasture for sheep whose wool was exported to Europe or turned to cloth in mill towns such as Bradford-on-Avon. Meanwhile the rich cow-grazed pastures of the valleys produced the Cheddar cheese for which the region has become famous.

The area's potential for wealth was first exploited by prehistoric chieftains whose large, mysterious monuments, such as Stonehenge and Maiden Castle, are striking features of the landscape. From this same soil sprang King Arthur *(see p273)* and King Alfred the Great, about whom there are numerous fascinating legends. It was King Arthur who is thought to have led British resistance to the Saxon invasion in the 6th century. The Saxons finally emerged the victors and one of them, King Alfred, first united the West Country into one political unit, called the Kingdom of Wessex *(see p47)*.

Wilton House and Lacock Abbey, both former monasteries, were turned into splendid stately homes during the 16th century, due to the Dissolution of the Monasteries *(see pp50–51)*. Today, their previous wealth can be gauged by the size and grandeur of their storage barns.

Matching the many man-made splendours of the region, Wessex is rich in rare wildlife and plants.

Two visitors enjoying the Elizabethan gardens of Montacute House, Somerset

◁ **Eighteenth-century cottages lining Gold Hill, Shaftesbury**

Exploring Wessex

FROM THE ROLLING CHALK PLAINS around Stonehenge to the rocky cliffs of Cheddar Gorge and the heather-covered uplands of Exmoor, Wessex is a scenically varied microcosm of England. Reflecting the underlying geology, each part of Wessex contributes its own distinctive architecture, with the Neo-Classically inspired buildings of Bath giving way to the mellow brick and timber of Salisbury and the thatched flint-and-chalk cottages of the Dorset landscape.

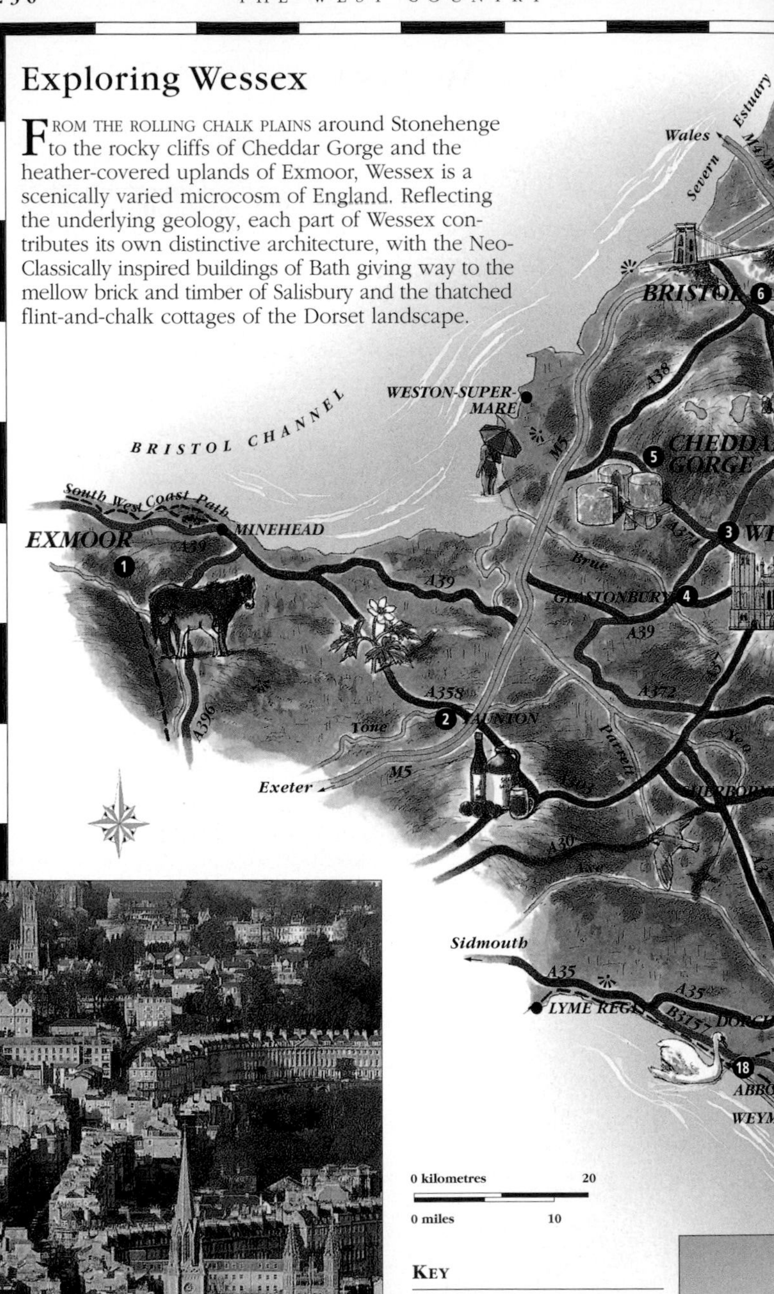

Bath's abbey and Georgian townscape

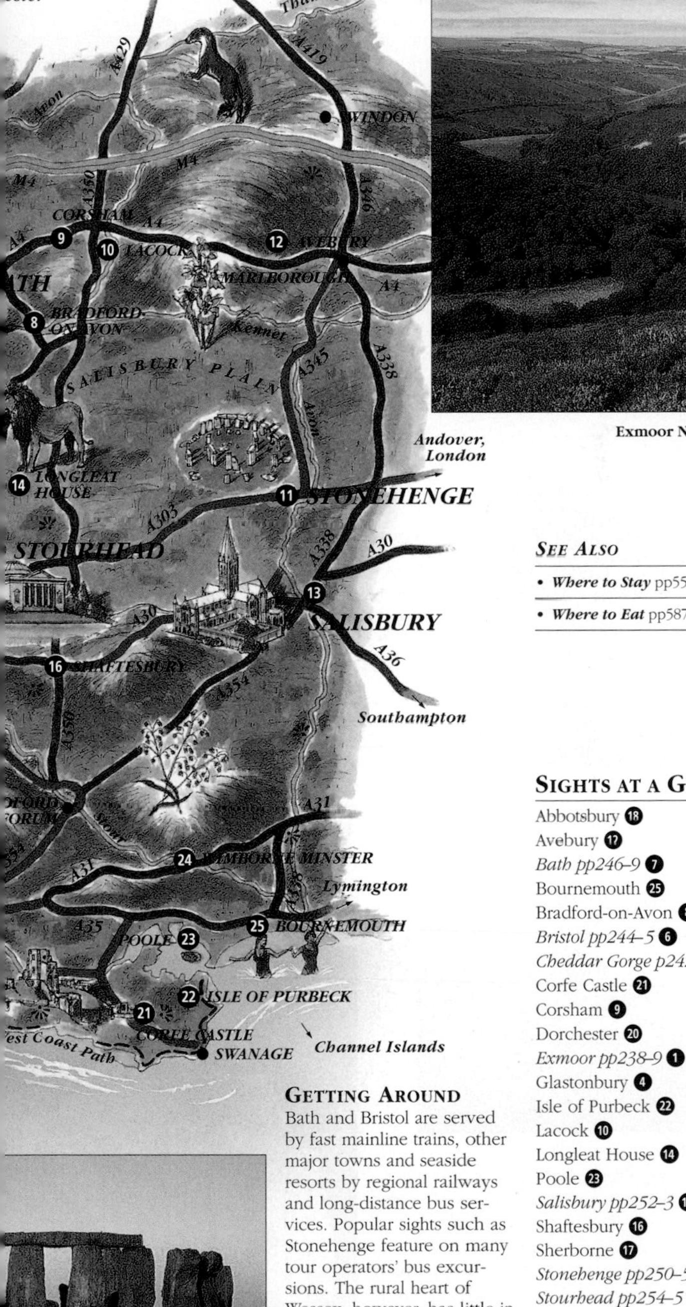

Exmoor National Park

Huge sarsen stones of Stonehenge, dating from around 3000 BC

See Also

- ***Where to Stay*** pp551–52
- ***Where to Eat*** pp587–9

Sights at a Glance

Abbotsbury 18
Avebury 12
Bath pp246–9 7
Bournemouth 25
Bradford-on-Avon 8
Bristol pp244–5 6
Cheddar Gorge p242 5
Corfe Castle 21
Corsham 9
Dorchester 20
Exmoor pp238–9 1
Glastonbury 4
Isle of Purbeck 22
Lacock 10
Longleat House 14
Poole 23
Salisbury pp252–3 13
Shaftesbury 16
Sherborne 17
Stonehenge pp250–51 11
Stourhead pp254–5 15
Taunton 2
Wells pp240–41 3
Weymouth 19
Wimborne Minster 24

Getting Around

Bath and Bristol are served by fast mainline trains, other major towns and seaside resorts by regional railways and long-distance bus services. Popular sights such as Stonehenge feature on many tour operators' bus excursions. The rural heart of Wessex, however, has little in the way of public transport and unless you have the time to walk the region's footpaths, you will need a car.

Exmoor National Park ❶

Curlew

THE MAJESTIC CLIFFS plunging into the Atlantic along Exmoor's northern coast are interrupted by lush, wooded valleys carrying rivers from the high moorland down to sheltered fishing coves. Inland, wild rolling hills are grazed by sturdy Exmoor ponies, horned sheep and the local wild red deer. Buzzards are also a common sight wheeling over the bracken-clad terrain looking for prey. For walkers, Exmoor offers 1,000 km (620 miles) of wonderful footpaths and varied, dramatic scenery, while the tamer perimeters of the National Park offer less energetic attractions – everything from traditional seaside entertainments to picturesque villages and ancient churches.

View east along the Southwest Coast Path

Parracombe church has a Georgian interior with a complete set of wooden furnishin

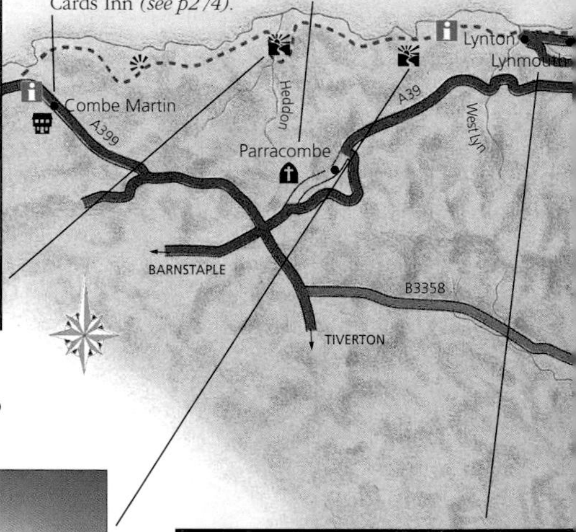

Combe Martin is a pretty setting for the Pack of Cards Inn *(see p274).*

Combe Martin
A399
Heddon
Parracombe
A39
West Lyn
Lynton
Lynmouth
BARNSTAPLE
B3358
TIVERTON

Heddon's Mouth
The River Heddon passes through woodland and meadows down to this attractive point on the coast.

The Valley of Rocks
Gritstone outcrops, eroded into fantastical shapes, characterize this natural gorge.

KEY

- Tourist information
- A road
- B road
- Minor road
- Coast path
- Viewpoint

Lynmouth
Above the charming fishing village of Lynmouth stands hill-top Lynton. The two villages are connected by a cliff railway (see p274).

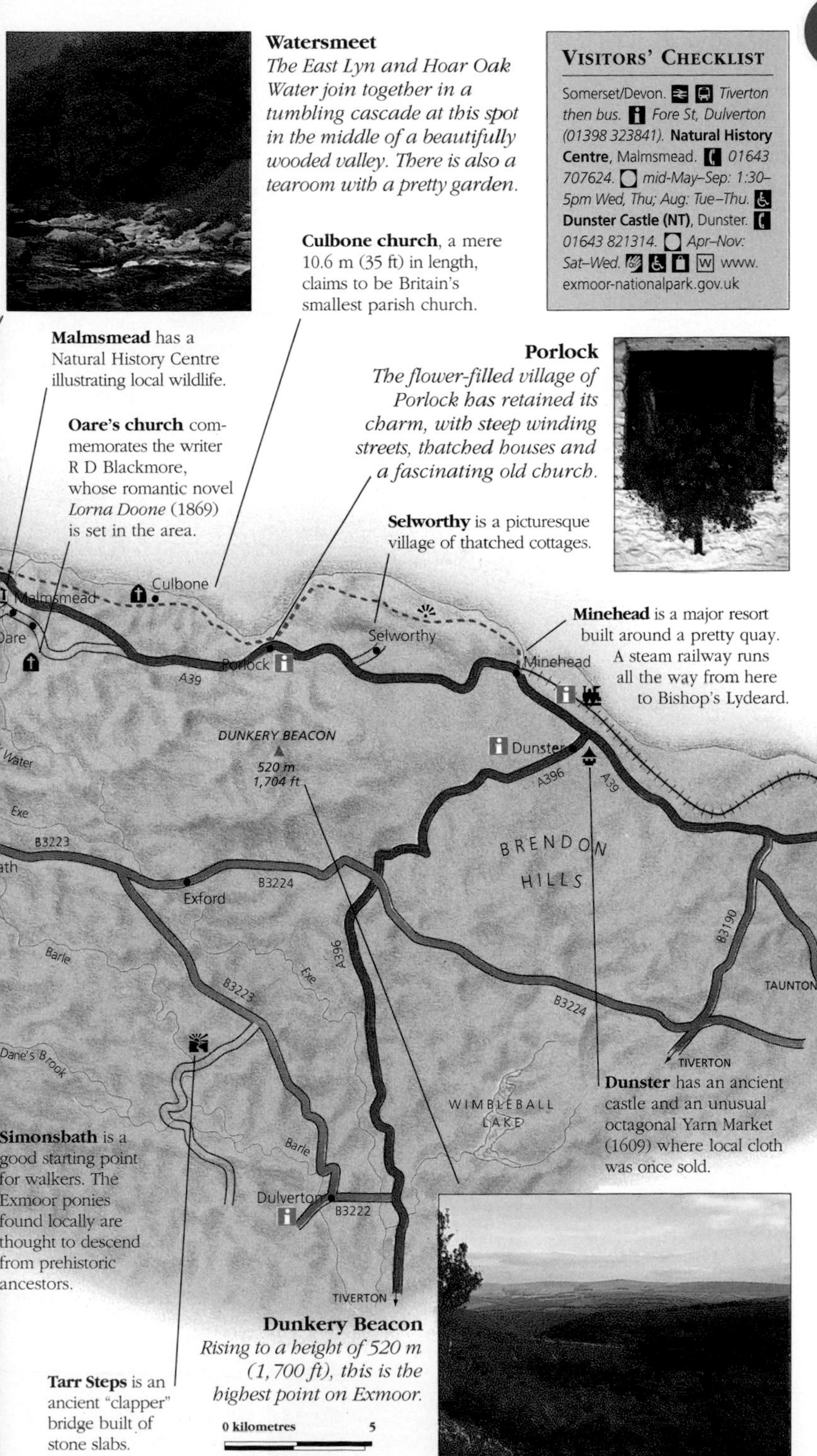

Watersmeet
The East Lyn and Hoar Oak Water join together in a tumbling cascade at this spot in the middle of a beautifully wooded valley. There is also a tearoom with a pretty garden.

Visitors' Checklist

Somerset/Devon. Tiverton then bus. Fore St, Dulverton (01398 323841). **Natural History Centre**, Malmsmead. 01643 707624. mid-May–Sep: 1:30–5pm Wed, Thu; Aug: Tue–Thu. **Dunster Castle (NT)**, Dunster. 01643 821314. Apr–Nov: Sat–Wed. www.exmoor-nationalpark.gov.uk

Culbone church, a mere 10.6 m (35 ft) in length, claims to be Britain's smallest parish church.

Malmsmead has a Natural History Centre illustrating local wildlife.

Porlock
The flower-filled village of Porlock has retained its charm, with steep winding streets, thatched houses and a fascinating old church.

Oare's church commemorates the writer R D Blackmore, whose romantic novel *Lorna Doone* (1869) is set in the area.

Selworthy is a picturesque village of thatched cottages.

Minehead is a major resort built around a pretty quay. A steam railway runs all the way from here to Bishop's Lydeard.

Dunster has an ancient castle and an unusual octagonal Yarn Market (1609) where local cloth was once sold.

Simonsbath is a good starting point for walkers. The Exmoor ponies found locally are thought to descend from prehistoric ancestors.

Dunkery Beacon
Rising to a height of 520 m (1,700 ft), this is the highest point on Exmoor.

Tarr Steps is an ancient "clapper" bridge built of stone slabs.

0 kilometres 5
0 miles 3

Taunton ❷

Somerset. 77,000. Paul St (01823 336 344). Tue & Sat (livestock).
www.heartofsomerset.com

TAUNTON LIES at the heart of a fertile region famous for its apples and cider, but it was the prosperous wool industry that financed the massive church of **St Mary Magdalene** (1488–1514) with its glorious tower. Taunton's **castle** was the setting for the notorious Bloody Assizes of 1685 when "Hanging" Judge Jeffreys dispensed harsh retribution on the Duke of Monmouth and his followers for an uprising against King James II. The 12th-century building now houses the **Somerset County Museum**. A star exhibit is the Roman mosaic from a villa at Low Ham, Somerset, showing the story of Dido and Aeneas.

ENVIRONS: Hestercombe Garden is one of Sir Edwin Lutyens and Gertrude Jekyll's great masterpieces.

Somerset County Museum
Castle Green. 01823 355504. Tue–Sat, public hols. ground floor. www.somersetgov.uk/museums

Hestercombe Garden
Cheddon Fitzpaine. 01823 413923. daily. www.hestercombegardens.com

SOMERSET CIDER

Somerset is one of the few English counties where real farmhouse cider, known as "scrumpy", is still made using the traditional methods. Cider once formed part of the farm labourer's wages and local folklore has it that various unsavoury additives, such as iron nails, were added to give strength. Cider-making can be seen at **Sheppy's** farm, on the A38 near Taunton.

Scrumpy cider

Wells ❸

Somerset. 10,000. Market Place (01749 672552). Wed, Sat.

WELLS IS NAMED after St Andrew's Well, the sacred spring that bubbles up from the ground near the 13th-century **Bishop's Palace**, residence of the Bishop of Bath and Wells. A tranquil city, Wells is famous for its magnificent cathedral which was begun in the late 1100s. Penniless Porch, where beggars once received alms, leads from the bustling market place to the calm of the cathedral close. **Wells Museum** has prehistoric finds from nearby Wookey Hole and other caves.

Cathedral clock (1386–92)

ENVIRONS: To the northeast of Wells lies the impressive cave complex of **Wookey Hole**, which has an extensive range of popular amusements.

Wells Museum
8 Cathedral Green. 01749 673477. Easter–Oct: daily; Nov–Easter: Wed–Mon. limited.

Wookey Hole
Off A371. 01749 672243. daily. www.wookey.co.uk

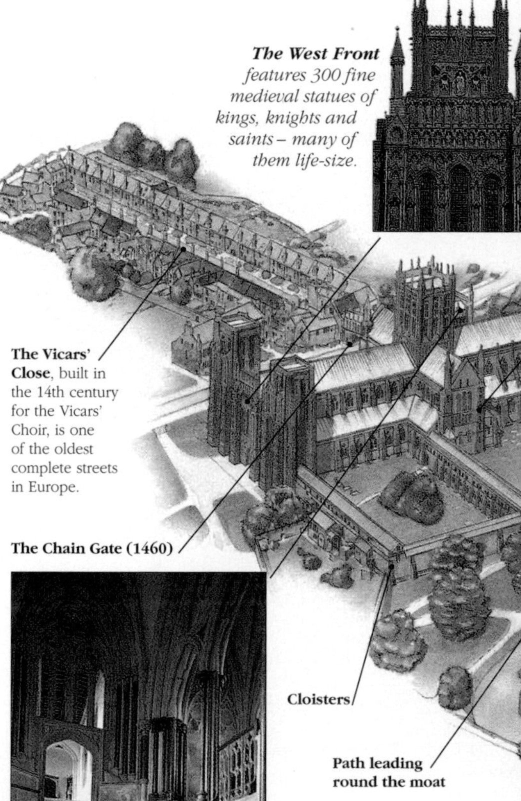

***The West Front** features 300 fine medieval statues of kings, knights and saints – many of them life-size.*

The Vicars' Close, built in the 14th century for the Vicars' Choir, is one of the oldest complete streets in Europe.

The Chain Gate (1460)

Cloisters

Path leading round the moat

***This graceful flight of steps** curves up to the octagonal Chapter House which has delicate vaulting dating from 1306. The 32 ribs springing from the central column create a beautiful palm-tree effect.*

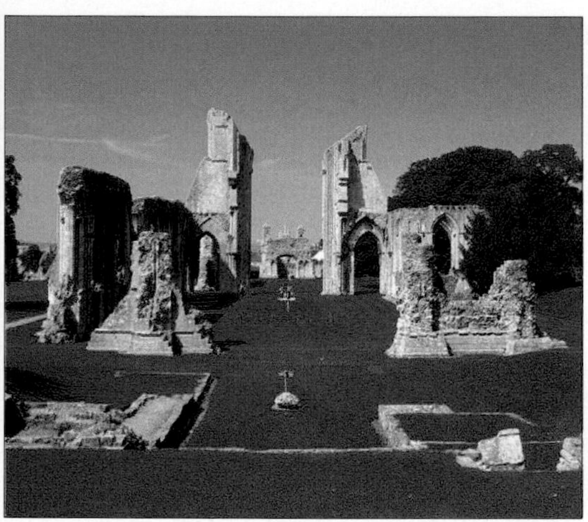

Glastonbury Abbey, left in ruins in 1539 after the Dissolution

Bishops' tombs *circle the chancel. This sumptuous marble tomb, in the south aisle, is that of Bishop Lord Arthur Hervey, who was Bishop of Bath and Wells (1869–94).*

The palace moat *is home to swans which ring a bell by the gatehouse when they want to be fed. Feeding times are at 11am and 4pm.*

The Bishop's Palace (1230–40)

13th-century ruins of the Great Hall

Wells Cathedral and the Bishop's Palace

The Close. 01749 674483. daily. limited.
Bishop's Palace 01749 678691. Apr–Oct: Tue– Fri, Sun & public hols (Aug: daily).

Wells has maintained much of its medieval character with its cathedral, Bishop's Palace and other buildings around the close forming a harmonious group. The most striking features of the cathedral are the west front and the "scissor arches" installed in 1338 to support the tower.

Glastonbury 4

Somerset. 9,000. Tribunal, High St (01458 832954). Tue.
www.glastonbury.co.uk

Shrouded in Arthurian myth and rich in mystical association, the town of Glastonbury was once one of the most important destinations for pilgrims in England. Now thousands flock here for the annual rock festival *(see p63)* and for the summer solstice on Midsummer's Day (21 June).

Over the years history and legend have become intertwined, and the monks who founded **Glastonbury Abbey**, around 700, found it profitable to encourage the association between Glastonbury and the mythical "Blessed Isle" known as Avalon – alleged to be the last resting place of King Arthur and the Holy Grail *(see p273)*.

The great abbey was left in ruins after the Dissolution of the Monasteries *(see p50)*. Even so, some magnificent relics survive, including parts of the vast Norman abbey church, the unusual Abbot's Kitchen, with its octagonal roof, and the Victorian farmhouse, now the **Somerset Rural Life Museum**.

Growing in the abbey grounds is a cutting from the famous Glastonbury thorn which is said to have miraculously grown from the staff of St Joseph of Arimathea. According to myth, he was sent around AD 60 to convert England to Christianity. The English hawthorn flowers at Christmas as well as in May.

The **Lake Village Museum** has some interesting finds from the Iron Age settlements that once fringed the marshlands around **Glastonbury Tor**. Seen for miles around, the Tor is a hill crowned by the remains of a 14th-century church.

Somerset Rural Life Museum
Chilkwell St. 01458 831197. Apr–Oct: Tue–Sun; Nov–Apr: Tue–Sat & public hols. 24–26 Dec, 1 Jan, Good Fri. limited. closed winter.

Lake Village Museum
Tribunal, High St. 01458 832954. daily. 25, 26 Dec.

Cheddar Gorge ❺

Described as a "deep frightful chasm" by novelist Daniel Defoe in 1724, Cheddar Gorge is a spectacular ravine cut through the Mendip plateau by fast-flowing streams during the glacial phases of the last Ice Age. Cheddar has given its name to a rich cheese which originates from here and is now produced worldwide. The caves in the gorge once provided the perfect environment of constant temperature and high humidity for storing and maturing the cheese.

Visitors' Checklist

On B3135, Somerset. 01934 744071. from Wells. www.somersetbythesea.co.uk
Cheddar Man & the Cannibals Museum 01934 742343. daily. limited. www.cheddarcaves.co.uk
Cheddar Gorge Cheese Co. 01934 742810. daily. www.cheddargorgecheeseco.co.uk

***The Cheddar Gorge Cheese Company** is part of the Cheddar Gorge Rural Village, where you can visit a 1920s working dairy, among many other attractions, and see cheesemakers at work.*

The B3135 road winds round the base of the 3 mile (5 km) gorge.

***"Cheddar Man"**, a 9,000-year-old skeleton, is on display in the museum.*

A footpath follows the top of the gorge on its southern edge.

***The gorge** is a narrow, winding ravine with limestone rocks rising almost vertically on either side to a height of 120 m (400 ft).*

Gough's Cave is noted for its cathedral-like proportions.

Tourist information

Cox's Cave contains unusually shaped stalactites and stalagmites.

Jacob's Ladder has 274 steps leading to the top of the gorge

***The rare Cheddar Pink** is among the astonishing range of plant and animal life harboured in the rocks.*

Lookout Tower has far-reaching views over the area to the south and west.

Bristol 6

See pp244–5.

Bath 7

See pp246–9.

Bradford-on-Avon 8

Wiltshire. *9,500.* *St Margaret St (01225 865797).* *Thu.* www.bradfordonavontown.com

THIS LOVELY COTSWOLD-STONE town with its steep flagged lanes is full of flamboyant houses built by wealthy wool and cloth merchants in the 17th and 18th centuries. One fine Georgian example is **Abbey House**, on Church Street. A little further along, **St Laurence Church** is a remarkably complete Saxon building founded in 705 *(see p47)*. The church was converted to a school and cottage in the 12th century and was rediscovered in the 19th century when a vicar recognized the characteristic cross-shaped roof.

Typical Cotswold-stone architecture in Bradford-on-Avon

At one end of the medieval **Town Bridge** is a small stone cell, built as a chapel in the 13th century but later used as a lock-up for 17th-century vagrants. A short walk away, near converted mill buildings and a stretch of the Kennet and Avon Canal, is the massive 14th-century **Tithe Barn** *(see p28)*.

Tithe Barn
Pound Lane. *daily.* *25, 26 Dec.*

Corsham 9

Wiltshire. *12,000.* *High St (01249 714660).* www.northwilts.gov.uk

THE STREETS of Corsham are lined with stately Georgian houses in Cotswold stone. **St Bartholomew's Church** has an elegant spire and a lovely carved alabaster tomb (1960) to the late Lady Methuen, whose family founded Methuen publishers. The family acquired **Corsham Court** in 1745 with its picture gallery and a remarkable collection of Flemish, Italian and English paintings, including works by Van Dyck, Lippi and Reynolds. Peacocks wander through the grounds, adding their colour and elegance to the façade of the Elizabethan mansion.

Peacock in grounds, Corsham Court

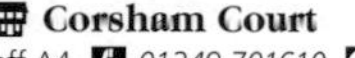

Corsham Court
off A4. *01249 701610.* *mid-Mar– Sep: Tue–Sun (pm); Oct–mid-Mar: Sat, Sun (pm).* *Dec.* *limited.*

Lacock 10

Wiltshire. *1,000.*

MAINTAINED in its pristine state by the National Trust, with very few modern intrusions, Lacock is a picturesque and delightful village to explore. The meandering River Avon forms the boundary to the north side of the churchyard, while humorous stone figures look down from **St Cyriac Church**. Inside the 15th-century church is the splendid Renaissance-style tomb of Sir William Sharington (1495–1553). He acquired **Lacock Abbey** after the Dissolution of the Monasteries *(see p50)*, but it was a later owner, John Ivory Talbot, who had the buildings remodelled in the Gothic revival style, in vogue in the early 18th century.

The abbey is famous for the window (in the south gallery) from which his descendant William Henry Fox Talbot, an early pioneer of photography, took his first picture in 1835, and for the sheets of snowdrops which cover the abbey grounds in early spring. A 16th-century barn at the abbey gates has been converted to the **Fox Talbot Museum**, which has displays on his experiments.

ENVIRONS: Designed by Robert Adam *(see pp24–5)* in 1769, **Bowood House** includes the laboratory where Joseph Priestley discovered oxygen in 1774, and a rich collection of sculpture, costumes and paintings. Italianate gardens surround the house while the lake-filled grounds, landscaped by Capability Brown *(see p22)*, contain a Doric temple, grotto, cascade and now a large adventure playground.

Lacock Abbey
(NT) Lacock. *01249 730227.* *Mar–Oct: Wed–Mon (pm).* *Good Fri.* *limited in house.*

Fox Talbot Museum
(NT) Lacock. *01249 730459.* *Mar–Oct: daily.* *Good Fri.*

Bowood House
Derry Hill, nr Calne. *01249 812102.* *Apr–Oct: daily.*

William Henry Fox Talbot (1800–77)

Bristol ❻

King Brennus, St John's Gate

It was in 1497 that John Cabot sailed from Bristol on his historic voyage to North America. The city, at the mouth of the Avon, became the main British port for transatlantic trade, pioneering the era of the ocean-going steam liner with the construction of SS *Great Britain*. The city flourished as a major trading centre, growing rich on the distribution of wine, tobacco and, in the 17th century, slaves.

Because of its docks and aero-engine factories, Bristol was heavily bombed during World War II and the city centre bears witness to the ideas of post-war planners. The docks have been shifted to deeper waters at Avonmouth and the old dock area has been transformed, taking on new life characterized by waterside cafés, shops and art galleries.

Exploring Bristol

The most interesting part of the city lies around Broad, King and Corn streets, known as the Old Quarter. There is a lively covered market, part of which occupies the **Corn Exchange**, built by John Wood the Elder *(see p246)* in 1743. Outside are the famous Bristol Nails, four bronze 16th–17th-century pedestals which Bristol merchants used as tables when paying for goods – hence the expression "to pay on the nail". **St John's Gate**, at the head of Broad Street, has medieval statues of Bristol's two mythical founders, King Brennus and King Benilus. Between Lewins Mead and Colston Street, **Christmas Steps** is a steep lane lined with specialist shops and cafés. The **Chapel of the Three Kings** at the top was founded in 1504.

A group of buildings around the cobbled King Street include the 17th-century timber-framed **Llandoger Trow** inn. It is here that Daniel Defoe is said to have met Alexander Selkirk, whose true-life island exile served as the inspiration for Defoe's novel *Robinson Crusoe* (1719). Just up from here is the **Theatre Royal**, built in 1766, and home to the famous Bristol Old Vic.

The bow of SS *Great Britain*

The Two Sisters (c.1889) by Renoir, City Museum and Art Gallery

Not far away the renowned **Arnolfini Gallery** on Narrow Quay is a showcase for contemporary art, drama, dance and cinema (closed for refurbishment until spring 2005).

On the Harbourside, **At-Bristol** combines the interactive science centre Explore, the wildlife centre Wildwalk and an IMAX cinema.

To the west of the city, the elegant suburbs of **Clifton** revel in ornate Regency crescents. The impressive **Clifton Suspension Bridge** by Brunel, completed in 1864, perfectly complements the drama of the steep Avon gorge. **Bristol Zoo Gardens**, nearby, concentrate on breeding and conserving endangered species.

Memorial to William Canynge the Younger (1400–74)

St Mary Redcliffe

Redcliffe Way. *0117 9291487. daily. by arrangement.*

This magnificent 14th-century church was claimed by Queen Elizabeth I to be "the fairest in England". The church owes much to the generosity of William Canynge the Elder and Younger, both famous mayors of Bristol. Inscriptions on the tombs of merchants and sailors tell of lives devoted to trade in Asia and the West Indies. Look out for the Bristol maze in the north aisle.

SS *Great Britain*

Gas Ferry Rd. *0117 9260680. daily. 24, 25 Dec. limited. by arrangement.*

www.ss-great-britain.com

Designed by Isambard Kingdom Brunel, this is the world's first large iron passenger ship. Launched in 1843, she travelled 32 times round the world before she was abandoned in the Falkland Islands in 1886. The ship is being restored until 2005 but remains open, with hard-hat tours to see work in progress.

Georgian House

7 Great George St. *0117 9211362. Apr–Oct: Sat–Wed.*

Life in a wealthy Bristol merchant's house of the 1790s is illustrated by furnishings in the elegant drawing room and the servants' area.

British Empire & Commonwealth Museum

Station Approach, Temple Meads. *0117 9254980. daily. 25, 26 Dec.*

www.empiremuseum.co.uk

This major new national museum is located in the 1841 railway terminus by Brunel, and presents the dramatic 500-year history of the British empire and the emergence of the modern Commonwealth, in over 20 themed galleries, special exhibitions, a library and archive.

Warehouses overlooking the Floating Harbour

Bristol Industrial Museum

Prince's Wharf. *0117 9251470.* *Apr–Oct: Sat–Wed; Nov–Mar: Sat–Sun.* *25, 26 Dec.* www.bristol-city.gov.uk/museums

The museum's collection of vehicles and models illustrates the huge range of products made in Bristol over the last 300 years. Among them are luxurious Bristol cars, the Bristol bus, the world's first touring caravan and Concorde, represented by a full-scale model of the pilot's cockpit.

City Museum and Art Gallery

Queen's Rd. *0117 922 3571.* *daily.* *24, 25 Dec.* *limited.* www.bristol-city.gov.uk/museums

Varied collections include Egyptology, dinosaur fossils, Roman tableware, the largest collection of Chinese glass outside China and a fine collection of European paintings including works by Renoir and Bellini. Bristol artists include Sir Thomas Lawrence and Francis Danby.

Visitors' Checklist

Bristol. *450,000.* *7 miles (11 km) SW Bristol.* *Temple Meads.* *Marlborough St.* *The Annexe, Wildscreen Walk, Harbourside (0906-586 2313).* *daily.* *Harbour Festival: Jul–Aug; Balloon Festival: Aug.* www.visitbristol.co.uk

Bristol Cathedral

College Green. *0117 9264879.* *daily.* **Donation.** *limited.* www.bristol-cathedral.co.uk

Bristol's cathedral, begun in 1140, took an unusually long time to build. Rapid progress was made between 1298 and 1330, when the inventive choir was rebuilt; the transepts and tower were finished in 1515, and another 350 years passed before the Victorian architect, G E Street, built the nave. Humorous medieval carving abounds – a snail crawling across the stone foliage in the Berkeley Chapel, musical monkeys in the Elder Lady Chapel, and a fine set of wooden misericords in the choir.

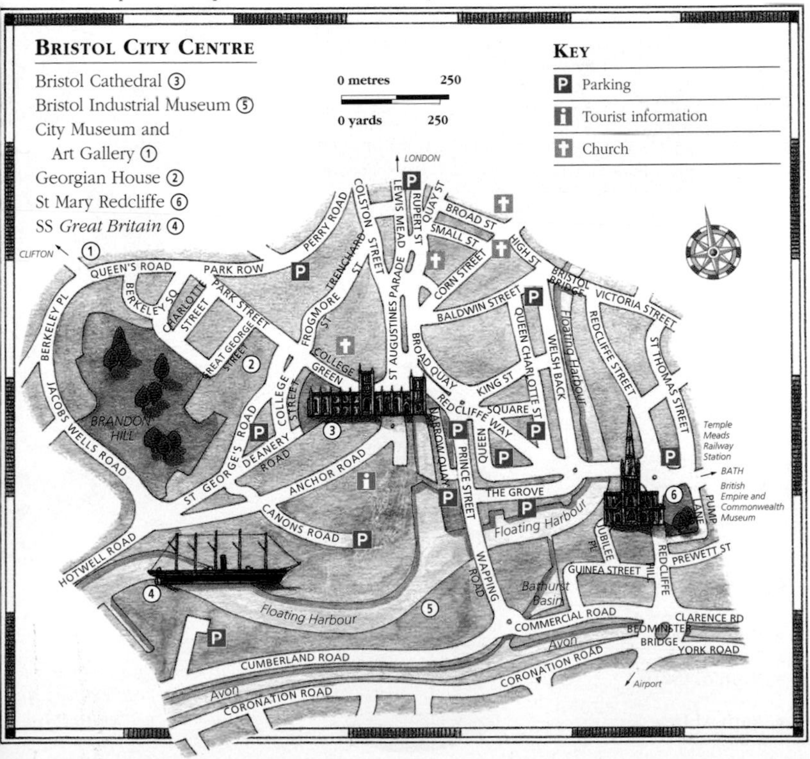

Bristol City Centre

Bristol Cathedral ③
Bristol Industrial Museum ⑤
City Museum and Art Gallery ①
Georgian House ②
St Mary Redcliffe ⑥
SS *Great Britain* ④

0 metres 250
0 yards 250

Key

Parking
Tourist information
Church

Street-by-Street: Bath ❼

BATH OWES ITS MAGNIFICENT Georgian townscape to the bubbling pool of water at the heart of the Roman Baths. The Romans transformed Bath into England's first spa resort and it regained fame as a spa town in the 18th century. At this time the two brilliant John Woods (Elder and Younger), both architects, designed the city's fine Palladian-style buildings. Many houses bear plaques recording the numerous famous people who have resided here.

The Circus
This is a daring departure from t typical Georgian square, by John V the Elder (1705–

No. 1 Royal Crescent

No. 17 is where the 18th-century painter Thomas Gainsborough lived *(see p151)*.

Assembly Rooms and Museum of Costume

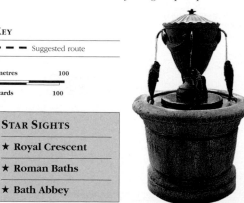

★ Royal Crescent
Hailed the most majestic street in Britain, this graceful arc of 30 houses (1767–74) is the masterpiece of John Wood the Younger. West of the Royal Crescent, Royal Victoria Park (1830) is the city's largest open space.

Jane Austen *(see p150)*, the writer, stayed at No. 13 Queen Square on one of many visits to Bath in her youth.

Milsom Street and New Bond Street contain some of Bath's most elegant shops.

Theatre Royal (1805)

KEY

– – – Suggested route

0 metres 100

0 yards 100

STAR SIGHTS

★ Royal Crescent

★ Roman Baths

★ Bath Abbey

Pump Rooms
These tearooms once formed the social hub of the 18th-century spa community. They contain this decorative drinking fountain.

Visitors' Checklist

Bath. 85,000. Bristol International Airport, 20 miles (32 km) W Bath. Dorchester St. Manvers St. Abbey Chambers, Abbey Church Yard (0906-7112000). daily. International Festival: May–Jun. www.visitbath.co.uk

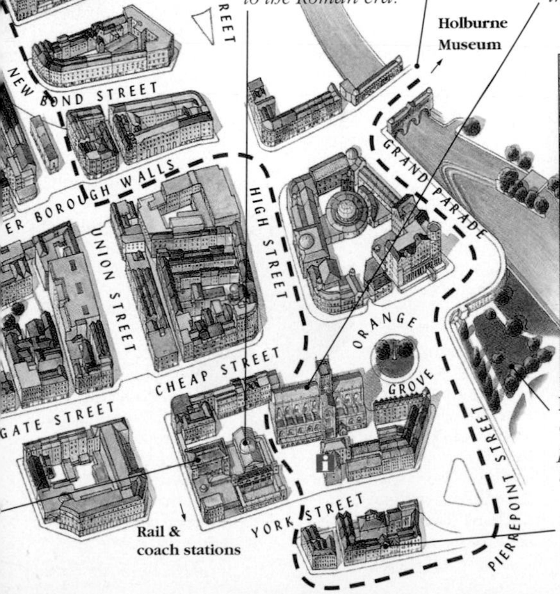

Pulteney Bridge

This charming bridge (1769–74), designed by Robert Adam, is lined with shops and links the centre with the magnificent Great Pulteney Street. Look out for a rare Victorian pillar box on the east bank.

The Building of Bath Museum

★ Roman Baths

Built in the 1st century, this bathing complex is one of Britain's greatest memorials to the Roman era.

★ Bath Abbey

The splendid abbey stands at the heart of the old city in the Abbey Church Yard, a paved courtyard enlivened by buskers. Its unique façade features stone angels climbing Jacob's Ladder to heaven.

Holburne Museum

Parade Gardens

Courting couples came to this pretty riverside park for secret liaisons in the 18th century.

Rail & coach stations

Sally Lunn's House (1482) is one of Bath's oldest houses.

Exploring Bath

Piazza cellist

THE BEAUTIFUL AND COMPACT CITY OF BATH is set among the rolling green hills of the Avon valley, and wherever you walk you will enjoy spendid views of the surrounding countryside. The traffic-free heart of this lively city is full of street musicians, museums, cafés and enticing shops, while the elegant honey-coloured Georgian houses, so characteristic of Bath, form an elegant backdrop to city life.

Bath Abbey, at the heart of the old city, begun in 1499

Bath Abbey

13 Kingston Bldgs, Abbey Churchyard. *01225 422462. daily. during services.* **Donation.**
www.bathabbey.org

This splendid abbey was supposedly designed by divine agency. According to legend, God dictated the form of the church to Bishop Oliver King in a dream; this story has been immortalized in the wonderfully eccentric carvings on the west front. The bishop began work in 1499, rebuilding a church that had been founded in the 8th century. Memorials cover the walls and the varied Georgian inscriptions make fascinating reading. The spacious interior is remarkable for the fan vaulting of the nave, an addition made by Sir George Gilbert Scott in 1874.

Assembly Rooms and Museum of Costume

Bennett St. *01225 477789. daily. 25, 26 Dec.*
www.museumofcostume.co.uk

The Assembly Rooms were built by Wood the Younger in 1769, as a meeting place for the fashionable elite and as an elegant backdrop for many glittering balls. Jane Austen's novel *Northanger Abbey* (1818) describes the atmosphere of gossip and flirtation here.

In the basements is a collection of costumes in authentic period settings. The display illustrates changing fashions from the 16th century to the present day.

No. 1 Royal Crescent

Royal Crescent. *01225 428 126. Tue–Sun & public hols. Dec, Jan, Good Fri.*
www.bath-preservation-trust.org.uk

This museum lets you inside the first house of this beautiful Georgian crescent, giving a glimpse of what life was like for 18th-century aristocrats, such as the Duke of York, who probably lived here. It is furnished down to such details as the dog-powered spit used to roast meat in front of the fire.

Holburne Museum of Art

Great Pulteney St. *01225 466669. daily (Nov–Easter: Tue–Sat, Sun pm). mid-Dec–mid-Feb.*
www.bath.ac.uk/holburne

This historic building is named after William Holburne of Menstrie (1793–1874), whose collections form the nucleus of the display of fine and decorative arts. Paintings can be seen by British artists such as Gainsborough and Stubbs.

Roman Baths Museum

Entrance in Abbey Churchyard. *01225 477784. daily. 25, 26 Dec. limited.*
www.romanbaths.co.uk

According to legend, Bath owes its origin to the Celtic King Bladud who discovered the curative properties of its natural hot springs in 860 BC. Cast out from his kingdom as a leper, Bladud cured himself by imitating his swine and rolling in the hot mud at Bath.

In the first century, the Romans built baths around the spring, and a temple dedicated to the goddess Sulis Minerva, who combined the attributes of the Celt water goddess Sulis and the Roman goddess Minerva. Among the Roman relics is a bronze head of the goddess.

Gilded bronze head of Sulis Minerva

Medieval monks of Bath Abbey also exploited the springs' properties, but it was when Queen Anne visited in 1702–3 that Bath reached its zenith as a fashionable watering place.

Building of Bath Museum

The Vineyards. *01225 333895.* *Tue–Sun & public hols.* *end-Nov–mid-Feb.* *limited.* www.bath-preservation-trust.org.uk

This museum, housed in an old Methodist chapel, is an excellent starting point for exploring the city. It shows how, in the 18th century, Bath was transformed from a medieval wool town into one of Europe's most elegant spas. John Wood and his son designed the Classically inspired stone fronts of the Royal Crescent and the Circus, leaving individual property speculators to develop the houses behind. While the façades speak of harmony and order, the houses behind show the result of rampant individualism, with no two houses alike. The museum looks at every aspect of the buildings, from their construction to a new gallery of Georgian interiors.

American Museum

Claverton Manor, Claverton Down. *01225 460503.* *Aug: daily (pm); Mar–Oct, mid-Nov–mid-Dec: Tue–Sun (pm).* *limited.* www.americanmuseum.org

Founded in 1961, this was the first American museum to be established in this country. Rooms in the 1820 manor house are decorated in many styles, from the rudimentary dwellings of the first settlers to opulent 19th-century homes. There are special sections on Shaker furniture, quilts and Native American art, and a replica of George Washington's Mount Vernon garden of 1785.

A 19th-century American Indian weathervane

Richard "Beau" Nash (1674–1762)

Elected in 1704 as Master of Ceremonies, "Beau" Nash played a crucial role in transforming Bath into the fashionable centre of Georgian society. During his long career, he devised a never-ending round of games, balls and entertainment (including gambling) that kept the idle rich amused and ensured a constant flow of visitors.

The Great Bath

The open-air Great Bath, which stands at the heart of the Roman spa complex, was not discovered until the 1870s. Leading off this magnificent pool were various bathing chambers which became increasingly sophisticated over the four centuries the Romans were here. The baths fell into ruin, but extensive excavations have revealed the remarkable skill of Roman engineering.

he dome (1897) is based on St ephen Walbrook church in London see p114).

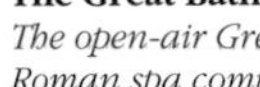

Around the edges of the bath are the bases of piers that once supported a barrel-vaulted roof.

York Street

A late 19th-century terrace bears statues of famous Romans such as Julius Caesar.

The sacred spring is enclosed by a resevoir now named the King's Bath.

The water flows from the spring into the corner of the bath at a constant temperature of 46° C (115° F).

The lead-lined bath, steps, column bases and paving stones around the edge all date from Roman times.

Stonehenge ⓫

Built in several stages from about 3000 BC, Stonehenge is Europe's most famous prehistoric monument. We can only guess at the rituals that took place here, but the alignment of the stones leaves little doubt that the circle is connected with the sun and the passing of the seasons, and that its builders possessed a sophisticated understanding of both arithmetic and astronomy.

Despite popular belief, the circle was not built by the Druids, an Iron Age priestly cult that flourished in Britain from around 250 BC – more than 1,000 years after Stonehenge was completed.

Finds from a burial mound near Stonehenge (Devizes Museum)

Stonehenge as it is today

The Heel Stone casts a long shadow straight to the heart of the circle on Midsummer's day.

The Avenue forms a ceremonial approach to the site.

The Slaughter Stone, named by 17th-century antiquarians who believed Stonehenge to be a place of human sacrifice, was in fact one of a pair forming a doorway.

The Outer Bank, dug around 3000 BC, is the oldest part of Stonehenge.

Reconstruction of Stonehenge

This illustration shows what Stonehenge probably looked like about 4,000 years ago.

Building of Stonehenge

Stonehenge's monumental scale is more impressive given that the only tools available were made of stone, wood and bone. The labour involved in quarrying, transporting and erecting the huge stones was such that its builders must have been able to command immense resources and vast numbers of people. One method is explained below.

A sarsen stone *was moved on rollers and levered into a pit.*

With levers *supported by timber packing, it was gradually raised.*

The stone *was then pulled upright by about 200 men hauling on ropes.*

The pit *round the [cut off] was packed tightly [cut off] stones and chalk.*

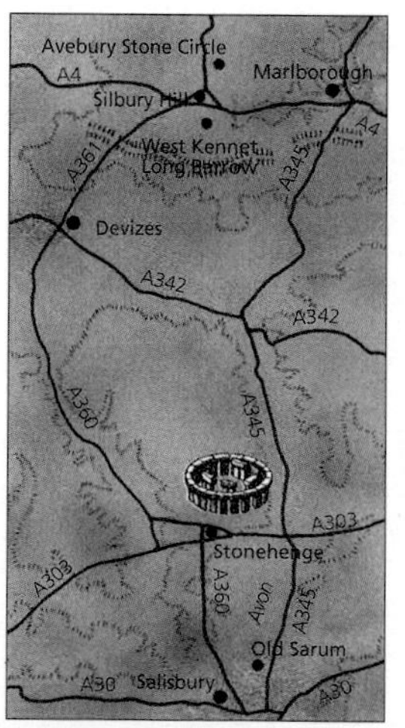

Wiltshire's Other Prehistoric Sites

The open countryside of the Salisbury Plain made this area an important centre of prehistoric settlement, and today it is covered in many ancient remains. Ringing the horizon around Stonehenge are scores of circular barrows, or burial mounds, where members of the ruling class were honoured with burial close to the temple site. Ceremonial bronze weapons and other finds excavated around Stonehenge and the other local prehistoric sites can be seen in the museum at Salisbury *(see pp252–3)* and the main museum at Devizes.

Silbury Hill (NT) is Europe's largest prehistoric earthwork,

Silbury Hill

but despite extensive excavations its purpose remains a mystery. Built out of chalk blocks around 2750 BC, the hill covers 2 ha (5 acres) and rises to a height of 40 m (131 ft). Nearby **West Kennet Long Barrow** (NT) is the biggest

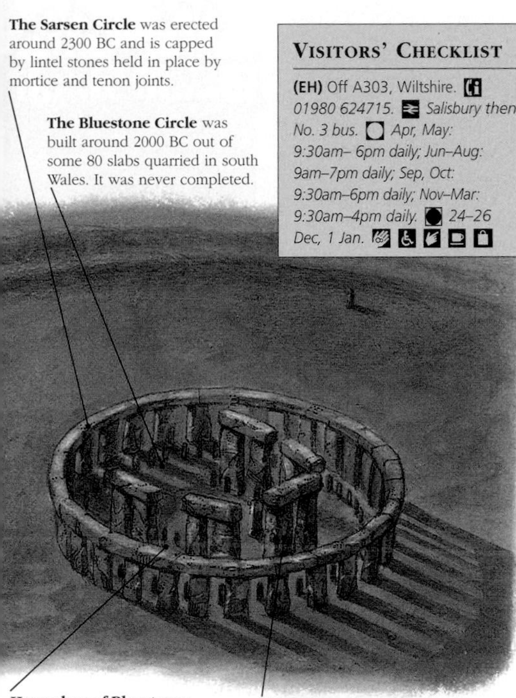

The Sarsen Circle was erected around 2300 BC and is capped by lintel stones held in place by mortice and tenon joints.
The Bluestone Circle was built around 2000 BC out of some 80 slabs quarried in south Wales. It was never completed.
Horseshoe of Bluestones
Horseshoe of Sarsen Trilothons

Visitors' Checklist

(EH) Off A303, Wiltshire. *01980 624715. Salisbury then No. 3 bus. Apr, May: 9:30am– 6pm daily; Jun–Aug: 9am–7pm daily; Sep, Oct: 9:30am–6pm daily; Nov–Mar: 9:30am–4pm daily. 24–26 Dec, 1 Jan.*

***lternate ends** f the lintel were vered up.*

***The weight** of the lintel was supported by a timber platform.*

***The lintel** was then levered sideways on to the uprights.*

chambered tomb in England, with numerous stone-lined "rooms" and a monumental entrance. Built as a communal cemetery around 3250 BC, it was in use for several centuries – old bodies were taken away to make room for newcomers.

Old Sarum is set within the massive ramparts of a 1st-century Romano-British hill fort. The Norman founders of Old Sarum built their own motte and bailey castle inside this ready-made fortification, and the remains of this survive along with the foundations of the huge cathedral of 1075. Above ground nothing remains of the town that once sat within the ramparts. The town's occupants moved to the fertile river valley site that became Salisbury during the early 12th century *(see pp252–3)*.

Old Sarum

(EH) Castle Rd. *01722 335398. daily. 24–26 Dec, 1 Jan.*

The chambered tomb of West Kennet Long Barrow (c.3250 BC)

Sarsen stone forming part of the Avebury Stone Circle

Avebury ⓬

Wiltshire. *600. Swindon then bus.* Green St *(01672 539424).*

Built around 2500 BC, the **Avebury Stone Circle** (EH/NT) surrounds the village of Avebury and was probably once some form of religious centre. Although the stones used are smaller than those at Stonehenge, the circle itself is wider. Superstitious villagers smashed many of the stones in the 18th century, believing the circle to have been a place of pagan sacrifice.

The original form of the circle is best appreciated by a visit to the excellent **Alexander Keiller Museum** to the west of the site, which illustrates in detail the construction of the circle. There is also a fascinating exhibition entitled "6,000 Years of Mystery", which explains the changing landscape of Avebury.

St James's Church has a Norman font carved with sea monsters, and a rare 15th-century choir screen.

Environs: A few minutes drive east, **Marlborough** is an attractive town with a long and broad High Street lined with colonnaded Georgian shops.

Alexander Keiller Museum

(NT) Off High St. *01672 539250. daily. 24, 25 Dec.*

Salisbury ⓭

SALISBURY WAS FOUNDED IN 1220, when the old hill-top settlement of Old Sarum *(see p251)* was abandoned, being too arid and windswept, in favour of a new site among the lush water meadows where the rivers Avon, Nadder and Bourne meet. Purbeck marble may have been floated down the Nadder from Chilmark, 12 miles (20 km) west of Salisbury, for the construction of a new cathedral which was built mostly in the early 13th century, over the remarkably short space of 38 years. Its magnificent landmark spire – the tallest in England – was an inspired afterthought added in 1280–1310.

The 15th-century house of John A'Port, Queen's Street

Bishop's Walk and a sculpture by Elisabeth Frink (1930–93), Cathedral Close

Exploring Salisbury

The spacious and tranquil **Close**, with its schools, almshouses and clergy housing, makes a fine setting for Salisbury's cathedral. Among the numerous elegant buildings here are the **Matrons' College**, built in 1682 as a home for clergy widows, and 13th-century **Malmesbury House** with its splendid early Georgian façade (1719), fronted by lovely wrought-iron gates. Other buildings of interest include the 13th-century **Deanery**, the 13th-century **Wardrobe**, now a regimental museum, and the **Cathedral School**, housed in the 13th-century Bishop's Palace and famous for the quality of its choristers.

Beyond the walls of the Cathedral Close, Salisbury developed its chessboard layout, with areas devoted to different trades, perpetuated in street names such as Fish Row and Butcher Row. Leaving the Close through **High Street Gate,** you reach the busy High Street leading to the 13th-century **Church of St Thomas**, which has a lovely carved timber roof (1450), and a late 15th-century Doom painting, showing Christ seated in judgement and demons seizing the damned. Nearby in Silver Street, **Poultry Cross** was built in the 15th century as a covered poultry market. An intricate network of alleys fans out from this point with a number of fine timber-framed houses. In the large bustling **Market Place** the **Guildhall** is an unusual cream stone building from 1788–95, used for civic functions. More attractive are the brick and tile-hung houses on the north side of the square, many with Georgian façades concealing medieval houses.

FISH ROW

Street signs reflecting trades of 13th-century Salisbury

The Cloisters are the largest in England. They were added between 1263 and 1284 in the Decorated style.

The Chapter House has an original of the *Magna Carta*. Its walls have stone friezes of the Old Testament.

The Trinity Chapel contains the grave of St Osmund who was bishop of Old Sarum from 1078–1099.

Choir stalls

Bishop Audley's Chantry, a magnificent 16th-century monument to the bishop, is one of several small chapels clustered round the altar.

Mompesson House

(NT) The Close. *01722 335659.* *Apr–Oct: 11am–5pm Sat–Wed.* *limited.*

Built by a wealthy Wiltshire family in 1701, the handsomely furnished rooms of this house give an indication of life for the Close's inhabitants in the 18th century. The delightful garden, bounded by the north wall of the Close, has fine herbaceous borders.

Salisbury and South Wiltshire Museum

The Close. *01722 332151.* *Mon–Sat (Jul–Aug: Sun pm).* www.salisburymuseum.org.uk

In the medieval King's House, this museum has displays on early man, Stonehenge and nearby Old Sarum *(see p251)*.

The graceful spire soars to a height of 123 m (404 ft).

***The West Front** is decorated by rows of lavish symbolic figures and saints in niches.*

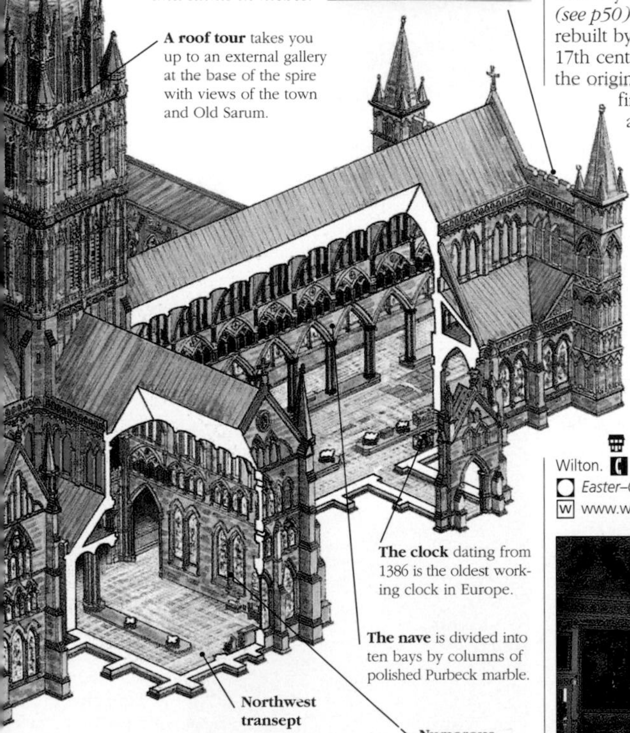

A roof tour takes you up to an external gallery at the base of the spire with views of the town and Old Sarum.

The clock dating from 1386 is the oldest working clock in Europe.

The nave is divided into ten bays by columns of polished Purbeck marble.

Northwest transept

Numerous windows add to the airy and spacious atmosphere of the interior.

Salisbury Cathedral

The Close. *01722 555120.* *daily.* **Donation.** www.salisburycathedral.org.uk

The cathedral was mostly built between 1220 and 1258. It is a fine example of Early English Gothic architecture, typified by tall, sharply pointed lancet windows.

Visitors' Checklist

Wiltshire. 40,000. South Western Rd. Endless St. Fish Row (01722 334956). Tue, Sat. Salisbury Festival: end May. www.visitsalisbury.com

Environs: The town of Wilton is renowned for its carpet industry, founded by the 8th Earl of Pembroke using French Huguenot refugee weavers. The town's ornate **church** (1844) is a brilliant example of Neo-Romanesque architecture, incorporating genuine Roman columns, Flemish Renaissance woodwork, German and Dutch stained glass and Italian mosaics.

Wilton House has been home to the Earls of Pembroke since it was converted from a nunnery after the Dissolution *(see p50)*. The house, largely rebuilt by Inigo Jones in the 17th century, includes one of the original Tudor towers, a fine collection of art and a landscaped park with a Palladian bridge (1737). The glories of the house are the Single and Double Cube State Rooms. Both have magnificently frescoed ceilings and gilded stucco work and were designed to hang a series of family portraits by Van Dyck.

Wilton House

Wilton. *01722 746729.* *Easter–Oct: daily.* www.wiltonhouse.com

Double Cube room, designed by Inigo Jones in 1653

***The Longleat Tree* tapestry (1980) depicting a 400-year history**

Longleat House ⓮

Warminster, Wiltshire. *01985 844400.* *Warminster then taxi.*
House *daily.* *25 Dec.*
Safari Park *Apr–Nov: daily.*
www.longleat.co.uk

THE ARCHITECTURAL HISTORIAN John Summerson coined the term "prodigy house" to describe the exuberance and grandeur of Elizabethan architecture that is so well represented at Longleat. The house was started in 1540, when John Thynne bought the ruins of a priory on the site for £53. Over the centuries subsequent owners have added their own touches. These include the Breakfast Room and Lower Dining Room (dating from the 1870s), modelled on the Venetian Ducal Palace, and erotic murals painted by the present owner, the 7th Marquess of Bath. Today, the Great Hall is the only remaining room which belongs to Thynne's time.

In 1949, the 6th Marquess was the first landowner in Britain to open his stately home to the public, in order to fund the maintenance and preservation of the house and its estate. Parts of the grounds, landscaped by Capability Brown *(see p22)*, were turned into an expansive safari park in 1966, where lions, tigers and other wild animals roam freely. This, along with other additions such as the world's longest hedge maze, the Adventure Castle and Blue Peter Maze, and special events, now draw even more visitors than the house.

Stourhead ⓯

STOURHEAD IS AMONG THE FINEST EXAMPLES of 18th-century landscape gardening in Britain *(see pp22–3)*. The garden was begun in the 1740s by Henry Hoare (1705–85), who inherited the estate and transformed it into a breathtaking work of art. Hoare created the lake, surrounding it with rare trees and plants, and Neo-Classical Italianate temples, grottoes and bridges. The Palladian-style house, built by Colen Campbell *(see p24)*, dates from 1724.

Pantheon
Hercules is among the statues of Roman gods housed in the elegant Pantheon (1753).

Gothic Cottage (1806)

Iron Bridge

A walk of 2 miles (3 km) round the lake provides artistically contrived vistas.

The lake was created from a group of medieval fishponds. Hoare dammed the valley to form a single expanse of water.

Turf Bridge

Temple of Flora (1744)

★ Temple of Apollo
The Classical temples that dot the garden were all designed by influential architect Henry Flitcroft (1679–1769).

Grotto
Tunnels lead to an artificial cave with a pool and a life-size statue of the guardian of the River Stour, sculpted by John Cheere in 1748.

VISITORS' CHECKLIST

(NT) Stourton, Wiltshire. *01747 841152. 0891 335205. Gillingham (Dorset) then taxi.* **House** *Apr–Oct: 11am–5pm Fri–Tue (last adm: 4:30pm).* **Gardens** *9am–7pm (or dusk if earlier) daily. limited.*

★ Stourhead House
Reconstructed after a fire in 1902, the house contains fine Chippendale furniture. The art collection reflects Henry Hoare's Classical tastes and includes The Choice of Hercules *(1637) by Nicolas Poussin.*

Colourful shrubs around the house include fragrant rhododendrons in spring.

Stourton village was incorporated into Hoare's overall design.

Pelargonium House is a historical collection of over 100 species and cultivars.

The reception contains exhibitions illustrating the story of Stourhead.

Entrance and car park

St Peter's Church
The parish church contains monuments to the Hoare family. The medieval monument nearby was brought from Bristol in 1765.

STAR SIGHTS

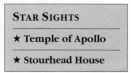

★ Temple of Apollo

★ Stourhead House

Shaftesbury 16

Dorset. 8,000. 8 Bell St (01747 853514). Thu.
www.shaftesburydorset.co.uk

HILLTOP SHAFTESBURY, with its cobbled streets and 18th-century cottages is often used as a setting for films to give a flavour of Old England. Picturesque **Gold Hill** is lined on one side by a wall of the demolished **abbey**, founded by King Alfred in 888. Only the excavated remains of the abbey church survive, and many masonry fragments are found in the local museum.

The Almshouse (1437) adjoining the Abbey Church, Sherborne

Sherborne 17

Dorset. 9,500. Digby Rd (01935 815341). Thu, Sat.
www.westdorset.com

FEW OTHER TOWNS in Britain have such a wealth of unspoilt medieval buildings. Edward VI *(see p41)* founded the famous Sherborne School in 1550, saving intact the splendid **Abbey Church** and other monastic buildings that might otherwise have been demolished in the Dissolution *(see p50)*. Remains of the Saxon church can be seen in the abbey's façade, but the most striking feature is the 15th-century fan-vaulted ceiling.

Sherborne Castle, built by Sir Walter Raleigh *(see p51)* in 1594, is a wonderfully varied building that anticipates the flamboyant Jacobean style. Raleigh also lived briefly in the early 12th-century **Old Castle**, which now stands in ruins, demolished during the Civil War *(see p52)*.

ENVIRONS: West of Sherborne, past Yeovil, is the magnificent Elizabethan **Montacute House** *(see p233)*, set in 120 ha (300 acres) of grounds. It is noted for tapestries, and for the Tudor and Jacobean portraits in the vast Long Gallery.

Sherborne Castle
Off A30. *01935 813182.* **Castle** *Apr–Oct: Tue–Thu, Sat, Sun & bank hols (pm).* **Grounds** *Apr–Oct: Thu–Tue.*
www.sherbornecastle.com

Old Castle
(EH) Off A30. *01935 812730.* *Easter–Oct: daily; Nov–Easter: Wed–Sun.* *25, 26 Dec, 1 Jan.*

Montacute House
(NT) Montacute. *01935 823289.* **Grounds** *Apr–Nov: Wed–Mon.*

Abbotsbury 18

Dorset. *400.* *Bakehouse, Market St.* www.abbotsbury-tourism.co.uk

THE NAME ABBOTSBURY recalls the town's 11th-century Benedictine abbey of which little but the huge tithe barn, built around 1400, remains.

Nobody knows when the **Swannery** here was founded, but the earliest record dates to 1393. Mute swans come to nest in the breeding season, attracted by the reed beds which spread along the Fleet, a brackish lagoon protected from the sea by a high ridge of pebbles called **Chesil Bank** *(see p230)*. Its wild atmosphere makes an appealing contrast to the south coast resorts, although strong currents make swimming too dangerous. **Abbotsbury Sub-Tropical Gardens** are the frost-free home to many new plants, discovered by botanists travelling in South America and Asia in the last 30 years.

The Swannery at Abbotsbury

Swannery
New Barn Rd. *01305 871858.* *Apr–Nov: daily.*

Abbotsbury Sub-Tropical Gardens
Off B3157. *01305 871387.* *daily.* *25, 26 Dec, 1 Jan.*

Weymouth 19

Dorset. *62,000.* *King's Statue, The Esplanade (01305 785747).* *Thu.*
www.jurassiccoast.com

WEYMOUTH'S POPULARITY as one of Britain's earliest seaside resorts began in 1789 when George III paid the first of many summer visits here. The king's bathing machine

Weymouth Quay, Dorset's south coast

can be seen in the **The Esplanade**, and his statue is a prominent feature on the seafront. Here gracious Georgian terraces and hotels look across to the beautiful expanse of Weymouth Bay. Different in character is the old town around Custom House Quay with its fishing boats and old seamen's inns.

The Esplanade
Hope Sq. 01305 777622. *daily.* *25, 26 Dec, 2 wks in Jan.*

A 55 m (180 ft) giant carved on the chalk hillside, Cerne Abbas (NT)

Dorchester 20

Dorset. *16,000.* *Antelope Walk (01305 267992).* *Wed.* www.westdorset.com

DORCHESTER, the county town of Dorset, is still recognizably the town in which Thomas Hardy based his novel *The Mayor of Casterbridge* (1886). Here, among the many 17th- and 18th-century houses lining the High Street, is the **Dorset County Museum**, where the original manuscript of the novel is displayed. Dorchester has the only example of a **Roman town house** in Britain. The remains reveal architectural details including a fine mosaic. There are also finds from Iron Age and Roman sites on the outskirts of the town. **Maumbury Rings** (Weymouth Avenue), is a Roman amphitheatre, originally a Neolithic henge. To the west, many Roman graves have been found below the Iron Age hill fort, **Poundbury Camp**.

ENVIRONS: Just southwest of Dorchester, **Maiden Castle** *(see p43)* is a massive monument dating from around 100 BC. In AD 43 it was the scene of a battle when the Romans fought the Iron Age people of southern England.

To the north lies the charming village of **Cerne Abbas** with its magnificent medieval tithe barn and monastic buildings. The huge chalk figure of a giant on the hillside here is a fertility figure thought to represent either the Roman god Hercules or an Iron Age warrior.

East of Dorchester are the churches, thatched villages and rolling hills immortalized in Hardy's novels. Picturesque **Bere Regis** is the Kingsbere of *Tess of the D'Urbervilles*, where the tombs of the family whose name inspired the novel may be seen in the Saxon **church**. **Hardy's Cottage** is where the writer was born and **Max Gate** is the house he designed and lived in from 1885 until his death. His heart is buried with his family at **Stinsford** church – his body was given a public funeral at Westminster Abbey *(pp94–5)*.

Hardy's statue, Dorchester

There are beautiful gardens *(see p233)* and a magnificent medieval hall at 15th-century **Athelhampton House**.

Dorset County Museum
High West St. 01305 262735. *Nov–Apr: Mon–Sat; May–Oct: daily.* *25, 26 Dec.* *limited.* www.dorsetcountymuseum.org

Hardy's Cottage
(NT) Higher Bockhampton. 01305 262366. *Apr–Oct: Thu–Mon.* *garden only.*

Max Gate
(NT) Alington Ave, Dorchester. 01305 262538. *Apr–Sep: Sun, Mon & Wed (pm).*

Athelhampton House
Athelhampton. 01305 848363. *Mar–Oct: Sun–Fri.* *gardens only.*

THOMAS HARDY (1840–1928)

The vibrant, descriptive novels and poems of Thomas Hardy, one of England's best-loved writers, are set against the background of his native Dorset. The Wessex countryside provides a constant and familiar stage against which his characters enact their fate. Vivid accounts of rural life record a key moment in history, when mechanization was about to destroy ancient farming methods, just as the Industrial Revolution had done in the towns a century before *(see pp54–5)*. Hardy's powerfully visual style has made novels such as *Tess of the D'Urbervilles* (1891) popular with modern film-makers, and drawn literary pilgrims to the villages and landscapes that inspired his fiction.

Nastassja Kinski in Roman Polanski's film *Tess* (1979)

Corfe Castle 21

(NT) Corfe Castle, Dorset. *01929 481294.* *Wareham then bus.* *daily.* *25, 26 Dec.* *limited.* *Mar–Oct: free; Nov–Feb: by arrangement.*

THE SPECTACULAR RUINS of Corfe Castle romantically crown a jagged pinnacle of rock above the charming unspoilt village that shares its name. The castle has dominated the landscape since the 11th century, first as a royal fortification, then as the dramatic ruins seen today. In 1635 the castle was purchased by Sir John Bankes, whose wife and her retainers – mostly women – courageously held out against 600 Parliamentary troops, in a six-week siege during the Civil War *(see pp52–3)*. The castle was eventually taken through treachery and in 1646 Parliament voted to have it "slighted" – deliberately blown up to prevent it being used again. From the ruins there are far-reaching views over the Isle of Purbeck and its coastline.

The ruins of Corfe Castle, dating mainly from Norman times

Isle of Purbeck 22

Dorset. *Wareham.* *Shell Bay, Studland.* *Swanage (01929 422885).* www.swanage.gov.uk

THE ISLE OF PURBECK, which is in fact a peninsula, is the source of the grey shelly limestone, known as Purbeck marble, from which the castle and surrounding houses were built. The geology changes to the southwest at **Kimmeridge**, where the muddy shale is rich in fossils and recently discovered oil reserves. The Isle is fringed with unspoilt beaches. **Studland Bay** (NT) – with its white sand and its sand-dune nature reserve, rich in birdlife – has been rated one of Britain's best beaches. Sheltered **Lulworth Cove** is almost encircled by white cliffs and there is a fine clifftop walk to Durdle Door *(see p231)*, a natural chalk arch eroded by the waves.

The main resort in the area is **Swanage**, the port where Purbeck stone was transported by ship to London, to be used for everything from street paving to church building. Unwanted masonry from demolished buildings was shipped back and this is how Swanage got its wonderfully ornate **Town Hall** façade, designed by Wren around 1668.

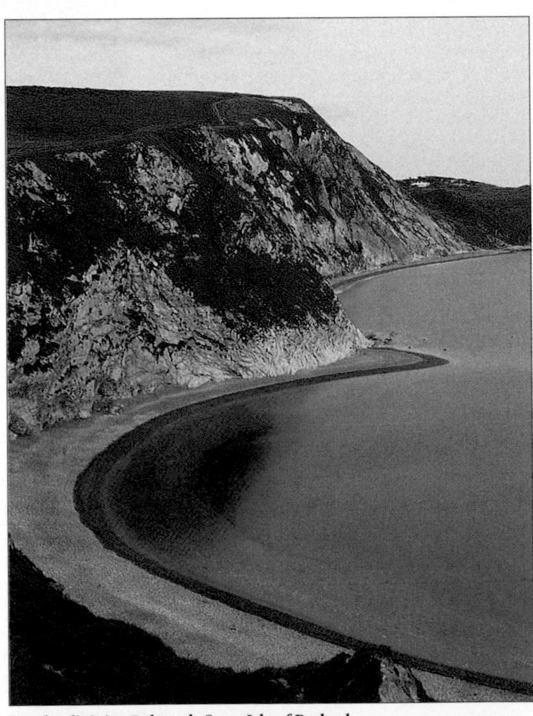

Beach adjoining Lulworth Cove, Isle of Purbeck

Poole 23

Dorset. *142,000.* *High St (01202 253253).* www.pooletourism.com

SITUATED ON ONE of the largest natural harbours in the world, Poole is an ancient, still thriving, seaport. The quay is lined with old warehouses, modern apartments and a marina, overlooking a safe sheltered bay. The **Waterfront Museum**, partly housed in 15th-century cellars on the quay, tells the seafaring history of the port and town, and has a range of changing exhibitions. Nearby **Brownsea Island** (reached by boat from the quay) is given over to a woodland nature reserve with a waterfowl and heron sanctuary. The fine views of the Dorset coast add to the appeal of the island.

Waterfront Museum
High St. 01202 262600.
daily. 25, 26 Dec, 1 Jan.
www.poole.gov.uk

Brownsea Island
(NT) Poole. *01202 707744.* *Apr–Nov: daily (boat trips leave the quayside every 30 mins during the season).*

Boats in Poole harbour

Wimborne Minster 24

Dorset. *6,500.* *29 High St (01202 886116).* *Fri–Sun.*
www.visiteastdorset.com

The fine collegiate church of Wimborne's **Minster** was founded in 705 by Cuthburga, sister of King Ina of Wessex. It fell prey to marauding Danish raiders in the 10th century, and the imposing grey church we see today dates from the refounding by Edward the Confessor *(see p47)* in 1043. Stonemasons made use of the local Purbeck marble, carving beasts, biblical scenes, and a mass of zig-zag decoration.

The 16th-century **Priest's House Museum** has rooms furnished in the style of different periods and an enchanting hidden garden.

Environs: Designed for the Bankes family after the destruction of Corfe Castle, **Kingston Lacy** was acquired by the National Trust in 1981. The estate has always been farmed by traditional methods and is astonishingly rich in wildlife, rare flowers and butterflies. This quiet, forgotten corner of Dorset is grazed by rare Red Devon cattle and can be explored using paths and "green lanes" that date back to Roman and Saxon times. The fine 17th-century house on the estate contains an outstanding collection of paintings, including works by Rubens, Velázquez and Titian.

Priest's House Museum
High St. *01202 882533.* *Apr–Oct: Mon–Sat.* *limited.*

Kingston Lacy
(NT) on B3082. *01202 883402.*
House *Apr–Oct: Sun–Wed.*
Gardens *Apr–Oct: daily; Nov–Mar: Sat & Sun.* *gardens only.*

Bournemouth 25

Dorset. *165,000.*
Westover Rd (0906 8020234).
www.bournemouth.co.uk

Bournemouth's popularity as one of England's favourite seaside resorts is due to an almost unbroken sweep of sandy beach, extending from the mouth of Poole Harbour to Hengistbury Head. Most of the seafront is built up, with many large seaside villas and exclusive hotels. To the west there are numerous clifftop parks and gardens, interrupted by beautiful wooded river ravines, known as "chines". The varied and colourful garden of **Compton Acres** was conceived as a museum of many different garden styles.

In central Bournemouth the amusement arcades, casinos, nightclubs and shops cater for the city's many visitors. During the summer, pop groups, TV comedians and the highly regarded Bournemouth Symphony Orchestra perform at various venues in the city. The **Russell-Cotes Art Gallery and Museum**, housed in a late Victorian villa, has an extensive collection with many fine Oriental and Victorian artefacts.

A toy train on the popular seafront at Bournemouth

***Marchesa Maria Grimaldi* by Sir Peter Paul Rubens (1577–1640), Kingston Lacy**

Environs: The magnificent **Christchurch Priory**, east of Bournemouth, is 95 m (310 ft) in length – the longest church in England. It was rebuilt between the 13th and 16th centuries and presents a sequence of different styles. The original nave, built around 1093, is an impressive example of Norman architecture, but the highlight is the intricate stone reredos which features a Tree of Jesse, tracing the lineage of Christ. Next to the Priory are the ruins of a Norman **castle**.

Between Bournemouth and Christchurch, **Hengistbury Head** is well worth climbing for grassland flowers, butterflies and sea views, while **Stanpit Marsh**, to the west of Bournemouth, is an excellent spot for viewing herons and other wading birds.

Compton Acres
Canford Cliffs Rd. *01202 700 778.* *daily.*
www.comptonacres.co.uk

Russell-Cotes Art Gallery and Museum
Eastcliff. *01202 451800.* *Tue–Sun.* www.russell-cotes.bournemouth.gov.uk

PW 33
PW 33

Devon and Cornwall

Devon · Cornwall

Miles of magnificently varied coastline *dominate this magical corner of Britain. Popular seaside resorts alternate with secluded coves and unspoilt fishing villages rich in maritime history. In contrast there are lush, exotic gardens and the wild terrain of the moorland interior, dotted with tors and historic remains.*

Geographical neighbours, the counties of Devon and Cornwall are very different in character. Celtic Cornwall, with its numerous villages named after early Christian missionaries, is mostly stark and treeless at its centre. In many places it is still scarred by the remains of tin and copper mining that has played an important part in the economy for some 4,000 years. Yet this does not detract from the beauty and variety of the coastline dotted with lighthouses and tiny coves, and penetrated by deep tidal rivers.

Devon, by contrast, is a land of lush pasture divided into a patchwork of tiny fields and threaded with narrow lanes, whose banks support a mass of flowers from the first spring primroses to summer's colourful mixture of campion, foxglove, oxeye daisies and blue cornflowers. The leisurely pace of rural life here, and in Cornwall, contrasts with life in the bustling cities. Exeter with its magnificent cathedral, historic Plymouth, elegant Truro and Elizabethan Totnes are urban centres brimming with life and character.

The spectacular coastline and the mild climate of the region attract families, boating enthusiasts and surfers. For those in search of solitude, the Southwest Coastal Path provides access to the more tranquil areas. There are fishing villages and harbours whose heyday was in the buccaneering age of Drake and Raleigh *(see p51)*, and inland the wild moorland of Bodmin and Dartmoor, which provided inspiration for many romantic tales. Many of these are associated with King Arthur *(see p273)* who, according to legend, was born at Tintagel on Cornwall's dramatically contorted north coast.

Beach huts on the seafront at Paignton, near Torquay

◁ **Fishing boats in Port Isaac, on Cornwall's north coast**

Exploring Devon and Cornwall

ROMANTIC MOORLAND dominates the inland parts of Devon and Cornwall, ideal walking country with few roads and magnificent views stretching for miles. By contrast the extensive coastline is indented by hundreds of sheltered river valleys, each one seemingly isolated from the rest of the world – one reason why Devon and Cornwall can absorb so many visitors and yet still seem uncrowded. Wise tourists get to know one small part of Devon or Cornwall intimately, soaking up the atmosphere of the region, rather than rushing to see everything in the space of a week.

KEY

- Motorway
- Major road
- Minor road
- Scenic route
- Scenic path
- River
- Viewpoint

SIGHTS AT A GLANCE

AppledNore 16
Barnstaple 17
Bideford 15
Bodmin 11
Buckfastleigh 23
Buckland Abbey 26
Bude 13
Burgh Island 24
Clovelly 14
Cotehele 27
Dartmoor pp282–3 29
Dartmouth 21
Eden Project pp270–71 9
Exeter 19
Falmouth 6
Fowey 10
Helston and the Lizard Peninsula 5
Lynton and Lynmouth 18
Morwellham Quay 28
Penzance 3
Plymouth 25
St Austell 8
St Ives 2
St Michael's Mount pp266–7 4
Tintagel 12
Torbay 20
Totnes 22
Truro 7

Walks and Tours

Penwith Tour 1

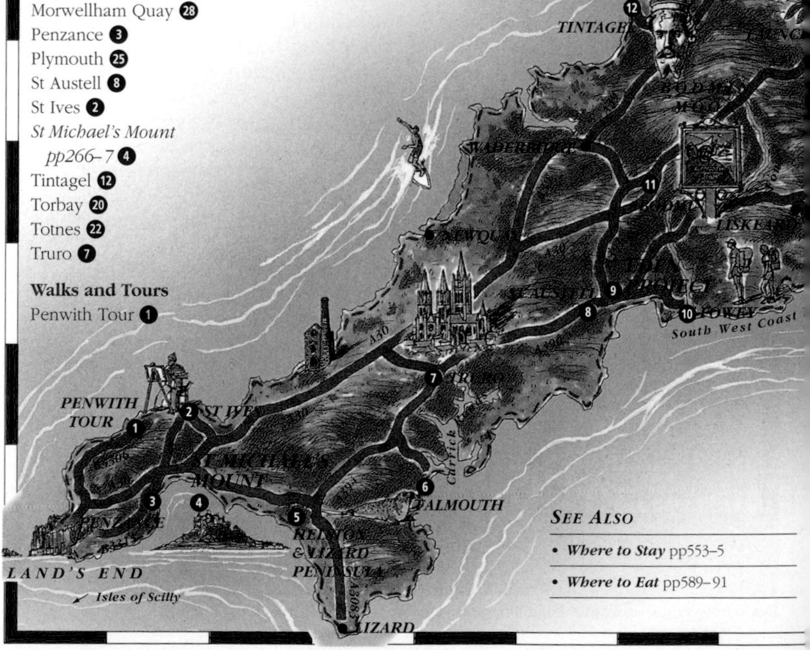

The dramatic cliffs of Land's End, England's most westerly point

SEE ALSO

- ***Where to Stay*** pp553–5
- ***Where to Eat*** pp589–91

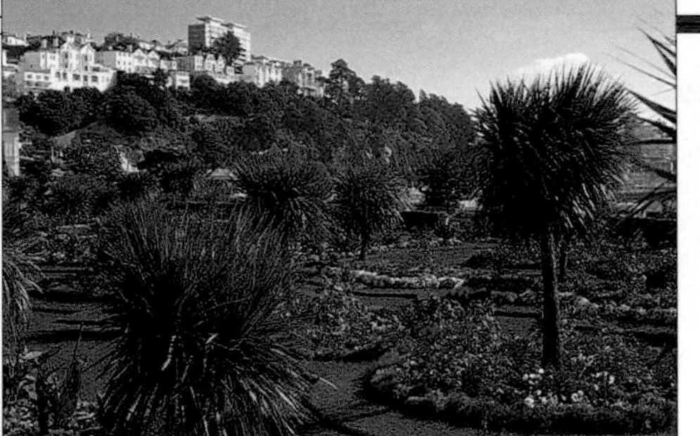

Sub-tropical gardens at Torquay, the popular seaside resort

GETTING AROUND

Large numbers of drivers, many towing caravans (trailers), travel along the M5 motorway and A30 trunk road from mid-July to early September and travel can be slow, especially on Saturdays. Once in Devon and Cornwall, allow ample time if you are travelling by car along the region's narrow and high-banked lanes.

The regular train services, running from Paddington to Penzance, along Brunel's historic Great Western Railway, stop at most major towns. Aside from this, you are dependent on taxis or infrequent local buses.

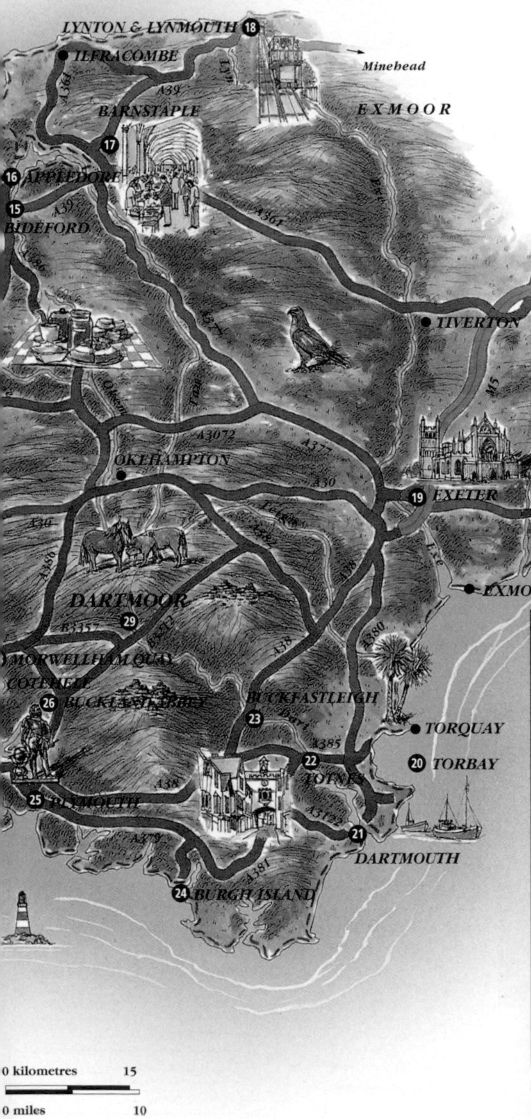

LYNTON & LYNMOUTH 18
ILFRACOMBE
Minehead
A39
BARNSTAPLE
17
EXMOOR
16 APPLEDORE
15 BIDEFORD
A361
A38
Taunton
TIVERTON
Yeovil
M5
HONITON
A358
A3072
OKEHAMPTON
A377
A30
19 EXETER
A3052
SIDMOUTH
EXMOUTH
DARTMOOR
29
MORWELLHAM QUAY
26
BUCKFASTLEIGH
23
TORQUAY
20 TORBAY
A385
22
TOTNES
25 PLYMOUTH
A3122
21
DARTMOUTH
A379
A381
24 BURGH ISLAND
0 kilometres 15
0 miles 10

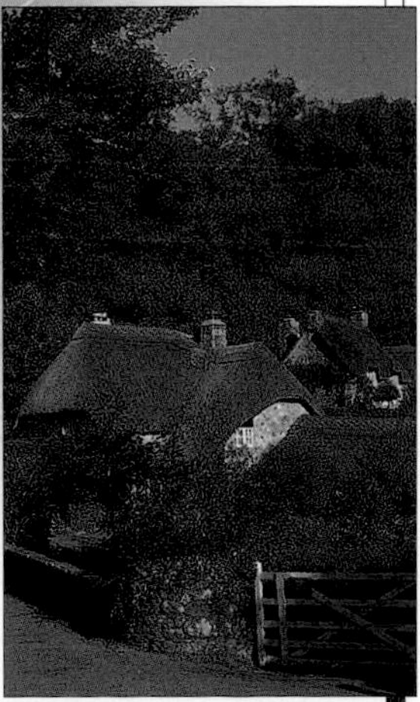

Typical thatched, stone cottages, Buckland-in-the-Moor, Dartmoor

Penwith Tour ❶

THIS TOUR PASSES THROUGH a spectacular, remote Cornish landscape, dotted with relics of the tin mining industry, picturesque fishing villages and many prehistoric remains. The magnificent coastline varies between the gentle rolling moorland in the north and the rugged, windswept cliffs that characterize the dramatic south coast. The beauty of the area, combined with the clarity of light, has attracted artists since the late 19th century. Their work can be seen in Newlyn, St Ives and Penzance.

Tips for Drivers

***Tour length**: 31 miles (50 km)*
***Stopping-off points**: There are pubs and cafés in most villages. Sennen Cove makes a pleasant mid-way stop.* (See also pp636–7.)

Zennor ①
The carved mermaid in the church recalls the legend of the mermaid who lured the local squire's son to her ocean lair.

Lanyon Quoit ②
One of many prehistoric monuments, this chambered tomb is visible on the left from the road to Madron.

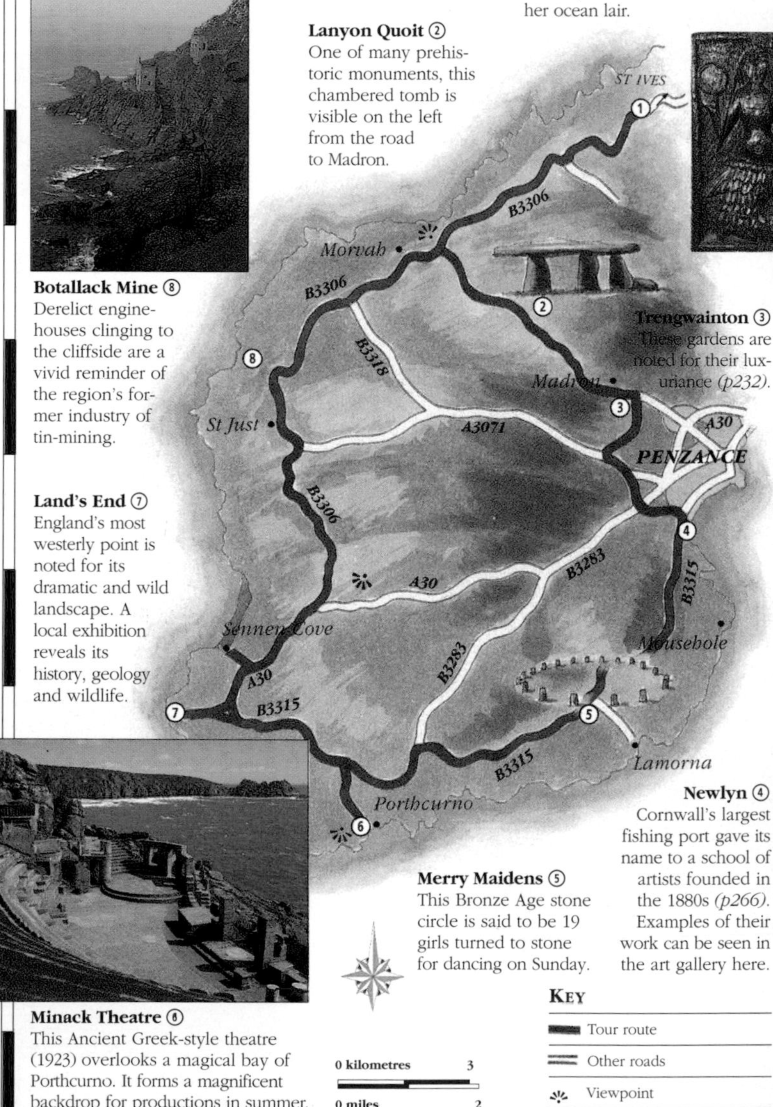

Botallack Mine ⑧
Derelict engine-houses clinging to the cliffside are a vivid reminder of the region's former industry of tin-mining.

Trengwainton ③
These gardens are noted for their luxuriance *(p232)*.

Land's End ⑦
England's most westerly point is noted for its dramatic and wild landscape. A local exhibition reveals its history, geology and wildlife.

Newlyn ④
Cornwall's largest fishing port gave its name to a school of artists founded in the 1880s *(p266)*. Examples of their work can be seen in the art gallery here.

Merry Maidens ⑤
This Bronze Age stone circle is said to be 19 girls turned to stone for dancing on Sunday.

Minack Theatre ⑥
This Ancient Greek-style theatre (1923) overlooks a magical bay of Porthcurno. It forms a magnificent backdrop for productions in summer.

Key

- Tour route
- Other roads
- Viewpoint

St Ives ❷

Cornwall. 11,000.
Street-an-Pol (01736 796297).
www.go-cornwall.com

St Ives is renowned for the **Barbara Hepworth Museum and Sculpture Garden** and **Tate St Ives**, which together celebrate the work of a group of artists who set up a seaside art colony here from the 1920s. Tate St Ives, designed to frame a panoramic view of Porthmeor Beach, reminds visitors of the natural surroundings that inspired the art on display within. The Barbara Hepworth Museum presents the sculptor's work in the house and garden where she lived and worked for many years.

The town of St Ives remains a typical English seaside resort, surrounded by a crescent of golden sands. Popular taste rules in the many other art galleries tucked down winding alleys with names such as Teetotal Street, a legacy of the town's Methodist heritage. Many galleries are converted cellars and lofts where fish were once salted and packed. In between are whitewashed cottages with tiny gardens brimming with marigolds, sunflowers and trailing lobelia, their vibrant colours made intense by the unusually clear light that first attracted artists to St Ives.

The Lower Terrace, Tate St Ives

Barbara Hepworth Museum and Sculpture Garden

Barnoon Hill. 01736 796226.
Mar–Oct: daily; Nov–Feb: Tue–Sun. 24–26 Dec. by arrangement.

Tate St Ives

Porthmeor Beach. 01736 796226.
Mar–Oct: daily; Nov–Feb: Tue–Sun. 24–26 Dec.
www.tate.org.uk

Twentieth-Century Artists of St Ives

Ben Nicholson and Barbara Hepworth formed the nucleus of a group of artists that made a major contribution to the development of abstract art in Europe. In the 1920s, St Ives together with Newlyn *(see p264)* became a place for aspiring artists. Among the prolific artists associated with the town are the potter Bernard Leach (1887–1979) and the painter Patrick Heron (1920–99), whose *Coloured Glass Window (see p228)* dominates the Tate St Ives entrance. Much of the art on display at Tate St Ives is abstract and illustrates new responses to the rugged Cornish landscape, the human figure and the ever-changing patterns of sunlight on sea.

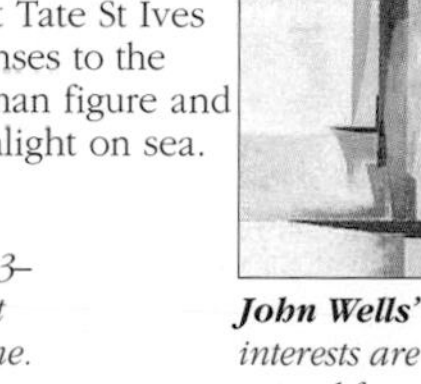
John Wells' *(b.1907) key interests are in light, curved forms and birds in flight, as revealed in* Aspiring Forms *(1950).*

Barbara Hepworth *(1903–75) was one of the foremost abstract sculptors of her time.* Madonna and Child *(1953) can be seen in the church of St Ia.*

Ben Nicholson's *(1894–1982) work shows a change in style from simple scenes, such as the view from his window, to a preoccupation with shapes – as seen in this painting* St Ives, Cornwall *(1943–5). Later, his interest moved towards pure geometric blocks of colour.*

Penzance ❸

Cornwall. 15,000.
Station Approach (01736 362207).
www.go-cornwall.com

PENZANCE IS A BUSTLING resort with a climate so mild that palm trees and sub-tropical plants grow happily in the lush **Morrab Gardens**. The town commands fine views of St Michael's Mount and a great sweep of clean sandy beach.

The main road through the town is Market Jew Street, at the top of which stands the magnificent domed Market House (1837), fronted by a statue of Sir Humphrey Davy (1778–1829). Davy, who came from Penzance, invented the miner's safety lamp which detected lethal gases.

Chapel Street is lined with curious buildings, none more striking than the flamboyant **Egyptian House** (1835), with its richly painted façade and lotus bud decoration. Just as curious is **Admiral Benbow Inn** (1696) on the same street, which has a pirate perched on the roof looking out to sea. The town's **Museum and Art Gallery** has pictures by the Newlyn School of artists.

ENVIRONS: A short distance south of Penzance, **Newlyn** *(see p264)* is Cornwall's largest fishing port, which has given its name to the local school of artists founded by Stanhope Forbes (1857–1947). They painted outdoors, aiming to capture the fleeting impressions of wind, sun and sea. Continuing south, the coastal road ends at **Mousehole** (pronounced Mowzall), a pretty, popular village with a tiny harbour, tiers of cottages and a maze of narrow alleys.

The Egyptian House (1835)

North of Penzance, overlooking the magical Cornish coast, **Chysauster** is a fine example of a Romano-British village. The site has remained almost undisturbed since it

St Michael's Mount ❹

(NT) Marazion, Cornwall. *01736 710507.* *from Marazion (Apr–Oct) or on foot at low tide.* *Apr–Oct: Mon–Fri; Nov–Mar guided tours only (phone to arrange).*
www.stmichaelsmount.co.uk

ST MICHAEL'S MOUNT emerges dramatically from the waters of Mount Bay, opposite the small village of Marazion.

According to ancient Roman historians, the mount was the island of Ictis, an important centre for the Cornish tin trade during the Iron Age. It is dedicated to the archangel St Michael who, according to legend, appeared here in 495.

When the Normans conquered England in 1066 *(see pp46–7)*, they were struck by the island's resemblance to their own Mont-St-Michel, whose Benedictine monks were invited to build a small abbey here. The abbey was absorbed into a fortress at the Dissolution *(see p339)*, when Henry VIII set up a chain of coastal defences to counter an expected attack from France.

In 1659 St Michael's Mount was purchased by Sir John St Aubyn whose descendants subsequently turned the fortress into a magnificent house.

Harbourside village
Access to the island is by boat from Marazion or on foot by a cobbled causeway at low tide.
The rocky slopes were planted with sub-tropical trees and shrubs by the St Aubyn family.

View of St Michael's Mount from Marazion

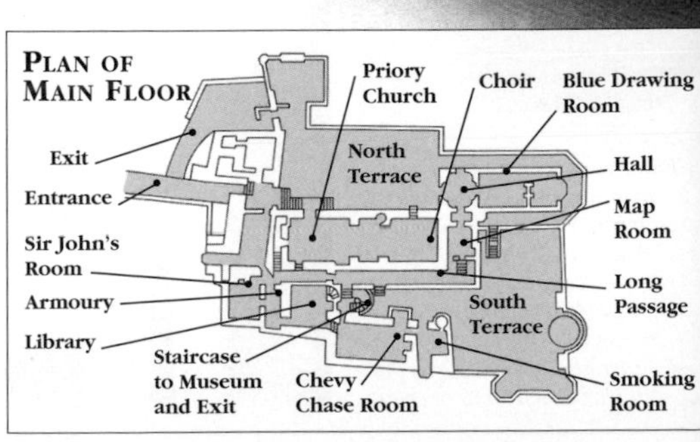

was abandoned during the 3rd century.

From Penzance, regular boat and helicopter services depart for the **Isles of Scilly**, a beautiful archipelago forming part of the same granite mass as Land's End, Bodmin Moor and Dartmoor. Along with tourism, flower-growing forms the main source of income here.

Penlee House Gallery and Museum
Morrab Rd.
01736 363625. May–Sep: 10am–5pm Mon–Sat; Oct–Apr: 10:30am–4:30pm Mon–Sat.
25–26 Dec, 1 Jan.
www.penleehouse.org.uk

Chysauster
Off B3311.
07831 757934.
Apr–Oct: daily.

THE GROWTH OF METHODISM

John Wesley (1703–91)

The hard-working and independent mining and fishing communities of the West Country had little time for the established church, but they were won over by the new Methodist religion, with its emphasis on hymn singing, open-air preaching and regular or "methodical" Bible reading. When John Wesley, the founder of Methodism, made the first of many visits to the area in 1743, sceptical Cornishmen pelted him with stones. His persistence, however, led to many conversions and by 1762 he was preaching to congregations of up to 30,000 people. Simple places of worship were built throughout the county; one favoured spot was the amphitheatre **Gwennap Pit**, at Busveal, south of Redruth. Methodist memorabilia can be seen in the Royal Cornwall Museum in Truro *(see p269)*.

stle
trance

The South Terrace forms the roof of the large Victorian wing. Beneath it there are five floors of private quarters.

The Blue Drawing Room *was formed from the Lady Chapel in the mid-18th century and is decorated in charming Rococo Gothic style. It contains fine plaster work, furniture and paintings by Gainsborough and Thomas Hudson.*

The Armoury displays sporting weapons and military trophies brought back by the St Aubyn family from various wars.

The Priory Church*, rebuilt in the late 14th century, forms the summit of the island. Beautiful rose windows are found at both ends.*

The Chevy Chase Room *takes its name from a plaster frieze (1641) representing hunting scenes.*

Pinnacles of serpentine rock at Kynance Cove (NT), Lizard Peninsula

Helston and the Lizard Peninsula ❺

Cornwall. *from Penzance.*
79 Meneage St (01326 565431).
www.go-cornwall.com

THE ATTRACTIVE TOWN of Helston makes a good base for exploring the windswept coastline of the Lizard Peninsula. The town is famous for its Furry Dance which welcomes spring with dancing through the streets *(see p62);* the **Folk Museum** explains the history of this ancient custom. The Georgian houses and inns of Coinagehall Street are a reminder that Helston was once a thriving stannary town where tin ingots were brought for weighing and stamping before being sold. Locally mined tin was brought down river to a harbour at the bottom of this street until access to the sea was blocked in the 13th century by a sand and shingle bar which formed across the estuary. The bar created the freshwater lake, Loe Pool, and an attractive walk skirts its wooded shores. In 1880, Helston's trade was taken over by a new harbour created to the east on the River Helford, at Gweek. Today, Gweek is the home of the **National Seal Sanctuary**, where sick seals are nursed back to health before being released into the sea.

Cornwall's tin mining industry, from Roman to recent times, is covered at the **Poldark Mine** where underground tours reveal the working conditions of miners in the 18th century. Another major attraction is **Flambards Village Theme Park,** with its recreation of a Victorian village and of Britain during the Blitz.

Further south, huge satellite dishes rise from the heathland. The **Goonhilly Earth Station** visitors' centre here explores the world of satellite communications.

Local shops sell souvenirs carved from serpentine, a soft greenish stone which forms the unusual-shaped rocks that rise from the sandy beach at picturesque **Kynance Cove**.

Cornish Smugglers

In the days before income tax was invented, the main form of government income came from tax on imported luxury goods, such as brandy and perfume. Huge profits were to be made by evading these taxes, which were at their height during the Napoleonic Wars (1780–1815). Remote Cornwall, with its coves and rivers penetrating deep into the mainland, was prime smuggling territory; estimates put the number of people involved, including women and children, at 100,000. Some notorious families resorted to deliberate wrecking, setting up deceptive lights to lure vessels onto the sharp rocks, in the hope of plundering the wreckage.

Folk Museum
Market Place, Helston. *01326 564027.* *Mon–Sat* *Christmas Week.* *limited.*

National Seal Sanctuary
Gweek. *01326 221361.* *daily* *25 Dec.*
www.sealsanctuary.co.uk

Poldark Mine
Wendron. *01326 573173.*
Nov–Mar, Jul, Aug: daily; May, Jun, Sep, Oct: Sun–Fri.
www.poldark-mine.co.uk

Flambards Village Theme Park
Culdrose Manor, Helston. *01326 573404.* *Easter–Oct: daily.*
www.flambards.co.uk

Goonhilly Earth Station
Nr Helston, off B3293. *0800 679593.* *Apr-Oct: daily.*
www.goonhilly.bt.com

Falmouth ❻

Cornwall. *22,000.*
28 Killigrew St (01326 312300).
www.go-cornwall.com

FALMOUTH stands at the point where seven rivers flow into a long stretch of water called the **Carrick Roads**. The drowned river valley is so deep that huge ocean going ships can sail up almost as far as Truro. Numerous creeks are ideal for boating excursions to view the varied scenery and birdlife.

Falmouth has the third largest naturally deep harbour after Sydney and Rio de Janeiro, and it forms the most interesting part of this seaside resort. On the harbour waterfront stands the recently constructed **National Maritime Museum Cornwall**, part of a projected large new waterside complex, to include cafés, shops and restaurants. With an exterior that is oak-clad to reflect the history of wooden boat sheds in the area, the museum is dedicated to the great maritime tradition of Cornwall, and contains Britain's finest public collection of historic and contemporary small craft. The building is designed to bring to life the stories of boats, maritime themes and Cornwall's heritage, as well as the story of the people whose lives depended on the sea. It aims to be accessible to the whole family.

The many old houses on the harbour include the striking **Customs House** and the chimney alongside, known as the "King's Pipe" because it was used for burning contraband tobacco seized from smugglers in the 19th century. **Pendennis Castle** and St Mawes Castle opposite, were built by King Henry VIII.

Environs: To the south, **Glendurgan** *(see p232)* and **Trebah** gardens are both set in sheltered valleys leading down to delightful sandy coves on the Helford River.

Truro Cathedral, designed by J L Pearson and completed in 1910

National Maritime Museum Cornwall
Discovery Quay, Falmouth. *01326 313388.* *daily.* *public hols.*
www.nmmc.co.uk

Ship's figure-head, Falmouth

Pendennis Castle
(EH) The Headland. *01326 316594.* *daily.* *24–26 Dec, 1 Jan.* *limited.*

Glendurgan
(NT) Mawnan Smith. *01326 250906.* *mid-Feb–mid-Nov: Tue–Sat & public hols.* *Good Fri.*
www.nationaltrust.org.uk

Trebah
Mawnan Smith. *01326 250448.* *daily.*
www.trebah-garden.co.uk

Truro ❼

Cornwall. *19,000.*
Boscawen St (01872 274555). *Wed (cattle), Wed & Sat (farmers' market).* www.truro.gov.uk

Once a market town and port, Truro is now the administrative capital of Cornwall. Truro's many gracious Georgian buildings reflect its prosperity during the tin mining boom of the 1800s. In 1876 the 16th-century parish church was rebuilt to create the first new **cathedral** to be built in England since Wren built St Paul's *(see pp116–17)* in the 17th century. With its central tower, lancet windows and spires, the cathedral is an exuberant building that looks more French than English.

Truro's cobbled streets and alleys lined with craft shops are also a delight to explore. The **Royal Cornwall Museum** provides an excellent intro-duction to the history of the county with displays on tin mining, Methodism *(see p267)*, and smuggling.

Environs: On the outskirts of the city lie **Trewithen** and **Trelissick** gardens *(see p232)*. The former has a rich collection of Asiatic plants.

Royal Cornwall Museum
River St. *01872 272205.* *Mon–Sat.* *public hols.*
www.royalcornwallmuseum.org.uk

Trewithen
Grampound Rd. *01726 883647.* *Mar–Sep: Mon–Sat (Apr, May: daily).* *by arrangement.*
www.trewithengardens.co.uk

Trelissick
(NT) Feock. *01872 862090.* *mid-Feb–Oct: daily.*
www.nationaltrust.org.uk

The "Cornish Alps": china-clay spoil tips north of St Austell

St Austell ❽

Cornwall. *20,000.*
BP Service Station, Southbourne Rd (01726 879500). *Fri–Sun.*
www.cornish-riviera.co.uk

The busy industrial town of St Austell is the capital of the local china-clay industry which rose to importance in the 18th century. Clay is still a vital factor here; until recently, China was the only other place where such quality and quantity of clay could be found. Spoil tips are a prominent feature; on a sunny day they look like snow-covered peaks, meriting the local name the "Cornish Alps".

Environs: The famous **Lost Gardens of Heligan** are an amazing restoration project to recreate the extraordinary gardens created by the Tremayne family from the 16th century to World War I. At the **Wheal Martyn China Clay Museum**, nature trails weave through clay works that operated from 1878 until the 1920s.

Lost Gardens of Heligan
Pentewan. *01726 845100.* *daily.* *limited.*
www.heligan.com

Wheal Martyn China Clay Museum
Carthew. *01726 850362.* *daily.* *limited.*
www.wheal-martyn.com

Eden Project ⑨

Built into the walls of an abandoned china clay pit, the Eden Project is a global garden for the 21st century and a dramatic setting in which to tell the fascinating story of mankind's dependence on plants. Two futuristic conservatories called biomes have been designed to mimic the environments of warmer climes: one hot and humid, the other warm and dry. Outside, the walls of the pit are planted with species that thrive in the Cornish climate. Unlike a standard conservatory where plants are set out to be admired as species, the Eden Project seeks to educate by telling the story of plants and habitats. The relationship between humans and nature is interpreted by storytellers and artists throughout the site.

④ Tropical South America
Some plants in Amazonia reach massive proportions. The giant waterlilies (Victoria cruziana) *will stretch to 2 m (6 ft) wide.*

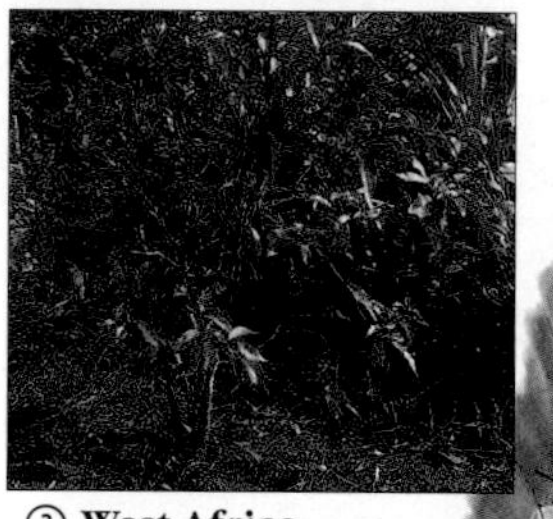

③ West Africa
Iboga is central to the African religion Bwiti. Highly hallucinogenic, it is an integral part of initiation ceremonies.

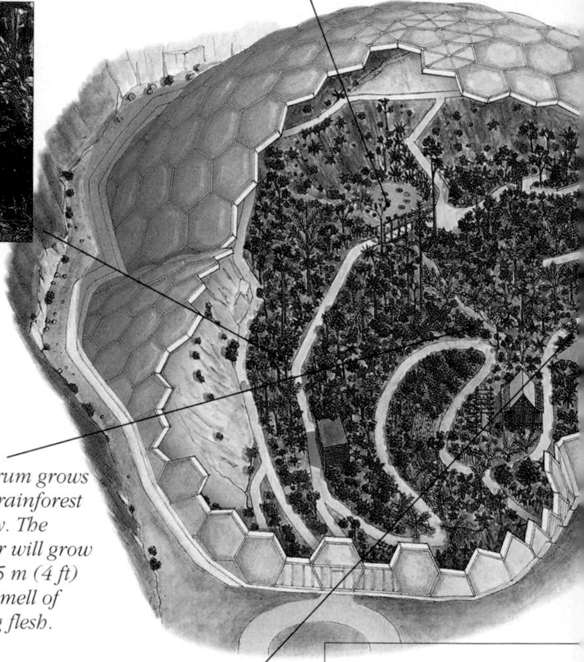

② Malaysia
The Titan arum grows within this rainforest display. The flower will grow to 1.5 m (4 ft) and smell of rotting flesh.

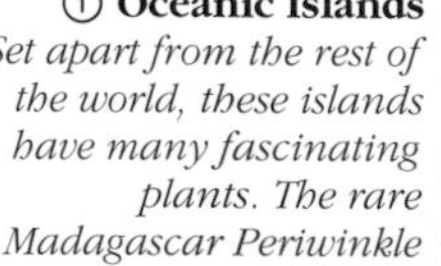

① Oceanic Islands
Set apart from the rest of the world, these islands have many fascinating plants. The rare Madagascar Periwinkle (Catharanthus roseus) *is thought to help cure leukemia.*

The Site

Access to the landscape and the biomes is via the visitor centre.

Humid Tropics Biome
① Oceanic Islands
② Malaysia
③ West Africa
④ Tropical South America
⑤ Crops & cultivation

Warm Temperate Biome
⑥ The Mediterranean
⑦ South Africa
⑧ California
⑨ Crops & cultivation

Visitors' Checklist

Bodelva, St Austell, Cornwall. 01726 811911. St Austell. dedicated bus service from St Austell. Apr–Oct: 10am–6pm daily (last adm 5pm); Nov–Mar: 10am–4:30pm daily (last adm 3pm). 24, 25 Dec.

www.edenproject.com

Building Eden

Cornwall's declining china clay industry has left behind many abandoned pits. The Eden Project makes ingenious use of this industrial landscape. After partly infilling a pit, the massive biomes were nestled into its base and walls.

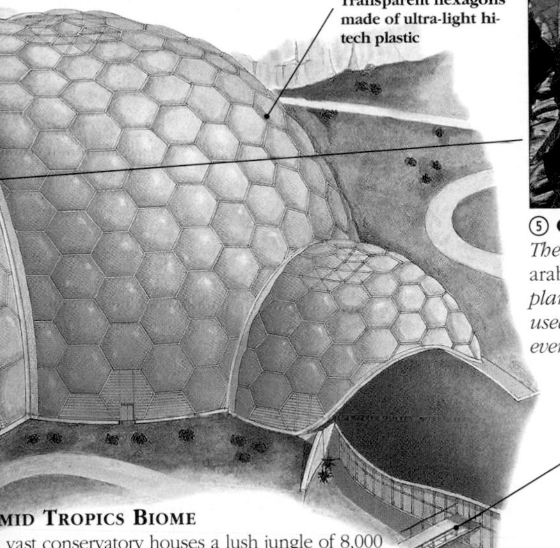

⑤ Crops and cultivation

The coffee plant (Coffea arabica) *is one of the many plants on display that are used in the manufacture of everyday products.*

The entrance to both the Humid Tropics and Warm Temperate Biomes is via The Link, where two restaurants are located.

mid Tropics Biome

; vast conservatory houses a lush jungle of 8,000 s and plants. The dome is high enough to allow rainforest trees to grow to their full height.

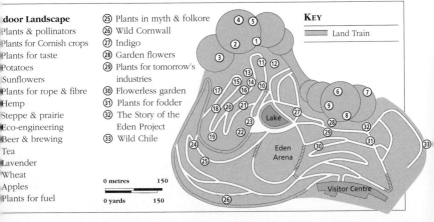

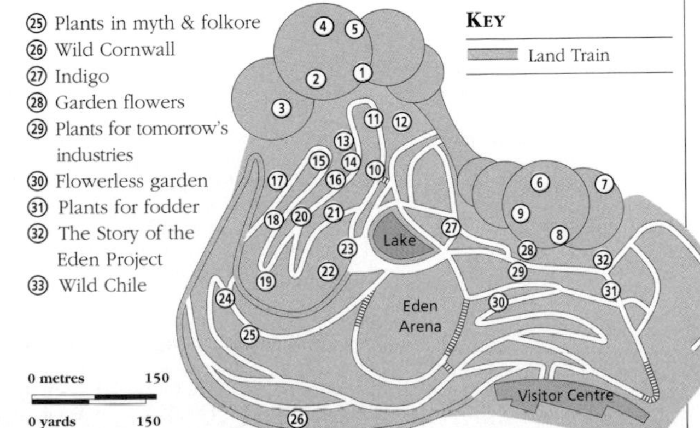

View of Polruan across the estuary from Fowey

Fowey ⑩

Cornwall. 2,000. 4 Custom House Hill (01726 833616). www.fowey.co.uk

Fowey (pronounced Foy), has been immortalized under the name of Troy Town in the humorous novels of Sir Arthur Quiller-Couch (1863–1944), who lived here in a house called **The Haven**. A resort favoured by many wealthy Londoners with a taste for yachting and expensive seafood restaurants, Fowey is the most gentrified of the Cornish seaside towns. The picturesque charm of the flower-filled village is undeniable, with its tangle of tiny steep streets and its views across the estuary to Polruan. The church of **St Fimbarrus** marks the end of the ancient Saint's Way footpath from Padstow – a reminder of the Celtic missionaries who arrived on the shores of Cornwall to convert people to Christianity. Its flower-lined path leads to a majestic porch and carved tower. Inside there are some fine 17th-century memorials to the Rashleigh family whose seat, Menabilly, became Daphne du Maurier's home and featured as Manderley in *Rebecca* (1938).

Environs: For a closer look at the town of **Polruan** and the ceaseless activity of the harbour there is a number of river trips up the little creeks. At the estuary mouth are the twin towers from which chains were once hung to demast invading ships – an effective form of defence.

A fine stretch of coast leads further east to the picturesque fishing villages of **Polperro**, nestling in a narrow green ravine, and neighbouring **Looe**.

Upriver from Fowey is the tranquil town of **Lostwithiel**. Perched on a hill just to the north are the remains of the Norman **Restormel Castle**.

Restormel Castle

(EH) Lostwithiel. 01208 872687.
Apr–Oct: daily.

Daphne du Maurier

The period romances of Daphne du Maurier (1907–89) are inextricably linked with the wild Cornish landscape where she grew up. *Jamaica Inn* established her reputation in 1936, and with the publication of *Rebecca* two years later she found herself one of the most popular authors of her day. *Rebecca* was made into a film directed by Alfred Hitchcock, starring Joan Fontaine and Lord Laurence Olivier.

Bodmin ⑪

Cornwall. *Bodmin Parkway.* *Bodmin.* *Mount Folly Sq, Bodmin (01208 76616).* www.bodminlive.com

Bodmin, Cornwall's ancient county town, lies on the sheltered western edge of the great expanse of moorland that shares its name. The history and archaeology of the town and moor is covered by **Bodmin Town Museum**, while **Bodmin Jail**, where public executions took place until 1909, has been turned into a gruesome tourist attraction. The churchyard is watered by the ever-gushing waters of a holy spring, and it was here that St Guron established a Christian cell in the 6th century. The **church** is dedicated to St Petroc, a Welsh missionary who founded a monastery here in the same period, as well as many others in the region. The monastery has disappeared, but the bones of St Petroc remain, housed in a splendid 12th-century ivory casket in the church.

Jamaica Inn, Bodmin Moor

South of Bodmin is the **Lanhydrock** estate. Amid its extensive wooded acres and formal gardens *(see p232)* lies the massive house, rebuilt after a fire in 1881, but retaining some Jacobean features. The labyrinth of corridors and rooms illustrates life in a Victorian manor house and the fine 17th-century plaster ceiling in the Long Gallery depicts scenes from the Bible.

The desolate wilderness of Bodmin Moor is noted for its network of prehistoric field boundaries. The main attraction, however, is the 18th-century **Jamaica Inn**, made famous by Daphne du Maurier's tale of smuggling and romance. Today there is a restaurant and bar based on du Maurier's novel, and a small museum. A 30-minute walk from the Inn is **Dozmary Pool**, reputed to be bottomless until it dried up in 1976.

The ruins of Tintagel Castle on the north coast of Cornwall

According to legend, the dying King Arthur's sword Excalibur was thrown into the pool.

To the east is **Altarnun**. Its spacious 15th-century church of **St Nonna** is known as the "Cathedral of the Moor".

Bodmin Town Museum
Mt Folly Sq, Bodmin. *01208 77067.* *Easter–Oct: Mon–Sat, Good Fri.* *public hols.* *limited.*

Bodmin Jail
Berrycombe Rd, Bodmin. *01208 76292.* *daily.* *25 Dec.*

Lanhydrock
(NT) Bodmin. *01208 73320.* **House** *Apr–Oct: Tue–Sun & public hols.* **Gardens** *daily.*

Tintagel ⓬

Cornwall. *1,700.* *01840 779084.* *Thu (summer).*

THE ROMANTIC and mysterious ruins of **Tintagel Castle**, built around 1240 by Earl Richard of Cornwall, sit high on a hill-top surrounded by crumpled slate cliffs and yawning black caves. Access to the castle is by means of two steep staircases clinging to the cliff-side where pink thrift and purple sea lavender abound.

The earl was persuaded to build in this isolated, windswept spot by the popular belief, derived from Geoffrey of Monmouth's fictitious *History of the Kings of Britain*, that this was the birthplace of the legendary King Arthur.

Large quantities of fine eastern Mediterranean pottery dating from around the 5th century have been discovered, indicating that the site was an important trading centre, long before the medieval castle was built. Whoever lived here, perhaps the ancient Kings of Cornwall, could evidently afford a luxurious lifestyle.

A clifftop path leads from the castle to Tintagel's **church** which has Norman and Saxon masonry. In Tintagel village the **Old Post Office** is a rare example of a 14th-century Cornish manor house, restored and furnished with 17th-century oak furniture.

ENVIRONS: A short distance to the east, **Boscastle** is another pretty National Trust village. The River Valency runs down the middle of the main street to the fishing harbour, which is sheltered from the sea by high slate cliffs. Access from the harbour to the sea is via a channel cut through the rocks.

Tintagel Castle
Off High St. *01840 770328.* *daily.* *24–26 Dec, 1 Jan.*

Old Post Office
(NT) Fore St. *01840 770024.* *Apr–Oct: daily.*

KING ARTHUR

King Arthur, from a 14th-century chronicle by Peter of Langtoft

Historians think the legendary figure of King Arthur has some basis in historical fact. He was probably a Romano-British chieftain or warrior who led British resistance to the Saxon invasion of the 6th century *(see pp46–7)*. Geoffrey of Monmouth's *History of the Kings of Britain* (1139) introduced Arthur to literature with an account of the many legends connected with him – how he became king by removing the sword Excalibur from a stone, his final battle with the treacherous Mordred, and the story of the Knights of the Round Table *(see p158)*. Other writers, such as Alfred, Lord Tennyson, took up these stories and elaborated on them.

Bude ⓭

Cornwall. *9,000.* *Crescent car park (01288 354240).* *Fri (summer).* www.visitbude.co.uk

WONDERFUL beaches around this area make Bude a popular resort for families. The expanse of clean golden sand that attracts visitors today once made Bude a bustling port. Shelly, lime-rich sand was transported along a canal to inland farms where it was used to neutralize the acidic soil. The canal was abandoned in 1880 but a short stretch survives, providing a haven for birds such as kingfishers and herons.

Kingfisher

Clovelly 14

Devon. 350. 01237 431781.
Town & Visitors' Centre *daily.*
25 Dec. *Visitors' Centre.*
www.clovelly.co.uk

CLOVELLY has been a noted beauty spot since the novelist Charles Kingsley (1819–75) wrote about it in his stirring story of the Spanish Armada, *Westward Ho!* (1855). The whole village is privately owned and has been turned into a tourist attraction, with little sign of the flourishing fishing industry to which it owed its birth. It is a charming, picturesque village with steep, traffic-free cobbled streets rising up the cliff from the harbourside, white-washed houses and gardens brimming with brightly coloured flowers. There are superb views from the lookout points and fine coastal paths to explore from the tiny quay.

Hobby Drive is a scenic 3-mile (5-km) approach on foot to the village which runs through woodland along the coast. The road was constructed in 1811–29 to give employment to local men who had been made redundant at the end of the Napoleonic Wars *(see pp54–5).*

Bideford's medieval bridge, 203 m (666 ft) long with 24 arches

Bideford 15

Devon. 14,000. *Victoria Park (01237 477676).* *Tue, Sat.*

STRUNG OUT along the boat-filled estuary of the River Torridge, Bideford grew and thrived on importing tobacco from the New World. Some 17th-century merchants' houses survive in Bridgeland Street, including the splendid bay-windowed house at No. 28 (1693). Beyond is Mill Street, leading to the parish church and the fine medieval bridge. The quay stretches from here to a pleasant park and a statue which commemorates Charles Kingsley, whose novels helped bring visitors to the area in the 19th century.

ENVIRONS: To the west of Bideford, the village **Westward Ho!** was built in the late 19th century and named after Kingsley's popular novel. The development failed and the Victorian villas and hotels are now part of a holiday resort. Rudyard Kipling *(see p151)* was at school here and the hill to the south, known as **Kipling Tors**, was the background for *Stalky & Co* (1899).

Also to the west is **Hartland Abbey**, built as a monastery c.1157, now a family home. Visitors can enjoy a museum, art and antiques collections as well as informal gardens and a woodland walk.

Henry Williamson's *Tarka the Otter* (1927) describes the otters of the **Torridge Valley** and naturalists are hoping to reintroduce otters here. Part of a Tarka Trail has been laid out along the Torridge and bicycles can be hired from the old railway station. The trail passes close to the magnificent **Rosemoor Garden**.

Day trips run from either Bideford or Ilfracombe (depending on the tide) to **Lundy** island, which is abundant in birds and wildlife.

RHS Rosemoor Garden
Great Torrington. 01805 624067.
daily. *25 Dec.*
www.rhs.org.uk

Hartland Abbey nr. Bideford.
01237 441264. *Apr–Oct: 2–5:30pm Tue (Jul–Aug only), Wed, Thu, Sun, public hols.*

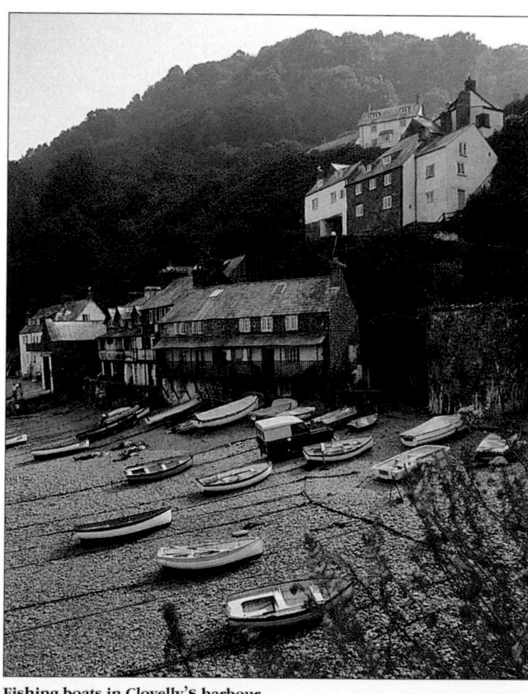

Fishing boats in Clovelly's harbour

Fishermen's cottages, Appledore

Appledore 16

Devon. 3,000. Bideford (01237 477676).

APPLEDORE'S remote position at the tip of the Torridge Estuary has helped to preserve its charms intact. Busy boatyards line the long riverside quay, which is also the departure point for fishing trips and ferries to the sandy beaches of Braunton Burrows on the opposite shore. Timeworn Regency houses line the main street which runs parallel to the quay, and behind is a network of narrow cobbled lanes with 18th-century fishermen's cottages. Several shops retain their original bow-windows and sell an assortment of crafts, antiques and souvenirs.

Uphill from the quay is the **North Devon Maritime Museum**, with an exhibition on the experiences of Devon emigrants in Australia and displays explaining the work of local shipyards. The tiny **Victorian Schoolroom** which is affiliated to the museum, shows various documentary videos on local trades such as fishing and shipbuilding.

North Devon Maritime Museum
Odun Rd. 01237 474852. May–Sep: daily; Apr, Oct: pm. limited. www.devonmuseums.net

Barnstaple 17

Devon. 33,000. The Square (01271 375000). Mon–Sat. www.staynorthdevon.co.uk

ALTHOUGTH BARNSTAPLE is an important distribution centre for the whole region, its town centre remains calm due to the exclusion of traffic. The massive glass-roofed **Pannier Market** (1855) has stalls of organic fruit and vegetables, honey and eggs, much of it produced by farmers' wives to supplement their income. Nearby is **St Peter's Church** with its twisted broach spire, said to have been caused by a lightning strike which warped the timbers in 1810.

On the Strand is a wonderful arcade topped with a statue of Queen Anne, now the **Heritage Centre**. This was built as an exchange where merchants traded the contents of their cargo boats moored on the River Taw alongside. Nearby is the 15th-century bridge and the **Museum of North Devon**, where displays cover local history and the 700-year-old pottery industry, as well as local wildlife, such as the otters that are returning to rivers in the area. The 180-mile (290-km) Tarka Trail circuits around Barnstaple; 35 miles (56 km) of it can be cycled.

Statue of Queen Anne (1708)

Barnstaple's Pannier Market

ENVIRONS: Just to the west of Barnstaple, **Braunton "Great Field"** covers over 120 ha (300 acres) and is a well-preserved relic of medieval open-field cultivation. Beyond lies **Braunton Burrows**, one of the most extensive wild-dune reserves in Britain. It is a must for plant enthusiasts who would like to spot sea kale, sea holly, sea lavender and horned poppies growing in their natural habitat. The sandy beaches and pounding waves at nearby Croyde and Woolacombe, are favourites among surfing enthusiasts, but there are also calmer areas of warm shallow water and rock pools.

Arlington Court, north of Barnstaple, has a collection of model ships, magnificent perennial borders and a lake. The stables house a collection of horse-drawn vehicles. Carriage rides are available.

Museum of North Devon
The Square. 01271 346747. Mon–Sat. 24 Dec–1 Jan. limited.

Arlington Court
(NT) Arlington. 01271 850296. Apr–Oct: Wed–Mon. limited.

DEVONSHIRE CREAM TEAS

Devon people claim all other versions of a cream tea are inferior to their own. The essential ingredient is Devonshire clotted cream which comes from Jersey cattle fed on rich Devon pasture – anything else is second best, or so it is claimed. Spread thickly on freshly baked scones, with lashings of homemade strawberry jam, this makes a seductive, delicious, but fattening, tea-time treat.

A typical cream tea with scones, jam and clotted cream

The village of Lynmouth

Lynton and Lynmouth ⓲

Devon. 2,000. Town Hall, Lee Rd (015987 52225). See pp238–9. www.lyntourism.co.uk

SITUATED AT THE POINT where the East and West Lyn rivers meet the sea, Lynmouth is a picturesque, though rather commercialized, fishing village. The pedestrianized main street, lined with shops selling clotted cream and seaside souvenirs, runs parallel to the Lyn, now made into a canal with high embankments as a precaution against flash floods. One flood devastated the town at the height of the holiday season in 1952. The scars caused by the flood, which was fuelled by heavy rain on Exmoor, are now overgrown by trees in the pretty **Glen Lyn Gorge**, which leads north out of the village. Lynmouth's sister town, Lynton, is a mainly Victorian village perched on the clifftop 130 m (427 ft) above, giving lovely views across the Bristol Channel to the Welsh coast. It can be reached from the harbour front by a cliff railway, by road or by a steep path.

ENVIRONS: Lynmouth makes an excellent starting point for walks on Exmoor. There is a 2 mile (3 km) trail that leads southeast to tranquil **Watersmeet** *(see p239)*. On the western edge of Exmoor, **Combe Martin** *(see p238)* lies in a sheltered valley. On the main street, lined with Victorian villas, is the 18th-century Pack of Cards Inn, built by a gambler with 52 windows, for each card in the pack.

Exeter ⓳

EXETER IS DEVON'S CAPITAL, a bustling and lively city with a great deal of character, despite the World War II bombing that destroyed much of its city centre. Built high on a plateau above the River Exe, the city is encircled by substantial sections of Roman and medieval wall, and the street plan has not changed much since the Romans first laid out what is now the High Street. Elsewhere the Cathedral Close forms a pleasant green, and there are cobbled streets and narrow alleys which invite leisurely exploration. For shoppers there is a wide selection of big stores and smaller speciality shops.

Exploring Exeter

The intimate green and the close surrounding Exeter's distinctive cathedral were the setting for Anthony Trollope's novel *He Knew He Was Right* (1869). Full of festive crowds listening to buskers in the summer, the close presents an array of architectural styles. One of the finest buildings here is the Elizabethan **Mol's Coffee House**. Among the other historic buildings that survived World War II are the magnificent **Guildhall** (1330) on the High Street (one of Britain's oldest civic buildings), the opulent **Custom House** (1681) by the quay, and the elegant 18th-century **Rougement House** which stands near the remains of a Norman **castle** built by William the Conqueror *(see pp46–7)*.

The port area has been transformed into a tourist attraction with its early 19th-century warehouses converted into craft shops, antique galleries and cafés. Boats can be hired for cruising down the short stretch of canal. The **Quay House Interpretation Centre** (open daily April–October; weekends November–March) has audio-visual and other displays on the history of Exeter.

The timber-framed Mol's Coffee House (1596), Cathedral Close

West front and south tower, Cathedral Church of St Peter

Cathedral Church of St Peter

Cathedral Close. 01392 255573. daily.

Exeter's cathedral is one of the most gloriously ornamented in Britain. Except for the two Norman towers, the cathedral is mainly 14th century and built in the style aptly known as Decorated because of the swirling geometric patterns of the stone work. The West Front, the largest single collection (66) of medieval figure sculptures in England, includes kings, apostles and prophets. Started in the 14th century, it was completed by 1450. Inside, the splendid Gothic vaulting sweeps from one end of the church to the other, impressive in its uniformity and punctuated by gaily painted ceiling bosses.

Among the tombs around the choir is that of Edward II's treasurer, Walter de Stapledon (1261–1326), who was murdered by a mob in London. Stapledon raised much of the money needed to fund the building of this cathedral

Collection of shells and other objects in the library of A La Ronde

and for Exeter College in Oxford *(see pp210–15)*.

Underground Passages

Roman Gate Passage. 01392 665 887. Jul–Sep: Mon–Sat; Oct–Jun: Tue–Fri (pm), Sat. 25, 26 Dec, 1 Jan.

Under the city centre lie the remains of Exeter's medieval water-supply system. An excellent video and guided tour explain how the stone-lined tunnels were built in the 14th and 15th centuries on a slight gradient to bring in fresh water from springs outside the town.

19th-century head of an Oba, Royal Albert Museum

St Nicholas Priory

The Mint. 01392 265858. Easter–Oct: Mon, Wed & Sat pm.

Built in the 12th century, this building has retained many original features and rooms. These trace its fascinating history from austere monastic beginnings, through its secular use as a Tudor residence for wealthy merchants, to its 20th-century incarnation as five separate premises occupied by various tradesmen including a bootmaker and an upholsterer.

Royal Albert Memorial Museum and Art Gallery

Queen St. 01392 265858. *Mon–Sat.* *24–26 Dec, 1 Jan, Good Fri, public hols.*

This museum has a wonderfully varied collection, including Roman remains, a zoo of stuffed animals, West Country art and a particularly good ethnographic display. Highlights include displays on silverware, watches and clocks.

Environs: South of Exeter on the A376, the eccentric **A La Ronde** is a 16-sided house built in 1796 by two spinster cousins, who decorated the interior with shells, feathers and souvenirs gathered while on tour in Europe.

Further east, the unspoilt Regency town of **Sidmouth** lies in a sheltered bay. There is an eclectic array of architecture, the earliest buildings dating from the 1820s when Sidmouth became a popular summer resort. Thatched cottages stand opposite huge Edwardian villas, and elegant terraces line the seafront. In summer the town hosts the famous International Festival of Folk Arts *(see p63)*.

Visitors' Checklist

Devon. 111,000. 5 miles (8 km) east. Exeter St David's, Bonhay Rd; Exeter Central, Queen St. Paris St. Paris St (01392 265700). daily. www.exeter.gov.uk

North of Sidmouth lies the magnificent church at **Ottery St Mary**. Built in 1338–42 by Bishop Grandisson, the church is clearly a scaled-down version of Exeter Cathedral, which he also helped build. A memorial in the churchyard wall recalls the fact the poet Coleridge was born in the town in 1772.

Nearby **Honiton** is famous for its extraordinarily intricate and delicate lace, made here since Elizabethan times.

To the north of Exeter, **Killerton** is home to the National Trust's costume collection. Here, displays of bustles and corsets and vivid tableaux illustrate aristocratic fashions from the 18th century to the present day.

Further north near Tiverton, is **Knightshayes Court**, a Victorian Gothic mansion with fine gardens *(see p233)*.

A La Ronde

(NT) Summer Lane, Exmouth. *01395 265514. Apr–Oct: Sun–Thu.*

Killerton

(NT) Broadclyst. *01392 881345.* **House** *Apr–Oct: daily.* **Garden** *daily all year.*

Knightshayes Court

(NT) Bolham. *01884 254665. Apr–Nov: Sat–Thu, Good Fri (gardens Apr–Nov daily). limited.*

Mexican dancer at Sidmouth's International Festival of Folk Arts

Torbay 20

Torbay. *Torquay, Paignton.* *Vaughan Parade, Torquay (01803 297428).* www.theenglishriviera.co.uk

THE THREE SEASIDE TOWNS of Torquay, Paignton and Brixham form an almost continuous resort around the great sweep of sandy beach and calm blue waters of Torbay. Because of its mild climate, extensive semi-tropical gardens and exuberant Victorian hotel architecture, this popular coastline has been dubbed the English Riviera. In its heyday, Torbay was patronized by the wealthy, especially during Victorian times. Today, mass entertainment is the theme and there are plenty of attractions of this type, mostly in and around Torquay.

Torre Abbey includes the remains of a monastery founded in 1196 and now serves as an art gallery. There is a magnificent barn in the grounds where prisoners captured from the Spanish Armada of 1588 were once held. **Torquay Museum** nearby covers natural history and archaeology, including finds from **Kents Cavern**, on the outskirts of the town. This is one of England's most important prehistoric sites and the spectacular caves serve as the background for displays on people and animals who lived here up to 350,000 years ago.

The charming miniature town of **Babbacombe Model Village** lies to the north of Torquay, while a mere mile (1.5 km) inland is the lovely little village of **Cockington**. Visitors travel by horse-drawn carriage to view the preserved Tudor manor house, church, thatched cottages and forge.

In Paignton, the celebrated **Paignton Zoo** teaches children about the planet's wildlife, and from here you can take the steam railway – an ideal way to visit Dartmouth.

Continuing south from Paignton, the pretty town of Brixham was once England's most prosperous fishing port.

Torquay, on the "English Riviera"

Bayards Cove, Dartmouth

Torre Abbey
King's Drive, Torquay. *01803 293593.* *Apr–Oct: daily.*

Torquay Museum
Babbacombe Rd, Torquay. *01803 293975.* *daily (Nov–Easter: Mon–Sat).* *Christmas wk.*

Kents Cavern
Ilsham Rd, Torquay. *01803 294059.* *daily.* *25 Dec.*

Babbacombe Model Village
Hampton Ave, Torquay. *01803 315315.* *daily.*

Paignton Zoo
Totnes Rd, Paignton. *01803 557479.* *daily.*

Dartmouth 21

Devon. *5,500.* *Mayors Ave (01803 834224).* *Tue–Fri am.* www.dartmouth-information.co.uk

SITTING HIGH ON THE HILL above the River Dart is the **Royal Naval College**, where British naval officers have trained since 1905. Dartmouth has always been an important port and it was from here that English fleets set sail to join the Second and Third Crusades. Some 18th-century houses adorn the cobbled quay of Bayards Cove, while carved timber buildings line the 17th-century Butterwalk, home to **Dartmouth Museum**. To the south is **Dartmouth Castle** (1388).

Dartmouth Museum
Butterwalk. *01803 832923.* *Mon–Sat.* *25, 26 Dec, 1 Jan.* www.devonmuseums.net

Dartmouth Castle
(EH) Castle Rd. *01803 833588.* *daily (Nov–Easter: Wed–Sun).* *24–26 Dec, 1 Jan.*

Stained glass window in Blessed Sacrament Chapel, Buckfast Abbey

Totnes 22

Devon. 7,500.
Coronation Rd (01803 863168).
Tue am (May–Sep), Fri, Sat.
www.totnesinfo.org.uk

TOTNES SITS at the highest navigable point on the River Dart with a Norman **castle** perched high on the hill above. Linking the two is the steep High Street, lined with bow-windowed Elizabethan houses. Bridging the street is the **Eastgate**, part of the medieval town wall. Life in the town's heyday is explored in the **Totnes Elizabethan Museum**, which also has a room devoted to the mathematician Charles Babbage (1791–1871), who is regarded as the pioneer of modern computers. There is a **Guildhall**, and a **church** with a delicately carved and gilded rood screen. On Tuesdays in the summer, market stallholders dress in Elizabethan costume.

ENVIRONS: A few miles north of Totnes, **Dartington Hall** has 10 ha (25 acres) of lovely gardens and a famous music school where concerts are held in the timbered 14th-century Great Hall.

Stallholders in Totnes market

Totnes Castle
(EH) Castle St. *01803 864406.*
Apr–Oct: daily.

Totnes Elizabethan Museum
Fore St. *01803 863821.*
Easter–Oct: Mon–Fri. *limited.*

Guildhall
Rampart Walk. *01803 862147.*
Apr–Oct: Mon–Fri.

Dartington Hall Gardens
01803 862367. *daily.*
www.dartingtonhalltrust.com

Buckfastleigh 23

Devon. *3,300.* *Fore St (01364 644522).*

THIS MARKET TOWN, situated on the edge of Dartmoor *(see pp282–3)*, is dominated by **Buckfast Abbey**. The original abbey, founded in Norman times, fell into ruin after the Dissolution of the Monasteries and it was not until 1882 that a small group of French Benedictine monks set up a new abbey here. Work on the present building was financed by donations and carried out by the monks. The abbey was completed in 1938 and lies at the heart of a thriving community. The fine mosaics and modern stained glass window are also the work of the monks.

Nearby is the **Buckfast Butterfly Farm and Otter Sanctuary,** and the **South Devon Steam Railway** terminus where steam trains leave for Totnes.

Buckfast Abbey
Buckfastleigh. *01364 645500.*
daily. *25–27 Dec, Good Fri.*
www.buckfast.org.uk

Buckfast Butterfly Farm and Otter Sanctuary
Buckfastleigh. *01364 642916.*
Easter–Nov: daily.
www.ottersandbutterfliestrust.com

Burgh Island 24

Devon. *Plymouth, then taxi.*
Kingsbridge (01548 853195).
www.kingsbridgeinfo.co.uk

THE SHORT WALK across the sands at low tide from Bigbury-on-Sea to Burgh Island takes you back to the era of the 1920s and 1930s. It was here that the millionaire Archibald Nettlefold built the luxury **Burgh Island Hotel** *(see p553)* in 1929. Created in Art Deco style with a natural rock sea-bathing pool, this was the exclusive retreat of figures such as the Duke of Windsor and Noel Coward. The restored hotel is worth a visit for the photographs of its heyday and the Art Deco fittings. You can also explore the island and **Pilchard Inn** (1336), reputed to be haunted by the ghost of a smuggler.

The Art Deco style bar in Burgh Island Hotel

Plymouth ㉕

Plymouth. 250,000. *Island House, The Barbican. (01752 304849).* *daily.* www.plymouth.gov.uk

THE TINY PORT from which Drake, Raleigh, the Pilgrim Fathers, Cook and Darwin all set sail on pioneering voyages has now grown to a substantial city, much of it boldly rebuilt after wartime bombing. Old Plymouth clusters around the **Hoe**, the famous patch of turf on which Sir Francis Drake is said to have calmly finished his game of bowls as the Spanish Armada approached the port in 1588 *(see pp50–51)*. Today the Hoe is a pleasant park and parade ground surrounded by memorials to naval men, including Drake himself. Alongside is Charles II's **Royal Citadel**, built to guard the harbour in the 1660s. A popular attraction is **Plymouth Dome**, a visitor centre which uses high-tech displays to explain Plymouth's past and present, including live satellite weather pictures and radar screens for monitoring ships. On the harbour is the **National Marine Aquarium**. Nearby is the **Mayflower Stone and Steps**, the spot where the Pilgrim Fathers set sail for the New World in England's third and successful attempt at colonization in 1620.

Drake's coat of arms

ENVIRONS: A boat tour of the harbour is the best way to see Plymouth's dockyards where warships have been built since the Napoleonic Wars. There are also splendid views of various fine gardens, such as **Mount Edgcumbe Park** *(see p232)*, scattered around the coastline of the Plymouth Sound. East of the city, the 18th-century **Saltram House** has two rooms by Adam *(see pp24–5)* and portraits by Reynolds, who was born in nearby Plympton.

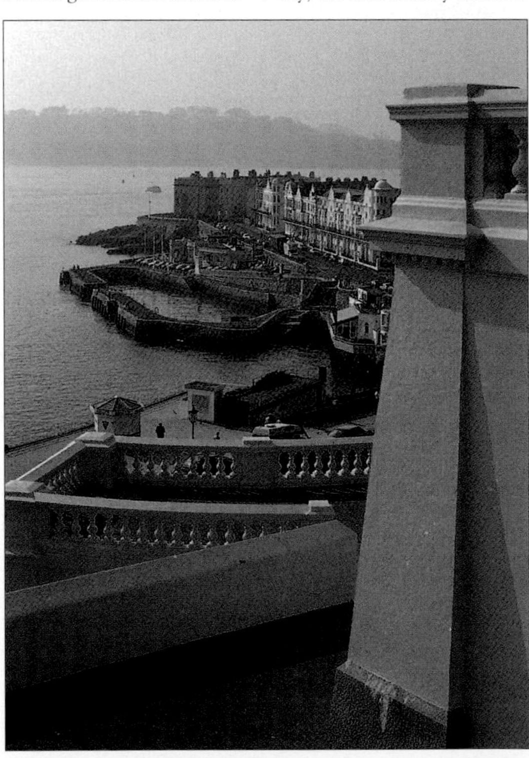

View of Plymouth Harbour from the Hoe

Mid-18th-century carved wood chimneypiece, Saltram House

Royal Citadel
(EH) The Hoe. *0117 9750700.* *call for details.* *only.*

Plymouth Dome
The Hoe. *01752 603300.* *Apr–Oct: daily; Nov–Mar: Tue–Sat.*

National Marine Aquarium
Rope Walk, Coxside. *01752 600301.* *daily.* *25 Dec.* www.national-aquarium.co.uk

Mount Edgcumbe Park
Cremyll, Torpoint. *from Torpoint car park.* *01752 822236.* **House** *Mar–Nov: Sun–Thu.* **Grounds** *all year.*

Saltram House
(NT) Plympton. *01752 333500.* **Gallery** *Mar–Dec: Sat–Thu; Jan, Feb: Sat, Sun.* **Gardens** *all year.* *open all year.*

Buckland Abbey ㉖

(NT) Yelverton, Devon. *01822 853607.* *from Yelverton.* *Fri–Wed (Nov–Mar: Sat & Sun pm).* *call for details.*

FOUNDED BY the Cistercian monks in 1278, Buckland Abbey was converted to a house after the Dissolution of the Monasteries and became the home of Drake from 1581–96. Many of the monastic buildings survive in a garden setting, the most impressive being the 14th-century tithe barn *(see p28)*. Part of the house explains Drake's life and times through paintings and memorabilia.

Cotehele 27

(NT) St Dominick, Cornwall. 01579 351346. Calstock. **House** *Apr–Oct: Sat–Thu & Good Fri.* **Grounds** *daily.* *limited.*

MAGNIFICENT WOODLAND and lush river scenery make Cotehele (pronounced Coteal) one of the most delightful spots on the River Tamar and a rewarding day can be spent exploring the estate. Far from civilization, tucked into its wooded fold in the Cornish countryside, Cotehele has slumbered for 500 years. The main attraction is the house and valley garden at its centre. Built mainly between 1489 and 1520, it is a rare example of a medieval house, set around three courtyards with a magnificent open hall, kitchen, chapel and a warren of private parlours and chambers. The romance of the house is enhanced by colourful terraced gardens to the east, leading via a tunnel into a richly planted valley garden. The path through this garden passes a large domed medieval dovecote and descends to a quay, to which lime and coal were once shipped. There are fine views up and down the winding reed-fringed Tamar from Prospect Tower, and a gallery on the quayside specializes in local arts and crafts. The estate includes a village, a quay with a small maritime museum, working mill buildings, ancient lime kilns and workshops with 19th-century equipment.

Medieval dovecote in the gardens of Cotehele estate

Spanish Armada and British fleets in the English Channel, 1588

SIR FRANCIS DRAKE

Sir Francis Drake (c.1540–1596) was the first Englishman to circumnavigate the globe and he was knighted by Elizabeth I in 1580. Four years later he introduced tobacco and potatoes to England, after bringing home 190 colonists who had tried to establish a settlement in Virginia. To many, however, Drake was no more than an opportunistic rogue, renowned for his exploits as a "privateer", the polite name for a pirate. Catholic Spain was the bitter enemy and Drake further endeared himself to queen and people by his part in the victory over Philip II's Armada *(see pp50–51)*, defeated by bad weather and the buccaneering spirit of the English.

Morwellham Quay 28

Near Tavistock, Devon. 01822 832766. Gunnislake. *Easter–Oct: daily; Nov–Mar: groups only.* *limited.*
www.morwellham-quay.co.uk

MORWELLHAM QUAY was a neglected and overgrown industrial site until 1970, when members of a local trust began restoring the abandoned cottages, schoolhouse, farmyards, quay and copper mines to their original condition.

Today, Morwellham Quay is a thriving and rewarding industrial museum, where you can easily spend a whole day partaking in the typical activities of a Victorian village, from preparing the shire horses for a day's work, to riding a tramway deep into a copper mine in the hillside behind the village. The museum is brought to life by characters in costumes, some of whom give demonstrations throughout the day. You can watch, or lend a hand to the cooper while he builds a barrel, attend a lesson in the schoolroom, take part in Victorian playground games or dress up in 19th-century hooped skirts, bonnets, top hats or jackets. The staff, who convincingly play the part of villagers, lead you through their lives and impart a huge amount of information about the history of this small copper-mining community.

Industrial relics at Morwellham Quay in the Tamar Valley

Dartmoor National Park ㉘

Buzzard

THE WILD AND OPEN MOORLAND of Dartmoor's bleak and isolated heart provided the eerie background for Conan Doyle's thriller, *The Hound of the Baskervilles* (1902). Here at Princetown, surrounded by gaunt weathered outcrops of granite tors is Britain's most secure prison. Also dotting the landscape are scores of prehistoric remains which have survived because of the durability of granite. Elsewhere the mood is very different. Streams tumble through wooded and boulder-strewn ravines forming pretty cascades and waterfalls, and cosy thatched cottages nestle in the sheltered valleys around the margins of the moor offering cream teas and warming fires to weary walkers.

Characteristic moorland near Drewsteignton

Okehampton has the Museum of Dartmoor Life and a ruined 14th-century castle.

Brentor
This volcanic hill crowned by a tiny church (first built in 1130) is visible for miles.

Lydford Gorge (open Apr–Oct) is a dramatic wooded ravine, leading to a waterfall.

The Ministry of Defence uses much of this area for training but access is available most days.

Main information centre

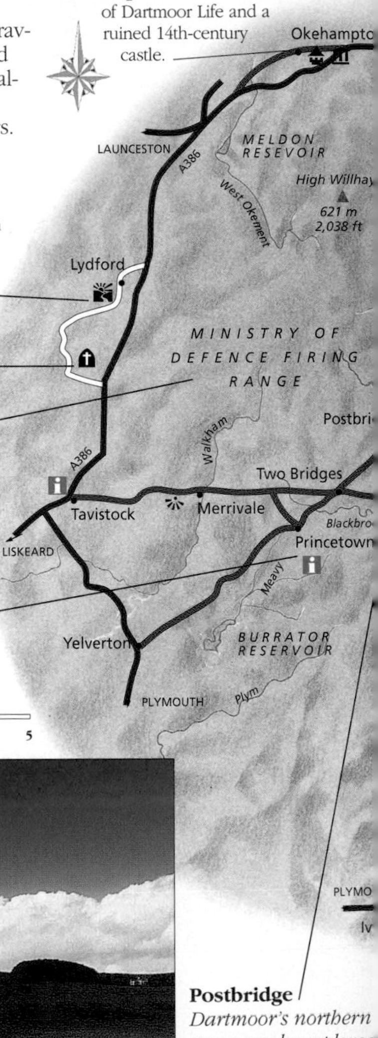

KEY

i	Tourist information
▬	A road
▬	B road
═	Minor road
⁂	Viewpoint

0 kilometres 5

0 miles 5

Postbridge
Dartmoor's northern moor can be explored from the village of Postbridge. The gently rolling moorland is crossed by many dry-stone walls.

Dartmoor Ponies
These small, tough ponies have lived wild on the moor since at least the 10th century.

Visitors' Checklist

Devon. 🚂 🚌 *Exeter, Plymouth, Totnes then bus.* ℹ *High Moorland, Princetown (01822 890414).* **Okehampton Castle**, Castle Lane, Okehampton. ☎ *01837 52844.* ○ *Apr–Oct: daily.* ● *Nov–Mar.* **Museum of Dartmoor Life**, West St, Okehampton. ☎ *01837 52295.* ○ *Easter–Oct: Mon–Sat (Jun–Sep: daily); Nov–Easter: Mon–Fri.* ● *24 Dec–1 Jan.* ♿ *limited.* **Castle Drogo (NT)**, Drewsteignton. ☎ *01647 433306.* ○ *Apr–Nov: Wed–Mon.* **Gardens** ○ *daily.* ♿ *gardens only.* W www.dartmoor-npa.gov.uk

Grimspound is the impressive site of Bronze Age huts built nearly 4,000 years ago.

Castle Drogo is a magnificent mock-castle built by the architect Sir Edwin Lutyens *(see p25)* in 1910–30.

Becky Falls is a 22 m (72 ft) waterfall set in delightful woodlands.

Hound Tor
This tor (a pile of rocks, probably Celtic in origin) includes the remains of a medieval settlement which was inhabited from Saxon times until around 1300.

Bovey Tracey has an extensive woodland reserve.

Haytor Rocks is one of the most accessible of the many tors.

South Devon Steam Railway

Buckfast Abbey was founded by King Canute *(see p159)* in 1018.

Dartmoor Butterfly and Otter Sanctuary

artmeet arks the lovely onfluence point the East and est Dart rivers.

Buckland-in-the-Moor
This is one of the most picturesque thatch-and-granite villages on Dartmoor.

THE MIDLANDS

INTRODUCING THE MIDLANDS 286-293
THE HEART OF ENGLAND 294-317
EAST MIDLANDS 318-331

The Midlands at a Glance

THE MIDLANDS IS AN AREA that embraces wonderful landscapes and massive industrial cities. Visitors come to discover the wild beauty of the rugged Peaks, cruise slowly along the Midlands canals on gaily painted narrowboats and explore varied and enchanting gardens. The area encompasses the full range of English architecture from mighty cathedrals and humble churches to charming spa towns, stately homes and country cottages. There are fascinating industrial museums, many in picturesque settings.

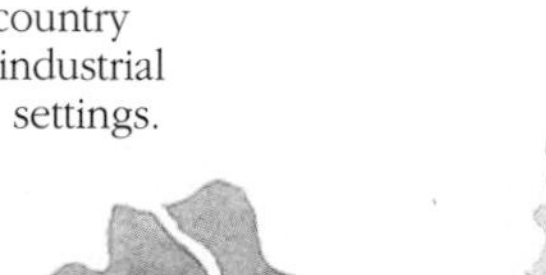

Tissington Trail (see p325) *combines a walk through scenic Peak District countryside with an entertaining insight into the ancient custom of well-dressing.*

Ironbridge Gorge (see pp302–3) *was the birthplace of the Industrial Revolution* (see pp336–7). *Now a World Heritage Centre, the site is a reminder of the lovely countryside in which the original factories were located.*

The Cotswolds (see pp292–93) *are full of delightful houses built from local limestone, on the profits of the medieval wool trade. Snowshill Manor (left) is situated near the unspoilt village of Broadway.*

The front of the half-timbered Lord Leycester Hospital, Warwick

Chatsworth House (see pp322–3), *a magnificent Baroque edifice, is famous for its gorgeous gardens. The "Conservative" Wall, a greenhouse for exotic plants, is pictured above.*

Lincoln Cathedral (see p329), *a vast, imposing building, dominates the ancient town. Inside are splendid misericords and the superb 13th-century Angel Choir, which has 30 carved angels.*

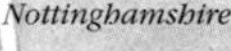

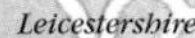

Burghley House (see pp330–31) *is a dazzling landmark for miles around in the flat East Midlands landscape, with architectural motifs from the European Renaissance.*

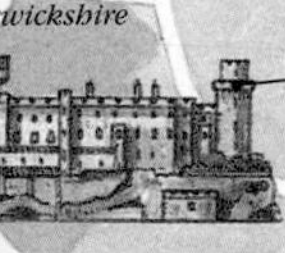

Warwick Castle (see pp310–11) *is an intriguing mixture of medieval power base and country house, complete with massive towers, battlements, a dungeon and state apartments, such as the Queen Anne Bedroom.*

Stratford-upon-Avon (see pp312–15) *has many picturesque houses connected with William Shakespeare's life, some of which are open to visitors. These black and white timber-framed buildings, which abound in the Midlands, are a typical example of Tudor architecture* (see pp290–91).

Canals of the Midlands

One of England's first canals was built by the 3rd Duke of Bridgewater in 1761 to link the coal mine on his Worsley estate with Manchester's textile factories. This heralded the start of a canal-building boom and by 1805, a 3,000 mile (4,800 km) network of waterways had been dug across the country, linking into the natural river system. Canals provided the cheapest, fastest way of transporting goods, until competition began to arrive from the railways in the 1840s. Cargo transport ended in 1963 but today nearly 2,000 miles (3,200 km) of canals are still navigable, for travellers who wish to take a leisurely cruise on a narrowboat.

The Grand Union Canal *(pictured in 1931) is 300 miles (485 km) long and was dug in the 1790s to link London with the Midlands.*

The Farmer's Bridge *is a flight of 13 locks in Birmingham. Locks are used to raise or lower boats from one level of the canal to another. The steeper the gradient, the more locks are needed.*

Lock-keepers were provided with canalside houses.

Lockside inns cater for narrowboats.

Heavy V-shaped timber gates close off the lock.

Water pressing against the gate keeps it shut.

The towpath is where horses pulled the canal boats before engines were invented. They were changed periodically for fresh animals.

Narrowboats *have straight sides and flat bottoms and are pointed at both ends. Cargo space took up most of the boat, with a small cabin for the crew. Exteriors were brightly painted.*

Midlands Canal Network

The industrial Midlands was the birthplace of the English canal system and still has the biggest concentration of navigable waterways.

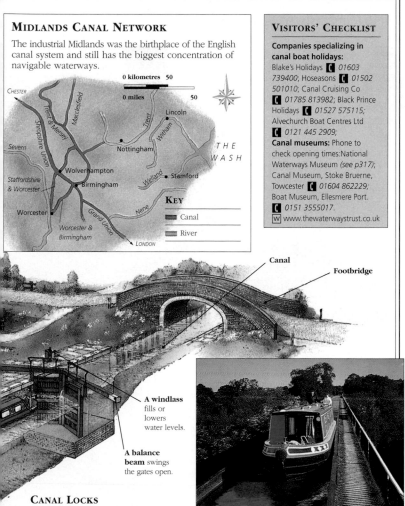

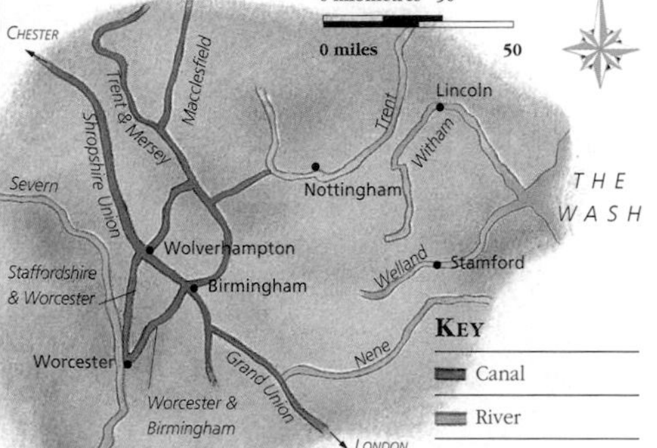

Visitors' Checklist

Companies specializing in canal boat holidays: Blake's Holidays *01603 739400*; Hoseasons *01502 501010*; Canal Cruising Co *01785 813982*; Black Prince Holidays *01527 575115;* Alvechurch Boat Centres Ltd *0121 445 2909;*
Canal museums: Phone to check opening times:National Waterways Museum *(see p317)*; Canal Museum, Stoke Bruerne, Towcester *01604 862229;* Boat Museum, Ellesmere Port. *0151 3555017.* www.thewaterwaystrust.co.uk

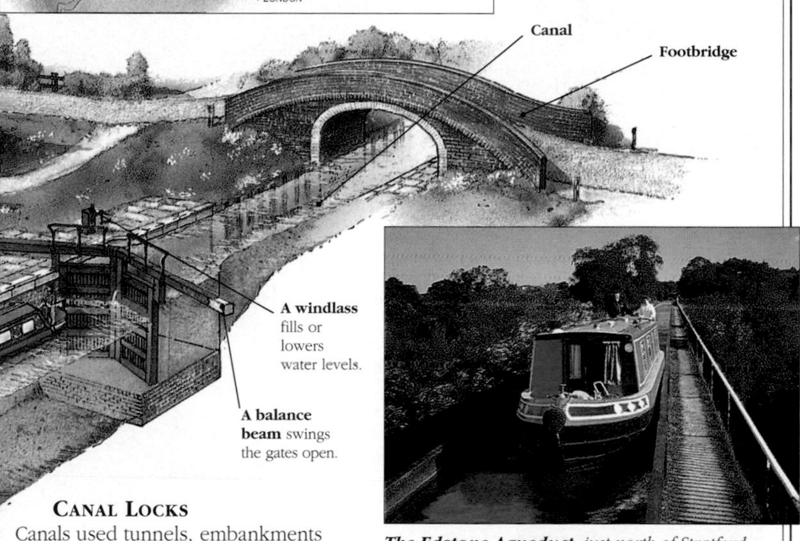

Canal Locks

Canals used tunnels, embankments and locks for the speedy transportation of goods across country. Locks were used to convey boats up or down hills.

***The Edstone Aqueduct**, just north of Stratford-upon-Avon, carries the canal in a cast iron trough. This is supported on brick piers for 180 m (495 ft), over roads and a busy railway line.*

Canal Art

Canal boat cabins are very small and every inch of space is utilized to make a comfortable home for the occupants. Interiors were enlivened with colourful paintings and attractive decorations.

Furniture was designed to be functional and to brighten up the cramped cabin.

Narrowboats are often decorated with ornamental brass.

Water cans were also painted. The most common designs were roses and castles, with local variations in style.

Tudor Manor Houses

MANY STRIKING MANOR HOUSES were built in central England during the Tudor Age *(see pp50–51)*, a time of relative peace and prosperity. The abolition of the monasteries meant that vast estates were broken up and sold to secular landowners, who built houses to reflect their new status *(see p24)*. In the Midlands, wood was the main building material, and the gentry flaunted their wealth by using timber panelling for flamboyant decorative effect.

The Lucy family arms

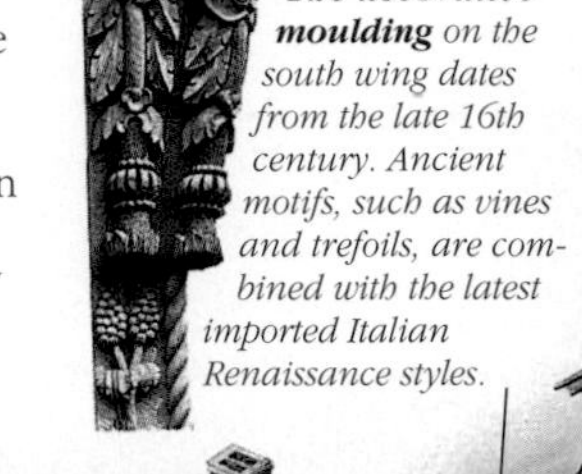

***The decorative moulding** on the south wing dates from the late 16th century. Ancient motifs, such as vines and trefoils, are combined with the latest imported Italian Renaissance styles.*

***The rectangular moat** was for decoration rather than defence. It surrounds a recreated knot garden* (see p22) *that was laid out in 1975 using plants known to have been available in Tudor times.*

***The Long Gallery**, the last part of the Hall to be built (1580), was used for exercise. It has original murals portraying* Destiny *(left) and* Fortune.

Brickwork chimney

Jetties (overhanging upper stories)

Tudor Mansions and Tudor Revival

There are many sumptuously decorated Tudor mansions in the Midlands. In the 19th century Tudor Revival architecture became a very popular "Old English" style, intended to invoke family pride and values rooted in the past.

***Hardwick Hall** in Derbyshire, whose huge kitchen is pictured, is one of the finest Tudor mansions in the country. These buildings are known as "prodigy" houses* (see p330) *due to their gigantic size.*

***Charlecote Park**, Warwickshire, is a brick mansion built by Sir Thomas Lucy in 1551–59. It was heavily restored in Tudor style in the 19th century, but has a fine original gatehouse. According to legend, the young William Shakespeare* (see pp312–15) *was caught poaching deer in the park.*

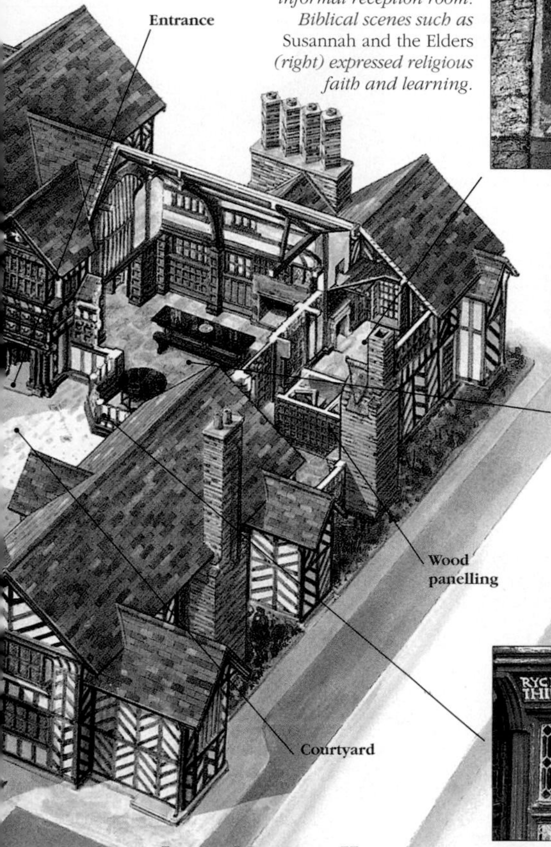

***The Parlour** was an informal reception room. Biblical scenes such as* Susannah and the Elders *(right) expressed religious faith and learning.*

Entrance

***The Great Hall** (c.1440) is the oldest part of the house, and in Tudor times was the most important. The open-plan hall was the main communal area for dining and entertainment.*

Wood panelling

Courtyard

LITTLE MORETON HALL
The Moreton family home *(see p299)* was built between 1440 and 1580, from a number of box-shapes, fitted together. Wood panelling and jetties displayed the family's wealth.

***The patterned glazing** in the great bay window is typically 16th century: small pieces of locally made glass were cut into diamond shapes and held in place by lead glazing bars.*

***Packwood House** in Warwickshire is a timber-framed mid-Tudor house with extensive 17th-century additions. The unusual garden of clipped yew trees dates from the 17th century and is supposed to represent the Sermon on the Mount.*

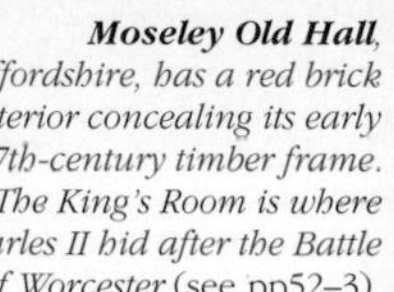

***Moseley Old Hall**, Staffordshire, has a red brick exterior concealing its early 17th-century timber frame. The King's Room is where Charles II hid after the Battle of Worcester* (see pp52–3).

***Wightwick Manor**, West Midlands, was built in 1887–93. It is a fine example of Tudor Revival architecture and has superb late 19th-century furniture and decorations.*

Building with Cotswold Stone

Dragon, Deerhurst Church

THE COTSWOLDS are a range of limestone hills running over 50 miles (80 km) in a northeasterly direction from Bath *(see pp246–9)*. The thin soils are difficult to plough but ideal for grazing sheep, and the wealth engendered by the medieval wool trade was poured into building majestic churches and opulent town houses. Stone quarried from these hills was used to build London's St Paul's Cathedral *(see pp116–17)*, as well as the villages, barns and manor houses that make the landscape so picturesque.

***Arlington Row Cottages** in Bibury, a typical Cotswold village, were built in the 17th century for weavers whose looms were set up in the attics.*

Windows were taxed and glass expensive. Workers' cottages had only a few, not very large windows made of small panes of glass.

A drip mould keeps rain off the chimney.

The roof is steeply pitched to carry the weight of the tiles. These were made by master craftsmen who could split blocks of stone into sheets by using natural fault lines.

Timber lintels and doors

Timber framing was cheaper than stone, and was used for the upper rooms in the roof.

COTSWOLD STONE COTTAGE

The two-storey Arlington Row Cottages are asymmetrical and built of odd-shaped stones. Small windows and doorways make them quite dark inside.

VARIATIONS IN STONE

Cotswold stone is warmer-toned in the north, pearly in central areas and light grey in the south. The stone seems to glow with absorbed sunlight. It is a soft stone that is easily carved and can be used for many purposes, from buildings to bridges, headstones and gargoyles.

"Tiddles" is a cat's gravestone in Fairford churchyard.

***Lower Slaughter** gets its name from the Anglo-Saxon word* slough, *or muddy place. It has a low stone bridge, over the River Eye.*

Cotswold Stone Towns and Villages

The villages and towns on this map are prime examples of places built almost entirely from stone. By the 12th century almost all of the villages in the area were established. Huge deposits of limestone resulted in a wealth of stone buildings. Masons worked from distinctive local designs that were handed down from generation to generation.

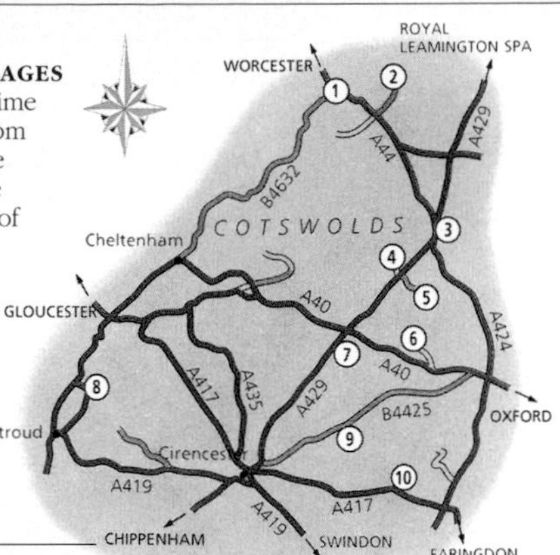

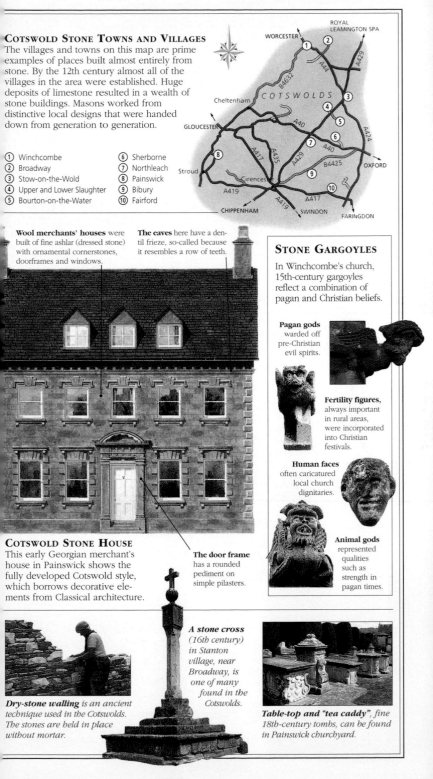

1. Winchcombe
2. Broadway
3. Stow-on-the-Wold
4. Upper and Lower Slaughter
5. Bourton-on-the-Water
6. Sherborne
7. Northleach
8. Painswick
9. Bibury
10. Fairford

Wool merchants' houses were built of fine ashlar (dressed stone) with ornamental cornerstones, doorframes and windows.

The eaves here have a dentil frieze, so-called because it resembles a row of teeth.

The door frame has a rounded pediment on simple pilasters.

Cotswold Stone House

This early Georgian merchant's house in Painswick shows the fully developed Cotswold style, which borrows decorative elements from Classical architecture.

Stone Gargoyles

In Winchcombe's church, 15th-century gargoyles reflect a combination of pagan and Christian beliefs.

Pagan gods warded off pre-Christian evil spirits.

Fertility figures, always important in rural areas, were incorporated into Christian festivals.

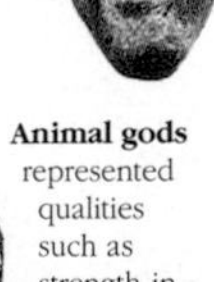

Human faces often caricatured local church dignitaries.

Animal gods represented qualities such as strength in pagan times.

***Dry-stone walling** is an ancient technique used in the Cotswolds. The stones are held in place without mortar.*

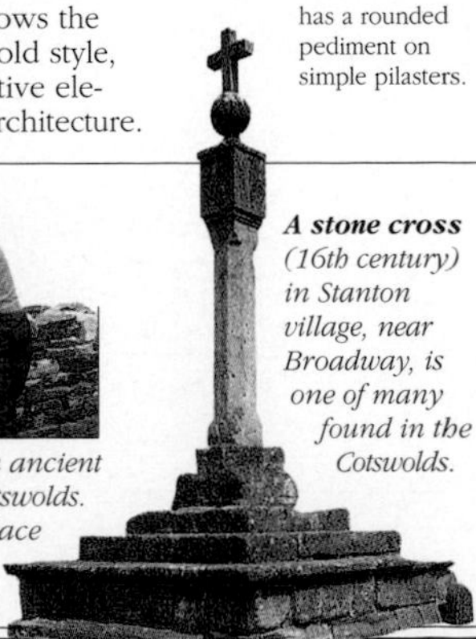

***A stone cross** (16th century) in Stanton village, near Broadway, is one of many found in the Cotswolds.*

***Table-top and "tea caddy"**, fine 18th-century tombs, can be found in Painswick churchyard.*

The Cotswold
Restaurant
Beer Garden
Morning Coffee

THE HEART OF ENGLAND

CHESHIRE · GLOUCESTERSHIRE · HEREFORDSHIRE
SHROPSHIRE · STAFFORDSHIRE · WARWICKSHIRE · WORCESTERSHIRE

BRITAIN'S GREAT ATTRACTION *is its variety, and nowhere is this more true than at the heart of the country, where the Cotswold hills, enfolding stone cottages and churches, give way to the flat, fertile plains of Warwickshire. Shakespeare country borders on the industrial heart of England, once known as the workshop of the world.*

Coventry, Birmingham, the Potteries and their hinterlands have been manufacturing iron, textiles and ceramics since the 18th century. In the 20th century these industries have declined, and a new type of museum has developed to commemorate the towns' industrial heyday and explain the manufacturing processes which were once taken for granted. Ironbridge Gorge and Quarry Bank Mill, Styal, where the factories are now living museums, are fascinating industrial sites and enjoy beautiful surroundings.

These landscapes may be appreciated from the deck of a narrowboat, making gentle progress along the Midlands canals, to the region on the border with Wales known as the Marches. Here the massive walls of Chester and the castles at Shrewsbury and Ludlow recall the Welsh locked in fierce battle with Norman barons and the Marcher Lords. The Marches are now full of rural communities served by the peaceful market towns of Leominster, Malvern, Ross-on-Wye and Hereford. The cities of Worcester and Gloucester both have modern shopping centres, yet their majestic cathedrals retain the tranquillity of an earlier age.

Cheltenham has Regency terraces, Cirencester a rich legacy of Roman art and Tewkesbury a solid Norman abbey. Finally, there is Stratford-upon-Avon, where William Shakespeare, the Elizabethan dramatist, lived and died.

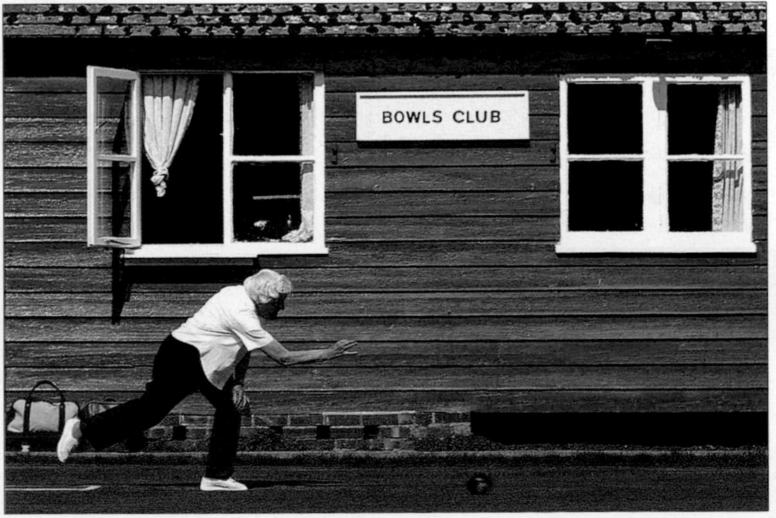

Leisurely village pastimes, reminiscent of a more tranquil age

◁ **Cotswold stone: an extremely popular building material in the Heart of England**

Exploring the Heart of England

THE HEART OF ENGLAND, more than any other region, takes its character from the landscape. Picturesque houses, pubs and churches, made from timber and Cotswold stone, create a harmonic appearance that delights visitors and adds greatly to the pleasures of exploration. The area around Birmingham and Stoke-on-Trent, however – once the industrial hub of England – contrasts sharply. The bleak concrete skyline may not appeal, but the area has a fascinating history that is reflected in the self-confident Victorian art and architecture, and a series of award-winning industrial heritage museums.

Arlington Row: stone cottages in the Cotswold village of Bibury

SIGHTS AT A GLANCE

Birmingham 13
Cheltenham 20
Chester 2
Chipping Campden 18
Cirencester 22
Coventry 14
Gloucester 21
Great Malvern 11
Hereford 8
Ironbridge pp302–3 5
Ledbury 10
Leominster 7
Ludlow 6
Quarry Bank Mill, Styal 1
Ross-on-Wye 9
Shrewsbury 4
Stoke-on-Trent 3
Stratford-upon-Avon pp312–15 17
Tewkesbury 19
Warwick pp309–11 16
Worcester 12

Walks and Tours

Midlands Garden Tour 15

GETTING AROUND

The Heart of England is easily reached by train, with mainline rail services to Cheltenham, Worcester, Birmingham, and Coventry. The M5 and M6 motorways are the major road routes but are frequently congested. Long-distance buses provide regular shuttle services to Cheltenham and Birmingham. Travelling within the region is best done by car. Rural roads are delightfully empty, although major attractions, such as Stratford-upon-Avon, may be very crowded during the summer.

SEE ALSO

- ***Where to Stay*** pp555–8
- ***Where to Eat*** pp591–3

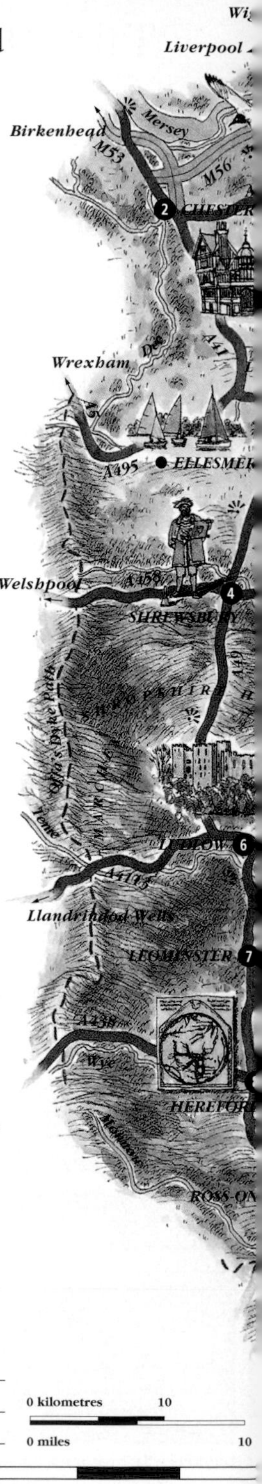

Liverpool
Birkenhead
Mersey
M53
M56
2 CHESTER
Wrexham
A41
A495
ELLESMERE
Welshpool
A458
4 SHREWSBURY
A49
Offa's Dyke Path
Teme
6 LUDLOW
A4113
Llandrindod Wells
LEOMINSTER 7
A438
Wye
HEREFORD
ROSS-ON

0 kilometres 10

0 miles 10

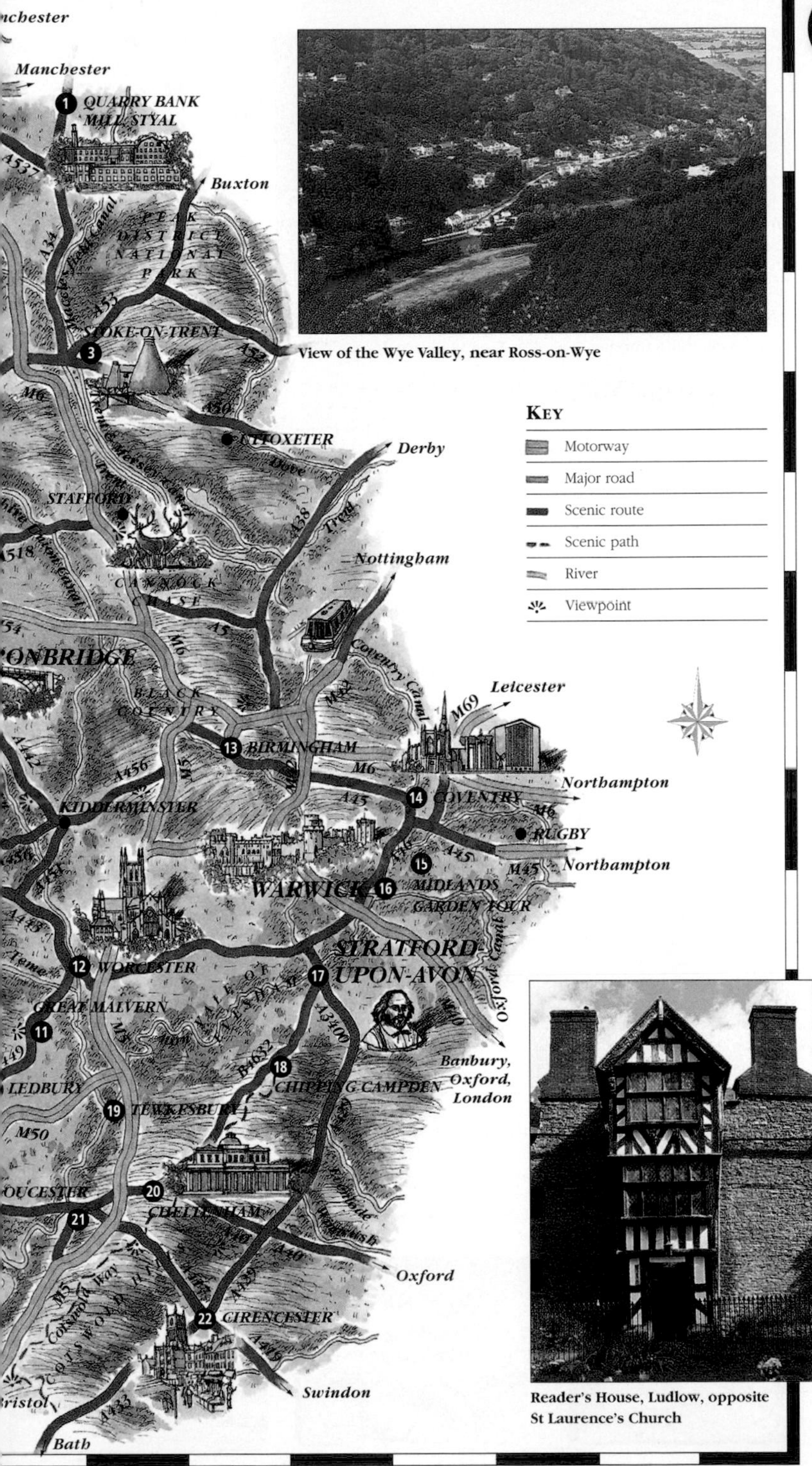

View of the Wye Valley, near Ross-on-Wye

Reader's House, Ludlow, opposite St Laurence's Church

Quarry Bank Mill, a working reminder of the Industrial Revolution

Quarry Bank Mill, Styal ❶

(NT) Cheshire. *01625 527468.* *Wilmslow then bus.* *Apr–Sep: daily; Oct–Mar: Tue–Sun.* *23-25 Dec.* *limited.* www.quarrybankmill.org.uk

THE HISTORY of the Industrial Revolution *(see pp54–5)* is brought vividly to life at Quarry Bank Mill, an early factory now transformed into a museum. Here, mill master Samuel Greg first used the waters of the Bollin Valley in 1784 to power the water frame, a machine for spinning raw cotton fibres into thread. By the 1840s, the Greg cotton empire was one of the biggest in Britain, and the mill produced bolts of material to be exported all over the world.

Today the massive old mill buildings have been restored to house a living museum of the cotton industry. This dominated the Manchester area for nearly 200 years, but was finally destroyed by foreign competition. The entire process, from the spinning and weaving to the bleaching, printing and dyeing, is shown through a series of reconstructions, demonstrations and hands-on displays. The weaving shed is full of clattering looms producing textiles. There are fascinating contraptions that demonstrate how water can be used to drive machinery, including an enormous wheel, 50 tons in weight and 7 m (24 ft) high, that is still used daily to provide power for the looms.

The Greg family realized the importance of having a healthy, loyal and stable workforce. A social history exhibition explains how the mill workers were housed in the purpose-built village of Styal, in spacious cottages which had vegetable gardens and toilets. Details of their wages, working conditions and medical facilities are displayed on information boards.

There are guided tours of the nearby **Apprentice House**. Local orphans lived here, and were sent to work up to 12 hours a day at the mill when they were just six or seven years old. Visitors can try the beds in the house and even sample the medicine they were given. Quarry Bank Mill is surrounded by over 115 ha (284 acres) of woodland.

Chester ❷

Cheshire. *125,000.* *Town Hall, Northgate St (01244 402111).* *Mon–Sat.* www.chestertourism.com

FIRST SETTLED BY THE ROMANS *(see pp44–5)*, who established a camp in AD 79 to defend fertile land near the River Dee, the main streets of Chester are now lined with timber buildings. These are the **Chester Rows**, which, with their two tiers of shops and continuous upper gallery, anticipate today's multi-storey shops by several centuries.

Although their oriel windows and decorative timber-work are mostly 19th century, the Rows were first built in the 13th and 14th centuries, and the original structures can be seen in many places. The façade of the 16th-century **Bishop Lloyd's House** in Watergate Street is the most richly carved in Chester. The Rows are at their most varied and attractive where Eastgate Street meets Bridge Street. Here, views of the cathedral and the town walls give the impression of a perfectly preserved medieval city. This illusion is helped by the Town Crier, who calls the hour and announces news in summer from the Cross, a reconstruction of the 15th-century stone crucifix that was destroyed in the Civil War *(see pp52–3)*.

Chester's 1897 clocktower

The **Grosvenor Museum**, south of the Cross, explains the town's history. To the north is the **cathedral**. The choir stalls have splendid misericords *(see p329)*, with

Examples of the intricate carving on Bishop Lloyd's House, a Tudor building in Watergate Street, Chester

The Chester Rows, where shops line the first-floor galleries

scenes including a quarrelling couple. In sharp contrast are the delicate spire-lets on the stall canopies. The cathedral is surrounded on two sides by the **city walls**, originally Roman but rebuilt at intervals. The best stretch is from the cathedral to Eastgate, where a wrought-iron **clock** was erected in 1897. The route to Newgate leads to a **Roman amphitheatre** built in AD 100.

Grosvenor Museum
Grosvenor St. *01244 402008.*
Mon–Sat, Sun pm. *24–26 Dec, 1 Jan, Good Fri.*
limited.

Roman Amphitheatre
Little St John St. *01244 402009.*
daily.

Stoke-on-Trent ❸

Stoke-on-Trent. *252,000.*
Quadrant Rd, Hanley (01782 236000). *Mon–Sat.*
www.visitstoke.co.uk

From the mid-18th century, Staffordshire became a leading centre for mass-produced ceramics. Its fame arose from the fine bone china and porcelain products of Wedgwood, Minton, Doulton and Spode, but the Staffordshire potteries also make a wide range of utilitarian products such as baths, toilets and wall tiles.

In 1910 a group of six towns – Longton, Fenton, Hanley, Burslem, Tunstall and Stoke – merged to form the conurbation of Stoke-on-Trent, also known as the Potteries. Fans of the writer Arnold Bennett (1867–1931) may recognise this area as the "Five Towns", a term he used in a series of novels about the region (Fenton was excluded).

The **Gladstone Pottery Museum** is a Victorian complex of workshops, kilns, galleries and an engine house. There are demonstrations of traditional pottery techniques. The **Potteries Museum and Art Gallery** in Hanley has historic and modern ceramics.

Josiah Wedgwood began his earthenware firm in 1769 and built a workers' village, Etruria. The last surviving steam-powered pottery mill is on display at the **Etruria Industrial Museum**.

Environs: About 10 miles (16 km) north of Stoke-on-Trent is **Little Moreton Hall** *(see p291)*, a half-timbered early Tudor manor house.

Gladstone Pottery Museum
Uttoxeter Rd, Longton. *01782 319232.* *daily.*
www.stoke.gov.uk/gladstone

Potteries Museum and Art Gallery Bethesda St, Hanley. *01782 232323.* *daily.*
www.stoke.gov.uk/museums

Etruria Industrial Museum
Lower Bedford St, Etruria. *01782 233144.* *Jan–Mar: Mon–Wed; Apr–Dec: Sat–Wed.* *25 Dec–1 Jan.* *by arrangement.*

Little Moreton Hall
(NT) Congleton, off A34. *01260 272018.* *Mar–Oct: Wed–Sun & public hols; last week Nov–22 Dec: Sat, Sun.* *limited.*

Staffordshire Pottery

An abundance of water, marl, clay and easily mined coal to fire the kilns enabled Staffordshire to develop as a ceramics centre; and local supplies of iron, copper and lead were used for glazing. In the 18th century, pottery became widely accessible and affordable. English bone china, which used powdered animals' bones for strength and translucence, was shipped all over the world, and Josiah Wedgwood (1730–95) introduced simple, durable crockery – though his best known design is the blue jasperware decorated with white Classical themes. Coal-powered bottle kilns fired the clay until the 1950s Clean Air Acts put them out of business. They have been replaced by electric or gas-fired kilns.

Wedgwood candlesticks, 1785

Timber-framed, gabled mansions in Fish Street, Shrewsbury

Shrewsbury ❹

Shropshire. *96,000.* *The Square (01743 281200).* *Tue, Wed, Fri, Sat.* www.shrewsbury.ws

SHREWSBURY is almost an island, enclosed by a great loop of the River Severn. A gaunt **castle** of red sandstone, first built in 1083, guards the entrance to the town, standing on the only section of land not surrounded by the river. Such defences were necessary on the frontier between England and the wilder Marches of Wales, whose inhabitants fiercely defied Saxon and Norman invaders *(see pp46–7)*. The castle, rebuilt over the centuries, now houses the Shropshire Regimental Museum.

In AD 60 the Romans *(see pp44–5)* built the garrison town of Viroconium, modern Wroxeter, 5 miles (8 km) east of Shrewsbury. Finds from the excavations are displayed at **Shrewsbury Museum and Art Gallery**, including a decorated silver mirror from the 2nd century and other luxury goods imported by the Roman army.

The town's medieval wealth as a centre of the wool trade is evident in the many timber-framed buildings found along the High Street, Butcher Row, and Wyle Cop. Two of the grandest High Street houses, **Ireland's Mansions** and **Owen's Mansions**, are named after Robert Ireland and Richard Owen, the wealthy wool merchants who built them in 1575 and 1570 respectively. Similarly attractive buildings in Fish Street frame a view of the **Prince Rupert Hotel**, which was briefly the headquarters of Charles I's nephew, Rupert, in the English Civil War *(see pp52–3)*.

Outside the loop of the river, the **Abbey Church** survives from the medieval monastery. It has a number of interesting memorials, including one to Lieutenant WES Owen MC, better known as the war poet Wilfred Owen (1893–1918), who taught at the local Wyle Cop school and was killed in the last days of World War I.

Roman silver mirror in Rowley's House Museum

ENVIRONS: To the south of Shrewsbury, the road to Ludlow passes through the landscapes celebrated in the 1896 poem by AE Housman (1859–1936), *A Shropshire Lad*. Highlights include the bleak moors of **Long Mynd,** with 15 prehistoric barrows, and **Wenlock Edge**, wonderful walking country with glorious, far-reaching views.

Shrewsbury Castle
Castle St. *01743 358516.* *Easter–Sep: daily; Oct–Easter: Wed–Sat.* *22 Dec–mid-Feb.*

Shrewsbury Museum and Art Gallery
Barker St. *01743 361196.* *Oct–May: Tue–Sat; Jun–Sep: daily.* *2 wks over Christmas.* *limited.* www.shrewsburymuseums.com

Ironbridge Gorge ❺

See pp302–3.

Ludlow ❻

Shropshire. *10,000.* *Castle St (01584 875053).* *Mon, Fri, Sat.* www.ludlow.org.uk

LUDLOW ATTRACTS large numbers of visitors to its splendid castle, but there is much else to see in this town, with its small shops and its lovely Georgian and half-timbered Tudor buildings. Ludlow is an important area of geological research and the **museum**, just off the town centre, has fossils of the oldest known animals and plants.

The ruined **castle** is sited on cliffs high above the River Teme. Built in 1086, it was damaged in the Civil War *(see pp52–3)* and abandoned in 1689. *Comus,* a court masque using music and drama and a precursor of opera, by John Milton (1608–74) was first performed here in 1634 in the Great Hall.

The 13th-century south tower and hall of Stokesay Castle, near Ludlow

Prince Arthur (1486–1502), elder brother of Henry VIII *(see pp50–51)*, died at Ludlow Castle. His heart is buried in **St Laurence Church** at the other end of Castle Square, as are the ashes of the poet A E Housman. The east end of the church backs onto the **Bull Ring**, with its ornate timber buildings. Two inns vie for attention across the street: **The Bull**, with its Tudor back yard, and **The Feathers**, with its flamboyant façade, whose name recalls the feathers used in arrow-making, once a local industry.

ENVIRONS: About 5 miles (8 km) north of Ludlow, in a lovely setting, is **Stokesay Castle**, a fortified manor house with a colourful moated garden.

Ludlow Castle
The Square. 01584 873355. daily (Jan: Sat, Sun only). limited. www.ludlowcastle.com

Ludlow Museum
Castle St. 01584 873857. Apr–Oct: Mon–Sat (Jun–Aug: daily).

Stokesay Castle
Craven Arms, A49. 01588 672544. Apr–Oct: daily; Nov–Mar: Wed–Sun. 24–26 Dec, 1 Jan.

Leominster ❼

Herefordshire. 11,000. Corn Sq (01568 616460). Fri. www.visitorlinks.com

FARMERS COME TO LEOMINSTER (pronounced "Lemster") from all over this rural region to buy supplies. There are two buildings of note in the town, which has been a wool-manufacturing centre for 700 years. In the town centre stands the magnificent **Grange Court**, carved with bold and bizarre figures in 1633. Nearby is the **priory**, whose imposing Norman portal is carved with an equally strange mixture of mythical birds and beasts. The lions, at least, can be explained: medieval monks believed the name of Leominster was derived from *monasterium leonis*, "the monastery of the lions". In fact, *leonis* probably comes from medieval, rather than Classical Latin, and it means "of the marshes". The aptness of this description can readily be seen in the green lanes around the town, following the lush river valleys.

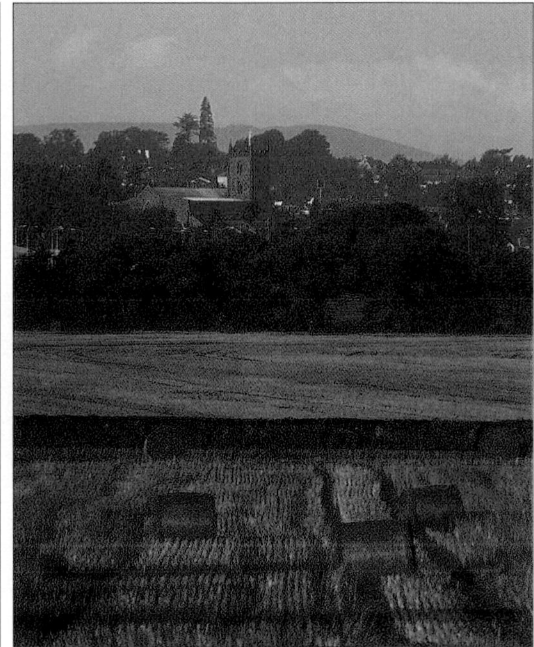

A view of Leominster, set on the River Lugg in rolling border country

ENVIRONS: South of the town, the magnificent gardens and parkland at **Hampton Court** have recently been restored and include island pavilions and a maze. To the west of the town, along the River Arrow, are the villages of **Eardisland** and **Pembridge**, with their well-kept gardens and timber-framed houses. **Berrington Hall**, 3 miles (5 km) north of Leominster, is a Neo-Classical house set in grounds by Capability Brown. Inside are beautifully preserved ceiling decorations and period furniture.

To the northeast of Leominster is **Tenbury Wells**, which enjoyed brief popularity as a spa in the 19th century. The River Teme flows through it, full of minnows, trout and other fish and beloved of the composer Sir Edward Elgar *(see p305)*, who came to seek inspiration on its banks. The river also feeds **Burford House Gardens**, on the western outskirts of Tenbury Wells, where the water is used to create streams, fountains and pools that are rich in unusual moisture-loving plants.

Gatehouse of Stokesay Castle, near Ludlow

Hampton Court Gardens
nr Hope Under Dinmore. 01568 797 777. Apr–21 Dec: 11am–5pm (to 4pm Nov–Dec) Tue–Sun. www.hamptoncourt.org.uk

Berrington Hall
Berrington. 01568 615721. Apr–Oct: daily.

Burford House Gardens
Tenbury Wells. 01584 810777. daily. 1 Jan, 25, 26 Dec. www.burford.co.uk

Ironbridge Gorge ❺

IRONBRIDGE GORGE was one of the most important centres of the Industrial Revolution *(see pp54–5)*. It was here, in 1709, Abraham Darby I (1678–1717) pioneered the use of inexpensive coke, rather than charcoal, to smelt iron ore. The use of iron in bridges, ships and buildings transformed Ironbridge Gorge into one of the world's great iron-making centres. Industrial decline in the 20th century led to the Gorge's decay, although today it has been restored as an exciting complex of industrial archaeology, with several museums strung along the wooded banks of the River Severn.

Visitors' Checklist

Shropshire. 2,900. Telford then bus (Telford Travelink 01952 200005). 01952 433522. Ironbridge town (01952 432166). mid-Apr–Oct: daily; Nov–mid-Apr: call for details. 1 Jan, 24, 25 Dec. Some sites closed Nov–Apr, call for details. most sites. by arrangement. www.ironbridge.org.uk

Wrought-iron clock (1843) on the roof of the Museum of Iron

Museum of Iron

THE HISTORY OF IRON and the men who made it is traced in this remarkable museum. Abraham Darby I's discovery of how to smelt iron ore with coke allowed the mass production of iron, paving the way for the rise of large-scale industry. His original blast furnace forms the museum's centrepiece.

One of the museum's themes is the history of the Darby dynasty, a Quaker family who had a great impact on the Coalbrookdale community. The social and working conditions faced by the labourers, who sometimes had to toil for 24 hours at a stretch, are also illustrated.

Ironbridge led the world in industrial innovation, producing the first iron wheels and cylinders for the first steam engine. A restored locomotive and cast-iron statues, many of them commissioned for the 1851 Great Exhibition *(see pp56–7)*, are among the many Coalbrookdale Company products on display.

One of the Darby family's homes in the nearby village of Coalbrookdale, **Rosehill House**, has been furnished in mid-Victorian style.

Museum of the Gorge

THIS PARTLY CASTELLATED, Victorian building was a warehouse for storing products from the ironworks before they were shipped down the River Severn. The warehouse is now home to the Museum of the Gorge, and has displays illustrating the history of the Severn and the development of the water industry.

Until the arrival of the railways in the mid-19th century, the Severn was the main form of transport and communication to and from the Gorge. Sometimes too shallow, at other times in flood, the river was not a particularly reliable means of transportation; by the 1890s river trading had stopped completely.

The highlight of the museum is a wonderful 12 m (40 ft) model of the Gorge as it would have appeared in 1796, complete with foundries, cargo boats and growing villages.

***Europe* (1860), statue in the Museum of Iron**

Jackfield Tile Museum

THERE HAVE BEEN POTTERIES in this area since the 17th century, but it was not until the Victorian passion for decorative tiles that Jackfield became famous. There were two tile-making factories here – Maw and Craven Dunnill – that produced a tremendous variety of tiles from clay mined nearby.

Peacock Panel (1928), one of the tile museum's star attractions

Talented designers created an astonishing range of images. The newly refurbished Jackfield Tile Museum, in the old Craven Dunnill works, has a collection of the decorative floor and wall tiles that were produced here from the 1850s to the 1960s. Visitors can watch small-scale demonstrations of traditional methods of tile-making in the old factory buildings, including the kilns and the decoration workshops.

Ironbridge Gorge Sights

Blists Hill Museum ⑥
Coalport China Museum ⑤
Iron Bridge ③
Jackfield Tile Museum ④
Museum of Iron ①
Museum of the Gorge ②

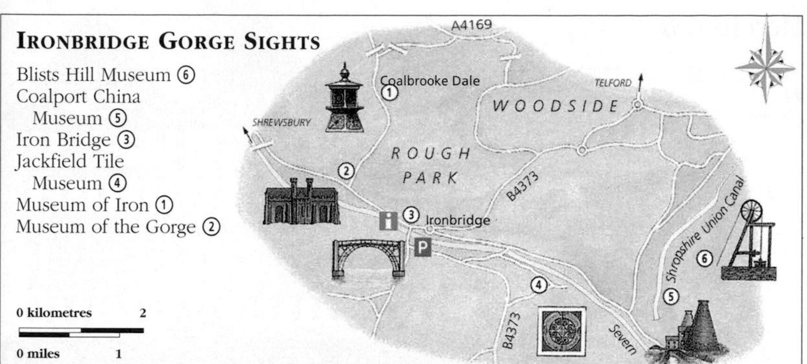

Coalport China Museum

In the mid-19th century the Coalport Works was one of the largest porcelain manufacturers in Britain, and its name was synonymous with fine china. The Coalport Company still makes porcelain but has long since moved its operations to Stoke-on-Trent *(see p299)*. Today the china workshops have been converted into a museum, where visitors can watch demonstrations of the various stages of making porcelain, including the skills of pot-throwing, painting and gilding. There is a superb collection of 19th-century china housed in one of the museum's distinctive bottle-shaped kilns.

Coalport China Museum with its bottle-shaped kiln

Nearby is the **Tar Tunnel**, an important source of natural bitumen discovered 110 m (360 ft) underground in the 18th century. It once yielded 20,500 litres (4,500 gal) of tar every week; visitors can still explore part of the tunnel.

The Iron Bridge

Abraham Darby III (grandson of the first man to smelt iron with coke) cast the world's first iron bridge in 1779, revolutionizing building methods in the process. Spanning the Severn, the bridge is a monument to the ironmasters' skills. The toll-house on the south bank charts its construction.

Blists Hill Museum

This enormous open-air museum recreates Victorian life as it would have been in an Ironbridge Gorge town. A group of 19th-century buildings has been reconstructed on the 20 ha (50 acre) site of Blists Hill, an old coal mine that used to supply the ironworks in the Gorge. Here, people in period costume enact roles and perform tasks such as iron forging.

The site has period housing, a church and even a Victorian school. Visitors can change money into old coinage to buy items from the baker or even pay for a drink in the local pub.

The centrepiece of Blists Hill is a complete foundry that still produces wrought iron. One of the most spectacular sights is the Hay Inclined Plane, which was used to transport canal boats up and down a steep slope. Other attractions include steam engines, a saddlers, a doctors, a chemist, a candlemakers and a sweetshop.

Hereford 8

Herefordshire. 50,000.
King St (01432 268430).
Wed (cattle, general), Sat (general).
www.visitorlinks.com

ONCE THE CAPITAL of the Saxon kingdom of West Mercia, Hereford is today an attractive town which serves the needs of a primarily rural community. A cattle market is held here every Wednesday, and local produce is sold at the covered market in the town centre. Almost opposite, the timber-framed **Old House** of 1621 is now a museum of local history.

In the **cathedral**, only a short stroll away, interesting features include the Lady Chapel, in richly ornamented Early English style, the *Mappa Mundi* (see below) and the Chained Library, whose 1,500 books are tethered by iron chains to bookcases as a precaution against theft. The story of these national treasures is told through models, original artifacts and interactive computer technology. The best place for an overall view of the cathedral is at the Bishop's Meadow, south of the centre, leading down to the banks of the Wye.

Hereford's many rewarding museums include the **City Museum and Art Gallery**, noted for its Roman mosaic and for watercolours by local artists, and the **Cider Museum and King Offa Distillery**. In the museum, visitors can discover the history of traditional cider making. The King Offa Distillery, which is open for visits and tastings, is the first distillery licensed to produce cider brandy for 200 years.

Hereford's 17th-century Old House, furnished in period style

Detail of figures on Kilpeck Church

ENVIRONS: During the 12th century, Oliver de Merlemond made a pilgrimage from Hereford to Spain. Impressed by several churches he saw on the way, he brought French masons over to England and introduced their techniques to this area. One result was **Kilpeck Church**, 6 miles (10 km) southwest, covered in lustful figures showing their genitals, and tail-biting dragons. At **Abbey Dore**, 4 miles (6 km) west, the Cistercian abbey church is complemented by the serene riverside gardens of **Abbey Dore Court**.

MEDIEVAL VIEW

Hereford Cathedral's most celebrated treasure is the *Mappa Mundi*, the Map of the World, drawn in 1290 by a clergyman, Richard of Haldingham. The world is depicted here on Biblical principles: Jerusalem is at the centre, the Garden of Eden figures prominently and monsters inhabit the margins of the world.

Central detail, *Mappa Mundi*

Old House
High Town. 01432 260694. *Apr–Sep: Tue–Sun; Oct–Mar: Tue–Sat; public hols.* *25, 26 Dec, 1 Jan, Good Fri.* *limited.* www.herefordshire.gov.uk/museums

City Museum and Art Gallery
Broad St. *01432 260692.* *Apr–Sep: Tue–Sun; Oct–Mar: Tue–Sat, public hols.* *25, 26 Dec, 1 Jan, Good Fri.* www.cidermuseum.com

Cider Museum and King Offa Distillery
Ryelands St.
01432 354207.
Apr–Oct: daily; Jan–Mar: Tue–Sun & public hols. *25, 26 Dec, 1 Jan.* *limited.* *by arrangement.*

Ross-on-Wye 9

Herefordshire. 10,000.
Eddie Cross St (01989 562768).
Thu, Sat.
www. countrysideatitsbest.com

THE FINE TOWN of Ross sits on a cliff of red sandstone above the water meadows of the River Wye. There are wonderful views over the river from the cliff-top gardens,

The wooded Wye Valley near Ross

given to the town by a local benefactor, John Kyrle (1637–1724). Kyrle was lauded by the poet Alexander Pope (1688–1744) in his *Moral Essays on the Uses of Riches* (1732) for using his wealth in a practical way, and he came to be known as "The Man of Ross". There is a memorial to Kyrle in **St Mary's Church**.

ENVIRONS: From Hereford to Ross, the **Wye Valley Walk** follows 16 miles (26 km) of gentle countryside. From Ross it continues south for 33 miles (54 km), over rocky ground in deep, wooded ravines.

Goodrich Castle, 5 miles (8 km) south of Ross, is a 12th-century red sandstone fort on a rock above the river.

Goodrich Castle
(EH) Goodrich. *01600 890538.* *daily (Nov–Mar: Wed–Sun).* *24–26 Dec, 1 Jan.* *(Apr–Sep).*

Ledbury ⑩

Herefordshire. *8,000.* *The Homend (01531 636147).* www.countrysideatitsbest.com

LEDBURY'S MAIN STREET is lined with timbered houses, including the **Market Hall** which dates from 1655. Church Lane, a cobbled lane running up from the High Street, has lovely 16th-century buildings: the **Heritage Centre** and **Butcher Row House** are both now museums. **St Michael and All Angels Church** has a massive detached bell tower, ornate Early English decoration and interesting monuments.

Medieval tile from the Priory at Great Malvern

Heritage Centre
Church Lane. *Easter–Oct: daily.*

Butcher Row House
Church Lane. *Easter–Oct: daily.*

Great Malvern and the Malverns ⑪

Worcestershire. *35,000.* *21 Church St (01684 892289).* *Fri.* www.malvernhills.gov.uk

THE ANCIENT GRANITE ROCK of the Malvern Hills rises from the plain of the River Severn, its 9 miles (15 km) of glorious scenery visible from afar. Composer Sir Edward Elgar (1857–1934) wrote many of his greatest works here, including the oratorio *The Dream of Gerontius* (1900), inspired by what the diarist John Evelyn (1620–1706) described as "one of the goodliest views in England". Elgar's home was in **Little Malvern**, whose truncated Church of St Giles, set on a steep, wooded hill, lost its nave when the stone was stolen during the Dissolution (*see p339*). **Great Malvern**, capital of the hills, is graced with 19th-century buildings which look like Swiss sanitoria: patients would stay at institutions such as Doctor Gulley's Water Cure Establishment. The water gushing from the hillside at St Ann's Well, above the town, is bottled and sold throughout Britain. The town is home to the famous Morgan cars (contact Tourist Information to arrange a factory visit).

Malvern's highlight is the **Priory**, with its 15th-century stained-glass windows and medieval misericords. The old monastic fishponds below the church form the lake of the **Winter Gardens**. Here the theatre hosts performances of Elgar's music and plays by George Bernard Shaw.

A view of the Malverns range, formed of hard Pre-Cambrian rock

Worcester ⓬

Worcestershire. 95,000.
High St (01905 722480).
Mon–Sat.
www.cityofworcester.gov.uk

WORCESTER is one of many English cities whose character has been transformed by modern development. The architectural highlight remains the **cathedral**, off College Yard, which suffered a collapsed tower in 1175 and a disastrous fire in 1203, before the present structure was started in the 13th century.

The nave and central tower were completed in the 1370s, after building was severely interrupted by the Black Death, which decimated the labour force *(see p48)*. The most recent and ornate addition was made in 1874, when Sir George Gilbert Scott *(see p451)* designed the High Gothic choir, incorporating 14th-century carved misericords.

There are many interesting tombs, including King John's, a masterpiece of medieval carving, in front of the altar. Prince Arthur, Henry VIII's brother *(see p301)*, who died at the age of 15, is buried in the chantry chapel south of the altar. Underneath, the huge Norman crypt survives from the first cathedral (1084).

Charles I holding a symbol of the Church on Worcester's Guildhall

From the cathedral cloister, a gate leads to College Green and out into Edgar Street and its Georgian houses. Here the **Museum of Worcester Porcelain** displays Royal Worcester porcelain dating back to 1751. On the High Street, north of the cathedral, the **Guildhall** of 1723 is adorned with statues of Stuart monarchs, reflecting the city's Royalist allegiances. In Cornmarket is **Ye Olde King Charles House**, in which Prince Charles, later Charles II, hid after the Battle of Worcester in 1651 *(see pp52–3)*.

Some of Worcester's finest timber buildings are found in Friar Street: **Greyfriars**, built around 1480, has been restored in period style. The **Commandery** was originally an 11th-century hospital. It was rebuilt in the 15th century and used by Prince Charles as a base during the Civil War. Now a museum, it has a fine hammerbeam roof.

Elgar's Birthplace was the home of composer Sir Edward Elgar *(see p305)* and contains memorabilia of his life.

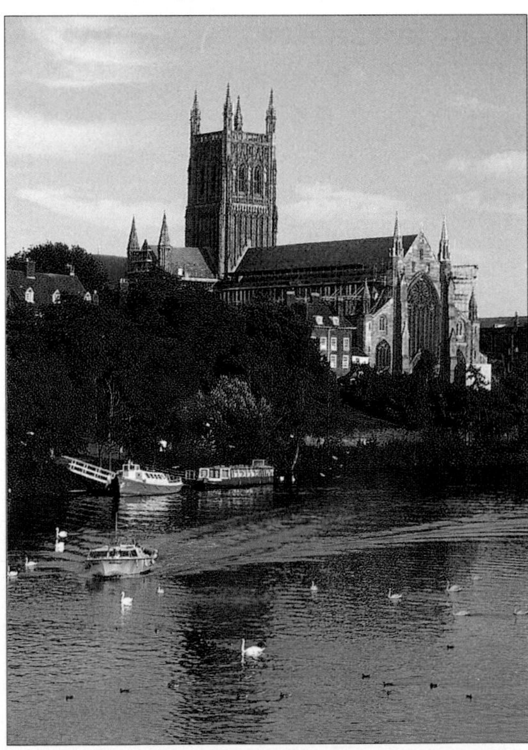

Worcester Cathedral, overlooking the River Severn

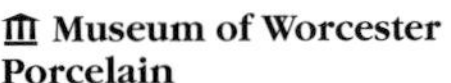

Museum of Worcester Porcelain
Severn St. 01905 23221.
daily.
www.royalworcester.com

Greyfriars
(NT) Friar St. 01905 23571.
Apr–Oct: Wed–Sat (public hols pm only).

Commandery
Sidbury. 01905 361821.
daily (Sun: pm). *25–26 Dec, 1 Jan.*

Elgar's Birthplace
Lower Broadheath. 01905 333224.
daily. *24 Dec–mid-Jan.*
www.elgarmuseum.org

Birmingham ⓭

Birmingham. 1,000,000.
0121 2025099. Mon–Sat.
www.birmingham.org.uk

BRUM, as it is affectionately known to its inhabitants, grew up as a major centre of the Industrial Revolution in the 19th century. A vast range of manufacturing trades was based in Birmingham and was responsible for the rapid development of grim factories and cramped housing. Since the clearance of several of

***The Last of England*, Ford Madox Brown, Birmingham Art Gallery**

these areas after World War II, Birmingham has raised its cultural profile. The city succeeded in enticing Sir Simon Rattle to conduct the City of Birmingham Symphony Orchestra, and persuaded the former Royal Sadler's Wells Ballet (now the Birmingham Royal Ballet) to leave London for the more up-to-date facilities of Birmingham. The **National Exhibition Centre**, 8 miles (13 km) east of the centre, draws thousands of people to its conference, lecture and exhibition halls.

Set away from the massive Bullring shopping centre, Birmingham's 19th-century civic buildings are excellent examples of Neo-Classical architecture. Among them are the **City Museum and Art Gallery**, where the collection includes outstanding works by pre-Raphaelite artists such as Sir Edward Burne-Jones (1833–98), who was born in Birmingham, and Ford Madox Brown (1821–93). The museum also organizes some interesting temporary exhibitions of art, such as works by J M W Turner (1775–1851).

Birmingham's extensive canal system is now used mainly for leisure boating *(see pp288–9)*, and several former warehouses have been converted into museums and galleries. **Thinktank – the Birmingham Museum of Science and Discovery** celebrates the city's contributions to the world of railway engines, aircraft, and the motor trade. The old jewellery quarter has practised its traditional crafts here since the 16th century.

Suburban Birmingham has many attractions, including the **Botanical Gardens** at Edgbaston, and **Cadbury World** at Bournville, where there is a visitor centre dedicated to chocolate (booking ahead is advisable). Bournville village was built in 1890 by the Cadbury brothers for their workers and is a pioneering example of a garden suburb.

City Museum and Art Gallery
Chamberlain Sq. *0121 303 2834.* *daily (Sun: pm).*

Thinktank
Millennium Point. *0121 202222.* *Sat–Thu.* *24–26 Dec.*

Botanical Gardens
Westbourne Rd, Edgbaston. *0121 454 1860.* *daily.* *25 Dec.* *by arrangement.*

Cadbury World
Linden Rd, Bournville. *0121 4514159.* *20 Jan–Oct: daily; Nov, Dec: call for details.* *first two weeks Jan.*

Stately civic office buildings in Victoria Square, Birmingham

Coventry 14

Coventry. 300,000. Bayley Lane (024 7622 7264). Mon–Sat. www.visitcoventry.co.uk

As an armaments centre, Coventry was a prime target for German bombing raids in World War II, and in 1940 the **cathedral** in the city centre was hit. After the war the first totally modern cathedral by Sir Basil Spence (1907–76) was built alongside the ruins. It includes sculptures by Sir Jacob Epstein (1880–1959) and a tapestry by Graham Sutherland (1903–80).

Epstein's *St Michael Subduing the Devil*, on Coventry Cathedral

The **Herbert Gallery and Museum** has displays on the 11th-century legend of Lady Godiva, who rode naked through the streets. The recently renovated **Museum of British Road Transport** has the largest collection of Britain's road transport in the world, including cars, cycles and models, and features the fastest car in the world as well as interactive displays.

Herbert Gallery and Museum
Jordan Well. *024 7683 2381.* *daily (Sun: pm) 1 Jan.*

Museum of British Road Transport
Hales St. *024 7683 2425.* *daily.* www.mbrt.co.uk

Midlands Garden Tour ⓯

Plum tree in blossom

THE CHARMING COTSWOLD stone buildings perfectly complement the lush gardens for which the region is famous. This picturesque route from Warwick to Cheltenham is designed to show every type of garden, from tiny cottage plots, brimming with bell-shaped flowers and hollyhocks, to the deer-filled, landscaped parks of stately homes. The route follows the escarpment of the Cotswold Hills, taking in spectacular scenery and some of the prettiest Midlands villages on the way.

Tips for Drivers

Tour length: *35 miles (50 km).*
Stopping-off points: *Hidcote Manor has excellent lunches and teas; there are refreshments at Kiftsgate Court and Sudeley Castle. Travellers will find a good choice in Broadway, from traditional pubs and tea shops to the de luxe Lygon Arms.* (See also pp636–7.)

Cheltenham Imperial Gardens ⑨
These colourful public gardens on the Promenade were laid out in 1817–18 to encourage people to walk from the town to the spa *(see p316).*

Sudeley Castle ⑧
The restored castle is complemented by box hedges, topiary and an Elizabethan knot garden *(see p22).* Catherine Parr, Henry VIII's widow, died here in 1548.

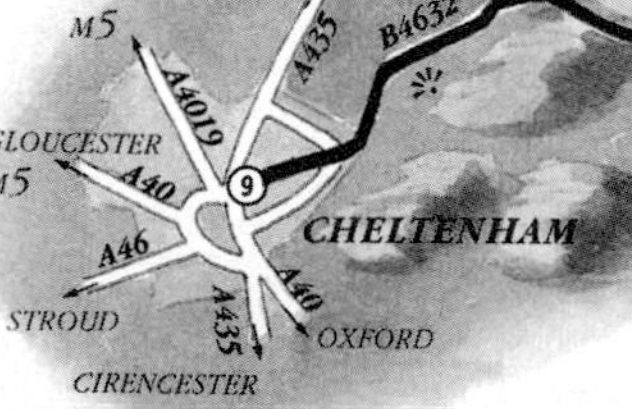

Broadway ⑤
Wisteria and cordoned fruit trees cover 17th-century cottages, fronted by immaculate gardens.

Stanway House ⑦
This Jacobean manor has many lovely trees in its grounds and a pyramid above a cascade of water.

Snowshill Manor ⑥
This Cotswold stone manor contains an extraordinary collection, from bicycles to Japanese armour. There are walled gardens and terraces full of *objets d'art* such as the clock (left). The colour blue is a recurrent theme.

Varwick Castle ①
'he castle's gardens *e pp310–11)* include Mound, planted in nedieval style, with ıss, oaks, yew trees and box hedges.

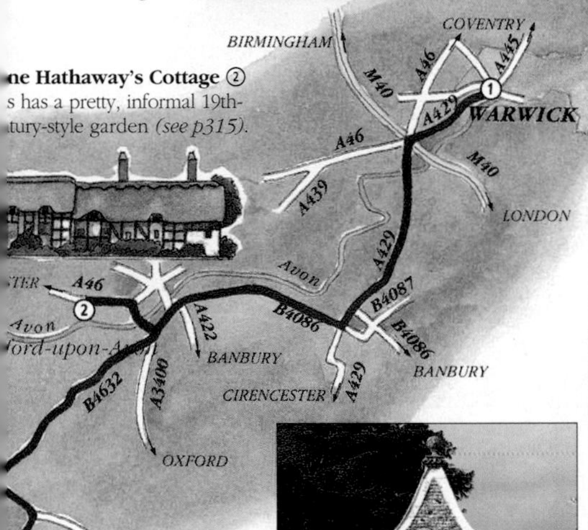

ne Hathaway's Cottage ②
s has a pretty, informal 19th- ıtury-style garden *(see p315)*.

Hidcote Manor Gardens ③
Started in the early years of this century, these beautiful gardens pioneered the idea of a garden as a series of outdoor "rooms", enclosed by high yew hedges and planted according to themes.

Kiftsgate Court Garden ④
This charmingly naturalistic garden lies opposite Hidcote Manor. It has many rare and unusual plants on a series of hillside terraces, including the enormous "Kiftsgate" Rose, nearly 30 m (100 ft) high.

KEY

	Motorway
	Tour route
	Other roads
	Viewpoint

0 kilometres 5

0 miles 5

Warwick ⑯

Warwickshire. 28,000. The Courthouse, Jury St (01926 492212). Sat. www.warwick-uk.co.uk

THOUGH WARWICK suffered a major fire in 1694, some spectacular medieval buildings survived. The **Warwick Doll Museum** in Castle Street (1573) displays rare toys and dolls from all over the world. At the west end of the High Street, a row of medieval guild buildings were transformed in 1571 by the Earl of Leicester (1532–88), who founded the **Lord Leycester Hospital** as a refuge for his old soldiers.

The arcaded **Market Hall** (1670) is part of the Warwickshire Museum, renowned for its unusual tapestry map of the county, woven in 1558.

In Church Street, to the south of St Mary's Church, is the **Beauchamp Chapel** (1443–64). It is a superb example of Perpendicular architecture and has tombs of the Earls of Warwick. There is a view of **Warwick Castle** *(see pp310–11)* from St Mary's tower.

Warwick Doll Museum
Castle St. *01926 495546. Easter–Oct: daily (Sun: pm): (Nov–Easter: Sat).* www.warwickshire.gov.uk/museum

Lord Leycester Hospital
High St. *01926 491422. Tue–Sun & public hols. 25 Dec, Good Fri.* **Gardens** *same as house but Easter–Sep only. limited.*

Market Hall Market Place. *01926 412500. Mon–Sat (May–Sep: daily). limited.*

The Lord Leycester Hospital, now a home for ex-servicemen

Warwick Castle

Neville family at prayer (c.1460)

WARWICK'S MAGNIFICENT CASTLE is a splendid medieval fortress which is also one of the country's finest stately homes. The original Norman castle was rebuilt in the 14th century, when huge outer walls and towers were added, mainly to display the power of the great feudal magnates, the Beauchamps and the Nevilles, the Earls of Warwick. The castle passed in 1604 to the Greville family who, in the 17th and 18th centuries, transformed it into a great country house. In 1978 the owners of Madame Tussaud's *(see p106)* bought the castle and set up tableaux of wax figures to illustrate its history.

The Ghost Tower is where the ghost of Sir Fulke Greville, murdered by a servant in 1628, is said to walk.

The Mound has remains the motte and bailey c *(see p472)* and the 1 century kee

Royal Weekend Party
The waxwork valet is part of the award-winning exhibition of the Prince of Wales's visit in 1898.

★ Great Hall and State Rooms
Medieval apartments were transformed into the Great Hall and State Rooms. A mark of conspicuous wealth, they display a collection of family treasures from around the world.

The Mill and Engine House

Kingmaker Attraction
Dramatic displays recreate medieval life as "Warwick the Kingmaker", Richard Neville, prepared for battle in the Wars of the Roses .

View of Warwick Castle, south front, by Antonio Canaletto (1697–1768)

Visitors' Checklist

Castle Lane, Warwick. *0870 4422000.* *Apr–Sep: 10am–6pm daily; Oct–Mar: 10am–5pm daily (last adm: 30 mins before closing).* *25 Dec.* *limited.*

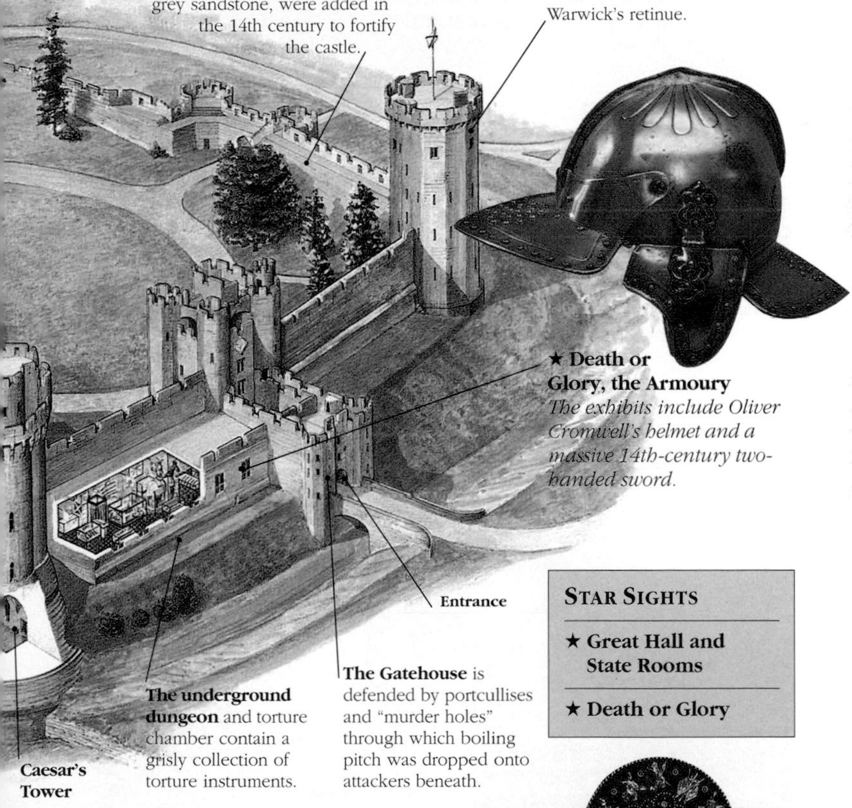

Guy's Tower (1393) had lodgings for guests and members of the Earl of Warwick's retinue.

Ramparts and towers, of local grey sandstone, were added in the 14th century to fortify the castle.

★ Death or Glory, the Armoury
The exhibits include Oliver Cromwell's helmet and a massive 14th-century two-handed sword.

Entrance

The Gatehouse is defended by portcullises and "murder holes" through which boiling pitch was dropped onto attackers beneath.

The underground dungeon and torture chamber contain a grisly collection of torture instruments.

Caesar's Tower

Star Sights

- **★ Great Hall and State Rooms**
- **★ Death or Glory**

Timeline

Shield (1745), Death or Glory

Richard Neville

1000 – 1200 – 1400 – 1600 – 1800

1068 Norman motte and bailey castle built

1264 Simon de Montfort, champion of Parliament against Henry III, sacks Warwick Castle

1356–1401 Present castle built by the Beauchamp family, Earls of Warwick

1449–1471 Richard Neville, Earl of Warwick, plays leading role in Wars of the Roses

1478 Castle reverts to Crown after murder of Richard Neville's son-in-law

1604 James I gives castle to Sir Fulke Greville

1600–1800 Interiors remodelled and gardens landscaped

1642 Royalists imprisoned in the castle

1871 Anthony Salvin (1799–1881) restores Great Hall and State Rooms after fire

1893–1910 Visits from future Edward VII

Street-by-Street: Stratford-upon-Avon ⓱

A 1930s jester

SITUATED ON THE WEST BANK of the River Avon, in the heart of the Midlands, is one of the most famous towns in England. Stratford-upon-Avon dates back to at least Roman times but its appearance today is that of a small Tudor market town, with mellow, half-timbered architecture and tranquil walks beside the tree-fringed Avon. This image belies its popularity as the most visited tourist attraction outside London, with eager hordes flocking to see buildings connected to William Shakespeare or his descendants.

Bancroft Gardens
There is an attractive boat-filled canal basin here and a 15th-century causeway.

★ Shakespeare's Birthplace
This building was almost entirely reconstructed in the 19th century, but in the style of the Tudor original.

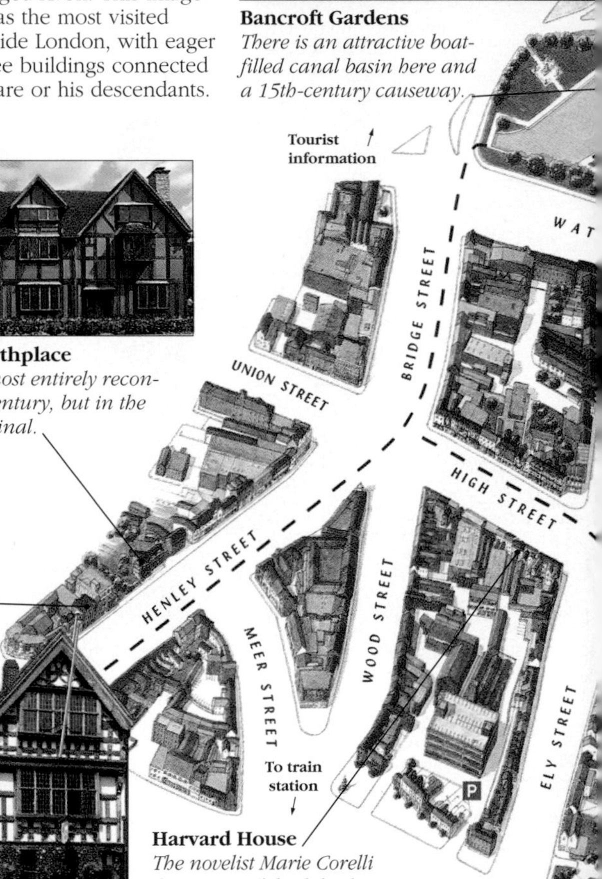

Harvard House
The novelist Marie Corelli (1855–1924) had this house restored. Next door is the 16th-century Garrick Inn.

STAR SIGHTS

- ★ Shakespeare's Birthplace
- ★ Hall's Croft
- ★ Holy Trinity Church

Town Hall
Built in 1767, there are traces of 18th-century graffiti on the front of the building saying God Save the King.

Royal Shakespeare Theatre
The highly acclaimed resident theatre company, the RSC, has staged all of Shakespeare's plays since it began in 1961.

Visitors' Checklist

Warwickshire. 22,000. 20 miles (32 km) NW of Stratford-upon-Avon. Alcester Rd. Bridge St. Bridge Foot (01789 293127); Shakespeare Centre, Henley St (01789 204016). Fri. Shakespeare's Birthday: Apr; Stratford Festival: Jul. www.shakespeare-country.co.uk

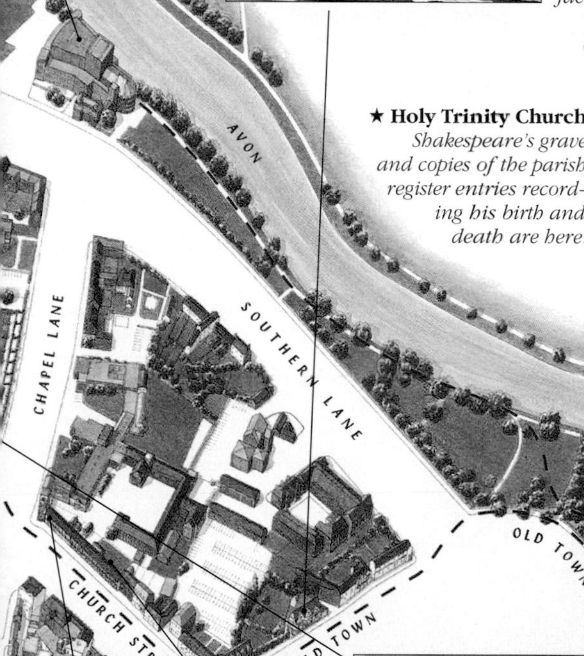

★ Hall's Croft
John Hall, Shakespeare's son-in-law, was a doctor. This delightful house has one room fitted out as a dispensary, with original Jacobean furniture.

★ Holy Trinity Church
Shakespeare's grave and copies of the parish register entries recording his birth and death are here.

Edward VI Grammar School

Nash's House
The foundations of New Place, where Shakespeare died, form the garden beside this house.

Guild Chapel

Key

— — — Suggested route

Exploring Stratford-upon-Avon

Mosaic of Shakespeare on the beautiful Old Bank (1810)

William Shakespeare was born in Stratford-upon-Avon on St George's Day, 23 April 1564. Admirers of his work have been coming to the town since his death in 1616. In 1847 a public appeal successfully raised the money to buy the house in which he was born. As a result Stratford has become a literary shrine to Britain's greatest dramatist. It also has a thriving cultural reputation as the provincial home of the prestigious Royal Shakespeare Company, whose dramas are usually performed in Stratford before playing a second season in London *(see pp126–7)*.

Anne Hathaway's Cottage, home of Shakespeare's wife

Around Stratford

The centre of Stratford-upon-Avon has many buildings that are connected with William Shakespeare and his descendants. On the High Street corner is the **Cage**, a 15th-century prison. It was converted into a house where Shakespeare's daughter Judith lived, and is now a shop. At the end of the High Street, the **Town Hall** has a statue of Shakespeare on the façade given by David Garrick (1717–79), the actor who in 1769 organized the first Shakespeare festival.

The High Street leads into Chapel Street where the half-timbered **Nash's House** is a museum of local history. It is also the site of **New Place**, where Shakespeare died in 1616, and which is now a herb and knot garden *(see p22)*. In Church Street opposite, the **Guild Chapel** (1496) has a *Last Judgement* painting (c.1500) on the chancel wall. Shakespeare is thought to have attended the **Edward VI Grammar School** (above the former Guildhall) next door.

A left turn into Old Town leads to **Hall's Croft**, home of Shakespeare's daughter Susanna, which displays 16th and 17th-century medical artefacts. An avenue of lime trees leads to **Holy Trinity Church**, where Shakespeare is buried. A walk along the river follows the Avon to **Bancroft Gardens**, which lies at the junction of the River Avon and the Stratford Canal.

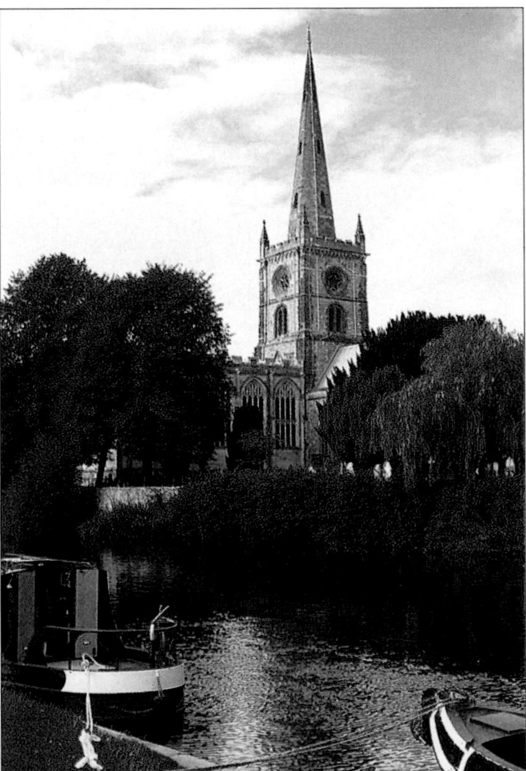

Holy Trinity Church, seen across the River Avon

Shakespeare's Birthplace

Henley St. 01789 204016. *daily.* *23–26 Dec.* *limited* www.shakespeare.org.uk

Bought for the nation in 1847 when it was a public house, Shakespeare's Birthplace was converted back to Elizabethan style. Objects associated with Shakespeare's father, John, a glovemaker and wool merchant, are on display. There is a birth room, in which Shakespeare was supposedly born, and another room has a window etched with visitors' autographs, including that of Sir Walter Scott *(see p498)*.

Harvard House

High St. 01789 204016. May–Sep: Fri–Sun, bank hol Mon. limited. www.shakespeare.org.uk

Built in 1596, this ornate house was the home of Katherine Rogers, whose son, John Harvard, emigrated to America and in 1638 left his estate to a new college, later renamed Harvard University. The house contains a Museum of British Pewter and displays relating to John Harvard.

ENVIRONS: No tour of Stratford would be complete without a visit to **Anne Hathaway's Cottage**. Before her marriage to William Shakespeare she lived at Shottery, 1 mile (1.5 km) west of Stratford. Despite fire damage in 1969, the cottage is still impressive, with some original 16th-century furniture. The Hathaway descendants lived here until the early 20th century *(see p309)*.

Anne Hathaway's Cottage

Cottage Lane. 01789 292100. daily. 23–26 Dec. www.shakespeare.org.uk

Kenneth Branagh in *Hamlet*

THE ROYAL SHAKESPEARE COMPANY

The Royal Shakespeare Company is renowned for its new interpretations of Shakespeare's work. The company performs at the 1932 Royal Shakespeare Theatre, a windowless brick building adjacent to the Swan Theatre, built in 1986 to a design based on an Elizabethan playhouse. Next to it is a building displaying sets, props and costumes. The RSC also performs at the 150-seat theatre, known as the Other Place, and in London *(see pp126–7)*.

Grevel House, the oldest house in Chipping Campden

Chipping Campden ⓲

Gloucestershire. 2,500. Hollis House, Stow-on-the-Wold (01451 831082). www.cotswold.gov.uk

THIS PERFECT Cotswold town is kept in pristine condition by the Campden Trust. Set up in 1929, the Trust has kept alive the traditional skills of stonecarving and repair that make Chipping Campden such a unified picture of golden-coloured and lichen-patched stone. Visitors travelling from the northwest along the B4035 first see a group of ruins: the remains of **Campden Manor**, begun around 1613 by Sir Baptist Hicks, 1st Viscount Campden. The manor was burned by Royalist troops to stop it being sequestered by Parliament at the end of the Civil War *(see pp52–3)*, but the almshouses opposite the gateway were spared. They were designed in the form of the letter "I" (which is Latin for "J"), a symbol of the owner's loyalty to King James I.

The town's **Church of St James**, one of the finest in the Cotswolds, was built in the 15th century, financed by merchants who bought wool from Cotswold farmers and exported it at a high profit. Inside the church there are many elaborate tombs, and a magnificent brass dedicated to William Grevel, describing him as "the flower of the wool merchants of England". He built **Grevel House** (c.1380) in the High Street, the oldest in a fine row of buildings, which is distinguished by a double-storey bay window.

Viscount Campden donated the **Market Hall** in 1627. His contemporary, Robert Dover, founded in 1612 the "Cotswold Olimpicks", long before the modern Olympic Games had been established. The 1612 version included such painful events as the shin-kicking contest. It still takes place on the first Friday after each Spring Bank Holiday, followed by a torchlit procession into town ready for the Scuttlebrook Wake Fair on the next day. The setting for the games is a spectacular natural hollow on **Dover's Hill** above the town, worth climbing on a clear day for the marvellous views over the Vale of Evesham.

The 17th-century Market Hall in Chipping Campden

Tewkesbury's abbey church overlooks the town, crowded onto the bank of the River Severn

Tewkesbury 19

Gloucestershire. 11,000.
Barton St (01684 295027).
Wed, Sat. www.
visitcotswoldsandsevernvale.gov.uk

THIS LOVELY TOWN sits on the confluence of the rivers Severn and Avon. It has one of England's finest Norman abbey churches, **St Mary the Virgin**, which locals saved during the Dissolution of the Monasteries *(see p50)* by paying Henry VIII £453. Around the church, with its bulky tower and Norman façade, timbered buildings are crammed within the bend of the river. Warehouses are a reminder of past wealth, and Borough Mill on Quay Street, the only mill left harnessed to the river's energy, still grinds corn.

ENVIRONS: Boat trips can be taken from the river to **Upton-on-Severn**'s riverside pubs, 6 miles (10 km) north.

Cheltenham 20

Gloucestershire. 107,000.
77 Promenade (01242 522878).
Sun. www.visitcheltenham.info

CHELTENHAM'S REPUTATION for elegance was first gained in the late 18th century, when high society flocked to the spa town to "take the waters", following the example set by George III *(see pp54–5)*. Many gracious terraced houses were built, in a Neo-Classical style, along broad avenues. These survive around the Queen's Hotel, near **Montpellier**, a lovely Regency arcade lined with craft and antique shops, and in the **Promenade**, with its smart department stores and couturiers. A more modern atmosphere prevails in the newly built Regency Arcade, where the star attraction is the 1987 **clock** by Kit Williams: visit on the hour to see fish blowing bubbles over the onlookers' heads. The **Museum and Art Gallery** is worth a visit to see its unusual collection of furniture and other crafts made by members of the influential Arts and Crafts Movement (*see p25*), whose strict principles of utilitarian design were laid down by William Morris (*see p208*).

Pump Room detail, Cheltenham

The **Pitville Pump Room** (1825–30), modelled on the Greek Temple of Ilissos in Athens, is frequently used for performances during the town's renowned annual festivals of music (July) and literature (October).

The event that really attracts the crowds is the Cheltenham Gold Cup – the premier event of the National Hunt season – held in March (*see p66*).

Museum and Art Gallery

Clarence St. *01242 237431.*
daily. *25 Dec, 1 Jan & public hols.* *by arrangement.*
www.
cheltenham.artgallery.museum

Pitville Pump Room

Pitville Park. *01242 523852.*
Wed–Mon. *25, 26 Dec, 1 Jan, public hols & frequently for functions: call to check.*

Fantasy clock, by Kit Williams, in Cheltenham's Regency Arcade

Gloucester Cathedral's nave

Gloucester 21

Gloucestershire. *110,000.* *28 Southgate St (01452 421188).* *Wed, Sat.* www.gloucester.gov.uk/tourism

GLOUCESTER has played a prominent role in the history of England. It was here that William the Conqueror ordered a vast survey of all the land in his kingdom, that was to be recorded in the *Domesday Book* of 1086 *(see p48)*.

The city was popular with the Norman monarchs and in 1216 Henry III was crowned in its magnificent **cathedral**. The solid, dignified nave was begun in 1089. Edward II *(see p425)*, who was murdered in 1327 at Berkeley Castle, 14 miles (22 km) to the south-west, is buried in a tomb near the high altar. Many pilgrims came to honour Edward's tomb, leaving behind generous donations, and Abbot Thoky was able to begin rebuilding in 1331. The result was the wonderful east window and the cloisters, where the fan vault was developed and then copied in other churches all over the country.

The impressive buildings around the cathedral include College Court, with its **House of the Tailor of Gloucester** museum, in the house that the children's author Beatrix Potter used as the setting *(see p355)* for her illustrations of that story. A museum complex has been created in the **Gloucester Docks**, part of which is still a port, linked to the Bristol Channel by the Gloucester and Sharpness Canal (opened in 1827). In the old port, and housed in a Victorian warehouse, the **National Waterways Museum** incorporates hands-on displays to relate the history of canals.

House of the Tailor of Gloucester
College Court. *01452 422856.* *Mon–Sat.* *public hols.*

National Waterways Museum
Llanthony Warehouse, Gloucester Docks.
01452 318054. *daily.* *25 Dec.*
www.nwm.org.uk

Cirencester 22

Gloucestershire. *20,000.* *Market Place (01285 654180).* *Mon, Tue (cattle) & Fri.*
www.cotswold.gov.uk

KNOWN AS THE CAPITAL of the Cotswolds, Cirencester has as its focus a market place, where there is a market every Monday and Friday. Overlooking the market is the **Church of St John Baptist**, whose "wineglass" pulpit (1515) is one of the few pre-Reformation pulpits to survive in England. To the west, **Cirencester Park** was laid out by the 1st Earl of Bathurst from 1714, with help from the poet Alexander Pope *(see p305)*. The mansion is surrounded by a massive yew hedge, claimed to be the tallest in the world. Clustering round the park entrance are the 17th- and 18th-century wool merchants' houses of Cecily Hill, built in grand Italianate style. Much humbler Cotswold houses are to be found in Coxwell Street, and underlying this is a Roman town, evidence of which emerges whenever the ground is dug.

The **Corinium Museum** (*Corinium* was the Latin name) features excavated objects in a series of tableaux illustrating life in a Roman household.

Cirencester Park
Cirencester Park. *01285 653135.* *daily.*
www.cirencesterpark.co.uk

Corinium Museum
Park St. *01285 655611.* *until 2004; call for details.*

Cirencester's fine parish church, one of the largest in England

Art and Nature in the Roman World

Cirencester was an important centre of mosaic production in Roman days. Fine examples of the local style are shown in the Corinium Museum and mosaics range from Classical subjects, such as Orpheus taming lions and tigers with the music of his lyre, to the naturalistic depiction of a hare. At Chedworth Roman Villa, 8 miles (13 km) north, mosaics are inspired by real life. In the *Four Seasons* mosaic, *Winter* shows a peasant, dressed in a woollen hood and a wind-blown cloak, clutching a recently caught hare in one hand and a branch for fuel in the other.

Hare mosaic, Corinium Museum

EAST MIDLANDS

DERBYSHIRE · LEICESTERSHIRE · LINCOLNSHIRE
NORTHAMPTONSHIRE · NOTTINGHAMSHIRE

THREE VERY DIFFERENT KINDS OF LANDSCAPE *greet visitors to the East Midlands. In the west, wild moors rise to the craggy heights of the Peak District. These give way to the low-lying plain and the massive industrial towns at the region's heart. In the east, hills and limestone villages stretch to a long, flat seaboard.*

The East Midlands owes much of its character to a conjunction of the pastoral with the urban. The spa resorts, historical villages and stately homes coexist within a landscape shaped by industrialization. Throughout the region there are swathes of scenic countryside – and grimy industrial cities.

The area has been settled since prehistoric times. The Romans mined lead and salt, and they built a large network of roads and fortresses. Anglo-Saxon and Viking influence is found in many of the place names. During the Middle Ages profits from the wool industry enabled the development of towns such as Lincoln, which still has many fine old buildings. The East Midlands was the scene of ferocious battles during the Wars of the Roses and the Civil War, and insurgents in the Jacobite Rebellion reached as far as Derby.

In the west of the region is the Peak District, Britain's first national park. Created in 1951, it draws crowds in search of the wild beauty of the heather-covered moors, or the wooded dales of the River Dove. The peaks are very popular with rock climbers and hikers.

The eastern edge of the Peaks descends through stone-walled meadows to sheltered valleys. The Roman spa of Buxton adds a final note of elegance before the flatlands of Derbyshire, Leicestershire and Nottinghamshire are reached. An area of coal mines and factories since the late 18th century, the landscape is set to be transformed over the next century into a new national forest.

Well-dressing dance, an ancient custom at Stoney Middleton in the Peak District

West front of Chatsworth House, a superb Baroque stately home in the Peak District

Exploring the East Midlands

THE EAST MIDLANDS is a popular tourist destination, easily accessible by road, but best explored on foot. Numerous well-marked trails pass through the Peak District National Park. There are superb country houses at Chatsworth and Burghley and the impressive historic towns of Lincoln and Stamford to discover.

SIGHTS AT A GLANCE

Burghley pp330–31 8
Buxton 1
Chatsworth pp322–3 2
Lincoln pp328–9 7
Matlock Bath 3
Northampton 10
Nottingham 6
Stamford 9

Walks and Tours

Peak District Tour 5
Tissington Trail 4

View of Burghley House from the north courtyard

GETTING AROUND

The M6, M1 and A1 are the principal road routes to the East Midlands, but they are subject to frequent delays because of the volume of traffic they carry. It can be faster and more interesting to find cross-country routes to the region, for example through the attractive countryside and villages around Stamford and Northampton. Roads in the Peak District become very congested during the summer and an early start to the day is advisable. Lincoln and Stamford are well served by fast mainline trains from London. Rail services in the Peak District are far more limited, but local lines run as far as Matlock and Buxton.

SEE ALSO

• ***Where to Stay*** pp558–59
• ***Where to Eat*** pp593–95

KEY

Motorway
Major road
Scenic route
Scenic path
River
Viewpoint

Peak District countryside seen from the Tissington Trail

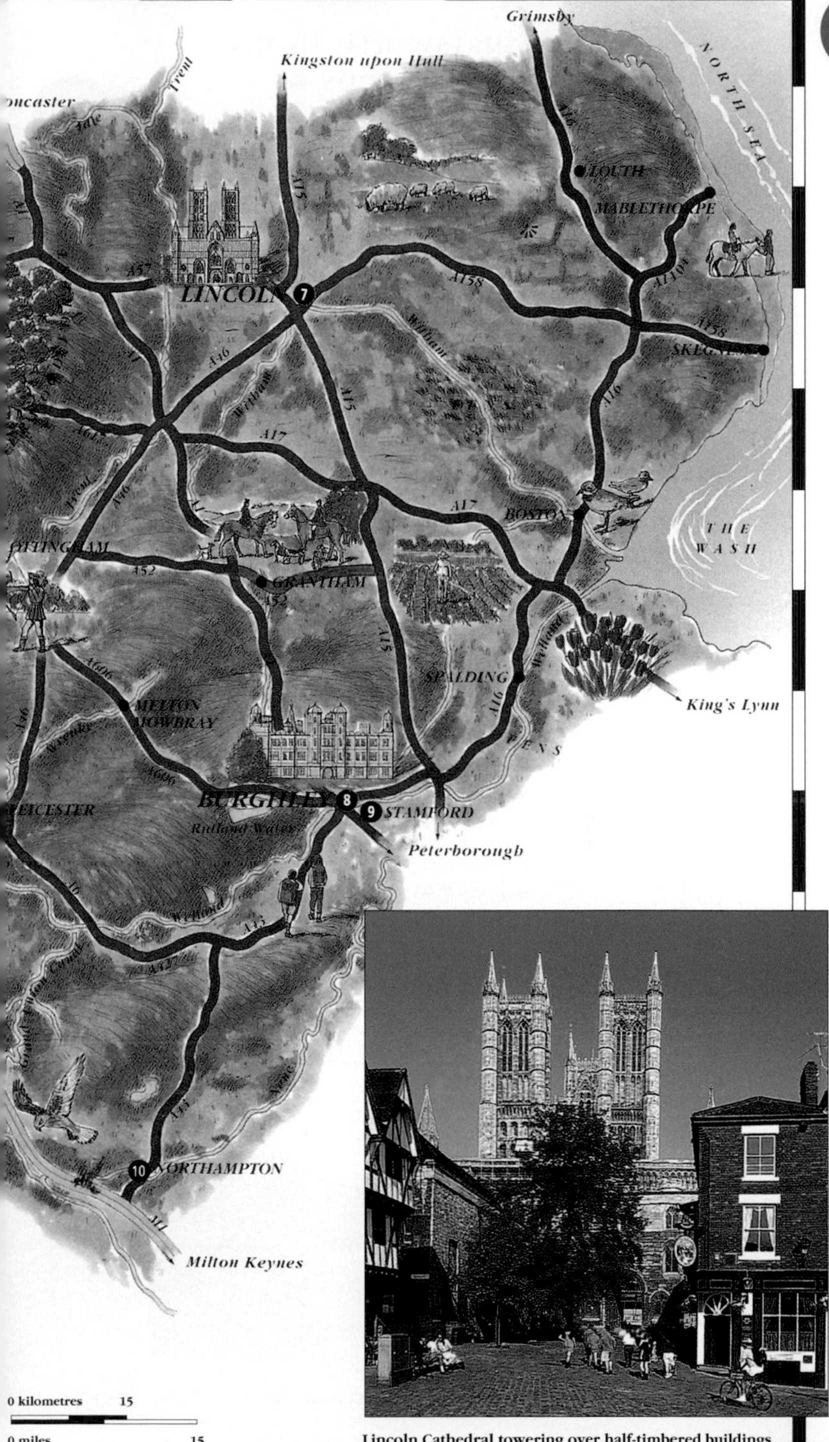

Lincoln Cathedral towering over half-timbered buildings

Buxton Opera House, a late 19th-century building restored in 1979

Buxton ❶

Derbyshire. 20,000.
The Crescent (01298 25106).
Tue, Sat. www.highpeak.gov.uk

BUXTON was developed as a spa town by the 5th Duke of Devonshire during the late 18th century. It has many fine Neo-Classical buildings, including the **Devonshire Royal Hospital** (1790), originally stables, at the entrance to the town. The **Crescent** was built (1780–90) to rival Bath's Royal Crescent *(see p246)*.

At its southwest end, the tourist information office is housed in the former town baths. Here, a spring where water surges from the ground at a rate of 7,000 litres (1,540 gallons) an hour can be seen. Buxton water is bottled and sold but there is a public fountain at **St Ann's Well**, opposite.

Steep gardens known as the Slopes lead from the Crescent to the small, award-winning **Museum and Art Gallery**, with geological and archaeological displays. Behind the Crescent, overlooking the Pavilion Gardens, is the striking 19th-century iron and glass **Pavilion**, and the splendidly restored **Opera House**, where a Music and Arts Festival is held in summer.

Buxton Museum and Art Gallery
Terrace Rd. 01298 24658. Easter–Sep: Tue–Sun; Oct–Easter: Tue–Sat. 25 Dec–2 Jan.
www.derbyshire.gov.uk

Pavilion and Gardens
St John's Rd. 01298 23114.
daily. 25 Dec.

Chatsworth House and Gardens ❷

CHATSWORTH IS ONE of Britain's most impressive stately homes. Between 1687 and 1707, the 4th Earl of Devonshire replaced the old Tudor mansion with this Baroque palace. The house has beautiful gardens, landscaped in the 1760s by Capability Brown *(see p22)* and developed by the head gardener, Joseph Paxton *(see pp56–7)*, in the mid-19th century.

First house built in 1552 by Bess of Hardwick

Summerhouse

Round ponds, known as the Spectacles

★ Cascade
Water tumbles down the steps of the Cascade, built in 1696 to a French design.

STAR SIGHTS

★ Cascade

★ Chapel

Garden entrance

House entrance

Paxton's "Conservative" Wall
This iron-and-glass conservatory wall was designed in 1848 by Joseph Paxton, the creator of Chatsworth's Great Conservatory (now demolished).

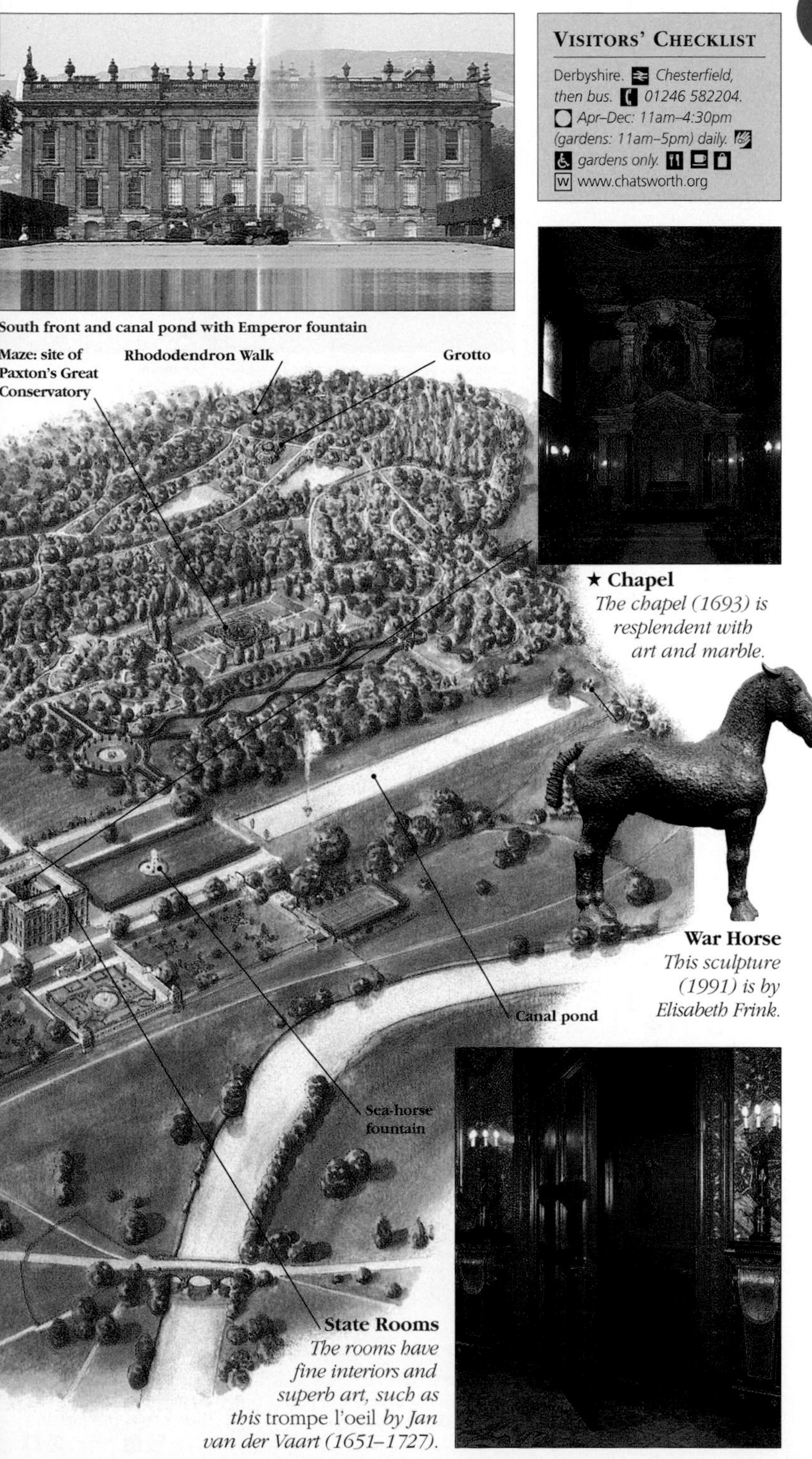

South front and canal pond with Emperor fountain

★ Chapel
The chapel (1693) is resplendent with art and marble.

War Horse
This sculpture (1991) is by Elisabeth Frink.

State Rooms
The rooms have fine interiors and superb art, such as this trompe l'oeil *by Jan van der Vaart (1651–1727).*

VISITORS' CHECKLIST

Derbyshire. *Chesterfield, then bus.* *01246 582204.* *Apr–Dec: 11am–4:30pm (gardens: 11am–5pm) daily.* *gardens only.* www.chatsworth.org

Matlock ❸

Derbyshire. 23,000.
Crown Square (01629 583388).
www.derbyshiredales.gov.uk

Matlock was developed as a spa from the 1780s. Interesting buildings include the massive structure (1853) on the hill above the town, built as a hydrotherapy centre but now council offices. On the hill opposite is the mock-Gothic **Riber Castle**.

From Matlock, the A6 winds through the outstandingly beautiful **Derwent Gorge** to **Matlock Bath**. Here, cable cars ascend to the **Heights of Abraham** pleasure park, with caves, nature trail and extensive views. Lead-mining is the subject of the **Peak District Mining Museum**, and visitors can inspect the old **Temple Mine** nearby. **Sir Richard Arkwright's Cromford Mill** (1771), a world heritage site and the first ever water-powered cotton spinning mill, lies at the southern end of the gorge *(see p327)*.

Heights of Abraham On A6. 01629 582365. *Feb–Mar: Sat, Sun; Easter–Nov: daily. limited.*
Peak District Mining Museum The Pavilion, off A6. 01629 583834. *daily.* www.peakmines.co.uk
Temple Mine Temple Rd, off A6. 01629 583834. *call for details. 25 Dec.*
Cromford Mill Mill Lane, Cromford. 01629 824297. *daily. 25 Dec.* www.cromfordmill.co.uk

Cable cars taking visitors to the Heights of Abraham

Tissington Trail ❹

See p325.

Peak District Tour ❺

See pp326–7.

Nottingham ❻

Nottinghamshire. 269,000.
Smithy Row (0115 9155330). *daily.*
www.profilenottingham.co.uk

The name of Nottingham often conjures up the image of the evil Sheriff, adversary of Robin Hood. **Nottingham Castle** stands on a rock riddled with underground passages. The castle houses a museum, with displays on the city's history, and what was Britain's first municipal art gallery, featuring works by Sir Stanley Spencer (1891–1959) and Dante Gabriel Rossetti (1828–82). At the foot of the castle, Britain's oldest tavern, the **Trip to Jerusalem** (1189), is still in business. Its name may refer to the 12th- and 13th-century crusades, but much of it is 17th-century.

There are several museums near the castle, ranging from the **Tales of Robin Hood**, which tells the story of the outlaw, to the **Museum of Costume and Textiles**, explaining Nottingham's role as a leading centre for embroidery, lace-making, tapestries and knitted textiles.

Environs: Stately homes within a few miles of Nottingham include the Neo-Classical **Kedleston Hall** *(see pp24–5)*. "Bess of Hardwick", Countess of Shrewbury *(see p322)*, built the spectacular **Hardwick Hall** *(see p290)*.

Nottingham Castle and Museum Castle Rd. 0115 9153700. *daily. 24–27 Dec, 1 Jan. Sat, Sun & public hols.*
Tales of Robin Hood 30–38 Maid Marion Way. 0115 9483284. *daily. 24–26 Dec.*
Museum of Costume and Textiles 51 Castle Gate. 0115 9153500. *Wed–Mon, public hols. 24 Dec–1 Jan.*
Kedleston Hall (NT) off A38. 01332 842191. *Apr–Oct: Sat–Wed (pm).*
Hardwick Hall (NT) off A617. 01246 850430. *Apr–Oct: Wed, Thu, Sat, Sun & public hols. limited.*

Robin Hood of Sherwood Forest

England's most colourful folk hero was a legendary swordsman, whose adventures are depicted in numerous films and stories. He lived in Sherwood Forest, near Nottingham, with a band of "merry men", robbing the rich to give to the poor. As part of an ancient oral tradition, Robin Hood figured mainly in ballads; the first written records of his exploits date from the 15th century. Today historians think that he was not one person, but a composite of many outlaws who refused to conform to medieval feudal constraints.

Victorian depiction of Friar Tuck and Robin Hood

Tissington Trail ❹

THE FULL-LENGTH Tissington Trail runs for 13 miles (22 km), from the village of Ashbourne to Parsley Hay, where it meets the High Peak Trail. This is a short version, taking an easy route along a dismantled railway line around Tissington village and providing good views of the beautiful White Peak countryside. The Derbyshire custom of well-dressing is thought to have originated in pre-Christian times. It was revived in the early 17th century, when the Tissington village wells were decorated in thanksgiving for deliverance from the plague, in the belief that the fresh water had had a medicinal effect. Well-dressing is still an important event in the Peakland calendar, and can be seen in other villages where the water supplies were prone to dry up.

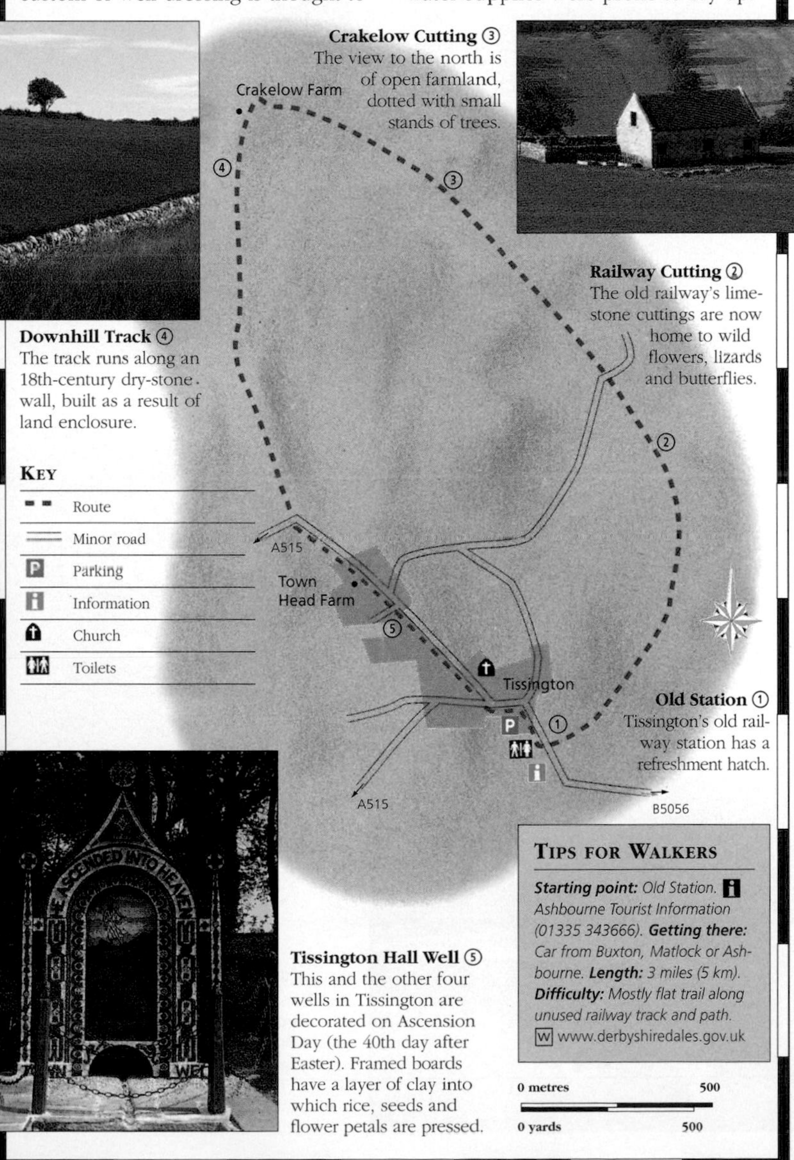

Crakelow Cutting ③
The view to the north is of open farmland, dotted with small stands of trees.

Railway Cutting ②
The old railway's limestone cuttings are now home to wild flowers, lizards and butterflies.

Downhill Track ④
The track runs along an 18th-century dry-stone wall, built as a result of land enclosure.

Old Station ①
Tissington's old railway station has a refreshment hatch.

Tissington Hall Well ⑤
This and the other four wells in Tissington are decorated on Ascension Day (the 40th day after Easter). Framed boards have a layer of clay into which rice, seeds and flower petals are pressed.

TIPS FOR WALKERS

Starting point: *Old Station.* *Ashbourne Tourist Information (01335 343666).* ***Getting there:*** *Car from Buxton, Matlock or Ashbourne.* ***Length:*** *3 miles (5 km).* ***Difficulty:*** *Mostly flat trail along unused railway track and path.*
www.derbyshiredales.gov.uk

Peak District Tour ❺

Detail, Buxton Opera House

THE PEAK DISTRICT's natural beauty and sheep-grazed crags contrast with the factories of nearby valley towns. Designated Britain's first National Park in 1951, the area has two distinct types of landscape. In the south are the gently rolling hills of the limestone White Peak. To the north, west and east are the wild, heather-clad moorlands of the Dark Peak peat bogs, superimposed on millstone grit.

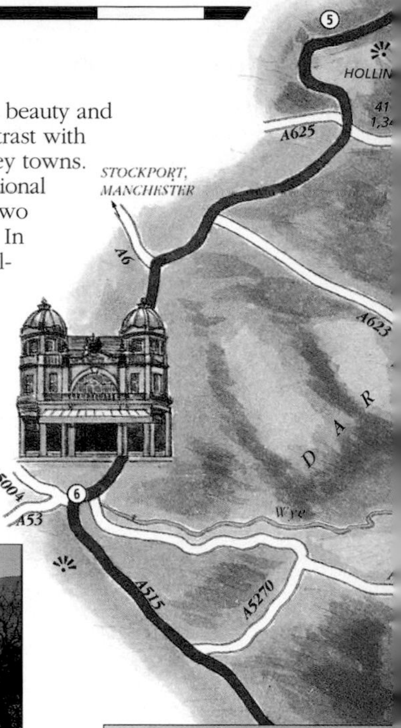

STOCKPORT, MANCHESTER
A625
A6
A623
A5004
A53
A515
A5270
Wye

Edale ⑤
The high plateau of scenic Edale mark the starting point of the 256 mile (412 km) Pennine Way footpath *(see p32)*.

Buxton ⑥
This lovely spa town's opera house *(see p322)* is known as the "theatre in the hills" because of its magnificent setting.

TIPS FOR DRIVERS

Tour length: *40 miles (60 km).*
Stopping-off points: *There are refreshments at Crich Tramway Village and Arkwright's Mill in Cromford. Eyam has good old-fashioned tea shops. The Nag's Head in Edale is a charming Tudor inn. Buxton has many pubs and cafés.* (See also pp636–7.)

Arbor Low ⑦
This stone circle, known as the "Stonehenge of the North", dates from around 2000 BC and consists of 46 recumbent stones enclosed by a ditch.

KEY

- Tour route
- Other roads
- Viewpoint

Dovedale ⑧
Popular Dovedale is one of the prettiest of the Peak District's river valleys, with its stepping stones, thickly wooded slopes and wind-sculpted rocks. Izaac Walton (1593–1683), author of *The Compleat Angler*, used to fish here.

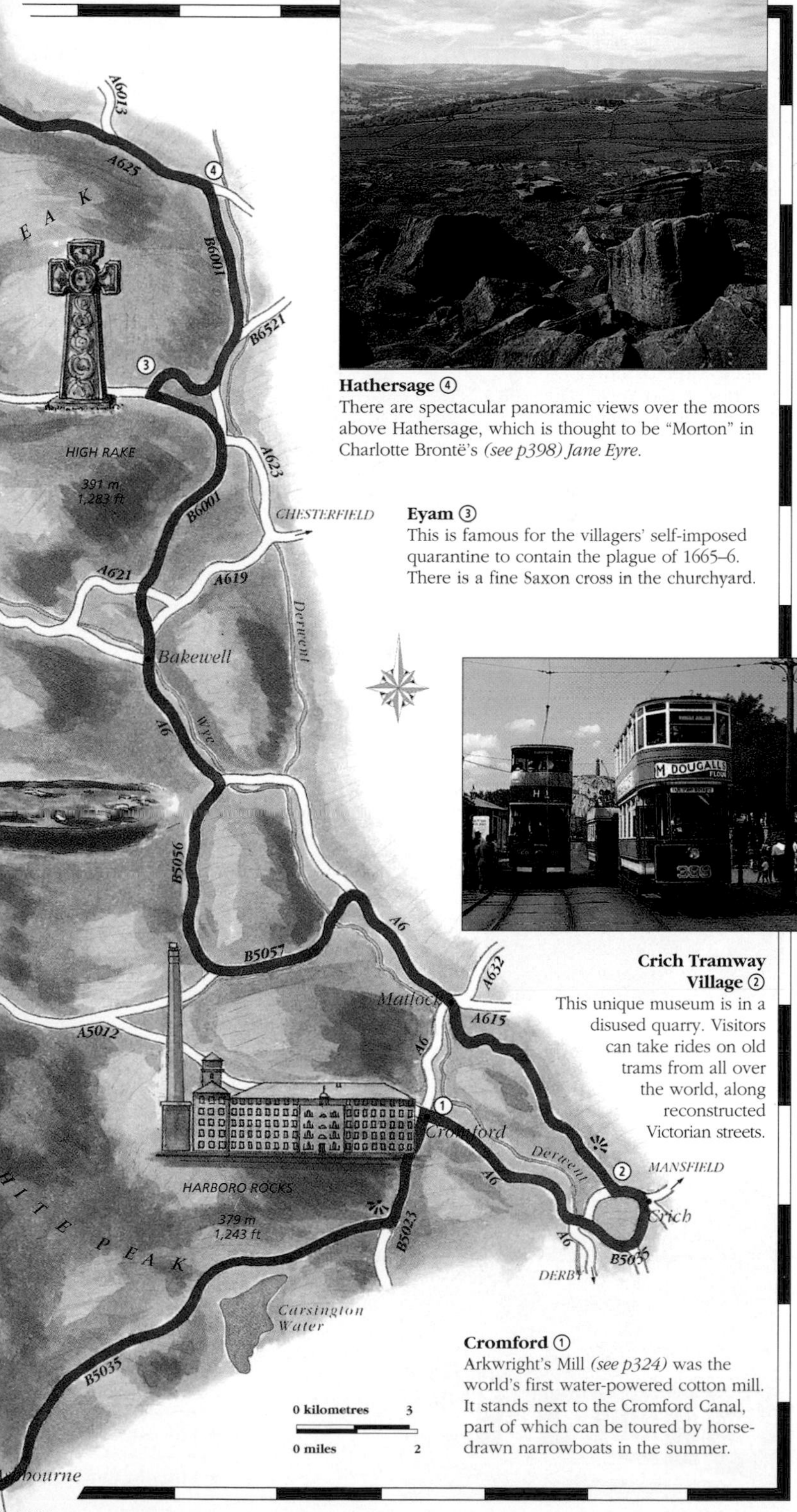

Hathersage ④
There are spectacular panoramic views over the moors above Hathersage, which is thought to be "Morton" in Charlotte Brontë's *(see p398) Jane Eyre.*

Eyam ③
This is famous for the villagers' self-imposed quarantine to contain the plague of 1665–6. There is a fine Saxon cross in the churchyard.

Crich Tramway Village ②
This unique museum is in a disused quarry. Visitors can take rides on old trams from all over the world, along reconstructed Victorian streets.

Cromford ①
Arkwright's Mill *(see p324)* was the world's first water-powered cotton mill. It stands next to the Cromford Canal, part of which can be toured by horse-drawn narrowboats in the summer.

Street-by-Street: Lincoln ❼

Carving in Angel Choir

SURROUNDED BY the flat landscape of the Fens, Lincoln rises dramatically on a cliff above the River Witham, the three towers of its massive cathedral visible from afar. The Romans *(see pp44–5)* founded the first fortress here in AD 50. By the time of the Norman Conquest *(see p47)*, Lincoln was one of the most important cities in England (after London, Winchester and York). The city's wealth was due to its strategic importance for the export of wool from the Lincolnshire Wolds to Europe. Lincoln has managed to retain much of its historic character. Many remarkable medieval buildings have survived, most of which are along the aptly named Steep Hill, leading to the cathedral.

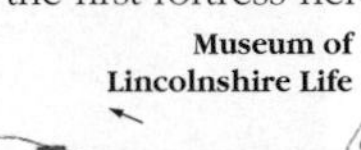

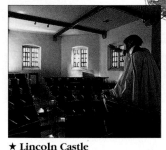

★ Lincoln Castle
The early Norman castle, rebuilt at intervals, acted as the city prison from 1787–1878. The chapel's coffin-like pews served to remind felons of their fate.

KEY

 Suggested route

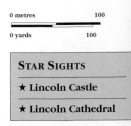

0 metres 100

0 yards 100

Jew's House
Lincoln had a large medieval Jewish community. This mid-12th-century stone house, one of the oldest of its kind, was owned by a Jewish merchant.

STAR SIGHTS

- ★ Lincoln Castle
- ★ Lincoln Cathedral

Visitors' Checklist

Lincolnshire. 85,000. Humberside, 30 miles (48 km); E Midlands, 51 miles (82 km). St Mary St. Melville St. Castle Hill (01522 873214). www.lincoln.gov.uk

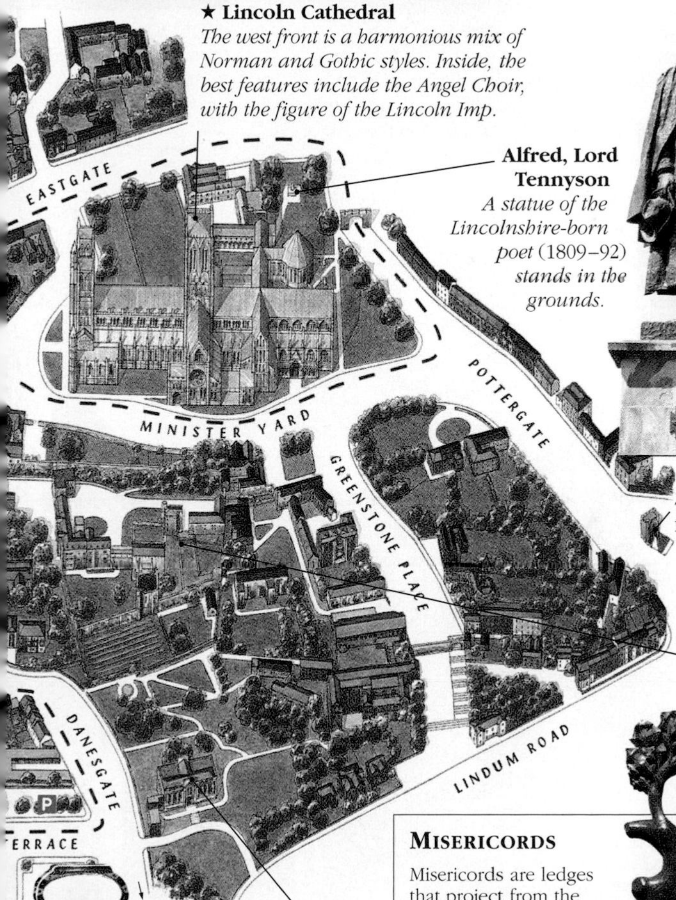

★ Lincoln Cathedral
The west front is a harmonious mix of Norman and Gothic styles. Inside, the best features include the Angel Choir, with the figure of the Lincoln Imp.

Alfred, Lord Tennyson
A statue of the Lincolnshire-born poet (1809–92) *stands in the grounds.*

EASTGATE
MINISTER YARD
POTTERGATE
GREENSTONE PLACE
DANESGATE
LINDUM ROAD
ERRACE

The 14th-century Pottergate Arch

Arboretum

Ruins of Bishop's Palace

Coach station

Usher Art Gallery
This is packed with clocks, ceramics, and silver. There are paintings by Peter de Wint (1784–1849) and J M W Turner (see p93).

Misericords

Misericords are ledges that project from the underside of the hinged seat of a choir stall, which provide support while standing. Lincoln Cathedral's misericords in the early Perpendicular-style canopied choir stalls are some of the best in England. The wide variety of subjects includes parables, fables, myths, biblical scenes and irreverent images from daily life.

St Francis of Assisi

One of a pair of lions

Burghley House 8

Portrait of Sir Isaac Newton, Billiard Room

William Cecil, 1st Lord Burghley (1520–98) was Queen Elizabeth I's adviser and confidant for 40 years. He built the wonderfully dramatic Burghley House in 1555–87, probably designing it himself. The roof line bristles with stone pyramids, chimneys disguised as Classical columns and towers shaped like pepper pots. The busy skyline only resolves itself into a symmetrical pattern when viewed from the west, where a lime tree stands, one of many planted by Capability Brown *(see p22)* when the surrounding deer park was landscaped in 1760. Burghley's interior is lavishly decorated with Italian paintings of Greek gods enacting their dramas across the walls and ceiling.

★ Old Kitchen
Gleaming copper pans hang from the walls of the fan-vaulted kitchen, little altered since the Tudor period.

North Gate
Intricate examples of 19th-century wrought-iron work adorn the principal entrances.

The Billiard Room has many fine portraits inset in oak panelling.

Cupolas were very fashionable details, inspired by European Renaissance architecture.

A chimney has been disguised as a Classical column.

Mullioned windows were added in 1683 when glass became less expensive.

The Gatehouse, with its side turrets, is a typical feature of the "prodigy" houses of the Tudor era *(see p290)*.

West Front
Featuring the Burghley crest, the West Front was finished in 1577 and formed the original main entrance.

Star Sights

- **★ Old Kitchen**
- **★ Heaven Room**
- **★ Hell Staircase**

The Fourth George Room, one of a suite, is panelled in oak stained with ale.

★ Hell Staircase
Verrio painted the ceiling to show Hell as the mouth of a cat crammed with tormented sinners. The staircase, of local stone, was installed in 1786.

The wine cooler (1710) is thought to be the largest in existence.

The Great Hall has a double hammer-beam roof and was a banqueting hall in Elizabethan days.

★ Heaven Room
Gods tumble from the sky, and satyrs and nymphs play on the walls and ceiling in this masterpiece by Antonio Verrio (1639–1707).

VISITORS' CHECKLIST

Off A1 SE of Stamford, Lincolnshire. *01780 752451. Stamford. Apr–Oct: 11am–4:30pm daily. one day Sep (for horse trials). limited.*

Stamford ❾

Lincolnshire. *18,000.* *27 St Mary's St (01780 755611). Fri.* www.stamfordonline.co.uk

STAMFORD is a showpiece town, famous for its many churches and its Georgian townhouses. Stamford retains a medieval street plan, with a warren of winding streets and cobbled alleys.

The spires of the medieval churches (five survive of the original 11) give Stamford the air of a miniature Oxford.

Barn Hill, leading up from All Saints Church, is the best place for a view of Stamford's Georgian architecture in all its variety. Below it is Broad Street, where the **Stamford Museum** covers the history of the town. By far the most popular exhibit is a waxwork of Britain's fattest man, Daniel Lambert, who was 336 kg (53 stone) and died while attending Stamford Races in 1809.

Stamford Museum
Broad St. *01780 766317. Apr–Sep: daily (Sun: pm); Oct–Mar: Mon–Sat. limited.* www.lincolnshire.gov.uk/stamfordmuseum

Northampton ❿

Northamptonshire. *187,000. Guildhall Rd (01604 622677). Tue–Sat (Thu: antiques).* www.northampton.gov.uk

THIS MARKET TOWN was once a centre for shoe-making, and the **Central Museum and Art Gallery** holds the world's largest collection of footwear. One of many fine old buildings is the Victorian Gothic **Guildhall**. Six miles west of the town is **Althorp House**, family home of Diana Princess of Wales. Visitors can tour the house, grounds, and see her island resting place.

Central Museum and Art Gallery
Guildhall Rd. *01604 238548. daily (Sun: pm). 25, 26 Dec.* www.northampton.gov.uk/museums

Althorp House
Great Brington (off A428). *0870 1679000. Jul–Sep daily. 30 Aug.* www.althorp.com

The North Country

Introducing the North Country 334-341
Lancashire and the Lakes 342-365
Yorkshire and the Humber Region 366-399
Northumbria 400-415

The North Country at a Glance

Rugged coastlines, spectacular walks and climbs, magnificent stately homes and breathtaking cathedrals all have their place in the north of England, with its dramatic history of Roman rule, Saxon invasion, Viking attacks and border skirmishes. Reminders of the industrial revolution are found in towns such as Halifax, Liverpool and Manchester, and peace and inspiration in the dramatic scenery of the Lake District, with its awe-inspiring mountains and waters.

Hadrian's Wall (see pp408–9), *built around 120 to protect Roman Britain from the Picts to the north, cuts through rugged Northumberland National Park scenery.*

The Lake District (see pp342–57) *is a combination of superb peaks, tumbling rivers and falls and shimmering lakes such as Wast Water.*

Yorkshire Dales National Park (see pp370–72) *creates a delightful environment for walking and touring the farming landscape, scattered with attractive villages such as Thwaite, in Swaledale.*

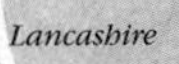

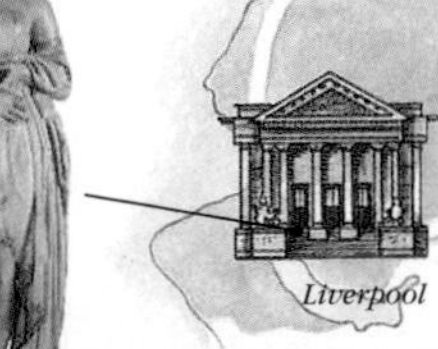

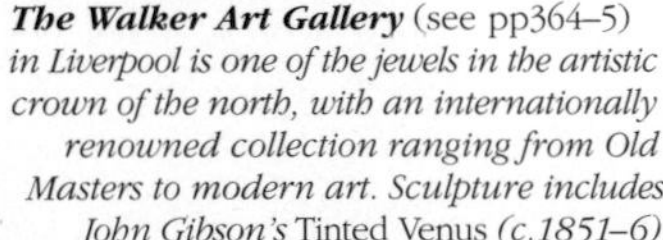

The Walker Art Gallery (see pp364–5) *in Liverpool is one of the jewels in the artistic crown of the north, with an internationally renowned collection ranging from Old Masters to modern art. Sculpture includes John Gibson's* Tinted Venus *(c.1851–6).*

◁ **The 11th-century Alnwick Castle, Alnwick, Northumberland, from across the River Aln**

Durham Cathedral (see pp414–5), *a striking Norman structure with an innovative southern choir aisle and fine stained glass, has towered over the city of Durham since 995.*

Fountains Abbey (see pp376–7), *one of the finest religious buildings in the north, was founded in the 12th century by monks who desired simplicity and austerity. Later the abbey became extremely wealthy.*

Castle Howard (see pp384–5), *a triumph of Baroque architecture, offers many magnificent settings, including this Museum Room (1805–10), designed by CH Tatham.*

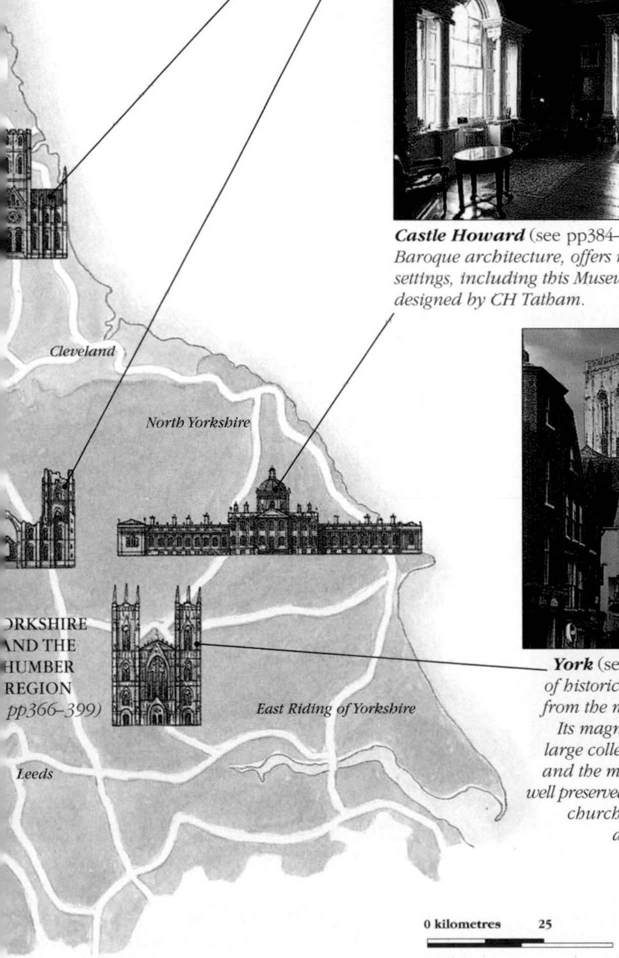

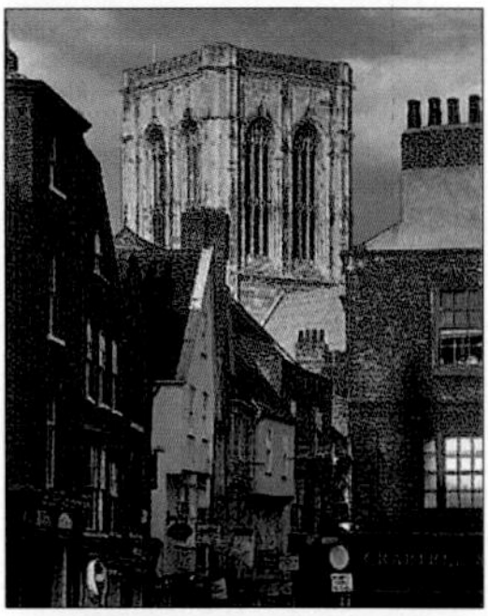

Cleveland

North Yorkshire

ORKSHIRE
AND THE
HUMBER
REGION
pp366–399)

East Riding of Yorkshire

Leeds

York (see pp390–95) *is a city of historical treasures, ranging from the medieval to Georgian. Its magnificent minster has a large collection of stained glass and the medieval city walls are well preserved. Other sights include churches, narrow alleyways and notable museums.*

0 kilometres **25**

0 miles **25**

The Industrial Revolution in the North

THE FACE OF NORTHERN ENGLAND in the 19th century was dramatically altered by the development of the coal mining, textile and shipbuilding industries. Lancashire, Northumberland and the West Riding *(see p367)* of Yorkshire all experienced population growth and migration to cities. The hardships of urban life were partly relieved by the actions of several wealthy industrial philanthropists, but many people lived in extremely deprived conditions. Although most traditional industries have now declined sharply or disappeared as demand has moved elsewhere, a growing tourist industry has developed in many of the former industrial centres.

Back-to-backs *or colliers' rows, suc as these houses at Easington, wer provided by colliery owners from th 1800s onwards. They comprise two small rooms for cooking an sleeping, and an outside toile*

Coal mining *was a family industry in the North of England with women and children working alongside the men.*

1815 Sir Humphrey Davy invented a safety oil lamp for miners. Light shone through a cylindrical gauze sheet which prevented the heat of the flame igniting methane gas in the mine. Thousands of miners benefited from this device.

1750	**1800**
PRE-STEAM	**STEAM AGE**
1750	**1800**

1781 Leeds–Liverpool Canal opened. The building of canals facilitated the movement of raw materials and finished products, and aided the process of mechanization immeasurably.

1830 Liverpoo Manchester r opened, connecting the biggest cities c London. Within a mor railway carried passe

Halifax's Piece Hall (see p399), *restored in 1976, is the most impressive surviving example of industrial architecture in northern England. It is the only complete 18th-century cloth market building in Yorkshire. Merchants sold measures of cloth known as "pieces" from rooms lining the cloisters inside.*

Hebden Bridge (see p398), *a typical West Riding textile mill town jammed into the narrow Calder Valley, typifies a pattern of workers' houses surrounding a central mill. The town benefited from its position when the Rochdale Canal (1804) and then the railway (1841) took advantage of this relatively low-level route over the Pennines.*

Saltaire (see p397) *was a model village built by the wealthy cloth merchant and mill-owner Sir Titus Salt (1803–76), for the benefit of his workers. Seen here in the 1870s, it included houses and facilities such as shops, gardens and sportsfields, with almshouses, a hospital, school and chapel. A disciplinarian, Salt banned alcohol and pubs from Saltaire.*

George Hudson *(1800–71) built the first railway station in York* (see p394) *in 1840–42. In the 1840s he owned more than a quarter of the railways in Britain and was known as the "railway king".*

Port Sunlight (see p365) *was founded by William Hesketh Lever (1851–1925) to provide housing for workers at his Sunlight soap factory. Between 1889 and 1914 he built 800 cottages. Amenities included a pool.*

Strikes to improve working conditions were common. Violence flared in July 1893 when colliery owners locked miners out of their pits and stopped their pay after the Miners' Federation resisted a 25 per cent wage cut. Over 300,000 men struggled without pay until November, when work resumed at the old rate.

1842 Coal Mines Act prevented women and children from working in harsh conditions in the mines.

1850 **1900**

FULL MECHANIZATION

1850 **1900**

Power loom weaving *transformed the textile industry while creating unemployment among skilled hand loom weavers. By the 1850s, the West Riding had 30,000 power looms, used in cotton and woollen mills. Of 79,000 workers, over half were to be found in Bradford alone.*

Furness dry dock *was built in the 1890s when the shipbuilding industry moved north, in search of cheap labour and materials. Barrow-in-Furness, Glasgow* (see pp502–5) *and Tyne and Wear* (see p410) *were the new centres.*

Joseph Rowntree *(1836–1925) founded his chocolate factory in York in 1892, having formerly worked with George Cadbury. As Quakers, the Rowntrees believed in the social welfare of their workers (establishing a model village in 1904), and, with Terry's confectionary (1767), they made a vast contribution to York's prosperity. Today, Nestlé Rowntree is the world's largest chocolate factory and York is Britain's chocolate capital.*

North Country Abbeys

Northern England has some of the finest and best preserved religious houses in Europe. Centres of prayer, learning and power in the Middle Ages, the larger of these were designated abbeys and were governed by an abbot. Most were located in rural areas, considered appropriate for a spiritual and contemplative life. Viking raiders had destroyed many Anglo-Saxon religious houses in the 8th and 9th centuries *(see pp46–7)* and it was not until William the Conqueror founded the Benedictine Selby Abbey in 1069 that monastic life revived in the north. New orders, Augustinians in particular, arrived from the Continent and by 1500 Yorkshire had 83 monasteries.

Cistercian monk

Ruins of St Mary's Abbey today

St Mary's Abbey

Founded in York in 1086, this Benedictine abbey was one of the wealthiest in Britain. Its involvement in the wool trade in York and the granting of royal and papal privileges and land led to a relaxing of standards by the early 12th century. The abbot was even allowed to dress in the same style as a bishop, and was raised by the pope to the status of a "mitred abbot". As a result, 13 monks left in 1132, to found Fountains Abbey *(see pp376–7)*.

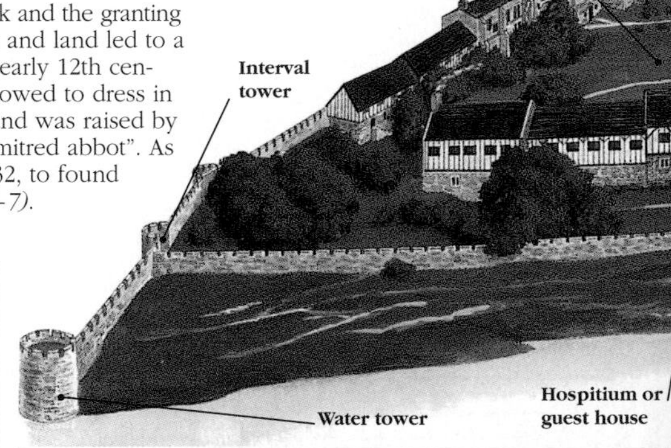

The Liberty of St Mary was the name given to the land around the abbey, almost a city within a city. Here, the abbot had his own market, fair, prison and gallows – all exempt from the city authorities.

Gatehouse and St Olave's church

Interval tower

Water tower

Hospitium or guest house

Monasteries and Local Life

As one of the wealthiest landowning sections of society, the monasteries played a vital role in the local economy. They provided employment, particularly in agriculture, and dominated the wool trade, England's largest export during the Middle Ages. By 1387 two thirds of all wool exported from England passed through St Mary's Abbey, the largest wool trader in York.

Cistercian monks tilling their land

Where to See Abbeys Today

Fountains Abbey *(see pp376–7)*, founded by Benedictine monks and later taken over by Cistercians, is the most famous of the numerous abbeys in the region. Rievaulx *(see p379)*, Byland *(see p378)* and Furness *(see p356)* were all founded by the Cistercians, and Furness became the second wealthiest Cistercian house in England after Fountains. Whitby Abbey *(see p382)*, sacked by the Vikings, was later rebuilt by the Benedictine order. Northumberland is famous for its early Anglo-Saxon monasteries, such as Ripon, Lastingham and Lindisfarne *(see pp404–5)*.

Mount Grace Priory (see p380), *founded in 1398, is the best-preserved Carthusian house in England. The former individual gardens and cells of each monk are still clearly visible.*

The Dissolution of the Monasteries (1536–40)

By the early 16th century, the monasteries owned one-sixth of all English land and their annual income was four times that of the Crown. Henry VIII ordered the closure of all religious houses in 1536, acquiring their wealth in the process. His attempt at dissolution provoked a large uprising of Catholic northerners led by Robert Aske later that year. The rebellion failed and Aske and others were executed for conspiracy. The dissolution continued under Thomas Cromwell, who became known as "the hammer of the monks".

Thomas Cromwell (c.1485–1549)

The large Abbot's House testified to the grand lifestyle that late medieval abbots adopted.

The Chapter House, an assembly room, was the most important building after the church.

Lavatory

Kitchen

The Warming House was the only room in the monastery, apart from the kitchen, which had a fire.

Refectory

The Abbey Wall had battlements added in 1318 to protect it against raids by Scottish armies.

Common parlour

Cloister

Kirkham Priory*, an Augustinian foundation of the 1120s, enjoys a tranquil setting on the banks of the River Derwent, near Malton. The finest feature of the ruined site is the 13th-century gatehouse which leads into the priory complex.*

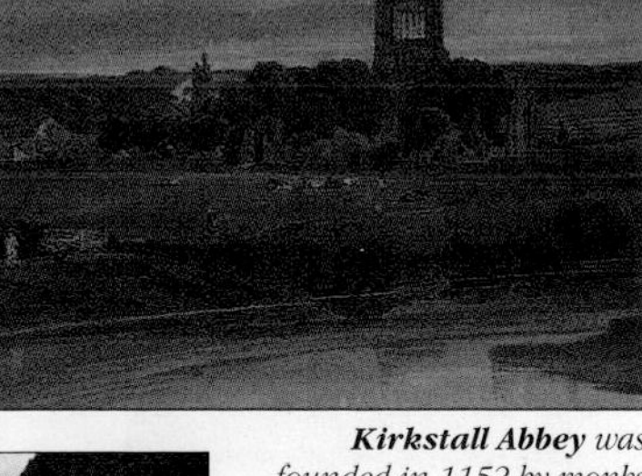

Kirkstall Abbey *was founded in 1152 by monks from Fountains Abbey. The well-preserved ruins of this Cistercian house near Leeds include the church, the late Norman chapter house and the abbot's lodging. This evening view was painted by Thomas Girtin (1775–1802).*

sby Abbey *lies beside the River Swale, outside the pretty market town of Richmond. Among the nains of this Premonstratensian ouse, founded in 1155, are the -century refectory and sleeping ters and 14th-century gatehouse.*

The Geology of the Lake District

THE LAKE DISTRICT contains some of England's most spectacular scenery. Concentrated in just 900 sq miles (231 sq km) are the highest peaks, deepest valleys and longest lakes in the country. Today's landscape has changed little since the end of the Ice Age 10,000 years ago, the last major event in Britain's geological history. But the glaciated hills which were revealed by the retreating ice were once part of a vast mountain-chain whose remains can also be found in North America. The mountains were first raised by the gradual fusion of two ancient landmasses which, for millions of years, formed a single continent. Eventually the continent broke into two, forming Europe and America, separated by the widening Atlantic Ocean.

Piece of Lake District slate

Honister Pass, *with its distinctive U-shape, is an example of a glaciated valley, once completely filled with ice.*

Geological History

The oldest rock formed as sediment under an ocean called Iapetus. Some 450 million years ago, Earth's internal movements made two continents collide, and the ocean disappear.

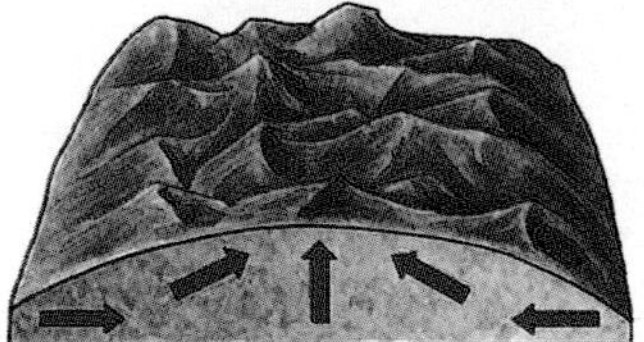

1 ***The collision*** *buckled the former sea bed into a mountain range. Magma rose from Earth's mantle, altered the sediments and cooled into volcanic rock.*

2 ***In the Ice Age,*** *glaciers slowly excavated huge rock basins in the mountainsides, dragging debris to the valley floor. Frost sculpted the summits.*

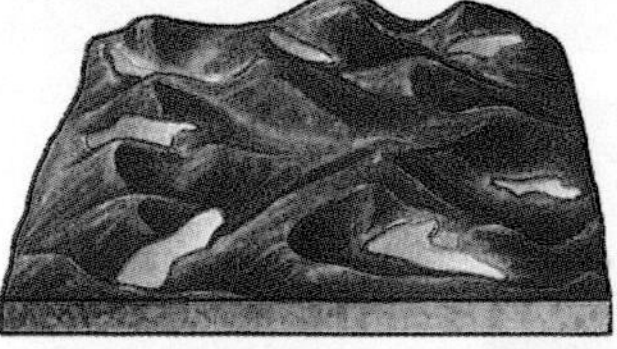

3 ***The glaciers retreated*** *10,000 years ago, their meltwaters forming lakes in valleys dammed by debris. As the climate improved, plants colonized the fells.*

Radiating Lakes

The diversity of lakeland scenery owes much to its geology: hard volcanic rocks in the central lakes give rise to rugged hills, while soft slates to the north produce a more rounded topography. The lakes form a radial pattern, spreading out from a central volcanic rock zone.

Scafell Pike is the highest peak in England. One of the three Scafell Pikes, its two neighbours are Broad Crag and Ill Crag.

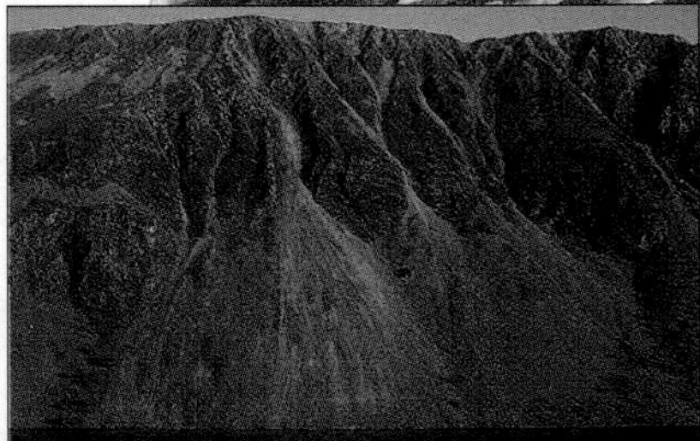

Wast Water *is the deepest of the lakes. Its south-eastern cliffs are streaked with granite scree – the debris formed each year as rock shattered by the winter frost tumbles down during the spring thaw.*

MAN ON THE MOUNTAIN

The sheltered valley floors with their benign climate and fertile soils are ideal for settlement. Farmhouses, dry-stone walls, pasture and sheep pens are an integral part of the landscape. Higher up, the absence of trees and bracken are the result of wind and a cooler climate. Old mine workings and tracks are the relics of once-flourishing industries.

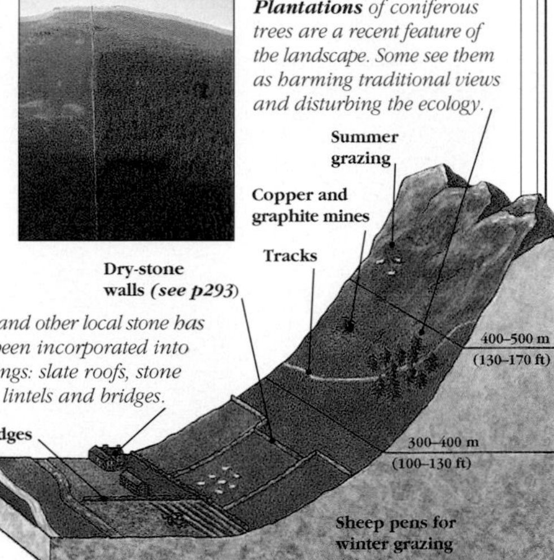

Plantations *of coniferous trees are a recent feature of the landscape. Some see them as harming traditional views and disturbing the ecology.*

Slate *and other local stone has long been incorporated into buildings: slate roofs, stone walls, lintels and bridges.*

Skiddaw *is composed of slate, formed when the muddy sediment of the ancient ocean floor was altered by extreme pressure.*

Striding Edge *is a long, twisting ridge which leads to the summit of Helvellyn. It was sharpened by the widening of the valleys on either side caused by the build up of glaciers.*

The Langdale Pikes *are remnants of the volcanic activity which once erupted in the area. They are made of hard igneous rocks, known as Borrowdale Volcanics. Unlike the Skiddaw Slates, they have not eroded smoothly, so they leave a craggy skyline.*

Merseyside
Maritime
Museum

Lancashire and the Lakes

Cumbria · Lancashire

The landscape painter John Constable (1776–1837) declared that the Lake District, now visited by 18 million people annually, had "the finest scenery that ever was". The Normans built many religious houses here, and William II created estates for English barons. Today, the National Trust is its most important landowner.

Within the 30 mile (45 km) radius of the Lake District lies an astonishing number of fells and lakes. Today, all looks peaceful, but from the Roman occupation to the Middle Ages, the northwest was a turbulent area, as successive kings and rulers fought over the territory. Historians can revel in the various Celtic monuments, Roman remains, stately homes and monastic ruins. Although the scenery is paramount, there are many outdoor activities as well as spectator sports, such as Cumbrian wrestling, and wildlife to observe.

Lancashire's portfolio of tourist attractions includes the fine county town of Lancaster, bright Blackpool with its autumn illuminations and fairground attractions, and the peaceful seaside beaches to the south. Inland, the most appealing regions are the Forest of Bowland, a sparse expanse of heathery grouse moor, and the picturesque Ribble Valley.

Further south still are the industrial conurbations of Manchester and Merseyside, where the attractions are more urban. There are many fine Victorian buildings in Manchester, where the industrial quarter of Castlefield has been revitalized. Liverpool, with its restored Albert Dock, is best known as the seaport city of the Beatles. It has a lively club scene and is increasingly used as a film location. Both cities have good art galleries and museums.

Jetty at Grasmere, one of the most popular regions of the Lake District

Restored Albert Dock, lining the River Mersey in Liverpool

Exploring Lancashire and the Lakes

THE LAKE DISTRICT's natural scenery outweighs any of its man-made attractions. Its natural features are the result of geological upheavals over millennia *(see pp340–41)*, and four of its peaks are more than 1,000 m (3,300 ft). Human influences have left their mark too: the main activities are quarrying, mining, farming and tourism.

The Lakes are most crowded in summer when activities include lake trips and hill-walking. The best bases are Keswick and Ambleside, while there are also good hotels on the shores of Windermere and Ullswater and in the Cartmel area.

Lancashire's Bowland Forest is an attractive place to explore on foot, with picturesque villages. Further south, Manchester and Liverpool have excellent museums and galleries.

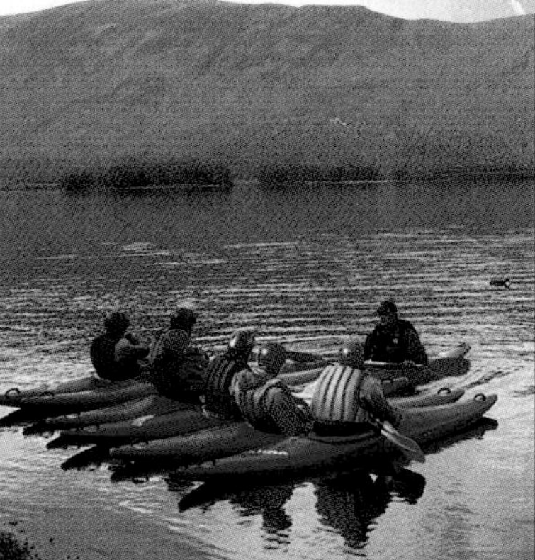

Watersports on Derwentwater in the Northern Fells and Lakes area

GETTING AROUND

For many, the first glimpse of the Lake District is from the M6 near Shap Fell, but the A6 is a more dramatic route. You can reach Windermere by train, but you need to change at Oxenholme, on the mainline route from Euston to Carlisle. Penrith also has rail services and bus links into the Lakes. L'al Ratty, the miniature railway up Eskdale, and the Lakeside & Haverthwaite railway, which connects with the steamers on Windermere, make for enjoyable outings. Regular buses link all the main centres where excursions are organized. One of the most enterprising is the Mountain Goat minibus, in Windermere and Keswick.

Lancaster, Liverpool and Manchester are on the main rail and bus routes and also have airports. For Blackpool, you need to change trains in Preston. Wherever you go in the area, one of the best means of getting around is on foot.

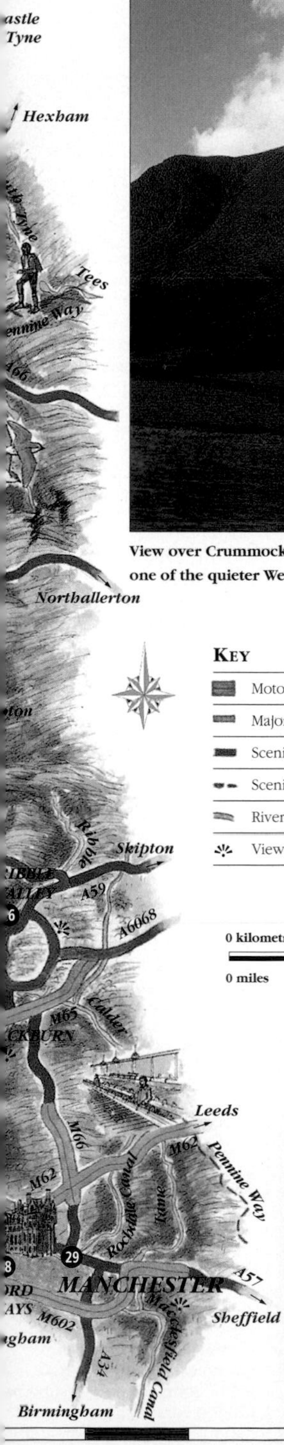

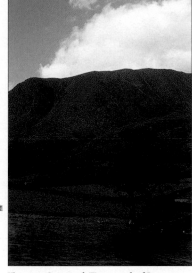

View over Crummock Water, north of Buttermere, one of the quieter Western Lakes

Sights at a Glance

Ambleside 16
Blackpool 27
Borrowdale 10
Buttermere 9
Carlisle 1
Cartmel 21
Cockermouth 7
Coniston Water 18
Dalemain 3
Duddon Valley 13
Eskdale 12
Furness Peninsula 20
Grasmere and Rydal 15
Kendal 19
Keswick 5
Lancaster 25
Langdale 14
Leighton Hall 24
Levens Hall 22
Liverpool pp362–5 30
Manchester pp360–61 29
Morecambe Bay 23
Newlands Valley 8
Northern Fells and Lakes pp348–9 6
Penrith 2
Ribble Valley 26
Salford Quays 28
Ullswater 4
Wastwater 11
Windermere 17

Key

- Motorway
- Major road
- Scenic route
- Scenic path
- River
- Viewpoint

0 kilometres 20

0 miles 10

See Also

• ***Where to Stay*** pp559–61

• ***Where to Eat*** pp595–7

Preserved docks and Liver Building, Liverpool

Carlisle ❶

Cumbria. *102,000.* *mainly private.* *The Old Town Hall, Green Market (01228 625600).* www.historic-carlisle.org.uk

DUE TO ITS proximity to the Scottish border, this city has long been a defensive site. Known as Luguvalium by the Romans, it was an outpost of Hadrian's Wall *(see pp408–9)*. Carlisle was sacked and pillaged repeatedly by the Danes, the Normans and border raiders, and suffered damage as a Royalist stronghold under Cromwell *(see p52)*.

Today, Carlisle is the capital of Cumbria. In its centre are the timber-framed Guildhall and market cross, and fortifications still exist around its West Walls, drum-towered gates and its Norman **castle**. The castle tower has a small museum devoted to the King's Own Border Regiment. The cathedral dates from 1122 and features a decorative east window. Carlisle's **Tullie House Museum** recreates the city's past with sections on Roman history and Cumbrian wildlife. Nearby lie the evocative ruins of **Lanercost Priory** (c.1166) and the remains of the unique **Birdoswald Roman Fort**.

Saxon iron sword in the Tullie House Museum

Façade of Hutton-in-the-Forest with medieval tower on the right

Carlisle Castle
(EH) Castle Way. *01228 591922.* *daily.* *limited.*

Tullie House Museum
Castle St. *01228 534781.* *daily (Sun: pm).* *1 Jan, 25, 26 Dec.*

Lanercost Priory
(EH) Nr Brampton. *016977 3030.* *Apr–Oct: daily.* *limited.*

Birdoswald Roman Fort
(EH) Gilsland, Brampton. *016977 47602.* *Mar–Oct: daily.* *limited.*
www.birdoswaldromanfort.org.uk

Penrith ❷

Cumbria. *15,000.* *Robinson's School, Middlegate (01768 867466).* *Tue, Sat.* www.visiteden.co.uk

TIMEWARP SHOPFRONTS on the market square and a 14th-century **castle** of sandstone are Penrith's main attractions. There are some strange hog-back stones in St Andrew's churchyard, allegedly a giant's grave, and the 285 m (937 ft) Beacon provides stunning views of distant fells.

ENVIRONS: Just northeast of Penrith at Little Salkeld is a famous Bronze Age circle (with 66 tall stones) known as **Long Meg and her Daughters**. Six miles (9 km) northwest of Penrith lies **Hutton-in-the-Forest**. The oldest part of this house is the 13th-century tower. Inside is a magnificent Italianate staircase, a sumptuously panelled 17th-century Long Gallery, a delicately stuccoed Cupid Room dating from the 1740s, and several Victorian rooms. Outside, you can walk around the walled garden and topiary terraces, or explore the woods.

Penrith Castle
Ullswater Rd. *daily.* *in grounds.*

Hutton-in-the-Forest
Off B5305. *017684 84449.*
House *Easter–Sep: Thu, Fri, Sun & public hols (pm).* **Grounds** *Apr–Oct: Sun–Fri.* *25 Dec.* *limited.*

TRADITIONAL CUMBRIAN SPORTS

Cumberland wrestling is one of the most interesting sports to watch in the summer months. The combatants, often clad in longjohns and embroidered velvet pants, clasp one another in an armlock and attempt to topple each other over. Technique and good balance outweigh physical force. Other traditional Lakeland sports include fell-racing, a gruelling test of speed and stamina up and down local peaks at ankle-breaking speed. Hound-trailing is also a popular sport in which specially bred hounds follow an aniseed trail over the hills. Sheep-dog trials, steam fairs, flower shows and gym-khanas take place in summer. The Egremont Crab Fair in September holds events such as greasy-pole climbing.

Cumberland wrestlers

Dalemain ❸

Penrith, Cumbria. *017684 86450.* *Penrith then taxi.* *Apr–Sep: Sun–Thu.* *limited.*

A SEEMLY GEORGIAN façade gives this fine house near Ullswater the impression of architectural unity, but hides a greatly altered medieval and Elizabethan structure with a maze of rambling passages. Public rooms include a superb Chinese drawing room with hand-painted wallpaper, and

Sheep resting at Glenridding, on the southwest shore of Ullswater

a panelled 18th-century drawing room. Several small museums occupy various outbuildings, and the gardens contain a fine collection of fragrant shrub roses and a huge silver fir.

Sumptuous Chinese drawing room at Dalemain

Ullswater ❹

Cumbria. *Penrith.* *Main car park, Glenridding, Penrith (017684 82414).* www.lake-district.gov.uk

Often considered the most beautiful of all Cumbria's lakes, Ullswater stretches from gentle farmland near Penrith to dramatic hills and crags at its southern end. The main western shore road can be very busy. In summer, two restored Victorian steamers ply regularly from Pooley Bridge to Glenridding. One of the best walks crosses the eastern shore from Glenridding to Hallin Fell and the moorland of Martindale. The western side passes Gowbarrow, where Wordsworth's immortalized "host of golden daffodils" bloom in spring *(see p354)*.

Keswick ❺

Cumbria. *5,000.* *Moot Hall, Market Sq (017687 72645).* www.keswick.org

Popular as a tourist venue since the advent of the railway in Victorian times, Keswick now has guest houses, a summer repertory theatre, outdoor equipment shops and a serious parking problem in high season. Its most striking central building is the **Moot Hall**, dating from 1813, now used as the tourist office. The town prospered on wool and leather until, in Tudor times, deposits of graphite were discovered. Mining then took over as the main industry and Keswick became an important centre for pencil manufacture. In World War II, hollow pencils were made to hide espionage maps on thin paper. The factory includes the **Pencil Museum** with interesting audiovisual shows. Among the many fine exhibits at the **Keswick Museum and Art Gallery** are the original manuscripts of Lakeland writers, musical stones and many other curiosities.

To the east of the town lies the ancient stone circle of Castlerigg, thought to be older than Stonehenge.

Pencil Museum

Carding Mill Lane. *017687 73626.* *daily.* *25, 26 Dec, 1 Jan.* www.pencil.co.uk

Keswick Museum and Art Gallery

Fitz Park, Station Rd. *017687 73263.* *call for details.*

Outdoor equipment shop in Keswick

Northern Fells and Lakes ❻

The rare red squirrel, native to the area

MANY VISITORS praise this northern area of the Lake District National Park for its scenery and geological interest *(see pp340–41)*. It is ideal walking country, and nearby Derwentwater, Thirlmere and Bassenthwaite provide endless scenic views, rambles and opportunities for watersports. Large areas surrounding the regional centre of Keswick *(see p347)* are accessible only on foot, particularly the huge mass of hills known as Back of Skiddaw – located between Skiddaw and Caldbeck – or the Helvellyn range, east of Thirlmere.

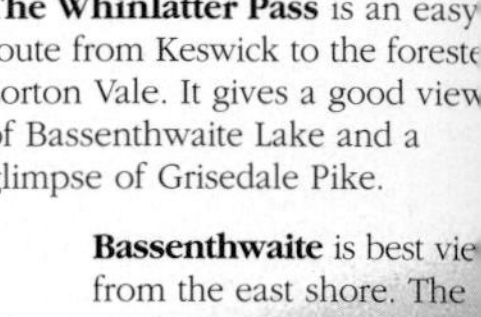

The Whinlatter Pass is an easy route from Keswick to the foreste Lorton Vale. It gives a good view of Bassenthwaite Lake and a glimpse of Grisedale Pike.

Bassenthwaite is best vie from the east shore. The road passes through Dod Wood at the foot of Skidc

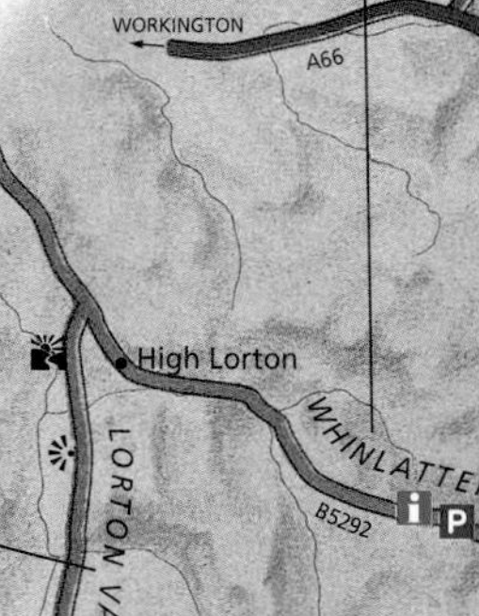

Lorton Vale
The lush, green farmland south of Cockermouth creates a marked contrast with the more rugged mountain landscapes of the central Lake District. In the village of Low Lorton is the private manor house of Lorton Hall, dating from the 15th century.

Derwentwater
Surrounded by woodland slopes and fells, this attractive oval lake is dotted with tiny islands. One of these was inhabited by St Herbert, a disciple of St Cuthbert (see p405)*, who lived there as a hermit until 687. A boat from Keswick provides a lake excursion.*

THE MAJOR PEAKS

The Lake District hills are the highest in England. Although they seem small by Alpine or world standards, the scale of the surrounding terrain makes them look extremely grand. Some of the most important peaks are shown on the following pages. Each peak is regarded as having its own personality. This section shows the Skiddaw fells, which are north of Keswick.

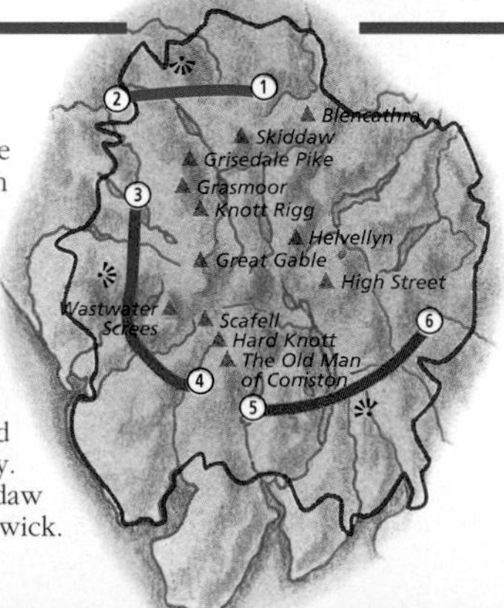

KEY

- From ① Blencathra to ② Cockermouth *(see opposite)*
- From ③ Grisedale Pike to ④ the Old Man of Coniston *(see pp350–51)*
- From ⑤ the Old Man of Coniston to ⑥ Windermere and Tarn Crag *(see pp352–3)*
- National Park boundary

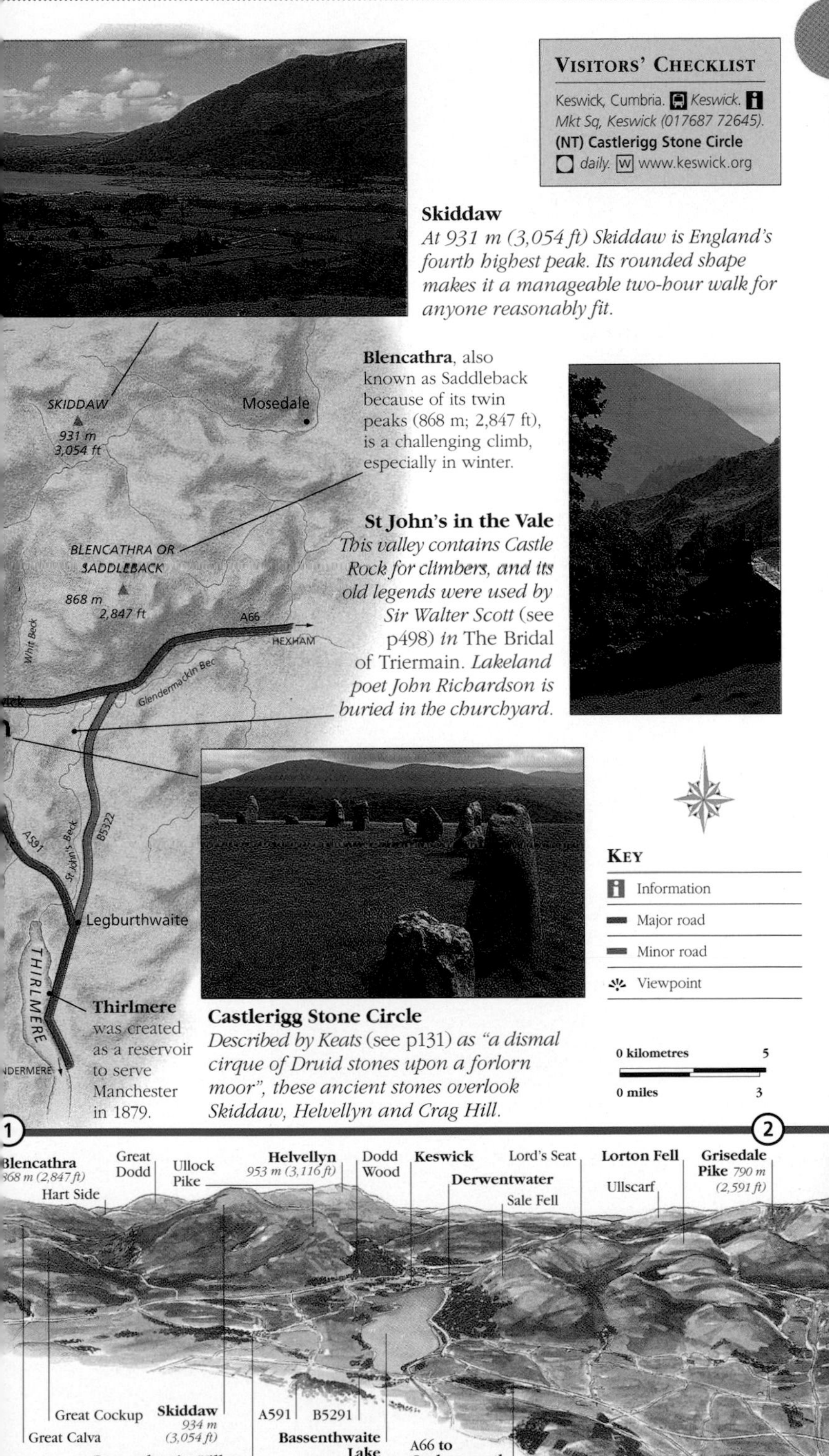

Visitors' Checklist

Keswick, Cumbria. *Keswick.* *Mkt Sq, Keswick (017687 72645).* **(NT) Castlerigg Stone Circle** *daily.* www.keswick.org

Skiddaw
At 931 m (3,054 ft) Skiddaw is England's fourth highest peak. Its rounded shape makes it a manageable two-hour walk for anyone reasonably fit.

Blencathra, also known as Saddleback because of its twin peaks (868 m; 2,847 ft), is a challenging climb, especially in winter.

St John's in the Vale
This valley contains Castle Rock for climbers, and its old legends were used by Sir Walter Scott (see p498) *in* The Bridal of Triermain. *Lakeland poet John Richardson is buried in the churchyard.*

Thirlmere was created as a reservoir to serve Manchester in 1879.

Castlerigg Stone Circle
Described by Keats (see p131) *as "a dismal cirque of Druid stones upon a forlorn moor", these ancient stones overlook Skiddaw, Helvellyn and Crag Hill.*

Crummock Water, one of the quieter "western lakes"

Cockermouth 7

Cumbria. 8,000. Workington. Town Hall, Market St (01900 822634).
www.western-lakedistrict.co.uk

COLOURWASHED TERRACES and restored workers' cottages beside the river are especially attractive in the busy market town of Cockermouth, which dates from the 12th century. The place not to miss is the handsome **Wordsworth House**, in the Main Street, where the poet was born *(see p354)*. This fine Georgian building still contains a few of the family's possessions, and is furnished in the style of the late 18th century. Wordsworth mentions the attractive terraced garden, which overlooks the River Derwent, in his *Prelude*. The local parish church contains a Wordsworth memorial window.

Cockermouth **castle** is partly ruined but still inhabited and closed to the public. The town has small museums of printing, toys and a mineral collection, and an art gallery. The **Jennings Brewery** invites visitors for tours and tastings.

Wordsworth House
(NT) Main St. *01900 824805.*
for refurbishment. Call for details.

Jennings Brewery
Castle Brewery. *01900 821011.*
Mon–Sat (Jul, Aug: daily).
1 Jan, 25, 26 Dec.
www.jenningsbrewery.co.uk

Kitchen, with an old range and tiled floor, at Wordsworth House

Newlands Valley 8

Cumbria. *Workington then bus.* *Cockermouth.* *Town Hall, Market St, Cockermouth (01900 822634); Market Sq, Keswick (017687 72645).*
www.western-lakedistrict.co.uk

FROM THE gently wooded shores of Derwentwater, the Newlands Valley runs through a scattering of farms towards rugged heights of 335 m (1,100 ft) at the top of the pass, where steps lead to the waterfall, Moss Force. Grisedale Pike, Grasmoor and Knott Rigg all provide excellent fell walks. Local mineral deposits of copper, graphite, lead and even small amounts of gold and silver were extensively mined here from Elizabethan times onwards. **Little Town** was used as a setting by Beatrix Potter *(see p355)* in *The Tale of Mrs Tiggywinkle*.

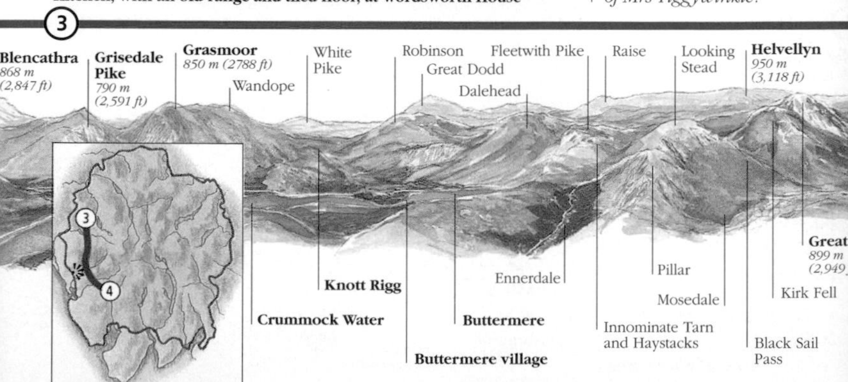

Buttermere ❾

Cumbria. 🚉 *Penrith.* 🚌 *Cockermouth.* 🚌 *Penrith to Keswick; Keswick to Buttermere.* ℹ *Town Hall, Market St, Cockermouth (01900 822634).*

INTERLINKING WITH Crummock Water and Loweswater, Buttermere and its surroundings contain some of the most appealing countryside in the region. Often known as the "western lakes", the three are remote enough not to become too crowded. Buttermere is a jewel amid grand fells: High Stile, Red Pike and Haystacks. Here the ashes of the celebrated hill-walker and author of fell-walking books, A W Wainwright, are scattered.

The village of Buttermere, with its handful of houses and inns, is a popular starting point for walks round all three lakes. Loweswater is hardest to reach and therefore the quietest, surrounded by woods and hills. Nearby Scale Force is the highest waterfall in the Lake District, plunging 36 m (120 ft).

Verdant valley of Borrowdale, a favourite with artists

Borrowdale ❿

Cumbria. 🚉 *Workington.* 🚌 *Cockermouth.* ℹ *Town Hall, Market St, Cockermouth (01900 822634).*

THIS ROMANTIC VALLEY, subject of a myriad sketches and watercolours before photography stole the scene, lies beside the densely wooded shores of Derwentwater under towering crags. It is a popular trip from Keswick and a great variety of walks are possible along the valley.

The tiny hamlet of **Grange** is one of the prettiest spots, where the valley narrows dramatically to form the "Jaws of Borrowdale". Nearby Castle Crag has superb views.

From Grange you can complete the circuit of Derwentwater along the western shore, or move southwards to the more open farmland around Seatoller. As you head south by road, look out for a National Trust sign *(see p25)* to the **Bowder Stone**, a delicately poised block weighing nearly 2,000 tonnes, which may have fallen from the crags above or been deposited by a glacier millions of years ago.

Two attractive hamlets in Borrowdale are **Rosthwaite** and **Stonethwaite**. Also worth a detour, preferably on foot, is Watendlath village, off a side road near the famous beauty spot of **Ashness Bridge**.

WALKING IN THE LAKE DISTRICT

Typical Lake District stile over dry-stone wall

Two long-distance footpaths pass through the Lake District's most spectacular scenery. The 70 mile (110 km) Cumbrian Way runs from Carlisle to Ulverston via Keswick and Coniston. The western section of the Coast-to-Coast Walk *(see pp32–3)* passes through this area. There are hundreds of shorter walks along lake shores, nature trails or following more challenging uphill routes. Walkers should stick to paths to avoid erosion, and check weather conditions at National Park information centres.

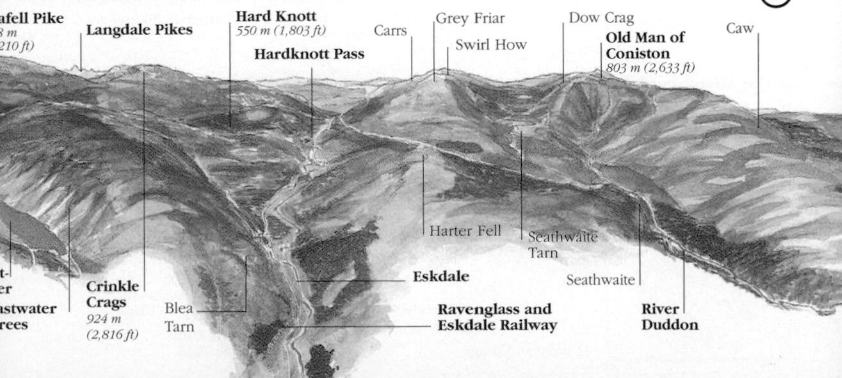

Convivial Wasdale Head Inn *(see p561)* at Wasdale Head

Wastwater ⓫

Cumbria. *Whitehaven.* *12 Main St, Egremont (01946 820693).*

A SILENT REFLECTION of truly awesome surroundings, black, brooding **Wastwater** is a mysterious, evocative lake. The road from Nether Wasdale continues along its northwest side. Along its eastern flank loom walls of sheer scree over 600 m (2,000 ft) high. Beneath them the water looks inky black, whatever the weather, plunging an icy 80 m (260 ft) from the waterline to the bottom to form England's deepest lake. You can walk along the screes, but it is an uncomfortable and dangerous scramble. Boating on the lake is banned for conservation reasons, but fishing permits are available from the nearby National Trust camp site.

At **Wasdale Head** lies one of Britain's grandest views: the austere pyramid of **Great Gable**, centrepiece of a fine mountain composition, with the huge forms of Scafell and **Scafell Pike**. The scenery is utterly unspoilt, and the only buildings lie at the far end of the lake: an inn and a tiny church commemorating fallen climbers. Here the road ends, and you must turn back or take to your feet, following signs for Black Sail Pass and Ennerdale, or walk up the grand fells ahead. Wasdale's irresistible backdrop was the inspiration of the first serious British mountaineers, who flocked here during the 19th century, insouciantly clad in tweed jackets, carrying little more than a length of rope slung over their shoulders.

Eskdale ⓬

Cumbria. *Ravenglass then narrow-gauge railway to Eskdale (Easter–Oct: daily; Dec–Feb: Sat, Sun).* *12 Main St, Egremont (01946 820693).* www.eskdale.info.co.uk

THE PASTORAL DELIGHTS of Eskdale are best encountered over the gruelling **Hardknott Pass**, which is the most taxing drive in the Lake District, with steep gradients. You can pause at the 393-m (1,291-ft) summit to explore the Roman **Hardknott Fort** or enjoy the lovely view. As you descend into Eskdale, rhododendrons and pines flourish in a landscape of small hamlets, narrow lanes and gentle farmland. The main settlements below are the attractive village of Boot and coastal Ravenglass, both with old corn mills.

Just south of Ravenglass is the impressive **Muncaster Castle**, the richly furnished home of the Pennington family. Another way to enjoy the scenery is to take the miniature railway (La'l Ratty) from Ravenglass to Dalegarth.

Eskdale Mill

Boot. *019467 23335.*

Apr– Sep: Tue–Sun, public hols.

Muncaster Castle

Ravenglass. *01229 717614.*

Castle *mid-Mar–mid-Nov: Sun–Fri (pm) & public hols.* **Garden** *daily.*

ground floor and garden.

www.muncaster.co.uk

Remains of the Roman Hardknott Fort, Eskdale

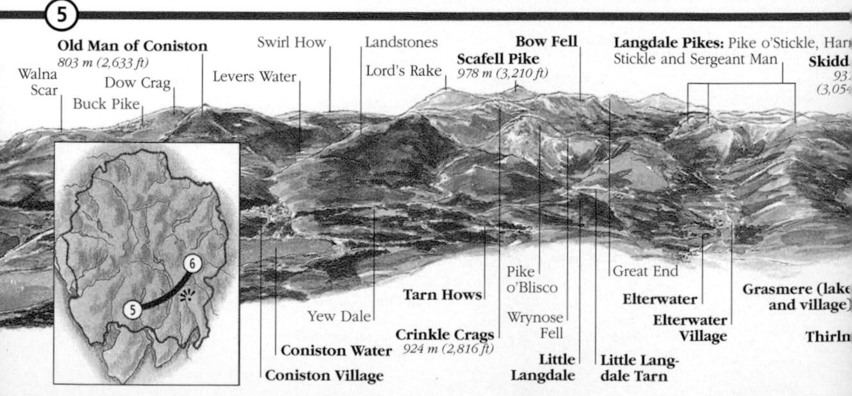

Autumnal view of Seathwaite, in the Duddon Valley, a popular centre for walkers and climbers

Duddon Valley ⓭

Cumbria. 🚉 *Foxfield, Ulverston.* ℹ *The Square, Broughton-in-Furness (01229 716115).* W www.lakelandgateway.info

ALSO KNOWN as Dunnerdale, this picturesque tract of countryside inspired 35 of Wordsworth's sonnets *(see p354)*. The prettiest stretch lies between Ulpha and Cockley Beck. In autumn the colours of heather moors and a light sprinkling of birch trees are particularly beautiful. Stepping stones and bridges span the river at intervals, the most charming being Birk's Bridge, near Seathwaite. At the southern end of the valley, where the River Duddon meets the sea at Duddon Sands, is the pretty village of Broughton-in-Furness. Note the stone slabs used for fish on market day in the square.

Langdale ⓮

Cumbria. 🚉 *Windermere.* ℹ *Market Cross, Ambleside (015394 32582).* W www.amblesideonline.co.uk

STRETCHING FROM Skelwith Bridge, where the Brathay surges powerfully over waterfalls, to the summits of Great Langdale is the two-pronged Langdale Valley. Walkers and climbers throng here to take on **Pavey Ark, Pike o'Stickle, Crinkle Crags** and **Bow Fell**. The local mountain rescue teams are the busiest in Britain.

Great Langdale is the more spectacular valley and it is often crowded, but quieter **Little Langdale** has many attractions too. It is worth completing the circuit back to Ambleside via the southern route, stopping at Blea Tarn. Reedy **Elterwater** is a picturesque spot, once a site of the gunpowder industry. Wrynose Pass, west of Little Langdale, climbs to 390 m (1,281 ft), a warm-up for Hardknott Pass further on. At its top is Three Shires Stone, marking the former boundary of the old counties of Cumberland, Westmorland and Lancashire.

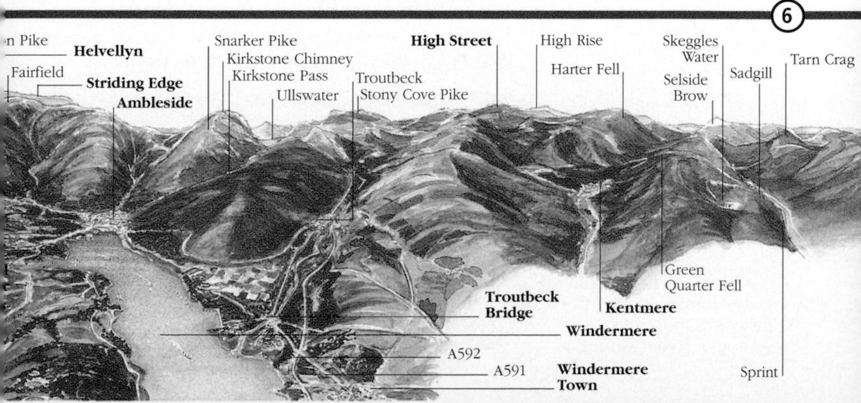

Rydal Water, one of the major attractions of the Lake District

Grasmere and Rydal 15

Cumbria. **Grasmere** *700.* **Rydal** *100.* *Grasmere.* *Redbank Rd, Grasmere (015394 35245).* www.lake-district.gov.uk

The poet William Wordsworth lived in both these pretty villages on the shores of two sparkling lakes. Fairfield, Nab Scar and Loughrigg Fell rise steeply above their reedy shores and offer good opportunities for walking. Grasmere is now a sizable settlement and the famous Grasmere sports *(see p346)* attract large crowds every August.

The Wordsworth family is buried in St Oswald's Church, and crowds flock to the annual ceremony of strewing the church's earth floor with fresh rushes. Most visitors head for **Dove Cottage**, where the poet spent his most creative years. The museum in the barn behind includes such artefacts as the great man's socks. The Wordsworths moved to a larger house, **Rydal Mount**, in Rydal in 1813 and lived here until 1850. The grounds have waterfalls and a summerhouse. Dora's Field nearby is a blaze of daffodils in spring and Fairfield Horseshoe offers an energetic, challenging walk.

Dove Cottage and the Wordsworth Museum
Off A591 nr Grasmere. *015394 35544.* *daily.* *24–26 Dec, mid-Jan–mid-Feb.*
www.wordsworth.org.uk

Rydal Mount
Rydal. *015394 33002.* *Mar–Oct: daily; Nov–Feb: Wed–Mon.* *25 Dec; Jan.* *limited.*

Ambleside 16

Cumbria. *3,400.* *Central Buildings, Market Cross (015394 32582).* *Wed.*
www.amblesideonline.co.uk

Ambleside has good road connections to all parts of the Lakes and is an attractive base, especially for walkers and climbers. Mainly Victorian in character, it has a good range of outdoor clothing, crafts and specialist food shops. An enterprising little cinema and a summer classical music festival add life in the evenings. Sights in town are small-scale: the remnants of the Roman fort of Galava, AD 79, Stock Ghyll Force waterfall and **Bridge House**, now a National Trust information centre.

Environs: Within easy reach are the wooded Rothay valley and the **Kirkstone Galleries** at Skelwith Bridge, with their contemporary design products. At nearby Troutbeck is the restored farmhouse of **Townend**, dating from 1626,

The tiny Bridge House over Stock Beck in Ambleside

William Wordsworth (1770–1850)

Best known of the Romantic poets, Wordsworth was born in the Lake District and spent most of his life there. After school in Hawkshead and a period at Cambridge, a legacy enabled him to pursue his literary career. He settled at Dove Cottage with his sister Dorothy and in 1802 married an old school friend, Mary Hutchinson. They lived simply, walking, bringing up their children and receiving visits from poets such as Coleridge and de Quincey. Wordsworth's prose works include one of the earliest guidebooks to the Lake District.

Beatrix Potter and the Lake District

Although best known for her children's stories with characters such as Peter Rabbit and Jemima Puddleduck, which she also illustrated, Beatrix Potter (1866–1943) became a champion of conservation in the Lake District after moving there in 1906. She married William Heelis, devoted herself to farming, and was an expert on Herdwick sheep. To conserve her beloved countryside, she donated land to the National Trust.

Cover illustration of *Jemima Puddleduck* (1908)

whose interior gives an insight into Lakeland domestic life.

Kirkstone Galleries
Skelwith Bridge. *015394 34002.* *daily.* *24–26 Dec.*

Townend
(NT) Troutbeck, Windermere. *015394 32628.* *Apr–Oct: Tue–Fri, Sun & bank hol Mon; pm.*

Windermere 17

Cumbria. *Windermere.* *Victoria St.* *Victoria St (015394 46499) or Glebe Rd, Bowness-on-Windermere (015394 42895).* www.lakelandgateway.info

At over 10 miles (16 km) long, this dramatic watery expanse is England's largest mere. Industrial magnates built mansions around its shores long before the railway arrived. Stately **Brockhole**, now a national park visitor centre, was one such grand estate. When the railway reached Windermere in 1847, it enabled crowds of workers to visit the area on day trips.

Today, a year-round car ferry service connects the lake's east and west shores (it runs between Ferry Nab and Ferry House), and summer steamers link Lakeside, Bowness and Ambleside on the north-south axis. Belle Isle, a wooded island on which a unique round house stands, is one of the lake's most attractive features, but landing is not permitted. **Fell Foot Park** is at the south end of the lake, and there are good walks on the northwest shore. A quite stunning viewpoint is Orrest Head 238 m (784 ft) northeast of Windermere town.

Environs: Bowness-on-Windermere, on the east shore, is a hugely popular centre. Many of its buildings display Victorian details, and St Martin's Church dates back to the 15th century. The **Windermere Steamboat Museum** has a collection of superbly restored craft, and one of these, *Swallow*, makes regular lake trips. The **World of Beatrix Potter** recreates her characters in an exhibition, and a film tells her life story.

Beatrix Potter wrote many of her books at **Hill Top**, the 17th-century farmhouse at Near Sawrey, northwest of Windermere. Hill Top is furnished with many of Potter's possessions, and left as it was in her lifetime. The **Beatrix Potter Gallery** in Hawkshead holds annual exhibitions of her manuscripts and illustrations.

Brockhole Visitor Centre
On A591. *015394 46601.* *Apr–Oct: daily.*

Fell Foot Park
(NT) Newby Bridge. *015395 31273.* *daily.*

Windermere Steamboat Museum
Rayrigg Rd, Windermere. *015394 45565.* *late Mar–Nov: daily.* www.steamboat.co.uk

World of Beatrix Potter
The Old Laundry, Crag Brow. *015394 88444.* *daily.* *25 Dec, last three wks in Jan.* *limited.* www.hop-skip-jump.com

Hill Top
(NT) Near Sawrey, Ambleside. *015394 36269.* *Apr–Oct: Sat–Wed.*

Beatrix Potter Gallery
(NT) The Square, Hawkshead. *015394 36355.* *Apr–Oct: Sat–Wed.*

Boats moored along the shore at Ambleside, the north end of Windermere

Peaceful Coniston Water, the setting of Arthur Ransome's novel, *Swallows and Amazons* (1930)

Coniston Water 18

Cumbria. *Windermere then bus.* *Ambleside then bus.* *Coniston car park, Ruskin Ave (015394 41533).* www.coniston-net.com

For the finest view of this stretch of water just outside the Lake District, you need to climb. The 19th-century art critic, writer and philosopher John Ruskin, had a fine view from his house, **Brantwood**, where his paintings and memorabilia can be seen today. Contemporary art exhibitions and events take place throughout the year.

An enjoyable excursion is the summer lake trip from Coniston Pier on the National Trust steam yacht, *Gondola*, calling at Brantwood. Coniston was also the scene of Donald Campbell's fatal attempt on the world water speed record in 1967. The green slate village of Coniston, once a centre for copper-mining, now caters for local walkers.

Also interesting is the traffic-free village of **Hawkshead** to the northwest, with its quaint alleyways and timber-framed houses. To the south is the vast Grizedale Forest, dotted with woodland sculptures.

Just north of Coniston Water is the man-made **Tarn Hows**, a landscaped tarn surrounded by woods. There is a pleasant climb up the 803 m (2,635 ft) Old Man of Coniston.

Brantwood
Off B5285, nr Coniston. *015394 41396.* *mid-Mar–mid-Nov: daily; mid-Nov–mid-Mar: Wed–Sun.* www.brantwood.org.uk

Kendal 19

Cumbria. *26,000.* *Town Hall, Highgate (01539 725758).* *Mon–Sat.* www.kendaltown.org.uk

A busy market town, Kendal is the administrative centre of the region and the southern gateway to the Lake District. Built in grey limestone, it has an arts centre, the **Brewery**, and a central area which is best enjoyed on foot. **Abbot Hall**, built in 1759, has paintings by Turner and Romney as well as Gillows furniture. In addition, the hall's stable block contains the **Museum of Lakeland Life**, with occasional lively workshops demonstrating local crafts and trades. There are dioramas of geology and wildlife in the **Museum of Natural History and Archaeology**. About 3 miles (5 km) south of the town is 14th-century **Sizergh Castle**, with a fortified tower, carved fireplaces and a lovely garden.

Kendal mint cake, the famous lakeland energy-booster for walkers

Abbot Hall Art Gallery & Museum of Lakeland Life
Kendal. *01539 722464.* *mid-Feb–20 Dec: Mon–Sat.* *gallery.* *by arrangement.* www.abbothall.org.uk

Kendal Museum of Natural History and Archaeology
Station Rd. *01539 721374.* *mid-Feb–20 Dec: Mon–Sat.* www.kendalmuseum.org.uk

Sizergh Castle
(NT) off A591 & A590. *015395 60070.* *Apr–Oct: Sun–Thu.* *ground floor & grounds.*

Furness Peninsula 20

Cumbria. *Barrow-in-Furness.* *28 Duke St, Barrow-in-Furness (01229 894784).*

Barrow-in-Furness *(see p337)* is the peninsula's main town. Its **Dock Museum**, cleverly built over a Victorian dock where ships were repaired, traces the history of Barrow using interactive computer displays.

Ruins of the red sandstone walls of **Furness Abbey** remain in the wooded Vale of Deadly Nightshade, with a small exhibition of monastic life. The historic town of Ulverston received its charter in 1280. **Ulverston Heritage**

Centre charts its development from market town to port. Stan Laurel, of Laurel and Hardy fame, was born here in 1890. His memorabilia **museum** has a cinema.

Dock Museum
North Rd, Barrow-in-Furness. *01229 894444.* *Easter–Oct: Tue–Sun; Nov–Easter: Wed–Sun (Sat, Sun: pm); public hols.*
www.dockmuseum.org.uk

Furness Abbey
Vale of Deadly Nightshade. *01229 823420.* *Easter–Sep: daily; Oct–Easter: Wed–Sun.* *24–26 Dec, 1 Jan.* *limited.*

Ulverston Heritage Centre
Lower Brook St. *01229 580820.* *Apr–Dec: Mon–Sat; Jan–Mar: Mon, Tue, Thu–Sat.* *25, 26 Dec, 1 Jan.* *limited.*

Laurel and Hardy Museum
Upper Brook St, Ulverston. *01229 582292.* *daily.* *25 Dec; Jan.*

Staircase at Holker Hall

Cartmel 21

Cumbria. *700.* *Main St, Grange-over-Sands (015395 34026).* www.grangetic@southlakeland.gov.uk

THE HIGHLIGHT of this pretty village is its 12th-century **priory**, one of the finest Cumbrian churches. Little remains of the original priory except the gatehouse in the village centre. The restored church has an attractive east window, a stone-carved 14th-century tomb, and beautiful misericords.

Cartmel also boasts a small racecourse. The village has given its name to its surroundings, a hilly district of green farmland with mixed woodland and limestone scars.

A major local attraction is **Holker Hall**, former residence of the Dukes of Devonshire. Inside are lavishly furnished rooms, with fine marble fireplaces, and a superb oak staircase. Outside are stunning gardens and a deer park.

Holker Hall
Cark-in-Cartmel. *015395 58328.* *Apr–Nov: Sun–Fri.* *limited.* *by arrangement.*
www.holker-hall.co.uk

Levens Hall 22

Nr Kendal, Cumbria. *015395 60321.* *from Kendal or Lancaster.* *Apr–mid-Oct: Sun–Thu.* *gardens only.*
www.levenshall.co.uk

THE OUTSTANDING attraction of this Elizabethan mansion is its topiary, but the house itself has much to offer. Built around a 13th-century tower, it contains a fine collection of Jacobean furniture and watercolours by Peter de Wint (1784–1849). Also of note are the ornate ceilings, Charles II dining chairs, the earliest example of English patchwork and the gilded hearts on the drainpipes.

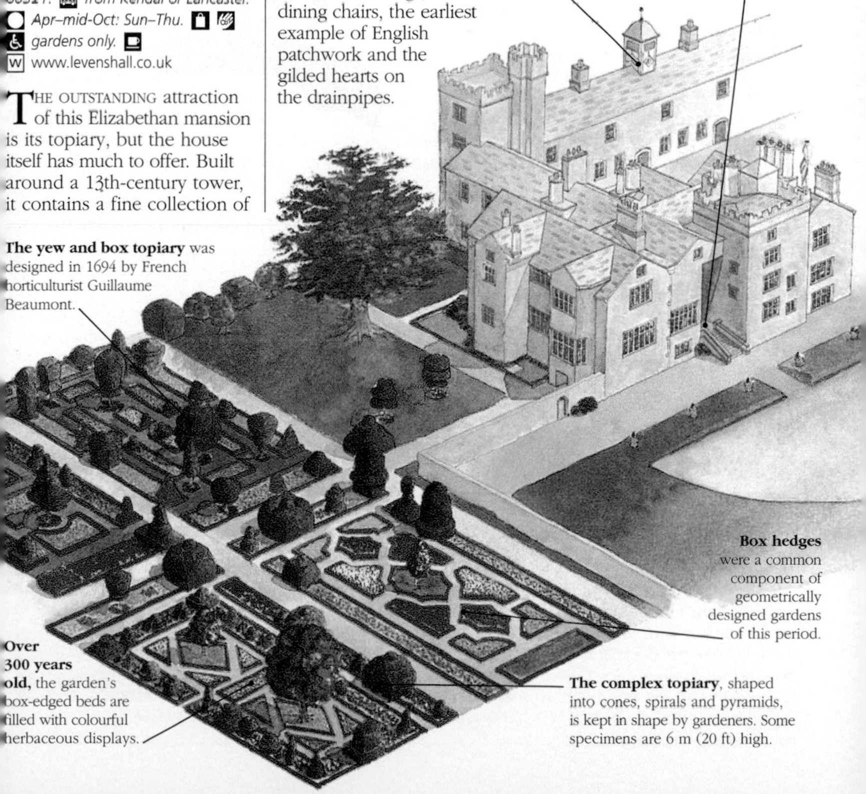

The 18th-century Turret Clock has a single hand, a common design of the period.

Main entrance

The yew and box topiary was designed in 1694 by French horticulturist Guillaume Beaumont.

Box hedges were a common component of geometrically designed gardens of this period.

Over 300 years old, the garden's box-edged beds are filled with colourful herbaceous displays.

The complex topiary, shaped into cones, spirals and pyramids, is kept in shape by gardeners. Some specimens are 6 m (20 ft) high.

Morecambe Bay, looking northwest towards Barrow-in-Furness

Morecambe Bay ㉓

Lancashire. *Morecambe.*
Heysham (to Isle of Man).
Marine Rd. (01524 582808).
www.lancaster.gov.uk

THE BEST WAY to explore Morecambe Bay is by train from Ulverston to Arnside. The track follows a series of low viaducts across a huge expanse of glistening tidal flats where thousands of wading birds feed and breed. The bay is one of the most important bird reservations in the country. On the Cumbrian side of the bay, retirement homes have expanded the sedate Victorian resort of Grange-over-Sands, which grew up after the arrival of the railway in 1857. Its best feature is its natural setting. Nearby, **Hampsfield Fell** and **Humphrey Head Point** give fine views along the bay.

Leighton Hall ㉔

Carnforth, Lancashire. *01524 734474.* *to Yealand Conyers (from Lancaster).* *by appointment.* *ground floor only.* *pm only.*
www.leightonhall.com

LEIGHTON HALL'S estate dates back to the 13th century, but most of the building is 19th-century, including its Neo-Gothic façade. It is owned by the Gillow family, of the Lancastrian furniture business, whose products are now prized antiques. Excellent pieces can be seen here, including a ladies' work-box inlaid with biblical scenes. In the afternoon, weather permitting, the hall's large collection of birds of prey display their aerial prowess.

Lancaster ㉕

Lancashire. *50,000.* *Castle Hill (01524 32878).* *Mon–Sat.*
www.lancaster.gov.uk

THIS COUNTY TOWN of Lancashire is tiny compared to Liverpool or Manchester (now counties in their own right), but it has a long history. The Romans named it after their camp over the River Lune. Originally a defensive site, it developed into a prosperous port largely on the proceeds of the slave trade. Today, its university and cultural life still thrive. The Norman **Lancaster Castle** was expanded in the 14th and 16th centuries. It has been a crown court and a prison since the 13th century. The Shire Hall is decorated with 600 heraldic shields. Some fragments from Hadrian's Tower (which has a collection of torture instruments) are 2,000 years old.

The nearby priory church of **St Mary** is on Castle Hill. Its main features include a Saxon doorway and carved 14th-century choir stalls. There is an outstanding museum of furniture in the 17th-century **Judge's Lodgings**, while the **Maritime Museum**, in the Georgian custom house on St George's Quay, contains displays on the port's history. The **City Museum**, based in the old town hall, concentrates on the history of Lancaster.

Tawny eagle at Leighton Hall

The splendid **Lune Aqueduct** carries the canal over the River Lune on five wide arches. Other attractions are found in **Williamson Park**, site of the 1907 Ashton Memorial. This folly was built by the local linoleum magnate and politician, Lord Ashton.

CROSSING THE SANDS

Morecambe Bay sands are very dangerous. Travellers used to cut across the bay at low tide to shorten the long trail around the Kent estuary. Many perished as they were caught by rising tides or quicksand, and sea fogs hid the paths. Locals who knew the bay became guides, and today you can travel with a guide from Kents Bank to Hest Bank near Arnside.

The High Sheriff of Lancaster Crossing Morecambe Sands **(anon)**

'here are fine views from the op of this 67 m (220 ft) domed tructure. Opposite is the ropical butterfly house and he pavilion café.

Lancaster Castle
'astle Parade. *01524 64998.* *laily.* *1 Jan, 25 Dec.* *only imited when court is in session).*
www. lancastercastle.com

Judge's Lodgings
'hurch St. *01524 32808.* *Apr–un, Oct: daily (Sat, Sun: pm only); Jul–ep: daily.* *Nov–Good Fri.*

Maritime Museum
'ustom House, St George's Quay. *1524 64637.* *daily (Nov–Easter: m).* *24–26, 31 Dec, 1 Jan.*
www.nettingthebay.org.uk

City Museum
Aarket Sq. *01524 64637.* *Aon–Sat.* *24 Dec–2 Jan.*

Williamson Park
Vyresdale Rd. *01524 33318.* *daily.* *limited.*
www.williamsonpark.u-net.com

Ribble Valley 26

ancashire. *Clitheroe.* *Market 'lace, Clitheroe (01200 425566).* *Tue, Thu, Sat.*
www.ribblevalley.gov.uk

CLITHEROE, A SMALL market town with a hilltop astle, is a good centre for xploring the Ribble Valley's ivers and old villages, such s Slaidburn. Ribchester has a **Roman Museum**, and there s a ruined **Cistercian abbey** t Whalley. To the east is 560 n (1,830 ft) Pendle Hill, with Bronze Age burial mound t its peak.

Roman Museum
'ibchester. *01254 878261.* *laily.* *by arrangement.*

Whalley Abbey
Vhalley. *01254 828400.* *daily.* *24 Dec–2 Jan.*
www.whalleyabbey.org

Blackpool 27

ancashire. *150,000.* *Clifton St (01253 478222).*
www.blackpooltourism.com

BRITISH HOLIDAY patterns have changed in the past few lecades, and Blackpool is no onger the apogee of seaside ntertainment, but it remains a

***Coming from the Mill* (1930) by L S Lowry**

unique experience. A wall of amusement arcades, piers, bingo halls and fast-food stalls stretch behind the sands. At night, entertainers strut their stuff under the bright lights. The town attracts thousands of visitors in September and October when the Illuminations trace the skeleton of the 158 m (518 ft) Blackpool Tower. Blackpool's resort life dates back to the 18th century, but it burst into prominence when the railway first arrived in 1840, bringing Lancastrian workers to their holiday resort.

Blackpool Tower, painted gold for its centenary in 1994

Salford Quays 28

Salford. *Harbour City (from Manchester).* *City Council (0161 848 8601).*
www.salford.gov.uk

THE QUAYS, to the west of Manchester city centre, were once the terminal docks for the **Manchester Ship Canal**. However, after the docks closed in 1982 the area became sadly run down. Since the 1990s all this has changed dramatically, with the creation of new residential and leisure facilities. In 2000 **The Lowry** opened, a spectacular new arts complex with theatres and galleries, including one dedicated to the world's largest collection of works by Salford-born artist L S Lowry. Across the footbridge over the canal is Trafford (Manchester United Football Club's ground at Old Trafford is nearby), where you will find the **Imperial War Museum North**, which opened in 2002. Sited in a striking building by architect Daniel Libeskind, its collection emphasizes war as seen from the point of view of the people caught up in it.

The Lowry
Pier 8, Salford Quays. *0161 876 2000.* *daily.* *25 Dec.*
www.thelowry.com

Imperial War Museum North
Trafford Wharf. *0870 220 3435.* *daily.* *25, 26 Dec.*
www.iwm.org.uk/north

Manchester ㉙

Sign for the John Rylands Library

MANCHESTER'S HISTORY dates back to Roman times, when, in AD 79, Agricola's legions set up a base camp called Mancunium on the site of the present city. It rose to prominence in the late 18th century, when Richard Arkwright's steam-powered spinning machines introduced the brave new world of cotton processing. By 1830, the first railway linked Manchester and Liverpool, and in 1894 the Manchester Ship Canal *(see p359)* opened, allowing cargo vessels 36 miles (55 km) inland. Confident civic buildings sprang up from the proceeds of cotton wealth, but these were in stark contrast to the over-crowded slums of the millworkers. Social discontent led writers, politicians and reformers to espouse liberal or radical causes. One result was the foundation in 1821 of the forthright local newspaper, the *Manchester Guardian*, a forerunner of today's national paper, the *Guardian*. The city was the first to introduce massive slum clearance and smokeless zones during the 1950s.

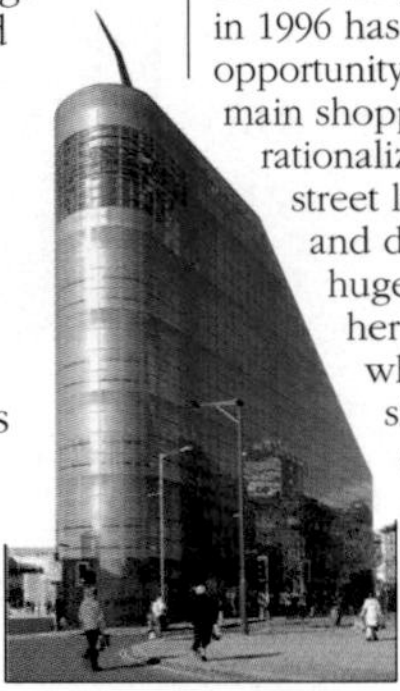

Urbis, a new interactive museum on life in cities

Exploring Manchester

Manchester is a fine, compact city with much to see in its central areas. It has a lively club scene, one of the largest Chinatowns in the world outside China and a wide range of restaurants. The restoration of the tram system has helped ease the pressures of urban transport, and the car-bombing of the city centre in 1996 has been seized as an opportunity to redevelop the main shopping areas and rationalize some of the street layouts. The mills and docks have left a huge architectural heritage, much of which is providing sites for imaginative development, including, on the west side of the city, **Salford Quays** *(see p359)*. Among the fine 19th-century buildings

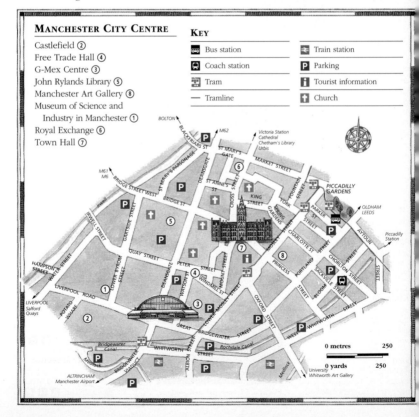

Manchester City Centre

Castlefield ②
Free Trade Hall ④
G-Mex Centre ③
John Rylands Library ⑤
Manchester Art Gallery ⑧
Museum of Science and Industry in Manchester ①
Royal Exchange ⑥
Town Hall ⑦

Key

- Bus station
- Coach station
- Tram
- Tramline
- Train station
- Parking
- Tourist information
- Church

0 metres 250
0 yards 250

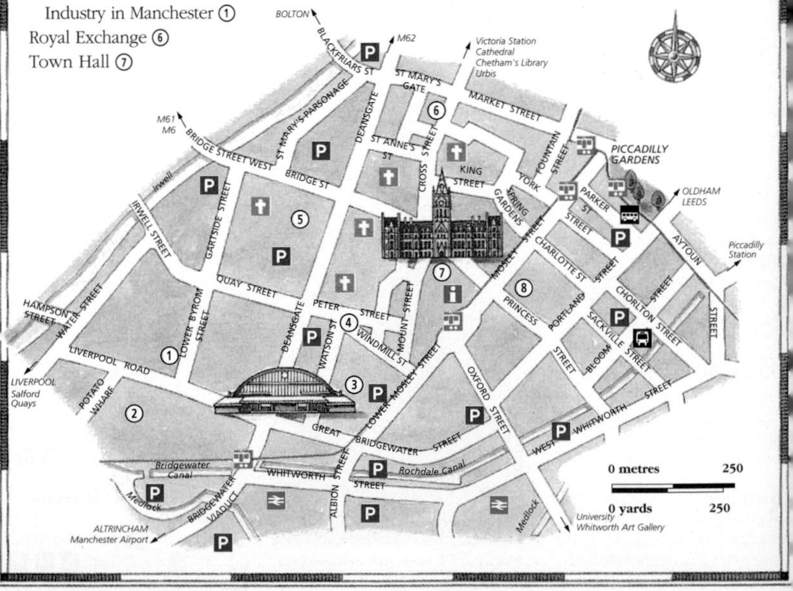

The Neo-Gothic Town Hall by Alfred Waterhouse, opened 1877

are the **John Rylands Library** founded over a hundred years ago by the widow of a local cotton millionaire, the **Town Hall**, the **Royal Exchange**, now a theatre and restaurant, and the **Free Trade Hall**. Behind the **cathedral** is **Chetham's Library**, housed in part of a well-preserved group of late-medieval buildings. The former central railway station, closed in 1969, is now the **G-Mex Centre**, a huge exhibition and conference complex. The once derelict industrial site of **Castlefield** has come back to life as a thriving office, residential and leisure area, offering museums, narrowboat trips and the worlds' first ever passenger railway station, now home to the Museum of Science and Industry *(below)*.

Museum of Science and Industry in Manchester

Liverpool Rd. *0161 832 2244.* *daily.* *24–26 Dec.*
www.msim.org.uk

One of the largest science museums in the world, the spirit of scientific enterprise and industrial might of Manchester's heyday is conveyed here. Among the best sections are the Power Hall, a collection of working steam engines, the Electricity Gallery, tracing the history of domestic power, and an exhibition on the Liverpool and Manchester Railway. A collection of planes that made flying history are displayed in the Air and Space Gallery.

Manchester Art Gallery

Mosley St & Princess St. *0161 235 8888.* *Tue–Sun.* *Mondays except Bank Holidays, 24–26, 31 Dec, 1 Jan, Good Fri.*
www.manchestergalleries.org

The gallery reopened in summer 2002, doubling its display space after a £35 million makeover and a brand new extension by architect Sir Michael Hopkins. The original building was designed by Sir Charles Barry (1795–1860) in 1824, and contains an excellent collection of British art, notably Pre-Raphaelites such as Holman Hunt and Dante Gabriel Rossetti. Early Italian, Flemish and French Schools are also represented. The gallery has a fine collection of decorative arts, from the Greeks to Picasso to contemporary craftworkers, in the Gallery of Craft & Design.

Urbis

Cathedral Gdns. *0161 605 8200.* *daily.* *25 Dec.* *0161 605 8282.*
www.urbis.org.uk

The Urbis museum, opened in 2002, is set in a dramatic high-rise glass building, and explores life in different cities around the world through interactive exhibits. The visit begins with a one-minute sky glide in a glass elevator, then proceeds through four cascading floors of themed exhibitions.

VISITORS' CHECKLIST

Manchester. *2.5 million.* *Off M56 11 miles (18 km) S Manchester.* *Oxford Rd, Victoria, Piccadilly.* *Chorlton St.* *Lloyd St (0161 234 3157).* *daily.*
www.manchester.gov.uk

Whitworth Art Gallery

University of Manchester, Oxford Rd. *0161 275 7450.* *daily (Sun: pm).* *24 Dec–2 Jan, Good Fri.*
www.whitworth.man.ac.uk

The Manchester machine tool manufacturer and engineer Sir Joseph Whitworth bequeathed money for this gallery, originally intended to be a museum of industrial art and design that would inspire the city's textile trade. The fine red-brick building is Edwardian, while the modern interior dates from the 1960s. It houses a superb collection of contemporary art, textiles and prints. Jacob Epstein's *Genesis* nude occupies the entrance, and there is an important collection of British watercolours by Turner *(see p93)*, Girtin and others. Look out for the Japanese woodcuts and a collection of historic and modern wallpapers.

Jacob Epstein's *Genesis* (1930–1) in the Whitworth Art Gallery

THE PETERLOO MASSACRE

In 1819, the working conditions of Manchester's factory workers were so bad that social tensions reached breaking point. On 16 August, 50,000 people assembled in St Peter's Field to protest at the oppressive Corn Laws. Initially peaceful, the mood darkened and the poorly trained mounted troops panicked, charging the crowd with their sabres. Eleven were killed and many wounded. The incident was called Peterloo (the Battle of Waterloo had taken place in 1815). Reforms such as the Factory Act came in that year.

G Cruikshank's *Peterloo Massacre* cartoon

Liverpool ㉚

Traces of settlement on Merseyside date back to the 1st century. In 1207 "Livpul", a fishing village, was granted a charter by King John. The population was only 1,000 in Stuart times, but during the 17th and 18th centuries Liverpool's westerly seaboard gave it a leading edge in the lucrative Caribbean slave trade. The first docks opened in 1715 and eventually stretched 7 miles (11 km) along the Mersey. Liverpool's first ocean steamer set out from here in 1840, and would-be emigrants to the New World poured into the city from Europe, including a flood of Irish refugees from the potato famine. Many settled permanently in Liverpool and a large, mixed community developed. Today, the port handles even greater volumes of cargoes than in the 1950s and 1960s, but container ships use Bootle docks. Despite economic and social problems, the irrepressible "Scouse" or Liverpudlian spirit re-emerged in the Swinging Sixties, when four local lads stormed the pop scene. Many people still visit Liverpool to pay homage to the Beatles, but the city is also known for its orchestra, the Liverpool Philharmonic, its sport (football and the Grand National steeplechase) and its universities.

Liver Bird on the Royal Liver Building

Victorian ironwork, restored and polished, at Albert Dock

Exploring Liverpool

Liverpool's waterfront by the Pier Head, guarded by the mythical Liver Birds (a pair of cormorants with seaweed in their beaks) on the **Royal Liver Building**, is one of the most easily recognized in Britain. Nearby are the famous ferry terminal across the River Mersey and the revitalized

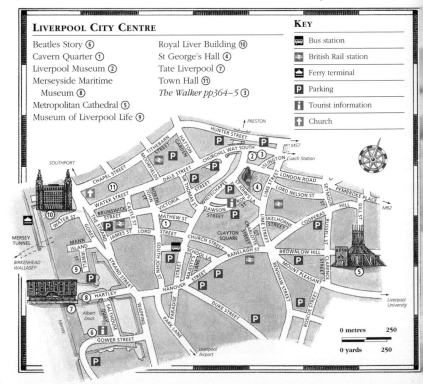

Liverpool City Centre

- Beatles Story ⑥
- Cavern Quarter ①
- Liverpool Museum ②
- Merseyside Maritime Museum ⑧
- Metropolitan Cathedral ⑤
- Museum of Liverpool Life ⑨
- Royal Liver Building ⑩
- St George's Hall ④
- Tate Liverpool ⑦
- Town Hall ⑪
- *The Walker pp364–5* ③

Key

- Bus station
- British Rail station
- Ferry terminal
- Parking
- Tourist information
- Church

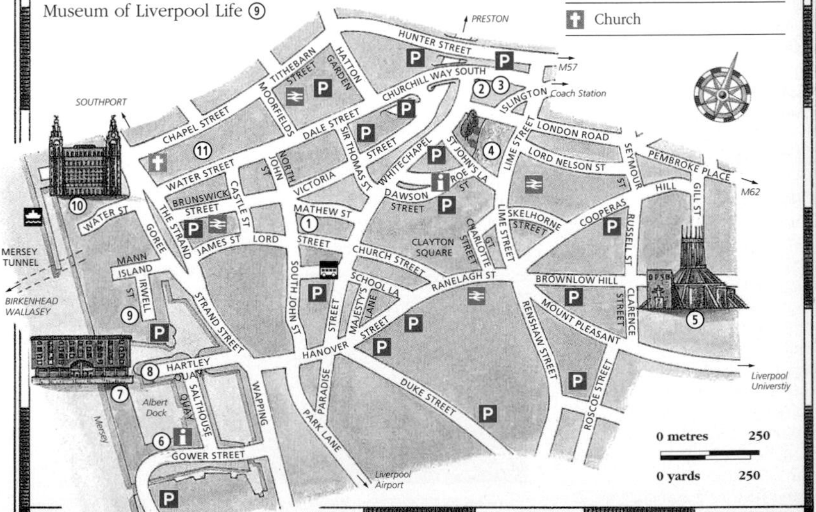

0 metres 250

0 yards 250

docklands. Other attractions include top-class museums and fine galleries, such as the **Walker** *(see pp364–5)*. Its wealth of interesting architecture includes some fine Neo-Classical buildings in the city centre, such as the gargantuan **St George's Hall**, and two cathedrals.

Albert Dock

0151 708 7334. daily. 25 Dec, 1Jan. some attractions. www.albertdock.com

There are five warehouses surrounding Albert Dock, all designed by Jesse Hartley in 1846. The docks were closed by 1972. After a decade of dereliction, these Grade I listed buildings were restored in a development that includes museums, galleries, shops, restaurants, bars and businesses.

Albert Dock quay beside the River Mersey

Merseyside Maritime Museum

Albert Dock. *0151 478 4499. daily. limited.* www.merseysidemaritimemuseum.org.uk

Devoted to the history of the Port of Liverpool, this large complex has good sections on shipbuilding and the Cunard and White Star liners as well as a Transatlantic Slavery gallery. The area on the Battle of the Atlantic in World War II includes models and charts. Another gallery deals with emigration to the New World. The **HM Customs and Excise National Museum** is also located here, and examines the history of the subject, including smuggling, as well as customs and excise today. Across the quayside is the rebuilt Piermaster's House and the Cooperage.

Ship's bell in the Maritime Museum

Museum of Liverpool Life

Pier Head, Albert Dock. *0151 478 4499. daily.* www.museumofliverpoollife.org.uk

Many aspects of Liverpool culture converge here. Exhibits cover the history of Liverpool, its people and their contribution to international life. The *City Soldier's* gallery explores life in the King's Regiment in times of war and peace. Other interactive exhibits and accounts of daily life tell stories of sporting and political events since the 1800s.

Visitors' Checklist

Liverpool. 450,000. 7 miles (11 km) SE Liverpool. Lime St. Norton St. from Pier Head to the Wirral, also sightseeing trips; to Isle of Man & N Ireland. Queens Sq (09066 806886). Sun (heritage market). 0906 680 6886; Liverpool Show: May; River Festival: Jun; Beatles Week: Aug. www.visitliverpool.com

Beatles Story

Britannia Vaults. *0151 709 1963. daily. 25, 26 Dec.* www.beatlesstory.com

In a walk-through exhibition, this museum records the history of The Beatles' meteoric rise to fame, from their first record, *Love Me Do,* through Beatlemania to their last live appearance together in 1969, and their eventual break-up. The hits that mesmerized a generation can be heard.

Tate Liverpool

Albert Dock. *0151 702 7400. Tue–Sun, public hols. Mon; Good Fri, 24–26 Dec, 1 Jan. some exhibitions. by arrangement.* www.tate.org.uk/liverpool

Tate Liverpool has one of the best contemporary art collections outside London. Marked by bright blue and orange panels and arranged over three floors, the gallery was converted from an old warehouse by architect James Stirling. It opened in 1988 as Tate Britain's *(see p93)* first outstation.

The Beatles

Liverpool has produced many good bands and a host of singers, comedians and entertainers before and since the 1960s. But the Beatles – John Lennon, Paul McCartney, George Harrison and Ringo Starr – were the most sensational, and locations associated with the band, however tenuous, are revered as shrines in Liverpool. Bus and walking tours trace the hallowed ground of the Salvation Army home at *Strawberry Fields* and *Penny Lane* (both outside the city centre), as well as the boys' old homes. The most visited site is Mathew Street, near Moorfields Station, where the Cavern Club first throbbed to the Mersey Beat. The original site is now a shopping arcade, but the bricks have been used to create a replica. Nearby are statues of the Beatles and *Eleanor Rigby.*

Liverpool: The Walker

Italian dish (c.1500)

FOUNDED IN 1873 by Sir Andrew Barclay Walker, a local brewer and Mayor of Liverpool, this gallery houses one of the finest art collections in the North. Paintings range from early Italian and Flemish works to Rubens, Rembrandt, Poussin, and French Impressionists such as Degas's *Woman Ironing* (c.1892–5). Among the strong collection of British artists from the 18th century onward are works by Millais and Turner and Gainsborough's *Countess of Sefton* (1769). There is 20th-century art by Hockney and Sickert, and the sculpture collection includes works by Henry Moore.

Seashells *(1874) Albert Moore paint female figures base on antique statues. Influenced by Whistler* (see p505)*, he adopted subtle shading.*

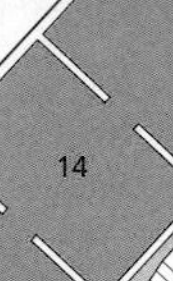

Interior at Paddington *(1951) Lucian Freud's friend Harry Diamond posed for six months for this picture, intended by the artist to "make the human being uncomfortable".*

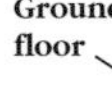

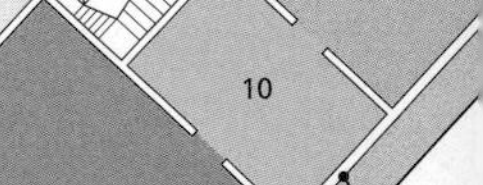

Façade was designed by H H Vale and Cornelius Sherlock.

Main entrance

GALLERY GUIDE

All the picture galleries are on the first floor. Rooms 1–2 house medieval and Renaissance paintings; Rooms 3 and 4 have 17th-century Dutch, French, Italian and Spanish art. British 18th- and 19th-century works are in Rooms 5–9. Rooms 11–15 have 20th-century and contemporary British art, and Room 10 has Impressionists and Post-Impressionists.

The Sleeping Shepherd Boy *(c.1835) The great Neo-Classic sculptor of the mid-19th century John Gibson (1790–1866), use traditional colours to give his statuary a smooth appearance.*

Visitors' Checklist

William Brown St. *0151 478 4199. Lime St. Empire Theatre or Lime St. 10am–5pm Mon–Sat; noon–5pm Sun. 23–26 Dec, 1 Jan.* www.thewalker.org.uk

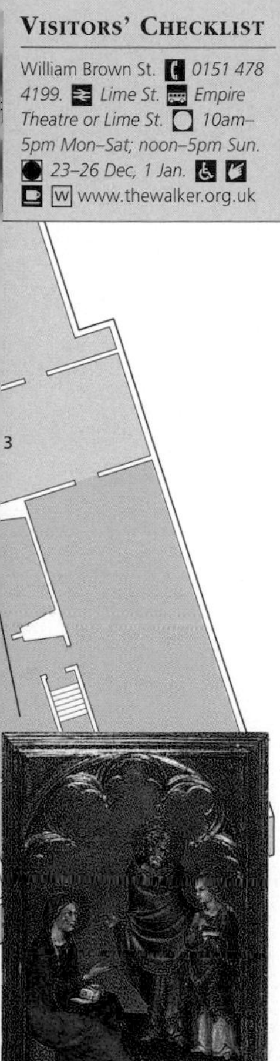

Christ Discovered in the Temple *(1342)*
Simone Martini's Holy Family conveys emotional tension through highly expressive body language.

Key to Floorplan

- 13th–17th-century European
- 18th–19th-century British, Pre-Raphaelites and Victorian
- Impressionist/Post-Impressionist
- 20th-century and contemporary British
- Sculpture gallery
- Craft and design gallery
- Special exhibitions
- Non-exhibition space

The 7th-century Kingston Brooch in Liverpool Museum

Liverpool Museum

William Brown St. *0151 478 4399. closed for renovation until spring 2005.* www.liverpoolmuseum.org.uk

Five floors of exhibits in this excellent museum include collections of Egyptian, Greek and Roman pieces, natural history, archaeology, space and time. Highlights include hands-on Exploration Zones, a Planetarium and a Discovery Centre. The museum is being extensively renovated to create a new aquarium, gallery of world cultures and Bug House.

Anglican Cathedral

St James' Mount. *0151 709 6271. daily.* www.liverpoolcathedral.org.uk

Although Gothic in style, this building was only completed in 1978. The largest Anglican cathedral in the world is a fine red sandstone edifice designed by Sir Giles Gilbert Scott. The foundation stone was laid in 1904 by Edward VII but, dogged by two world wars, building work dragged on to modified designs.

Metropolitan Cathedral of Christ the King

Mount Pleasant. *0151 709 9222. daily.* **Donation.** www.liverpoolmetrocathedral.org.uk

Liverpool's Roman Catholic cathedral rejected traditional forms in favour of a striking modern design. Early plans, drawn up by Pugin and later by Lutyens *(see p25)* in the 1930s, proved too expensive. The final version, brainchild of Sir Frederick Gibberd and built from 1962–7, is a circular building surmounted by a stylized crown of thorns 88 m (290 ft) high. It is irreverently known as "Paddy's Wigwam" by non-Catholics (a reference to Liverpool's large Irish population). Inside, the stained glass lantern, designed by John Piper and Patrick Reyntiens, floods the circular nave with diffused blueish light. There is a fine bronze of Christ by Elisabeth Frink (1930–94).

Environs: A spectacular richly timbered building dating from 1490, **Speke Hall** lies 6 miles (10 km) east of Liverpool's centre, surrounded by lovely grounds. The oldest parts of the hall enclose a cobbled courtyard dominated by two yew trees, Adam and Eve.

Birkenhead on the Wirral peninsula has been linked to Liverpool by ferry for over 800 years. Now, road and rail tunnels supplement access. The Norman Priory is still in use on Sundays, and stately Hamilton Square was designed from 1825–44 by J Gillespie Graham, one of the architects of Edinburgh's New Town.

On the Wirral side is **Port Sunlight Village** *(see p337)*, a Victorian garden village built by enlightened soap manufacturer William Hesketh Lever for his factory workers. He also founded the **Lady Lever Art Gallery** here for his collection of works of art, including Pre-Raphaelite paintings.

Speke Hall

(NT) The Walk, Speke. *0151 427 7231. Apr–Oct: Wed–Sun (pm); Nov–mid-Dec: Sat, Sun (pm); public hols. limited.*

Port Sunlight Village & Heritage Centre

95 Greendale Rd, Port Sunlight, Wirral. *0151 644 6466. Apr–Oct: 10am–4pm; Nov–Mar: 11am–4pm daily. Christmas wk.* www.portsunlightvillage.com

Entrance to the half-timbered manor house of Speke Hall

YORKSHIRE AND THE HUMBER REGION

NORTH YORKSHIRE · EAST RIDING OF YORKSHIRE

WITH THE HISTORIC CITY *of York at its heart, this is an area of picturesque moorland and valleys. To the north lie the Yorkshire Dales and the North York Moors; eastwards, a coastline of beaches; and southwards, a landscape of lush meadows.*

Yorkshire was originally made up of three separate counties, formerly known as "Ridings". Today it covers over 5,000 sq miles (12,950 sq km). The northeast section has dramatic limestone scenery that was carved by glaciers in the Ice Age. Farming was the original livelihood, and the dry-stone walls weaving up precipitous scars and fells were used to divide the land. Imposed on this were the industries of the 19th century; blackened mill chimneys and crumbling viaducts are as much a part of the scenery as the grand houses of those who profited from them.

Close to the Humber, the landscape is very different, dominated historically by the now flagging fishing industry, and geographically by lush, sprawling meadows. Its coastline is exceptional, and further north are the attractions of wide, sandy beaches and bustling harbour towns. Yet it is the contrasting landscapes that make the area so appealing, ranging from the bleak moorland of the Brontë novels to the ragged cliff coast around Whitby, and the flat expanse of Sunk Island.

The city of York, where Roman and Viking relics exist side by side, is second only to London in the number of visitors that tread its streets. Indeed the historical centre of York is the region's foremost attraction. Those in search of a real taste of Yorkshire, however, should head for the countryside. In addition to excellent touring routes, a network of rewarding walking paths range from mellow ambles along the Cleveland Way to rocky scrambles over the Pennine Way at Pen-y-Ghent.

Lobster pots on the quayside at the picturesque fishing port of Whitby

◁ **The peaceful valley of Rosedale, North York Moors**

Exploring Yorkshire and the Humber Region

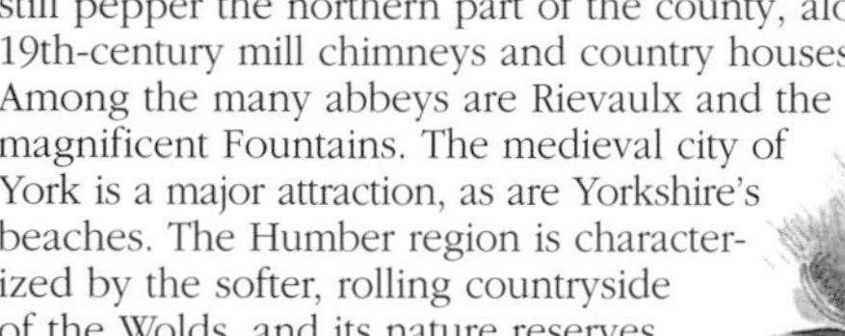

YORKSHIRE COVERS A WIDE AREA, once made up of three counties or "Ridings". Until the arrival of railways, mining and the wool industry in the 19th century, the county was a farming area. Dry-stone walls dividing fields still pepper the northern part of the county, alongside 19th-century mill chimneys and country houses. Among the many abbeys are Rievaulx and the magnificent Fountains. The medieval city of York is a major attraction, as are Yorkshire's beaches. The Humber region is characterized by the softer, rolling countryside of the Wolds, and its nature reserves attract enormous quantities of birds.

Rosedale village in the North York Moors

SIGHTS AT A GLANCE

- Bempton and Flamborough Head 26
- Beverley 27
- Bradford 35
- Burton Agnes 25
- Burton Constable 28
- Byland Abbey 10
- *Castle Howard pp384–5* 22
- Coxwold 11
- Eden Camp 23
- *Fountains Abbey pp376–7* 7
- Grimsby 31
- Halifax 38
- Harewood House 33
- Harrogate 3
- Haworth 36
- Hebden Bridge 37
- Helmsley 13
- Holderness and Spurn Head 30
- Hutton-le-Hole 16
- Kingston upon Hull 29
- Knaresborough 4
- Leeds 34
- Magna 41
- Mount Grace Priory 15
- National Coal Mining Museum 39
- Newby Hall 6
- North York Moors 17
- North York Moors Railway 18
- Nunnington Hall 12
- Rievaulx Abbey 14
- Ripley 5
- Ripon 8
- Robin Hood's Bay 20
- Scarborough 21
- Sutton Bank 9
- Whitby 19
- Wharram Percy 24
- *York pp390–95* 32
- Yorkshire Dales National Park 1
- Yorkshire Sculpture Park 40

Walks

- Malham Walk 2

SEE ALSO

- ***Where to Stay*** pp562–3
- ***Where to Eat*** pp597–9

Section of Lendal Bridge (1863) crossing the Ouse in York

Getting Around

The area is served by the A1, the M1, the M62 and the A59. Trains run to major cities such as York and Leeds, and there are train or coach (bus) links between many towns and hamlets. The Yorkshire Dales and North York Moors national parks are good for walkers, and cyclists can enjoy rides around York and the river Humber.

Yorkshire Dales National Park ❶

THE YORKSHIRE DALES is a farming landscape, formed from three principle dales, Swaledale, Wharfedale and Wensleydale, and a number of small ones, such as Deepdale. Glaciation in the Ice Age helped carve out these steep-sided valleys, and this scenery contrasts with the high moorlands. However, 12 centuries of settlement have altered the landscape in the form of cottages, castles and villages which create a delightful environment for walking. A national park since 1954, the area provides recreation while serving local community needs.

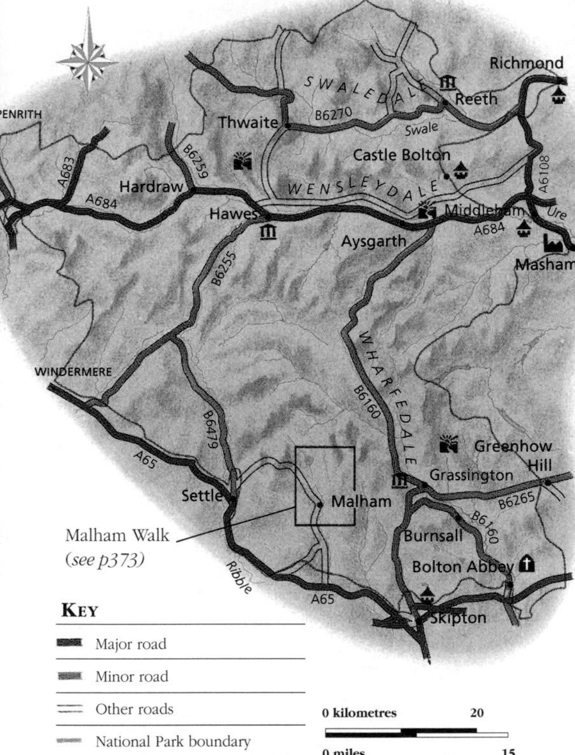

The green, rolling landscape of Deepdale, near Dent

Monk's Wynd – one of Richmond's narrow, winding streets

Exploring Swaledale

Swaledale's prosperity was founded largely on wool, and it is famous for its herd of sheep that graze on the wild higher slopes in the harshest weather. The fast-moving river Swale that gives the northernmost dale its name travels from bleak moorland down magnificent waterfalls into the richly wooded lower slopes, passing through the village of Reeth and the town of Richmond.

Richmond Castle

(EH) Tower Street. 01748 822493. daily. limited.

Swaledale's main point of entry is the medieval market town of Richmond, which has the largest cobbled marketplace in England. Alan Rufus, the Norman 1st Earl of Richmond, began building the castle in 1071, and some of the masonry on the curtain walls probably dates from that time. It has a fine Norman keep, 30 m (100 ft) high with walls 3.3 m (11 ft) thick. An 11th-century arch leads into a courtyard containing Scolland's Hall (1080), one of England's oldest buildings.

Richmond's marketplace was once the castle's outer bailey. Its quaint, narrow streets gave rise to the song, *The Lass of Richmond Hill* (1787), written by Leonard McNally for his wife, Frances I'Anson, who was brought up in Hill House, on Richmond Hill. Turner *(see p93)* depicted the town many times. The Georgian Theatre (1788), which was restored in 1962, is the only one of its age still surviving.

Swaledale Folk Museum
Reeth Green. *01748 884373.* *Easter–Oct: daily.*
Reeth, a town that became known as the centre of the lead-mining industry and helped bring prosperity to the region, houses this museum in a former Methodist Sunday school (1830). Included in it are mining and wool-making artifacts (wool from the hardy Swaledale sheep was another mainstay of the economy) and brass band memorabilia.

Buttertubs
Near Thwaite, on the B6270 Hawes road, are a series of potholes that streams fall into. These became known as the Buttertubs when farmers going to market lowered their butter into the holes to keep it cool.

Buttertubs, near Thwaite

Exploring Wensleydale

The largest of the Yorkshire dales, Wensleydale is famous for its cheese and more recently for James Herriot's books and the television series, *All Creatures Great and Small.* It is easy walking country for anyone seeking an alternative to major moorland hikes.

Dales Countryside Museum
Station Yard, Hawes. *01969 667450.* *daily.*
In a former railway goods warehouse in Hawes, capital of Upper Wensleydale, is a

Barrels at the Theakston Brewery

fascinating museum, filled with items from life and industry in the 18th- and 19th-century Upper Dales. This includes cheese- and butter-making equipment. Wensleydale cheese was created by monks at nearby Jervaulx Abbey. There is also a rope-making works a short walk away.

Hawes itself is the highest market town in England, at 259 m (850 ft) above sea level. It is a thriving centre where thousands of sheep and cattle are auctioned each summer.

Hardraw Force
at Green Dragon Inn, Hardraw.
At the tiny village of Hardraw, nearby, is England's tallest single-drop waterfall, with no outcrops to interrupt its 29 m (96 ft) fall. It became famous in Victorian times when the daredevil Blondin walked across it on a tightrope. Today, you can walk right under this fine waterfall, against the rock face, and look through the stream without getting wet.

Aysgarth Waterfalls
National Pk Centre (01969 663424) *Fri–Sun.*
An old packhorse bridge gives a clear view of the point at which the previously placid River Ure suddenly begins to plunge in foaming torrents over wide limestone shelves. Turner painted the impressive lower falls in 1817.

Theakston Brewery
Masham. *01765 680000.* *Apr–Nov: call for details.*
www.theakstons.co.uk
The pretty town of Masham is the home of Theakston brewery, creator of the potent ale Old Peculier. The history

VISITORS' CHECKLIST
N Yorkshire. *Skipton.* *01756 752774 (Wed, Fri–Mon).*
www.destinationdales.org.uk

of this local family brewery from its origin in 1827 is on display in the visitors' centre. Masham village itself has an attractive square once used for sheep fairs, surrounded by 17th- and 18th-century houses. There is a medieval church.

Bolton Castle
Castle Bolton, nr Leyburn. *01969 623981.* *daily.*
www.boltoncastle.co.uk
Situated in the village of Castle Bolton, this castle was built in 1379 by the 1st Lord Scrope, Chancellor of England. It was used as a fortress from 1568 to 1569 when Mary, Queen of Scots *(see p497)* was held prisoner here by Elizabeth I *(see pp50–51)*.

Middleham Castle
Middleham, nr Leyburn. *01969 623899.* *Jan–Mar: 10am–4pm Wed–Sun; Apr–Sep: 10am–6pm daily; Oct: 10am–5pm daily; Nov–Dec: 10am–4pm daily.* *24–26 Dec.*
Owned by Richard Neville, Earl of Warwick, it was built in 1170. The castle is better known as home to Richard III *(see p49)* when he was made Lord of the North. It was once one of the strongest fortresses in the north but became uninhabited during the 15th century, when many of its stones were used for nearby buildings. The keep provides a fine view of the landscape.

Remains of Middleham Castle, once residence of Richard III

Extensive ruins of Bolton Priory, dating from 1154

Exploring Wharfedale

This dale is characterized by gritstone moorland, contrasting with quiet market towns along meandering sections of river. Many consider Grassington a central point for exploring Wharfedale, but the showpiece villages of Burnsall, overlooked by a 506 m (1,661 ft) fell, and Buckden, 701 m (2,302 ft), near Buckden Pike, also make excellent bases.

Nearby are the Three Peaks of Whernside, 736 m (2,416 ft), Ingleborough, 724 m (2,376 ft) and Pen-y-Ghent 694 m (2,278 ft). They are known for their potholes and tough terrain, but this does not deter keen walkers from attempting to climb them all in one day. If you sign in at the Pen-y-Ghent café at Horton-in-Ribblesdale, at the centre of the Three Peaks, and complete the 20 mile (32 km) course, reaching the summit of all three peaks in less than 12 hours, you can qualify for membership of the Three Peaks of Yorkshire Club.

Burnsall

St Wilfrid's, Burnsall. *01756 720331. Apr–Oct: daily to dusk.*

Preserved in St Wilfrid's church graveyard are the original village stocks, gravestones from Viking times and a headstone carved in memory of the Dawson family by sculptor Eric Gill (1882–1940). The village has a five-arched bridge and hosts Britain's oldest fell race every August.

Upper Wharfedale Museum

The Square, Grassington. *Mar–Oct: daily (pm). limited.*

This folk museum is set in two 18th-century lead miners' cottages. Its exhibits illustrate the domestic and working history of the area, including farming and lead mining.

Bolton Priory

Bolton Abbey, Skipton. *01756 718009. daily.*

One of the most beautiful areas of Wharfedale is around the village of Bolton Abbey, set in an estate owned by the Dukes of Devonshire. While preserving its astounding beauty, its managers have incorporated over 30 miles (46 km) of footpaths, many suitable for the disabled and young families.

The ruins of Bolton Priory, established by Augustinian canons in 1154 on the site of a Saxon manor, are extensive. They include a church, chapter house, cloister and prior's lodging. These all demonstrate the wealth accumulated by the canons from the sale of wool from their flocks of sheep. The priory nave is still used as a parish church. Another attraction of the estate is the "Strid", a point where the River Wharfe surges spectacularly through a gorge, foaming yellow and gouging holes out of the rocks.

Stump Cross Caverns

Greenhow Hill, Pateley Bridge. *01756 752780 or 01423 711282. Apr–Oct: daily; Nov–Mar: Sat, Sun & public hols (call for details).*

www.stumpcrosscaverns.co.uk

These caves were formed over a period of half a million years: trickles of underground water formed intertwining passages and carved them into fantastic shapes and sizes. Sealed off in the last Ice Age, the caves were only discovered in the 1850s when lead miners sank a mine shaft into the caverns.

Skipton Castle

High St. *01756 792442. daily (Sun: pm). 25 Dec.*

www.skiptoncastle.co.uk

The market town of Skipton is still one of the largest auctioning and stockraising centres in the north. Its 11th-century castle was almost entirely rebuilt by Robert de Clifford in the 14th century. Beautiful Conduit Court was added by Henry, Lord Clifford, in Henry VIII's reign. The central yew tree was planted by Lady Anne Clifford in 1659 to mark restoration work to the castle after Civil War damage.

Conduit Court (1495) and yew tree at Skipton Castle

Malham Walk ❷

THE MALHAM AREA, shaped by glacial erosion 10,000 years ago, has one of Great Britain's most dramatic limestone landscapes. The walk from Malham village can take over four hours if you pause to enjoy the viewpoints and take a detour to Gordale Scar. Those who are short of time tend to go only as far as Malham Cove. This vast natural amphitheatre, formed by a huge geological tear, is like a giant boot-heel mark in the landscape. Above lie the deep crevices of Malham Lings, where rare flora such as hart's-tongue flourishes. Unusual plants grow in the lime-rich Malham Tarn, said to have provided inspiration for Charles Kingsley's *The Water Babies* (1863). Coot and mallard visit the tarn in summer and tufted duck in winter.

Sandpiper at Malham Tarn

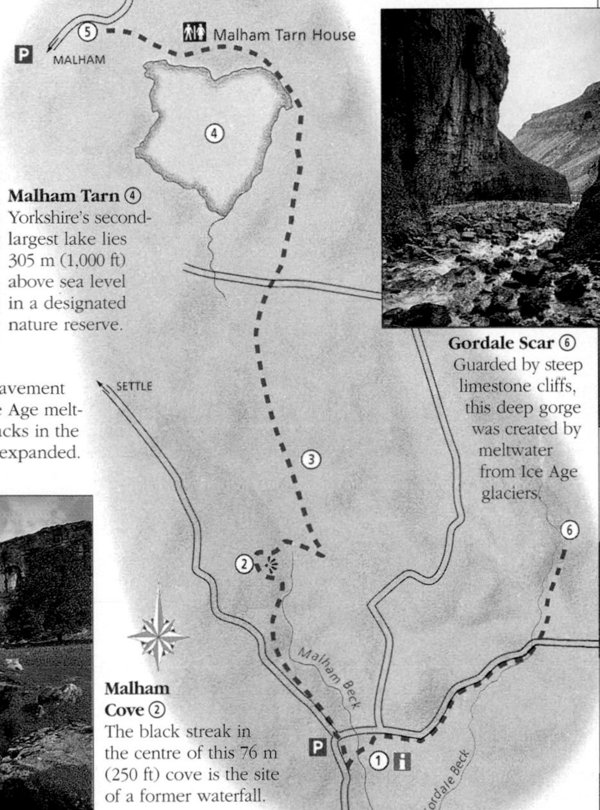

Where the path meets the road ⑤
From here, you can catch a bus back to Malham village.

Malham Tarn ④
Yorkshire's second-largest lake lies 305 m (1,000 ft) above sea level in a designated nature reserve.

Malham Lings ③
This fine limestone pavement was formed when Ice Age meltwater seeped into cracks in the rock, then froze and expanded.

Gordale Scar ⑥
Guarded by steep limestone cliffs, this deep gorge was created by meltwater from Ice Age glaciers.

Malham Cove ②
The black streak in the centre of this 76 m (250 ft) cove is the site of a former waterfall.

Malham ①
An attractive riverside village, it has an information centre with details of drives and walks.

KEY

- Walk route
- Minor road
- Viewpoint
- Parking
- Tourist information
- Toilets

0 kilometres 1

0 miles ½

TIPS FOR WALKERS

Starting point: *Malham.* ***Getting there:*** *Leave M65 at Junction 14 and take A56 to Skipton, then follow signs to Malham which is off A65.* ***Length:*** *7 miles (11 km).* ***Difficulty:*** *Malham Cove is steep but the Tarn area is flatter.*
01729 830363.

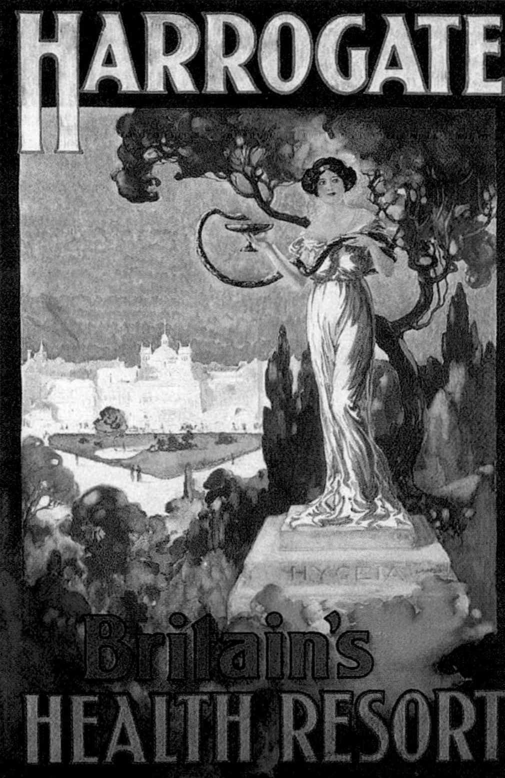

A 1920s poster advertising the spa town of Harrogate

Harrogate ❸

North Yorkshire. 69,000. *Assembly Rooms, Crescent Rd (01423 537300).* www.harrogate.gov.uk

Between 1880 and World War I, Harrogate was the north's leading spa town, with nearly 90 medicinal springs. It was ideal for aristocrats who, after a tiring London season, were able to stop for a health cure before journeying on to grouse-shooting in Scotland.

Today, Harrogate's main attractions are its spa town atmosphere, fine architecture, public gardens and its convenience as a centre for visiting North Yorkshire and the Dales.

The naturally welling spa waters may not currently be in use, but you can still go for a Turkish bath in one of the country's most attractive steam rooms. The entrance at the side of the Royal Bath Assembly Rooms (1897) is unassuming, but once inside, the century-old **Harrogate Turkish Baths** are a visual feast of tiled Victoriana.

The town's spa history is recorded in the **Royal Pump Room Museum**. At the turn of the century, the waters were thought to be rich in iron early in the day. So, between 7am and 9am the 1842 octagonal building would have been filled with rich and fashionable people drinking glasses of water. Poorer people could take water from the pump outside. Today you can sample the waters and enjoy the museum's exhibits, including a Penny Farthing bicycle.

Harrogate is also known for the rainbow-coloured flower-beds in **The Stray**, a common space to the south of the town centre, and for the ornamental **Harlow Car Gardens**, owned by the Royal Horticultural Society. Visitors can enjoy the delicious cakes at **Betty's Café Tea Rooms** *(see p598)*.

Harrogate Turkish Baths
Assembly Rooms, Crescent Rd. *01423 556746.* ***Men**: Mon, Wed & Fri: (pm); Sat. **Women**: Mon (am); Tue & Thu: (pm); Fri (am); Sun. **Mixed** (in bathing suits): Tue (am); (couples only in bathing suits): Fri (eve); Sun (eve).*

Royal Pump Room Museum
Crown Pl. *01423 556188.* *daily.* *24–26 Dec, 1 Jan.*

Betty's Café Tea Rooms
1 Parliament St. *01423 502746.* *daily.* *25–26 Dec, 1 Jan.* www.bettysandtaylors.co.uk

Harlow Car Gardens
Crag Lane. *01423 565418.* *daily* www.rhs.org.uk

Knaresborough ❹

North Yorkshire. *14,000.* *from Harrogate.* *9 Castle Courtyard, Market Place (01423 866886).* *Wed.*

Perched precipitously above the River Nidd is one of England's oldest towns, mentioned in the Domesday Book of 1086 *(see p48)*. Its historic streets – which link the church, John of Gaunt's ruined castle, and the market place with the river – are now lined with fine 18th-century houses.

Nearby is **Mother Shipton's Cave**, reputedly England's oldest tourist attraction. It first went on show in 1630 as the birthplace of Ursula Sontheil,

Mother Shipton's cave, with objects encased in limestone

The south front of Newby Hall

a famous local prophetess. Today, people can view the effect the well near her cave has on objects hung below the dripping surface. Almost any item, from umbrellas to soft toys, will become encased in limestone within a few weeks.

Mother Shipton's Cave
Prophesy House, High Bridge. 01423 864600. *Easter–Oct: daily; Nov, Feb–Easter: Sat, Sun.* *Dec, Jan.*

Ripley 5

North Yorkshire. *150.* *from Harrogate or Ripon.* *01423 537300.* www.harrogate.gov.uk

SINCE THE 1320s, when the first generation of the Ingilby family lived in an early incarnation of **Ripley Castle**, the village has been made up almost exclusively of castle employees. The influence of one 19th-century Ingilby had the most visual impact. In the 1820s, Sir William Amcotts Ingilby was so entranced by a village in Alsace Lorraine that he created a similar one in French Gothic style, complete with an *Hotel de Ville*. Present-day Ripley has a cobbled market square, and quaint cottages line the streets.

Ripley Castle, with its 15th-century gatehouse, was where Oliver Cromwell *(see p52)* stayed following the Battle of Marston Moor. The 28th generation of Ingilbys live here, and it is open for tours. The attractive grounds contain two lakes and a deer park, as well as more formal gardens.

Ripley Castle
Ripley. *01423 770152.* *Sep–May: Tue, Thu, Sat, Sun; Jun–Aug: daily.* *25 Dec.*

Newby Hall 6

Nr Ripon, North Yorkshire. *01423 322583.* *Apr–Sep: Tue–Sun and Bank Holiday Mondays.* www.newbyhall.com

NEWBY HALL stands on land once occupied by the de Nubie family in the 13th century, and has been in the hands of the current family since 1748. The central part of the present house was built in the late 17th century in the style of Sir Christopher Wren.

Visitors will find 25 acres of gardens to explore. Laid out in a series of compartmented areas off a main axis, each garden is planted to come into flower during a different season. There is also a Woodland Discovery Walk, where contemporary scultpture is displayed.

For children, there is an adventure garden with activities and a miniature railway that runs through the gardens alongside the river Ure. River boat rides are also available. Each year a number of special events are staged, including Plant Fairs, a Historic Vehicle Rally and two Craft Fairs.

Fountains Abbey 7

See pp376–7.

Ripon 8

North Yorkshire. *14,000.* *from Harrogate.* *Minster Rd (01765 604625).* *Thu.* www.riponcity.info

RIPON, A CHARMING small city, is best known for the cathedral and "the watch", which has been announced since the Middle Ages by the Wakeman. In return for protecting Ripon citizens, he would charge an annual toll of two pence per household. Today, a man still blows a horn in the Market Square each evening at 9pm, and every Thursday a handbell is rung to open the market.

The **Cathedral of St Peter and St Wilfrid** is built above a 7th-century Saxon crypt. At less than 3 m (10 ft) high and just over 2 m (7 ft) wide, it is held to be the oldest complete crypt in England. The cathedral is known for its collection of misericords *(see p329)*, which include both pagan and Old Testament examples. The architectural historian Sir Nikolaus Pevsner (1902–83) considered the cathedral's West Front the finest in England.

Ripon's **Prison and Police Museum**, housed in the 1686 "House of Correction", looks at police history and the conditions in Victorian prisons.

Prison and Police Museum
St Marygate. 01765 690799. *Apr–Oct: daily.* *Nov–Mar.* www.riponmuseums.co.uk

Ripon's Wakeman, blowing his horn in the Market Square

Fountains Abbey 7

NESTLING in the wooded valley of the River Skell are the extensive sandstone ruins of Fountains Abbey and the outstanding water garden of Studley Royal. Fountains Abbey was founded by Benedictine monks in 1132 and taken over by Cistercians three years later. By the mid-12th century it had become the wealthiest abbey in Britain, though it fell into ruin during the Dissolution *(see p50)*. In 1720, John Aislabie, the MP for Ripon and Chancellor of the Exchequer, developed the land and forest of the abbey ruins. He began work, continued by his son William, on the famous water garden, the statuary and Classical temples in the grounds. This makes a dramatic contrast to the simplicity of the abbey.

Fountains Hall
Built by Sir Stephen Proctor around 1611, with stones from the abbey ruins, its design is attributed to architect Robert Smythson. It included a great hall with a minstrels' gallery and an entrance flanked by Classical columns.

THE ABBEY

The abbey buildings were designed to reflect the Cistercians' desire for simplicity and austerity. The abbey frequently dispensed charity to the poor and the sick, as well as travellers.

The Chapel of Nine Altars *at the east end of the church was built from 1203 to 1247. It is ornate, compared to the rest of the abbey, with an 18-m (60-ft) high window complemented by another at the western end of the nave.*

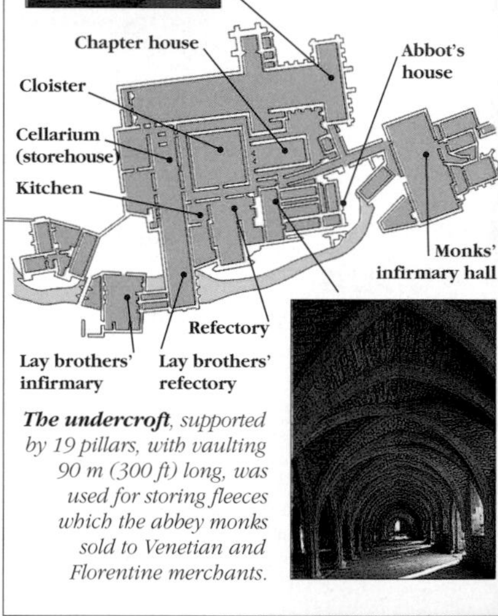

The undercroft*, supported by 19 pillars, with vaulting 90 m (300 ft) long, was used for storing fleeces which the abbey monks sold to Venetian and Florentine merchants.*

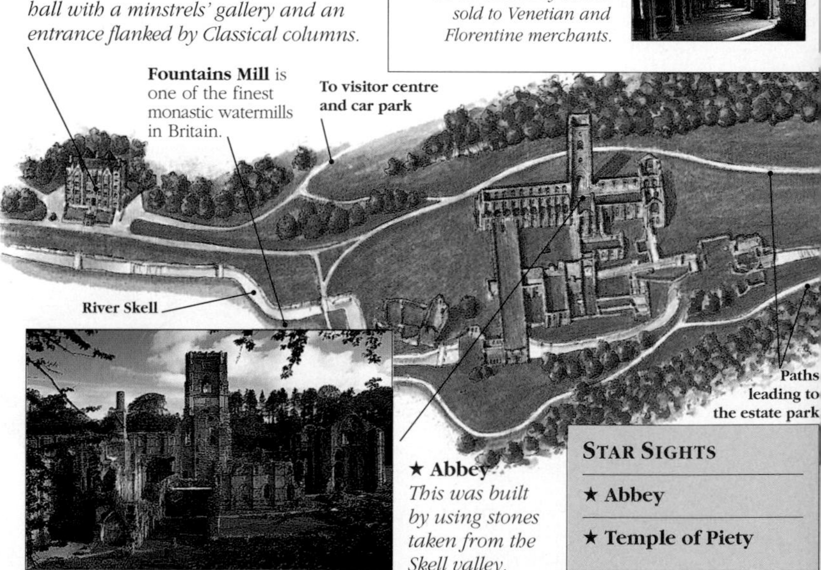

Fountains Mill is one of the finest monastic watermills in Britain.

★ Abbey
This was built by using stones taken from the Skell valley.

STAR SIGHTS

★ **Abbey**

★ **Temple of Piety**

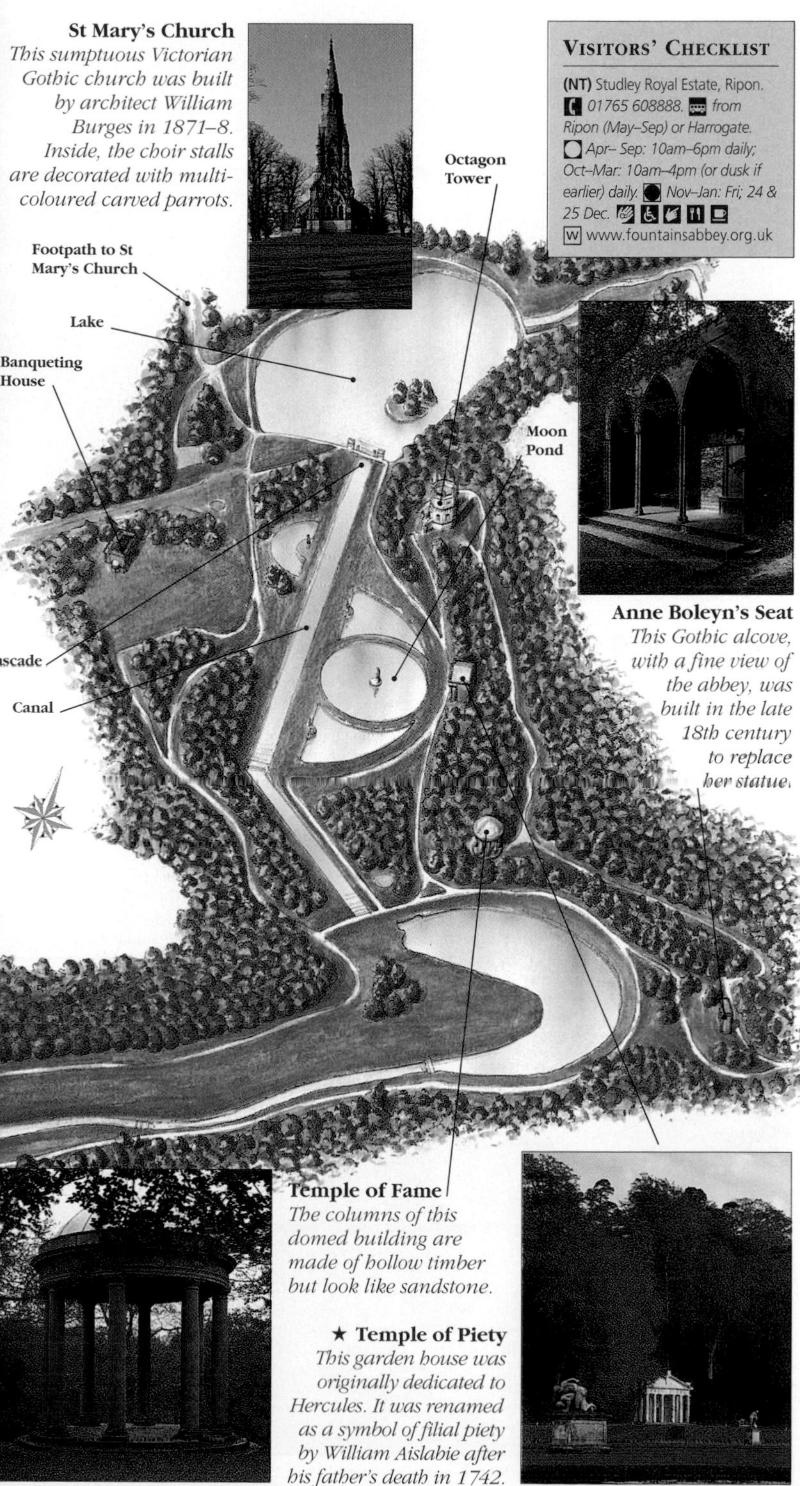

St Mary's Church
This sumptuous Victorian Gothic church was built by architect William Burges in 1871–8. Inside, the choir stalls are decorated with multi-coloured carved parrots.

Anne Boleyn's Seat
This Gothic alcove, with a fine view of the abbey, was built in the late 18th century to replace her statue.

Temple of Fame
The columns of this domed building are made of hollow timber but look like sandstone.

★ Temple of Piety
This garden house was originally dedicated to Hercules. It was renamed as a symbol of filial piety by William Aislabie after his father's death in 1742.

VISITORS' CHECKLIST

(NT) Studley Royal Estate, Ripon. *01765 608888.* *from Ripon (May–Sep) or Harrogate.* *Apr– Sep: 10am–6pm daily; Oct–Mar: 10am–4pm (or dusk if earlier) daily.* *Nov–Jan: Fri; 24 & 25 Dec.*
w www.fountainsabbey.org.uk

The 19th-century white horse, seen on one of the walks around Sutton Bank

Sutton Bank ⑨

North Yorkshire. *Thirsk.* *Sutton Bank (01845 597426).*

NOTORIOUS AMONG motorists for its 1 in 4 gradient, which climbs for about 107 m (350 ft), Sutton Bank itself is well known for its panoramic views. On a clear day you can see from the Vale of York to the Peak District *(see pp326–7).* William and his sister Dorothy Wordsworth stopped here to admire the vista in 1802, on their way to visit his future wife, Mary Hutchinson, at Brompton. Apart from Sutton Bank, where you can walk round the white horse, the area is less wild than the coastal side, and suitable for children.

Byland Abbey ⑩

(EH) Coxwold, York. *01347 868614.* *from York or Helmsley.* *Thirsk.* *Apr–Oct: daily.* *Nov–Mar.* *limited.*

THIS CISTERCIAN monastery was founded in 1177 by monks from Furness Abbey in Cumbria. It featured what was then the largest Cistercian church in Britain, 100 m (328 ft) long and 41 m (135 ft) wide across the transepts. The layout of the entire monastery, including extensive cloisters and the west front of the church, is still visible, as is the green and yellow glazed tile floor. Fine workmanship is shown in carved stone details and in the capitals, kept in the small museum.

In 1322 the Battle of Byland was fought nearby, and King Edward II *(see p40)* narrowly escaped capture when the invading Scottish army learned that he was dining with the Abbot. In his hurry to escape, the king had to leave many treasures behind, which were looted by the invading soldiers.

Shandy Hall, home of author Laurence Sterne, now a museum

Coxwold ⑪

North Yorkshire. *160.* *49 Market Place, Thirsk (01845 522755).* www.herriotcountry.com

SITUATED JUST inside the bounds of the North York Moors National Park *(see p381)*, this charming village nestles at the foot of the Howardian Hills. Its pretty houses are built from local stone, and the 15th-century church has some fine Georgian box pews and an impressive octagonal tower. But Coxwold is best known as the home of the author Laurence Sterne (1713–68), whose writings include *Tristram Shandy* and *A Sentimental Journey*.

Sterne moved here in 1760 as the church curate. He rented a rambling house that he named **Shandy Hall** after a Yorkshire expression meaning eccentric. Originally built as a timber-framed, open-halled house in the 15th century, it was modernized in the 17th century and Sterne later added a façade. His grave lies beside the porch at Coxwold's church.

Shandy Hall
Coxwold. *01347 868465.* *May–Sep: Wed & Sun (pm).* *limited.* **Gardens** *Sun–Fri.*

Nunnington Hall ⓬

(NT) Nunnington, York. *01439 748283.* *Malton, then bus or taxi.* *Apr–May, Sep–Oct: Wed–Sun (pm); Jun–Aug: Tue–Sun, public hols (pm).* *ground floor.*

SET IN ALLURING surroundings, this 17th-century manor house is a combination of architectural styles, including features from the Elizabethan and Stuart periods. Both inside and outside, a notable architectural feature is the use of the broken pediment (the upper arch is left unjoined).

Nunnington Hall was a family home until 1952, when Mrs Ronald Fife donated it to the National Trust. A striking feature is the panelling in the Oak Hall. Formerly painted, it extends over the three-arched screen to the Great Staircase. Nunnington's collection of 22 miniature furnished period rooms is popular with visitors.

A mid-16th-century tenant Dr Robert Huickes, physician to Henry VIII *(see p50–51)*, is best known for advising Elizabeth I that she should not, at the age of 32, consider having any children.

The miniature Queen Anne drawing room at Nunnington Hall

Helmsley ⓭

North Yorkshire. *2,000.* *from Malton or Scarborough.* *Town Hall, Market Place (01439 770173).* *Fri.* www.ryedale.gov.uk/tourism

THIS PRETTY MARKET TOWN is noted for its **castle**, now an imposing ruin. Built from 1186 to 1227, its main function and strength as a fortress is illustrated by the remaining keep, tower and curtain walls. The original D-shaped keep had one part blasted away in the Civil War *(see p52)*, but remains the dominant feature. The castle was so impregnable that there were few attempts to force entry. However, in 1644, after holding out for a three-month seige against Sir Thomas Fairfax, the Parliamentary general, the castle was finally taken.

Helmsley church tower

Rievaulx Abbey ⓮

(EH) Nr Helmsley, North Yorkshire. *01439 798228.* *Thirsk or Scarborough, then bus or taxi.* *daily.* *limited.*

RIEVAULX IS PERHAPS the finest abbey in the area, partly due to its dramatic setting in the steep wooded valley of the River Rye and partly to its extensive remains. It is almost entirely surrounded by steep banks that form natural barriers from the outside world. Monks of the French Cistercian order from Clairvaux founded this, their first major monastery in Britain, in 1132. The main buildings, which include the Cistercian nave, were finished before 1200. The layout of the chapel, kitchens and infirmary give an idea of monastic life.

Rievaulx Abbey, painted by Thomas Girtin (1775–1802)

Mount Grace Priory ruins, with farm and mansion in foreground

Mount Grace Priory 15

(EH/NT) Northallerton, North Yorkshire. *01609 883494.* Northallerton then bus. *Apr–Oct: daily; Nov–Mar: Wed–Sun.* ground floor, shop & grounds.

FOUNDED BY Thomas Holland, Duke of Surrey, and in use from 1398 until 1539, this is the best-preserved Carthusian or charterhouse monastery *(see pp338–9)* in England. The monks, just 20 of them at the beginning, took a vow of silence and lived in solitary cells, each with his own garden and an angled hatch so that he would not even see the person serving his food. They only met at matins, vespers and feast-day services. Attempts at escape by those who could not endure the rigour of the rules were punished by imprisonment.

The ruins of the priory include the former prison, gatehouse and outer court, barns, guesthouses, cells and the church. The 14th-century church, the best-preserved section of the site, is particularly small, as it was only rarely used by the community. A cell has been reconstructed to give an impression of monastic life.

Hutton-le-Hole 16

North Yorkshire. *400.* *Malton then bus.* *The Ropery, Pickering (01751 473791).*
www.ryedale.gov.uk

THIS PICTURESQUE VILLAGE is characterized by a spacious green, grazed by roaming sheep, and surrounded by houses, an inn and shops. Lengths of white wood, replacing stone bridges, span the moorland stream. Its cottages, some with date panels over the doors, are made from limestone, with red pantiled roofs. In the village centre is the excellent **Ryedale Folk Museum**, which records the lifestyle of an agricultural community using Romano-British artifacts and reconstructed buildings.

Ryedale Folk Museum
Hutton-le-Hole. *01751 417367.* *mid-Mar–mid-Nov: daily.*

Wheelwright's workshop at Ryedale Folk Museum

North York Moors Tour 17

See p381.

North Yorkshire Moors Railway 18

Pickering & Grosmont, North Yorkshire. *01751 472580.* *Apr–Oct: daily, Nov–Mar: some weekends (call for details).* www.northyorkshiremoorsrailway.com

DESIGNED in 1831 by George Stephenson as a route along the North York Moors and links with the Esk Valley, Pickering and Whitby *(see p382)*, this railway was considered an engineering miracle. Due to budget constraints, Stephenson was not able to build a tunnel, so had to lay the route down the mile-long (1.5 km) incline between Beck Hole and Goathland. The area around Fen Bog had to be stabilized using timber, heather brushwood and fleeces so that a causeway could be built over it. A horse was used to pull a coach along the track at 10 miles (16 km) per hour. After horsepower came steam, and for almost 130 years the railway linked Whitby to the rest of the country. In the early 1960s the line was closed but in 1967, a group of locals began a campaign to relaunch it, and in 1973 it was officially reopened. Today, the 18 mile (29 km) line runs from Pickering via Levisham, Newtondale Halt and Goathland before stopping at Grosmont, through the scenic heart of the North York Moors.

North York Moors ⓱

The area between Cleveland, the Vale of York and the Vale of Pickering is known as the North York Moors National Park. The landscape consists of bleakly beautiful moors interspersed with lush green valleys. Agriculture is still the main source of income here as it has been for centuries, and until the advent of coal, the communities' local source of fuel was turf. In the 19th century, the geology of the area created extractive industries which included ironstone, lime, coal and building stone.

Farndale
During springtime, this area is famous for the beauty and profusion of its daffodils.

Mallyan Spout
A footpath leads to this waterfall from Goathland.

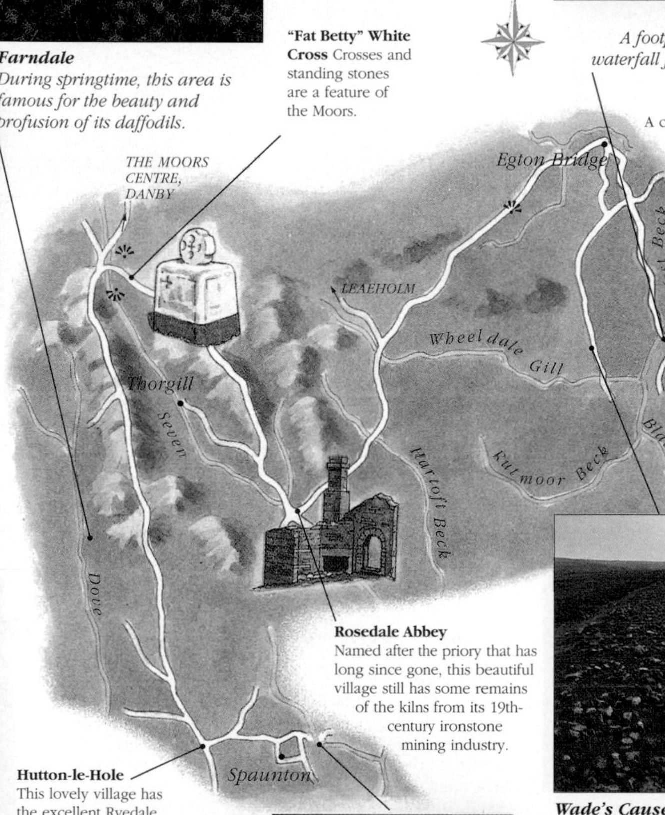

"Fat Betty" White Cross Crosses and standing stones are a feature of the Moors.

Goathland
A centre for forest and moorland walks, it has 19th-century houses and good accommodation.

Rosedale Abbey
Named after the priory that has long since gone, this beautiful village still has some remains of the kilns from its 19th-century ironstone mining industry.

Hutton-le-Hole
This lovely village has the excellent Ryedale Folk Museum.

THE MOORS CENTRE, DANBY
Egton Bridge
WHITBY
LEAEHOLM
West Beck
Wheeldale Gill
Thorgill
Seven
Hartoft Beck
Rutmoor Beck
Blawarth Beck
Dove
Spaunton

Wade's Causeway
Often called the Roman Road, its origins and destination are unknown. Long considered Roman in date, this is now less certain, although it may date from towards the end of the Roman occupation.

Lastingham
Lastingham's church, dating from 1078, has a Norman crypt with stone carving.

0 kilometres 2
0 miles 2

VISITORS' CHECKLIST

North Yorkshire. *Pickering.* *Pickering.* **Moorsbus** *01845 597426.* *Eastgate, Pickering (01751 473791); Moors Centre (01287 660540).* www.northyorkmoors-npa.gov.uk

Whitby 19

WHITBY'S KNOWN HISTORY dates back to the 7th century, when a Saxon monastery was founded on the site of today's famous 13th-century abbey ruins. In the 18th and early 19th centuries it became an industrial port and shipbuilding town, as well as a whaling centre. In the Victorian era, the red-roofed cottages at the foot of the east cliff were filled with workshops crafting jet into jewellery and ornaments. Today, the tourist shops that have replaced them sell antique-crafted examples of the distinctive black gem.

Jet comb (c.1870)

VISITORS' CHECKLIST

North Yorkshire. *13,500.* *Teeside, 50 miles (80 km) NW Whitby.* *Station Sq.* *Langborne Rd (01947 602674).* *Tue, Sat.* *Whitby Festival: Jun; Angling Festival: Jul; Lifeboat Day: Jul or Aug; Folk Week: 17–23 Aug; Whitby Regatta: Aug.* www.discoveryorkshirecoast.com

Exploring Whitby

Whitby is divided into two by the estuary of the River Esk. The Old Town, with its pretty cobbled streets and pastel-hued houses, huddles round the harbour. High above it is St Mary's Church with a wood interior reputedly fitted by ships' carpenters. The ruins of the 13th-century Whitby Abbey, nearby, are still used as a landmark by mariners. From them you get a fine view over the still-busy harbour, strewn with colourful nets. A pleasant place for a stroll, the harbour is overlooked by an imposing bronze clifftop statue of the explorer Captain James Cook (1728–79), who was apprenticed as a teenager to a Whitby shipping firm.

Medieval arches above the nave of Whitby Abbey

Whitby Abbey

(EH) Abbey Lane. *01947 603568.* *daily.*

The monastery that Abbess Hilda founded in 657 was sacked by Vikings in 870. In the 11th century it was rebuilt as a Benedictine Abbey. The present ruins date mainly from the 13th-century. A visitor centre has recently been added.

Lobster pots lining the quayside of Whitby's quaint harbour

St Mary's Parish Church

East Cliff. *01947 603421.* *daily.*

Stuart and Georgian alterations to this Norman church have left a mixture of twisted wood columns and maze-like 18th-century box pews. The 1778 triple-decker pulpit has rather avant-garde decor – ear-trumpets used by a Victorian rector's deaf wife.

Captain Cook Memorial Museum

Grape Lane. *01947 601900.* *Mar: Sat & Sun; Apr–Oct: daily.* www.cookmuseumwhitby.co.uk

The young James Cook slept in the attic of this 17th-century harbourside house when he was apprenticed nearby. The museum has displays of period furniture in the style described in the inventories of the house, and watercolours by artists who travelled on his voyages.

Whitby Museum and Pannett Art Gallery

Pannett Park. *01947 602908.* *May–Sep: daily (Sun: pm); Oct–Apr: Tue–Sun (Sun: pm).* *Sun: am; 24 Dec–2 Jan.* *museum.* *limited.*

The Pannett park grounds, museum and gallery were a gift of Whitby solicitor, Robert Pannett (1834–1920), to house his art collection. Among the museum's treasures are objects illustrating local history, such as jet jewellery, and Captain Cook artifacts.

Museum of Victorian Whitby

Entrance through Venus Trading shop, Sandgate. *01947 601221.* *daily.*

Amongst the exhibits on Victorian life in Whitby is the animated wheel-house of a whaling ship.

Caedmon's Cross

East Cliff.

On the path side of the abbey's clifftop graveyard is the cross of Caedmon, an illiterate labourer who worked at the abbey in the 7th century. He had a vision that inspired him to compose cantos of Anglo-Saxon religious verse still sung today.

Cross of Caedmon (1898)

Robin Hood's Bay 20

North Yorkshire. 1,400. Whitby. Langbourne Rd, Whitby (01947 602674). www.discoveryorkshirecoast.com

LEGEND HAS IT that Robin Hood *(see p324)* kept his boats here in case he needed to make a quick getaway. The village has a history as a smugglers' haven, and many houses have ingenious hiding places for contraband. The cobbled main street is so steep that visitors need to leave their vehicles in the car park. In the village centre, attractive, narrow streets full of colour-washed stone cottages huddle around a quaint quay. There is a rocky beach with rock pools for children to play in. At low tide, the pleasant walk south to Boggle Hole takes 15 minutes, but you need to keep an eye on the tides.

Cobbled alley in the Bay Town area of Robin Hood's Bay

The fishing port and town of Scarborough nestling round the harbour

Scarborough 21

North Yorkshire. 54,000. Pavilion House, Valley Bridge Rd (01723 373333). Mon–Sat. www.discoveryorkshirecoast.com

THE HISTORY OF Scarborough as a resort can be traced back to 1626, when it became known as a spa. In the Industrial Revolution *(see pp336–7)* it was nicknamed "the Queen of the Watering Places", but the post-World War II trend for holidays abroad has meant fewer visitors. The town has two beaches; the South Bay amusement arcades contrast with the quieter North Bay.

Playwright Alan Ayckbourn premiers his work at the Stephen Joseph theatre, and Anne Brontë *(see p398)* is buried in St Mary's Church.

Bronze and Iron Age relics have been found on the site of **Scarborough Castle**, and **Wood End Museum** exhibits local geology and history. The **Rotunda** (1828–9) was one of Britain's first purpose-built museums. Works by local artist Atkinson Grimshaw (1836–93) hang in **Scarborough Art Gallery**. The **Sea-Life and Marine Sanctuary**'s baby seals are its main attraction.

Scarborough Castle
(EH) Castle Rd. 01723 372451. daily. 1 Jan, 24–26 Dec.

Wood End Museum
The Crescent. 01723 367326. Jun–Sep: Tue–Sun; Oct–May: Wed, Sat, Sun & public hols. 25, 26 Dec, 1 Jan.

Rotunda Museum
Vernon Rd. 01723 374839. Jun–Sep: Tue–Sun; Oct–May: Tue, Sat, Sun & public hols. 25, 26 Dec, 1 Jan.

Scarborough Art Gallery
The Crescent. 01723 374753. Jun–Sep: Tue–Sun; Oct–May: Thu, Fri, Sat & public hols. 25, 26 Dec, 1 Jan.

Sea-Life and Marine Sanctuary
Scalby Mills Rd. 01723 376125. daily. 25 Dec. www.sealife.co.uk

THE GROWING POPULARITY OF SWIMMING

During the 18th century, sea-bathing came to be regarded as a healthy pastime, and from 1735 onwards men and women, on separate stretches of the coast, could be taken out into the sea in bathing huts, or "machines". In the 18th century, bathing was segregated although nudity was permitted. The Victorians brought in fully clothed bathing, and 19th-century workers from Britain's industrial heartlands used the new steam trains to visit the coast for their holidays. At this time, British seaside resorts such as Blackpool *(see p359)* and Scarborough expanded to meet the new demand.

A Victorian bathing hut on wheels

Castle Howard 22

Pillar detail in the Great Hall, carved by Samuel Carpenter

STILL OWNED and lived in by the Howard family, Castle Howard was created by Charles, 3rd Earl of Carlisle. In 1699, he commissioned Sir John Vanbrugh, a man of dramatic ideas but with no previous architectural experience, to design a palace for him. Vanbrugh's grand designs of 1699 were put into practice by architect Nicholas Hawksmoor *(see p24)* and the main body of the house was completed by 1712. The West Wing was built in 1753–9, using a design by Thomas Robinson, son-in-law of the 3rd Earl. Castle Howard was used as the location for the television version of Evelyn Waugh's novel *Brideshead Revisited* (1945).

Temple of the Four Winds
Vanbrugh's last work, designed in 1724, has a dome and four Ionic porticoes. Situated in the grounds at the end of the terrace, it is typical of an 18th-century "landscape building".

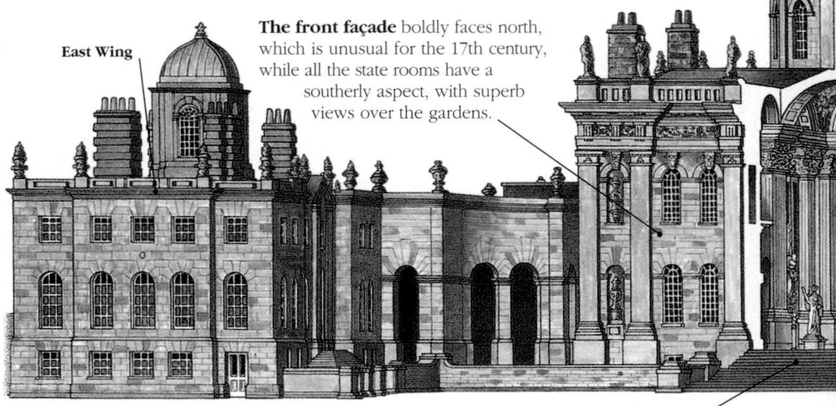

The front façade boldly faces north, which is unusual for the 17th century, while all the state rooms have a southerly aspect, with superb views over the gardens.

★ Great Hall
Rising 20 m (66 ft), from its 515 sq m (5,500 sq ft) floor to the dome, the Great Hall has columns by Samuel Carpenter (1660-1713), wall paintings by Pellegrini and a circular gallery.

SIR JOHN VANBRUGH

Vanbrugh (1664–1726) trained as a soldier, but became better known as a playwright, architect and member of the Whig nobility. He collaborated with Hawksmoor over the design of Blenheim Palace, but his bold architectural vision, later greatly admired, was mocked by the establishment. He died while working on the garden buildings and grounds of Castle Howard.

Chapel Stained Glass
Admiral Edward Howard ered the chapel in 1870–75. e windows were designed by Edward Burne-Jones and ade by William Morris & Co.

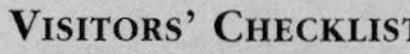

VISITORS' CHECKLIST

A64 from York, Yorkshire. *01653 648333.* *York then bus, or Malton then taxi.* **House** *Feb–Nov: 11am–4pm daily.* **Grounds** *10am–6pm daily.*

Bust of the 7th Earl
J H Foley sculpted this portrait bust, which stands at the top of the Grand Staircase in the West Wing, in 1870.

★ Long Gallery
The Howard lineage is illustrated here by a large number of portraits, including works by Reynolds and Pannini.

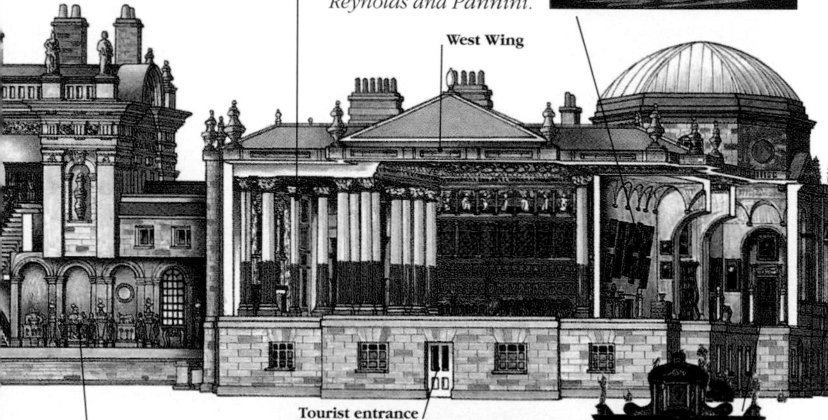

Antique Passage
Antiquities collected in the 18th and 19th centuries by the various earls of Carlisle are on display here. The plethora of mythical figures and gods reflects contemporary interest in Classical civilizations.

Museum Room
Furniture here includes Regency chairs, Persian rugs and this 17th-century cabinet.

STAR SIGHTS

- ★ **Great Hall**
- ★ **Long Gallery**

Eden Camp ㉓

Malton, North Yorkshire. *01653 697777.* *Malton then taxi.* *mid-Jan–late Dec: daily.* www.edencamp.co.uk

THIS IS AN UNUSUAL, award-winning theme museum which pays tribute to the British people during World War II. Italian and German prisoners of war were kept at Eden Camp between 1939 and 1948. Today, some original huts built by Italian prisoners in 1942 are used as a museum, with period tableaux and a soundtrack. Each hut adopts a theme to take the visitor through civilian life in wartime, from Chamberlain's radio announcement of the outbreak of hostilities to the coming of peace. Visitors, including schoolchildren and nostalgic veterans, can see the Doodlebug V-1 bomb which crashed outside the Officers' Mess, take tea in the canteen or experience a night in the Blitz. A tour can last for several hours.

British and American flags by the sign for Eden Camp

Wharram Percy ㉔

(EH) North Yorkshire. *01904 601901 (English Heritage).* *Malton, then taxi.* *daily.*

THIS IS ONE of England's most important medieval village sites. Recent excavations have unearthed evidence of a 30-household community, with two manors, and the remains of a medieval church. There is also a millpond which has beautiful wild flowers in late spring. Wharram Percy is set in a pretty valley, signposted off the B1248 from Burdale, in the heart of the green, rolling Wolds. It is about 20 minutes' walk from the car park, and makes an ideal picnic stop.

Alabaster carving on the chimney-piece at Burton Agnes

Burton Agnes ㉕

On A614, nr Driffield, East Yorkshire. *01262 490324.* *Driffield, then bus.* *Apr–Oct: daily.* *limited in house.* www.burton-agnes.com

OF ALL the grand houses in this area, Burton Agnes Hall is a firm favourite. This is partly because the attractive, red-brick Elizabethan mansion has such a homely atmosphere. One of the first portraits you see in the Small Hall is of Anne Griffith, whose father, Sir Henry, built the house. There is a monument to him in the local church.

Burton Agnes has remained in the hands of the original family and has changed little since it was built, between 1598 and 1610. You enter it by the turreted gatehouse, and the entrance hall has a fine Elizabethan alabaster chimney piece. The massive oak staircase is an impressive example of Elizabethan woodcarving.

In the library is a collection of Impressionist and Post-Impressionist art, pleasantly out of character with the rest of the house, including works by André Derain, Renoir and Augustus John. The extensive grounds include a purpose-built play area for children.

Bempton and Flamborough Head ㉖

East Yorkshire. *4,300.* *Bempton.* *Bridlington.* *25 Prince St, Bridlington (01262 673474).* www.eastriding.gov.uk

BEMPTON, which consists of 5 miles (8 km) of steep chalk cliffs between Speeton and Flamborough Head, is the largest seabird-breeding colony in England, and is famous for its puffins. The ledges and fissures provide ideal nest-sites for more

Nesting gannet on the chalk cliffs at Bempton

than 100,000 pairs of birds. Today, eight different species, including skinny black shags and kittiwakes, thrive on the Grade 1 listed *(see p617)* Bempton cliffs. Bempton is the only mainland site for goose-sized gannets, well known for their dramatic fishing techniques. May, June and July are the best bird-watching months.

The spectacular cliffs are best seen from the north side of the Flamborough Head peninsula.

Beverley ㉗

East Riding of Yorkshire. 30,000.
34 Butcher Row (01482 867430).
Sat. www.inbeverley.co.uk

THE HISTORY of Beverley dates back to the 8th century, when Old Beverley served as a retreat for John, later Bishop of York, who was canonized for his healing powers. Over the centuries Beverley grew as a medieval sanctuary town. Like York, it is an attractive combination of both medieval and Georgian buildings.

The best way to enter Beverley is through the last of five town gates, the castellated North Bar that allowed the medieval inhabitants in and out of the town's surrounding walls. It was rebuilt in 1409–10.

The skyline is dominated by the twin towers of the magnificent **minster**. This was co-founded in 937 by Athelstan, King of Wessex, in place of the church that John of Beverley had chosen as his final resting place in 721. The decorated nave is the earliest surviving building work which dates back to the early 1300s. It is particularly famous for its 16th-century choir stalls and 68 misericords *(see p329)*.

The minster contains many early detailed stone carvings, including a set of four from about 1308 that illustrate figures with ailments such as toothache and lumbago. On the north side of the altar is the richly carved 14th-century Gothic Percy tomb, thought to be that of Lady Idoine Percy, who died in 1365. Also on the north side is the Fridstol, or Peace Chair, said to date from 924-39, the time of Athelstan. Anyone who sat on it would then be granted 30 days' sanctuary.

Minstrel Pillar in St Mary's Church

Within the North Bar, **St Mary's Church** has a 13th-century chancel and houses Britain's largest number of medieval stone carvings of musical instruments. The brightly painted 16th-century Minstrel Pillar is particularly notable. Painted on the panelled chancel ceiling are portraits of monarchs after 1445. On the richly sculpted doorway of St Michael's Chapel is the grinning pilgrim rabbit said to have inspired Lewis Carroll's White Rabbit in *Alice in Wonderland*.

The inspiration for Lewis Carroll's White Rabbit, St Mary's Church

Southeast of the minster, the **Museum of Army Transport** contains over 100 exhibits of army vehicles. A Saturday market takes place near here.

Museum of Army Transport

Flemingate. 01482 860445.
daily. www.museum-of-army-transport.co.uk

Beverley Minster, one of Europe's finest examples of Gothic architecture

Burton Constable 28

Nr Hull, East Yorkshire. 01964 562400. Hull then taxi. Easter–Oct: Sat–Thu. www.burtonconstable.com

The constable family have been leading landowners since the 13th century, and have lived at Burton Constable since work began on it in 1570. It is an Elizabethan house, altered in the 18th century by Thomas Lightholer, Thomas Atkinson and James Wyatt. Today, its 30 rooms include Georgian and Victorian interiors. It has a fine collection of Chippendale furniture and family portraits dating from the 16th century. Most of the collections of prints, textiles and drawings belong to Leeds City Art Galleries. The family still lives in the south wing.

Painting of Burton Constable (c.1690) by an anonymous artist

The Princes' Dock in Kingston upon Hull's restored docks area

Kingston upon Hull 29

Kingston upon Hull. 270,000. Paragon St. (01482 223559). Tue, Fri, Sat. www.hullcc.gov.uk

There is a lot more to Hull than the heritage of a thriving fishing industry. The restored town centre docks are attractive, and Hull's Old Town, laid out in medieval times, is all cobbled, winding streets and quaintly askew red-brick houses. You can follow the "Seven Seas" Fish Trail, a path of inlaid metal fishes on the city's pavements that illustrates the many different varieties that have been landed in Hull, from anchovy to shark.

In Victoria Square is the **Maritime Museum**. Built in 1871 as the offices of the Hull Dock Company, it traces the city's maritime history. Among its exhibits are an ornate whalebone and vertebrae bench and a display of complicated rope knots such as the Eye Splice and the Midshipman's Hitch.

An imposing Elizabethan building, **Hands on History**, explores Hull's story through a collection of some of its families' artifacts.

In the heart of the Old Town, on a street that often reeks of salty sea air, is the **William Wilberforce House**, one of the surviving examples of the High Street's brick merchants' dwellings. Its first-floor oak-panelled rooms date from the 17th century, but most of the house is dedicated to the Wilberforce family, whose connection began in 1732 with the grandfather of the abolitionist. Among the more gruesome museum exhibits are iron ankle fetters for slaves. A fine Victorian doll collection strikes a lighter note.

Nearby is the **Streetlife Transport Museum**, Hull's most popular and noisiest museum, loved by children. It features Britain's oldest tramcar, a simulated mailcoach ride, amd breathtaking period street scenes.

Maritime Museum
Queen Victoria Sq. 01482 613903. daily (Sun: pm). www.hullcc.gov.uk/museums

Hands on History
South Churchside. 01482 613952. daily (Sun: pm). 23–27 Dec, 1 Jan, Good Fri.

William Wilberforce (1758–1833)

William Wilberforce, born in Hull to a merchant family, was a natural orator. After studying Classics at Cambridge, he entered politics and in 1784 gave one of his first public addresses in York. The audience was captivated, and Wilberforce realized the potential of his powers of persuasion. From 1785 onwards, adopted by the Pitt government as spokesman for the abolition of slavery, he conducted a determined and conscientious campaign. But his speeches won him enemies, and in 1792, threats from a slave-importer meant that he needed a constant armed guard. In 1807 his bill to abolish the lucrative slave trade became law.

A 19th-century engraving of Wilberforce by J Jenkins

William Wilberforce House

High St, Hull. *01482 613921.* *daily (Sun: pm).* *24–27 Dec, 1 Jan, Good Fri.* *limited.*

Streetlife Transport Museum

High St, Hull. *01482 613902.* *Mon–Sat, Sun pm.* *1 Jan, Good Fri, 25–26 Dec.*

Holderness and Spurn Head 30

East Riding of Yorkshire. *Hull (Paragon St) then bus.* *120 Newbegin, Hornsea (01964 536404).*

THIS CURIOUS FLAT AREA east of Hull, with straight roads and delicately waving fields of oats and barley, in many ways resembles Holland, except that its mills are derelict. Beaches stretch for 30 miles (46 km) along the coastline. The main resort towns are **Withernsea** and **Hornsea**, well known for its pottery.

The Holderness landscape only exists because of erosion higher up the coast. The sea continues to wash down tiny bits of rock which accumulate. Around 1560, this began to form a sandbank, and by 1669 it had became large enough to be colonized as Sonke Sand. The last bits of silting mud and debris joined the island to the mainland as recently as the 1830s. Today, you can drive through the eerie, lush wilderness of Sunk Island on the way east to Spurn Head. This is located at the tip of the Spurn Peninsula, a 3.5 mile (6 km) spit of land that has also built up as the result of coastal erosion elsewhere. Flora, fauna and birdlife have been protected here by the Yorkshire Wildlife Trust since 1960. Walking here gives the eerie feeling that the land could be eroded from under your feet at any time. A surprise discovery at the end of Spurn Head is a tiny community of pilots and lifeboat crew, constantly on call to guide ships into Hull harbour, or help cope with disasters.

Fishing boat at Grimsby's National Fishing Heritage Centre

Grimsby 31

NE Lincs. *92,000.* *42–43 Alexandra Rd, Cleethorpes (01472 323111).* www.nelincs.gov.uk

PERCHED at the mouth of the River Humber, Grimsby was founded in the Middle Ages by a Danish fisherman by the name of Grim, and rose to prominence in the 19th century as one of the world's largest fishing ports. Its first dock was opened in 1800 and, with the arrival of the railways, the town secured the means of transporting its catch all over the country. Even though the traditional fishing industry had declined by the 1970s, dock area redevelopment has ensured that Grimsby's unique heritage is retained.

This is best demonstrated by the award-winning **National Fishing Heritage Centre**, a museum that recreates the industry in its 1950s heyday, capturing the atmosphere of the period. Visitors sign on as crew members on a trawler and, by means of a variety of vivid interactive displays, travel from the back streets of Grimsby to the Arctic fishing grounds. On the way, they can experience the roll of the ship, the smell of the fish and the heat of the engine. The tour can be finished off with a guided viewing of the restored 1950s trawler, the *Ross Tiger*.

Other attractions in Grimsby include an International Jazz Festival every September, a restored Victorian shopping street called Abbeygate, a market, a wide selection of restaurants, and the nearby seaside resorts of Cleethorpes, Mablethorpe and Skegness.

National Fishing Heritage Centre

Heritage Sq, Alexandra Dock. *01472 323345.* *Easter–Oct: daily.*

Isolated lighthouse at Spurn Head, at the tip of Spurn Peninsula

Street-by-Street: York ㉜

Monk Bar coat of arms

The city of York has retained so much of its medieval structure that walking into its centre is like entering a living museum. Many of the ancient timbered houses, perched on narrow, winding streets, such as the Shambles, are protected by a conservation order. Cars are banned from the centre, so there are always student bikes bouncing over cobbled streets. Its strategic position led to its development as a railway centre in the 19th century.

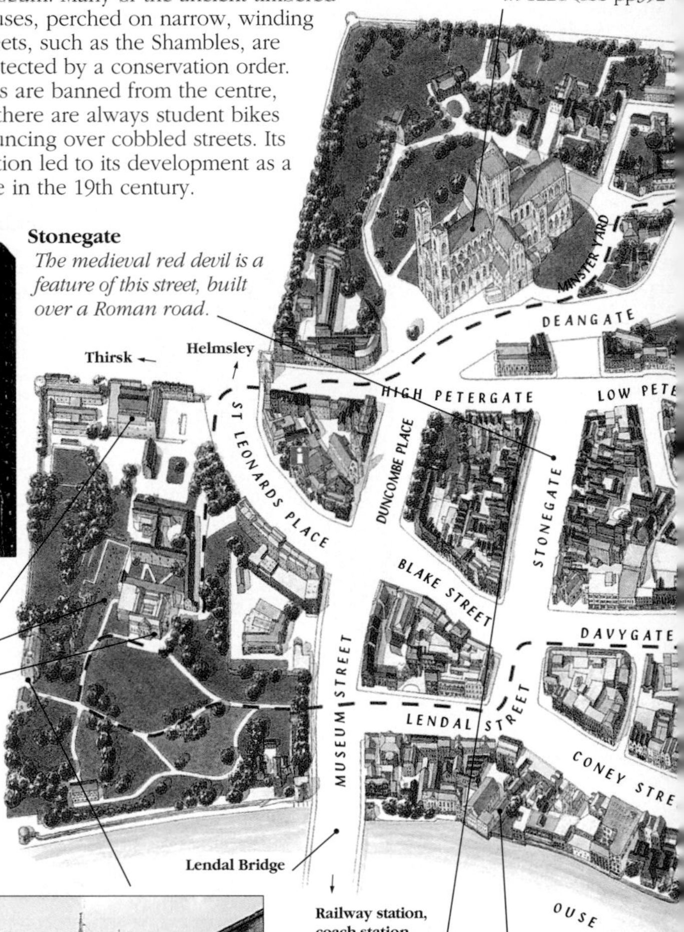

★ York Minster
England's largest me... eval church was beg... in 1220 (see pp392–

Stonegate
The medieval red devil is a feature of this street, built over a Roman road.

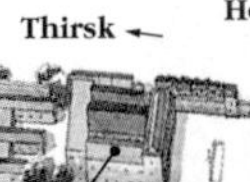

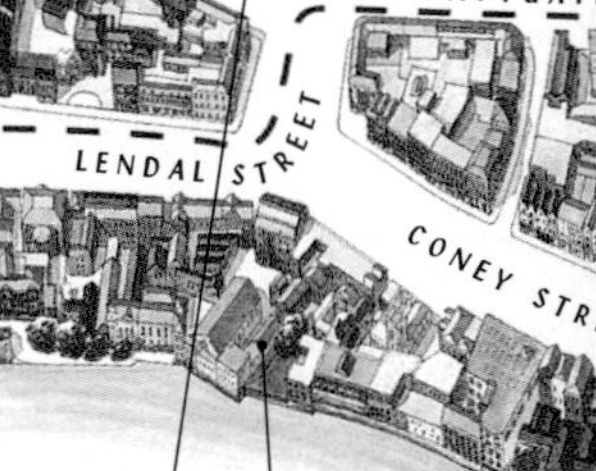

York City Art Gallery

St Mary's Abbey

Yorkshire Museum contains a fine collection of fossils, discovered at Whitby in the 19th century.

Lendal Bridge

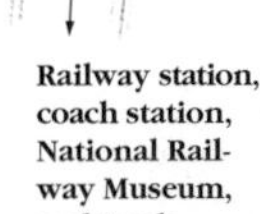

Railway station, coach station, National Railway Museum, and Leeds

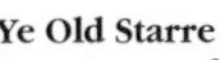

Ye Old Starre Inne is one of the oldest pubs in York.

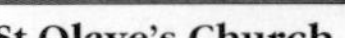

St Olave's Church
The 11th-century church, next to the gatehouse of St Mary's Abbey (see p338), *was founded by the Earl of Northumbria in memory of St Olaf, King of Norway. To the left is the Chapel of St Mary on the Walls.*

Guildhall
This two-headed medieval roof boss is on the 15th-century Guildhall, situated beside the River Ouse and restored after bomb damage during World War II.

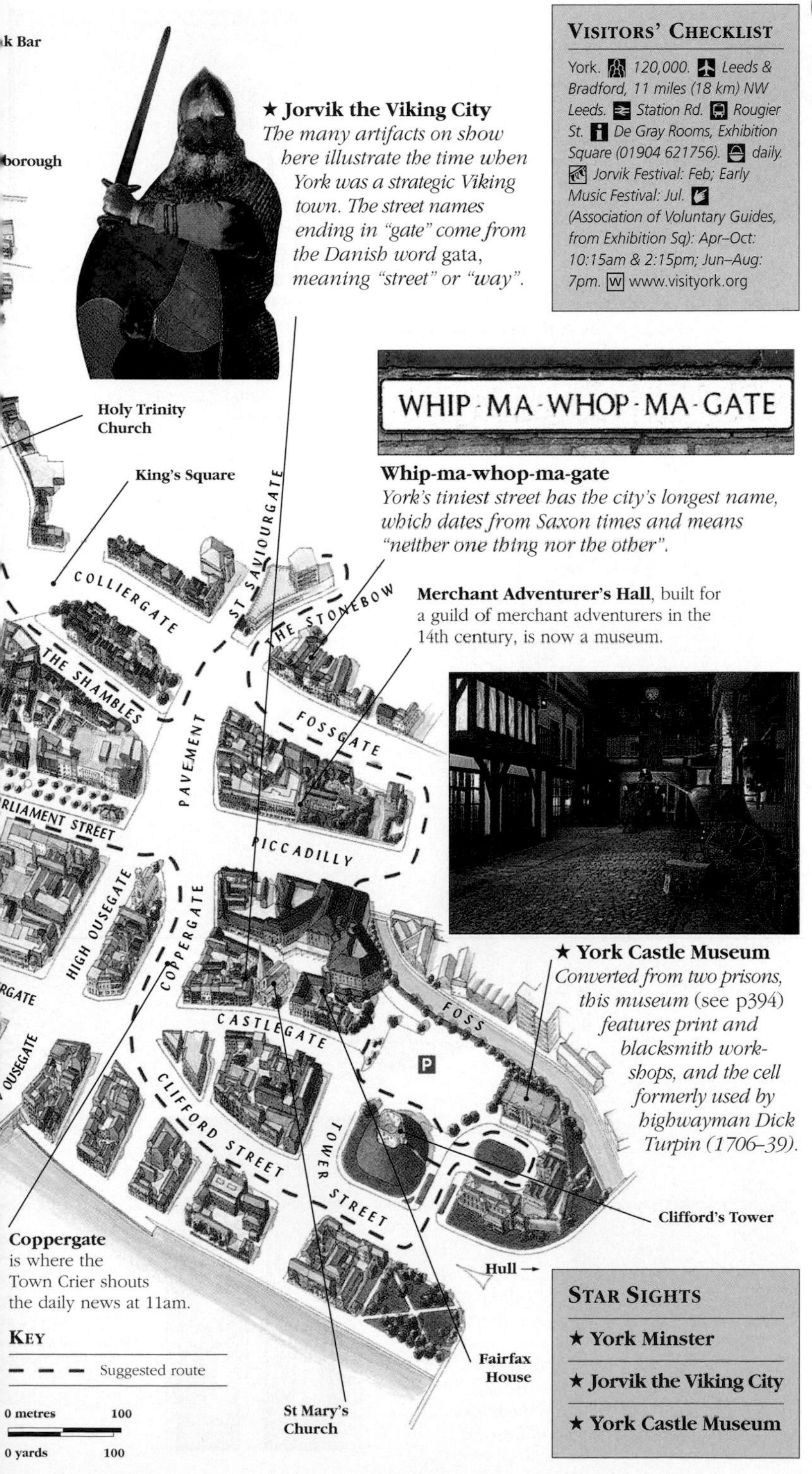

★ Jorvik the Viking City
The many artifacts on show here illustrate the time when York was a strategic Viking town. The street names ending in "gate" come from the Danish word gata, *meaning "street" or "way".*

Whip-ma-whop-ma-gate
York's tiniest street has the city's longest name, which dates from Saxon times and means "neither one thing nor the other".

Merchant Adventurer's Hall, built for a guild of merchant adventurers in the 14th century, is now a museum.

★ York Castle Museum
Converted from two prisons, this museum (see p394) *features print and blacksmith workshops, and the cell formerly used by highwayman Dick Turpin (1706–39).*

Coppergate is where the Town Crier shouts the daily news at 11am.

KEY

– – – Suggested route

VISITORS' CHECKLIST

York. 120,000. Leeds & Bradford, 11 miles (18 km) NW Leeds. Station Rd. Rougier St. De Gray Rooms, Exhibition Square (01904 621756). daily. Jorvik Festival: Feb; Early Music Festival: Jul. (Association of Voluntary Guides, from Exhibition Sq): Apr–Oct: 10:15am & 2:15pm; Jun–Aug: 7pm. www.visityork.org

STAR SIGHTS

★ **York Minster**

★ **Jorvik the Viking City**

★ **York Castle Museum**

York Minster

Central sunflower in rose window

THE LARGEST Gothic church north of the Alps, York Minster is 158 m (519 ft) long and 76 m (249 ft) wide across the transepts, and houses the largest collection of medieval stained glass in Britain *(see p395)*. The word "minster" usually means a church served by monks, but priests always served at York. The first minster began as a wooden chapel used to baptize King Edwin of Northumbria in 627. There have been several cathedrals on or near the site, including an 11th-century Norman structure. The present minster was begun in 1220 and completed 250 years later. In July 1984, the south transept roof was destroyed by fire. Restoration cost £2.25 million.

Central Tower
Reconstructed in 1420–65 (after partial collapse in 1407) from a design by the master stonemason William Colchester, its geometrical roof design has a central lantern.

Great East Window *(p395)*

The Choir has a vaulted entrance with a 15th-century boss of the Assumption of the Virgin.

Exit in south transept

The 16th-century rose window

★ Choir Screen
Sited between the choir and the nave, this 15th-century stone screen depicts kings of England from William I to Henry VI, and has a canopy of angels.

The Nave, built i 1291, was severe damaged by fire i 1840. Rebuildin costs were heav but it was re-opene with a new peal c bells in 184

★ Chapter House
A Latin inscription near the entrance of the wooden-vaulted Chapter House (1260–85) reads: "As the rose is the flower of flowers, so this is the house of houses".

Visitors' Checklist

Deangate, York. 01904 557216. *Apr–Oct: 9am–6pm daily (Sun pm only); Nov–Mar: 10am–4pm daily (Sun pm only).* **Donation.** *to Undercroft & Central Tower.* *7:30am, 7:50am Mon–Fri; 8am, 8:45am, 10am Sun; choral matins: 11:30am Sun; choral evensong: 5pm Mon–Fri, 4pm Sat & Sun.* *main floors.* *when available.* *in St William's College.* www.yorkminster.org

The western towers, with their 15th-century decorative panelling and elaborate pinnacles, contrast with the simpler design of the north transept. The southwest tower is the minster belfry.

Star Sights

★ Chapter House

★ Choir Screen

Timbered interior of the Merchant Adventurers' Hall

Monk Bar

This is one of York's finest original medieval gates, situated at the end of Goodramgate. It is vaulted on three floors, and the portcullis still works. In the Middle Ages, the rooms above it were rented out, and it was a prison in the 16th century. Its decorative details include men holding stones ready to drop on intruders.

York City Art Gallery

Exhibition Sq. *01904 697979.* *daily.* *24–26 Dec, 1 Jan.* www.york.art.museum

This Italianate building of 1879 holds a wide-ranging collection of paintings from western Europe dating from the early 14th century. There is also a collection of British and foreign studio pottery, including work by Bernard Leach, William Staite Murray and Shoji Hamada.

A 15th-century French portrait of St Anthony in York City Art Gallery

Clifford's Tower

(EH) Clifford's St. *01904 646940.* *daily.* *24–26 Dec, 1 Jan.* www.english-heritage.org

Sited on top of a mound that William the Conqueror built for his original wooden castle, destroyed by fire during anti-Jewish riots in 1190, Clifford's Tower dates from the 13th century. Built by Henry III, it was named after the de Clifford family, who were constables of the castle.

ARC

St Saviourgate. *01904 654324.* *Mon–Fri.* *mid-Dec–5 Jan, Good Fri.*

Housed in a restored medieval church off the Shambles, the ARC is a centre for exploring archaeology. Visitors become archaeological detectives and can discover how archaeologists have pieced together clues from the past to unravel the history of the Viking age in York.

Merchant Adventurers' Hall

Fossgate. *01904 654818.* *Easter–Sep: daily; Oct–Easter: Mon–Sat.* *24 Dec–3 Jan.*

Built by the York Merchants' Guild, which controlled the northern cloth trade in the 15th–17th centuries, this building has fine timberwork. The Great Hall is probably the best example of its kind in Europe. Among its paintings is an unattributed 17th-century copy of Van Dyck's portrait of Charles I's queen, Henrietta Maria. Below the Great Hall is the hospital, which was used by the guild until 1900, and a private chapel.

Exploring York

The appeal of York is its many layers of history. A medieval city constructed on top of a Roman one, it was first built in AD 71, when it became capital of the northern province and was known as Eboracum. It was here that Constantine the Great was made emperor in 306, and reorganized Britain into four provinces. A hundred years later, the Roman army had withdrawn. Eboracum was renamed Eoforwic, under the Saxons, and then became a Christian stronghold. The Danish street names are the reminder that it was a Viking centre from 867, and one of Europe's chief trading bases. Between 1100 and 1500 it was England's second city. The glory of York is the minster *(see pp392–3)*. The city also boasts 18 medieval churches, 3 mile long (4.8 km) medieval city walls, elegant Jacobean and Georgian architecture and fine museums.

The Middleham Jewel, Yorkshire Museum

York Castle Museum

The Eye of York. 01904 650333. daily. ground floor only. www.york.castle.museum

Housed in two 18th-century prisons, the museum has a fine folk collection, started by Dr John Kirk of the market town of Pickering. Opened in 1938, its period displays include a Jacobean dining room, a moorland cottage, and a 1950s front room. It also contains an exhibition on the traditions of birth, marriages and death in Britain from 1700 to 2000.

The most famous exhibits include the reconstructed Victorian street of Kirkgate, complete with shopfronts, and the Anglo Saxon York Helmet, discovered in 1982.

York Minster

See pp392–3.

Jorvik, The Viking City

Coppergate. 01904 643211. daily. ring first. www.vikingjorvik.com

This popular centre is built on the site of the original Viking settlement which archaeologists uncovered at Coppergate. It is most famous for recreating the smells of Viking York. A dynamic vision of 10th-century York combines with new technology to transform archaeological evidence and bring the hub of the Viking world to life.

Yorkshire Museum and St Mary's Abbey

Museum Gardens. 01904 551800. daily.

Yorkshire Museum was in the news when it purchased the 15th-century Middleham Jewel for £2.5 million, one of the finest pieces of English Gothic jewellery found this century. Other exhibits include 2nd-century Roman mosaics and an Anglo-Saxon silver gilt bowl.

St Mary's Abbey *(see p338)* in the riverside grounds is where the medieval York Mystery Plays are set every few years.

Grand staircase and fine plaster ceiling at Fairfax House

Fairfax House

Castlegate. 01904 655543. daily (Sun: pm, Fri: booked tour only 11am, 2pm). 6 Jan–20 Feb. limited. www.fairfaxhouse.co.uk

From 1755 to 1762 Viscount Fairfax built this fine Georgian town house for his daughter, Anne. The house was designed by John Carr *(see p24)*, and restored in the 1980s. Between 1920 and 1965 it was a cinema and dancehall. Today, visitors can see the bedroom of Anne Fairfax (1725–93), and a fine collection of 18th-century furniture, porcelain and clocks.

National Railway Museum

Leeman Rd. 01904 621261. daily. www.nrm.org.uk

The world's largest railway museum and the 2001 European Museum of the Year, covers nearly 200 years of history using a variety of visual aids. Visitors can try wheel-tapping and shunting in the interactive gallery, or find out what made Stephenson's *Rocket* so successful. Exhibits include uniforms, rolling stock from 1797 onward and Queen Victoria's Royal Train carriage, as well as the very latest rail innovations.

Reproduction of Stephenson's *Rocket* (right) and 1830s first-class carriage in York's National Railway Museum

The Stained Glass of York Minster

YORK MINSTER houses the largest collection of medieval stained glass in Britain, some of it dating from the late 12th century. The glass was generally coloured during production, using metal oxides to produce the desired colour, then worked on by craftsmen on site. When a design had been produced, the glass was first cut, then trimmed to shape. Details were painted on, using iron oxide-based paint which was fused to the glass by firing in a kiln. Individual pieces were then leaded together to form the finished window.

Window detail

Part of the fascination of the minster glass is its variety of subject matter. Some windows were paid for by lay donors who specified a particular subject, others reflect ecclesiastical patronage.

Miracle of St Nicholas *(late 12th century) was put in the nave over 100 years after it was made. It shows a Jew's conversion.*

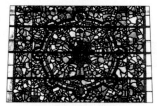

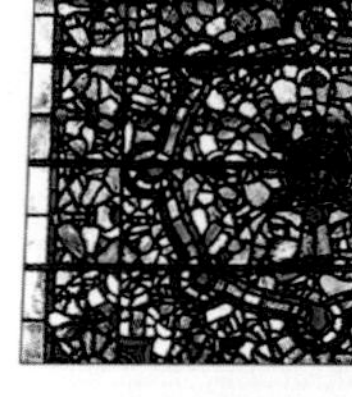
The Five Sisters *in the north transept are the largest examples of* grisaille *glass in Britain. This popular 13th-century technique involved creating fine patterning on clear glass and decorating it with black enamel.*

St John the Evangelist*, in part of the Great West Window (c.1338), is holding an eagle, itself an example of stickwork, where paint is scraped off to reveal clear glass.*

Noah's Ark *with its distinct boat-like shape is easily identified in the Great East Window.*

The Great East Window *(1405-8), the size of a tennis court, is the largest area of medieval painted glass in the world. The Dean and Chapter paid master glazier John Thornton four shillings a week for this celebration of the Creation.*

Edward III *is a fine example of the 14th-century "soft" style of painting, achieved by stippling the paint.*

Walter Skirlaw*, whose bishopric was revoked in favour of Richard Scrope, donated this window on its completion in 1408.*

Harewood House 33

Leeds. *0113 2181010.* *Leeds then bus.* *Mar– Nov: daily.* *by arrangement.* www.harewood.org

DESIGNED BY John Carr in 1759, Harewood House is the Yorkshire home of the Earl and Countess of Harewood.

The grand Palladian exterior is impressive, with interiors created by Robert Adam and an unrivalled collection of 18th-century furniture made specifically for Harewood by Yorkshire-born Thomas Chippendale (1711–79). There is a collection of paintings by Italian and English artists, including Reynolds and Gainsborough, and two watercolour rooms. The grounds by Capability Brown *(see p22)* include the **Harewood Bird Garden**, which has exotic species and a breeding programme of certain endangered varieties.

Bali starling, one of Harewood's rare birds

Leeds 34

Leeds. *750,000.* *Leeds City Station (0113 2425242).* *Mon–Sat.* www.leeds.gov.uk

THE THIRD LARGEST of Britain's provincial cities, Leeds was at its most prosperous during the Victorian period. The most impressive legacy from this era is a series of ornate, covered shopping arcades. Also of note is the **Town Hall**, designed by Cuthbert Brodrick and opened by Queen Victoria in 1858.

Today, although Leeds is primarily an industrial city, it also offers a thriving cultural scene. Productions at **The Grand** by Opera North, one of Britain's top operatic companies, are of a high quality.

The **City Art Gallery** has an impressive collection of British 20th-century art and fine examples of Victorian paintings including works by local artist Atkinson Grimshaw (1836–93). Among the late 19th-century French art are works by Signac, Courbet and Sisley. The Henry Moore Institute, added in 1993, is devoted to the research, study and display of sculpture of all periods. It comprises a reading room, study centre, library and video gallery, as well as galleries and an archive of material on and by Moore and other sculptural pioneers.

The **Armley Mills Museum**, in a 19th-century woollen mill, explores the industrial heritage of Leeds. Filled with original equipment, recorded sounds and models in 19th-century workers' clothes, it traces the history of the ready-to-wear industry.

A striking waterfront development by the River Aire has attracted two museums. The **Royal Armouries Museum**, from the Tower of London, tells the story of arms and armour around the world in battle, sport, self-defence and fashion, using live demonstrations, film, music and poetry. The **Thackray Medical Museum**, the largest of its kind in Europe, is a fascinating interactive display of medical advances, from a re-created vision of Victorian slum life to modern-day medical challenges.

Leeds has two sights that are especially suitable for children. **Tropical World** features crystal pools, a rainforest house, butterflies and tropical fish. There is also a farm and a Rare Breeds centre in the grounds of the Tudor-Jacobean **Temple Newsam House**, which has major art and furniture collections including Chippendale pieces.

The County Arcade, one of Leeds' restored shopping arcades

City Art Gallery
The Headrow. *0113 2478248.* *daily (Sun: pm).*

Armley Mills Museum
Canal Rd, Armley. *0113 2637861.* *Tue–Sun (Sun: pm), public hols.* *25, 26 Dec, 1 Jan.*

Royal Armouries
Armouries Drive. *0113 2201999.* *daily.* *24, 25 Dec.*

Thackray Medical Museum
Beckett St. *0113 2457084.* *daily.* *24–26, 31 Dec, 1 Jan.*

Tropical World
Canal Gdns, Princes Ave. *0113 266 1850.* *daily.* *25, 26 Dec.*

Temple Newsam House
Off A63. *0113 2647321.* *Tue–Sun.* *25, 26 Dec, Jan.*

Working loom at the Armley Mills Museum in Leeds

The Other Side (1990–93) by David Hockney at Bradford's 1853 Gallery in Saltaire

Bradford ㉟

Bradford. 492,000.
City Hall, Centenary Square (01274 753678). Mon–Sat.
W www.visitbradford.com

IN THE 16TH CENTURY, Bradford was a thriving market town, and the opening of its canal in 1774 boosted trade. By 1850, it was the world's capital for worsted (fabric made from closely twisted wool). Many of the city's well-preserved civic and industrial buildings date from this period, such as the Wool Exchange on Market Street. In the 1800s a number of German textile manufacturers settled in what is now called Little Germany. Their houses are characterized by decora-tive stone carvings that illustrated the wealth and standing of the occupants.

The **National Museum of Photography, Film and Television**, founded in 1983, explores the technology and art of these media. There is a television section called TV Heaven, where visitors can ask to watch their favourite programme. They are also encouraged to see themselves read the news on TV. The giant IMAX screen uses the world's largest film format. Film subjects include journeys into space, the ocean and the natural world.

The **Colour Museum** traces dyeing and textile printing from ancient Egypt to the present day with an emphasis on hands-on elements. **Bradford Industrial Museum** is housed in an original spinning mill. As well as seeing and hearing all the mill machinery, you can ride on a horse-drawn tram. Saltaire, a Victorian industrial village *(see p337)*, is on the outskirts of the city. Built by Sir Titus Salt for his Salts Mill workers, it was completed in 1873. The **1853 Gallery** has the world's largest collection of works by David Hockney, born in Bradford.

Daguerreotype camera by Giroux (1839)

National Museum of Photography, Film and Television
Pictureville. 01274 202030. daily (school hols); Tue–Sun (school terms); public holidays. 24–26 Dec.
W www.nmpft.org.uk

Colour Museum
1 Providence St. 01274 390955. Tue–Sat. 24 Dec–2 Jan.
W www.sdc.org.uk

Bradford Industrial Museum
Moorside Mills, Moorside Rd. 01274 435900. Tue–Sat, Sun (pm), public hols. 25, 26 Dec.

1853 Gallery
Salts Mill, Victoria Rd. 01274 531163. daily. 25–26 Dec, 1 Jan.
W www.saltsmill.org.uk

BRADFORD'S INDIAN COMMUNITY

Immigrants from the Indian subcontinent originally came to Bradford in the 1950s to work in the mills, but with the decline of the textile industry many began small businesses. By the mid-1970s there were 1,400 such enterprises in the area. Almost one fifth were in the food sector, born out of simple cafés catering for mill-workers whose families were far away. As Indian food became more popular, these restaurants thrived, and today there are over 200 serving the highly spiced dishes of the Indian subcontinent.

Balti in a Bradford restaurant

Haworth Parsonage, home to the Brontë family, now a museum

Haworth 36

Bradford. 5,000. Keighley.
2–4 West Lane (01535 642329).
www.yorkshirevisitor.com

THE SETTING OF HAWORTH, in bleak Pennine moorland dotted with farmsteads, has changed little since it was home to the Brontë family. The village boomed in the 1840s, when there were more than 1,200 hand-looms in operation, but it is more famous today for the Brontë connection.

You can visit the **Brontë Parsonage Museum**, home from 1820–61 to novelists Charlotte, Emily and Anne, their brother Branwell and their father, the Revd Patrick Brontë. Built in 1778–9, the house remains decorated as it was during the 1850s. Eleven rooms, including the children's study and Charlotte's room, display letters, manuscripts, furniture and personal objects.

The nostalgic Victorian **Keighley and Worth Valley Railway** runs through Haworth. It stops at Oakworth station, where parts of *The Railway Children* were filmed. At the end of the line is the Railway Museum at Oxenhope.

Brontë Parsonage Museum

Church St. 01535 642323.
daily. 24–27 Dec; Jan.
limited. www.bronte.info

Charlotte Brontë's childhood story book, for her sister, Anne

The Brontë Sisters

Charlotte Brontë (1816–55)

During a harsh, motherless childhood, Charlotte, Emily and Anne retreated into fictional worlds of their own, writing poems and stories. As adults, they had to work as governesses, but still published a poetry collection in 1846. Only two copies were sold, but in the following year Charlotte's *Jane Eyre*, became a bestseller, arousing interest in Emily's *Wuthering Heights* and Anne's *Agnes Grey*. After her siblings' deaths in 1848–9, Charlotte published her last novel, *Villette*, in 1852. She married the Revd Nicholls, her father's curate, in 1854, but died shortly afterwards.

Hebden Bridge 37

Calderdale. 12,500.
1 Bridgegate (01422 845266). Thu
www.hebdenbridge.co.uk

HEBDEN BRIDGE is a delightful South Pennines former mill town, surrounded by steep hills and former 19th-century mills. The houses seem to defy gravity as they cling to the valley sides. Due to the gradient, one house is made from two bottom floors, and the top two floors form another unit. To separate ownership of these "flying freeholds", an Act of Parliament was devised.

There is a superb view of Hebden Bridge from nearby **Heptonstall**, where the poet Sylvia Plath (1932–63) is buried. The village contains a Wesleyan chapel (1764).

Halifax 38

Calderdale. 88,000.
Piece Hall (01422 368725).
Thu–Sat.
www.calderdale.gov.uk

HALIFAX'S HISTORY has been influenced by textiles since the Middle Ages, but today's visual reminders date mainly from the 19th century. The town inspired William Blake's vision of "dark Satanic mills" in his poem *Jerusalem* (1820). The wool trade helped to make the Pennines into Britain's industrial backbone.

Until the mid-15th century cloth production was modest, but vital enough to inspire the 11th-century Gibbet Law, which stated that anyone caught stealing cloth could be hanged. There is a replica of the gibbet used for decapitation at the bottom of Gibbet Street. Many of Halifax's 18th- and 19th-century buildings owe their existence to wealthy cloth traders. Sir Charles Barry (1795–1860), architect of the Houses of Parliament, was commissioned by the Crossley family to design the Town Hall. They also paid for the landscaping of the People's Park by the creator of the Crystal Palace, Sir Joseph Paxton (1801–65). Thomas Bradley's

Large Two Forms **(1966–9) by Henry Moore in Bretton Country Park**

18th-century **Piece Hall** was where wool merchants once sold their cloth, trading in one of the 315 "Merchants' Rooms". It has a massive Italianate courtyard, now beautifully restored. Today, Halifax's market takes place here.

Eureka! is a hands-on children's museum, with exhibits such as the Giant Mouth Machine. **Shibden Hall Museum** is a fine period house, parts of which date to the 15th century.

Environs: The nearby village of **Sowerby Bridge** was an important textile centre from the Middle Ages to the 1960s. Today visitors come to enjoy the scenic canals.

Eureka!
Discovery Rd. 01422 330069.
daily. 24–26 Dec.
www.eureka.org.uk

Shibden Hall Museum
Listers Rd. 01422 352246.
daily (Sun: pm). 24 Dec–2 Jan.

National Coal Mining Museum 39

Wakefield. *01924 848806.*
Wakefield then bus. *daily.*
24–26 Dec, 1 Jan.
www.ncm.org.uk

Housed in the old Caphouse Colliery, this museum gives visitors the chance to go into a real mine shaft: warm clothing is advised. An underground tour takes you 137 m (450 ft) down, equipped with a hat and a miner's lamp. You can enter some of the narrow seams and see exhibits such as life-size working models. Other displays depict mining methods and conditions from 1820 to the present day.

Yorkshire Sculpture Park 40

Wakefield. *01924 830302.*
Wakefield then bus. *daily.*
24, 25, 29–31 Dec.
www.ysp.co.uk

This is one of Europe's leading open-air galleries, situated in 45 ha (110 acres) of 18th-century parkland. Each year a series of large exhibitions of sculpture by international artists is organized alongside the main collection, which includes work by Barbara Hepworth and Sol LeWitt. Bretton Country Park, next to the sculpture park, has the largest collection of Henry Moore sculptures in Europe.

Magna 41

Rotherham. *01709 720002.*
Rotherham Central or Sheffield then bus (No. 69). *daily.*
24–25 Dec.
www.magnatrust.org.uk

A former steel works has been imaginatively converted into a huge science adventure centre, with an emphasis on interactive exhibits, noise and spectacle designed to appeal to 4–15-year-olds. In the Air, Fire, Water and Earth Pavilions visitors can get close to a tornado, operate real diggers or discover what it's like to detonate a rock face. There are also multimedia displays on the lives of steelworkers and on how a giant furnace operated, as well as a show that features robots with artificial intelligence that evolve and learn as they hunt each other down.

The Face of Steel display at Magna

NORTHUMBRIA

NORTHUMBERLAND · COUNTY DURHAM

ENGLAND'S NORTHEAST *extremity is a tapestry of moorland, ruins, castles, cathedrals and huddled villages. With Northumberland National Park and Kielder Water reservoir to the north, a rugged eastern coastline, and the cities of Newcastle and Durham to the south, the area combines a dramatic history with abundant natural beauty.*

The empty peaceful hills, elusive wildlife and panoramic vistas of Northumberland National Park belie the area's turbulent past. Warring Scots and English, skirmishing tribes, cattle drovers and whisky smugglers have all left traces on ancient routes through the Cheviot Hills. Slicing through the southern edge of the park is the famous reminder of the Romans' 400-year occupation of Britain, Hadrian's Wall, the northern boundary of their empire.

Conflict between Scots and English continued for 1,000 years after the Romans departed, and even after the 1603 union between the two crowns. A chain of massive crenellated medieval castles punctuates the coastline, while other forts that once defended the northern flank of England along the River Tweed lie mostly in ruins. Seventh-century Northumbria was the cradle of Christianity under St Aidan, but this was sharply countered by Viking violence from 793 onward, as the Scandinavian invaders raided the monasteries. But a reverence for Northumbrian saints is in the local psyche, and St Cuthbert and the Venerable Bede are both buried in Durham Cathedral. The influence of the Industrial Revolution, concentrated around the mouths of the rivers Tyne, Wear and Tees, made Newcastle upon Tyne the north's main centre for coal mining and shipbuilding. Today, the city is famous for its "industrial heritage" attractions and urban regeneration schemes.

Section of Hadrian's Wall, built by the Romans in about 120, looking east from Cawfields

◁ **The towers of Durham Cathedral, rising above the River Wear**

Exploring Northumbria

HISTORIC SITES ARE PLENTIFUL along Northumbria's coast. South of Berwick-upon-Tweed, a causeway leads to the ruined priory and castle on Lindisfarne, and there are major castles at Bamburgh, Alnwick and Warkworth. The hinterland is a region of wide open spaces, with wilderness in the Northumberland National Park, and fascinating Roman remains of Hadrian's Wall at Housesteads and elsewhere. The glorious city of Durham is dominated by its castle and cathedral, and Newcastle upon Tyne has a lively nightlife.

SIGHTS AT A GLANCE

Alnwick Castle 5
Bamburgh 4
Barnard Castle 17
Beamish Open Air Museum 13
Berwick-upon-Tweed 1
Cheviot Hills 8
Corbridge 10
Durham pp414–15 14
Farne Islands 3
Hadrian's Wall pp408–409 11
Hexham 9
Kielder Water 7
Lindisfarne 2
Middleton-in-Teesdale 16
Newcastle upon Tyne 12
Warkworth Castle 6

Walks and Tours
North Pennines Tour 15

SEE ALSO

- ***Where to Stay*** pp563–4
- ***Where to Eat*** pp599–601

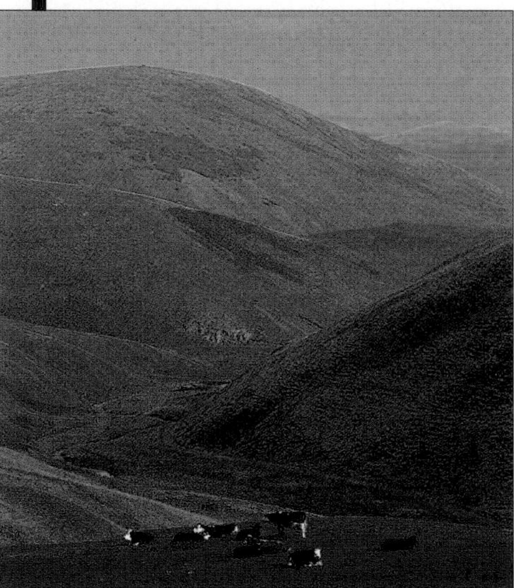

The wilderness of Upper Coquetdale in the sparsely populated Cheviot Hills

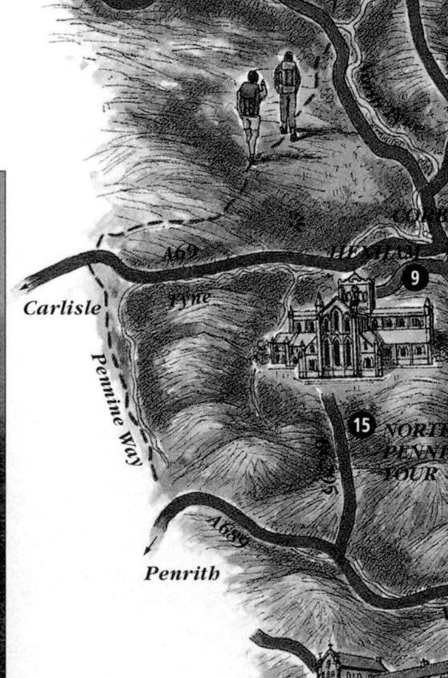

0 kilometres 10
0 miles 10

Penrith
A66

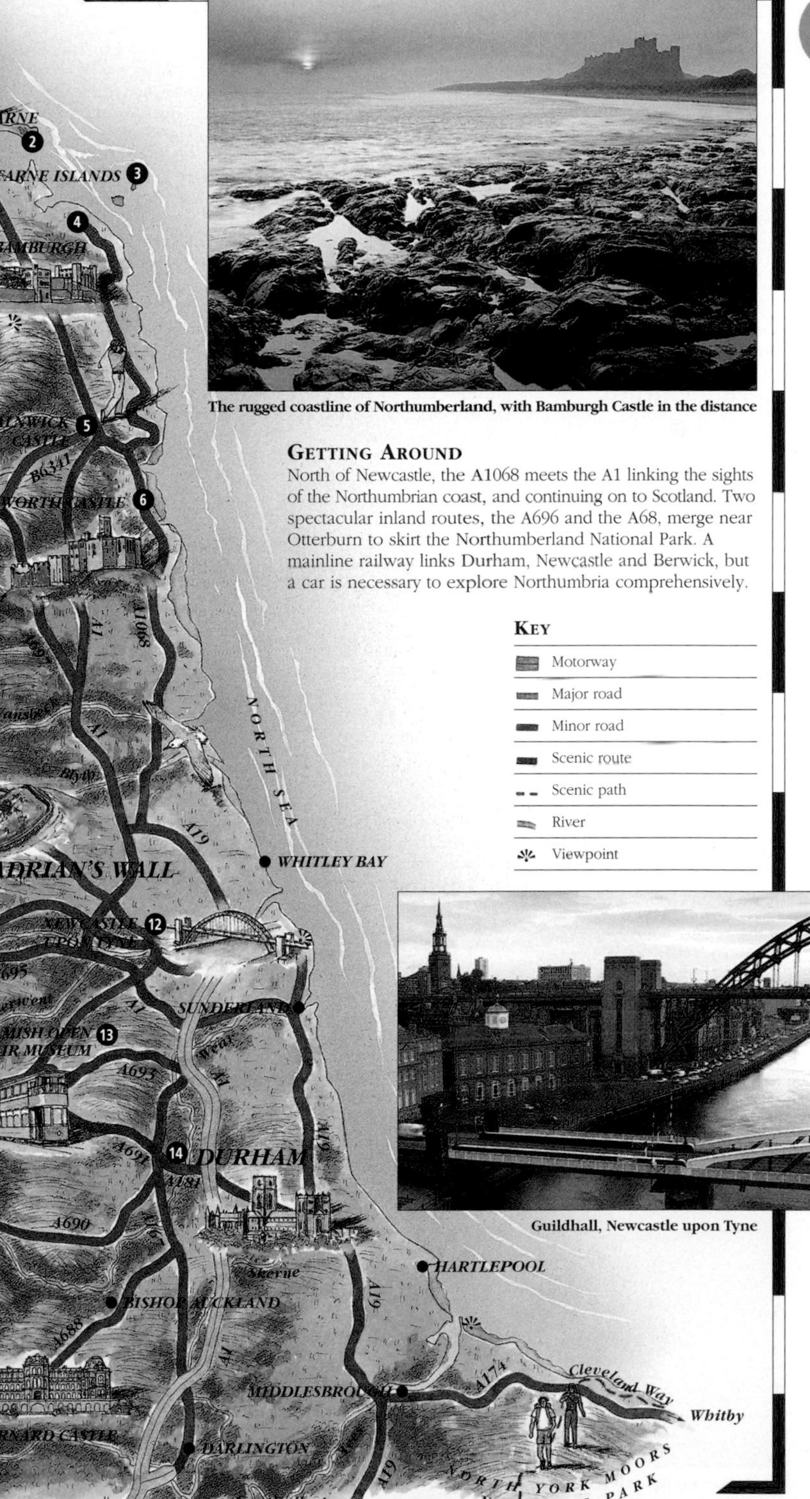

The rugged coastline of Northumberland, with Bamburgh Castle in the distance

Getting Around

North of Newcastle, the A1068 meets the A1 linking the sights of the Northumbrian coast, and continuing on to Scotland. Two spectacular inland routes, the A696 and the A68, merge near Otterburn to skirt the Northumberland National Park. A mainline railway links Durham, Newcastle and Berwick, but a car is necessary to explore Northumbria comprehensively.

Key

- Motorway
- Major road
- Minor road
- Scenic route
- Scenic path
- River
- Viewpoint

Guildhall, Newcastle upon Tyne

View over Berwick-upon-Tweed's three bridges

Berwick-upon-Tweed ❶

Northumberland. 13,000. 106 Mary Gate (01289 330733). Wed, Sat. www.berwickonline.org.uk

Between the 12th and 15th centuries Berwick-upon-Tweed changed hands 14 times in the wars between the Scots and English. Its position, at the mouth of the river which divides the two nations, made the town strategically vital.

The English finally gained permanent control in 1482 and maintained Berwick as a fortified garrison. Ramparts dating from 1555, 1.5 miles (2.5 km) long and 7 m (23 ft) thick, offer superb views over the Tweed. Within the 18th-century barracks are the **King's Own Scottish Borderers Regimental Museum**, an **art gallery**, and **By Beat of Drum**, charting the history of British infantrymen.

King's Own Scottish Borderers Regimental Museum
The Barracks. *01289 307427.* *Mon–Sat.* *22 Dec–3 Jan, public hols.*

Lindisfarne ❷

Northumberland. *Berwick-upon-Tweed then bus.* *106 Mary Gate, Berwick-upon-Tweed (01289 330733).*

Twice daily a long, narrow neck of land sinks under the North Sea tide for five hours, separating Lindisfarne, or Holy Island, from the coast. At low tide, visitors stream over the causeway to the island made famous by St Aidan, St Cuthbert and the Lindisfarne gospels. Nothing remains of the Celtic monks' monastery, finally abandoned in 875 after successive Viking attacks, but the magnificent arches of the 11th-century **Lindisfarne Priory** are still visible.

After 1540, stones from the priory were used to build **Lindisfarne Castle**, which was restored and made into a private home by Sir Edwin Lutyens *(see p25)* in 1903. It includes an attractive walled garden created by Gertrude Jekyll *(see p23)*.

Lindisfarne Castle
(NT) Holy Island. *01289 389244* *Mar–Nov: Sat–Thu & Good Fri (pm).*

Farne Islands ❸

(NT) Northumberland. *from Seahouses (Apr–Oct).* *106 Mary Gate, Berwick-upon-Tweed (01289 330733).*

There are between 15 and 28 Farne Islands off the coast from Bamburgh, some of them periodically covered by sea. Nature wardens and lighthouse keepers share them with seals, puffins and other seabirds. Boat tours depart from **Seahouses** harbour and can land on Staple and Inner Farne, site of St Cuthbert's 14th-century chapel, or Longstone, where Grace Darling's lighthouse is located.

Lindisfarne Castle (1540), the main landmark on the island of Lindisfarne

Celtic Christianity

St Cuthbert on a sea voyage

The Irish monk St Aidan arrived in Northumbria in 635 from the island of Iona, off western Scotland, to evangelize the north of England. He founded the monastery on the island of Lindisfarne, and it became one of the most important centres for Christianity in England. This and other monastic communities thrived in Northumbria, becoming rich in scholarship, although the monks lived simply. It also emerged as a place of pilgrimage after miracles were reported at the shrine of St Cuthbert, Lindisfarne's most famous bishop. But the monks' pacifism made them defenceless against 9th-century Viking raids.

St Aidan's Monastery *was added to over the centuries to become Lindisfarne Priory. This 8th-century relic with interlaced animal decorations is from a cross at the site.*

The Venerable Bede *(673–735), the most brilliant early medieval scholar, was a monk at the monastery of St Paul in Jarrow. He wrote* The Ecclesiastical History of the English People *in 731.*

St Aidan *(600–651), an Irish missionary, founded a monastery at Lindisfarne and became Bishop of Northumbria in 635. This 1960 sculpture of him, by Kathleen Parbury, is in Lindisfarne Priory grounds.*

St Cuthbert *(635–87) was the monk and miracle worker most revered of all. He lived as a hermit on Inner Farne (a chapel was built there in his memory) and later became Bishop of Lindisfarne.*

Lindisfarne Priory *was built by Benedictines in the 11th century, on the site of St Aidan's earlier monastery.*

The Lindisfarne Gospels

This book of richly illustrated portrayals of Gospel stories is one of the masterpieces of the "Northumbrian Renaissance" which left a permanent mark on Christian art and history-writing. The work was carried out by monks at Lindisfarne under the direction of Bishop Eadfrith, around 700. Monks managed to save the book and carried it with them when they fled from Lindisfarne in 875 after suffering repeated Viking raids. Other treasures were plundered.

Elaborately decorated initial to the *Gospel of St Matthew* (c.725)

Illustration of Grace Darling from the 1881 edition of *Sunday at Home*

Bamburgh ❹

Northumberland. 1,100. Berwick. Seahouses (01665 720884; Apr–Oct); 106 Mary Gate, Berwick-upon-Tweed (01289 330733).

DUE TO NORTHUMBRIA'S history of hostility against the Scots, there are more strongholds and castles here than in any other part of England. Most were built from the 11th to the 15th centuries by local warlords, as was Bamburgh's red sandstone **castle**. Its coastal position had been fortified since prehistoric times, but the first major stronghold was built in 550 by a Saxon chieftain, Ida the Flamebearer.

In its heyday between 1095 and 1464, Bamburgh was the royal castle that was used by the Northumbrian kings for coronations. By the end of the Middle Ages it had fallen into obscurity, then in 1894 it was bought by Newcastle arms tycoon Lord Armstrong, who restored it. Works of art are exhibited in the cavernous Great Hall, and there are suits of armour and medieval artifacts in the basement.

Bamburgh's other main attraction is the tiny **Grace Darling Museum** which celebrates the bravery of the 23-year-old, who, in 1838, rowed through tempestuous seas with her father, the keeper of the Longstone lighthouse, to rescue nine people from the wrecked *Forfarshire* steamboat.

Bamburgh Castle
Bamburgh. *01668 214515.*
Mar–Nov: daily.
www.bamburghcastle.com

Grace Darling Museum
Radcliffe Rd. *Easter–Oct: daily.*

Alnwick Castle ❺

Alnwick, Northumberland. 01665 510777. Alnmouth. April–Oct: daily. limited.

DOMINATING THE MARKET town on the River Aln is another great fortress, Alnwick Castle. Described by the Victorians as the "Windsor of the north", it is the main seat of the Duke of Northumberland, whose family, the Percys, have lived here since 1309. This border stronghold has survived many battles, but now peacefully dominates the pretty market town of Alnwick, overlooking landscape designed by Capability Brown. The stern medieval exterior belies the fine treasure house within, furnished in palatial Renaissance style with an exquisite collection of Meissen china and paintings by Titian, Van Dyck and Canaletto. The Postern Tower contains a collection of early British and Roman relics. The **Regimental Museum of Royal Northumberland Fusiliers** is in the Abbot's Tower. Among other attractions are the Percy State coach, the dungeon, the gun terrace and superb countryside views.

Carrara marble fireplace (1840) at Alnwick Castle

Warkworth Castle ❻

(EH) Warkworth, nr Amble. *01665 711423. daily. 24–2 Dec, 1 Jan. limited.*

WARKWORTH CASTLE sits on green hill overlooking the River Coquet. It was one of the Percy family homes. Shakespeare's *Henry IV* features the castle in the scenes between the Earl of Northumberland and his son, Harry Hotspur.

Much of the present-day castle remains date from the 14th century. The unusual turreted, cross-shaped keep, which was also added in the 14th century, is a central feature of the castle tour.

Warkworth Castle reflected in the River Coquet

Kielder Water ❼

Yarrow Moor, Falstone, Hexham. *0870 2403549. daily.*
www.kielder.org

ONE OF THE top attractions of Northumberland, Kielder Water lies close to the Scottish border, surrounded by spectacular scenery. With a perimeter of 27 miles (44 km), it is Europe's largest man-made lake, and offers facilities for sailing, windsurfing, canoeing, water-skiing and fishing. In summer, the cruiser *Osprey* departs from Leaplish on trips around the lake. The Kielder Water Exhibition, next to the Tower Knowe Visitor Centre, depicts the history of the valley from the Ice Age to the present day.

Cheviot Hills 8

These bare, lonely moors, smoothed into rounded humps by Ice Age glaciers, form a natural border with Scotland. Walkers and outdoor enthusiasts find a near-wilderness unmatched anywhere else in England. This remotest extremity of the Northumberland National Park nevertheless has a long and vivid history. Roman legions, warring Scots and English border raiders, cattle drovers and whisky smugglers have all left traces along the ancient routes and tracks they carved out here.

Visitors' Checklist

Northumberland. *Hexham.* *Wooler (01668 282123), Eastburn, South Park.* 01434 605555.

The Cheviots' *isolated burns and streams are among the last habitats in England for the shy, elusive otter.*

Chew Green Camp*, which to the Romans was* ad fines, *or, "towards the last place", has fine views from the remaining fortified earthworks.*

The Pennine Way *starts in Derbyshire and ends at Kirk Yetholm in Scotland. The final stage (shown here) goes past Byrness, crosses the Cheviots and traces the Scottish border.*

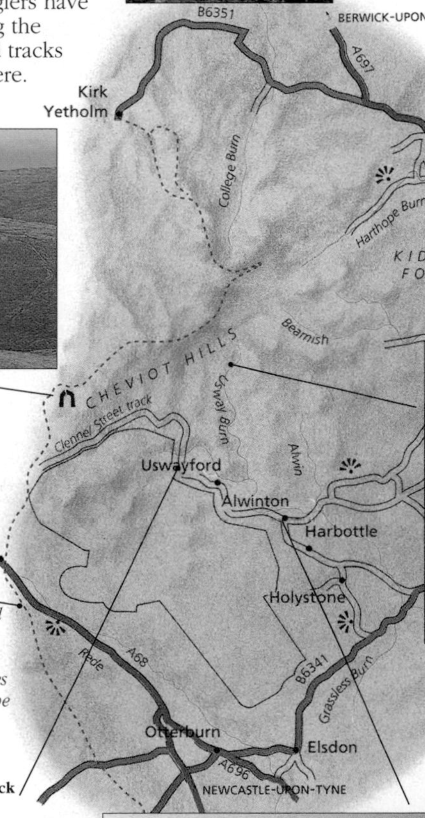

Uswayford Farm track

Uswayford Farm*, is perhaps the most remote farm in England, and one of the hardest to reach. It is set in deserted moorland.*

Key

- A roads
- B roads
- Minor roads
- Pennine Way
- Viewpoint

kilometres 5

miles 5

Alwinton*, a tiny village built mainly from grey stone, is situated beside the River Coquet. It is an access point for many fine walks in the area, and the wild landscape is deserted except for sheep.*

Hexham 9

Northumberland. 14,000. Wentworth Car Park (01434 652220). Tue. www.hadrianswallcountry.org

THE BUSY MARKET TOWN of Hexham was established in the 7th century, growing up around the church and monastery built by St Wilfrid, but the Vikings sacked and looted it in 876. In 1114, Augustinians began work on a priory and abbey on the original church ruins to create **Hexham Abbey**, which still towers over the market square. The Saxon crypt, built partly with stones from the former Roman fort at Corbridge, is all that remains of St Wilfrid's Church. The south transept has a 12th-century night stair: stone steps leading from the dormitory. In the chancel is the Frith Stool, a Saxon throne in the centre of a circle which protected fugitives.

Ancient stone carvings at Hexham Abbey

Medieval streets, many with Georgian and Victorian shopfronts, spread out from the market square, The 15th-century Moot Hall was once a council chamber and the old gaol (jail) contains a **museum** of border history.

Hadrian's Wall 11

ON THE ORDERS of Emperor Hadrian, work began in AD 120 on a 73 mile (117 km) wall to be erected across northern England, to mark and defend the northern limits of the British province and the northwest border of the Roman Empire. Troops were stationed at milecastles along the wall, and large turrets, later forts, were built at 5 mile (8 km) intervals. The wall, now the responsibility of English Heritage, was abandoned in 383 as the Empire crumbled, but much of it remains.

Location of Hadrian's Wall

Vindolanda *is the site of several fort[s]. The first timber fort dated from AD 9[…] and a stone fort was not built until t[…] 2nd century. The museum has a colle[c]tion of Roman writing tablets provid[…] details of food, clothes and work.*

Great Chesters Fort was built facing east to guard Caw Gap, but there are few remains today. To the south and east of the fort are traces of a civil settlement and a bathhouse.

Carvoran Fort is probably pre-Hadrianic. Little of the fort survives, but the Roman Army museum nearby covers the wall's history.

Housesteads Se[ttle]ment includes t[h]e remains of terrac[ed] shops or taverns

Emperor Hadrian *(76–138) came to Britain in 120 to order a stronger defence system. Coins were often cast to record emperors' visits, such as this bronze* sestertius. *Until 1971, the penny was abbreviated to* d, *short for* denarius, *a Roman coin.*

Cawfields, *2 m[…] (3 km) north o[f] Haltwhistle, is t[…] access point to […] of the highest a[…] most rugged sec[…] of the wall. To t[…] east, the remain[…] a milecastle sit […] Whin Sill crag.*

Hexham Abbey
Market Place. *01434 602031.* *daily.*

Border History Museum
Old Gaol, nr Hallgate. *01434 652349.* *for renovation until mid-2004: call for details.*

Corbridge ⑩

Northumberland. *4,000.* *Hill St (01434 632815).*

THIS QUIET TOWN conceals a few historic buildings constructed with stones from the Roman garrison town of nearby Corstopitum. Among these are the thickset Saxon tower of St Andrew's Church and the 14th-century fortified tower house built to protect the local clergyman. Excavations of Corstopitum, now known as **Corbridge Roman Site and Museum**, have exposed earlier forts, a well-preserved granary, temples, fountains and an aqueduct.

The parson's 14th-century fortified tower house at Corbridge

Corbridge Roman Site and Museum
(EH) *01434 632349.* *Apr–Oct: daily; Nov–Mar: Wed–Sun.* *24–26 Dec, 1 Jan.* *limited.*

The Wall Coast-to-Coast

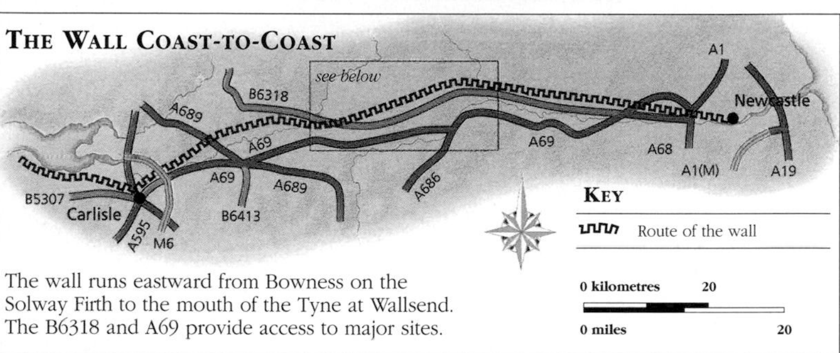

The wall runs eastward from Bowness on the Solway Firth to the mouth of the Tyne at Wallsend. The B6318 and A69 provide access to major sites.

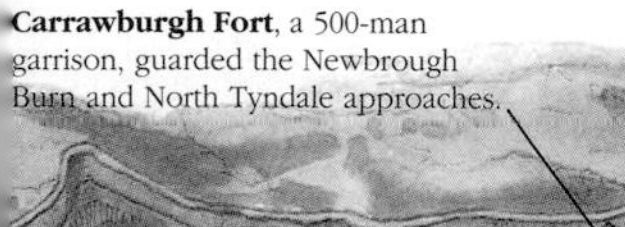

Carrawburgh Fort, a 500-man garrison, guarded the Newbrough Burn and North Tyndale approaches.

Limestone Corner Milecastle is sited at the northernmost part of the wall and has magnificent views of the Cheviot Hills *(see p407).*

***Sewingshields Milecastle**, with magnificent views west to Housesteads, is one of the best places for walking. This reconstruction shows the layout of a Roman milecastle on the wall.*

Chesters Fort was a bridgehead over the North Tyne. In the museum are altars, sculptures and inscriptions.

Chesters Bridge crossed the Tyne. The original Hadrianic bridge was rebuilt in 207. The remains of this second bridge abutment can still be seen.

***Housesteads Fort** is the best-preserved site on the wall, with fine views over the countryside. The excavated remains include the commanding officer's house and a Roman hospital.*

0 metres 500
0 yards 500

Newcastle upon Tyne ⓬

Newcastle upon Tyne. 273,000. Railway station; *132 Granger St (0191 2610610).* *Sun.* www.newcastle.gov.uk

NEWCASTLE OWES ITS NAME to its Norman **castle** which was founded in 1080 by Robert Curthose, the eldest son of William the Conqueror *(see p47)*. The Romans had bridged the Tyne and built a fort on the site 1,000 years earlier. During the Middle Ages it was used as a base for English campaigns against the Scots. From the Middle Ages, the city flourished as a coal mining and exporting centre. It was known in the 19th century for engineering, steel production and later as the world's foremost shipyard. The city's industrial base has recently declined, but "Geordies", as inhabitants of the city are known, have refocused their civic pride on the ultra-modern Metro Centre shopping mall at Gateshead, southwest of the city, and Newcastle United soccer team. The city's lively night scene includes clubs, pubs and ethnic restaurants. The visible trappings of its past are reflected in the magnificent **Tyne Bridge** and in **Earl Grey's Monument**, as well as the grand façades in the city centre thoroughfares, such as Grey Street. On the quayside there are some dramatic new features, notably **Baltic**, the contemporary art centre, **The Sage Gateshead**, the international centre for music, and the tilting **Gateshead Millennium Bridge**.

Bridges crossing the Tyne at Newcastle

The Castle

St Nicholas St. *0191 232 7938.* *daily.*

Curthose's original wooden "new castle" was rebuilt in stone in the 12th century. Only

Beamish Open Air Museum ⓭

THIS GIANT OPEN AIR MUSEUM, spread over 120 ha (300 acres) of County Durham, recreates an authentic picture of family, working and community life in the northeast in the 19th and early 20th centuries. It has a High Street, a colliery village, a disused mine, a school, chapel and farm, all with guides in period costume. A restored tramline serves the different parts of the museum, which carefully avoids romanticizing the past.

Tram symbol

Home Farm *recreates the atmosphere of an old-fashioned farmyard. Rare breeds of cattle and sheep, more common before the advent of mass breeding, can be seen.*

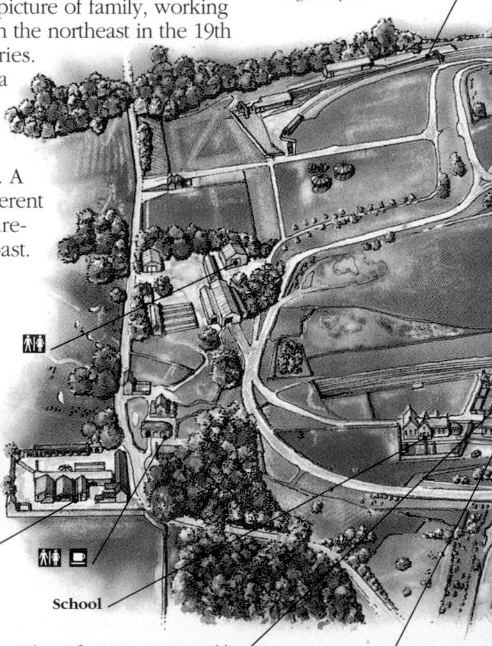

The station, which dates back to 1913, has a platform, a signal box, a wrought-iron footbridge and a goods yard.

School

Miners' houses were tiny, oil-lit dwellings, backing onto vegetable plots and owned by the colliery.

Chapel

he thickset, crenellated keep 'emains intact with two suites)f royal apartments. A series)f staircases spiral up to the 'enovated battlements, from vhich there are fine views)ver the city and the Tyne.

St Nicholas Cathedral

;t Nicholas Sq. 0191 2321939.
daily.

Chis is one of Britain's tiniest :athedrals. There are remnants nside of the original 11th-:entury Norman church on vhich the present 14th- and 15th-century structure was 'ounded. Its most striking 'eature is its ornate "lantern ower" – half tower, half spire –)f which there are only three)thers in Britain.

Bessie Surtees' House

11–44 Sandhill. 0191 2611585.
Mon–Fri. 25 Dec–2 Jan,)ublic hols. limited.

Che story of beautiful, wealthy 3essie, who lived here before eloping with penniless John Scott, later Lord Chancellor of England, is the romantic tale behind these half-timbered 16th- and 17th-century houses. The window through which Bessie escaped now has a blue glass pane.

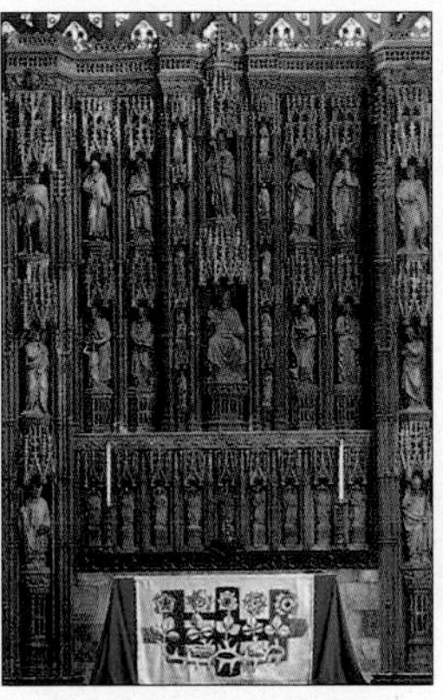

Reredos of the Northumbrian saints in St Nicholas Cathedral

Tyne Bridge

Newcastle–Gateshead.
daily.

Opened in 1928, this steel arch was the longest of its type in Britain with a span of 162 m (531 ft). Designed by Mott, Hay and Anderson, it soon became the city's most potent symbol.

Earl Grey's Monument

Grey St.

Benjamin Green created this memorial to the 2nd Earl Grey, Liberal Prime Minister from 1830 to 1834.

Baltic

The Centre for Contemporary Art
Gateshead. 0191 478 1810.
daily. www.balticmill.com

This former grain warehouse has been converted by architect Dominic Williams into a major new international centre for contemporary art, one of the biggest in Europe, with amazing views of Tyneside from its rooftop restaurant.

The Town *has a sweet shop, newspaper office, solicitor, dentist and music teacher. There is also a pub.*

Visitors' Checklist

Beamish, County Durham. *0191 370 4000. Durham, then bus. Apr–Oct: 10am–5pm daily (last adm 3pm); Nov–Mar: High Street only 10am–4pm Tue–Thu, Sat, Sun. Christmas (phone to check).*

The Co-op *stocked everything a family needed at the turn of the century. A full range of foods available in 1913 is displayed.*

Pockerley Manor farm

The 1825 Railway

Steam Winding Engine

Mahogany Drift mine*, a tunnel driven into coal seams near the surface, was here long before the museum and was worked from the 1850s to 1958. Visitors are given guided tours to underground pits.*

Entrance

Houses built by the London Lead Company in Middleton-in-Teesdale

Durham ⓮

See pp414–5.

North Pennines Tour ⓯

See p413.

Cotherstone cheese, a speciality of the Middleton-in-Teesdale area

Middleton-in-Teesdale ⓰

County Durham. *1,100.* *Darlington.* *10 Market Place (01833 641001).*

CLINGING TO A HILLSIDE amid wild Pennine scenery on the River Tees is this old lead mining town. Many of its rows of grey stone cottages were built by the London Lead Company, a paternalistic, Quaker-run organization who influenced every corner of its employees' daily lives.

The company began mining in 1753, and soon it virtually owned the town. Workers were expected to observe strict temperance, send their children to Sunday school and conform to the many company maxims. Today, mining has all but ceased in Teesdale, with Middleton standing as a monument to the 18th-century idea of the "company town". The offices of the London Lead Company can still be seen, as well as Nonconformist chapels from the era and a memorial fountain made of iron.

The crumbly Cotherstone cow's milk cheese, a speciality of the surrounding dales, is available in the shops.

Barnard Castle ⓱

County Durham. *5,000.* *Darlington.* *Woodleigh, Flatts Rd (01833 690909).* *Wed.*

BARNARD CASTLE, known in the area as "Barney", is a little town full of character, with old shopfronts and a cobbled market overlooked by the ruins of the Norman castle from which it takes its name. The original Barnard Castle was built around 1125–40 by Bernard Balliol, ancestor of the founder of Balliol College, Oxford *(see p210)*, to guard a river crossing point. Later, the market town grew up around the fortification.

Today, Barnard Castle is known for the extraordinary French-style château to the east of the town, surrounded by acres of formal gardens. Started in 1860 by the local aristocrat John Bowes and his French wife Josephine, an artist and actress, it was never a private residence, but always intended as a museum and public monument. The château finally opened in 1892, by which time the couple were both dead. Nevertheless, the **Bowes Museum** stands as a monument to his wealth and her extravagance.

The museum houses a strong collection of Spanish art which includes El Greco's *The Tears of St Peter*, dating from the 1580s, and Goya's *Don Juan Meléndez Váldez*, painted in 1797. Clocks, porcelain, furniture, musical instruments, toys and tapestries are among its treasures, with a mechanical silver swan as a showpiece.

Bowes Museum
Barnard Castle. *01833 690606.* *daily.* *(summer).* www.bowesmuseum.org.uk

The Bowes Museum, a French-style château near Barnard Castle

North Pennines Tour ⓯

STARTING JUST TO THE SOUTH of Hadrian's Wall, this tour explores the South Tyne Valley, and Upper Weardale. It crosses one of England's wildest and most remote tracts of moorland, then heads north again. The high ground is mainly blanketed with heather, dotted with sheep or criss-crossed with dry-stone walls, a feature of this region. Harriers and other birds hover above, and streams tumble into valleys of tightly huddled villages.

Sheep grazing on the moors

Celts, Romans and other settlers have left imprints on the North Pennines. The wealth of the area was based on lead mining and stone quarrying which has long co-existed with farming.

Haltwhistle ①
In the Church of the Holy Cross is the tombstone of John Ridley, brother of Protestant martyr, Nicholas Ridley, burnt at the stake in 1555 *(see p210)*.

Haydon Bridge ③
There are some delightful walks near this spa town where the painter John Martin was born in 1789. Nearby Langley Castle is worth a visit.

Hexham ④
A pretty old town *(see p408)*, Hexham has a fine abbey.

Blanchland ⑤
Some houses in this lead-mining village are built on the site of a 12th-century abbey, using the original stone.

Bardon Mill ②
To the north is the Roman fort and civilian settlement of Vindolanda *(see p408)*.

Allendale ⑦
With its capital at Allendale Town, this is an area of spectacular scenery, with many walking and trout fishing opportunities.

Stanhope ⑥
An 18th-century castle overlooks the market square. The giant stump of a fossilized tree, said to be 250 million years old, guards the graveyard.

Tips for Drivers

Length: *50 miles (80 km)*
Stopping-off points: *Several pubs in Stanhope serve bar meals, and the Durham Dales Centre provides teas all year round. Horsley Hall Hotel at Eastgate serves meals all day. (See also pp636–7.)*

Key

- Tour route
- Other roads
- Viewpoint

0 kilometres 5

0 miles 5

Durham ⓮

Cathedral Sanctuary knocker

THE CITY OF DURHAM was built on Island Hill or "Dunholm" in 995. This rocky peninsula, which defies the course of the River Wear's route to the sea, was chosen as the last resting place for the remains of St Cuthbert. The relics of the Venerable Bede were brought to the site 27 years later, adding to its attraction for pilgrims. Durham Cathedral was treated by architects as an experiment for geometric patterning, while the Castle served as the Episcopal Palace until 1832, when Bishop William van Mildert gave it up and surrendered part of his income to found Britain's third university. The 23 ha (57 acre) peninsula has many footpaths, views and fine buildings.

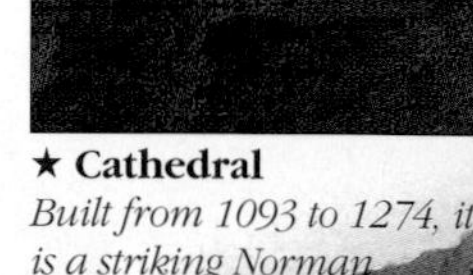

★ Cathedral
Built from 1093 to 1274, it is a striking Norman structure.

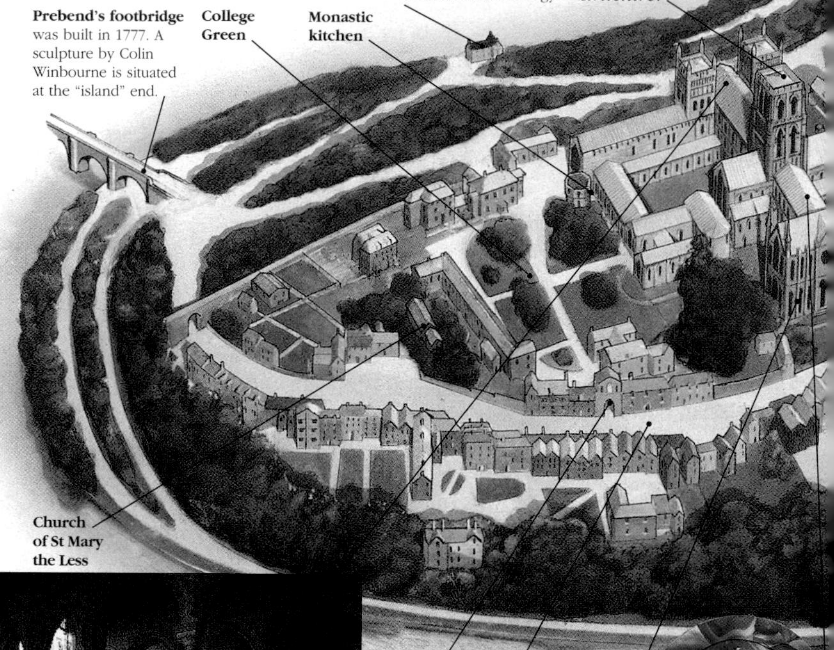

Old Fulling Mill, a largely 18th-century building, houses a museum of archaeology.

Prebend's footbridge was built in 1777. A sculpture by Colin Winbourne is situated at the "island" end.

College Green

Monastic kitchen

Church of St Mary the Less

College gatehouse

South Bailey

St Cuthbert's Tomb

Galilee Chapel
Architects began work on the exotic Galilee Chapel in 1170, drawing inspiration from the Great Mosque of Cordoba in Andalusia. It was altered by Bishop Langley (d.1437) whose tomb is by the west door.

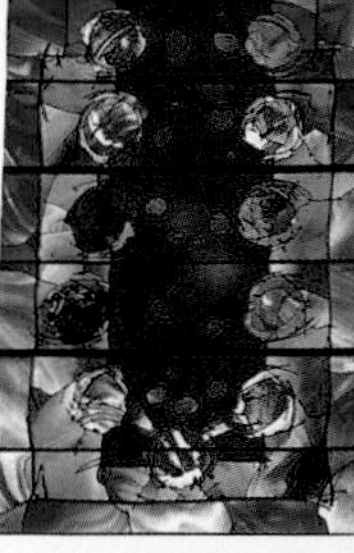

"Our Daily Bread" Window
This modern stained glass window in the north nave aisle was donated in 1984 by a local department store.

STAR SIGHTS

- **★ Cathedral**
- **★ Castle**

★ Castle
Begun in 1072, the castle is a fine Norman fortress. The keep, sited on a mound, is now part of the university.

Visitors' Checklist

County Durham. Station Approach. North Rd. Millennium Pl (0191 384 3720). **Cathedral** 9:30am–6:15pm daily (to 5pm Sun). 11:15am, 3:30pm Sun. **Castle** 0191 374 3800. univ hols: daily; term: Mon, Wed, Sat (pm).

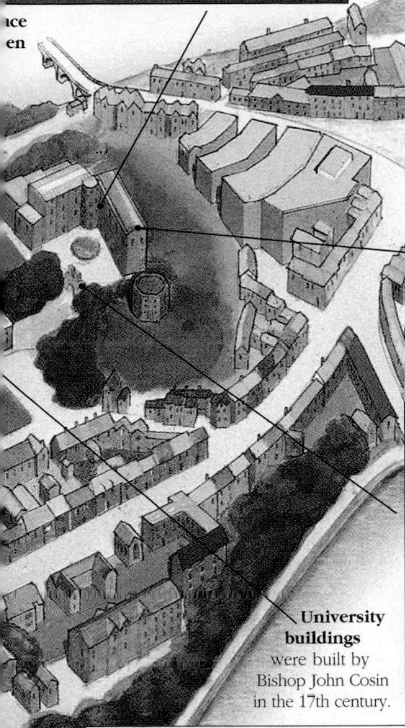

Town Hall (1851)

St Nicholas' Church (1857)

ace
en

Tunstal's Chapel
Situated at the end of the Tunstal's Gallery, the castle chapel was built c.1542. Its fine woodwork includes this unicorn misericord (see p329).

Castle Gatehouse
Traces of Norman stonework can be seen in the outer arch, while the sturdy walls and upper floors are 18th century, rebuilt in a style dubbed "gothick" by detractors.

University buildings were built by Bishop John Cosin in the 17th century.

rch of St
le Bow

ingsgate
otbridge,
built from
–3, leads
to North
Bailey.

Cathedral Architecture

The vast dimensions of the 900-year-old columns, piers and vaults, and the inventive giant lozenge and chevron, trellis and dogtooth patterns carved into the stone columns, are the main innovative features of Durham Cathedral. It is believed that 11th- and 12th-century architects such as Bishop Ranulph Flambard tried to unify all parts of the structure. This can be seen in the south aisle of the nave below.

Ribbed vaults*, criss-crossing above the nave, are now common in church ceilings. One of the major achievements of Gothic architecture, they were first built at Durham.*

The lozenge *shape is a pattern from prehistoric carving, but never before seen in a cathedral.*

Chevron patterns *on some of the piers in the nave are evidence of Moorish influence.*

BH11

Wales

Introducing Wales 418–425

North Wales 426–441

South and Mid-Wales 442–461

Wales at a Glance

WALES IS A COUNTRY of outstanding natural beauty with varied landscapes. Visitors come to climb dramatic mountain peaks, go walking in the forests, fish in the broad rivers and enjoy the miles of unspoilt coastline. The country's many seaside resorts have long been popular with English holidaymakers. As well as outdoor pursuits there is the vibrancy of Welsh culture, with its strong Celtic roots, to be experienced. Finally there are many fine castles, ruined abbeys, mansions and cities full of magnificent architecture.

***Beaumaris Castle** was intended to be a key part of Edward I's "iron ring" to contain the rebellious Welsh* (see p422). *Begun in 1295 but never completed, the castle* (see p424) *has a sophisticated defence structure that is unparalleled in Wales.*

Anglesey

Caernarfonshire & Merionethshire

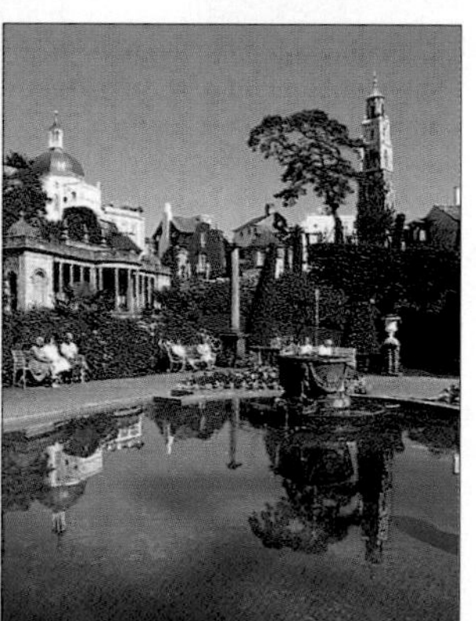

Portmeirion (see pp440–41) *is a private village whose astonishing buildings seem rather incongruous in the Welsh landscape. The village was created by the architect Sir Clough Williams-Ellis to fulfill a personal ambition. Some of the buildings are assembled from pieces of architecture taken from sites around the country.*

Card

Carmarthensh

Pembrokeshire

***St David** is the smallest city in Britain. The cathedral* (see pp450–51) *is the largest in Wales, and its nave is noted for its carved oak roof and beautiful rood screen. Next to the cathedral is the medieval Bishop's Palace, now a ruin.*

◁ **Caernarfon's colourful quayside marina**

Llanberis and Snowdon (see p437) *is an area famous for dangerous, high peaks, long popular with climbers. Mount Snowdon's summit is most easily reached from Llanberis. Its Welsh name,* Yr Wyddfa Fawr, *means "great tomb" and it is the legendary burial place of a giant slain by King Arthur* (see p273).

Conwy Castle *guards one of the best-preserved medieval fortified towns in Britain* (see pp432–3). *Built by Edward I, the castle was besieged and came close to surrender in 1294. It was taken by Owain Glyndŵr's supporters in 1401.*

Flintshire

rconwy
'olwyn

Denbighshire

NORTH WALES
(see pp426–41)

Wrexham

The Brecon Beacons (see pp454–5) *is a national park, a lovely area of mountains, forest and moorland in South Wales, which is a favourite with walkers and naturalists. Pen-y-Fan is one of the principal summits.*

Powys

SOUTH AND MID-WALES
(see pp442–61)

Cardiff Castle's (see pp458–9) *Clock Tower is just one of many 19th-century additions by the eccentric but gifted architect William Burges. His flamboyant style still delights and amazes visitors.*

Monmouthshire

rdiff, Swansea & Environs

0 kilometres **25**

0 miles **25**

A Portrait of Wales

LONG POPULAR WITH BRITISH HOLIDAYMAKERS, *the many charms of Wales are now becoming better known internationally. They include spectacular scenery and a vibrant culture specializing in male-voice choirs, poetry and a passionate love of team sports. Governed from Westminster since 1536, Wales has its own distinct Celtic identity and in 1999 finally gained partial devolution.*

Much of the Welsh landmass is covered by the Cambrian Mountain range, which effectively acts as a barrier from England. Wales is warmed by the Gulf Stream and has a mild climate, with more rain than most of Britain. The land is unsuitable for arable farming, but sheep and cattle thrive; the drove roads, along which sheep used to be driven across the hills to England, are now popular walking trails. It is partly because of the rugged terrain that the Welsh have managed to maintain their separate identity and their ancient language.

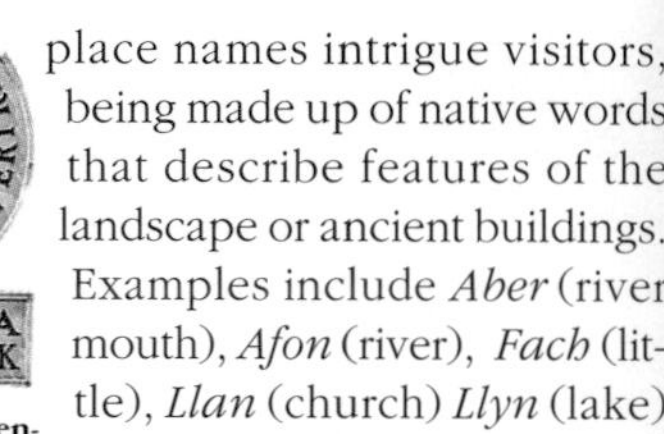

One of Wales's splendid National Parks

Welsh is an expansive, musical language, spoken by only one-fifth of the 2.7 million inhabitants, but in parts of North Wales it is still the main language of conversation. There is an official bilingual policy: road signs are in Welsh and English, even in areas where Welsh is little spoken. Welsh place names intrigue visitors, being made up of native words that describe features of the landscape or ancient buildings. Examples include *Aber* (river mouth), *Afon* (river), *Fach* (little), *Llan* (church) *Llyn* (lake) and *Nant* (valley).

Mountain sheep: a familiar sight in rural Wales

Wales was conquered by the Romans, but not by the Saxons. The land and the people therefore retained Celtic patterns of settlement and husbandry for six centuries before the Norman Conquest in 1066. This allowed time for the development of a distinctive Welsh nation whose homogeneity continues to this day.

Rugby: the popuiar Welsh sport

The early Norman kings subjugated the Welsh by appointing "Marcher Lords" to control areas bordering England. A string of massive castles provides evidence of the turbulent years when Welsh insurrection was a constant threat. It was not until 1535 that Wales formally became part of Britain, and it would take nearly 500 years before the people of Wales regained partial autonomy.

Religious non-conformism and radical politics are deeply rooted in Welsh consciousness. Saint David converted the country to Christianity in the 6th century. Methodism, chapel and teetotalism became firmly entrenched in

A *gorsedd* (assembly) of bards at the eisteddfod

the Welsh psyche during the 19th century. Even today some pubs stay closed on Sundays (alcohol is not sold at all in the Llŷn Peninsula). A longstanding oral tradition in Wales has produced many outstanding public speakers, politicians and actors. Welsh labour leaders have played important roles in the British trade union movement and the development of socialism.

Welsh lovespoon

Welsh heritage is steeped in song, music, poetry and legend rather than handicrafts, although one notable exception is the carved Welsh lovespoon – a craft recently revived. The well-known Welsh love of music derives from the ancient bards: minstrels and poets, who may have been associated with the Druids. Bardic tales of quasi-historical figures and magic were part of the oral tradition of the Dark Ages. They were first written down in the 14th century as the *Mabinogion,* which has inspired Welsh poets up to the 20th century's Dylan Thomas. The male-voice choirs found in many towns, villages and factories, particularly in the industrial south, express the Welsh musical heritage. Choirs compete in eisteddfods: festivals that celebrate Welsh culture.

In the 19th century, the opening of the South Wales coalfield in Mid-Glamorgan – for a time the biggest in the world – led to an industrial boom, with mass migration from the countryside to the iron and steelworks. This prosperity was not to last: apart from a brief respite in World War II, the coal industry has been in terminal decline for decades, causing severe economic hardship. Today tourism is being promoted in the hope that the wealth generated, by outdoor activities in particular, will be able to take "King Coal's" place.

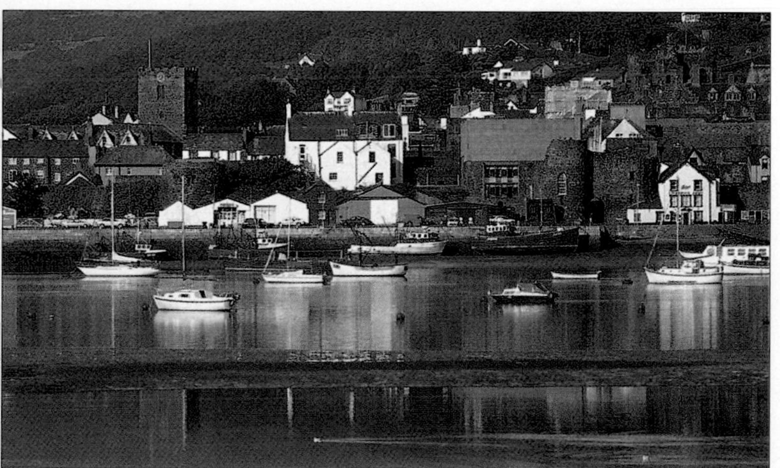

Conwy's picturesque, medieval walled town, fronted by a colourful harbour

The History of Wales

St David, patron saint of Wales

WALES HAS BEEN SETTLED since prehistoric times, its history shaped by many factors, from invasion to industrialization. The Romans set up bases in the mountainous terrain, but it was effectively a separate Celtic nation when Offa's Dyke was built as the border with England in 770. Centuries of cross-border raids and military campaigns followed before England and Wales were formally united by the Act of Union in 1535. The rugged northwest, the former stronghold of the Welsh princes, remains the heartland of Welsh language and culture.

Owain Glyndwr, heroic leader of Welsh opposition to English rule

THE CELTIC NATION

Ornamental Iron Age bronze plaque from Anglesey

WALES WAS SETTLED by waves of migrants in prehistoric times. By the Iron Age *(see pp42–3)*, Celtic farmers had established hillforts and their religion, Druidism. From the 1st century AD until the legions withdrew around 400, the Romans built fortresses and roads, and mined lead, silver and gold. During the next 200 years, Wales was converted to Christianity by missionaries from Europe. St David *(see pp450–51)*, the Welsh patron saint, is said to have turned the leek into a national symbol. He persuaded soldiers to wear leeks in their hats to distinguish themselves from Saxons during a 6th-century skirmish.

The Saxons *(see pp46–7)* failed to conquer Wales, and in 770 the Saxon King Offa built a defensive earthwork along the unconquered territory *(see p447)*. Beyond Offa's Dyke the people called themselves *Y Cymry* (fellow countrymen) and the land *Cymru*. The Saxons called the land "Wales" from the Old English *wealas*, meaning foreigners. It was divided into kingdoms of which the main ones were Gwynedd in the north, Powys in the centre and Dyfed in the south. There were strong trade, cultural and linguistic links between each.

MARCHER LORDS

THE NORMAN INVASION of 1066 *(see p47)* did not reach Wales, but the border territory ("the Marches") was given by William the Conqueror to three powerful barons based at Shrewsbury, Hereford and Chester. These Marcher Lords made many incursions into Wales and controlled most of the lowlands. But the Welsh princes held the mountainous northwest and exploited English weaknesses. Under Llywelyn the Great (d.1240), North Wales was almost completely independent; in 1267 his grandson, Llywelyn the Last, was acknowledged as Prince of Wales by Henry III.

Edward I designating his son Prince of Wales in 1301

In 1272 Edward I came to the English throne. He built fortresses and embarked on a military campaign to conquer Wales. In 1283 Llywelyn was killed in a skirmish, a shattering blow for the Welsh. Edward introduced English law and proclaimed his son Prince of Wales *(see p430)*.

OWAIN GLYNDŴR'S REBELLION

WELSH RESENTMENT against the Marcher Lords led to rebellion. In 1400 Owain Glyndŵr (c.1350–1416), a descendant of the Welsh princes, laid waste to English-dominated towns and castles. Declaring himself Prince of Wales, he found Celtic allies in Scotland, Ireland, France and Northumbria. In 1404 Glyndŵr captured Harlech and Cardiff, and formed a parliament in Machynlleth *(see p448)*. In 1408 the French made a truce with the English king, Henry IV. The rebellion then failed and Glyndŵr went into hiding until his death.

Union with England

Wales suffered greatly during the Wars of the Roses *(see p49)* as Yorkists and Lancastrians tried to gain control of the strategically important Welsh castles. The wars ended in 1485, and the Welshman Henry Tudor, born in Pembroke, became Henry VII. The Act of Union in 1535 and other laws abolished the Marcher Lordships, giving Wales parliamentary representation in London instead. English practices replaced inheritance customs and English became the language of the courts and administration. The Welsh language survived, partly helped by the church and by Dr William Morgan's translation of the Bible in 1588.

Vernacular Bible, which helped to keep the Welsh language alive

Miners from South Wales pictured in 1910

Industry and Radical Politics

The industrialization of south and east Wales began with the development of open-cast coal mining near Wrexham and Merthyr Tydfil in the 1760s. Convenient ports and the arrival of the railways helped the process. By the second half of the 19th century open-cast mines had been superseded by deep pits in the Rhondda Valley.

Living and working conditions were poor for industrial and agricultural workers. A series of "Rebecca Riots" in South Wales between 1839 and 1843, involving tenant farmers (dressed as women) protesting about tithes and rents, was forcibly suppressed. The Chartists, trade unions and the Liberal Party had much Welsh support.

The rise of Methodism *(see p267)* roughly paralleled the growth of industry: 80 per cent of the population was Methodist by 1851. The Welsh language persisted, despite attempts by the British government to discourage its use, which included punishing children caught speaking it.

Wales Today

In the 20th century the Welsh, for the first time, became a power in British politics. David Lloyd George, although not born in Wales, grew up there and was the first British Prime Minister to come from a Welsh family. Aneurin Bevan, a miner's son who became a Labour Cabinet Minister, helped create the National Health Service *(see p59)*.

Welsh nationalism continued to grow: in 1926 Plaid Cymru, the Welsh Nationalist Party, was formed. In 1955 Cardiff was recognized as the capital of Wales *(see p456)* and four years later the ancient symbol of the red dragon became the emblem on Wales' new flag. Plaid Cymru won two parliamentary seats at Westminster in 1974, and in a 1998 referendum the Welsh espoused limited home rule.

The Welsh language has declined: whereas half the population could speak it in 1901, the figure was down to 21 per cent 70 years later. The 1967 Welsh Language Act gave it protection by making Welsh compulsory in schools and the television channel S4C (Sianel 4 Cymru), formed in 1982, broadcasts many programmes in Welsh.

From the 1960s the steel and coal industries declined, creating mass unemployment. This has been only partly alleviated by the emergence of new, high-tech industries, and by the recent growth in tourism and higher education.

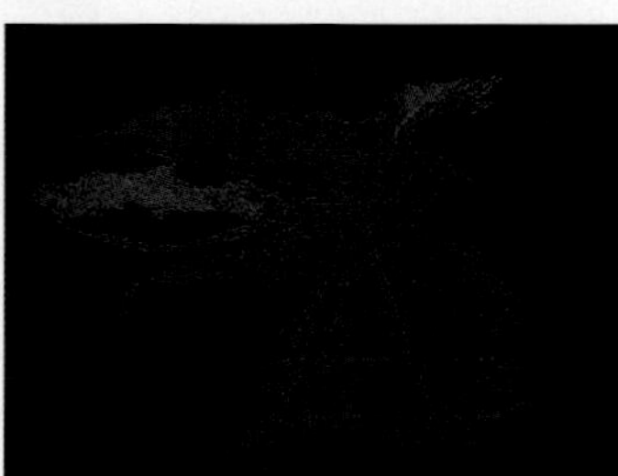

The logo of S4C, Wales's own television station

Castles of Wales

A French 15th-century painting of Conwy Castle

WALES IS RICH in romantic medieval castles. Soon after the Battle of Hastings, in 1066 *(see p47)*, the Normans turned their attentions to Wales. They built earth and timber fortifications, later replaced by stone castles, initiating a building programme that was pursued by the Welsh princes and invading forces. Construction reached its peak during the reign of Edward I *(see p422)*. As the need for security lessened in the later Middle Ages, some castles became stately homes.

The north gatehouse was planned to be 18 m (60 ft) high, providing lavish royal accommodation, but its top storey was never built.

The inner ward was lined with a hall, granary, kitchens and stables.

Rounded towers, with fewer blind spots than square ones, gave better protection.

Arrow slit

Moat

Curtain wall

Beaumaris Castle

The last of Edward I's Welsh castles *(see p430)*, this perfectly symmetrical, concentric design was intended to combine impregnable defence with comfort. Invaders would face many obstacles before reaching the inner ward.

Where to See Welsh Castles

In addition to Beaumaris, in North Wales there are medieval forts at Caernarfon *(see p430)*, Conwy *(see p432)* and Harlech *(see p440)*. Edward I also built Denbigh, Flint (near Chester) and Rhuddlan (near Rhyll). In South and mid-Wales, Caerphilly (near Cardiff), Kidwelly (near Carmarthen) and Pembroke were built between the 11th and 13th centuries. Spectacular sites are occupied by Cilgerran (near Cardigan), Criccieth (near Porthmadog) and Carreg Cennen *(see p454)*. Chirk Castle, near Llangollen, is a good example of a fortress that has since become a stately home.

***Caerphilly**, 6 miles (10 km) north of Cardiff, is a huge castle with concentric stone and water defences that cover 12 ha (30 acres).*

***Harlech Castle** (see p440) is noted for its massive gatehouse, twin towers and the fortified stairway to the sea. It was the headquarters of the Welsh resistance leader Owain Glyndŵr (see p422) from 1404–8.*

Castell-Ŷ-Bere

This native Welsh castle at the foot of Cader Idris *(see p440)* was founded by Llywelyn the Great in 1221 *(see p422)*, to secure internal borders rather than to resist the English.

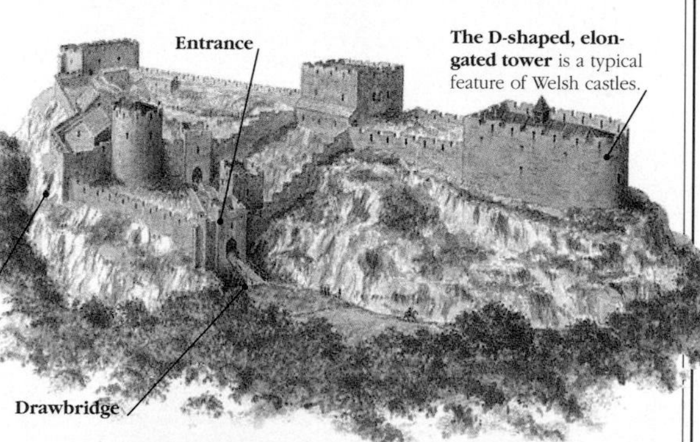

Entrance

The D-shaped, elongated tower is a typical feature of Welsh castles.

The castle's construction follows the shape of the rock. The curtain walls are too low and insubstantial to be of much practical use.

Drawbridge

The Chapel Tower has a utiful medieval chapel.

The protected dock, on a channel that originally led to the sea, received supplies during sieges.

nner wall, with an passage, was higher he curtain wall to t simultaneous firing.

Twin-towered gatehouse

Edward I and Master James of St George

In 1278 Edward I brought over from Savoy a master stonemason who became a great military architect, James of St George. Responsible for planning and building at least 12 of Edward's fine Welsh castles, James was paid well and liberally pensioned off, indicating the esteem in which he was held by the king.

Edward I (see p422) *was the warrior king whose castles played a key role in the subjugation of the Welsh people.*

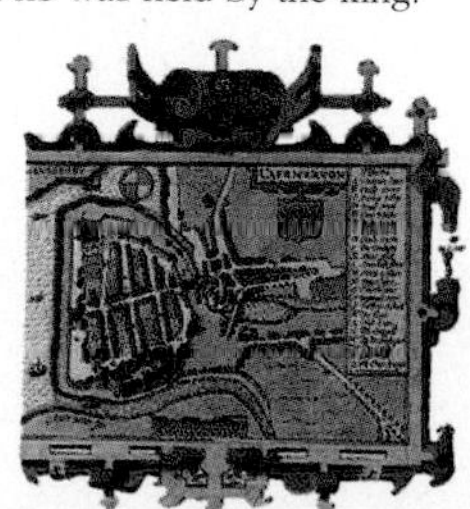

A plan of Caernarfon Castle *illustrates how its position, on a promontory surrounded by water, has determined the building's shape and defence.*

Caernarfon Castle (see p430), *birthplace of the ill-fated Edward II* (see p315), *was intended to be the official royal residence in North Wales, and has palatial private apartments.*

Castell Coch *was restored in Neo-Gothic style by Lord Bute and William Burges* (see p458). *Mock-castles were built by many Victorian industrialists.*

Conwy Castle (see p433), *like many other castles, required forced labour on a massive scale for its construction.*

North Wales

Aberconwy & Colwyn · Anglesey · Caernarfonshire & Merionethshire · Denbighshire · Flintshire · Wrexham

The North Wales landscape *has a dramatic quality reflected in its history. In prehistoric times, Anglesey was a stronghold of the religious elite known as the Druids. Roman and Norman invasions concentrated on the coast, leaving the mountains to the Welsh. These wild areas are the centre of Welsh language and culture.*

Defence and conquest have been constant themes in Welsh history. North Wales was the scene of ferocious battles between the Welsh princes and Anglo-Norman monarchs determined to establish English rule. The string of formidable castles which still stand in North Wales are as much a testament to Welsh resistance as to the wealth and strength of the invaders. Several massive fortresses, including Beaumaris, Caernarfon and Harlech, almost surround the rugged high country of Snowdonia, an area that even today maintains an untamed quality.

Sheep and cattle farming are the basis of the rural economy here, though there are also large areas of forestry. Along the coast, tourism is a major activity. Llandudno, a purpose-built Victorian resort, popularized the sandy northern coastline in the 19th century. The area continues to attract large numbers of visitors, though major development is confined to the narrow coastal strip that lies between Prestatyn and Llandudno, leaving the island of Anglesey and the remote Llŷn Peninsula largely untouched. The Llŷn Peninsula remains one of the strongholds of the Welsh language, along with rather isolated inland communities, such as Dolgellau and Bala.

No part of North Wales can truly be called industrial, though there are still remnants of the once-prosperous slate industry in Snowdonia, where the stark, grey quarries provide a striking contrast to the natural beauty of the surrounding mountains. At the foot of Snowdon (the highest mountain in Wales), the villages of Beddgelert, Betws-y-Coed and Llanberis are popular bases for walkers who come to enjoy the spectacular views and striking beauty of this remote region.

Caernarfon Castle, one of the forbidding fortresses built by Edward I

◁ The River Dee at Llangollen, still an area of unspoilt natural beauty

Exploring North Wales

THE DOMINANT FEATURE of North Wales is Snowdon, the highest mountain in Wales. Snowdonia National Park extends dramatically from the Snowdon massif south beyond Dolgellau, with thickly wooded valleys, mountain lakes, moors and estuaries. To the east are the softer Clwydian Hills, and unspoilt coastlines can be enjoyed on Anglesey and the beautiful Llŷn Peninsula.

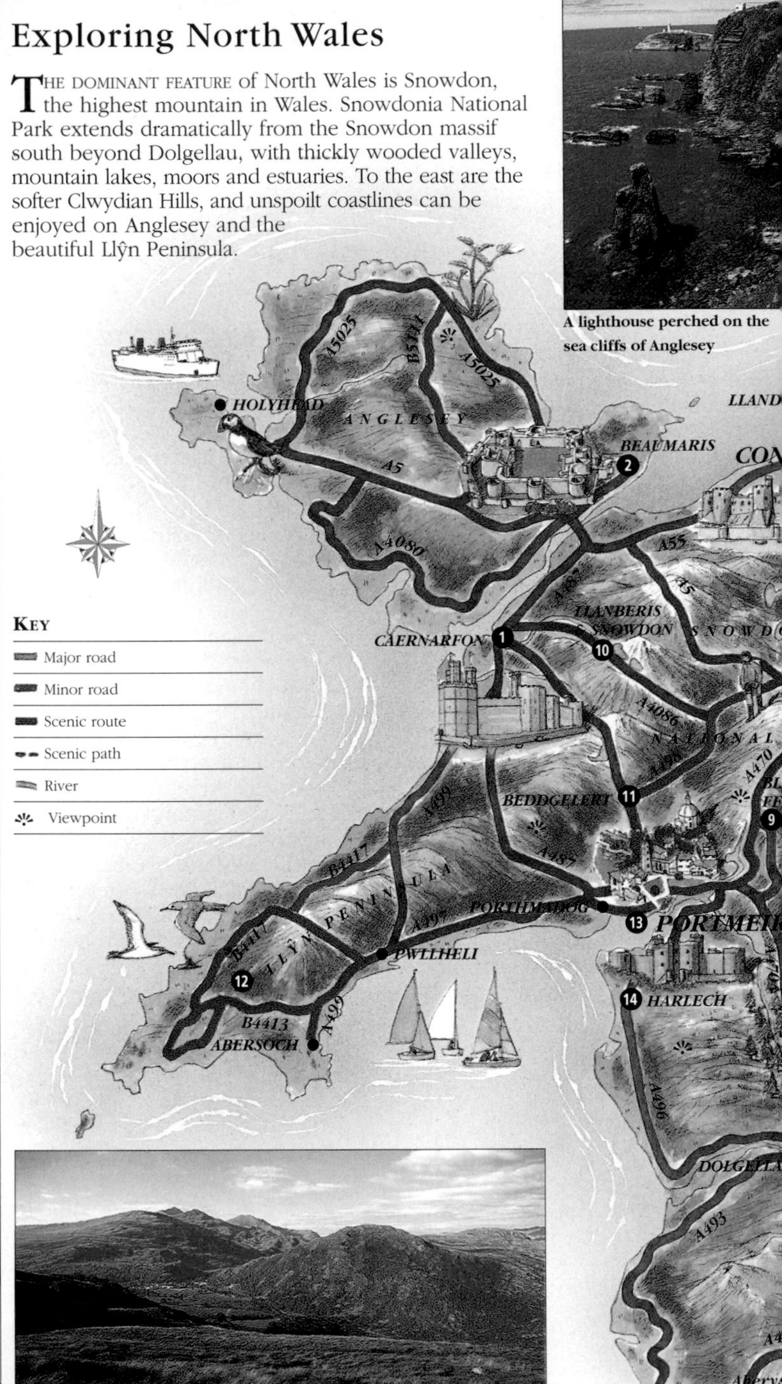

A lighthouse perched on the sea cliffs of Anglesey

The peaks and moorland of Snowdonia

Getting Around

The main route into North Wales from the northwest of England is the A55, a good dual carriageway which bypasses several places that used to be traffic bottlenecks, including Conwy. The other main route through the region is the A5 Shrewsbury to Holyhead road, which follows a trail through the mountains pioneered by the 19th-century engineer Thomas Telford *(see p433)*. Rail services run along the coast to Holyhead, connecting with ferries across the Irish Sea to Dublin and Dun Laoghaire. Scenic branch lines travel from Llandudno Junction to Blaenau Ffestiniog (via Betws-y-Coed) and along the southern Llŷn Peninsula.

Sights at a Glance

Aberdyfi 16
Bala 7
Beaumaris 2
Beddgelert 11
Betws-y-Coed 8
Blaenau Ffestiniog 9
Caernarfon 1
Conwy pp432–3 3
Dolgellau 15
Harlech 14
Llanberis and Snowdon 10
LLandudno 4
LLangollen 6
Llŷn Peninsula 12
Portmeirion pp440–41 13
Ruthin 5

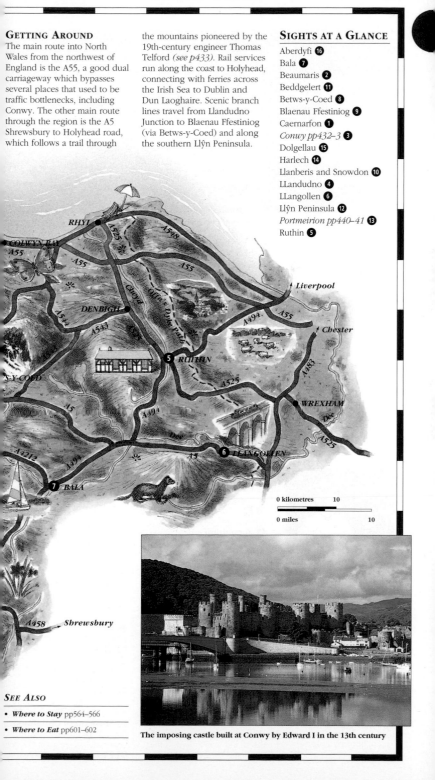

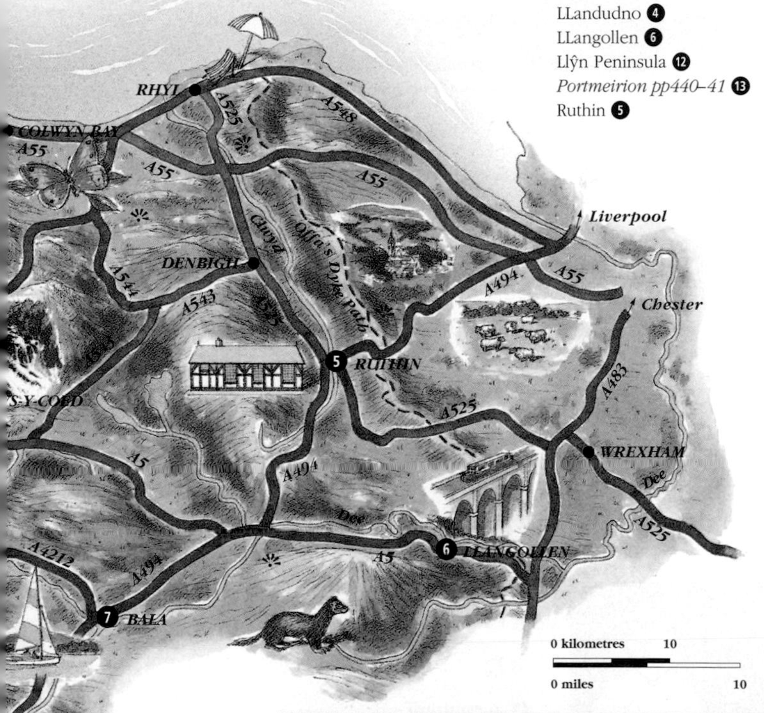

0 kilometres 10
0 miles 10

The imposing castle built at Conwy by Edward I in the 13th century

See Also

- ***Where to Stay*** pp564–566
- ***Where to Eat*** pp601–602

Caernarfon Castle, built by Edward I as a symbol of his power over the conquered Welsh

Caernarfon ❶

Caernarfonshire & Merionethshire (Gwynedd). 10,000. *Castle St (01286 672232).* *Sat.* www.gwynedd.gov.uk

One of the most famous castles in Wales looms over this busy town. Both were created after Edward I's defeat of the last native Welsh prince, Llywelyn ap Gruffydd (Llywelyn the Last) in 1283 *(see p422)*. The town walls merge with modern streets that spread beyond the medieval centre to a market square.

Overlooking the town and its harbour, **Caernarfon Castle** *(see p425)*, with its polygonal towers, was built as a seat of government for North Wales. Caernarfon was a thriving port in the 19th century, and during this period the castle ruins were restored by the architect Anthony Salvin. Displays in the castle include the Royal Welch Fusiliers Museum, and exhibitions tracing the history of the Princes of Wales and exploring the theme "Chieftains and Princes".

On the hill above the town are the ruins of **Segontium**, a Roman fort built in about AD 78. Local legend claims that the first Christian Emperor of Rome, Constantine the Great, was born here in 280.

The Investiture

In 1301 the future Edward II became the first English Prince of Wales *(see p422)*, a title since held by the British monarch's eldest son. In 1969 the investiture in Caernarfon Castle of Prince Charles *(above)* as Prince of Wales drew 500 million TV viewers.

Caernarfon Castle
Y Maes. *01286 677617.* *daily.* *call for details.* www.cadw.wales.gov.uk

Segontium
Beddgelert Rd. *01286 675625.* *daily (Sun: pm).* *24, 26 Dec, 1 Jan.* *limited.* www.nmgw.ac.uk

Beaumaris ❷

Anglesey (Gwynedd). *2,000.* *Llanfair PG, Station Site, Holyhead Rd, Anglesey (01248 713177).* www.anglesey.gov.uk

Handsome Georgian and Victorian architecture gives Beaumaris the air of a resort on England's southern coast. The buildings reflect this sailing centre's past role as Anglesey's chief port, before the island was linked to the mainland by the road and railway bridges built across the Menai Strait in the 19th century. This was the site of Edward I's last, and possibly greatest, **castle** *(see p424)*, which was built to command this important ferrying point to the mainland of Wales.

Ye Olde Bull's Head inn, on Castle Street, was built in 1617. Its celebrated literary patrons have included Dr Samuel Johnson (1709–84) and Victorian novelist Charles Dickens *(see p177)*.

The town's **Courthouse**, was built in 1614 and the recently restored 1829 **Gaol** preserves its soundproofed punishment room and a huge treadmill for prisoners. Two public hangings took place here. Richard Rowlands, the last victim, protested his innocence and cursed the church clock as he was led to the gallows, declaring that its four faces would never show the same times again. It failed to show consistent times until it had an overhaul in 1980.

Beaumaris's award-winning **Museum of Childhood** contains a collection of toys from the 19th and 20th centuries.

Beaumaris Castle
Castle St. *01248 810361.* *daily.* www.cadw.wales.gov.uk

Courthouse
Castle. *01248 810921.* *Apr–Sep: daily.*

Gaol
Bunkers Hill. *01248 810921.* *Apr–Sep: daily.* *limited.*

Museum of Childhood
Castle St. *01248 712498.* *2 wks before Easter–Nov: daily (Sun: pm).* www.cadw.wales.gov.uk

Alice in Wonderland

The Gogarth Abbey Hotel, Llandudno, was the summer home of the Liddells. Their friend, Charles Dodgson (1832–98), would entertain young Alice Liddell with stories of characters such as the White Rabbit and the Mad Hatter. As Lewis Carroll, Dodgson wrote his magical tales in *Alice's Adventures in Wonderland* (1865) and *Through the Looking-Glass* (1871).

Arthur Rackham's illustration (1907) of *Alice in Wonderland*

Conwy ❸

See pp432–3.

Llandudno ❹

Gwynedd. 19,000. 1–2 Chapel St (01492 876413).
www.llandudno-tourism.co.uk

Llandudno's crescent-shaped bay

LLANDUDNO retains much of the holiday spirit of the 19th century, when the new railways brought crowds to the coast. Its **pier**, more than 700 m (2,295 ft) long, and its canopied walkways recall the heyday of seaside holidays. The town is proud of its association with the author Lewis Carroll. **The Alice in Wonderland Centre** is a grotto decorated with life-sized scenes from his books.

Llandudno's cheerful seaside atmosphere owes much to a strong sense of its Victorian roots – unlike many British seaside towns, which embraced the flashing lights and funfairs of the 20th century. To take full advantage of its sweeping beach, Llandudno was laid out between its two headlands, Great Orme's Head and Little Orme's Head.

Great Orme's Head, now a Country Park and Nature Reserve, rises to 207 m (670 ft) and has a long history. In the Bronze Age copper was mined here; the **copper mines** and their excavations are open to the public. The **church** on the headland was built from timber in the 6th century by St Tudno, rebuilt in stone in the 13th century, restored in 1855 and is still in use. Local history and wildlife can be traced in an information centre on the summit.

There are two effortless ways to reach the summit: on the **Great Orme Tramway**, one of only three cable-hauled street tramways in the world (the others are in San Francisco and Lisbon), or by the **Llandudno Cable Car**. Both operate only in summer.

The Alice in Wonderland Centre
Trinity Sq. *01492 860082.* *Easter–Oct: daily; Nov–Easter: Mon–Sat.* *1 Jan, 2 wks in Nov, 25–26 Dec.*
www.wonderland.co.uk

Great Orme Copper Mines
Off A55. *01492 870447.* *Feb–Oct: daily.* *limited.*

Ruthin ❺

Denbighshire (Clwyd). 5,000. Craft Centre, Park Rd (01824 703992). 1st Tue of every month; Thu (indoor).
www.borderlands.co.uk

RUTHIN'S LONG-STANDING prosperity as a market town is reflected in its fine half-timbered medieval buildings. These include the National Westminster and Barclays banks in St Peter's Square. The former was a 15th-century courthouse and prison, the latter the home of Thomas Exmewe, Lord Mayor of London in 1517–18. **Maen Huail** ("Huail's stone"), a boulder outside Barclays, is said to be where King Arthur *(see p273)* beheaded Huail, his rival in a love affair.

St Peter's Church, on the edge of St Peter's Square, was founded in 1310 and has a Tudor oak roof in the north aisle, with 500 carved panels. Next to the Castle Hotel is the 17th-century **Myddleton Arms** pub, whose seven unusual, Dutch-style, dormer windows are known locally as the "eyes of Ruthin".

The "eyes of Ruthin", an unusual feature in Welsh architecture

Street-by-Street: Conwy ❸

CONWY IS ONE OF BRITAIN'S most underrated historic towns. Until the early 1990s it was famous as a traffic bottleneck, but thanks to a town bypass, its concentration of architectural riches – unparalleled in Wales – can now be appreciated. The castle dominates: a brooding, intimidating monument built by Edward I *(see p424)*. But Conwy is set apart from other medieval towns by its amazingly well-preserved town walls. Fortified with 21 towers and three gateways, the walls form an almost unbroken shield around the old town.

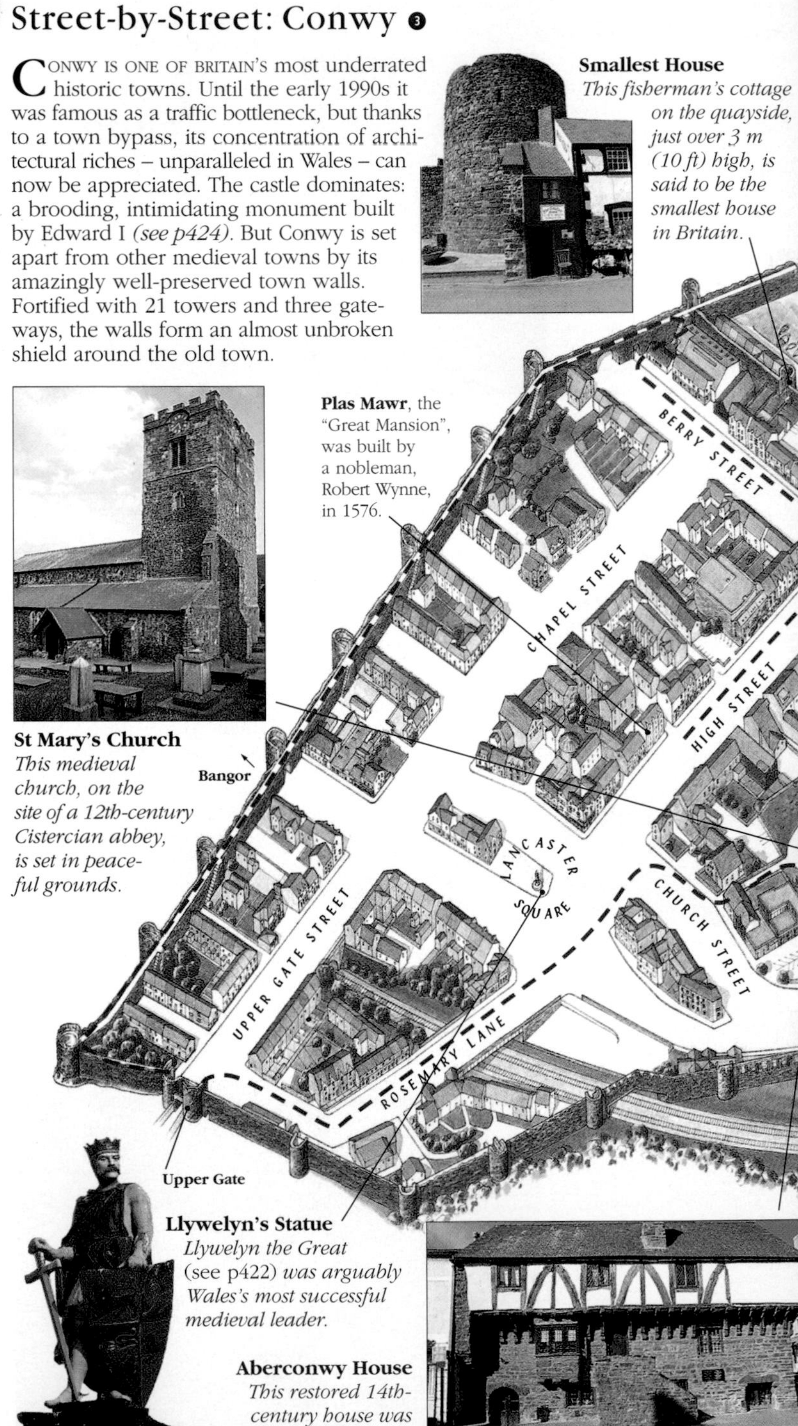

Smallest House
This fisherman's cottage on the quayside, just over 3 m (10 ft) high, is said to be the smallest house in Britain.

Plas Mawr, the "Great Mansion", was built by a nobleman, Robert Wynne, in 1576.

St Mary's Church
This medieval church, on the site of a 12th-century Cistercian abbey, is set in peaceful grounds.

Llywelyn's Statue
Llywelyn the Great (see p422) *was arguably Wales's most successful medieval leader.*

Aberconwy House
This restored 14th-century house was once the home of a wealthy merchant.

Thomas Telford

Thomas Telford (1757–1834) was the gifted Scottish engineer responsible for many of Britain's roads, bridges and canals. The Menai Bridge *(see p430)*, the Pontcysyllte Aqueduct *(see p436)* and Conwy Bridge are his outstanding works in Wales. Telford's graceful bridge at Conwy has aesthetic as well as practical qualities. Completed in 1826 across the mouth of the Conwy estuary, it was designed in a castellated style to blend with the castle. Before the bridge's construction the estuary could only be crossed by ferry.

Visitors' Checklist

Conwy. 8,000. Conwy. 01492 592248. **Aberconwy House (NT)** 01492 592246. Wed–Mon. Nov–Mar. **Conwy Castle** 01492 592358. daily. **Smallest House** 01492 593484. Apr–Oct: daily. www.stayinnorthwales.com

★ **Town Walls**
These remarkably well-preserved medieval walls are 1,280 m (4,200 ft) long and over 9 m (30 ft) high.

Key

— — — Suggested route

Star Sights

★ **Town Walls**

★ **Conwy Castle**

★ **Conwy Castle**
This atmospheric watercolour, Conwy Castle (c.1770), *is by the Nottingham artist Paul Sandby.*

Pontcysyllte Aqueduct, built in 1795–1805, carrying the Llangollen Canal

Llangollen 6

Denbighshire. 5,000. *Town Hall, Castle St (01978 860828).* *Tue.* www.llangollen.org.uk

BEST KNOWN for its annual Eisteddfod (festival), this pretty town sits on the River Dee, which is spanned by a 14th-century bridge. The town became notorious in the 18th century, when two eccentric Irishwomen, Lady Eleanor Butler and Sarah Ponsonby, the "Ladies of Llangollen", set up house together in the half-timbered **Plas Newydd**. Their unconventional dress and literary enthusiasms attracted such celebrities as the Duke of Wellington *(see p150)* and William Wordsworth *(see p354)*. The ruins of a 13th-century castle, **Castell Dinas Brân**, occupy the summit of a hill overlooking the house.

ENVIRONS: Boats on the **Llangollen Canal** sail from Wharf Hill in summer and cross the spectacular 300 m (1,000 ft) long Pontcysyllte Aqueduct, built by Thomas Telford *(see p433)*.

Plas Newydd

Hill St. 01978 861314.
Easter–Oct: daily. *limited.*

Bala 7

Gwynedd. 2,000. *from Llangollen.* *Penllyn, Pensarn Rd (01678 521021).*

BALA LAKE, Wales's largest natural lake, lies between the Aran and Arenig mountains at the fringes of Snowdonia National Park. It is popular for water-sports and boasts a unique fish called a *gwyniad*, which is related to the salmon.

The little grey-stone town of Bala is a Welsh-speaking community, its houses strung out along a single street at the eastern end of the lake. Thomas Charles (1755–1814), a Methodist church leader, once lived here. A plaque on his former home recalls Mary Jones who, in 1800, walked 28 miles (42 km) barefoot from Abergynolwyn to buy a Bible. This prompted Charles to establish the Bible Society, to provide cheap bibles to the working class.

The narrow-gauge **Bala Lake Railway** follows the lake shore from Llanuwchllyn, 4 miles (6 km) southwest.

Betws-y-Coed 8

Conwy. 600. *The Old Stables (01690 710426).*

THIS VILLAGE near the peaks of Snowdonia has been a hill-walking centre since the 19th century. To the west are the **Swallow Falls**, where the River Llugwy flows through a wooded glen. The bizarre **Tŷ Hyll** ("Ugly House"), is a *tŷ unnos* ("one-night house"); traditionally, houses erected between dusk and dawn on common land were entitled to freehold rights, and the owner could enclose land as far as he could throw an axe from the door. To the east is **Waterloo Bridge**, built by Thomas Telford to celebrate the victory against Napoleon.

Tŷ Hyll

Capel Curig. *01690 720287.*
House *Easter–Sep: daily.* **Grounds** *Easter–Sep: daily; Oct–Easter: Mon–Fri.* *limited.*

World Cultures in Llangollen

Llangollen's International Eisteddfod *(see p63)* in the first half of July draws musicians, singers and dancers from around the world. First held in 1947 as a gesture of post-war international unity, it now attracts over 12,000 performers from nearly 50 countries to the six-day-long competition-cum-fair.

Choristers at the Eisteddfod, a popular Welsh festival

The ornate Waterloo Bridge, built in 1815 after the famous battle

◁ The picturesque village of Beddgelert in Snowdonia National Park

A view of the Snowdonia countryside from Llanberis Pass, the most popular route to Snowdon's peak

Blaenau Ffestiniog 9

Gwynedd. 5,500. Betws-y-Coed (01690 710426); Jun–Sep: 01766 830360. Tue (Jun–Sep).

BLAENAU FFESTINIOG, once the slate capital of North Wales, sits among mountains riddled with quarries. The **Llechwedd Slate Caverns**, overlooking Blaenau, opened to visitors in the early 1970s, marking a new role for the declining industrial town. The electric Miners' Tramway takes passengers on a tour into the original caverns.

On the Deep Mine tour, visitors descend on Britain's steepest passenger incline railway to the underground chambers, while sound effects recreate the atmosphere of a working quarry. The dangers included landfalls and floods, as well as the more gradual threat of slate dust breathed into the lungs.

There are slate-splitting demonstrations on the surface, a quarryman's cottage and a re-creation of a Victorian village to illustrate the cramped and basic living conditions endured by workers between the 1880s and 1945.

The popular narrow-gauge **Ffestiniog Railway** *(see pp438–9)* runs from Blaenau to Porthmadog.

Llechwedd Slate Caverns
Off A470. *01766 830306. daily. except the Deep Mine.* www.llechwedd.co.uk

Llanberis and Snowdon 10

Gwynedd. 2,100. High St, Llanberis (01286 870765). www.gwynedd.gov.uk

SNOWDON, which at 1,085 m (3,560 ft) is the highest peak in Wales, is the main focus of the vast Snowdonia National Park, whose scenery ranges from this rugged mountain country to moors and sandy beaches.

The easiest route to Snowdon's summit begins in Llanberis: the 5 mile (8 km) **Llanberis Track**. From Llanberis Pass, the Miners' Track (once used by copper miners) and the Pyg Track are alternative paths. Walkers should beware of sudden weather changes and dress accordingly. The narrow-gauge **Snowdon Mountain Railway**, which opened in 1896, is an easier option.

Llanberis was a major 19th-century slate town, with grey terraces hewn into the hills. Other attractions are the 13th-century shell of **Dolbadarn Castle**, and, above Lake Peris, the **Electric Mountain**, which has tours of Europe's biggest hydro-electric pumped storage station.

Dolbadarn Castle
Off A4086 nr Llanberis. *01286 870765. Jul–Sep: daily; Oct–Jun: call for details.*

Electric Mountain
Llanberis. *01286 870636. Feb–Mar: Thu–Sun; Easter–20 Dec: daily.*

BRITAIN'S CENTRE OF SLATE

Welsh slates provided roofing material for Britain's new towns in the 19th century. In 1898, the slate industry employed nearly 17,000 men, a quarter of whom worked at Blaenau Ffestiniog. Foreign competition and new materials later took their toll. Quarries such as Dinorwig in Llanberis and Llechwedd in Blaenau Ffestiniog now survive on the tourist trade.

The dying art of slate-splitting

The village of Beddgelert, set among the mountains of Snowdonia

Beddgelert 11

Gwynedd. 500. *High St, Porthmadog (01766 512981); Jun–Aug: 01766 890615.* www.gwynedd.gov.uk

BEDDGELERT enjoys a spectacular location in Snowdonia. The village sits on the confluence of the Glaslyn and Colwyn rivers at the approach to two mountain passes: the beautiful Nant Gwynant Pass, which leads to Snowdonia's highest reaches, and the Aberglaslyn Pass, a narrow wooded gorge which acts as a gateway to the sea.

Business was given a boost by Dafydd Pritchard, the landlord of the Royal Goat Hotel, who in the early 19th century adapted an old Welsh legend to associate it with Beddgelert. Llywelyn the Great *(see p422)* is said to have left his faithful hound Gelert to guard his infant son while he went hunting. He returned to find the cradle overturned and Gelert covered in blood. Thinking the dog had savaged his son, Llywellyn slaughtered Gelert, but then discovered the boy, unharmed, under the cradle. Nearby was the corpse of a wolf, which Gelert had killed to protect the child. To support the tale, Pritchard created **Gelert's Grave** (*bedd Gelert* in Welsh) by the River Glaslyn a mound of stones a short walk south of the village.

ENVIRONS: There are many fine walks in the area: one leads south to the Aberglaslyn Pass and along a disused part of the Welsh Highland Railway. The **Sygun Copper Mine**, 1 mile (1.5 km) northeast of Beddgelert, offers self-guided tours of caverns recreating the life of Victorian miners.

Sygun Copper Mine

On A498. *01766 890595/510100. Mar–Nov: daily; Oct–Feb: call for opening hours.* *limited.* www.syguncoppermine.co.uk

Ffestiniog Railway

Engine plaque

THE FFESTINIOG narrow-gauge railway takes a scenic 14 mile (22 km) route from Porthmadog Harbour to the mountains and the slate town of Blaenau Ffestiniog *(see p437)*. Designed to carry slate from the quarries to the quay, the railway replaced a horse-drawn tramway constructed in 1836, operating on a 60 cm (2 ft) gauge. After closure in 1946, it was reconstructed by volunteers and re-opened in sections from 1955–82.

Steam traction *trains were first used on the Ffestiniog Railway in 1863. There are some diesel engines but most trains on the route are still steam-hauled.*

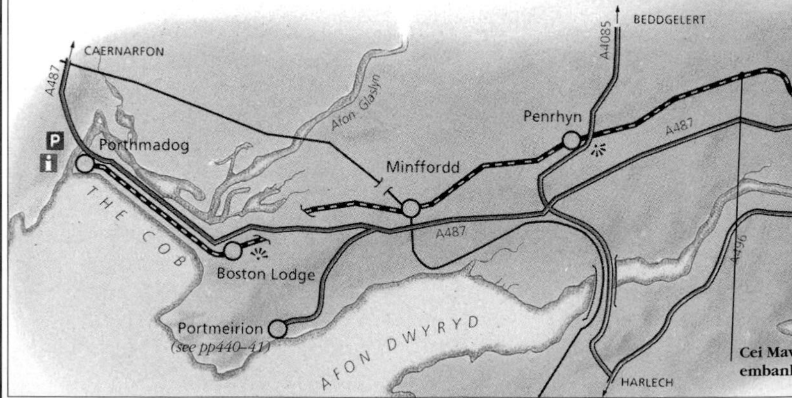

ʟlŷn Peninsula ⓬

ɜwynedd. Pwllheli.
Aberdaron to Bardsey Island.
Min-y-don, Station Sq, Pwllheli
)1758 613000).
www.nwt.co.uk

THIS 24 MILE (38 km) finger of land points southwest ·rom Snowdonia into the Irish ;ea. Although it has popular ɔeaches, notably at Pwllheli, ;riccieth, Abersoch and Nefyn, he coast's overriding feature is ts untamed beauty. Views are ıt their most dramatic in the far vest and along the mountain-ɔacked northern shores.

The windy headland of **Braich-y-Pwll**, to the west of \berdaron, looks out towards Bardsey Island, the "Isle of 20,000 Saints". This became a ɔlace of pilgrimage in the 6th century, when a monastery was founded here. Some of he saints are said to be buried in the churchyard of the ruined 13th-century **St Mary's Abbey**. Close by is **Porth Oer**, a small bay also known as "Whistling Sands" (the sand is meant to squeak, or whistle, underfoot).

East of Aberdaron is the 4 mile (6.5 km) bay of **Porth Neigwl**, known in English as Hell's Mouth, the scene of many shipwrecks due to the bay's treacherous currents. Hidden in sheltered grounds above Porth Neigwl bay, 1 mile (1.5 km) northeast of Aberdaron, is **Plas-yn-Rhiw**, a small, medieval manor house with Tudor and Georgian additions and lovely gardens.

The former quarrying village and "ghost town" of **Llithfaen**, tucked away below the sheer cliffs of the mountainous north coast, is now a centre for Welsh language studies.

Plas-yn-Rhiw
(NT) off B4413. 01758 780219.
Apr–mid-May: Thu–Mon; mid-May–Sep: Wed–Mon. limited.

Llithfaen village, now a language centre, on the Llŷn Peninsula

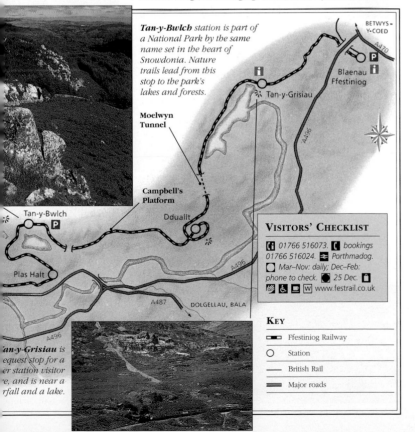

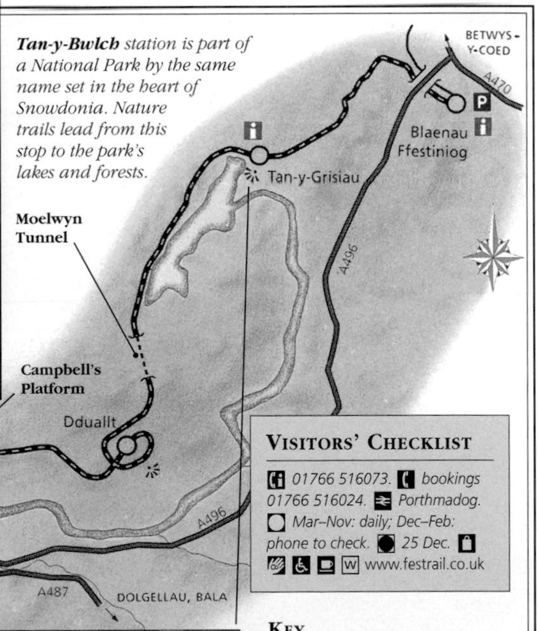

Tan-y-Bwlch *station is part of a National Park by the same name set in the heart of Snowdonia. Nature trails lead from this stop to the park's lakes and forests.*

Moelwyn Tunnel

Campbell's Platform

Tan-y-Bwlch
Dduallt
Tan-y-Grisiau
Blaenau Ffestiniog
BETWYS-Y-COED
A470
A496
A487
DOLGELLAU, BALA
Plas Halt

ʼan-y-Grisiau *is equest stop for a er station visitor ·e, and is near a rfall and a lake.*

VISITORS' CHECKLIST

01766 516073. bookings 01766 516024. Porthmadog. Mar–Nov: daily; Dec–Feb: phone to check. 25 Dec. www.festrail.co.uk

KEY

- Ffestiniog Railway
- Station
- British Rail
- Major roads

Portmeirion ⓭

Gwynedd. 01766 770000.
Minffordd. daily. 25 Dec.
limited.
www.portmeirion-village.com

THIS BIZARRE ITALIANATE village on a private peninsula at the top of Cardigan Bay was created by Welsh architect Sir Clough Williams-Ellis (1883–1978). He fulfilled a childhood dream by building a village "to my own fancy on my own chosen site". About 50 buildings surround a central piazza, in styles from Oriental to Gothic. Visitors can stay at the luxurious hotel or in one of the charming village cottages. Portmeirion has been an atmospheric location for many films and television programmes, including the popular 1960s television series *The Prisoner*.

Sir Clough Williams-Ellis at Portmeirion

Hercules *is a life-size 19th-century copper statue near the Town Hall, where a 17th-century ceiling, rescued from a demolished mansion, depicts his legend.*
Fountain Cottage is where Noel Coward (1899–1973) wrote *Blithe Spirit*.
The ***Amis Reunis*** is a stone replica of a boat that sank in the bay
Swimn pool
The Portmeirion Hotel *has many exotic interiors: the furniture in the Jaipur Bar comes from Rajasthan, India.*

Harlech ⓮

Gwynedd. 1,300. High St (01766 780658). Sun (summer).
www.gwynedd.gov.uk

THIS SMALL TOWN with fine beaches is dominated by **Harlech Castle**, a medieval fortress *(see p424)* built by Edward I between 1283 and 1289. The castle sits on a precipitous crag, with superb views of Tremadog Bay and the Llŷn Peninsula to the west, and Snowdonia to the north. When the castle was built, the sea reached a fortified stairway cut into the cliff, so that supplies could arrive by ship, but now the sea has receded. A towering gatehouse protects the inner ward, enclosed by walls and four round towers.

Despite its defences, Harlech Castle fell to Owain Glyndŵr *(see p422)* in 1404, and served as his court until its recapture four years later. The song *Men of Harlech* is thought to have been inspired by the castle's heroic resistance during an eight-year siege in the Wars of the Roses *(see p49)*.

Harlech Castle's strategic site overlooking mountains and sea

Harlech Castle

Castle Sq. 01766 780552. daily
www.cadw.wales.gov.uk

Dolgellau ⓯

Gwynedd. 2,650. Eldon Sq (01341 422888). Fri (livestock).
www.gwynedd.gov.uk

THE DARK LOCAL STONE gives a stern, solid look to this market town, where the Welsh language and customs are still very strong. It lies in the long shadow of the 892 m (2,927 ft) mountain of Cader Idris where, according to legend, anyone who spends a night on its summit will awake a poet or a madman – or not at all.

Dolgellau was gripped by gold fever in the 19th century, when high-quality gold was

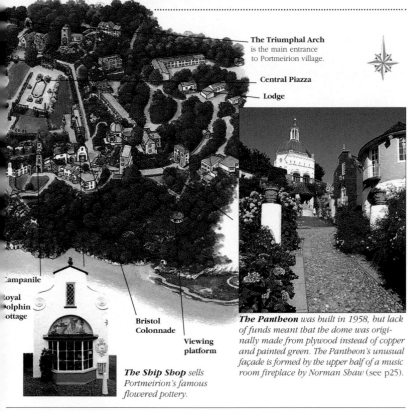

The Triumphal Arch is the main entrance to Portmeirion village.

Central Piazza

Lodge

__The Pantheon__ was built in 1958, but lack of funds meant that the dome was originally made from plywood instead of copper and painted green. The Pantheon's unusual façade is formed by the upper half of a music room fireplace by Norman Shaw (see p25).

Campanile

Royal Dolphin Cottage

Bristol Colonnade

Viewing platform

__The Ship Shop__ sells Portmeirion's famous flowered pottery.

Dolgellau's grey-stone buildings, dwarfed by the mountain scenery

discovered in the Mawddach Valley nearby. The deposits were not large enough to sustain an intensive mining industry for long. Nevertheless, up until 1999, small amounts were mined and crafted locally into fine jewellery.

Dolgellau is a good centre for walking, whether you wish to take gentle strolls through beautiful leafy countryside or strenuous hikes across extreme terrain with dramatic mountain views. The lovely **Cregennen lakes** are set high in the hills above the thickly wooded **Mawddach Estuary** to the northwest; north are the harsh, bleak **Rhinog moors**, one of Wales's last true wildernesses.

Aberdyfi ⓰

Gwynedd. 900. *Wharf Gardens (01654 767321).*
www.gwynedd.gov.uk

PERCHED ON THE MOUTH of the Dyfi Estuary, this little harbour resort and sailing centre makes the most of its splendid but rather confined location, its houses occupying every yard of a narrow strip of land between mountain and sea. In the 19th century, local slate was exported from here, and between the 1830s and the 1860s about 100 ships were built in the port. *The Bells of Aberdovey*, a song by Charles Dibdin for his opera *Liberty Hall* (1785), tells the legend of Cantref-y-Gwaelod, thought to have been located here, which was protected from the sea by dykes. One stormy night, the sluice gates were left open by Prince Seithenyn, when he was drunk, and the land was lost beneath the waves. The submerged church bells are said to peal under the water to this day.

Neat Georgian houses by the sea, Aberdyfi

SOUTH AND MID-WALES

CARDIFF, SWANSEA & ENVIRONS · CARDIGANSHIRE
CARMARTHENSHIRE · MONMOUTHSHIRE · POWYS · PEMBROKESHIRE

SOUTH AND MID-WALES *are less homogeneous regions than North Wales. Most of the population lives in the southeast corner. To the west is Pembrokeshire, the loveliest stretch of Welsh coastline. To the north the industrial valleys give way to the wide hills of the Brecon Beacons and the rural heartlands of central Wales.*

South Wales's coastal strip has been settled for many centuries. There are prehistoric sites in the Vale of Glamorgan and Pembrokeshire. The Romans established a major base at Caerleon, and the Normans built castles all the way from Chepstow to Pembroke. In the 18th and 19th centuries, coal mines and ironworks opened in the valleys of South Wales, attracting immigrants from all over Europe. Close communities developed here, focused on the coal trade, which turned Cardiff from a sleepy coastal town into the world's busiest coal-exporting port.

The declining coal industry has again changed the face of this area: slag heaps have become green hills, and the valley towns struggle to find alternative forms of employment. Coal mines such as Blaenafon's Big Pit are now tourist attractions; today, many of the tour guides taking visitors underground are ex-miners, who can offer a first-hand glimpse of the hard life found in mining communities before the pits closed.

The southern boundary of the Brecon Beacons National Park marks the beginning of rural Wales. With a population sparser than anywhere in England, this is an area of small country towns, hill-sheep farms, forestry plantations and spectacular man-made lakes.

The number of Welsh-speakers increases and the sense of Welsh culture becomes stronger as you travel further from the border with England, with the exception of an English enclave in south Pembrokeshire.

The changing face of the coal industry: former miners take visitors down the Big Pit in Blaenafon

◁ **Magnificent coastal scenery near St David's, Pembrokeshire**

Exploring South and Mid-Wales

Magnificent coastal scenery marks the Pembrokeshire Coast National Park and cliff-backed Gower Peninsula, while Cardigan Bay and Carmarthen Bay offer quieter beaches. Walkers can enjoy grassy uplands in the Brecon Beacons and gentler country in the leafy Wye Valley. Urban life is concentrated in the southeast of Wales, where old mining towns line the valleys north of Cardiff, the capital.

Cliffs of the Pembrokeshire Coast National Park

Getting Around

The M4 motorway is the major route into Wales from the south of England, and there are good road links west of Swansea running to the coast. The A483 and A488 give access to mid-Wales from the Midlands. Frequent rail services connect London with Swansea, Cardiff and the ferry port of Fishguard.

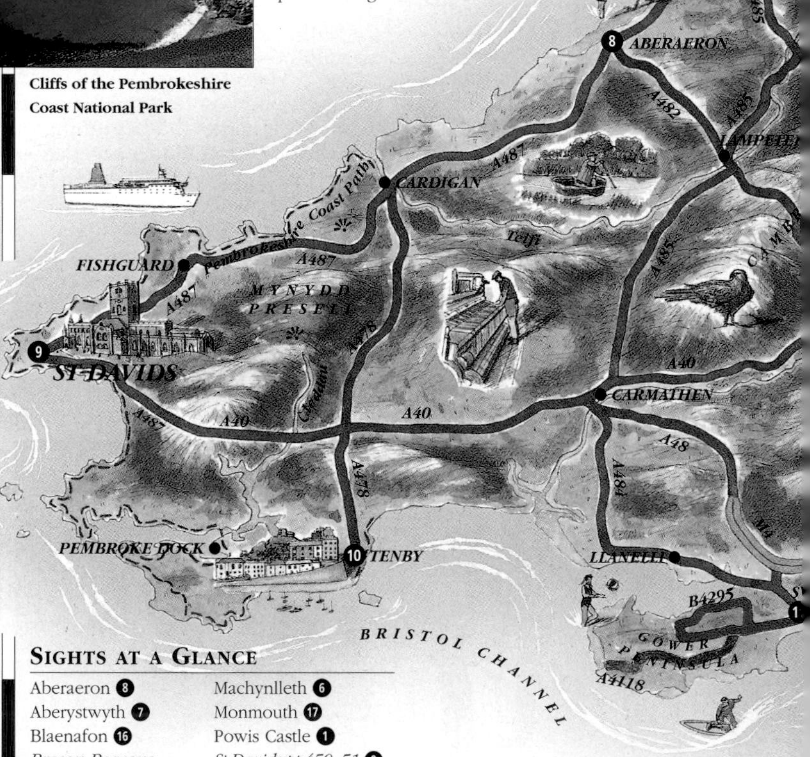

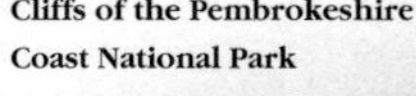

Sights at a Glance

Aberaeron 8
Aberystwyth 7
Blaenafon 16
Brecon Beacons pp454–5 13
Caerleon 15
Cardiff pp456–9 14
Elan Valley 5
Hay-on-Wye 3
Knighton 2
Llandrindod Wells 4
Machynlleth 6
Monmouth 17
Powis Castle 1
St Davids pp450–51 9
Swansea and the Gower Peninsula 11
Tenby 10
Tintern Abbey 18

Walks and Tours

Wild Wales Tour 12

See Also

- ***Where to Stay*** pp566–8
- ***Where to Eat*** pp602–4

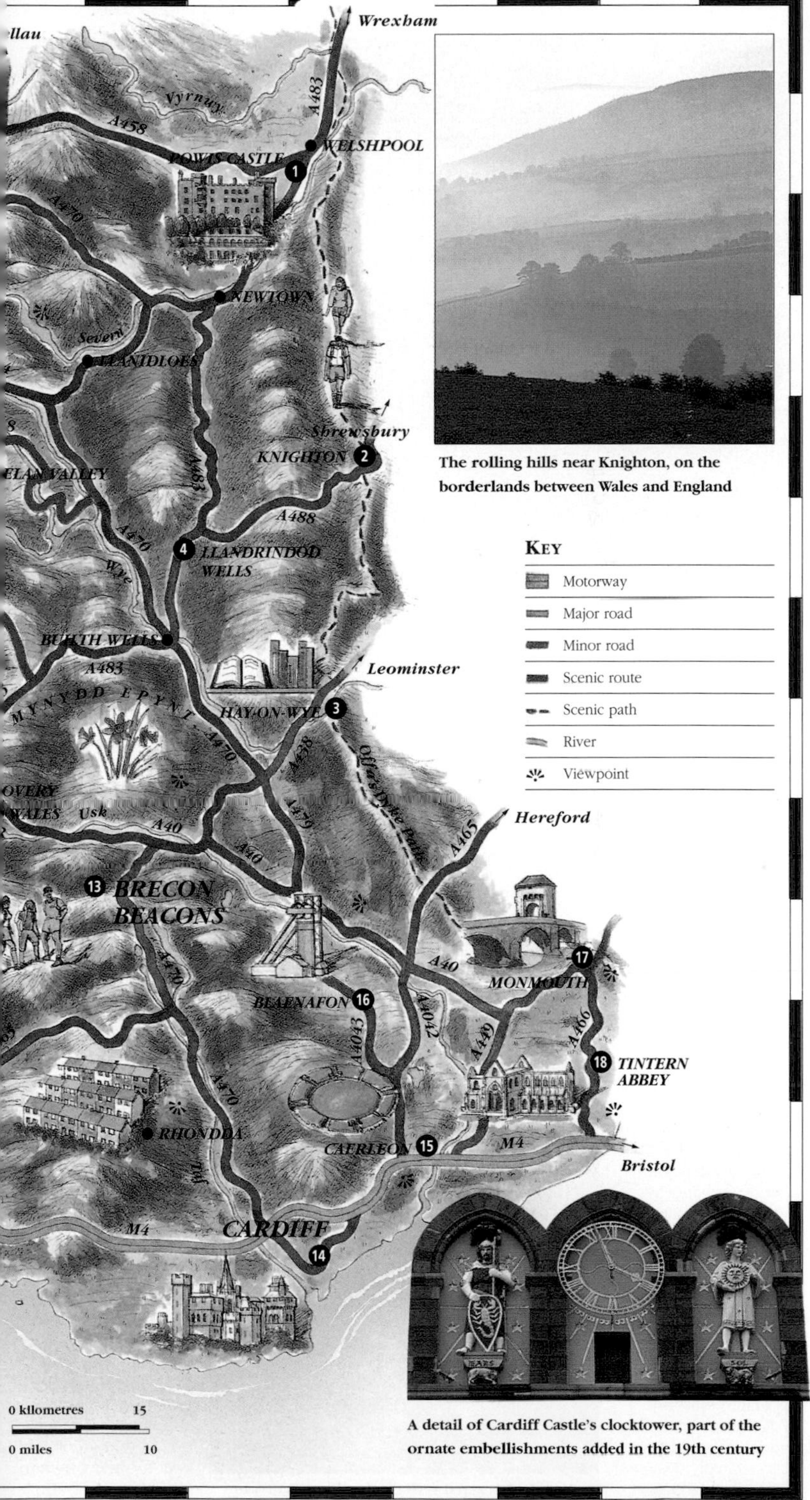

The rolling hills near Knighton, on the borderlands between Wales and England

KEY

- Motorway
- Major road
- Minor road
- Scenic route
- Scenic path
- River
- Viewpoint

A detail of Cardiff Castle's clocktower, part of the ornate embellishments added in the 19th century

Italianate terraces and formal gardens at Powis Castle, adding a Mediterranean air to the Welsh borderlands

Powis Castle ❶

(NT) Welshpool, Powys. *01938 551944.* *Welshpool then bus.* *Apr–Jun & Sep–Oct: Wed–Sun; Jul–Aug: Tue–Sun & public hols.* *limited.*

POWIS CASTLE – the spelling is an archaic version of "Powys" – has outgrown its military roots. Despite its sham battlements and dominant site, 1 mile (1.6 km) to the southwest of the town of Welshpool, this red-stone building has served as a country mansion for centuries. It began life in the 13th century as a fortress, built by the princes of Powys to control the border with England.

The castle is entered through one of few surviving medieval features: a gateway, built in 1283 by Owain de la Pole. The gate is flanked by two round towers with arrow slits and portcullis slots.

The castle's lavish interiors soon banish all thoughts of war. A **Dining Room**, decorated with fine 17th-century panelling and family portraits, was originally designed as the castle's Great Hall. The **Great Staircase**, added in the late 17th century and elaborately decorated with carved fruit and flowers, leads to the main apartments: an early 19th-century library, the panelled **Oak Drawing Room** and the Elizabethan **Long Gallery**, where ornate plasterwork on the fireplace and ceiling date from the 1590s. In the **Blue Drawing Room** there are three 18th-century Brussels tapestries.

The Herbert family bought the property in 1587 and were proud of their Royalist connections; the panelling in the **State Bedroom** bears the royal monogram. Powis Castle was defended for Charles I in the Civil War *(see pp52–3)*, but fell to Parliament in 1644. The 3rd Baron Powis, a supporter of James II, had to flee the country when William and Mary took the throne in 1688 *(see pp52–3)*.

The castle's **Clive Museum** has an exhibition concerning "Clive of India" (1725–74), the general and statesman who helped strengthen British control in India in the mid-18th century. The family's link with Powis Castle was established by the 2nd Lord Clive, who married into the Herbert family and became the Earl of Powis in 1804.

The gardens at Powis are among the best-known in Britain, with their series of elegant Italianate terraces, adorned with statues, niches, balustrades and hanging gardens, all stepped into the steep hillside beneath the castle walls. Created between 1688 and 1722, these are the only formal gardens of this period in Britain that are still kept in their original form *(see pp22–3)*.

The richly carved 17th-century Great Staircase

Knighton ❷

Powys. 3,500. *West St (01547 528753).* *Thu.*
www.offasdyke.demon.co.uk

KNIGHTON'S WELSH NAME, Tref y Clawdd ("The Town on the Dyke"), reflects its status as the only original settlement on **Offa's Dyke**. In the 8th century, King Offa of Mercia (central and southern England) constructed a ditch and bank to mark out his territory, and to enable the enforcement of a Saxon law: "Neither shall a Welshman cross into English land without the appointed man from the other side, who should meet him at the bank and bring him back again without any offence being committed." Some of the best-preserved sections of the 6 m (20 ft) high earthwork lie in the hills around Knighton. The Offa's Dyke Footpath runs for 177 miles (285 km) along the border between England and Wales.

Knighton's clock

Knighton is set on a steep hill, sloping upwards from **St Edward's Church** (1877) with its medieval tower, to the summit, where a castle once stood. The main street leads via the market square, marked by a 19th-century clock tower, along **The Narrows**, a Tudor street with little shops. **The Old House** on Broad Street is a medieval "cruck" house (curved timbers form a frame to support the roof), with a hole in the ceiling instead of a chimney.

Hay-on-Wye ❸

Powys. 1,300. *Oxford Rd (01497 820144).* *Thu.*
www.hay-on-wye.co.uk

BOOK-LOVERS from all over the world come to this quiet border town in the Black Mountains. Hay-on-Wye has over 30 second-hand bookshops stocking millions of titles, and in early summer hosts a prestigious Festival of Literature. The town's love affair with books began when a bookshop was opened in the 1960s by Richard Booth, who claims the (fictitious) title of King of Independent Hay and lives in **Hay Castle**, a 17th-century mansion in the grounds of the original 13th-century castle. Hay's oldest inn, the 16th-century **Three Tuns** on Bridge Street, is still functioning and has an attractive half-timbered façade.

ENVIRONS: Hay sits on the approach to the Black Mountains and is surrounded by rolling hills. To the south are the heights of Hay Bluff and the Vale of Ewyas, where the 12th-century ruins of **Llanthony Priory** *(see p455)* retain fine pointed arches.

Hay Castle
01497 820503. *daily.* *25 Dec.* *grounds only.*

Llandrindod Wells ❹

Powys. 5,000. *Memorial Gardens (01597 822600).* *Fri.*
www.visitllandrindod.co.uk

LLANDRINDOD is a perfect example of a Victorian town, with canopied streets, delicate wrought ironwork, gabled villas and ornamental parklands. This purpose-built spa town became Wales's premier inland resort of the 19th century. Its sulphur and magnesium spring waters were taken to treat skin complaints and a range of other ailments.

One of Hay-on-Wye's bookshops

The town now makes every effort to preserve its Victorian character, with a lake and the well-tended **Rock Park Gardens**. The **Heritage Centre** houses a heritage exhibition and a restored 19th-century **Pump Room** is now a restaurant and is the focus of the summer Victorian Festival, when residents don period costume and cars are banned from the town centre.

The **Radnorshire Museum** traces the town's past as one of a string of 19th-century Welsh spas which included Builth, Llangammarch and **Llanwrtyd** (now a pony trekking centre).

Heritage Centre
Rock Park. *01597 829267.* *Tue–Sat.* *Christmas week.*

Radnorshire Museum
Memorial Gardens. *01597 824513.* *Tue–Sat & public hols (& Sun pm Apr–Oct).* *25, 26 Dec, 1 Jan.* *limited.*

Victorian architecture on Spa Road, Llandrindod Wells

Craig Goch, one of the original chain of Elan Valley reservoirs

Elan Valley ❺

Powys. *Llandrindod.*
Rhayader (01597 810898).
www.elanvalley.org.uk

A STRING OF SPECTACULAR reservoirs, the first of the country's man-made lakes, has made this one of Wales's most famous valleys. **Caban Coch**, **Garreg Ddu**, **Pen-y-Garreg** and **Craig Goch**, were created between 1892 and 1903 to supply water to Birmingham, 73 miles (117 km) away. They form a chain of lakes about 9 miles (14 km) long, holding 50 billion litres (13 billion gallons) of water. Victorian engineers selected these high moorlands on the Cambrian Mountains, for their high annual rainfall of 1,780 mm (70 inches). The choice created bitter controversy and resentment: more than 100 people had to move from the valley that was flooded in order to create Caban Coch.

Unlike their more utilitarian modern counterparts, these dams were built during an era when decoration was seen as an integral part of any design. Finished in dressed stone, they have an air of grandeur which is lacking in the huge **Claerwen** reservoir, a stark addition built during the early 1950s to double the lakes' capacity. Contained by a 355 m (1,165 ft) dam, it lies 4 miles (6 km) along the B4518 that runs through Elan Valley and offers magnificent views.

The remote moorlands and woodlands surrounding the lakes are an important habitat for wildlife; the red kite can often be seen here. The **Elan Valley Visitors' Centre**, beside the Caban Coch dam, describes the construction of the lakes, as well as the valley's own natural history. **Elan Village**, set beside the centre, is an unusual example of a model workers' village, built during the 1900s to house the waterworks staff. Outside the centre is a statue of the poet Percy Bysshe Shelley *(see p210)*, who stayed in the valley at the mansion of Nantgwyllt in 1810 with his wife, Harriet. The house now lies underneath the waters of Caban Coch, along with the rest of the old village. Among the buildings submerged were the village school and a church.

The trail from Machynlleth to Devil's Bridge, near Aberystwyth

Machynlleth ❻

Powys. 2,200. *Canolfan Owain Glyndŵr (01654 702401).* *Wed.*

HALF-TIMBERED BUILDINGS and Georgian façades appear among the grey-stone houses in Machynlleth. It was here that Owain Glyndŵr, Wales's last native leader *(see p422)*, held a parliament in 1404. The restored **Parliament House** has displays on his life and a brass-rubbing centre.

The ornate **Clock Tower**, in the middle of Maengwyn Street, was erected in 1874 by the Marquess of Londonderry to mark the coming of age of his heir, Lord Castlereagh. The Marquess lived in **Plas Machynlleth**, a 17th-century house in parkland off the main street, which is now a centre of Celtic heritage and culture.

Parliament House sign, Machynlleth

ENVIRONS: In an old slate quarry 2.5 miles (4 km) to the north, a "village of the future" is run by the **Centre for Alternative Technology**. A water-balanced cliff railway takes summer visitors to view low-energy houses and organic gardens, to see how to make the best of Earth's resources.

Parliament House
Maengwyn St. *01654 702827.* *Easter–Oct: Mon–Sat.*
Centre for Alternative Technology On A487. *01654 702400.* *daily.* *early Jan.* www.cat.org.uk

Aberystwyth ❼

Ceredigion. 11,000. *Terrace Rd (01970 612125).*
www.ceredigion.gov.uk

THIS SEASIDE AND UNIVERSITY town claims to be the cultural capital of mid-Wales. By the standards of this rural area, "Aber" is a big place, its population increased for much of the year by students.

To Victorian travellers, Aberystwyth was the "Biarritz

of Wales". There have been no great changes along the promenade, with its gabled hotels, since the 19th century. **Constitution Hill**, a steep outcrop at the northern end, can be scaled in summer on the electric **Cliff Railway**, built in 1896. At the top, in a ***camera obscura***, a lens

Buskers on Aberystwyth's seafront

projects views of the town. The ruined **Aberystwyth Castle** (1277) is located south of the promenade. In the town centre, the **Ceredigion Museum**, set in a former music hall, traces the history of the town.

To the northeast of the town centre, **The National Library of Wales**, next to Aberystwyth University, has a valuable collection of ancient Welsh manuscripts.

Savin's Hotel

When the Cambrian Railway opened in 1864, businessman Thomas Savin put £80,000 into building a new hotel in Aberystwyth for package tourists. The scheme made him bankrupt, but the seafront building, complete with mock-Gothic tower, was bought by campaigners attempting to establish a Welsh university. The "college by the sea" opened in 1872, and is now the Theological College.

Mosaics on the college tower

Environs: During the summer the narrow-gauge Vale of Rheidol Railway runs 12 miles (19 km) to **Devil's Bridge**, where a dramatic series of waterfalls plunges through a wooded ravine and a steep trail leads to the valley floor.

Ceredigion Museum
Terrace Rd. 01970 633088. Mon–Sat. 25 Dec–2 Jan, Good Fri.

Aberaeron 8

Ceredigion. *1,500.*
Aberystwyth, then bus. The Quay (01545 570602).
www.ceredigion.gov.uk

Aberaeron's harbour, lined with Georgian houses, became a trading port and shipbuilding centre in the early 19th century. Its orderly streets were laid out in pre-railway days, when the ports along Cardigan Bay enjoyed considerable wealth. The last boat was built here in 1994 and its harbour is now full of holiday sailors. The harbour can be crossed via a wooden footbridge.

On the quayside, the popular Honey Bee Ice Cream Parlour serves world-renowned ice creams to a loyal clientele. There is also a centre of local crafts in the town, Clos Pengarreg.

Rows of brightly painted Georgian houses lining the purpose-built harbour at Aberaeron

St Davids 9

Icon of Elijah, south transept

St David, the patron saint of Wales, founded a monastic settlement in this remote corner of southwest Wales in about 550, which became one of the most important Christian shrines. The present cathedral, built in the 12th century, and the Bishop's Palace, added a century later, are set in a grassy hollow below St Davids town, officially Britain's smallest city. The date of St David's death, 1 March, is commemorated throughout Wales.

St David's Cathedral, the largest in Wales

★ Great Hall
The open arcade and decorated parapet were added by Bishop Gower (1328–47) to unify different sections of the palace.

The Private Chapel was a late 14th-century addition, built, like the rest of the palace, over a series of vaults.

Entrance

Bishop's Palace

The bishop's residence, built between 1280 and 1350 and now in ruins, had lavish private apartments.

Palace latrines

Rose window

The Bishop's Hall, smaller than the Great Hall, may have been reserved for private use.

Great Hall

This reconstruction shows the hall before the lead was stripped from the roof. Bishop Barlow, St David's first Protestant bishop (1536–48), is thought to have been responsible for the lead's removal.

Star Sights

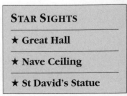

- ★ Great Hall
- ★ Nave Ceiling
- ★ St David's Statue

★ Nave Ceiling
The roof of the nave is lowered and hidden by an early 16th-century oak ceiling. A beautiful 14th-century rood screen divides the nave from the choir.

Visitors' Checklist

Cathedral Close, St Davids. *01437 720199.* *Haverfordwest then bus.* *9am–6pm daily (Sat, Sun: pm).* *7:30am, 8am, 6pm, Mon–Sat; 8am, 9:30am, 11:15am, 6pm Sun.*

Cathedral

St David was one of the founders of the 6th-century monastic movement, so this was an important site of pilgrimage. Three visits here equalled one to Jerusalem.

Stained Glass Window
In the nave's west end, eight panels, produced in the 1950s, radiate from a central window showing the dove of peace.

St Mary's College Chapel

Bishop Vaughan's Chapel has a fine fan-vaulted early Tudor roof.

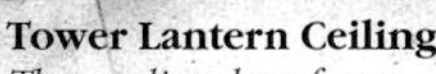

Entrance

Tower Lantern Ceiling
The medieval roof was decorated with episcopal insignia when restored in the 1870s by Sir George Gilbert Scott.

★ St David's Statue
A statue of the saint is placed near the shrine. Thought to symbolize the Holy Spirit, a dove is said to have landed on David's shoulder as he spoke to a gathering of bishops.

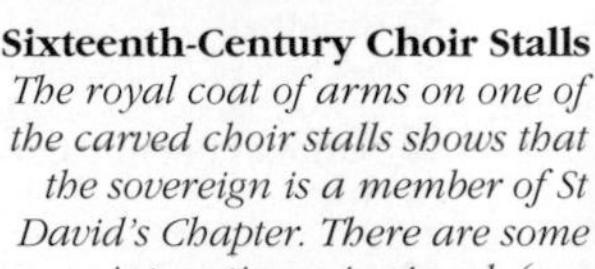

Sixteenth-Century Choir Stalls
The royal coat of arms on one of the carved choir stalls shows that the sovereign is a member of St David's Chapter. There are some interesting misericords (see p329) *in these stalls.*

Tenby ⑩

Pembrokeshire (Dyfed). *5,000.* *The Croft (01834 842402).*

Tenby has successfully trodden the fine line between over-commercialization and popularity, refusing to submit its historic character to the garish excesses of some seaside towns. Georgian houses overlook its handsome harbour, which is backed by a well-preserved medieval clifftop town of narrow streets and passages. The old town was defended by a headland fortress, now ruined, flanked by two wide beaches and a ring of 13th-century walls. These survive to their full height in places, along with a fortified gateway, the **Five Arches**.

The three-storeyed **Tudor Merchant's House** is a 15th-century relic of Tenby's highly prosperous seafaring days, with original fireplaces and chimneys. There are regular boat trips from the harbour to **Caldey Island**, 3 miles (5 km) offshore, home of a perfume-making monastic community.

Tudor Merchant's House
(NT) Quay Hill. *01834 842279.* *Apr–Sep: Thu–Tue; Oct: Thu, Fri, Sun–Tue (Sun: pm).* *Nov-Mar.* *for pre-booked parties.*

A partly medieval restaurant next to the Tudor Merchant's House

Swansea and the Gower Peninsula ⑪

Swansea. *230,000.* *Plymouth St (01792 468321).* *Mon–Sat.* www.visitswanseabay.com.

Swansea, Wales's second city, is set along a wide, curving bay. The city centre was rebuilt after heavy bombing in World War II but, despite the modern buildings, a traditional Welsh atmosphere prevails. This is particularly noticeable in the excellent food market, full of Welsh delicacies such as laverbread *(see p36)* and locally caught cockles.

The award-winning **Maritime Quarter** redevelopment has transformed the old docklands, and is worth a visit. A statue of copper magnate John Henry Vivian (1779–1855) overlooks the marina. The Vivians, a leading Swansea family, founded the **Glynn Vivian Art Gallery**, which has exquisite Swansea pottery and porcelain. Archaeology and Welsh history feature at the **Swansea Museum**, the oldest museum in Wales.

Swansea's most celebrated son, the poet Dylan Thomas

The life and work of local poet Dylan Thomas (1914–53) is celebrated in the recently opened **Dylan Thomas Centre**. A permanent exhibition, Man and Myth, includes the original drafts of his poems, letters and memorabilia. His statue overlooks the Maritime Quarter. Thomas spent his childhood in the city's suburbs. **Cwmdonkin Park** was the scene of an early poem, *The Hunchback in the Park*, and its water garden has a memorial stone quoting from his *Fern Hill*.

Swansea's austere **Guildhall** (1934) has a surprisingly rich interior. The huge panels, by Sir Frank Brangwyn (1867–1956), on the theme of the British Empire, were originally painted for the House of Lords.

Picturesque fishermen's cottages at the Mumbles seaside resort

Swansea Bay leads to the **Mumbles**, a popular watersports centre at the gateway to the 19 mile long (30 km) Gower Peninsula, which in 1956 was the first part of Britain to be declared an Area of Outstanding Natural Beauty. A string of sheltered, south-facing bays leads to Oxwich and Port-Eynon beaches.

Rhossili's enormous beach leads to north Gower and a coastline of low-lying burrows, salt marshlands and cockle beds. The peninsula is littered with ancient sites such as **Parc Le Breose**, a prehistoric burial chamber.

Near Camarthen is the **National Botanic Garden of Wales**, with formal gardens centred on The Great Glasshouse which contains a Mediterranean ecosystem.

Glynn Vivian Art Gallery
Alexandra Rd. *01792 655006.* *Tue–Sun & public hols.* *23–26 Dec, 1 Jan.* *limited.* *by arrangement.*

Swansea Museum
Victoria Rd. *01792 653763.* *Tue–Sun & public hols.* *25, 26 Dec, 1 Jan.* *limited.*

Dylan Thomas Centre
Somerset Pl. *01792 463980.* *Tue–Sun, bank hols.* *by arrangement.*
www.dylanthomas.com

Guildhall
St Helen's Rd. *01792 636000.* *Mon–Fri.* *public hols.*

National Botanic Garden of Wales
Middleton Hall, Llanarthne. *01558 668768.* *daily.*

Wild Wales Tour ⓬

THIS TOUR WEAVES ACROSS the Cambrian Mountains' windswept moors, green hills and high, deserted plateaux. New roads have been laid to the massive Llyn Brianne Reservoir, north of Llandovery, and the old drover's road across to Tregaron has a tarmac surface. But the area is still essentially a "wild Wales" of hidden hamlets, isolated farmsteads, brooding highlands and traditional, quiet market towns.

Llanidloes ⑥
The town was a centre of religious and social unrest in the 17th and 18th centuries *(see p423)*. There is a rare example of a free-standing Tudor market hall. The medieval church was restored in the late 19th century.

Devil's Bridge ④
This is a popular, romantic beauty spot with waterfalls, rocks, wooded glades and an ancient stone bridge – built by the Devil, according to legend.

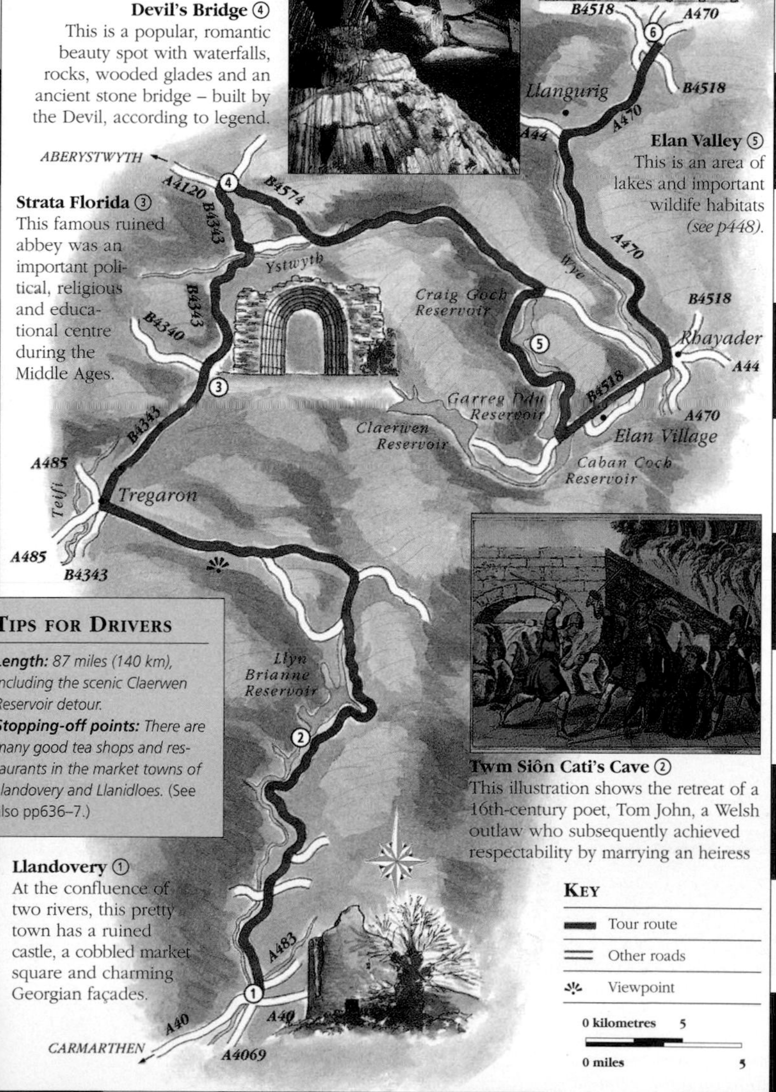

Elan Valley ⑤
This is an area of lakes and important wildlife habitats *(see p448)*.

Strata Florida ③
This famous ruined abbey was an important political, religious and educational centre during the Middle Ages.

TIPS FOR DRIVERS

Length: *87 miles (140 km), including the scenic Claerwen Reservoir detour.*
Stopping-off points: *There are many good tea shops and restaurants in the market towns of Llandovery and Llanidloes.* (See also pp636–7.)

Twm Siôn Cati's Cave ②
This illustration shows the retreat of a 16th-century poet, Tom John, a Welsh outlaw who subsequently achieved respectability by marrying an heiress

Llandovery ①
At the confluence of two rivers, this pretty town has a ruined castle, a cobbled market square and charming Georgian façades.

KEY

- Tour route
- Other roads
- Viewpoint

0 kilometres 5

0 miles 5

Brecon Beacons 13

Trekking in the Beacons

THE BRECON BEACONS National Park covers 520 sq miles (1,345 sq km) from the Wales–England border almost all the way to Swansea. There are four mountain ranges within the park: the Black Mountain (to the west), Fforest Fawr, the Brecon Beacons and the Black Mountains (to the east). Much of the area consists of high, open country with smooth, grassy slopes on a bedrock of red sandstone. The park's southern rim has limestone crags, wooded gorges, waterfalls and caves. Visitors can enjoy many outdoor pursuits, from fishing in the numerous reservoirs to pony trekking, caving and walking.

Llyn y Fan Fach
This remote, myth-laden glacial lake is a 4 mile (6.5 km) walk from Llanddeusant.

BUILTH WELLS
LAMPETER
Llandovery
A40
Sennybridge
Usk
USK RESERVOIR
Crai
A4067
A40
A42
Llanddeusant
Senni
A4069
A40
Tywi
CARMARTHEN
Llandeilo
Trapp
BLACK MOUNTAIN
YSTRADFELL RESERVO
A483
A4069
A4067
FFOREST FAWR
Mellte
Hepste
Twrch
Gïed
Llandybie
A471
LLANELLI
Ammanford
A4068
Tawe
A4221
A4109
A40
SWANSEA
Ystradgynlais
A465
NEATH
Hirwaun

The Black Mountain, a largely unexplored wilderness of knife-edged ridges and high, empty moorland, fills the western corner of the National Park.

0 kilometres 10

0 miles 5

Fforest Fawr ("Great Forest") is named after an area that was a medieval royal hunting ground.

Carreg Cennen Castle
Spectacularly sited, the ruined medieval fortress of Carreg Cennen (see p424) *stands on a sheer limestone cliff near the village of Trapp.*

Dan-yr-Ogof Caves
A labyrinth of caves runs through the Brecon Beacons. Guided tours of two large caves are offered here.

Key

- A road
- B road
- Minor road
- Footpath
- Viewpoint

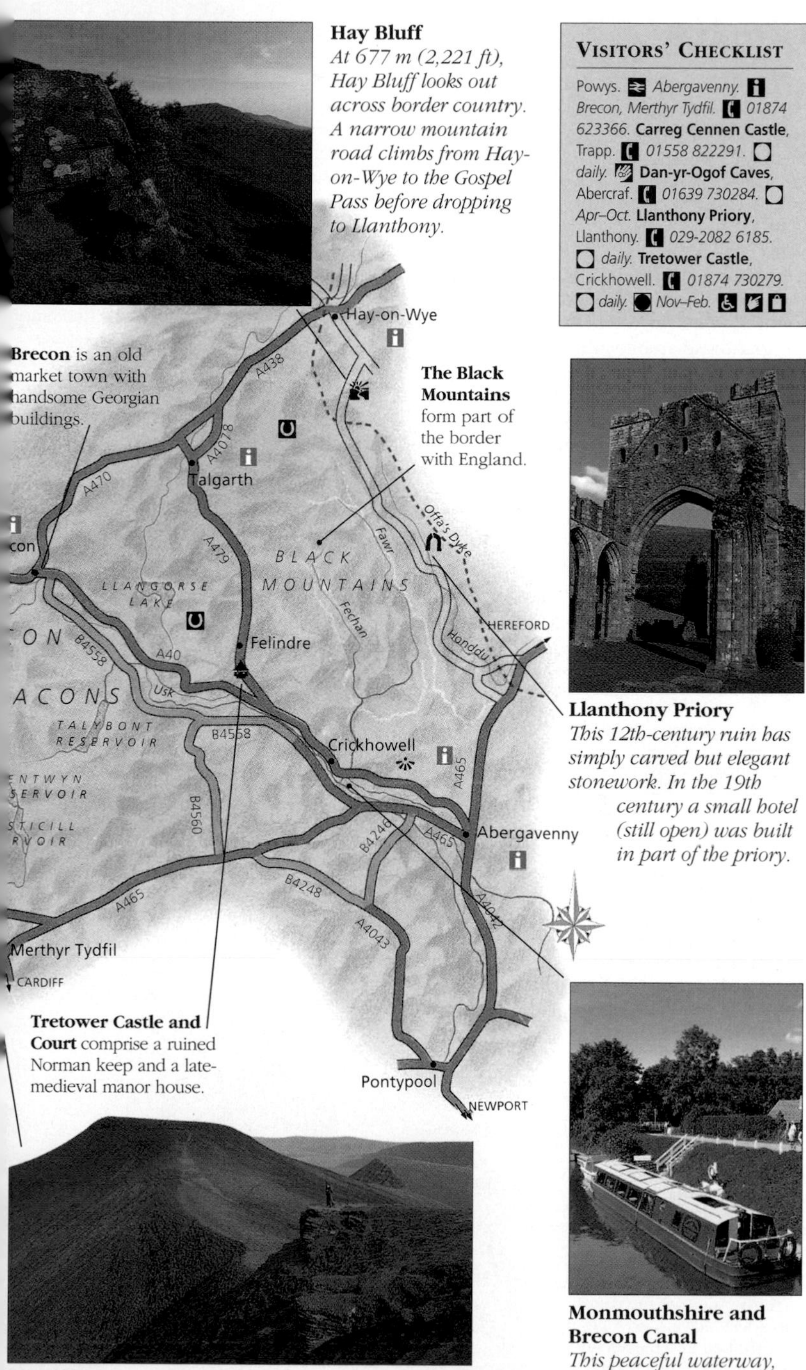

Hay Bluff
At 677 m (2,221 ft), Hay Bluff looks out across border country. A narrow mountain road climbs from Hay-on-Wye to the Gospel Pass before dropping to Llanthony.

Brecon is an old market town with handsome Georgian buildings.

The Black Mountains form part of the border with England.

Tretower Castle and Court comprise a ruined Norman keep and a late-medieval manor house.

Pen y Fan
At 886 m (2,907 ft), Pen y Fan is the highest point in South Wales. Its distinctive, flat-topped summit, once a Bronze Age burial ground (see pp42–3), *can be reached by footpaths from Storey Arms on the A470.*

VISITORS' CHECKLIST

Powys. *Abergavenny.* *Brecon, Merthyr Tydfil.* *01874 623366.* **Carreg Cennen Castle**, Trapp. *01558 822291.* *daily.* **Dan-yr-Ogof Caves**, Abercraf. *01639 730284.* *Apr–Oct.* **Llanthony Priory**, Llanthony. *029-2082 6185.* *daily.* **Tretower Castle**, Crickhowell. *01874 730279.* *daily.* *Nov–Feb.*

Llanthony Priory
This 12th-century ruin has simply carved but elegant stonework. In the 19th century a small hotel (still open) was built in part of the priory.

Monmouthshire and Brecon Canal
This peaceful waterway, completed in 1812, was once used to transport raw materials between Brecon and Newport. It is now popular with leisure boats.

Cardiff ⓮

CARDIFF WAS FIRST OCCUPIED by the Romans, who built a fort here in AD 75 *(see pp44–5)*. Little is known of its subsequent history until Robert FitzHamon *(see p458)*, a knight in the service of William the Conqueror, was given land here in 1093. By the 13th century, the settlement was substantial enough to be granted a royal charter, but it remained a quiet country town until the 1830s when the Bute family, who inherited land in the area, began to develop it as a port. By 1913 this was the world's busiest coal-exporting port, profiting from rail links with the South Wales mines. Its wealth paid for grandiose architecture, while the docklands became a raucous boom-town. Cardiff was confirmed as the first Welsh capital in 1955, by which time demand for coal was falling and the docks were in decline. The city is now dedicated to commerce and administration, and is being transformed by urban renewal programmes.

Fireplace detail in the Banqueting Hall, Cardiff Castle *(see pp458–9)*

City Hall's dome, adorned with a dragon, the emblem of Wales

Exploring Cardiff

Cardiff is a city with two focal points. The centre, laid out with Victorian and Edwardian streets and gardens, is the first of these. There is a Neo-Gothic castle and Neo-Classical civic buildings, as well as indoor shopping malls and a 19th-century **covered market**. Canopied arcades, lined with shops, lead off the main streets, the oldest being the **Royal Arcade** of 1856. The **Millennium Stadium** (on the site of Cardiff Arms Park, the first home of Welsh rugby) opened in 1999 with the Rugby World Cup, and is open for tours every day.

To the south of the centre, the docklands are now being transformed into the second focal point by the creation of a marina and waterfront. A new Cardiff is taking shape, especially around the Inner Harbour area. The **Pier Head Building**, constructed on Cardiff Bay in 1896 for the Cardiff Railway Company, is a reminder of the city's heyday. Its intricate decoration and terracotta detail was partly influenced by the red Mogul buildings of India. Another attraction in the area is **Techniquest**, a hands-on science museum.

The wooden **Norwegian Church** on Waterfront Park was first erected in 1868 for Norwegian sailors bringing wooden props for use in the coal pits of the South Wales valleys. Once surrounded by warehouses, it was taken apart and rebuilt during the dockland development. The **Cardiff Bay Visitor Centre**, near the Pier Head Building, has displays on the various building projects that are uniting the civic centre with the maritime district.

Cardiff Castle

See pp458–9.

City Hall and Civic Centre

Cathays Park. *029-2087 1727.* *Mon–Fri.* *public hols.*

Cardiff's civic centre of Neo-Classical buildings in white Portland stone is set among parks and avenues around Alexandra Gardens. The City Hall (1905), one of its first buildings, is dominated by its 60 m (200 ft) dome and clock tower. Members of the public can visit the first-floor Marble Hall, which is furnished with Siena marble columns and statues of Welsh heroes, among them St David, Wales's patron saint *(see pp450–51)*. The Crown Building, at the northern end of the complex,

The Pier Head Building overlooking the redeveloped area of Cardiff Bay

now houses the Welsh Office, which is responsible for all Welsh government affairs.

National Museum and Gallery of Wales

Cathays Park. 029-2039 7951. Tue–Sun, public hols. 24, 25 Dec. by arrangement. www.nmgw.ac.uk

Opened in 1927, the museum occupies an impressive civic building with a colonnaded portico, guarded by a statue of David Lloyd George *(see p423)*. Displays include a fine collection of Impressionist art by Renoir, Monet and Van Gogh, donated by two local sisters Gwendoline and Margaret Davies.

Statue of Welsh politician David Lloyd George

Crafts in the Bay

The Flourish, Lloyd George Ave., Cardiff Bay. 029-2048 4611. daily.

An extensive new crafts gallery, organized by the Makers' Guild in Wales, opened here in March 1996. The building now houses a wide variety of craft displays and demonstrations, including textile weaving and ceramic making.

As well as the permanent displays, there are frequently changing exhibitions on crafts-related themes. Visitors are free to browse around the centre or to book up for one of the workshops (www.makersguildinwales.org.uk).

ENVIRONS: Established during the 1940s at St Fagans, on the western edge of the city, the open-air **Museum of Welsh Life** was one of the first of its kind. Buildings from all over Wales, including workers' terraced cottages, farmhouses, a tollhouse, a row of shops, a chapel and an old schoolhouse have been carefully reconstructed within the 40 ha (100 acre) parklands, along with a recreated Celtic village. There is also a Tudor mansion which can be visited, boasting its own beautiful gardens in the grounds.

Llandaff Cathedral lies in a deep, grassy hollow beside the River Taf at Llandaff – a pretty "village suburb" which is 2 miles (3 km) northwest of the city centre. The cathedral was first a medieval building, occupying the site of a 6th-century monastic community.

Restored after suffering severe bomb damage during World War II, it was eventually reopened in 1957 with the addition of Sir Jacob Epstein's huge, stark statue, *Christus*, which is mounted on a concrete arch.

Museum of Welsh Life

St Fagans. 029-2057 3500. daily. www.nmgw.ac.uk

> **VISITORS' CHECKLIST**
>
> Cardiff. 285,000. Rhoose. Central Sq. Wood St. Wood St (029-2022 7281). Cardiff Festival: Aug. www.visitcardiff.info

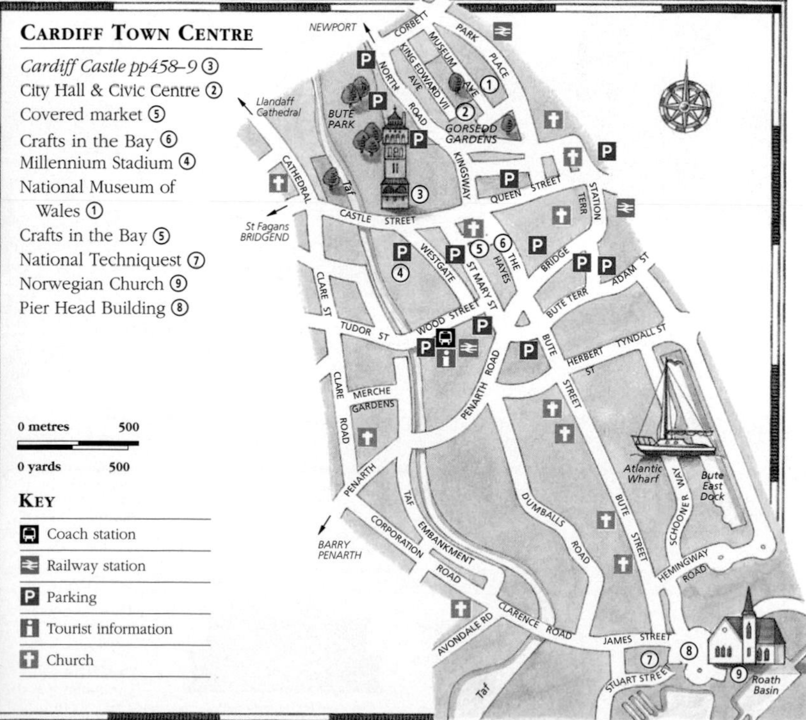

Cardiff Castle

Cardiff castle began life as a Roman fort, whose remains are separated from later work by a band of red stone. A keep was built within the Roman ruins in the 12th century. Over the following 700 years, the castle passed to several powerful families and eventually to John Stuart, son of the Earl of Bute, in 1776. His great-grandson, the 3rd Marquess of Bute, employed the "eccentric genius", architect William Burges, who created an ornate mansion between 1869 and 1881, rich in medieval images and romantic detail.

Arab Room
The gilded ceiling, with Islamic marble and lapis lazuli decorations, was built in 1881.

Animal Wall
A lion and other creatures guard the wall to the west of the castle. They were added between 1885 and 1930.

★ Summer Smoking Room
This was part of a complete bachelor suite in the Clock Tower, that also included a Winter Smoking Room.

Timeline

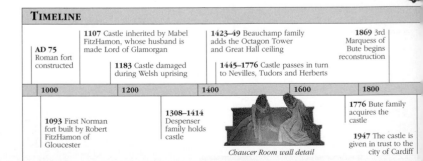

AD 75 Roman fort constructed

1093 First Norman fort built by Robert FitzHamon of Gloucester

1107 Castle inherited by Mabel FitzHamon, whose husband is made Lord of Glamorgan

1183 Castle damaged during Welsh uprising

1308–1414 Despenser family holds castle

1423–49 Beauchamp family adds the Octagon Tower and Great Hall ceiling

1445–1776 Castle passes in turn to Nevilles, Tudors and Herberts

1776 Bute family acquires the castle

1869 3rd Marquess of Bute begins reconstruction

1947 The castle is given in trust to the city of Cardiff

1000 | 1200 | 1400 | 1600 | 1800

Chaucer Room wall detail

Visitors' Checklist

Castle St, Cardiff. *029-2087 8100.* *Mar–Oct: 9:30am–6pm daily; Nov–Feb: 9:30am–4:30pm daily.*
www.cardiffcastle.com

★ Banqueting Hall
The design and decoration of this room depicts the castle's history, making impressively ingenious use of the murals and castellated fireplace.

The Octagon Tower, also called the Beauchamp Tower, is the setting for Burges's Chaucer Room, decorated with themes from the *Canterbury Tales* *(see p174)*.

★ Roof Garden
Using tiles, shrubs and a central fountain, Burges aimed to create a Mediterranean feel in this indoor garden, turning it into the crowning glory of the castle's apartments.

The Bute Tower had a suite of private rooms added in 1873, including a dining room, bedroom and sitting room.

★ Library
Carved figures representing ancient characters of Greek, Assyrian, Hebrew and Egyptian alphabets decorate the library's chimneypiece.

Star Sights

- ★ **Banqueting Hall**
- ★ **Library**
- ★ **Summer Smoking Room**
- ★ **Roof Garden**

Remains of Caerleon's amphitheatre, built in the 2nd century

Caerleon ⓯

Newport (Gwent). 11,000.
5 High St (01633 422656).
www.caerleon.net

TOGETHER WITH YORK *(see pp390–91)* and Chester *(see pp298–9)*, Caerleon was one of only three fortress settlements in Britain built for the Romans' elite legionary troops. From AD 74 Caerleon (*Isca* to the Romans, after the River Usk, which flows beside the town) was home to the 2nd Augustan Legion, which had been sent to Wales to crush the native Silures tribe. The remains of their base now lie between the modern town and the river.

An altar at Caerleon's Legionary Museum

The excavations at Caerleon are of great social and military significance. The Romans built not just a fortress for their crack 5,500-strong infantry division but a complete town to service their needs, including a stone amphitheatre. Judging by the results of the excavation work carried out since the archaeologist Sir Mortimer Wheeler unearthed the amphitheatre in 1926, Caerleon is one of the largest and most important Roman military sites in Europe. The defences enclosed an area of 20 ha (50 acres), with 64 rows of barracks, arranged in pairs, a hospital, and a bath-house complex.

Outside the settlement, the amphitheatre's large stone foundations have survived in an excellent state of preservation. Six thousand spectators could enjoy the blood sports and gladiators' combat.

More impressive still is the fortress baths complex, which opened to the public in the mid-1980s. The baths were designed to bring all the home comforts to an army posted to barbaric Britain. The Roman troops could take a dip in the open-air swimming pool, play sports in the exercise yard or covered hall, or enjoy a series of hot and cold baths.

Nearby are the foundations of the only Roman legionary barracks on view in Europe. The many excavated artifacts, including a collection of engraved gemstones, are displayed at the **Roman Legionary Museum**.

Roman Legionary Museum
High St. 01633 423134. *Mon–Sat, Sun (pm).* *24–26 Dec, 1 Jan.* www.nmgw.ac.uk

Big Pit Mining Museum, reminder of a vanished industrial society

Blaenafon ⓰

Torfaen. *6,000.* *Blaenafon Ironworks, North St.* *01495 792615.* www.blaenafontic.com

COMMERCIAL COAL-MINING has now all but ceased in the South Wales valleys – an area which only 100 years ago was gripped by the search for its "black gold". Though coal is no longer produced at **Big Pit** in Blaenafon, the **Mining Museum** provides a vivid reminder of this tough industry. The Big Pit closed as a working mine in 1980, and opened three years later as a museum. Visitors follow a marked-out route around the mine's surface workings to the miners' baths, the blacksmith's forge, the workshops and the engine house. There is also a replica of an underground gallery, where mining methods are explained. But the climax of any visit to Big Pit is beneath the ground. Kitted out with helmets, lamps and safety batteries, visitors descend by cage 90 m (300 ft) down the mineshaft and then are guided by ex-miners on a tour of the underground workings and pit ponies' stables.

Blaenafon also has remains of the iron-smelting industry. Across the valley from Big Pit stand the 18th-century smelting furnaces and workers' cottages that were once part of the **Blaenafon Ironworks**, and which are now a museum.

Big Pit Mining Museum
Blaenafon. *01495 790311.* *mid-Feb–Nov: daily.* *phone first.* www.nmgw.ac.uk

Blaenafon Ironworks
North St. *01495 792615.* *Apr–Oct: daily.*

Monmouth ⓱

Monmouthshire (Gwent). *12,000.* *Shire Hall (01600 713899).* *Fri, Sat.* www.visitwyevalley.com

THIS MARKET TOWN, which sits at the confluence of the Wye and Monnow rivers, has many historical associations. The 11th-century castle, behind Agincourt Square, is in ruins but the **Regimental Museum**,

Monnow Bridge in Monmouth, once a watchtower and jail

beside it, remains open to the public. The castle was the birthplace of Henry V *(see p49)* in 1387. Statues of Henry V (on the façade of Shire Hall) and Charles Stewart Rolls stand in the Square. Rolls, born at nearby Hendre, co-founded Rolls-Royce cars, and died in a flying accident in 1910.

Lord Horatio Nelson *(see p54)*, the famous admiral, visited Monmouth in 1802. An excellent collection of Nelson memorabilia, gathered by Lady Llangattock, mother of Charles Rolls, is displayed at the **Nelson Museum**.

Monmouth was the county town of the old Monmouthshire. The wealth of elegant Georgian buildings, including the elaborate **Shire Hall**, which dominates Agincourt Square, reflect its former status. The most famous architectural feature in Monmouth is **Monnow Bridge**, a narrow 13th-century gateway on its western approach, thought to be the only surviving fortified bridge gate in Britain.

For a lovely view over the town, climb the Kymin, a 256 m (840 ft) hill crowned by a **Naval Temple** built in 1801.

Monmouth Castle and Regimental Museum
The Castle. *01600 772175.* *Apr–Oct: daily (pm); Nov–Mar: Sat & Sun (pm).* *25 Dec.* www.monmouthcastlemuseum.org.uk

Nelson Museum
Priory St. *01600 710630.* *daily (Sun: pm).*

Tintern Abbey 18

Monmouthshire (Gwent). *01291 689251.* *Chepstow then bus.* *daily.* *24–26 Dec, 1 Jan.* www.cadw.wales.gov.uk

Ever since the 18th century, travellers have been enchanted by Tintern's setting in the steep and wooded Wye Valley and by the majestic ruins of its abbey. Poets were often inspired by the scene. Wordsworth's sonnet, *Lines composed a few miles above Tintern Abbey*, embodied his romantic view of landscape:

once again
Do I behold these steep and lofty cliffs,
That on a wild, secluded scene impress
Thoughts of more deep seclusion

The abbey was founded in 1131 by Cistercian monks, who cultivated the surrounding lands (now forest), and developed it as an influential religious centre. By the 14th century this was the richest abbey in Wales, but along with other monasteries it was dissolved in 1536. Its skeletal ruins are now roofless and exposed, the soaring arches and windows giving them a poignant grace and beauty.

Tintern Abbey in the Wye Valley, in the past a thriving centre of religion and learning, now a romantic ruin

Scotland

Introducing Scotland 464-475
The Lowlands 476-509
The Highlands And Islands 510-535

Scotland at a Glance

STRETCHING from the rich farmlands of the Borders to a chain of isles only a few degrees south of the Arctic Circle, the Scottish landscape has a diversity without parallel in Britain. As you travel northwest from Edinburgh, the land becomes more mountainous and its archaeological treasures more numerous. In the far northwest, Scotland's earliest relics stand upon the oldest rock on Earth.

Skye (see pp520–21), *renowned for its dramatic scenery, has one of Scotland's most striking coastlines. On the east coast, a stream plunges over Kilt Rock, a cliff of hexagonal basalt columns named after its likeness to an item of Scottish national dress.*

The Trossachs (see pp480–81) *are a beautiful range of hills straddling the border between the Highlands and the Lowlands. At their heart, the forested slopes of Ben Venue rise above the still waters of Loch Achray.*

Culzean Castle (see pp508–9) *stands on a cliff's edge on the Firth of Clyde, amid an extensive country park. One of the jewels of the Lowlands, Culzean is a magnificent showcase of work by the Scottish-born architect, Robert Adam* (see p24).

◁ **Loch Lomond, the Lowlands**

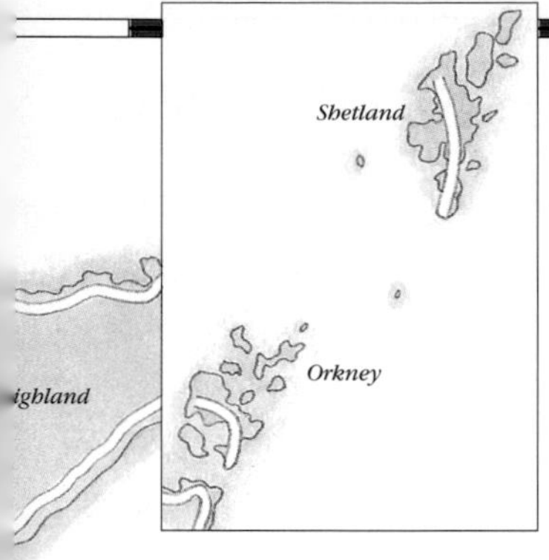

The Cairngorms (see pp530–31) *cover an area prized for its beauty and diversity of wildlife, though there are also many historical relics to be found, such as this early 18th-century arch at Carrbridge.*

Royal Deeside (see pp526–7) *in the Grampians has been associated with British royalty since Queen Victoria bought Balmoral Castle in 1852.*

Edinburgh (see pp490–97) *is the capital of Scotland. Between its medieval castle and the Palace of Holyroodhouse stretches the Royal Mile – a concentration of historic sights, ranging from the old Scottish Parliament buildings to the house of John Knox. Georgian terraces predominate in the New Town.*

The Burrell Collection (see pp506–7), *on the southern outskirts of Glasgow, is a museum of some of the city's greatest art treasures. It is housed in a spacious, glass building opened in 1983.*

0 kilometres 50

0 miles 50

A Portrait of Scotland

FROM THE GRASSY HILLS *of the Borders to the desolate Cuillin Ridge of Skye, the landscape of Scotland is breathtaking in its variety. Lonely glens, sparkling lochs and ever-changing skies give the land a challenging character, which is reflected in the qualities of the Scottish people. Tough and self-reliant, they have made some of Britain's finest soldiers, its boldest explorers and most astute industrialists.*

The Scots are proud of their separate identity and their own systems of law and education and, in 1998, voted overwhelmingly for their own parliament. Many Scots welcomed this as a long-awaited reversal of the Act of Union that united the English and Scottish parliaments in 1707. But despite their national pride, they are not a homogeneous people, the main division is between traditionally Gaelic-speaking Highlanders, and the Lowlanders who spoke Scots, a form of Middle English which is now extinct. Today, though Gaelic survives (chiefly in the Western Isles), most people speak regional dialects or richly accented English. Many Scottish surnames derive from Gaelic: the prefix "mac" means "son of". A Norse heritage can be found in the far north, where Shetlanders welcome the annual return of the sun during the Viking fire festival, Up Helly Aa.

A hammer-thrower at the Braemar Games

In the 16th century, a suspicion of authority and dislike of excessive flamboyance attracted many Scots to the Presbyterian church with its absence of bishops and its stress on simple worship. The Presbyterian Church of Scotland was established in 1689, though a substantial Catholic minority remained which today predominates in the crofting (small-scale farming) communities of the Western Isles. Now sparsely populated, the Isles preserve a rural culture that once dominated the Highlands, a region that is the source of much that is distinctively Scottish. The clan system originated there, along with the tartans, the bagpipes and such unique sports as tossing the caber – a large tree trunk. Highland sports, along with traditional dances, are still performed at annual games *(see p64)*.

Edinburgh bagpiper

Resourcefulness has always been a prominent Scottish virtue, and Scotland has produced a disproportionately high number of Britain's geniuses. James Watt designed the first effective steam engine to power the Industrial Revolution, while Adam Smith became the 18th century's most influential economist. In the 19th century, James Simpson discovered the anaesthetic qualities of

The Viking festival, Up Helly Aa, in Lerwick, Shetland

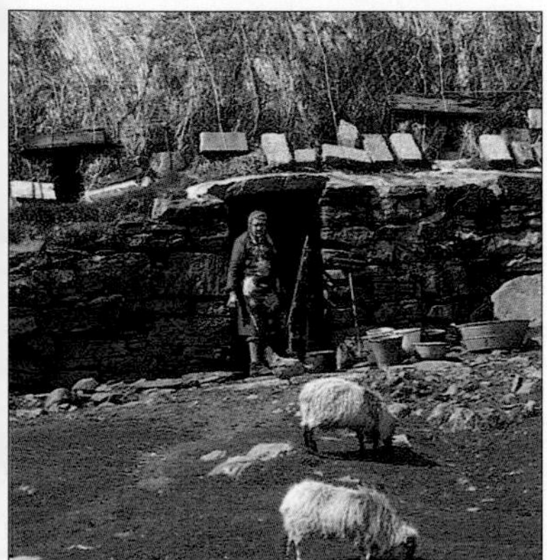

A traditional stone croft on the Isle of Lewis

chloroform, James Young developed the world's first oil refinery and Alexander Bell revolutionized communications by inventing the telephone. The 20th century saw one of the greatest advances in medicine with the discovery of penicillin by Alexander Fleming.

The Scots are also known for being shrewd businessmen, and have always been prominent in finance: both the Bank of England and the Royal Bank of France were founded by Scots, while Andrew Carnegie created one of 19th century-America's biggest business empires.

Detail of Edinburgh's Festival Fringe office

With some of the harshest weather conditions in Europe it is perhaps less surprising that Scotland has bred numerous great explorers, the most famous being Robert Scott (of the Antarctic) and African missionary David Livingstone. There is also a strong intellectual and literary tradition, from the 18th-century philosopher David Hume, through novelists Sir Walter Scott and Robert Louis Stevenson, to the poetry of Robert Burns. Today Scotland hosts a variety of arts festivals, such as Edinburgh's.

With a population density only one-fifth of England and Wales, Scotland has vast tracts of untenanted land which offer numerous outdoor pleasures. It is richly stocked with game, and the opening of the grouse season on 12 August is a highlight on the social calendar. Fishing and hill-walking are popular and in winter thousands flock to the Cairngorms and Glencoe for skiing. Though the weather may be harsher than elsewhere, the Scots will claim that the air is purer – and that enjoying rugged conditions is what distinguishes them from their soft southern neighbours.

The blue waters of Loch Achray in the heart of the Trossachs, north of Glasgow

The History of Scotland

***Bonnie Prince Charlie*, by G Dupré**

SINCE THE ROMAN INVASION of Britain, Scotland's history has been characterized by its resistance to foreign domination. The Romans never conquered the area, and when the Scots extended their kingdom to its present boundary in 1018, a long era of conflict began with England. After many wars, the Scots finally accepted union with the "auld enemy": first with the union of crowns, and then with the Union of Parliament in 1707. In 1999 the inauguration of the Scottish Parliament was a dramatic change.

An elaborately carved Pictish stone at Aberlemno, Angus

Early History

THERE IS MUCH EVIDENCE in Scotland of important prehistoric population centres, particularly in the Western Isles, which were peopled mostly by Picts who originally came from the Continent. By the time Roman Governor Julius Agricola invaded in AD 81, there were at least 17 independent tribes, including the Britons in the southwest, for him to contend with.

The Romans reached north to the Forth and Clyde valleys, but the Highlands deterred them from going further. By 120, they had retreated to the line where the Emperor Hadrian had built his wall to keep the Picts at bay (not far from today's border). By 163 the Romans had retreated south for the last time. The Celtic influence began when "Scots" arrived from Ireland in the 6th century, bringing the Gaelic language with them.

The Picts and Scots united under Kenneth McAlpin in 843, but the Britons remained separate until 1018, when they became part of the Scottish kingdom.

The English Claim

THE NORMAN KINGS regarded Scotland as part of their territory but seldom pursued the claim. William the Lion of Scotland recognized English sovereignty by the Treaty of Falaise (1174), though English control never spread to the northwest. In 1296 William Wallace, supported by the French (the start of the Auld Alliance, which lasted two centuries), began the long war of independence. During this bitter conflict, Edward I seized the sacred Stone of Destiny from Scone *(see p484)*, and took it to Westminster Abbey. The war lasted for more than 100 years. Its great hero was Robert the Bruce, who defeated the English in 1314 at Bannockburn. The English held the upper hand after that, even though the Scots would not accept their rule.

John K statue Edinbu

The Road to Union

THE SEEDS OF UNION between the crowns were sown in 1503 when James IV of Scotland married Margaret Tudor, daughter of Henry VII. When her brother, Henry VIII, came to the throne, James sought to assert independence but was defeated and killed at Flodden Field in 1513. His granddaughter, Mary, Queen of Scots *(see p497)*, married the French Dauphin in order to cement the Auld Alliance and gain assistance in her claim to

***Bruce in Single Combat at Bannockburn* (1906) by John Hassall**

the throne of her English cousin, Elizabeth I. She had support from the Catholics wanting to see an end to Protestantism in England and Scotland. However, fiery preacher John Knox won support for the Protestants and established the Presbyterian Church in 1560. Mary's Catholicism led to the loss of her Scottish throne in 1568, and her subsequent flight to England, following defeat at Langside. Finally, after nearly 20 years of imprisonment she was executed for treason by Elizabeth in 1587.

The factories on Clydeside, once creators of the world's greatest ships

Union and Rebellion

On Elizabeth I's death in 1603, Mary's son, James VI of Scotland, succeeded to the English throne and became James I, king of both countries. Thus the crowns were united, though it was 100 years before the formal Union of Parliaments in 1707. During that time, religious differences within the country reached boiling point. There were riots when the Catholic-influenced Charles I restored bishops to the Church of Scotland and authorized the printing of a new prayer book. This culminated in the signing, in Edinburgh in 1638, of the National Covenant, a document that condemned all Catholic doctrines. Though the Covenanters were suppressed, the Protestant William of Orange took over the English throne in 1688 and the crown passed out of Scottish hands.

Articles of Union between England and Scotland, 1707

In 1745, Bonnie Prince Charlie *(see p521)*, descended from the Stuart kings, tried to seize the throne from the Hanoverian George II. He marched far into England, but was driven back and defeated at Culloden field *(see p523)* in 1746.

Industrialization and Social Change

In the late 18th and 19th centuries, technological progress transformed Scotland from a nation of crofters to an industrial powerhouse. In the notorious Highland Clearances *(see p517)*, from the 1780s on, landowners ejected tenants from their smallholdings and gave the land over to sheep and other livestock. The first ironworks was established in 1760 and was soon followed by coal mining, steel production and shipbuilding on the Clyde. Canals were cut, railways and bridges built.

A strong socialist movement developed as workers sought to improve their conditions. Keir Hardie, an Ayrshire coal miner, in 1892 became the first socialist elected to parliament, and in 1893 founded the Independent Labour Party. The most enduring symbol of this time is the spectacular Forth rail bridge *(see p488)*.

Scotland Today

Although the status of the country appeared to have been settled in 1707, a strong nationalist sentiment remained and was heightened by the Depression of the 1920s and '30s which had severe effects on the heavily industrialized Clydeside. This was when the Scottish National Party formed, advocating self-rule. The Nationalists asserted themselves in 1950 by stealing the Stone of Scone from Westminister Abbey.

The discovery of North Sea oil in 1970 encouraged a nationalist revival and, in 1979, the Government promised to establish a separate assembly if 40 per cent of the Scottish electorate endorsed the plan in a referendum. This figure was finally surpassed in 1998, and the Scottish Parliament was duly inaugurated in 1999.

A North Sea oil rig, helping to provide prosperity in the 1970s

Clans and Tartans

THE CLAN SYSTEM, by which Highland society was divided into tribal groups led by autocratic chiefs, can be traced to the 12th century, when clans were already known to wear the chequered wool cloth later called tartan. All members of the clan bore the name of their chief, but not all were related by blood. Though they had noble codes of hospitality, the clansmen had to be warriors to protect their herds, as can be seen from their mottoes. After the Battle of Culloden *(see p523)*, all the clan lands were forfeited to the Crown, and the wearing of tartan was banned for nearly 100 years.

***The Mackays**, also known as the Clan Morgan, won lasting renown during the Thirty Years War.*

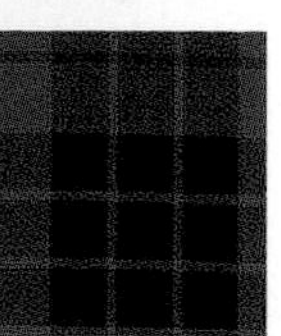

***The MacLeods** are of Norse heritage. The clan chief still lives in Dunvegan Castle, Skye* (see p520).

***The MacDonalds** were the most powerful of all the clans, holding the title of Lords of the Isles.*

***The Mackenzies** received much of the lands of Kintail* (see p516) *from David II in 1362.*

CLAN CHIEF

The chief was the clan's patriarch, judge and leader in war, commanding absolute loyalty from his clansmen who gave military service in return for his protection. The chief summoned his clan to do battle by sending a runner across his land bearing a burning cross.

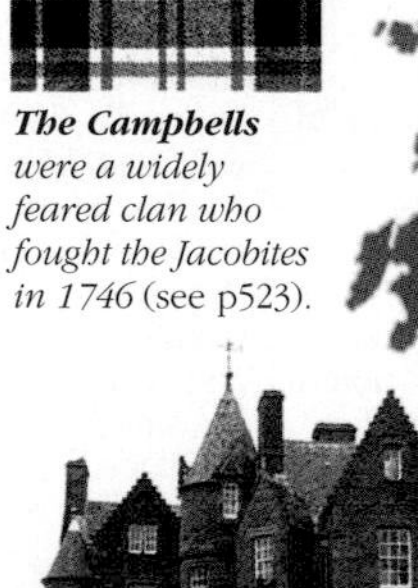

***The Campbells** were a widely feared clan who fought the Jacobites in 1746* (see p523).

***The Black Watch**, raised in 1729 to keep peace in the Highlands, was one of the Highland regiments in which the wearing of tartan survived. After 1746, civilians were punished by exile for up to seven years for wearing tartan.*

***The Sinclairs** came from France in the 11th century and became Earls of Caithness in 1455.*

***The Frasers** came to Britain from France with William the Conqueror* (see p47) *in 1066.*

***George IV**, dressed as a Highlander, visited Edinburgh in 1822, the year of the tartan revival. Many tartan "setts" (patterns) date from this time, as the original ones were lost.*

***The Gordons** were famously good soldiers; the clan motto is "by courage, not by craft".*

***The Stuarts** were Scotland's royal dynasty. Their motto was "no one harms me with impunity".*

***The Douglas** clan were prominent in Scottish history, though their origin is unknown.*

Clan Territories

The territories of 10 prominent clans are marked here with their clan crests. Dress tartans tend to be colourful, while hunting tartans are darker.

Plant Badges

Each clan had a plant associated with its territory. It was worn on the bonnet, especially on the day of battle.

Scots pine was worn by the MacGregors of Argyll.

Rowan berries were worn by the Clan Malcolm.

Ivy was worn by the Clan Gordon of Aberdeenshire.

Spear thistle, now a national symbol, was a Stuart badge.

Cotton grass was worn by the Clan Henderson.

Highland Clans Today

Once the daily dress of the clansmen, the kilt is now largely reserved for formal occasions. The one-piece *feileadh-mor* has been replaced by the *feileadh-beag*, or "small plaid", made from approximately 7 m (23 ft) of material with a double apron fastened at the front with a silver pin. Though they exist now only in name, the clans are still a strong source of pride for Scots, and many still live in areas traditionally belonging to their clans. Many visitors to Britain can trace their Scots ancestry *(see p27)* to the Highlands.

Modern Highland formal dress

Evolution of the Scottish Castle

THERE ARE FEW more romantic sights in the British Isles than a Scottish castle on an island or at a lochside. These formidable retreats, often in remote settings, were essential all over the Highlands, where incursions and strife between the clans were common. From the earliest Pictish *brochs (see p43)* and Norman-influenced motte and bailey castles, the distinctively Scottish tower-house evolved, first appearing in the 14th century. By the mid-17th century fashion had become more important than defence, and there followed a period in which numerous huge Scottish palaces were built.

Detail of the Baroque façade, Drumlanrig

Motte and Bailey

These castles first appeared in the 12th century. They stood atop two adjacent mounds enclosed by a wall, or palisade, and defensive ditches. The higher mound, or motte, was the most strongly defended as it held the keep and chief's house. The lower bailey was where the people lived. Of these castles little more than earthworks remain today.

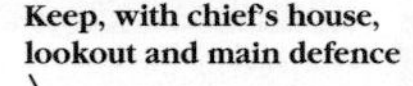

All that remains today of Duffus Castle, Morayshire

***Duffus Castle**, (c.1150), was atypically made of stone rather than wood. Its fine defensive position dominates the surrounding flatlands north of Elgin.*

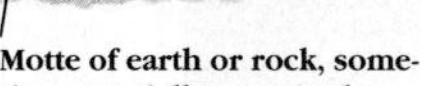

Early Tower-House

Designed to deter local attacks rather than a major assault, the first tower-houses appeared in the 13th century, though their design lived on for 400 years. They were built initially on a rectangular plan, with a single tower divided into three or four floors. The walls were unadorned, with few windows. Defensive structures were on top, and extra space was made by building adjoining towers. Extensions were made as vertically as possible, to minimize the area open to attack.

***Neidpath Castle**, standing upon a steep rocky crag above the River Tweed, is an L-shaped tower-house dating from the late 14th century. Once a stronghold for Charles II, its walls still bear damage from a siege conducted by Oliver Cromwell* (see p52).

Claypotts Castle (c.1570) with uniquely projecting garrets above its towers

Braemar Castle (c.1630), a conglomeration of extended towers

LATER TOWER-HOUSE

Though the requirements of defence were being replaced by those of comfort, the style of the early tower-house remained popular. By the 17th century, wings for accommodation were being added around the original tower (often creating a courtyard). The battlements and turrets were kept more for decorative than defensive reasons.

Drum Castle *(see p527)*, a 13th-century keep with a mansion house extension from 1619

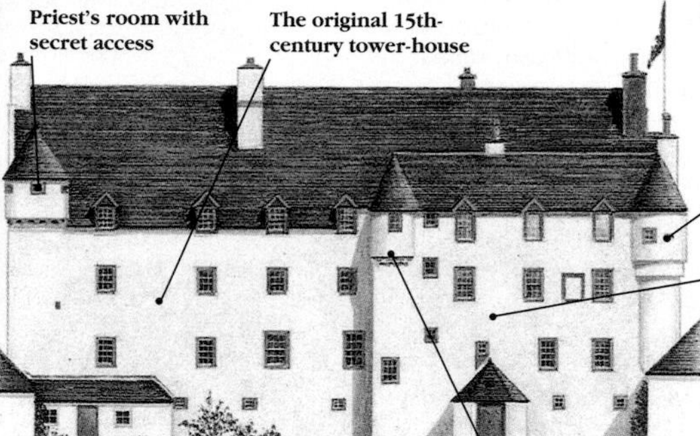

Traquair House (see p499), *by the Tweed, is reputedly the oldest continuously inhabited house in Scotland. The largely unadorned, roughcast exterior dates to the 16th century, when a series of extensions were built around the original 15th-century tower-house.*

Blair Castle *(see p529)*, incorporating a medieval tower

CLASSICAL PALACE

By the 18th century, the defensive imperative had passed and castles were built in the manner of country houses, rejecting the vertical tower-house in favour of a horizontal plan (though the building of imitation fortified buildings continued into the 19th century with the mock-Baronial trend). Outside influences came from all over Europe, including Renaissance and Gothic revivals, and echoes of French châteaux.

Dunrobin Castle (c.1840), Sutherland

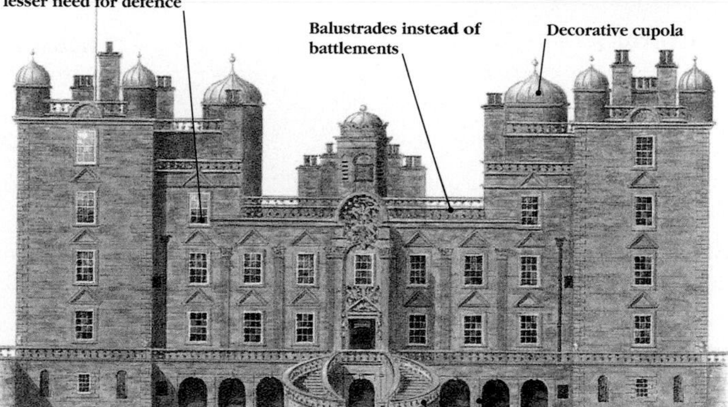

Drumlanrig Castle (see p500) *was built in the 17th century. There are many traditional Scots aspects as well as such Renaissance features as the decorated stairway and façade.*

Scottish Food and Drink

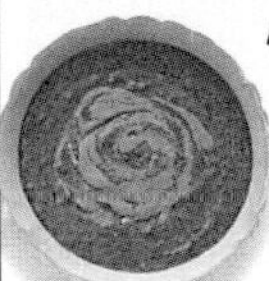

Porridge *is a breakfast of oats, boiled in water and milk, with salt or sugar.*

THE SCOTTISH LARDER is generous in meat and fish, which are usually served simply, without heavy sauces. Grouse and deer range the hills, Aberdeen Angus beef is world famous, and the rivers are renowned for their salmon and trout. With Scotland's cold, wet climate and shallow soil, wheat was grown less than oats, which are still present in traditional Scottish foods, such as porridge and oatcakes (rather than bread) and, of course, haggis.

Kippers*, eaten at breakfast, are fresh herring split down the back, salted and cured by smoking over a fire.*

Poached salmon *tastes best when cooked whole in a bouillon of water, wine and vegetables, during which its deep red flesh turns a delicate pink. Salmon are caught in all Scotland's rivers.*

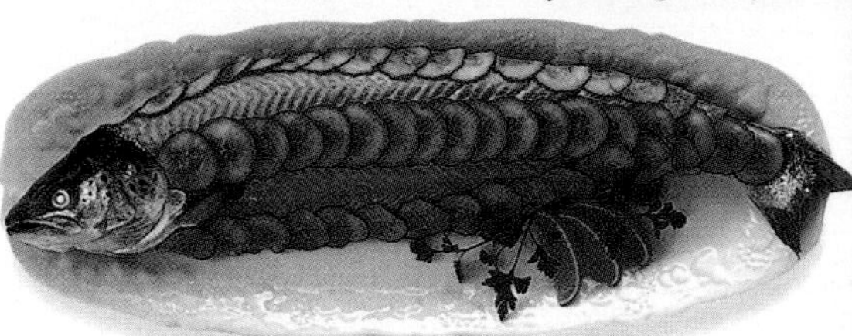

Scotch broth *is a light, thin soup based on neck of mutton, to which pearl barley and vegetables are added.*

Venison *is allowed to hang for ten days before being seasoned with mixed spices, wine and vinegar, and then roasted.*

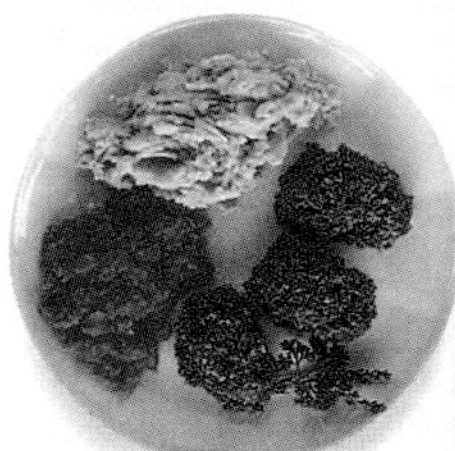

Haggis*, served boiled with swedes, or "neeps", and potatoes, is spiced sheep's innards, here mixed with oatmeal.*

MARMALADE

Marmalade was created in Dundee *(see p485)* in the 1700s after a rash purchase left grocer James Keiller with a large cargo of bitter Seville oranges. He was unable to re-sell them, so his wife Janet added them to a preserve. Word soon spread about her delicious creation which now appears on breakfast tables throughout the world.

Traditional orange

Grapefruit and ginger

Dundee cake *is a rich, sweet cake made of dried fruits and spices topped with almonds.*

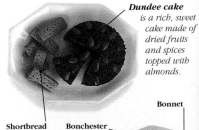

Shortbread

Bonchester

Bonnet

Scottish oatcakes *are flat biscuits of fine oatmeal which accompany sweets or savouries. Hard Bonnet and soft Bonchester are popular among the Scottish cheeses.*

How Whisky is Made

Traditionally made from just barley, yeast and stream water, Scottish whisky (from the Gaelic *usquebaugh*, or the "water of life") takes a little over three weeks to produce, though it must be given at least three years to mature. Maturation usually takes place in oak casks, often in barrels previously used for sherry. The art of blending was pioneered in Edinburgh in the 1860s.

Barley grass

1 Malting is the first stage. Barley grain is soaked in water and spread on the malting floor. With regular turning the grain germinates, producing a "green malt". Germination stimulates the production of enzymes which turn the starches into fermentable sugars.

2 Drying of the barley halts germination after 12 days of malting. This is done over a peat fire in a pagoda-shaped malt-kiln. The peat-smoke gives flavour to the malt and eventually to the mature whisky. The malt is gleaned of germinated roots and then milled.

3 Mashing of the ground malt, or "grist", occurs in a large vat, or "mash tun", which holds a vast quantity of hot water. The malt is soaked and begins to dissolve, producing a sugary solution called "wort", which is then extracted for fermentation.

4 Fermentation occurs when yeast is added to the cooled wort in wooden vats, or "washbacks". The mixture is stirred for hours as the yeast turns the sugar into alcohol, producing a clear liquid called "wash".

5 Distillation involves boiling the wash twice so that the alcohol vaporizes and condenses. In copper "pot stills", the wash is distilled – first in the "wash still", then in the "spirit still". Now purified, with an alcohol content of 57 per cent, the result is young whisky.

Traditional drinking vessels, or *quaichs*, made of silver

6 Maturation is the final process. The whisky mellows in oak casks for a legal minimum of three years. Premium brands give the whisky a 10- to 15-year maturation, though some are given up to 50 years.

***Blended whiskies** are made from a mixture of up to 50 different single malts.*

***Single malts** vary according to regional differences in the peat and stream water used.*

The Lowlands

Clyde Valley · Central Scotland · Fife · The Lothians
Ayrshire · Dumfries and Galloway · The Borders

SOUTHEAST *of the Highland boundary fault line lies a part of Scotland very different in character from its northern neighbour. If the Highlands embody the romance of Scotland, the Lowlands have traditionally been her powerhouse. Lowlanders have always prospered in agriculture and, more recently, in industry and commerce.*

Being the region of Scotland closest to the English border, the Lowlands inevitably became the crucible of Scottish history. For centuries after the Romans built the Antonine Wall *(see p44)* across the Forth–Clyde isthmus, the area was engulfed in conflict. The Borders are scattered with the castles of a territory in uneasy proximity to rapacious neighbours, and the ramparts of Stirling Castle overlook no fewer than seven different battlefields fought over in the cause of independence.

The ruins of medieval abbeys, such as Melrose, also bear witness to the dangers of living on the invasion route from England, though the woollen trade founded by their monks still flourishes in Peebles and Hawick.

North of the Borders lies Edinburgh, the cultural and administrative capital of Scotland. With its Georgian squares dominated by a medieval castle, it is one of Europe's most elegant cities. While the 18th and 19th centuries saw a great flowering of the arts in Edinburgh, the city of Glasgow became a merchant city second only to London. Fuelled by James Watt's development of the steam engine in the 1840s, Glasgow became the cradle of Scotland's Industrial Revolution, which created a prosperous cotton industry and launched the world's greatest ships.

Both cities retain this dynamism today: Edinburgh annually hosts the world's largest arts festival, and Glasgow is acclaimed as a model of industrial renaissance.

A juggler performing at the annual arts extravaganza, the Edinburgh Festival

◁ **Glamis Castle, 12 miles (19 km) north of Dundee, with its typically Scottish turreted exterior**

Exploring the Lowlands

The lowlands are traditionally all the land south of the fault line stretching northeast from Loch Lomond to Stonehaven. Confusingly, they include plenty of wild upland country. The region illustrates the diversity of Scotland's scenery. The wooded valleys and winding rivers of the borders give way to the stern hills of the Cheviots and Lammermuirs. Fishing villages cling to the rocky east coast, while the Clyde coast and its islands are dotted with holiday towns. Inland lies the Trossachs, a romantic area of mountain, loch and woodland east of Loch Lomond that is a magnet for walkers *(see pp32–3)* and well within reach of Glasgow.

Loch Katrine seen from the Trossachs

See Also

- ***Where to Stay*** pp568-70
- ***Where to Eat*** pp604-6

Sights at a Glance

Abbotsford House 20
Biggar 22
Burns Cottage 31
Culross 11
Culzean Castle pp508–9 30
Doune Castle 3
Drumlanrig Castle 27
Dundee 6
Dunfermline 10
East Neuk 8
Edinburgh pp490–97 16
Falkirk Wheel 13
Falkland Palace 9
Forth Bridges 15
Glamis Castle 5
Glasgow pp502–7 25
Hopetoun House 14
Linlithgow Palace 12
Melrose Abbey 19
New Lanark 24
Pentland Hills 23
Perth 4
St Abb's Head 17
St Andrews 7
Sanquhar 26
Stirling pp482–3 2
Threave Castle 28
Traquair House 21
Trossachs pp480–81 1
Whithorn 29

Walks and Tours

Tour of the Borders 18

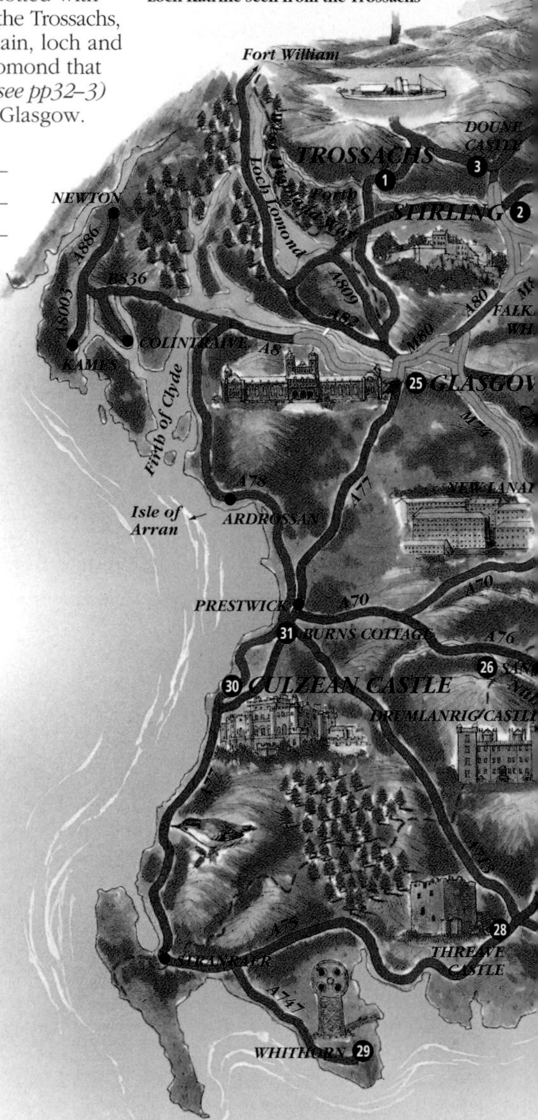

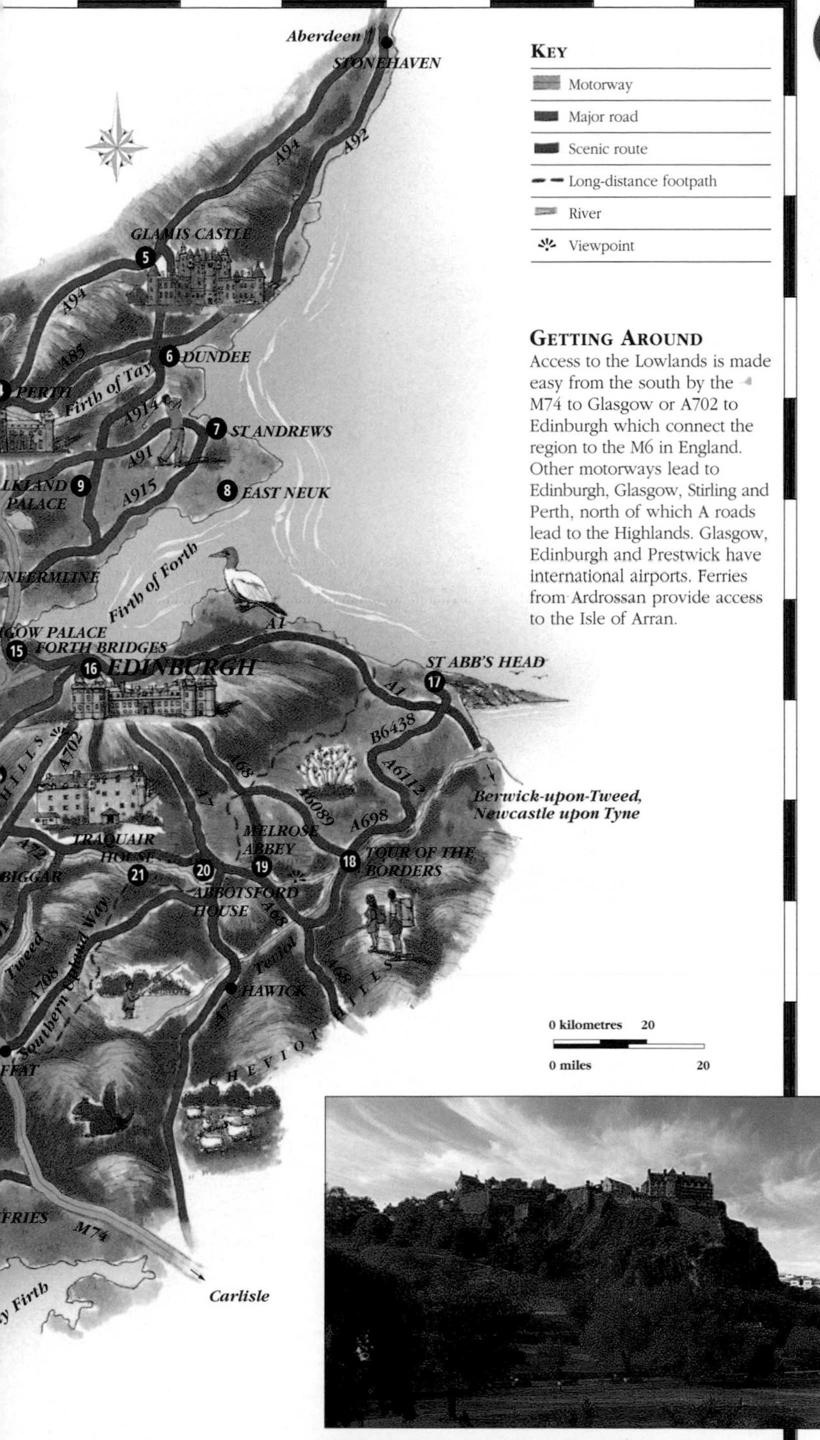

Getting Around

Access to the Lowlands is made easy from the south by the M74 to Glasgow or A702 to Edinburgh which connect the region to the M6 in England. Other motorways lead to Edinburgh, Glasgow, Stirling and Perth, north of which A roads lead to the Highlands. Glasgow, Edinburgh and Prestwick have international airports. Ferries from Ardrossan provide access to the Isle of Arran.

Edinburgh Castle viewed from Princes Street

The Trossachs ❶

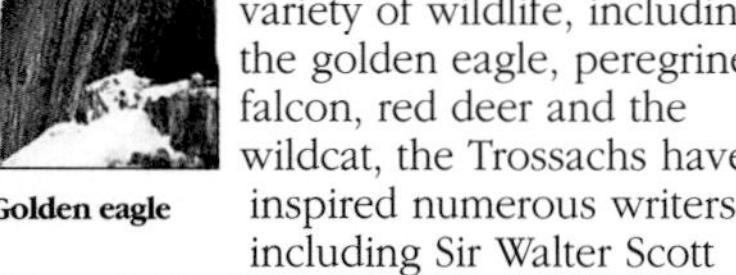

Golden eagle

COMBINING THE RUGGEDNESS of the Grampians with the pastoral tranquillity of the Borders, this beautiful region of craggy hills and sparkling lochs is the colourful meeting place of the Lowlands and Highlands. Home to a wide variety of wildlife, including the golden eagle, peregrine falcon, red deer and the wildcat, the Trossachs have inspired numerous writers, including Sir Walter Scott *(see p498)* who made the area the setting for several of his novels. It was the home of Scotland's folk hero, Rob Roy, who was so well known that, in his own lifetime, he was fictionalized in *The Highland Rogue* (1723), a novel attributed to Daniel Defoe.

Loch Katrine
The setting of ... *Walter Scott's* ... of the Lake *(1*... *this freshwater loch can be explored on the Victorian steam*... *SS* Sir Walter S... *which cruises f*... *the Trossachs F*...

Loch Lomond
Britain's largest freshwater lake was immortalized in a ballad composed by a local Jacobite soldier, dying far from home. He laments that though he will return home before his companions who travel on the high road, he will be doing so on the low road (of death).

The West Highland Way provides a good footpath through the area.

KEY

Tourist information

A road

B road

Minor road

Footpath

Viewpoint

0 kilometres 5

0 miles 5

Luss
With its exceptionally picturesque cottages, Luss is one of the prettiest villages in the Lowlands. Surrounded by grassy hills, it occupies one of the most scenic parts of Loch Lomond's western shore.

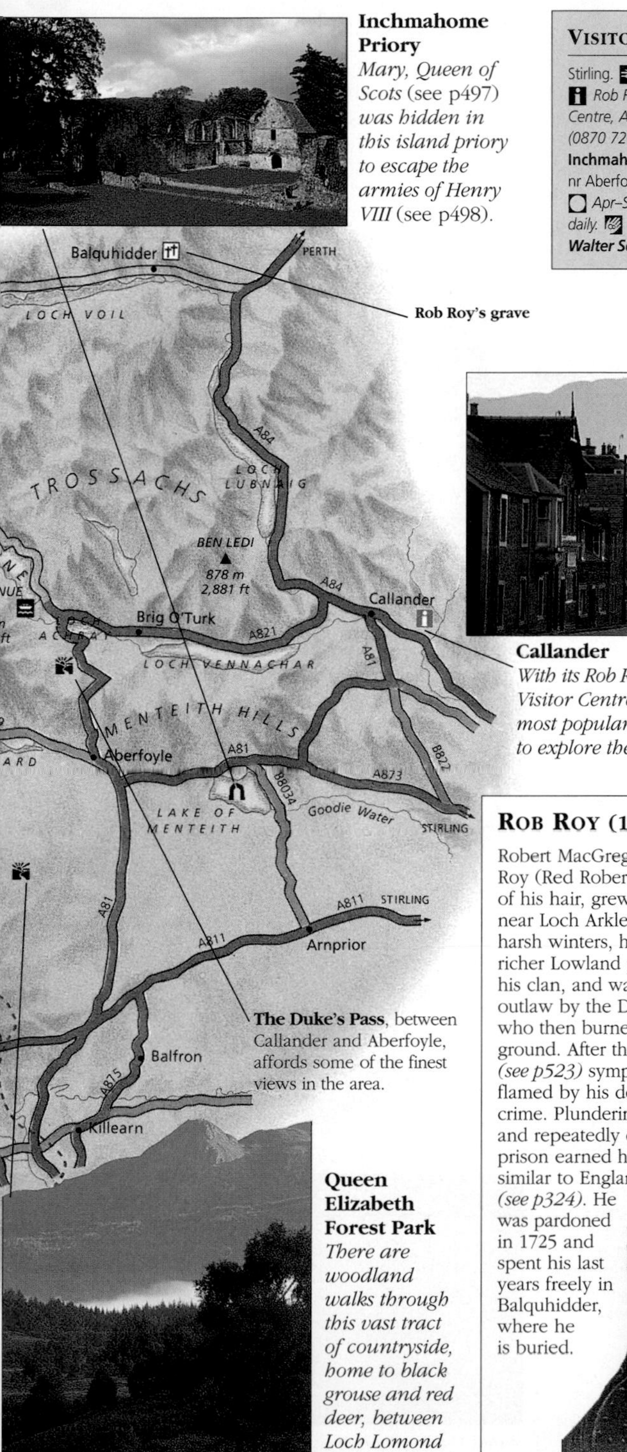

Inchmahome Priory
Mary, Queen of Scots (see p497) *was hidden in this island priory to escape the armies of Henry VIII* (see p498).

Callander
With its Rob Roy and Trossachs Visitor Centre, Callander is the most popular town from which to explore the Trossachs.

The Duke's Pass, between Callander and Aberfoyle, affords some of the finest views in the area.

Queen Elizabeth Forest Park
There are woodland walks through this vast tract of countryside, home to black grouse and red deer, between Loch Lomond and Aberfoyle.

Visitors' Checklist

Stirling. *Stirling.* *Callander.* *Rob Roy & Trossachs Visitor Centre, Ancaster Sq, Callander (0870 7200628).* *Mar–Dec.*
Inchmahome Priory, off A81, nr Aberfoyle. *0870-7200628.* *Apr–Sep: 9:30am–6:30pm daily.* *limited.* ***SS Sir Walter Scott****: ring Visitor Centre.*

Rob Roy (1671–1734)

Robert MacGregor, known as Rob Roy (Red Robert) from the colour of his hair, grew up as a herdsman near Loch Arklet. After a series of harsh winters, he took to raiding richer Lowland properties to feed his clan, and was declared an outlaw by the Duke of Montrose who then burned his house to the ground. After this, Rob's Jacobite *(see p523)* sympathies became inflamed by his desire to avenge the crime. Plundering the duke's lands and repeatedly escaping from prison earned him a reputation similar to England's Robin Hood *(see p324)*. He was pardoned in 1725 and spent his last years freely in Balquhidder, where he is buried.

The 17th-century town house of the Dukes of Argyll, Stirling

Stirling ❷

Stirling. 28,000.
41 Dunbarton Rd (0870 7200620).
www.visitscottishheartlands.org

SITUATED BETWEEN the Ochil Hills and the Campsie Fells, Stirling grew up around its castle, historically one of Scotland's most important fortresses. Below the castle the Old Town is still protected by the original 16th-century walls, built to keep Mary Queen of Scots safe from Henry VIII. The medieval **Church of the Holy Rude**, on Castle Wynd, where the infant James VI was crowned in 1567, has one of Scotland's few surviving hammerbeam oak roofs. The ornate façade of **Mar's Wark** is all that remains of a grand palace which, though never completed, was commissioned in 1570 by the 1st Earl of Mar. It was destroyed by the Jacobites *(see p523)* in 1746. Opposite stands the beautiful 17th-century town house of the Dukes of Argyll.

ENVIRONS: Two miles (3 km) south, the **Bannockburn Heritage Centre** stands by the field where Robert the Bruce defeated the English *(see p468)*. After the battle, he dismantled the castle so it would not fall back into English hands. A bronze equestrian statue commemorates the man who is an icon of Scottish independence.

Bannockburn Heritage Centre
(NTS) Glasgow Rd. *01786 812664.* *Apr–Sep: 10am–5:30pm daily; Oct–Mar: 11am–4:30pm daily.* *24 Dec–Feb.*

Stirling Castle

RISING HIGH on a rocky crag, this magnificent castle, which dominated Scottish history for centuries, now remains one of the finest examples of Renaissance architecture in Scotland. Legend says that King Arthur *(see p273)* wrested the original castle from the Saxons, but there is no evidence of a castle before 1124. The present building dates from the 15th and 16th centuries and was last defended, against the Jacobites *(see p523)*, in 1746. From 1881 to 1964 the castle was a depot for recruits into the Argyll and Sutherland Highlanders, though now it serves no military function.

Gargoyle on castle wall

Robert the Bruce
In the esplanade, this modern statue shows Robert the Bruce sheathing his sword after the Battle of Bannockburn in 1314.

***Stirling Castle in the Time of the Stuarts*, painted by Johannes Vorsterman (1643–99)**

★ Palace
The otherwise sparse interiors of the royal apartments contain the Stirling Heads. These Renaissance roundels depict 38 figures, thought to be contemporary members of the royal court.

Visitors' Checklist

Castle Wynd, Stirling. *01786 450000.* *Apr–Sep: 9:30am–6pm daily; Oct–Mar: 9:30am–5pm daily (last adm: 45 mins before closing).* *25–26 Dec, 1–2 Jan.* except museum. limited. www.historic-scotland.gov.uk

The King's Old Building houses the Regimental Museum of the Argyll and Sutherland Highlanders.

★ Chapel Royal
Seventeenth-century frescoes by Valentine Jenkins adorn the chapel, reconstructed in 1594.

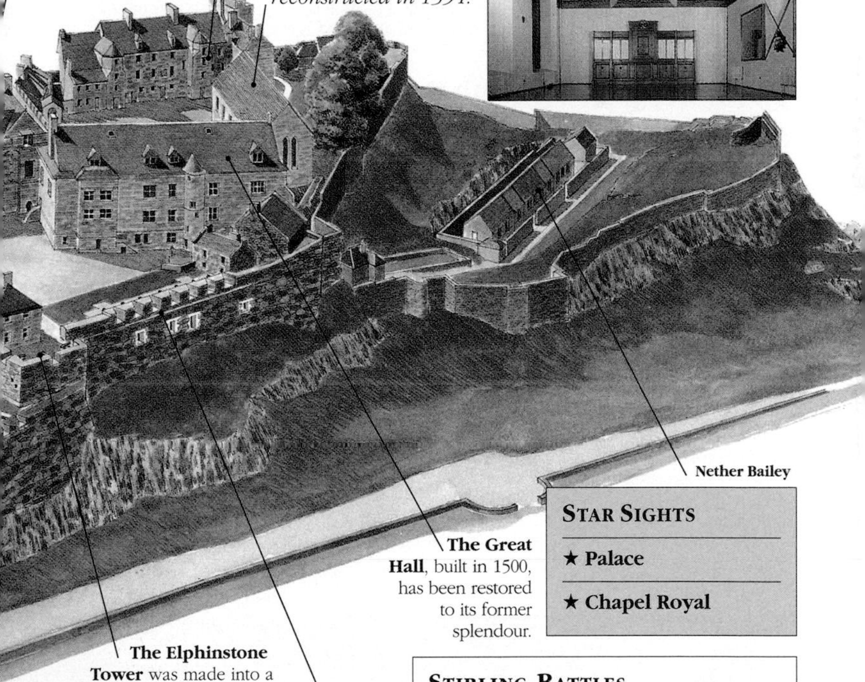

Nether Bailey

Star Sights

★ Palace

★ Chapel Royal

The Great Hall, built in 1500, has been restored to its former splendour.

The Elphinstone Tower was made into a gun platform in 1714.

Grand Battery
Seven guns stand on this parapet, built in 1708 during a strengthening of defences following the revolution of 1688 (see p53).

Stirling Battles

At the highest navigable point of the Forth and holding the pass to the Highlands, Stirling occupied a key position in Scotland's struggles for independence. Seven battlefields can be seen from the castle; the 67 m (220 ft) Wallace Monument at Abbey Craig recalls William Wallace's defeat of the English at Stirling Bridge in 1297, foreshadowing Bruce's victory in 1314 *(see p468)*.

The Victorian Wallace Monument

Perth seen from the east across the Tay

Doune Castle ❸

Doune, Stirling. 01786 841742. Stirling then bus. *Apr–Sep: 9:30am–6:30pm, daily; Oct–Mar: 9:30am–4pm, Sat–Thu.* *21 Dec–8 Jan.* *limited.*

BUILT AS THE residence of Robert, Duke of Albany, in the 14th century, **Doune Castle** was a Stuart stronghold until it fell into ruin in the 18th century. Now fully restored, it is one of the most complete castles of its time and offers a unique insight into the medieval royal household.

The Gatehouse, once a self-sufficient residence, leads through to the central courtyard from which the Great Hall can be entered. Complete with its reconstructed open-timber roof, minstrels' gallery and central fireplace, the Hall adjoins the Lord's Hall and Private Room with its original privy and well-hatch. A number of private stairs and narrow passages illustrate the ingenious means by which the royal family tried to protect itself during times of danger.

Perth ❹

Perthshire. 45,000. *West Mill St (01738 450600).* www.perthshire.co.uk

ONCE THE CAPITAL of medieval Scotland, Perth's rich heritage is reflected in many of its buildings. It was in the **Church of Saint John**, founded in 1126, that John Knox *(see p469)* delivered many of his fiery sermons. The Victorianized **Fair Maid's House**, on North Port, is one of the oldest houses in town (c.1600) and was the fictional home of the heroine of Sir Walter Scott's *(see p498) The Fair Maid of Perth* (1828).

In **Balhousie Castle**, the Museum of the Black Watch commemorates the first Highland regiment, while the **Art Gallery and Museum** has displays on local industry and exhibitions of Scottish painting.

ENVIRONS: Two miles (3 km) north of Perth, the Gothic mansion of **Scone Palace** stands on the site of an abbey destroyed in 1559. Between the 9th and 13th centuries, Scone guarded the sacred Stone of Destiny *(see pp468–9)*, now kept in Edinburgh Castle *(see pp492–3)*. Some of Mary, Queen of Scots' *(see p497)* embroideries are on display within.

Balhousie Castle
RHQ Black Watch, Hay St. *0131 310 8530.* *May–Sep: 10am–4:30pm, Mon–Sat; Oct–Apr: 10am–3:30pm, Mon–Fri.* *23 Dec–6 Jan.*

Art Gallery and Museum
78 George St. *01738 632488.* *10am–5pm Mon–Sat.* *24 Dec–4 Jan.*

Scone Palace
A93 to Braemar. *01738 552300.* *Easter–Oct: 9:30am–5:30pm daily; Nov–Easter: Fri (grounds only).*

Glamis Castle ❺

Forfar, Angus. *01307 840242.* *Dundee then bus.* *Apr–Oct: 10:30am–5:30pm daily.* www.glamiscastle.co.uk

WITH THE pinnacled fairy-tale outline of a Loire chateau, the imposing medieval tower-house of **Glamis**

Glamis Castle with statues of James VI (left) and Charles I (right)

Castle began as a royal hunting lodge in the 11th-century but underwent extensive reconstruction in the 17th century. It was the childhood home of Queen Elizabeth the Queen Mother, and her former bedroom can be seen with a youthful portrait by Henri de Laszlo (1878–1956).

Many rooms are open to the public, including Duncan's Hall, the oldest in the castle and Shakespeare's setting for the king's murder in *Macbeth*. Together, the rooms present an array of china, paintings, tapestries and furniture spanning five centuries. In the grounds stand a pair of wrought-iron gates made for the Queen Mother on her 80th birthday in 1980.

View of St Andrews over the ruins of the cathedral

Dundee 6

Dundee City. 150,000. 21 Castle Street (01382 527527). Tue, Fri–Sun. www.angusanddundee.co.uk

FAMOUS FOR ITS cake, marmalade and the DC Thomson publishing empire (creators of children's magazines *Beano* and *Dandy*), **Dundee** was also a major ship-building centre in the 18th and 19th centuries, a period which can be atmospherically recreated by a trip to the Victoria Docks.

HMS *Unicorn*, built in 1824, is the oldest British-built warship still afloat and is still fitted as it was on its last voyage. Berthed at Riverside is the royal research ship ***Discovery***, built here in 1901 for Captain Scott's first voyage to the Antarctic. Housed in a Victorian Gothic building, the **McManus Galleries** provide a glimpse of Dundee's industrial heritage, as well as exhibitions on archaeology and Victorian art. The **Howff Burial Ground**, near City Square, has intriguing Victorian tombstones.

HMS *Unicorn*
Victoria Docks, City Quay. *01382 200900. Apr–Oct: 10am–5pm daily: Nov–Mar: 10am–4pm Wed–Sun. late Dec–early Jan. limited.*

Discovery
Discovery Point. *01382 201245. Apr–Oct: 11am–5pm; Nov–Mar: 11am–4pm (Sun pm). by appointment.*

McManus Galleries
Albert Sq. *01382 432084. 10:30am–5pm daily (7pm Thu, 12:30–4pm Sun). 25, 26 Dec, 1–3 Jan.*

The Ancient Game of Golf

Scotland's national game was pioneered on the sandy links around St Andrews. The earliest record dates from 1457, when golf was banned by James II on the grounds that it was interfering with his subjects' archery practice. Mary, Queen of Scots *(see p497)* enjoyed the game and was berated in 1568 for playing straight after the murder of her husband Darnley.

Mary, Queen of Scots at St Andrews in 1563

St Andrews 7

Fife. 14,000. Leuchars. Dundee. 70 Market St (01334 472021). www.standrews.co.uk

SCOTLAND'S OLDEST UNIVERSITY town and one-time ecclesiastical capital, **St Andrews** is now a shrine to golfers from all over the world *(see below)*. Its three main streets and numerous cobbled alleys, full of crooked housefronts, dignified university buildings and medieval churches, converge on the venerable ruins of the 12th-century **cathedral**. Once the largest in Scotland, the cathedral was later pillaged for stones to build the town. **St Andrew's Castle** was built for the bishops of the town in 1200. The dungeon can still be seen. The city's golf courses to the west are each open for a modest fee. The **British Golf Museum**, tells how the city's Royal and Ancient Golf Club became the ruling arbiter of the game.

St Mary's College insignia, St Andrews University

St Andrew's Castle
The Scores. *01334 477196. Apr–Sep: 9:30–6pm; Oct–Mar: 9:30–4pm daily. 25, 26 Dec, 1, 2 Jan.*

British Golf Museum
Bruce Embankment. *01334 478880. Easter–mid-Oct: 9:30am–5:30pm daily; mid-Oct–Easter: 11am–3pm Thu–Mon.*

The central courtyard of Falkland Palace, bordered by rose bushes

East Neuk 8

Fife. Leuchars. Glenrothes & Leuchars. 70 Market Street, St Andrews (01334 472021).

A STRING of pretty fishing villages scatters the shoreline of the **East Neuk** (the eastern "corner") of Fife, stretching from Earlsferry to Fife Ness. Much of Scotland's medieval trade with Europe passed through these ports, a connection reflected in the Flemish-inspired crow-stepped gables of many of the cottages. Although the herring industry has declined and the area is now a peaceful holiday centre, the sea still dominates village life. Until the 1980s, fishing boats were built at St Monans, a charming town of narrow twisting streets, while Pittenweem is the base for the East Neuk fishing fleet.

The town is also known for **St Fillan's Cave**, the retreat of a 9th-century hermit whose relic was used to bless the army of Robert the Bruce *(see p468)* before the Battle of Bannockburn. A church stands among the cobbled lanes and colourful cottages of Crail; the stone by the church gate is said to have been hurled to the mainland from the Isle of May by the Devil.

Several 16th- to 19th-century buildings in the village of Anstruther contain the **Scottish Fisheries Museum** which tells the area's history with the aid of interiors, boats and displays on whaling. From the village you can also embark for the nature reserve on the **Isle of May** which teems with seabirds and grey seals. The statue of Alexander Selkirk in Lower Largo recalls the local boy whose adventures inspired Daniel Defoe's *Robinson Crusoe* (1719). Disagreeing with his captain, he was dumped on a desert island for four years.

Scottish Fisheries Museum

Harbour Head, St Ayles, Anstruther. *01333 310628. 10am–5:30pm daily. 25, 26 Dec, 1, 2 Jan.*

The Palace Keeper

Due to the size of the royal household and the necessity for the king to be itinerant, the office of Keeper was created by the medieval kings who required custodians to maintain and replenish the resources of their many palaces while they were away. Now redundant, it was a hereditary title and gave the custodian permanent and often luxurious lodgings.

James VI's bed in the Keeper's Bedroom, Falkland Palace

Falkland Palace 9

(NTS) Falkland, Fife. *01337 857397. Ladybank, Kirkcaldy, then bus. Mar–Oct: 10am-6pm daily (Sun: pm).* www.nts.org

THIS STUNNING Renaissance palace was designed as a hunting lodge of the Stuart kings. Although its construction was begun by James IV in 1500, most of the work was carried out by his son, James V *(see p496)*, in the 1530s. Under the influence of his two French wives he employed French workmen to redecorate the façade of the East Range with dormers, buttresses and medallions, and to build the beautifully proportioned South Range. The palace fell into ruin during the years of the Commonwealth *(see p52)* and was occupied briefly by Rob Roy *(see p481)* in 1715.

After buying the estates in 1887, the 3rd Marquess of Bute became the Palace Keeper and restored it. The richly panelled interiors are filled with superb furniture and portraits of the Stuart monarchs. The royal tennis court, the oldest in Britain, was built in 1539 for James V.

Dunfermline 10

Fife. *45,000.* *1 High St (01383 720999).* www.standrews.com/fife

SCOTLAND'S CAPITAL until 1603, Dunfermline is dominated by the ruins of the 12th-century abbey and palace which recall its royal past. In the 11th century, the town was the seat of King Malcolm III, who founded a priory on the present site of the **Abbey Church**. With its Norman nave and 19th-century choir, the church contains the tombs of 22 Scottish kings and queens, including Robert the Bruce *(see p468)*.

The ruins of King Malcolm's **palace** soar over the beautiful gardens of Pittencrieff Park. Dunfermline's most famous son, philanthropist Andrew Carnegie (1835–1919), had been forbidden entrance to the park as a boy. After making his fortune, he bought the entire Pittencrieff estate and gave it to the people of Dunfermline. He was born in the town, though moved to Pennsylvania in his teens. There he made a vast fortune in the iron and steel industry. The **Carnegie Birthplace Museum** is still furnished as it was when he lived there, and tells the story of his meteoric career.

Carnegie Birthplace Museum
Moodie St. 01383 724302. *Apr–Oct: daily (Sun: pm).*

The 12th-century Norman nave of Dunfermline Abbey Church

Culross ⓫

(NTS) Fife. *450.* *Dunfermline.* *Dunfermline.* *National Trust for Scotland, The Palace (01383 880359).* *Apr–Jun, Sep, Oct: noon–5pm daily; Jul, Aug: 10am–6pm; daily.* *limited.*

An important religious centre in the 6th century, the town of Culross is said to have been the birthplace of St Mungo in 514. Now a beautifully preserved 16th- and 17th-century village, Culross prospered in the 16th century with the growth of its coal and salt industries, most notably under Sir George Bruce. He took charge of the Culross colliery in 1575 and created a drainage system called the "Egyptian Wheel" which cleared a mile-long (1.5 km) mine beneath the River Forth.

During its subsequent decline Culross stood unchanged for over 150 years. The National Trust for Scotland began restoring the town in 1932 and now provides a guided tour, which starts at the **Visitors' Centre**.

Built in 1577, Bruce's **palace** has the crow-stepped gables, decorated windows and red pantiles typical of the period. The interior retains its original early 17th-century painted ceilings. Crossing the Square, past the **Oldest House**, dating from 1577, head for the **Town House** to the west. Behind it, a cobbled street known as the Back Causeway (with its raised section for nobility) leads to the turreted **Study**, built in 1610 as a house for the Bishop of Dunblane. The main room is open to visitors and should be seen for its original Norwegian ceiling. Continuing northwards to the ruined abbey, fine church and Abbey House, don't miss the Dutch-gabled **House with the Evil Eyes**.

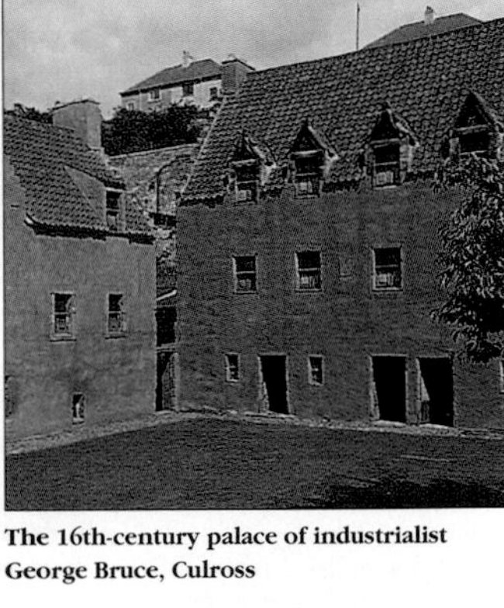

The 16th-century palace of industrialist George Bruce, Culross

Linlithgow Palace ⓬

Linlithgow, West Lothian. *01506 842896.* *Apr-Sep: 9:30am–6:30pm daily; Oct-Mar: 9:30am–4:30pm Mon–Sat, 2–4:30pm Sun.* *25, 26 Dec, 1, 2 Jan.* *limited.* www.historic-scotland.gov.uk

On the edge of Linlithgow Loch stands the former royal palace of **Linlithgow**. Today's remains are mostly of the palace of James I in 1425. The scale of the building is demonstrated by the 28 m (94 ft) long Great Hall, with its huge fireplace and windows. Mary, Queen of Scots *(see p497)*, was born here in 1542.

Falkirk Wheel ⓭

Lime Rd, Tamfourhill, Falkirk. *01324 619888; booking line: 08700 500208.* *Falkirk.* *Mar–mid-Jan: 9am–6pm daily.* *boat trip.* www.thefalkirkwheel.co.uk

This impressive, elegant boat lift is the first ever to revolve, and the centrepiece of Scotland's ambitious canal regeneration scheme. Once important for commercial transport, the Union and the Forth and Clyde canals were blocked by numerous roads in the 1960s. Now the Falkirk Wheel gently swings boats between the two waterways creating an uninterrupted link between Glasgow and Edinburgh. Visitors can ride the wheel on boats that leave the visitor's centre every half hour.

The rotating Falkirk Wheel boat lift

Hopetoun House ⓮

West Lothian. 0131 225 3858. *Dalmeny then taxi.* *mid-Apr–Sep: 10am-5:30pm daily.* *limited.* www.hopetounhouse.com

An extensive parkland by the Firth of Forth, designed in the style of Versailles, is the setting for one of Scotland's finest stately homes. The original house was built by 1707; it was later absorbed into William Adam's grand extension. The dignified, horseshoe-shaped plan and lavish interior plasterwork represent Neo-Classical 18th-century architecture at its finest. The red and yellow drawing rooms, with their Rococo plasterwork and highly ornate mantelpieces, are particularly impressive. The Marquess of Linlithgow, whose family still occupies part of the house, is a descendant of the 1st Earl of Hopetoun, for whom the house was built.

A wooden panel above the main stair, depicting Hopetoun House

Forth Bridges ⓯

Edinburgh. *Dalmeny, Inverkeithing.* *Queensferry Lodge Hotel, N Queensferry (01383 417759).*

The small town of South Queensferry is dominated by the two great bridges that span the mile (1.6 km) across the River Forth to North Queensferry. The spectacular rail bridge, the first major steel-built bridge in the world, was opened in 1890 and remains one of the greatest engineering achievements of the late Victorian era. Its massive cantilevered sections are held together by more than 6.5 million rivets, and the painted area adds up to some 55 ha (135 acres). The saying "it's like painting the Forth Bridge" has become a byword for non-stop, repetitive endeavour. It also inspired *The Bridge* (1986) by the writer Iain Banks.

The neighbouring road bridge was the largest suspension bridge outside the USA when it was opened in 1964, a distinction now held by the Humber Bridge in England. The two bridges make an impressive contrast, best seen from South Queensferry promenade. The town received its name from the 11th-century Queen Margaret *(see p493)*, who used the ferry here on her journeys between Edinburgh and the royal palace at Dunfermline *(see p487)*.

The shattered crags and cliffs of St Abb's Head

Edinburgh ⓰

See pp490–97.

St Abb's Head ⓱

Scottish Borders. *Berwick-upon-Tweed.* *from Edinburgh.*

The jagged cliffs of St Abb's Head, rising 91 m (300 ft) from the North Sea near the southeastern tip of Scotland, offer a spectacular view of thousands of seabirds wheeling and diving below. This 80 ha (200 acre) nature reserve is an important site for cliff-nesting sea birds and becomes, during the May to June breeding season, the home of more than 50,000 birds, including fulmars, guillemots, kittiwakes and puffins that throng the headland near the fishing village of St Abbs. The village has one of the few unspoiled working harbours on Britain's east coast. A clifftop trail begins at the **Visitors' Centre**, where displays include identification boards and a touch table where young visitors can get to grips with wings and feathers.

Visitors' Centre
St Abb's Head. 018907 71443. *Easter–Oct: 10am-5pm daily.*

The huge, cantilevered Forth Rail Bridge, seen from South Queensferry

A Tour of the Borders ⓲

Because of their proximity to England, the Scottish Borders are scattered with the ruins of many ancient buildings destroyed in the conflicts between the two nations. Most poignant of all are the Border abbeys, whose magnificent architecture bears witness to their former spiritual and political power. Founded during the 12th-century reign of David I, the abbeys were destroyed by Henry VIII *(see p498)*.

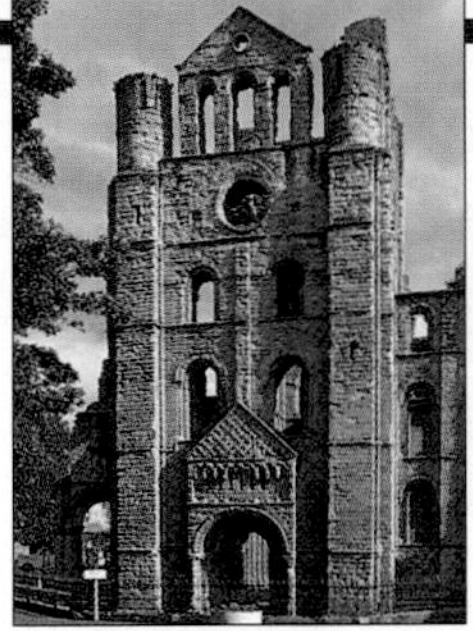

Kelso Abbey ②
The largest of the Border Abbeys, Kelso was once the most powerful ecclesiastical establishment in Scotland.

Melrose Abbey ⑥
Once one of the richest abbeys in Scotland, it is here that Robert the Bruce's heart is buried *(see p498)*.

Floors Castle ①
Open in summer, the Duke of Roxburgh's ancestral home was built in the 18th century by William Adam.

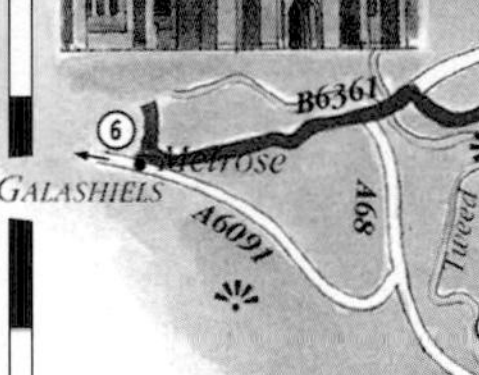

Scott's View ⑤
This was Sir Walter Scott's favourite view of the Borders. During his funeral, the hearse stopped here briefly as Scott had done so often in life.

Dryburgh Abbey ④
Set on the banks of the Tweed, Dryburgh is considered the most evocative monastic ruin in Scotland. Sir Walter Scott is buried here.

Jedburgh Abbey ③
Though established in 1138, fragments of 9th-century Celtic stonework survive from an earlier structure. A Visitors' Centre illustrates the lives of the Augustinian monks who once lived here.

Tips for Drivers

Length: *32 miles (50 km).*
Stopping-off points: *There is a delightful walk northwards from Dryburgh Abbey to the footbridge over the River Tweed.*

0 kilometres 5

0 miles 3

Edinburgh ⑯

Royal Scots soldiers from the castle

WITH ITS STRIKING medieval and Georgian districts, overlooked by the extinct volcano of Arthur's Seat and, to the northeast, Calton Hill, Edinburgh is widely regarded as one of Europe's most handsome capitals. The city is famous for the arts (it was once known as "the Athens of the North"), a pre-eminence reflected in its hosting every year of Britain's largest arts extravaganza, the Edinburgh Festival *(see p495)*. Its museums and galleries display the riches of many cultures.

Exploring Edinburgh

Edinburgh falls into two main sightseeing areas, divided by Princes Street, the city's most famous thoroughfare and commercial centre. The Old Town straddles the ridge between the castle and the Palace of Holyroodhouse, with most of the city's medieval history clustered in the alleys of the Grassmarket and Royal Mile areas. The New Town, to the north, evolved after 1767 when wealthy merchants expanded the city beyond its medieval walls. This district contains Britain's finest concentration of Georgian architecture.

🏛 National Gallery of Scotland

The Mound. ☎ *0131 624 6200.* ◯ *10am–5pm Mon–Sat, noon–5pm Sun.* ♿ *by appointment.* W www.nationalgalleries.org

One of Scotland's finest art galleries, the National Gallery of Scotland is worth visiting for its 15th- to 19th-century British and European paintings alone, though plenty more can be found to delight the art-lover. Ranks of paintings hang on deep red walls behind a profusion of statues and other works. Highlights among the Scottish works include portraits by Allan Ramsay and Henry Raeburn, such as his *Reverend Robert Walker Skating on Duddingston Loch* (c.1800). The Early German collection includes Gerard David's almost comic-strip treatment of the *Three Legends of Saint Nicholas* (c.1500). Works by Raphael, Titian and Tintoretto accompany southern European paintings such as Velázquez's *An Old Woman Cooking Eggs* (1620) and the entire room devoted to *The Seven Sacraments* (c.1640) by Nicholas Poussin. Flemish painters represented include Rembrandt, Van Dyck and Rubens while, among the British, important works by Reynolds, Ramsay and Gainsborough can be seen.

Raeburn's *Rev. Robert Walker Skating on Duddingston Loch*

The doorway of the Georgian House, 7 Charlotte Square

Georgian House

(NTS) 7 Charlotte Sq. ☎ *0131 226 3318.* ◯ *daily.* ● *mid-Dec–mid-Jan.* ♿ *limited.* W www.nts.org.uk

In the heart of the New Town, Charlotte Square is a superb example of Georgian architecture, its north side, built in the 1790s, being a masterwork by the architect Robert Adam *(see pp24–5)*. The Georgian House at No. 7 has been furnished and repainted in its original 18th-century colours which provide a memorable introduction to the elegance of wealthy New Town life. The dining room table is arranged with Sheffield plate, Wedgwood china and mid-18th-century glasses, while the chairs are mainly Edinburgh "brander backs". The formal drawing room is in stately contrast to the intimacy of the parlour with its Staffordshire and Spode china services.

The view from Duncan's Monument on Calton Hill, looking west towards the castle

Scottish Gallery of Modern Art & Dean Gallery

Belford Rd. *0131 624 6200.* *10am-5pm Mon-Sat, noon-5pm Sun.* *25, 26 Dec, 1, 2 Jan.*

Situated in extensive grounds to the northwest of the city centre, a classical 19th-century school is home to this gallery. Most European and American 20th-century greats are represented here, from Vuillard and Picasso, to Magritte and Lichtenstein. Work by John Bellany can be found among the Scottish painters. Sculpture by Henry Moore is on display in the garden.

Lichtenstein's *In the Car*, National Gallery of Modern Art

Medieval chessmen, Museum of Scotland

Museum of Scotland

Chambers St. *0131 225 7534.* *10am-5pm Mon-Sat, noon–5pm Sun.* *25 Dec.* www.nms.ac.uk

This purpose-built museum houses the Scottish Collections of the National Museums of Scotland. Exhibitions tell the story of Scotland, the land and its people, dating from its geological beginnings right up to the constitutionally exciting events of today.

Key exhibits include the famous medieval *Lewis Chessmen*; *Pictish Chains*, known as Scotland's earliest crown jewels; the *Ellesmere* railway locomotive and icons of the 20th century selected both by famous Scots and the public. Children's guidebooks and activities are available.

Visitors' Checklist

Edinburgh. *420,000.* *8 miles (13 km) W Edinburgh.* *North Bridge (Waverley Station).* *St Andrew Sq.* *3 Princes St (0131 473 3800).* *Edinburgh International: Aug; Military Tattoo: Aug; Fringe: Aug.* www.edinburgh.org

Scottish National Portrait Gallery

1 Queen St. *0131 556 8921.* *10am-5pm Mon-Sat, noon-5pm Sun.* *25, 26 Dec.* *by appointment.*

The National Portrait Gallery contains a rich and informative exhibition on the royal house of Stuart, explaining the turbulent history of 12 generations of Scottish monarchs from Robert the Bruce *(see p468)* to Queen Anne. Memorabilia from many reigns include Mary, Queen of Scots' *(see p497)* jewellery and a silver travelling canteen abandoned by Bonnie Prince Charlie *(see p521)* at Culloden *(see p523)*. The upper gallery has portraits of famous Scots, including Robert Burns *(see p501)* by Alexander Nasmyth.

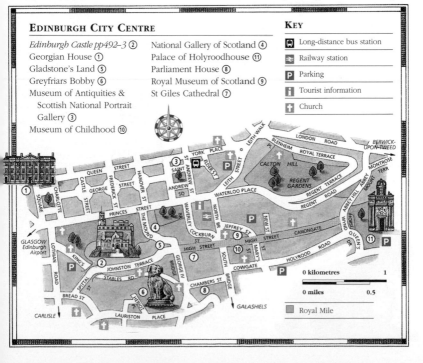

Edinburgh City Centre

Edinburgh Castle pp492–3 ②
Georgian House ①
Gladstone's Land ⑤
Greyfriars Bobby ⑥
Museum of Antiquities & Scottish National Portrait Gallery ③
Museum of Childhood ⑩
National Gallery of Scotland ④
Palace of Holyroodhouse ⑪
Parliament House ⑧
Royal Museum of Scotland ⑨
St Giles Cathedral ⑦

Key

- Long-distance bus station
- Railway station
- Parking
- Tourist information
- Church

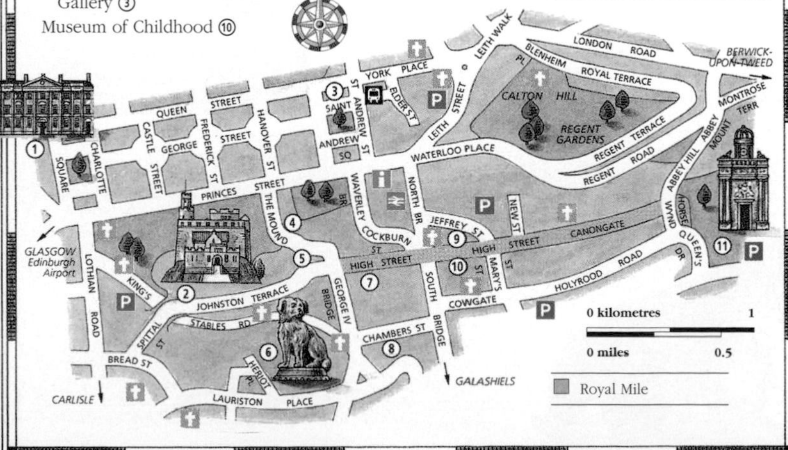

0 kilometres 1

0 miles 0.5

Royal Mile

Edinburgh Castle

Beam support in the Great Hall

STANDING UPON the basalt core of an extinct volcano, Edinburgh Castle is an assemblage of buildings dating from the 12th to the 20th centuries, reflecting its changing role as fortress, royal palace, military garrison and state prison. Though there is evidence of Bronze Age occupation of the site, the original fortress was built by the 6th-century Northumbrian King Edwin, from whom the city takes its name. The castle was a favourite royal residence until the Union of Crowns *(see p469)* in 1603, after which the king resided in England. After the Union of Parliaments in 1707, the Scottish regalia were walled up in the Palace for over a hundred years. The castle is now the zealous possessor of the so-called Stone of Destiny, a relic of ancient Scottish kings which was seized by the English and not returned until 1996.

Scottish Crown
Now on display in the palace, the Crown was restyled by James V of Scotland in 1540.

Military Prison

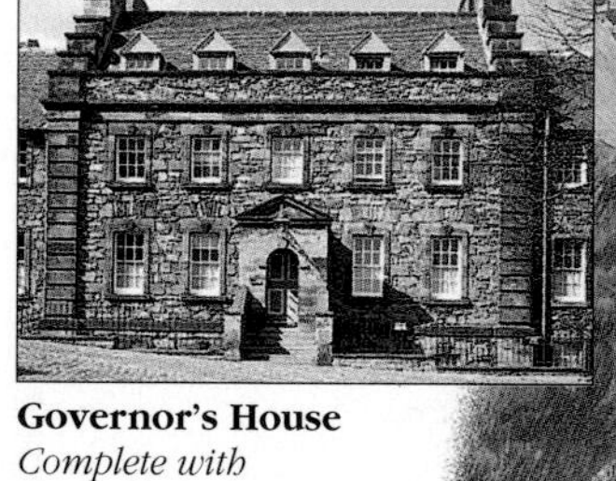

Governor's House
Complete with Flemish-style crow-stepped gables, this building was constructed for the governor in 1742 and now serves as the Officers' Mess for the castle garrison.

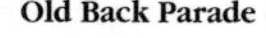
Old Back Parade

Vaults
This French graffiti, dating from 1780, recalls the many prisoners who were held in the vaults during the wars with France in the 18th and 19th centuries.

Mons Meg

Positioned outside St Margaret's Chapel, the siege gun (or *bombard*) Mons Meg was made in Belgium in 1449 for the Duke of Burgundy, who gave it to his nephew, James II of Scotland. It was used by James against the Douglas family in their stronghold of Threave Castle *(see p501)* in 1455, and later by James IV against Norham Castle in England. After exploding during a salute to the Duke of York in 1682, it was kept in the Tower of London until it was returned to Edinburgh in 1829, at Sir Walter Scott's request.

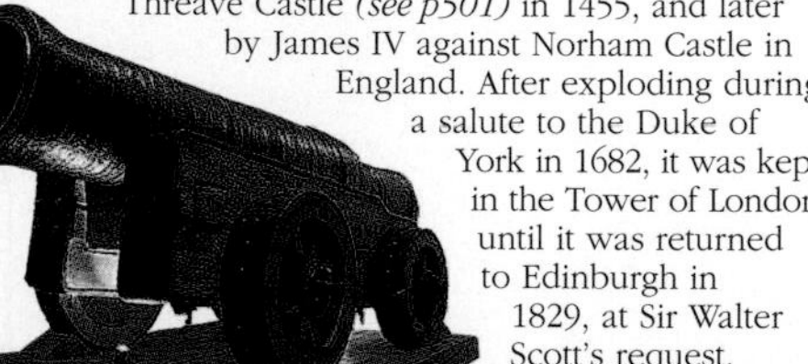

Star Sights

- ★ **Great Hall**
- ★ **Palace**

Argyle Battery
This fortified wall commands a spectacular view to the north beyond the city's Georgian district of New Town.

VISITORS' CHECKLIST

Castle Hill. *0131 225 9846.* *Apr–Oct: 9:30am–6pm daily; Nov–Mar: 9:30am–5pm daily (last adm: 45 mins before closing).* 25, 26 Dec. www.historic-scotland.gov.uk

★ Palace
Mary, Queen of Scots (see p497) *gave birth to James VI in this 15th-century palace, where the Scottish regalia are on display.*

Entrance

Royal Mile

The Esplanade is the location of the Military Tattoo *(see p495).*

The Half Moon Battery was built in the 1570s as a platform for the artillery defending the northeastern wing of the castle.

St Margaret's Chapel
This stained glass window depicts Malcolm III's saintly queen, to whom the chapel is dedicated. Probably built by her son, David I, in the early 12th century, the chapel is the castle's oldest existing building.

★ Great Hall
With its restored open-timber roof, the Hall dates from the 15th century and was the meeting place of the Scottish parliament until 1639.

Exploring the Royal Mile: Castlehill to High Street

Eagle sign outside Gladstone's Land

THE ROYAL MILE is a stretch of four ancient streets (from Castlehill to Canongate) which formed the main thoroughfare of medieval Edinburgh, linking the castle to the Palace of Holyroodhouse. Confined by the city wall, the "Old Town" grew upwards, with some tenements climbing to 20 storeys. It is still possible, among the 66 alleys and closes off the main street, to sense the city's medieval past.

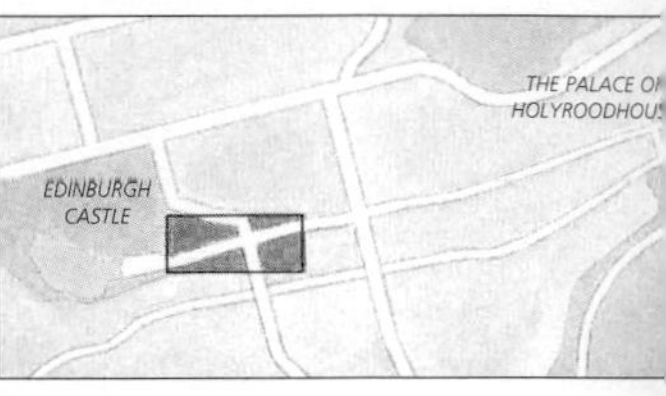

Locator map

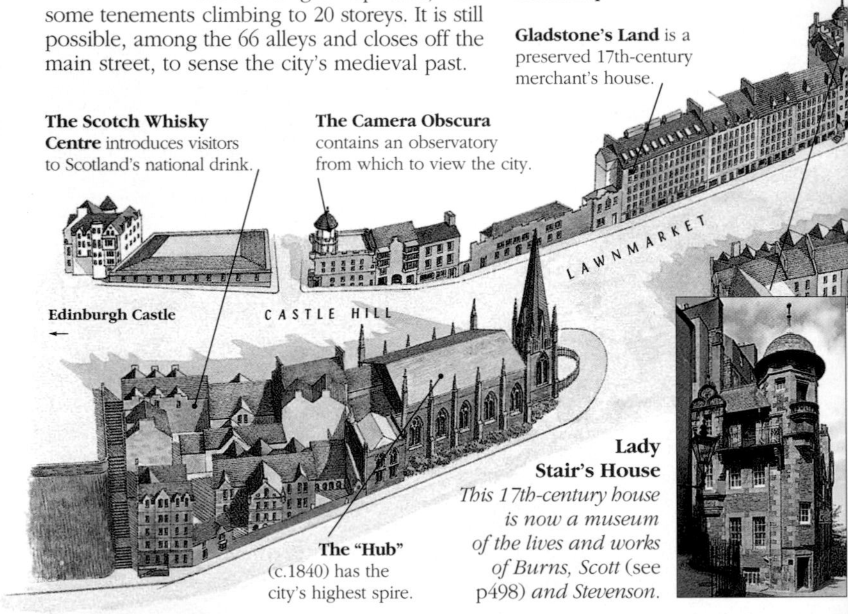

Gladstone's Land is a preserved 17th-century merchant's house.

The Scotch Whisky Centre introduces visitors to Scotland's national drink.

The Camera Obscura contains an observatory from which to view the city.

LAWNMARKET

Edinburgh Castle ←

CASTLE HILL

Lady Stair's House
This 17th-century house is now a museum of the lives and works of Burns, Scott (see p498) *and Stevenson.*

The "Hub" (c.1840) has the city's highest spire.

Gladstone's Land

(NTS) 477B Lawnmarket. *0131 2265856. Apr–Oct: 10am–5pm Mon–Sat, 2–5pm Sun*

This 17th-century merchant's house, recently restored, provides a window on life in a typical Old Town house before overcrowding drove the rich to the Georgian New Town. "Lands", as they were known, were tall, narrow buildings erected on small plots of land. The six-storey Gladstone's Land was named after Thomas Gledstanes, the merchant who built it in 1617. The house still has the original arcade booths on the street front and a painted ceiling with fine Scandinavian floral designs. Though extravagantly furnished, it also contains items which are a reminder of the less salubrious side of the old city, such as wooden overshoes which had to be worn in the dirty streets. A chest in the beautiful Painted Chamber is said to have been given by a Dutch sea captain to a Scottish merchant who saved him from a shipwreck. A similar house, Morocco Land, can be found on Canongate *(see p497)*.

The bedroom of Gladstone's Land

Parliament House

Parliament Sq, High St. *0131 2252595. 9am–5pm Mon–Fri. public hols. limited.*

This majestic, Italianate building was constructed in the 1630s for the Scottish parliament. Parliament House has been home to the Court of Session and the Supreme Court since the Union of Parliaments *(see p469)* in 1707. It is worth seeing, as much for the spectacle of its gowned and wigged advocates as for the stained-glass window in its Great Hall, commemorating the inauguration of the Court of Session by James V, in 1532.

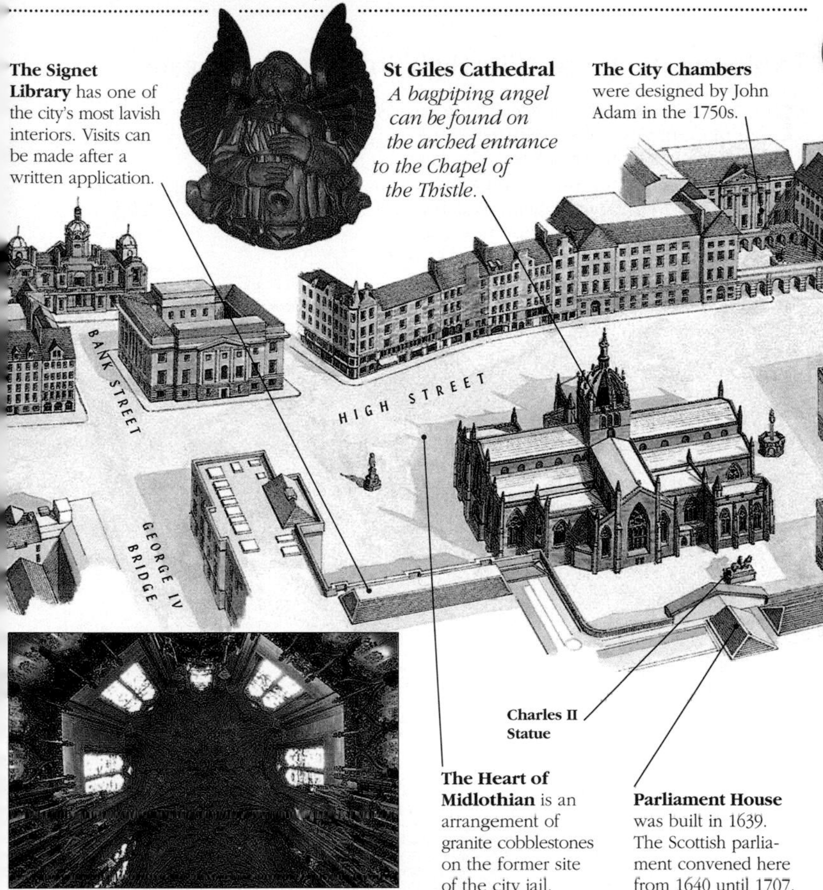
The Signet Library has one of the city's most lavish interiors. Visits can be made after a written application.
St Giles Cathedral *A bagpiping angel can be found on the arched entrance to the Chapel of the Thistle.*
The City Chambers were designed by John Adam in the 1750s.
BANK STREET
HIGH STREET
GEORGE IV BRIDGE
Charles II Statue
The Heart of Midlothian is an arrangement of granite cobblestones on the former site of the city jail.
Parliament House was built in 1639. The Scottish parliament convened here from 1640 until 1707.

Rib-vaulting in the Thistle Chapel, St Giles Cathedral

St Giles Cathedral

Royal Mile. 0131 2259442. *Oct–Apr: 9am–5pm Mon–Sat (Sun pm); May–Sep: 9am–7pm Mon–Fri, 9am–5pm Sat (Sun: pm).* *25, 26 Dec, 1 Jan.* www.stgiles.net

Properly known as the High Kirk (church) of Edinburgh, it is ironic that St Giles is popularly known as a cathedral. Though it was twice the seat of a bishop in the 17th century, it was from here that John Knox *(see p469)* directed the Scottish Reformation with its emphasis on individual worship freed from the authority of bishops. A tablet marks the place where Jenny Geddes, a stallholder from a local market, scored a victory for the Covenanters *(see p469)* by hurling her stool at a preacher reading from an English prayer book in 1637.

The Gothic exterior is dominated by a 15th-century tower. Inside, the impressive Thistle Chapel can be seen, with its elaborate rib-vaulted roof and carved heraldic canopies. The chapel honours the knights, past and present, of the Order of the Thistle. The carved royal pew in the Preston Aisle is used by the Queen when she stays in Edinburgh.

Edinburgh Festival

Every year, for three weeks in late summer *(see p63)*, Edinburgh hosts one of the world's most important arts festivals, with every available space (from theatres to street corners) overflowing with international artists and performers. It has been held in Edinburgh since 1947 and brings together the best in contemporary theatre, music, dance and opera. The alternative Festival Fringe, with some 600 companies involved, balances the classic productions with a host of innovative performances. The most popular event is the Edinburgh Tattoo, held on the Castle Esplanade – a spectacle of Scottish infantry battalions marching to pipe bands from all over the world.

Street performer from the Edinburgh Festival Fringe

Exploring the Royal Mile: High Street to Canongate

THE SECOND SECTION of the Royal Mile passes two monuments to the Reformation: John Knox's House and the Tron Kirk. The latter is named after a medieval *tron* (weighing beam) that stood nearby. The Canongate was once an independent district, owned by the canons of the Abbey of Holyrood, and sections of its south side have been restored. Beyond Morocco's Land, the road stretches for the final half-mile (800 m) to the Palace of Holyroodhouse.

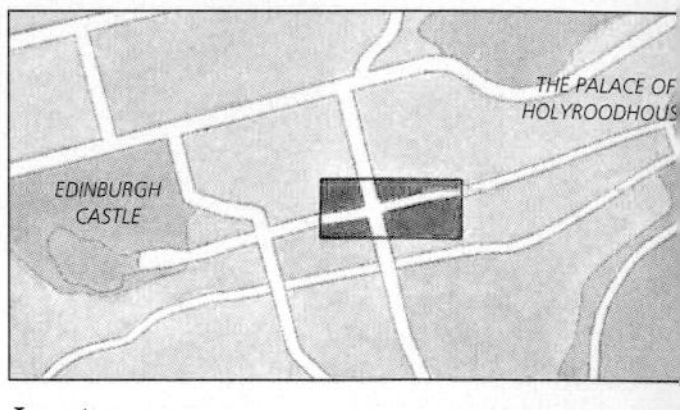

Locator map

The Mercat Cross marks the city centre. It was here that Bonnie Prince Charlie *(see p521)* was proclaimed king in 1745.

The Tron Kirk was built in 1630 for the Presbyterians who left St Giles Cathedral when it came under the Bishop of Edinburgh's control.

Museum of Childhood

42 High St. 0131 529 4142. *10am–5pm Mon–Sat (& Sun pm during Festival).* *25–27 Dec.* *limited.*

This lovely museum is not merely a toy collection but a magical insight into childhood, with all its joys and trials. Founded in 1955 by a city councillor, Patrick Murray (who claimed to enjoy eating children for breakfast), it was the first museum in the world to be devoted to the history and theme of childhood. The collection includes medicines, school books and prams as well as galleries full of old-fashioned toys. With its nickel-odeon, antique slot machines and the general enthusiasm of visitors, this has been called the world's noisiest museum.

An 1880 automaton of the Man on the Moon, Museum of Childhood

The entrance to the Palace of Holyroodhouse, seen from the west

Palace of Holyroodhouse

East end of Royal Mile. *0131 556 7371.* *9:30am–4:45pm daily.* *phone first for seasonal closures.* *limited.*

Now the Queen's official Scottish residence, the Palace of Holyroodhouse is named after the "rood", or cross, which King David I is said to have seen between the antlers of a stag he was hunting here in 1128. The present palace was built in 1529 to accommodate James V *(see p487)* and his French wife, Mary of Guise, though it was remodelled in the 1670s for Charles II. The Royal Apartments (including the Throne Room and Royal Dining Room) are used for investitures and banquets whenever the Queen visits the palace, though they are otherwise open to the public. A chamber in the James V tower is associated with the unhappy reign of Mary, Queen of Scots. It was here, in 1566, that she saw the murder of her trusted Italian secretary, David Rizzio, by her jealous husband, Lord Darnley. She had married Darnley a year earlier in Holyroodhouse chapel.

Bonnie Prince Charlie held court here in 1745 in the Jacobite *(see p523)* rising.

John Knox's House
Dating from 1490, the oldest house in the city was the home of John Knox (see p469) *in the 1560s. He is said to have died in an upstairs room. Open daily, it contains relics of his life.*

Morocco Land is a reproduction of a 17th-century tenement house. It takes its name from the statue of a Moor which adorns the entrance.

→ **The Palace of Holyroodhouse**

CANONGATE

Museum of Childhood
Though created as a museum for adults by a city councillor who was known to dislike children, this lively musem now attracts flocks of young visitors.

Moubray House was to be the signing place of the Treaty of Union in 1707 *(see p469)*, until a mob forced the authorities to retreat to another venue.

Royal Museum of Scotland

Chambers St. *0131 225 7534.* *10am–5pm Mon–Sat, noon–5pm Sun.* *25 Dec.* www.nms.ac.uk

This elegant museum, purpose-built in 1861, houses the National Museum of Scotland's international collections. Exhibits include examples from the applied arts and sciences. The Main Hall's fine collection of Asian sculpture includes a beautiful 13th-century statue of the Hindu goddess Parvati. European Art from 1200 to 1800 is on the first floor, while the second floor exhibits rare scientific instruments. Geological specimens and Eastern decorative arts are on the top floor.

Parvati, at the Royal Museum of Scotland

Greyfriars Bobby

On an old drinking fountain near the gateway to Greyfriars Church stands the statue of a little Skye terrier. This commemorates the dog who, for 14 years, guarded the grave of his master, John Gray, who died in 1858. The people of Edinburgh fed him until his death in 1872. He was also granted citizenship to prevent him being destroyed as a stray.

Mary, Queen of Scots (1542–87)

Born only days before the death of her father, James V, the young Queen Mary spent her childhood in France, after escaping Henry VIII's invasion of Scotland *(see p498)*. A devout Catholic, she married the French Dauphin, and made claims on the English throne. This alarmed Protestants throughout England and Scotland, and when she returned as a widow to Holyroodhouse, aged 18, she was harangued for her faith by John Knox *(see p469)*. In 1567 she was accused of murdering her second husband, Lord Darnley. Two months later, when she married the Earl of Bothwell (also implicated in the murder), rebellion ensued. She lost her crown and fled to England where she was held prisoner for 20 years, before being charged with treason and beheaded at Fotheringhay.

The ruins of Melrose Abbey, viewed from the southwest

Melrose Abbey 19

Abbey Street, Melrose, Scottish Borders. *01896 822562.* *Oct–Mar: 9:30am–4:30pm Mon–Sat, 2–4:30pm Sun; Apr–Sep: 9:30am–6:30pm daily.* *25, 26 Dec, 1, 2 Jan.* *limited.*

THE ROSE-PINK RUINS of one of the most beautiful of the border abbeys *(see p489)* bear testimony to the hazards of standing in the path of successive English invasions. Built by David I in 1136 for Cistercian monks from Yorkshire, and also to replace a 7th-century monastery, Melrose was repeatedly ransacked by English armies, notably in 1322 and 1385. The final blow, from which none of the abbeys recovered, came in 1545 during Henry VIII's destructive Scottish policy known as the "Rough Wooing". This resulted from the failure of the Scots to ratify a marriage treaty between Henry VIII's son and the infant Mary, Queen of Scots *(see p497)*. What remains of the abbey are the outlines of cloisters, the kitchen and other monastic buildings and the shell of the abbey church with its soaring east window and profusion of medieval carvings. The rich decorations of the south exterior wall include a gargoyle shaped like a pig playing the bagpipes.

An embalmed heart, found here in 1920, is probably that of Robert the Bruce *(see p468)*, who had decreed that his heart be taken on a crusade to the Holy Land. It was returned to Melrose after its bearer, Sir James Douglas *(see p501)*, was killed in Spain.

SIR WALTER SCOTT

Sir Walter Scott (1771–1832) was born in Edinburgh and trained as a lawyer. He is best remembered as a major champion and literary figure of Scotland, whose poems and novels (most famously his *Waverley* series) created enduring images of a heroic wilderness filled with the romance of the clans. His orchestration, in 1822, of the state visit of George IV to Edinburgh *(see p471)* was an extravaganza of Highland culture that helped re-establish tartan as the national dress of Scotland. He served as Clerk of the Court in Edinburgh's Parliament House *(see p494)* and for 30 years was Sheriff of Selkirk in the Scottish Borders, which he loved. He put the Trossachs *(see pp480–81)* firmly on the map with the publication of the *Lady of the Lake* (1810). His final years were spent writing to pay off a £114,000 debt following the failure of his publisher in 1827. He died with his debts paid, and was buried at Dryburgh Abbey *(see p489)*.

Abbotsford House 20

Galashiels, Scottish Borders. *01896 752043.* *from Galashiels.* *mid-Mar–May & Oct: 9:30am–5pm daily (Sun: 2–5pm); Jun–Sep: daily.* *limited.* www.melrose.bordernet.co.uk/abbotsford

FEW HOUSES bear the stamp of their creator so intimately as Abbotsford House, the home of Sir Walter Scott for the last 20 years of his life. He bought a farm here in 1811, known as Clarteyhole ("dirty hole" in Scots), though he soon renamed it Abbotsford, after the monks of Melrose Abbey who used to cross the River Tweed nearby. He later demolished the house to make way for the turreted building we see today, funded by the sales of his novels.

Scott's library contains more than 9,000 rare books and his collections of historic relics reflect his passion for the heroic past. An extensive collection of arms and armour includes Rob Roy's broadsword *(see p481)*. Stuart mementoes include a crucifix that belonged to Mary, Queen of Scots and a lock of Bonnie Prince Charlie's *(see p521)* hair. The small study in which he wrote his *Waverley* novels can be visited as can the room, overlooking the river, in which he died in 1832.

The Great Hall at Abbotsford, adorned with arms and armour

Traquair House ㉑

Peebles, Scottish Borders. *01896 830 323.* *from Peebles.* *Easter–Jun, Sep, Oct: noon–5:30pm; Jul–Aug: 10:30am–5:30pm; daily.* *limited.* www.traquair.co.uk

As Scotland's oldest continuously inhabited house, Traquair has deep roots in Scottish religious and political history, stretching back over 900 years. Evolving from a fortified tower to a stout-walled 17th-century mansion *(see p473)*, the house was a Catholic Stuart stronghold for 500 years. Mary, Queen of Scots *(see p497)* was among the many monarchs to have stayed here and her bed is covered by a counterpane which she made. Family letters and engraved Jacobite *(see p523)* drinking glasses are among relics recalling the period of the Highland rebellions.

After a vow made by the 5th Earl, Traquair's Bear Gates (the "Steekit Yetts"), which closed after Bonnie Prince Charlie's *(see p521)* visit in 1745, will not reopen until a Stuart reascends the throne. A secret stairway leads to the Priest's Room which attests to the problems faced by Catholic families until Catholicism was legalized in 1829. Traquair House Ale is still produced in the 18th-century brewhouse.

Mary, Queen of Scots' crucifix, Traquair House

Biggar ㉒

Clyde Valley. *2,000.* *High St (01899 221066).*

This typical Lowland market town has a number of museums worth visiting. The **Gladstone Court Museum** boasts a reconstructed Victorian street complete with a milliner's, printer's and a village library, while the grimy days of the town's industrial past are recalled at the **Gasworks Museum**, with its collection of engines, gaslights and appliances. Established in 1839 and preserved in the 1970s, the Biggar Gasworks is the only remaining rural gasworks in Scotland.

Gladstone Court Museum
Northback Rd. *01899 221050.* *Apr–Oct: 10:30am–5pm daily (Sun: 2–5pm).*

Gasworks Museum
Gasworks Rd. *01899 221070.* *Jun–Sep: 2–5pm daily.*

Pentland Hills ㉓

The Lothians. *Edinburgh, then bus.* *Regional Park Headquarters, Biggar Rd, Edinburgh (0131 4453383).*

The Pentland Hills, stretching for 16 miles (26 km) southwest of Edinburgh, offer some of the best hill-walking country in the Lowlands. Leisurely walkers can saunter along the many signposted footpaths, while the more adventurous can take the chairlift at the Hillend dry ski slope to reach the higher ground leading to the 493 m (1,617 ft) hill of Allermuir. Even more ambitious is the classic scenic route along the ridge from Caerketton to West Kip.

To the east of the A703, in the lee of the Pentlands, stands the exquisite and ornate 15th-century **Rosslyn Chapel**. It was originally intended as a church, but after the death of its founder, William Sinclair, it was also used as a burial ground for his descendants. The delicately wreathed Apprentice Pillar recalls the legend of the apprentice carver who was killed by the master stonemason in a fit of jealousy at his pupil's superior skill.

Rosslyn Chapel
Roslin. *0131 4402159.* *10am–5pm daily (Sun: pm only).*

Details of the decorated vaulting in Rosslyn Chapel

The Classical 18th-century tenements of New Lanark on the banks of the Clyde

New Lanark 24

Clyde Valley. 150. Lanark. *Horsemarket, Ladyacre Rd (01555 661661).* *Mon.* www.newlanark.org

SITUATED BY THE falls of the River Clyde, the village of New Lanark was founded in 1785 by the industrial entrepreneur David Dale. Ideally located for the working of its water-driven mills, the village had become Britain's largest cotton producer by 1800. Dale and his successor, Robert Owen, were philanthropists whose reforms proved that commercial success need not undermine the wellbeing of the workforce. Now a museum, New Lanark is a window on to working life in the early 19th century. The **New Millennium Experience** provides a special-effects ride through time, from the life of a mill girl in 1820 to the 23rd century.

ENVIRONS: 15 miles (24 km) north, Blantyre has a memorial to the famous Scottish explorer David Livingstone.

DAVID LIVINGSTONE

Scotland's great missionary doctor and explorer was born in Blantyre where he began working life as a mill boy at the age of ten. Livingstone (1813–73) made three epic journeys across Africa, from 1840, promoting "commerce and Christianity". He became the first European to see Victoria Falls and died in 1873 while searching for the source of the Nile. He is buried in Westminster Abbey *(see pp94–5)*.

New Millennium Experience
New Lanark Visitor Centre. *01555 661345.* *11am–5pm daily.* *25 Dec, 1 Jan.* *by appt.*

Glasgow 25

See pp502–7.

Sanquhar 26

Dumfries & Galloway. *2,500.* *64 Whitesands, Dumfries (01387 253862).*

NOW OF CHIEFLY historic interest, the town of **Sanquhar** was famous in the history of the Covenanters *(see p469)*. In the 1680s, two declarations opposing the rule of bishops were pinned to the Mercat Cross, the site of which is now marked by a granite obelisk. The first protest was led by a local teacher, Richard Cameron, whose followers became the Cameronian regiment. The Georgian **Tolbooth** was designed by William Adam *(see p534)* in 1735 and houses a local interest museum and tourist centre. The Post Office, opened in 1763, is the oldest in Britain, predating the mail coach service.

Drumlanrig Castle 27

Thornhill, Dumfries & Galloway. *01848 330248.* *Dumfries, then bus.* *May–Sep: 11am–5pm Mon–Sat, noon–5pm Sun.*

RISING SQUARELY from a grassy platform, the massive fortress-palace of **Drumlanrig** *(see p473)* was built from pink sandstone between 1679 and 1691 on the site of a 15th-century Douglas

The Baroque front steps and doorway of Drumlanrig Castle

stronghold. A formidable multi-turreted exterior contains a priceless collection of art treasures as well as such Jacobite relics as Bonnie Prince Charlie's camp kettle and sash. Hanging within oak-panelled rooms are paintings by Da Vinci, Holbein and Rembrandt. The emblem of a crowned and winged heart, shown throughout the castle, recalls Sir James, the "Black Douglas", who bore Robert the Bruce's *(see p468)* heart while on crusade to fulfil a vow made by the king. After being mortally wounded he threw the heart at his enemies with the words "forward brave heart!"

The sturdy island fortress of Threave Castle on the Dee

Threave Castle ㉘

(NTS) Castle Douglas, Dumfries & Galloway. *07711 223101 or 01556 502611.* *Dumfries.* *Apr–Sep: 9:30am–6:30pm daily (last boat leaves island 6pm); Oct: phone for details.*

THIS MENACING GIANT of a tower, a 14th-century Black Douglas *(see above)* stronghold standing on an island in the Dee, commands the most complete medieval riverside harbour in Scotland. Douglas's struggles against the early Stewart kings culminated in his surrender here after a two-month siege in 1455 – but only after James II had brought the cannon Mons Meg *(see p492)* to batter the castle. Threave was dismantled after Protestant Covenanters *(see p469)* defeated its Catholic de-fenders in 1640. Inside the tower, only the shell of the kitchen, great hall and domestic levels remains. Over the 15th-century doorway is the "gallows knob", a reminder of when the owners are said to have boasted that it never lacked its noose. Access to the castle is by small boat.

Whithorn ㉙

Dumfries & Galloway. *1,000.* *Stranraer.* *Dashwood Sq, Newton Stewart (01671 402431).* www.dumfriesandgalloway.co.uk

THE EARLIEST SITE of continuous Christian worship in Scotland, Whithorn (meaning white house) takes its name from the white chapel built here by St Ninian in 397. Though nothing remains of his chapel, a guided tour of the archaeological dig reveals evidence of Northumbrian, Viking and Scottish settlements ranging from the 5th to the 19th centuries. A visitors' centre, **The Whithorn Story**, provides information on the excavations and contains a collection of carved stones. One, dedicated to Latinus, dates to 450, making it Scotland's earliest Christian monument.

The Whithorn Story
The Whithorn Trust, 45–47 George St. *01988 500508.* *Apr–Oct: 10:30am–5pm daily.*

Culzean Castle ㉚

See pp508–9.

Robert Burns surrounded by his creations, by an unknown artist

Burns Cottage ㉛

Alloway, South Ayrshire. *01292 443700.* *Ayr, then bus.* *Oct–Apr: 10am–5pm daily; May–Sep: 9:30am–5:30pm daily.* *25, 26 Dec, 1, 2 Jan.* *by appt.* www.burnsheritagepark.co.uk

ROBERT BURNS (1759–96), Scotland's favourite poet, was born and spent his first seven years in this small thatched cottage in Alloway. Built by his father, the cottage still contains much of its original furniture. There is also a small museum next door displaying many of Burns's manuscripts along with early editions of his works. Much of his poem *Tam o' Shanter* (1790) is set in Alloway, which commemorates him with a huge monument on the outskirts of the village.

Burns became a celebrity following the publication in 1786 of the Kilmarnock Edition of his poems. Scots everywhere gather to celebrate Burns Night *(see p65)* on his birthday, 25 January.

Scottish Textiles

Weaving in the Scottish Borders goes back to the Middle Ages, when monks from Flanders established a thriving woollen trade with the Continent. Cotton became an important source of wealth in the Clyde Valley during the 19th century, when handloom weaving was overtaken by power-driven mills. The popular Paisley patterns were based on Indian designs.

A colourful pattern from Paisley

Glasgow ㉕

The coat of arms of Glasgow city

THOUGH ITS CELTIC NAME, *Glas cu*, means "dear green place", Glasgow is more often associated with its industrial past, and once enjoyed the title of Second City of the Empire (after London). Glasgow's architectural standing, as Scotland's finest Victorian city, reflects its era of prosperity, when ironworks, cotton mills and shipbuilding were fuelled by Lanarkshire coal. The Science Centre now sits on the Clyde's revitalized south bank. Glasgow rivals Edinburgh *(see pp490–97)* in the arts, with galleries such as the Kelvingrove and the Burrell Collection *(see pp506–7)*.

Glasgow's medieval cathedral viewed from the southwest

Exploring Glasgow

With some relics of its grimy industrial past and glossy new image, modern Glasgow is a city of contrasts. The deprived area of the East End, with its busy weekend market, "the Barras", stands by the restored 18th-century Merchant City and Victorian George Square. The more affluent West End prospered in the 19th century as a retreat for wealthy merchants escaping the heavily industrialized Clydeside, and it is here that Glasgow's chief galleries and museums can be found. South of the river, the Govan and Gorbals districts give way to the Pollok Country Park, site of the Burrell Collection. An underground network provides easy travel around the city.

Glasgow Cathedral

Cathedral Square. *0141 5526891*
Easter–Oct: 9:30am–6pm Mon–Sat, 2–5pm Sun; Nov–Easter: 9:30am–4pm Mon–Sat, 2–4pm Sun.

As one of the only cathedrals to escape destruction during the Scottish Reformation *(see pp468–9)* – by adapting itself to Protestant worship – this is a rare example of an almost complete 13th-century church. It was built on the site of a chapel founded by the city's patron saint, St Mungo, a 6th-century bishop of Strathclyde. According to legend, Mungo placed the body of a holy man named Fergus on a cart yoked to two wild bulls, telling them to take it to the place ordained by God. In the "dear green place" at which the bulls stopped he built his church. Because of its sloping site, the cathedral is on two levels.

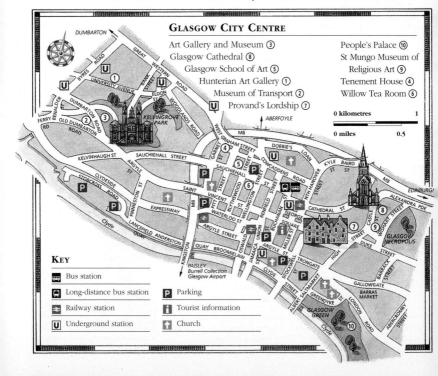

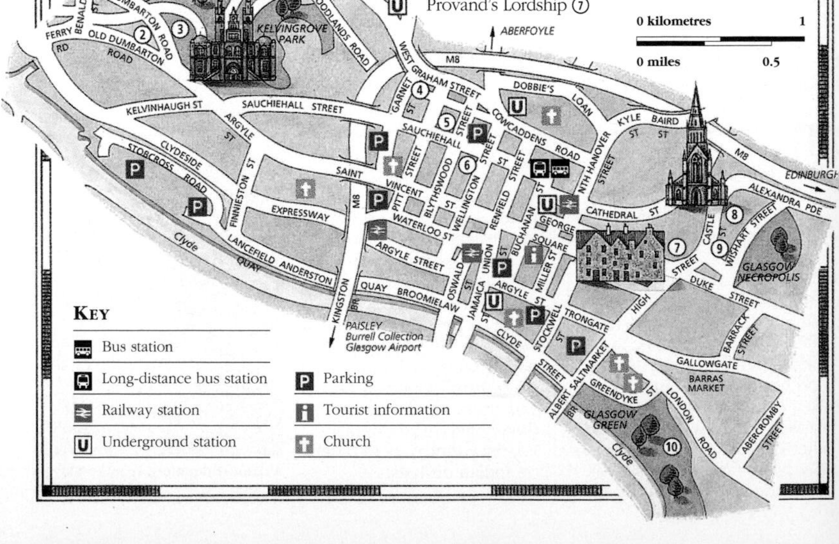

Glasgow City Centre

Art Gallery and Museum ③
Glasgow Cathedral ⑧
Glasgow School of Art ⑤
Hunterian Art Gallery ①
Museum of Transport ②
Provand's Lordship ⑦
People's Palace ⑩
St Mungo Museum of Religious Art ⑨
Tenement House ④
Willow Tea Room ⑥

0 kilometres 1
0 miles 0.5

Key

- Bus station
- Long-distance bus station
- Railway station
- Underground station
- Parking
- Tourist information
- Church

Dalí's *Christ of St John of the Cross* at the St Mungo Museum of Religious Life and Art

The crypt contains the tomb of St Mungo, surrounded by an intricate forest of columns springing up to end in delicately carved rib-vaulting. The Blackadder Aisle, reputed to have been built over a cemetery blessed by St Ninian *(see p501)*, has a ceiling thick with decorative bosses.

St Mungo Museum of Religious Life and Art

2 Castle St. *0141 5532557.* *10am–5pm daily.* *25, 26 Dec, 1 Jan.* *by appointment.*

Situated in the cathedral precinct, this new museum is a world first. The main exhibition illustrates religious themes with superb artifacts, including a 19th-century dancing Shiva and an Islamic painting entitled the *Attributes of Divine Perfection* (1986) by Ahmed Moustafa. An exhibition on religion in Glasgow throws light on the life of the missionary David Livingstone *(see p500)*. Recently moved from the Kelvingrove Art Gallery and Museum *(see p505)*, Salvador Dalí's powerful work *Christ of St John of the Cross* (1951) is now here. Outside you can visit Britain's only permanent Zen Buddhist garden.

Tenement House

(NTS) 145 Buccleuch St. *0141 3330183.* *Mar–Oct: 2–5pm daily.* *by appointment.*

Less a museum than a time capsule, the Tenement House is an almost undisturbed record of life in a modest Glasgow flat in a tenement estate during the early 20th century. Glasgow owed much of its vitality and neighbourliness to tenement life, though many of these Victorian and Edwardian apartments were to earn a bad name for poverty and overcrowding, and many have now been pulled down. The Tenement House was first owned by Miss Agnes Toward who lived here from 1911 until 1965. It remained largely unaltered and, since Agnes threw very little away, it is now a treasure-trove of social history. The parlour, previously used only on formal occasions, has afternoon tea laid out on a white lace cloth. The kitchen, with its coal-fired range and box bed, is filled with the tools of a vanished era such as a goffering iron for crisping waffles, a washboard and a stone hot-water bottle.

Agnes's lavender water and medicines are still in the bathroom, as though she had stepped out for a minute 70 years ago, and forgotten to return home.

Visitors' Checklist

City of Glasgow. *735,000.* *Argyle St (Glasgow Central).* *Buchanan St.* *11 George Square (0141 2044400).* *Sat, Sun.* www.seeglasgow.com

The preserved Edwardian kitchen of the Tenement House

The Kelvingrove Art Gallery and the Glasgow University buildings, viewed from the south

Glasgow's medieval house, Provand's Lordship

Provand's Lordship

3 Castle St. 0141 5528819.
10am–5pm daily (11am Fri & Sun).

Now a museum, Provand's Lordship was built as a canon's house in 1471, and is the city's oldest surviving house. Its low ceilings and austere wooden furnishings create a vivid impression of life in a wealthy 15th-century household. It is thought that Mary, Queen of Scots *(see p497)* may have stayed here when she made a visit to Glasgow in 1566 to see her cousin and husband, Lord Darnley.

Mackintosh's interior of the Willow Tea Room

Willow Tea Room

217 Sauchiehall St. 0141 332 0521.
9am–4:30pm Mon–Sat, noon–4pm Sun. 25, 26 Dec, 2 Jan.

This is the sole survivor of a series of delightfully frivolous tea rooms created by Charles Rennie Mackintosh at the turn of the century for the celebrated restaurateur Miss Kate Cranston. Everything from the high-backed chairs to the tables and cutlery was of his own design. In particular, the 1904 Room de Luxe sparkles with eccentricity: striking mauve and silver furniture, coloured glass and a flamboyant leaded door create a remarkable venue in which to enjoy afternoon tea.

Museum of Transport

1 Bunhouse Rd. 0141 2872000.
10am-5pm Mon-Thu, Sat, 11am-5pm Fri, Sun. 25, 26 Dec, 1 Jan.

Housed in Kelvin Hall, this imaginative museum conveys the optimism and vigour of the city's industrial heyday. Model ships and ranks of gleaming Scottish-built steam engines, cars and motorcycles recall the 19th and early 20th centuries, when Glasgow's supremacy in shipbuilding, trade and manufacturing made her the "second city" of the British Empire. Old Glasgow can be seen through fascinating footage of the town in the cinema and through a reconstruction of a 1938 street, with Art Deco shop fronts, a cinema and an Underground station.

The Museum of Transport's reconstructed 1938 street, with Underground station

Glasgow Necropolis

Cathedral Sq. 0141 2873961.
daily. limited.

Behind the cathedral, the reformer John Knox *(see p469)* surveys the city from his Doric pillar overlooking a Victorian cemetery. It is filled with crumbling monuments to the dead of Glasgow's wealthy merchant families.

Charles Rennie Mackintosh

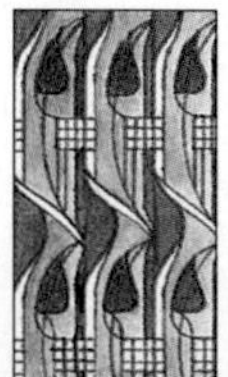
A Mackintosh floral design

Glasgow's most celebrated designer, Charles Rennie Mackintosh (1868–1928), entered Glasgow School of Art at 16. After his first big break with the Willow Tea Room, he became a leading figure in the Art Nouveau movement, developing a unique style that borrowed from Gothic and Scottish Baronial designs. He believed a building should be a fully integrated work of art, creating furniture and fittings that complemented the overall construction. Nowhere is this total design better seen than in the Glasgow School of Art, which he designed in 1896. Unrecognized in his lifetime, Mackintosh's work is now widely imitated. Its characteristic straight lines and flowing detail are the hallmark of early 20th-century Glasgow style, in all fields of design from textiles to architecture.

People's Palace

Glasgow Green. 0141 5540223. 10am–5pm Mon–Sat, 11am–5pm Sun. 25, 26 Dec, 1 Jan.

This Victorian sandstone structure was purpose-built in 1898 as a cultural museum for the people of Glasgow's East End. It houses everything from temperance tracts to trade-union banners, suffragette posters to comedian Billy Connolly's banana-shaped boots, providing a social history of the city from the 12th to the 20th century. A superb conservatory at the back contains an exotic winter garden.

Glasgow School of Art

167 Renfrew St. 0141 3534526. by appointment only. limited. www.gsa.ac.uk

Widely considered to be Charles Rennie Mackintosh's greatest architectural work, the Glasgow School of Art was built between 1897 and 1909 to a design he submitted in a competition. It was built in two periods due to financial constraints. The later, western wing displays a softer design than the more severe eastern half, built only a few years earlier and compared by a contemporary critic to a prison.

A student guide takes you through the building to the Furniture Gallery, Board Room and the Library, the latter a masterpiece of spatial composition. Each room is an exercise in contrasts between height, light and shade with innovative details echoing the architectural themes of the structure. How much of the school can be viewed depends on curricular requirements at the time of visiting.

Hunterian Art Gallery

82 Hillhead St. 0141 3305431. 9:30am–5pm Mon–Sat. 24 Dec–5 Jan & public hols. limited. www.hunterian.gla.ac.uk

Built to house a number of paintings bequeathed to Glasgow University by ex-student and physician Dr William Hunter (1718–83), the Hunterian Art Gallery contains Scotland's largest print collection and works by major European artists stretching back to the 16th century. A collection of work by Charles Mackintosh is supplemented by a complete reconstruction of No. 6 Florentine Terrace, where he lived from 1906 to 1914. A major collection of 19th- and 20th-century Scottish art includes work by William McTaggart (1835–1910), but the gallery's most famous collection is of work by the painter James McNeill Whistler (1834–1903).

George Henry's *Japanese Lady with a Fan* (1894), Art Gallery and Museum

Whistler's *Sketch for Annabel Lee* (c.1869), Hunterian Art Gallery

Kelvingrove Art Gallery and Museum

Argyle St, Kelvingrove. 0141 287 2699. until mid-2006. **McLellan Galleries** 270 Sauchiehall St. 0141 565 4100. 10am–5pm Mon–Sat, 11am–5pm Fri & Sun. www.glasgow.gov.uk

An imposing red sandstone building, Scotland's most popular gallery houses a magnificent art collection. The gallery is currently closed for refurbishment, but more than 200 exhibits can be viewed at the McLellan Galleries. Kelvingrove's 17th-century Dutch and Flemish masters including Rembrandt can be seen, as well as 19th-century British artists such as Turner and Constable. Scottish art and design is well represented with rooms dedicated to the Scottish Colourists and the Glasgow Style. Also included here are two recently acquired works by Charles Rennie Mackintosh: a fine gesso panel and a 1904 writing cabinet.

The Georgian Pollok House, viewed from the south

Pollock House

(NTS) 2060 Pollokshaws Rd. *(0141) 616 6410.* *10am–5pm daily.* *25, 26 Dec, 1, 2 Jan.* *Apr–Oct only.* www.nts.org.uk

Pollok house is Glasgow's finest 18th-century domestic building and contains one of Britain's best collections of Spanish paintings. The Neo-Classical central block was finished in 1750, the sobriety of its exterior contrasting with the exuberant plasterwork within. The Maxwells have lived at Pollok since the mid-13th century, but the male line ended with Sir John Maxwell, who added the grand entrance hall in the 1890s and designed most of the terraced gardens and parkland beyond.

Hanging above the family silver, porcelain, hand-painted Chinese wallpaper and Jacobean glass, the Stirling Maxwell collection is strong on British and Dutch schools, including William Blake's *Sir Geoffrey Chaucer and the Nine and Twenty Pilgrims* (1745) and William Hogarth's portrait of James Thomson, who wrote the words to *Rule Britannia*.

Spanish 16th- to 19th-century art predominates: El Greco's *Lady in a Fur Wrap* (1541) hangs in the library, while the drawing room contains works by Francisco de Goya and Esteban Murillo. In 1966 Anne Maxwell Macdonald gave the house and 146 ha (361 acres) of parkland to the City of Glasgow. The park provides the site for the city's fascinating Burrell Collection.

Glasgow: The Burrell Collection

Given to the city in 1944 by Sir William Burrell (1861–1958), a wealthy shipping owner, this internationally acclaimed collection is the star of Glasgow's renaissance, with objects of major importance in numerous fields of interest. The building was purpose-built in 1983. In the sun, the stained glass blazes with colour, while the shaded tapestries seem a part of the surrounding woodland.

Figure of a Loha

This sculpture of Buddha's disciple dates from the Mir Dynasty (1484).

Hutton Castle Drawing Room

This is a reconstruction of the Drawing Room at Burrell's own home – the 16th-century Hutton Castle, near Berwick-upon-Tweed. The Hall and Dining Room can also be seen nearby.

Bull's Head

Dating from the 7th century BC, this bronze head from Turkey was once part of a cauldron handle.

Hornby Portal

This detail shows the arch's heraldic display. The 14th-century portal comes from Hornby Castle in Yorkshire.

Main entrance

Star Exhibits

★ **Stained Glass**

★ **Tapestries**

Rembrandt van Rijn
This self-portrait, signed and dated 1632, has pride of place among the Dutch paintings hanging in the 17th- and 18th-century room.

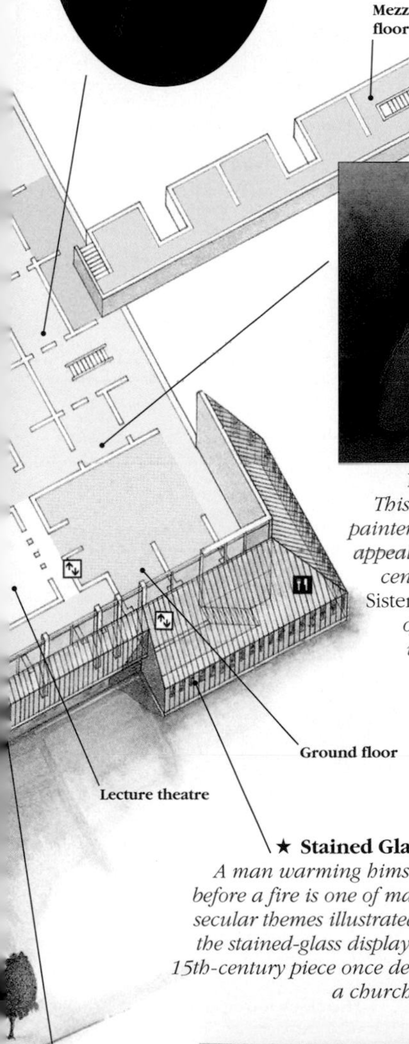

Mezzanine floor

Matthijs Maris
This popular Dutch painter's ethereal style appealed to late 19th-century tastes. The Sisters *(1875) is one of over 50 Maris works acquired by Burrell.*

Ground floor

Lecture theatre

★ Stained Glass
A man warming himself before a fire is one of many secular themes illustrated in the stained-glass display. This 15th-century piece once decorated a church in Suffolk.

★ Tapestries
Scenes from the Life of Christ and of the Virgin *(c.1450), a Swiss work in wool, is one of many tapestries on show.*

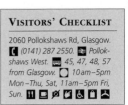

Visitors' Checklist

2060 Pollokshaws Rd, Glasgow. *(0141) 287 2550. Pollokshaws West. 45, 47, 48, 57 from Glasgow. 10am–5pm Mon–Thu, Sat, 11am–5pm Fri, Sun.*

Gallery Guide

Except for a mezzanine-floor display of paintings, the exhibitions are on the ground floor. Right of the entrance hall, rooms are devoted to tapestries, stained glass and sculpture, while ancient civilizations, Oriental art and the period galleries are ahead.

Key to Floorplan

- Ancient civilizations
- Oriental art
- Medieval and post-medieval European art, stained glass and tapestries
- Period galleries
- Hutton Castle Rooms
- Paintings and drawings
- Temporary exhibition area

Culzean Castle ㉚

Robert Adam **by George Willison**

STANDING ON A CLIFF'S EDGE in an extensive parkland estate, the 16th-century keep of Culzean (pronounced Cullayn), home of the Earls of Cassillis, was remodelled between 1777 and 1792 by the Neo-Classical architect Robert Adam *(see p24)*. Restored in the 1970s, it is now a major showcase of his later work. The grounds became Scotland's first public country park in 1969 and, with farming flourishing alongside ornamental gardens, they reflect both the leisure and everyday activities of a great country estate.

View of Culzean Castle **(c.1815), by Nasmyth**

Lord Cassillis' Rooms contain typical mid-18th-century furnishings, including a gentleman's wardrobe of the 1740s.

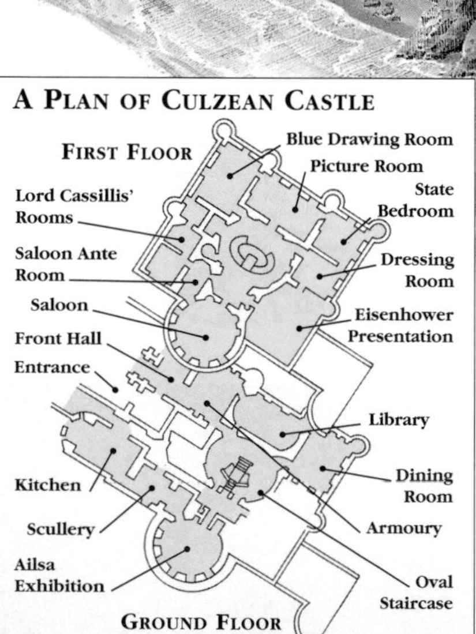

The clock tower, fronted by the circular carriageway, was originally the coach house and stables. The clock was added in the 19th century, and today the buildings are used for residential and educational purposes and a shop.

STAR SIGHTS

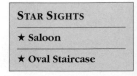

- ★ **Saloon**
- ★ **Oval Staircase**

Armoury
Displayed on the walls is the world's most important collection of flintlock pistols, used by the British Army and Militia between the 1730s and 1830s.

The Eisenhower Presentation honours the general who was given the top floor of Culzean in gratitude for his role in World War II.

Fountain Court
This sunken garden is a good place to begin a tour of the grounds to the east.

VISITORS' CHECKLIST

(NTS) 4 miles (6 km) West of Maybole. *01655 884400.* *Ayr, then bus.* **Castle** *Apr–Oct: 10am–5:30pm daily (last adm: 5pm).* **Grounds** *dawn until dusk daily.*

★ Saloon
With its restored 18th-century colour scheme and Louis XVI chairs, this elegant saloon perches on the cliff's edge 46 m (150 ft) above the Firth of Clyde. The carpet is a copy of the one designed by Adam.

★ Oval Staircase
Illuminated by an overarching skylight, the staircase, with its Ionic and Corinthian pillars, is considered one of Adam's finest achievements.

THE HIGHLANDS AND ISLANDS

ABERDEENSHIRE · MORAY · ARGYLL & BUTE · PERTH & KINROSS
SHETLAND · ORKNEY · WESTERN ISLES · HIGHLANDS · ANGUS

MOST OF THE STOCK IMAGES *of Scottishness – clans and tartans, whisky and porridge, bagpipes and heather – originate in the Highlands and enrich the popular picture of Scotland as a whole. But for many centuries the Gaelic-speaking, cattle-raising Highlanders had little in common with their southern neighbours.*

Clues to the non-Celtic ancestors of the Highlanders lie scattered across the Highlands and Islands in the form of stone circles, brochs and cairns some over 5,000 years old. By the end of the 6th century, the Gaelic-speaking Celts had arrived from Ireland, along with St Columba who taught Christianity. Its fusion with Viking culture in the 8th and 9th centuries produced St Magnus Cathedral in the Orkney Isles.

For over 1,000 years, Celtic Highland society was founded on a clan system, built on family ties to create loyal groups dependent on a feudal chief.

However, the clans were systematically broken up by England after 1746, following the defeat of the Jacobite attempt on the British crown, led by Bonnie Prince Charlie *(see p521)*. A more romantic vision of the Highlands started in the early 19th century. Its creation was largely due to Sir Walter Scott, whose novels and poetry depicted the majesty and grandeur of a country previously considered merely poverty-stricken and barbaric. Another great popularizer was Queen Victoria, whose passion for Balmoral helped to establish the trend for acquiring Highland sporting estates. But behind the sentimentality lay harsh economic realities that drove generations of Highlanders to seek a new life overseas.

Today, over half the inhabitants of the Highlands and Islands still live in communities of less than 1,000. Oil and tourism have supplemented fishing and whisky as the main businesses and population figures are rising.

A wintry dawn over the Cairngorms, the home of Britain's only herd of reindeer

◁ The stunningly sited castle of Eilean Donan, Loch Duich in Glen Shiel

Exploring the Highlands and Islands

To the north and west of Stirling (the historic gateway to the Highlands) lie the magnificent mountains and glens, fretted coastlines and lonely isles that are the epitome of Scottish scenery. Inverness, the Highland capital, makes a good starting point for exploring Loch Ness and the Cairngorms, while Fort William holds the key to Ben Nevis. Inland from Aberdeen lie Royal Deeside and the Spey Valley whisky heartland. The romantic Hebrides can be reached by ferry from Oban or Ullapool.

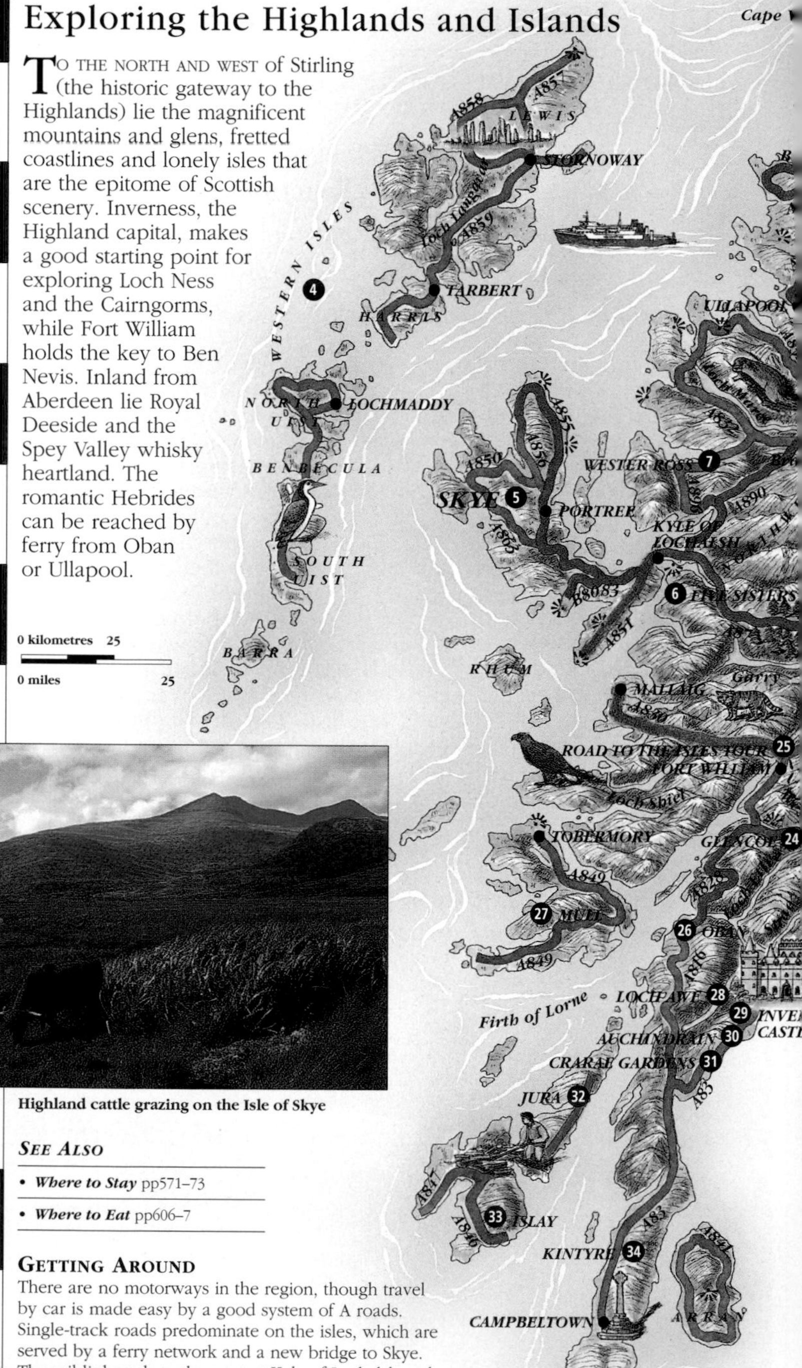

Highland cattle grazing on the Isle of Skye

See Also

- ***Where to Stay*** pp571–73
- ***Where to Eat*** pp606–7

Getting Around

There are no motorways in the region, though travel by car is made easy by a good system of A roads. Single-track roads predominate on the isles, which are served by a ferry network and a new bridge to Skye. The rail link ends to the west at Kyle of Lochalsh and to the north at Wick and Thurso. There are regular flights from London to Inverness, Aberdeen and Wick.

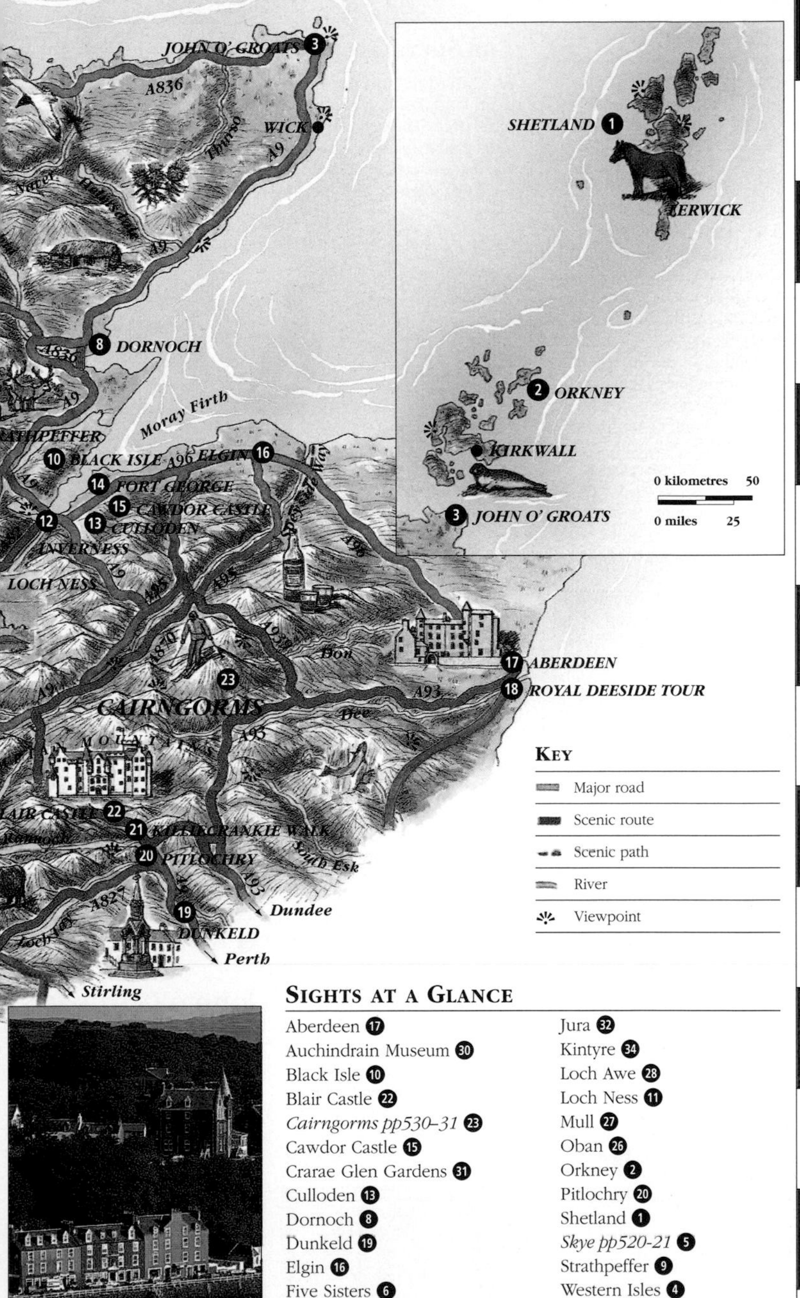

Key

- Major road
- Scenic route
- Scenic path
- River
- Viewpoint

Colour-washed houses at the harbour of Tobermory, Mull

Sights at a Glance

Aberdeen 17
Auchindrain Museum 30
Black Isle 10
Blair Castle 22
Cairngorms pp530–31 23
Cawdor Castle 15
Crarae Glen Gardens 31
Culloden 13
Dornoch 8
Dunkeld 19
Elgin 16
Five Sisters 6
Fort George 14
Glencoe 24
Inveraray Castle 29
Inverness 12
Islay 33
John o'Groats 3
Jura 32
Kintyre 34
Loch Awe 28
Loch Ness 11
Mull 27
Oban 26
Orkney 2
Pitlochry 20
Shetland 1
Skye pp520-21 5
Strathpeffer 9
Western Isles 4
Wester Ross 7

Walks and Tours

Killiecrankie Walk 21
Road to the Isles Tour 25
Royal Deeside Tour 18

Shetland ❶

Shetland. 23,000. from Aberdeen and Stromness on mainland Orkney. Lerwick (01595 693434).
www.visitshetland.com

LYING SIX DEGREES SOUTH of the Arctic Circle, the rugged Shetland islands are Britain's most northerly region and were, with Orkney, part of the kingdom of Norway until 1469. In the main town of Lerwick, this Norse heritage is remembered during the ancient midwinter festival Up Helly Aa *(see p466)*, in which costumed revellers set fire to a replica Viking longship. Also in the town, the **Shetland Museum** tells the story of a people dependent on the sea, right up to modern times with the discovery of North Sea oil and gas in the 1970s.

One of Shetland's greatest treasures is the Iron Age tower, **Mousa Broch**, which can be visited on its isle by boat from Sandwick. There is more ancient history at Jarlshof where a museum explains the sprawling sea-front ruins which span 3,000 years.

A boat from Lerwick sails to the isle of Noss where grey seals bask beneath sandstone cliffs crowded with Shetland's seabirds – a spectacle best seen between May and June.

Shetland Museum
The Hillhead, Lerwick. 01595 695057. 10am–7pm Mon, Wed, Fri; 10am–5pm Tue, Thu, Sat.

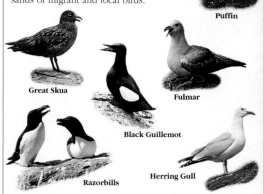

THE SHETLAND SEABIRD ISLES

As seabirds spend most of their time away from land, nesting is a vulnerable period in their lives. The security provided by the inaccessible cliffs at such sites as Noss and Hermaness on Unst finds favour with thousands of migrant and local birds.

Puffin

Great Skua

Fulmar

Black Guillemot

Razorbills

Herring Gull

Orkney ❷

Orkney. 19,800. from Gills Bay, Caithness; John o'Groats (May–Sep); Scrabster, Aberdeen. Broad St, Kirkwall (01856 872856).
www.visitorkney.com

THE FERTILE ISLES of Orkney are remarkable for the wealth of prehistoric monuments which place them among Europe's most treasured archaeological sites. In the town of Kirkwall, the sandstone **St Magnus Cathedral** stands amid a charming core of narrow streets. Its many interesting tombs include that of its 12th-century patron saint. Nearby, the early 17th-century **Earl's Palace** is widely held to be one of Scotland's finest Renaissance buildings. To the west of Kirkwall lies Britain's most impressive chambered tomb, the cairn of **Maes Howe**. Dating from 2000 BC, the tomb has runic graffiti on its walls believed to have been left by Norsemen returning from the crusades in 1150.

Nearby, the great **Standing Stones of Stenness** may have been associated with Maes Howe rituals, though these still remain a mystery. Further west, on a bleak heath, stands the Bronze Age **Ring of Brodgar**.

Another archaeological treasure can be found in the Bay of Skail – the complete Stone Age village of **Skara Brae**. It was unearthed by a storm in 1850, after lying buried for 4,500 years. Further south, the town of Stromness was a vital centre of Scotland's herring industry in the 18th century. Its story is told in the local museum, while the **Pier Arts Centre** displays British and international art.

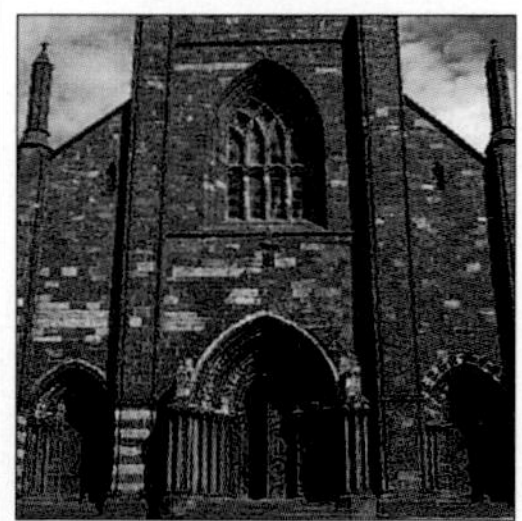

The Norman façade of the St Magnus Cathedral, Orkney

Earl's Palace
Palace Rd, Kirkwall. 0131 668 8800. Apr–Sep: 9:30am–6:30pm daily. limited.

Pier Arts Centre
Victoria St, Stromness. 01856 850209. 10:30am–5pm Tue–Sat. 24 Dec–10 Jan. limited.

John o'Groats ❸

Highland. 500. Wick John o'Groats to Burwick, Orkney (May–Sep). John o'Groats (01955 611373).

SOME 876 miles (1,409 km) north from Land's End, Britain's most northeasterly mainland village faces Orkney, 8 miles (13 km) across the turbulent Pentland Firth. The village takes its name from a 15th-century Dutchman John de Groot, who, to avoid accusations of favouritism, is said to have built an octagonal house here with one door for each of his eight heirs. The spectacular cliffs and rock stacks of Duncansby Head lie a few miles further east.

Western Isles ❹

WESTERN SCOTLAND ENDS with this remote chain of islands, made of some of the oldest rock on Earth. Almost treeless landscapes are divided by countless waterways, the western, windward coasts edged by miles of white sandy beaches. For centuries, the eastern shores, composed largely of peat bogs, have provided the islanders with fuel. Man has been here for 6,000 years, living off the sea and the thin turf, though such monuments as an abandoned Norwegian whaling station on Harris attest to the difficulties in commercializing the islanders' traditional skills. Gaelic, part of an enduring culture, is widely spoken.

The monumental Standing Stones of Callanish in northern Lewis

Lewis and Harris

Western Isles. 22,000. Stornoway. Uig (Skye), Ullapool, Kyle of Lochalsh. Stornoway, Lewis (01851 703088); Tarbert, Harris (01859 502011). www.witb.co.uk

Black House Museum *01851 710395. Mon–Sat.*

Forming the largest landmass of the Western Isles, Lewis and Harris are a single island, though Gaelic dialects differ between the two areas. From **Stornoway**, with its bustling harbour and colourful house fronts, the ancient **Standing Stones of Callanish** are only 16 miles (26 km) to the west. Just off the road on the way to Callanish are the ruins of **Carloway Broch**, a Pictish *(see p468)* tower over 2,000 years old. The more recent past can be explored at Arnol's **Black House Museum** – a showcase of crofting life as it was until only 50 years ago.

South of the rolling peat moors of Lewis, a range of mountains marks the border with Harris, which one enters as one passes Aline Lodge at the head of Loch Seaforth. Only a little less spectacular than the "Munros" (peaks over 914 m; 3,000 ft) of the mainland and the Isle of Skye *(see pp520–21)*, the mountains of Harris are a paradise for the hillwalker and, from their summits on a clear day, the distant Isle of St Kilda can be seen 50 miles (80 km) to the west.

The ferry port of Tarbert stands on a slim isthmus separating North and South Harris. The tourist office provides addresses for local weavers of the tough Harris Tweed. Some still use plants to make their dyes.

From the port of Leverburgh, close to the southern tip of Harris, a ferry can be taken to the isle of North Uist, where a causeway has been built to Berneray.

The Black House Museum, a traditional croft on Lewis

The Uists, Benbecula and Barra

Western Isles. 7,200. Barra, Benbecula. Uig (Skye), Ullapool, Oban, Mallaig. Oban, Mallaig, Kyle of Lochalsh. Lochmaddy, North Uist (01876 500321); Lochboisdale, South Uist (01878 700286); Castlebay, Barra (01871 810336). www.witb.co.uk

After the dramatic scenery of Harris, the lower-lying, largely waterlogged southern isles may seem an anticlimax, though they nurture secrets well worth discovering. Long, white, sandy beaches fringe the Atlantic coast, edged with one of Scotland's natural treasures: the lime-rich soil known as *machair*. During the summer months, the soil is covered with wild flowers.

From **Lochmaddy**, North Uist's main village, the A867 crosses 3 miles (5 km) of causeway to Benbecula, the isle from which Flora MacDonald smuggled Bonnie Prince Charlie *(see p521)* to Skye. Another causeway leads to South Uist, with its golden beaches renowned as a National Scenic Area. From Lochboisdale, a ferry sails to the tiny isle of Barra. The ferry docks in Castlebay, affording an unforgettable view of **Kisimul Castle**, the ancestral stronghold of the MacNeils of Barra.

The remote and sandy shores of South Uist

The western side of the Five Sisters of Kintail, seen from above Loch Duich

Skye 5

See pp520–21.

The Five Sisters 6

Skye & Lochalsh. *Kyle of Lochalsh.* *Glenshiel.* *Bayfield Lane, Portree, Isle of Skye (01478 612137).* www.highlandfreedom.com

Dominating one of Scotland's most haunting regions, the awesome summits of the Five Sisters of Kintail rear into view at the northern end of Loch Cluanie as the A87 enters Glen Shiel. The **Visitor Centre** at Morvich offers ranger-led excursions in the summer. Further west, the road passes **Eilean Donan Castle**, connected by a bridge. A Jacobite *(see p523)* stronghold, it was destroyed in 1719 by English warships. In the 19th century it was restored and now contains Jacobite relics.

Eilean Donan Castle
Off A87, nr Dornie. *01599 555202.* *Apr–Sep: 10am–6pm; Oct, Nov: 10am–3:30pm; daily.*

Wester Ross 7

Ross & Cromarty. *Achnasheen, Strathcarron.* *Gairloch (01445 712130).*

Leaving Loch Carron to the south, the A890 suddenly enters the northern Highlands and the great wilderness of Wester Ross. The Torridon Estate includes some of the oldest mountains on Earth (Torridonian rock is over 600 million years old), and is home to red deer, wild cats and wild goats. Peregrine falcons and golden eagles nest in the towering sandstone mass of Liathach, above the village of Torridon with its breathtaking views over Applecross to Skye. The **Torridon Countryside Centre** provides guided walks in season and essential information on the natural history of the region.

To the north, the A832 cuts through the Beinn Eighe National Nature Reserve in which remnants of the ancient Caledonian pine forest still stand on the banks and isles of Loch Maree.

Along the coast, exotic gardens thrive in the warming currents of the Gulf Stream, most impressive being **Inverewe Garden** created in 1862 by Osgood Mackenzie (1842–1922). May and June are the months to see the display of rhododendrons and azaleas; July and August for the herbaceous borders.

Typical Torridonian mountian scenery in the Wester Ross

Torridon Countryside Centre
(NTS) Torridon. *01445 791221.* *May–Sep: 10am–6pm Mon–Sat, 2–5pm Sun.* www.nts.org.uk

Inverewe Garden
(NTS) off A832, nr Poolewe. *01445 781200.* *mid-Mar–Oct: 9:30am–dusk daily.*

Dornoch 8

Sutherland. *2,200.* *Golspie, Tain.* *The Square, Dornoch (01862 810916).* www.dornoch.com

With its first-class golf course and extensive sandy beaches, **Dornoch** is a popular holiday resort, though it has retained a peaceful atmosphere. Now the parish church, the medieval cathedral was all but destroyed in a clan dispute in 1570; it was finally restored in the 1920s for its 700th anniversary. A stone at the beach end of River Street marks the place where Janet Horne, the last woman to be tried in Scotland for witchcraft, was executed in 1722.

Environs: Twelve miles (19 km) northeast of Dornoch is the stately Victorianized pile of **Dunrobin Castle**, magnificently situated in a great park with formal gardens overlooking the sea. Since the 13th century, this has been the seat of the Earls of Sutherland.

Many of its rooms are open to visitors. A steam-powered fire engine is among the miscellany of objects on display.

South of Dornoch stands the town of **Tain**. Though patronized by medieval kings as a place of pilgrimage, it became an administrative centre of the Highland Clearances. All is explained in the heritage centre, **Tain Through Time**.

Dunrobin Castle
Nr Golspie. *01408 633177.*
Apr–mid-Oct: 10:30am–4:30pm, noon–4:30pm Sun.

Tain Through Time
Tower St. *01862 894089.*
Apr–Oct: 10am–6pm Mon–Sat; Nov–Mar: by arrangement.

The serene cathedral precinct in the town of Dornoch

Strathpeffer 9

Ross & Cromarty. *1,400.*
Dingwall, Inverness. *Inverness.*
North Kessock (01463 731505; Easter–Oct).

STANDING 5 miles (8 km) from the Falls of Rogie and to the east of the Northwest Highlands, the popular town of Strathpeffer still has the refined charm for which it was well known in Victorian times, when it flourished as a spa and health resort. The grand hotels and gracious layout of Strathpeffer recall the days when royalty from all over Europe used to flock to the chalybeate- and sulphur-laden springs, which were believed to help in the cure of tuberculosis.

The shores of the Black Isle in the Moray Firth

The Black Isle 10

Ross & Cromarty. *Inverness.*
North Kessock (01463 731505; Easter–Oct).

THOUGH THE DRILLING platforms in the Cromarty Firth are reminders of how oil has changed the local economy, the peninsula of the Black Isle is still largely composed of farmland and fishing villages. The town of **Cromarty** was an important port in the 18th century, with thriving rope and lace industries. Many of its merchant houses still stand; the award-winning museum in the **Cromarty Courthouse** provides heritage tours of the town. The thatched **Hugh Miller's Cottage** is a museum to the theologian and geologist Hugh Miller (1802–56), who was born here. **Fortrose** boasts a ruined 14th-century cathedral, while a stone on Chanonry Point commemorates the Brahan Seer, a 17th-century prophet burnt alive in a tar barrel by the Countess of Seaforth after he foresaw her husband's infidelity. For local archaeology, visit **Groam House Museum** in Rosemarkie.

Cromarty Courthouse
Church St, Cromarty. *01381 600418.* *Apr–Oct: 10am–5pm daily; Nov–Mar: noon–4pm daily.* *23 Dec–25 Feb.*

Hugh Miller's Cottage
(NTS) Church St, Cromarty. *01381 600245.* *May–Sep: 11am–5pm daily (Sun: noon–5pm).* *limited.*

Groam House Museum
High St, Rosemarkie. *01381 620961.* *May–Sep: 10am–5pm daily (Sun: 2–4:30pm); Oct–Apr: Sat & Sun (pm).* *ground floor only.*

THE HIGHLAND CLEARANCES

During the heyday of the clan system *(see p470)* tenants paid their clan chiefs rent for their land in the form of military service. However, with the decline of the clan system after the Battle of Culloden *(see p523)* and the coming of sheep from the borders, landowners were able to command a financial rent their tenants were unable to afford and the land was bought up by Lowland and English farmers. In what became known as "the year of the sheep" (1792), thousands of tenants were evicted to make way for sheep. Many emigrated to Australia, America and Canada. Ruins of their crofts can still be seen in Sutherland and Wester Ross.

***The Last of the Clan* (1865) by Thomas Faed**

Isle of Skye 36

Otter by the coast at Kylerhea

THE LARGEST of the Inner Hebrides, Skye can be reached by the bridge linking Kyle of Lochalsh and Kyleakin. A turbulent geological history has given the island some of Britain's most varied and dramatic scenery. From the rugged volcanic plateau of northern Skye to the ice-sculpted peaks of the Cuillins, the island is divided by numerous sea lochs, leaving the traveller never more than 8 km (5 miles) from the sea. Limestone grasslands predominate in the south, where the hillsides, home of sheep and cattle, are scattered with the ruins of crofts abandoned during the Clearances *(see p517)*. Historically, Skye is best known for its association with Bonnie Prince Charlie.

Skeabost has the ruins of a chapel which is associated with St Columba. Medieval tombstones can be found in the graveyard.

Grave of Flora MacDonald

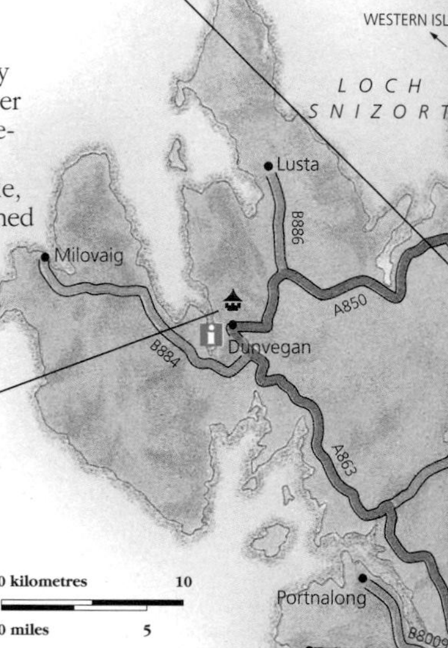

0 kilometres 10

0 miles 5

Dunvegan Castle

For over seven centuries, Dunvegan Castle has been the seat of the chiefs of the Clan MacLeod. It contains the Fairy Flag, a fabled piece of magical silk treasured for its protection.

The Talisker Distillery produces one of the best Highland malts, often described as "the lava of the Cuillins".

Cuillins

Britain's finest mountain range is within walking distance of Sligachan, and in summer a boat sails from Elgol to the desolate inner sanctuary of Loch Coruisk. As he fled across the surrounding moorland, Bonnie Prince Charlie is said to have claimed: "even the Devil shall not follow me here!"

KEY

- Tourist information
- Major road
- Minor road
- Narrow lane
- Viewpoint

◁ **Dawn over the desolate tablelands of northern Skye, viewed from the Quiraing**

Quiraing
A series of landslides has exposed the roots of this volcanic plateau, revealing a fantastic terrain of spikes and towers. They are easily explored off the Uig to Staffin road.

Kilt Rock

The Storr
The erosion of this basalt plateau has created the Old Man of Storr, a monolith rising to 49 m (160 ft) by the Portree road.

Portree
With its colourful harbour, Portree (meaning "port of the king") is Skye's metropolis. It received its name after a visit by James V in 1540.

Loch Coruisk

Luib has a beautiful thatched cottage, preserved as it was 100 years ago.

Bridge to mainland

Otters can be seen from the haven in Kylerhea.

Armadale Castle Gardens and Museum of the Isles houses the Clan Donald visitor centre.

Kilchrist Church
This ruined pre-Reformation church's last service was held in 1843. It once served Skye's most populated areas, though the surrounding moors are now deserted.

Visitors' Checklist

The Highlands. *11,500.* *Kyle of Lochalsh.* *Portree.* *from Mallaig or Glenelg.* Bayfield House, Portree *(01478 612137).* www.host.co.uk
Dunvegan Castle, *Dunvegan.* *01470 521206.* *daily.* *limited.* **Armadale Castle,** *Armadale.* *01471 844227.* *Apr–Oct: daily (gardens open all year).* **Talisker Distillery,** *Carbost.* *01478 614308.* *daily: call for details.* *limited.*

Bonnie Prince Charlie

The last of the Stuart claimants to the Crown, Charles Edward Stuart (1720–88), came to Scotland from France in 1745 to win the throne. After marching as far as Derby, his army was driven back to Culloden where it was defeated. Hounded for five months through the Highlands, he escaped to Skye, disguised as the maidservant of a woman called Flora MacDonald, from Uist. From the mainland, he sailed to France in September 1746, and died in Rome. Flora was buried in 1790 at Kilmuir, on Skye, wrapped in a sheet taken from the bed of the "bonnie" (handsome) prince.

The prince, disguised as a maidservant

The ruins of Urquhart Castle on the western shore of Loch Ness

Loch Ness ⓫

Inverness. *Inverness.* *Castle Wynd, Inverness (01463 234353).*
www.loch-ness-scotland.com

At 24 miles (39 km) long, one mile (1.5 km) at its widest and up to 305 m (1,000 ft) deep, **Loch Ness** fills the northern half of the Great Glen fault from Fort William to Inverness. It is joined to lochs Oich and Lochy by the 22 mile (35 km) Caledonian Canal, designed by Thomas Telford *(see p433)*. On the western shore, the A82 passes the ruins of the 16th-century **Urquhart Castle**, which was blown up by government supporters in 1692 to prevent it falling into Jacobite hands. A short distance to the west, **The Official Loch Ness Exhibition Centre** provides a wealth of audio-visual information.

The Loch Ness Monster

First sighted by St Columba in the 6th century, "Nessie" has attracted increasing attention since ambiguous photographs were taken in the 1930s. Though serious investigation is often undermined by hoaxers, sonar techniques continue to yield enigmatic results: plesiosaurs, giant eels and too much whisky are the most popular explanations. Nessie appears to have a close relative in the waters of Loch Morar *(see p532)*.

Urquhart Castle
Nr Drumnadrochit. *01456 450551.* *Easter–Oct: 9:30am–6:30pm; Nov–Easter: 9:30am–4:30pm; daily.*

The Official Loch Ness Exhibition Centre
Drumnadrochit. *01456 450573.* *Easter–May: 9:30am–5pm; Jun, Sep: 9am–6pm; Jul, Aug: 9am–8pm; Oct: 9:30am–5:30pm; daily.*

Kilt maker with royal Stuart tartan

Inverness ⓬

Highland. *60,000.* *Castle Wynd (01463 234353).*
www.host.co.uk

As the Highland capital, Inverness makes an ideal base from which to explore the surrounding countryside. The Victorian castle dominates the town centre, the oldest buildings of which are found in nearby Church Street. Today the castle is used as law courts. The **Inverness Museum and Art Gallery** provides a good introduction to the history of the Highlands with exhibits including a lock of Bonnie Prince Charlie's *(see p521)* hair and a fine collection of Inverness silver. The **Scottish Kiltmaker Visitor Centre** explores the history and tradition of Scottish kilts as well as workshops, while those in search of tartans and knitwear should visit the **James Pringle Weavers of Inverness**.

Jacobite Cruises runs regular summer cruises along the Caledonian Canal and on to Loch Ness. The unfolding scenery makes this a most pleasant and tranquil way to spend a sunny afternoon.

Museum and Art Gallery
Castle Wynd. *01463 237114.* *9am–5pm Mon–Sat.* *25, 26 Dec, 1, 2 Jan.*

James Pringle Weavers of Inverness
Holm Woollen Mill, Dores Rd. *01463 223311.* *9am–5pm Mon–Sat, 11am–4pm Sun.* *25 Dec, 1 Jan.*

Scottish Kiltmaker Visitor Centre
Huntly St. *01463 222781.* *9am–5pm daily.* *25 Dec, 1 Jan.*

Jacobite Cruises
Glenurquhart Road. *01463 233999.* *Easter–Oct: daily.*

Culloden ⓭

(NTS) Inverness. *Inverness.*
www.nts.org.uk

A DESOLATE STRETCH of moorland, Culloden looks much as it did on 16 April 1746, the date of the last battle to be fought on British soil *(see p469)*. Here the Jacobite cause, with Bonnie Prince Charlie's *(see p521)* leadership, finally perished under the onslaught of Hanoverian troops led by the Duke of Cumberland. All is explained in the excellent **NTS Visitor Centre**.

ENVIRONS: Signposted for a mile (1.5 km) or so east are the outstanding Neolithic burial sites, the **Clava Cairns**.

NTS Visitor Centre
On the B9006 east of Inverness.
01463 790607. Apr–Oct: 9am–6pm; Nov–Mar: 10am–4pm daily. Jan.

Fort George ⓮

Inverness. *01667 462777.*
Inverness, Nairn. 9:30am–6:30pm Mon–Sat, 2–5pm Sun.
25, 26 Dec.
www.historicscotland.co.uk

ONE OF THE FINEST works of European military architecture, Fort George stands on a windswept promontory jutting into the Moray Firth, ideally located to suppress the Highlanders. Completed in 1769, the fort was built after the Jacobite risings to discourage further rebellion in the Highlands and has remained a military garrison ever since. The Fort houses the **Regimental Museum** of the Queen's Own Highlanders, and some of its barrack rooms reconstruct the conditions of the common soldiers stationed here more than 200 years ago. The **Grand Magazine** contains an outstanding collection of arms and military equipment. The battlements also make an excellent place from which to watch dolphins in the Moray Firth.

THE JACOBITE MOVEMENT

James II, by Samuel Cooper (1609–72)

The first Jacobites (mainly Catholic Highlanders) were the supporters of James II of England (James VII of Scotland) who was deposed by the "Glorious Revolution" of 1688 *(see p53)*. With the Protestant William of Orange on the throne, the Jacobites' desire to restore the Stuart monarchy led to the uprisings of 1715 and 1745. The first, in support of James VIII, the "Old Pretender", ended at the Battle of Sheriffmuir (1715). The failure of the second uprising, with the defeat at Culloden, saw the end of Jacobite hopes and led to the end of the clan system and the suppression of Highland culture for over a century *(see p471)*.

The drawbridge on the eastern side of Cawdor Castle

A contemporary picture, *The Battle of Culloden* (1746), by D Campbell

Cawdor Castle ⓯

On B9090 (off A96). *01667 404615. Nairn, then bus. from Inverness. May–mid-Oct: 10am–5pm daily. gardens & ground floor only.*
www.cawdorcastle.com

WITH ITS TURRETED central tower, moat and drawbridge, Cawdor Castle is one of the most romantic stately homes in the Highlands. Though the castle is famed for being the 11th-century home of Shakespeare's *(see p310)* Macbeth and the scene of his murder of King Duncan, it is not historically proven that either came here.

An ancient holly tree preserved in the vaults is said to be the one under which, in 1372, Thane William's donkey, laden with gold, stopped for a rest during its master's search for a place to build a fortress. According to legend, this was how the site for the castle was chosen. Now, after 600 years of continuous occupation (it is still the home of the Thanes of Cawdor) the house is a treasury of family history, containing a number of rare tapestries and portraits by the 18th-century painters Joshua Reynolds (1723–92) and George Romney (1734–1802). Furniture in the Pink Bedroom and Woodcock Room includes work by Chippendale and Sheraton. In the Old Kitchen, the huge Victorian cooking range stands as a shrine to below-stairs drudgery. The grounds provide nature trails and a nine-hole golf course.

Elgin 16

Moray. 25,000.
17 High St, Moray (01343 542666).

With its cobbled market-place and crooked lanes, the popular holiday centre of Elgin still retains much of its medieval layout. The 13th-century **cathedral** ruins next to King Street are all that remain of one of Scotland's architectural triumphs, the design of its tiered windows reminiscent of the cathedral at St Andrews *(see p485)*. Once known as the Lantern of the North, the cathedral was severely damaged in 1390 by the Wolf of Badenoch (the son of Robert II) in revenge for his excommunication by the Bishop of Moray. Even worse damage came in 1576 when the Regent Moray ordered the stripping of its lead roofing. Among its outstanding remains is a Pictish cross-slab in the nave, and a basin in a

Details of the central tower of Elgin Cathedral

corner where one of Elgin's benefactors, Andrew Anderson, was kept as a baby by his homeless mother. As well as local history, the **Elgin Museum** has anthropological, geological displays, while the **Moray Motor Museum** has over 40 vehicles.

Elgin Museum

1 High St. *01343 543675.* *Apr–Oct: 10am–5pm daily (Sun: pm). Phone to check times.* *limited.*

Moray Motor Museum

Bridge St, Bishopmill. *01343 544933.* *Easter–Oct: 11am–5pm daily.*

Aberdeen 17

Scotland's third largest city and Europe's offshore oil capital, Aberdeen has prospered since the discovery of petroleum in the North Sea in 1970. The sea bed has now yielded 50 oilfields. Widely known as the Granite City, its rugged outlines are softened by sumptuous year-round floral displays in its public parks and gardens, the Duthie Park Winter Gardens being the largest indoor garden in Europe. The picturesque village of Footdee, which sits at the end of the city's 2 mile (3 km) beach, has good views back to the busy harbour.

The spires of Aberdeen, rising behind the city harbour

Exploring Aberdeen

The city centre flanks the mile-long (1.5 km) Union Street ending to the east at the Mercat Cross. The cross stands in Castlegate, the one-time site of the city castle. From here the cobbled Shiprow winds southwest and passes Provost Ross's House *(see p526)* on its way to the harbour with its fish market. A bus can be taken a mile (1.5 km) north of the centre to Old Aberdeen which, with its medieval streets and wynds, has the peaceful character of a separate village. Driving is restricted in some streets.

King's College

College Bounds, Old Aberdeen. *01224 273702.* *9:30am–5pm Mon–Fri, 11am–5pm Sat.* *24 Dec–3 Jan.* www.abdn.ac.uk/kcc

Founded in 1495 as the city's first university, the college now has a Visitor Centre. The inter-denominational chapel, in the past consecutively Catholic and Protestant, has a lantern tower rebuilt after a storm in 1633. Stained-glass windows by Douglas Strachan add a contemporary touch to the interior which contains a 1540 pulpit, later carved with heads of Stuart monarchs.

St Andrew's Cathedral

King St. *01224 640290.* *May–Sep: 10am–4pm Mon–Sat.* *by appointment.*

The Mother Church of the Episcopal Communion in America, St Andrew's has a memorial to Samuel Seabury, the first Episcopalian bishop in the United States, who was consecrated in Aberdeen in 1784. Coats of arms adorn the ceiling above the north and south aisles, contrasting colourfully with the white walls and pillars. They represent the American States and local Jacobite *(see p523)* families.

The elegant lantern tower of the chapel at King's College

Provost Skene's House

Guestrow. ☎ *01224 641086.* ○ *10am–5pm Mon–Sat, 1–4pm Sun.* ● *25, 26, 31 Dec–2 Jan.* W www.aagm.co.uk

Once the home of Sir George Skene, a 17th-century provost (mayor) of Aberdeen, the house was built in 1545. Inside, period rooms span 200 years of design. The Duke of Cumberland stayed here before the Battle of Culloden *(see p523)*.

Visitors' Checklist

City of Aberdeen. *212,000.* *Guild St.* *Union St (01224 288828).* W www.aberdeen-grampian.com

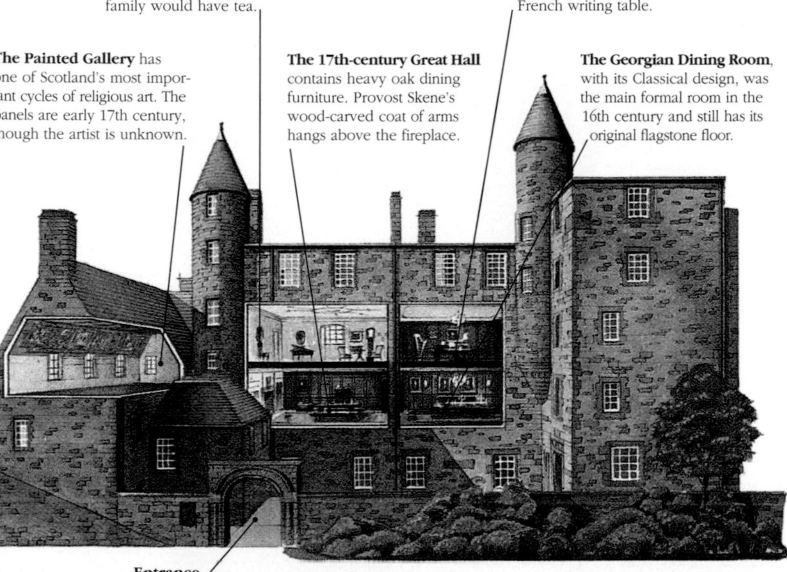

The 18th-century Parlour, with its walnut harpsichord and covered chairs by the fire, was the informal room in which the family would have tea.
The Regency Room typifies early 19th-century elegance. A harp dating from 1820 stands by a Grecian-style sofa and a French writing table.
The Painted Gallery has one of Scotland's most important cycles of religious art. The panels are early 17th century, though the artist is unknown.
The 17th-century Great Hall contains heavy oak dining furniture. Provost Skene's wood-carved coat of arms hangs above the fireplace.
The Georgian Dining Room, with its Classical design, was the main formal room in the 16th century and still has its original flagstone floor.
Entrance

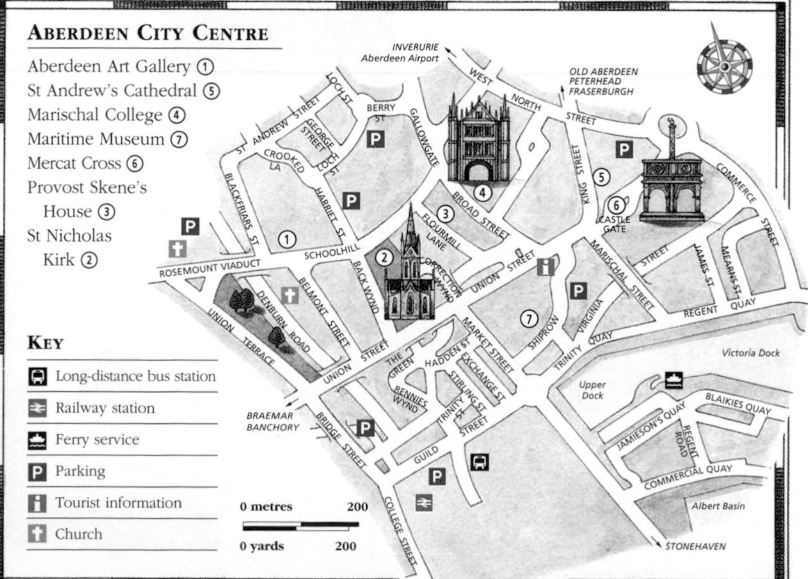

Aberdeen City Centre
Aberdeen Art Gallery ①
St Andrew's Cathedral ⑤
Marischal College ④
Maritime Museum ⑦
Mercat Cross ⑥
Provost Skene's House ③
St Nicholas Kirk ②
Key
Long-distance bus station
Railway station
Ferry service
Parking
Tourist information
Church
0 metres 200
0 yards 200
INVERURIE
Aberdeen Airport
OLD ABERDEEN
PETERHEAD
FRASERBURGH
WEST NORTH STREET
LOCH ST
BERRY ST
GALLOWGATE
ST ANDREW STREET
GEORGE STREET
LOCH ST
CROOKED LA
BLACKFRIARS ST
HARRIET ST
SCHOOLHILL
ROSEMOUNT VIADUCT
UNION TERRACE
DENBURN ROAD
BELMONT STREET
BACK WYND
CORRECTION WYND
FLOURMILL LANE
BROAD STREET
UNION STREET
KING STREET
CASTLE GATE
COMMERCE STREET
MARISCHAL STREET
JAMES ST
MEARNS ST
REGENT QUAY
VIRGINIA
SHIPROW
TRINITY QUAY
MARKET STREET
HADDEN ST
EXCHANGE ST
THE GREEN
BENNIES WYND
STIRLING ST
TRINITY ST
UNION STREET
BRAEMAR
BANCHORY
BRIDGE STREET
GUILD STREET
COLLEGE STREET
Victoria Dock
Upper Dock
BLAIKIES QUAY
JAMIESON'S QUAY
REGENT ROAD
COMMERCIAL QUAY
Albert Basin
STONEHAVEN

Art Gallery

Schoolhill. 01224 523700. 10am–5pm Mon–Sat, 2–5pm Sun. 25 Dec–2 Jan. www.aagm.co.uk

Housed in a Neo-Classical building, purpose-built in 1884, the Art Gallery has a wide range of exhibitions, with an emphasis on contemporary work. A fine collection of Aberdonian silver can be found among the decorative arts on the ground floor, and is the subject of a video presentation. A permanent collection of 18th–20th-century fine art features such names as Toulouse-Lautrec, Reynolds and Zoffany. Several of the works were bequeathed in 1900 by a local granite merchant, Alex Macdonald. He commissioned many of the paintings in the Macdonald Room, which displays 92 self-portraits by British artists. Occasional poetry-readings, music recitals and films are on offer.

Aberdonian silver in the Art Gallery

St Nicholas Kirk

Union St. 01224 643494. May–Sep: 10am–4pm daily; Oct–Apr: Mon–Fri (am).

Founded in the 12th century, St Nicholas is Scotland's largest parish church. Though the present structure dates from 1752, many relics of earlier times can be seen inside. After being damaged during the Reformation, the interior was divided into two. A chapel in the East Church contains iron rings used to secure witches in the 17th century, while in the West Church there are some embroidered panels attributed to one Mary Jameson (1597–1644).

Maritime Museum

Shiprow. 01224 337700. 10am–5pm Mon–Sat.

Overlooking the harbour is Provost Ross's House, which dates back to 1593 and is one of the oldest residential buildings in the town. This museum traces the history of Aberdeen's long seafaring tradition. Exhibitions include shipwrecks, rescues, shipbuilding and the many oil installations off Scotland's east coast.

St Machar's Cathedral

The Chanonry. 01224 485988. 9am–5pm daily.

Dominating Old Aberdeen, the 15th-century edifice of St Machar's is the oldest granite building in the city. The stonework of one arch even dates as far back as the 14th century. The impressive nave now serves as a parish church and its magnificent oak ceiling is adorned with the coats of arms of 48 popes, emperors and princes of Christendom.

Royal Deeside Tour 18

SINCE QUEEN VICTORIA'S purchase of the Balmoral estate in 1852, Deeside has been best known as the summer home of the British Royal Family, though it has been associated with royalty since the time of Robert the Bruce *(see p468)*. The route follows the Dee, formerly a prolific salmon river, through some magnificent Grampian scenery.

Muir of Dinnet Nature Reserve ④

An information centre on the A97 provides an excellent place from which to explore this beautiful mixed woodland area, formed by the retreating glaciers of the last Ice Age.

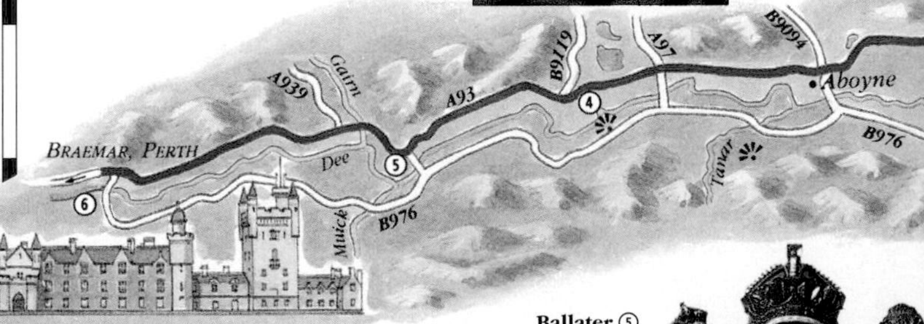

Ballater ⑤

The old railway town of Ballater has royal warrants on many of its shop fronts. It grew as a 19th-century spa town, its waters reputedly providing a cure for tuberculosis.

Balmoral ⑥

Bought by Queen Victoria for 30,000 guineas in 1852, after its owner choked to death on a fishbone, the castle was rebuilt in the Scottish Baronial style at Prince Albert's request.

Dunkeld ⓳

Perth & Kinross. 2,500. Birnam. The Cross (01350 727688). www.perthshire.co.uk

SITUATED BY the River Tay, this ancient and charming village was all but destroyed in the Battle of Dunkeld, a Jacobite *(see p523)* defeat, in 1689. The **Little Houses** lining Cathedral Street were the first to be rebuilt, and are fine examples of imaginative restoration. The ruins of the 14th-century **cathedral** enjoy an idyllic setting on shady lawns beside the Tay, against a backdrop of steep and wooded hills. The choir is used as the parish church and its north wall contains a Leper's Squint: a hole through which lepers could see the altar during mass. It was while on holiday in the Dunkeld countryside that Beatrix Potter *(see p355)* found the location for her Peter Rabbit stories.

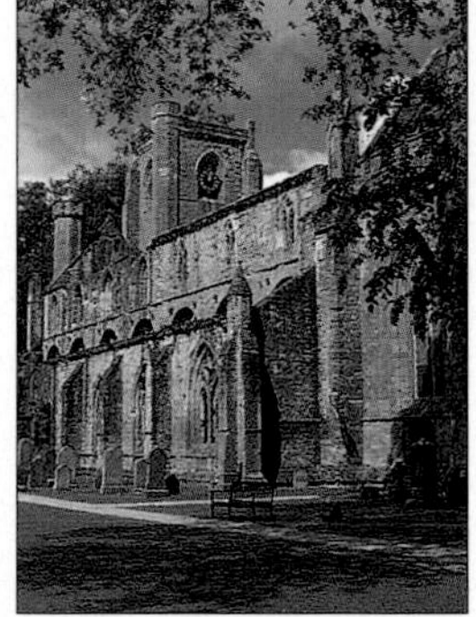

The ruins of Dunkeld Cathedral

Pitlochry ⓴

Perth & Kinross. 2,500. 22 Atholl Rd (01796 472215). www.pitlochry.org.uk

SURROUNDED BY the pine-forested hills, Pitlochry became famous after Queen Victoria *(see p56)* described it as one of the finest resorts in Europe. In early summer, salmon swim up the ladder built into the Power Station Dam, on their way to spawning grounds upriver. The **Power Station Visitor Centre** outlines the hydro-electric scheme which harnesses the waters of the River Tummel. The home of Bell's whisky, the **Blair Athol Distillery**, gives an insight into whisky making *(see p475)* and is open for tours. The **Festival Theatre**, one of Scotland's most famous, puts on a summer season when the programme changes daily.

Power Station Visitor Centre
Pitlochry. *01796 473152.* *late Mar–Oct: 10am–5:30pm daily.*

Festival Theatre
Port-na-Craig. *01796 472680.* *mid-May–Oct: daily.*

Blair Athol Distillery
Perth Rd. *01796 482003.* *Apr–Sep: Mon–Sat (& Sun pm Jun–Sep); Oct: Mon–Fri; Nov–Mar: Mon–Fri pm.* *22 Dec–3 Jan.* *limited.*

TIPS FOR DRIVERS

Length: *69 miles (111 km).*
Stopping-off points: *Crathes Castle café (May–Sep: daily); Station Restaurant, Ballater (food served all day).* (See also pp636–7)

Drum Castle ①
This impressive 13th-century keep was granted by Robert the Bruce to his standard bearer in 1323, in gratitude for his services.

Banchory ③
Local lavender is a popular attraction here. From the 18th-century Brig o' Feugh, salmon can be seen.

Crathes Castle and Gardens ②
This is the family home of the Burnetts, who were made Royal Foresters of Drum by Robert the Bruce. Along with the title, he gave Alexander Burnett the ivory Horn of Leys which is still on display.

0 kilometres 5
0 miles 4

KEY

Tour route
Other roads
Viewpoint

Killiecrankie Walk ㉑

In an area famous for its scenery and historical connections, this circular walk offers typical Highland views. The route is fairly flat, though ringed by mountains, and follows the River Garry south to Loch Faskally, meandering through a wooded gorge, passing the Soldier's Leap and a Victorian viaduct. There are several ideal picnic spots along the way. Returning along the River Tummel, the walk crosses one of Queen Victoria's favourite Highland areas, before doubling back along the rivers to complete the circuit.

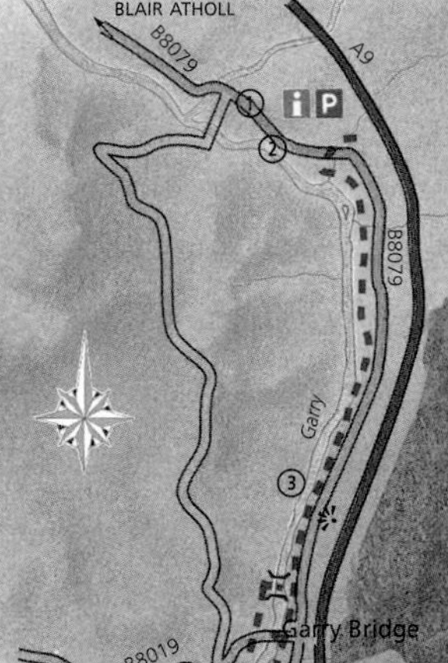

Killiecrankie ①
A Visitor Centre provides information on the Battle of Killiecrankie, fought in 1689.

Soldier's Leap ②
The Redcoat soldier Donald Macbean leapt over the river here to avoid capture by Jacobites during the 1689 battle.

Killiecrankie Pass ③
A 17th-century military road built by General Wade follows the gorge.

Clunie Foot Bridge ④
This bridge crosses the artificial Loch Faskally, created by the damming of the River Tummel for hydro-electric power in the 1950s.

Memorial Arch ⑤
The workers killed in the construction of the Clunie Dam are commemorated here.

Coronation Bridge ⑥
Spanning the River Tummel, this footbridge was built in 1860 in honour of George IV.

Linn of Tummel ⑦
The path passes a pool beneath the Falls of Tummel and leads through a beautiful forest trail.

Key

- Route
- Major road
- B road
- Minor road
- Viewpoint
- Parking
- Visitor Centre

0 kilometres 1
0 miles 0.5

Tips for Walkers

Starting point: *NTS Visitor Centre Killicrankie. ☎ 01796 473233.*
Getting there: *Bus from Pitlochry or Aberfeldy.*
Length: *10 miles (16 km).*
Difficulty: *Very easy.*

The Three Sisters, Glencoe, in late autumn

Blair Castle ㉒

Blair Atholl, Perthshire. *01796 481207.* *Blair Atholl.* *Apr–Oct: 10am–6pm daily.* *limited.* *www.blair-castle.co.uk*

THIS RAMBLING, turreted castle has been altered and extended so often in its 700-year history that it now provides a unique insight into the history of Highland aristocratic life. The 18th-century wing, with its draughty Victorian passages hung with antlers, has a display containing the gloves and pipe of Bonnie Prince Charlie *(see p521)* who spent two days here gathering Jacobite *(see p523)* support. Family portraits cover 300 years and include paintings by such masters as Johann Zoffany and Sir Peter Lely. Sir Edwin Landseer's priceless *Death of a Stag in Glen Tilt* (1850) was painted nearby. In 1844 Queen Victoria visited the castle and conferred on its owners, the Dukes of Atholl, the distinction of being allowed to maintain a private army. The Atholl Highlanders still flourish.

THE MASSACRE OF GLENCOE

In 1692, the chief of the Glencoe MacDonalds was five days late in registering an oath of submission to William III, giving the government an excuse to root out a nest of Jacobite *(p523)* supporters. For ten days 130 soldiers, captained by Robert Campbell, were hospitably entertained by the unsuspecting MacDonalds. At dawn on 13 February, in a terrible breach of trust, the soldiers fell on their hosts, killing some 38 MacDonalds. Many more died in their wintry mountain hideouts. The massacre, unsurprisingly, became a political scandal, though there were to be no official reprimands for three years.

Detail of *The Massacre of Glencoe* by James Hamilton

The Cairngorms ㉓

See pp530–31.

Glencoe ㉔

Highland. *Fort William.* *Glencoe.* *Cameron Sq, Fort William (01397 703781).*

RENOWNED for its awesome scenery and savage history, Glencoe was compared by Dickens to "a burial ground of a race of giants". The precipitous cliffs of Buachaille Etive Mor and the knife-edged ridge of Aonach Eagach (both over 900 m; 3,000 ft) present a formidable challenge even to experienced mountaineers.

Against a dark backdrop of craggy peaks and the tumbling River Coe, the Glen offers superb hill-walking in the summer. Stout footwear, waterproofs and attention to safety warnings are essential. Details of routes, ranging from the easy half-hour between the **NTS Visitor Centre** and Signal Rock (from which the signal was given to commence the massacre) to a stiff 6 mile (10 km) haul up the Devil's Staircase can be had from the Visitor Centre. Guided walks are offered in summer by the NTS Ranger service.

NTS Visitor Centre
Ballachulish. *01855 811307.*
Mar–Oct: 10am–5pm daily.

The Cairngorms ㉒

Wild goat

Rising to a height of 1,309 m (4,296 ft), the Cairngorm mountains form the highest landmass in Britain. Cairn Gorm itself is the site of one of Britain's first ski centres. A weather station at the mountain's summit provides regular reports, essential in an area known for sudden changes of weather. Walkers should be sure to follow the mountain code without fail. The funicular railway that climbs Cairn Gorm affords superb views over the Spey Valley. Many estates in the valley have centres which introduce the visitor to Highland land use.

Strathspey Steam Railway
This track between Aviemore and Broomhill dates from 1863.

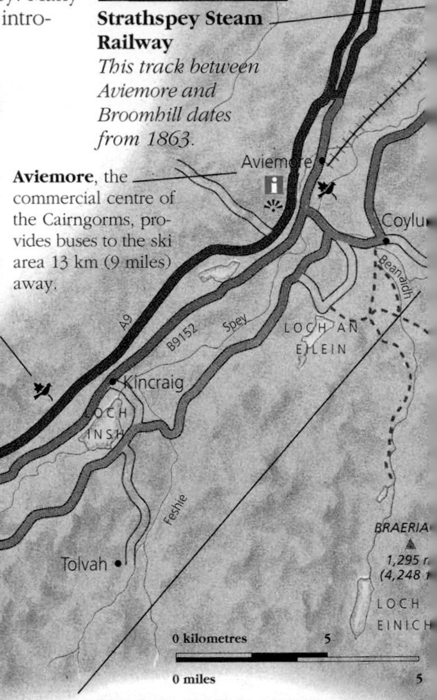

Aviemore, the commercial centre of the Cairngorms, provides buses to the ski area 13 km (9 miles) away.

Kincraig Highland Wildlife Park
Driving through this park, the visitor can see bison alongside wolves and wild boar. All of these animals were once common in the Highlands.

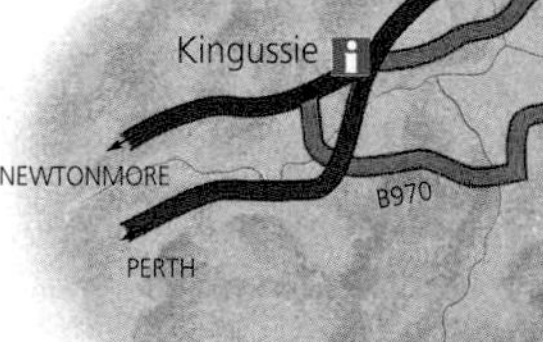

Rothiemurchus Estate
Highland cattle can be seen among many other creatures at Rothiemurchus. A visitor centre provides guided walks and illustrates life on a Highland estate.

The Cairngorms by Aviemore

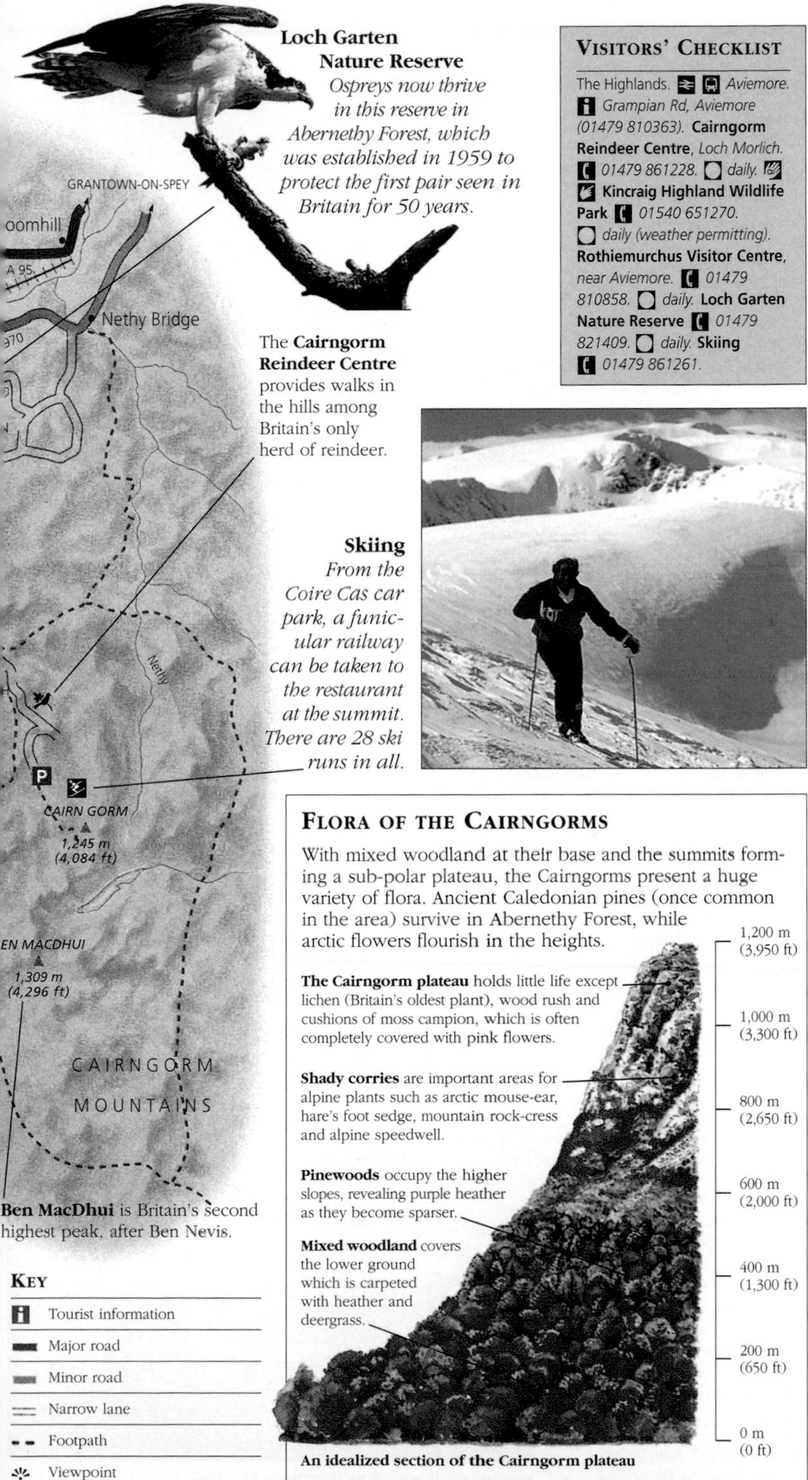

Loch Garten Nature Reserve

Ospreys now thrive in this reserve in Abernethy Forest, which was established in 1959 to protect the first pair seen in Britain for 50 years.

The **Cairngorm Reindeer Centre** provides walks in the hills among Britain's only herd of reindeer.

Skiing

From the Coire Cas car park, a funicular railway can be taken to the restaurant at the summit. There are 28 ski runs in all.

Ben MacDhui is Britain's second highest peak, after Ben Nevis.

Visitors' Checklist

The Highlands. *Aviemore.* *Grampian Rd, Aviemore (01479 810363).* **Cairngorm Reindeer Centre**, *Loch Morlich.* *01479 861228.* *daily.* **Kincraig Highland Wildlife Park** *01540 651270.* *daily (weather permitting).* **Rothiemurchus Visitor Centre**, *near Aviemore.* *01479 810858.* *daily.* **Loch Garten Nature Reserve** *01479 821409.* *daily.* **Skiing** *01479 861261.*

Flora of the Cairngorms

With mixed woodland at their base and the summits forming a sub-polar plateau, the Cairngorms present a huge variety of flora. Ancient Caledonian pines (once common in the area) survive in Abernethy Forest, while arctic flowers flourish in the heights.

The Cairngorm plateau holds little life except lichen (Britain's oldest plant), wood rush and cushions of moss campion, which is often completely covered with pink flowers.

Shady corries are important areas for alpine plants such as arctic mouse-ear, hare's foot sedge, mountain rock-cress and alpine speedwell.

Pinewoods occupy the higher slopes, revealing purple heather as they become sparser.

Mixed woodland covers the lower ground which is carpeted with heather and deergrass.

An idealized section of the Cairngorm plateau

Key

- Tourist information
- Major road
- Minor road
- Narrow lane
- Footpath
- Viewpoint

Road to the Isles Tour 25

THIS SCENIC ROUTE goes past vast mountain-corridors, breathtaking beaches of white sand and tiny villages, to the town of Mallaig, one of the ferry ports for the isles of Skye, Rum and Eigg. As well as the stunning scenery, the area is steeped in Jacobite history *(see p523)*.

TIPS FOR DRIVERS

Tour length: *45 miles (72 km).*
Stopping-off points: *Glenfinnan NTS Visitors' Centre (01397 722 250) explains the Jacobite risings and serves refreshments; the Old Library Lodge, Arisaig, has good Scottish food.* (See also pp636–7.)

Mallaig ⑦
The Road to the Isles ends at Mallaig, an active little fishing port with a very good harbour and one of the ferry links to Skye *(see pp520-21)*.

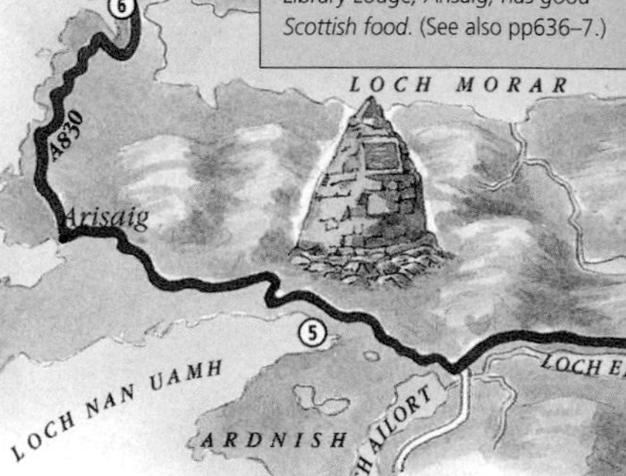

Morar ⑥
The road continues through Morar, an area renowned for its white sands, and Loch Morar, rumoured to be the home of a 12 m (40 ft) monster known as Morag.

Prince's Cairn ⑤
Crossing the Ardnish Peninsu to Loch Nan Uamh, a cairn marks the spot from which Bonnie Prince Charlie finally left Scotland for France in 174

Oban 26

Argyll & Bute. *8,500.* *Argyll Sq (01631 563122).* www.scottish-heartlands.org

LOCATED ON the Firth of Lorne and commanding a magnificent view of the Argyll coast, the bustling port of Oban is a popular destination for travellers on their way to Mull and the Western Isles *(see p515)*.

Dominating the skyline is McCaig's Tower, an unfinished Victorian imitation of the Colosseum in Rome. It is worth making the 10-minute climb from the town centre for the sea views alone. Attractions in the town include working centres for glass, pottery and whisky; the Oban distillery produces one of the country's finest malt whiskies *(see p475)*. The **Scottish Sealife Sanctuary** rescues injured and orphaned seals and has displays of underwater life. A busy harbour shelters car ferries going to Barra and South Uist, Mull, Tiree and Colonsay islands.

Scottish Sealife Sanctuary
Barcaldine. *01631 720386.* *daily (winter: phone to check).* www.sealsanctuary.co.uk

Mull 27

Argyll & Bute. *2,800.* *from Oban, Kilchoan, Lochaline.* *Main Street, Tobermory (01688 302182).*

MOST ROADS on this easily accessible Hebridean island follow the sharply indented rocky coastline, affording wonderful sea views. From Craignure, the Mull and West Highland Railway serves the baronial **Torosay Castle**. A pathway through its gardens is lined with statues, while inside, 19th-century furniture and paintings can be found. On a promontory to the east lies **Duart Castle**, home of the chief of Clan Maclean. Visitors can see the Banqueting Hall and State Rooms in the 13th-century keep. Its dungeons once held prisoners from a Spanish Armada galleon sunk by a Donald Maclean in 1588.

Looking out to sea across Tobermory Bay, Mull

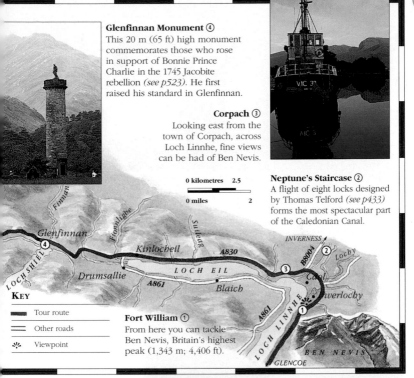

Glenfinnan Monument ④
This 20 m (65 ft) high monument commemorates those who rose in support of Bonnie Prince Charlie in the 1745 Jacobite rebellion *(see p523)*. He first raised his standard in Glenfinnan.

Corpach ③
Looking east from the town of Corpach, across Loch Linnhe, fine views can be had of Ben Nevis.

Neptune's Staircase ②
A flight of eight locks designed by Thomas Telford *(see p433)* forms the most spectacular part of the Caledonian Canal.

0 kilometres 2.5
0 miles 2

KEY

Tour route

Other roads

Viewpoint

Fort William ①
From here you can tackle Ben Nevis, Britain's highest peak (1,343 m; 4,406 ft).

ENVIRONS: From Fionnphort, a ferry goes to **Iona**, where St Columba *(see p511)* began his mission in Scotland in 563. North of Iona, the Isle of Staffa should be visited for its magnificent **Fingal's Cave**.

Torosay Castle
Off A849, Nr Craignure. *01680 812421.* **Castle** *Apr–mid-Oct: 10:30am–5:30pm daily.* **Gardens** *Apr–Sep: 9am–7pm; Oct–Mar: dawn–dusk; daily.* *for groups.*

Duart Castle
Off A849, nr Craignure. *01680 812309.* *May–mid-Oct: 10:30am–6pm daily.*

The ruins of Kilchurn Castle on the shore of Loch Awe

Loch Awe ㉘

Argyll & Bute. *Dalmally.* *Inveraray (01499 302063).*

ONE OF the longest of Scotland's freshwater lochs, Loch Awe fills a 25 mile (40 km) glen in the south-western Highlands. A short drive east of the village of Lochawe leads to the lochside remains of **Kilchurn Castle**, which was abandoned after being struck by lightning in the 18th century. Dwarfing the castle is the huge bulk of Ben Cruachan, whose summit can be reached by the narrow Pass of Brander, in which Robert the Bruce *(see p468)* fought the Clan MacDougal in 1308. From the A85, a tunnel leads to the cavernous Cruachan Power Station.

Near the village of Taynuilt the preserved Lorn Furnace at Bonawe is a reminder of the iron-smelting industry that caused the destruction of much of the area's woodland in the 18th and 19th centuries.

Marked prehistoric cairns are found off the A816 between Kilmartin and Dunadd. The latter boasts a 6th-century hill fort from which the Stone of Destiny *(see p468)* originated.

Inveraray Castle ㉙

Inveraray, Argyll & Bute. Arrochar, then bus. 01499 302203. Apr–Jun, Sep, Oct: Sat–Thu; Jul–Aug: daily 10am–5:45pm (Sun: pm). limited.

www.inveraray-castle.com

THIS MULTI-TURRETED mock Gothic palace is the family home of the powerful Clan Campbell who have been the Dukes of Argyll since 1701. The castle was built in 1745 by architects Roger Morris and William Adam on the ruins of a 15th-century castle, and the conical towers added later, after a fire in 1877. Magnificent interiors, designed by Robert Mylne in the 1770s, form a backdrop to a huge collection of Oriental and European porcelain and Regency furniture and portraits by Ramsay, Gainsborough and Raeburn. The Armoury Hall features a display of weaponry collected by the Campbells to fight the Jacobites *(see p523)*.

The pinnacled, Gothic exterior of Inveraray Castle

Auchindrain Museum ㉚

Inveraray, Argyll & Bute. 01499 500235. Inveraray, then bus. Apr–Sep: 10am–5pm daily. limited.

THE FIRST OPEN-AIR museum in Scotland, Auchindrain illuminates the working lives of the kind of farming community that was typical of the Highlands until the late 19th century. Originally a township of some 20 thatched buildings, the site was communally farmed by its tenants until the last one retired in 1962. Visitors can wander through the buildings, many of which combine living space, kitchen and cattle shed under one roof. Some of them are furnished with box beds and old rush lamps. The homes of Auchindrain are a quite fascinating memorial to the time before the transition from subsistence to commercial farming.

An old hay turner at the Auchindrain Museum

Crarae Gardens ㉛

Crarae, Argyll & Bute. 01546 886614 or NTS (0131 243 9300). Inveraray, then bus. Easter–Oct: 9am–6pm; Nov–Easter: 10am-dusk daily. limited.

www.crarae-gardens.org

CONSIDERED the most beguiling of the many gardens of the West Highlands, the **Crarae Gardens** were created in the 1920s by Lady Grace Campbell. She was the aunt of explorer Reginald Farrer, whose specimens from Tibet were the beginnings of a collection of exotic plants. The gardens are nourished by the warmth of the Gulf Stream and the high rainfall of the region. Although there are many unusual Himalayan rhododendrons flourishing here, the gardens are also home to exotic plants from Tasmania, New Zealand and the USA. Plant collectors still contribute to the gardens which are best seen in spring and early summer, against the blue waters of Loch Fyne.

Jura ㉜

Argyll & Bute. 200. from Kennacraig to Islay, then Islay to Jura. Bowmore (01496 810254).

BARREN, MOUNTAINOUS and overrun by red deer, the isle of Jura has only one road which connects the single village of Craighouse to the Islay ferry. Though walking is restricted during the stalking (deer hunting) season between August and October, the island offers superb hill-walking, especially on the slopes of the three main peaks, known as the Paps of Jura. The tallest of these is Beinn An Oir at 784 m (2571 ft). Beyond the northern tip of the isle are the notorious whirlpools of Corryvreckan. The novelist George Orwell (who came to the island to write his final novel, *1984*) nearly lost his life here in 1946 when he fell into the water. A legend tells

Lagavulin distillery, producer of one Scotland's finest malts, on Islay

Mist crowning the Paps of Jura, seen at sunset across the Sound of Islay

of Prince Breackan who, to win the hand of a princess, tried to keep his boat anchored in the whirlpool for three days, held by ropes made of hemp, wool and maidens' hair. The Prince drowned when a single rope, containing the hair of a girl who had been untrue, finally broke.

Islay ❸❸

Argyll & Bute. *3,500.* *from Kennacraig.* *The Square, Bowmore (0870-7200617).* www.isle-of-islay.com

THE MOST SOUTHERLY of the Western Isles, Islay (pronounced 'Eyeluh') is the home of respected Highland single malt whiskies Lagavulin and Laphroaig. Most of the island's distilleries produce heavily peated malts with a distinctive tang of the sea. The Georgian village of Bowmore has the island's oldest distillery and a circular church designed to minimize the Devil's possible lurking-places. The **Museum of Islay Life** in Port Charlotte contains fascinating information on social and natural history. Seven miles (11 km) east of Port Ellen stands the Kildalton Cross. A block of local green stone adorned with Old Testament scenes, it is one of the most impressive 8th-century Celtic crosses in Britain. Worth a visit for its archaeological and historical interest is the medieval stronghold of the Lords of the Isles, **Finlaggan**. Islay's beaches support a variety of bird life, some of which can be observed at the RSPB reserve at Gruinart.

Museum of Islay Life
Port Charlotte. *01496 850358.*
Easter–Oct: 10am–5pm Mon–Sat, 1–4pm Sun.

Kintyre ❸❹

Argyll & Bute. *6,000.* *Oban.* *Campbeltown.* *MacKinnon House, The Pier, Campbeltown (01586 552056).*

A LONG, NARROW PENINSULA stretching far south of Glasgow, Kintyre has superb views across to the islands of Gigha, Islay and Jura. The 9 mile (14 km) Crinan Canal, opened in 1801, is a delightful inland waterway, its 15 locks bustling with pleasure craft in the summer. The town of Tarbert (meaning "isthmus" in Gaelic) takes its name from the neck on which it stands, which is narrow enough to drag a boat across between Loch Fyne and West Loch Tarbert. This feat was first achieved by the Viking King Magnus Barfud who, in 1198, was granted by treaty as much land as he could sail around. Travelling south past Campbeltown, the B842 ends at the headland known as the Mull of Kintyre, which was made famous when former Beatle Paul McCartney commercialized a traditional pipe tune of the same name. Westward lies the isle of Rathlin, where Robert the Bruce *(see p468)* learned patience in his struggles against the English by watching a spider weaving a web in a cave.

Fishing boats and yachts moored at Tarbert harbour, Kintyre

THE GREYHOU

Travellers' Needs

Where to Stay 538-573

Where to Eat 574-611

Where to Stay

Whatever your budget or accommodation preferences, you should be able to find somewhere to suit you from the large choice given in the hotel listings section that follows *(see pp542–73)*. The listings include over 370 suggestions, ranging from palatial five-star establishments to humble guest-houses. The common factor in this selection is that they are all, we believe, good of their kind, offering distinctive character or exceptional qualities of hospitality, facilities or value for money. Location is another prime consideration for inclusion. All the hotels and guesthouses listed make convenient touring bases for one or more of the destinations featured in this book, or have attractive or interesting settings enjoyable in their own right. On the next few pages we outline some of the types of accommodation available in Britain, along with various aspects of choosing, booking and paying for somewhere to stay.

Hilton doorman, London

Country-House Hotels

The quintessentially British country-house hotel has proliferated in the last few decades. Many indifferent hotels try and claim the title with a cursory decorative makeover, but the genuine article stands head and shoulders above them. Individual examples vary widely, but the best country-house hotels are usually set in buildings of architectural or historic interest filled with antiques or high-quality traditional furnishings. They generally have extensive grounds, but are not always in deeply rural locations. Comfort, even luxury, is assured, along with good food and service – frequently with a high price tag. Many such hotels are still owned and personally managed by resident proprietors; others belong to groups or chains.

Boutique and Designer Hotels

There is a new breed of sophisticated, contemporary hotel that has been making waves in Britain for some years now. These ultra-cool temples of style revel in innovative architecture, funky décor and hip high-tech gadgetry. Most exude an air of uncluttered minimalism, and some have outstanding restaurants. The best-known examples are perhaps in London (the Hempel, *p542*, for instance, or the Sanderson, *p544*), but they can be found elsewhere too, usually in city centres. Trend-setting, upmarket micro-chains like Malmaison or **Hotel du Vin** could perhaps be included in this category. Most of these hotels are expensive, but facilities, furnishings, service and privacy justify the cost.

Buckland Manor *(see p555)*, Worcestershire

Atholl Palace Hotel *(see p572)*

Hotel Groups

New hotel groups have taken the place of many of the long-established names, providing reliably standardized accommodation at all price levels in most parts of Britain. The majority of chain hotels (operated by the same company under identical corporate branding) lie in accessible, convenient locations. Though lacking in much individuality, they are practical and efficiently run, and usually represent good value for money.

Budget chains offering no-frills, motel-lodge-style accommodation include **Ibis**, Travelodge and Premier Lodge; further up the scale are mid-market chains like Holiday Inn or **Novotel.** Chain-hotel rates generally don't include breakfast, but look out for inclusive leisure-

◁ **The 11th-century ruins of Corfe Castle, Dorset**

The Swan, Suffolk *(see p548)*, a converted coaching inn

break rates at pricier chains like De Vere or Moat House.

Hotel consortiums – groups of similar but individually owned hotels which market themselves under the same umbrella – include **Best Western** and **Pride of Britain.** There's also **Wolsey Lodges**, a group of private houses, many beautifully furnished and often sited in buildings of notable architectural or historic interest.

Inns and Pubs with Rooms

The coaching inn is a familiar concept in Britain. Many of these fine old hostelries date from the 18th century, though some are even older, such as The George of Stamford *(see p559)*, and often provide reliable restaurants, traditional décor and a warm and friendly atmosphere.

Other types of pub or inn now offer accommodation and reputable food, and many have become much more welcoming to families. Britain's best inns are very comfortable and stylish and bear comparison with any good hotel. Some budget hotel chains, such as Travel Inn or Innkeeper's Lodge, specialize in adding purpose-built accommodation blocks to existing branded dining pubs like Beefeater or Vintage Inns.

Bed-and-Breakfasts and Guest Houses

The B*B is probably the best-known and certainly the most widely used type of budget accommodation in Britain. These establishments are generally family-owned private homes or farmhouses. Accommodation and facilities tend to be simple (bedrooms may not have TV, telephones, or en-suite bathrooms, for instance), but the best can be quite sophisticated. Prices include breakfast (generally a traditional British fry-up, but other options are usually available as well).

Many B&Bs are reluctant to accept credit cards or travellers' cheques, or may charge a premium for doing so. It's advisable to have some alternative method of payment, preferably cash or, for British nationals, a personal cheque backed by a cheque guarantee card. Any regional tourist office should be able to supply a list of local registered B&Bs on request, though they cannot make specific recommendations, and may charge a fee or a commission for making bookings on your behalf.

Hotel Gradings

Recent but only partially successful attempts have been made to harmonize the confusing and often conflicting systems of accommodation classification used by the various tourist boards and motoring organizations, such as the AA and RAC. In England, hotel gradings are now based on a system of one to five stars awarded for facilities and service (the more stars, the more luxurious you can expect your hotel to be). Guesthouses and B&Bs are graded with one to five diamonds, a quality score which is based on various aspects of the accommodation, including cleanliness and hospitality. Special awards (gold and silver, ribbons, rosettes, eggcups, etc) are given for excellence in certain categories, such as an exceptional breakfast or a warm welcome. Scotland and Wales have their own quality-based gradings.

Hintlesham Hall, Suffolk *(see p548)*

Prices and Bookings

Make sure you understand clearly what terms you are being offered when you book. Some hotels just quote room rates, others quote a B&B or half board (dinner, bed and breakfast) rate per person. Rates are generally inclusive of VAT and service but some top-range hotels make additional charges; most charge hefty single-person supplements.

Prices in London start at around £80 per night for a standard en-suite double room, including breakfast, but could be well over £200 (without breakfast) at the top end of the scale. Outside London, expect to pay upward of around £60 for facilities of a similar standard.

The elegant hallway of the Gore Hotel in London ***(see p542)***

Bed-and-breakfast accommodation outside London starts from around £35 per person per night (though prices vary seasonally and regionally). Farm guesthouses (which often include dinner) can be very good value, at around £30 for half board per person.

Most hotels request confirmation in writing and a deposit in advance (a credit card number will generally do). E-mail bookings are now commonplace, and some hotels have an on-line booking facility. Websites are usually updated more often than hotel brochures and tariffs. Business or chain hotels often give big discounts; contact central reservations as well as the hotel itself to see which one will give you the best deal.

The folly of Doyden Castle, Cornwall, now a National Trust holiday cottage

A hotel booking, whether made by telephone or in writing, is a legally binding contract. If you don't show up, the full cost of your stay may be charged. Most hotels will refund your deposit if they are able to relet the room, but some will charge a penalty, depending how close to your stay you cancel. Most annual travel insurance policies cover cancellation charges for pre-booked UK hotel stays of more than two days, provided you have a satisfactory reason.

Watch out for those hidden extras. Telephone charges from hotel rooms are a very common cause of complaint; most hotels charge a high mark-up, and rates quoted per unit do not always indicate too clearly how much time you get for your money. Consider using a lobby payphone instead. Certain chains have a regrettable policy of charging meals or other extras to your credit card weeks after you have left the hotel; check your card statement carefully.

Roadside signboard for bed-and-breakfast

There is no need to tip staff unless they go out of their way to perform some very exceptional duty, such as booking theatre tickets or restaurants for you.

Self Catering

Self catering has many attractions, especially for families on a budget and with young children. Tourist boards give accommodation a one to five star rating for quality and facilities, much the same as for hotels. The range of places to let for holiday rentals is huge, from luxury apartments to log cabins or converted farm buildings. Character properties are available from conservation organizations such as the **Landmark Trust**, which restores buildings of historic or architectural interest and makes them available for short-term lets, or the **National Trust** *(see p25)*, which has a number of holiday cottages on its estates. They tend to be very popular, so book well ahead.

Annually updated self-catering guides are a useful source of listings. Also try specialist agencies, tour operators and the small ads in newspapers. Tourist offices can supply up-to-date regional lists and can also offer a booking service.

Confirm what is included in the price (cleaning, electricity, etc.) and check whether any extra fees, deposits or insurance charges will be added to the bill.

Caravanning, Camping and Motor Homes

Most of Britain's campsites and caravan (trailer) parks open only for about six months of the year (typically from Easter to October), but you will need to make reservations in advance. Helpful organizations in Britain include the **Camping and Caravanning Club** and the Caravan Club, which publish lists of their member parks and operate their own grading systems. Camping or caravanning pitches typically cost between £6 and £10 per night. The **Forestry Commission** operates a number of sites in scenic woodland locations throughout the UK.

Motor homes give greater freedom to explore at your own pace and a wider choice of places to stay – including most campsites and caravan parks. Some operators will let you pick up your vehicle directly from an airport or ferry terminal. The **Motor Caravanners' Club** produces a useful monthly magazine.

Campsite, Ogwen Valley, Snowdonia

Disabled Travellers

All the UK's tourist boards now provide detailed information about disabled access in their accommodation and sight-seeing guides, and can send further information on request. National Accessible Scheme gradings are awarded to properties inspected and approved under the Tourism for All initiative for various categories of disability.

For more information on these gradings, or other advice on accommodation and travel for disabled visitors, contact **Holiday Care**. Another useful organization is **RADAR** (the Royal Association for Disability and Rehabilitation), which publishes a yearly *Holidays in the British Isles: A Guide for Disabled People*. The listings on pp542–73 indicate which hotels have wheelchair access, but you are strongly advised to check when booking that it matches your needs. The same is true of camping and caravan sites.

Directory

For useful information on all types of accommodation, see
W www.visitbritain.com

Hotels

Accor Hotels
(Ibis, Novotel)
T *020-8237 7474.*
W www.accorhotels.com

Best Western
Amy Johnson Way, Clifton Moor, York, YO30 4GP.
T *08457 747474.* *(central reservations).*
W www.bestwestern.co.uk

Hilton International
Hilton Reservations Worldwide, 4 Cadogan Sq., Cadogan St Glasgow G2 7PH.
T *020-8897 6644.*
W www.hilton.com

Hotel du Vin
12 Southgate Street, Winchester, Hants, SO23 9EF. T *01962 850676.*
W www.hotelduvin.com

Pride of Britain
Cowage Farm, Foxley Wiltshire, SN16 0JH.
T *0870-609 3012.*
W www.prideofbritainhotels.com

Wolsey Lodges
9 Market Place, Hadleigh, Ipswich, Suffolk, IP7 5DL.
T *01473 822058.*
W www.wolsey-lodges.co.uk

Caravanning, Camping and Motor Homes

Camping and Caravanning Club
Westwood Way, Coventry, West Midlands, CV4 8JH.
T *01203 694995.*
W www.campingandcaravanningclub.co.uk

Forestry Commission
231 Corstorphine Road, Edinburgh, EH12 7AT.
T *0131 334 0303.*
W www.forestry.gsi.gov.uk

Motor Caravanners' Club
Freepost, TK1292 Twickenham TW2 5BR.
T *020-8893 3883.*
W www.motorcaravanners.org.uk

Self-Catering

Landmark Trust
Shottesbrooke, Maidenhead, Berkshire SL6 3SW.
T *01628 825925.*
W www.landmarktrust.co.uk

National Trust
PO Box 39, Bromley, Kent BR1 3XL.
T *0870 458 4000.*
W www.nationaltrust.org.uk

National Trust for Scotland
Wemyss Hse, 28 Charlotte Square, Edinburgh EH2 4ET.
T *0131 243 9300.*
W www.nts.org.uk

Snowdonia Tourist Services
High Street, Porthmadog, Gwynedd LL49 9PG.
T *01766 513829.*
W www.sts-holidays.com

Disabled Travellers

Holiday Care
7th flr, Sunley Hse, 4 Bedford Pk, Croydon CR0 2AP.
T *0845 124 9971.*
W www.holidaycare.org.uk

RADAR
Unit 12, City Forum, 250 City Road, London, EC1V 8AF.
T *020-7250 3222.*
W www.radar.org.uk

Choosing a Hotel

THE HOTELS in this guide have been selected across a wide price range for their excellent facilities and locations. Many also have a recommended restaurant. The chart lists the hotels by region, starting with London; colour-coded thumb tabs indicate the regions covered on each page. For restaurant listings, see pp574–607.

LONDON

Hotel	Credit Cards	Restaurant	Children Welcome	Garden/Terrace	Number of Rooms
PADDINGTON: *Delmere.* **Map** 2 E1. www.delmerehotels.com ££ 130 Sussex Gardens W2. *020 7706 3344.* FAX *020 7262 1863.* A well-managed welcoming hotel that stands out in a street packed with budget accommodation. Bedrooms are small but tidy.	AE DC MC V	■			36
PADDINGTON: *Mornington.* **Map** 2 E1. www.mornington.com £££ 12 Lancaster Gate, W2. *020 7262 7361.* FAX *020 7706 1028.* Cool bedrooms contrast with the masculine clubbiness of the bar at this Swedish hotel which offers *Smorgasbord* buffet breakfasts.	AE DC MC V		●		66
PADDINGTON: *Hempel.* **Map** 2 E1. www.the-hempel.co.uk £££££ 31 Craven Hill Gardens, W2. *020 7298 9000.* FAX *020 7402 4666.* Anouska Hempel's ultra-chic design statement combines innovative decor, superb service and state-of-the-art technology.	AE DC	■	●		46
NOTTING HILL: *Abbey Court.* **Map** 1 B2. www.abbeycourthotel.co.uk £££ 20 Pembridge Gardens, W2. *020 7221 7518.* FAX *020 7720 0858.* Quiet rooms furnished with books and personal touches mark this Victorian townhouse near Notting Hill Gate.	AE DC MC V		●	■	24
NOTTING HILL: *Pembridge Court.* **Map** 1 B2. www.pemct.co.uk ££££ 34 Pembridge Gardens, W2. *020 7229 9977.* FAX *020 7727 4982.* A family-run hotel full of Victorian curios. A ginger cat, Churchill, welcomes visitors.	AE DC MC V		●		20
NOTTING HILL: *Portobello.* **Map** 1 A2. www.portobello-hotel.co.uk ££££ 22 Stanley Gardens, W11. *020 7727 2777.* FAX *020 7792 9641.* Eccentric place that has an exotic, sophisticated decor – a mix of Victorian and Edwardian periods. Rooms range from tiny to lavish. *23 Dec–1 Jan.*	AE MC V	■	●		24
KENSINGTON: *Abbey House.* **Map** 1 C3. www.abbeyhousekensington.com £ 11 Vicarage Gate, W8. *020 7727 2594.* FAX *020 7727 1873.* Once a Victorian family home, now a no-frills bed-and-breakfast. Rooms though spacious are simply furnished without *en suite* bathrooms.			●		16
KENSINGTON: *Kensington House.* **Map** 2 D5. www.kenhouse.com £££ 15–16 Prince of Wales Terrace, W8. *020 7937 2345.* FAX *020 7368 6700.* This smart, newly opened townhouse hotel combines period interest with understated contemporary style.	AE DC MC V	■	●		41
KENSINGTON: *The Gore.* **Map** 2 D5. www.gorehotel.com £££££ 189 Queen's Gate, SW7. *020 7584 6601.* FAX *020 7589 8127.* This idiosyncratic Victorian hotel is over a pair of chic restaurants. Bedrooms vary from tiny singles to Tudor fantasies with their own minstrels' galleries. Charming service.	AE DC MC V	■	●		53
KNIGHTSBRIDGE: *Basil Street.* **Map** 5 A3. www.thebasil.com £££££ 8 Basil St, SW3. *020 7581 3311.* FAX *020 7581 3693.* An enduringly popular hotel just off Sloane Street. It has a long history and lots of personality. Its brasserie-wine bar is superb and very good value for this expensive area.	AE DC MC V	■	●		80
KNIGHTSBRIDGE: *Beaufort.* **Map** 5 A3. www.thebeaufort.co.uk £££££ 33 Beaufort Gardens, SW3. *020 7584 5252.* FAX *020 7589 2834.* An aristocratic hideaway in a quiet square with beautifully decorated rooms. Room service and free health club membership.	AE MC V		●		29
KNIGHTSBRIDGE: *Halkin.* **Map** 5 A3. www.halkin.co.uk £££££ 5 Halkin St, SW1. *020 7333 1000.* FAX *020 7333 1100.* Sophisticated Italian design with Oriental touches makes this hotel a startling experience. The Thai restaurant overlooks a courtyard.	AE DC MC V	■	●	■	41

Price categories for a standard double room per night, inclusive of breakfast, service charges and any additional taxes such as VAT:

- £ under £65
- ££ £65–£100
- £££ £100–£150
- ££££ £150–£200
- £££££ £200 plus

RESTAURANT
Hotel restaurant or dining room serving more than just breakfast; often open to non-residents.

CHILDREN WELCOME
Especially welcoming to families. May have children's facilities such as cots, babysitting, family rooms, etc.

GARDEN/TERRACE
Hotels with a garden, courtyard or terrace, often providing tables for eating outside.

CREDIT CARDS
Indicates which credit cards are accepted: *AE* American Express; *DC* Diners Club; *MC* Master Card/Access; *V* Visa.

Hotel	Credit Cards	Restaurant	Children Welcome	Garden/Terrace	Number of Rooms
SOUTH KENSINGTON: *Five Sumner Place.* **Map** 2 E5. £££ 5 Sumner Place, SW7. Tel. *020 7584 7586.* W www.sumnerplace.com A small, award-winning hotel with a quiet, courteous welcome and good facilities. Breakfast is served with complimentary newspapers. TV	AE MC V		●		13
SOUTH KENSINGTON: *Blakes.* **Map** 2 E5. W www.blakeshotels.com £££££ 33 Roland Gardens, SW7. Tel. *020 7370 6701.* Fax *020 7373 0442.* Opulent hotel, each room a fantasy of natural materials and antiques. Secluded gardens and an Oriental-style restaurant. TV	AE MC V	■	●	■	49
VICTORIA: *Morgan House.* **Map** 5 B4. W www.morganhouse.co.uk £ 120 Ebury St, SW1. Tel. *020 7730 2384.* Fax *020 7730 8442.* This stylish budget B&B in a Georgian terrace has light, modern decor; just four rooms have private bathrooms. TV	MC V		●		11
VICTORIA: *Tophams Belgravia.* **Map** 5 B4. W www.tophams.co.uk £££ 28 Ebury St, SW1. Tel. *020 7730 8147.* Fax *020 7823 5966.* Several adjacent townhouses make up this classy hotel. Family heirlooms deck cosy public rooms. TV	AE DC MC V	■	●		39
VICTORIA: *Windermere.* **Map** 5 C4. W www.windermere-hotel.co.uk £££ 142–144 Warwick Way, SW1. Tel. *020 7834 5163.* Fax *020 7630 8831.* Inexpensive, friendly hotel, ten minutes' walk from Victoria Station. Lovely breakfast room which doubles as a dining room. Light, clean bedrooms. Helpful service. TV	AE MC V	■	●		22
VICTORIA: *Goring.* **Map** 5 B4. W www.goringhotel.co.uk £££££ 15 Beeston Place, SW1. Tel. *020 7396 9000.* Fax *020 7834 4393.* Fine Belgravia hotel with elegant furnishings and a warm welcome. Immaculate gardens make a pleasant backdrop. TV P	AE DC MC V	■		■	74
WESTMINSTER: *Dolphin Square.* **Map** 6 D5. ££££ Chichester St, SW1. Tel. *020 7834 3800.* W www.dolphinsquarehotel.co.uk A smart complex of suites and studios near the Tate Britain. Facilities include gardens, sports courts, a swimming pool, a shopping mall, a Gary Rhodes restaurant and a brasserie. TV P	AE DC MC V	■	●	■	148
ST JAMES'S: *22 Jermyn Street.* **Map** 6 D1. W www.22jermyn.com £££££ 22 Jermyn St, SW1. Tel. *020 7734 2353.* Fax *020 7734 0750.* A luxurious complex of suites and studios with round-the-clock service, a video library and use of the nearby health club. TV	AE DC MC V		●		18
MAYFAIR: *Chesterfield.* **Map** 6 D1. W www.redcarnationhotels.com ££££ 35 Charles St, W1. Tel. *020 7491 2622.* Fax *020 7491 4793.* This quiet, well-kept place near Berkeley Square is decked with fruit and flowers, bedrooms are deluxe and staff welcoming. TV P	AE DC MC V	■	●		110
MAYFAIR: *Brown's.* **Map** 6 D1. W www.brownshotel.com £££££ Albemarle St, W1. Tel. *020 7493 6020.* Fax *020 7493 9381.* A long-established and highly traditional hotel which rambles through 11 townhouses and offers classic bedrooms. TV	AE DC MC V	■	●		118
OXFORD STREET & SOHO: *Edward Lear.* **Map** 3 5A. W www.edlear.com ££ 28–30 Seymour St, W1. Tel. *020 7402 5401.* Fax *020 7706 3766.* Clean, simple bed-and-breakfast, once the home of the author Edward Lear. Single travellers and families are made very welcome. TV	MC V		●		31
OXFORD STREET & SOHO: *Durrants.* **Map** 3 A4. £££ George St, W1. Tel. *020 7935 8131.* Fax *020 7487 3510.* W www.durrantshotel.co.uk Georgian hotel that still has the feel of the old coaching inn it once was. The look is of old leather and wood. Bedrooms are unfussy. TV	AE MC V	■	●		92

For key to symbols see back flap

Price categories for a standard double room per night, inclusive of breakfast, service charges and any additional taxes such as VAT:
£ under £65
££ £65–£100
£££ £100–£150
££££ £150–£200
£££££ £200 plus

RESTAURANT
Hotel restaurant or dining room serving more than just breakfast; often open to non-residents.

CHILDREN WELCOME
Especially welcoming to families. May have children's facilities such as cots, babysitting, family rooms, etc.

GARDEN/TERRACE
Hotels with a garden, courtyard or terrace, often providing tables for eating outside.

CREDIT CARDS
Indicates which credit cards are accepted: *AE* American Express; *DC* Diners Club; *MC* Master Card/Access; *V* Visa.

	Credit Cards	Restaurant	Children Welcome	Garden/Terrace	Number of Rooms
OXFORD STREET & SOHO: *Hazlitt's.* **Map** 3 A4. £££££ 6 Frith St, W1. *020 7434 1771.* FAX *020 7439 1524.* W www.hazlittshotel.com Three 18th-century houses in the heart of Soho make a peaceful bolthole, for artistic temperaments of many kinds. The interior is furnished with Victorian antiques with mod cons unobtrusively incorporated. TV	AE DC MC V				23
OXFORD STREET & SOHO: *Sanderson.* **Map** 3 A4. £££££ 50 Berners St, W1. *020 7300 1400.* FAX *020 7300 1401.* W www.lanschragerhotels.com One of London's sleekest hotels. Decor is truly eye-catching with courtyard, fountains and voguish bedrooms. TV	AE DC MC V	■	●	■	150
BLOOMSBURY: *Generator.* **Map** 4 D3. W www.the-generator.co.uk £ 37 Tavistock Place, WC1. *020 7388 7666.* FAX *020 7388 7644.* Somewhere between sci-fi and industrial chic, this youth-orientated hostel provides budget solutions for impecunious travellers.	MC V	■	●		200
BLOOMSBURY: *Academy.* **Map** 4 D3. W www.etontownhouse.com £££ 21 Gower St, WC1. *020 7631 4115.* FAX *020 7636 3442.* Five Georgian townhouses near the heart of London University. Inside, the ambience is sophisticated without excess. TV	AE DC MC V		●		49
BLOOMSBURY: *Charlotte Street.* **Map** 4 E4. £££££ 15 Charlotte St, W1. *020 7806 2000.* W www.firmdale.com The "Bloomsbury" theme incorporates original period art in the spacious. public areas, while bedrooms run to mini-TV screens in the granite bathrooms and exemplary high-tech facilities. TV	AE DC MC V	■	●	■	52
COVENT GARDEN & STRAND: *Fielding.* **Map** 4 F5. ££ 4 Broad Court, Bow St, WC2. *020 7836 8305.* W www.the-fielding-hotel.co.uk A good-value hotel near the Royal Opera House with limited but clean facilities. No meals served; no children under 12. TV	AE DC MC V				24
COVENT GARDEN & STRAND: *Covent Garden.* **Map** 4 E5. £££££ 10 Monmouth St, WC2. *020 7806 1000.* FAX *020 7806 1100.* W www.firmdale.com A discreet but theatrical hotel on one of Covent Garden's most interesting streets. A tour-de-force of dramatic interior design. TV	AE MC V	■	●		58
COVENT GARDEN & STRAND: *One Aldwych.* **Map** 4 F5. £££££ Aldwych, WC2. *020 7300 1000.* FAX *020 7300 1001.* W www.onealdwych.co.uk Filled with contemporary works of art, every inch of this hotel is imaginative, with well-thought out rooms. Underwater classical music plays in the swimming pool. TV P	AE DC MC V	■	●		105
COVENT GARDEN & STRAND: *Savoy.* **Map** 4 F5. £££££ Strand, WC2. *020 7836 4343.* FAX *020 7240 6040.* W www.savoy-group.co.uk Flamboyant Art Deco hotel with glorious waterfront views, combining period character with modern comforts. TV P	AE DC MC V	■	●	■	265
REGENTS PARK & MARYLEBONE: *Dorset Square.* **Map** 3 A3. ££££ 39–40 Dorset Sq, NW1. *020 7723 7874.* FAX *020 7724 3328.* W www.firmdale.com Beautifully restored Regency building with antiques, overlooking an 18th-century square. Rooms have character; service is friendly. TV	AE MC V	■	●		38
WATERLOO & SOUTHWARK: *Travel Inn County Hall.* **Map** 6 F3. £ Belvedere Rd, SE1. *0870 238 3300.* FAX *020 7902 1619.* W www.travelinn.co.uk Excellent value in the old GLC building next to the London Eye. Practical and spacious rooms (breakfast not included). Book in advance. TV	AE DC MC V	■	●		313
WATERLOO & SOUTHWARK: *Novotel Waterloo.* **Map** 6 F3. £££ 113 Lambeth Rd, SE1. *020 7793 1010.* FAX *020 7793 0202.* W www.novotel.com Good for families – two children stay free when they share parents' rooms. Front rooms have views of Lambeth Palace and Westminster.	AE DC MC V	■	●		187

Hotel	Cards				
CITY: *Novotel Tower Bridge.* **Map** 8 E3. W www.novotel.com ££££ 10 Pepys St, EC3. *020 7265 6000.* FAX *020 7265 6060.* This newly opened chain hotel in a fascinating part of London has well-equipped pleasing bedrooms. Good value for families. TV	AE DC MC V	■	●	■	203
CITY: *Great Eastern.* **Map** 8 E2. W www.great-eastern-hotel.co.uk £££££ Liverpool St, EC2. *020 7618 5000.* FAX *020 7618 5001.* A restoration of Liverpool Street's grand railway hotel with smart restaurants and elegant bedrooms. TV	AE DC MC	■	●		267
CITY: *Rookery.* **Map** 8 E2. W www.rookeryhotel.com £££££ Peter's Lane, Cowcross St, EC1. *020 7336 0931.* FAX *020 7336 0932.* Lovingly restored B&B in several 18th-century town houses near Smithfield market. All rooms have handsome period furnishings. TV	AE DC MC V		●		33
CANARY WHARF: *Four Seasons Canary Wharf* £££££ 46 Westferry Circus, E14. *020 7510 1999.* W www.fourseasons.com A stunning complex with superb waterfront views and facilities. The Holmes Place leisure centre is just next door. TV P	AE DC MC V	■	●		142
HAMPSTEAD: *La Gaffe* W www.lagaffe.co.uk ££ 107–111 Heath St, NW3. *020 7435 8965.* FAX *020 7794 7592.* A cheerful, family-run Italian restaurant-with-rooms, in the heart of Hampstead village. Bedrooms are simple but pretty. TV	AE MC V	■	●		18
THE DOWNS AND CHANNEL COAST					
BATTLE: *Fox Hole Farm* £ Kane Hythe Rd, Battle, E Sussex TN33 9QU. & FAX *01424 772053.* Deep in the Sussex countryside, this delightful farmhouse offers a bucolic but stylish B&B experience, with light evening meals by arrangement. Self-catering cottages available. *Christmas.* TV P	MC V			■	3
BEAULIEU: *Master Builder's House* W www.themasterbuilders.co.uk ££££ Buckler's Hard, Beaulieu, Hampshire SO42 7XB. *01590 616253.* FAX *01590 616297.* The former home of a ship builder enjoys a stunning waterfront location. Recently refurbished, it is comfortable and charming inside. Bedrooms in the main building have most character. TV P	AE MC V	■		■	25
BILLINGSHURST: *Old Wharf* @ david.mitchell@farming.co.uk ££ Newbridge, Wisborough Green, Billingshurst, W Sussex RH14 0HG. & FAX *01403 784096.* A fascinating canal-side warehouse imaginatively converted into a B&B. Tasteful décor, immaculate bedrooms and restful views. Swimming pool, tennis, fishing. Cash and cheques only. *Christmas & New Year.* TV P				■	3
BRIGHTON: *Dove Waldorf* £ 18 Regency Sq, Brighton, E Sussex BN1 2FG. 01273 779222. FAX 01273 746912. A bright and friendly guesthouse in an elegant square near the seafront. Bedrooms vary; best are at the front. TV	AE MC V		●		9
BRIGHTON: *Pelirocco* W www.hotelpelirocco.co.uk £££ 10 Regency Sq, Brighton, E Sussex BN1 2 FG. *01273 327055.* FAX *01273 733845.* Funkily themed bedrooms and hip young staff attract a trendy clientele to this unconventional interpretation of a Georgian townhouse. TV	AE DC MC V				19
CANTERBURY: *Magnolia House* W freespace.virgin.net/magnolia.canterbury ££ 36 St Dunstans Terrace, Canterbury, Kent CT2 8AX. & FAX *01227 765121.* High standards are constantly maintained in this trim B&B. Dinner by arrangement in winter. TV P	AE DC MC V			■	7
CANTERBURY: *The Falstaff* W www.corushotels.com/thefalstaff £££ 8–10 St Dunstan's St, Canterbury, Kent CT2 8AF. *01227 462138.* FAX *01227 463525.* This 15th-century coaching inn by the West Gate barbican has been efficiently but sympathetically modernized with contemporary colour-schemes and business facilities. TV P	AE DC MC V	■		■	47
EASTBOURNE: *Grand* W www.grandeastbourne.com ££££ King Edwards Parade, Eastbourne, E Sussex BN21 4EQ. *01323 412345.* FAX *01323 412233.* This splendid institution, after recent renovation, maintains the same dignity and high standards as always. It now has indoor and outdoor pools and a spa. Acclaimed restaurant, and welcoming staff. TV P	AE DC MC V	■	●	■	152

For key to symbols see back flap

Price categories for a standard double room per night, inclusive of breakfast, service charges and any additional taxes such as VAT:
£ under £65
££ £65–£100
£££ £100–£150
££££ £150–£200
£££££ £200 plus

Restaurant
Hotel restaurant or dining room serving more than just breakfast; often open to non-residents.

Children Welcome
Especially welcoming to families. May have children's facilities such as cots, babysitting, family rooms, etc.

Garden/Terrace
Hotels with a garden, courtyard or terrace, often providing tables for eating outside.

Credit Cards
Indicates which credit cards are accepted: *AE* American Express; *DC* Diners Club; *MC* Master Card/Access; *V* Visa.

	Credit Cards	Restaurant	Children Welcome	Garden/Terrace	Number of Rooms
East Grinstead: *Gravetye Manor* www.gravetyemanor.co.uk £££££ Vowels Lane, East Grinstead, W Sussex RH19 4LJ. *01342 810567.* FAX *01342 810080.* A truly splendid country house, tastefully furnished and surrounded by glorious gardens. Save this one for a real treat – you'll remember it for more than the bill, especially its superb cooking *(see also p583).* TV P	MC V	■	●	■	18
Guildford: *Angel Posting House & Livery* www.slh.com ££££ 91 High St, Guildford, Surrey GU1 3DP. *01483 564555.* FAX *01483 533770.* A historic hostelry on the London–Portsmouth coaching route. The interior is traditional, atmospheric, handsome. Vaulted cellar restaurant. TV	AE DC MC V		●		21
Lewes: *Millers* www.hometown.aol.com/millers134 ££ 134 High St, Lewes, E Sussex BN7 1XS. *01273 475631.* With just two rooms, it's advisable to book ahead for this idiosyncratic bed-and-breakfast in the town centre. The house dates from the 16th century. TV		■	●	■	2
Lewes: *Shelleys* www.shelleys-hotel-lewes.com ££££ 137 High St, Lewes, E Sussex BN7 1XS. *01273 472361.* FAX *01273 483152.* Once an aristocratic manor house, Shelleys has more than a touch of class, especially during the Glyndebourne opera season. TV P	AE DC MC V	■	●	■	19
New Milton: *Chewton Glen* www.chewtonglen.com £££££ Christchurch Rd, New Milton, Hampshire BH25 6QS. *01425 275341.* FAX *01425 272310.* Everything is geared towards pampering at this luxury establishment deep in the forest. For energetic activity, wonderful food or sybaritic relaxation, this hotel is hard to match. Indoor and outdoor pools *(see also p583).* TV P	AE DC MC V	■	●	■	59
Ringlestone: *Ringlestone Inn* www.ringlestone.com £££ Ringlestone, Maidstone, Kent ME17 1NX. *01622 859900.* FAX *01622 859966.* A cosy village inn, popular with non-residents for its food and old-world charm. Bedrooms are in separate annexes. Extensive, attractively landscaped grounds. Handy for exploring North Kent and the Medway Valley. TV P	AE DC MC V	■	●	■	9
Ringwood: *Moortown Lodge* www.moortownlodge.co.uk ££ 244 Christchurch Rd, Ringwood, Hampshire BH24 3AS. *01425 471404.* FAX *01425 476052.* This attractively decorated restaurant-with-rooms in an early Georgian building makes a convenient base for Bournemouth and the New Forest. Rear rooms are quieter. *24 Dec–mid-Jan; 1 week in July.* TV P	AE MC V	■	●		6
Royal Tunbridge Wells: *Hotel du Vin* www.hotelduvin.com ££ Crescent Rd, Tunbridge Wells, Kent TN1 2LY. *01892 526455.* FAX *01892 512044.* This vivacious, stylish place belies the town's staid, conservative image. The interior is voguishly contemporary, and the atmosphere constantly buzzing. Brilliant food and wine. TV P	AE DC MC V	■		■	36
Rye: *Jeake's House* www.jeakeshouse.com ££ Mermaid St, Rye, E Sussex TN31 7ET. *01797 222828.* FAX *01797 222623.* A delightful B&B in one of the town's quaintest streets, occupying what was once a 17th-century Quaker meeting house. Bedrooms are full of character. A wood-panelled parlour provides space to relax in the evenings. TV P	MC V				11
Rye: *Old Vicarage* www.oldvicaragerye.co.uk ££ 66 Church Sq, Rye, E Sussex TN31 7HF. *01797 222119.* FAX *01797 227466.* A friendly place by the church in a charming Georgian cottage filled with antiques and fresh country furnishings. Delicious breakfasts; sherry in the evenings. *Christmas.* TV P				■	4
Sandgate: *Sandgate* www.sandgatehotel.com ££ The Esplanade, Sandgate, Folkestone, Kent CT20 3DY. *01303 220444.* FAX *01303 220496.* A charming family-owned seafront hotel ten minutes' drive from the Channel Tunnel. The rooms are immaculate and the service exemplary. It includes a restaurant and bar, and serves all-day breakfast at weekends. TV P	AE DC MC V	■	●	■	14

Hotel	Cards				Rooms
SEAVIEW: *Seaview* www.seaviewhotel.co.uk ££££ High St, Seaview, Isle of Wight PO34 5EX. *01983 612711.* FAX *01983 613729.* This long-established hotel combines warm and well-practised hospitality with superb seafood, in a modest Victorian villa close to the sea near Ryde. *Christmas.*	AE DC MC V	■	●	■	16
SWAY: *Nurse's Cottage* www.nursescottage.co.uk £££ Station Rd, Sway, Lymington, Hampshire SO41 6BA. & FAX *01590 683402.* An unassuming bungalow in a quiet New Forest village, now firmly established as a dazzling restaurant-with-rooms. Bedroom facilities run to CD and video players. *3 weeks in Nov, 2 in Mar.*	AE MC V	■		■	3
WINCHESTER: *Wykeham Arms* ££ 75 Kingsgate St, Winchester, Hamphire SO23 9PE. *01962 853834.* FAX *01962 854411.* A successful blend of historic inn, stylish bar-restaurant and smart central hotel, just behind the cathedral. Full of character and memorabilia; always popular with locals and visitors *(see also p608).* 25 Dec.	AE DC MC V	■		■	14
YARMOUTH: *George* www.thegeorge.co.uk ££££ Quay St, Yarmouth, Isle of Wight PO41 0PE. *01983 760331.* FAX *01983 760425.* Next to the Lymington ferry terminal on the old town square, this smart historic inn dates from the 17th century. Accomplished restaurant and a simpler brasserie. Parking can be tricky.	AE MC V	■		■	17

EAST ANGLIA

Hotel	Cards				Rooms
ALDEBURGH: *Wentworth* www.wentworth-aldeburgh.com £££ Wentworth Rd, Aldeburgh, Suffolk IP15 5BD. *01728 452312.* FAX *01728 454343.* A solid Victorian seaside hotel with well-decorated bedrooms and tasty dinners. Sea views are worth the extra charge. *27 Dec–5 Jan.*	AE DC MC V	■	●	■	37
BLAKENEY: *White Horse* www.blakeneywhitehorse.co.uk ££ 4 High St, Blakeney, Holt, Norfolk NR25 7AI. *01263 740574.* FAX *01263 741303.* A friendly, down-to-earth pub offering distinctly above-average food in an upmarket coastal village. Recently refurbished. *1 Jan.*	AE MC V	■	●	■	10
BUCKDEN: *Lion* www.lionhotel.co.uk ££ High Street, Buckden, Cambridgeshire PE19 5XA. *01480 810313.* FAX *01480 811070.* A fine old building full of oak timbers and panelling, just off the A1. Well-furnished bedrooms, some in an annexe. *1 Jan.*	AE MC V	■	●		15
BURNHAM MARKET: *Hoste Arms* www.hostearms.co.uk £££ The Green, Burnham Market, King's Lynn, Norfolk PE31 8HD. *01328 738777.* An important part of the social fabric of a pretty Norfolk village, this excellent Georgian inn provides a splendid array of bistro-style food and tastefully furnished rooms – some in an annexe.	MC V	■	●	■	43
BURY ST EDMUNDS: *Ounce House* www.ouncehouse.co.uk ££ Northgate St, Bury St Edmunds, Suffolk IP33 1HP. *01284 761779.* FAX *01284 768315.* A thoroughly civilized, family-run B&B within easy walking distance of the historic centre. Classy furnishings; friendly welcome.	AE DC MC V		●	■	3
CAMBRIDGE: *Meadowcroft* www.meadowcrofthotel.co.uk £££ Trumpington Rd, Cambridge CB2 2EX. *01223 346120.* FAX *01223 346138.* This smartly furnished Victorian hotel lies about a mile from the centre. Décor enhances its handsome period features. *Christmas & New Year.*	AE MC V		●	■	18
CAMPSEA ASHE: *Old Rectory* ££ Campsea Ashe, Woodbridge, Suffolk IP13 0PU. & FAX *01728 746524.* This comfortable, antique-and-print-filled house offers tranquil Wolsey Lodge hospitality, and some excellent cooking. Bedrooms are light and pleasing. Lovely big gardens. *Christmas.*	DC MC V	■	●	■	7
COGGESHALL: *White Hart* www.oldenglish.co.uk ££ Market End, Coggeshall, Essex CO6 1NH. *01376 561654.* FAX *01376 561789.* This fine 15th-century guildhall-cum-coaching inn is a local landmark. The interior is furnished with antiques. Good Italian food.	AE DC MC V	■	●	■	18
DEDHAM: *Dedham Hall* www.dedhamhall.demon.co.uk ££ Brook St, Dedham, Colchester, Essex CO7 6AD. *01206 323027.* FAX *01206 323293.* An idyllic base for Constable Country. Partly 15th-century, this friendly place offers residential art courses as well as very cosy accommodation and elegant fixed-price dinners. Large gardens. *Christmas.*	MC V	■	●	■	6

Price categories for a standard double room per night, inclusive of breakfast, service charges and any additional taxes such as VAT:
£ under £65
££ £65–£100
£££ £100–£150
££££ £150–£200
£££££ £200 plus

RESTAURANT
Hotel restaurant or dining room serving more than just breakfast; often open to non-residents.

CHILDREN WELCOME
Especially welcoming to families. May have children's facilities such as cots, babysitting, family rooms, etc.

GARDEN/TERRACE
Hotels with a garden, courtyard or terrace, often providing tables for eating outside.

CREDIT CARDS
Indicates which credit cards are accepted: *AE* American Express; *DC* Diners Club; *MC* Master Card/Access; *V* Visa.

Hotel	Credit Cards	Restaurant	Children Welcome	Garden/Terrace	Number of Rooms
DEDHAM: *Maison Talbooth* W www.talbooth.com ££££ Stratford Rd, Dedham, Colchester, Essex CO7 6HN. *01206 322367.* FAX *01206 322752.* The Victorian accommodation wing of Dedham's top-flight restaurant (Le Talbooth is a short walk – *see p584*). Lavish country-house décor. TV P	AE DC MC V	■	●	■	10
DUNWICH: *Ship Inn* W www.shipinndunwich.co.uk ££ St James St, Dunwich, Suffolk IP 17 3DT. *01728 648219.* FAX *01728 648675.* A popular brick-built village pub with cosy bars and a conservatory. Pretty, rustic bedrooms, some with sea views. Super breakfasts. ● *25 Dec.* TV P	MC V	■		■	3
GREAT DUNMOW: *The Starr* W www.the-starr.co.uk £££ Market Place, Great Dunmow, Essex CM6 1AX. *01371 874321.* FAX *01371 876337.* The food's the thing at this historic 16th-century inn, but there are some ritzy bedrooms in the adjacent converted stable-block. Ask for the four-poster Oak Room. ● *first week Jan.* TV P	AE DC MC V	■	●		8
GRIMSTON: *Congham Hall* W www.conghamhallhotel.co.uk ££££ Lynn Rd, Grimston, King's Lynn, Norfolk PE32 1AH. *01485 600250.* FAX *01485 601191.* Though grand, this Georgian country house surrounded by parkland is unpretentious and relaxing. TV P	AE DC MC V	■	●	■	14
HINTLESHAM: *Hintlesham Hall* W www.hintleshamhall.com £££ George St, Hintlesham, Ipswich, Suffolk IP8 3NS. *01473 652268.* FAX *01473 652463.* A blend of Tudor and Georgian architecture set in 175 acres of grounds. Décor and food are unashamedly lavish, as are the posher suites. Loads of leisure facilities. *(See also p585.)* TV P	AE DC MC V	■	●	■	33
HUNTINGDON: *Old Bridge* W www.huntsbridge.com £££ 1 High St, Huntingdon, Cambridgeshire PE29 3TQ. *01480 424300.* FAX *01480 411017.* It's difficult to miss this handsome 18th-century building on its eponymous bridge over the Ouse. Spacious and smartly furnished, its attractive gardens shield it from passing traffic. *(See also p585.)* TV P	AE DC MC V	■	●	■	24
IPSWICH: *Marlborough* W www.themarlborough.co.uk ££ Henley Rd, Ipswich, Suffolk IP1 3SP. *01473 257677.* FAX *01473 226927.* A Victorian town house in a residential area near a park, with a solid reputation for high standards of service, food and furnishings. TV P	AE DC MC V	■	●	■	22
LAVENHAM: *Lavenham Priory* W www.lavenhampriory.co.uk ££ Water St, Lavenham, Suffolk CO10 9RW. *01787 247404.* FAX *01747 248472.* One of picturesque Lavenham's less pricy options, this delightful listed B&B has beautifully furnished rooms with character. ● *Christmas, New Year.* TV P	MC V			■	6
LAVENHAM: *Swan* W www.macdonaldhotels.co.uk £££ High St, Lavenham, Suffolk CO10 9QA. *01787 247477.* FAX *01787 248286.* This well-known hostelry was built on the proceeds of the wool trade. The recently refurbished bedrooms are stylish and very comfortable. TV P	AE DC MC V	■	●	■	51
LOWESTOFT: *Ivy House Farm* W www.ivyhousefarm.co.uk ££ Ivy Lane, Oulton Broad, Lowestoft, Suffolk NR33 8HY. *01502 501353.* FAX *01502 501539.* Located in a quiet backwater, these converted farm buildings house rustic but sophisticated units. Super food; lovely gardens. TV P	AE DC MC V	■	●	■	19
NORTH WALSHAM: *Beechwood* W www.beechwood-hotel.co.uk £££ 20 Cromer Rd, North Walsham, Norfolk NR28 0HD. *01692 403231.* FAX *01692 407284.* A stylish small hotel with enthusiastic, attentive hosts. A handy base for exploring north-west Norfolk and the Broads. TV P	MC V	■		■	10
NORWICH: *By Appointment* ££ 25–29 St George's St, Norwich, Norfolk NR3 1AB. & FAX *01603 630730.* The food is irresistible at this delightfully eccentric restaurant-with-rooms. Bedrooms are designed to pamper; lots of personal touches. TV P	MC V	■			4

Hotel	Cards				Rooms
NORWICH: *Catton Old Hall* W www.catton-hall.co.uk ££ Lodge Lane, Catton, Norwich, Norfolk NR6 7HG. ☎ *01603 419379.* FAX *01603 400339.* North-east of the centre, this welcoming 17th-century farmhouse is full of character and family mementoes. Fine dinners by arrangement. TV P	AE DC MC V	■		■	7
PETERBOROUGH: *Express by Holiday Inn* W www.hiexpress.co.uk ££ East of England Way, Alwalton, Peterborough PE2 6HE. ☎ *01733 284450.* FAX *01733 284451.* An unusually appealing chain hotel beside the East of England Showground. Excellent value, especially for families sharing a room. TV P	AE DC MC V		●		80
SOUTHWOLD: *Swan* W www.adnams.co.uk ££££ Market Place, Southwold, Suffolk IP18 6EG. ☎ *01502 722186.* FAX *01502 724800.* This elegant and comfortable hotel stands near Adnams' brewery, a focal point for centuries. Some bedrooms in garden annexe. TV P	MC V	■	●	■	43
SWAFFHAM: *Strattons* W www.strattons-hotel.co.uk £££ 4 Ash Close, Swaffham, Norfolk PE37 7NH. ☎ *01760 723845.* FAX *01760 720458.* An eco-friendly, award-winning venture in a neo-classical villa near the town centre. The interior is dashingly decorated; regional produce is on the menu. *(See also p585.)* ● *Christmas.* TV P	AE MC V	■	●	■	7
WELLINGHAM: *Manor House Farm* ££ Wellingham, nr Fakenham, Norfolk PE32 2IH. ☎ *01328 838227.* FAX *01328 838348.* This bed and breakfast is an 18th-century farmhouse with good views over the countryside. Two rooms are in a converted stable block with a kitchenette and large sitting room. Food includes farm produce. Horse-riding available nearby. Family room; children over 12 preferred. TV P				■	4
WOODBRIDGE: *Seckford Hall* W www.seckford.co.uk £££ Woodbridge, Suffolk IP13 6NU. ☎ *01394 385678.* FAX *01394 380610.* Off the A12 in peaceful grounds, this Elizabethan house is crammed with historic interest, as well as every modern comfort. ● *25 Dec.* TV P	AE DC MC V	■	●	■	32

THAMES VALLEY

Hotel	Cards				Rooms
AYLESBURY: *Hartwell House* W www.hartwell-house.com £££££ Oxford Rd, Aylesbury, Oxfordshire HP17 8NL. ☎ *01296 747444.* FAX *01296 747450.* Impeccably restored, this palatial country house's unabashed luxury is tastefully restrained. Superb Capability Brown grounds *(see p22)*, spa, indoor pool, tennis courts. TV P	AE MC V	■		■	46
BURFORD: *Burford House* W www.burfordhouse.co.uk £££ 99 High St, Burford, Oxfordshire OX18 4QA. ☎ *01993 823151.* FAX *01993 823240.* Classic gold-stone and timbered building with a smart interior. Light lunches and traditional teas are available, but no evening meals. ● *25–26 Dec, 2 weeks Jan.* TV P	AE MC V	■		■	8
CHIPPERFIELD: *Two Brewers* ££ The Common, Chipperfield, King's Langley, Hertfordshire WD4 9BS. ☎ *01923 265266.* A huddle of cottages on the edge of the village cricket pitch presents a timeless English scene. Inside, the bucolic idyll continues in firelit, low-ceilinged bars. Bedrooms are in outbuildings away from the noise. ● *25–26 Dec.* TV P	AE DC MC V	■		■	20
CLANFIELD: *Plough at Clanfield* W www.theplough-tablesir.com £££ Bourton Rd, Clanfield, Bampton, Oxfordshire OX18 2RB. ☎ *01367 810222.* Striking Elizabethan manor with traditional country furnishings, beams and creaky floorboards. Well known for its food. ● *Christmas.* TV P	AE DC MC V	■		■	12
GREAT TEW: *Falkland Arms* W www.falklandarms.org.uk ££ Great Tew, Chipping Norton, Oxfordshire OX7 4DB. ☎ *01608 683653.* FAX *01608 683656.* Stone-built, creeper-covered pub full of old-world charm. Snug bedrooms and good home cooking. *(See also p609.)* ● *24–27 Dec, 31 Dec–1 Jan.* TV P	AE MC V	■		■	5
HARPENDEN: *Harpenden House* ££££ 18 Southdown Rd, Harpenden, Hertfordshire AL5 1PE. ☎ *01582 449955.* FAX *01582 769858.* W www.corushotels.co.uk/harpendenhouse This handsome Georgian house is an efficient business hotel with easy access to the North London motorway network. TV P	AE DC MC V	■	●	■	76
HENLEY-ON-THAMES: *Red Lion* W www.redlionhenley.co.uk £££ Hart St, Henley-on-Thames, Oxfordshire RG9 2AR. ☎ *01491 572161.* FAX *01491 410039.* Overlooking the Thames, this fine old building is one of Henley's dominant features. Plenty of antiques and rowing memorabilia scattered about. TV P	AE MC V	■	●		26

Price categories for a standard double room per night, inclusive of breakfast, service charges and any additional taxes such as VAT:
£ under £65
££ £65–£100
£££ £100–£150
££££ £150–£200
£££££ £200 plus

RESTAURANT
Hotel restaurant or dining room serving more than just breakfast; often open to non-residents.

CHILDREN WELCOME
Especially welcoming to families. May have children's facilities such as cots, babysitting, family rooms, etc.

GARDEN/TERRACE
Hotels with a garden, courtyard or terrace, often providing tables for eating outside.

CREDIT CARDS
Indicates which credit cards are accepted: *AE* American Express; *DC* Diners Club; *MC* Master Card/Access; *V* Visa.

KINGSTON BAGPUIZE: *Fallowfields* W www.fallowfields.com £££
Farringdon Rd, Southmoor, Kingston Bagpuize, Abingdon, Oxfordshire OX13 5BH. *01865 820416.* FAX *01865 821275.*
Family-run country house in a sensitively updated historic building. Home-grown produce features on the menu. Most rooms have jacuzzis.

LONG CRENDON: *Angel* W www.angelsrestaurant.co.uk ££
47 Bicester Rd, Long Crendon, Aylesbury, Buckinghamshire HP18 9EE. *01844 208268.* FAX *01844 202497.*
The food's the thing at this chic 16th-century inn, but there are quaint bedrooms with uneven floors upstairs (often booked). *(See also p586.)*

MARLOW: *Compleat Angler* W www.compleatangler-hotel.co.uk £££££
Marlow Bridge, Marlow, Buckinghamshire SL17 1RG. *0870 400 8100.* FAX *01628 486388.*
A spectacular riverbank setting overlooking Marlow Weir draws the crowds to this traditional hostelry. Good-value leisure breaks.

MOULSFORD: *Beetle & Wedge* W www.beetle&wedgehotel.co.uk ££££
Ferry Lane, Moulsford on Thames, Wallingford, Oxfordshire OX10 9JF. *01491 651381.*
Jerome K Jerome used to live in this idyllic waterfront hideaway. Today visitors beat a path to its door for sophisticated food and smartly furnished rooms. Best river views are from the main building. *(See also p587.)*

OXFORD: *Burlington House* W www.burlington-house.co.uk ££
374 Banbury Rd, Oxford OX2 7PP. *01865 513513.* FAX *01865 311785.*
This upmarket guesthouse in north Oxford is acquiring a loyal following for its great breakfasts and reasonable prices. ● *Christmas.*

OXFORD: *Old Bank* W www.oxford-hotels-restaurants.co.uk ££££
92–94 High St, Oxford OX1 4BN. *01865 799599.* FAX *01865 799598.*
Located in a former bank, this hotels's contemporary interior is sleek and stylish, with lots of modern gadgetry. ● *25–26 Dec.*

OXFORD: *Old Parsonage* W www.oxford-hotels-restaurants.co.uk ££££
1 Banbury Rd, Oxford OX2 6NN. *01865 310210.* FAX *01865 311262.*
This ancient creeper-clad building, with its central location and steepish tariffs, is smartly decked out and hard to resist. ● *25–26 Dec.*

ST ALBANS: *Comfort* W www.choicehotels.com ££
Ryder House, Holywell Hill, St Albans, Hertfordshire AL1 1HG. *01727 848849.*
This central hotel occupies an attractive historic building. It retains some character inside as well. Simple meals; helpful staff.

SHEFFORD WOODLANDS: *Fishers Farm* W www.fishersfarm.co.uk £
Shefford Woodlands, Hungerford, Berkshire RG17 7AB. *01488 648466.* FAX *01488 648706.*
Welcoming B&B on a family farm. From the open-plan kitchen (meals prepared on request) views extend over the fields. Indoor swimming pool.

STADHAMPTON: *Crazy Bear* W www.crazybearhotel.co.uk £££
Bear Lane, Stadhampton, nr Oxford OX44 7UR. *01865 890714.* FAX *01865 400481.*
Wacky country pub with outré décor and a choice of Thai or modern British cooking. The zany bedrooms cater for sophisticates.

WINDSOR: *Sir Christopher Wren's House* W www.wrensgroup.com ££££
Thames St, Windsor, Berkshire SL4 1PX. *01753 861354.* FAX *01753 860172.*
A riverside location near Eton Bridge and Windsor Castle. A genuine Wren pedigree (1676) with streamlined facilities. *charge; book ahead.*

WOODSTOCK: *Feathers* W www.feathers.co.uk £££
Market St, Woodstock, Oxfordshire OX20 1SX. *01993 812291.* FAX *01993 813158.*
Smart central hotel in 17th-century premises. Interior décor is dashing and upbeat; the cooking is accomplished modern British.

Hotel	Credit Cards	Restaurant	Children Welcome	Garden/Terrace	Number of Rooms
Kingston Bagpuize: Fallowfields	AE MC V	■	●	■	10
Long Crendon: Angel	MC V	■	●	■	3
Marlow: Compleat Angler	AE DC MC V	■	●	■	64
Moulsford: Beetle & Wedge	AE DC MC V	■	●	■	10
Oxford: Burlington House	AE MC V			■	11
Oxford: Old Bank	AE DC MC V	■	●	■	42
Oxford: Old Parsonage	AE DC MC V	■	●	■	30
St Albans: Comfort	AE DC MC V	■	●		60
Shefford Woodlands: Fishers Farm			●	■	3
Stadhampton: Crazy Bear	AE MC V	■	●	■	12
Windsor: Sir Christopher Wren's House	AE DC MC V	■	●	■	92
Woodstock: Feathers	AE DC MC V	■	●	■	20

Hotel					
YATTENDON: *Royal Oak* W www.corushotels.com/royaloak £££ The Square, Yattendon, Thatcham, Berkshire RG18 0UG. *01635 201325.* A great country pub in a pretty village, with a sophisticated but informal atmosphere and immaculate bedrooms. Award-winning food.	AE DC MC V	■		■	5
WESSEX					
ABBOTSBURY: *Abbey House* W www.theabbeyhouse.co.uk £ Church St, Abbotsbury, Dorset DT3 4JJ. *01305 871330.* FAX *01305 871088.* This charming guesthouse was once the infirmary for the Benedictine abbey nearby. Lunch only served (Apr–Oct). Occasional concerts.		■	●	■	5
BATH: *Villa Magdala* W www.villamagdala.co.uk ££ Henrietta Rd, Bath BA2 6LX. *01225 466329.* FAX *01225 483207.* A Victorian villa overlooking Bath's delightful Henrietta Park make a quiet, relaxing stay. ● *Christmas week.*	AE MC V			■	18
BATH: *Royal Crescent* W www.royalcrescent.co.uk £££££ 16 Royal Crescent, Bath BA1 2LS. *01225 823333.* FAX *01225 339401.* For the ultimate Regency experience, this ultra-discreet establishment is truly sumptuous inside *(see p246)*. Staff are friendly; luxury spa.	AE DC MC V	■	●	■	45
BATHFORD: *Eagle House* W www.eaglehouse.co.uk ££ Church St, Bathford, Bath BA1 7RS. *01225 859946.* FAX *01225 859430.* Understated Georgian elegance just outside Bath. Family-friendly and a sociable black Labrador. Cooked breakfast extra. ● *20 Dec–3 Jan.*	MC V		●	■	8
BOURNEMOUTH: *Miramar* W www.miramar-bournemouth.com £££ East Overcliff Dr, Bournemouth, Dorset BH1 3AL. *01202 556581.* FAX *01202 291242.* Views from the clifftops are the main appeal of this smart, traditionally furnished Edwardian hotel. Ask for a sea-view room.	AE MC V	■	●	■	43
BRADFORD-ON-AVON: *Bradford Old Windmill* ££ 4 Masons Lane, Bradford-on-Avon, Wiltshire BA15 1QN. *01225 866842.* FAX *01225 866648.* W www.bradfordoldwindmill.co.uk B&B in a stone-built, 19th-century windmill with quirky bedrooms – the circular tower room has a round bed. Vegetarian cooking. ● *Jan–Feb.*	MC V	■		■	3
BRISTOL: *Hotel du Vin* W www.hotelduvin.com £££ The Sugar House, Narrow Lewins Mead, Bristol BS1 2NU. *0117 925 5577.* Several converted warehouses create an interesting setting for this trendy hotel-restaurant. Dynamic décor, exemplary facilities and bistro food.	AE DC MC V	■	●		40
CALNE: *Chilvester Hill House* W www.chilvesterhillhouse.co.uk ££ Calne, Wiltshire SN11 0LP. *01249 813981.* FAX *01249 814217.* A civilized welcome is guaranteed at this quiet Victorian country home (a long-established Wolsey Lodge) just off the A4. Good cooking.	AE DC MC V			■	3
DORCHESTER: *Casterbridge* W www.casterbridgehotel.co.uk ££ 49 High St, Dorchester, Dorset DT1 1HU. *01305 264043.* FAX *01305 260884.* Family-run B&B in a Georgian townhouse, offering a smart but unpretentious stay. Breakfast served in the conservatory. ● *25–26 Dec.*	AE DC MC V		●	■	14
DULVERTON: *Ashwick House* W www.ashwickhouse.co.uk ££ Dulverton, Somerset TA22 9QD. & FAX *01398 323868.* Tranquil Edwardian house in the heart of Exmoor. The terrace makes a splendid vantage point for summertime breakfasts.		■		■	6
EVERSHOT: *Summer Lodge* W www.summerlodgehotel.com £££££ Evershot, Dorchester, Dorset DT2 0JR. *01935 83424.* FAX *01935 83005.* This gorgeous Georgian dower house in deepest Wessex countryside is perfect for a peaceful, pampered stay. Wonderful food and caring service.	AE DC MC V	■	●	■	18
GILLINGHAM: *Stock Hill House* W www.stockhillhouse.co.uk £££££ Stock Hill, Gillingham, Dorset SP8 5NR. *01747 823626.* FAX *01747 825628.* A flamboyant interior stuffed with antiques makes this 19th-century gentleman's residence an entertaining stay. Superb cooking and fine wines.	MC V	■		■	8
GLASTONBURY: *Number 3* W www.numberthree.co.uk ££ 3 Magdalene St, Glastonbury, Somerset BA6 9EW. *01458 832129.* FAX *01458 834227.* An ideal B&B base in central Glastonbury, this elegant Georgian house was once home to Winston Churchill's mother. ● *Dec–Jan.*	AE DC MC V		●	■	5

Price categories for a standard double room per night, inclusive of breakfast, service charges and any additional taxes such as VAT:
(£) under £65
(£)(£) £65–£100
(£)(£)(£) £100–£150
(£)(£)(£)(£) £150–£200
(£)(£)(£)(£)(£) £200 plus

RESTAURANT
Hotel restaurant or dining room serving more than just breakfast; often open to non-residents.
CHILDREN WELCOME
Especially welcoming to families. May have children's facilities such as cots, babysitting, family rooms, etc.
GARDEN/TERRACE
Hotels with a garden, courtyard or terrace, often providing tables for eating outside.
CREDIT CARDS
Indicates which credit cards are accepted: *AE* American Express; *DC* Diners Club; *MC* Master Card/Access; *V* Visa.

	Credit Cards	Restaurant	Children Welcome	Garden/Terrace	Number of Rooms
KIMMERIDGE: *Kimmeridge Farmhouse* kimmeridgefarmhouse@hotmail.com (£) Kimmeridge, Wareham, Dorset BH20 5PE. *01929 480990.* FAX *01929 481503.* Super B&B on a working farm, perfect for exploring Purbeck and the Coastal Path. Parts of the house date from the 14th century. *Christmas.* TV P				■	3
LACOCK: *At the Sign of the Angel* www.lacock.co.uk (£)(£)(£) 6 Church St, Lacock, Wiltshire SN15 2LB. *01249 730230.* FAX *01249 730527.* Antique, half-timbered inn (a former wool-merchant's house) in a showcase Wiltshire village. The restaurant is a focal point *(see also p588)*, but the quaint bedrooms are full of character. *23–31 Dec.* TV P	AE DC MC V	■	●	■	10
MIDDLE WINTERSLOW: *The Beadles* www.guestaccom.co.uk/754.htm (£) Middleton, Middle Winterslow, Salisbury, Wiltshire SP5 1QS. *01980 862922.* A friendly guesthouse near Salisbury. The house is modern neo-Georgian, skilfully decorated in period style. Dinners by arrangement. TV P	MC V			■	3
MONTACUTE: *Milk House* (£) The Borough, Montacute, Somerset TA15 6XB. *01935 823823.* A captivating 15th-century B&B with country furnishings – a real home-from-home. Appetizing dinners by arrangement. *Nov–Mar.*			●	■	3
PORLOCK WEIR: *Andrews on the Weir* (£)(£) Porlock Weir, Minehead, Somerset TA24 8PB. *01643 863300.* www.andrewsontheweir.co.uk In a picturesque hamlet where Exmoor meets the sea, this stylish restaurant-with-rooms has immaculate bedrooms. *2nd–3rd weeks of Jan.* TV P	AE DC MC V	■		■	5
SHEPTON MALLET: *Charlton House* www.charltonhouse.com (£)(£)(£)(£) Charlton Rd, Shepton Mallet, Somerset BA4 4PR. *01749 342008.* FAX *01749 346362.* Interior design is the watchword at this 17th-century manor. A showcase of luscious fabrics and daring colour-schemes. Top-quality cooking. TV P	AE DC MC V	■	●	■	25
SHIPTON GORGE: *Innsacre Farmhouse* www.innsacre.com (£)(£) Shipton Lane, Shipton Gorge, Bridport, Dorset DT6 4LJ. & FAX 01308 456137. This delightful farm guesthouse has inglenook fires and plenty of imaginative home cooking. Recently refurbished bedrooms have dashing rustic décor (duvets and dark oak beds). No showers. *24 Dec–3 Jan.* TV P	MC V	■		■	4
TEFFONT EVIAS: *Howard's House* www.howardshousehotel.co.uk (£)(£)(£) Teffont Evias, Salisbury, Wiltshire SP3 5RJ. *01722 716392.* FAX *01722 716820.* This relaxing hideaway west of Salisbury is a 17th-century dower house in pretty gardens. Dinners are memorably excellent. *Christmas.* TV P	AE DC MC V	■	●	■	9
WAREHAM: *Priory* www.theprioryhotel.co.uk (£)(£)(£)(£) Church Green, Wareham, Dorset BH20 4ND. *01929 551666.* FAX *01929 554519.* Beautiful old priory in gorgeous riverside gardens. Ambitious cooking in an atmospheric cellar restaurant. TV P	DC MC V	■		■	18
WEYMOUTH: *Seaham Guesthouse* www.theseaham.co.uk (£) 3 Waterloo Place, Weymouth, Dorset DT4 7NU. *01305 782010.* Impeccable B&B with friendly, informal owners. Bedrooms are cosy, some with sea views. Early-bird breakfasts for ferry travellers. *Christmas week.* TV	AE MC V				5
WIMBORNE MINSTER: *Beechleas* www.beechleas.com (£)(£) 17 Poole Rd, Wimborne Minster, Dorset BH21 1QA. *01202 841684.* FAX *01202 849344.* The dining room is the focal point at this welcoming place – a Georgian townhouse with a graciously furnished interior. Some bedrooms are in a quieter coach-house annexe. *24 Dec–12 Jan.* TV P	AE DC MC V	■	●	■	9
WOOKEY HOLE: *Glencot House* www.glencothouse.co.uk (£)(£) Glencot Lane, Wookey Hole, Wells, Somerset BA5 1BH. *01749 677160.* FAX *01749 670210.* A Victorian mansion in Jacobean style, set in parkland. Ornate panelling, antique furnishings and curios make it a fascinating stay. TV P	AE DC MC V	■	●	■	13

DEVON AND CORNWALL

Hotel	Price	Cards				Rooms
ASHBURTON: *Tugela* @ paul@tugelahotel.freeserve.co.uk 68 East St, Ashburton, Devon TQ13 7AX. 01364 652206. FAX 01364 652 477. A positive welcome for families with children is a major attraction of this Georgian townhouse, but it also offers tasty home cooking, stylish décor and lots of toys and games. *Christmas & 3 weeks in Jan.* TV P	£	MC V	■	●	■	7
BELSTONE: *Tor Down House* W www.tordownhouse.co.uk Belstone, Okehampton, Devon EX20 1QY. & FAX 01837 840731. Idyllic B&B in a thatched longhouse on the edge of Dartmoor. Super gardens, welcoming hosts and loads of character. *Nov–Mar.* TV P	££	MC V			■	2
BIGBURY-ON-SEA: *Burgh Island* W www.burghisland.com Bigbury-on-Sea, Kingsbridge, Devon TQ7 4BG. 01548 810514. FAX 01548 810243. Romantic Art Deco-themed hotel on a tidal island. Visitors arrive by sea tractor to find themselves in a glamorous 1930s time warp. Rates include extravagant suites and a lavish dinner. *(See also p277.)* *first 3 weeks Jan.* TV P	£££££	MC V	■	●	■	15
BISHOP'S TAWTON: *Halmpstone Manor* W www.halmpstonemanor.co.uk Bishop's Tawton, Barnstaple, Devon EX32 0EA. 01271 830321. FAX 01271 830826. This manor house is an elegant country-house hotel with charming, professional staff. *Christmas, New Year & Feb.* TV P	£££	AE DC MC V	■		■	5
BOSCASTLE: *The Old Rectory* W www.stjuliot.com St Juliot, Boscastle, Cornwall PL35 0BT. 01840 250 225. Thomas Hardy stayed in this Victorian rectory, which has large gardens and is near the beach. Breakfasts with home produce. TV P	££	MC		●	■	4
BOTALLACK: *Botallack Manor* Botallack, St Just, Penzance, Cornwall TR19 7QG. 01736 788525. Joyce Cargeeg has been offering her hospitable style of B&B in this granite house near Land's End for more than 50 years. Great breakfasts. TV P	£				■	3
CHILLATON: *Quither Mill* W www.quithermill.co.uk Quither, Tavistock, Devon PL19 0PZ. & FAX 01822 860160. A converted mill is the setting for this relaxed Wolsey Lodge. Mouthwatering dinners served house-party style at a single table. TV P	££	MC V	■		■	4
CRACKINGTON HAVEN: *Manor Farm* Crackington Haven, Bude, Cornwall EX23 0JW. 01840 230 304. An historic farmhouse close to a dramatic stretch of Heritage Coast. Beautifully furnished interior and delicious dinners. *Christmas & New Year.* P	££		■		■	3
EXETER: *Barcelona* W www.hotelbarcelona-uk.com Magdalen St, Exeter, Devon EX2 4HY. 01392 281000. FAX 01392 281001. Voguish conversion of a former eye hospital, the bistro buzzes with a trendy crowd, and bedrooms are fitted with electronic extras. TV P	££	AE DC MC V	■	●	■	46
FOWEY: *Marina* W www.themarinahotel.co.uk 17 The Esplanade, Fowey, Cornwall PL23 1HY. 01726 833315. FAX 01726 832779. Dazzling estuary views from a former bishop's residence with considerable style and good food. TV P	£££	AE MC V	■	●	■	13
GALMPTON: *Maypool Park* W www.maypoolpark.co.uk Maypool, Galmpton, Devon TQ5 0ET. 01803 842442. FAX 01803 845782. This tranquil retreat stands high above the River Dart, next to Agatha Christie's former home, and within easy reach of Torbay. TV P	££	MC V	■		■	10
GITTISHAM: *Combe House* W www.thishotel.com Gittisham, Nr Honiton, Devon EX14 3AD. 01404 540400. FAX 01404 46004. This fascinating country house set amid parklands has been restored with antiques and period fittings. Friendly hosts, ambitious cooking. TV P	£££	AE DC MC V	■	●	■	15
HELSTON: *Nansloe Manor* W www.nansloe-manor.co.uk Meneage Rd, Helston, Cornwall TR13 0SB. 01326 574691. FAX 01326 564680. A friendly family welcome and good cooking make this quietly grand Georgian building special. The atmosphere is relaxing. TV P	£££	AE MC V	■		■	8
KINGSWEAR: *Nonsuch House* W www.nonsuch-house.co.uk Church Hill, Kingswear, Devon TQ6 0BX. 01803 752829. FAX 01803 752357. Breathtaking views towards Dartmouth from this superior Edwardian guest-house. Elegant décor and welcoming family hosts. TV	££	MC V	■		■	3

For key to symbols see back flap

Price categories for a standard double room per night, inclusive of breakfast, service charges and any additional taxes such as VAT:
£ under £65
££ £65–£100
£££ £100–£150
££££ £150–£200
£££££ £200 plus

RESTAURANT
Hotel restaurant or dining room serving more than just breakfast; often open to non-residents.

CHILDREN WELCOME
Especially welcoming to families. May have children's facilities such as cots, babysitting, family rooms, etc.

GARDEN/TERRACE
Hotels with a garden, courtyard or terrace, often providing tables for eating outside.

CREDIT CARDS
Indicates which credit cards are accepted: *AE* American Express; *DC* Diners Club; *MC* Master Card/Access; *V* Visa.

LANDEWEDNACK: *Landewednack House* ££
Church Cove, Landewednack, The Lizard, Cornwall TR12 7PQ. *01326 290909.* FAX *01326 290192.* @ landewednackhouse@amserve.com
Beautiful gardens and elegantly furnished rooms in a quiet Georgian rectory. Heated outdoor pool; close to the sea. Meals to order. *Christmas.* TV P

MAWNAN SMITH: *Meudon* W www.meudon.co.uk ££££
Mawnan Smith, Falmouth, Cornwall TR11 5HT. *01326 250541.* FAX *01326 250543.*
Traditional hospitality at this long-established, family-run hotel. Sub-tropical gardens running down to the sea provide a stunning backdrop. Excellent value for lone travellers. *3 Jan–early Feb.* TV P

MEMBURY: *Lea Hill* W www.leahill.co.uk £££
Membury, Axminster, Devon EX13 7AQ. *01404 881881.* FAX *01404 881890.*
Idyllic complex of thatched buildings in rolling countryside. Immaculate; bold but tasteful décor. Super breakfasts. TV P

MORTEHOE: *Cleeve House* W www.cleevehouse.co.uk £
North Morte Rd, Mortehoe, Woolacombe, Devon EX34 7ED. *01271 870719.*
A civilized welcome in an extended modern house on a stunning bit of coastline. Afternoon teas and home-laid breakfast eggs. *Nov–Mar.* TV P

NEWQUAY: *Sands* W www.sandsresort.co.uk £££
Watergate Rd, Porth, Newquay, Cornwall TR7 3LX. *01637 872864.* FAX *01637 876365.*
A large, well-equipped family resort near North Cornwall's wonderful surfing beaches. Bedrooms are light and spacious. *end Nov–Feb.* TV P

NORTH BOVEY: *Blackaller* W www.blackaller.co.uk ££
North Bovey, Moretonhampstead, Devon TQ13 8QY. *01647 440322.* FAX *01647 441131.*
A 17th-century woollen mill in a wooded Dartmoor valley run on relaxed, unassuming, eco-friendly lines. Décor is tastefully rustic. *Jan–Feb.* TV P

PELYNT: *Jubilee Inn* W www.jubileeinn.com ££
Jubilee Hill, Pelynt, Nr Looe, Cornwall PL13 2JZ. *01503 220312.* FAX *01503 220920.*
A cheerful, unpretentious pub-with-rooms. A wide range of meals is served, sometimes in the sheltered beer gardens. Bedrooms are cottagey. TV P

PENZANCE: *Summer House* W www.summerhouse-cornwall.com ££
Cornwall Terrace, Penzance, Cornwall TR18 4HL. *01736 363744.* FAX *01736 360959.*
Mediterranean cooking and chic bedrooms make a winning combination in this charming venture just behind the promenade. *Nov–Feb.* TV P

PERRANUTHNOE: *Ednovean Farm* W www.ednoveanfarm.co.u ££
Perranuthnoe, Nr Penzance, Cornwall TR20 9LZ. *01736 711883.* FAX *01736 710480.*
A flair for interior décor and sumptuous breakfasts distinguish this converted farmhouse B&B with vistas of St Michael's Mount. *Christmas.* TV P

PLYMOUTH: *Athenaeum Lodge* W www.athenaeumlodge.co.uk £
4 Athenaeum St, The Hoe, Plymouth, Devon PL1 2RQ. *& FAX 01752 665005.*
This well-kept townhouse B&B, with pink-and-pretty bedrooms, stands near Drake's famous bowling green *(see p278)*. *Christmas & New Year.* TV P

ROCK: *St Enodoc* W www.enodoc-hotel.co.uk ££££
Rock, Nr Wadebridge, Cornwall PL27 6LA. *01208 863394.* FAX *01208 863970.*
This breezily designed place overlooks the Camel estuary. It's cheerful, well-managed and very stylish. New World cooking. *Jan–mid-Feb.* TV P

ST BLAZEY: *Nanscawen Manor* W www.nanscawen.com ££
Prideaux Rd, Luxulyan Valley, St Blazey, Cornwall PL24 2SR. *01726 814488.*
A secluded B&B in gardens lush enough to evoke the nearby Eden Project *(see pp270–71)*. The cottagey façade is deceptive; it's smartly spacious. TV P

Hotel	Credit Cards	Restaurant	Children Welcome	Garden/Terrace	Number of Rooms
Landewednack House	MC V	■		■	3
Meudon	AE DC MC V	■	●	■	29
Lea Hill	AE MC V			■	11
Cleeve House	MC V	■		■	7
Sands	MC V	■	●	■	70
Blackaller		■		■	3
Jubilee Inn	MC V	■	●	■	11
Summer House	MC V	■		■	5
Ednovean Farm	AE MC V			■	3
Athenaeum Lodge	MC V				9
St Enodoc	AE MC V	■	●	■	20
Nanscawen Manor	MC V			■	3

ST HILARY: *Ennys* W www.ennys.co.uk ££ Trewhella Lane, St Hilary, Penzance, Cornwall TR20 9BZ. *01736 740262.* FAX *01736 740055.* The perfect rustic B&B: a 17th-century farmhouse with delightful gardens and a pool. Family suites in converted barn. *Nov–Mar.* TV P	MC V			■	5
ST KEYNE: *Well House* W www.wellhouse.co.uk £££ St Keyne, Liskeard, Cornwall PL14 4RN. *01579 342001.* FAX *01579 343891.* In the tranquil Looe Valley, this Victorian tea-planter's home makes a sophisticated retreat. Good food and fine wines; tennis and swimming. TV P	MC V	■	●	■	9
ST MAWES: *Rising Sun* W www.innsofcornwall.co.uk £££ The Square, St Mawes, Truro, Cornwall TR2 5DJ. *01326 270233.* FAX *01326 270198.* This classy harbourfront pub makes a valuable contribution to St Mawes' upmarket image. The bedrooms exude an air of casual chic. TV P	MC V	■	●	■	8
ST MAWES: *Hotel Tresanton* W www.tresanton.com £££££ St Mawes, Truro, Cornwall TR2 5DR. *01326 270055.* FAX *01326 270053.* This exceptional hotel, redesigned in 1997 by its present owner, was originally a cluster of old houses overlooking the sea. Beautiful views, an elegant and casual atmosphere and an excellent restaurant. TV P	AE MC V	■	●	■	29
SALCOMBE: *Soar Mill Cove* W www.makepeacehotels.co.uk £££££ Soar Mill Cove, Salcombe, Devon TQ7 3DS. *01548 561566.* FAX *01548 561223.* It's hard to imagine a more peaceful coastal hideaway. This family-run hotel provides excellent cooking and supreme comfort. *Jan.* TV P	AE MC V	■	●	■	20
TEIGNMOUTH: *Thomas Luny House* W www.thomas-luny-house.co.uk ££ Teign St, Teignmouth, Devon TQ14 8EG. *01626 772976.* A quiet, upmarket B&B in a charming Regency house, beautifully kept and full of personality. Summer breakfasts in the walled garden. TV P	MC V			■	4
VERYAN: *Nare* W www.narehotel.co.uk £££££ Carne Beach, Veryan, Truro, Cornwall TR2 5PF. *01872 501111.* FAX *01872 501856.* This gloriously located hotel keeps visitors of all ages satisfied. Lots to do, plus space to relax. Two heated swimming pools; lovely gardens. TV P	MC V	■	●	■	39
WIDEGATES: *Coombe Farm* W www.coombefarmhotel.co.uk ££ Widegates, Looe, Cornwall PL13 1QN. *01503 240223.* FAX *01503 240895.* A rural guesthouse offering a great welcome to families. Large grounds and plenty of animals and activities. *Nov–Feb.* TV P	AE MC V		●	■	3

HEART OF ENGLAND

ARMSCOTE: *Fox & Goose* W www.aboveaverage.co.uk ££ Armscote, Stratford-upon-Avon, Warwickshire CV37 8DD. & FAX *01608 682293.* This charming village pub-with-rooms is catching on fast since a new owner took it several rungs upmarket. Now it fizzes with life. *25–26 Dec.* TV P	AE MC V	■		■	4
BIBURY: *Swan* W www.swanhotel.co.uk ££££ Bibury, Cirencester, Gloucestershire GL7 5NW. *01285 740695.* FAX *01285 740473.* This riverside coaching inn is extremely photogenic; inside, the Swan is comfortably smart with well-equipped bedrooms. TV P	AE DC MC V	■	●	■	20
BIRMINGHAM: *Hotel du Vin & Bistro* W www.hotelduvin.com £££ 25 Church St, Birmingham B3 2NR. *0121-200 0600.* FAX *0121-236 0889.* A temple of style in a redundant eye hospital. This witty, glamorous, centrally placed hotel-brasserie oozes casual chic. TV	AE DC MC V	■	●	■	66
BLACKWELL: *Blackwell Grange* W www.blackwellgrange.co.uk ££ Blackwell, Shipston-on-Stour, Warwickshire CV36 4PF. *01608 682357.* FAX *01608 682856.* Historic working farm in tranquil Cotswold surroundings. A beautifully furnished and personal family home. *Christmas & New Year.* TV P	AE MC V			■	4
BLOCKLEY: *Old Bakery* ££££ High St, Blockley, Moreton-in-Marsh, Gloucestershire GL56 9EU. & FAX 01386 700408. Smart, sociable hotel in converted Victorian cottage. Showcase Cotswold surroundings. Room rates include dinner. *Dec–Jan, 2 weeks Jun.* TV P	AE MC V			■	3
BROAD CAMPDEN: *Malt House* W www.malt-house.co.uk £££ Broad Campden, Chipping Campden, Gloucestershire GL55 6UU. *01386 840295.* Idyllic Cotswold guesthouse with charming gardens. Generous breakfasts make use of home-grown produce. Elegant bedrooms. *23–27 Dec.* TV P	AE MC V	■	●	■	7

Price categories for a standard double room per night, inclusive of breakfast, service charges and any additional taxes such as VAT:
£ under £65
££ £65–£100
£££ £100–£150
££££ £150–£200
£££££ £200 plus

RESTAURANT
Hotel restaurant or dining room serving more than just breakfast; often open to non-residents.
CHILDREN WELCOME
Especially welcoming to families. May have children's facilities such as cots, babysitting, family rooms, etc.
GARDEN/TERRACE
Hotels with a garden, courtyard or terrace, often providing tables for eating outside.
CREDIT CARDS
Indicates which credit cards are accepted: *AE* American Express; *DC* Diners Club; *MC* Master Card/Access; *V* Visa.

Hotel	Credit Cards	Restaurant	Children Welcome	Garden/Terrace	Number of Rooms
BROADWAY: *Barn House* @ barnhouse@btinternet.com £ 152 High St, Broadway, Worcestershire WR12 7AJ. Tel & FAX *01386 858633.* Quiet B&B in large, beautiful grounds on the edge of a popular Cotswold village. Simple, cottagey bedrooms. Swimming pool. TV P			●	■	4
BUCKLAND: *Buckland Manor* W www.bucklandmanor.com £££££ Buckland, Broadway, Gloucestershire WR12 7LY. Tel *01386 852626.* FAX *01386 853557.* Archetypal Cotswold manor dating back to Domesday times. Glorious gardens. Exquisitely furnished in country-house style. TV P	*AE DC MC V*	■		■	13
CHELTENHAM: *Georgian House* W www.georgianhouse.net ££ 77 Montpellier Terrace, Cheltenham, Gloucestershire GL50 1XA. Tel *01242 515577.* A classic sandstone terrace gives an authentic air of Georgian living to this reasonably priced B&B. Hearty breakfasts. ● *Christmas–New Year.* TV P	*AE DC MC V*				3
CHELTENHAM: *Kandinsky* W www.hotelkandisky.com ££ Bayshill Rd, Cheltenham, Gloucestershire GL50 3AS. Tel *01242 527788.* FAX *01242 226412.* The exterior is conventional Regency, but inside this is a delightfully funky place with eccentricities galore. Unobtrusive service and a pizzeria. TV P	*AE DC MC V*	■	●	■	48
CHIPPING CAMPDEN: *Cotswold House* W www.cotswoldhouse.co ££££ The Square, Chipping Campden, Gloucestershire GL55 6AN. Tel *01386 840330.* Townhouse architecture and attractive décor in a Cotswold location. The restaurant attracts many non-residents. Charming rear garden. TV P	*AE MC V*	■	●	■	20
EVESHAM: *Evesham* W www.eveshamhotel.com £££ Cooper's Lane, off Waterside, Evesham, Worcestershire WR11 6DA. Tel *01386 765566.* This entertaining, unconventional place is family-friendly, with themed bedrooms and loads to do in the grounds. Indoor swimming pool. Very popular at weekends – book well ahead. ● *25–26 Dec.* TV P	*AE DC MC V*	■	●	■	40
GLEWSTONE: *Glewstone Court* W www.glewstonecourt.com ££ Glewstone, Ross-on-Wye, Herefordshire HR9 6AW. Tel *01989 770367.* FAX *01989 770282.* A relaxed air pervades this rambling country house overlooking the Wye Valley. Good cooking (regional and organic produce). ● *25–27 Dec.* TV P	*AE MC V*	■	●	■	8
HEREFORD: *Castle House* W www.castlehse.co.uk ££££ Castle St, Hereford HR1 2NW. Tel *01432 356321.* FAX *01432 365909.* This dynamic venture utilizes two secluded Georgian villas in the city centre. The interior is extravagantly luxurious. Local specialities feature. TV P	*AE MC V*	■	●	■	15
HOPWAS: *Oak Tree Farm* ££ Hints Rd, Hopwas, Tamworth, Staffordshire B78 3AA. Tel & FAX *01827 56807.* Just off the M42, these converted farm buildings enjoy views of open countryside. This high-quality B&B offers immaculate bedrooms, excellent breakfasts and an indoor swimming pool. ● *Christmas & New Year.* TV P	*AE MC V*			■	7
ILMINGTON: *Howard Arms* W www.howardarms.com ££ Lower Green, Ilmington, Shipston-on-Stour, Warwickshire CV36 4LT. Tel & FAX *01608 682226.* A classy dining pub in a charming Cotswold village. The building is ancient, the interior furnished with taste. Real ales and fine wines. TV P	*MC V*	■		■	3
IRONBRIDGE: *Library House* W www.libraryhouse.com £ Severn Bank, Ironbridge, Shropshire TF8 7AN. Tel *01952 432299.* FAX *01952 433967.* A charming Georgian B&B cottage (formerly the local library) by the famous iron bridge. Crammed with books. Pretty garden. ● *Jan.* TV				■	4
LEDBURY: *Feathers* W www.feathers-ledbury.co.uk ££ High St, Ledbury, Herefordshire HR8 1DS. Tel *01531 635266.* FAX *01531 638955.* This striking timbered coaching inn offers a comfortably furnished, traditional interior. Streetside bedrooms may be noisy. Gym; indoor pool. TV P	*AE DC MC V*	■	●	■	19

Hotel	Cards				Rooms
LEYSTERS: *Hills Farm* W www.thehillsfarm.co.uk £ Leysters, Leominster, Herefordshire HR6 0HP. *01568 750205.* FAX *01568 750306.* This farmhouse B&B is a delightful place to unwind. Several rooms are in converted outbuildings. Masses of books, boardgames and magazines. Dinner if pre-booked. *Nov–Feb & 2 weeks in June.*	MC V			■	5
LITTLE MALVERN: *Holdfast Cottage* W www.holdfast-cottage.co.uk ££ Marlbank Rd, Little Malvern, Worcestershire WR13 6NA. *01684 310288.* FAX *01684 311117.* Quintessential country cottage in rural location overlooking the Malvern Hills. Cosy bedrooms full of thoughtful extras.	MC V	■	●	■	8
LUDLOW: *Mr Underhill's* W www.mr-underhills.co.uk £££ Dinham Weir, Ludlow, Shropshire SY8 1EH. *01584 874431.* Acclaimed restaurant-with-rooms in a beautifully located mill on the River Teme. All the crisp, simple bedrooms enjoy good views. Brilliant modern European cooking. *Christmas week & 1 week Jan.*	MC V	■	●	■	6
MALVERN WELLS: *Cottage in the Wood* W www.cottageinthewood.co.uk ££ Holywell Rd, Malvern Wells, Worcestershire WR14 4LG. *01684 575859.* FAX *01684 560662.* Surrounded by rolling, wooded countryside, this family-run Georgian dower house is an ideal Malvern touring base.	AE MC V	■	●	■	31
NORTON: *Hundred House* W www.hundredhouse.co.uk £££ Bridgnorth Rd, Norton, Shropshire TF11 9EE. *01952 730353.* FAX *01952 730355.* Effortfully decorated, family-run inn with a cosy, homespun feel. The brasserie features wide-ranging menus and home-brewed ales.	MC V	■	●	■	10
OAKAMOOR: *Bank House* W www.smoothhound.co.uk/hotels/bank.html ££ Farley Lane, Oakamoor, Stoke-on-Trent, Staffordshire ST10 3BD. & FAX *01538 702810.* Outstanding B&B accommodation in the quiet Churnet Valley near Alton Towers Theme Park. Large lovely garden *Christmas week.*	DC MC V		●	■	3
PAINSWICK: *Painswick* W www.painswickhotel.com £££ Kemps Lane, Painswick, Gloucestershire GL6 6YB. *01452 812160.* FAX *01452 814059.* A grandly elegant Palladian-style rectory in a charming village near Gloucester. Despite its splendour, it is entirely unstuffy and informal.	AE MC V	■	●	■	19
PRESTBURYı *White House Manor* W www.thewhitehouse.uk.com £££ New Rd, Prestbury, Macclesfield, Cheshire SK10 4HP. *01625 829376.* FAX *01625 828627.* Romantic bedrooms team up with some talented cooking in this picturesque village. A useful base for Quarry Bank Mill. *25–26 Dec.*	AE MC V	■		■	11
SHREWSBURY: *Albright Hussey* W www.albrighthussey.co.uk £££ Ellesmere Rd, Shrewsbury, Shropshire SY4 3AF. *01939 290571.* FAX *01939 291143.* Historic moated-and-mullioned manor house, with wide-ranging international menus. Characterful bedrooms in the original house.	AE DC MC V	■	●	■	26
STRATFORD-UPON-AVON: *Victoria Spa Lodge* ££ Bishopton Lane, Stratford-upon-Avon, Warwickshire CV37 9QY. *01789 267985.* FAX *01789 204728.* W www.stratford-upon-avon.co.uk/victoriaspa.htm A friendly canalside B&B just outside Stratford, set in a grand, gabled building with tall chimneys (the former pump-room of a spa). Light, fresh bedrooms and plenty of period features.	MC V		●	■	7
SUTTON COLDFIELD: *New Hall* W www.newhallhotel.net £££££ Walmley Rd, Sutton Coldfield, West Midlands B76 1QX. *0121 378 2442.* FAX *0121 378 4637.* Romantic escapism on the northern fringes of the Black Country. This ancient moated manor in gorgeous grounds has fine period features.	AE DC MC V	■	●	■	60
TEWKESBURY: *Abbey Antiques* @ brazdys@amserve.net £ 61 Church St, Tewkesbury, Gloucestershire GL20 5RZ. & FAX *01684 298145.* An antique shop B&B, with plenty of interesting bits and bobs. The abbey bells peal out across the road, and hens scuffle round the garden.				■	3
ULLINGSWICK: *The Steppes* W www.steppeshotel.co.uk ££ Ullingswick, Hereford HR1 3JG. *01432 820424.* FAX *01432 820042.* Rustic charm and superb home cooking in skilfully converted farm buildings of great character and antiquity. A delightfully peaceful base for exploring rural Herefordshire. *Nov–mid-Feb.*	MC V	■		■	6
WILMCOTE: *Pear Tree Cottage* W www.peartreecot.co.uk £ Church Rd, Wilmcote, Stratford-upon-Avon, Warwickshire CV37 9UX. *01789 205889.* B&B in a gorgeous timbered cottage with Shakespearean associations. Good breakfasts; super gardens; self-catering apartment. *23 Dec–10 Jan.*				■	5

For key to symbols see back flap

Price categories for a standard double room per night, inclusive of breakfast, service charges and any additional taxes such as VAT:
- £ under £65
- ££ £65–£100
- £££ £100–£150
- ££££ £150–£200
- £££££ £200 plus

RESTAURANT
Hotel restaurant or dining room serving more than just breakfast; often open to non-residents.

CHILDREN WELCOME
Especially welcoming to families. May have children's facilities such as cots, babysitting, family rooms, etc.

GARDEN/TERRACE
Hotels with a garden, courtyard or terrace, often providing tables for eating outside.

CREDIT CARDS
Indicates which credit cards are accepted: *AE* American Express; *DC* Diners Club; *MC* Master Card/Access; *V* Visa.

Hotel	Credit Cards	Restaurant	Children Welcome	Garden/Terrace	Number of Rooms
WINCHCOMBE: *Wesley House* www.wesleyhouse.co.uk ££ High St, Winchcombe, Gloucestershire GL54 5LJ. Tel *01242 602366.* FAX *01242 609046.* A historic restaurant-with-rooms in a fine Cotswold wool town. Bedrooms are shoehorned into improbably small spaces, but very classy and cosy.	AE MC V	■	●	■	6

EAST MIDLANDS

Hotel	Credit Cards	Restaurant	Children Welcome	Garden/Terrace	Number of Rooms
ASWARBY: *Tally Ho Inn* £ Aswarby, Sleaford, Lincolnshire NG34 8SA. Tel *01529 455205.* FAX *01529 455773.* Unassuming roadside inn offering quiet bedrooms in a barn conversion. Good bar meals; pretty gardens. A useful base for the Lincolnshire fens.	MC V	■	●	■	6
BABWORTH: *The Barns* www.thebarns.co.uk £ Morton Fram, Babworth, Retford, Nottinghamshire DN22 8HA. Tel *01777 706336.* Good-value, welcoming B&B in appealing farm conversion near the A1. Fresh, stylish rooms; immaculate gardens; rural setting.	AE DC MC V		●	■	6
BASLOW: *Cavendish* www.cavendish-hotel.net £££ Baslow, Bakewell, Derbyshire DE45 1SP. Tel *01246 582311.* FAX *01246 582312.* A graciously furnished hotel on the Chatsworth estate where antiques mingle with works of modern art. Gorgeous views; super cooking.	AE DC MC V	■	●	■	24
BIGGIN-BY-HARTINGTON: *Biggin Hall* www.bigginhall.co.uk ££ Biggin, Buxton, Derbyshire SK17 0DH. Tel *01298 84451.* FAX *01298 84681.* A 17th-century stone house of great character in the Peak District National Park. Light, calm interior, with open views and open fires.	AE MC V	■		■	19
BUXTON: *Buxton's Victorian Guesthouse* www.buxtonvictorian.co.uk £ 3A Broad Walk, Buxton, Derbyshire SK17 6JE. Tel *01298 78759.* FAX *0101298 74732.* An elegant B&B overlooking the Pavilion Gardens, a short stroll from the town centre. Interior décor is themed on Gilbert & Sullivan operas.	MC V		●		9
CASTLE ASHBY: *Falcon* @ falcon.castleashby@oldenglishinns.co.uk £££ Castle Ashby, Northamptonshire NN7 1LF. Tel *01604 696200.* FAX *01604 696673.* An ancient estate village provides an attractive backdrop for this inn. Smartly furnished, cottagey bedrooms and large gardens.	AE MC V	■	●	■	16
EAST BARKWITH: *Bodkin Lodge* £ Grange Farm, Torrington Lane, East Barkwith, Lincolnshire LN8 5RY. Tel & FAX *01673 858249.* This outstandingly hospitable B&B has views of the Lincolnshire Wolds. If it's full, try The Grange farmhouse nearby (same family) – children accepted; no wheelchair access. Light supper available. ● *Christmas & New Year.*		■		■	2
GLOSSOP: *Wind in the Willows* www.windinthewillows.co.uk £££ Derbyshire Level, Glossop, Derbyshire SK13 7PT. Tel *01457 868001.* FAX *01457 853354.* Spacious, welcoming hotel in large gardens, with views of the Snake Pass. Handsome antique beds in some rooms. Traditional English cooking.	AE DC MC V	■		■	12
HOPE: *Underleigh House* www.underleighhouse.co.uk ££ Off Edale Road, Hope, Derbyshire S33 6RF. Tel *01433 621272.* FAX *01433 621324.* Set high above Edale, this welcoming B&B enjoys peaceful panoramas. Ideal walking base; light, floral bedrooms. ● *Christmas & New Year.*	MC V			■	6
LANGAR: *Langar Hall* www.langarhall.com ££££ Langar, Nottingham NG13 9HG. Tel *01949 860559.* FAX *01949 861045.* Gracious hospitality in a charming Regency-style house in a rural village setting. Stylish, individual bedrooms; top-notch cooking.	AE DC MC V	■	●	■	12
LINCOLN: *D'Isney Place* www.disneyplacehotel.co.uk ££ Eastgate, Lincoln LN2 4AA. Tel *01522 538881.* FAX *01522 511321.* Superior B&B in a fine 18th-century house close to the cathedral. No public rooms; breakfast is served in the well-equipped, comfortable bedrooms. Welcoming, unobtrusive service; secluded garden.	AE DC MC V		●	■	17

MATLOCK BATH: *Hodgkinson's* www.hodgkinsons-hotel.co.uk ££
150 South Parade, Matlock Bath, Derbyshire DE4 3NR. *01629 582170.* FAX *01629 584891.*
Idiosyncratic, well-placed hotel attractively furnished in Victorian style. Italian chef-patron. Interesting gardens. *24–26 Dec.* TV P
AE MC V — 7

NOTTINGHAM: *Greenwood Lodge* www.greenwoodlodgecityguesthouse.co.uk £
Third Ave, Sherwood Rise, Nottingham NG7 6JH. & FAX *0115-962 1206.*
A mile north of the city centre, this secluded 19th-century guesthouse is flamboyantly decked with period antiques. Welcoming owners. TV P
MC V — 6

NOTTINGHAM: *Lace Market* www.lacemarkethotel.co.uk £££
29–31 High Pavement, The Lace Market, Nottingham NG1 1HE. *0115-852 3232.*
A contemporary hotel in the city's fascinating lace-making district. Trendy restaurant; bedrooms full of bold colours and gadgetry. TV *limited.*
AE DC MC V — 42

OAKHAM: *Barnsdale Lodge* www.barnsdalelodge.co.uk ££
The Avenue, Rutland Water North Shore, Rutland LE15 8AH. *01572 724678.*
A handy base for Rutland Water and Burghley, this attractively extended stone farmhouse is now a cheerful, thriving hotel with good facilities. TV P
AE DC MC V — 45

OAKHAM: *Lord Nelson's House* www.nelsons-house.com ££
11 Market Place, Oakham, Rutland LE15 6DT. & FAX *01572 723199.*
Classy but informal restaurant-with-rooms in the centre of Rutland's historic county town. Quaint, half-timbered building. Attentive service. *24 Dec–9 Jan, 10 days Easter, 2 weeks late July.* TV P
MC V — 4

PAULERSPURY: *Vine House* www.vinehouse-hotel.com ££
100 High St, Paulerspury, Northamptonshire NN12 7NA. *01327 811267.* FAX *01327 811309.*
The restaurant reigns supreme *(see also p595)*, but bedrooms are charming and elegantly personalized too. Just off the A5, this welcoming place makes a convenient touring base near Northampton. *24 Dec–7 Jan.* TV P
MC V — 6

SARACEN'S HEAD: *Pipwell Manor* www.smoothhound.co.uk/hotels/pipwell £
Washway Rd, Saracen's Head, Holbeach, Lincolnshire PE12 8AL. & FAX *01406 423119.*
A great B&B in an early Georgian house, furnished with style and care. Bedrooms are simple but charming. Excellent breakfasts; gorgeous gardens. A perfect base for exploring the Fens. *Christmas & New Year.* P
— 4

STAMFORD: *George of Stamford* www.georgehotelofstamford.com £££
71 St Martins, Stamford, Lincolnshire PE9 2LB. *01780 750750.* FAX *01780 750701.*
This ancient coaching inn has beckoned travellers off the Great North Road since medieval times. Its handsome, rambling interior contains extensive bar-dining space, and lavishly individual bedrooms. *(See also p610.)* TV P
AE DC MC V — 47

UPPER HAMBLETON: *Finch's Arms* www.finchsarms.co.uk ££
Oakham Rd, Upper Hambleton, Oakham, Rutland LE15 TL. *01572 756575.*
This upmarket pub-with-rooms is set in a charming village surrounded by Rutland Water. Interesting cooking. TV P
AE DC MC V — 6

UPPINGHAM: *Lake Isle* www.lakeisle.com ££
16 High St East, Uppingham, Rutland LE15 9PZ. & FAX *01572 822951.*
Friendly restaurant-with-rooms in Georgian townhouse on historic Uppingham's classy main street. Some rooms in annexe cottages. TV P
AE DC MC V — 10

LANCASHIRE AND THE LAKES

AMBLESIDE: *Drunken Duck* www.drunkenduckinn.co.uk ££
Barngates, Ambleside, Cumbria LA22 0NG. *015394 36347.* FAX *015394 36781.*
A lively, dining-pub-with-rooms in a South Lakeland setting. Bedrooms are stylish and inviting. Room rates include afternoon tea. *25 Dec.* TV P
AE MC V — 16

AMBLESIDE: *Rowanfield* www.rowanfield.com ££
Kirkstone Rd, Ambleside, Cumbria LA22 9ET. *015394 33686.* FAX *015394 31569.*
Superior farmhouse accommodation with spectacular views near the Kirkstone Pass. Beautifully decorated rooms. *end Nov–mid-Mar.* TV P
MC V — 8

AMBLESIDE: *Wateredge Inn* www.wateredgeinn.co.uk ££
Waterhead Bay, Ambleside, Cumbria LA22 0EP. *015394 32332.* FAX *015394 31878.*
Inn-with-rooms with a glamorous waterfront setting at the northern tip of Lake Windermere. Stylish dining; bright, neat bedrooms in all sizes. TV P
AE DC MC V — 21

BASSENTHWAITE: *Pheasant* www.the-pheasant.co.uk £££
Bassenthwaite Lake, Cockermouth, Cumbria CA13 9YE. *017687 76234.* FAX *017687 76002.*
The snug bar is a focal point at this well-loved hostelry. Plenty of lounge space; great cooking. Refurbished bedrooms are bright and sleek. *25 Dec.* P
MC V — 13

Price categories for a standard double room per night, inclusive of breakfast, service charges and any additional taxes such as VAT:
£ under £65
££ £65–£100
£££ £100–£150
££££ £150–£200
£££££ £200 plus

Restaurant
Hotel restaurant or dining room serving more than just breakfast; often open to non-residents.
Children Welcome
Especially welcoming to families. May have children's facilities such as cots, babysitting, family rooms, etc.
Garden/Terrace
Hotels with a garden, courtyard or terrace, often providing tables for eating outside.
Credit Cards
Indicates which credit cards are accepted: *AE* American Express; *DC* Diners Club; *MC* Master Card/Access; *V* Visa.

Hotel	Credit Cards	Restaurant	Children Welcome	Garden/Terrace	Number of Rooms
Blackpool: *Raffles* W www.raffleshotelblackpool.co.uk £ 73–76 Hornby Rd, Blackpool, Lancashire FY1 4QJ. *01253 294713.* FAX *01253 294240.* Near the Tower, this flower-decked, blue-and-white B&B is easy to spot. It's very neat, with refurbished bedrooms. Traditional dinners; tearooms. TV P	AE MC V	■	●		17
Bowness-on-Windermere: *Lindeth Fell* W www.lindethfell.co.uk £££ Lyth Valley Rd, Bowness-on-Windermere, Cumbria LA23 3JP. *015394 43286.* A relaxing country-house hotel with glorious lakeland views and beautiful gardens. Fresh, tasteful décor and lots of personality. TV P	MC V	■	●	■	14
Bowness-on-Windermere: *Linthwaite House* W www.linthwaite.com £££ Crook Rd, Bowness-on-Windermere, Cumbria LA23 3JA. *015394 88600.* Dazzling Windermere views grace the beautiful grounds of this smart country-house hotel. Sophisticated menus; fishing and croquet. TV P	AE DC MC V	■	●	■	26
Buttermere: *Wood House* W www.wdhse.co.uk ££ Buttermere, Cockermouth, Cumbria CA13 9XA. *017687 70208.* FAX *017687 70241.* Tranquil National Trust property on the shores of Crummock Water. Beautifully furnished and decorated. Splendid home cooked dinners served house-party style. *mid-Nov–mid-Feb.* P		■		■	3
Carlisle: *Number Thirty-One* W www.number31.freeservers.com ££ 31 Howard Place, Carlisle, Cumbria CA1 1HR. & FAX *01228 597080.* Outstanding Victorian townhouse run with enthusiasm. Décor is bold and full of panache. Carefully considered, soundproofed bedrooms. *Nov–Feb.* TV	AE MC V	■		■	3
Cartmel Fell: *Lightwood* W www.lightwoodguesthouse.co.uk £ Cartmel Fell, Grange-over-Sands, Cumbria LA11 6NP. & FAX *015395 31454.* 17th-century farmhouse of great character with charming cottagey bedrooms, attractive gardens and good home cooking. *Christmas.* TV P	MC V	■	●	■	6
Cockermouth: *The Trout* W www.trouthotel.co.uk £££ Crown St, Cockermouth, Cumbria CA13 0EJ. *01900 823591.* FAX *01900 827514.* 17th-century building in a unique setting on the banks of the River Derwent. Short walk to Cockermouth. Lovely, extensive gardens. TV *limited.* P	AE MC V	■	●	■	43
Coniston: *Bankground* W www.bankground.com ££ East of Lake Rd, Coniston, Cumbria LA21 8AA. *015394 41264.* FAX *015394 41900.* 15th-century farmhouse across the lake from Coniston village and adjoining Grizedale Forest. Family-run B&B that is a good base for walking trips. P	MC V		●	■	15
Cowan Bridge: *Hipping Hall* W www.kirby-lonsdale.com ££ Cowan Bridge, Kirkby Lonsdale, Carnforth, Lancashire LA6 2JJ. *015242 71187.* An elegant, rambling country house in lovely grounds. Beautifully furnished. Cooking makes ambitious use of local produce. *Christmas.* TV P	AE MC V	■	●	■	7
Grange-in-Borrowdale: *Borrowdale Gates* £££ Grange-in-Borrowdale, Keswick, Cumbria CA12 5UQ. *01768 777204.* FAX *017687 77254.* W www.borrowdale-gates.com This soundly managed hotel enjoys glorious views. Spacious and smart. Tariffs include an excellent, satisfying dinner. *Jan.* TV P	AE MC V	■	●	■	31
Grasmere: *Howfoot Lodge* W www.howfoot.co.uk ££ Town End, Grasmere, Cumbria LA22 9SH. *015394 35366.* FAX *015394 35268.* This Victorian villa, owned by the Wordsworth Trust, is furnished with period features, and set in landscaped gardens. Excellent base for walkers. TV P	MC V	■	●	■	6
Keswick: *The Grange* W www.grangekeswick.com ££ Manor Brow, Keswick, Cumbria CA12 4BA. & FAX *017687 72500.* This well-established B&B on the outskirts of town has lovely views and gardens. *Mid-Nov–mid-Mar.* TV P	MC V			■	10

LORTON: *New House Farm* W www.newhouse-farm.co.uk ££
Lorton, nr Cockermouth, Cumbria CA13 9UU. Tel & FAX *01900 85404.*
A lovely Vale of Lorton location makes this characterful farm guesthouse a winner. Organized teas in the barn and superb suppers.

MANCHESTER: *Eleven Didsbury Park* W www.elevendidsburypark.com £££
11 Didsbury Park, Didsbury Village, Manchester M20 5LH. Tel *0161 448 7711.*
Stylish Victorian townhouse in a smart conservation suburb. Contemporary décor and high-quality gadgetry. Hot-tub in the garden. No restaurant, but evening deli service in rooms. TV P

MANCHESTER: *Crowne Plaza Midland* ££££
Peter St, Manchester M60 2DS. Tel *0161 236 3333.* FAX *0161 932 4100.*
W www.manchester-themidland.crowneplaza.com
This sumptuous, palatial hotel harkens back to the golden era of railway travel. Neoclassical, Louis XIII and art nouveau styles. TV P

MANCHESTER: *The Lowry* W www.thelowryhotel.com £££££
50 Dearmans Pl, Chapel Wharf, Salford, Manchester M3 5LH. Tel *0161 827 4000.*
Located in the heart of the city, this luxury contemporary hotel is in a quiet riverside location. Restaurant run by Marco Pierre White. TV P

MELLOR: *Millstone* W www.shirehotels.co.uk ££
3 Church Lane, Mellor, Blackburn, Lancashire BB2 7JR. Tel *01254 813333.* FAX *01254 812628.*
This former coaching inn makes a good base for rural Lancashire. Bedrooms are neat and practical. Beamed and panelled public areas. TV P

MUNGRISDALE: *Mill Hotel* W www.themillhotel.com £££
Mungrisdale, Penrith, Cumbria CA11 0XR. Tel *017687 79659.* FAX *017687 79155.*
Not to be confused with the neighbouring Mill Inn, this small hotel makes a delightful stay. Good restaurant. Closed *Nov–Feb.* TV P

NEWLANDS: *Swinside Lodge* W www.swinsidelodge-hotel.co.uk £££
Grange Rd, Newlands, Keswick, Cumbria CA12 5UE. Tel & FAX *017687 72948.*
A gorgeous, isolated setting near Cat Bells. Smart décor; lots of books and maps, and excellent cooking (rates include dinner). TV P

PENRITH: *North Lakes* W www.shireinns.co.uk £££
Ullswater Rd, Penrith, Cumbria CA11 8QT. Tel *01768 868111.* FAX *01768 868291.*
Unimpressive setting, but this modern block beside the M6 has an attractive chalet-style interior. Indoor pool and fitness centre. TV P

SEATOLLER: *Seatoller House* W www.seatollerhouse.co.uk ££
Seatoller, Borrowdale, Keswick, Cumbria CA12 5XN. Tel *017687 77218.* FAX *017687 77189.*
This delightfully laid-back walking base near the Honister Pass is a place to mix and mingle. Communal meals. Closed *Dec–Feb.* P

SELSIDE: *Low Jock Scar* @ ljs@avmail.co.uk £
Selside, Kendal, Cumbria LA8 9LE. Tel & FAX *01539 823259.*
An utterly secluded but easily accessible location north of Kendal makes this delightful guesthouse an ideal springboard for the southern Lakes. Super gardens; tasty suppers. Simple, cosy bedrooms. Closed *Nov–mid-Mar.* P

ULLSWATER: *Sharrow Bay* W www.sharrow-bay.com £££££
Ullswater, Penrith, Cumbria CA10 2LZ. Tel *017684 86301.* FAX *017684 86349.*
Britain's first proper country-house hotel is still a Lakeland legend. An incomparable lakeshore setting, exquisite décor, perfect service and wonderful cooking. *(See also p597.)* Closed *Dec–Feb.* TV P

ULVERSTON: *Bay Horse* W www.furness.co.uk/bayhorse ££££
Canal Foot, Ulverston, Cumbria LA12 9EL. Tel *01229 583972.* FAX *01229 580502.*
At the edge of Morecambe Bay, this smartly comfortable inn provides bedroom binoculars for birdwatching. Splendid food (rates include dinner). TV P

WASDALE HEAD: *Wasdale Head* W www.wasdale.com ££
Wasdale Head, nr Gosforth, Seascale, Cumbria CA20 1X. Tel *019467 26229.*
This famous climbing inn occupies a remote, spectacular setting near Wast Water. Microbrewery on site; loads of character. P

WHITEWELL: *Inn at Whitewell* ££
Whitewell, Forest of Bowland, Clitheroe, Lancashire BB7 3AT. Tel *01200 448222.* FAX *01200 448298.*
This wittily sophisticated riverside inn makes a splendid base for exploring the Ribble Valley. The building has enormous character. Stylishly spectacular bedrooms. Wonderful food and wines. *(See also p597.)* TV P

Hotel	Cards				Rooms
New House Farm	MC V	■		■	5
Eleven Didsbury Park	AE DC MC V		●	■	17
Crowne Plaza Midland	AE DC MC V	■	●		303
The Lowry	AE DC MC V	■	●		165
Millstone	AE DC MC V	■	●		24
Mill Hotel		■	●	■	8
Swinside Lodge	MC V	■		■	7
North Lakes	AE DC MC V	■	●	■	84
Seatoller House	MC V	■	●	■	10
Low Jock Scar	MC V	■		■	5
Sharrow Bay	AE MC V	■		■	26
Bay Horse	AE MC V	■			9
Wasdale Head	AE MC V	■	●	■	14
Inn at Whitewell	MC V	■	●	■	20

Price categories for a standard double room per night, inclusive of breakfast, service charges and any additional taxes such as VAT:
£ under £65
££ £65–£100
£££ £100–£150
££££ £150–£200
£££££ £200 plus

RESTAURANT
Hotel restaurant or dining room serving more than just breakfast; often open to non-residents.

CHILDREN WELCOME
Especially welcoming to families. May have children's facilities such as cots, babysitting, family rooms, etc.

GARDEN/TERRACE
Hotels with a garden, courtyard or terrace, often providing tables for eating outside.

CREDIT CARDS
Indicates which credit cards are accepted: *AE* American Express; *DC* Diners Club; *MC* Master Card/Access; *V* Visa.

Hotel	Credit Cards	Restaurant	Children Welcome	Garden/Terrace	Number of Rooms
WINDERMERE: *Gilpin Lodge* www.gilpinlodge.com ££££ Crook Rd, Windermere, Cumbria LA23 3NE. *015394 88818.* FAX *015394 88058.* An elegant and comfortable hotel, both spacious and beautifully furnished. Some split-level suites with jacuzzi baths. Extensive grounds.	DC MC V	■		■	14

YORKSHIRE AND THE HUMBER REGION

Hotel	Credit Cards	Restaurant	Children Welcome	Garden/Terrace	Number of Rooms
AMPLEFORTH: *Shallowdale House* www.shallowdalehouse.demon.co.uk ££ Ampleforth, nr York YO62 4DY. *01439 788325.* FAX *01439 788885.* Refined guesthouse within easy reach of Rievaulx and Byland abbeys. Simple but stylish rooms with lovely views. *Christmas & New Year.*	MC V	■		■	3
BRADFORD: *Beeties* www.beeties.co.uk £ 7 Victoria Rd, Saltaire Village, Shipley, Bradford, W Yorkshire BD18 3LA. *01274 581718.* Located in a converted fish shop, this restaurant-with-rooms is well placed for visiting the arty village of Saltaire. Tastefully furnished bedrooms.	AE MC V	■			5
EAST WITTON: *Blue Lion* www.thebluelion.co.uk ££ East Witton, Leyburn, N Yorkshire DL8 4SN. *01969 624273.* FAX *01969 624189.* Classy coaching inn near the ruins of Jervaulx Abbey. Smart food attracts non-residents; it gets busy at weekends and front bedrooms may be noisy.	MC V	■	●	■	12
FLAMBOROUGH: *Manor House* www.flamboroughmanor.co.uk ££ Flamborough, Bridlington, E Yorkshire YO15 1PD. & FAX *01262 850943.* This elegant Georgian house is a private home and a Wolsey Lodge. Book ahead; dinners feature local seafood. *Christmas.*	MC V	■		■	2
GRASSINGTON: *Ashfield House* www.ashfieldhouse.co.uk ££ Summers Fold, Grassington, N Yorkshire BD23 5AE. & FAX *01756 752584.* This cluster of 17th-century cottages makes a good base for neighbouring Malhamdale. Stylish interiors with simple bedrooms. *Jan.*	MC V	■		■	7
HALIFAX: *Holdsworth House* www.holdsworthhouse.co.uk £££ Holdsworth Rd, Holmfield, Halifax, W Yorkshire HX2 9TG. *01422 240024.* FAX *01422 245174.* Period features survive intact in this rambling Jacobean manor in the Calder Valley near Halifax. Bedrooms, in a modern wing, are as attractive as the main house. Elaborate menus. *Christmas & New Year.*	AE DC MC V	■	●	■	40
HARROGATE: *Balmoral* www.balmoralhotel.co.uk £££ Franklin Mount, Harrogate, N Yorkshire HG1 5EJ. *01423 508208.* FAX *01423 530652.* Eccentric memorabilia gives this mock-Tudor hotel edge over its rivals. Straightforward business facilities and some ornate bedrooms.	AE MC V	■	●	■	21
HELM: *Helm* www.helmyorkshire.com ££ Helm, nr Askrigg, Leyburn, N Yorkshire DL8 3JF. & FAX *01969 650443.* This guesthouse occupies a handsome stone building in one of Wensleydale's best-known villages. Beautifully kept bedrooms. *mid-Nov–Dec.*	MC V	■		■	3
HELMSLEY: *Feversham Arms* reception@feversham-helmsley.fsnet.co.uk ££££ 178 High St, Helmsley, Yorks YO62 5AG. *01439 770766.* Comfortable refurbished coaching inn in small historic market town near Castle Howard *(pp384–5).* Pool and gym. Room rate includes dinner.	AE MC V	■	●	■	22
INGLEBY GREENHOW: *Manor House Farm* mbloom@globalnet.co.uk ££ Ingleby Greenhow, nr Great Ayton, N Yorkshire TS9 6RB. *01642 722384.* Remote, charming farmhouse on the edge of the North York Moors. Cottagey bedrooms with views. Rates include a five-course dinner. *Dec.*	MC V	■		■	3
LEEDS: *Malmaison Leeds* www.malmaison.com £££ Sovereign Quay, Leeds LS1 1DQ. *0113 398 1000.* FAX *0113 398 1002.* This ultra-contemporary hotel occupying an old tram-shed offers themed bedrooms and brasserie food. Views of the city skyline.	DC MC V	■	●		100

Hotel	Credit cards				Rooms
MYTHOLMROYD: *Redacre Mill* W www.redacremill.freeserve.co.uk £ Mytholmroyd, Hebden Bridge, W Yorkshire HX7 5DQ. & FAX *01422 885563.* A friendly English guesthouse in a converted canalside cotton mill, with South Indian cuisine. Meals by arrangement TV P	MC V		●	■	5
OSMOTHERLY: *Three Tuns* ££ 9 South End, Osmotherley, N Yorkshire DL6 3BN. *01609 883301.* Recently transformed into a quirkily inviting restaurant-with-rooms, this long-established hostelry lies near Mount Grace Priory. TV P	AE MC V	■		■	7
PICKERING: *White Swan* W www.white-swan.co.uk £££ Market Place, Pickering, N Yorkshire YO18 7AA. *01751 472288.* FAX *01751 475554.* Central Georgian inn with a breezy modern interior. Bedrooms are plain and practical. A useful base for the North York Moors Railway. TV P	AE MC V	■	●	■	12
RAMSGILL: *Yorke Arms* W www.yorke-arms.co.uk ££££ Ramsgill-in-Nidderdale, N Yorkshire HG3 5RL. *01423 755243.* FAX *01423 755330.* Top cooking in this restaurant-with-rooms. A former shooting lodge, the building is ancient and full of character. Bedrooms are elegant. TV P	AE DC MC V	■		■	14
REETH: *Arkleside* W www.arklesidehotel.co.uk ££ Reeth, nr Richmond, N Yorkshire DL11 6SG. & FAX *01748 884200.* Set in a village amid dazzling Swaledale scenery, this guesthouse is a popular walking base. Bedrooms are smart but variable. *24–25 Dec, Jan.* TV P	MC V	■		■	10
ROYDHOUSE: *Three Acres Inn* @ 3acres@globalnet.co.uk ££ Roydhouse, Shelley, Huddersfield, W Yorkshire HD8 8LR. *01484 602606.* FAX *01484 608411.* Moorland views grace this inn near the Yorkshire Sculpture Park and National Coal Mining Museum *(see p399)*. The bar-restaurant evokes turn-of-the-century style. Bedrooms have period character too. *25, 31 Dec, 1 Jan.* TV P	AE MC V	■	●	■	20
SCARBOROUGH: *Interludes* W www.interludeshotel.co.uk £ 32 Princess St, Scarborough, N Yorkshire YO11 1QR. *01723 360513.* FAX *01723 368597.* A refined guesthouse in the old town with sea views from some rooms. Simple dinners and theatre packages available. Tricky parking. TV	MC V	■			5
WHITBY: *White Horse & Griffin* W www.whitehorseandgriffin.co.uk ££ Church St, Whitby, N Yorkshire YO22 4BH. & FAX *01947 604857.* A quaint old inn on the cobbled main street, furnished with antiques. Local fish on the menu. Quieter rooms in self-contained annexe cottages. TV	MC V	■	●		17
WINTERINGHAM: *Winteringham Fields* W www.winteringhamfields.com £££ Winteringham, Scunthorpe, Lincolnshire DN15 9PF. *01724 733096.* FAX *01724 733898.* A superb restaurant-with-rooms and the most elegant touring base near the Humber Bridge. Worth the journey for its cooking; excellent bedrooms too. *(See also p599.)* *last week Mar & Oct, first week Aug, 2 weeks Christmas.* TV P	AE MC V	■		■	10
YORK: *The Hazelwood* W www.thehazelwoodyork.com ££ 24–25 Portland St, York YO21 7EH. *01904 626548.* FAX *01904 628032.* Central but secluded townhouse B&B providing unobtrusive service and opulent, spacious bedrooms. Small rear garden. TV P	MC V			■	12
YORK: *Middlethorpe Hall* W www.middlethorpe.com ££££ Bishopthorpe Rd, York YO23 2GB. *01904 641241.* FAX *01904 620176.* Grand historic house-hotel near the racecourse. Period features blend with luxurious furnishings. Gourmet restaurant; health spa; croquet. TV P	MC V	■		■	30

NORTHUMBRIA

Hotel	Credit cards				Rooms
BERWICK-UPON-TWEED: *Number One Sallyport* & FAX *01289 308827.* £ Off Bridge St, Berwick-upon-Tweed TD15 1EZ. W www.1sallyport-bedandbreakfast.com Charming 17th-century B&B in central Berwick. The owner is an ex-restaurateur, and serves delicious French Provençal suppers. TV P	AE MC V	■	●	■	3
CHESTER-LE-STREET: *Lumley Castle* W www.lumleycastle.com £££ Chester-le-Street, Durham DH3 4NX. *0191 389 1111.* FAX *0191 387 1437.* With a Norman pedigree, this flamboyantly turreted building is predictably grand. Elizabethan banquets attract many visitors. Beamish Museum lies nearby *(see pp410–11)*. *24–26 Dec, 1 Jan.* TV P	AE DC MC V	■	●	■	59
CROOKHAM: *Coach House* W www.coachhousecrookham.com ££ Crookham, Cornhill-on-Tweed, Northumberland TD12 4TD. *01890 820293.* FAX *01890 820284.* Close to the Borders, this welcoming guesthouse offers peace, unpretentious comfort and hearty home cooking. *Nov–Easter.* TV P	MC V	■	●	■	9

Price categories for a standard double room per night, inclusive of breakfast, service charges and any additional taxes such as VAT:
£ under £65
££ £65–£100
£££ £100–£150
££££ £150–£200
£££££ £200 plus

RESTAURANT
Hotel restaurant or dining room serving more than just breakfast; often open to non-residents.

CHILDREN WELCOME
Especially welcoming to families. May have children's facilities such as cots, babysitting, family rooms, etc.

GARDEN/TERRACE
Hotels with a garden, courtyard or terrace, often providing tables for eating outside.

CREDIT CARDS
Indicates which credit cards are accepted: *AE* American Express; *DC* Diners Club; *MC* Master Card/Access; *V* Visa.

	Credit Cards	Restaurant	Children Welcome	Garden/Terrace	Number of Rooms
DURHAM: *Georgian Town House* W www.thegeorgiantownhouse.co.uk ££ 10–11 Crossgate, Durham DH1 4PS. & FAX *0191 386 8070.* A friendly, family-run B&B in the heart of the city. Cathedral views from some rooms. Pancake house and café downstairs. ● *Christmas & New Year.* TV				■	8
HALTWHISTLE: *Centre of Britain* W www.centre-of-britain.org.uk ££ Main St, Haltwhistle, Northumberland NE49 0BH. *01434 322422.* FAX *01434 322655.* A stylish conversion of a 15th-century defensive tower near Hadrian's Wall. Exposed stonework and beams. Bedrooms are light and tasteful. TV P	*AE DC MC V*	■	●		9
HAMSTERLEY FOREST: *Grove House* W www.grovehouse.biz ££ Hamsterley Forest, Bishop Auckland, Durham DL13 3NL. *01388 488203.* FAX *01388 488174.* Once a Georgian hunting lodge, portraits and objets d'art decorate this much-loved private home set in protected woodlands. ● *mid-Dec–mid-Jan.* P		■		■	3
HEXHAM: *Langley Castle* W www.langleycastle.com £££ Langley on Tyne, Hexham, Northumberland NE47 5LU. *01434 688888.* FAX *01434 684019.* A Medieval castellated stronghold with baronial interiors. Coach house rooms are cheaper, but just as comfortable. TV P	*AE DC MC V*	■	●	■	18
HIGH BUSTON: *High Buston Hall* W www.highbuston.com ££ High Buston, Alnmouth, Alnwick, Northumberland NE66 3QH. *01665 830606.* This fine Georgian villa surveys sweeping countryside near Warkworth Castle. Warm, unobtrusive welcome. ● *Christmas & New Year.* P				■	3
NEWCASTLE UPON TYNE: *Malmaison Newcastle* W www.malmaison.com £££ 104 Quayside, Newcastle upon Tyne NE1 3DX. *0191 245 5000.* FAX *0191 245 4545.* Sophisticated warehouse conversion on the central waterfront next to the Millennium Bridge and opposite Baltic *(see pp410–11).* TV	*AE DC MC V*	■	●		116
ROMALDKIRK: *Rose & Crown* W www.rose-and-crown.co.uk £ Romaldkirk, Barnard Castle, Durham DL12 9EB. *01833 650213.* FAX *01833 650828.* The village green makes a quintessentially English backdrop for this delightful inn on the fringes of Teesdale. Inside, it's exceptionally smart but reassuringly traditional. Accomplished cooking. *(See also p600.)* ● *Christmas.* TV P	*MC V*	■	●		12
SEAHOUSES: *Olde Ship* W www.seahouses.co.uk ££ 7–9 Main St, Seahouses, Northumberland NE68 7RD. *01665 720200.* FAX *01665 721383.* This inn overlooks the harbour, departure point for the Farne Islands *(see p404).* Best rooms are in the annexe. *(See also p611.)* ● *Dec–Jan.* TV P	*JCB MC V*	■		■	18
STANNERSBURN: *Pheasant* W www.thepheasantinn.com ££ Stannersburn, Kielder Water, Northumberland NE48 1DD. *01434 240382.* FAX *01434 240382.* Creeper-covered inn near Kielder Water's visitor centre *(see p406).* A friendly place, full of character, with unassuming, cosy bedrooms in an adjoining barn conversion. Good food (regional produce). ● *25 Dec.* TV P	*MC V*	■	●	■	8

NORTH WALES

	Credit Cards	Restaurant	Children Welcome	Garden/Terrace	Number of Rooms
ABERDYFI: *Penhelig Arms* W www.penheligarms.com ££ Aberdyfi, Gwynedd LL35 0LT. *01654 767215.* FAX *01654 767690.* A whitewashed inn on the seafront. Most rooms have estuary views; those in the annexe have private terraces. *(See also p601.)* ● *25–26 Dec.* TV P	*MC V*	■	●	■	14
ABERDYFI: *Trefiddian* W www.trefwales.com £££ Tywyn Rd, Aberdyfi, Gwynedd LL35 0SB. *01654 767213.* FAX *01654 767777.* This large, friendly hotel enjoys coastal views. Long owned by the same family, it's an energetic place with lots to do. ● *3 weeks Nov–Dec.* TV P	*MC V*	■	●	■	59
ABERSOCH: *Porth Tocyn* W www.porth-tocyn-hotel.co.uk £££ Bwylch Tocyn, Abersoch, Gwynedd LL53 7BU. *01758 713303.* FAX *01758 713538.* A comfortable country-house hotel with family hospitality and traditional cooking. Heated pool; tennis court. *(See also p601.)* ● *mid-Nov–Mar.* TV P	*MC V*	■	●	■	17

Hotel	Credit cards				Rooms
BEAUMARIS: *Olde Bull's Head* W www.bullsheadinn.co.uk ££ Castle St, Beaumaris, Anglesey LL58 8AP. *01248 810329.* FAX *01248 811294.* This ancient inn near the castle makes an ideal base for exploring Anglesey. Furnishings evoke the Victorian era (Dickens stayed here in 1859). Inventive cooking. *(See also p601 and p611.)* ● *25–26 Dec, 1 Jan.* TV P	AE MC V	■	●		13
BEDDGELERT: *Sygun Fawr* W www.sygunfawr.co.uk ££ Beddgelert, Caernarfon, Gwynedd LL55 4NE. & FAX *01766 890258.* Tremendous views at this friendly 17th-century manor. Lots of beams and stonework. Good cooking and cosy bedrooms. ● *Jan.* P		■	●	■	9
CAPEL GARMON: *Tan-y-Foel* W www.tyfhotel.co.uk £££ Capel Garmon, Betws-y-Coed, Conwy LL26 0RE. *01690 710507.* FAX *01690 710681.* A quiet country retreat set in woodland with fine views along the Conwy Valley. Stylish contemporary décor. ● *mid-Dec–mid-Feb.* TV P	AE DC MC V	■		■	7
CRICCIETH: *Mynydd Ednyfed* W www.criccieth.net ££ Caernarfon Rd, Criccieth, Gwynedd LL52 0PH. *01766 523269.* FAX *01766 522929.* A secluded, 400-year-old country house in grounds near the sea. Rustic décor and cottagey bedrooms. Gym and tennis court. ● *23 Dec–4 Jan.* TV P	MC V	■	●	■	9
GANLLWYD: *Plas Dolmelynllyn* W www.dolly-hotel.co.uk ££ Ganllwyd, Dolgellau, Gwynedd LL40 2HP. *01341 440273.* FAX *01341 440273.* The respectable comfort of the Victorian era is evoked at this historic country house in quiet countryside near Dolgellau. ● *Nov–Feb.* TV P	AE DC MC V	■		■	10
HARLECH: *Castle Cottage* W www.castlecottageharlech.co.uk ££ Pen Llech, Harlech, Gwynedd LL46 2YL. & FAX *01766 780479.* This quaint old restaurant-with-rooms near the castle has lovely sea and mountain vistas. Be prepared to share these cosy quarters with a vast array of ornamental pigs. Talented cooking. *(See also p601.)* ● *3 weeks in Jan.* TV	MC V	■	●		9
LLANABER: *Llwyndu Farmhouse* W www.llwyndu-farmhouse.co.uk ££ Llanaber, Barmouth, Gwynedd LL42 1RR. *01341 280144.* FAX *01341 281231.* This splendidly restored farmhouse dates back several centuries. Antiques and unusual curios; exposed stonework and timbers. ● *25–26 Dec.* TV P	MC V	■	●	■	7
LLANARMON DYFFRYN CEIRIOG: *West Arms* W www.thewestarms.co.uk £££ Llanrmon Dyffryn Ceiriog, Llangollen, Wrexham LL20 7LD. *01691 600665.* FAX *01691 600622.* This fine hostelry in the tranquil Ceiriog valley has a welcoming ambience and beamy comfortable bedrooms. 10% service charge. *(See also p601.)* TV P	MC V	■	●	■	15
LLANDRILLO: *Tyddyn Llan* W www.tyddynllan.co.uk £££ Llandrillo, Corwen, Denbigh LL21 0ST. *01490 440264.* FAX *01490 440414.* A rambling Georgian house near Bala Lake. Tastefully furnished and spacious. Restaurant uses fine local produce. *(See also p602.)* ● *2 weeks Jan.* TV P	DC MC V	■	●	■	12
LLANDDEINIOLEN: *Ty'n Rhos* W www.tynrhos.co.uk ££ Seion, Llanddeiniolen, Caernarfon LL55 3AE. *01248 670489.* FAX *01248 670079.* Gourmet B&B in converted farm buildings, overlooking the quiet countryside near the Menai Straits. Dinner for residents only. ● *23–30 Dec.* TV P	AE MC V			■	11
LLANDUDNO: *St Tudno* W www.st-tudno.co.uk £££ Promenade, Llandudno, Conwy LL30 2LP. *01492 874411.* FAX *01492 860407.* A welcoming seafront hotel in a smart Victorian terrace. Bay windows overlook the bay. Colourful, spacious rooms; indoor swimming pool. TV P	AE DC MC V	■	●	■	19
LLANDUDNO: *Bodysgallen Hall* W www.bodysgallen.com ££££ Llandudno, Conwy LL30 1RS. *01492 584466.* FAX *01492 582519.* Impressive, historic country-house hotel in a parkland setting with stunning views. Immaculate and refined inside and out; wonderful food. TV P	MC V	■		■	34
LLANFACHRETH: *Ty Isaf Farmhouse* W www.tyisaf78.freeserve.co.uk £ Llanfachreth, nr Dolgellau, Gwynedd LL40 1EA. & FAX *01341 423261.* This friendly 17th-century longhouse has cosy bedrooms and stacks of chacter and rural charm. Good Welsh dinners served communally at an oak table. Resident llamas. ● *mid-Dec–Jan.* P		■		■	3
PENMAENPOOL: *George III* W www.george-3rd.co.uk ££ Penmaenpool, Dolgellau, Gwynedd LL40 1YD. *01341 422525.* FAX *01341 423565.* Unusual waterfront hotel converted from a chandlery, a railway station and a pub. Atmospheric cellar bar and beamed dining room. TV P	MC V	■	●		11

Price categories for a standard double room per night, inclusive of breakfast, service charges and any additional taxes such as VAT:
£ under £65
££ £65–£100
£££ £100–£150
££££ £150–£200
£££££ £200 plus

RESTAURANT
Hotel restaurant or dining room serving more than just breakfast; often open to non-residents.

CHILDREN WELCOME
Especially welcoming to families. May have children's facilities such as cots, babysitting, family rooms, etc.

GARDEN/TERRACE
Hotels with a garden, courtyard or terrace, often providing tables for eating outside.

CREDIT CARDS
Indicates which credit cards are accepted: *AE* American Express; *DC* Diners Club; *MC* Master Card/Access; *V* Visa.

Hotel	Credit Cards	Restaurant	Children Welcome	Garden/Terrace	Number of Rooms
PENMAENPOOL: *Penmaenuchaf Hall* W www.penhall.co.uk £££ Penmaenpool, Dolgellau, Gwynedd LL40 1YB. *01341 422129.* FAX *01341 422787.* Peace and relaxation are assured at this elegant Victorian mansion, along with ambitious menus and magnificent views of Snowdonia. TV P	DC MC V	■		■	14
PORTMEIRION: *Portmeirion* W www.portmeirion-village.com £££ Portmeirion, Penrhyndeudraeth, Gwynedd LL48 6ET. & FAX *01766 770000.* A Mediterranean architectural fantasy transported to a wooded estuary above Cardigan Bay. The village-like complex includes a sumptuous hotel and self-catering cottage suites. *(See also p440.)* *6 Jan–1 Feb.* TV P	AE DC MC V	■	●	■	51
TALSARNAU: *Maes-y-Neuadd* W www.neuadd.com ££££ Talsarnau, Gwynedd LL47 6YA. *01766 780200.* FAX *01766 780211.* A graciously relaxing and stylish country house in glorious gardens. A 14th-century building with sensitive stone and glass additions. TV P	AE DC MC V	■	●	■	16
TYN-Y-GROES: *Groes Inn* W www.groesinn.com ££ Tyn-y-Groes, Conwy LL32 8TN. *01492 650545.* FAX *01492 650855.* An ancient coaching inn with masses of character and bric-à-brac. Service is pleasantly relaxed but efficient. Good-value bar meals. TV P	AE DC MC V	■	●	■	14
SOUTH AND MID-WALES					
ABERYSTWYTH: *Conrah Country House* W www.conrah.co.uk £££ Chancery, Aberystwyth, Cered SY23 4DF. *01970 617941.* FAX *01970 624546.* Traditional country-house hotel with extensive woodland grounds and lovely gardens. Grand views and an indoor pool. *Christmas.* TV P	AE DC MC V	■		■	17
BRECON: *Cantre Selyf* W www.cantreselyf.co.uk £ 5 Lion St, Brecon, Powys LD3 7AU. *01874 622904.* FAX *01874 622315.* Refined but relaxed townhouse in Brecon's attractive old centre. Timbered 17th-century interior. Guests are consulted about dinner menus. *Dec–Jan.* P		■	●	■	3
BROAD HAVEN: *Druidstone* W www.druidstone.co.uk ££ Druidston Haven, Broad Haven, Pembrokeshire SA62 3NE. *01437 781221.* Perched high above a quiet beach, this slightly bohemian hotel arouses ferocious loyalty. Several en-suite loft rooms. *(See also p602.)* P	AE MC V	■	●	■	11
CARDIFF: *Big Sleep* W www.thebigsleephotel.com £ Bute Terrace, Cardiff CF10 2FE. *029-2063 6363.* FAX *029-2063 6364.* A stylish, imaginative budget venture in a ten-storey office block. The interior is streamlined and contemporary. *25–26 Dec.* TV P	AE DC MC V		●		81
CARDIFF: *St David's* W www.thestdavidshotel.com £££££ Havannah St, Cardiff CF10 5SD. *029 2045 4045.* FAX *029 2031 3075.* This luxury spa hotel makes a sleek, contemporary statement on the shores of Cardiff Bay. State-of-the-art health and fitness facilities. TV P	AE DC MC V	■	●	■	132
CLYTHA: *Clytha Arms* W www.clytha-arms.com ££ Clytha, Abergavenny, Monmouth NP7 9BW. *01873 840206.* FAX *01873 840209.* Deliciously inventive cooking is the highpoint of this charming country pub near Abergavenny. Several tastefully furnished bedrooms. The Big Pit is an easy drive. Kitchen closed Mondays. *(See also p603.)* *25 Dec.* TV P	AE DC MC V	■	●	■	4
CRICKHOWELL: *Gliffaes Country House* W www.gliffaeshotel.com £££ Crickhowell, Powys NP8 1RH. *01874 730371.* FAX *01874 730463.* Gorgeous gardens and Usk Valley scenery at this creeper-clad, Victorian country house. The spacious, refined interior feels equally serene. TV P	AE DC MC V	■	●	■	22
EGLWYSFACH: *Ynyshire Hall* W www.ynyshire-hall.co.uk ££££ Eglwysfach, Machynlleth, Powys SY20 8TA. *01654 781209.* FAX *01654 781366.* This fine Georgian mansion by the mouth of the Dovey was once owned by Queen Victoria. Mature gardens with velvety lawns. TV P	AE DC MC V	■		■	9

FISHGUARD: *Manor Town House* ££
11 Main St, Fishguard, Pembroke SA65 9HG. & FAX *01348 873260.*
This excellent guesthouse stands in the heart of Fishguard's attractive upper town. Splendid harbour views. *restricted winter opening.* TV

MC V | ■ | ● | ■ | 6

LAKE VYRNWY: *Lake Vyrnwy* W www.lakevyrnwy.com £££
Lake Vyrnwy, Llanwddyn, Powys SY10 0LY. *01691 870692.* FAX *01691 870259.*
A lakeshore setting distinguishes this Victorian fishing lodge. Most bedrooms have lake views. Lots of outdoor activities. TV P

AE DC MC V | ■ | ● | ■ | 35

LLANDEILO: *Cawdor Arms* W www.cawdor-arms.co.uk £
Rhosmaen St, Llandeilo, Carmarthen SA19 6EN. *01558 823500.* FAX *01558 822399.*
A fine touring base on the west side of the Brecon Beacons, this Georgian inn boasts accomplished food and smart bedrooms. TV P

MC V | ■ | ● | | 17

LLANFIHANGEL-YNG-NGWYNFA: *Cyfie Farm* ££
Llanfihangel, Llanfyllin, Powys SY22 5JE. & FAX *01691 648451.*
Top-range B&B in a 17th-century farmhouse, with spectacular views over the Meifod Valley. Roomy suites in converted outbuildings. *Jan–Feb.* TV P

| ■ | ● | ■ | 3

LLANGAMMARCH WELLS: *Lake Country House* ££££
Llangammarch Wells, Powys LD4 4BS. *01591 620202.* W www.lakecountryhouse.co.uk
This mellow, mainly Edwardian building lies in 52-acre grounds. The interior is grandly tasteful, warm and welcoming. Fishing. TV P

AE DC MC V | ■ | ● | ■ | 19

LLANIGON: *Old Post Office* W www.oldpost-office.co.uk £
Llanigon, Hay-on-Wye, Powys HR3 5QA. *01497 820008.*
Delightful cottage B&B in a quiet National Park village just outside Hay. Though small and simple, it is immaculate and stylish inside. P

| | ● | | 3

LLANTHONY: *Llanthony Priory* W www.llanthonypriory.supanet.com ££
Llanthony, Abergavenny, Monmouthshire NP7 7NN. *01873 890487.* FAX *01873 890844.*
A 12th-century Augustinian Priory forms part of this retreat-like hotel in a beautiful quiet location surrounded by hills. Rooms (some with 4-poster beds) are reached by a spiral staircase; real ale and home-cooked food.

AE DC MC V | ■ | | ■ | 5

LLANWRTYD WELLS: *Carlton House* W www.carltonrestaurant.co.uk ££
Dolycoed Rd, Llanwrtyd Wells, Powys LD5 4RA. *01591 610248.* FAX *01591 610242.*
Food is taken seriously at this restaurant-with-rooms in a Cambrian spa town. A relaxed, cheerful style of budget B&B prevails. *10–28 Dec.* TV

MC V | ■ | ● | | 6

LLYSWEN: *Llangoed Hall* W www.llangoedhall.com ££££
Llyswen, Brecon, Powys LD3 0YP. *01874 754525.* FAX *01874 754545.*
A grand, part-Jacobean mansion owned by Sir Bernard Ashley (widower of Laura). Recently refurbished interior and extensive grounds. TV P

AE DC MC V | ■ | | ■ | 23

MILEBROOK: *Milebrook House* W www.milebrookhouse.co.uk ££
Milebrook, Knighton, Powys LD7 1LT. *01547 528632.* FAX *01547 520509.*
Poised beside Offa's Dyke and the River Teme, this stone-built Georgian house, in large, attractive gardens, is very close to the English border. TV P

AE DC MC V | ■ | | ■ | 10

THE MUMBLES: *Hillcrest House* W www.hillcresthousehotel.com ££
1 Higher Lane, Langland, The Mumbles, Swansea SA3 4NS. *01792 363700.*
This welcoming small hotel has a quiet setting. Tastefully decorated, with strikingly themed bedrooms. Pleasing restaurant. TV P

AE MC V | ■ | ● | ■ | 6

NANTGAREDIG: *Cwmtwrch Farm* W www.tourlink.co.uk ££
Nantgaredig, Carmarthen SA31 7NY. *01267 290238.* FAX *01267 290808.*
An ideal country stay is promised in this stylishly renovated farm in twelve acres of grounds. Gym and indoor pool. *23–28 Dec.* TV P

MC V | ■ | ● | ■ | 6

NEWPORT: *Cnapan* W www.online-holidays.netcnapan ££
East St, Newport, Pembroke SA42 0SY. *01239 820575.*
This Georgian house has a cheerful and welcoming air. Compact, rustic bedrooms with plenty to read. *(See also p603.)* *25–26 Dec, Jan–Feb.* TV P

MC V | ■ | ● | ■ | 5

PENALLY: *Penally Abbey* W www.penally-abbey.com £££
Penally, Tenby, Pembroke SA70 7PY. *01834 843033.* FAX *01834 844714.*
Neo-Gothic architectural flourishes give this fine country house considerable character. Located on the Pembrokeshire Coast Path near Tenby. TV P

AE MC V | ■ | ● | ■ | 17

PORTHKERRY: *Egerton Grey* W www.egertongrey.co.uk £££
Porthkerry, Barry, Glamorgan CF62 3BZ. *01446 711666.* FAX *01446 711690.*
Handy for Cardiff airport, this refined Victorian rectory boasts original plasterwork and mahogany panelling. Traditional menus and service. TV P

AE MC V | ■ | ● | ■ | 10

Price categories for a standard double room per night, inclusive of breakfast, service charges and any additional taxes such as VAT:
£ under £65
££ £65–£100
£££ £100–£150
££££ £150–£200
£££££ £200 plus

RESTAURANT
Hotel restaurant or dining room serving more than just breakfast; often open to non-residents.

CHILDREN WELCOME
Especially welcoming to families. May have children's facilities such as cots, babysitting, family rooms, etc.

GARDEN/TERRACE
Hotels with a garden, courtyard or terrace, often providing tables for eating outside.

CREDIT CARDS
Indicates which credit cards are accepted: *AE* American Express; *DC* Diners Club; *MC* Master Card/Access; *V* Visa.

Hotel	Credit Cards	Restaurant	Children Welcome	Garden/Terrace	Number of Rooms
REYNOLDSTON: *Fairyhill* W www.fairyhill.net £££ Reynoldston, Swansea SA3 1BS. *01792 390139.* FAX *01792 391358.* This isolated country house in wooded grounds makes a fine place to unwind. Attentive service and interesting food. ● *Christmas, 1–18 Jan.* TV P	AE MC V	■		■	8
ST BRIDES WENTLOOGE: *Inn at the Elm Tree* W www.the-elm-tree.co.uk ££ St Brides Wentlooge, Newport NP10 8SQ. *01633 680225.* FAX *01633 681035.* This roadside dining inn, a 19th-century barn conversion, boasts an imaginative contemporary look. Highly regarded food. TV P	AE MC V	■	●	■	10
ST BRIDES WENTLOOGE: *West Usk Lighthouse* ££ Lighthouse Rd, St Brides Wentlooge, Newport NP10 8SF. *01633 810126.* FAX *01633 815582.* W www.westusklighthouse.co.uk This lighthouse B&B on the salt flats by the Severn boasts a warm welcome. Simple, cosy interior; alternative therapy available. ● *Christmas.* TV P	AE DC MC V		●	■	4
SPITTAL: *Lower Haythog Farm* W www.lowerhaythogfarm.co.uk £ Spittal, Haverfordwest, Pembroke SA62 5QL. & FAX *01437 731279.* B&B on a working farm in central Pembrokeshire offering tremendous value. Good home cooking and cottagey bedrooms. TV P		■	●	■	6
TINTERN: *Parva Farmhouse* W www.hoteltintern.co.uk ££ Tintern, Chepstow, Monmouth NP16 6SQ. *01291 689411.* FAX *01291 689557.* An ideal base for exploring Tintern's abbey and the surrounding Wye Valley, this stonebuilt 17th-century building is furnished in rustic style. TV P	AE MC V	■	●	■	9
WHITEBROOK: *Crown at Whitebrook* W www.crownatwhitebrook.co.uk ££ Whitebrook, Monmouth NP25 4TX. *01600 860254.* FAX *01600 860607.* This restaurant-with-rooms lies in a leafy stretch of Wye Valley. Secluded, but the cooking is popular. The interior is bright and comfortable, with neat, practical bedrooms. *(See also p604.)* ● *Christmas & New Year.* TV P	AE DC MC V	■		■	10
WOLF'S CASTLE: *The Wolfe* W www.the-wolfe.co.uk ££ Wolf's Castle, Haverfordwest, Pembroke SA62 5LS. *01437 741662.* FAX *01437 741676.* This typical stonebuilt, creeper-clad roadside inn not far from St David's has an unexpected Italianate interior, along with the odd wolfish touch. TV P	MC V	■	●	■	3

THE LOWLANDS

Hotel	Credit Cards	Restaurant	Children Welcome	Garden/Terrace	Number of Rooms
ABERDOUR: *Hawkcraig House* ££ Hawkcraig Point, Aberdour, Fife KY3 0TZ. *01383 860335.* An amazing waterfront setting at this charming guesthouse in an old ferryman's house. Book ahead. Excellent dinners. ● *Nov–Mar.* TV P		■	●	■	2
ALLOWAY: *Ivy House* W www.theivyhouse.uk.com ££££ 2 Alloway, Ayrshire KA7 4NL. *01292 442336.* FAX *01292 445572.* A makeover has given this restaurant-with-rooms near Robbie Burns' cottage an upbeat, contemporary feel. Culzean Castle is an easy drive. TV P	AE MC V	■	●	■	5
AUCHTERARDER: *Gleneagles* W www.gleneagles.com £££££ Auchterarder, Perth & Kinross. *01764 662231.* FAX *01764 662134.* Luxury château-style resort hotel with tip-top service, championship golf courses and a health spa. It's surprisingly family-friendly. TV P	AE DC MC V	■	●	■	220
BALQUHIDDER: *Monachyle Mhor* W www.monachylemhor.com £££ Balquhidder, Lochearnhead, Stirling FK19 8PQ. *01877 384622.* FAX *01877 384305.* A beautiful setting at the end of a remote, lochside glen makes this upbeat, family-run farmhouse memorable. Stylishly rustic bedrooms. TV P	MC V	■		■	10
BLAIRGOWRIE: *Kinloch House* W www.kinlochhouse.com ££££ By Blairgowrie, Perth & Kinross PH10 6SG *01250 884237.* FAX *01250 884333.* A traditional country-house hotel in extensive parkland, ideal for a restful break. Lots of activities and a heated indoor pool. ● *18–30 Dec.* TV P	MC V	■	●	■	18

Hotel	Cards				Rooms
CALLANDER: *Leny House* www.lenyestate.com ££££ Leny Estate, Callander, Perthshire FK17 8HA. & *01877 331078.* This delightful B&B is a great base for exploring the Trossachs. Originally 16th-century, its present incarnation is largely Victorian. Luxurious and stylish inside, it retains many period features. *Nov–Apr.*	MC V	■		■	3
CLINTMAINS: *Clint Lodge* www.clintlodge.co.uk ££ Clintmains, St Boswells, Borders TD6 0DZ. *01835 822027.* *01835 822656.* Views of the Tweed grace this attractive Victorian guesthouse close to Melrose Abbey. The ambience is restful; breakfasts outstanding. *25 Dec, 1 Jan.*	MC V	■		■	5
CUPAR: *Peat Inn* www.thepeatinn.co.uk ££££ Peat Inn, Cupar, Fife KY25 5LH. *01334 840206.* *01334 840530.* Primarily renowned for its food, the Peat Inn also boasts luxury suites set in a separate annexe. A romantic base for sightseeing around St Andrews. *(See also p605.)* *25–26 Dec, Sun–Mon.*	AE MC V	■	●	■	8
DOLLAR: *Castle Campbell* www.castle-campbell.co.uk ££ 11 Bridge St, Dollar, Clackmannan FK14 7DE. *01259 742519.* *01259 743742.* A simple but dignified Georgian building in the town centre, inoffensively upholstered in tartan and leather.	AE DC MC V	■	●		8
DUNOON: *Enmore* www.enmorehotel.co.uk ££ Marine Parade, Dunoon, Argyll & Bute PA23 8HH. *01369 702230.* *01369 702148.* Modern Scottish cooking in an attractive Georgian house with views over the Firth of Clyde. Several bedrooms feature jacuzzis. *mid-Nov–mid-Feb.*	AE MC V	■	●	■	9
EDINBURGH: *19 St Bernard's Crescent* £££ 19 St Bernard's Crescent, Edinburgh EH4 1NR. & *0131 332 6162.* www.aboutscotland.com/edin/stbernards.html An imposing neoclassical townhouse B&B with a distinguished artistic background; inside, it's crammed with antiques, books, porcelain and works of art. *Nov–Mar.* *throughout.*	MC V				2
EDINBURGH: *The Bonham* www.thebonham.com ££££ 35 Drumsheugh Gardens, Edinburgh EH3 7RN. *0131 226 6050.* *0131 226 6080.* Ultra-smart townhouse boasting rich interior décor with touches of whimsy. The oak-panelled restaurant serves serious modern European fare. Opulent, hi-tech bedrooms.	AE DC MC V	■	●		48
EDINBURGH: *The Scotsman* www.thescotsmanhotel.co.uk ££££ 20 North Bridge, Edinburgh EH1 1YT. *0131 556 5565.* *0131 652 3652.* An unusual hotel venture set in the plush Edwardian offices of the eponymous newspaper. Leisure club and fashionable brasserie dining.	AE DC MC V	■	●		68
EDNAM: *Edenwater House* www.edenwaterhouse.co.uk ££ Ednam, Kelso, Borders TD5 7QL. *01573 224070.* *01573 226615.* A quiet stone guesthouse on the edge of the village. Cheviot views from some rooms. Appetizing dinners served. Good wine list. *1–14 Jan.*	MC V	■		■	4
GLASGOW: *Langs* www.langshotels.co.uk £££ 2 Port Dundas Place, Glasgow G2 3LD. *0141 333 1500.* *0141 333 5700.* A style-conscious glamorous boutique hotel with two trendy restaurants. Bedrooms are comfortably minimalist. Gym.	AE DC MC V	■	●		100
GLASGOW: *One Devonshire Gardens* ££££ 1 Devonshire Gardens, Glasgow G12 0UX. *0141 339 2001.* *0141 337 1663.* www.onedevonshiregardens.co.uk The ultimate luxury townhouse, glamorously refurbished and opulently decorated, with cooking to match and plenty of hi-tech gadgetry in the bedrooms. A place for a serious treat. *(See also p605.)*	AE DC MC V	■	●		38
GLENROTHES: *Balbirnie House* www.balbirnie.co.uk ££££ Balbirnie Park, Markinch, Glenrothes, Fife KY7 6NE. *01592 610066.* *01592 610529.* This elegant Georgian mansion evokes an air of tastefully restrained hedonism. A certain amount of business and conference trade is tactfully separated from the main building. Bedrooms are luxuriously individual.	AE DC MC V	■	●	■	32
GULLANE: *Golf Inn* ££ Main St, Gullane, East Lothian EH31 2AB. *01620 843259.* *01620 842066.* Smartly refurbished village inn with crisp colour schemes and pine furnishings – even a little trompe l'oeil. Simple, appetizing menus. Good value.	AE MC V	■	●	■	14

Price categories for a standard double room per night, inclusive of breakfast, service charges and any additional taxes such as VAT:
£ under £65
££ £65–£100
£££ £100–£150
££££ £150–£200
£££££ £200 plus

RESTAURANT
Hotel restaurant or dining room serving more than just breakfast; often open to non-residents.

CHILDREN WELCOME
Especially welcoming to families. May have children's facilities such as cots, babysitting, family rooms, etc.

GARDEN/TERRACE
Hotels with a garden, courtyard or terrace, often providing tables for eating outside.

CREDIT CARDS
Indicates which credit cards are accepted: *AE* American Express; *DC* Diners Club; *MC* Master Card/Access; *V* Visa.

GULLANE: *Greywalls* www.greywalls.co.uk £££££
Muirfield, Gullane, E Lothian EH31 2EG. *01620 842144.* FAX *01620 842241.*
Despite its name, this photogenic Lutyens house overlooking the famous golf course is built of warm golden stone. The Jekyll-designed gardens are gorgeous, and the interior suitably refined. *mid-Oct–mid-Apr.*

HEITON: *Roxburghe* www.roxburghe.net ££££
Heiton, Kelso, Borders TD5 8JZ. *01573 450331.* FAX *01573 450611.*
This grand Jacobean-style house in extensive parkland makes a supremely comfortable, if highly traditional, Borders base, with lots of on-site outdoor activities.

INVERSNAID: *Inversnaid Lodge* www.inversnaidphoto.com ££
Inversnaid, Aberfoyle, Stirling FK8 3TU. *01877 386254.*
A photogenic setting on the eastern shores of Loch Lomond makes an ideal base for a hotel owned by and geared towards photographers. Simple cottagey bedrooms and straightforward dinners. *Nov–Mar.*

JEDBURGH: *Hundalee House* www.accommodation-scotland.org £
Jedburgh, Borders TD8 6DA. & FAX *01835 863011.*
Refined B&B in a handsome Georgian manor in 15-acre grounds. Classic interior and a warm welcome. Remarkable value. *Nov–Mar.*

KIRKCUDBRIGHT: *Gladstone House* hilarygladstone@aol.com ££
48 High St, Kirkcudbright, Dumfrs & Gall DG6 4JX. & FAX *01557 331734.*
Charming, simple B&B in an attractive townhouse set back from the Solway waterfront. The interior is light and stylish. Excellent breakfasts.

LINLITHGOW: *Champany Inn* www.champany.com £££
Champany, Linlithgow, W Lothian EH49 7LU. *01506 834532.* FAX *01506 834302.*
This restaurant boasts stylish accommodation. Décor and furnishings are classy; bathrooms sparklingly efficient. *(See p605.)* *25–26 Dec, 1–2 Jan.*

ST ANDREWS: *Old Course* www.oldcoursehotel.co.uk £££££
Old Station Rd, St Andrews, Fife KY16 9SP. *01334 474371.* FAX *01334 477668.*
The legendary seaside links course is effectively the garden of this luxury hotel. Its 1960s exterior wins no beauty contests, but its glamorously stylish interior and exemplary facilities are unsurpassed. *Christmas.*

ST BOSWELLS: *Dryburgh Abbey* www.dryburgh.co.uk £££
St Boswells, Melrose, Borders TD6 0RQ. *01835 822261.* FAX *01835 823945.*
A ruined abbey beside the River Tweed makes an atmospheric setting for this hotel. Formal restaurant; comfortable, spacious bedrooms.

ST FILLANS: *Four Seasons* www.thefourseasonshotel.co.uk ££
St Fillans, Perthshire PH6 2NF. *01764 685333.* FAX *01764 685444.*
This welcoming hotel enjoys a glorious waterfront location. Plenty of comfortable lounge and dining space. Practical bedrooms. *Feb.*

STRATHKINNESS: *Fossil House* www.fossil-guest-house.co.uk £
12–14 Main St, Strathkinness, St Andrews, Fife KY16 9RU. & FAX *01334 850639.*
A family-friendly B&B in a converted smallholding (bedrooms are in the court-yard stable-block). Conservatory lounge. *limited.* *throughout.*

TROON: *Lochgreen House* www.costleyhotels.co.uk £££
Monktonhill Rd, Southwood, Troon, S. Ayrshire KA10 7EN. *01292 313343.* FAX *01292 318661.*
Elegant, antique-filled Edwardian hotel with excellent cooking, served in a baronial-looking modern restaurant. Bedrooms are luxurious.

YARROW: *Tibbie Shiels Inn* www.tibbieshielsinn.com £
Yarrow, by Selkirk TD7 5LH. *01750 42231.* FAX *01750 42302.*
Once a hostelry favoured by Sir Walter Scott, this 18th-century inn offers good food and a warm welcome. Beautiful setting on St Mary's Loch.

Hotel	Credit Cards	Restaurant	Children Welcome	Garden/Terrace	Number of Rooms
Gullane: Greywalls	AE DC MC V	■	●	■	23
Heiton: Roxburghe	AE DC MC V	■	●	■	19
Inversnaid: Inversnaid Lodge		■		■	9
Jedburgh: Hundalee House			●	■	5
Kirkcudbright: Gladstone House	MC V			■	3
Linlithgow: Champany Inn	AE DC MC V	■	●	■	16
St Andrews: Old Course	AE DC MC V	■	●		150
St Boswells: Dryburgh Abbey	AE MC V	■	●	■	38
St Fillans: Four Seasons	AE MC V	■	●	■	18
Strathkinness: Fossil House	AE MC V		●	■	4
Troon: Lochgreen House	AE MC V	■		■	40
Yarrow: Tibbie Shiels Inn	MC V	■		■	5

Highlands and Islands

Hotel	Cards				Rooms
Aberdeen: *Marcliffe at Pitfodels* W www.marcliffe.com £££ North Deeside Rd, Aberdeen AB15 9YA. *01224 861000.* FAX *01224 868860.* A smoothly managed, upmarket hotel in large grounds just ten minutes' drive from the city centre. Beautifully kept inside, it has a warm and welcoming air. TV P	AE DC MC V	■	●	■	42
Achiltibuie: *Summer Isles* W www.summerisleshotel.co.uk £££ Achiltibuie, Ullapool, Highland IV26 2YG. *01854 622282.* FAX *01854 622251.* A remote and picturesque setting overlooking the Summer Isles makes this disarmingly low-key place an idyllic retreat. Quietly sophisticated inside, it has first class food and lovely bedrooms. ● *Oct–Easter.* TV P	MC V	■		■	13
Arisaig: *Old Library Lodge* W www.oldlibrary.co.uk £££ Arisaig, Highland PH39 4NH. *01687 450651.* FAX *01687 450219.* A modest restaurant-with-rooms on the Road to the Isles, offering five choices at each course, and much fresh, locally sourced produce. Peaceful, spacious bedrooms, mostly in a modern rear extension. ● *Dec–Feb.* TV	AE MC V	■		■	6
Auldearn: *Boath House* W www.boath-house.com ££££ Auldearn, Nairn, Highland IV12 5TW. *01667 454896.* FAX *01667 455469.* Close to the Moray Firth, this imposing Georgian mansion stands in secluded 20-acre grounds. The strikingly decorated contemporary interior is cool and spacious. Outstanding food (organic and seasonal). ● *25, 26 Dec.* TV P	AE MC V	■	●	■	6
Ballater: *Balgonie Country House* W www.royaldeesidehotels.com £££ Braemar Place, Ballater, Aberdeen AB35 5NQ. & FAX *013397 55482.* Welcoming hosts play a major role in the success of this secluded Deeside property, which offers excellent cooking and bright, comfortable rooms. A good place to unwind. ● *5 Jan–10 Feb.* TV P	AE DC MC V	■	●	■	9
Ballater: *Darroch Learg* W www.darrochlearg.co.uk £££ Braemar Rd, Ballater, Aberdeen AB35 5UX. *013397 55443.* FAX *013397 55252.* Two interesting Victorian houses in hilly gardens provide top-notch cooking and very comfortable rooms. Splendid views towards Lochnagar. Formidable wine-list. *(See also p606.)* ● *Christmas & 3 weeks in Jan.* TV P	AE DC MC V	■	●	■	18
Clachan-Seil: *Willowburn* W www.willowburn.co.uk £££ Clachan-Seil, Isle of Seil, Oban, Argyll & Bute PA34 4TJ. *01852 300276.* FAX *01852 300597.* Set on a mini-islet connected by bridge to the mainland south of Oban, this idyllic retreat is a whitewashed cottage with lochside views, and simple, cheerful décor. Good seafood. ● *Dec–Feb.* TV P	MC V	■	●	■	7
Crinan: *Crinan* W www.crinanhotel.com £££££ Crinan, Lochgilphead, Argyll & Bute PA31 8SR. *01546 830261.* FAX *01546 830292.* Vistas over Loch Fyne and the Jura Sound enhance this simple white building. Seafood is on the menus. Room rate includes dinner. ● *Christmas.* TV P	AE MC V	■	●	■	20
Dunkeld: *The Pend* W www.thepend.com ££ 5 Brae St, Dunkeld, Perth & Kinross PH8 0BA. *01350 727586.* FAX *01350 727173.* High-quality accommodation in a quiet Georgian townhouse just off the main street. Beautifully kept interior with antiques and period features. Excellent breakfasts served at flexible times; imaginative dinners available. TV P	AE DC MC V	■	●		3
Dunkeld: *Kinnaird* W www.kinnairdestate.com £££££ Kinnaird Estate, Dunkeld, Perth & Kinross PH8 0LB. *01796 482440.* FAX *01796 482289.* Superb country-house accommodation on a huge Tayside sporting estate. Tranquil setting; seriously smart but relaxing interior. Highly regarded cooking. *(See also p607.)* Room rate includes dinner. ● *Mon–Wed in Jan–Feb.* TV P	AE MC V	■		■	9
Eriska: *Isle of Eriska* W www.eriska-hotel.co.uk £££££ Eriska, Ledaig, Oban, Argyll & Bute PA37 1SD. *01631 720371.* FAX *01631 720531.* Family-run luxury hideaway in Scots Baronial style with impressive leisure facilities on an island in the Firth of Lorne. Elaborate dinners. ● *Jan.* TV P	AE MC V	■	●	■	17
Fort William: *Ashburn House* W www.highland5star.co.uk ££ 4 Achintore Rd, Fort William, Highland PH33 6RQ. *01397 706000.* FAX *01397 702024.* Expect a proper Highland welcome and an excellent breakfast at this Victorian B&B overlooking Loch Linnhe. Bedrooms are well furnished and equipped for a thoroughly comfortable stay. ● *Dec–Jan.* TV *throughout.* P	AE MC V		●	■	7

For key to symbols see back flap

Price categories for a standard double room per night, inclusive of breakfast, service charges and any additional taxes such as VAT:
£ under £65
££ £65–£100
£££ £100–£150
££££ £150–£200
£££££ £200 plus

RESTAURANT
Hotel restaurant or dining room serving more than just breakfast; often open to non-residents.

CHILDREN WELCOME
Especially welcoming to families. May have children's facilities such as cots, babysitting, family rooms, etc.

GARDEN/TERRACE
Hotels with a garden, courtyard or terrace, often providing tables for eating outside.

CREDIT CARDS
Indicates which credit cards are accepted: *AE* American Express; *DC* Diners Club; *MC* Master Card/Access; *V* Visa.

	Credit Cards	Restaurant	Children Welcome	Garden/Terrace	Number of Rooms
FORT WILLIAM: *The Grange* W www.thegrange-scotland.co.uk ££ Grange Rd, Fort William, Highland PH33 6JF. *01397 705516.* FAX *01397 701595.* Skillfully restored B&B overlooking the loch. Its beautifully furnished bedrooms are spacious and stylish, with antique beds and luxurious bathrooms. Generous breakfasts. ● *Nov–mid-Mar.* TV *throughout.* P				■	4
GLENLIVET: *Minmore House* W www.minmorehouse.com £££ Glenlivet, Moray AB37 9DB. *01807 590378.* FAX *01807 590472.* A tranquil,elegant country house on the Glenlivet estate (former home of the distillery's founder). Glorious Speyside surroundings. Traditionally comfortable bedrooms (some very grand). ● *Feb–mid-Mar.* P	*AE MC V*	■	●	■	10
GRANTOWN-ON-SPEY: *Culdearn House* W www.culdearn.com £££ Woodlands Terrace, Grantown-on-Spey, Highland PH26 3JU. *01479 872106.* Exemplary hospitality in a Victorian house on the Speyside whisky trail. Comfortable, well-equipped bedrooms and tasty four-course dinners. Rates include dinner. ● *Dec–Jan.* TV *throughout.* P	*AE MC V*	■		■	9
INVERNESS: *Glenmoriston Town House* W www.glenmoriston.com ££ 20 Ness Bank, Inverness, Highland IV2 4SF. *01463 223777.* FAX *01463 712378.* Riverside hotel with tasteful, contemporary décor. Bedrooms attain high standards, with marble bathrooms and lavish furnishings. TV P	*AE DC MC V*	■	●	■	15
INVERNESS: *Millwood House* W www.millwoodhouse.co.uk ££ 36 Old Mill Rd, Inverness, Highland IV2 3HR. *01463 237254.* FAX *0870-4296806.* A charming B&B in a private home, quietly set in a lovely residential district. Welcoming and civilized, with attractive, well-equipped bedrooms. Guests may use its beautiful gardens. ● *Jan–Feb.* TV P	*MC V*			■	3
ISLE OF HARRIS: *Leachin House* W www.leachin-house.com £££ Tarbert, Isle of Harris HS3 3AH. & FAX *01859 502157.* Victorian stone building by Norman MacLeod, "father" of the Harris tweed industry, with many period features. On shores of West Loch Tarbert and good base for shooting (arranged by hotel) and fishing. Rates include dinner. TV P	*MC V*			■	3
ISLE OF IONA: *Argyll* W www.argyllhoteliona.co.uk £££ Isle of Iona, Argyll & Bute PA76 6SJ. *01681 700334.* FAX *01681 700510.* A relaxing retreat with bright simple bedrooms and a sunny conservatory overlooking the sound. Good local cooking. ● *19 Oct–24 Mar.* P	*MC V*	■	●	■	16
ISLE OF LEWIS: *Galson Farm* W www.galsonfarm.co.uk ££ South Galson, Isle of Lewis, Western Isles HS2 0SH. & FAX *01851 850492.* Simple, homely accommodation on a working farm. This traditional 18-acre coastal croft dates back to the 18th century. Neat bedrooms and good home cooking (interesting vegetarian options). TV P	*MC V*	■	●	■	3
ISLE OF MULL: *Druimard Country House* W www.druimard.co.uk £££ Dervaig, Tobermory, Isle of Mull PA75 6QW. *01688 400345.* FAX *01688 400345.* Stonebuilt Victorian hotel in a quiet glenside setting. Mull's Little Theatre stands in its grounds. Good cooking. Polished service. Rates include dinner. ● *Nov–Mar.* TV P	*MC V*	■	●	■	7
ISLE OF SKYE: *Duisdale* W www.duisdale.com ££ Sleat, Isle Ornsay, Isle of Skye IV43 8QW. *01471 833202.* FAX *01471 833404.* Friendly Victorian house with magnificent views across the Sound of Sleat. Flamboyantly decorated; stacks of personality. The owner is a Paris-trained chef, so expect some good cooking. Lovely gardens. ● *Nov–mid-Mar.* P	*AE MC V*	■	●	■	19
ISLE OF SKYE: *Three Chimneys* W www.threechimneys.co.uk ££££ Colbost, Dunvegan, Isle of Skye IV55 8ZT. *01470 511258.* FAX *01470 511358.* Spectacular coastal location, superlative cooking and startlingly voguish bedrooms make these converted crofters' cottages the talk of the isles. Perfection without pretension. ● *3 weeks in Jan.* TV *throughout.* P	*AE MC V*	■	●	■	6

KILLIECRANKIE: *Killiecrankie* W www.killiecrankiehotel.co.uk ££££
Killiecrankie, Pitlochry, Perth & Kinross PH16 5LG. Tel *01796 473220.* FAX *01796 472451.*
A relaxing, informal place by the scenic wooded cliffs of the Killiecrankie Pass (an RSPB bird reserve). Décor is bright and stylish. Acclaimed cooking – light meals available. Well-kept gardens. *(See also p607.)* ● *Jan.* TV P

MC V	■	●	■	10

KINGUSSIE: *The Cross* W www.thecross.co.uk ££££
Tweed Mill Brae, Ardbroilach Road, Kingussie, Highland PH21 1LB. Tel *01540 661166.*
Acclaimed restaurant-with-rooms in a converted tweed mill near the Cairngorms. The smartly refurbished interior is light and bright with lots of modern paintings. Brilliant cooking. ● *23 Dec–Jan.* TV P

MC V	■		■	8

LOCHINVER: *Albannach* W www.thealbannach.co.uk ££££
Baddidarroch, Lochinver, Highland IV27 4LP. Tel *01571 844407.* FAX *01571 844285.*
This welcoming house has a wonderful atmosphere and fine views. Home-grown produce and Lochinver seafood go into its seasonal menus. Rates include dinner. ● *Mon, Dec–mid-Mar.* *throughout.* P

MC V	■		■	5

LOCHRANZA: *Apple Lodge* ££
Lochranza, Isle of Arran KA27 8HJ. Tel & FAX *01770 830229.*
A charming base on the Isle of Arran, handy for the Kintyre ferry, with views over the nearby castle. Bedrooms are prettily floral; several in a self-contained cottage annexe. Excellent cooking. ● *Christmas & New Year.* TV P

	■		■	4

MUIR OF ORD: *The Dower House* @ info@thedowerhouse.co.uk ££
Highfield, Muir of Ord, Ross-shire IV6 7XN. Tel & FAX *01463 870090.*
An extremely agreeable small hotel that is attractively decorated. Pleasing bedrooms and a first-rate restaurant. TV *limited.* P

MC V	■	●	■	5

ORKNEY ISLANDS: *Foveran* W www.foveranhotel.co.uk ££
St Ola, Kirkwall, Orkney KW15 1SF. Tel *01856 872389.* FAX *01856 876430.*
A family-run hotel-restaurant with a fine outlook over Scapa Flow. Recently refurbished under new ownership, it is practical and stylish. Good home cooking. TV P

MC V	■	●	■	8

PITLOCHRY: *Atholl Palace* W www.athollpalace.com ££££
Pitlochry, Perthshire PH16 5LY. Tel *01796 472400.* FAX *01796 473036.*
Though somewhat overbearing, this grandiose hotel is an excellent example of Scottish Baronial architecture. Vast rooms. TV P

AE DC MC V	■	●	■	97

POOLEWE: *Pool House* W www.poolhousehotel.com £££££
Poolewe, by Achnasheen, Highland IV22 2LD. Tel *01445 781272.* FAX *01445 781403.*
This traditional-looking lochside building has undergone a startling transformation into a series of exotic luxury suites, ideal for a honeymoon or special occasion. Inverewe Gardens lie just across the bay. ● *Jan.* TV P

AE MC V	■		■	5

PORT APPIN: *Airds* W www.airds-hotel.com £££££
Port Appin, Appin, Argyll & Bute PA38 4DF. Tel *01631 730236.* FAX *01631 730535.*
The views over Loch Linnhe are stunning from this classy old ferry inn. Country-house furnishings and well-chosen antiques. Accomplished cooking. *(See also p607.)* ● *Christmas, 6–26 Jan.* TV P

MC V	■	●	■	12

SPEAN BRIDGE: *Old Pines* W www.oldpines.co.uk ££££
Spean Bridge, Fort William, Highland PH34 4EG. Tel *01397 712324.* FAX *01397 712433.*
A Scandinavian house is the setting for this restaurant-with-rooms in a grove of Scots pines. Bedrooms are neat and pretty; acclaimed home-cooking with organic local produce. Rates include dinner. *throughout.* P

MC V	■	●	■	8

STRONTIAN: *Kilcamb Lodge* W www.kilcamblodge.com £££
Strontian, Highland PH36 4HY. Tel *01967 402257.* FAX *01967 402041.*
This comfortable, tastefully furnished country house on the quiet Ardnamurchan peninsula enjoys a wonderful outlook over a winding sea loch. A lovely place to relax. Excellent food. ● *Dec–Feb.* TV P

MC V	■	●	■	11

TORLUNDY: *Inverlochy Castle* W www.inverlochycastlehotel.com £££££
Torlundy, Fort William, Highland PH33 6SN. Tel *01397 702177.* FAX *01397 702953.*
A grand, luxurious Victorian mansion in palatial parkland. Traditional, classic interior with very high standards of food, accommodation and service. Fishing, tennis and croquet in the grounds. ● *Jan–Feb.* TV P

AE MC V	■	●	■	17

ULLAPOOL: *Tanglewood House* W www.tanglewoodhouse.co.uk ££
Ullapool, Highland IV26 2TB. Tel & FAX *01854 612059.*
This tastefully furnished, highly individual modern house commands panoramic vistas of Loch Broom from its huge picture windows. Inventive dinners available on request. ● *Christmas & New Year.* TV *throughout.* P

MC V	■		■	3

For key to symbols see back flap

Where to Eat

British food need strike no terrors to the visiting gourmet's heart; the UK's restaurant scene has moved far from its once dismal reputation. This is partly due to an influx of foreign chefs and cooking styles; you can now sample a wide range of international cuisine throughout Britain, with the greatest choice in London and the other major cities. Home-grown restaurateurs have risen to the challenge of redeeming British food too, and our indigenous cooking (once thought to consist only of fish and chips, overcooked vegetables, meat pies and lumpy custard) has improved out of all recognition in the last decade. You can now also eat extremely well in Britain whatever your budget – and at most times of day in the towns. Much less elaborate, but well-prepared, affordable food is making a mark in all types of brasseries, restaurants and cafés throughout the country; more modern approaches combine fresh produce and dietary common sense with influences from around the world. The restaurant listings *(see pp578–607)* feature some of the very best places as well as those with a steady track record.

Michelin Man at Bibendum, London

What's on the Menu?

The choice seems endless in large cities, particularly London. Cuisines from all over the world are represented, as well as their infinite variations – Thai and Tex-Mex, Turkish and Tuscan, Tandoori, Bhel Poori and Balti. There are many more unusual styles of cooking such as Hungarian, Polish, Caribbean and Pacific Rim. French and Italian restaurants are still highly regarded, offering everything from pastries and espresso coffee to the highest standards of *haute cuisine*. Outside the major cities the food scene is more limited, but most towns will have at least a couple of Italian, Indian and Chinese restaurants. The vague term "modern-international cuisine" adopted by many restaurants disguises a diverse rag-bag of styles. The spectrum ranges from French to Asian recipes, loosely characterized by the imaginative use of fresh, high-quality ingredients, which are cooked simply with imaginative seasonings.

Nostalgic yearnings for British food have produced a revival of hearty traditional dishes such as steak and kidney pie and treacle pudding *(see p37)*, though "Modern British" cooking adopts a lighter, more innovative approach to old-fashioned stodge. The distinctions between this and Modern International food are starting to blur, which is mostly a change for the better as young chefs apply Oriental and Mediterranean flavours to home-grown ingredients.

The Gay Hussar, London, a top Hungarian restaurant ***(see p580)***

Breakfast

It used to be said that the best way to enjoy British food was to eat breakfast three times a day. Traditional British breakfast starts with cereal and milk followed by bacon, eggs and tomato, perhaps with fried black pudding *(see p36)* in the North and Scotland. It is finished off with toast and marmalade washed down with tea. Or you can just have black coffee and fruit juice, with a croissant or two (known as Continental breakfast in hotels). The price of breakfast is often included in hotel tariffs in Britain.

Lunch

Many restaurants offer light lunches at fixed prices, sometimes of only two courses. The most popular lunchtime foods are sandwiches, salads, baked potatoes with fillings and ploughman's lunches, the latter found mainly in pubs. A traditional Sunday lunch of roast chicken, lamb or beef is served in some pubs and restaurants.

Afternoon Tea

No visitor should miss the experience of a proper English afternoon tea, which rivals breakfast as the most enjoyable meal of the day *(see p36)*. Some of the most palatial teas are offered by country-house and top London hotels such as the Ritz or Browns. The area that is best known for its classic "cream teas" is the West Country; these always include scones, spread with clotted cream, butter and jam. Wales, Scotland, Yorkshire and the Lake District also offer tasty teas with regional variations; in the North Country a slice of apple pie or fruit cake is served hot with a piece of North Yorkshire Wensleydale cheese on top.

An afternoon tea including sandwiches, cakes and scones

Dinner

At dinner time, the grander restaurants and hotels offer elaborately staged meals, sometimes billed as five or six courses (though one may be simply a sorbet, or coffee with *petits fours*). Dessert is often followed by cheese and crackers. Confusingly, in the North of England and Scotland "lunch" can be called "dinner" and "dinner" may be called "tea".

Generally, you can choose to take your dinner before 6pm or after 9pm only in larger towns, where there is a broad choice of ethnic restaurants, bars and all-day brasseries, which often have long opening hours.

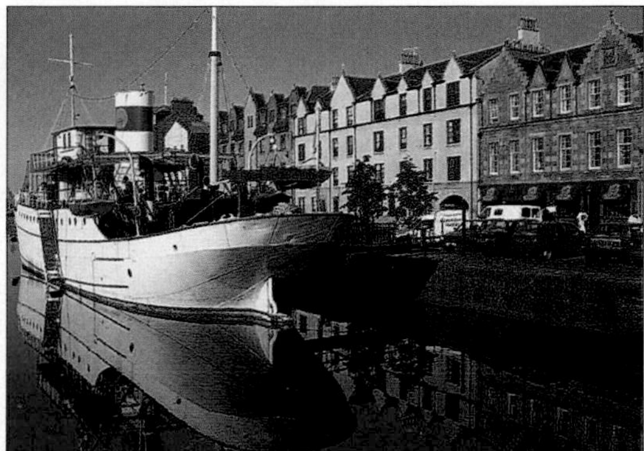

Leith Docks in Edinburgh, a centre of good pubs, bars and restaurants

Places to Eat

Eating venues are extremely varied, with brasseries, bistros, wine bars, tearooms, *tapas* bars and theatre cafés now competing with the more conventional cafés and restaurants. Many pubs also now serve excellent bar food at often reasonable prices *(see p608–11)*.

Brasseries, Bistros and Cafés

French-style café-brasseries are now popular in Britain. Sometimes they stay open all day, serving coffee, snacks and fairly simple dishes along with a selection of beers and wines. Alcoholic drinks, however, may only be available at certain times of day. The atmosphere is usually young and urbane, with decor to match. Drinks such as imported bottled beers, exotic spirits or cocktails may be fairly expensive.

***The café at Tate St Ives, Cornwall** (see p591)*

Wine bars are similar to brasseries, but with a better selection of wines, which may include English varieties *(see p148)*. Some bars have a good range of ciders and real ales as well *(see p34)*. Bistros are another French import, serving full meals at lunch and dinner time with less formality and more moderate prices than you would expect at a restaurant. You should expect to pay anything from £12 to £30 for a standard three-course meal in a bistro.

Restaurants-with-Rooms and Hotels

Restaurants-with-rooms are a new breed of small establishments with only a handful of bedrooms and usually excellent food. They tend to be expensive and are usually in a rural location.

Many hotel restaurants happily serve non-residents. They tend to be expensive, but the best can be unparalleled. Hotels serving a high standard of food are also included in the hotel listings.

Restaurant Etiquette

As a rule of thumb, the more expensive the restaurant, the more formal the dress code – though few restaurants nowadays will expect men to wear a shirt and tie. If you are not sure, ring first.

Some establishments do not allow smoking at all, while others now have separate sections or tables for people who wish to smoke.

Raymond Blanc's Le Manoir Aux Quat'Saisons *(see p586)*, one of Britain's most acclaimed restaurants-with-rooms

Alcohol

Britain's laws concerning the sale of alcohol, the "licensing laws", were once among the most restrictive in Europe. Now they are more relaxed, but some establishments may still only serve alcohol at set times with food. Some unlicensed restaurants operate a "Bring Your Own" policy. A corkage fee is often charged. The Scottish laws are different to the rest of Britain, most apparent in the later closing times of pubs.

Vegetarian Food

Britain is ahead of many of its European counterparts in providing vegetarian alternatives to meat dishes. A few of our selections serve only vegetarian meals, but most cater for carnivores as well. Vegetarians who want a wider choice should seek out South Indian, Chinese and other ethnic restaurants which have a tradition of vegetarian cuisine.

Fast Food

Fast food comes much cheaper, usually well under £10. Apart from the numerous individually owned fish and chip shops, there are many fast food chains in Britain, such as McDonald's, Burger King, Pizza Hut and KFC. Sandwich bars are very popular, and are often good value; some also have seating. Budget cafés, nicknamed "greasy spoons", serve simple, inexpensive food, often in the form of endless variations of the breakfast fry-up (see p36).

Betty's Café in Harrogate *(see p598)*

Booking Ahead

It is always safer to book a table first before making a special journey to a restaurant; city restaurants can be very busy and some of the more renowned establishments can be fully booked a month in advance. If you cannot keep a reservation, you should ring up and cancel. A lot of restaurants operate on knife-edge profit margins, and customers not turning up can threaten their livelihood.

Checking the Bill

All restaurants are required by law to display their current prices outside the door. These amounts include Value Added Tax (VAT), currently at 17.5 per cent. Service and cover charges (if any) are also specified. So you should have a rough idea of what a meal may cost beforehand.

Wine is always pricey in Britain, and extras like coffee or bottled water can be disproportionately expensive.

Service charges (usually between 10 per cent and 15 per cent) are sometimes automatically added to your bill. If you feel that the service has been poor, you are entitled to subtract this service charge. If no service charge has been added, you are expected to add 10 to 15 per cent to the bill, but it is your decision.

Some restaurants may leave the "total" box of credit card slips blank, hoping customers will add something extra to the service charge. Another growing trend is for smart restaurants to boost their sagging profit margins with a "cover charge" for flowers, bread and butter, etc. Live entertainment may also be costed. The majority of restaurants accept credit cards, or cheques with a guarantee card, but pubs and cafés expect cash – do not rely on plastic.

Mealtimes

Breakfast is a moveable feast. It may be as early as 6:30am in a city business hotel (most hoteliers will make special arrangements if you have a plane to catch or some other reason for checking out early) or as late as 10:30am in relaxed country house establishments. Few hoteliers relish cooking bacon and eggs that late, however, and some insist you are up and about by 9:00 sharp if you want anything to eat. But you can find breakfast all day long in some urban restaurants. The American concept of Sunday "brunch" (a leisurely halfway house between breakfast and lunch) is becoming increasingly popular in some hotels, restaurants and cafés.

Lunch in pubs and restaurants is usually served between noon and 2:30pm. Try to arrive in time to order the main course before 1:30pm, or you may find choice restricted and service peremptory. Most tourist areas have plenty of cafés, fast-food diners and coffee bars where you can have a snack at any time of day. During peak hours there may be a minimum charge.

If you are lucky enough to be in one of the places where you can get a traditional afternoon tea, it is usually served between 3pm and 5pm.

Dinner is usually served from 7pm until 10pm; some places, especially ethnic restaurants, stay open later. In guest houses or small hotels, dinner may be served at a specific time (sometimes uncomfortably early).

Children

The continental norm of dining out *en famille* is steadily becoming more acceptable in Britain, and visiting a restaurant may no longer entail endless searches for a babysitter. Many places welcome junior diners, and some actively encourage families, at least during the

L'Artiste Musclé wine bar-bistro *(see p579)*, London

day or early evening. Formal restaurants sometimes cultivate a more adult ambience at dinner time, and some impose age limits. If you want to take young children to a restaurant, check when you book. Italian, Spanish, Indian, fast-food restaurants and ice-cream parlours nearly always welcome children, and sometimes provide special menus or high chairs for them. Even traditional English pubs, which were once a strictly adult preserve, are now relaxing their rules to accommodate families and may even provide special rooms or play areas.

Ice-cream parlour sign

The places that welcome children are indicated in the pubs guide *(see pp608–11)*. The restaurant listings also indicate which establishments cater for children's needs.

Disabled Access

As in most walks of life, restaurant facilities in Britain could be better for disabled visitors, but things are gradually improving. Modern premises usually take account of mobility problems, but it's always best to check first if you have special needs.

Picnics

Eating outside is becoming more popular in Britain, though it is more likely that you will find tables outside pubs in the form of a beer garden, than outside restaurants. One inexpensive option is to make up your own picnic; most towns have good delicatessens and bakeries where you can collect provisions, and in Britain you do not usually have to worry about shops closing at mid-day as they often do on the Continent.

Look out for street markets to pick up fresh fruit and local cheeses at bargain prices. Department stores like Marks & Spencer and supermarkets such as Sainsbury's and Tesco often sell an excellent range of pre-packed sandwiches and snacks; large towns usually have several sandwich bars to choose from. Your hotel or guest house may also be able to provide a packed lunch. Ask for it the night before.

An option for a chillier day is a hot takeaway meal; fish and chips with salt and vinegar all wrapped in paper is not only a British cliché but a national institution.

Eating alfresco at Grasmere in the Lake District

Choosing a Restaurant

THE RESTAURANTS in this guide have been selected across a wide range of price categories for their good value, exceptional food and interesting location. This chart lists the restaurants by region, starting with London. Use the colour-coded thumb tabs, which indicate the regions covered on each page, to guide you to the relevant sections of the chart.

London

Restaurant	Credit Cards	Children Welcome	Fixed-Price Menu	Vegetarian	Outdoor Tables
BAYSWATER & PADDINGTON: *40 Degrees at Veronicas.* **Map** 1 C2. ££ 3 Hereford Rd, W2. *020 7229 5079.* Specializing in both classic and modern international cuisine. Choice of dining room includes Victorian style and a modern room with leather tablecloths.	AE DC MC V	●	■	●	
NOTTING HILL: *Mandola* **Map** 1 C1. ££ 139-143 Westbourne Grove W11. *020-7229 4734.* Sudanese cuisine, including a seven salad starter, in a "Khartoum" setting.	MC V	●		●	
NOTTING HILL: *Cortina* **Map** 1 B1. £££ 33a All Saint's Road, W11. *020-7221 4477.* A split-level, cleverly converted terraced house, tastefully decorated. Contemporary modern Italian cuisine, with weekend brunch a highlight.	AE DC MC V		■	●	■
KENSINGTON: *Sticky Fingers* **Map** 2 D2. ££ 1a Phillimore Gdns, W8. *020-7938 5338.* www.stickyfingers.co.uk American staples like great burgers and plenty of Rolling Stones memorabilia.	AE DC MC V	●		●	
KENSINGTON: *Kensington Place* **Map** 1 C4. £££ 205 Kensington Church St W8. *020-7727 3184.* Minimalist venue attracting a dedicated crowd. Excellent Modern International cuisine includes chicken and goat's cheese mousse with olives.	AE DC MC V	●	■	●	
KENSINGTON: *Wódka* **Map** 1 C4. £££ 12 St Alban's Grove W8. *020-7937 6513.* A mixture of classic and modern Polish food (blini with smoked salmon, roast duck), served in a modern but friendly setting. Great range of vodkas.	AE DC MC V		■	●	
KENSINGTON: *Bombay Brasserie* **Map** 2 D5. ££££ Courtfield Close, Courtfield Rd SW7. *020-7370 4040.* Acclaimed restaurant with an impressive colonial atmosphere, including conservatory, cocktail bar and pianist. Bombay and regional cuisine.	AE DC MC V	●		●	
KNIGHTSBRIDGE & VICTORIA: *Café Fish* **Map** 5 B4. £££ 36-40 Rupert St SW1. *020-7287 8989.* A classic French approach is applied to the fish and seafood, with favourites including fish and chips and seafood platter.	AE DC MC V	●	■	●	
KNIGHTSBRIDGE & VICTORIA: *Boisdale* **Map** 5 B4. ££££ 15 Eccleston St, SW1. *020-7730 6922.* www.boisdale.uk.com Traditional and Modern British with Scottish specialities such as haggis and salmon, served in a traditional, clubby atmosphere.	AE DC MC V	●	■	●	
KNIGHTSBRIDGE & VICTORIA: *The Fifth Floor* **Map** 5 A2. ££££ Fifth Floor, Harvey Nichols, 109-125 Knightsbridge, SW1. *020-7235 5250.* At the top of London's most fashionable department store, Modern British food in a contemporary setting. Also a café, sushi counter and foodmarket.	AE DC MC V	●	■	●	
KNIGHTSBRIDGE & VICTORIA: *L'Incontro* **Map** 5 B4. ££££ 87 Pimlico Rd, SW1. *020-7730 5062.* Wonderful Italian dishes with a leaning towards Venetian cuisine.	DC MC V	●	■	●	
KNIGHTSBRIDGE & VICTORIA: *Rhodes in the Square* **Map** 6 D5. ££££ Dolphin Sq, Chichester St, SW1. *020-7798 6767.* Inspired Modern British dishes (red wine beef lasagne with a chestnut mushroom cream sauce), served in an Art Deco setting. *Sun–Mon.*	AE DC MC V		■	●	
KNIGHTSBRIDGE & VICTORIA: *Pétrus* **Map** 5 C4. £££££ The Berkeley Hotel, Wilton Place SW1. *020-7930 4272.* www.petrus-restaurant.com Classical French cuisine in this elegant restaurant run by chef Marcus Wareing and owned by Gordon Ramsay. *Sun, public hols.*	AE DC MC V	●	■	●	

Price categories include a three-course meal for one, half a bottle of house wine, and all unavoidable extra charges such as cover, service, VAT:
£ under £15
££ £15-£25
£££ £25-£35
££££ £35-£50
£££££ over £50

CHILDREN WELCOME
Restaurants which offer smaller portions and high-chairs for children. Special menus sometimes available.

FIXED-PRICE MENU
A good value fixed-price meal, at lunch, dinner or both, usually of three courses.

VEGETARIAN
Vegetarian specialities served, sometimes for both starters and main courses.

CREDIT CARDS
Indicates which credit cards are accepted: *AE* American Express; *DC* Diners Club; *MC* Master Card/Access; *V* Visa.

	Credit Cards	Children Welcome	Fixed-Price Menu	Vegetarian	Outdoor Tables
KNIGHTSBRIDGE & VICTORIA: *Zafferano* **Map** 5 B3. £££££ 15 Lowndes St SW1. *020-7235 5800.* One of London's finest Modern Italian restaurants, with white truffle dishes among the numerous specialities. The wine list includes grappa.	AE DC MC V	●	■	●	
CHELSEA & FULHAM: *Chutney Mary* £££ 535, Kings Rd SW10. *020-7351 3113.* www.realindianfood.com An Indian term for women crossing two cultures, "Chutney Mary" serves a delicious blend of Indian and Western cuisine. Attractive colonial Raj decor.	AE DC MC V		■	●	
CHELSEA & FULHAM: *Bluebird* ££££ 350 King's Rd SW3. *020-7559 1000.* www.conran.com Inspired conversion of a 1923 garage, renovating the original mix of Classical Neo-Georgian and Art Deco elements. Game and crustacea a speciality.	AE DC MC V	●	■	●	
CHELSEA & FULHAM: *Aubergine* £££££ 11 Park Walk SW10. *020-7352 3449.* Provençale decor, charming service and faultless cuisine: salad of quail, foie gras, sweetbreads and truffle dressing. *Sun, 19 Dec–6 Jan, 2 wks Aug.*	AE DC MC V	●	■	●	
CHELSEA & FULHAM: *Bibendum* £££££ 1st Floor, Michelin House, 81 Fulham Rd, SW3. *020-7581 5817.* www.bibendum.co.uk A retro-chic showcase for Modern British cuisine, including bistro dishes, game and offal.The ground floor features an Oyster Bar and separate café.	AE MC V	●	■		
PICCADILLY & MAYFAIR: *L'Artiste Musclé* **Map** 5 C1. ££ 1 Shepherd Mkt, W1. *020-7493 6150.* French bistro cuisine: boeuf Bourguignon, Toulouse sausage, in a classic bistro setting, with pavement tables overlooking Shepherd Market.	AE MC V			●	■
PICCADILLY & MAYFAIR: *Sofra* **Map** 2 D2. ££ 18 Shepherd St W1. *020-7493 3320.* One of London's best-value chains of Turkish restaurants.	AE MC V	●	■	●	■
PICCADILLY & MAYFAIR: *Carluccio's* **Map** 3 B5. £££ 3-5 Barrett St, St Christopher's Pl, W1. *020-7935 5927.* Authentic Italian dishes available throughout the day, including soup and pasta, with a shop stocking Carluccio's range of Italian foodstuffs.	AE MC V	●		●	
PICCADILLY & MAYFAIR: *Chor Bizarre* **Map** 5 C1. £££ 16 Albemarle St W1. *020-7629 9802.* Amid numerous Indian antiques (all for sale), the menu has a Kashmiri focus, such as *gostaba* (minced lamb with cardamom and yogurt).	AE DC MC V	●	■	●	
PICCADILLY & MAYFAIR: *Hard Rock Café* **Map** 5 B1. £££ 150 Old Park Lane W1. *020-7629 0382.* www.hardrock.com No reservations means queues, but the reward is classic American fare (great burgers and a daily changing special) amid music videos and memorabilia.	AE DC MC V	●		●	■
PICCADILLY & MAYFAIR: *Criterion Brasserie* **Map** 6 D1. ££££ Piccadilly Circus W1. *020-7930 0488.* www.white.starline.org.uk Stunning, historic interiors culminate in a glittering neo-Byzantine mosaic ceiling. French dishes with Mediterranean influences.	AE DC MC V	●	■	●	
PICCADILLY & MAYFAIR: *Momo* **Map** 5 C1. ££££ 25 Heddon St, W1. *020-7434 4040.* Housed within a wonderful "antique Moroccan palace", the cuisine is North African, balancing tradition with a more modern approach.	AE DC MC V		■	●	■
PICCADILLY & MAYFAIR: *Quaglino's* **Map** 5 C1. ££££ 16 Bury St, SW1. *020-7930 6767.* www.conran.com Modern British brasserie, thriving on Conran design. Classic dishes include calves' liver and bacon, roast guinea fowl with buttered spinach and almonds.	AE DC MC V	●	■	●	

For key to symbols see back flap

Price categories include a three-course meal for one, half a bottle of house wine, and all unavoidable extra charges such as cover, service, VAT:
£ under £15
££ £15-£25
£££ £25-£35
££££ £35-£50
£££££ over £50

Children Welcome
Restaurants which offer smaller portions and high-chairs for children. Special menus sometimes available.

Fixed-Price Menu
A good value fixed-price meal, at lunch, dinner or both, usually of three courses.

Vegetarian
Vegetarian specialities served, sometimes for both starters and main courses.

Credit Cards
Indicates which credit cards are accepted: *AE* American Express; *DC* Diners Club; *MC* Master Card/Access; *V* Visa.

Restaurant	Credit Cards	Children Welcome	Fixed-Price Menu	Vegetarian	Outdoor Tables
Piccadilly & Mayfair: *The Sugar Club* **Map** 5 C1. ££££ 21 Warwick St W1. *020-7437 7776.* Pacific Rim cuisine, served in a streamlined setting: spicy kangaroo salad with mint, peanuts and lime chilli dressing, and plenty of New World wines.	AE DC MC V			●	
Piccadilly & Mayfair: *Veeraswamy* **Map** 3 C5. ££££ Mezzanine Floor, Victory House, 99 Regent St W1. *020-7734 1401.* London's oldest Indian (established 1927) it is also one of the most modern. Inspiring, original and authentic Indian dishes, with great service.	AE DC MC	●	■	●	
Piccadilly & Mayfair: *Deca* **Map** 3 C5. £££££ 23 Conduit St W1. *020-7493 7070.* A new, elegant setting for superstar chef, Nico Ladenis, to exercise his classical French gastronomic artistry. *public hols.*	AE DC MC V	●	■	●	
Piccadilly & Mayfair: *Le Gavroche* **Map** 5 C1. £££££ 43 Upper Brook St W1. *020-7408 0881.* www.le-gavroche.co.uk Superlative modern and classical French cuisine (lobster mousse with caviar and champagne sauce) in a sophisticated setting. Smart bar for aperitifs and lounge for coffee and cigars. Dress code. *Christmas.*	AE DC MC V		■	●	
Piccadilly & Mayfair: *Green's Restaurant & Oyster Bar* £££££ **Map** 5 C1. 36 Duke St St James's, SW1. *020-7930 4566.* Classic English "gentleman's club" decor, with banquettes and booths, serving a range of British classics, with fish and oysters a feature. *Sun.*	AE DC MC V	●	■	●	
Piccadilly & Mayfair: *The Grill Room* **Map** 2 D2. £££££ The Dorchester Hotel, Park La, W1. *020-7317 6336.* www.dorchesterhotel.com Traditional British cuisine (home-smoked breast of Norfolk duck with pimento and onion compote), a separate vegetarian menu. Opulent decor.	AE DC MC V	●	■	●	
Piccadilly & Mayfair: *Nobu* **Map** 5 B1. £££££ 19 Old Park Lane, W1. *020-7447 4747.* Views over Hyde Park and great staff serve sensational Japanese, South American fusion cuisine, with black cod in miso a signature dish.	AE DC MC V	●	■	●	
Regent's Park & Marylebone: *Blandford St Restaurant* ££££ **Map** 3 B4. 5-7 Blandford St W1. *020-7486 9696.* Stylishly modern, streamlined but colourful venue, offering a daily changing menu of Modern British fine dining (marinated loin of Scottish venison). *Sun.*	AE DC MC V	●	■	●	■
Soho: *Yo! Sushi* **Map** 4 E5. £ 52-53 Poland St, W1. *020-7287 0443.* Sushi, sashimi, salads, soups and noodles pass by on a conveyor belt, in this modern, minimalist setting. Yo! Below bar in the basement.	AE MC V	●		●	
Soho: *Mildred's* **Map** 4 D5. ££ 45 Lexington St W1. *020-7494 1634.* Global vegetarian cuisine accompanied by an all-organic wine list. *Sun.*				●	■
Soho: *The Gay Hussar* **Map** 4 E5. £££ 2 Greek St W1. *020-7437 0973.* Bohemian library setting serving various politicians, media and literary figures: chilled wild cherry soup, Transylvanian stuffed cabbage. *Sun.*	AE DC MC V		■	●	
Soho: *Sri Siam* **Map** 4 E5. £££ 16 Old Compton St W1. *020-7434 3544.* This stylish restaurant is the place for your first taste of Thai food; the heat is toned down, but the flavours aren't: seafood dishes, as well as satay and curries.	AE DC MC V				
Soho: *Alastair Little* **Map** 4 E5. ££££ 49 Frith St W1. *020-7734 5183.* Modern International cooking with a distinct Italian accent: Tuscan fish casserole, grilled seabass with flageolet and lemon minestra. *Sun.*	AE MC V	●	■	●	

Soho: *Mezzo* **Map** 4 E5. ££££ 100 Wardour St W1. *020-7314 4000.* A Soho landmark, housed in an elegant, mirrored basement, modern European dishes such as bruschetta of goat's cheese, fig and San Daniele ham.	AE DC MC V		■	●	
Covent Garden & Strand: *Belgo Centraal* **Map** 4 F5. £ 50 Earlham St WC2. *020-7813 2233.* An industrial lift takes you down to this modern, monastic basement with refectory seating and booths. Belgian mussel pots and platters a speciality.	AE DC MC V	●	■	●	
Covent Garden & Strand: *Bertorelli's* **Map** 4 F5. £££ 44a Floral St WC2. *020-7836 3969.* Modern Italian cuisine with traditional favourites, including pizza, pasta, meat and fish dishes. Relaxed and inviting decor. ● *Sun.*	AE DC MC V	●	■	●	
Covent Garden & Strand: *Chez Gerard* **Map** 4 F5.. £££ Opera Terrace, The Market, Covent Garden Piazza, WC2. *020-7379 0666.* A French selection encompasses grills, fish and vegetarian dishes, while renowned for classic Parisian *steak frites*. Terrace overlooking the piazza.	AE DC MC V		■	●	■
Covent Garden & Strand: *Simpson's-in-the-Strand* **Map** 4 F5. £££ 100 Strand WC2. Map 13 C2. *020-7836 9112.* For a truly traditional English experience, with Victorian interiors, the menu includes a superb traditional breakfast. A smart cocktail bar is ideal for aperitifs.	AE DC MC V	●	■	●	
Covent Garden & Strand: *The Ivy* **Map** 4 F5. ££££ 1 West St WC2. *020-7836 4751.* An institution of the theatre district, you need to book weeks ahead for this Art Deco style restaurant. Crispy duck salad and fish cakes are classics.	AE DC MC V	●	■	●	
Covent Garden & Strand: *Orso* **Map** 4 F5. ££££ 27 Wellington St WC2. *020-7240 5269.* W www.joeallen.co.uk A media, theatre-goers rendezvous, with soft terracotta walls, white linen tablecloths and and Italianate pictures, serving Italian regional cuisine.	AE MC V		■	●	
Covent Garden & Strand: *Rules* **Map** 4 F5. ££££ 35 Maiden La WC2. *020-7836 5314.* W www.rules.co.uk London's oldest surviving restaurant serving traditional British fare since 1798. Dishes include Dover sole, rib of beef, game, amid Edwardian decor.	AE DC MC V	●		●	
Bloomsbury & Fitzrovia: *Wagamama* **Map** 4 E4. £ 4 Streatham St WC1. *020-7323 9223.* W www.wagamama.com Modern refectory-style, within a spacious, bustling basement, serving various types of noodles. Queues are fast-moving. Several branches.	AE DC MC V	●		●	
Bloomsbury & Fitzrovia: *Villandry* **Map** 3 C4 £££ 170 Great Portland St, W1. *020-7631 3131.* W www.villandry.com Chic and thoroughly comprehensive Euro-deli and grocery store with a stylish modern restaurant. The bar has a separate all-day menu.	AE DC MC V	●		●	■
Bloomsbury & Fitzrovia: *Hakkasan* **Map** 4 D4. ££££ 8 Hanway Pl, W1. *020-7907 1888.* *Dim sum* is served all day, changing to à la carte for dinner, with the lounge bar also serving snacks in the evening. Modern ethnic decor.	AE MC V			●	
Spitalfields & Clerkenwell: *Quality Chop House* £££ 94 Farringdon Road EC1. *020-7837 5093.* Beautiful Victorian diner with its original 1869 fittings. Sausage and mash, and salmon fish cakes are appealing staples.	AE MC V	●		●	
Spitalfields & Clerkenwell: *Maison Novelli* £££££ 29 Clerkenwell Green EC1. *020-7251 6606.* Jean-Christophe Novelli's background is *haute cuisine*, and it shows in his modern French cuisine; the chocolate plate dessert is legendary. ● *Sun.*	AE DC MC V	●		●	■
City & Southbank: *Wine Wharf at Vinopolis* **Map** 8 D4. ££ Stoney Street, Borough Market, SE1. *020-7940 8335.* Graze on tapas-type dishes including salads and cheeses, or tackle the fuller menu, within this converted Victorian warehouse. Great choice of wines.	AE MC V			●	
City & Southbank: *Club Gascon* **Map** 7 C2. £££ 57 West Smithfield, EC1. *020-796 0699.* Regional cuisine from southwest France, with foie gras, truffle and seafood dishes a speciality. Also served tapas-style in the bar. ● *Sun.*	AE MC V		■	●	

For key to symbols see back flap

Price categories include a three-course meal for one, half a bottle of house wine, and all unavoidable extra charges such as cover, service, VAT:
£ under £15
££ £15-£25
£££ £25-£35
££££ £35-£50
£££££ over £50

Children Welcome
Restaurants which offer smaller portions and high-chairs for children. Special menus sometimes available.
Fixed-Price Menu
A good value fixed-price meal, at lunch, dinner or both, usually of three courses.
Vegetarian
Vegetarian specialities served, sometimes for both starters and main courses.
Credit Cards
Indicates which credit cards are accepted: *AE* American Express; *DC* Diners Club; *MC* Master Card/Access; *V* Visa.

Restaurant	Credit Cards	Children Welcome	Fixed-Price Menu	Vegetarian	Outdoor Tables
City & Southbank: *Livebait* **Map** 7 B4. £££ 43 The Cut SE1. *020-7928 7211.* www.santeonline.co.uk/livebait Retaining the original Victorian ceramic tiles, mirrors and chrome, the fish and shellfish repertoire includes traditional fish and chips. *Sun.*	AE DC MC V			●	
City & Southbank: *Tate Britain Restaurant* **Map** 7 C3. £££ Tate Britain, Millbank, SE1. *020-7887 8825.* www.tate.org.uk Modern English cuisine, and over 300 wines to choose from. Witty, whimsical murals by Rex Whistler date from 1925 and provide an enchanting setting.	AE DC MC V	●	●	●	●
City & Southbank: *The Oxo Tower* **Map** 7 B3. ££££ Oxo Tower Wharf, Barge House St, SE1. *020-7803 3888.* www.harveynichols.com Set on the eighth floor of this landmark 1930s building, with stunning views along the Thames. Exemplary Modern British cuisine.	AE DC MC V	●	●	●	●
City & Southbank: *Le Pont de la Tour* **Map** 8 F4. £££££ Butlers Wharf SE1. *020-7403 8403.* www.conran.com Riverside marvel with great views, a separate crustacea bar, pianist nightly, and French cuisine with Euro-Mediterranean influences. Decor is classic Conran.	AE DC MC V	●	●	●	●
Further Afield: *River Café* £££££ Thames Wharf Studios, Rainville Rd W6. *020-7386 4200.* A modern style that also provides river views, serving interpretations of traditional Italian cuisine such as chargrilled squid with chilli and rocket.	AE DC MC V	●			●

The Downs and Channel Coast

Restaurant	Credit Cards	Children Welcome	Fixed-Price Menu	Vegetarian	Outdoor Tables
Amberley: *Queen's Room, Amberley Castle* ££££ On B2139, Amberley, W Sussex. *01798 831992.* www.amberleycastle.co.uk A romantic medieval fortress provides a dramatic backdrop for "castle cuisine", a mix of ancient and Modern British recipes.	AE DC MC V		●	●	
Boughton Lees: *Eastwell Manor* www.marstonhotels.com ££££ Eastwell Park, Boughton Lees, nr Ashford, Kent. *01233 219955.* A grand parkland setting graces this dynamic hotel restaurant where the service is formal but friendly.	AE DC MC V	●	●	●	●
Brighton: *Food for Friends* ££ 17–18 Prince Albert St, Brighton. *01273 202310.* www.foodforfriends.com This vegetarian wholefood café in the Lanes offers friendly service, generous helpings and imaginative cooking amid pine and pot plants. *25, 26 Dec.*	DC MC V	●		●	
Brighton: *Black Chapati* £££ 12 Circus Parade, New England Rd, Brighton. *01273 699011.* Adventurous and eclectic Asian cooking fizzes with original ideas in a stark café setting just outside the town centre. The service is efficient, and the atmosphere friendly and welcoming. *L; Sun, Mon.*	AE MC V			●	
Brighton: *Terre à Terre* £££ 71 East St, Brighton. *01273 729051.* Close to the pavilion, pier and the Lanes, this vegetarian retaurant has an imaginative international menu. *Mon L.*	AE DC MC V	●		●	
Brockenhurst: *Simply Poussin* ££ The Courtyard, Brookley Rd, Brockenhurst, Hants. *01590 623063.* New Forest produce such as venison and wild pork appears on the menu in robust provincial French-style fare. *Sun, Mon.*	MC V		●		●
Chichester: *Comme Ça* £££ 67 Broyle Rd, Chichester, W Sussex. *01243 788724.* This French restaurant is situated close to the Festival Theatre and pre- and post- performance meals are available. Fish specialities such as local seabass. *Christmas.*	AE DC MC V	●	●	●	●

CUCKMERE: *Golden Galleon* info@goldengalleon.co.uk ££
Exceat Bridge, Cuckmere Haven, E Sussex. *01323 892247.*
This pub-restaurant has its own brewery and smokery; try the smoked salmon and duck breast. Conservatory and terrace with sea views. *Sun D winter.*
MC V

EAST GRINSTEAD: *Gravetye Manor* £££££
Vowels Lane, East Grinstead, W Sussex. *01342 810567.* www.gravetyemanor.co.uk
Classic food is served in this plush Elizabethan mansion, a luxury hotel in gorgeous grounds.
MC V

EDENBRIDGE: *Honours Mill* ££££
87 High St, Edenbridge, Kent. *01732 866757.* www.honoursmill.co.uk
Mind your head: the beams are low. Well-tried French classics are daringly adapted in this quiet, friendly restaurant. *Sat L, Sun D, Mon.*
MC V

EMSWORTH: *36 on the Quay* £££££
47 South St, Emsworth, Hants. *01243 375592.* www.36onthequay.co.uk
Restaurant-with-rooms by the waterfront. Food is innovative but disciplined. Local fish features on the menu. *Sat L, Sun, Mon L, bank hols (except Good Fri).*
AE DC MC V

FERNHURST: *King's Arms* £££
Midhurst Road, Fernhurst, Surrey. *01428 652005.*
The accomplished modern-British cooking always includes fish dishes, the chef's speciality, at this 17th-century country dining pub. *Sun D, 25 Dec, 1 Jan.*
MC V

HAMPTON HILL: *Monsieur Max* ££££
133 High St, Hampton Hill, Middx. *020-8979 5546.* monsmax@aol.com
First-class ingredients and proficient cooking are all part of the package of this Michelin-starred French restaurant. *Sat L.*
AE DC MC V

HASTINGS: *Bonapartes* phyl@pjbone.freeserve.co.uk £££
64 Eversfield Pl, St Leonards, Hastings, E Sussex. *01424 712218.*
Freshness is the watchword here: bread is made on the premises. Fish and game are specialities. *Mon.*
MC V

HAYWARDS HEATH: *Jeremy's at Borde Hill* *01444 441102.* £££
Balcombe Rd, Haywards Heath, W. Sussex. www.houseofgoodfood.co.uk
Vivaciously modern European cooking produces memorable results in this civilized modern interior overlooking a walled garden. *Sun D, Mon.*
AE MC V

HURSTBOURNE TARRANT: *Esseborne Manor* *01264 736444.* £££
On A343, N of Hurstbourne Tarrant, Hants. www.essebornemanor.com
Well-flavoured and sophisticated English country cooking is offered in this stylish Victorian manor-house hotel. Good-value set lunch.
AE DC MC V

JEVINGTON: *Hungry Monk* www.hungrymonk.co.uk £££
Between Polegate and Alfriston, E Sussex. *01323 482178.*
This restaurant's popularity rests partly on its 15th-century setting and on innovative food. All fresh home produce on the menu. *Mon–Sat L.*
MC V

NEW MILTON: *Marryat, Chewton Glen* £££££
Christchurch Rd, New Milton, Hants. *01425 275341.* www.chewtonglen.com
A gastronomic shrine in a tranquil New Forest country-house hotel. The conservatory restaurant overlooks lovely gardens.
AE DC MC V

RICHMOND: *Nightingales* www.petershamhotel.co.uk ££££
Petersham Hotel, Nightingale Lane, Richmond upon Thames, Surrey. *020 8940 7471.*
A superb Thames view adds to the pleasure of mostly traditional English cooking at this Victorian hotel. *Sun D.*
AE DC MC V

RIPLEY: *Michels'* £££££
High St, Ripley, Surrey. *01483 224777.* www.michelsrestaurant.co.uk
Ambitious menus change with the seasons. Picturesque setting. In summer you can have drinks in a walled garden. *Sat L, Sun D, Mon.*
AE MC V

RYE: *Landgate Bistro* £££
5–6 Landgate, Rye, E Sussex. *01797 222829.* www.landgatebistro.co.uk
Local produce like Romney Marsh lamb or freshly caught fish figures imaginatively in this pleasant informal restaurant. *Sun, Mon.*
MC V

STORRINGTON: *Fleur de Sel* ££££
Manleys Hill, Storrington, W Sussex. *01903 742331.*
French cooking at this cottage restaurant where service is calm and efficient. Seafood is a speciality. *Sat L, Sun D, Mon.*
AE MC V

For key to symbols see back flap

Price categories include a three-course meal for one, half a bottle of house wine, and all unavoidable extra charges such as cover, service, VAT:
Ⓕ under £15
ⒻⒻ £15-£25
ⒻⒻⒻ £25-£35
ⒻⒻⒻⒻ £35-£50
ⒻⒻⒻⒻⒻ over £50

Children Welcome
Restaurants which offer smaller portions and high-chairs for children. Special menus sometimes available.

Fixed-Price Menu
A good value fixed-price meal, at lunch, dinner or both, usually of three courses.

Vegetarian
Vegetarian specialities served, sometimes for both starters and main courses.

Credit Cards
Indicates which credit cards are accepted: *AE* American Express; *DC* Diners Club; *MC* Master Card/Access; *V* Visa.

	Credit Cards	Children Welcome	Fixed-Price Menu	Vegetarian	Outdoor Tables
Tunbridge Wells: *Sankeys* www.crabsatsankeys.co.uk ⒻⒻⒻ 39 Mount Ephraim, Tunbridge Wells, Kent. 01892 511422. A smart wine bar specializing in seafood from all parts of Britain, from Scotland to Cornwall. *25, 26 Dec.*	MC V	●		●	■
Tunbridge Wells: *Thackeray's* ⒻⒻⒻⒻ 85 London Rd, Tunbridge Wells, Kent. 01892 511921. www.thackeraysrestaurant.com The novelist's home is now a restaurant and wine bar where local produce is given a Gallic touch. *Sun, Mon.*	AE DC MC V	●	■	●	■
Whitstable: *Whitstable Oyster Fishery Co* ⒻⒻⒻ Royal Native Oyster Stores, Whitstable, Kent. 01227 276856. The name suggests what it does best, but other fishy things appear on the menu in this Victorian building on the beach. *Sun D (winter), Mon.*	AE DC MC V	●		●	■
Wickham: *Old House* ⒻⒻⒻⒻ The Square, Wickham, Hants. 01329 833049. enq@theoldhousehotel.co.uk British/European-inspired food with exotic touches, served in the timber-framed former stable-block of a Georgian house. *Mon L, Sun D.*	AE MC V	●		●	

East Anglia

	Credit Cards	Children Welcome	Fixed-Price Menu	Vegetarian	Outdoor Tables
Aldeburgh: *Regatta* ⒻⒻ 171–173 High St, Aldeburgh, Suff. 01728 452011. www.regattaaldeburgh.com Seafaring decor reflects the fish specialities which are always cooked with care. Sometimes there's local game on the menu. The ingredients are always top quality, and the service is friendly. *Wed.*	AE MC V	●	■	●	
Burnham Market: *Fishes'* ⒻⒻⒻ Market Pl, Burnham Market, Norf. 01328 738588. www.burnhammarket.co.uk Located on the 18th-century village green, this restaurant provides reliable fish specialities: the best of the catch at fair prices. Try the Brancaster oysters, mussels or a seafood platter. *Sun D, Mon.*	DC MC V	●	■		
Bury St Edmunds: *Maison Bleu* ⒻⒻ 31 Churchgate St, Bury St Edmunds, Suff. 01284 760623. www.maisonbleu.co.uk Straightforward seafood fresh from the market. There's a huge menu and good white wines. Can get very busy. *Sun–Mon.*	AE MC V	●	■	●	
Cambridge: *Restaurant Twenty-two* ⒻⒻⒻ 22 Chesterton Rd, Cambs. 01223 351880. www.restaurant22.co.uk Courteous service complements pleasingly inventive food in Victorian setting. Three-course menus change every month. *L; Sun & Mon.*	AE DC MC V		■	●	
Cambridge: *Midsummer House* ⒻⒻⒻⒻⒻ Midsummer Common, Cambs. 01223 369299. www.midsummerhouse.co.uk An intimate restaurant serving fixed-price menus of great complexity. Puddings are luscious and elaborate. *Sun–Mon.*	AE MC V		■	●	■
Colchester: *Warehouse Brasserie* ⒻⒻ 12A Chapel St North, Colchester, Essex. 01206 765656. A popular restaurant with Modern British and Continental home-cooked dishes. Lots of local produce; some light main courses. *Sun–Mon.*	MC V	●	■	●	
Dedham: *Le Talbooth* ⒻⒻⒻⒻⒻ Gun Hill, Dedham, nr Colchester, Essex. 01206 323150. talbooth@talbooth.co.uk Standards stay high at this long-established Tudor restaurant by the River Stour. Creative cooking that is popular with locals and visitors alike.	AE DC MC V	●		●	■
Diss: *Weaver's Wine Bar* ⒻⒻ Market Hill, Diss, Norf. 01379 642411. A charming timbered setting for a cheerful, ad hoc restaurant. *Sat L, Sun, Mon L, public hols.*	AE DC MC V	●	■	●	

ELY: *Old Fire Engine House* £££
25 St Mary's St, Ely, Cambs. *01353 662582.* W www.theoldfireenginehouse.co.uk
Local produce inspires hearty British cooking in the old fire station by the cathedral. Friendly, unfussy atmosphere.
MC V

FRESSINGFIELD: *Fox and Goose* £££
On B1116, Fressingfield, Suff. *01379 586247.* W www.foxandgoose.net
This remote country pub serves a wide range of inventive British and international dishes. Children are welcomed.
MC V

HARWICH: *Pier at Harwich* £££
The Quay, Harwich, Essex. *01255 241212.* W www.milsomhotels.com
A bustling harbourside stop-over with nautical decor and excellent fish. Comfortable rooms are also available.
AE DC MC V

HINTLESHAM: *Hintlesham Hall* ££££
On A1071, Hintlesham, Suff. *01473 652268.* W www.hintleshamhall.com
Presentation is the key to success at this hotel west of Ipswich. Excellent cheese-board. *(See also p548.)* *Sat L.*
AE DC MC V

HUNTINGDON: *Old Bridge* £££
1 High St, Huntingdon, Cambs. *01480 424300.* W www.huntsbridge.com
A handsome riverside inn with an airy restaurant proffering British and Mediterranean fare, and splendid English cheeses. Good teas too.
AE DC MC V

ICKLINGHAM: *Red Lion* £££
The Street, Icklingham, Suff. *01638 717802.*
Attractive, 16th-century inn with exposed beams and log fires. Choose from the wide range of seafood, or try game dishes such as wild boar. *25 Dec.*
MC V

KELSALE: *Harrison's* £££
Main Road (A12), Kelsale, Suff. *01728 604444.*
This charming thatched restaurant near Aldeburgh uses seasonal local ingredients in imaginative, Modern British cooking. *Sun & Mon.*
MC V

NORWICH: *Adlard's* ££££
79 Upper St Giles St, Norwich, Norf. *01603 633522.* W www.adlards.co.uk
A deceptively elegant setting belies high-quality cooking of great flair. The cuisine is Modern British with French overtones. *Sun, Mon.*
AE MC V

ORFORD: *Butley Orford Oysterage* £££
Market Hill, The Square, Orford, Woodbridge, Suff. *01394 450277.*
Café-restaurant with its own smokehouse and oyster-beds. Enjoy a snack or meal in a delightful Suffolk village. *Oct–Mar: Fri & Sat D.*
MC V

SNAPE: *Plough and Snail* W www.snapemaltings.com £££
Snape Maltings Riverside Centre, Snape, Suff. *01728 688413.*
Sprats and other local fish are the specialities at this popular pub with restaurant – part of a concert hall/craft shop/art gallery complex.
AE DC MC V

SUDBURY: *Great House Hotel* W www.greathouse.co.uk £££
Market Place, Lavenham, Sudbury, Suff. *01787 247431.*
This family restaurant combines the finest French and Continental cuisine. Lovely garden for children outside. Amazing cheese board. Rooms. *Sun D, Mon.*
AE DC MC V

SWAFFHAM: *Stratton House* ££££
4 Ash Close, Swaffham, Norf. *01760 723845.* W www.strattons-hotel.co.uk
Lady Hamilton once stayed in this 18th-century house, which is now a hotel. The changing menu includes local organic produce. *L; 25, 26 Dec.*
MC V

THORPE MARKET: *Green Farm Restaurant* *01263 833602.* £££
North Walsham Road, Thorpe Market, Norf. W www.greenfarmhotel.co.uk
This restaurant in a 16th-century farmhouse has an excellent reputation for top-class dishes made from fresh local ingredients. Try the crab, sea trout or venison.
AE DC MC V

WELLS-NEXT-THE-SEA: *The Crown* *01328 710209.* ££££
The Crown, The Butlands, Wells-Next-The-Sea, Norf. W www.thecrownhotelwells.co.uk
This formal Michelin-star restaurant overlooks the delightful Butlands green, and uses varied and local produce in a Modern British menu.
AE DC MC V

WOODBRIDGE: *Captain's Table* ££
3 Quay Street, Woodbridge, Suff. *01394 383145.* W www.captainstable.co.uk
Set in a 16th-century building, this restaurant presents an eclectic British and European menu cooked with flair. *Sun D, Mon (except bank hols).*
MC V

Price categories include a three-course meal for one, half a bottle of house wine, and all unavoidable extra charges such as cover, service, VAT:
Ⓛ under £15
ⓁⓁ £15-£25
ⓁⓁⓁ £25-£35
ⓁⓁⓁⓁ £35-£50
ⓁⓁⓁⓁⓁ over £50

Children Welcome
Restaurants which offer smaller portions and high-chairs for children. Special menus sometimes available.

Fixed-Price Menu
A good value fixed-price meal, at lunch, dinner or both, usually of three courses.

Vegetarian
Vegetarian specialities served, sometimes for both starters and main courses.

Credit Cards
Indicates which credit cards are accepted: *AE* American Express; *DC* Diners Club; *MC* Master Card/Access; *V* Visa.

Thames Valley

Restaurant	Credit Cards	Children Welcome	Fixed-Price Menu	Vegetarian	Outdoor Tables
Bray: *Waterside Inn* ⓁⓁⓁⓁⓁ Ferry Rd, Bray, Windsor & Maidenhead. *01628 620691.* www.waterside-inn.co.uk Renowned pillar of French classic cuisine in an idyllic riverside setting. The set lunches are excellent. *Mon; Jan; Jun–Aug: Tue L.*	*AE DC MC V*	●	■	●	
Chinnor: *Sir Charles Napier* ⓁⓁⓁⓁ Spriggs Alley, nr Chinnor, Oxon. *01494 483011.* Service is informal, but the food is good in this Chiltern pub-restaurant. The garden has eccentric sculptures. *Sun D, Mon.*	*AE MC V*	●	■	●	■
Cookham: *Manzano's* ⓁⓁⓁ 19–21 Station Hill Parade, Cookham, Windsor & Maidenhead. *01628 525775.* Intimate, family-run restaurant full of friendly enthusiasm and specialities such as suckling pig and roast lamb. A takeaway tapas menu is also available. *Sat L, Sun, bank hols.*	*AE MC V*	●	■	●	■
Dinton: *La Chouette* ⓁⓁⓁⓁ Westlington Green, Dinton, Bucks. *01296 747422.* Belgian gastronomic flair in this beautiful 16th-century building. The *patron* also offers a selection of Belgian and Trappist beers. *Sat L, Sun.*	*MC V*	●	■		■
Easington: *Mole & Chicken* ⓁⓁⓁ Easington Terrace, Chilton Rd, Bucks. *01844 208387.* www.moleandchicken.co.uk Adventurous cooking is the hallmark of this friendly and efficient restaurant. Specialities include duckling in orange sauce. Now also a B&B.	*AE MC V*	●	■	●	
Godstow: *Trout* ⓁⓁ Godstow, Wolvercote, Oxon. *01865 302071.* A trout stream runs past this charming creeper-covered medieval pub north of Oxford. Peacocks strut outside; inside, it is always civilized.	*MC V*	●		●	■
Goring: *Leatherne Bottel* ⓁⓁⓁⓁ On B4009, Goring, Oxon. *01491 872667.* www.leathernebottel.co.uk A glorious riverside setting accounts for the popularity of this relaxing place. Fresh local ingredients are presented with Pacific Rim touches. *Sun D.*	*AE MC V*		■	●	■
Great Milton: *Le Manoir aux Quat'Saisons* ⓁⓁⓁⓁⓁ Church Rd, Great Milton, Oxon. *01844 278881.* www.manoir.com Raymond Blanc's gastronomic pleasure palace is a rural idyll. The superb food is fresh, inventive and fully flavoured. A memorable experience, though at a price. Luxurious rooms available.	*AE DC MC V*	●	■	●	
Great Missenden: *La Petite Auberge* ⓁⓁⓁⓁ 107 High St, Great Missenden, Bucks. *01494 865370.* An intimate restaurant producing reliable provincial French cooking. Service is efficient but unobtrusive. *L, Sun, public hols.*	*DC MC V*	●			
Haddenham: *Green Dragon* ⓁⓁⓁ 8 Church Way, Haddenham, Bucks. *01844 291403.* www.eatatthedragon.co.uk A village dining pub with wide range of home-made British food such as scallops. The big dining rooms are open to the bar. *Sun D.*	*AE MC V*	●	■	●	■
Kintbury: *Dundas Arms* ⓁⓁⓁ 53 Station Rd, Kintbury, Newbury. *01488 658263.* www.dundasarms.co.uk This old riverside pub serves an imaginative range of bar snacks and traditional dishes. Fresh fish supplied daily. *Sun, Mon D.*	*AE MC V*	●		●	■
Long Crendon: *Angel Inn* ⓁⓁⓁ Bicester Rd, Long Crendon, Bucks. *01844 208268.* www.angelrestaurant.co.uk Antique, listed 16th-century inn offering fresh fish, blackboard specials, mouth-watering puddings and good-value wines. *Sun D.*	*MC V*	●	■	●	■

MELBOURN: *Pink Geranium* www.pinkgeranium.co.uk ££££
Station Rd, Melbourn, nr Royston, Herts. *01763 260215.*
Assured cooking is served in this pretty thatched cottage by the church. The atmosphere is welcoming, the decor pink. *Sun D, Mon.* *limited.*
AE MC V

MOULSFORD: *Beetle and Wedge* ££££
Ferry Lane, Moulsford, Oxon. *01491 651381.* www.beetleandwedge.co.uk
On the Thames in *Wind in the Willows* country. Eat in the informal Boathouse or sophisticated dining room. Booking essential.
AE DC MC V

OXFORD: *Nosebag* £
6–8 St Michael's St, Oxford. *01865 721033.*
Excellent salads, soups and imaginative light dishes are served to queues of hungry students on the upper floor of a quaint building. *25, 26 Dec.*
MC V

OXFORD: *Al-Shami* ££
25 Walton Crescent, Oxford. *01865 310066.* www.al-shami.co.uk
This bustling Lebanese restaurant serves *falafel, tabouleh, ful medames* and other favourites, with authentic desserts to follow.
MC V

OXFORD: *Browns* £££
5–11 Woodstock Rd, Oxford. *01865 511995.* www.browns-restaurant.com
A lively, informal restaurant serving a tempting range of snacks and fuller meals amid bentwood furnishings and potted plants. *25, 26 Dec.*
AE MC V

OXFORD: *Cherwell Boathouse* £££
Bardwell Rd, Oxford. *01865 552746.* www.cherwellboathouse.co.uk
A romantic punting spot on the River Cherwell. The fixed-price menus are British with a European twist. *Sun D.*
AE DC MC V

SHINFIELD: *L'Ortolan* www.l'ortolan.com £££££
Old Vicarage, Church Lane, Shinfield, Reading. *0118 9883783.*
L'Ortolan is one of Britain's best restaurants. The setting is charming, though the modern French and British dishes are very pricey. Set menus and lunches represent better value. *Sun D, Mon.*
AE DC MC V

SPEEN: *Old Plow* £££
Flowers Bottom, Speen, Bucks. *01494 488300.*
An informal bistro in a picturesque former pub. Much is home-made, and all of it is fresh. *Sat L, Sun D, Mon.* *limited.*
AE MC V

STONOR: *The Flying Pig at the Stonor Hotel* £££
On B480, Stonor, Oxon. *01491 638345.* www.mystonor.com
A restaurant near Henley-on-Thames. Good local organic produce is cooked with flair then served in the conservatory or outside deck (seats 80).
AE MC V

STREATLEY: *The Swan at Streatley* £££
High St, Streatley, Berks. *01491 878800.* www.theswanatstreatley.com
A Thames-side business and leisure hotel serving carefully prepared dishes using the finest local ingredients in a delightful setting. *Sat L.*
AE DC MC V

WINDSOR: *Al Fassia* ££
27 St Leonards Rd, Windsor, Berks. *01753 855370.*
Highly sought after Moroccan restaurant with traditional North African decor. Try filo parcels of chicken and almonds, or the lamb tagine. *Sun.*
AE DC MC V

WOBURN: *Paris House* £££££
Woburn Park, Woburn, Beds. *01525 290692.* www.parishouse.co.uk
Modern French food stars at this smart mock-Tudor building in the grounds of Woburn Abbey. Try the hot raspberry soufflé. *Sun D, Mon, Feb.*
AE DC MC V

WOBURN SANDS: *Spooners* www.spooners.co.uk £££
61 High St, Woburn Sands, Milton Keynes, Bucks. *01908 584385.*
This Victorian terraced house makes an agreeable place for a light lunch or a substantial meal in the evenings. The steaks are especially tasty. Warm, friendly atmosphere. *Sun, Mon.*
AE MC V

WESSEX

AVEBURY: *The Circle Restaurant* £
Avebury, Wilts. *01672 539514*
Wholefood fans rave about the dishes at this counter-service vegetarian restaurant beside the ancient stone circle. Some lovely soups on the menu. Vegan and gluten-free diets are catered for. *D.*
MC V

Price categories include a three-course meal for one, half a bottle of house wine, and all unavoidable extra charges such as cover, service, VAT:
£ under £15
££ £15-£25
£££ £25-£35
££££ £35-£50
£££££ over £50

Children Welcome
Restaurants which offer smaller portions and high-chairs for children. Special menus sometimes available.

Fixed-Price Menu
A good value fixed-price meal, at lunch, dinner or both, usually of three courses.

Vegetarian
Vegetarian specialities served, sometimes for both starters and main courses.

Credit Cards
Indicates which credit cards are accepted: *AE* American Express; *DC* Diners Club; *MC* Master Card/Access; *V* Visa.

Restaurant	Credit Cards	Children Welcome	Fixed-Price Menu	Vegetarian	Outdoor Tables
Barwick: *Little Barwick House* £££ Off A37, Barwick, Som. *01935 423902.* www.littlebarwickhouse.co.uk Non-residents can dine at this Georgian dower-house hotel. The quality of the local ingredients underpins the Modern British menu. *limited.*	AE MC V	●	■	●	
Bath: *Hole in the Wall* £££ 16 George St, Bath, B & NE Som. *01225 425242.* The new management has made dynamic changes in this famous cellar. Sample modern British cooking at its best. *Sun, public hols.*	AE MC V		■	●	
Bath: *Moon and Sixpence* £££ 6A Broad St, Bath, B & NE Som. *01225 460962.* www.moonandsixpence.co.uk This popular bistro and wine bar serves inexpensive lunchtime dishes and good-value dinners. The downstairs conservatory is particularly pleasant in summer. *26 Dec, 1 Jan.*	AE MC V	●	■	●	
Bath: *The Bath Priory* £££££ Weston Rd, Bath, B & NE Som. *01225 331922.* www.thebathpriory.co.uk This palatial but relaxing country-house hotel in lovely gardens offers French and English Michelin-star cooking in a variety of themed rooms.	AE DC MC V	●	■	●	■
Beaminster: *Bridge House* £££ 3 Prout Bridge, Beaminster, Dorset. *01308 862200.* www.bridge-house.co.uk This ancient clergy house dishes up old favourites and inventive adaptations in a civilized setting. Good-value rooms.	AE DC MC V		■	●	
Bournemouth: *Chez Fred* £ 10 Seamoor Rd, Westbourne, Bournemouth. *01202 761023.* www.chezfred.co.uk Fred's fish and chips and wicked puddings, such as treacle sponge, are his claim to fame. The service is friendly, the atmosphere lively. *Sun L.*	MC V	●	■	●	
Bradford-on-Avon: *Woolley Grange* ££££ Woolley Green, Bradford-on-Avon, Wilts. *01225 864705.* www.woolleygrange.com A delightful Jacobean country-house hotel with everything from children's chicken nuggets to enterprising international cuisine. The atmosphere is informal, and the service excellent.	DC MC V	●	■	●	■
Bristol: *Riverstation* £££ The Grove, Bristol. *01179 144434.* www.riverstation.co.uk A former river police station on the docks near the city centre, this light and airy restaurant and deli specializes in Modern European cuisine. *25, 26 Dec.*	DC MC V	●	■	●	■
Bristol: *Lords* ££££ 43 Corn Street, Bristol. *01179 262658.* French and Mediterranean influences combine in the delicious creations on offer in the basement of a bank building. The fish dishes are good, as is the choice of desserts. *Sat L, Sun, 25 Dec–2 Jan, Easter week, last 2 weeks Aug.*	AE MC V	●		●	
Clevedon: *Junior Poon* £££ 16 Hill Rd, Clevedon, Som. *01275 341900.* www.juniorpoon.com A relaxed Peking and Szechuan restaurant and wine bar, set in a Grade II listed Georgian building. Try the tiger prawns in garlic butter sauce. *Sun.*	AE MC V	●	■	●	
Colerne: *Lucknam Park* £££££ Off A420, Colerne, Wilts. *01225 742777.* www.lucknampark.co.uk A luxurious country-house hotel offering suitably posh cooking. The atmosphere is discreet and formal. Men are required to wear a jacket and tie. A memorable experience. *Mon–Sat L.*	AE DC MC V			●	
Lacock: *At the Sign of the Angel* ££££ 6 Church St, Lacock, Wilts. *01249 730230.* www.lacock.co.uk The 14th-century hotel with low beams, wood panelling and open fires serves superb traditional British fare, including steak and kidney pie. *Mon L.*	AE DC MC V	●		●	■

MAIDEN NEWTON: *Le Petit Canard* ££££
Dorchester Rd, Maiden Newton, Dorset. *01300 320536.* www.le-petit-canard.co.uk
Modern British dishes prepared using fresh local produce feature in this candlelit restaurant. *Mon, Tue–Sat L, 2nd & 4th Sun of month.*
AE MC V

MONTACUTE: *The King's Arms Inn* ££
Off A303, Som. *01935 822513.*
This 16th-century inn houses the award-winning Abbey Room, offering superb modern British cuisine in cosy surroundings.
AE MC V

POOLE: *The Mansion House* £££
Thames St, Poole, Dorset. *01202 685666.* www.themansionhouse.co.uk
Located in a cobbled mews just off Poole Quay, this Georgian townhouse restaurant uses local produce in good Modern British fare.
AE DC MC V

SALISBURY: *Harpers* www.harpers.restaurant.co.uk ££
6–7 Ox Row, Market Place, Salisbury, Wilts. *01722 333118.*
Light, friendly, family restaurant offers unpretentious roasts, casseroles as well as daily specials. Worth a visit for the wonderful views over historic Salisbury. *Sun D (Oct–May).*
AE DC MC V

SHAFTESBURY: *La Fleur de Lys* ££££
25 Salisbury St, Shaftesbury, Dorset. *01747 853717.* www.lafleursdelys.co.uk
This unobstrusive place (a wood panelled loft conversion above a stable block) conceals some accomplished cooking. *Sun D, Mon L, 2 weeks Jan.*
AE MC V

SHEPTON MALLET: *Bowlish House* £££
Wells Rd, Shepton Mallet, Som. *01749 342022.* www.bowlishhouse.com
A Georgian merchant's house with peaceful gardens. Relaxed dinners; afternoon teas too. Modern British cuisine.
MC V

STON EASTON: *Ston Easton Park* ££££
On A37, Ston Easton, Som. *01761 241631.* stoneastonpark@stoneaston.co.uk
Straightforward menus characterize this splendid country-house hotel. The modern European cookery justifies the expense. An experience that will not be a disappointment.
AE DC MC V

STURMINSTER NEWTON: *Plumber Manor* www.plumbermanor.com £££
Hazelbury Bryan Rd, Sturminster Newton, Dorset. *01258 472507.*
Oil paintings adorn this hotel dining room, but they won't distract from the food. The fish is superb, and the desserts are very tempting. *Mon–Sat L.*
AE DC MC V

TAUNTON: *Castle* £££££
Castle Green, Taunton, Som. *01823 272671.* www.the-castle-hotel.com
A dignified but unostentatious wisteria-clad hotel makes a fine setting for consistently excellent modern British fare.
AE DC MC V

WARMINSTER: *Bishopstrow House* ££££
On B3414, Warminster, Wilts. *01985 212312.* www.vonessenhotels.com/bishopstrow
Light lunches and dinners in the elegant Georgian surroundings of this country-house hotel.
AE DC MC V

WEST BAY: *Riverside* ££
Off A35 nr Bridport, Dorset. *01308 422011.* www.riverside-restaurant.co.uk
Fish is the mainstay of this long-established restaurant, but there's a good selection of casual snacks. Book ahead. *Sun D, Mon, Dec–mid-Feb.*
MC V

WEST BEXINGTON: *Manor Hotel* £££
Beach Rd, West Bexington, Dorset. *01308 897785.* www.themanorhotel.com
A delightful range of bar and restaurant food in an old stone inn with nice guestrooms and a garden for children. Close to Chesil Beach. *25 Dec D.*
AE DC MC V

DEVON AND CORNWALL

AVONWICK: *Avon Inn* £££
Avonwick, nr South Brent, Devon. *01364 73475.*
A dining pub on the banks of the Avon. The restaurant is English with a Continental twist, using fish and local meat.
MC V

BARNSTAPLE: *Lynwood House* *01271 343695.* £££
Bishops Tawton Rd, Barnstaple, Devon. www.thelynwood.freeserve.co.uk
Family-run Victorian house hotel offering real home cooking. Good fish soup and seafood dishes. Comfortable rooms.
AE MC V

For key to symbols see back flap

Price categories include a three-course meal for one, half a bottle of house wine, and all unavoidable extra charges such as cover, service, VAT:
£ under £15
££ £15-£25
£££ £25-£35
££££ £35-£50
£££££ over £50

Children Welcome
Restaurants which offer smaller portions and high-chairs for children. Special menus sometimes available.

Fixed-Price Menu
A good value fixed-price meal, at lunch, dinner or both, usually of three courses.

Vegetarian
Vegetarian specialities served, sometimes for both starters and main courses.

Credit Cards
Indicates which credit cards are accepted: *AE* American Express; *DC* Diners Club; *MC* Master Card/Access; *V* Visa.

Restaurant	Credit Cards	Children Welcome	Fixed-Price Menu	Vegetarian	Outdoor Tables
Chagford: *22 Mill Street* ££££ 22 Mill St, Chagford, Devon. *01647 432244.* www.22millstreet.co.uk Exquisite Modern European cooking, such as crab lasagne or seabass roasted with pickled ginger and basil. ● *Sun–Tue L, 2 wks Jan, 1st wk in Jun.*	MC V		■	●	
Chagford: *Gidleigh Park* £££££ Chagford, Devon. *01647 432367.* www.gidleigh.com Imaginative details mark out from the crowd this first-class country-house hotel and restaurant. Pricey; a place for special occasions.	AE DC MC V		■	●	
Dartington: *Cott Inn* ££ Dartington, Devon. *01803 863777.* www.thecottinn.co.uk A restaurant-with-rooms in a 14th-century inn. Good British home cooking with a daily changing menu and a nice garden.	AE MC V			●	■
Dartmouth: *Carved Angel* ££££ 2 South Embankment, Dartmouth, Devon. *01803 832465.* www.thecarvedangel.com One of Britain's best restaurants occupies a quayside Tudor building. The menu features local fish and shellfish, and in winter makes use of local game, like wild duck. ● *Sun D, Mon L, 24–26 Dec.*	AE MC V	●	■	●	
Doddiscombsleigh: *Nobody Inn* £££ Doddiscombsleigh, nr Exeter, Devon. *01647 252394.* www.nobodyinn.co.uk The traditional, beamed restaurant in this dining pub has a stunning wine list and an amazing choice of local cheeses.	AE MC V			●	■
Exeter: *Thai Orchid* ££ 5 Cathedral Yard, Exeter, Devon. *01392 214215.* Authentic Thai cuisine is expertly served within a 15th-century listed building which originally housed the stonemasons working on the cathedral. Fresh orchids on every table add to the elegance. ● *Sun, 25, 26 Dec, 1 Jan.*	MC V	●	■	●	
Kingsbridge: *Buckland-Tout-Saints Hotel* ££££ Goveton, Kingsbridge, Devon. *01548 853055.* www.tout-saints.co.uk Refined cuisine served in a handsome Queen Anne house in lovely grounds. British produce is cooked with Gallic finesse. ● *3 wks in Jan.* *limited.*	MC V	●	■	●	■
Lewdown: *Lewtrenchard Manor* ££££ Off A30, Lewdown, Devon. *01566 783256.* www.lewtrenchard.co.uk This Elizabethan manor-house hotel with mouthwatering fixed-price menus makes a gloriously romantic retreat.	AE DC MC V		■		
Lifton: *Arundell Arms* ££££ Off A30, Lifton, Devon. *01566 784666.* www.arundellarms.com An attractive sporting inn in a peaceful village. Local fish and game appear on the fixed-price menus. Bar snacks are also available for lunch and dinner. Convivial atmosphere.	AE DC MC V	●	■	●	
Lynmouth: *The Rising Sun* ££££ Harbourside, Lynmouth, Devon. *01598 753223.* www.risingsunlynmouth.co.uk Fish is unloaded almost on the doorstep of this 14th-century smugglers' haunt, but it excels in cooking other things as well.	AE DC MC V		■	●	■
Padstow: *Seafood Restaurant* £££££ Riverside, Padstow, Corn. *01841 532700.* www.rickstein.com A favourite with fish-lovers, this restaurant has a wonderful harbourside location. Plainer, but good, food in sister hotel-restaurant St Petroc's House. ● *22–26 Dec, 1 May, 1st Sun in Jul.*	MC V		■	●	
Penzance: *Harris's* £££ 46 New St, Penzance, Corn. *01736 364408.* www.harrissrestaurant.co.uk Game, when in season, and locally farmed meat are a match for the fish dishes. The lunch menu is good value. ● *Sun; Mon (winter).* *limited.*	AE MC V		■		

POLPERRO: *Kitchen* ££££

The Coombes, Polperro, Corn. 01503 272780. kitchen@polperro.aol.com

A tiny restaurant specializing in fresh local fish which is a sound choice for the tourists who flock to Polperro in summer. *L; Oct–Easter.*

MC V

PORT ISAAC: *Slipway* £££

Harbour Front, Port Isaac, Corn. 01208 880264. www.portisaac.com

In season, this 16th-century chandlery offers a perfect sample of North Cornwall's fishy fare. *Jan–mid-Feb; mid-Feb–Easter: Sat & Sun.*

AE MC V

PORTREATH: *Tabb's* ££

Tregea Terrace, Portreath, Corn. 01209 842488.

A small restaurant in an old forge. Everything on the deliciously eclectic menu is home-made. *Mon–Sat L, Tue D, 26 Dec, 1 Jan.*

MC V

ST IVES: *Tate St Ives Coffee Shop and Restaurant* ££

Porthmeor Beach, St Ives, Corn. 01736 791122. www.tate.org.uk

Admire the views from this art-gallery brasserie while tucking into wholefood dishes made with fresh local produce, including fish and shellfish. *D; Mon (winter).*

MC V

ST IVES: *Russets* £££

18A Fore St, St Ives, Corn. 01736 794700. www.russets.co.uk

This seafood restaurant in St Ives main thoroughfare is casual, laid-back and yet surprisingly lively. Local artists' work hangs from the walls. *Jan.*

AE MC V

ST MAWES: *Hotel Tresanton* ££££

Lower Castle Rd, St Mawes, Corn. 01326 270055. www.tresanton.com

This restaurant in one of the best hotels in Cornwall specializes in local fish and has wonderful views over the sea from the terrace.

AE MC V

TAVISTOCK: *The Horn of Plenty* www.thehornofplenty.co.uk £££££

Gulworthy, Tavistock, Devon. & FAX 01822 832528.

A 200-year-old building set in almost five acres of gardens. TV cook Peter Gorton is executive head chef. *Mon L, 23–26 Dec.*

AE MC V

TORQUAY: *Mulberry Room* £££

1 Scarborough Rd, Torquay, Torbay. 01803 213639.

This friendly restaurant-with-rooms offers snacks and delicious lunches (dinners on Fri to Sun). Try the bread and cakes. *Mon & Tue (residents only).*

TOTNES: *Willow* £

87 High St, Totnes, Devon. 01803 862605.

Vegetarian specialities from around the globe, including Mexican, Indian, Caribbean and Italian, make this place cosmopolitan and eclectic. Warm welcoming atmosphere. *Sun, Mon D, Tues D.* *Thurs D (summer only).*

TREBURLEY: *Springer Spaniel* £££

Treburley, nr Launceston, Cornwall. 01579 370424.

A friendly dining pub with an attractive, beamed restaurant. The menu changes frequently, reflecting the owners' desire to use local produce, including home-grown vegetables and salads. *limited.*

MC V

VIRGINSTOW: *Percy's* ££££

Virginstow, Devon. 01409 211236. FAX 01409 211275. www.percys.co.uk

Contemporary country cuisine is the fare of this very rural restaurant, situated some 9 miles from Launceston in the midst of a 130 acre estate.

AE MC V

THE HEART OF ENGLAND

ABBERLEY: *Brooke Room, The Elms* £££££

Stockton Rd, Abberley, Worcs. 01299 896666. www.theelmshotel.com

Finest organic home-grown produce and local specialities at this elegant Queen Anne mansion. Lovely decor and rooms.

AE DC MC V

BIRMINGHAM: *Chung Ying Garden* ££

17 Thorp St, Birmingham. 0121 6666622. www.chungying.co.uk

A flamboyant Cantonese food palace offering a giant range of specialities, including *dim sum*. Karaoke on request.

AE DC MC V

BISHOP'S TACHBROOK: *Mallory Court* £££££

Off B4087 nr Leamington Spa, Warw. 01926 330214. www.mallory.co.uk

Classic French and British cuisine feature at this manor-house hotel, with impressive results. Beautiful gardens.

AE DC MC V

For key to symbols see back flap

Price categories include a three-course meal for one, half a bottle of house wine, and all unavoidable extra charges such as cover, service, VAT:
£ under £15
££ £15-£25
£££ £25-£35
££££ £35-£50
£££££ over £50

CHILDREN WELCOME
Restaurants which offer smaller portions and high-chairs for children. Special menus sometimes available.

FIXED-PRICE MENU
A good value fixed-price meal, at lunch, dinner or both, usually of three courses.

VEGETARIAN
Vegetarian specialities served, sometimes for both starters and main courses.

CREDIT CARDS
Indicates which credit cards are accepted: *AE* American Express; *DC* Diners Club; *MC* Master Card/Access; *V* Visa.

BRIMFIELD: *The Roebuck Inn* £££
Brimfield, Here. *01584 711230.* www.theroebuckinn.com
A deceptively simple setting (a village pub) and a relaxed atmosphere conceal highly sophisticated British cooking. *Mon–Fri (dining room).*

BURTON UPON TRENT: *Dovecliff Hall* *01283 531818.* £££££
Dovecliff Rd, Stretton, Burton upon Trent, Staffs. www.dovecliffhallhotel.co.uk
A Georgian country house in extensive grounds by the River Dove. An elegant setting. Modern British food. *Sat L, Sun D, Mon L, bank hols.*

CHELTENHAM: *Le Champignon Sauvage* £££££
24 Suffolk Rd, Cheltenham, Glos. *01242 573449.*
A two Michelin-starred restaurant serving Gallic dishes with startling ingredient combinations: sardine and *tapenade* (olive and anchovy paste), rabbit and black pudding. A delight to the palate. *Sun, Mon, 24 Dec–3 Jan, 3 weeks in June.*

CHESTER: *Francs* £££
14 Cupping St, Chester, Ches. *01244 317952.* www.francs.co.uk
An ever-popular brasserie where French rock beats out over tasty *plats du jour*. Sundays are family days; special low price for children. Book ahead.

COVENTRY: *Browns* £
Earl St, Coventry. *024 76221100.* www.browns-cafebar.co.uk
Located next to Coventry Cathedral, this restaurant and bar have a wide-ranging menu of traditional English food. There is a late-night bar and live music on Friday and Saturday nights. *Sun D, 25 Dec.*

COVENTRY: *Ryton Organic Gardens Restaurant* www.hdra.org.uk ££
Henry Doubleday Research Assoc., Ryton Organic Gardens, off A45. *024 76307142.*
Set within 10 acres of organic display gardens, this restaurant offers meat, fish, vegetarian and vegan meals. Many of the vegetables are grown on site. *24 Dec–2 Jan.*

DORRINGTON: *Country Friends* ££££
On A49 nr Shrewsbury, Shrops. *01743 718707.*
Simple, reliable English cooking in a pleasant mock-Tudor setting. Fixed-price menu available. Log fires burn in winter. *Sun–Tue.*

KENILWORTH: *Restaurant Bosquet* ££££
97A Warwick Rd, Kenilworth, Warw. *01926 852463.*
This Victorian house offers serious classic French food with rich sauces and fresh seasonal produce. *Sat L, Sun, Mon.*

LEAMINGTON SPA: *Piccolino's Pizzeria* ££
9 Spencer St, Leamington Spa, Warw. *01926 422988.*
A jovial family-owned place serving home-cooked Italian favourites – pizza and pasta, of course, and other dishes at inexpensive prices.

LEAMINGTON SPA: *Flynns* ££
14 The Parade, Leamington Spa, Warw. *01926 421620.*
Italian dishes predominate in this relaxed brasserie. Stylish decor.

LOWER SLAUGHTER: *Lower Slaughter Manor* £££££
Off A429, Lower Slaughter, Glos. *01451 820456.* www.lowerslaughter.co.uk
Renowned restaurant in a beautiful Cotswolds manor. The menu is based on French and British classics, modernized by the latest influences from all over the globe. Highly recommended.

LUDLOW: *Unicorn Inn* ££
66 Corve St, Ludlow, Shrops. *01584 873555.*
The emphasis is on local produce in the restaurant of this 17th-century inn. The home-made puddings are good. Great bar food available too.

	Credit Cards	Children Welcome	Fixed-Price Menu	Vegetarian	Outdoor Tables
Brimfield: The Roebuck Inn	MC V	●		●	■
Burton upon Trent: Dovecliff Hall	AE MC V		■	●	
Cheltenham: Le Champignon Sauvage	AE DC MC V	●	■		
Chester: Francs	AE MC V	●	■	●	
Coventry: Browns	DC MC V			●	■
Coventry: Ryton Organic Gardens Restaurant	MC V	●		●	■
Dorrington: Country Friends	MC V	●	■	●	
Kenilworth: Restaurant Bosquet	AE MC V	●	■		
Leamington Spa: Piccolino's Pizzeria	MC V	●		●	
Leamington Spa: Flynns	AE MC V	●	■	●	
Lower Slaughter: Lower Slaughter Manor	AE MC V		■	●	
Ludlow: Unicorn Inn	AE MC V	●		●	■

LUDLOW: *Merchant House* ££££
62 Lower Corve St, Ludlow. 01584 875438. www.merchanthouse.org
This highly acclaimed restaurant is based in a charming Jacobean building which backs on to the River Corve. The eclectic menu is mostly organic. Vegetarians should call in advance. *Sun, Mon; Tue–Thu L.*
DC MC V

PRESTBURY: *White House* £££
The Village, Prestbury, Ches. 01625 829376. www.whitehouse.co.uk
The smart and elegant decor matches the up-market cosmopolitan food here. There's a conservatory for warm summer evenings. Attractive rooms. *Sun D, Mon L.*
AE DC MC V

ROSS-ON-WYE: *Meader's* ££
1 Copse Cross St, Ross-on-Wye, Here. 01989 562803.
Friendly Hungarian business; you can sample authentic goulash and *galuska* (dumplings) without breaking the bank. *Sun, Mon.*
MC V

ROSS-ON-WYE: *The Pheasant* ££££
52 Edde Cross St, Ross-on-Wye, Here. 01989 565751.
www.pheasant-at-ross.co.uk
A cheerful, homely restaurant in a former Tudor tavern offers fine British cuisine, ancient and modern, and personal service. *Sun–Wed.*
AE DC MC V

SHREWSBURY: *Floating Thai Restaurant* 01743 243123. ££
Welsh Bridge, Frankwell, Shrewsbury. www.floatingthairestaurant.co.uk
This atmospheric Thai restaurant is located near the city centre, on a boat as the name suggests. It has an extensive seafood menu. Advanced reservation is recommended. *L.*
AE MC V

SHREWSBURY: *Cromwells Hotel* £££
11 Dogpole, Shrewsbury. 01743 361440. www.cromwellsinn.com
A wine bar/restaurant located in a small hotel in the town centre, opposite the Guildhall. *throughout.*
AE MC V

STRATFORD-UPON-AVON: *The Opposition* ££
13 Sheep St, Stratford-upon-Avon, Warw. 01789 269980. www.theopposition.co.uk
A bustling bistro offering simple pre-theatre suppers. The day's specials are chalked on blackboards. *(Fri–Sat).*
MC V

STRATFORD-UPON-AVON: *Russons* £££
8 Church St, Stratford-upon-Avon, Warw. 01789 268822.
This rustic 16th-century setting fits the Shakespearean location. A varied menu, with fish a speciality. Pre-theatre dinners and lunches available and varied inexpensive meals. *Sun, Mon.*
AE MC V

TETBURY: *Gumstool Inn* £££
Calcot Manor, Tetbury, Gloucs. 01666 890391. www.calcotmanor.co.uk
The dining area and bar are combined in this popular gastro dining pub. The eclectic menu ranges from local beer sausages to Moroccan specialities.
AE DC MC V

EAST MIDLANDS

BAKEWELL: *Renaissance* £££
Bath St, Bakewell, Derbs. 01629 812687.
French-style cuisine enjoyed in this traditionally beamed house. Despite lavish ingredients, (truffles and *foie gras*), the prices are reasonable.
Sun D, Mon, 1–15 Jan, early Aug.
AE MC V

BASLOW: *Fischer's at Baslow* £££££
Baslow Hall, Calver Rd, Baslow, Derbs. 01246 583259.
www.fischers-baslowhall.co.uk
Whether you eat in the smart dining room or more casually at the adjoining Café Max, the cooking is top notch. Handy for Chatsworth.
AE DC MC V

BECKINGHAM: *Black Swan* ££
Hillside, Beckingham, Lincs. 01636 626474.
This award-winning 17th-century coaching inn is intimate, the quality of the modern British dishes on the gourmet menu or the less formal café menu is high and the service is always friendly and efficient.
Mon, Sun D.
MC V

For key to symbols see back flap

Price categories include a three-course meal for one, half a bottle of house wine, and all unavoidable extra charges such as cover, service, VAT:
- £ under £15
- ££ £15-£25
- £££ £25-£35
- ££££ £35-£50
- £££££ over £50

CHILDREN WELCOME
Restaurants which offer smaller portions and high-chairs for children. Special menus sometimes available.

FIXED-PRICE MENU
A good value fixed-price meal, at lunch, dinner or both, usually of three courses.

VEGETARIAN
Vegetarian specialities served, sometimes for both starters and main courses.

CREDIT CARDS
Indicates which credit cards are accepted: *AE* American Express; *DC* Diners Club; *MC* Master Card/Access; *V* Visa.

Restaurant	Credit Cards	Children Welcome	Fixed-Price Menu	Vegetarian	Outdoor Tables
BIRCH VALE: *Waltzing Weasel* ££££ New Mills Rd, Birch Vale, High Peak, Derbs. *01663 743402.* www.w-weazel.co.uk Hearty English fare (roasts, chops, game pie and Stilton) is served, accompanied by panoramic views of Kinder Scout. Attractive rooms.	AE MC V	●	■	●	■
BOTTESFORD: *Paul's Contemporary Cuisine* £££ 1 Market St, Bottesford, Leics. *01949 842375.* www.paulsrestaurant.co.uk Local supplies of game in season is one reason for this bistro's success; attractive beamed decor is another. *Sun D, Mon.*	MC V	●	■	●	■
BURTON ON THE WOLDS: *Langs* £££ 147 Melton Rd, Burton on the Wolds, Leics. *01509 880980.* www.langsrestaurant.com Smartly furnished barn conversion offering inventive dishes and startling arrays of classic treatments of fish and meat. *Sun D.*	AE MC V	●	■	●	■
CASTLETON: *Castle Inn* £££ Castle St, Castleton, Derbs. *01433 620578.* Relaxing pub restaurant in the heart of the Peak District. Traditional British food with Mediterranean influences served in an oak-beamed room.	AE MC V	●		●	■
COLSTON BASSETT: *Martins Arms Inn* £££ School Lane, Colston Bassett, Notts. *01949 81361.* Situated in a former farmhouse, this traditional English pub includes a comfortable dining room that serves much more than standard pub fare. The cooking is in the modern British style. *Sun D, 25 Dec.*	AE MC V			●	
EMPINGHAM: *White Horse* ££ Empingham, Rutland. *01780 460221.* www.the-white-horse.co.uk This delightful, 17th-century stone-built courthouse now holds a bar and bistro. It also serves morning croissants and afternoon teas.	AE DC MC V	●		●	■
GAUNTON NEWARK: *Gaunton Beck* £££ Main St, Gaunton Newark, Notts. *01636 636793.* An eclectic menu of French, British and Eastern dishes are served in this 1750s beamed building. Nice patio in summer.	AE DC MC V	●	■	●	■
HAMBLETON: *Hambleton Hall* £££££ Off A606 nr Oakham, Rutland. *01572 756991.* www.hambletonhall.com Splendid views over Rutland Water are a good start to the menu of outstanding fresh cooking with lobsters and *foie gras*. Such memorable feasts don't come cheap. Smart accommodation.	AE MC V	●	■	●	■
KEYSTON: *The Pheasant Inn* £££ Off A14, Keyston, Northants. *01832 710241.* www.huntsbridge.co.uk Light or full-menu options are available in this delightful thatched inn. The menu is eclectic and modern; the home-made ices are delicious. *limited.*	AE DC MC V	●		●	■
LEICESTER: *Bobby's* ££ 154–156 Belgrave Rd, Leicester. *0116 2660106.* www.eatatbobbys.com Vegetarian Gujarati and South Indian dishes make an interesting, good-value treat. The combinations of freshly ground spices make this place unique. Licensed, but you can also bring your own wine. *Mon.*	MC V	●	■	●	
LEICESTER: *The Case* ££££ 4–6 Hotel St, Leicester. *01162 517675.* www.thecase.co.uk Stylish, light restaurant serving Modern European dishes such as home-made brie *Sun, 24–27 Dec, 1, 2 Jan.*	AE DC V	●		●	
LINCOLN: *Wig and Mitre* £££ 30–32 Steep Hill, Lincoln. *01522 535190.* www.wigandmitre.com This operates on similar lines to its sibling, Gaunton Beck, in Newark. French and British dishes. Diners appreciate its flexibility and long opening hours.	AE DC MC V	●	■	●	

LINCOLN: *Jew's House* ££££
15 The Strait, Lincoln. *01522 524851.* www.thejewshouse.co.uk
A fascinating old building close to the cathedral, serving Modern European and international food. Wonderful, calorific hand-made chocolates. *Sun & Mon.*
AE DC MC V

NEWARK: *Gannets Café* £
35 Castlegate, Newark, Notts. *01636 702066.*
A cheery ground-floor café by the castle with a garden extension and an upstairs bistro. It is plain, simple and affordable. The staff are very friendly and the atmosphere is bohemian. *D, 25–26 Dec, 1 Jan.*

NOTTINGHAM: *Saagar* ££
473 Mansfield Rd, Sherwood, Nottingham. *0115 9622014.*
North "Indian" cookery from the Punjab, Kashmir and Pakistan. Menus change frequently and new recipes spice up the choice. *Sun L.*
AE MC V

NOTTINGHAM: *Sonny's* £££
3 Carlton St, Hockley, Nottingham. *0115 9473041.*
Blend of simple snack-bar and restaurant offering Modern European food with Eastern touches. The atmosphere is laid-back and fashionable.
AE MC V

PAULERSPURY: *Vine House* ££££
100 High St, Paulerspury, Northnts. *01327 811267.* www.vinehousehotel.com
Seventeenth-century house just off the A5. Unusual ingredients, modern British influences and informal, pleasant rooms. *Sat L, Sun, Mon–Wed L.*
MC V

PLUMTREE: *Perkins Restaurant* ££
Old Railway Station, Plumtree, Notts. *0115 9373695.* www.perkinsrestaurant.co.uk
This bistro serves a mix of British game and fish with French sauces. Good bar snacks. *Sun D, Mon.*
AE DC MC V

REDMILE: *Peacock* ££££
Church Corner, Redmile, Leics. *01949 842554.*
An excellent dining pub offering a changing menu of modern and traditional British and European dishes. Menu changes regularly.
AE MC V

RIDGEWAY: *Old Vicarage* ££££
Ridgeway Moor, Ridgeway, Derbs. *0114 2475814.* www.theoldvicarage.co.uk
High-quality meat, vegetables and fresh herbs produce insistent flavours at this stone-built Victorian house. With three- and four-course menus, and plenty of vegetarian choices. *Sun D, Mon.*
AE MC V

ROADE: *Roade House* www.roadehousehotel.co.uk ££££
16 High St, Roade, Northnts. *01604 863372.*
This family business offers seasonal British cooking. Most dishes have complex sauces. Game features during winter. *Sat L, Sun D, Mon L.*
AE MC V

STOKE BRUERNE: *Bruerne's Lock* ££££
5 The Canalside, Stoke Bruerne, Northnts. *01604 863654.* www.bruerneslock.co.uk
A fast-evolving modern British restaurant by the side of the Grand Union Canal. Personal service is the keynote. *Sat L, Sun D, Mon.*
AE MC V

STRETTON: *Ram Jam Inn* £££
Great North Rd, Stretton, Rutland. *01780 410776.* rji@ratnet.co.uk
This roadside haven has provided hospitality since 1750. Hearty snacks and freshly prepared hot dishes are served all day, every day. *25 Dec.*
AE MC V

LANCASHIRE AND THE LAKES

AMBLESIDE: *Sheila's Cottage* ££
The Slack, Ambleside, Cumbria. *015394 33079.*
Tasty baking takes place in this converted stable-block cottage. Tea breads and cakes supplements savoury dishes such as Cumbrian sugar-baked ham or Westmorland ramekin. Children at lunchtimes only. *25, 26 Dec, 2 wks in Jan.*
MC V

AMBLESIDE: *Zeffirelli's* ££
Compston Rd, Ambleside, Cumbria. *015394 33845.* www.zeffirellis.co.uk
An unusual enterprise combining shops, café, a cinema and a trendily decorated pizzeria serving pizzas, salads and pasta. *Mon–Fri L.*
MC V

AMBLESIDE: *Rothay Manor* ££££
Rothay Bridge, Ambleside, Cumbria. *015394 33605.* www.rothaymanor.co.uk
This elegant Regency hotel mainly serves traditional English dishes. Lunch and splendid teas are excellent value.
AE DC MC V

For key to symbols see back flap

Price categories include a three-course meal for one, half a bottle of house wine, and all unavoidable extra charges such as cover, service, VAT:
£ under £15
££ £15-£25
£££ £25-£35
££££ £35-£50
£££££ over £50

Children Welcome
Restaurants which offer smaller portions and high-chairs for children. Special menus sometimes available.

Fixed-Price Menu
A good value fixed-price meal, at lunch, dinner or both, usually of three courses.

Vegetarian
Vegetarian specialities served, sometimes for both starters and main courses.

Credit Cards
Indicates which credit cards are accepted: *AE* American Express; *DC* Diners Club; *MC* Master Card/Access; *V* Visa.

Restaurant	Credit Cards	Children Welcome	Fixed-Price Menu	Vegetarian	Outdoor Tables
Applethwaite: *Underscar Manor* £££££ Off A66 nr Keswick, Cumbria. *017687 75000.* A sumptuous Italianate house in peaceful gardens sets the scene for ambitious food. Beautifully decorated rooms make a romantic retreat.	AE MC V		■	●	
Blackpool: *September Brasserie* £££ 15–17 Queen St, Blackpool. *01253 623282.* pat.wood@cyberscape.net Amid the flotsam of Blackpool's eateries, this brasserie is a beacon of hope. It produces some highly innovative robust dishes. *Mon, Sun.*	AE DC MC V	●	■	●	
Bowness-on-Windermere: *Porthole Eating House* £££ 3 Ash St, Bowness-on-Windermere, Cumbria. *015394 42793.* Summer crowds fail to jade this Italian restaurant. It maintains its pleasing simplicity of style and provides good value. *Sat L, Tue, mid-Dec–mid-Feb.*	AE DC MC V	●		●	■
Braithwaite: *Ivy House* £££ Off A66 nr Keswick, Cumbria. *017687 78338.* www.ivy-house.co.uk This Georgian hotel is in the centre of the village. Striking decor. Dinners have panache. Comfortable accommodation. *Jan.*	AE DC MC V		■	●	
Cartmel: *Uplands* £££ Haggs Lane, Cartmel, Cumbria. *015395 36248.* www.uplands.uk.com This peaceful hotel serves excellent-value set lunches of local produce; the views towards Morecambe Bay are delightful. A place to come back to, year after year. *Mon; Tue–Thu L.*	AE MC V		■		
Cartmel: *L'Enclume* £££££ Cavendish St, Cartmel, Cumbria. *015395 36362.* reservations@lenclume.co.uk This much-talked of Michelin-star restaurant run by chef Simon Rogan offers ultra-modern Continental cuisine. Open for breakfast. *Mon, 1st 2 wks Jan.*	AE DC MC V	●	■		■
Cockermouth: *Quince and Medlar* £££ 13 Castlegate, Cockermouth, Cumbria. *01900 823579.* Adventurous vegetarian cooking in a modest house near the castle. The award-winning menu is well worth sampling. *L, Sun, Mon.*	MC V			●	
Crosthwaite: *Punch Bowl Inn* enquiries@punchbowl.fsnet.co.uk ££ Crosthwaite, nr Kendal, Cumbria. *01539 568237.* People come from miles around to eat at this 17th-century coaching inn. There is a choice of several rooms. The menu is eclectic and special diets are catered for. *Sun & Mon (except bank hols), 25 Dec, 26 Dec D, 1 Jan D.*	MC V	●	■	●	■
Grasmere: *White Moss House* ££££ On A591 at Rydal Water, Cumbria. *01539 435295.* www.whitemoss.com Classy set dinners are served unpompously in this comfortable country-house hotel. A traditional setting and attentive service in a house that once belonged to William Wordsworth. *L, Sun.*	MC V	●	■		
Kendal: *Moon* *01539 729254.* ££ 129 Highgate, Kendal, Cumbria. moon@129highgate.freeserve.co.uk Modern contemporary cuisine using fresh local produce. The atmosphere is pleasantly informal and relaxed. *L; Mon, Tue; 25, 26 Dec.*	MC V	●	■	●	
Langho: *Northcote Manor* £££££ On A59 nr Blackburn, Blackb with Darwen. *01254 240555.* www.northcotemanor.com Nigel Howarth cooks with regional flair including several Lancashire specialities. Also more gastronomic dishes served in the evenings. Highly recommended food and wine.	AE MC V	●	■	●	
Liverpool: *Left Bank* £££ 1 Church Rd, Liverpool. *0151 734 5040.* French restaurant located off Penny Lane of Beatles fame, in a wood-panelled intimate setting. Book well in advance for weekend meals. *Sat D.*	AE MC V	●	■	●	

LIVERPOOL: *60 Hope St* ££££
60 Hope St, Liverpool. *0151 707 6060.* FAX *0151 707 6016.* W www.60hopestreet.com
Spread over three floors of a Georgian building with a modern interior. Quality service, superb food. *Sun, Mon; 25, 26 Dec, 1 Jan, bank hols.*
MC V

LONGRIDGE: *The Longridge Restaurant* ££££
104–106 Higher Rd, Longridge, Lancs. *01772 784969.* W www.heathcotes.co.uk
The relaxed style of this British restaurant is deceptive, as the food is prepared with slick technique and innovative talent. *Mon L.* *limited.*
AE DC MC V

MANCHESTER: *Siam Orchid* ££
54 Portland St, Manchester. *0161 236 1388.*
Manchester's best Thai restaurant has a great range of dishes, including many vegetarian choices. There are also influences from other parts of south-east Asia. Beware the fiery sauces; quell them with Singha beer. *Sat L, Sun L.*
AE MC V

MANCHESTER: *Restaurant Bar & Grill* £££
14 John Dalton St, Manchester. *0161 839 1999.*
This modern eaterie offers fine Modern European dishes in impressive surroundings, with glass walls and a long bar downstairs. *25 & 26 Dec.*
AE MC V

MANCHESTER: *Moss Nook* £££££
B5166 nr airport, Manchester. *0161 437 4778.*
Moss Nook offers a superb presentation of gastronomic medleys. Try the vast *menu surprise*, or one of the many desserts. *Sat L, Sun, Mon.*
AE MC V

MELMERBY: *Village Bakery* ££
On A686 nr Penrith, Cumbria. *01768 881811.* W www.village-bakery.com
An 18th-century barn is the setting for this shop and eaterie. Organic and vegetarian meals are available all day. *D.*
DC MC V

NEAR SAWREY: *Ees Wyke* £££
On B52 nr Hawkshead, Cumbria. *015394 36393.* W www.eeswyke.co.uk
The views towards Esthwaite Water are one attraction; charming hosts and excellent, good-value dinners are others. This country house hotel is a place that you will not forget in a hurry. *L; Jan–Feb.*
MC V

POULTON-LE-FYLDE: *River House* ££££
Skippool Creek, Thornton-le-Fylde, Lancs. *01253 883497.* W www.hotel-lakedistrict.com
This restaurant-with-rooms prides itself on its details (cheeses, teas and *petits fours*) being as good as the main courses. *L, Sun; 25, 26 Dec.*
MC V

SADDLEWORTH: *The Old Bell Inn Hotel* £££
Huddersfield Rd, Delph, Oldham. *01457 870130.*
A seasonally changing menu is offered in the main restaurant, with informal meals and snacks served in the bar.
AE MC V

ULLSWATER: *Sharrow Bay* £££££
Nr Pooley Bridge, Ullswater, Cumbria. *017684 86301.* W www.sharrow-bay.com
This is one of Britain's greatest country-house hotels. Even the teas are a banquet. *Dec–Feb.*
MC V

WATERMILLOCK: *Rampsbeck Country House Hotel* £££££
On A592 nr Pooley Bridge, Cumbria. *017684 86442.*
Rampsbeck's dining room occupies a fine stretch of lakeshore, but the modern British food is ambitious enough to hold the attention and the service is pleasant. Book for lunch. *4 Jan–mid-Feb.*
MC V

WHITEWELL: *Inn at Whitewell* £££
Whitewell, Forest of Bowland, Clitheroe, Lancs. *01200 448222.*
Full of atmosphere and very friendly, this old coaching inn's restaurant offers an above-average menu of predominantly English dishes.
MC V

WINDERMERE: *Miller Howe* £££££
Rayrigg Rd, Windermere, Cumbria. *015394 42536.* W www.millerhowe.com
This restaurant is also a beautiful hotel, but the elaborate and theatrical dishes are the main reason for visiting.
AE MC V

WITHERSLACK: *Old Vicarage* £££
Church Rd, Witherslack, Cumbria. *015395 52381.*
W www.oldvicarage.com
Dinner at this idyllic country-house hotel is a mouthwatering affair using local produce. Book ahead. Early bird half-price dinner until 7pm. *L.*
AE MC V

For key to symbols see back flap

Price categories include a three-course meal for one, half a bottle of house wine, and all unavoidable extra charges such as cover, service, VAT:
£ under £15
££ £15-£25
£££ £25-£35
££££ £35-£50
£££££ over £50

CHILDREN WELCOME
Restaurants which offer smaller portions and high-chairs for children. Special menus sometimes available.

FIXED-PRICE MENU
A good value fixed-price meal, at lunch, dinner or both, usually of three courses.

VEGETARIAN
Vegetarian specialities served, sometimes for both starters and main courses.

CREDIT CARDS
Indicates which credit cards are accepted: *AE* American Express; *DC* Diners Club; *MC* Master Card/Access; *V* Visa.

YORKSHIRE AND THE HUMBER REGION

Restaurant	Credit Cards	Children Welcome	Fixed-Price Menu	Vegetarian	Outdoor Tables
ASENBY: *Crab and Lobster* £££ Off A168 nr Thirsk, N Yorks. *01845 577286.* www.crabandlobster.com A great seafood pub just off the A1. Blackboards reflect the unpredictability of fresh catches. The place hums with activity. Rooms available.	AE MC V		■	●	■
BOLTON ABBEY: *Devonshire Arms Country House Hotel* £££££ Just off A59 nr Ilkley, N Yorks. *01756 710441.* www.thedevonshirearms.co.uk A luxurious country-house hotel. All types flock in to enjoy the smart restaurant, excellent bar snacks and luscious teas. ● *Mon–Sat L.*	AE DC MC V	●	■	●	
BRADFORD: *Koh-I-Noor* £ Simes St, Bradford. *01274 737564.* www.kohinoor.co.uk This up-market Indian restaurant specializes in Balti and vegetarian dishes, although the menu offers plenty of variety for all. Tandooris are an especially strong point. ● *Mon–Sat L.*	MC V	●	■	●	
BRADFORD: *Guide Post Hotel* £££ Common Rd, Low Moor, Bradford BD12 0ST. *01274 607866.* www.guideposthotel.net The location of this restaurant may not be ideal – a warehouse district surrounds the building – but it is definitely worth a visit for the quality of the English and continental food and for the service. ● *Sat L, Sun D.*	AE DC MC V	●		●	
BREARTON: *The Malt Shovel* £ Brearton, N Yorks. *01423 862929.* Varied blackboard menu featuring British, European and Oriental influences, served in a 16th-century beamed pub. ● *Mon; Sun D; 25, 26 Dec.*		●		●	■
ELLAND: *La Cachette* ££ 31 Huddersfield Road, Elland, Calderdale. *01422 378833.* Modern British food served in an Edwardian interior from an extensive menu, which may include deep-fried brie, rib-eye steaks, game and sticky toffee pudding. Fish a speciality. ● *Sun, bank hol Mon, last 2 weeks of Aug.*	MC V		■	●	
HARROGATE: *Betty's* ££ 1 Parliament St, Harrogate, N Yorks. *01423 502746.* www.bettysandtaylors.co.uk Betty's serves breakfasts, lunches and dinners as well as an eye-popping range of cakes, teas and coffees, all in a refined atmosphere of Edwardian living. ● *25, 26 Dec, 1 Jan.*	MC V	●		●	
HARROGATE: *Drum and Monkey* ££ 5 Montpellier Gardens, Harrogate, N Yorks. *01423 502650.* The Drum and Monkey is a town-centre pub which has now achieved a more elevated status as a smart seafood restaurant. It's fish or nothing here. ● *Sun.*	MC V	●			
HAWORTH: *Weaver's* ££ 15 West Lane, Haworth, W Yorks. *01535 643822.* www.weaversmallhotel.co.uk Hearty Yorkshire home cooking is given a modern accent at Weaver's, to the delight of literary pilgrims seeking sustenance after tramping Heathcliff's moors. ● *Sun D, Mon; 26 Dec–1 Jan.*	AE DC MC V	●	■	●	
HEADINGLEY: *Bryan's* £ 9 Weetwood Lane, Headingley, Leeds. *0113 2785679.* A traditional fish and chip restaurant of the best Yorkshire sort. Beef dripping and fresh fish are the secrets behind perfect results. Traditional, delicious desserts like treacle pudding round off the meal.	MC V	●	■	●	
HETTON: *Angel Inn* ££££ Off B6265 nr Skipton, N Yorks. *01756 730263.* www.angelhetton.co.uk This convivial beamed restaurant-with-rooms is more than a village pub, but the bar and brasserie food stay down to earth. ● *25 Dec.*	AE MC V	●	■	●	

ILKLEY: *Box Tree* £££
35–37 Church St, Ilkley, W Yorks. *01943 608484.* www.theboxtree.co.uk
Cuisine is definitely haute in this 18th-century farmhouse, recently revitalized by a new and creative chef. Desserts and cheeses do not disappoint. *Sun D, Mon.*
AE MC V

KNARESBOROUGH: *Carriages Wine Bar* £££
89 High St, Knaresborough, N Yorks. *01423 867041.* www.carriageswinebar.co.uk
The Australian owner and chef serves mainly Pacific Rim cuisine in summer and French and Mediterranean food in winter. A lovely garden overlooks the quiet, pretty railway station and the viaduct over the Nidd Gorge. *25, 26 Dec, 1 Jan.* *limited.*
MC V

LEEDS: *Brasserie Forty-four* ££££
44 The Calls, Leeds. *0113 2343232.* www.brasserie44.com
This waterfront warehouse complex combines bright, sophisticated cooking with stylish accommodation at No. 42. The lively atmosphere makes this a fun night out. Especially pleasant in summer. *Sat L, Sun.* *limited.* *Fri & Sat.*
AE DC MC V

LEEDS: *Haley's* £££
Shire Oak Rd, Headingley, Leeds. *0113 2784446.* www.haleys.co.uk
A peaceful Victorian hotel in the university district produces Anglo-French cuisine with exquisite presentation. Light, modern bedrooms. *L.* *limited.*
AE MC V

RIPLEY: *Boar's Head* £££
Ripley Castle Estate, Ripley, N Yorks. *01423 771888.* www.boarsheadripley.co.uk
This coaching inn provides luxury accommodation and fine dining as well as a bistro. Fine wines and a great selection of ales.
AE DC MC V

SHEFFIELD: *Greenhead House* ££££
84 Burncross Rd, Chapeltown, Sheffield. *0114 2469004.*
Four-course menus give a taste of France in the smart dining room of this stone house. Home-made soups a speciality. *Sun–Tue, Wed L, Sat L.*
AE MC V

WATH IN NIDDERDALE: *Sportsman's Arms* £££
Wath in Nidderdale, Pateley Bridge, nr Harrogate, N Yorks. *01423 711306.*
This restaurant-with-rooms also has a bar, but it is the well-cooked food that attracts customers. Local produce features on the menu. *25 Dec.*
MC V

WHITBY: *Magpie Café* £
14 Pier Rd, Whitby, N Yorks. *01947 602058.* www.magpiecafe.co.uk
This house by the harbour serves superlative fish and chips with good cheer. Don't miss the diverse and unusual puddings. *Jan–early-Feb.*
MC V

WINTERINGHAM: *Winteringham Fields* £££££
Winteringham, N Lincs. *01724 733096.* www.winteringhamfields.com
Superlative modern British cooking is served in this restaurant-with-rooms, in a setting of opulent Victoriana. *(See also p563.)* *Sun, Mon.*
AE MC V

YORK: *Little Betty's* ££
46 Stonegate, York. *01904 622865.* www.bettysbypost.com
A wide range of Yorkshire and Swiss specialities, home-made cakes and light lunches are served in this medieval building.
MC V

YORK: *Melton's* £££
7 Scarcroft Rd, York. *01904 634341.* www.meltonsrestaurant.co.uk
This small restaurant in a Victorian terrace is good value and welcoming, serving varied Anglo-French food. *Sun; Mon L.* *limited.*
MC V

NORTHUMBRIA

BELFORD: *The Blue Bell Hotel* ££
Market Place, Belford, Northum. *01668 213543.* www.bluebellhotel.com
The walled gardens of this old coaching inn shelter a profusion of organic produce, complementing local meat and fish on seasonally changing menus.
AE MC V

CONSETT: *Pavilion* ££
Iveston, Consett, Durham. *01207 503388.*
Bustling Cantonese restaurant serving generous helpings from an extensive Chinese menu. Friendly atmosphere and good value.
AE DC MC V

Price categories include a three-course meal for one, half a bottle of house wine, and all unavoidable extra charges such as cover, service, VAT:
£ under £15
££ £15-£25
£££ £25-£35
££££ £35-£50
£££££ over £50

CHILDREN WELCOME
Restaurants which offer smaller portions and high-chairs for children. Special menus sometimes available.

FIXED-PRICE MENU
A good value fixed-price meal, at lunch, dinner or both, usually of three courses.

VEGETARIAN
Vegetarian specialities served, sometimes for both starters and main courses.

CREDIT CARDS
Indicates which credit cards are accepted: *AE* American Express; *DC* Diners Club; *MC* Master Card/Access; *V* Visa.

Restaurant	Credit Cards	Children Welcome	Fixed-Price Menu	Vegetarian	Outdoor Tables
DARLINGTON: *Cottage Thai* £££ 94–96 Parkgate, Darlington, Durham. *01325 361717.* Handy for the station and theatre, this simple place offers Thai classics like *tom yum* soups, and red and green curries.	AE MC V	●		●	
DURHAM: *Bistro 21* £££ Aykley Heads House, Aykley Heads, Durham. *0191 3844354.* Eclectic modern cooking with menus that include enough variety to satisfy just about any taste. Relaxed atmosphere. *Sun, 25 Dec, bank hols.*	AE DC MC V	●	■	●	■
DURHAM: *Shaheens Indian Bistro* shaheens_durham@yahoo.com ££ Old Post Office, 48 North Bailey, Durham. *0191 386 0960.* This Indian bistro is located in the historic part of Durham, with a range of good traditional Indian dishes on its menu. *L.*	DC MC V	●	■	●	
EAST BOLDON: *Forsters* www.forsters-restaurant.co.uk £££ 2 St Bedes, Station Rd, East Boldon, Tyne and Wear. *0191 5190929.* A family enterprise run on classic British lines, welcoming and unpretentious but with plenty of sparkle. The food is never disappointing. *Sun, Mon, Tue–Sat L.*	AE DC MC V		■	●	
GATESHEAD: *Eslington Villa* £££ On A6127, Low Fell, Gateshead. *0191 4876017.* Reliable classic cooking figures in this attractive, graciously furnished hotel. Guests are greeted with bonhomie. *Sat L, Sun D.*	AE DC MC V	●	■	●	
HAYDON BRIDGE: *General Havelock Inn* ££ Radcliffe Rd, Haydon Bdge, Northum. *01434 684376.* www.northumberlandrestaurants.co.uk Good food at sensible prices, both for the evening four-course menu and the lunchtime specials. Gardens run down to the River Tyne. *Mon, Sun D.*	DC MC V	●	■	●	■
HEXHAM: *The Valley Connection 301* £££ 19 Market Pl, Hexham, Northum. *01434 601234.* www.thevalleyrestaurant.co.uk Luxurious interior and top-quality Indian cuisine using unusual herbs and spices. Good views of Hexham Abbey, floodlit at night. *Mon; L; 25 Dec.*	MC V			●	
NEWCASTLE UPON TYNE: *Café 21* www.cafetwentyone.co.uk £££ 19–21 Queen St, Princes Wharf, Quayside, Newcastle upon Tyne. *0191 2220755.* Much more than just a café, this is a warm, welcoming bistro with a cosy feel. The menu changes on a daily basis. Unruffled service. *Sun.*	AE DC MC V		■	●	
NEWCASTLE UPON TYNE: *Treacle Moon* ££££ 5–7 The Side, Newcastle upon Tyne. *0191 2325537.* www.treaclemoonrestaurant.com Fresh local meat, game and exotic fish feature in this brasserie. Modern-international cuisine gives flavour and colour. A laid-back atmosphere with jazz in the background. *L; Sun.* *limited.*	AE MC V	●		●	
NEWCASTLE UPON TYNE: *Fisherman's Lodge* £££££ Jesmond Dene, Jesmond, N'castle upon Tyne. *0191 2813281.* www.fishermanslodge.co.uk Situated in the centre of Jesmond Dene park, serving excellent food of the highest quality. Fish is a speciality. *Sun, 25, 26 Dec, bank hols.*	AE MC V	●	■	●	■
ROMALDKIRK: *Rose and Crown* £££ On B6277 nr Barnard Castle, Durham. *01833 650213.* www.rose-and-crown.co.uk This handsome coaching inn offers a splendid mix of pub with good-value bar meals and undaunting restaurant. Well worth making a detour for. Good selection of ales. *24, 26 Dec.*	MC V	●	■	●	■
SEATON BURN: *Horton Grange* *01661 860686.* ££££ Off A1 at Ponteland, Northum. www.hortongrangehotel.sageweb.co.uk This pleasant country house hotel offers local English produce. Decor and cooking are sophisticated, light and elegant. *L, Sun.*	AE MC V		■	●	

STOKESLEY: *Chapters* ££££
27 High St, Stokesley, N Yorks. *01642 711888.* www.chaptershotel.co.uk
A successful duo of informal bistro and more serious dining room. Cooking is French with global cross-currents. *Sun, 25 Dec, 1 Jan.*

NORTH WALES

ABERDYFI: *Penhelig Arms* £££
Aberdyfi, Gwynedd. *01654 767215.* www.penheligarms.com
Freshly caught fish features strongly on the menu at this hotel-restaurant right by the sea. *(See also p564.)* *25, 26 Dec.*

ABERSOCH: *Riverside Hotel* £££
On A499 nr Pwllheli, Gwynedd. *01758 712419.* www.riversideabersoch.co.uk
Morning coffee, light lunches and afternoon teas are served in the lounge and garden. Restaurant evening meals ooze with Mediterranean charm. *Nov–Easter.*

ABERSOCH: *Porth Tocyn* ££££
Abersoch, Gwynedd. *01758 713303.* www.porth-tocyn-hotel.co.uk
Few fail to be charmed by this coastal hotel. There are light alternatives to the menu on offer. *(See also p564.)* *Nov–wk before Easter.*

BEAUMARIS, ANGLESEY: *Ye Olde Bulls Head* ££££
Castle St, Beaumaris, Anglesey. *01248 810329.* www.bullsheadinn.co.uk
This handsome coaching inn has a restaurant and a brasserie, both of which feature its wonderful fish specialities. Book ahead. *brasserie only.*

CAPEL COCH: *Tre-Ysgawen Hall* £££
On B5111 nr Llangefni, Anglesey. *01248 750750.* www.treysgawen-hall.co.uk
A firm classical training tailors the modern French cooking at this massive country-house hotel. Service is courteous and attentive.

COLWYN BAY: *Café Niçoise* £££
124 Abergele Rd, Colwyn Bay, Conwy. *01492 531555.*
This French-style bistro comes complete with jazz and blues and Parisian scenes. Modern European cooking inspires the menus. *Mon; Tue L, Sun.*

CONWY: *Old Rectory* www.oldrectorycountryhouse.co.uk ££££
Llanrwst Rd, Llansanffraid Glan, Glan Conwy. *01492 580611.*
Great care is lavished on the three-course dinners here. Inside, there are many paintings and antiques. Rooms available. *30 Nov–1 Feb.*

DEGANWY: *Paysanne* ££
Station Rd, Deganwy, Conwy. *01492 582079.*
This bustling Gallic bistro serves daily specials and three-course provincial dinners. Special dietary needs catered for by arrangement. *L, Sun, Mon.*

DOLGELLAU: *Dylanwad Da* £££
2 Ffôs-y-Felin, Dolgellau, Gwynedd. *01341 422870.* dylanwadda@aol.com
Bistro serving Welsh lamb and port, plum and ginger pie. Serves coffee and cakes during day. *L; Nov–Apr: Sun–Wed; Feb–mid-Mar; May–Oct: Mon.* *limited.*

EYTON: *The Plassey Shippon Restaurant* ££
Eyton, nr Wrexham. *01978 780905.* www.theplassey.co.uk
Set amid a complex of Edwardian farm buildings and craft workshops, Plassey offers good bar snacks and blackboard specials. Slow-roasted Welsh lamb is a delicious speciality. *Sun & Mon D.*

GLANWYDDEN: *Queen's Head* ££
Off B5115 nr Llandudno Junction, Conwy. *01492 546570.*
Popular country pub offering Welsh lamb, local mussels and soups. Traditional puddings appear on a long list of sweets. *limited.*

HARLECH: *Castle Cottage* £££
Pen Llech, Harlech, Gwynedd. *01766 780479.* www.castlecottageharlech.co.uk
This is one of the oldest buildings in Harlech. Menus have Welsh and English elements. Fresh local produce gives the dishes an authentic flavour. Bedrooms available. *L, Jan.*

LLANARMON DYFFRYN CERIOG: *West Arms Hotel* ££££
Llanarmon Dyffryn Ceriog, nr Llangollen, Denbighs.
01691 600665. www.thewestarms.co.uk
Superb cooking and excellent presentation await at this restaurant in an idyllic 16th-century inn. Local fish dishes are good. Afternoon teas available. *limited.*

Stokesley: Chapters	AE DC MC V	●		●	■
Aberdyfi: Penhelig Arms	MC V	●	■	●	
Abersoch: Riverside Hotel	MC V	●		●	■
Abersoch: Porth Tocyn	MC V	●	■	●	■
Beaumaris, Anglesey: Ye Olde Bulls Head	AE MC V	●	■	●	
Capel Coch: Tre-Ysgawen Hall	AE MC V	●	■	●	
Colwyn Bay: Café Niçoise	AE MC V		■	●	
Conwy: Old Rectory	MC V		■		
Deganwy: Paysanne	MC V		■		
Dolgellau: Dylanwad Da		●		●	
Eyton: The Plassey Shippon Restaurant	DC MC V	●		●	■
Glanwydden: Queen's Head	MC V			●	■
Harlech: Castle Cottage	MC V	●	■	●	
Llanarmon Dyffryn Ceriog: West Arms Hotel	MC V	●	■	●	

Price categories include a three-course meal for one, half a bottle of house wine, and all unavoidable extra charges such as cover, service, VAT:
£ under £15
££ £15-£25
£££ £25-£35
££££ £35-£50
£££££ over £50

Children Welcome
Restaurants which offer smaller portions and high-chairs for children. Special menus sometimes available.

Fixed-Price Menu
A good value fixed-price meal, at lunch, dinner or both, usually of three courses.

Vegetarian
Vegetarian specialities served, sometimes for both starters and main courses.

Credit Cards
Indicates which credit cards are accepted: *AE* American Express; *DC* Diners Club; *MC* Master Card/Access; *V* Visa.

Restaurant	Credit Cards	Children Welcome	Fixed-Price Menu	Vegetarian	Outdoor Tables
Llanberis: *Y Bistro* £££ 43–45 High St, Llanberis, Gwynedd. *01286 871278.* www.ybistro.co.uk Hungry walkers flock to this restaurant at the foot of the Snowdon railway. A good range of hearty main courses. ● *L, Sun.*	MC V			●	
Llandrillo: *Tyddyn Llan* ££££ On B4401 nr Corwen, Denbigh. *01490 440264.* www.tyddynllan.co.uk This Georgian country house hotel produces distinctive, high-quality cooking using local ingredients such as Welsh Black beef and fish. *(See also p565.)* ● *Mon L.*	MC V	●	■	●	■
Llandudno: *Richard's* £££ 7 Church Walks, Llandudno, Conwy. *01492 877924.* This bistro in a Victorian town house is deservedly popular. The menu has plenty of options. ● *L, Sun–Mon, 25–26 Dec.*	AE DC MC V	●	■	●	
Llangollen: *Gales* ££ 18 Bridge St, Llangollen, Denbighs. *01978 860089.* www.galesofllangollen.co.uk A wine bar, restaurant and guesthouse. Cosmopolitan menu changes daily, and is served in a panelled bar with church pews. ● *Sun, 25 Dec–2 Jan.* *limited.*	AE DC MC V	●		●	
Northop: *Soughton Hall* £££ Off A5119, Northop, Flint. *01352 840811.* www.soughtonhall.co.uk Grand cooking matches this hotel's palatial setting: an 18th-century bishop's palace in parkland. Restaurant in bar and hotel restaurant.	MC V			●	■
Portmeirion: *Hotel Portmeirion* www.portmeirionvillage.com ££££ Off A487, signposted from Minffordd, Portmeirion. *01766 770000.* Elegant restaurant in a smart seaside hotel using local produce in a Modern British menu. The nearby Castell Deudraeth brasserie is an offshoot.	AE DC MC V	●		●	■
Pwllheli: *Plas Bodegroes* ££££ Nefyn Rd, Pwllheli, Gwynedd. *01758 612363.* www.bodegroes.co.uk This elegant Georgian country house takes full advantage of excellent local ingredients to produce accomplished British cooking for its three-course dinners. Fish especially good. ● *Tue–Sat L; Mon, Dec–Feb.*	MC V	●	■		

South and Mid-Wales

Restaurant	Credit Cards	Children Welcome	Fixed-Price Menu	Vegetarian	Outdoor Tables
Aberaeron: *Hive on the Quay* ££ Cadwgan Pl, Aberaeron, Cardiganshire. *01545 570445.* www.hiveonthequay.co.uk Honey ice-cream is the speciality at this summertime café, which serves wholesome teas and lunches (dinners too, in high summer) in a welcoming setting of stripped pine and lots of pot plants. ● *mid-Sep–Apr.*	MC V	●		●	■
Brechfa: *Ty Mawr* £££ Brechfa, Carmarthen. *01267 202332.* www.tymawrhotel.co.uk Small, luxury rural hotel with fine dining. Local produce is treated to international flourishes.	MC V	●	■	●	
Broad Haven: *Druidstone Hotel* www.druidstone.co.uk £££ Druidston Haven, Broad Haven, Pembroke. *01437 781221.* This informal family hotel combines local produce with international spices. Set in vast grounds with clifftop views. ● *Sun D (phone for winter opening hours).*	AE MC V	●		●	■
Cardiff: *La Brasserie/Champers/Le Monde* ££ 60–62 St Mary St, Cardiff. *029 20234134.* www.le-monde.co.uk Bustling complex of French brasserie (fish and grills), tapas bar and seafood restaurant with friendly atmosphere and good wines.	AE DC MC V	●	■	●	
Cardiff: *Woods Brasserie* £££ Pilotage Building, Stuart St, Cardiff. *029 20492400.* Minimalist but comfortable, serving Modern British food, with an emphasis on fish and Welsh chicken and lamb. ● *Sun D, 25, 26, 31 Dec, 1 Jan.*	AE DC MC V	●		●	■

CLYTHA: *Clytha Arms* £££
Nr Abergavenny, Monmouth. *01873 840206.* www.clytha-arms.com
Country pub where France and Wales meet in fare such as laverbread *(see p36)* or oysters with leeks. *Sun D, Mon.*
AE DC MC V

COWBRIDGE: *Off the Beeton Track* ££
1 Town Hall Sq, Cowbridge, V of Glam. *01446 773599.*
Home-baked cakes, simple lunches and afternoon teas. *Sun & Mon.*
DC MC V

CRICKHOWELL: *Nantyffin Cider Mill Inn* £££
Brecon Rd, Crickhowell, Powys. *01873 810775.* www.cidermill.co.uk
This unpretentious, 16th-century stone-built inn proffers Modern British and European dishes, plus local game and seafood. *Mon or Tue (phone first).*
AE MC V

CRICKHOWELL: *The Bear* £££
High St, Crickhowell, Powys. *01873 810408.* www.bearhotel.co.uk
Traditional British food using local produce, especially fish and game. Bar meals or dining room. Rooms available. *25 Dec.* *limited.*
AE MC V

FISHGUARD: *Three Main Street* ££££
3 Main St, Fishguard, Pembroke. *01348 874275.*
In a Georgian building overlooking the harbour the Modern British menu may include crab soufflé and roast breast of guinea fowl. *Sun–Mon, Feb, 2 weeks end Nov.*

GWAUN VALLEY, NR FISHGUARD: *Tregynon Country Farmhouse* £££
Off B4313, Gwaun Valley, Newport. *01239 820531.* www.online-holidays.net/tregynon
The food here is delicious and carefully considered (home-smoked bacon and wholefoods). Best to book. *L, Sun, Thu.*
MC V

LAMPHEY: *Dial Inn* £££
The Ridgeway, Lamphey, Pembroke. *01646 672426.*
Hearty fare such as Lamphey lamb and home-made beef and Guinness pie keeps the customers happy. Fish and vegetarian choices too. *25 Dec.*
MC V

LLANDEWI SKIRRID: *Walnut Tree Inn* £££
On B4521 nr Abergavenny, Monmouth. *01873 852797.* www.thewalnuttree.com
This popular, informal bistro offers a vast selection of Italian cuisine, unpretentiously served but carefully prepared. *Sun D & Mon (except bank hols).*
MC V

LLYSWEN: *Griffin Inn* £££
On A470, Llyswen, Powys. *01874 754241.* www.griffin-inn.co.uk
Shooting and fishing are the attractions in the Wye Valley, home of this 15th-century inn; the fare reflects this. Rooms available. *Sun D.*
AE DC MC V

MUMBLES: *Claude's* ££
93 Newton Rd, Mumbles. *01792 366006.* FAX *01792 368931.* www.claudes.org.uk
Modern European cuisine is the style of fare here, using fresh local produce. *Mon & Sun D, 26 Dec–1 Jan.*
AE MC V

NANTGAREDIG: *Four Seasons, Cwmtwrch Farm* £££
On B4310, Carmarthen. *01267 290238.*
Local produce receives honest farmhouse treatment in this family-run restaurant. Welsh lamb and smoked salmon feature prominently. *Sun, Mon.*
MC V

NEWPORT: *Cnapan* £££
East St, Newport, Pembroke. *01239 820575.* www.online-holidays.net/cnapan
This Georgian restaurant-with-rooms includes Welsh specialities in its lunch and dinner menus. *Tue, Jan–Feb.*
MC V

ST DAVID'S: *Morgan's Brasserie* £££
20 Nun St, St David's, Pembroke. *01437 720508.* www.morgan-in-stdavids.co.uk
Fish is the main attraction at this family-run brasserie. Local beef and lamb also feature. *Jan & Feb: daily; Mar: Sun–Tue; Nov & Dec: Mon–Thu.*
AE MC V

SWANSEA: *La Braseria* £££
28 Wind St, Swansea. *01792 469683.* www.labraseria.com
This Spanish restaurant is especially popular at lunchtime for good-value set lunches garnished with chips, salads and garlic bread. *Sun.*
AE DC MC V

TENBY: *The Plantagenet* £££
Plantagenet Hse, Quay Hill, Tenby. *01834 842350.*
This partly medieval restaurant next to the Tudor Merchant's House is also open for breakfast and snacks. It specializes in seafood, serves organic meat and is very child-friendly. *L Mon–Fri, D Sat & Sun; Jan–mid-Feb.* *limited.*
AE MC V

For key to symbols see back flap

Price categories include a three-course meal for one, half a bottle of house wine, and all unavoidable extra charges such as cover, service, VAT:
£ under £15
££ £15-£25
£££ £25-£35
££££ £35-£50
£££££ over £50

CHILDREN WELCOME
Restaurants which offer smaller portions and high-chairs for children. Special menus sometimes available.

FIXED-PRICE MENU
A good value fixed-price meal, at lunch, dinner or both, usually of three courses.

VEGETARIAN
Vegetarian specialities served, sometimes for both starters and main courses.

CREDIT CARDS
Indicates which credit cards are accepted: *AE* American Express; *DC* Diners Club; *MC* Master Card/Access; *V* Visa.

Restaurant	Credit Cards	Children Welcome	Fixed-Price Menu	Vegetarian	Outdoor Tables
WELSH HOOK: *Stone Hall* £££ Off A40 nr Wolf's Castle, Pembroke. *01348 840212.* www.stonehall-mansion.co.uk French cooking with unusual touches reigns in this hotel-restaurant in wooded grounds. *L, 25 & 26 Dec.*	*AE DC MC V*	●	■	●	
WHITEBROOK: *Crown at Whitebrook* ££££ Whitebrook, Monmouth. *01600 860254.* crown@eightywhitebrook.co.uk This 17th-century outpost of modern French and British cuisine in the Wye Valley is now run as a restaurant-with-rooms. *Sun D, Mon L, Christmas & New Year.*	*AE DC MC V*		■	●	

THE LOWLANDS

Restaurant	Credit Cards	Children Welcome	Fixed-Price Menu	Vegetarian	Outdoor Tables
ANSTRUTHER: *Cellar* ££££ 24 East Green, Anstruther, Fife. *01333 310378.* One of this fishing port's oldest buildings. Only top-quality produce is used; fresh seafood dominates the menu. *Sun & Mon in Nov–Mar; 24–28 Dec.*	*AE MC V*		■	●	
AYR: *Fouters Bistro* ££ 2A Academy St, Ayr, S Ayrshire. *01292 261391.* www.fouters.co.uk Lively bistro in a vaulted basement. Ingredients are Scottish, cooking mostly provincial-French, with vegetarian dishes. *Sun, Mon.*	*AE DC MC V*	●	■	●	
CUPAR: *Ostlers Close* £££ Bonnygate, Cupar, Fife. *01334 655574.* www.ostlersclose.co.uk Fish plays a large part in the menus at this tiny place, but plenty of meat or game dishes get expert French treatment too. Wild mushrooms are one of their delicious specialities. *Sun, Mon, Tue–Thu L.* *limited*	*AE MC V*	●		●	
DIRLETON: *Open Arms Hotel* £££ Dirleton, E Lothian. *01620 850241.* www.openarmshotel.com On the edge of the village green overlooking the 13th-century castle the well-established hotel-restaurant enjoys a deserved reputation for good food. Choose between formal restaurant or the brasserie.	*MC V*	●	■	●	■
EDINBURGH: *Henderson's* ££ 94 Hanover St, Edinburgh. *0131 2252131.* www.hendersonsofedinburgh.co.uk This institution has a wide range of vegetarian specialities. Cakes and unusual cheeses accompany filling salads and hot dishes.	*AE MC V*	●	■	●	
EDINBURGH: *The Lost Sock Diner* ££ 11 East London St, Edinburgh. *0131 5576097.* This eatery is one of the best in the area. Interesting menu, including New York tortilla "wraps". Breakfast served until 4pm.		●	■	●	
EDINBURGH: *Susie's Diner* £ 53 West Nicolson St, Edinburgh. *0131 6678729.* www.ednet.co.uk/susies A friendly wholefood vegetarian café centrally located near Edinburgh University. Good-quality ingredients, impeccably flavoured. *limited.*		●		●	■
EDINBURGH: *Daniel's* ££ 88 Commercial St, Leith, Edinburgh. *0131 5535933.* www.edinburghrestaurant.co.uk One of the best of the new conservatory restaurants, situated opposite the Scottish Office. Serves hearty Alsace cuisine.	*AE MC V*	●	■	●	
EDINBURGH: *Kalpna* ££ 2–3 St Patrick Sq, Edinburgh. *0131 6679890.* Indian vegetarian cookery in a calming environment near the university. Flavours are mild and service variable. *Sun L.*	*MC V*	●	■	●	
EDINBURGH: *Atrium & Blue Bar Café* £££ 10 Cambridge St, Edinburgh. *0131 2288882.* www.atriumrestaurant.co.uk A stylish interior by the Traverse Theatre complements the simple but exciting cooking here. Modern British with a Mediterranean influence. *Sat L, Sun.*	*AE MC V*	●		●	

EDINBURGH: *Martin's* martinirons@fsbdial.co.uk £££
70 Rose St (between Frederick St and Castle St), North Lane, Edinburgh. *0131 2253106.*
This central restaurant offers a range of imaginative, contemporary Scottish cooking. *Sat L, Sun, Mon; Christmas & New Year, end May, beg. Oct.*
AE DC MC V

EDINBURGH: *Vintners Rooms* £££
87 Giles St, Leith, Edinburgh. *0131 5546767.* www.thevintnersrooms.demon.co.uk
This unusual candlelit restaurant is housed in a wine warehouse. Both cooking and service are admirably unpretentious. Light lunches are served in the wine bar. *Sun, last week Dec, first week Jan.*
AE MC V

EDINBURGH: *Waterfront Wine Bar* £££
1C Dock Place, Leith, Edinburgh. *0131 5547427.* www.sjf.co.uk
Best of the Leith waterfront bar-restaurants with a cosy bar, excellent wine list, and conservatory restaurant serving modish fare. *25 & 26 Dec.*
MC V

GLASGOW: *The Buttery* ££££
652 Argyle St, Glasgow. *0141 2218188.*
Attractive turn-of-the-century pub converted into an elegant dining room. *Sat L, Sun, 25 Dec, 1 Jan.*
AE DC MC V

GLASGOW: *Camerons, Glasgow Hilton* ££££
1 William St, Glasgow. *0141 2045511.* www.hilton.com
This is theme-park Scotland, but both food and service are beyond reproach at this business hotel and restaurant. *Sat L, Sun.*
AE DC MC V

GLASGOW: *One Devonshire Gardens* ££££
1 Devonshire Gardens, Glasgow. *0141 3392001.* www.onedevonshiregardens.com
French and British inspiration at this sumptuous hotel-restaurant. The atmosphere is pleasantly relaxed. *(See also p569.)* *L.*
AE DC MC V

GLASGOW: *Ubiquitous Chip* ££££
12 Ashton Lane, Glasgow. *0141 3345007.* www.ubiquitouschip.co.uk
The lighthearted individuality suggested by the name reveals itself most in the upstairs bistro. The food throughout is good, with well-rehearsed and hugely varied treatments of Scottish fare.
AE DC MC V

KIPPFORD: *The Anchor Hotel* ££
Kippford, Dalbeattie, Kirkcudbrightshire. *01556 620205*
Situated on the waterfront, with views of the boating activity, this friendly hotel and pub offers good bar food. *25 Dec.* *limited.*
MC V

LARGS: *Nardini's* £
The Esplanade, Largs, N Ayrshire. *01475 674555.* www.nardini.co.uk
A splendid Art Deco interior sets the scene of this seafront lounge café. Breakfasts, cakes, Italian and British dishes are served all day. This is the perfect place in which to sit back, read the paper and relax.
AE DC MC V

LINLITHGOW: *Champany Inn* ££££
Champany, nr Linlithgow, W Lothian. *01506 834532.* www.champany.com
Wines spring to the fore here, but the food is good too, whether a perfect Angus steak, or more ornate dishes with sauces. *Sat L, Sun.*
AE DC MC V

MOFFAT: *Well View* £££
Ballplay Rd, Moffat, Dumfries & Galloway. *01683 220184.* www.wellview.co.uk
Modern French cooking with some Scottish elements is served in this family-run hotel. Peaceful atmosphere. No children under five at night. *Sat L.*
AE MC V

PORTPATRICK: *Knockinaam Lodge* *01776 810471.* ££££
Off A77 nr Portpatrick, Dumfries & Galloway www.prideofbritainhotels.com
An idyllic location overlooking the sea. Modern British cooking with international touches. *limited.*
AE DC MC V

ST ANDREWS: *Brambles* ££
5 College St, St Andrews, Fife. *01334 475380.*
Popular self-service café specializing in wholefood and vegetarian recipes, though meat and fish also appear. Cakes are freshly baked on the premises.
MC V

ST ANDREWS: *The Peat Inn* ££££
On B940 nr St Andrews, Fife. *01334 840206.* www.thepeatinn.co.uk
Highly accomplished modern cooking with regional produce and seasonal vegetables has established this fine hotel-restaurant as one of the best in Britain. Lunch is a bargain. *Sun, Mon.*
AE MC V

For key to symbols see back flap

Price categories include a three-course meal for one, half a bottle of house wine, and all unavoidable extra charges such as cover, service, VAT:
£ under £15
££ £15-£25
£££ £25-£35
££££ £35-£50
£££££ over £50

Children Welcome
Restaurants which offer smaller portions and high-chairs for children. Special menus sometimes available.

Fixed-Price Menu
A good value fixed-price meal, at lunch, dinner or both, usually of three courses.

Vegetarian
Vegetarian specialities served, sometimes for both starters and main courses.

Credit Cards
Indicates which credit cards are accepted: *AE* American Express; *DC* Diners Club; *MC* Master Card/Access; *V* Visa.

	Credit Cards	Children Welcome	Fixed-Price Menu	Vegetarian	Outdoor Tables
Swinton: *Wheatsheaf* £££ Main St, Swinton, Borders. ☎ *01890 860257.* W www.wheatsheaf-swinton.co.uk This country inn offers imaginative cooking served in a traditional dining room or conservatory. Bedrooms available. ● *Mon.* ♿ 🚭	MC V	●		●	■
Troon: *Highgrove House* £££ Old Loans Rd, Troon, S Ayrshire. ☎ *01292 312511.* W www.costley-hotels.co.uk Watery prospects over the Firth of Clyde accompany informal meals from a wide-ranging menu in this retired sea-captain's house. Bedrooms available.	AE MC V	●	■	●	■
The Highlands and Islands					
Aberdeen: *The Silver Darling* £££ Pocra Quay, Footdee, North Pier, Aberdeen. ☎ *01224 576229.* Located on the noth side of Aberdeen Harbour, this restaurant offers superb seafood, which varies with the daily catch. ● *Sat L, Sun, 24 Dec–mid-Jan.* 🍷	AE DC MC V	●			
Alexandria: *Georgian Room, Cameron House* £££££ Off A82, Loch Lomond, Alexandria, W Dunbar. ☎ *01389 755565.* W www.cameronhouse.co.uk This large, comfortable hotel caters for the well-heeled leisure market of fishing and golf with three fine restaurants. ● *Mon.* ♿ 🚭	AE DC MC V		■	●	
Alyth: *Drumnacree House* ££ St Ninian's Rd, Alyth, Perthshire. ☎ *01828 632194.* W www.drumnacreehouse.co.uk The smokehouse and garden provide produce for a mixed bag of cooking styles used with great enthusiasm and flair. An eclectic range of original ideas to tempt any palate. ● *Mon.* ♿ 🚭 🍷	MC V	●		●	
Auchmithie: *But 'n' Ben* ££ Off A92 nr Arbroath, Angus. ☎ *01241 877223.* Twin cottages in a working fishing village. The day's catch figures at lunch and dinner, and there are splendid high teas. ● *Tue.* ♿ 🚭	MC V	●		●	
Ballater: *Green Inn* £££ 9 Victoria Rd, Ballater, Aberdeenshire. ☎ *013397 55701.* W www.green-inn.com Scottish produce is given the full works at this refurbished restaurant-with-rooms. Service is friendly and informed. ● *L, 25–27 Dec.* ♿ 🚭	AE MC V	●		●	
Ballater: *Darroch Learg* ££££ Braemar Rd, Ballater, Aberdeenshire. ☎ *013397 55443.* W www.darroch-learg.co.uk A Victorian shooting lodge with a fine restaurant. The food is Modern British using a wide range of ingredients. ● *23–27 Dec, 10 Jan–1 Feb.* ♿ 🚭 🍷	AE DC MC V	●	■	●	
Cairndow: *Loch Fyne Oyster Bar* W www.loch-fyne.com ££ Clachan Farm, Ardkinglas, Cairndow, Argyll & Bute. ☎ *01499 600236.* This splendid place offers a warm welcome with platters of shellfish, overlooking the lochside oyster beds. ♿ 🚭	DC MC V	●		●	
Colbost by Dunvegan: *The Three Chimneys* ££££ Colbost, nr Dunvegan, Isle of Skye. ☎ *01470 511258.* W www.threechimneys.co.uk Situated a few miles from Dunvegan, on the western shore of Loch Dunvegan. Once a stone-built crofter's cottage, this award-winning restaurant offers seafood and game lovingly prepared with fresh local ingredients. The atmosphere is peaceful and relaxed. Accommodation is also available. ● *Jan.* ♿ 🚭 *throughout.* 🍷	AE MC V	●		●	
Drymen: *The Pottery* £ The Square, Drymen, Stirlingshire. ☎ *01360 660458.* Friendly restaurant and coffee shop, serving good home-cooked food all day and delicious afternoon teas. Delightful terrace. ● *1 Jan, 25 Dec.* ♿ 🚭 *throughout.*	AE DC MC V	●		●	■

DUNKELD: *Kinnaird* www.kinnairdestate.com ££££££
Kinnaird Estate, off B898 nr Dunkeld, Perthshire. 01796 482440.
This estate hotel produces ornate food of great originality. Lunch is more affordable. *Jan–Feb: Mon, Tues, Wed.*
AE MC V

FORT WILLIAM: *Crannog Seafood Restaurant* ££
Town Pier, Fort William, Highland. 01397 705589. www.crannog.net
Nothing detracts from the simple pleasure of eating exquisitely fresh seafood overlooking a panoramic loch view. Helpings are generous. The atmosphere is warm and welcoming, and the service efficient.
MC V

INVERNESS: *Culloden House* ££££
Off A96 at Culloden, Highland. 01463 790461. www.cullodenhouse.co.uk
The food is Scottish country-house style, with sauces, jellies, sorbets and mousses interspersing hearty meat, game and fish dishes. Rooms available.
AE DC MC V

KILBERRY: *Kilberry Inn* ££
Kilberry by Tarbert, Argyll & Bute. 01880 770223. www.kilberryinn.com
This low, white croft (former post office, now pub) in a quiet coastal village serves traditional British home cooking at its best, with a constantly changing blackboard menu. Rooms available. *Sun D, Mon (except public hols).* *throughout.*
MC V

KILLIECRANKIE: *The Killiecrankie Hotel* £££
Off A9 nr Pitlochry, Perthshire. 01796 473220. www.killiecrankiehotel.co.uk
Excellent bar meals supplement more ambitious dinnertime fare in this attractive hotel. It's hearty stuff, with a few Oriental dishes. *limited.*
MC V

KINCLAVEN: *Ballathie House* ££££
Off B9099 nr Stanley, Perthshire. 01250 883268. www.ballathiehousehotel.com
A warm, hearty hotel in a huge estate on the Tay. The restaurant serves appropriate fare like venison and, of course, salmon.
AE DC MC V

KINCRAIG: *The Boathouse Restaurant* £
Loch Insh, Kincraig, Invernesshire, Highland. 01540 651272. www.lochinsh.com
Food is served all day at this log-cabin restaurant overlooking the loch – fresh fish, haggis or steak. A bar and a gift shop can also be found here.
MC V

KYLE OF LOCHALSH: *Seagreen Restaurant and Book Shop* ££
Plockton Rd, Kyle of Lochalsh, Highland. 01599 534388. www.seagreenkyle.f9.co.net
All-day waitress service offering snacks or lunch. A pleasant vegetarian and fish menu that even the most hardened meat-eater will enjoy.
Jan–beg. Apr; Sat & Sun Nov–Dec.
MC V

KYLESKU: *Kylesku Hotel* £££
On A894 by Lairg, Highland. 01971 502231. kylesku@lycos.co.uk
Lochs and mountains provide a splendid backdrop to this hotel. The menu is extensive, with fresh fish always a good option.
MC V

OBAN: *Knipoch Hotel* ££££
On A816 nr Oban, Argyll & Bute. 01852 316251. www.knipochhotel.co.uk
Dinners range from three to five courses. Huge arrays of vegetables and flamboyant puddings are features.
AE DC MC V

PERTH: *Let's Eat* £££
77 Kinnoull St, Perth. 01738 643377. www.letseatperth.co.uk
Local ingredients – fish, game, beef and lamb – are the mainstay of the modern cooking here. *Sun, Mon, 25–26 Dec, 1–2 Jan, 2 weeks mid-Jan, 2 weeks mid-Jul.*
AE MC V

PORT APPIN: *The Airds Hotel* ££££
Port Appin, Appin, Argyll & Bute. 01631 730236. www.airds-hotel.com
This hotel restaurant has a fine waterfront location and cheerful interior to complement the splendidly flavoured dinners. *(See also p573.)*
MC V

ST MARGARET'S HOPE: *The Creel Restaurant* £££
Front Rd, St Margaret's Hope, S. Ronaldsay, Orkney. 01856 831311. www.thecreel.co.uk
Excellent, honest cooking. Seafood predominates, but you might try the seaweed-fed lamb. *Jan–Feb, 2 weeks mid-Oct.*
MC V

ULLAPOOL: *Ceilidh Place* £££
14 West Argyle St, Ullapool, Highland. 01854 612103. info@theceilidhplace.com
An interesting building with great atmosphere, incorporating a restaurant, bars and bookshop, as well as rooms above. Imaginative menus at various prices. *throughout.*
AE DC MC V

British Pubs

No tour of Britain could be complete without some exploration of its public houses *(see pp34–5)*. These are a great social institution, descendants of centuries of hostelries, ale-houses and stagecoach halts. Some have colourful histories or fascinating contents, and still occupy a central role in the community, staging quiz games and folk dancing. Many of those listed below are lovely buildings, or have attractive settings. Most serve a variety of beers, spirits and wine by the glass.

A "free house" is independent and will stock several leading regional beers, but most pubs are "tied" – this means that they are owned by a brewery and only stock that brewery's selection.

Many pubs offer additional attractions such as live music and beer gardens with picnic tables. Traditional pub food is often served at lunchtime, and increasingly food is served in the evenings too. Traditional pub games take many forms, including cribbage, shove ha'penny, skittles, dominoes and darts.

London

Bloomsbury: *Lamb*
94 Lamb's Conduit St, WC1.
Unspoilt Victorian pub with cut-glass "snob screens" and theatrical photographs. Small courtyard at the rear.

City: *Black Friar*
174 Queen Victoria St, EC4.
Eccentric inside and out, with intriguing Art Nouveau decor. Attentive service.

City: *Olde Cheshire Cheese*
Wine Office Court, Fleet St EC4.
Authentic 17th-century inn haunted by the shades of Johnson, Pope and Dickens. Restored to its plain, bareboarded glory with open fires in winter.

Hammersmith: *Dove*
19 Upper Mall, W6.
One of the most attractive of West London's riverside pubs, where you can watch rowing crews from the terrace. Very crowded in fine weather.

Hampstead: *Spaniards Inn*
Spaniards Lane, NW3.
Famous Hampstead landmark dating from the 18th century, once part of a tollgate. Attractive garden.

Kensington: *Windsor Castle*
114 Campden Hill Rd, W8.
A civilized Georgian inn with traditional oak furnishings and open fires. The walled garden attracts well-heeled, youngish crowds in summer. Hearty English food.

Southwark: *George Inn*
77 Borough High St, SE1.
Quaint coaching inn with unique galleried courtyard, now owned by the National Trust. Rooms ramble upstairs and downstairs, and the overspill sits outside. Morris men and Globe Players may be seen at times *(see p122)*.

The Downs and Channel Coast

Alciston: *Rose Cottage*
Off A27 nr Lewes, Sussex.
Charming, creeper-covered cottage inn decorated with rustic bygones. Limited room inside.

Alfriston: *Star*
Alfriston, Sussex.
This quaint old inn, once a pilgrim hostel, is now a smart hotel but is full of character.

Chale: *Wight Mouse Inn*
On B3399, Chale, Isle of Wight.
Cheerful, family-oriented inn with large gardens. Bric-a-brac dangles from the ceilings.

Fletching: *Griffin*
Off A272, Fletching, Sussex.
Sophisticated but very laid-back country inn with a 1930s air, which serves imaginative food. Attractive accommodation.

Rye: *Mermaid*
Mermaid St, Rye, Sussex.
Famous historic building in a steep cobbled street, full of panelling, frescoes and antiques.

Smarden: *Bell*
Off A274, Smarden, Kent.
An ancient brick-and-beam pub among orchards. Traditional games, inglenook fireplaces and flagstone floors.

Walliswood: *Scarlett Arms*
Off A29 nr Ewhurst, Surrey.
Workers' cottages converted into a relaxing pub with beams, log fires and trestle tables.

Winchester: *Wykeham Arms*
75 Kingsgate St, Winchester, Hants.
Classy, idiosyncratic town centre pub/hotel with fascinating decor. Excellent food, wine and accommodation *(see p547)*.

East Anglia

Cambridge: *Boathouse*
14 Chesterton Rd, Cambridge.
One of the best of Cambridge's waterside pubs, overlooking Jesus Green. For entertainment in summer, sit and watch barges and punts glide past; oars hang in the bars.

Holywell: *Olde Ferry Boat*
Off A1123 at Needingworth, Cambs.
The Great Ouse reaches almost to the door of this picturesque thatched pub. Inside it is comfortably modernized, with cosy bedrooms. Wide range of food, and a resident ghost called Juliette.

Littlebury: *Queens Head Inn*
High St, Littlebury, Essex.
This Tudor village pub has kept plenty of its original character. It offers outstanding real ales and food in a welcoming atmosphere.

Snape: *Golden Key*
Priory Lane, Snape, Suffolk.
Pretty gardens, stylish interior and appetizing food are a draw at this inn. Very popular during the Aldeburgh Festival *(see p63)*.

Snettisham: *Rose & Crown*
Off A149 nr Heacham, Norfolk.
Former coaching inn with three attractive bars and plenty of room for children to play in the garden.

Southwold: *Crown*
High Street, Southwold, Suffolk.
Popular seaside haunt with nautical decor and oak panelling. Excellent food and Adnam beers.

STIFFKEY: *Red Lion*
On A149, Norfolk.
Traditional English pub with open fires in winter and the garden overlooking the Stiffkey River on the North Norfolk Coastal Path.

TILLINGHAM: *Cap & Feathers*
South St, Tillingham, Essex.
Smoked meat, homemade pies and sausages, and fish are on offer at this 16th-century pub near the salt marshes.

THAMES VALLEY

BARLEY: *Fox & Hounds*
High St, Barley, Herts.
Look for the tall chimney and the hunting scene sign. Both food and real ales are excellent. Disabled visitors welcome.

BROOM: *Cock*
23 High St, Broom, Bedfordshire.
Charming 17th-century inn called "the pub with no bar" (place your orders at the hatch, and the beer comes straight from the cellar casks).

BURFORD: *Lamb*
Sheep St, Burford, Oxon.
This picture-postcard Cotswolds inn has roses round the door and mullioned windows. Food is good, as is the service and atmosphere.

FAWLEY: *Walnut Tree*
Off B4155 nr Henley, Buckinghamshire.
A splendid base for enjoying the Chilterns. You can even hitch your horse up in the car park.

GREAT TEW: *Falkland Arms*
Off B4022 nr Chipping Norton, Oxon.
This partly thatched and creeper-covered inn is in an idyllic corner of rural England. It is delightfully straightforward and simply decorated, with mugs and jugs and gleaming horsebrasses.

OXFORD: *Turf Tavern*
Bath Pl, St Helen's Passage, Oxford.
Tiny pub in the heart of the old collegiate quarter gives you an idea of cloistered quadrangles. Sit outside in fine weather.

WATTON-AT-STONE: *George & Dragon*
High St, Watton-at-Stone, Herts.
Attractive pink building dating back to 1603. Smart but also welcoming; plenty of locals use it, and there are newspapers to read.

WEST ILSLEY: *Harrow*
Off A34 nr Newbury, Berkshire.
A stylish, white, tiled inn by the village pond, catering for walkers and racing folk. Up-market food.

WESSEX

ABBOTSBURY: *Ilchester Arms*
Market St, Abbotsbury, Dorset.
The pub is a main feature of this honey-coloured village near Chesil Beach. Warm, rambling rooms are smartly done up with prints. The restaurant has a conservatory extension.

BATHFORD: *Crown*
2 Bathford Hill, Bathford, Avon.
This hilly village has enjoyed its namesake hostelry since its 18th-century heyday. Now it is stylish inside, with ambitious food.

CROSCOMBE: *Bull Terrier*
On A371 nr Wells, Somerset.
One of Somerset's oldest pubs (originally a priory), this inn is much loved for good food, and has welcoming service. Try the Bull Terrier best bitter, and the walk to the Bishop's Palace at Wells.

FORD: *White Hart*
On A420 nr Chippenham, Wiltshire.
A delightful trout-stream setting adds a lot to this lovely 16th-century pub-hotel. It is very popular in summer. Good walks nearby.

NORTON ST PHILIP: *George*
On A366, Somerset.
This famous old pub sheltered the Duke of Monmouth before the Battle of Sedgemoor. It is a splendid half-timbered building with good food and an ancient galleried courtyard.

SALISBURY: *Haunch of Venison*
1 Minster St, Salisbury, Wiltshire.
Once the church house for St Thomas's, this ancient pub dates back 650 years. The severed, mummified hand of an 18th-century card-player is on display among more cheerful clutter in its genuinely antique interior.

STANTON WICK: *Carpenters Arms*
Off A368, Avon.
A row of pretty converted miners' cottages contain this welcoming place with log fires. Excellent food is a major attraction.

DEVON AND CORNWALL

BROADHEMBURY: *Drewe Arms*
Off A373, Devon.
Fresh fish is one reason to come to this thatched village pub, but the West Country ales, garden and atmosphere add to its appeal.

DARTMOUTH: *Cherub*
13 High St, Dartmouth, Devon.
Dartmouth's oldest building, dating from 1380 and once a wool-merchant's house. Local fish prominent on the menu.

KNOWSTONE: *Masons Arms*
Off A361 nr South Molton, Devon.
One of Devon's favourite inns, with plenty of local life and welcoming hosts. The rustic decor includes farm tools. The big fireplace has a bread oven. Good bar food.

LYDFORD: *Castle Inn*
Off A386, Devon.
Pretty, pink-washed Tudor inn by a ruined castle and scenic river gorge. Staff are friendly, food is imaginative, and there's lots of historic interest. Good value rooms.

MYLOR BRIDGE: *Pandora Inn*
Off A39 nr Penryn, Cornwall.
Medieval thatched pub by the waterside. Popular with boating folk and crowded in summer. Bags of atmosphere.

PORT ISAAC: *Port Gaverne Hotel*
Off B3314 nr Pendoggett, Cornwall.
Gorgeous seafront setting. A 17th-century building with panelling and maritime decor. Local seafood and excellent wine list. Good rooms available.

TREGADILLETT: *Eliot Arms*
Off A30 nr Launceston, Cornwall.
Cluttered with horsebrasses, old postcards, prints, books and china, and a curious collection of clocks.

THE HEART OF ENGLAND

ALDERMINSTER: *Bell*
On A34 nr Stratford-upon-Avon, Warwickshire.
Coaching inn conveniently near Stratford. A civilized place to stop for a meal with well-kept beers. Good wines too.

For key to symbols see back flap

BICKLEY MOSS: *Cholmondeley Arms*
On A49, Cholmondeley, Cheshire.
Food draws the crowds to this Victorian school room pub near the castle grounds. Lots of period interest inside.

BLOCKLEY: *Crown*
High St, Blockley, Gloucestershire.
Smart Elizabethan pub in a gorgeous Cotswolds village. The food and courtyard gardens are a great draw.

BRETFORTON: *Fleece*
The Cross, Bretforton, Hereford & Worcester.
Astonishing medieval house owned by the National Trust, first licensed in 1848. A living museum of rural antiquities such as dough-proving tables and cheese moulds. Food is simple, but beers are excellent. Lots of community gatherings for Morris dancing.

CAULDON: *Yew Tree*
Off A523 Waterhouses, Stoke-on-Trent, Staffs.
An extraordinary collection of musical machines is on display (working polyphones, pianolas, symphonions), along with many other fascinating bygones. The interior is homely, with traditional pub games. Simple snacks and beers.

TUTBURY: *Dog & Partridge*
On A50 nr Burton-on-Trent, Staffs.
Imposing Tudor coaching inn, agreeably modernized into bars and family-oriented eating areas. Pleasant service.

WENLOCK EDGE: *Wenlock Edge Inn*
Hilltop, Much Wenlock, Shropshire.
There's a wood-burning stove and friendly bar owner; Monday night is story night. Good walks nearby and rooms available.

EAST MIDLANDS

BIRCHOVER: *Druid Inn*
Main St, Birchover, Derbyshire.
Creeper-covered village pub with a large menu of good fresh food. Excellent walking centre with Row Tor Rocks (allegedly a place of Druid rituals) and Stanton Moor nearby.

FOTHERINGHAY: *Falcon*
Main St, Fotheringhay, Northants.
A splendid pub, now modernized to serve a range of excellent food. The public bar keeps its original character and local clientele.

GLOOSTON: *Old Barn Inn*
Andrews Lane, Glooston, Leicestershire.
Sixteenth-century inn with tastefully renovated interior and several cosy rooms. A la carte menu and hand-pumped ales. Rooms available.

MONSAL HEAD: *Monsal Head Hotel*
On B6465, Derbyshire.
Former stable block with horsy decor. Magnificent view of the steep Wye valley from the hotel lounge; good walks all round.

NOTTINGHAM: *Olde Trip to Jerusalem*
Brewhouse Yard, Nottingham.
Unique pub built into sandstone caverns once used as a meeting place for crusaders. One of the oldest in Britain.

STAMFORD: *George*
St Martins, Stamford, Lincolnshire.
Splendid old coaching inn with vestiges of a Norman pilgrim hospice. Now very elegant, it offers an excellent range of food with Italian wines. Pretty cobbled courtyard and gardens.

UPTON: *Cross Keys*
Main St, Upton, Nottinghamshire.
Beamed pub with hanging baskets and pictures. Good bar food with fresh fish. The restaurant is in the old dovecote.

LANCASHIRE AND THE LAKES

CARTMEL FELL: *Mason's Arms*
Off A5074 at Bowland Bridge sign, Cumbria.
Lively, characterful pub with an immense range of bottled beers, real ales, cider and country wines. Good walks nearby.

ELTERWATER: *Britannia Inn*
Off A593 nr Ambleside, Cumbria.
Unadorned rustic interior and open fires in the Langdale valley. An excellent walking or touring base with rooms.

GARSTANG: *Th'Owd Tithebarn*
Off Church St, Garstang, Lancashire.
A converted barn by the canal with rustic decor, popular with walkers.

GREAT LANGDALE: *Old Dungeon Ghyll*
On B5343, Langdale, Cumbria.
Dramatic setting near waterfalls in the Langdale Pikes. A walking and climbing base with rooms, plain but cosy.

LIVERPOOL: *Philharmonic*
36 Hope St, Liverpool.
One of the most characterful Merseyside haunts, a Victorian setting with plasterwork, stained glass and mahogany.

MANCHESTER: *Lass o' Gowrie*
36 Charles St, Manchester.
Popular student dive with a gaslit bar and its own brewery in the cellar. Lively at weekends.

NEAR SAWREY: *Tower Bank Arms*
B5285, Near Sawrey, Cumbria.
This pretty village is a mecca for Beatrix Potter fans. The pub backs on to her house, Hill Top. Well-preserved interior.

YORKSHIRE AND HUMBERSIDE

ASKRIGG: *Kings Arms*
Off A684 nr Bainbridge, N Yorks.
The rustic interior is used as the set in a TV series. Good bar food, wines and beers are other reasons to find it.

COXWOLD: *Fauconberg Arms*
Coxwold, N Yorks.
"Olde worlde" pub with antique oak settles and Windsor armchairs to sit on, and plenty of beer, wine, and good food.

FLAMBOROUGH: *Seabirds*
On B1255, Flamborough, E Yorks.
The white chalk cliffs nearby are a marvellous place for birdwatching. Interesting interior. The fish is the highlight of the menu.

GOATHLAND: *Mallyan Spout*
Off A169, Goathland, N Yorks.
Traditional moorland inn with a relaxing air and good food. The open fires make it popular with walkers. Good rooms.

HULL: *Olde White Harte*
Off 25 Silver St, Hull, E Yorks.
This ancient tavern lies behind a modern "White Hart". The interior sports inglenook fireplaces and copper-topped bar.

LOW CATTON: *Gold Cup*
Off A166 at Stamford Bridge, E Yorks.
The farm animals around add an authentic touch to this rural pub with comfortable, relaxing bars and good food.

MOULTON: *Black Bull*
Off A1 nr Scotch Corner, N Yorks.
This pleasant old place puts masses of energy into the food, bar snacks and good wines. The atmosphere is upmarket.

NORTHUMBRIA

BLANCHLAND: *Lord Crewe Arms*
Blanchland, Northumb.
Moorland hotel with priests' holes, 13th-century fireplaces and ghosts. Popular with walkers; good food and rooms.

CRASTER: *Jolly Fisherman*
Off B1339 nr Alnwick, Northumb.
Unassuming local pub with beautiful sea views. Home-made crab soup and seafood are specialities. Excellent cliff-top walks.

GRETA BRIDGE: *Morritt Arms*
Off A66 nr Scotch Corner, Co Durham.
A fine stone coaching inn with a splendid, spacious interior with oak settles. Attractive riverside setting.

NEW YORK: *Shiremoor House Farm*
Off A191, New York, Tyne & Wear.
A skilful conversion from some derelict farm buildings, it is now comfortable and stylish. Has interesting food, and families welcome.

NEWCASTLE UPON TYNE: *Crown Posada*
31 The Side, Newcastle upon Tyne.
A Victorian real ale pub with an ornate interior of gilt mirrors and stained glass. It is a city pub for drinkers, so no children are allowed.

SEAHOUSES: *Olde Ship*
On B1340, Seahouses, Northumb.
Maritime curiosities festoon this harbour-front inn. From the window you can see the Farne Islands. Good coastal walks.

NORTH WALES

BEAUMARIS: *Olde Bulls Head*
Castle St, Beaumaris, Anglesey.
A 500-year-old building with fascinating details inside including a 17th-century water clock, cutlasses and a witch's ducking stool.

BODFARI: *Dinorben Arms*
Off A541, Bodfari, Denbighshire.
Hillside pub with excellent bar food, lots of whiskies and a pleasant range of terraces for admiring the views.

CAPEL CURIG: *Bryn Tyrch Hotel*
On A5 nr Betws-y-Coed, A & C.
This inn is popular with walkers and climbers exploring the Snowdonia National Park.

GLANWYDDEN: *Queen's Head*
Off B5115, The Glanwydden, A & C.
Excellent pub food is a major draw at this village pub. It can get crowded in season.

MAENTWROG: *Grapes Hotel*
On A496, Maentwrog, A & C.
Coaching inn with lovely views and a walled garden. Much of the furniture was salvaged from disused chapels.

SOUTH AND MID-WALES

ABERYSTWYTH: *Halfway Inn*
On A4120, Pisgah, Cardiganshire.
Rheidol Valley pub with stunning views. Comfy rooms, and free camping for customers.

CRICKHOWELL: *Bear*
Brecon Rd, Crickhowell, Powys.
Old inn with splendid food and excellent range of drinks. Period features and interesting decor. Bedrooms available.

EAST ABERTHAW: *Blue Anchor*
On B4265, East Aberthaw, V of Glam.
Charming thatched pub with low-ceilinged, intimate warren-like rooms and open fires. Estuary walks nearby.

HAY-ON-WYE: *Old Black Lion*
26 Lion St, Hay-on-Wye, Powys.
A 13th-century inn with restaurant food and 10 rooms. Lots of local sporting activities (fishing, riding, golf), plus bookshops.

NEVERN: *Trewern Arms*
On B4582, Nevern, Pembrokeshire.
Appealing riverside inn in a pretty village. The slate-floored bar is crammed with agricultural and domestic bygones.

PENALLT: *Boat Inn*
Long Lane, Penallt, Monmouthshire.
A mecca for music and ale right on the border; drinks are served in Wales. Disused railway cycle tracks and canoeing.

THE LOWLANDS

EDINBURGH: *Bow Bar*
80 West Bow, Edinburgh.
Bar of mahogany and mirrorglass, with malts and real ales. No children, games or music.

EDINBURGH: *Cafe Royal Circle Bar*
West Register St, Edinburgh.
Refurbished in Victorian style – tiled portraits of Scottish worthies, leather seating and chandeliers. Oyster bar and restaurant.

ELIE: *Ship Inn*
The Harbour, Elie, Fife.
Atmospheric quayside pub with nautical decor and attractive views. Summer barbecues are a feature.

GLASGOW: *Horseshoe*
17–19 Drury St, Glasgow.
Busy Victorian pub with a long bar and plenty of period features. Good value bar snacks. Karaoke in the evenings.

ISLE OF WHITHORN: *Steam Packet*
Isle of Whithorn, Dumfries & Galloway.
Superb setting on a lovely harbour scene. Pleasant eating areas and real ales. Boat trips from the harbour.

THE HIGHLANDS AND ISLANDS

APPLECROSS: *Applecross Inn*
Shore St, Applecross, Wester Ross, Highland.
Spectacularly located beyond Britain's highest mountain pass, this pub overlooks Skye. Local seafood is served, and there is music some evenings.

DUNDEE: *Fishermans Tavern*
10-16 Fort St, Broughty Ferry, Tayside.
Award-winning real ales and lots of malts too. Good seafront and Tay rail bridge views. Rooms available.

ISLE OF SKYE: *Tigh Osda Eilean Iarmain*
Off A851, Isle Ornsay, Isle of Skye.
Welcoming hotel bar. Lots of malts and good bar food. Gorgeous setting.

LOCH LOMOND: *Oak Tree Inn*
Balmaha, Loch Lomond (east side).
Traditional stone inn with bar, restaurant and bed & breakfast; open fires in winter and good bar food served all day.

PORTSOY: *The Shore Inn*
The Old Harbour, Portsoy, Banffshire.
A 300-year-old seafaring inn nestling in a picturesque harbour. Traditional cask ale and a real open fire.

ULLAPOOL: *Ferry Boat*
Shore St, Ullapool, Highland.
Good whiskies and bar lunches, and fine views over the harbour. Coal fires and big windows overlooking the loch.

For key to symbols see back flap

SH21

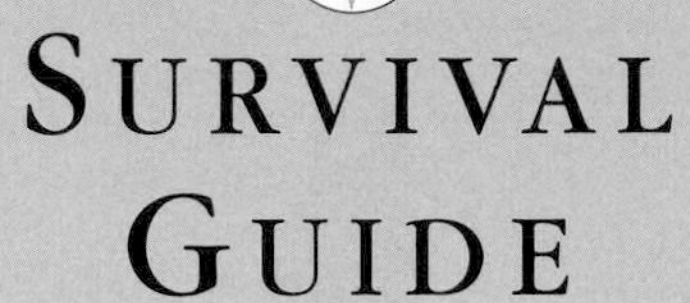

Survival Guide

Practical Information 614-631

Travel Information 632-643

General Index 644-669

Practical Information

Millions annually seek out what the British often take for granted – the country's ancient history, colourful pageantry, and spectacularly varied countryside. The range of facilities on offer to visitors in Britain has expanded and improved considerably over the last few years. To enjoy Britain fully it is best to know something about the nuts and bolts of British life: when to visit, how to get around, where to find information and what to do if things go wrong. Whether or not you find Britain an expensive country will depend a lot on the exchange rate between the pound and your own currency. Prices vary within Britain; regional differences in some items are very noticeable. London, not surprisingly, is the most expensive. The knock-on effect extends to most of southern England, Britain's most affluent region. Entertainment, food, hotels, transport and consumer items in shops are generally cheaper in other parts of the country.

A mounted sentry, London

Weymouth beach, Dorset, on a busy public holiday weekend

When to Visit

Britain's temperate maritime climate does not produce many temperature extremes *(see p68)*. There are many fine days but it is impossible to predict rain or shine reliably in any season. Weather patterns shift constantly, and the climate can differ widely in places only a short distance apart. The southeast is generally drier than elsewhere. But wherever you are going be sure to pack a mix of warm and cool clothes and an umbrella. Always get an up-to-date weather forecast before you set off on foot to remote mountain areas or moorland. Walkers can be surprised by the weather, and the Mountain Rescue services are often called out due to unexpectedly severe conditions. Weather reports are given on television and radio, in newspapers, or by phone services *(see p637)*.

Britain's towns and cities are all-year destinations, but many attractions open only between Easter and October. Some hotels are crammed at Christmas and New Year. The main family holiday months, July and August, and public holidays *(see p65)* are always busy. Spring and autumn offer a compromise between some good weather and a relative lack of crowds. The information at the beginning of each attraction listed in this guide gives opening days.

Insurance

It is sensible to take out travel insurance to cover cancellation or curtailment of your holiday, theft or loss of money and possessions, and the cost of any medical treatment *(see p620)*. It is better to arrange this in advance, although you can organize it once on your trip if necessary. If your country has a reciprocal medical arrangement with Britain (for example Australia, New Zealand and the EU), you can obtain free treatment under the National Health Service, but there are a number of forms to fill in. Certain benefits covered by medical insurance will not be included. North American and Canadian health plans or student identity cards may give you some protection against costs, but check the small print. If you want to drive a car in Britain, it is illegal to drive without third-party insurance and it is advisable to take out fully comprehensive insurance.

A sign for the Mountain Rescue

Advance Booking

Out of season, you should have few problems booking accommodation or transport at short notice, but in the high season, if you have set your heart on a popular West End show, luxury hotel, well-known restaurant, or specific flight or tour, always try to book ahead. Contact **VisitBritain** in your country, or a travel agent for advice and general information.

Tourist Information

Tourist information is available in many towns and public places, including airports, main rail and coach stations and at some places of historical interest. These bureaux will be able to help you on almost anything in their area. Look out for the tourist information symbol, which can indicate anything from a large and busy central

The most common English tourist information sign

◁ **Fishing boats in Scarborough port, North Yorkshire**

office to a simple kiosk or even an information board in a parking area.

Free leaflets are generally offered but a charge may be made for more detailed maps and booklets. Most tourist offices can suggest guided walks, places of interest and nearly all will reserve accommodation for you on request. During the busy holiday periods it is worth asking about the *Book-a-bed-ahead* scheme to places you intend to visit. Tourist office addresses and phone numbers are listed wherever possible in this guide. **VisitBritain**'s monthly magazine *In Britain,* available from tourist offices, contains articles about worthwhile places to visit and also includes a useful events diary.

VisitBritain's magazine

Disabled Travellers

The facilities on offer for disabled visitors to Britain are steadily improving: recently designed or newly renovated buildings and public spaces now offer lifts and ramps for wheelchair access (information given in the headings for each entry in this book); specially designed toilets; grab rails, and for the hearing impaired, earphones. Given advance notice, British Rail *(see p638)*, ferry or bus staff will help any disabled passengers. Ask a travel agent about the Disabled Persons Railcard, which entitles you to discounted rail fares. Many banks, theatres and museums can now provide aids for the visually or hearing impaired. Specialist tour operators, such as **Holiday Care Service**, cater for the physically handicapped visitor. If renting a car, Hertz offers hand-controlled vehicles for hire without any extra cost *(see p637)*. For permission to use any of the disabled parking spaces, you need to display a special sign in your car. For more general information contact **RADAR** or **Mobility International**.

One of the best series for disabled travellers is *Access* by Pauline Hephaistos, published by Survey Projects. You could also try *Holidays in the British Isles: a Guide for Disabled People* (RADAR), and *The World Wheelchair Traveller* by Ann Tyrrell and Susan Abbott (AA).

RADAR
020-7250 3222.
www.radar.org.uk

Mobility International
North America 541 343 1284.

Holiday Care Service
08451 249971.
www.holidaycare.org.uk

Lorna Doone Cottage and National Trust Information Centre, Somerset

Directory

For all VisitBritain information in the UK and overseas:
www.visitbritain.com

International Tourist Information

VisitBritain Australia
02 9021 4400 or 1300 85 8589.

VisitBritain Canada
1 888 847 4885 or 1 905 405 1720.

VisitBritain Ireland
01 670 8000 or 01 670 8100.

VisitBritain USA
1 800 462 2748 or 1 212 986 2266.

Regional Tourist Boards

Britain
1 Lower Regent St, London W1.
020-8846 9000.
www.visitbritain.com

Cumbria
01539 444444.
www.gocumbria.co.uk

East of England
01473 822922. www.eastofenglandtouristboard.com

Heart of England
01905 763436.
www.visitheartofengland.com

London
020-7932 2000.
www.londontouristboard.com

Northumbria
0191 375 3000.
www.visitnorthumbria.com

Northwest
01942 821222.
www.visitnorthwest.com

Scotland
0131 332 2433.
www.visitscotland.com

Southeast
01892 540766. www.southeastengland.uk.com

Wales
020 7808 3838.
www.visitwales.com

West Country
01392 360050.
www.westcountrynow.com

Yorkshire and the Humber region
01904 707961.
www.yorkshirevisitor.com

A visit to HMS Victory *(p157)*

Travelling with Children

BRITAIN IS NOT the easiest or most welcoming place for young children, but things are slowly changing.

Peak holiday times – Easter, July and August – and school holidays have most to offer in the way of entertainment for children. Many places have something child-centred going on at Christmas too, particularly pantomimes. Discounts for children, or family tickets, are now widely available for travel, theatre shows and other entertainments.

Choose accommodation that welcomes children, or opt for self-catering solutions with hard-wearing furnishings and room in which to run around. Many hotels now provide baby-sitting or baby-listening services, and may offer reductions or free accommodation for very young children *(see pp538–73)*.

Restaurants are becoming less child-phobic than they used to be and many now provide highchairs and special child menus *(see pp574–607)*. Italian eateries are often the most friendly and informal, but even the British pub, once resolutely child-free, is now relenting with beer gardens and family rooms. Under-18s are not permitted near the bars and must not buy or consume alcohol. The annual publication *Family Welcome* (HarperCollins) is available from newsagents and lists those places where children are made welcome.

Public Toilets

ALTHOUGH MANY older-style supervised public toilets still exist, these have largely been replaced by the modern free-standing, coin-operated "Superloos". Young children should never use these toilets on their own.

Student Travellers

FULL-TIME STUDENTS who have an International Student Identity Card (ISIC), are often entitled to discounts on things like travel, sports facilities and entrance fees. North American students can also get medical cover but it may be very basic *(see p620)*. If you don't have an ISIC, they are available from **STA Travel**, or the **National Union of Students**.

An **International Youth Hostel Federation** card enables you to stay in Britain's hundreds of youth hostels. Inexpensive accommodation is also available (out of term) at many of the university halls of residence – such as the **University of London** – a good way of staying in city centres on a tight budget. If you are exploring the wilder regions of Britain, sleeping quarters can be found in camping barns (dormitory-style bunkhouses) which, though spartan, cost very little. For information on working in Britain, contact **BUNAC**.

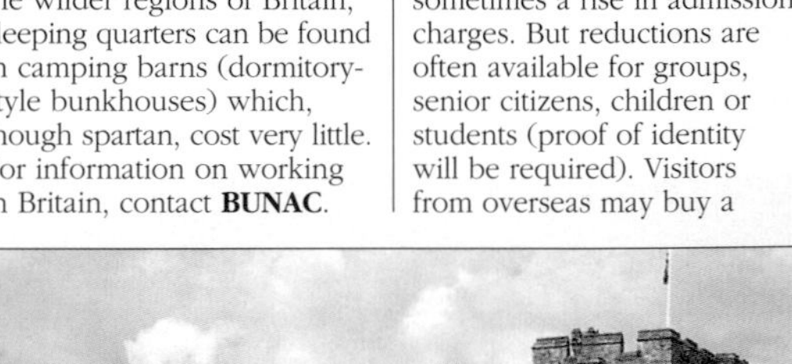

Great British Heritage Pass

Business Hours

MANY BUSINESSES and shops are closed on Sundays, though trading is now legal. Monday to Friday hours are generally 9 or 10am to 5 or 5:30pm, but shop hours can vary, with late shopping one evening a week, and lunch-time or even half-day closing – usually a Wednesday.

Museums in London often open late one day a week, but those outside the capital may have more inflexible hours, sometimes closing during the morning, or for one day a week – often on Mondays.

On public holidays, known as bank holidays in Britain, banks, offices, most shops, restaurants and attractions will generally close.

Admission Charges

THESE VARY WIDELY from a nominal 50p to over £10 for the popular attractions, although many of the major national museums are now free. Museums now combine entertainment with education, and are livelier than ever before. Alongside this move, however, there is sometimes a rise in admission charges. But reductions are often available for groups, senior citizens, children or students (proof of identity will be required). Visitors from overseas may buy a

The privately owned, admission-charging, Hever Castle *(see p177)*

A Cotswold church, one of hundreds of parish churches open to the public free of charge

Great British Heritage Pass, which gives access to over 600 sights, available from VisitBritain offices abroad and, in the UK, from the Britain Visitor Centre in London's Lower Regent Street and some ports of entry and Tourist Information Centres *(see p615)*. A few local authority museums and art galleries are free, but donations are always welcome. Other sights are in private hands, run either as a commercial venture or on a charitable basis. Stately homes open to the public may still belong to the gentry who have lived there for centuries; a charge is made to defray the enormous costs of upkeep. Many of these beautiful houses have added safari parks or garden centres to encourage and attract more visitors, such as Woburn Abbey (*see p218*).

Britain's thousands of small parish churches are among the country's greatest architectural treasures. None of the churches charge an entrance fee, although some, sadly, are locked because of vandalism. Increasingly, many of the great cathedrals expect a donation from visitors.

English Heritage and the National Trust

Many of Britain's historic buildings, parks, gardens, and vast tracts of countryside and coastline are cared for by **English Heritage** (EH), the **National Trust** (NT) or the **National Trust for Scotland** (NTS).We identify EH, NT and NTS properties at the beginning of each entry. Entrance fees are often high, so if you wish to visit several stately homes it may be worth taking out annual membership, which allows free access thereafter to any of their properties (remember many are closed in winter).

Information leaflets, National Trust

Many of the NT's properties are "listed". These are buildings or sites that are recognized as having special architectural or historical interest and therefore fully protected from alterations and demolition.

The sign and symbol of English Heritage

Useful Addresses

BUNAC
16 Bowling Green Lane, London EC1R 0QH. Tel *020-7251 3472.*
W www.bunac.org

English Heritage (EH)
PO Box 569, Swindon SN2 2YP.
Tel *01793 414910.*
W www.english-heritage.org.uk

International Youth Hostel Federation
Tel *01707 324 170.*
W www.hihostels.com

National Trust (NT)
PO Box 39, Bromley, Kent, BR1 3XL. Tel *0870-458 4000.*
W www.nationaltrust.org.uk

National Trust for Scotland (NTS)
28 Charlotte Sq, Edinburgh EH2 4ET. Tel *0131 243 9300.*
W www.nts.org.uk

National Union of Students
Tel *020-7561 6500.*
W www.nusonline.co.uk

STA Travel
Priory Hse, 6 Wrights Lane, London W8 6TA.
Tel *020-7361 6161 (Europe).*
Tel *020-7361 6262 (worldwide).*
W www.statravel.co.uk

University of London Union
Malet St, London WC1.
Tel *020-7862 8000.*
W www.ulu.lon.ac.uk

Useful Publications

Both the regional and national tourist boards produce comprehensive lists of local attractions and registered accommodation. For route planning, excellent, clear, large-format motoring atlases are produced by the RAC and AA *(see p637)*. For rural exploration, *Ordnance Survey* maps are ideal.

Media

British national newspapers fall into two categories: broadsheets – quality papers, such as *The Times* or *The Guardian* – and tabloids, heavy on gossip, such as *The Sun* or *The Daily Mirror*.

The weekend newspapers are more expensive than dailies but are packed with supplements of all kinds, including sections on the arts, motoring, entertainment, travel, listings and reviews.

Specialist periodicals are available from newsagents on just about every topic from hamster-keeping to hi-fi. For a more in-depth analysis of current events buy *The Economist, New Statesman & Society* or *The Spectator,* while *Private Eye* cocks a satirical snook at public figures. There are a few foreign magazines and newspapers available in large towns, often at main railway stations, but mostly in London. One of the most popular is the *International Herald Tribune,* which is available on the day of issue.

Television is undergoing an upheaval in Britain as satellite and cable networks invade the airwaves. Still more influential,

Some of Britain's national newspapers

A local newsagent and sub-post office at Arisaig, Scotland

however, is the state-run BBC (British Broadcasting Corporation), which operates two terrestrial channels and maintains its reputation for producing some of the best television in the world without commercial breaks. The BBC's three commercial rivals are ITV, Channel Four and Channel 5, the first tending toward popular soap operas and game-shows, Channel Four catering for trendy and minority tastes (art films, offbeat chat shows, game-shows and documentaries), and the last relying on US imports and TV movies. There are also regional variations.

The BBC has a number of radio stations, ranging from pop music (Radio One) to the middlebrow Radio Four. There are many local commercial radio stations.

Full TV and radio schedules are listed in daily newspapers and several listings magazines; one of the best is the *Radio Times*, a weekly publication found in most newsagents.

Smoking

It is now forbidden to smoke in many public places in Britain. These include most public transport systems, taxis, theatres and cinemas. The exception to the anti-smoking trend is pubs. ASH (Action on Smoking and Health) can advise on smoke-free venues (020-7935 3519).

Working Restrictions

Residents of the EU can work in Britain with no permit, while Commonwealth citizens under the age of 27 may work part-time for up to two years in the UK. North American students can get a blue card through their university, which enables them to work for up to six months – get this before arrival in Britain. BUNAC *(see p617)* is a student club which will organize exchange schemes for students to work abroad.

Electricity

The voltage in Britain is 220/240 AC, 50 Hz. Electrical plugs have three square pins and take fuses of 3, 5 and 13 amps. Visitors will need an adaptor for North American or continental appliances which have been bought from home, such as portable computers, hairdriers and tape recorders. Most hotels will have two-pronged European-style sockets for shavers only.

Standard British three-pin plug

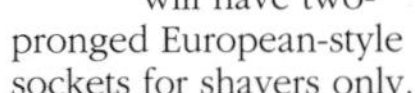

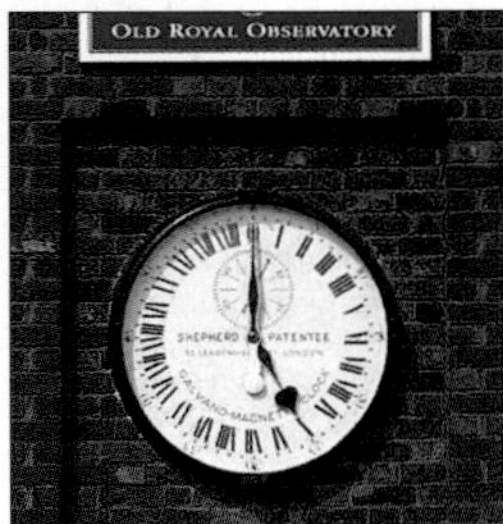

Clock, the Royal Observatory, Greenwich *(see p133)*

Time

Britain is on Greenwich Mean Time (GMT) during the winter months, five hours ahead of Eastern Standard Time and ten hours behind Sydney. From the middle of March to October, the clocks go forward one hour to British Summer Time (equivalent to Central European Time). To check the correct time, you can dial 123 to contact the Speaking Clock service.

CUSTOMS AND IMMIGRATION

A VALID PASSPORT is needed to enter Britain. Visitors from the European Union (EU), the United States, Canada, New Zealand and Australia do not require visas to enter the country. Nor are inoculations or vaccinations necessary. When you arrive at any British air or seaport you will find separate queues at immigration control – one for European Union nationals, and several others for everyone else. As a result of Britain's membership of the European Union, anyone who arrives in Britain from a member country can pass through a blue channel – but random checks are still being made to detect entry of any prohibited goods, particularly drugs, indecent material and weapons. Never, under any circumstances, carry luggage or parcels through customs for someone else.

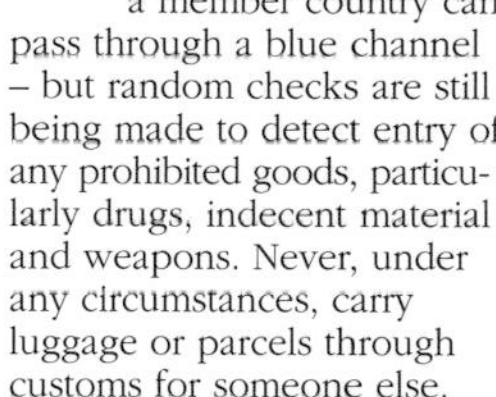

Highland malt

Travellers entering from outside the EU still have to pass through customs channels. Go through the green channel if you have nothing to declare over the customs allowances for overseas visitors, and the red channel if you have goods to declare. If you are unsure of importation restrictions go through the red channel.

Limits on the quantities of alcohol are: two litres of still table wine plus one litre of alcoholic drink over 22 per cent vol or two litres of alcoholic drink not over 22 per cent vol; for tobacco products the limits are: 200 cigarettes or 50 cigars. You are allowed up to £145 worth of other goods including gifts, souvenirs, cider and beer. No live animals may be imported without a permit as Britain is free of rabies. Any animals found will be impounded and may be destroyed. Non-EU residents can obtain a VAT refund on goods bought in Britain *(see p626)*.

Green and red customs channels at Heathrow airport *(see p634)*

HM Customs and Excise
Thomas Paine House, Angel Square, Torrens St, London EC1.
020-7865 3000; advice line 0845 0109000. Contact for information regarding import or export restrictions. www.hmce.gov.uk

The mosque in Regent's Park *(see p105)*, London

RELIGIOUS ORGANIZATIONS

Baptist
London Baptist Assn, 235 Shaftesbury Ave., London WC2. *020-7692 5592.* www.londonbaptist.org.uk

Buddhist
Buddhist Society, 58 Eccleston Sq, London SW1.
020-7834 5858.

Church of England
Great Smith St, London SW1.
020-7898 1000.
www.cofe.anglican.org

Evangelical Alliance
Whitefield Hse, 186 Kennington Park Rd, London SE11.
020-7207 2100. www.eauk.org

Jewish
Liberal Jewish Synagogue, 28 St John's Wood Rd, London NW8.
020-7286 5181. www.ljs.org

United Synagogue (Orthodox), Adler House, 735 High Rd, North Finchley, London, N12.
020-8343 8989.
www.unitedsynagogue.org.uk

Moslem
Islamic Cultural Centre, 146 Park Rd, London NW8.
020-7724 3363.

Quakers
Friends Hse, 173–177 Euston Rd, London NW1. *020-7663 1000.*
www.quaker.org.uk

Roman Catholic
Westminster Cathedral, Victoria St, London SW1.
020-7798 9055.
www.westminstercathedral.org.uk

EMBASSIES AND CONSULATES

Australian High Commission
Australia Hse, the Strand, London WC2.
020-7379 4334.
www.australia.org.uk

Canadian High Commission
Canada Hse, Trafalgar Sq, London SW1.
020-7258 6600.
www.canada.gc.ca

New Zealand High Commission
New Zealand Hse, 80 Haymarket, London SW1.
020-7930 8422.
www.nzembassy.com

United States Embassy
24 Grosvenor Sq, London W1.
020-7499 9000.
www.usembassy.org.uk

CONVERSION CHART

Britain is officially metricated in line with the rest of Europe, but imperial measures are still in common usage, including road distances (measured in miles). Imperial pints and gallons are 20 per cent larger than US measures.

Imperial to metric
1 inch = 2.5 centimetres
1 foot = 30 centimetres
1 mile = 1.6 kilometres
1 ounce = 28 grams
1 pound = 454 grams
1 pint = 0.6 litres
1 gallon = 4.6 litres

Metric to imperial
1 millimetre = 0.04 inch
1 centimetre = 0.4 inch
1 metre = 3 feet 3 inches
1 kilometre = 0.6 mile
1 gram = 0.04 ounce
1 kilogram = 2.2 pounds

Personal Security and Health

Britain is a densely populated country which, like any other, has its share of social problems. However, it is very unlikely that you will come across any violence. If you do encounter difficulties, never hesitate to contact the police for help. Britain's National Health Service can be relied upon for both emergency and routine treatment. However, you may have to pay if your country has no reciprocal arrangement with Britain.

Hospitals and Medical Treatment

All visitors to Britain are strongly advised to take out medical insurance against the cost of any emergency hospital care, repatriation and specialists' fees, especially for those visitors from outside the European Union (EU). Emergency medical treatment in a British National Health Service (NHS) casualty ward is free, but any kind of additional medical care could prove very expensive.

Residents of the European Union and nationals of some other Commonwealth and European countries are entitled to free medical treatment under the NHS, though the process is bureaucratic. Before travelling, you should obtain a form confirming that your country of origin has adequate reciprocal health arrangements with Britain. But some treatments are not covered and repatriation is not included, so medical insurance is preferable.

If you need to see a dentist while staying in Britain, you will have to pay. The cost varies, depending on your entitlement to NHS treatment, and whether you can find an NHS dentist to treat you. Emergency dental treatment is available in some hospitals, but if you would prefer a private dentist, try looking in the *Yellow Pages* *(see p622)*.

Pharmacists

You can buy a wide range of proprietary medicines without prescription from chemists in Britain. Boots is the best-known and largest supplier, with branches in most towns. Many medicines, however, are only available with a doctor's prescription, which you must take to a chemist or pharmacist. If you are likely to need drugs, either bring your own or get your doctor to write out the generic (as opposed to the brand) name of the drug. If you are entitled to an NHS prescription, you will be charged a standard rate; without this you will be charged the full cost of the drug. Do ask for a receipt for any insurance claim. Some pharmacies are open until midnight; for emergencies contact the local hospital. Doctors' surgeries are normally open mornings and early evenings. You can call NHS Direct 24-hour helpline (0845 4647), or go to a hospital casualty department any time. In an emergency, dial 999 for an ambulance.

Pharmacy sign

Crime

Britain is not a dangerous place for visitors, and it is most unlikely that your stay will be blighted by crime. Practical advice to help you avoid loss or injury is given below. Due to past terrorist attacks, there are occasional security alerts, especially on the Underground, but these are mainly false alarms often due to people accidentally leaving a bag or parcel lying around. Always co-operate with the authorities if your bag has to be searched or if you are asked to evacuate a building.

Suitable Precautions

Take good care of your belongings at all times. Make sure your possessions are adequately insured before you arrive. Never leave them unattended in public places.

Keep your valuables well concealed (particularly mobile phones), especially in crowds. In all public places, keep handbags on your lap, not on the floor. It is always advisable not to carry too much cash or jewellery with you; leave it in your hotel safe instead. Pickpockets love crowded places like markets, busy shops and all modes of transport during rush-hour.

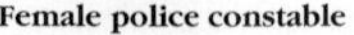

Female police constable

Traffic police officer

Male police constable

If you are travelling alone at night try to avoid deserted and poorly lit buildings and places such as back streets and car parks. By far the safest way of carrying large amounts of cash around is in traveller's cheques *(see p625)*.

Begging is an increasingly common sight in many British cities, and foreign visitors are frequent targets for hard-luck stories. Requests for money are usually polite; but any abuse should be reported to the police immediately.

Women Travelling Alone

It is not unusual in Great Britain for women to travel unaccompanied, or visit a bar or restaurant with a group of female friends. Nor is it especially dangerous, but caution is advisable in deserted places, especially after dark. Try to avoid using public transport when there is just one other passenger or a group of young men. Summon a licensed taxi *(see p642)* rather than walk through a lonely area at night, especially if you do not know the district very well.

Legally, you cannot carry any offensive weapons around with you in Britain, even for self-defence. This include knives, coshes, guns or tear-gas; however, personal alarm systems are allowed.

Police

The sight of a traditional British bobby patrolling the streets in a tall hat is now less common than the police patrol car, sometimes with wailing sirens and flashing lights. But the old-fashioned police constable does still exist, particularly in rural areas and in crowded city centres, and continues to be courteous, approachable and helpful.

Unlike in many countries, the police force in Great Britain do not carry guns. If you are lost, the advice to ask a policeman or woman still applies. Traffic wardens may also be able to help you with directions.

Police car

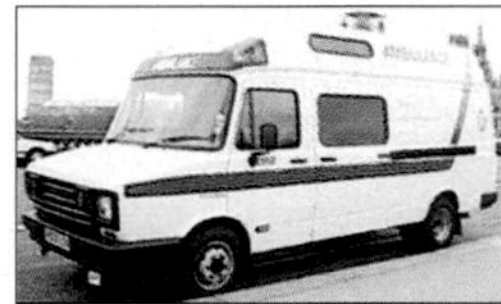
Ambulance

Fire engine

In a crisis, dial 999 to get the police, fire and ambulance services which are on call 24-hours a day. Calls are free from any public or private phone, but they should only be made in real emergencies. Along the coastal areas of Great Britain this number will also put you in touch with Britain's voluntary coastguard rescue service, the Royal National Lifeboat Institute.

Royal National Lifeboat Institute logo

Lost Property

If you are unlucky enough to lose anything or have anything stolen, go straight to the nearest police station and make a report of your loss. If you plan to make a claim on your insurance for any theft, you will need a written report from the local police. All of the main bus or rail stations have lost property offices. Don't leave your valuables on display in your room: hotels usually disclaim all responsibility for valuables not kept in their safe.

Directory

Crisis Information

Police, Fire and Ambulance services
999. Calls are free (24-hr phoneline).

Accident and Emergency Departments
For the nearest unit check in phone directory or contact the police.

Childline
0800 1111. Calls free for children in need of help (24-hr phoneline). W www.childline.org.uk

Emergency Dental Care
020-7837 3646 (24-hour phoneline; children only); 020–7955 4317 (Guy's Hosp, London).

Rape Crisis Centre
0115 900 3560 (Rape Crisis Federation of England & Wales).
W www.rapecrisis.co.uk

Samaritans
0845 7909090 (24-hr phoneline for all emotional problems).
W www.samaritans.org.uk

Helplines

Alcoholics Anonymous
0845 7697555. W www.alcoholics-anonymous.org.uk

Disabled Helplines
DIAL UK. *01302 310123.*
W www.dialuk.org.uk
Disabled Living Foundation.
020-7289 6111.

Late-opening Chemists
Contact your local police station or hospital for a list.

Lost Property
Contact your local police station.

National Helpline for Drugs
0800 776600 (24-hr helpline).
W www.nhd.org.uk

National Helpline for the Blind
0845 766 9999.
W www.rnib.org.uk

British Deaf Association
0870 770 3300. W www.britishdeafassociation.org.uk

British Pregnancy Advisory Service
08457 304030.
W www.bpas.org

Victim Support
0845 3030900.
W www.victimsupport.org

Communications

Modern BT phone box

WITH CONTINUOUSLY IMPROVING telecommunication systems and the spread of e-mail, staying in contact and making plans while travelling has never been easier. The telephone system in Britain is efficient and inexpensive. Charges depend on when, where and for how long you talk. The cheapest time to call is between 6pm and 8am Monday to Friday, and throughout the weekend. Local calls made on public payphones, however, are charged at a fixed rate per minute.

PAYPHONES

YOU CAN PAY for a payphone using coins or a card. Payphones accept 10p, 20p, 50p and £1 pieces, while newer phones also accept £2 coins. The minimum cost of a call is 20p. If you expect a call to be short, use 10p or 20p pieces, as payphones only return unused coins. You may find a phone card more convenient than coins. BT (formerly British Telecom) has now stopped issuing its own prepaid phone cards, but other phone companies' cards are available from newsagents and post offices. If you use a credit card, be warned that it carries a minimum charge and your phone calls will be charged at a higher rate.

TELEPHONE DIRECTORIES

DIRECTORIES, SUCH as *Yellow Pages* and *Thomson Local*, list local businesses and services. They can be found at local Post Office branches, libraries and often at your hotel.

USING A CARD AND COIN PHONE

1 Lift the receiver and wait for the dial tone.

2 Insert your phone card into the slot or deposit any of the following coins: 10p, 20p, 50p, £1, £2. The minimum amount is 20p.

3 Dial the number and wait to be connected.

4 The display indicates how much credit you have left. A rapid bleeping noise means your money has run out. Deposit more coins or insert another phone card.

5 If you want to make another call and you have money left in credit, do not replace the receiver, press the follow-on-call button.

6 When you have finished speaking, replace the receiver and retrieve your card or collect your change. Only wholly unused coins are refunded.

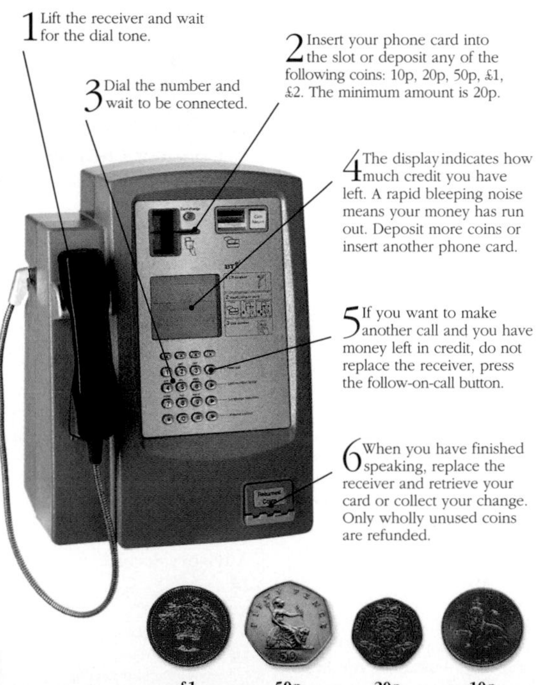

USEFUL NUMBERS

A number of telephone services exist to help you find or reach a specific phone number. You will be charged more for enquiries if calling from a mobile phone.

Emergency Calls
999. Police, Fire, Ambulance, Coastguard, Mountain and Cave Rescue.

Directory Enquiries
118 500 (charge applies).

International Directory Enquiries
118 505 (charge applies).

International Operator
118 505 (charge applies).

Operator Assistance
100.

Overseas Calls
00 followed by country code: Australia (61), Canada (1), Ireland (353), New Zealand (64), South Africa (27), United States (1).

Talking Pages
(0800) 600900. Provides numbers for specific kinds of shops or services in any area.

ACCESSING THE INTERNET

MOST CITIES AND towns now have some form of public access to computers and the Internet. Free Internet access is often available at main library branches, although you may have to book a time slot. Internet cafés usually charge by the minute for computer use. Charges tend to build up quickly, especially when including the cost of printed pages. EasyEverything, a chain of massive Internet cafés, has branches in many cities including Edinburgh (58 Rose Street) and London (7 Strand). Internet access is very cheap and is most reasonable during off-peak times.

24-hour Internet access at the Europe-wide chain EasyEverything

Sending a Letter

Red and gold Post Office logo

BESIDES MAIN POST OFFICE branches that offer all the mail services available, there are many Post Office outlets in newsagents, grocery stores and general information centres, particularly in more isolated areas. In many villages the Post Office outlet is also the only shop. Post Office branches are usually open from 9am to 5:30pm Monday to Friday, and until 12:30pm on Saturday. Post boxes – in all shapes and sizes but always red – are found throughout cities, towns and villages.

A Cotswold Post Office outlet

Postal Services

STAMPS CAN BE BOUGHT at many outlets, including supermarkets and petrol stations. Hotels often have post boxes at their reception. When writing to a British address always include the postcode, which can be obtained from either the **Royal Mail** enquiry line or website. Letters and postcards can be sent either first or second class within the UK. First-class service is more expensive but quicker, with most letters reaching their destination the following day (except Sunday); second-class mail takes a day or two longer.

All air letters are 1st class

1st-class stamp 2nd-class stamp

Greetings stamps featuring characters from children's fiction

Royal Mail
0845 7740740.
www.royalmail.com

Poste Restante

LARGE URBAN Post Office branches have a *poste restante* service where letters can be sent for collection. To use the service be sure to print the surname (last name) clearly so it will be filed correctly. Send it to *Poste Restante* followed by the address of the Post Office branch. To collect your post you will have to show your passport or other form of identification. Post is kept for one month. London's main Post Office branch is in William IV Street, WC2. The American Express office at 30–31 Haymarket, London SW1 has a *poste restante* for customers.

Post Boxes

THESE MAY BE either free-standing "pillar boxes" or wall safes, both painted bright red. Some pillar boxes have separate slots, one for overseas and first-class mail, another for second-class mail.

Collections are usually made several times a day during weekdays (less often on Saturdays and Sundays); times are marked on the box.

A rural mailbox, embedded in a stone wall

Mailing Abroad

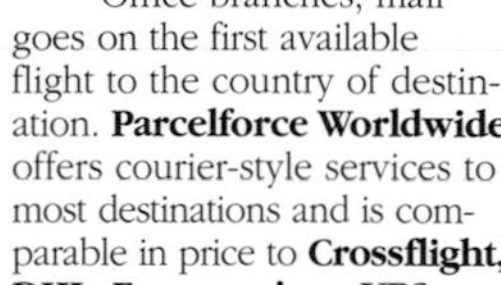

Pillar box

AIR LETTERS go by Royal Mail's fast airmail service anywhere in the world; the cost depends on the destination. On average, it usually takes three days for them to reach cities in Europe, and four to six days for destinations elsewhere. Sending post overseas by surface mail may be economical, but it can take up to eight weeks for it to reach its destination. Royal Mail offers an express airmail service called **Swiftair**. Available from all Post Office branches, mail goes on the first available flight to the country of destination. **Parcelforce Worldwide** offers courier-style services to most destinations and is comparable in price to **Crossflight, DHL**, **Expressair** or **UPS**.

Crossflight
01753 776000.
www.crossflight.co.uk

DHL
08701 100300. www.dhl.com

Expressair
020-8897 6568.

Parcelforce Worldwide
08708 501150.
www.parcelforce.com

Swiftair (Royal Mail)
08457 740740.
www.royalmail.com

UPS
08457 877877. www.ups.com

Banking and Local Currency

VISITORS TO BRITAIN usually find that the high-street banks offer them the best rates of exchange. However, if you do find yourself having to use one of the hundreds of privately owned bureaux de change that are found at nearly every major airport, rail station and tourist area, care should be taken to check the commission and minimum charges before completing any transaction. Traveller's cheques are by far the safest method of bringing currency to Britain with you.

Lloyds Bank with bureau de change facilities

Bureaux de Change

SMALL PRIVATE bureaux de change may be more conveniently located and open when banks are closed. But rates of exchange can vary considerably and commission charges can be high, so it may be worth looking around.

The reputable firms such as **Exchange International**, **Travelex**, **American Express** and **Chequepoint** usually offer good exchange facilities and have branches throughout Britain.

Banks

BANKS GENERALLY offer the best rates of exchange for visitors, though commissions may vary considerably.

Every large town and city in Britain will have a branch of at least one of these five high-street clearing banks – **Barclays**, **Lloyds TSB**, **HSBC**, **National Westminster**, and the **Royal Bank of Scotland**.

Many banks have an ATM (cash dispenser) from which you can obtain money with a credit card and your personal identification number (PIN); arrange this before you leave home. Some of the most modern machines have easy-to-read computerized instructions in several languages. American Express cards may be used at all ATM cash machines. Once again you will need a PIN number to access your personal account. There is a 2 per cent handling charge for each transaction that you make.

If you run out of funds, another way to get money is to contact your own bank and ask them to wire the cash to the nearest British bank. You can also ask branches of Travelex or American Express to do this for you. North American visitors can get cash dispatched through **Western Union** to a bank or post office. Take along your passport to claim the money.

Banking hours vary, but the minimum opening times are 10am to 3:30pm, Monday to Friday. Many will stay open longer, especially in cities, and some open Saturday mornings. All banks close on Public Holidays *(see p65)*.

Credit Cards

CREDIT AND STORE cards are widely accepted throughout Britain, and you will definitely need a credit card in order to rent a car and usually for hotel bookings. But many smaller shops, markets, guesthouses and cafés may not accept them, so it is always wise to check in advance. Cards that are accepted are usually displayed on the windows of the establishment. The main card used throughout Britain is Visa, but other credit cards include Diners Club, American Express, Access and Mastercard.

You can get cash advances with a credit card (up to your credit limit) at any bank and ATM cash machine displaying the appropriate card sign. You will be charged the credit card company's interest rate for obtaining cash, which will appear on your statement with the amount advanced when you return home.

British Banks

All these high-street banks have branches in most of Britain's towns and cities. Most will also offer exchange facilities, but proof of identity may be required.

BARCLAYS

Barclays Bank logo

HSBC Bank logo

National Westminster logo

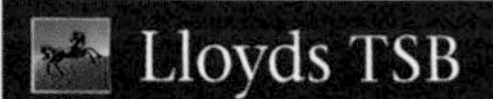

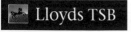

Lloyds TSB Bank logo

Royal Bank of Scotland logo

Exchange International
☎ 020-7630 1107.

Travelex
☎ 07333 18901.

American Express
☎ 020-7834 5555.
W www.americanexpress.co.uk

Chequepoint
☎ 020-7373 0111.
W www.chequepoint.com

Western Union
☎ 0800 833 833.
W www.westernunion.com

Currency and Traveller's Cheques

Britain's currency is the pound sterling (£), which is divided into 100 pence (p). There are no exchange controls in Britain, so you may bring in and take out as much cash as you like. Scotland has its own notes, which, though legal tender throughout Britain, are not always accepted in England and Wales. Traveller's cheques are the safest alternative to carrying large amounts of cash.

A Scottish one pound (£1) bank note

Always keep the receipts from your traveller's cheques separately from the cheques themselves because it makes it easier to obtain a refund if your cheques are lost or stolen. Some high-street banks issue traveller's cheques free of commission to their account holders, but the normal rate is about 1 per cent. When changing money ask for some smaller notes, as these are easier to use.

Bank Notes

English notes are produced in denominations of £5, £10, £20, and £50. Always get small denominations as some shops may refuse the larger notes.

£50 note

£20 note

£10 note

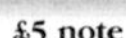

£5 note

Coinage

Coins currently in use are £2, £1, 50p, 20p, 10p, 5p, 2p and 1p (shown here at actual sizes).

2 pounds (£2) **1 pound (£1)** **50 pence (50p)** **20 pence (20p)**

10 pence (10p) **5 pence (5p)** **2 pence (2p)** **1 penny (1p)**

Shopping in Britain

WHILE THE WEST END OF LONDON *(see pp124–5)* is undeniably Britain's most exciting place to shop, many regional centres offer nearly as wide a range of goods. Moreover regional shopping can be less stressful, less expensive, and remarkably varied, with craft studios, farm shops, street markets and factory showrooms adding to the enjoyment of bargain-hunting. Britain is famous for its country clothing: wool, waxed cotton and tweed are all popular, along with classic prints such as Liberty or Laura Ashley and tartan. Other particularly British goods include antiques, floral soaps and scents, porcelain, glass and local crafts.

Antiques stall at Bermondsey Market

Shopping Hours

IN GENERAL, you can assume most shops in Britain will open during the week from 9am or 10am, and they will close after 5pm or 6pm. Hours on Saturdays may be shorter. Few town centre shops open on Sundays, unless it is near Christmas. Some stores open late for one evening a week – Thursday in London's West End – while village shops may close at lunch-time, or for one afternoon each week. Market days vary from town to town; some markets *(see pp124–5)* are held on Sundays.

How to Pay

MOST LARGE SHOPS all over the UK will accept well-known credit cards such as Access and VISA. Charge cards such as American Express or Diners Club are acceptable in some places, but Marks & Spencer, markets and some small shops will not take credit cards. Traveller's cheques can be used in larger stores, though exchange rates for non-sterling cheques may be poor. Take your passport with you for identification. Few places will accept cheques drawn on foreign banks. Cash is still the most popular way to pay for small purchases.

Rights and Refunds

IF SOMETHING YOU BUY is defective, you are entitled to a refund, provided you have kept your receipt as proof of purchase and return the goods in the same condition as when you bought them, and preferably in the same packaging. This may not always apply to sale goods clearly marked as seconds, imperfect, or shop-soiled. Inspect these carefully before you buy. You do not have to accept a credit note in place of a cash refund.

Vivienne Westwood's designer label

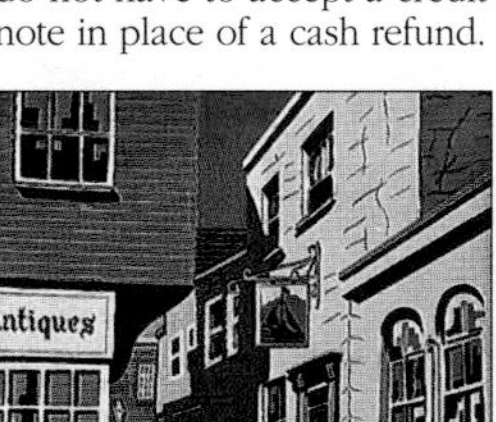

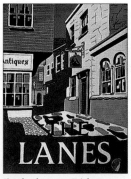

Sign for the Lanes, Brighton *(see p163)*

Annual Sales

TRADITIONALLY, sales take place during January, and in June and July, when nearly every shop cuts prices to get rid of slow-selling or imperfect stock. But you may well find special offers at any time of the year. Some shops begin their winter sales just before Christmas. Department stores and fashion houses have some excellent bargains for keen shoppers; one of the most prestigious sales is at Harrod's *(see p99)*, where queues will usually form long before opening time.

VAT and Tax-Free Shopping

VALUE ADDED TAX (VAT) is charged on most goods and services sold in Britain – exceptions include food, books and children's clothes. It is usually included in the advertised price. Visitors from outside the European Union who stay less than three months may claim this tax back. Take your passport with you whenever you go shopping. You must complete a form in the shop when you buy your goods and give a copy to the customs authorities when you leave the country. You may have to show your goods as proof of purchase. If you arrange to have the goods shipped from the store, the VAT should be deducted before you pay.

Out-of-Town Shopping Centres

THESE LARGE COMPLEXES, built along the lines of North American malls, are rapidly increasing around Britain. The advantages of car access and easy, cheap parking are undeniable, and most centres are accessible by public transport too. The centres usually feature clusters of popular high street stores, with many services on offer such as toilets, cafés, crèches, restaurants and cinemas.

A traditional shop front in Stonegate, York *(see p390)*

Department Stores

A FEW BIG DEPARTMENT stores, such as Harrod's, are only found in London, but others have provincial branches. John Lewis, for example, has shops in 22 locations. It sells a huge range of fabrics, clothing and household items, combining quality service with good value. Marks & Spencer, with branches in most major towns and cities in Britain, is famed for its good-value clothing and pre-prepared food. Debenhams and British Home Stores (BhS) are other well-known general stores with inexpensive clothing and home furnishings. Habitat is a reputable supplier of modern furniture. The sizes of all these stores, and the range of stock they carry, will differ from region to region.

Clothes Shops

ONCE AGAIN, London has the widest range, from *haute couture* to cheap and cheerful items ready-made. Shopping for clothing in the regions, however, can often be less tiring. Many towns popular with tourists – Oxford, Bath and York for instance – have independently owned clothes shops where you receive a more personal service. Or you could try one of the chain stores in any high street such as Principles or Next for smart, reasonably priced clothes, and Top Shop and Miss Selfridge for younger and cheaper fashions.

Supermarkets and Foodshops

SUPERMARKETS are a good way to shop for food. The range and quality of items in stock is usually excellent. Several large chains compete for market share and as a result prices are generally lower than smaller shops. Sainsbury, Tesco, Asda, Safeway and Waitrose are some of the national names. However, the smaller town-centre shops such as local bakeries, greengrocers or farm shops, may give you a more interesting choice of fresh regional produce, and more personal service.

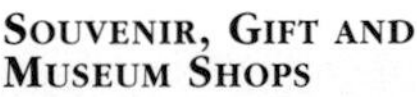

Local Teesdale cheeses

Souvenir, Gift and Museum Shops

BUYING PRESENTS is a must for most travellers. Most reputable large stores can arrange freight of high-value items. If you want to buy things you can carry back in your suitcase, the choice is wide. You can buy attractive, well-made, portable craft items all over the country, especially in areas tourists are likely to visit. For slightly more unusual presents, have a look in museum shops and the gifts available in National Trust *(see p25)* and English Heritage *(see p617)* properties.

The Mustard Shop *(see p189)*, Norwich

Secondhand and Antique Shops

BRITAIN'S LONG HISTORY means there are many interesting artifacts to be found. A visit to any of Britain's stately homes will reveal a national passion for antiques. Most towns will have an antique or bric-a-brac (miscellaneous second-hand items) shop or two. Look for auctions – tourist information centres *(see pp614–15)* can help you to locate them. You may like to visit a jumble or car boot sale in the hope of picking up a bargain.

Book stall, Hay-on-Wye, Wales *(see p447)*

Markets

LARGE TOWNS AND CITIES usually have a central covered market which operates most weekdays, selling everything from fresh produce to pots and pans. The information under each town entry in this guide lists market days. Many towns hold weekly markets in the main square. While you browse among the stalls, look out for local fresh produce and the jams and cakes of the Women's Institute stalls.

Entertainment in Britain

Punch and Judy show

LONDON IS WITHOUT DOUBT the entertainment capital of Britain *(see pp126–9)*, but many regional theatres, opera houses and concert halls have varied programmes. Edinburgh, Manchester, Birmingham, Leeds and Bristol in particular have a lot to offer and there are a number of summer arts festivals around the country such as those at Bath and Aldeburgh *(see pp62–3)*. Ticket prices are often cheaper outside the capital.

SOURCES OF INFORMATION

IN LONDON, check the listings magazines, such as *Time Out,* or the *Evening Standard,* London's evening newspaper. All of the quality broadsheet newspapers *(see p618)* provide comprehensive arts reviews and listings of the cultural events and shows throughout the country, with the largest sections at the weekends. Local newspapers, libraries, or tourist offices *(see p615)* can supply details of regional events. Specialist magazines such as *NME* or *Melody Maker* give up-to-date news of the pop music scene and are available from any newsagent.

THEATRES

BRITAIN HAS AN enduring theatrical tradition dating back to Shakespeare *(see pp312–15)* and beyond. All over the country, amateurs and professionals tread the boards in purpose-built auditoriums, pubs, clubs and village halls. Productions and performance standards are generally high, and British actors have an international reputation.

London is the place to enjoy theatre at its most varied and glamorous *(see p126)*. The West End alone has more than 50 theatres *(see p127)* ranging from elaborate Edwardian, upholstered in red plush, to exciting modern buildings such as the National Theatre on the South Bank in London.

In Stratford-upon-Avon, the Royal Shakespeare Company presents a year-round programme of Shakespeare, as well as avant-garde and experimental plays. Bristol also has a long dramatic tradition, the Theatre Royal *(see p244)* being the oldest working theatre in Britain. Some of the best productions outside the capital can be found at the West Yorkshire Playhouse in Leeds, the Royal Exchange in Manchester *(see p360)* and the Traverse in Edinburgh.

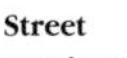

Street entertainer

Open-air theatre ranges from the free street entertainment that is to be found in many city centres, to student performances on the grounds of Cambridge or Oxford colleges or a production at Cornwall's spectacular clifftop amphitheatre, the Minack Theatre *(see p264)*. Every fourth year, York also stages a series of open-air medieval mystery plays called the York Cycle. Perhaps the liveliest theatrical tradition in Britain is the Edinburgh Festival *(see p495)*. Seaside resorts put on summer programmes of lighthearted entertainment, traditionally stand-up comedy.

Ticket availability varies from show to show. You may be able to buy a ticket at the door, especially for a mid-week matinee, but for the more popular West End shows tickets may have to be booked weeks or even months in advance. You can book through agencies and some travel agents, and most hotels will organize theatre tickets for you. Booking fees are often charged. Beware of tickets offered by touts *(see p67)* – these may be counterfeit. There are no age restrictions in Britain's theatres. It is left to your discretion to decide whether a show is suitable for children.

The Buxton Opera House, the Midlands

MUSIC

A DIVERSE musical repertoire can be found in a variety of venues. Church choral music is a great national tradition and many churches and cathedrals host concerts. London, Manchester, Birmingham, Liverpool, Bristol and Bournemouth all have their own excellent orchestras.

Rock, jazz, folk and country-and-western concerts are staged periodically in pubs, clubs and sometimes in outdoor auditoria. Wales has a strong musical tradition which you will come across in many Welsh pubs; northern England is renowned for its booming brass and silver bands; and Scotland, of course, has its famous bag-pipers *(see p466)*.

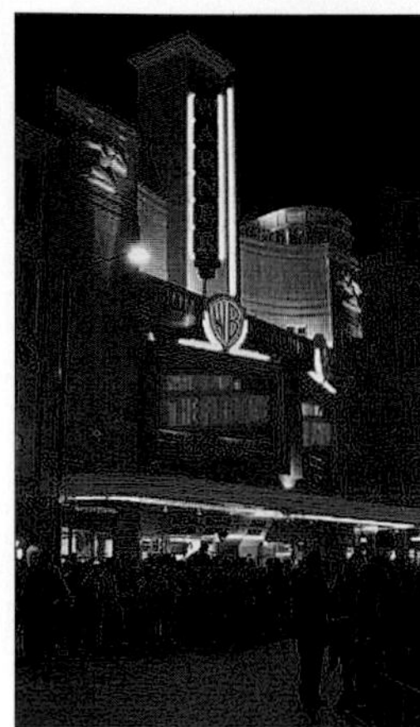

The multiplex Warner West End cinema, Leicester Square, London

Cinemas

THE LATEST FILMS can be seen in any large town. Check the local papers or the tourist office to find out what is on.

Cinemas are having a revival, with luxurious multi-screen cinemas taking over from the local, single-screen cinemas. In larger cities a more diverse range of films is often on offer including more foreign-language productions. These tend to be shown at arts or repertory cinemas. Mainstream English-speaking films are usually shown by the big chains. Age limits apply to certain films. Young children are allowed to see any feature film which is graded with a U (universal) or PG (parental guidance) certificate. Cinema prices vary widely; some are cheaper at off-peak times, such as Mondays or afternoons. For new releases it is advisable to book in advance.

Clubs

MOST CITIES have some sort of club scene, though London has the most famous venues *(see p129)*. These may feature live music, discos, or DJ or dance performances. Some insist on dress codes or members only, and most have doormen, or "bouncers". Apart from the major cities, Brighton and Bristol have lively clubs.

Dance

THIS COVERS a multitude of activities: everything from classical ballet and acid-house parties to traditional English Morris dancing or the Scottish Highland fling, which you may come upon in pubs and villages around the country.

Dance halls are rarer than they were, but ballroom dancing is alive and well. Other dance events you may find are ceilidhs (pronounced kay-lee), which is Celtic dancing and music; May Balls often held at universities (invitation only); dinner or tea dances and square dancing.

Birmingham is home to the Birmingham Royal Ballet and is the best place to see performances outside London. Avant-garde contemporary dance is also performed.

Gay

MOST LARGE communities will have some gay meeting places, mostly bars and clubs. You can find out about them from publications such as the free *Pink Paper* or *Gay Times* on sale in some newsagents, and in gay bars and clubs. London's gay life is centred around Soho *(see p82)* with its many European-style cafés and bars. Outside London, the most active gay scenes are in Manchester and Brighton. Gay Pride is the largest free outdoor festival in Europe.

Three revellers, Gay Pride Festival

Children

LONDON OFFERS children a positive goldmine of fun, excitement and adventure, though it can be expensive. From the traditional sights to something more unusual such as a discovery centre, London has a wide range of activities, many interactive, to interest children of all ages. The weekly magazine *Time Out* has details of children's events.

Outside London, activities for children range from nature trails to fun fairs. Your local tourist office or the local library will have information on things to do with children.

Pirate Ship, Chessington World of Adventures, Surrey

Theme Parks

THEME PARKS in Britain are enjoyed by children of all ages. Alton Towers has conventional rides plus a motor museum. Chessington World of Adventures is a huge complex south of London. Based on a zoo, it includes nine themed areas, such as Calamity Canyon and Circus World. Legoland, the latest park, opened in March 1996. Thorpe Park is a large watery theme park full of model buildings and a peaceful pet farm.

Alton Towers
Alton, Staffordshire.
0870 444 4455.
www.altontowers.com

Chessington World of Adventures
Leatherhead Rd, Chessington, Surrey.
08704 447777.
www.chessington.com

Legoland
Winkfield Rd, Windsor, Berkshire.
08705 040404.
www.legoland.co.uk

Thorpe Park
Staines Rd, Chertsey, Surrey.
08704 444466.
www.thorpepark.com

Specialist Holidays and Outdoor Activities

BRITAIN OFFERS MANY special interest holidays or courses where you can learn a new sport or skill, practise an activity you enjoy, or simply have fun and meet people. If you prefer less structured activities, there is a variety of sports you can participate in, from walking in Britain's national parks to sailing on the many waterways and skiing in Scotland, or exploring the country on horseback. Another option is volunteer work on a nature or bird reserve, or an archaeological dig or conservation project.

Horse riding on a country bridleway ***(see p33)***

Specialist Holidays

A GREAT ADVANTAGE to these holidays is that you can attend the courses alone but without feeling too solitary. There are hundreds of options: any kind of sport – boating, golf, skiing, riding, tennis; arts and crafts such as painting, pottery, calligraphy, jewellery-making; and educational courses on everything from Shakespeare to ecology.

The British Tourist Boards *(see p615)* have lists and pamphlets on some of these activities, and can tell you who to contact for more information. Look out for their publication, **Activity Holidays** (Jarrold), available from some bookshops.

You can book direct with the organizers, or through a travel agent. Introductory courses generally provide you with all the equipment you need plus accommodation and sometimes transport.

Courses are available at all levels of expertise, for all ages. If you are fit and interested in the countryside, you may like to work on a conservation project for a few days. It can be hard work but worthwhile. Contact the tourist board.

Walking and Cycling

WALKING ALLOWS YOU to experience at first hand the spectacular variety of the British landscape, by yourself or with a club. There is a network of long-distance footpaths and shorter trail routes all over Britain *(see pp32–3)*.

Cyclists may use designated cycle routes and bridleways *(see p643)* and the quieter rural roads can be a delight. Choose a flat or hilly one depending on your energy and fitness. Be sure to take spare parts with you.

Golf and Tennis

THERE ARE ABOUT 2,000 golf courses in Britain and many clubs welcome visiting players. Weekends are usually busy. Specialist operators will book packages for you. Green fees vary widely; many clubs offer temporary membership.

You will find tennis courts in every town and many hotels and some clubs offer temporary membership, but courts in summer are in demand. The **Lawn Tennis Association** can provide more information.

Sailing, Cardigan Bay, Welsh coast

Boating and Sailing

MESSING ABOUT IN BOATS is a British obsession. You can sail at many places – the Isle of Wight and the south coast are full of pleasure craft. Inland, the network of rivers, lakes and canals can offer a calmer sort of pleasure. Canal-cruising is very popular *(see p641)* and the Norfolk Broads *(see p186)* provides one of the best inland boating experiences (the **Broads Authority** will provide information). Elsewhere, the Thames and the canals slice through lovely landscape. The Lake District *(see pp342–57)* is another area which is popular with boating enthusiasts.

Other Water Sports

WITH SO MUCH coastline, Britain is a place for enjoying the water, even if temperatures are low. The best areas for surfing are the

Walkers and rock climbers, Yorkshire Dales National Park ***(see pp370–71)***

West Country and South Wales. Windsurfing is also popular, both on the coast and on lakes. Tuition and equipment hire are available at many resorts, and several also offer water-skiing facilities. Most towns and resorts have public swimming pools, many with water tunnels, slides and wave machines. Scuba diving is popular around rocky parts of the West Country.

Fishing

Fishing in the sea and on rivers is Britain's biggest participation sport. Regulations are very strict, so check for details of rod licences, close seasons and other restrictions at tourist offices or tackle shops. You may have to join a club, or buy a temporary permit. The best game fishing (salmon and trout) is in the West Country, the Northeast, Wales and Scotland.

Solitary sea fisherman, England's southeast coast

Spectator Sports

Football (soccer) is a passion for a large section of the population. League fixtures are held at many large towns once or twice a week in the season. If you want to see a game, ask at the local tourist office, or check the local papers. Rugby Football also has a good following and games are played in cities such as London, Cardiff and Edinburgh. Cricket is the English national game, and matches are played from April to September on village greens throughout the land. Both flat-racing and steeplechasing are very popular and betting is big business. You can find details of race meetings in most national newspapers.

Paragliding over the South Downs ***(see p169)***

Adventure Sports

Adventure sports are well-catered for and popular. Among the options are rock-climbing and mountaineering; aeronautical sports and gliding; ice-skating in many major cities and horse riding throughout the country. Although expensive, it is also possible to try go-karting. Facilities for skiing are limited in the UK but there are winter sports facilities at Scottish resorts such as the Cairngorms.

Directory

Aircraft Owners and Pilots Assoc.
☎ *020-7834 5631.*
W www.aopa.co.uk

Assoc. of Pleasure Craft Operators
☎ *01952 813572.* W www.canals.com/orgs/apco

Assoc. of British Riding Schools
38–40 Queen St, Penzance, Cornwall TR18. ☎ *01736 369440.* W www.abrs.org

British Activity Holiday Association
☎ *01932 252 994.*
W www.baha.org.uk

British Hang-Gliding and Paragliding Assoc.
The Old School Room, Loughborough Rd, Leicester LE4.
☎ *0870 8706490.*
W www.bhpa.co.uk

British Mountaineering Council
177–179 Burton Rd, Manchester M20.
☎ *08700 104878.*
W www.thebmc.co.uk

British Surfing Assoc.
Champions Yd, Penzance, Cornwall TR18.
☎ *01736 360250.*
W www.britsurf.co.uk

British Water Ski Federation
390 City Rd, London EC1V.
☎ *020-7833 2855.* W www.britishwaterski.co.uk

British Trust for Conservation Volunteers
36 St Mary's St, Wallingford, Oxon OX10 0EU. ☎ *01491 821600.*
W www.btcv.org

British Waterways
Willow Grange, Church Rd, Watford, Herts WD1. ☎ *01923 201120.* W www.britishwaterways.co.uk

Broads Authority
☎ *01603 610734.*
W www.broadsauthority.gov.uk

England & Wales Cricket Board
Lord's Cricket Ground, St John's Wood, NW8.
☎ *020-7432 1200.*
W www.ecb.co.uk

English Golf Union
☎ *01526 354500.* W www.englishgolfunion.org

Football Association
16 Lancaster Gate, London W2.
☎ *020-7262 4542.*
W www.thefa.com

Lawn Tennis Association
☎ *020-7381 7111.*
W www.lta.org.uk

National Federation of Anglers
☎ *01283 734735.*
W www.nfadirect.com

Environment Agency
☎ *01454 624411.*
W www.environment-agency.gov.uk

Outward Bound
☎ *08705 134227.* W www.outwardbound-uk.org

Racecourse Assoc.
Winkfield Rd, Ascot, Berks SL5. ☎ *01344 625912.*
W www.comeracing.com

Royal Yachting Assoc.
RYA Hse, Ensign Way, Hamble, Southampton, Hants SO31 4YA.
☎ *0845 345 0400.*
W www.rya.org.uk.

Rugby Football Union
Rugby Rd, Twickenham, Middx TW1.
☎ *020-8892 2000.*
W www.rfu.com

Ski Club of Great Britain
57–63 Church Rd, London SW19. ☎ *0845 458 0780.*
W www.skiclub.co.uk

Travel Information

As it is an international gateway for air and sea traffic, travelling to Britain poses few problems. By air, travellers have a very large choice of carriers serving North America, Australasia and Europe. Coach (bus) travel is a cheap, albeit rather slow, form of transport from Europe, while travelling by train has been transformed with the advent of the Channel Tunnel – three hours from Paris to London on Eurostar. Travelling within Britain itself is fairly easy. There is an extensive network of roads to all parts of the country and hiring a car is often the best way of travelling around. The rail network is efficient and the network to the smaller towns, especially around London, is good. Travelling by coach is the cheapest option; the coach network serves most areas but can be slow. If time is short, air travel is possible but expensive.

British Airways passenger jet

Passenger concourse, Waterloo Station, London

Travelling Around Britain

Choosing the best way to travel around Britain depends very much on where and when you want to go, although the quickest and most convenient methods are generally the most expensive.

Distances between any two points within mainland Britain are relatively small (at least by American or Australian standards) so air travel usually makes sense only between the extremes, such as London to Edinburgh. For shorter journeys, the time spent getting to and from airports often outweighs any savings in actual travelling time. Rail services are the best alternative if you want to visit Britain's major cities, though fares, especially at peak times, can be quite expensive. If you plan to do much travelling within Britain, a rail pass can be very good value. You can buy a pass before you arrive in the UK as several schemes cater for overseas visitors *(see p638)*.

Coach (bus) networks cover a wide number of UK destinations, and are cheaper than trains, but take longer and may be less comfortable *(see p640)*. Taxis are available at all main coach or rail stations to take you to your hotel; without a car you will avoid the stress of driving in city centres.

If you plan a more flexible touring holiday, hiring a car is more feasible than relying on public transport. Car rental can be arranged at major airports, large railway stations and city centre outlets *(see p637)*. To get the best deals, book from abroad. Small local firms often undercut the large operators in price, but may not be as reliable or convenient.

For detailed exploration of smaller areas such as Britain's National Parks or popular regions like the Lake District *(see pp342–57)* you may prefer more leisurely transportation offered by bike, horse or narrowboat. Sometimes there are picturesque local options like a rowing-boat ferry, such as the one between Southwold and Walberswick on the Blyth Estuary *(see p190)*. There are also larger car ferries which travel to Britain's islands.

Rowing-boat ferry on the River Blyth, Southwold, Suffolk

Channel Tunnel

This historic landlink between France and Britain opened for business in late 1994 and closed one of the "missing links" in the European transport system. The sleek new rolling-stock is high-tech and very comfortable, producing an experience more akin to air travel than rail. Passengers on buses and cars get onto a freight train run by **Eurotunnel** which takes 35 minutes to travel between Calais and Folkestone.

EURO TUNNEL

Eurotunnel logo

For those travelling by rail there are about 40 scheduled passenger-only **Eurostar** services, operated by the French, Belgian and British. They run direct services between Brussels, Lille, Paris, Frethun, Calais and London/Ashford. There are two passenger tunnels – and one service tunnel – which lie 25–45 m (82–147 ft) below the sea bed. All the tunnels are made of concrete and iron, and are 50 km (31 miles) long.

Arriving by Sea, Rail and Coach

If you are travelling from Europe by foot, car, coach (bus) or rail you will have to cross the English Channel or North Sea either by ferry or the Channel Tunnel. Ferry services operate from a huge number of ports on the European mainland and have good link-ups with international coaches, with services from most European cities to Britain. The Channel Tunnel has meant there is now a non-stop rail link between Europe and Britain. Prices between the ferries and the tunnel services remain competitive.

Ferry arriving at Dover

Ferry Services from Europe

A complex network of ferry services operate to over a dozen British ports, with around 20 car and passenger ferry services that travel regularly across the Channel and North Sea routes from many ports in northern and southern Europe *(see pp10–15)*.

Because of the number of areas they reach, ferries can be convenient and economical for those travelling in cars or on foot, depending on your destination. Fares vary greatly according to the season, time of travel and duration of stay. The shortest crossings are not always the cheapest: you pay for the speed of the journey.

Crossing Times

Crossing times vary from just over an hour on the shortest routes to a full 24 hours on services from Spain and Scandinavia. If you take an overnight sailing, you may have to pay extra for sleeping accommodation, but it is often worth booking a cabin on the longer trips to avoid feeling exhausted when you arrive. Fast **Seacat** (catamaran) services between Calais and Dover, Ostend and Dover, and Dieppe and Newhaven are run by **Hoverspeed**. These are the fastest routes across the Channel, taking just under an hour, and catamarans can carry vehicles. The crossings lack the dip and sway of a conventional ship, and so may be less painful for poor sailors.

Seaport Bureaucracy

Those visitors from outside the European Union should allow plenty of time for immigration control and customs clearance at British seaports *(see p619)*. You are not allowed to bring pets into Britain because of rabies.

International Coach Travel

Although coach (bus) travel is comparably cheaper than other methods of travel, it is not the most comfortable way of travelling across Europe. But if you have a lot of spare time and want to stop off en route it can be convenient. Once you have paid for your ticket you will not have to pay again to use the ferry or the Channel Tunnel.

A Eurostar train, which takes only three hours from Paris to London

International Rail Travel

With the advent of the Channel Tunnel, there is now access to Britain via **Eurostar** and **Eurotunnel** from the French and Belgian high-speed rail networks. Rail travel can be an efficient, comfortable and fast way of travelling across Europe to Britain – in France and Belgium, trains reach speeds of up to 186 mph (300 kmph). The cost is comparable to flying, although it is much more convenient.

Directory

Ferries, Rail and Coach Travel

Brittany Ferries
08705 360 360.
www.brittanyferries.com

European Rail Travel
08705 848 848 (for info).
www.raileurope.co.uk

Eurostar
08705 186186 (for foot & rail passengers).
www.eurostar.com

Eurotunnel/Le Shuttle
08705 353535 (for cars & coach travel).
www.eurotunnel.com

Hoverspeed/Seacat
08705 240241.
www.hoverspeed.com

International Coach Travel
020-7730 3466.

P&O Ferries
0870 6000600.
www.poferries.com

Arriving by Air

BRITAIN HAS ABOUT 130 licensed airports but only a handful of these are equipped for long-haul traffic. The largest is London's Heathrow, the world's busiest international airport and one of Europe's central routing points for international air travel. It is served by most of the world's leading airlines with direct flights from nearly all the major cities. The other major international airports include Gatwick, Stansted, Manchester, Glasgow, Newcastle, Birmingham and Edinburgh. Smaller airports such as London City, Bristol, Norwich and Cardiff have daily flights to European destinations.

A British Airways 747 jet at Heathrow Airport

BRITISH AIRPORTS

THE MAJORITY of Britain's largest and best known airports are run by the British Airports Authority – the rest are owned by a local authority or are in private hands. All BAA airports offer up-to-date facilities, including 24-hour banking, shops, cafés, hotels and restaurants. Security is strict at all British airports and it is important never to leave baggage unattended.

If you are starting your visit in London, flights to Gatwick, Heathrow or Stansted are equally convenient. But if you plan to visit northern England, there are an increasing number of flights going to Birmingham, Newcastle and Manchester, while for Scotland you can fly to Glasgow or Edinburgh.

Heathrow has four terminals and some others have two. Before you fly, check with the airport from which terminal your flight leaves.

During severe weather conditions in the winter months, your flight may be diverted to another airport. If this happens, the airline will organize transportation back to your original destination.

British Airways has flights to nearly all the world's important destinations. Other British international airlines include **Virgin Atlantic**, with routes to the USA and the Far East, and **British Midland**, which flies to Western Europe.

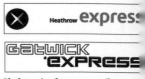

Platform sign for express railway service to London

The main American airlines offering scheduled services to Britain include **Delta**, **US Air** and **American Airlines**. From Canada, the main carrier is **Air Canada**. From Australasia, the national carriers **Qantas** and **Air New Zealand** vie with many Far Eastern rivals.

Britain imposes an airport tax on all departing passengers – currently £10 for domestic and EC routes, and £20 for non-EC and long-haul flights.

TRANSPORT FROM THE AIRPORT

BRITAIN'S INTERNATIONAL airports lie some way from city centres, but transport to

Arrival terminal at Heathrow Airport

AIRPORT	INFORMATION	DISTANCE TO CITY CENTRE	TAXI FARE TO CITY CENTRE	PUBLIC TRANSPORT TO CITY CENTRE
Heathrow	08700 000123	14 miles (23 km)	£40–45	Rail: 15 min Tube: 45 min
Gatwick	08700 002468	28 miles (45 km)	£75	Rail: 30 min Bus: 70 min
Stansted	08700 000303	37 miles (60 km)	£80	Rail: 45 min Bus: 75 min
Manchester	0161 4893000	10 miles (16 km)	£15–16	Rail: 15 min Bus: 30 min
Birmingham	0870 733 5511	8 miles (13 km)	£12–15	Bus: 30 min
Newcastle	0191 2860966	5 miles (8 km)	£10–12	Metro: 20 min Bus: 20 min
Glasgow	0141 8871111	8 miles (13 km)	£12–15	Bus: 20 min
Edinburgh	0131 3331000	8 miles (13 km)	£17–18	Bus: 25 min

and from them is efficient. Every airport has taxis and these are the most convenient form of door-to-door travel, but they are also expensive and can be slow if there is traffic congestion – very likely if you travel in the rush hour *(see p636)*. This can also be a problem with taking a coach or bus, although they are a lot cheaper than taxis.

Heathrow and Newcastle are both linked to the centre of the city by the Underground *(see p643)*. These are efficient, quick and cheap. Manchester, Stansted, Gatwick and Heathrow *(see p638)* have regular express trains which are not too expensive and are a reliable method for travelling into the heart of the city.

National Express Coaches *(see p640)* provide direct connections from major airports to many British destinations. They have a regular service between Gatwick and Heathrow.

CHOOSING A TICKET

FINDING THE RIGHT FLIGHT at the right price can be difficult. Promotional fares do come up and it is always worth checking with the airlines direct. Cheap deals are often available from package operators and are advertised in newspapers and travel magazines. Students and under 26s, senior citizens and regular or business travellers may be able to obtain a discount through student travel agencies. Children and babies also travel at cheaper rates.

The bar at the popular Posthouse Heathrow hotel

AIR FARES

FARES TO BRITAIN are usually seasonal, the highest being from June to September. The best deals are available from November to April, excluding the Christmas period – if you want to travel then, be sure to book well in advance.

APEX (Advance Purchase Excursion) fares are often the best value, though they must be booked up to a month ahead, and are subject to restrictions. Charter flights offer even cheaper seats, but are not usually flexible.

If you choose a discount fare, always buy from a reputable operator, and do not part with cash until you have seen your ticket and ensured your seat has been confirmed.

Packages may be worth considering, even if you enjoy independent travel, as sometimes car rental or rail travel is included. This can be cheaper than arranging it yourself when you have arrived in Britain.

Award-winning exterior of Stansted Airport

TRAVELLING WITHIN BRITAIN BY AIR

Britain's size means that internal air travel only makes sense over longish distances, where it can save a great deal of time – for example, London to Scotland, or to one of the many offshore islands. Air fares can be expensive, but if you book well ahead, fares can be up to three times cheaper than if you just turn up at the airport – although you are still always guaranteed a seat. The British Airways shuttle flights that operate between London and cities such as Glasgow, Edinburgh and Manchester are extremely popular with business travellers. At peak times of the day, flights leave every hour, while at other times there is usually a flight every two hours. Bad weather can cause delays or diversions during the winter months. Even on domestic flights, security is stringent, and you should never leave your bags unattended.

DIRECTORY

AIRLINE NUMBERS

Air Canada
08705 247226.

Air New Zealand
020-8741 2299.

American Airlines
08457 789789.

British Airways
08457 733377.

British Midland
020-8745 7321.

Continental Airlines
0800 776464.

Delta Airlines
0800 414767.

Qantas
020-8846 0321.

US Airways
08456 003300.

Virgin Atlantic
01293 747747.

Travelling Around by Car

THE MOST STARTLING difference for most foreign motorists is that in Britain you drive on the left, with corresponding adjustments at roundabouts and junctions. Distances are measured in miles. Once you adapt, rural Britain is an enjoyable place to drive, though traffic density in towns and at busy holiday times can cause long delays – public holiday weekends near the south coast can be particularly horrendous. An extensive network of toll-free motorways and trunk roads has now cut travelling time to most parts of the country.

What you Need

TO DRIVE IN BRITAIN you need a current driving licence with an international driving permit if required. In any vehicle you drive you must carry proof of ownership or a rental agreement, plus any insurance documents.

Roads in Britain

PEAK RUSH-HOUR traffic can last from 8–9:30am and 5–6:30pm on weekdays in the cities; at these times traffic can grind to a halt. In the country a good touring map is essential; the AA or RAC motoring atlases are fairly straightforward to use. For exploration of more rural areas, the Ordnance Survey series is the best. On all road maps B roads are secondary roads and A roads, often dual carriageways (two lanes in each direction), are main routes. B routes are often less congested and more enjoyable to use. Rural areas are crisscrossed by a web of tiny lanes. Motorways are marked with M followed by their identifying number.

The A30 dual carriageway going through Cornwall

Road Signs

SIGNS are now generally standardized in line with Europe. Directional signs are colour-coded: blue for motorways, green for major routes and white for minor routes. Signposting in Britain is not consistent and city suburbs can be confusing. Brown signs indicate places of interest. Advisory or warning signs are usually triangles in red and white, with easy to understand pictograms. Watch for electronic notices on motorways that warn of road works, accidents or patches of fog. Level crossings, found at rail lines, often have automatic barriers. If the lights are flashing red it means a train is coming and you must stop. The *UK Highway Code Manual* – available from most bookshops – is an up-to-date guide to all the current British driving regulations and traffic signs.

A motorway sign in miles

Rules of the Road

SPEED LIMITS are 30–40 mph (50–65 kmph) in built-up areas and 70 mph (110 kmph) on motorways or dual carriageways – look out for speed signs on other roads. It is compulsory to wear seat-belts in Britain. Drink-driving penalties are severe – see the *UK Highway Code Manual* for legal limits.

No stopping

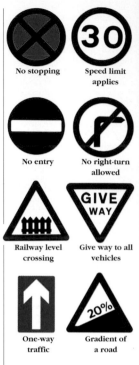

Speed limit applies

No entry

No right-turn allowed

Railway level crossing

Give way to all vehicles

One-way traffic

Gradient of a road

Parking

THIS IS THE BANE of the British motorist's life. Parking meters operate during working hours (usually 8am–6:30pm Mon–Sat); keep a supply of coins for them. Some cities have "park and ride" schemes, where you can take a bus from an out-of-city car park into the centre. Other towns have parking schemes where you buy a card at the tourist office or newsagents, fill in your parking times and display the card. Avoid double yellow lines at all times; single lines sometimes mean you can park in the evenings and at weekends, but check carefully. Traffic wardens will not hesitate to ticket, clamp or tow your car away. If in any doubt, find a car park *(see pp642–3)*. Outside urban areas and popular tourist zones, parking is easier. Look out for signs with a blue P, indicating parking spaces. Never leave any valuables or luggage in your car: thefts are common, especially in cities.

Sign for a car park

Petrol

North American visitors may find fuel (gas) very expensive in Britain. Large supermarkets often have the cheapest petrol; look out for branches of Tesco or Sainsbury with petrol stations. Motorway service areas are generally more expensive. Petrol is sold in three grades: diesel, LRP (lead replacement petrol) and unleaded. Most modern cars in Britain use unleaded petrol – any vehicle you hire will probably do so. Unleaded and diesel are cheaper than LRP. Most petrol stations in Britain are self-service but instructions at pumps are easy to follow.

Breakdown Services

Britain's major motoring organizations, the **AA** (Automobile Association) and the **RAC** (Royal Automobile Club), provide a comprehensive 24-hour breakdown service for members, as well as many other motoring services. Both offer reciprocal assistance for members of overseas motoring organizations – before arrival check with your own group to see if you are covered. You can contact the AA or RAC from the roadside SOS phones found on motorways. **Green Flag** is the other major rescue service in Britain, which can sometimes be quicker and cheaper since it makes greater use of local garages.

Most car hire agencies have their own cover, and their charges include membership of either the AA, the RAC or Green Flag while you are driving. Be sure to ask the rental company for the service's emergency number.

Even if you are not a member of an affiliated organization you can still call out a rescue service, although it will be expensive. Always follow the advice given on your insurance policy or rental agreement. If you have an accident that involves injury or another vehicle, call the police as soon as possible *(see p621)*.

A small rural petrol station in Goathland, North Yorkshire

Car Hire

Hiring a car in Britain can be expensive. One of the most competitive national companies is **Autos Abroad**, but small local firms may undercut even these rates. Many companies prefer you to leave a credit card number; otherwise you may have to part with a substantial cash deposit. You need your driving licence and a passport when you hire. Most companies will not hire to novice drivers, and set age limits (usually 21–74). Automatic cars are now generally available for hire. If you are touring Britain for three weeks or more, you may find a leasing arrangement cheaper than hiring. Remember to add VAT and insurance costs when you check hire rates.

Hitchhiking

Hitchhiking is a common practice in Britain, and you are likely to thumb a long-distance lift if you stand near a busy exit road junction. In rural or walking areas like the Lake District, tired hikers may well be offered a lift. It is illegal to hitch on motorways or their approach roads. As anywhere, there is a risk in hitchhiking alone, especially for a woman. Lift-sharing is now a common practice. The small-ads magazine *Loot* (sold in newsagents in London, Manchester and Bristol) has a large section for lift-seekers.

Directory

Breakdown

AA
📞 *0800 887 766.*

Green Flag
📞 *0800 400 600.*

RAC
📞 *0800 828 282.*

Car Hire

Autos Abroad
📞 *020-7287 6000.*
W www.autosabroad.com

Avis
📞 *08705 900 500.*
W www.avis.co.uk

Budget
📞 *0800 181 181.*
W www.budget.com

Europcar
📞 *08457 222 525.*
W www.europcar.co.uk

Hertz
📞 *08708 448 844.*
W www.hertz.co.uk

National Car Rentals
📞 *08705 365 365.*
W www.nationalcar.co.uk

General Information

AA Road Watch
📞 *09003 401 100.*

AA Disabled Line
📞 *0800 262 050.*

Emergency Calls
📞 *999.*

Weathercall
📞 *08706 004 242.*

Travelling Around by Rail

BRITAIN HAS a privatized rail network which covers the whole of the country. It is divided into regional sections which serve over 2,500 stations throughout Britain. The system is generally efficient and reliable with quiet, modernized rolling stock, particularly on the mainline services. Travelling across the country, rather than out of London, may involve a number of changes as most lines radiate from London, which has seven major terminals. There is now a rail link with Continental Europe on Eurostar, from Waterloo rail terminal in London *(see p632)*.

Mainline train speeding through countryside

Tickets

LARGE TRAVEL AGENTS and all railway stations sell rail tickets. First-class tickets cost about one-third more than standard fares, and generally return fares are cheaper than two singles.

Allow plenty of time to buy your ticket and always ask about any special offers or reduced fares. There are four types of discounted fares for adults. Apex tickets are available in limited numbers on some long-distance routes and have to be booked at least a week in advance. SuperApex fares have to be purchased 14 days in advance and again are available in limited numbers on a few mainline services. Savers can be used at weekends and on most weekday trains outside rush hours. Finally, Supersavers cannot be used on Fridays, or any peak-hour service to, from or through London.

Ticket offices in rural areas may close at weekends, but small branch lines have a conductor on board who sells tickets. Otherwise buy a ticket beforehand as inspectors can levy on-the-spot fines if you do not have a valid ticket. Many stations have automatic ticket machines.

Rail Passes

IF YOU PLAN to do much train travelling around Britain, buy a rail pass. These can be bought from many agents abroad, such as **Rail Europe** or **CIE Tours International**. An All Line Rail Rover gives adults unlimited travel throughout England, Scotland and Wales for 7 or 14 days. Children under 16 travel half price, or a Family Rail Card is available. It can be used for up to four adults and four children. Discounts are also available for 16- to 25-year-olds or full-time students attending a UK educational establishment with a Young Person's Rail Card. For those over the age of 60, the Senior Rail Card entitles you to a one-third price discount on most fares. There are special passes for London transport and a pass that covers London, Oxford, Canterbury and Brighton. Children of 5–15 years pay half fare; the under-5s travel free. Family tickets are also available. Disabled travellers qualify for many discounts. Keep a passport-sized photo handy for buying passes. If you have a pass, make sure you always show it when you buy a ticket.

General Tips

BRITAIN'S FASTEST and most comfortable trains are those on the mainline routes. These are very popular services and get booked up quickly. It is always advisable to reserve your seat in advance, especially if you want to travel at peak times such as Friday evenings. Mainline trains have dining cars, air-conditioning and are fast, travelling to Edinburgh from London, for example, in just over four hours.

For those arriving at Heathrow Airport and travelling into London *(see pp634–5)*, an alternative to the Underground *(see p643)* is the fast train to Paddington Station. Unlike the tube service, this operates 24 hours a day. Trains run frequently from 9am until midnight and then every hour between midnight and 5.30am, and every half hour thereafter until 9am.

Rail terminal, Liverpool Street Station

Porters are rare on British stations, although trolleys are often available for passengers to help themselves. If you are disabled and need help, call to book assistance at least 24 hours before your journey. A yellow line above a train window indicates a first class compartment. You cannot use these without paying the full fare, even if the train is full. Check which section of the train to join as they sometimes split through the journey and proceed to different destinations. Trains stop for only a minute at each station, so be ready to get on and off. Some stations are a little way from town centres, but are well signposted and nearly always on a bus route. Sunday trains and public holiday services are often a lot slower than normal.

Scenic Train Rides

As motor transport made many rural railways redundant in the mid-20th century, picturesque sections of track, as well as many old steam engines, were rescued and restored to working order by enthusiasts. These services are often privately run: the local tourist office, railway station ticket office or travel agents will provide you with information. Most of the lines are short – around 20 miles (32 km) – but cover some of the prettiest parts of the country and are one of the best ways to enjoy its spectacular scenery. Lines include: the Ffestiniog Railway *(see pp438–9)* in North Wales; the North York Moors Railway *(see p380)*; the Strathspey Steam Railway in the Cairngorm Mountains of the Scottish Highlands *(see p530)* and the La'l Ratty Railway in Cumbria *(see p352)*.

A reconditioned steam train, North Yorkshire

National Rail Network

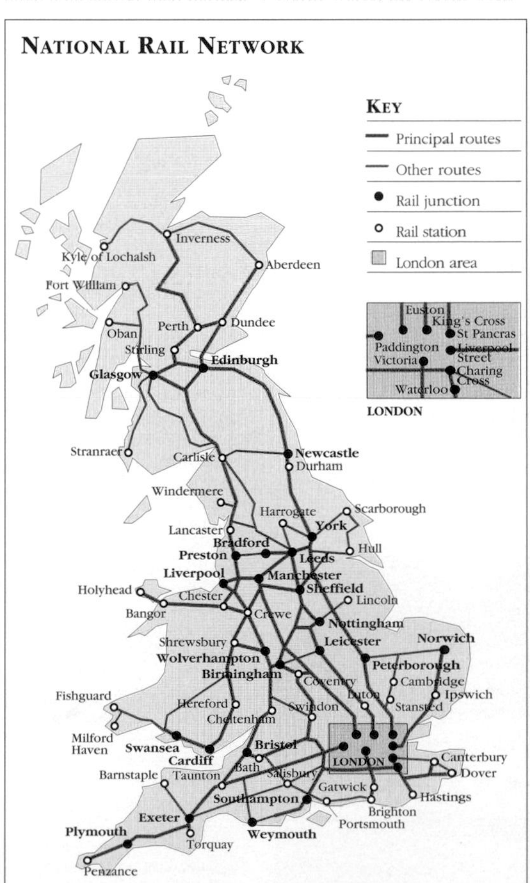

Directory

UK Rail Numbers

Disabled Travel
0845 744 3366 (call 24 hrs before journey to book help).

First North Eastern Railways
08459 505000 (bookings).

Great Western Trains
08457 000125 (bookings).

Lost Property
020-7387 8699 (Euston) or contact train company.

Midland Mainline
08457 221125 (bookings).

National Rail Enquiries Timetables
08457 484950.
www.nationalrail.co.uk

Rail Europe
08705 848848 (London).
www.raileurope.co.uk

Virgin Trains
08457 222333 (bookings).

Overseas Rail Numbers

CIE Tours International
(201) 292-3438 or (212) 319 0561 (United States); (800) 243 8687 (Canada).

Rail Europe
(914) 682-2999 (United States); (800) 848-7245 (Canada).

Travelling around by Coach

In Britain, coaches refer to the long-distance express buses and those used for sightseeing excursions. What the British refer to as buses, however, covers those vehicles that operate on regular routes with scheduled stops around or between villages, towns and cities. Many coach services duplicate rail routes, but are generally cheaper. Journey times, however, are longer and much less predictable on crowded roads. Modern coaches are comfortable, sometimes with refreshments and toilets on board. Some city to city routes, especially at weekends, are so popular that it is a good idea to buy a reserved journey ticket, which guarantees you a seat.

National Coach Network

There are a lot of regional coach companies, but by far the largest British coach operator is **National Express** with a nationwide network of over 1,200 destinations *(see pp12–15)*. On the more popular routes – particularly on Friday evenings – it is best to book ahead.

Discounts are available for full-time students or anyone under 25. Anyone aged 50 or over can also qualify for a discount coach card, saving up to 30 per cent on many fares. Britexpass cards lasting 30 days and Tourist Trail Passes are also available for those planning to cover many destinations in a limited period. You can buy these from most coach travel agents in North America – via **British Travel Associates** – or while in the UK, at the major international airports, **Victoria Coach Station** and most large travel agents. The **Oxford Tube** runs between Oxford and London, and is a frequent, wheelchair-friendly coach service. **Scottish Citylink** is a major operator running regular services between London, the North and Scotland. Some services run direct from Heathrow, Gatwick and Stansted airports. Allow plenty of time to buy your ticket before boarding. Luggage is stowed in the vehicle hold.

British Travel Associates
800 327 6097 (in North America).

National Express
08705 808080.
www.gobycoach.com

Oxford Tube
01865 772250.
www.stagecoach-oxford.co.uk

Scottish Citylink
08705 505050.
www.citylink.co.uk

Victoria Coach Station
020-7730 3466.
www.victoriacoachstation.com

A National Express coach

A coach tour, the Royal Mile, Edinburgh

Coach Tours

Dozens of coach tours are available in the UK, for all interests, age groups and destinations. Some include a tour guide. They may last anything from a couple of hours to two weeks or more, touring coast or countryside and visiting places of interest. Some are highly structured, organizing every last photo opportunity or cup of tea; others leave you to sightsee or shop at your own pace. You can opt for a prearranged route, or commission your own itinerary for a group.

Coach tours are popular, but may leave you feeling somewhat herded. Groups always travel at the pace of their slowest member, which can mean a lot of waiting. But at the same time all the stress of organizing a similar trip for yourself is taken away. Some coach operators will pick up passengers from their hotels and then drop them back.

Any large town will have a selection of coach companies. Check the local *Yellow Pages (see p622)*, or ask your hotel or the local tourist office. You can also book coach trips direct from overseas through a specialist travel agent.

Seaside resorts and tourist sites are destinations for many day trips, especially in high season. In some of the more popular rural areas, such as the Lake District, special small buses operate for ease of movement. You can book these in advance, or just turn up before the coach leaves, although the tour is likely to be fully booked, especially in high season. The local tourist information point or travel agent will be able to tell you where these trips leave from, the cost and may even sell you tickets. It is customary to tip the guide after your tour.

Regional Buses

Regional bus services are run by a large number of companies, some private and some operated by local authorities. Less economic services to remote rural areas tend to be sporadic and expensive, with some buses running just once a week and many isolated villages having no service at all. Only a few rural buses are equipped for wheelchairs.

As a general rule, you can assume that the further you get from a city, the fewer the buses and the more expensive the fare. It is therefore unwise to rely on local buses for transport, and if you want to see a lot of the country, renting a car is a better option. But if you do have the time, local buses can be a pleasant and often sociable way of travelling around Britain's lovely countryside.

Most buses run with just one operator – the driver. All drivers prefer you to have the correct fare, so always have a selection of low denomination coins handy. Some routes do not operate on Sundays and public holidays, and those that do are much reduced.

Always check your routes, schedules and fares at the local tourist office or bus station before you depart on a bus. This will prevent your being stranded somewhere with no return transport.

The Postbus provides transport in remote parts of the Highlands

Travelling Britain's Coasts and Waterways

Britain has thousands of miles of inland waterways and hundreds of islands scattered along its coastline. Cruising along a canal in the beautiful Midlands countryside or travelling on one of the small local ferries to a remote Scottish island are both wonderful experiences. Canal boats can be hired and scores of ferries run between Britain's offshore islands.

A barge on the Welsh Backs, Bristol, Avon

Canals

As industrial production grew in the 18th century, it became vital to find a cheap and effective way of transporting heavy loads. Canals fulfilled this need and a huge network was built, linking most industrial areas in the north and sea ports.

The arrival of the railways and their immediate success for freight made most canals redundant, but there are still some 3,200 km (2,000 miles) left, most in the old industrial heartland of the Midlands.

Today these canals lure the travellers who are content to cruise on old-fashioned, slow narrowboats, taking their time to enjoy the views and the canalside inns, originally built to satisfy the bargees' thirsts and to supply stabling for the barge horses. These canal holidays can be very relaxing if you have the time.

If you wish to hire a narrowboat, you can book with a specialist travel firm or contact **British Waterways**.

British Waterways
01442 235400.
www.britishwaterways.co.uk

Local Ferries

Britain's local ferries can offer anything from a ten-minute river journey to a seven-hour sea cruise.

Many of Scotland's ferries are operated by **Caledonian MacBrayne**. They sail to lots of different destinations, such as the Isle of Skye to the Kyle of Lochalsh, or the five-hour journey from Oban to Lochboisdale in the Western Isles. They offer a variety of different ticket types, from unlimited rover tickets for a specific period of time, to island-hop passes or all-inclusive coach tour and ferry tickets. Not all the island ferries take cars.

A car ferry travelling from Oban to Lochboisdale

River ferries make an interesting alternative to the more usual forms of transport. The ferry across the Mersey, between the cities of Liverpool and Birkenhead, is still used by many commuters. London's river trips, such as the one that runs from Westminster to Tower Bridge *(see p75)*, offer a different perspective on the city and make a change from tubes, buses and cars. Local tourist information centres can give you information about ferries in their area.

Caledonian MacBrayne
01475 650100.
www.calmac.co.uk

Travelling within Cities

URBAN PUBLIC TRANSPORT in Britain is efficient and can be fun – children love London's double-decker buses. Fares are good value, bearing in mind that you avoid the expense and difficulty of parking a car. Most of the larger cities have good bus services. London, Newcastle and Glasgow also have an underground system, while Manchester and Blackpool have trams. Taxis are available at every railway station and at ranks near hotels and city centres. The best way to see many cities is on foot, but whatever transport you choose, try to avoid the rush hours from 8am to 9:30am, and 4:30pm to 6:30pm.

Local buses travelling along Princes Street, Edinburgh

Local Buses

THE DEREGULATION of bus services has led to a complex system with many buses often duplicating services on the busiest routes. On most buses you pay the driver as you enter. They will not always accept notes so keep a selection of coins handy. Credit cards and cheques are not accepted. The fare depends on the distance you travel. If you are exploring a city by bus, a daily pass is a good idea. Many of the larger cities have daily or weekly passes that can be used on all public transport in that city; these can often be bought from newsagents. Check with the tourist office for schedules and fares. All-night services are only available in major cities, from about 11pm until early morning. You cannot use a day pass on these. In London night buses are prefixed with the letter N and all of them pass through Trafalgar Square.

A London double-decker bus

Be on your guard when travelling home alone late at night, when there may be few other passengers aboard.

Bus designs have become more innovative in the last few years. The old "big red bus" with a conductor still exists in London, but has been joined by a plethora of modern vehicles of all shapes, colours and sizes, with automatic doors and comfortable interiors. Many are small single-deckers, able to weave in and out of traffic more easily.

Many cities have bus lanes, intended to bypass car traffic jams during the rush hours. These can be effective but your journey could still take a long time. Schedules are hard to keep to, so regard timetables as advisory. At some stops, called request stops, the driver will not halt unless you signal that you want to get on or off. If you want to board, raise your arm as the bus approaches the stop; if you want to get off, ring the bell once before your stop.

Destinations are shown on the front of buses. If you are not sure which stop you need, ask the driver or conductor to alert you and stay on the lower deck. Always keep your ticket until the end of the journey in case an inspector boards, who can impose an on-the-spot fine if you are without a valid ticket. Stops can often be quite a long distance apart.

Driving in Cities

DRIVING IN CITY CENTRES is being increasingly discouraged, most notably in London with the introduction of the congestion charge in spring 2003. If you drive or park within the congestion zone covering central London from Monday to Friday, 7am to 6:30pm, you will need to pay a £5 fee before 10pm that day at a newsagent, petrol station or Post Office. Not paying the charge will lead to a large fine. Go to www.cclondon.com for more information. Other cities are considering similar steps to keep drivers out of the centres.

A traditional parking meter

Parking in city centres is also strictly controlled to prevent congestion *(see p636)*.

Taxis

IN LARGE TOWNS there are plenty of taxis to be found at taxi ranks and train stations. Some operate by radio so you have to phone. The local *Yellow Pages (see p622)*, pubs, restaurants and hotels will all have a list of taxi numbers. Prices are usually controlled. Always ask the price before you start your journey if there is no taxi meter. If you are not sure of the correct fare ask the local tourist information point.

Licensed taxi drivers undergo strict tests and all licensed cabs must carry a "For Hire" sign, which is lit up whenever they are free. Care is needed if you use unlicensed minicabs – some may be mechanically

An illegally parked car immobilized by a wheel clamp

unsound or even uninsured. Do not accept an unbooked minicab ride in the street. The famous London black cabs are almost as much of an institution as the big red bus. These are the safest cabs to use in London as all the drivers are licensed. They also know where they are going. Even these are changing, however, and you will see cabs of many colours, many covered with advertising. The newer cab designs are equipped to carry wheelchairs. If a cab stops for you in London, it must by law take you anywhere within a radius of 6 miles (10 km) so long as it is within the Metropolitan Police District. This includes most of London and Heathrow Airport.

One of London's black cabs

All licensed cabs have meters that start ticking as soon as the driver accepts your custom. The fare will increase minute by minute or for each 311 m (1,020 ft) travelled. Surcharges are added for each piece of luggage, each extra passenger or unsocial hours. Most drivers expect a tip of between 10 and 15 per cent of the fare. If you have a complaint, note the serial number found in the back of the cab.

Guided Bus Tours

In most major tourist cities, sightseeing bus tours are available. Weather permitting, a good way to see the cities is from a traditional open-topped double-decker bus. Private tours can be arranged with many companies. Contact the tourist information centre.

Trams

After a long absence (apart from a few nostalgic remnants in Blackpool), trams are making a comeback in clean, energy efficient and more modern guises. One of the best tram schemes in Britain is Manchester's Metrolink.

London Underground

The underground in London, known as the tube, is one of the largest systems of its kind in the world. It has over 270 stations, including the Docklands Light Railway (DLR), each of which are marked with the London Underground logo. The only other cities with an underground system are Glasgow and Newcastle, but both are small. London tube trains run every day, except Christmas Day, from about 5:30am until just after midnight. Fewer trains run on Sundays.

The 11 tube lines are colour-coded and maps called *Journey Planners* are posted at every station, while maps of the central section are displayed in each train. Most tube journeys between central destinations in London can be completed with only one or two changes of train. Smoking is not permitted on the Underground.

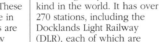

A London Underground sign outside a station

Newcastle's tube system is limited to the city centre but Glasgow's skirts around the centre. Both are clean and efficient, running the same hours as London's.

A tram along Blackpool's famous promenade

Walking in Cities

Once you get used to traffic on the left, Britain's cities can be safely and enjoyably explored on foot.

There are two types of pedestrian crossing: striped zebra crossings and push-button crossings at traffic lights. At a zebra crossing traffic should stop for you, but at push-button crossings cars will not stop until the lights change in your favour. Look for instructions written on the road; these will tell you from which direction you can expect the traffic to come. More and more cities and towns are creating traffic-free zones in the city centre for pedestrians.

Cycling under the Bridge of Sighs, Oxford

Cycling

Cycling is a popular pastime in Britain. Even in the smallest town there is often somewhere you can hire bikes. Whether you cycle in towns or the countryside, a helmet is recommended. Cyclists may not use motorways or their approach roads, nor can they ride on pavements, footpaths or pedestrianized zones. Many city roads have cycle lanes and their own traffic lights. You can take a bike on most trains (phone to check). Never leave your bike unlocked.

General Index

Page numbers in **bold** type refer to main entries

A

A La Ronde 277
AA 637
AA Disabled Line 637
AA Road Watch 637
Abberley, restaurants 591
Abbeys and priories
  Abbey Dore 304
  Anglesey Abbey **196**
  Bath Abbey 248
  Beaulieu Abbey 156
  Bolton Priory 372
  Buckfast Abbey 279, 283
  Buckland Abbey **280**
  Bury St Edmunds Abbey 194
  Byland Abbey **378**
  Cartmel Priory 357
  Castle Acre Priory 183
  Christchurch Priory 259
  Dryburgh Abbey 489
  Easby Abbey 339
  Fountains Abbey 335, **376–7**
  Furness Abbey **356**, 357
  Glastonbury Abbey 241
  Hartland Abbey 274
  Hexham Abbey **408**, 409
  Inchmahome Priory 481
  Jedburgh Abbey 489
  Kelso Abbey 489
  Kirkham Priory 339
  Kirkstall Abbey 339
  Lanercost Priory 346
  Lindisfarne Priory 404, 405
  Llanthony Priory 447, 455
  Melrose Abbey 489, **498**
  Mount Grace Priory 338, **380**
  North Country **338–9**
  Rievaulx Abbey **379**
  Rosedale Abbey 381
  St Mary's Abbey (York) 338–9, 394
  St Nicholas Priory (Exeter) 277
  Strata Florida Abbey 453
  Tintern Abbey **461**
  Torre Abbey 278
  Westminster Abbey (London) 73, 90, **94–5**
  Whalley Abbey 359
  Whitby Abbey 382
  Woburn Abbey **218**
Abbotsbury 28, **256**
  hotels 551
  pubs 609
Abbotsford House **498**
Aberaeron **449**
  restaurants 602
Aberconwy & Colwyn *see* North Wales
Aberdeen **524–6**
  hotels 571
  map 525
  restaurants 606
Aberdeenshire *see* Highlands and Islands
Aberdour, hotels 568
Aberdyfi **441**
  hotels 564
  restaurants 601
Abersoch
  hotels 564
  restaurants 601
Aberystwyth **448–9**
  hotels 566
  pubs 611
Achiltibuie, hotels 571
Achray, Loch 467
Act of Union (1535) 50
Act of Union (1707) 53, 466, 497
Adam, James 24
Adam, John 495
Adam, Robert 21, 55, 194
  Audley End 196
  Bowood House 243
  Culzean Castle 464, 508–9
  Georgian House (Edinburgh) 490
  Harewood House 396
  Kedleston Hall 24–5
  Kenwood House (London) 132
  portrait of 508
  Pulteney Bridge (Bath) 247
  Saltram House 280
  Syon House (London) 134
Adam, William 488, 489, 500, 534
Adelphi Theatre (London) 127
Admission charges 616–17
The Adoration of the Kings (Brueghel) 84
The Adoration of the Magi (Rubens) 201
Adventure sports 631
Afternoon tea 575, 577
  Devonshire cream teas 275
Agincourt, Battle of (1415) 49
Agricola, Julius 44, 360, 468
Aidan, St 46, 401, 404, 405
Air Canada 635
Air New Zealand 635
Air travel 632, **634–5**
Aircraft Owners and Pilots Association 631
Aislabie, John 376
Aislabie, William 376, 377
Alban, St 45, 221
Albany, Robert, Duke of 484
Albert, Prince Consort
  Albert Memorial (London) 99
  Balmoral 526
  Great Exhibition 57, 97, 98
  Osborne House 150, 156
  Victoria and Albert Museum (London) 100
  Windsor Castle 224
Albert Memorial (London)
  Street-by-Street map 99
Albery Theatre (London) 127
Alciston, pubs 608
Alcohol, in restaurants 576
Alcoholics Anonymous 621
Aldeburgh **190–91**
  festivals 63, 64, **191**
  hotels 547
  restaurants 584
Alderminster, pubs 609
Aldrich, Henry 214
Aldwych Theatre (London) 127
Alexandria, restaurants 606
Alfred the Great, King 47, 209, 235, 256
Alfriston 168
  pubs 608
All England Lawn Tennis Club (London) 129
All Souls College (Oxford) 49
All Souls, Langham Place (London) 107
Allendale, North Pennines tour 413
Allendale Baal Festival 65
Alloway, hotels 568
Alnwick Castle 334, **406**
Altarnun 273
Althorp House 331
Alton Towers 629
Alwinton 407
Alyth, restaurants 606
The Ambassadors (Holbein) 85
Amberley, restaurants 582
Ambleside 353, **354–5**
  hotels 559
  restaurants 595
Ambulances 621
American Airlines 635
American Express 624
American Revolution 54
Amigoni, Jacopo 202
Ampleforth, hotels 562
Anderson, Andrew 524
Anglesey 427, 428, 430
  restaurants 601
Anglesey Abbey **196**
Anglo-Saxons 39, **46–7**
Angus 511
Anne of Cleves 168
Anne, Queen 41, 54
  Bath 248
  Blenheim Palace 205, 216
  Hampton Court 161
  Kensington Gardens 103
  Kensington Palace 103
Anne Hathaway's Cottage 314, 315
  Midlands Garden tour 309
The Annunciation (Lippi) 84
Anstruther, restaurants 604
Anthony, St 393
Antique shops 627
Apollo Theatre (London) 127
Applecross, pubs 611
Appledore **275**
Applethwaite, restaurants 596
Aquariums
  National Marine Aquarium (Plymouth) 280
  Sea Life Centre (Brighton) 163
  see also Zoos
Arbor Low, Peak District tour 326
Architecture 20–21
  Cotswold stone **292–3**
  Rural architecture **28–9**
  Scottish castles **472–3**
  Stately homes **24–5**
  Tudor manor houses **290–91**
  Welsh castles **424–5**
Argyll, Dukes of 482, 534
Argyll & Bute *see* Highlands and Islands
Arisaig, hotels 571
Aristocracy **26–7**
Arkwright, Sir Richard 55, 324, 327, 360
Arlington Court 275
Armscote, hotels 555
Armstrong, Lord 406
Arnolfini Portrait (Van Eyck) 84
Art 20
Arthur, King 47, 235, **273**
  Dozmary Pool 272–3
  Glastonbury 241
  Maen Huail (Ruthin) 431
  Round Table 158
  Snowdon 419
  Stirling Castle 482
  Tintagel 261, **273**
Arthur, Prince 301
  tomb of 306
Arts and Crafts Movement 25, 316
Arundel Castle **160**
Asenby, restaurants 598
Ashburton, hotels 553
Ashmole, Elias 210, 212

Ashness Bridge 351
Ashton, Lord 358
Aske, Robert 339
Askrigg, pubs 610
Aspiring Forms (Wells) 265
Asquith, Henry 58
Association of British Riding Schools 631
Association of Pleasure Craft Operators 631
Astor, Nancy 150
Astor, William Waldorf 177
Aswarby, hotels 558
At the Theatre (Renoir) 85
Athelhampton House 233, 257
Athelstan, King of Wessex 387
Atholl, Dukes of 529
Atkinson, Thomas 388
Auchindrain Museum **534**
Auchmithie, restaurants 606
Auchterarder, hotels 568
Audley End **196–7**
Augustine, St 46, 174
Auldearn, hotels 571
Austen, Jane
  Bath 246, 248
  grave of 158
  Jane Austen's House (Chawton) 150, 160
Australian High Commission 619
Autos Abroad 637
Autumn in Great Britain 64
Avebury **251**
  restaurants 587
Aviemore 530
Avis 637
Avon *see* Wessex
Avon, River 17, 243, 252, 312, 314, 316
Avonwick, restaurants 589
Awe, Loch **533**
Ayckbourn, Alan 20, 383
Aylesbury, hotels 549
Ayr, restaurants 604
Ayrshire *see* Lowlands
Aysgarth Waterfalls 371

B

Babbacombe Model Village 278
Babbage, Charles 279
Babworth, hotels 558
Back of the New Mills (Crome) 189
Bacon, Sir Francis 220
Bacon, Francis 82, 189
Bakewell, restaurants 593
Bala **436**
Balhousie Castle 484
Ballater
  hotels 571
  restaurants 606
  Royal Deeside tour 526
Ballet 128
Balliol, Bernard 412
Balmoral 465
  Royal Deeside tour 526
Balquhidder, hotels 568
Bamburgh 403, **406**
Banbury 208
Banchory, Royal Deeside tour 527
Bank holidays 65
Bankes, Sir John 258
Bankes family 259
Banking 624
Banknotes 625
Banks, Iain 488
Bankside Power Station **123**
Bannockburn, Battle of (1314) 49, 468, 482
Banqueting House (London) **92**
  Street-by-Street map 91
Baptist Church 619
Barbican Concert Hall (London) 128
Bardon Mill, North Pennines tour 413
Bardsey Island 439
Barley, pubs 609
Barlow, Bishop of St David's 450
Barnard Castle **412**
Barnstaple **275**
  restaurants 589
Barra 515
Barrie, JM 103
Barrow-in-Furness 356
Barry, Sir Charles
  City Art Galleries (Manchester) 361
  Houses of Parliament (London) 74, 92
  Town Hall (Halifax) 398
Barwick, restaurants 588
Baslow
  hotels 558
  restaurants 593
Bassenthwaite 348, 349
  hotels 559
Batemans (Burwash) 151
Bath 229, 236, **246–9**
  hotels 551
  International Festival 63
  restaurants 588
  Street-by-Street map 246–7
Bath, Marquesses of 254
Bathford
  hotels 551
  pubs 609
Bathurst, 1st Earl of 317
Battersea Park (London) 77
Battle, hotels 545
Battle Abbey 169
Beaches, West Country 230–31
Beachy Head 168
Beaker People 42, 43
Beale, Gilbert 222
Beale Park, Thames River tour 222
Beaminster, restaurants 588
Beamish Open Air Museum **410–11**
The Beatles 27, 60, 362, **363**
Beatles Festival 63
Beauchamp family 310, 311, 458
Beaulieu **156**
  hotels 545
Beaumaris **430**
  Castle 418, **424–5**, 430
  Festival 63
  hotels 565
  pubs 611
  restaurants 601
Beaumont, Guillaume 357
Becket, Thomas à 48–9, 174, 175
Beckingham, restaurants 593
Becky Falls 283
Bed-and-breakfast 539
Beddgelert 436, **438**
  hotels 565
Bede, The Venerable 401, 405, 414
Bedford, Dukes of 218
Bedford Square (London) 109
Bedfordshire *see* Thames Valley
Bedingfeld, Sir Edmund 183
"Beefeaters" 120
Beer **34–5**
Belfast, HMS **119**
  river view of 75
Belford, restaurants 599
Bell, Alexander 467
Bell, Vanessa 151
Bellany, John 491
Bellini, Giovanni 212
Belstone, hotels 553
Bempton **386–7**
Benbecula 515
Bennett, Arnold 299
Bere Regis 257
Berkshire *see* Thames Valley
Bermondsey Market (London) 125
Berrington Hall (Leominster) 301
Berwick Street Market (London) 125
Berwick-upon-Tweed **404**
  hotels 563
Bess of Hardwick 322, 324
Bethnal Green Museum of Childhood (London) 133
Betws-y-Coed **436**
Beuys, Joseph 123
Bevan, Aneurin 423
Beverley **387**
Bible 52
Bibury 292, 296
  hotels 555
Bickley Moss, pubs 610
Bicycles 57, 630, 643
Bideford **274**
Big Ben 79
Bigbury-on-Sea, hotels 553
Biggar **499**
Biggin-by-Hartington, hotels 558
Billingshurst, hotels 545
Birch Vale, restaurants 594
Birchover, pubs 610
Birds
  Bempton **386–7**
  Harewood Bird Garden 396
  Loch Garten Nature Reserve 531
  Minsmere Reserve 190
  Morecambe Bay 358
  St Abb's Head **488**
  Shetland Seabird Isles **514**
  see also Wildlife reserves
Birkenhead 365
Birmingham **306–7**
  airport 634
  events 62
  hotels 555
  restaurants 591
Bishop's Tachbrook, restaurants 591
Bishop's Tawton, hotels 553
Bistros 575
Black Death 48, 49, 195
Black Isle **517**
Black Mountains 454–5
Blackmore, RD 239
Blackpool **359**
  hotels 560
  illuminations 64
  restaurants 596
Blackwell, hotels 555
Bladud, King 248
Blaenafon **460**
Blaenau Ffestiniog **437**
Blahnik, Manolo 119
Blair Atholl, festivals 62
Blair Castle 473, **529**
Blairgowrie, hotels 568
Blake, Peter 93
Blake, William 93, 398, 506
Blakeney, hotels 547
Blakeney Marshes, North Norfolk Coastal tour 185

Blanchland
North Pennines tour 413
pubs 611
Blencathra 349, 350
Blenheim Palace 146, 205, **216–17**
Blickling Hall **186**
Blockley
hotels 555
pubs 610
Blondin 371
Bloomsbury (London) **105–9**
area map 105
pubs 608
Bloomsbury Group 105, 109, 151, 168
Boadicea (Boudicca) 44, 179, **183**
Colchester 193
St Albans 220
Boatbuilding (Constable) 192
Boating 630
The Broads 186
Canals of the Midlands **288–9**
coast and waterway travel **641**
Oxford and Cambridge Boat Race 66
punting on the Cam 202
Tate to Tate river boats 93, 123
Touring the Thames 75, 223
Bodfari, pubs 611
Bodiam Castle **170**
Bodleian Library (Oxford) **215**
Bodley, Thomas 215
Bodmin **272–3**
Boer War 57
Boleyn, Anne
Anne Boleyn's Seat (Fountains Abbey) 377
Blickling Hall 186
execution 119, 120
Hever Castle 177
Bolton Abbey, restaurants 598
Bolton Castle 371
Bolton Priory 372
Booth, Richard 447
The Borders
Borders tour **489**
see also Lowlands
Borough Market (London) **122**, 125
Borromini, Francesco 116
Borrowdale **351**
Boscastle 273
hotels 553
Bosch, Hieronymus, *Christ Mocked* 73
Bossanyi, Erwin 175
Bosworth, Battle of (1485) 49
Botallack, hotels 553
Botallack Mine, Penwith tour 264
Bothwell, Earl of 497
Bottesford, restaurants 594
Boucher, François 106
Boughton Lees, restaurants 582
Bourgeois, Louise 123
Bournemouth **259**
hotels 551
restaurants 588
Bovey Tracey 283
Bow Fell 352, 353
Bowder Stone 351
Bowes, John 412
Bowness-on-Windermere 355
hotels 560
restaurants 596
Bowood House 243
Box Hill 160
Boxing Day 65
Boyne, Battle of the (1690) 53
Bradford **397**
hotels 562
Indian Community **397**
restaurants 598
Bradford-on-Avon **243**
hotels 551
restaurants 588
Bradley, Thomas 398–9
Braemar Castle 472
Braemar Games 64, 466
Brahan Seer 517
Braich-y-Pwll 439
Braithwaite, restaurants 596
Branagh, Kenneth 315
Brangwyn, Sir Frank 452
Brasseries 575
Braunton Burrows 275
Braunton "Great Field" 275
Brawne, Fanny 131
Bray, restaurants 586
Breakdown services 637
Breakfast 574, 577
Brearton, restaurants 598
Brechfa, restaurants 602
Brecon 455
festivals 63
hotels 566
Brecon Beacons 419, **454–5**
Brentor 282
Bretforton, pubs 610
Brick Lane Market (London) 125
Bridgewater, 3rd Duke of 288
Brighton 154, **162–7**
Festival 62
hotels 545
Palace Pier 162
restaurants 582
Royal Pavilion 147, 163, **166–7**
Street-by-Street map 162–3
Brimfield, restaurants 592
Bristol **244–5**
hotels 551
map 245
restaurants 588
British Activity Holiday Association 631
British Airways 635
British Airways London Eye **83**
river view of 74
British Broadcasting Corporation (BBC) 21
British Deaf Association 621
British Grand Prix 67
British Hang-Gliding and Paragliding Association 631
British International Antiques Fair 62
British Midland 635
British Mountaineering Council 631
British Museum (London) 73, **108–9**
British Open Golf Championship 67
British Pregnancy Advisory Service 621
British Surfing Association 631
British Travel Associates 640
British Trust for Conservation Volunteers 631
British Water Ski Federation 631
British Waterways 631, 641
Brittany Ferries 633
Britten, Benjamin 191
Brixham 278
Brixton Academy (London) 128
Broad Campden, hotels 555
Broad Haven
hotels 566
restaurants 602
Broadhembury, pubs 609
Broadlands (Southampton) 150
The Broads **186**
windmills 187
Broads Authority 631
Broadway
hotels 556
Midlands Garden tour 308
Brockenhurst, restaurants 582
Brodrick, Cuthbert 396
Brompton Oratory (London) **99**
Street-by-Street map 99
Brontë, Anne 383, 398
Brontë, Charlotte 327, 398
Brontë, Emily 398
Broom, pubs 609
Brown, Capability 22, 23
Alnwick Castle 406
Audley End 196
Berrington Hall (Leominster) 301
Blenheim Palace 217
Bowood House 243
Burghley House 330
Chatsworth House 322
Harewood House 396
Longleat House 254
Petworth House 160
Stowe 218
Brown, Ford Madox 49
The Last of England 307
Browns (London) 125
Brownsea Island 258–9
Bruce, Sir George 487
Bruce in Single Combat at Bannockburn (Hassall) 468
Brueghel, Pieter the Elder, *The Adoration of the Kings* 84
Brunel, Isambard Kingdom 244
Buckden, hotels 547
Buckfast Abbey 279, 283
Buckfastleigh **279**
Buckingham, Dukes of 218
Buckingham Palace (London) 72, **88–9**
Buckinghamshire *see* Thames Valley
Buckinghamshire, 2nd Earl of 186
Buckland, hotels 556
Buckland Abbey **280**
Buckland-in-the-Moor 263, 283
Buckler's Hard 156
Buddhism 619
Bude **273**
Budget (car hire) 637
BUNAC 617
Bunyan, John 219
Burberry (London) 125
Bureaux de change 624
Burford **208**
hotels 549
pubs 609
Burford House Gardens (Tenbury Wells) 301
Burges, William
Cardiff Castle 419, 458, 459
Castell Coch 425
St Mary's Church (Fountains Abbey) 377
Burgh Island **279**
The Burghers of Calais (Rodin) 90
Burghley, William Cecil, 1st Lord 330
Burghley House 287, 320, **330–31**
Burlington, 3rd Earl of 134
Burlington Arcade (London)
Street-by-Street map 86
Burne-Jones, Sir Edward 131, 307, 385

Burnham Market
hotels 547
restaurants 584
Burns, Robert 467, 491
Burns Cottage **501**
Burns Night 65
Burnsall 372
Burrell, Sir William 506
Burrell Collection (Glasgow) 465, **506–7**
Burton Agnes **386**
Burton Constable **388**
Burton on the Wolds, restaurants 594
Burton upon Trent, restaurants 592
Bury St Edmunds **194**
hotels 547
restaurants 584
Buses
guided tours 643
local 642
regional 640, **641**
Bute, 3rd Marquess of 425, 458, 486
Bute family 456
Butler, Lady Eleanor 436
Buttermere 350, **351**
hotels 560
Buttertubs 371
Buxton **322**
hotels 558
Peak District tour 326
Byland Abbey **378**
Byron, Lord 27

C

Caban Coch 448
Cabinet War Rooms (London) **91**
Street-by-Street map 90
Cabot, John 50, 244
Cadbury, George 337
Caedmon 382
Caerleon **460**
Caernarfon 418, **430**
Castle 425, 427
Caernarfonshire *see* North Wales
Caerphilly 424
Caesar, Julius 44
Cafés 575
Cairndow, restaurants 606
Cairngorms 465, 511, **530–31**
Caldey Island 452
Caledonian MacBrayne 641
Caley Mill, North Norfolk Coastal tour 184
Callander 481
hotels 569
Calne, hotels 551
Cam, River 17, 180, 198, 202
Camber Castle 173
Camber Sands 173
Cambridge 17, **198–203**
Folk Festival 63
hotels 547
King's College **200–201**
pubs 608
restaurants 584
Street-by-Street map 198–9
University 147, 198, **200–203**
Cambridge Theatre (London) 127
Cambridgeshire *see* East Anglia
Camden (London) **132**
Camden Lock Market (London) 125
Cameron, Richard 500
Campaign for Nuclear Disarmament (CND) 60
Campbell, Colen 24, 254
Campbell, D, *The Battle of Culloden* 523
Campbell, Donald 356
Campbell, Lady Grace 534
Campbell, Naomi 21, 60
Campbell, Robert 529
Campbell clan 470, 534
Campden, Sir Baptist Hicks, 1st Viscount 315
Camping 541
Campsea Ashe, hotels 547
Canada Tower (London) 61
Canadian High Commission 619
Canaletto, Antonio 106, 159, 311
Entrance to the Arsenal 218
Canals 55, 641
Falkirk Wheel **487**
Leeds-Liverpool Canal 336
Llangollen Canal 436
Midlands **288–9**
Monmouthshire and Brecon Canal 455
Canterbury **174–5**
Cathedral 147, 155, **174–5**
Festival 64
hotels 545
murder of Thomas à Becket 48–9
Canute, King 47
Buckfast Abbey 283
Bury St Edmunds 194
Holy Trinity Church 159
Canynge, William the Elder 244
Canynge, William the Younger 244
Capel Coch, restaurants 601
Capel Curig, pubs 611
Capel Garmon, hotels 565
Captain Thomas Lee (Gheeraerts) 93
Caravanning 541
Cardiff 443, 445, **456–9**
hotels 566
map 457
restaurants 602
Cardiff Castle 419, 445, **458–9**
Cardiganshire *see* South and Mid-Wales
Carlisle **346**
hotels 560
Carlisle, Charles, 3rd Earl of 384
Carloway Broch 515
Carlyle, Thomas 130
Carmarthenshire *see* South and Mid-Wales
Carnegie, Andrew 467, 486–7
Carol concerts 65
Caroline, Queen 103
Carpenter, Samuel 384
Carr, John 24, 394, 396
Carrawburgh Fort 409
Carreg Cennen Castle 454
Carrick Roads 268
Carroll, Lewis 213, 387, **431**
Cars **636–7**
driving in cities 642
hiring 632, **637**
mileage chart 14
see also Tours by car
Cartier International Polo 67
Cartmel **357**
restaurants 596
Cartmel Fell
hotels 560
pubs 610
Carvoran Fort 408
Cassillis, Earl of 508
Castell Coch 425
Castell-y-Bere 425
Castle Ashby, hotels 558
Castle Drogo 283
Castle Howard 24, 335, **384–5**
Castlereagh, Lord 448
Castlerigg Stone Circle 43, 347, 349
Castles 49
Scottish castles **472–3**
Welsh castles **424–5**
Aberystwyth 449
Alnwick 334, **406**
Arundel **160**
Balhousie 484
Balmoral 526
Bamburgh 403, 406
Barnard Castle 412
Beaumaris 418, **424–5**, 430
Blair 473, **529**
Bodiam **170**
Bolton 371
Braemar 472
Bramber 162
Caernarfon 425, 427, 430
Caerphilly 424
Camber 173
Cardiff 419, 445, **458–9**
Carisbrooke 156
Carlisle 346
Carreg Cennen 454
Castell Coch 425
Castell Dinas Brân 436
Castell-y-Bere 425
Cawdor **523**
Claypotts 472
Cockermouth 350
Colchester 193
Conwy 419, 425, 429, 432
Corfe **258**
Crathes 527
Culzean 464, **508–9**
Dartmouth 278
Dolbadarn 437
Doune **484**
Dover 170, 171
Drum 473, 527
Drumlanrig 472, 473, **500–501**
Duart **532**, 533
Duffus 472
Dunrobin 473, 516–17
Dunvegan 520
Durham 414, 415
Edinburgh 479, **492–3**
Eilean Donan 511, 516
Exeter 276
Floors 489
Framlingham **191**
Glamis 477, **484–5**
Goodrich 305
Harlech 424, 440
Helmsley 379
Hever **177**
Inverary **534**
Kilchurn 533
Kisimul 515
Lancaster **358**, 359
Leeds 153, **176**
Lewes 168
Lincoln 328
Lindisfarne 404
Ludlow **300**, 301
Middleham 371
Monmouth 460–61
Muncaster 352
Neidpath 472
Newcastle upon Tyne 410–11
Norwich 188

Castles (cont.)
Nottingham 324
Orford 191
Pendennis 269
Penrith 346
Portchester 157
Powis **446**
Restormel 272
Ripley 375
Rochester 176
St Andrews 485
Scarborough 383
Sherborne 256
Shrewsbury 300
Sizergh 356
Skipton 372
Stirling **482–3**
Taunton 240
Threave **501**
Tintagel **273**
Torosay **532**, 533
Totnes 279
Urquhart 522
Warkworth **406**
Warwick 287, 309, **310–11**
Winchester 158
Windsor 146, 223, **224–5**
Wolvesey 158
see also Palaces; Stately homes
Castleton, restaurants 594
Cathedrals
admission charges 617
Aberdeen 524, 526
Beverley Minster 387
Bristol 245
Bury St Edmunds 194
Canterbury 147, 155, **174–5**
Chester 298–9
Chichester 159
Coventry 307
Dunkeld 527
Durham 335, 401, 414, 415
Edinburgh 495
Elgin 524
Ely 147, 182–3
Exeter 276–7
Fortrose 517
Glasgow 502–3
Gloucester 317
Guildford 160
Hereford 304
Lincoln 287, 321, 329
Liverpool Anglican 365
Llandaff 457
Metropolitan Cathedral of Christ the King (Liverpool) 365
Newcastle upon Tyne 411
Norwich 188
Peterborough 182
Ripon 375
Rochester 176
St Albans 221
St Andrews 485
St David's 418, **450–51**
St Magnus 514
St Paul's (London) 73, 74, 111, 112, **116–17**
Salisbury 229, 252–3
Southwark (London) **122**
Truro 269
Wells 228, 240–41
Winchester 146, 158–9
Worcester 306
York Minster 390, **392–3**, **395**
Catherine of Aragon 50
tomb of 182
Catherine the Great 186
Cauldon, pubs 610
Cavell, Edith, grave of 188
Caves
Cheddar Gorge 242
Dan-yr-Ogof Caves 454
Fingal's Cave 533
Kents Cavern 278
Llechwedd Slate Caverns 437
Mother Shipton's Cave 374–5
St Fillan's Cave (East Neuk) 486
Stump Cross Caverns 372
Wookey Hole 240
Cawdor Castle **523**
Cawfields 408
Cecil, Robert 27, 219
Cedd, St 197
Celts 43
chalk figures 209
Christianity **405**
in Wales 422
Cemeteries, London 77
Cenotaph (London)
Street-by-Street map 91
Central Hall (London)
Street-by-Street map 90
Cenwulf 47
Cerne Abbas 257
Cézanne, Paul 123
Chagall, Marc 159
Chagford, restaurants 590
Chain stores, London **124**, 125
Chale, pubs 608
Chalk figures **209**
Cerne Abbas 257
Long Man of Wilmington 168
Sutton Bank 378
Chamberlain, Neville 91, 386
Chambers, William 82
Chanctonbury Ring 162
Changing of the Guard 89
Channel Coast **153–77**
climate 69
Exploring the Downs and Channel Coast 154–5
hotels 545–7
pubs 608
restaurants 582–4
Channel Tunnel 60, 61, 632
Chapman, John 183
Charlecote Park 290
Charles, Prince of Wales 61, 430
Charles I, King 41, 87
Banqueting House (London) 92
Bodiam Castle 170
Carisbrooke Castle 156
Civil War 205
execution 52–3, 115, 120
Oxford 212
Powis Castle 446
and Scotland 469
statue of 484
Worcester 306
Charles II, King 41
Audley End 196
Crown Jewels 120
Monument (London) 118
Moseley Old Hall 291
Neidpath Castle 472
Newmarket 195
Old Ship Hotel (Brighton) 162
Palace of Holyroodhouse 496
Restoration 52–3
Charles II, King (cont.)
Royal Citadel (Plymouth) 280
Worcester 306
Charles, Thomas 436
Charleston (Lewes) 151
Charlie, Bonnie Prince 491, 511, **521**
Battle of Culloden 54, 469, 523
Blair Castle 529
Glenfinnan Monument 533
Isle of Skye 520
mementoes 498, 501, 522
Palace of Holyroodhouse 496
portrait 468
Prince's Cairn 532
Traquair House 499
Western Isles 515
Charlotte, Queen 109
Chartists 423
Chartwell (Westerham) 151, 177
Chatham 176
Chatsworth House 287, 319, **322–3**
Chatto, Beth 193
Chaucer, Geoffrey 20, **174**
Canterbury Tales 49
memorial 95
Chawton, Jane Austen's House 150
Cheddar Gorge **242**
Chedworth Roman Villa 317
Cheere, John 255
Chelsea **130**
Chelsea Flower Show 62
Chelsea Physic Garden (London) 130
Cheltenham **316**
hotels 556
restaurants 592
Cheltenham and Gloucester Trophy 67
Cheltenham Imperial Gardens, Midlands Garden tour 308
Chequepoint 624
Cherwell, River 205, 212
Cheshire *see* Heart of England
Chesil Bank 230, 256
Chessington World of Adventures 629
Chester **298–9**
restaurants 592
Chester-le-Street, hotels 563
Chesters Bridge 409
Chesters Fort 409
Cheviot Hills 402, **407**
Chew Green Camp 407
Cheyne walk (London) 130
Chichester **159**
restaurants 582
Chiddingstone 154
Childline 621
Children
Bethnal Green Museum of Childhood (London) 133
entertainment 616, 629
in hotels 616
in restaurants 577, 616
Chillaton, hotels 553
Chinatown (London) **82**
Chinese New Year 65
Chinnor, restaurants 586
Chippendale, Thomas 55, 396, 523
Chipperfield, hotels 549
Chipping Campden **315**
hotels 556
Chisenhale Dance Space (London) 128
Chiswick (London) **134**
Chiswick House (London) 134
The Choice of Hercules (Poussin) 255
Christ Discovered in the Temple (Martini) 365

Christ Mocked (Bosch) 73
Christ of St John of the Cross (Dalí) 503
Christchurch Priory 259
Christianity, Celtic **405**
Christmas 65
Church of England 50, 619
Churches (general)
architecture 28–9
see also Cathedrals
Churches in London
All Souls, Langham Place 107
Brompton Oratory **99**
Queen's Chapel 87
St Bartholomew-the-Great **114–15**
St James Garlickhythe 112
St Margaret's 90
St Mary Abchurch 113
St Mary-le-Bow 112
St Nicholas Cole 112
St Paul's, Covent Garden 80
St Stephen Walbrook 113, **114**
Westminster Abbey (London) 73, 90, **94–5**
Churchill, Sir Winston 60
Blenheim Palace 216
Cabinet War Rooms (London) 90, 91
Chartwell (Westerham) 151, 177
World War II 59
Church's Shoes (London) 125
Chysauster 266–7
Cider 240
CIE Tours International 639
Cimabue 84
Cinema 21, 629
London 127
London Film Festival 64
Cinque Ports **170**
Cirencester **317**
Cissbury Ring 162
City of London **111–23**
area map 111
pubs 608
Street-by-Street map 112–13
Civil War 39, 52, 205
Clachan-Seil, hotels 571
Claerwen reservoir 448
Clanfield, hotels 549
Clans, Scottish **470–71**
Claude Lorrain 229
Claudius, Emperor 44, 171, 193
Clava Cairns 523
Claydon House (Winslow) 150
Claypotts Castle 472
Clevedon, restaurants 588
Cley windmill 179
North Norfolk Coastal tour 185
Clifford, Lady Anne 372
Clifford, Henry, Lord 372
Clifford, Robert de 372
Clifton 244
Climate **68–9**, 614
Clintmains, hotels 569
Clitheroe 359
"Clive of India", Clive Museum (Powis Castle) 446
Cliveden House (Maidenhead) 150
Cliveden Reach, Thames River tour 223
Clothes
in restaurants 575
shops **124**, 125, 627
Clovelly **274**
Clubs 629
Clunie Foot Bridge, Killiecrankie walk 528
Clyde, River 500, 502
Clyde Valley *see* Lowlands
Clydeside 469
Clytha
hotels 566
restaurants 603
Coach travel 632, **633**, **640–41**
Coal mining
Industrial Revolution in the North 336, 337
Mining Museum (Blaenafon) 460
National Coal Mining Museum **399**
Wales 423, 443
Coalbrookdale 302
Coast-to-Coast walk 33, 351
Cobbett, William 148
Cockermouth 349, **350**
hotels 560
restaurants 596
Cockington 278
Coggeshall **193**
hotels 547
Coins 625
Colbost by Dunvegan, restaurants 606
Colchester **193**
festivals 64
restaurants 584
Colchester, William 392
Coleridge, Samuel Taylor 277, 354
Colerne, restaurants 588
Colet, John 50
College of Arms (London) 26
Street-by-Street map 112
Colman's Mustard **189**
Colston Bassett, restaurants 594
Columba, St 511, 522
Iona 46, 533
Colwyn 427
Colwyn Bay, restaurants 601
Combe Martin 238, 276
Comedy Theatre (London) 127
Coming from the Mill (Lowry) 359
Commonwealth 52
Communications **622–3**
Concorde 61
Coniston, hotels 560
Coniston Water 352, **356**
Conran, Jasper 125
Conran, Terence 27
Conservative Party 61
Consett, restaurants 599
Constable, John 180, 343, 505
Boatbuilding 192
Christchurch Mansion (Ipswich) 191
Constable walk 192
The Hay-Wain 85
Salisbury Cathedral from the meadows 10, 229
Tate Britain (London) 93
Constable family 388
Constantine the Great, Emperor 45, 394, 430
Consulates 619
Continental Airlines 635
Conversion chart 619
Conwy 421
Castle 419, 425, 429
restaurants 601
Street-by-Street map 432–3
Conwy Castle (Sandby) 433
Cook, Captain James 213, 280
Captain Cook Memorial Museum (Whitby) 382
Cookham
restaurants 586
Thames River tour 223
Cooper, Samuel, *James II* 523
Coquet, River 406, 407
Corbridge **409**
Corelli, Marie 312
Corfe Castle **258**, 538
Cornwall **261–83**
climate 68
Exploring Devon and Cornwall 262–3
hotels 553–5
pubs 609
restaurants 589–91
Cornwall, Richard, Earl of 273
Coronation Bridge, Killiecrankie walk 528
Coronations 94
Corpach, Road to the Isles tour 533
Corsham **243**
Cosin, John, Bishop of Durham 415
Cotehele **281**
Cotman, John Sell 189
Cotswolds 286
stone buildings **292–3**
Countryside **30–31**
Walkers' Britain **32–3**
County Durham *see* Northumbria
Courbet, Gustave 396
Courtauld Institute (London) 82
Covenanters 469, 495, 500, 501
Covent Garden (London)
Market 125
Street-by-Street map 80–81
Coventry **307**
restaurants 592
Cowan Bridge, hotels 560
Coward, Noel 58, 279, 440
Cowbridge, restaurants 603
Coxwold **378–9**
pubs 610
Crackington Haven, hotels 553
Cragside 25
Craig Goch 448
Cranmer, Thomas, Martyrs' Memorial (Oxford) 210, 213
Cranston, Kate 504
Crarae Gardens **534**
Craster, pubs 611
Crathes Castle and Gardens, Royal Deeside tour 527
Credit cards 624, 626
in restaurants 576
Cregennen lakes 441
Criccieth, hotels 565
Crich Tramway Village, Peak District tour 327
Cricket 67, 631
Crickhowell
hotels 566
pubs 611
restaurants 603
Crime 620–21
Crimean War 56
Crinan, hotels 571
Crinkle Crags 351, 352, 353
Criterion Theatre (London) 127
Cromarty 517
Crome, John, *Back of the New Mills* 189
Cromford, Peak District tour 327
Cromwell, Oliver 41
Civil War 179
Commonwealth 52
Ely Cathedral 182
helmet 311
Huntingdon 196
Neidpath Castle 472

Cromwell, Oliver (cont.)
Oxford 205
Ripley Castle 375
Cromwell, Thomas 339
Crookham, hotels 563
Croscombe, pubs 609
Crossflight 623
Crosthwaite, restaurants 596
Crown Jewels **120**, 121
Crufts Dog Show 62
Cruikshank, G, *Peterloo Massacre* 361
Crummock Water 345, 350
Cuckmere, River 169
restaurants 583
Cuillins 520
Culbone church 239
Culloden, Battle of (1746) 54, 469, 470, **523**
Culross **487**
Culzean Castle 464, **508–9**
Cumberland, Duke of 523, 525
Cumberland Terrace (London) 107
Cumbria *see* Lancashire and the Lakes
Cupar
hotels 569
restaurants 604
Currency **624–5**
Curthose, Robert 410–11
Curzon, Lord 170
Curzon family 25
Customs and Excise, HM 619
Customs and immigration 619, 633
Cuthbert, St 348, 401
Farne Islands 404
Lindisfarne 404, 405
tomb of 414
Cuthburga 259
Cycling 57, 630, 643

D

Dale, David 500
Dalemain **346–7**
Dales Way 32
Dalí, Salvador, *Christ of St John of the Cross* 503
Dan-yr-Ogof Caves 454
Danby, Earl of 212
Danby, Francis 245
Dance 629
London 128
Dance, George the Elder 113
Darby, Abraham I 302
Darby, Abraham III 303
Darling, Grace 404, 406
Darlington, restaurants 600
Darnley, Lord 496, 497, 504
Dartington, restaurants 590
Dartington Hall 279
Dartmeet 283
Dartmoor National Park 228, **282–3**
Dartmouth **278**
pubs 609
restaurants 590
Darwin, Charles 151, 280
David, St 420, 422, 450, 451, 456
David I, King of Scotland 493, 496, 498
David, Gerard 490
Davies, Gwendolyn and Margaret 457
Davy, Sir Humphrey 266, 336
De Morgan, William 209
De Quincey, Thomas 354
De Wint, Peter 357
Dean, Tacita 93
Dean's Yard (London)
Street-by-Street map 90
Death Hope Life Fear (Gilbert and George) 123
Dedham
hotels 547–8
restaurants 584
Dedham Church, Constable walk 192
Dee, River 298, 427, 436, 501
Royal Deeside Tour **526–7**
Deepdale 370
Defoe, Daniel 242
The Highland Rogue 480
Robinson Crusoe 244, 486
Deganwy, restaurants 601
Degas, Edgar 364
Delta Airlines 635
Denbighshire *see* North Wales
Dennis Severs' House (London) 133
Dentists 620, 621
Department stores 627
London **124**, 125
Depression 58, 59
Derain, André 386
Derbyshire *see* East Midlands
Derwent Gorge 324
Derwentwater 344, 348, 349
Design Museum (London) **119**
Despenser family 458
Destailleur, Gabriel-Hippolyte 218
Devil's Bridge 449
Wild Wales tour 453
Devil's Dyke 169
Devon **261–83**
climate 68
Devonshire cream teas 275
Exploring Devon and Cornwall 262–3
hotels 553–5
pubs 609
restaurants 589–91
Devonshire, Dukes of 322, 357, 372
DHL 623
Diana, Princess of Wales
Althorp House 331
Kensington Gardens 103
Kensington Palace 103
marriage 61
Dibdin, Charles 441
Dickens, Charles 105, **177**, 529
Beaumaris 430
Bleak House (Broadstairs) 151
Charles Dickens Museum (Portsmouth) 157
Dickens House Museum (London) 109
George Inn (London) 122
Great Yarmouth 187
Dinner 575, 577
Dinton, restaurants 586
Directory enquiries 622
Dirleton, restaurants 604
Disabled Travel 639
Disabled travellers 615
helplines 621
hotels 541
in restaurants 577
travelling by train 639
Discounts
air travel 635
coach travel 640
rail travel 638
students 616
Disraeli, Benjamin 56, 57, 221
Diss, restaurants 584
Dissolution of the Monasteries 339
Docklands (London) **133**
Doctors 620
Doddiscombsleigh, restaurants 590
Dolgellau **440–41**
restaurants 601
Dollar, hotels 569
Domesday Book 28, 48, 317
Dominion Theatre (London) 127
Dorchester **257**
hotels 551
Dornoch **516–17**
Dorrington, restaurants 592
Dorset *see* Wessex
Douglas, Sir James "Black Douglas" 498, 501
Douglas clan 471, 492, 500–501
Doulton 299
Doune Castle **484**
Dovedale, Peak District tour 326
Dover 146, **171**
Dover, Robert 315
Downe House (Downe) 151
Downing Street (London) 90, **91**
Downs and Channel Coast **153–77**
climate 69
The Downs **169**
Exploring the Downs and Channel Coast 154–5
hotels 545–7
pubs 608
restaurants 582–4
Doyle, Sir Arthur Conan 282
Sherlock Holmes Museum (London) **106**
Dozmary Pool 272–3
Drake, Sir Francis 51, 280, **281**
Drinks *see* Food and drink
Druids 250, 421
Drum Castle 473
Royal Deeside tour 527
Drumlanrig Castle 472, 473, **500–501**
Dryburgh Abbey, Borders tour 489
Drymen, restaurants 606
Du Maurier, Daphne **272**
Duart Castle **532**, 533
Duchêne, Achille 216
Duchess Theatre (London) 127
Duddon Valley 351, **353**
Duffus Castle 472
Duke of York's Theatre (London) 127
Duke's Pass 481
Dulverton, hotels 551
Dumfries and Galloway *see* Lowlands
Duncan, King of Scotland 523
Dundee **485**
pubs 611
Dunfermline **486–7**
Dungeness 170–71
Dunkeld **527**
hotels 571
restaurants 607
Dunkery Beacon 239
Dunoon, hotels 569
Dunrobin Castle 473, 516–17
Dunster 239
Dunvegan Castle 520
Dunwich **190**
hotels 548
Dunwich Heath 190
Dupré, G, *Bonnie Prince Charlie* 468
Durdle Door 231, 258
Durham **414–15**
Cathedral 335, 401
hotels 564
restaurants 600
Durham, County *see* Northumbria

E

Eadfrith, Bishop 405
Eames, Charles 119
Eardisland 301
Easby Abbey 339
Easington 336
restaurants 586
East Aberthaw, pubs 611
East Anglia **179–203**
climate 69
Exploring East Anglia 180–81
hotels 547–9
pubs 608–9
restaurants 584–5
East Barkwith, hotels 558
East Boldon, restaurants 600
East End (London) **133**
East Grinstead, hotels 546
restaurants 583
East India Company 51
East Lambrook Manor 233
East Midlands **319–31**
climate 69
Exploring the East Midlands 320–21
hotels 558–9
pubs 610
restaurants 593–5
East Neuk **486**
East Witton, hotels 562
Eastbourne **168**
hotels 545
Easter 65
Edale, Peak District tour 326
Eden Camp **386**
Eden Project **270–71**
Edenbridge, restaurants 583
Edinburgh 465, **490–97**
airport 634
Castle 479, **492–3**
Festival 63, 477, **495**
Festival Fringe 63
hotels 569
map 491
pubs 611
restaurants 604–5
Royal Mile **494–7**
Edinburgh, Duke of 27
Edmund, St 194
Ednam, hotels 569
Edstone Aqueduct 289
Education Acts 57, 59
Edward, the Black Prince 175
Edward I, King 40, 49
Beaumaris Castle 418, 424–5, 430
Caernarfon Castle 430
conquers Wales 422
Conwy Castle 419, 429, 432
Eleanor crosses 213
Harlech Castle 440
Leeds Castle 176
and Stone of Destiny 468
Tower of London 120
Welsh castles 424–5
Winchelsea 173
Edward II, King 40
Byland Abbey 378
Caernarfon Castle 425
as Prince of Wales 422, 430
tomb of 317
Edward III, King 40
Order of the Garter 26
Windsor Castle 224
wool trade 195
York Minster 395
Edward IV, King 40, 120
Edward V, King 40
Edward VI, King 39, 41
death 51
Leeds Castle 176
Sherborne School 256
Edward VII, King 41
Liverpool Anglican Cathedral 365
Sandringham 185
Warwick Castle 311
Edward VIII, King *see* Windsor, Duke of
Edward the Confessor, King 47
Crown Jewels 120
Westminster Abbey (London) 95
Wimborne Minster 259
Edwin, King of Northumbria 392, 492
Eglwysfach, hotels 566
Eilean Donan 511, 516
Eisteddfod **436**
Elan Valley **448**
Wild Wales tour 453
Eleanor, Queen 221
Electricity 618
Elgar, Sir Edward 301, 305
Elgar's Birthplace 306
Elgin **524**
Elgin, Lord 108
Elgin Marbles 108
Elie, pubs 611
Eliot, George 130
tomb of 132
Eliot, TS 109, 130
memorial 95
Elizabeth, the Queen Mother 485
Elizabeth I, Queen 39, 41, 281
childlessness 379
Christchurch Mansion (Ipswich) 191
coat of arms 26
Epping Forest 197
Hatfield House 205, 219
Knole 176
and Mary, Queen of Scots 469
portraits of 83, 93
Spanish Armada 50–51
Elizabeth II, Queen 19, 41
Buckingham Palace 88–9
Coronation 60, 94
Edinburgh Cathedral 495
Honours List 27
Madame Tussaud's 106
Palace of Holyroodhouse 496
Windsor Castle 224
Elizabeth of York 158
Elland, restaurants 598
Elterwater 352, 353
pubs 610
Ely **182–3**
Cathedral 147, 182–3
restaurants 585
Ely, Reginald 200
Embassies 619
Emergencies 621, 622
Emin, Tracey 93
Empingham, restaurants 594
Emsworth, restaurants 583
England & Wales Cricket Board 631
English Golf Union 631
English Heritage 617
Entertainment **628–9**
London **126–9**
Entrance to the Arsenal (Canaletto) 218
Environment Agency 631
Epping Forest **197**
Epstein, Sir Jacob 457
Genesis 361
St Michael Subduing the Devil 307
Erasmus 50, 203
Eriska, hotels 571
Erpingham, Sir Thomas 188
Eskdale 351, **352**
Essex *see* East Anglia
Ethelwulf, King 162
Etiquette, in restaurants 575
Eton College, Thames River tour 223
Europcar 637
European Community 60
European Rail Travel 633
Eurostar 633
Eurotunnel 633
Evangelical Alliance 619
Evelyn, John 305
Evershot, hotels 551
Evesham, hotels 556
Exchange International 624
Exeter **276–7**
hotels 553
restaurants 590
Exmewe, Thomas 431
Exmoor National Park 228, 237, **238–9**
Expressair 623
Eyam, Peak District tour 327
Eyton, restaurants 601

F

Factory Act (1833) 56
Faed, Thomas, *The Last of the Clan* 517
Fairfax, Anne 394
Fairfax, Sir Thomas 379
Fairhaven, Lord 196
Faldo, Nick 67
Falkirk Wheel **487**
Falkland, Lord 208
Falkland Palace **486**
Falklands War (1982) 60, 61
Falmouth **268–9**
Family Records Centre (London) 27
Farmer's Bridge 288
Farndale, North York Moors tour 381
Farne Islands **404**
Farrer, Reginald 534
Fast food 576
"Fat Betty" White Cross, North York Moors tour 381
Fawkes, Guy 168
Fawley, pubs 609
Fens 182, **184**
windmills 187
Fernhurst, restaurants 583
Ferries 632, **633**, 641
Festival of Britain (1951) 60
Festivals 20, 62–5
Ffestiniog Railway **438–9**
Fforest Fawr 454
Fiennes, Ralph 20
Fife 477
Fife, Mrs Ronald 379
Films *see* Cinema
Fingal's Cave 533
Finlaggan 535
Fire services 621
First North Eastern Railways 639
Fishbourne Palace 44–5, 159
Fishguard
hotels 567
restaurants 603
Fishing 631
Fitzalan family 160
FitzHamon, Mabel 458

FitzHamon, Robert 456
Fitzherbert, Mrs 166, 167
Fitzwilliam, 7th Viscount 200
The Five Sisters of Kintail **516**
Flag Fen Bronze Age Centre 182
Flambard, Ranulph, Bishop of Durham 415
Flamborough
  hotels 562
  pubs 610
Flamborough Head **386–7**
Flaxman, John 195
Fleming, Alexander 467
Fletching, pubs 608
Flintshire *see* North Wales
Flitcroft, Henry 218, 254
Floors Castle, Borders tour 489
Flowers, Cairngorms 531
Foley, JH 385
Food and drink 21, **36–7**
  Devonshire cream teas 275
  Garden of England 148–9
  pubs **608–11**
  Scotland **474–5**
  shopping 627
  Somerset cider 240
  traditional British Pub **34–5**
  see also Restaurants
Football 66, 631
Football Association 631
Forbes, Stanhope 266
Ford, pubs 609
Forster, EM 151
Fort Amherst 176
Fort George **523**
Fort William
  hotels 571–2
  restaurants 607
Forth Bridges **488**
Fortnum & Mason (London) 125
  Street-by-Street map 86
Fortrose 517
Fortune Theatre (London) 127
Forum (London) 128
Foster, Norman 21, 189
Fotheringhay, pubs 610
Fountains Abbey 50, 335, **376–7**
Fowey **272**
  hotels 553
Fragonard, Jean Honoré 106
Framlingham Castle **191**
Frampton, George 103
Fraser clan 471
Fressingfield, restaurants 585
Freud, Anna 131
Freud, Lucian 20, 93
  Interior at Paddington 364
  Standing by the Rags 123
Freud, Sigmund
  Freud Museum (London) 131
Fridge (London) 128
Frink, Elisabeth 323, 365
Frobisher, Martin 51
Fruit 148–9
Furness 337
Furness Abbey **356**, 357
Furness Peninsula **356–7**
Furry Dancing Festival (Helston) 62

G

Gainsborough, Thomas 186
  Anglesey Abbey 196
  Bath 246
  Christchurch Mansion (Ipswich) 191
Gainsborough, Thomas (cont.)
  Gainsborough's House (Sudbury) 151, 194
  Inverary Castle 534
  Mr and Mrs Andrews 151
  National Gallery of Scotland (Edinburgh) 490
  Petworth House 160
  Sarah Siddons 54
  Tate Britain (London) 93
  Walker Art Gallery (Liverpool) 364
Galleries *see* Museums and galleries
Galmpton, hotels 553
Ganllwyd, hotels 565
Garden of England **148–9**
Gardens *see* Parks and gardens
Garreg Ddu 448
Garrick, David 314
Garrick Theatre (London) 127
Garstang, pubs 610
Gateshead, restaurants 600
Gatwick Airport 634
Gaunton Newark, restaurants 594
Gay meeting places 629
Geddes, Jenny 495
General Strike (1926) 59
Genesis (Epstein) 361
Geoffrey of Monmouth 273
Geology, Lake District **340–41**
George I, King 41, 54, 172
George II, King 41, 469
George III, King 41, 103
  Cheltenham 316
  Royal Mews (London) 89
  statue of 223
  Weymouth 256–7
George IV, King (Prince Regent) 41, 55
  Brighton 162–3, 166
  Buckingham Palace 88
  coronation 213
  Coronation Bridge (Killiecrankie) 528
  John Nash's Regency London 107
  and Mrs Fitzherbert 167
  National Gallery (London) 84
  Regent's Park (London) 105
  Royal Pavilion (Brighton) 147
  visits Edinburgh 471, 498
  Windsor Castle 224, 225
George V, King 41, 224
George VI, King 41
George Inn (London) **122**
Georgian Britain **54–5**
Gheeraerts, Marcus II, *Captain Thomas Lee* 93
Giacometti, Alberto 189
Gibberd, Sir Frederick 365
Gibbons, Grinling
  Blenheim Palace 217
  Hampton Court 161
  Petworth House 160
  St Mary Abchurch (London) 113
  St Paul's Cathedral (London) 117
Gibbs, James
  King's College (Cambridge) 200
  Radcliffe Camera (Oxford) 215
  Senate House (Cambridge) 202
  Stowe 218
Gibson, John
  The Sleeping Shepherd Boy 364
  Tinted Venus 334
Gielgud Theatre (London) 127
Gieves & Hawkes (London) 125
Gift shops 627
Gilbert and George 93
  Death Hope Life Fear 123
Gilbert Collection (London) 82
Gill, Eric 372
Gillingham, hotels 551
Gillow family 358
Girtin, Thomas 339, 361
  Rievaulx Abbey 379
Gittisham, hotels 553
Gladstone, William Ewart 57
Glamis Castle 477, **484–5**
Glanwydden
  pubs 611
  restaurants 601
Glasgow **502–7**
  airport 634
  hotels 569
  International Jazz Festival 63
  map 502
  pubs 611
  restaurants 605
Glastonbury **241**
  Festival 63
  hotels 551
Gledstanes, Thomas 494
Glencoe 65, **529**
Glencoe Massacre (1692) 53, **529**
Glendurgan 232, 269
Glenfinnan Monument, Road to the Isles tour 533
Glenlivet, hotels 572
Glenridding 347
Glenrothes, hotels 569
Glewstone, hotels 556
Globe Theatre (London) 50
Glooston, pubs 610
Glorious Revolution (1688) 53, 523
Glossop, hotels 558
Gloucester **317**
Gloucester, Humphrey, Duke of 215, 221
Gloucestershire *see* Heart of England
Glyndebourne Festival Opera 62
Glyndwr, Owain
  Conwy Castle 419
  Harlech Castle 424, 440
  Machynlleth 448
  Rebellion 422–3
Goathland
  North York Moors tour 381
  pubs 610
Godiva, Lady 307
Godstow, restaurants 586
Golf 67, **485**, 630
Good Friday 65
Goodrich Castle 305
Gordale Scar, Malham walk 373
Gordon, Douglas 93
Gordon clan 471
Goring, restaurants 586
Gossips (London) 129
Gower, Bishop of St David's 450
Gower, George 51
Gower, John, tomb of 122
Gower Peninsula **452**
Goya, Francisco de 412, 506
Graham, J Gillespie 365
Grahame, Kenneth 222
Grand Christmas Parade (London) 65
Grand Union Canal 288
Grandisson, Bishop 277
Grange-in-Borrowdale 351
  hotels 560
Grant, Duncan 151
  Vanessa Bell at Charleston 151
Grantown-on-Spey, hotels 572

Grasmere 343, 352, **354**
hotels 560
restaurants 596
Grasmoor 350
Grassington, hotels 562
Great Autumn Flower Show (Harrogate) 64
Great Britain, SS 244
Great Chesters Fort 408
Great Dunmow, hotels 548
Great Exhibition (1851) 56–7, 97, 98
Great Fire of London (1666) 53, 118
Great Gable 350, 352
Great Langdale, pubs 610
Great Malvern **305**
Great Milton, restaurants 586
Great Missenden, restaurants 586
Great Orme's Head 431
Great Tew **208**
hotels 549
pubs 609
Great Western Trains 639
Great Yarmouth **187**
Greater London, map 13
El Greco 214, 412, 506
Green, Benjamin 411
Green Flag 637
Green Park (London) 77
Greenwich (London) **133**
Greenwich Market (London) 125
Greenwich Park (London) 77
Greg, Samuel 298
Gresham, Sir Thomas 113
Greta Bridge, pubs 611
Grevel, William 315
Greville, Sir Fulke 310, 311
Grey, 2nd Earl 411
Greyfriars Bobby 497
Griffith, Sir Henry 386
Grimes Graves **182–3**
Grimsby **389**
Grimshaw, Atkinson 396
Grimspound 283
Grimston, hotels 548
Grisedale Pike 349, 350
Groot, John de 514
Guards Polo Club (London) 129
Guest houses 539
Guildford **160**
hotels 546
Gullane, hotels 569–70
Gunpowder Plot (1605) 52
Guron, St 272
Guy Fawkes Night 64
Gwaun Valley, restaurants 603

H

Haddenham, restaurants 586
Hadrian, Emperor 44, 408, 468
Hadrian's Wall 44, 334, 346, 401, **408–9**, 468
Halifax 336, **398–9**
hotels 562
Hall, John 312
Hallowe'en 64
Hals, Frans 106
Haltwhistle
hotels 564
North Pennines tour 413
Ham House (London) 134
Hamada, Shoji 393
Hambledon Mill, Thames River tour 222
Hambleton, restaurants 594
Hamilton, James, *The Massacre of Glencoe* 529
Hamilton, Richard 93
Hammersmith, pubs 608
Hampsfield Fell 358
Hampshire *see* Downs and Channel Coast
Hampstead (London) **131**
pubs 608
Hampstead Heath (London) 77, **132**
Hampton Court **161**
Flower Show 63
Privy Garden 22
Hampton Court (Leominster) 301
Hampton Hill, restaurants 583
Hamsterley Forest, hotels 564
Handel, George Frederick 200
Hard Knott 351
Hardie, Keir 469
Hardknott Pass 351, 352
Hardraw Force 371
Hardwick Hall 290, 324
Hardy, Thomas **257**
Hare, David 20
Harewood, Earl and Countess of 396
Harewood House **396**
Harlech **440**
Castle 424
hotels **565**
restaurants 601
Harold II, King
Battle of Hastings 169
Holy Trinity Church 159
Norman Conquest 46, 47
Harpenden, hotels 549
Harris, Isle of 515
hotels 572
Harrod, Henry Charles 99
Harrods (London) **99**, 125
Harrogate **374**
festivals 64
hotels 562
restaurants 598
Hartland Abbey 274
Hartley, Jesse 363
Harvard, John 202, 315
Harvest festivals 64
Harvey Nichols (London) 125
Harwich, restaurants 585
Hassall, John, *Bruce in Single Combat at Bannockburn* 468
Hastings **169**
restaurants 583
Hastings, Battle of (1066) 46, 47, **169**
Hatfield House 53, 205, **219**
Hathaway, Anne 315
Hathersage, Peak District tour 327
Hawkins, John 51
Hawkshead 353, 356
Hawksmoor, Nicholas 24
Blenheim Palace 216
Castle Howard 384
Haworth **398**
restaurants 598
Hay Bluff 455
Hay-on-Wye **447**
pubs 611
The Hay-Wain (Constable) 85
Haydon Bridge
North Pennines tour 413
restaurants 600
Haytor Rocks 283
Haywards Heath, restaurants 583
Heacham 179
Headingley, restaurants 598
Health care 620
Heart of England **295–317**
climate 68
Exploring the Heart of England 296–7
hotels 555–8
pubs 609–10
restaurants 591–3
Heathrow Airport 634
Heaven (London) 129
Hebden Bridge 336, **398**
Hebrides 520
Heddon's Mouth 238
Heiton, hotels 570
Helm, hotels 562
Helmsley **379**
hotels 562
Helplines 621
Helston **268**
festivals 62
hotels 553
Helvellyn 341, 349, 350, 353
Hengist 209
Hengistbury Head 259
Henley
hotels 549
Royal Regatta 63, 66
Thames River tour 222
Henrietta Maria, Queen
portrait 393
Queen's Chapel (London) 87
Queen's House (London) 133
Henry I, King 40
Henry II, King 40
coat of arms 26
Dover Castle 171
murder of Thomas à Becket 48–9
Orford Castle 191
Rosa Mundi 221
Windsor Castle 224
Henry III, King 40
Clifford's Tower (York) 393
Gloucester 317
Lewes 168
Westminster Abbey (London) 95
Henry IV, King 40, 422
Henry V, King 40
Battle of Agincourt 49
coat of arms 26
Monmouth Castle 461
Portchester Castle 157
Henry VI, King 40
All Souls College (Oxford) 214
Eton College 223
King's College (Cambridge) 200
St Albans 220
Henry VII, King 40, 423
coat of arms 26
King's College (Cambridge) 201
Richmond 134
Westminster Abbey (London) 94, 95
Henry VIII, King 39, 40, 119, 468
Camber Castle 173
Cambridge 199
Dissolution of the Monasteries 316, 339
Epping Forest 197
Hampton Court 161
Hever Castle 177
Hyde Park (London) 103
Knole 176
Leeds Castle 176
Mary Rose 50, 157
Pendennis Castle 269
portraits of 200
"Rough Wooing" 498

Henry VIII, King (cont.)
St James's Palace 86
St Michael's Mount 266
splits from church of Rome 50
Trinity College (Cambridge) 203
Henry of Eastry 175
Henry, George, *Japanese Lady with a Fan* 505
Henry Wood Promenade Concerts 63
Heptonstall 398
Hepworth, Barbara 20
Barbara Hepworth Museum and Sculpture Garden (St Ives) 265
Madonna and Child 265
Tate Britain 93
Yorkshire Sculpture Park 399
Her Majesty's Theatre (London) 127
Heraldry and the Aristocracy **26–7**
Herbert, St 348
Herbert family 446, 458
Hereford **304**
hotels 556
Herefordshire *see* Heart of England
Hereward the Wake 48, 182
Heriot, James 371
Hermitage Rooms (London) 82–3
Heron, Patrick 228, 265
Hertford, Marquesses of 106
Hertfordshire *see* Thames Valley
Hertz 637
Hervey, Arthur, Bishop of Bath and Wells 241
Herzog and de Meuron 123
Hestercombe Garden 240
Hetton, restaurants 598
Hever Castle **177**
Hexham **408–9**
hotels 564
North Pennines tour 413
restaurants 600
Hidcote Manor Gardens, Midlands Garden tour 309
High Buston, hotels 564
High Street 353
Highgate (London) **132**
Highgate Cemetery (London) 132
Highland Clearances 469, **517**
Highlands and Islands 466, **511–35**
climate 69
Exploring the Highlands and Islands 512–13
hotels 571–3
pubs 611
restaurants 606–7
Hiking *see* Walks
Hilda, Abbess 382
Hill, Octavia 25
Hilliard, Nicholas 93
Hintlesham
hotels 548
restaurants 585
Hippodrome (London) 129
Hirst, Damien 93
History **39–61**
Scotland **468–9**
Wales **422–3**
Hitchcock, Alfred 272
Hitchhiking 637
HMV (London) 125
Hoare, Henry 254, 255
Hobart, Sir Henry 186
Hobbema, Meindert 200
Hobbs (London) 125
Hobby Drive 274
Hockney, David 20, 364
Mr. and Mrs. Clark and Percy 93
The Other Side 397
Hodgkin, Howard 93
Hogarth, William 55, 93, 114, 506
Portrait of Richard James 200
Hogmanay 65
Holbein, Hans 501
The Ambassadors 85
Holburne of Menstrie, William 248
Holderness **389**
Holiday Care Service 615
Holidays, public 65
Holker Hall 357
Holkham Hall, North Norfolk Coastal Tour 185
Holland, Henry 24, 166, 218
Holland House (London) 130
Holland Park (London) 76, **130–31**
Holmes, Sherlock **106**
Holy Island (Lindisfarne) **404**
Holyroodhouse, Palace of 496
Holywell, pubs 608
Honister Pass 340
Honiton 277
Hoover, William 59
Hope, hotels 558
Hope, Emma 125
Hopetoun, 1st Earl of 488
Hopetoun House **488**
Hopkins, Anthony 20
Hopkins, Sir Michael 361
Hops and hopping 148–9
Hopwas, hotels 556
Horne, Janet 516
Hornsea 389
Horse Guards (London)
Street-by-Street map 91
Horses
Horse of the Year Show 64
racing 66, 195, 631
Royal Mews (London) 89
Hospitals 620
Hotels **538–73**
restaurants in 575
children in 616
Devon and Cornwall 553–5
Downs and Channel Coast 545–7
East Anglia 547–9
East Midlands 558–9
Heart of England 555–8
Lancashire and the Lakes 559–62
London 542–4
Northumbria 563–4
Scotland 568–73
Thames Valley 549–51
Wales 564–8
Wessex 551–2
Yorkshire and the Humber Region 562–3
Hound Tor 283
House of Lords 20
Houses of Parliament (London) 79, **92**
Gunpowder Plot (1605) 52
Opening of Parliament 64
river view of 74
Street-by-Street map 91
Housesteads Fort 409
Housesteads Settlement 408
Housman, AE 300, 301
Hoverspeed 633
Howard, Catherine 120
Howard, Sir Ebenezer 58
Howard, Admiral Edward 385
Howard, Lord 51
Howard family 196, 384, 385
Howell, Margaret 125
Hudson, George 337
Hudson, Thomas 267
Hughenden Manor **221**
Hughes, Thomas 209
Huguenots 133
Huickes, Dr Robert 379
Hull *see* Kingston upon Hull
Humber, River 389
Humber Region **367–99**
climate 69
Exploring Yorkshire and the Humber Region 368–9
hotels 562–3
pubs 610
restaurants 598–9
Hume, David 467
Humphrey Head Point 358
Hundred Years' War 49
Hunstanton Cliffs, North Norfolk Coastal tour 184
Hunt, Charles, *Life Below Stairs* 25
Hunt, Leigh 130
Hunt, William Holman 361
Hunter, Dr William 505
Huntingdon **196**
hotels 548
restaurants 585
Hurlingham Club (London) 129
Hurstbourne Tarrant, restaurants 583
Hutchinson, Mary 354, 378
Hutton-in-the-Forest 346
Hutton-le-Hole **380**
North York Moors tour 381
Hyde Park (London) 72, 77, **103**
area map 97

I

ICA (London) 128
Ice skating 67
Iceni **183**
Icklingham, restaurants 585
Icknield Way 33
Ickworth House 194–5
Ida the Flamebearer 406
Ideal Home Exhibition 62
Ightham Mote 176–7
Ilkley, restaurants 599
Ilmington, hotels 556
In the Car (Lichtenstein) 491
Inchmahome Priory 481
Indian Community, Bradford **397**
Industrial Revolution 54, 466, 477
Birmingham 306
Ironbridge Gorge 286, 302–3
North Country **336–7**
Quarry Bank Mill (Styal) 298
Industry 18–19
Ingilby, Sir William Amcotts 375
Ingleby Greenhow, hotels 562
Inns, accommodation in 539
Inns of Court (London), river view of 74
Insurance 614, 620
Interior at Paddington (Freud) 364
International Coach Travel 633
International Eisteddfod 63
International Festival of Folk Arts (Sidmouth) 63
International Henley Royal Regatta 63
International Highland Games (Blair Atholl) 62
International Sheepdog Trials 64

International Youth Hostel Federation 617
Internet 622
Inverary Castle **534**
Inverness **522**
  hotels 572
  restaurants 607
Inversnaid, hotels 570
Iona 533
  hotels 572
Ipswich **191**
  hotels 548
Ireland, Robert 300
Ironbridge Gorge 286, **302–3**
  hotels 556
  map 303
Isis, River 212
Islam 619
Islay **535**
Isle of Purbeck **258**
Isle of Skye 464, 512, **520–21**
  hotels 572
  map 520–21
  pubs 611
Isle of Wight **156**
Isle of Wight Coastal Path 33
Isles of Scilly 267
Islington (London) **132**

J

Jacobite movement 52, **523**
  Culloden 523
  Glencoe Massacre 53, 529
  Glenfinnan Monument 533
  Stirling Castle 482
James I, King (James VI, King of Scotland) 41, 51, 52
  Audley End 196
  Banqueting House (London) 92
  coronation 482
  Edinburgh Castle 493
  Epping Forest 197
  Hyde Park (London) 103
  Newmarket 195
  statue of 484
  union of England and Scotland 469
  Warwick Castle 311
James I, King of Scotland 487
James II, King 41, 52, 53, 176, 240
  Jacobite movement 523
  Threave Castle 501
James II, King of Scotland 485, 492
James IV, King of Scotland 468, 486, 492
James V, King of Scotland
  Crown 492
  Falkland Palace 486
  Holyroodhouse 496
  Parliament House (Edinburgh) 494
  Portree 521
James VIII (the "Old Pretender") 523
James of St George 425
James, Henry 130, 172
Jameson, Mary 526
Japanese Lady with a Fan (Henry) 505
Jazz
  festivals 63
  London 128–9
Jazz Café (London) 129
Jedburgh, hotels 570
Jedburgh Abbey, Borders tour 489
Jeffreys, Judge 240
Jekyll, Gertrude 23, 240, 404
Jenkins, Valentine 483
Jermyn Street (London)
  Street-by-Street map 87
Jevington, restaurants 583
Jews
  in Lincoln 328
  synagogues 619
John, King 40
  Beaulieu Abbey 156
  and Liverpool 362
  Magna Carta 48, 205, 221, 223
  tomb of 306
John, Augustus 386
John, Tom 453
John of Beverley 387
John of Gaunt 374
John o'Groats **514**
John Lewis (London) 125
Johnson, Dr Samuel 430
Jones, Sir Horace 118
Jones, Inigo 21
  Banqueting House (London) 91, 92
  Piazza and Central Market (London) 81
  Queen's Chapel (London) 87
  Queen's House (London) 133
  St Paul's Church (London) 80
  Wilton House 253
Jones, Mary 436
Joseph of Arimathea, St 241
Jura **534–5**

K

Kapoor, Anish 123
Katrine, Loch 478, 480
Keats, John 200, 349
  Keats House (London) 131
Kedleston Hall 24–5, 324
Keiller, James 474
Kelmscott **208–9**
Kelsale, restaurants 585
Kelso Abbey, Borders tour 489
Kendal **356**
  restaurants 596
Kenilworth, restaurants 592
Kennedy, Joseph Jr 190
Kenneth McAlpin, King of Scotland 47, 468
Kensal Green cemetery (London) 77
Kensington (London), pubs 608
Kensington Gardens (London) 21, 76, 77, **103**
Kensington Palace (London) **103**
Kent
  Garden of England **148–9**
  see also Downs and Channel Coast
Kent, William 24, 103
Kentmere 353
Kents Cavern 278
Kenwood House (London) 128, 132
Keswick **347**, 349
  hotels 560
Kew (London) **134**
Kew Gardens (London) 76, 134
Keynes, JM 151
Keyston, restaurants 594
Kielder Water **406**
Kiftsgate Court Garden, Midlands Garden tour 309
Kilberry, restaurants 607
Kilchurn Castle 533
Killerton 277
Killiecrankie
  hotels 573
  Killiecrankie walk **528**
  restaurants 607
Kilpeck Church 304
Kimmeridge 258
  hotels 552
Kinclaven, restaurants 607
Kincraig, restaurants 607
King, Oliver, Bishop of Bath 248
Kings and queens **40–41**
  coronations 94
  royal coat of arms 26
King's College (Cambridge) **200–201**
King's Lynn **184–5**
King's Road (London) 130
Kingsbridge, restaurants 590
Kingsley, Charles 274, 373
Kingston Bagpuize, hotels 550
Kingston Lacy 259
Kingston upon Hull **388–9**
  pubs 610
Kingswear, hotels 553
Kingussie, hotels 573
Kinski, Nastassja 257
Kintbury, restaurants 586
Kintyre **535**
Kipling, Rudyard 151, 274
Kipling Tors 274
Kippford, restaurants 605
Kirk, Dr John 394
Kirkcudbright, hotels 570
Kirkham Priory 339
Kirkstall Abbey 339
Kirkstone Galleries **354**, 355
Kisimul Castle 515
Kitaj, RB 93
Knaresborough **374–5**
  restaurants 599
Knebworth House **219**
Kneller, Sir Godfrey 216
Knighton 445, **447**
Knights Templar 114
Knightshayes Court 233, 277
Knole **176–7**
Knott Rigg 350
Knowstone, pubs 609
Knox, John 484
  John Knox's House (Edinburgh) 465, 497
  Presbyterian Church 469
  Scottish Reformation 495
  statues of 468, 504
Kyle of Lochalsh, restaurants 607
Kylesku, restaurants 607
Kynance Cove 268
Kyrle, John 305

L

Labour Party 61
Lacock **243**
  hotels 552
  restaurants 588
Laguerre, Louis 217
Lainé, Elie 218
Lake District 334, **343–65**
  climate 68
  Exploring Lancashire and the Lakes 344–5
  geology **340–41**
  hotels 559–62
  major peaks 348–53
  pubs 610
  restaurants 595–7
Lamb and Flag (London) 80
Lambert, Daniel 331
Lamphey, restaurants 603
Lancashire **343–65**
  climate 68

Lancashire (cont.)
Exploring Lancashire and the Lakes 344–5
hotels 559–62
pubs 610
restaurants 595–7
Lancaster **358–9**
Landewednack, hotels 554
Land's End 230, 262
Penwith tour 264
Landseer, Sir Edwin 529
Lanfranc, Archbishop of 174
Langar, hotels 558
Langdale **353**
Langdale Pikes 341, 351, 352
Langho, restaurants 596
Langley, Bishop of Durham 414
Languages
Gaelic 466
Welsh 420, 423
Lanhydrock 232, **272**, 273
Lanyon Quoit, Penwith tour 264
Large Two Forms (Moore) 399
Largs, restaurants 605
The Last of the Clan (Faed) 517
The Last of England (Brown) 307
Lastingham, North York Moors tour 381
Laszlo, Henri de 485
Latimer, Hugh, Martyrs' Memorial (Oxford) 210, 213
Lauderdale, Countess of 134
Laurel, Stan 357
Lavenham **194**
hotels 548
Lawn Tennis Association 631
Lawrence, Sir Thomas 245
Leach, Bernard 265, 393
Leamington Spa, restaurants 592
Ledbury **305**
hotels 556
Leeds **396**
hotels 562
restaurants 599
Leeds Castle 63, 153, **176**
Leeds-Liverpool Canal 336
Legoland 629
Leicester, Earl of 309
Leicester, restaurants 594
Leicestershire *see* East Midlands
Leighton, Lord 131
Leighton Hall **358**
Leighton House (London) 131
Leith Hill 160
Lely, Sir Peter 529
Leominster **301**
Leonardo da Vinci 89, 501
The Leonardo Cartoon 84
Levens Hall **357**
Lever, William Hesketh 337, 365
Lewdown, restaurants 590
Lewes **168**
hotels 546
Lewis, Isle of 467, 515
hotels 572
LeWitt, Sol 399
Leysters, hotels 557
Liberty (London) 125
Libeskind, Daniel 100, 359
Lichtenstein, Roy, *In the Car* 491
Life Below Stairs (Hunt) 25
Lifton, restaurants 590
Lightoler, Thomas 388
Limelight (London) 129
Limestone Corner Milecastle 409
Lincoln 287, **328–9**
Cathedral 321
hotels 558
restaurants 594–5
Street-by-Street map 328–9
Lincolnshire *see* East Midlands
Lindisfarne **404**, 405
Lindisfarne Gospels 405
Linley Sambourne House (London) 131
Linlithgow
hotels 570
restaurants 605
Linlithgow, Marquess of 488
Linlithgow Palace **487**
Linn of Tummel, Killiecrankie walk 528
Lippi, Fra Filippo, *The Annunciation* 84
Literature 20
Little Langdale 352
Little Malvern 305
hotels 557
Little Moreton Hall 290–91, 299
Little Town 350
Littlebury, pubs 608
Live Aid 61
Liverpool 343, 345, **362–5**
map 362
pubs 610
restaurants 596–7
Walker Art Gallery 334, **364–5**
Liverpool and Manchester railway 336
Livingstone, David 467, **500**, 503
Lizard Peninsula 228, **268**
Llanaber, hotels 565
Llanarmon Dyffryn Ceriog
hotels 565
restaurants 601
Llanberis 419, **437**
restaurants 602
Llandaff Cathedral 457
Llanddeiniolen, hotels 565
Llandeilo, hotels 567
Llandewi Skirrid, restaurants 603
Llandovery, Wild Wales tour 453
Llandrillo
hotels 565
restaurants 602
Llandrindod Wells **447**
Llandudno **431**
hotels 565
restaurants 602
Llanfachreth, hotels 565
Llanfihangel-Yng-Ngwynfa, hotels 567
Llangammarch Wells, hotels 567
Llangattock, Lady 461
Llangollen 427, **436**
restaurants 602
Llangollen Canal 436
Llanidloes, Wild Wales tour 453
Llanigon, hotels 567
Llanthony, hotels 567
Llanthony Priory 447, 455
Llanwrtyd Wells 447
hotels 567
Llithfaen 439
Lloyd, Christopher 170
Lloyd George, David 423
statue of 457
Lloyd's Building (London) **118**
Llyn Peninsula **439**
Llyn y Fan Fach 454
Llyswen
hotels 567
restaurants 603
Llywelyn the Great 422
Beddgelert 438
Llywelyn the Great (cont.)
Castell-y-Bere 425
statue of 432
Llywelyn the Last 422, 430
Lobb, John 125
Loch Ness Monster 522
Lochinver, hotels 573
Lochmaddy 515
Lochranza, hotels 573
Lombard Street (London)
Street-by-Street map 113
Lomond, Loch 464, 480
pubs 611
London **70–143**
City and Southwark **111–23**
climate 69
entertainment **126–9**, 628
events 62–5
Further Afield 130–34
hotels 542–4
London at a Glance 72–3
parks and gardens **76–7**
pubs 608
Regent's Park and Bloomsbury **105–9**
restaurants 578–82
river view of **74–5**
shops and markets **124–5**
South Kensington and Hyde Park **97–103**
street finder 135–43
Street-by-Street maps
City and Southwark 112–13
Covent Garden 80–81
Piccadilly and St James's 86–7
South Kensington and Hyde Park 98–9
Whitehall and Westminster 90–91
travel in 642–3
West End and Westminster **79–95**
London Coliseum 128
London Dungeon **119**
London Eye *see* British Airways London Eye
London Film Festival 64
London Lead Company 412
London Marathon 66
London Underground 20, 56, 643
London's Transport Museum
Street-by-Street map 81, **82**
Londonderry, Marquess of 448
Long, Richard 93, 123
Long Crendon
hotels 550
restaurants 586
Long Man of Wilmington 168
Long Meg and her Daughters 346
Long Mynd 300
Longleat House **254**
Longridge, restaurants 597
Looe 272
Lord Mayor's Procession and Show (London) 64
Lord Nelson pub (Burnham Market), North Norfolk Coastal tour 184
Lord's Cricket Ground (London) 129
Lorton, hotels 561
Lorton Fell 349
Lorton Vale 348
Losinga, Bishop 188
Lost Gardens of Heligan 269
Lost property 621, 639
Lostwithiel 272
Lothians 477
Low Catton, pubs 610

Lower Slaughter 292
restaurants 592
Lowestoft **187**
hotels 548
Lowlands (Scotland) **477–509**
climate 69
Exploring the Lowlands 478–9
hotels 568–70
pubs 611
restaurants 604–6
Lowry, LS, *Coming from the Mill* 359
Lucas, Sarah 93
Lucy, Sir Thomas 290
Ludlow 297, **300–301**
hotels 557
restaurants 592–3
Lulworth Cove 258
Lunch 574, 577
Lundy 274
Lune Aqueduct 358
Luss 480
Lutyens, Sir Edwin 365
Castle Drogo 25, 283
Cenotaph (London) 91
Great Dixter 170
Hestercombe Garden 240
Lindisfarne Castle 404
Queen Mary's Dolls' House 225
Lyceum Theatre (London) 127
Lydford, pubs 609
Lydford Gorge 282
Lynmouth 238, **276**
restaurants 590
Lynton **276**
Lyric Theatre (London) 127
Lytton, Lord 219

M

Macbean, Donald 528
Macbeth 523
McCartney, Paul 27, 535
see also Beatles
Macdonald, Alex 526
Macdonald, Anne Maxwell 506
MacDonald, Flora 515, 521
grave of 520
MacDonald clan 470, 529
Machynlleth **448**
Mackay clan 470
McKellen, Ian 20
Mackenzie, Osgood 516
Mackenzie clan 470
Mackintosh, Charles Rennie **504**, 505
Maclean clan 532
MacLeod clan 470, 520
McNally, Leonard 370
McTaggart, William 505
Madame Jojo's (London) 129
Madame Tussaud's (London) **106**
Madonna and Child (Hepworth,) 265
Madonna and Child (Michelangelo) 86
Maentwrog, pubs 611
Maes Howe 514
Magazines 618
Magna **399**
Magna Carta 48, 205, 221, 223
Magnus, St, tomb of 514
Magnus Barfud 535
Magritte, René 491
Maiden Castle 43, 257
Maiden Newton, restaurants 589
Mail services 623
Major, John 61
Malcolm III, King of Scotland 486, 493
Maldon **197**
Malham walk **373**
The Mall (London) **87**
Mallaig, Road to the Isles tour 532
Mallyan Spout, North York Moors tour 381
Malmshead 239
Malvern Wells, hotels 557
Malverns **305**
Manchester **360–61**
airport 634
hotels 561
map 360
pubs 610
restaurants 597
Manchester Ship Canal 359, 360
Mansfield, Isaac 216
Mansion House (London)
Street-by-Street map 113
Mantegna, Andrea 161
Mappa Mundi 304
Maps
Ordnance Survey 32
road maps 636
Aberdeen 525
Bath 246–7
Borders tour **489**
Brighton 162–3
Bristol 245
Cairngorms 530–31
Cambridge 198–9
Cardiff 457
Cheviot Hills 407
climate of Great Britain 68–9
Constable walk 192
Conwy 432–3
Cotswold stone towns and villages 293
Dartmoor National Park 282–3
Devon and Cornwall 262–3
Downs and Channel Coast 154–5
East Anglia 180–81
East Midlands 320–21
Edinburgh 491
Europe 11
Exmoor National Park 238–9
Ffestiniog Railway 438–9
Glasgow 502
Great Britain 10–11
Greater London 13
Hadrian's Wall 408–9
Heart of England 296–7
Highlands and Islands 512–13
houses of historical figures 150–51
Ironbridge Gorge 303
Killiecrankie walk 528
Lancashire and the Lakes 344–5
Lincoln 328–9
Liverpool 362
London 72–3
The City 112–13
City and Southwark 111
Covent Garden 80–81
parks and gardens **76–7**
Piccadilly and St James's 86–7
Regent's Park and Bloomsbury 105
river view of 74–5
South Kensington 98–9
South Kensington and Hyde Park 97
West End and Westminster 79
Whitehall and Westminster 90–91
Lowlands (Scotland) 478–9
Malham walk 373
Manchester 360
Maps (cont.)
Midlands 286–7
Midlands canal network 289
Midlands Garden tour 308–9
national rail network 639
North Country 334–5
North Norfolk Coastal tour 184–5
North Pennines tour 413
North Wales 428–9
North York Moors 381
Northern Fells and Lakes 348–9
Northumbria 402–3
Peak District tour 326–7
Penwith tour 264
Prehistoric Britain 42–3
Regional Great Britain 12–15
Road to the Isles tour 532–3
Royal Deeside tour 526–7
Rye 172–3
Scotland 464–5
Shetland and Orkney islands 11, 15
Skye 520–21
South and Mid-Wales 444–5
Southeast England 146–7
Stratford-upon-Avon 312–13
Thames River tour 222–3
Thames Valley 206–7
Tissington Trail 325
Trossachs 480–81
Wales 418–19
walkers' Britain 32–3
Wessex 236–7
West Country 228–9
West Country Gardens 232–3
Wild Wales tour 453
York 390–91
Yorkshire and the Humber Region 368–9
Yorkshire Dales National Park 370
Mar, 1st Earl of 482
Marble Hill House (London) 134
March, Earl of 159
Marcher Lords 422, 423
Marchesa Maria Grimaldi (Rubens) 259
Marconi, Guglielmo 58
Margaret, Queen of Scotland 488, 493
Margaret of Anjou 202
Margaret Tudor 468
Margate **171**
Maris, Matthijs, *The Sisters* 507
Markets 627
Borough Market (London) **122**
London 124–5
Marks & Spencer (London) 125
Marlborough 251
Marlborough, John Churchill, 1st Duke of 205, 216, 217
Marlow, hotels 550
Marney, Sir Henry 193
Martello towers 170
Martin, John 413
Martini, Simone, *Christ Discovered in the Temple* 365
Marx, Karl 105
tomb of 132
Mary, Queen, consort of George V 225
Mary, Queen of Scots 50, 51, 468–9, 491, **497**
Abbotsford House 498
Bolton Castle 371
Edinburgh Castle 493
golf 485
Inchmahome Priory 481
Linlithgow Palace 487

Mary, Queen of Scots (cont.)
Oxburgh Hall 183
Palace of Holyroodhouse 496
Provand's Lordship (Glasgow) 504
"Rough Wooing" 498
Scone Palace 484
Stirling 482
Traquair House 499
Mary I, Queen 39, 41, 114
Catholicism 50, 51
Framlingham Castle 191
Protestant martyrs 168, 213
tomb of 194
Mary II, Queen 41, 52, 161
Mary of Guise 496
Mary Rose 50, 157
The Massacre of Glencoe (Hamilton) 529
Matlock **324**
hotels 559
Maumbury Rings 257
Maundy Thursday 62
Mawddach Estuary 441
Mawnan Smith, hotels 554
Maxwell, Sir John 506
May, Isle of 486
May Day 65
Mayflower 52, 156–7, 280
Measurements, conversion chart 619
Medical treatment 620
Medway, River 176
Melbourn, restaurants 587
Mellor, hotels 561
Melmerby, restaurants 597
Melrose Abbey **498**
Borders tour 489
Membury, hotels 554
Merionethshire *see* North Wales
Merlemond, Oliver de 304
Merry Maidens, Penwith tour 264
Mersey, River 362
Methodism **267**, 423
Methuen, Lady 243
Michelangelo 212, 225
Madonna and Child 86
Mid-Wales **443–61**
climate 68
Exploring South and Mid-Wales 444–5
hotels 566–8
pubs 611
restaurants 602–4
Middle Ages **48–9**
Middle Winterslow, hotels 552
Middleham Castle 371
Middleton-in-Teesdale **412**
Midhurst 65
Midland Mainline 639
Midlands **285–331**
canals **288–9**
East Midlands **319–31**
Heart of England **295–317**
map 286–7
Midlands Garden tour **308–9**
Midnight Mass 65
Mildert, William van, Bishop of Durham 414
Mileage chart 14
Milebrook, hotels 567
Millais, Sir John Everett 93, 121, 131, 364
Ophelia 56–7
Miller, Hugh 517
Milton, John 219, 300
Minack Theatre, Penwith tour 264
Minehead 239
Mining *see* Coal mining
Ministry of Defence 282
Ministry of Sound (London) 129
Minsmere Reserve 190
Minton 299
Misericords 329
Mr and Mrs Andrews (Gainsborough) 151
Mr and Mrs Clark and Percy (Hockney) 93
Mobility International 615
Modigliani, Amadeo 189
Moffat, restaurants 605
Monarchy *see* Kings and queens
Monasteries 338
Dissolution of 50, 339
Mondrian, Piet 123
Monet, Claude 123, 200
Money **624–5**
Monmouth **460–61**
Monmouth, Duke of 240
Monmouthshire *see* South and Mid-Wales
Monmouthshire and Brecon Canal 455
Mons Meg **492**, 501
Monsal Head, pubs 610
Montacute
hotels 552
restaurants 589
Montacute House 233, 235, 256
Montagu, Lord 156
Montfort, Simon de 168, 311
Montgomery, Viscount 27
Montrose, Duke of 481
Monument (London) **118**
Moore, Albert, *Seashells* 364
Moore, Henry 20
Henry Moore Institute (Leeds) 396
Large Two Forms 399
Recumbent Figure 93
Sainsbury Centre for Visual Arts (Norwich) 189
St Stephen Walbrook (London) 113, 114
Scottish Gallery of Modern Art (Edinburgh) 491
Walker Art Gallery (Liverpool) 364
Morar, Road to the Isles tour 532
Moray 511
Moray, Bishop of 524
More, Sir Thomas 50, 130
Morecambe Bay **358**
Moreton family 291
Morgan, Dr William 423
Morris, Jane 208
Morris, Roger 534
Morris, William 316
Castle Howard 385
Jesus College (Cambridge) 202
Kelmscott Manor 208–9
Peterhouse (Cambridge) 203
Mortehoe, hotels 554
Morwellham Quay **281**
Moseley Old Hall 291
Moslem organizations 619
Mother Shipton's Cave 374–5
Motor homes 541
Mott, Hay and Anderson 411
Motte and bailey castles 472
Moulsford
hotels 550
restaurants 587
Moulton, pubs 610
Mount Edgcumbe Park 232, 280
Mount Grace Priory 338
Mountbatten, Earl 27, 150
Mousa Broch 514
Mousehole 266
Moustafa, Ahmed 503
Muir of Dinnet Nature Reserve, Royal Deeside tour 526
Muir of Ord, hotels 573
Mull, Isle of **532–3**
hotels 572
The Mumbles (Swansea) 452
hotels 567
restaurants 603
Muncaster Castle 352
Mungo, St 487, 502–3
Mungrisdale, hotels 561
Muñoz, Juan 123
Murillo, Esteban 506
Murray, Patrick 496
Museums and galleries
admission charges 616–17
opening hours 616
shops 627
Abbot Hall Art Gallery & Museum of Lakeland Life (Kendal) 356
Alexander Keiller Museum (Avebury) 251
Alice in Wonderland Centre (Llandudno) 431
American Museum (Bath) 249
Anne of Cleves House (Lewes) 168
ARC (York) 393
Armley Mills Museum (Leeds) 396
Art Gallery (Aberdeen) 526
Art Gallery and Museum (Perth) 484
Ashmolean Museum (Oxford) 210, 212
Assembly Rooms and Museum of Costume (Bath) 248
Auchindrain Museum **534**
Baltic (Newcastle upon Tyne) 410, **411**
Bannockburn Heritage Centre (Stirling) 482
Barbara Hepworth Museum and Sculpture Garden (St Ives) 265
Beamish Open Air Museum **410–11**
Beatles Story (Liverpool) 363
Beatrix Potter Gallery (Hawkshead) 355
Bethnal Green Museum of Childhood (London) 133
Black House Museum (Lewis) 515
Blaenafon Ironworks 460
Blists Hill Museum (Ironbridge Gorge) 303
Bodmin Town Museum **272**, 273
Border History Museum (Hexham) 408, 409
Bowes Museum (Barnard Castle) 412
Bradford Industrial Museum 397
Brantwood (Coniston) 356
Bridewell Museum (Norwich) 189
Bristol Industrial Museum 245
British Empire & Commonwealth Museum (Bristol) 244
British Golf Museum (St Andrews) 485
British Museum (London) 73, **108–9**
Brontë Parsonage Museum (Haworth) 398
Buckler's Hard 156
Building of Bath Museum (Bath) 249
Burns Cottage **501**

Museums and galleries (cont.)
Burrell Collection (Glasgow) 465, **506–7**
Butcher Row House (Ledbury) 305
Cadbury World (Bournville) 307
Captain Cook Memorial Museum (Whitby) 382
Carnegie Birthplace Museum (Dunfermline) 487
Castle Museum (Colchester) 193
Castle Museum (Norwich) 188–9
Central Museum and Art Gallery (Northampton) 331
Centre for Alternative Technology 448
Ceredigion Museum (Aberystwyth) 449
Charles Dickens Museum (Portsmouth) 157
Christchurch Mansion (Ipswich) 191
Cider Museum and King Offa Distillery (Hereford) 304
City Art Gallery (Leeds) 396
City Museum (Lancaster) **358**, 359
City Museum and Art Gallery (Birmingham) 307
City Museum and Art Gallery (Bristol) 245
City Museum and Art Gallery (Hereford) 304
Clive Museum (Powis Castle) 446
Coalport China Museum (Ironbridge Gorge) 303
Colour Museum (Bradford) 397
Commandery (Worcester) 306
Corbridge Roman Site and Museum 409
Corinium Museum (Cirencester) 317
Courtauld Institute (London) 82
Crafts in the Bay (Cardiff) 457
Crich Tramway Village 327
Cromarty Courthouse 517
Cromwell Museum (Huntingdon) 196
D-Day Museum 157
Dales Countryside Museum 371
Dartmouth Museum 278
Dennis Severs' House (London) 133
Design Museum (London) **119**
Dickens House Museum (London) 109
Discovery (Dundee) 485
Dock Museum (Barrow-in-Furness) **356**, 357
Dorset County Museum (Dorchester) 257
Dove Cottage and the Wordsworth Museum (Grasmere) 354
Dylan Thomas Centre (Swansea) 452
Eden Camp **386**
1853 Gallery (Bradford) 397
Elgar's Birthplace (Worcester) 306
Elgin Museum 524
Elizabethan House Museum (Great Yarmouth) 187
Etruria Industrial Museum 299
Eureka! (Halifax) 399
Fitzwilliam Museum (Cambridge) **200**
Flagship Portsmouth Victorygate 157
Flambards Village Theme Park 268
Folk Museum (Helston) 268
Fox Talbot Museum (Lacock) 243
Freud Museum (London) 131

Museums and galleries (cont.)
Gainsborough's House (Sudbury) 194
Gasworks Museum (Biggar) 499
Gilbert Collection (London) 82
Gladstone Court Museum (Biggar) 499
Gladstone Pottery Museum (Stoke-on-Trent) 299
Glasgow School of Art 505
Glynn Vivian Art Gallery (Swansea) 452
God's House Tower Museum of Archaeology 157
Goonhilly Earth Station 268
Grace Darling Museum (Bamburgh) 406
Groam House Museum (Rosemarkie) 517
Grosvenor Museum (Chester) **298**, 299
Hands on History (Hull) 388
Herbert Gallery and Museum (Coventry) 307
Heritage Centre (Ledbury) 305
Hermitage Rooms (London) 82–3
Historic Dockyard (Chatham) 176
HM Customs and Excise National Museum (Liverpool) 363
HMS *Unicorn* (Dundee) 485
Holburne Museum of Art (Bath) 248
Hollytrees Museum (Colchester) 193
House of the Tailor of Gloucester 317
Household Cavalry Museum (Windsor) 223
Hugh Miller's Cottage (Cromarty) 517
Hunterian Art Gallery (Glasgow) 505
Imperial War Museum North (Salford) 359
Inverness Museum and Art Gallery 522
Ipswich Museum 191
Jackfield Tile Museum (Ironbridge Gorge) 302
Jorvik, the Viking City (York) 391, **394**
Judge's Lodgings (Lancaster) **358**, 359
Keats House (London) 131
Kelvingrove Art Gallery (Glasgow) 503, **505**
Kendal Museum of Natural History and Archaeology 356
Keswick Museum and Art Gallery 347
King's Own Scottish Borderers Regimental Museum (Berwick-upon-Tweed) 404
Lady Lever Art Gallery (Port Sunlight) 365
Lake Village Museum (Glastonbury) 241
Laurel and Hardy Museum (Ulverston) 357
Leighton House (London) 131
Linley Sambourne House (London) 131
Little Hall (Lavenham) 194
Liverpool Museum 365
Llechwedd Slate Caverns 437
London Dungeon (London) **119**
London's Transport Museum (London) 81, **82**

Museums and galleries (cont.)
Lowestoft Museum 187
The Lowry (Salford) 359
Ludlow Museum **300**, 301
McManus Galleries (Dundee) 485
Madame Tussaud's (London) **106**
Maeldune Centre (Maldon) 197
Magna **399**
Manchester Art Gallery 361
Maritime Museum (Aberdeen) 526
Maritime Museum (Hull) 388
Maritime Museum (Lancaster) **358**, 359
Maritime Museum (Southampton) 157
Market Hall (Warwick) 309
Merseyside Maritime Museum (Liverpool) 363
Mining Museum (Blaenafon) 460
Mompesson House (Salisbury) 253
Moray Motor Museum (Elgin) 524
Morwellham Quay **281**
Moyse's Hall (Bury St Edmunds) **194**, 195
Museum and Art Gallery (Buxton) 322
Museum and Art Gallery (Cheltenham) 316
Museum and Art Gallery (Penzance) 266
Museum of Army Transport (Beverley) 387
Museum of British Road Transport (Coventry) 307
Museum of Canterbury 174
Museum of Childhood (Beaumaris) 430
Museum of Childhood (Edinburgh) 496, 497
Museum of Costume and Textiles (Nottingham) 324
Museum of the Gorge (Ironbridge Gorge) 302
Museum of Iron (Ironbridge Gorge) 302
Museum of Islay Life 535
Museum of Lakeland Life (Kendal) 356
Museum of Liverpool Life 363
Museum of London (London) **115**
Museum of North Devon (Barnstaple) 275
Museum of Oxford 213
Museum of Science and Industry in Manchester 361
Museum of Scotland (Edinburgh) 491
Museum of Transport (Glasgow) 504
Museum of Victorian Whitby 382
Museum of Welsh Life (Cardiff) 457
Museum of Worcester Porcelain 306
National Coal Mining Museum **399**
National Fishing Heritage Centre (Grimsby) 389
National Gallery (London) 72, 73, **84–5**
National Gallery of Scotland (Edinburgh) 490
National Horseracing Museum (Newmarket) 195
National Maritime Museum Cornwall 269
National Maritime Museum (London) 133
National Motor Museum 156

Museums and galleries (cont.)
National Museum and Gallery of Wales 457
National Museum of Photography, Film and Television (Bradford) 397
National Portrait Gallery (London) **83**
National Railway Museum (York) 394
National Waterways Museum (Gloucester) 317
Natural History Museum (London) 98, **102**
Nelson Museum (Monmouth) 461
New Lanark **500**
New Millennium Experience (New Lanark) 500
No. 1 Royal Crescent (Bath) 248
North Devon Maritime Museum (Appledore) 275
The Official Loch Ness Exhibition Centre 522
Oxford Story 213
Oxford University Museum 213
Parliament House (Machynlleth) 448
Peak District Mining Museum (Matlock) 324
Pencil Museum (Keswick) 347
Penlee House Gallery and Museum (Penzance) **266**, 267
People's Palace (Glasgow) 505
Pier Arts Centre (Orkney) 514
Pitt Rivers Museum (Oxford) 213
Plymouth Dome 280
Poldark Mine 268
Pollok House (Glasgow) **506**
Potteries Museum and Art Gallery (Hanley) 299
Priest's House Museum (Wimborne Minster) 259
Prison and Police Museum (Ripon) 375
Provand's Lordship (Glasgow) 504
Queen Elizabeth's Hunting Lodge (Epping Forest) 197
Queen's Gallery (London) 88, **89**
Radnorshire Museum (Llandrindod Wells) 447
Regimental Museum (Fort George) 523
Regimental Museum (Monmouth) 460–61
Regimental Museum of Royal Northumberland Fusiliers (Alnwick Castle) 406
Roman Baths Museum (Bath) 248
Roman Legionary Museum (Caerleon) 460
Roman Museum (Ribchester) 359
Rotunda (Scarborough) 383
Royal Academy (London) **83**
Royal Albert Memorial Museum and Art Gallery (Exeter) 277
Royal Armouries Museum (Leeds) 396
Royal Cornwall Museum (Truro) 269
Royal Museum of Scotland 497
Royal Naval Museum 157
Royal Pump Room Museum (Harrogate) 374
Russell-Cotes Art Gallery and Museum (Bournemouth) 259
Rydal Mount 354
Ryedale Folk Museum (Hutton-le-Hole) 380

Museums and galleries (cont.)
Sainsbury Centre for Visual Arts (Norwich) 189
St Mungo Museum of Religious Life and Art (Glasgow) 503
Salisbury and South Wiltshire Museum 253
Scarborough Art Gallery 383
Science Museum (London) 98, **102**
Scottish Fisheries Museum (East Neuk) 486
Scottish Gallery of Modern Art & Dean Gallery (Edinburgh) 491
Scottish Kiltmaker Visitor Centre (Inverness) 522
Scottish National Portrait Gallery (Edinburgh) 491
Sherlock Holmes Museum (London) **106**
Shetland Museum 514
Shibden Hall Museum (Halifax) 399
Shrewsbury Museum and Art Gallery 300
Sir John Soane's Museum (London) **114–15**
Somerset County Museum (Taunton) 240
Somerset Rural Life Museum (Glastonbury) 241
Southwold Museum 190
Stamford Museum 331
Strangers' Hall (Norwich) 189
Streetlife Transport Museum (Hull) **388**, 389
Swaledale Folk Museum 371
Swansea Museum 452
Tain Through Time 517
Tales of Robin Hood (Nottingham) 324
Tate Britain (London) 73, **93**
Tate Liverpool 363
Tate Modern (London) **123**
Tate St Ives 265
Techniquest (Cardiff) 456
Tenement House (Glasgow) 503
Thackray Medical Museum (Leeds) 396
Theakston Bewery (Masham) 371
Theatre Museum (London) 81, **82**
Thinktank – the Birmingham Museum of Science and Discovery 307
Tom Brown's School Museum (Uffington) 209
Torquay Museum 278
Torridon Countryside Centre 516
Totnes Elizabethan Museum 279
Tullie House Museum (Carlisle) 346
Tymperleys (Colchester) 193
Ulverston Heritage Centre 356–7
Upper Wharfedale Museum 372
Urbis (Manchester) 361
Usher Art Gallery (Lincoln) 329
Verulamium Museum (St Albans) 220
Victoria and Albert Museum (London) 72, 99, **100–101**
Walker Art Gallery (Liverpool) 334, **364–5**
Wallace Collection (London) **106**
Warwick Doll Museum 309
Waterfront Museum (Poole) **258**, 259
Wells Museum 240
West Gate Museum (Canterbury) 174
Westgate Museum (Winchester) **158**, 159

Museums and galleries (cont.)
Wheal Martyn China Clay Museum 269
Whitby Museum and Pannett Art Gallery 382
The Whithorn Story 501
Whitworth Art Gallery (Manchester) 361
William Wilberforce House (Hull) **388**, 389
Windermere Steamboat Museum 355
Wood End Museum (Scarborough) 383
Wordsworth House (Cockermouth) 350
World of Beatrix Potter 355
York Castle Museum 391, 394
York City Art Gallery 393
Yorkshire Museum (York) 390, 394
Yorkshire Sculpture Park **399**
Music 628
Aldeburgh Music Festival **191**
classical music, opera and dance 128
King's College Choir 200
rock, pop, jazz and clubs 128–9
Royal College of Music (London) 98
The Music Lesson (Vermeer) 88
Mylne, Robert 534
Mylor Bridge, pubs 609
Mytholmroyd, hotels 563

N

Nantgaredig
hotels 567
restaurants 603
Napoleon I, Emperor 171, 225, 436
Napoleon III, Emperor 225
Nash, John 21, 55
Buckingham Palace 88
Regency London **107**
Regent Street (London) 83
Regent's Park (London) 105
Royal Mews (London) 89
Royal Opera Arcade (London) 87
Royal Pavilion (Brighton) 147, 166
Nash, Paul 82, 93
Nash, Richard "Beau" **249**
Nasmyth, Alexander 491
National Car Rentals 637
National Coal Mining Museum **399**
National Covenant 52
National Exhibition Centre 307
National Express 640
National Federation of Anglers 631
National Gallery (London) 72, 73, **84–5**
National Health Service 59
National Helpline for the Blind 621
National Helpline for Drugs 621
National Maritime Museum (London) 133
National parks
Brecon Beacons 419, **454–5**
Dartmoor 228, **282–3**
Exmoor 228, 237, **238–9**
Lake District 348–9
North York Moors 381
Northumberland 407
Peak District 326–7
Pembrokeshire Coast 444
Snowdonia 428, 436, **437–8**
Yorkshire Dales 334, **370–72**
National Portrait Gallery (London) **83**
National Rail Enquiries 639
National Trust 24, **25**, 343, 617
National Trust for Scotland 617

National Union of Students 617
Natural History Museum (London) **102**
Street-by-Street map 98
Neal Street and Neal's Yard (London)
Street-by-Street map 80
Near Sawrey
pubs 610
restaurants 597
The Needles 156
Neidpath Castle 472
Nelson, Admiral Lord Horatio 54
Battle of Trafalgar 55
coat of arms 27
HMS *Victory* 157
Lord Nelson pub (Burnham Market) 184
Nelson Museum (Monmouth) 461
Nelson's Column (London) 72
Neptune's Staircase, Road to the Isles tour 533
Ness, Loch **522**
Nettlefold, Archibald 279
Nevern, pubs 611
Neville family 310, 458
Nevinson, CRW 93
New Change (London)
Street-by-Street map 112
New Forest **156**
New Lanark **500**
New London Theatre (London) 127
New Milton
hotels 546
restaurants 583
New Register House (Edinburgh) 27
New towns 58–9
New Year 65
New York (Northumbria), pubs 611
New Zealand High Commission 619
Newark, restaurants 595
Newby Hall **375**
Newcastle upon Tyne 403, **410–11**
airport 634
hotels 564
pubs 611
restaurants 600
slums 56
Newcomen, Thomas 102
Newlands, hotels 561
Newlands Valley **350**
Newlyn 266
Penwith tour 264
Newlyn School 266
Newman, Cardinal John Henry 99
Newmarket **195**
Newport
hotels 567
restaurants 603
Newquay, hotels 554
Newspapers 21, 618
Newton, Sir Isaac 52
portrait 330
statue of 203
Nicholson, Ben 93
St Ives, Cornwall 265
Nicolson, Harold 177
Nidd, River 374
Nightingale, Florence 56, 150
Ninian, St 501, 503
Norfolk *see* East Anglia
Norfolk, Dukes of 160
Norfolk, Earl of 191
Norfolk Coast Path 33
Normans
castles 48
invasion of Britain 39, 46, 422
Normans (cont.)
and Scotland 468
North Bovey, hotels 554
North Country **333–415**
abbeys **338–9**
Industrial Revolution **336–7**
Lancashire and the Lakes **343–65**
map 334–5
Northumbria **401–15**
Yorkshire and the Humber Region **367–99**
North Downs **169**
North Downs Way 33
North Norfolk Coastal tour **184–5**
North Pennines tour **413**
North Uist 515
North Wales **427–41**
climate 68
Exploring North Wales 428–9
hotels 564–6
pubs 611
restaurants 601–2
North Walsham, hotels 548
North York Moors 367, 368
North York Moors tour **381**
North Yorkshire Moors Railway **380**
Northampton **331**
Northamptonshire *see* East Midlands
Northern Ireland 20
Northop, restaurants 602
Northumberland *see* Northumbria
Northumberland, Dukes of 134, 406
Northumberland, Earls of 134
Northumbria **401–15**
climate 69
Exploring Northumbria 402–3
hotels 563–4
pubs 611
restaurants 599–601
Northumbria, Earl of 390
Norton, hotels 557
Norton St Philip, pubs 609
Norwich **188–9**
hotels 548–9
restaurants 585
Norwich School of painters 189
Notting Hill (London) **131**
Carnival 63
Nottingham **324**
Goose Fair 64
hotels 559
pubs 610
restaurants 595
Nottinghamshire *see* East Midlands
Nunnington Hall **379**

O

Oakamoor, hotels 557
Oakham, hotels 559
Oare 239
Oast houses 148–9
Oban **532**
restaurants 607
Offa, King of Mercia 46, 221, 422, 447
Offa's Dyke 422, 447
Offa's Dyke Footpath 32
Okehampton 282
Olaf, St, King of Norway 390
Old Man of Coniston 351, 352
Old Operating Theatre (London) **119**
Old Royal Naval College (London) 133
Old Sarum 251, 252
Old Spitalfields Market (London) 125
Oldenburg, Claes, *Soft Drainpipes – (Blue Cool)* 123
Oliver, Isaac 219
Olivier, Laurence 162, 272
Omega Workshops 151
100 Club (London) 128
Open-air theatre (London) 127
Opening hours 616
shops 626
Opera 128
Ophelia (Millais) 56–7
Ordnance Survey maps 32
Orford, restaurants 585
Orford Castle 191
Orkney 511, **514**
hotels 573
maps 11, 15
Orton, Joe 132
Orwell, George 132, 534
Osborne House 150, 156
Osmotherly, hotels 563
Osmund, St, grave of 252
The Other Side (Hockney) 397
Ottery St Mary 277
Ouse, River (East Anglia) 182, 184, 196
Ouse, River (York) 369
Outdoor activities **630–31**
Outward Bound 631
Oval Cricket Ground (London) 129
Overbecks 232
Owen, Richard 300
Owen, Robert 500
Owen, Wilfred, memorial 300
Oxburgh Hall and Garden 183
Oxford 204, 205, **210–15**
hotels 550
pubs 609
restaurants 587
Street-by-Street map 210–11
University 146, **214–15**
Oxford and Cambridge Boat Race 66
Oxford Tube 640
Oxfordshire *see* Thames Valley
Oyster Festival (Colchester) 64

P

P&O Ferries 633
Pacha London 129
Packwood House 291
Padstow, restaurants 590
Paignton 261
Paignton Zoo 278
Paine, Tom 183
Painswick 293
hotels 557
Paisley 501
Palace Keeper 486
Palace Theatre (London) 127
Palaces
Blenheim Palace 146, **216–17**
Buckingham Palace 72, **88–9**
Culross Palace 487
Dunfermline Palace 486–7
Falkland Palace **486**
Hampton Court **161**
Holyroodhouse 496
Kensington Palace **103**
Linlithgow Palace **487**
St James's Palace (London) 86
Scone Palace 484
Scotland 473
Stirling Castle 483
see also Castles; Stately homes
Pall Mall (London)
Street-by-Street map 87
Palladio, Andrea 80, 87, 134
Palmerston, Lord 203

Pangbourne, Thames River tour 222
Pannett, Robert 382
Parbury, Kathleen 405
Parcelforce Worldwide 623
Paris, Matthew 40
Park Crescent (London) 107
Parking 636
Parks and gardens **22–3**
  Abbotsbury Sub-Tropical Gardens 256
  Anglesey Abbey 196
  Anne Hathaway's Cottage 309
  Athelhampton House 257
  Audley End 196
  Battersea Park (London) 77
  Beth Chatto Garden (Colchester) 193
  Blenheim Palace 216, 217
  Botanical Gardens (Edgbaston) 307
  Burford House Gardens (Tenbury Wells) 301
  Burghley House 330
  Cambridge University Botanic Garden 203
  Chatsworth House 322–3
  Chelsea Physic Garden (London) 130
  Cheltenham Imperial Gardens 308
  Cirencester Park 317
  Compton Acres (Bournemouth) 259
  Cotehele 281
  Crarae Gardens **534**
  Crathes Castle and Gardens 527
  Dartington Hall 279
  Eden Project **270–71**
  Gardens of the Rose **221**
  Glendurgan 269
  Green Park (London) 77
  Greenwich Park (London) 77
  Hampstead Heath (London) 77, **132**
  Hampton Court 161
  Hampton Court (Leominster) 301
  Harewood House 396
  Harlow Car Gardens 374
  Hestercombe Garden 240
  Hidcote Manor Gardens 309
  Holland Park (London) 76, **130–31**
  Hyde Park (London) 72, 77, **103**
  Inverewe Garden 516
  Kensington Gardens (London) 76, 77, **103**
  Kew Gardens (London) 76, 134
  Kiftsgate Court Garden 309
  Knightshayes Court 277
  Levens Hall 357
  London's Parks and Gardens **76–7**
  Lost Gardens of Heligan 269
  Midlands Garden tour **308–9**
  Morrab Gardens (Penzance) 266
  Mount Edgcumbe Park 280
  National Botanical Garden of Wales 452
  Newby Hall 375
  Oxburgh Hall and Garden 183
  Oxford Botanic Garden 212
  Powis Castle 446
  Regent's Park (London) 77
  Richmond Park (London) 76, 134
  Rosemoor Garden 274
  St James's Park (London) 77
  Sissinghurst Castle Garden 177
  Snowshill Manor 308
  Somerleyton Hall 187
  Stanway House 308
  Stourhead 229, **254–5**
  Stowe **218**
Parks and gardens (cont.)
  Sudeley Castle 308
  Trebah 269
  Trelissick 269
  Trengwainton 264
  Trewithen 269
  Waddesdon Manor 218
  Warwick Castle 309
  West Country Gardens **232–3**
  Williamson Park (Lancaster) 358–9
  Windsor Great Park 223
Parliament *see* Houses of Parliament
Parliament Hill (London) 132
Parnham 233
Parr, Catherine 308
Parracombe 238
Passports 619
Paulerspury
  hotels 559
  restaurants 595
Pavarotti, Luciano 106
Pavey Ark 353
Paxton, Sir Joseph 57, 322, 398
Peacock Theatre (London) 128
Peak District 319, 320
  Peak District tour **326–7**
Pearson, JL 269
Peasants' revolt (1381) 49
Peddars Way 33
Peers of the realm 27
Pellegrini, Giovanni Antonio 384
Pelynt, hotels 554
Pembridge 301
Pembroke, 8th Earl of 253
Pembrokeshire *see* South and Mid-Wales
Pembrokeshire Coast National Park 444
Pembrokeshire Coastal Path 32
Pen y Fan 455
Pen-y-Garreg 448
Penallt, pubs 611
Penally, hotels 567
Penmaenpool, hotels 565–6
Penn, William 219
Pennines
  longhouses 29
  North Pennines tour **413**
  Pennine Way 32, 407
Penrith **346**
  hotels 561
Penshurst Place 177
Pentland Hills **499**
Pentre Ifan 42
Penwith tour 264
Penzance **266–7**
  hotels 554
  restaurants 590
Pepys, Samuel 203
Percy, Lady Idoine 387
Perranuthnoe, hotels 554
Personal security **620–21**
Perth **484**
  restaurants 607
Perth & Kinross *see* Highlands and Islands
Peter of Langtoft 273
Peter Jones (London) 125
Peterborough **182**
  hotels 549
Peterloo Massacre (1819) **361**
Petroc, St 272
Petrol 637
Petticoat Lane market (London) 19, 125
Petworth House 18, **160**
Pevsner, Sir Nikolaus 375
Pharmacists 620, 621
Philip II, King of Spain 51, 281
Phoenix Theatre (London) 127
Piazza and Central Market (London) **81**
Picasso, Pablo 189, 200, 212, 491
Piccadilly (London)
  Street-by-Street map 86–7
Piccadilly Circus (London) **83**
  Street-by-Street map 87
Piccadilly Theatre (London) 127
Pickering, hotels 563
Picnics 577
Picts 468
Pied à Terre (London) 125
Pike o'Stickle 353
Pilgrim Fathers 52, 53, 280
Piper, John 365
Pitlochry **527**
  hotels 573
Pizza on the Park (London) 129
The Place (London) 128
Plague 53
Plaid Cymru 423
Planetarium (London) **106**
Plath, Sylvia 398
Plumtree, restaurants 595
Plymouth **280**
  hotels 554
Pole, Owain de la 446
Police 620, 621
Politics 19–20
Pollok House (Glasgow) **506**
Polo 67
Polperro 272
  restaurants 591
Polruan 272
Ponsonby, Sarah 436
Pontcysyllte Aqueduct 436
Poole **258–9**
  restaurants 589
Poolewe, hotels 573
Pope, Alexander 305, 317
Porlock 239
Porlock Weir, hotels 552
Port Appin
  hotels 573
  restaurants 607
Port Isaac 261
  pubs 609
  restaurants 591
Port Sunlight 337, 365
Porth Neigwl 439
Porth Oer 439
Porthkerry, hotels 567
Portmeirion 418, **440–41**
  hotels 566
  restaurants 602
Portobello Road (London) **131**
Portobello Road Market (London) 125
Portpatrick, restaurants 605
Portrait of Richard James (Hogarth) 200
Portreath, restaurants 591
Portree 521
Portsmouth **157**
Portsoy, pubs 611
Post-Modernism 21
Postal services 623
Postbridge 282
Potter, Beatrix **355**
  Beatrix Potter Gallery (Hawkshead) 355
  Hill Top (Near Sawrey) 355
  House of the Tailor of Gloucester 317

Potter, Beatrix (cont.)
Little Town (Newlands Valley) 350
Peter Rabbit stories 527
World of Beatrix Potter (Windermere) 355
Potteries 299
Pottery
Jackfield Tile Museum (Ironbridge Gorge) 302
Staffordshire **299**
Poulton-le-Fylde, restaurants 597
Poundbury Camp 257
Poussin, Nicolas 229, 364, 490
The Choice of Hercules 255
Powis, 3rd Baron 446
Powis Castle **446**
Powys *see* South and Mid-Wales
Praxiteles 160
Pre-Raphaelites 93
Prehistoric Britain **42–3**
Arbor Low 326
Avebury Stone Circle **251**
Carloway Broch 515
Castlerigg stone circle 347, 349
Cerne Abbas 257
Clava Cairns 523
Flag Fen Bronze Age Centre 182
Grimes Graves **182–3**
Grimspound 283
hillside chalk figures 209
Kents Cavern 278
Lanyon Quoit 264
Long Meg and her Daughters 346
Maes Howe 514
Maiden Castle 257
Maumbury Rings 257
Merry Maidens 264
Mousa Broch 514
Old Sarum 251
Parc Le Breose 452
Peak District tour 326
Poundbury Camp 257
Ring of Brodgar 514
Rollright Stones 208
Salisbury Plain 250–1
Silbury Hill 250
Skara Brae 514
Standing Stones of Callanish 515
Standing Stones of Stenness 514
Stonehenge 229, **250–51**
Uffington Castle 209
Wayland's Smithy 209
West Kennet Long Barrow 250–1
Wiltshire **250–51**
Presbyterian Church of Scotland 466
Prestbury
hotels 557
restaurants 593
Priestley, Joseph 243
Prince Edward Theatre (London) 127
Prince of Wales Theatre (London) 127
Prince's Cairn, Road to the Isles tour 532
"Princes in the Tower" 120, 121
Priories *see* Abbeys and priories
Pritchard, Dafydd 438
Proctor, Sir Stephen 376
Public holidays 65
Public toilets 616
Pubs **608–11**
accommodation in 539
children in 616
traditional British pub **34–5**
Pugin, AWN 92, 365
Punk Rockers 61
Puritans **219**
Pwllheli, restaurants 602

Q

Qantas 635
Quakers 619
Quarry Bank Mill, Styal **298**
Queen Elizabeth Forest Park 481
Queen Square (London) 109
Queen's Chapel (London) **87**
Street-by-Street map 87
Queen's Club Real Tennis (London) 129
Queen's Gallery (London) 88, **89**
Queen's House (London) 133
Queen's Theatre (London) 127
Quiller-Couch, Sir Arthur 272
Quincey, Thomas de 82
Quiraing 521

R

RAC 637
RAC London to Brighton Veteran Car Rally 64
Racecourse Association 631
Rackham, Arthur 222, 431
RADAR 615
Radcliffe, Dr John 215
Radcot Bridge 209
Radio 618
Raeburn, Henry 534
Rev. Robert Walker Skating on Duddingston Loch 490
Rahere 115
Rail Europe 639
Railways 632, **638–9**
Bala Lake Railway 436
Ffestiniog Railway 437, **438–9**
international travel 633
Keighley and Worth Valley Railway 398
National Railway Museum (York) 394
North Yorkshire Moors Railway **380**
Ravenglass and Eskdale Railway 351
Romney, Hythe and Dymchurch Light Railway 171
Snowdon Mountain Railway 437
Strathspey Steam Railway 530
Rainfall 68–9
Raleigh, Sir Walter 51, 256, 280
Ramsay, Allan 490, 534
Ramsgill, hotels 563
Ransome, Arthur 356
Rape Crisis Centre 621
Raphael 212, 490
Rashleigh family 272
Rattle, Sir Simon 307
Ravenglass and Eskdale Railway 351
Reculver 171
Recumbent Figure (Moore) 93
Redgrave, Vanessa 20
Redmile, restaurants 595
Reeth, hotels 563
Reform Acts 56
Regency London, John Nash's **107**
Regent Street Christmas Lights 64
Regent's Park (London) 77, **105–9**
area map 105
open-air theatre 127
Reilly, Michael 82
Religion 619
Celtic Christianity **405**
Methodism **267**, 423
Rembrandt
Ashmolean Museum (Oxford) 212
Drumlanrig Castle 501
Kelvingrove Art Gallery and Museum 505
Kenwood House (London) 132
National Gallery of Scotland (Edinburgh) 490
Self-portrait 507
Walker Art Gallery (Liverpool) 364
Wallace Collection (London) 106
Remembrance Day 64
Renoir, Pierre Auguste 200, 386
At the Theatre 85
The Two Sisters 244
Restaurants 574–607
children in 616
Devon and Cornwall 589–91
Downs and Channel Coast 582–4
East Anglia 584–5
East Midlands 593–5
Heart of England 591–3
Lancashire and the Lakes 595–7
London 578–82
Northumbria 599–601
restaurants-with-rooms 575
Scotland 604–7
Thames Valley 586–7
Wales 601–4
Wessex 587–9
Yorkshire and the Humber Region 598–9
see also Food and drink
Restormel Castle 272
Rev. Robert Walker Skating on Duddingston Loch (Raeburn) 490
Reynolds, Sir Joshua
Art Gallery (Aberdeen) 526
Castle Howard 385
Cawdor Castle 523
Ickworth House 195
National Gallery of Scotland (Edinburgh) 490
Saltram House 280
Tate Britain 93
Woburn Abbey 218
Reynoldston, hotels 568
Reyntiens, Patrick 365
Rhinog moors 441
Ribble Valley **359**
Richard I, King 40
coat of arms 26
statue of 90
Richard II, King 40
Richard III, King 40, 49
Middleham Castle 371
Tower of London 121
Richard of Haldingham 304
Richardson, John 349
Richborough Roman Fort 171
Richmond (London) **134**
restaurants 583
Richmond (Yorkshire) 370–71
Richmond, Alan Rufus, 1st Earl of 370
Richmond Park (London) 76, 134
Ridgeway, restaurants 595
The Ridgeway (footpath) 33
Ridley, John 413
Ridley, Nicholas 413
Martyrs' Memorial (Oxford) 210, 213
Rievaulx Abbey **379**
Ring of Brodgar 514
Ringlestone, hotels 546
Ringwood, hotels 546

Ripley **375**
restaurants 583, 599
Ripon **375**
Ritz, César 83, 86
Ritz Hotel (London) **83**
Street-by-Street map 86
River view of London **74–5**
Rizzio, David 496
Road signs 636
Road to the Isles tour **532–3**
Roade, restaurants 595
Roads 636
Rob Roy **481**, 498
Falkland Palace 486
Trossachs 480
Robert II, King of Scotland 524
Robert the Bruce 491
Battle of Bannockburn 468, 482, 486
Drum Castle 527
embalmed heart 498, 501
Melrose Abbey 489
Pass of Brander 533
Rathlin 535
statue of 482
tomb of 486
Robin Hood **324**, 383
Robin Hood's Bay **383**
Robinson, Thomas 384
Rochester **176**
Rock, hotels 554
Rock music, London 128–9
Rodin, Auguste, *The Burghers of Calais* 90
Rogers, Katherine 315
Rogers, Richard 21, 118
Rokeby Venus (Velázquez) 85
Rollright Stones 208
Rolls, Charles Stewart 461
Romaldkirk
hotels 564
restaurants 600
Roman Britain 17, **44–5**
art and nature in the Roman World 317
Bath 247, 248
Birdoswald Roman Fort 346
Caerleon **460**
Chester 298
Chysauster 266–7
Colchester 193
Corbridge Roman Site and Museum 409
Dorchester 257
Fishbourne Roman Palace 159
Hadrian's Wall 334, **408–9**
Hardknott Fort 352
Manchester 360
Richborough Roman Fort 171
Scotland 468
Segontium 430
Shrewsbury 300
Verulamium 220
Roman Catholic Church 50, 619
Romney, George 132, 217, 523
Romney, Hythe and Dymchurch Light Railway 171
Romney Marsh **170–71**
Ronnie Scott's (London) 129
Rosedale 367, 368
North York Moors tour 381
Rosemoor Garden 274
Ross-on-Wye **304–5**
restaurants 593
Rossetti, Dante Gabriel 93, 208, 324, 361
Rosslyn Chapel 499
Rosthwaite 351
Rothiemurchus Estate 530
Rothschild, Baron Ferdinand de 218
Rotten Row (London) 103
Rotunda (Manchester) 57
Roubiliac, Louis François 203
Rowlands, Richard 430
Rowlandson, Thomas 212
Rowntree, Joseph 337
Royal Academy (London) **83**
Street-by-Street map 86
Summer Exhibitions 63
Royal Albert Hall (London) 128
Street-by-Street map 98
Royal Ascot 66
Royal College of Music (London)
Street-by-Street map 98
Royal Deeside 465
Royal Deeside tour **526–7**
Royal Exchange (London)
Street-by-Street map 113
Royal Highland Gathering (Braemar) 64
Royal Highland Show 63
Royal Hospital (London) 130
Royal Mews (London) **89**
Royal National Eisteddfod 63
Royal National Theatre (London) 127
Royal Observatory Greenwich (London) 133
Royal Opera Arcade (London)
Street-by-Street map 87
Royal Opera House (London) 128
Street-by-Street map 81
Royal Pavilion (Brighton) 147, 163, **166–7**
Royal Shakespeare Company (RSC) 127, 312, 314, **315**
Royal Show 63
Royal Tunbridge Wells *see* Tunbridge Wells
Royal Welsh Show 63
Royal Yachting Association 631
Roydhouse, hotels 563
Rubens, Peter Paul 364, 490
The Adoration of the Magi 201
Banqueting House (London) 92
Marchesa Maria Grimaldi 259
Rugby 66, 631
Rugby Football Union 631
Runnymede 223
Rupert, Prince 300
Rural architecture **28–9**
Ruskin, John 356
Russell Square (London) 109
Ruthin **431**
Rydal 354
Rydal Water 353
Rye
hotels 546
pubs 608
restaurants 583
Street-by-Street map 172–3
Rye, River 379
Rysbrack, Michael 216

S

Sackville, Thomas 176
Sackville-West, Vita 151, 176, 177
Saddleworth, restaurants 597
Sadler's Wells (London) 128
Sailing 630
St Abb's Head **488**
St Albans **220–21**
hotels 550
St Andrews **485**
hotels 570
restaurants 605
St Aubyn, Sir John 266
St Austell **269**
St Bartholomew-the-Great (London) **114–15**
St Blazey, hotels 554
St Boswells, hotels 570
St Brides Wentlooge, hotels 568
St David's 418, 443
Cathedral **450–51**
restaurants 603
St Fillans, hotels 570
St Fillan's Cave (East Neuk) 486
St George's Day 62
St Hilary, hotels 555
St Ives 228, **265**
restaurants 591
twentieth-century artists of St Ives **265**
St Ives, Cornwall (Nicholson) 265
St James's (London)
Street-by-Street map 86–7
St James Garlickhythe (London)
Street-by-Street map 112
St James's Palace (London)
Street-by-Street map 86
St James's Park (London) 77
St James's Piccadilly (London)
Street-by-Street map 86
St James's Square (London)
Street-by-Street map 87
St John's, Smith Square (London) 128
St John's in the Vale 349
St Keyne, hotels 555
St Leger, Sir Anthony 176
St Margaret's Church (London)
Street-by-Street map 90
St Margaret's Hope, restaurants 607
St Martin's Theatre (London) 127
Street-by-Street map 80
St Mary Abchurch (London)
Street-by-Street map 113
St Mary-le-Bow (London)
Street-by-Street map 112
St Mary's Abbey (York) 338–9
St Mawes
hotels 555
restaurants 591
St Michael Subduing the Devil (Epstein) 307
St Michael's Mount **266–7**
St Nicholas Cole (London)
Street-by-Street map 112
St Patrick's Day 62
St Paul's Cathedral (London) 73, 111, **116–17**
river view of 74
Street-by-Street map 112
St Paul's Covent Garden (London)
Street-by-Street map 80
St Stephen Walbrook (London) **114**
Street-by-Street map 113
St Thomas's Hospital (London) 119
Salcombe, hotels **555**
Sales 626
Salford Quays **359**
Salisbury 229, **252–3**
Cathedral 252–3
pubs 609
restaurants 589
Salisbury, Marquess of 27

Salisbury Cathedral from the meadows (Constable) 10, 229
Salt, Sir Titus 337, 397
Saltaire 337, 397
Saltram House 280
Salvin, Anthony 311, 430
Samaritans 621
Sambourne, Linley 131
Sandby, Paul, *Conwy Castle* 433
Sandgate, hotels 546
Sandringham **185**
Sanquhar **500**
Saracen's Head, hotels 559
Savin, Thomas 449
Saxons 420, 422
Scafell Pike 340, 351, 352
Scarborough **383**, 614
hotels 563
The Scarlet Sunset: A Town on a River (Turner) 93
Science Museum (London) **102**
Street-by-Street map 98
Scilly Isles 267
Scone Palace 484
Scotch House (London) 125
Scotland 17–18, **463–535**
castles **472–3**
clans and tartans **470–71**
climate 69
ferries 641
food and drink **474–5**
Highlands and Islands **511–35**
history **468–9**
hotels 568–73
The Lowlands **477–509**
maps 14–15, 464–5
A Portrait of **466–7**
pubs 611
restaurants 604–7
Scott, Sir George Gilbert
Bath Abbey 248
Martyrs' Memorial (Oxford) 213
St David's Cathedral 451
Worcester Cathedral 306
Scott, Sir Giles Gilbert 123, 365
Scott, John 411
Scott, Captain Robert 467, 485
Scott, Sir Walter 467, **498**
Abbotsford House **498**
Fair Maid's House (Perth) 484
grave 489
Highlands and Islands 511
Mons Meg 492
St John's in the Vale 349
Scott's View 489
Shakespeare's Birthplace (Stratford-upon-Avon) 314
The Trossachs 480
Wayland's Smithy 209
Scottish Citylink 640
Scottish National Party 469
Scottish Parliament 61
Scott's View, Borders tour 489
Scrope, Richard, Bishop of York 395
Seabury, Samuel 524
Seacat 633
Seaforth, Countess of 517
Seahouses 404
hotels 564
pubs 611
Seashells (Moore) 364
Seathwaite 353
Seatoller, hotels 561
Seaton Burn, restaurants 600
Seaview, hotels 547
Secondhand shops 627
Segontium 430
Seithenyn, Prince 441
Self-catering accommodation **540**, 541
Selfridges (London) 125
Selkirk, Alexander 244, 486
Selside, hotels 561
Selworthy 239
Serpentine (London) 103
Service charges, in restaurants 576
Seven Dials (London)
Street-by-Street map 80
Seven Sisters Country Park 168
Severn, River 316
Ironbridge Gorge 302
Severn, Robert 300
Severus, Septimius 45
Sewingshields Milecastle 409
Shaftesbury 235, **256**
restaurants 589
Shaftesbury Theatre (London) 127
Shakespeare, William 20, 50, 51, 100
Charlecote Park 290
Henry IV 122, 406
Macbeth 485, 523
memorials 95, 122
Shakespeare's Birthplace 314
Shakespeare's Globe (London) **122**
Southwark Cathedral (London) 122
Stratford-upon-Avon 287, 312–13
Sharington, Sir William 243
Shaw, George Bernard 105, **221**, 305
Shaw, Norman 25, 441
Sheffield, restaurants 599
Shefford Woodlands, hotels 550
Sheldon, Gilbert, Archbishop of Canterbury 213
Shell Mex House (London), river view of 74
Shelley, Percy Bysshe **210**
statue of 448
Shepard, Ernest 222
Shepton Mallet
hotels 552
restaurants 589
Sheraton, Thomas 523
Sherborne **256**
Sherlock, Cornelius 364
Sherlock Holmes Museum (London) **106**
Sherwood Forest 324
Shetland 511, **514**
maps 11, 15
Shetland Seabird Isles **514**
Up Helly Aa festival 466, 514
see also Highlands and Islands
Shinfield, restaurants 587
Shipton Gorge, hotels 552
Shoe shops, London **124**, 125
Shopping **626–7**
London **124–5**
opening hours 616
Shrewsbury **300**
hotels 557
restaurants 593
Shrewsbury, Countess of 322, 324
Shropshire *see* Heart of England
Le Shuttle 633
Sickert, Walter Richard 364
Siddons, Sarah 54
Sidmouth 277
festivals 63
Signac, Paul 396
Silbury Hill 250
Simonsbath 239
Simpson, James 466–7
Simpson, Wallis 59
Sinclair, William 499
Sinclair clan 471
Sir John Soane's Museum (London) **114–15**
Sisley, Alfred 396
Sissinghurst Castle Garden 177
The Sisters (Maris) 507
Six Nations Rugby Union 66
Sizergh Castle 356
Skara Brae 43, 514
Skeabost 520
Skene, Sir George 525
Sketch for Annabel Lee (Whistler) 505
Ski Club of Great Britain 631
Skiddaw 341, 349, 352
Skiing 531, 631
Skinners' Hall (London)
Street-by-Street map 113
Skipton Castle 372
Skirlaw, Walter, Bishop of York 395
Skye *see* Isle of Skye
Slate **437**
The Sleeping Shepherd Boy (Gibson) 364
Sloane, Sir Hans 108, 130
Sloane Square (London) 130
Smarden, pubs 608
Smirke, Robert 108
Smith, Adam 466
Smith, Paul 125
Smoking 575, 618
Smugglers, Cornish **268**
Smythson, Robert 376
Snape
pubs 608
restaurants 585
Snettisham, pubs 608
Snooker 66
Snowdon 419, **437**
Snowdonia National Park 428, 436, **437–8**
Snowshill Manor 286
Midlands Garden tour 308
Soane, Sir John 114
Society of Genealogists 27
Soft Drainpipes – (Blue Cool) (Oldenburg) 123
Soho (London) **82**
Soldier's Leap, Killiecrankie walk 528
Somerleyton Hall 187
Somerset *see* Wessex
Somerset House (London) **82–3**
Sonning Bridge, Thames River tour 222
South Bank Centre (London) 128
South Downs **169**
South Downs Way 33
South Kensington (London) **97–103**
area map 97
Street-by-Street map 98–9
"South Sea Bubble" (1720) 54
South Uist 515
South Wales **443–61**
climate 68
Exploring South and Mid-Wales 444–5
hotels 566–8
pubs 611
restaurants 602–4
Southampton **156–7**
Southeast England **144–225**
Downs and Channel Coast **153–77**
East Anglia **179–203**
Garden of England **148–9**

Southeast England (cont.)
houses of historical figures **150–51**
map 146–7
Thames Valley **205–25**
Southwark (London)
area map 111
Cathedral **122**
pubs 608
Southwest Coastal Path 32, 238, 261
Southwold **190**
hotels 549
pubs 608
Souvenir shops 627
Sowerby Bridge 399
Spanish Armada (1588) 39, 50–51, 280, 281
Speaker's Corner (London) 103
Spean Bridge, hotels 573
Specialist holidays 630
Speed limits 636
Speen, restaurants 587
Speke Hall 365
Spence, Sir Basil 307
Spencer, 1st Earl 86
Spencer, Sir Stanley 223, 324
Spencer House (London)
Street-by-Street map 86
Spittal, hotels 568
Spode 299
Sports 21, **630–31**
London 129
The Sporting Year **66–7**
traditional Cumberland Sports **346**
Spring in Great Britain 62
Spurn Head **389**
STA Travel 617
Stadhampton, hotels 550
Staffordshire *see* Heart of England
Staffordshire pottery **299**
Stained glass, York Minster **395**
Staite Murray, William 393
Stamford **331**
hotels 559
pubs 610
Standen 25
Standing by the Rags (Freud) 123
Standing Stones of Callanish 515
Standing Stones of Stenness 514
Stanhope, North Pennines tour 413
Stannersburn, hotels 564
Stanpit Marsh 259
Stansted Airport 634
Stanton Wick, pubs 609
Stanway House, Midlands Garden tour 308
Stapledon, Walter de 276–7
Stately homes **24–5**
admission charges 616–17
A La Ronde 277
Abbotsford House **498**
Althorp House 331
Anglesey Abbey **196**
Arlington Court 275
Audley End **196–7**
Beaulieu **156**
Berrington Hall (Leominster) 301
Blickling Hall **186**
Bowood House 243
Buckland Abbey **280**
Burghley House 287, 320, **330–31**
Burton Agnes **386**
Burton Constable **388**
Castle Drogo 283
Castle Howard 24, 335, **384–5**
Charlecote Park 290
Stately homes (cont.)
Charleston 168
Chartwell 177
Chatsworth House 287, 319, **322–3**
Chiswick House (London) 134
Clandon Park 160
Corsham Court 243
Cotehele **281**
Dalemain **346–7**
Fairfax House (York) 394
Georgian House (Edinburgh) 490
Gladstone's Land (Edinburgh) 494
Glynde Place 168
Goodwood House 159
Great Dixter 170
Ham House (London) 134
Hardwick Hall 290, 324
Harewood House **396**
Hatfield House 53, **219**
Hay Castle (Hay-on-Wye) 447
Holker Hall 357
Holkham Hall 185
Hughenden Manor **221**
Hutton-in-the-Forest 346
Ickworth House 194–5
Ightham Mote 176–7
Kedleston Hall 324
Kelmscott Manor 208–9
Kenwood House (London) 132
Kingston Lacy 259
Knebworth House **219**
Knole **176–7**
Lacock Abbey 243
Lanhydrock **272**, 273
Layer Marney Tower 193
Leighton Hall **358**
Levens Hall **357**
Little Moreton Hall 290–91, 299
Longleat House **254**
Marble Hill House (London) 134
Minster Lovell Hall (Swinbrook) 208
Montacute House 256
Moseley Old Hall 291
Muncaster Castle 352
Nunnington Hall **379**
Osborne House 156
Packwood House 291
Penshurst Place 177
Petworth House 18, **160**
Plas Newydd 436
Plas-yn-Rhiw 439
Quex House 171
Royal Pavilion (Brighton) 163, **166–7**
Saltram House 280
Sandringham **185**
Shandy Hall (Coxwold) 378, 379
Somerleyton Hall 187
Speke Hall 365
Spencer House (London) 86
Stokesay Castle 301
Stourhead 255
Syon House (London) 134
Temple Newsam House (Leeds) 396
Traquair House 473, **499**
Tudor manor houses **290–91**
Uppark House 169
Waddesdon Manor **218**
Warwick Castle 309, **310–11**
Wightwick Manor 291
Wilton House 253
Woburn Abbey **218**
see also Castles; Palaces
Stephen, King 40
Stephenson, George 380, 394
Sterne, Laurence 378, 379
Stevenson, Robert Louis 467
Steyning **162**
Stiffkey, pubs 609
Stirling **482**
Stirling, James 363
Stirling Castle **482–3**
Stirling Castle in the Time of the Stuarts (Vorsterman) 482
Stoke Bruerne, restaurants 595
Stoke-by-Nayland 195
Stoke-on-Trent **299**
Stokesay Castle 301
Stokesley, restaurants 601
Ston Easton, restaurants 589
Stone, Nicholas 212
Stone circles *see* Prehistoric Britain
Stonehenge 43, 229, 237, **250–51**
Stonethwaite 351
Stoney Middleton 319
Stonor, restaurants 587
Stoppard, Tom 20
Stornoway 515
The Storr 521
Storrington, restaurants 583
Story, Waldo 217
Stour, River 192
Stourhead 229, 233, **254–5**
festivals 63
Stowe **218**
Strachan, Douglas 173, 524
Strand Theatre (London) 127
Strata Florida, Wild Wales tour 453
Stratfield Saye 150
Stratford-upon-Avon 287, **312–15**
hotels 557
restaurants 593
Street-by-Street map 312–13
Strathkinness, hotels 570
Strathpeffer **517**
Streatley, restaurants 587
Street, GE 245
Stretton, restaurants 595
Striding Edge 341, 353
Stringfellows (London) 129
Strontian, hotels 573
Stuart, John 458
Stuart clan 471
Stuart dynasty **52–3**, 491, 523
Stubbs, George 159
Student travellers 616
Studland Bay 258
Stump Cross Caverns 372
Sturminster Newton, restaurants 589
Styal 298
Sudbury, restaurants 585
Sudeley Castle, Midlands Garden tour 308
Suffolk *see* East Anglia
Suffolk, Thomas Howard, 1st Earl of 196
Suffragettes 58
Summer in Great Britain 63
Summer Music Festival (Stourhead) 63
Summerson, John 254
Sunshine 68–9
Supermarkets 627
Surrey *see* Downs
Surrey, Thomas Holland, Duke of 380
Surtees, Bessie 411
Sussex *see* Channel Coast
Sutherland, Earls of 516
Sutherland, Graham 82, 159, 307
Sutton Bank **378**
Sutton Coldfield, hotels 557

Swaffham **183**
hotels 549
restaurants 585
Swaledale 370–71
Swanage 258
Swansea 443, **452**
restaurants 603
Sway, hotels 547
Swiftair 623
Swimming **383**
Swinbrook 208
Swinton, restaurants 606
Sygun Copper Mine 438
Synagogues 619
Syon House (London) 134

T

Tain 517
Talbot, John Ivory 243
Talbot, William Henry Fox 243
Talking Pages 622
Talsarnau, hotels 566
Tan-y-Bwlch 439
Tan-y-Grisiau 439
Tarbert 535
Tarn Hows 352, 356
Tarr Steps 239
Tartans **470–71**
Tate Britain (London) 73, **93**
Tate Liverpool 363
Tate Modern (London) **123**
Tate St Ives 265, 575, 591
Tate to Tate river boats 93, 123
Tatham, CH 335
Taunton **240**
restaurants 589
Tavistock, restaurants 591
Tax-free shopping 626
Taxis 632, 642–3
Teffont Evias, hotels 552
Teignmouth, hotels 555
Telephones 622
Television 21, 618
Telford, Thomas **433**
Caledonian Canal 522
Neptune's Staircase 533
Pontcysyllte Aqueduct 436
Waterloo Bridge (Betws-y-Coed) 436
Temperatures 68–9
Temple (London) **114**
river view of 74
Temple of Mithras (London)
Street-by-Street map 113
Tenbury Wells 301
Tenby **452**
restaurants 603
Tennis 66, 630
Tennyson, Alfred, Lord 273, 329
Tetbury, restaurants 593
Tettersells, Nicholas 162
Tewkesbury **316**
hotels 557
Textiles 337
Scotland **501**
tartans **470–71**
wool trade 195, 338
Thames, River
Radcot Bridge 209
river view of London **74–5**
Tate to Tate river boats 93, 123
Thames cruises 75
Thames Path 33
Touring the Thames 222–3
Thames Valley **205–25**
climate 68
Thames Valley (cont.)
Exploring the Thames Valley 206–7
hotels 549–51
pubs 609
restaurants 586–7
Thatcher, Margaret 20, 61, 83
Theatre 20, 628
London **126–7**
Shakespeare's Globe (London) **122**
Theatre Museum (London)
Street-by-Street map 81, **82**
Theatre Royal, Drury Lane Theatre (London) 127
Theatre Royal, Haymarket (London) 107, 127
Theme parks 629
Theresa, Mother 27
Thetford 183
Thirlmere 349, 352
Thoky, Abbot of Gloucester 317
Thomas, Dylan 82, 421
Dylan Thomas Centre (Swansea) 452
statue of 452
Thomas, Ewan 66
Thomson, James 506
Thornhill, Sir James 217
Thorpe Market, restaurants 585
Thorpe Park 629
Threave Castle **501**
333 (London) 129
Thynne, John 254
Tickets, sporting events 67
Tijou, Jean 117
Tillingham, pubs 609
Time zone 618
Tintagel **273**
Tinted Venus (Gibson) 334
Tintern, hotels 568
Tintern Abbey **461**
Tintoretto 490
Tipping, in restaurants 576
Tissington, festivals 62
Tissington Trail 286, 320, 325
Titian 106, 160, 195, 490
Tobermory 513
Toilets, public 616
Tolpuddle Martyrs 56
Torbay **278**
Torlundy, hotels 573
Torosay Castle **532**, 533
Torquay 263
restaurants 591
Torridge Valley 274
Totnes **279**
restaurants 591
Toulouse-Lautrec, Henri de 526
Tourist information 614–15
Tours by car
Borders tour **489**
Midlands Garden tour **308–9**
North Norfolk Coastal tour **184–5**
North Pennines tour **413**
North York Moors tour **381**
Peak District tour **326–7**
Penwith tour 264
Road to the Isles tour **532–3**
Royal Deeside tour **526–7**
Thames River tour **222–3**
Wild Wales tour **453**
Toward, Agnes 503
Tower Bridge (London) **118**
river view of 75
Tower-houses, Scotland **472–3**
Tower of London 73, **120–21**
river view of 75
Tower Records (London) 125
Townend (Troutbeck) 354–5
Tradescant, John 212, 219
Trafalgar, Battle of (1805) 55
Trains *see* Railways
Trams 643
Traquair House 473, **499**
Travel **632–43**
air **634–5**
buses 640, **641**, 642
cars **636–7**
in cities **642–3**
coaches 632, **633**, **640–41**
coasts and waterways **641**
Devon and Cornwall 263
Downs and Channel Coast 154
East Anglia 181
East Midlands 320
ferries 632, **633**, 641
Heart of England 296
Highlands and Islands 512
Lancashire and the Lakes 344
Lowlands (Scotland) 479
North Wales 429
Northumbria 403
railways 632, **633**, **638–9**
South and Mid-Wales 444
Thames Valley 206
Wessex 237
Yorkshire and the Humber Region 369
Travelex 624
Traveller's cheques **625**
Trebah 269
Treburley, restaurants 591
Tregadillett, pubs 609
Trelissick 232, 269
Trengwainton 232
Penwith tour 264
Trewithen 232, 269
Trollope, Anthony 276
Troon
hotels 570
restaurants 606
Trooping the Colour 63
The Trossachs 464, 467, **480–81**
Troutbeck Bridge 353
Truro **269**
Tudno, St 431
Tudor dynasty **50–51**, 458
Tudor manor houses **290–91**
Tummel, River 527, 528
Tunbridge Wells **177**
hotels 546
restaurants 584
Turner, JMW 132, 212, 307
Chelsea 130
Kelvingrove Art Gallery (Glasgow) 505
National Gallery (London) 85
Petworth House 160
Richmond 370–71
The Scarlet Sunset: A Town on a River 93
Tate Britain (London) 93
Turner Bequest 93
Whitworth Art Gallery (Manchester) 361
Walker Art Gallery (Liverpool) 364
Turpin, Dick 391
Tussaud, Madame 106
Tutbury, pubs 610

Twm Siôn Cati's Cave, Wild Wales tour 453
The Two Sisters (Renoir) 244
Tyler, Wat 114
Tyn-y-Groes, hotels 566

U

Uffington Castle 209
Uffington White Horse 43
Ullapool
 hotels 573
 pubs 611
 restaurants 607
Ullingswick, hotels 557
Ullswater **347**
 hotels 561
 restaurants 597
Ulverston 356–7
 hotels 561
United States Embassy 619
University of London Union 617
Upper Coquetdale 402
Upper Hambleton, hotels 559
Uppingham, hotels 559
UPS 623
Upton, pubs 610
Upton-on-Severn 316
Urban Outfitters (London) 125
Urquhart Castle 522
US Airways 635
Uswayford Farm 407

V

Vale, HH 364
Vale of the White Horse **209**
Valley of Rocks 238
Van der Plas, Pieter 219
Van der Vaart, Jan 323
Van Dyck, Sir Anthony
 Kenwood House (London) 132
 Merchant Adventurers' Hall (York) 393
 National Gallery of Scotland (Edinburgh) 490
 Petworth House 160
 Wallace Collection (London) 106
 Wilton House 253
Van Eyck, Jan, *Arnolfini Portrait* 84
Vanbrugh, Sir John 24, **384**
 Blenheim Palace 216
 Castle Howard 384
 Stowe 218
Vanessa Bell at Charleston (Grant) 151
VAT (Value Added Tax) 576, 626
Vaudeville Theatre (London) 127
Vegetarian food 576
Velázquez, Diego de Silva y 490
 Rokeby Venus 85
Vermeer, Johannes 89, 132
 The Music Lesson 88
Verrio, Antonio 331
Veryan, hotels 555
Victim Support 621
Victoria, Queen 41, 56, 57
 Balmoral 465, 526
 Blair Castle 529
 Buckingham Palace 88
 Crown Jewels 120
 Highlands and Islands 511
 Kensington Palace 103
 Osborne House 150, 156
 Pitlochry 527
 Royal Pavilion (Brighton) 166, 167
Victoria and Albert Museum (London) 72, 99, **100–101**
Victoria Coach Station 640
Victorian Britain **56–7**
Victory, HMS 157
Vikings 39, 46
Vindolanda 408
Virgin Atlantic 635
Virgin Megastore (London) 125
Virgin Trains 639
Virginstow, restaurants 591
Visas 619
Vivian, John Henry 452
Vorsterman, Johannes, *Stirling Castle in the Time of the Stuarts* 482
Vuillard, Edouard 491
Vyrnwy, Lake, hotels 567

W

Waddesdon Manor **218**
Wade's Causeway, North York Moors tour 381
Wainwright, AW 351
Walberswick 190
Wales 17–18, **417–61**
 castles **424–5**
 climate 68
 history **422–3**
 hotels 564–8
 map 418–19
 North Wales **427–41**
 A Portrait of **420–21**
 pubs 611
 restaurants 601–4
 South and Mid-Wales **443–61**
Walker, Sir Andrew Barclay 364
Walker, William 159
Walker Art Gallery (Liverpool) 334, **364–5**
Walks 630
 in cities 643
 Constable walk 192
 Killiecrankie walk **528**
 Lake District 351
 Malham walk **373**
 Tissington Trail 325
 Walkers' Britain **32–3**
Wallace, Sir Richard 106
Wallace, William 468, 483
Wallace Collection (London) **106**
Walliswood, pubs 608
Walpole, Sir Robert 54, 90
Walsingham, Alan de 182
Walton, Izaac 158, 326
Wanamaker, Sam 122
Wareham, hotels 552
Warkworth Castle **406**
Warminster, restaurants 589
Wars of the Roses 49, 423
Warwick 286, **309**
Warwick, Earls of 309, 310–11
Warwick, Richard Neville, Earl of 310, 311, 371
Warwick Castle 287, 309, **310–11**
 Midlands Garden tour 309
Warwickshire *see* Heart of England
Wasdale Head 352
 hotels 561
Wastell, John 200
Wastwater 340, 351, **352**
Water sports 630–31
Waterfalls
 Aysgarth Waterfalls 371
 Becky Falls 283
 Hardraw Force 371
 Scale Force 351
 Swallow Falls 436
Watermillock, restaurants 597
Watersmeet 239, 276
Waterway travel **641**
Wath in Nidderdale, restaurants 599
Watt, James 54, 466, 477
Watteau, Antoine 106
Watton-at-Stone, pubs 609
Waugh, Evelyn 132, 384
Wayland's Smithy 209
Wear, River 401, 414
Weather **68–9**, 614
Weathercall 637
Webb, Aston 87, 89, 101
Webb, Philip 25, 209
Wedgwood, Josiah 299
Well-dressing festivals (Tissington) 62
Wellingham, hotels 549
Wellington, Duke of 55, 150, 436
Wells 228, **240–41**
Wells, John, *Aspiring Forms* 265
Wells-next-the-Sea
 North Norfolk Coastal tour 185
 restaurants 585
Welsh Assembly 61
Welsh Hook, restaurants 604
Welwyn Garden City 58–9
Wenlock Edge 300
 pubs 610
Wensleydale 371
Wesley, John 189, 214, 267
Wessex **235–59**
 Exploring Wessex 236–7
 hotels 551–2
 pubs 609
 restaurants 587–9
West Bay, restaurants 589
West Bexington, restaurants 589
West Country **227–83**
 climate 68
 Coastal Wildlife 230–31
 Devon and Cornwall **261–83**
 map 228–9
 Wessex **235–59**
 West Country Gardens **232–3**
West End (London) **79–95**
 area map 79
West Highland Way 32, 480
West Ilsley, pubs 609
West Kennet Long Barrow 250–51
Wester Ross **516**
Western Isles 511, **515**
Western Union 624
Westminster (London) **79–95**
 area map 79
 Street-by-Street map 90–91
Westminster Abbey (London) 73, **94–5**
 Street-by-Street map 90
Westminster Pier (London)
 Street-by-Street map 91
Westward Ho! 274
Westwood, Vivienne 60, 125
Weymouth **256–7**
 hotels 552
Wharfedale 372
Wharram Percy **386**
Wheelchair access *see* Disabled travellers
Wheeler, Sir Mortimer 460
Whinlatter Pass 348
Whipsnade Wild Animal Park **219**
Whisky **475**
Whistler, James McNeill, *Sketch for Annabel Lee* 505

Whitby 21, 367, **382**
hotels 563
restaurants 599
Whitchurch Mill, Thames River tour 222
Whitebrook
hotels 568
restaurants 604
Whitehall (London)
Street-by-Street map 90–91
Whitewell
hotels 561
restaurants 597
Whithorn, Isle of **501**
pubs 611
Whitstable, restaurants 584
Whitworth, Sir Joseph 361
Wickham, restaurants 584
Widecombe-in-the-Moor 18
Widegates, hotels 555
Wightwick Manor 291
Wigmore Hall (London) 128
Wilberforce, William **388**
Wild Wales tour **453**
Wilde, Oscar 162
Wildlife
Braunton Burrows 275
Brownsea Island 258–9
Buckfast Butterfly Farm and Otter Sanctuary 279
The Countryside **30–31**
Elan Valley 448
Flora of the Cairngorms 531
Kincraig Highland Wildlife Park 530
National Seal Sanctury (Gweek) 268
Scottish Sealife Sanctuary (Oban) 532
Sea-Life and Marine Sanctuary (Scarborough) 383
Swannery (Abbotsbury) 256
West Country Coastal Wildlife 230–31
see also Aquariums; Birds; Zoos
Wilfrid, St 408
William II, King 40, 156, 343
William III, King 41, 52, 53
Glencoe Massacre 529
Hampton Court Palace 22, 161
Hyde Park (London) 103
Jacobite movement 523
and Scotland 469
William IV, King 41, 103
William the Conqueror, King 40
Battle Abbey 169
Battle of Hastings 169
coronation 94
Domesday Book 317
Exeter Castle 276
Gloucester 317
Lewes 168
New Forest 156
Norman Conquest 46, 47
Selby Abbey 338
Tower of London 120
and Wales 422
Winchester 158
Windsor Castle 224
York 393
William the Lion, King of Scotland 468
William of Wykeham 214
Williams, Dominic 411
Williams, Kit 316
Williams-Ellis, Sir Clough 418, 440
Williamson, Henry 274
Willison, George, *Robert Adam* 508
Willy Lott's Cottage, Constable walk 192
Wilmcote, hotels 557
Wilton 253
Wilton House 253
Wiltshire *see* Wessex
Wimbledon Lawn Tennis Tournament 66
Wimborne Minster **259**
hotels 552
Winbourne, Colin 414
Winchcombe 293
hotels 558
Winchelsea 173
Winchester **158–9**
Cathedral 19, 146
hotels 547
pubs 608
Windermere 353, **355**
hotels 562
restaurants 597
Windmills 187
Windsor **223–5**
Castle 146, 223, **224–5**
hotels 550
restaurants 587
Windsor, Duke of (Edward VIII) 41, 59, 279
Winter in Great Britain 65
Winteringham
hotels 563
restaurants 599
Withernsea 389
Witherslack, restaurants 597
Witney 208
Woburn Abbey **218**
restaurants 587
Woburn Sands, restaurants 587
Wolf of Badenoch 524
Wolf's Castle, hotels 568
Wolsey, Cardinal 161, 191, 214
Women travellers 621
Wood, John the Elder 229, 244, 246, 249
Wood, John the Younger 229, 246, 248, 249
Woodbridge
hotels 549
restaurants 585
Woodstock, hotels 550
Woodville, Elizabeth 202
Wookey Hole 240
hotels 552
Wool trade **195**, 338
Woolf, Virginia 151
Worcester **306**
Worcestershire *see* Heart of England
Wordsworth, Dorothy 378
Wordsworth, William **354**, 436
Dove Cottage (Grasmere) 354
Duddon Valley 353
Lake District 347
Rydal Mount 354
St John's College (Cambridge) 203
Sutton Bank 378
Tintern Abbey 461
Wordsworth House (Cockermouth) 350
Working restrictions 618
World War I 58
World War II 58, 59
Cabinet War Rooms (London) **91**
Eden Camp **386**
Wren, Sir Christopher 21, **116**, 258, 375
Christ Church College (Oxford) 214
Wren, Sir Christopher (cont.)
Emmanuel College (Cambridge) 202
Guildhall (Windsor) 223
Hampton Court 161
London churches 111, 112
Monument (London) 118
Old Royal Naval College (London) 133
Pembroke College (Cambridge) 202
Royal Hospital (London) 130
St James Garlickhythe (London) 112
St James's Piccadilly (London) 86
St Mary Abchurch (London) 113
St Nicholas Cole (London) 112
St Paul's Cathedral (London) 73, 112, 116–17
St Stephen Walbrook (London) 113, **114**
Sheldonian Theatre (Oxford) 210, 213
Wrexham 427
Wyatt, James 388
Wyatville, Sir Jeffry 225
Wycliffe, John 49
Wye, River 297, 304, 460, 461
Wye Valley walk 305
Wyndham's Theatre (London) 127
Wynne, Robert 432

Y

Yarmouth, hotels 547
Yarrow, hotels 570
Yattendon, hotels 551
Yeomen of the Guard 62
York 335, **390–95**
hotels 563
restaurants 599
Street-by-Street map 390–91
York Minster 390, **392–3**, **395**
York, Duke of 248
Yorkshire **367–99**
climate 69
Exploring Yorkshire and the Humber Region 368–9
hotels 562–3
pubs 610
restaurants 598–9
Yorkshire Dales National Park 334, **370–72**
Yorkshire Sculpture Park **399**
Young, James 467
Young British Artists (YBAs) 93

Z

Zennor, Penwith tour 264
Zoffany, Johann 526, 529
Zoos
Bristol Zoo Gardens 244
Paignton Zoo 278
Whipsnade Wild Animal Park **219**
see also Aquariums; Wildlife

Acknowledgments

DORLING KINDERSLEY would like to thank the following people whose contributions and assistance have made the preparation of this book possible.

MAIN CONTRIBUTOR
Michael Leapman was born in London in 1938 and has been a professional journalist since he was 20. He has worked for most British national newspapers and now writes about travel and other subjects for several publications, among them *The Independent, Independent on Sunday, The Economist* and *Country Life*. He has written 11 books, including the award-winning *Companion Guide to New York* (1983, revised 1995) and *Eyewitness Travel Guide to London*. In 1989 he edited the widely praised *Book of London*.

ADDITIONAL CONTRIBUTORS
Paul Cleves, James Henderson, Lucy Juckes, John Lax, Marcus Ramshaw.

ADDITIONAL ILLUSTRATIONS
Christian Hook, Gilly Newman, Paul Weston.

DESIGN AND EDITORIAL
MANAGING EDITOR Georgina Matthews
SENIOR ART EDITOR Sally Ann Hibbard
DEPUTY EDITORIAL DIRECTOR Douglas Amrine
DEPUTY ART DIRECTOR Gaye Allen
PRODUCTION David Proffit
PICTURE RESEARCH Ellen Root
DTP DESIGNER Ingrid Vienings
MAP CO-ORDINATORS Michael Ellis, David Pugh
RESEARCHER Pippa Leahy
Eliza Armstrong, Sam Atkinson, Moerida Belton, Josie Barnard, Hilary Bird, Louise Boulton, Julie Bowles, Roger Bullen, Deborah Clapson, Elspeth Collier, Gary Cross, Cooling Brown Partnership, Guy Dimond, Danny Farnham, Joy Fitzsimmons, Fay Franklin, Ed Freeman, Charlie Hawkings, Martin Hendry, Andrew Heritage, Paul Hines, Annette Jacobs, Gail Jones, Steve Knowlden, Nic Kynaston, Esther Labi, Kathryn Lane, Pippa Leahy, James Mills Hicks, Rebecca Milner, Elaine Monaghan, Marianne Petrou, Chez Picthall, Clare Pierotti, Andrea Powell, Mark Rawley, Jake Reimann, Carolyn Ryden, David Roberts, Mary Scott, Alison Stace, Hugh Thompson, Simon Tuite.

ADDITIONAL PHOTOGRAPHY
Max Alexander, Peter Anderson, Apex Photo Agency: Simon Burt, Steve Bere, Deni Bown, June Buck, Michael Dent, Philip Dowell, Mike Dunning, Chris Dyer, Andrew Einsiedel, Philip Enticknap, Jane Ewart, DK Studio/Steve Gorton, Frank Greenaway, Stephen Hayward, John Heseltine, Ed Ironside, Dave King, Neil Mersh, Robert O'Dea, Stephen Oliver, Vincent Oliver, Roger Phillips, Kim Sayer, Karl Shone, Chris Stevens, Jim Stevenson, Clive Streeter, Harry Taylor, David Ward, Mathew Ward, Alan Williams, Stephen Wooster, Nick Wright, Colin Yeates.

PHOTOGRAPHIC AND ARTWORK REFERENCE
Christopher Woodward of the Building of Bath Museum, Franz Karl Freiherr von Linden, Gendall Designs, NRSC Air Photo Group, The Oxford Mail and Times, and Mark and Jane Rees.

PHOTOGRAPHY PERMISSIONS
DORLING KINDERSLEY would like to thank the following for their assistance and kind permission to photograph at their establishments: Banqueting House (Crown copyright by kind permission of Historic Royal Palaces); Cabinet War Rooms; Paul Highnam at English Heritage; Dean and Chapter Exeter Cathedral; Gatwick Airport Ltd; Heathrow Airport Ltd; Thomas Woods at Historic Scotland; Provost and Scholars Kings College; Cambridge; London Transport Museum; Madame Tussaud's; National Museums and Galleries of Wales (Museum of Welsh Life); Diana Lanham and Gayle Mault at the National Trust; Peter Reekie and Isla Roberts at the National Trust for Scotland; Provost Skene House; Saint Bartholmew the Great; Saint James's Church; London St Paul's Cathderal; Masters and Wardens of the Worshipful Company of Skinners; Provost and Chapter of Southwark Cathderal; HM Tower of London; Dean and Chapter of Westminster; Dean and Chapter of Worcetser Cathedral and all the other churches, museums, hotels, restaurants, shops, galleries and sights too numerous to thank individually.

PICTURE CREDITS
t = top; tl = top left; tlc = top left centre; tc = top centre; tr = top right; cla = centre left above; ca = centre above; cra = centre right above; cl = centre left; c = centre; cr = centre right; clb = centre left below; cb = centre below; crb = centre right below; bl = bottom left; b = bottom; bc = bottom centre; bcl = bottom centre left; br = bottom right; d = detail.

Works of art have been reproduced with the permission of the following copyright holders: © ADAGP, Paris and DACS, London 1995: 159t; © Alan Bowness, Hepworth Estate 265bl; © DACS, London 1995: 93c; © Patrick Heron 1995 all rights reserved DACS: 228cb; © D Hockney: 1970–1 93tr, 1990–3 397t; © Estate of Stanley Spencer 1995 all rights reserved DACS 223t; © Angela Verren-Taunt 1995 all rights reserved DACS: 265br.

The work of Henry Moore, *Large Two Forms*, 1966, illustrated on page 399b has been reproduced by permission of the Henry Moore Foundation.

The publisher would like to thank the following individuals, companies and picture libraries for permission to reproduce their photographs:

ABBOT HALL ART GALLERY AND MUSEUM, Kendal: 358b(d); ABERDEEN ART GALLERIES 526t; ABERDEEN AND GRAMPIAN TOURIST BOARD 465ca; ACTION PLUS: 67t; 466t; Steve Bardens 66bl, 420c; David Davies 67cr; Glynn Kirk 66tl; Peter Tarry 66cla, 67bl; Printed by kind permission of MOHAMED AL FAYED: 99t; ALAMY: Gina Calvi 361tl; Angus Palmer 205b; AMERICAN MUSEUM, Bath: 249tl; ANCIENT ART AND ARCHITECTURE COLLECTION: 42cb, 44ca, 44clb, 45ca, 45clb, 46bl, 46br, 48crb, 51ca, 220tl, 223br, 425t; THE ARCHIVE & BUSINESS RECORDS CENTRE, University of Glasgow: 469t; T & R ANNAN AND SONS: 502b(d); ASHMOLEAN MUSEUM, OXFORD: 47t.

BARNABY'S PICTURE LIBRARY: 60tr; BEAMISH OPEN AIR MUSEUM: 410c, 401b, 411ca, 411cb, 411b; BRIDGEMAN ART LIBRARY, LONDON AND NEW YORK: Agnew and Sons, London 311t; Museum of Antiquities, Newcastle upon Tyne 44tl; Apsley House, The Wellington Museum, London 26tl; Bibliotheque Nationale, Paris *Neville Book of Hours* 310t(d); Birgmingham City Museums and Gallery 307t; Bonham's, London, *Portrait of Lord Nelson with Santa Cruz Beyond*, Lemeul Francis Abbot 54cb(d); Bradford Art Galleries and Museums 49clb; City of Bristol Museums and Art Galleries 244c; British Library, London, *Pictures and Arms of English Kings and Knights* 4t(d), 39t(d), *The Kings of England from Brutus to Henry* 26bl(d), *Stowe manuscript* 40tl(d), *Liber Legum Antiquorum Regum* 46t(d), *Calendar Anglo-Saxon Miscellany* 46–7t(d), 46–7c(d), 46–7b(d), *Decrees of Kings of Anglo-Saxon and Norman England* 47clb, 49bl(d), *Portrait of Chaucer*, Thomas Occleve 49br(d), *Portrait of Shakespeare*, Droeshurt 51bl(d), *Historia Anglorum* 40bl(d), 224tl(d), *Chronicle of Peter of Langtoft* 273b(d), *Lives and Miracles of St Cuthbert* 405tl(d), 405cl(d), 405cr(d), *Lindisfarne Gospels* 405br(d), *Commendatio Lamentabilis intransitu Edward IV* 422b(d), *Histoire du Roy d'Angleterre Richard II* 424t(d), 523b; Christies, London 431t; Claydon House, Bucks, *Florence Nightingale*, Sir William Blake Richmond 150t; Department of Environment, London 48tr; City of Edinburgh Museums and Galleries, *Chief of Scottish Clan*, Eugene Deveria 470bl(d); Fitzwilliam Museum, University of Cambridge, *George IV as Prince Regent*, Richard Cosway 167cb, 200bl, *Flemish Book of Hours* 338tl(d); Giraudon/Musee de la Tapisserie, with special authorization of the city of Bayeux 47b,169b; Guildhall Library, Corporation of London, *The Great Fire*, Marcus Willemsz

Doornik 53bl(d), *Bubbler's Melody* 54br(d), *Triumph of Steam and Electricity*, The Illustrated London News 57t(d), *Great Exhibition, The transept from Dickenson's Comprehensive Pictures* 56–7, *A Balloon View of London as seen from Hampstead* 107c(d); Harrogate Museum and Art Gallery, North Yorkshire 374t; Holburne Museum and Crafts Study Centre, Bath 53t; Imperial War Museum, *London Field Marshall Montgomery*, J Worsley 27cbr(d); Kedleston Hall, Derbyshire 24br; King Street Galleries, London, *Bonnie Prince Charlie*, G Dupré 468tl; Lambeth Palace Library, London, *St Alban's Chronicle* 49t; Lever Brothers Ltd, Cheshire 337cra; Lincolnshire County Council, Usher Gallery, Lincoln, *Portrait of Mrs Fitzherbert after Richard Cosway* 167b; London Library, *The Barge Tower from Ackermann's World in minature*, F Scoberl 55t; Manchester City Art Galleries 361b; David Messum Gallery, London 433b; National Army Museum, London, *Bunker's Hill*, R Simkin 54ca; National Gallery, London, *Mrs Siddons the Actress*, Thomas Gainsborough 54t(d), 151ca; National Museet, Copenhagen 46ca; Phillips, the International Fine Art Auctioneers, *James I*, John the Elder Decritz 52b(d); Private Collections: 8–9, 26ca(d), 34tl, 48–9, 55cla, 55bl, 56clb, Vanity Fair 57br, 151t, *Ellesmere Manuscript* 176b(d), *Armada: map of the Spanish and British Fleets*, Robert Adam 281t, 382t, 408b; Royal Geographical Society, London 151cb(d); Royal Holloway & Bedford New College, the *Princes Edward and Richard in the Tower*, Sir John Everett Millais 123b; Smith Art Gallery and Museum, Stirling 482b; Tate Gallery, London: 56crb, 225t; Thyssen-Bornemisza Collection, Lugo Casta, *King Henry VIII*, Hans Holbein the Younger 50b(d); Victoria and Albert Museum, London 24t(d), 56b, 99c, 192t, 339cr, 379b, *Miniature of Mary Queen of Scots*, by a follower of Francois Clouet 497br, 523t(d); Walker Art Gallery, Liverpool 364c; Westminster Abbey, London, *Henry VII Tomb effigy*, Pietro Torrigiano 26br(d), 40bc(d); The Trustees of the Weston Park Foundation, *Portrait of Richard III*, Italian School 49cla(d); Christopher Wood Gallery, London, *High Life Below Stairs*, Charles Hunt 25c(d); reproduced with permission of the British Airways: Adrian Meredith Photography 632t; BFI London IMAX Cinema Waterloo: Richard Holttum 127c; British Library Board: *Cotton Faustina BVII folio 85* 49cb, 111cl; © The British Museum: 42cr, 43cb, 73tl, 83c, 105, 108–9 all except 109t and 109bl; © The Bronte Society: 398 all; BT Payphones: 622tl, 622bla; Burton Constable Foundation: Dr David Connell 388t.

Cadogen Management: 86b; CADW – Welsh Historic Monuments (Crown Copyright), 460t; Camera Press: Cecil Beaton 94bl; Cardiff City Council: 458tr, 459t, 459c; Fkb Carlson: 35bcl; Castle Howard Estate Ltd: 385tl; Colin de Chaire: 185c; Trustees of the Chatsworth Settlement: 322b, 323b; Museum of Childhood, Edinburgh: 496b; Bruce Coleman Ltd: 31br; Stephen Bond 282b; Jane Burton 31cra; Mark N. Boulton 31cl; Patrick Clement 30clb; Peter Evans 530tl; Paul van Gaalen 238tl; Sir Jeremy Grayson 31bl; Harald Lange 30bc; Gordon Langsbury 531t; George McCarthy 30t, 31bl, 230b, 273br; Paul Meitz 514clb; Dr. Eckart Pott 30bl, 514t; Hans Reinhard 30cb, 31tc, 282t, 480tl; Dr Frieder Sauer 520t; N Schwiatz 31clb; Kim Taylor 31tl, 514cra; Konrad Wothe 514ca; Collections: Liz Stares 26tr,Yuri Lewinski 361tl; Corbis: Angelo Hornak 119tc, Bill Ross 633tr, John Heseltine 113br; Joe Cornish: 389b; Doug Corrance: 471b; John Crook: 159b.

EasyEverything: James Hamilton 622br; 1805 Club: 27t; 1853 Gallery, Bradford 397t; English Heritage: 134b, 196c, 196b, 197b, 236–7b, 251b, 338br, 339b, 380t, 405tr, 405c; Avebury Museum 42ca; Devizes Museum 42br, drawing by Frank Gardiner 409br; Salisbury Museum 42t, 42bl; Skyscan Balloon Photography 43t, 250b; 380t; 409bl; English Life Publications Ltd, Derby: 330tl, 330tr, 331t, 331b; Et Archive: 41tc, 41cr, 52cb, 53clb, 58crb, 150b; Bodleian Library, Oxford 48crb; British Library, London 48tl, 48ca; Devizes Museum 42cl, 43b, 250c; Garrick Club 422tl(d); Imperial War Museum, London 58clb(d), 59br; Labour Party Archives 60br; London Museum 43cla; Magdalene College 50ca; National Maritime Museum, London 39b; Stoke Museum Staffordshire Polytechnic 41bc, 52tl; Victoria & Albert Museum, London 50t(d); Mary Evans Picture Library: 9 inset, 34tr, 40br, 41tl, 41cl, 41bl, 41br, 44bl, 44br, 46cb, 47cla, 51t, 51cb, 51br, 53crb, 54bl, 55br, 56tl, 58ca, 59ca, 59clb, 59crb, 81cb, 106t, 107t, 145 inset, 150cb, 151b, 175c, 177c, 183b, 194c, 210bl, 216tl, 219c, 219bl, 219br, 222bl, 227 inset, 267t, 285 inset, 324b, 337t, 337cla, 406t, 433tl, 468b, 485b, 498bl, 500b, 501t, 521b, 613 inset. Chris Fairclough: 283b, 340b, 640b; Falkirk Wheel: 487b; Paul Felix: 222c; Ffotograff © Charles Aithie: 421t; Fishbourne Roman Villa: 45t; Louis Flood: 470br; Foreign and British Bible Society: Cambridge University Library 423c; Fotomas Index: 107cra. Garden Picture Library: J S Sira 23crt; John Glover 23rb; Steven Wooster 22–23t; Glasgow Museums: Burrell Collection 507ca, 506–7 all except 506tl; Art Gallery & Museum, Kelvingrove 505t, 517b, 529b(d); Saint Mungo Museum of Religious Life and Art 503tl; Museum of Transport 504cr; John Glover: 62cr, 148cb, 193b; The Gore Hotel, London: 540c.

Sonia Halliday and Laura Lushington Archive: 395t; Robert Harding Picture Library: 170t, 534t; Jan Baldwin 275b; M H Black 276t; Teresa Black 621cb; Nigel Blythe 632ca; L Bond 325b; Michael Botham 32br; C Bowman 629c; Lesley Burridge 292tr; Martyn F Chillman 293bc; Philip Craven 105t, 188b, 313b; Nigel Francis 207b, 635b; Robert Francis 66–7; Paul Freestone 214b; Brian Harrison 515b; Van der Hars 524t; Michael Jenner 45b, 515c; Norma Joseph 65b; Christopher Nicholson 241t; B O'Connor 33ca; Jenny Pate 149bc; Rainbird Collection 47crb; Roy Rainsford 33b, 156t, 286b, 326cr, 356t, 372t, 461b; Walter Rawling 21t; Hugh Routledge 2–3; Peter Scholey 287t; Michael Short 293br; James Strachen 370b; Julia K Thorne 472bl; Adina Tovy 61tl, 472br; Andy Williams 167t, 222br, 334c, 418t, 510; Adam Woolfitt 20t, 20c, 44tr, 45crb, 248b, 260, 275ca, 293bl, 425bl, 454tl, 530tr; Harewood House: 396c; Paul Harris: 32t, 62cl, 289bl(d), 326b, 355b, 612–3, 630c, 630b; Harrogate International Centre: 375b; Heathrow Airport Ltd: 619b; Crown copyright is reproduced with the permission of the Controller of HMSO: 73br, 120bl, 120br, 121tl; Cathedral Church of the Blessed Virgin Mary and St Ethelbert in Hereford: 304b; Hertfordshire County Council: Bob Norris 58–9; John Heseltine: 74t, 104, 109t, 110, 238tr, 238c, 455tl; Historic Royal Palaces (Crown Copyright): 161, 223 all; Historic Scotland (Crown Copyright): 483c, 492tr, 492c, 493bl; Peter Hollings: 336bl; Neil Holmes: 246b(d), 248c, 274t, 359b, 415tl, 415tr, 437b, 643t; Angelo Hornak Library: 392tl, 392bl, 392br, 395br; Reproduced by permission of the Clerk of Records, House of Lords: 469c; David Martin Hughes: 144–5, 152; Hulton-Deutsch Collection: 22c, 22tr, 27cl, 27cr, 53cla, 54c, 56c, 57cb, 58tl 58tr, 58b, 59t, 60ca, 60bl, 150ca, 157c, 221b, 288t, 336c, 337crb, 338bl, 363b, 383b, 384br, 423t, 481b, 508tl, 522b; Hunterian Art Gallery: 505b; Hutchison Library: Catherine Blacky 34cb; Bernard Gerad 467t; Hutton in the Forest: Lady Inglewood 346t.

The Image Bank, London: Derek Berwin 538t; David Gould 345b; Romilly Lockyer 74bl; Colin Molyneux 455bl; Stockphotos/Steve Allen360c, Trevor Wood 274b; Simon Wilkinson 168b; Terry Williams 114tc; Images Colour Library: 30cla, 43c, 209b, 222t, 237t, 238bl, 239b, 324t, 326cl, 327t, 341c, 638t, 638b; Horizon/Robert Estall 424c; Landscape Only 33cb, 236, 353, 425br; Ironbridge Museum: 303b. Jarrold Publishers: 200br, 217t(d), 292bl; Michael Jenner: 292tl, 328b, 514b; Jorvik Viking Centre, York: 391t.

Frank Lane Picture Agency: 386b(d); W Broadhurst 242b; Michael Callan 230crb; Andrew Lawson: 23c, 23cb, 232br, 233tl, 233tr, 233br; Leeds Castle Enterprises: 153b; Leighton House, Royal Borough of Kensington: 130br; published by kind permission Dean and Chapter of Lincoln 328t, 329cb, 329bl; Lincolnshire County Council: Usher Gallery, Lincoln: c 1820 by William Ilbery 329bl; Llangolen International Musical Eisteddfod 436c; London Ambulance Service: 621ca; London Film Festival: 62t; London Transport Museum: 82t; Longleat House: 254t; The Lowry Collection, Salford: *Coming From the Mill*, 1930, L.S. Lowry 359tr.

Madame Tussauds: 106b; Magna: 341b; Maldom Millenium Trust: 197t; Mansell Collection, London: 27clb, 40tr, 52ca,

55cb, 249tr, 311bl, 337clb, 388b; Nick Meers: 18t, 226–7; Metropolitan Police Service: 621t; Archie Miles: 228ca; Simon Miles: 340tr; Minack Theatre: Murray King 264b; Mirror Syndication International: 76b, 89b, 114; BTA/Juilian Nieman 34ca; Museum of London: 44crb, 115t; National Express Ltd: 640bl; National Fishing Heritage Centre, Grimsby: 389t; National Gallery, London: 73tr, 84–5 all; National Gallery Of Scotland: *The Reverend Walker Skating on Duddington Loch*, Sir Henry Raeburn 490c(d); National Library Of Wales: 422tr, 425c(d), 453b; National Museum Of Film And Television, Bradford: 397c; Board of Trustees of the National Museums and Galleries on Merseyside: Liverpool Museum 365t; Maritime Museum 363t; Walker Art Gallery 334b, 364tl, 364tr, 364b, 365c; National Museums of Scotland: 491t, 497bl; National Museum of Wales: 422c; By courtesy of the National Portrait Gallery, London: *First Earl of Essex*, Hans Peter Holbein 339t(d); National Tramway Museum, Crich: 327c; National Trust Photographic Library: *Bess of Hardwick (Elizabeth, Countess of Shrewsbury)*, Anon 322tl(d); Mathew Antrobus 290br, 376cl, 377bl; Oliver Benn 25br, 266c, 281bl, 376b; John Bethell 267c, 267bl, 267br, 291t; Nick Carter 243b; Joe Cornish 442; Prudence Cumming 255c; Martin Dohrn 50crb; Andreas Von Einsidedel 25bl, 290cb, 291ca; Roy Fox 259t; Geoffry Frosh 277t; Jerry Harpur 232t, 232bl; Derek Harris 232clb, 255t; Nadia MacKenzie 24cl; Nick Meers 254b, 255b, 308b, 615b; Rob Motheson 280t; Cressida Pemberton Piggot 540t; Ian Shaw 446t; Richard Surman 291br, 350b; Rupert Truman 291br, 365b; Andy Tryner 290bl; Charlie Waite 377t; Jeremy Whitaker 291bc, 379t, 446b; Mike Williams 290ca, 377c; George Wright 232crb, 280c; National Trust For Scotland: 464b, 486b, 487c, 494b, 508tr, 509tl, 509tr, 509br; Glyn Satterley 503tr; Lindsey Robertson 509bl; National Waterways Museum at Gloucester: 289bc, 289br; NHPA: Martin Garwood 381ca; Daniel Heuclin 270la; Nature Photographers: Andrew Cleave 230cla; E A James 31cla, 348t; Hugh Miles 407t; Owen Newman 31ca; William Paton 514crb; Paul Sterry 30crb, 30br, 31cb, 31crb, 222c, 243t, 373t, 514cla; Roger Tidman 185b; Network Photographers: Laurie Sparham 466b; New Shakespeare Theatre Co: 127t; Norfolk Museums Service: Norwich Castle Museum 189b; Oxford Scientific Films: Okapia 270lb.

'PA' News Photo Library: John Stillwell 61 cr. Palace Theatre Archive: 126c; Photos Horticultural: 149tlc, 149cra, 149cb, 149crb, 232ca, 233c; Pictures: 632t; Planet Earth Pictures: David Phillips 23crca; Popperfoto: 27br, 59bl, 60clb, 60crb, 61bl, 88tl, 148tr, 191t, 272cl, 430b; AFP/Eric Feferber 61br; SG Forester 67br; Port Merion Ltd: 440tl; The Post Office: 623tl, 641bl; Press Association: Martin Keene 62b; Public Record Office (Crown Copyright): 48b.

Rob Reichenfeld: 162t, 163c, 163b, 288b, 626b, 631t; Rex Features Ltd: 27ca, 41tr, 60tl, 61bc, 224c, 225br; Barry Beattie 247cl; Peter Brooke 27bc, 624br; Nils Jorgensen 26c, 629t, 636c; Eileen Kleinman 629br; Hazel Murray 61tr; Tess, Renn-Burrill Productions 257b; Brian Rasic 63t; Nick Rogers 61tc; Tim Rooke 64cr, 66tr; Sipa/Chesnot 27bl; Today 21c; Richard Young 60tl; The Ritz, London: 83t; Royal Academy Of Arts, London: 86ca; Royal Collection © 1995 Her Majesty Queen Elizabeth II: *The Family of Henry VIII*, Anon 38(d), 87c, 88tr, 88bl, 89t, 224tr, 225tl(d), 225tr, 225bl, *George IV, in full Highland dress*, Sir David Wilkie 471t; David Cripps 89c; John Freeman 88br; Royal College Of Music, London: 98c; Royal Pavilion, Art Gallery and Museums, Brighton: 166c, 166bl, 166br, 167cl, 167cr; Royal Botanic Gardens, Kew: 76ca;Royal Shakespeare Theatre Company: Donald Cooper 315c(d).

St. Alban's Museums: Verulamium Museum 220b; Sartaj Balti House: Clare Carnegie 397b; Scottish National Gallery of Modern Art: Roy Lichtenstein In the Car 493c; Scottish National Portrait Gallery: on loan from the collection of the Earl of Roseberry, *Execution of Charles I*, Unknown Artist 52–3; S4C (Channel 4 Wales): 423b; Sidmouth Folk Festival: Derek Brooks 277b; Skyscan Balloon Photography: 250t; John Snocken: 23cr, 23ra; Southbank Press Office: 128t; Sporting Pictures: 66cra, 66bc, 66br, 67cl, 346b; Still Moving Pictures: Doug Corrance 534b; Wade Cooper 469b; Derek Laird 468c; Robert Lees 65t; STB 530br, 531c, Paisley Museum 501b, Paul Tomkins 515tr; SJ Whitehorn 481t; David Tarn: 375tl; Tony Stone Images: 34–5, 536–7; Rex A.Butcher 83c; Richard Elliott 64b; Rob Talbot 341ca; David Woodfall 426; © Tate, London 2002: 73bl, 93 all except c and tl, 93c with kind permission of the Henry Moore Foundation, *Standing by the Rags*, 1988 © Lucian Freud 125tr; *Death from Death Hope Life Fear* (d) 1984 © Gilbert and George 125 cl; *Soft Drain Pipe – Blue (Cool) Version*, 1967 © Claes Oldenburg 125cr, 125br, 265c, 265bl, 265br; Rob Talbot: 341cb; Tuille House Museum, Carlisle: 346c; Urbis: 360c; courtesy of the Board of Trustees of the Victoria And Albert Musuem, London: 72b, 100–101.

Charlie Waite: 535t; © Wales Tourist Board: 419c, 420b, 424–5, 454br, 455tr, 455br; Roger Vitos 454tl, 454bl; The Wallace Collection, London: 106cb; David Ward: 511b, 529t; Frederick Warne & Co: 355t(d); Courtesy of the Trustees of The Wedgwood Museum, Barlaston, Staffordshire, England: 299b; Jeremy Whitaker: 216tr, 216c, 217b; Whitbread Plc: 34bl; Whitworth Art Gallery, University of Manchester: courtesy of Granada Television Arts Foundation 361c; Christopher Wilson: 390bl; Wilton House Trust: 253b; Winchester Cathedral: 159t; Woburn Abbey – by kind permission of the Marquess of Tavistock and Trustees of the Bedford Estate: 50–1, 218t; Timothy Woodcock Photolibrary: 5b; Photo © Woodmansterne, Watford, UK: Jeremy Marks 116t, 117t.

York Castle Museum: 391cb; York City Art Gallery: 393bl; Dean & Chapter York Minster: 395cla, 395ca, 395cl; Peter Gibson 395cra, 395cr, 395cl; Jim Korshaw 392tr; Reproduced couresty of the Yorkshire Museum: 394c; Yorkshire Sculpture Park: Jerry Hardman Jones 399t. ZEFA: 64t, 128b, 251t, 257t, 472c, 627t, 634c, 636bl; Bob Croxford 63cr; Weir 185t.

Front Endpaper: All special photography except Robert Harding Picture Library/Andy Williams tl, Adam Woolfitt bl; David Martin Hughes brl; National Trust Photographic Library/Joe Cornish clc; Tony Stone Images/David Woodfall cl. Back Endpaper: All special photography except John Heseltine tl, br.

Jacket
Front - Getty Images: main image; DK Picture Library: Peter Anderson crb; Rob Reichenfeld bc; Getty Images: Derek P. Redfearn clb. Back - Getty Images: Peter Irish t; Glyn Kirk b. Spine - Getty Images.

Central London

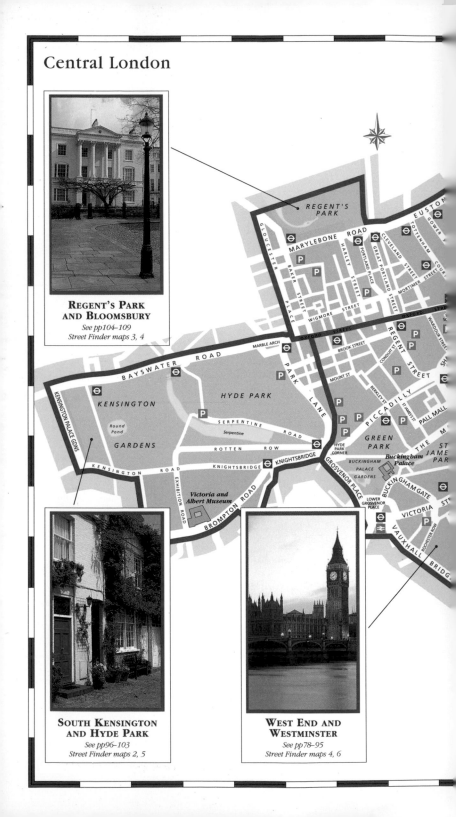

Regent's Park and Bloomsbury
See pp104–109
Street Finder maps 3, 4

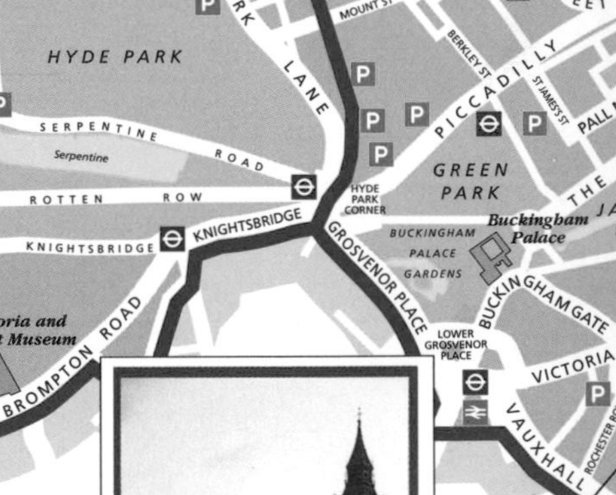

South Kensington and Hyde Park
See pp96–103
Street Finder maps 2, 5

West End and Westminster
See pp78–95
Street Finder maps 4, 6